GEOGRAPHICAL DISTRIBUTION OF FINANCIAL FLOWS

TO DEVELOPING COUNTRIES

◆

RÉPARTITION GÉOGRAPHIQUE DES RESSOURCES FINANCIÈRES

ALLOUÉES AUX PAYS EN DÉVELOPPEMENT

**DISBURSEMENTS
COMMITMENTS
ECONOMIC INDICATORS**

**VERSEMENTS
ENGAGEMENTS
INDICATEURS ÉCONOMIQUES**

1987/1990

ORGANISATION FOR ECONOMIC CO-OPERATION AND DEVELOPMENT
ORGANISATION DE COOPÉRATION ET DE DÉVELOPPEMENT ÉCONOMIQUES

D1276646

ORGANISATION FOR ECONOMIC CO-OPERATION AND DEVELOPMENT

ORGANISATION DE COOPÉRATION ET DE DÉVELOPPEMENT ÉCONOMIQUES

Pursuant to Article 1 of the Convention signed in Paris on 14th December 1960, and which came into force on 30th September 1961, the Organisation for Economic Co-operation and Development (OECD) shall promote policies designed:

— to achieve the highest sustainable economic growth and employment and a rising standard of living in Member countries, while maintaining financial stability, and thus to contribute to the development of the world economy;

— to contribute to sound economic expansion in Member as well as non-member countries in the process of economic development; and

— to contribute to the expansion of world trade on a multilateral, non-discriminatory basis in accordance with international obligations.

The original Member countries of the OECD are Austria, Belgium, Canada, Denmark, France, Germany, Greece, Iceland, Ireland, Italy, Luxembourg, the Netherlands, Norway, Portugal, Spain, Sweden, Switzerland, Turkey, the United Kingdom and the United States. The following countries became Members subsequently through accession at the dates indicated hereafter: Japan (28th April 1964), Finland (28th January 1969), Australia (7th June 1971) and New Zealand (29th May 1973). The Commission of the European Communities takes part in the work of the OECD (Article 13 of the OECD Convention). Yugoslavia has a special status at OECD (agreement of 28th October 1961).

En vertu de l'article 1er de la Convention signée le 14 décembre 1960, à Paris, et entrée en vigueur le 30 septembre 1961, l'Organisation de Coopération et de Développement Economiques (OCDE) a pour objectif de promouvoir des politiques visant :

— à réaliser la plus forte expansion de l'économie et de l'emploi et une progression du niveau de vie dans les pays Membres, tout en maintenant la stabilité financière, et à contribuer ainsi au développement de l'économie mondiale ;

— à contribuer à une saine expansion économique dans les pays Membres, ainsi que les pays non membres, en voie de développement économique ;

— à contribuer à l'expansion du commerce mondial sur une base multilatérale et non discriminatoire conformément aux obligations internationales.

Les pays Membres originaires de l'OCDE sont : l'Allemagne, l'Autriche, la Belgique, le Canada, le Danemark, l'Espagne, les Etats-Unis, la France, la Grèce, l'Irlande, l'Islande, l'Italie, le Luxembourg, la Norvège, les Pays-Bas, le Portugal, le Royaume-Uni, la Suède, la Suisse et la Turquie. Les pays suivants sont ultérieurement devenus Membres par adhésion aux dates indiquées ci-après : le Japon (28 avril 1964), la Finlande (28 janvier 1969), l'Australie (7 juin 1971) et la Nouvelle-Zélande (29 mai 1973). La Commission des Communautés européennes participe aux travaux de l'OCDE (article 13 de la Convention de l'OCDE). La Yougoslavie a un statut spécial à l'OCDE (accord du 28 octobre 1961).

TABLE OF CONTENTS – TABLE DES MATIÈRES

SECTION A

Summary Tables | **Tableaux récapitulatifs**

Pages

SECTION B

<table>
<tr><td>**Tables for Individual Recipient Countries and Territories**</td><td></td><td>**Tableaux par pays et territoires bénéficiaires**</td></tr>
</table>

Developing Countries and Territories Classified as: **Groupes des pays et territoires en développement :**

Of which: *Dont :*

SECTION C

Annex **Annexe**

Notes: The symbol in the tables:

    — (or a blank space) means nil, not available or not applicable;

    0.0 less than half the smallest unit shown;

    .. the sum of the components is not shown because it is incomplete.

Notes : Signification des signes utilisés dans les tableaux :

    — (ou un espace blanc) signifie néant, non disponible, ou non applicable ;

    0.0 moins de la moitié du plus petit chiffre indiqué ;

    .. la somme des composantes étant incomplète, aucun chiffre n'est donné.

INTRODUCTION

1. This report, the twelfth presenting the volume and sources of the external financial resources provided to individual developing countries and territories, contains detailed data on the geographical distribution of:

- Net and gross disbursements;
- Commitments;
- Terms; and
- The sector/purpose allocation of Official Development Financing (ODF) commitments.

for 133 developing countries and territories for 1987, 1988, 1989 and 1990 with data on per capita income and population to provide perspective in interpreting the resource flow information for each. The aim has been to achieve, within the compass of two pages, a comprehensive presentation of the external financing of each country shown.

2. The data show the transactions of each recipient country with:

i) DAC Member countries (individually or as a group)[1];
ii) Multilateral agencies (individually or as a group);
iii) Arab Countries Members of OPEC as a group, and for *commitments* and *gross disbursements* only, the Central Eastern European Countries (CEEC).

The Member countries of the OECD Development Assistance Committee for which data are presented are: Australia, Austria, Belgium, Canada, Denmark, Finland, France, Germany, Ireland, Italy, Japan, the Netherlands, New Zealand, Norway, Sweden, Switzerland, the United Kingdom and the United States. Data for the Commission of the European Communities, which is also a Member of the DAC, are included under "multilateral agencies". A further separate line (EEC + Members) gives the data for flows from the EEC as an institution and its DAC Member countries combined. No data are presented for Portugal and Spain, which became Members of the DAC in December 1991. The data on financial flows from multilateral sources cover the World Bank, IFC, IDA, IDB, AfDB, AfDF, AsDB, CarDB, IFAD, and the Social Loans programme of the European Resettlement Fund. Financial flows from Arab financed multilateral agencies, shown as a group, cover: BADEA, AFESD, the Islamic Development Bank and OFID. The Technical Assistance and Relief Agencies of the United Nations cover mainly the following programmes or agencies: UNTA, UNDP, UNHCR, UNRWA, UNICEF, WFP and UNFPA. Financial flows from Arab countries are shown as a combined total for the following countries: Algeria, Iraq, Kuwait, Libya, Qatar, Saudi Arabia and the United Arab Emirates. Flows from CEEC are shown as a combined total covering Bulgaria, Czechoslovakia, Hungary, Poland, Romania and the former USSR.

3. The data on changes in bank sector claims, given for information are for countries reporting to the Bank for International Settlements (BIS)[2] and the affiliates in the main financial centres of banks resident in the United States. They correspond to those in BIS publications, where they are shown adjusted to eliminate the effect of changes in exchange rates between quarters. In the present report, the adjusted quarterly figures have been summed to constitute calendar year estimates. (See Annex, paragraph A17).

Sources of Data

4. DAC bilateral flow figures are based on replies from Member countries to questionnaires issued by the OECD Secretariat. The data on multilateral flows are compiled from published reports of the agencies concerned, supplemented by additional information received directly from them. The bilateral aid figures for Arab countries are based on information provided by the Ministries of Finance of Kuwait, Saudi Arabia, United Arab Emirates, the Abu Dhabi Fund for Arab Economic Development, the Kuwait Fund for Arab Economic Development, the Saudi Fund for Development and the General Board for the South and Arabian Gulf. The remaining data are based on secondary sources and OECD Secretariat estimates. The data for Arab and CEEC countries have been classified and processed as far as possible according to DAC norms and definitions[3].

Data shown for per capita GNP and population in Section C were provided by IBRD.

Comprehensiveness

5. The resource flow data shown are based on records that are comprehensive for the majority of the individual categories shown. The omissions are essentially as follows:

i) Flows from countries that are neither developing countries nor members of the DAC (e.g., Luxemburg, South Africa).
ii) Flows from CEEC countries (with the exception of ODA commitments and gross disbursements); The 1990 geographical breakdown was not available when this report went to press.
iii) Private sector flows from Arab countries Members of OPEC.
iv) Intra-LDC flows, for which only limited data are available.

6. For developing countries combined, the net balance of payments effect of *iii)* and *iv)* is nil, since inflows to one country

are outflows of another. As regards *iv)* it would be misleading, for an individual recipient country, to show the incomplete figure corresponding to the data collected, since it could be treated as if it were the true total. The decision was taken not to show a country's receipts from other developing countries, except for ODA and OOF from Arab countries, until a satisfactory level of coverage has been achieved.

Unallocated Amounts

7. A comprehensive total reported by a source usually includes a "geographically unallocated" component. Administrative costs, which are mainly incurred on the territory of the donor country, are an example. They are excluded from the data for individual recipients in Section B, where, however, they are included under "unallocated" in the table for "all recipients combined" and in the totals in Section A. For the total amounts involved, see any recent issue of the DAC Chairman's Annual Report. A further portion of the amounts reported to DAC as geographically unallocated is properly classified thus e.g., amounts spent in the donor country on research performed for the benefit of developing countries (e.g., tropical diseases). Another portion reflects defective data collection procedures, or the effect of confidentiality restrictions requiring the non-disclosure of the identity of a partner country. For ODA and official sector transactions by DAC Members and multilateral organisations, geographically unallocated amounts are too small in aggregate to cause a substantial understatement of the figure for a given recipient country. However, the large amount of Arab ODA which is unallocated[4] and the incomplete coverage of bilateral non-concessional flows from Arab donor countries can involve serious distortion for some recipient countries. For certain categories of private sector flows, in particular private investment, there may be a fairly large understatement of a given country's net inflow. This is true of:

a) Countries hosting investment in the oil sector;
b) Countries whose investment inflows are derived in large part from source countries whose reporting includes large amounts not allocated by country. These source countries include in particular Canada, Denmark, Finland, New Zealand, Sweden and Switzerland.
c) Countries whose investment inflows from DAC Members have been channelled via an offshore centre which, while shown as the destination of the transactions concerned, is not itself a reporter to DAC.

PRESENTATION

8. The report consists of three sections:

Section A

9. This section contains eight tables covering the period 1984 to 1990. They show the receipts of each developing country or territory, including entities not shown separately in Section B, from DAC countries combined and, all sources combined, respectively, of:

i) Official Development Assistance: net disbursements;
ii) Official Development Assistance: commitments;
iii) Total resource flows: net disbursements.

Two tables show the receipts of each developing country of net disbursements of concessional assistance ("multilateral ODA") and total net disbursements from multilateral agencies combined.

Each table in this section contains a recapitulation of the resource receipts of selected developing country groups (see Annex, paragraph A21). These data are also illustrated graphically.

Section B

10. The tables in this section treat *each developing country* individually[5] showing its resource receipts by type and by donor, with separate sub-totals for DAC Members, multilateral agencies and Arab donors. Global data on commitments by CEEC countries are shown under "other aggregates". These tables are followed by tables of identical format showing the same information for *groups of developing countries* (see Annex, paragraph A21).

Coverage

Detailed Tables for Individual Recipients by Origin of Resources

11. The layout of each country table in Section B is identical. Two pages are used for each country. They contain three panels of tables showing the following types of flow by origin[6]:

1. Total receipts net (4 + 12 + Private);
2. ODA Loans gross;
3. Total Official Gross (7 + 9);
4. Total ODA Net (5 + 8);
5. ODA Loans Net;
6. Total Official Net (4 + 12);
7. Total ODA Gross;
8. Grants (including 11);
9. Total OOF Gross;
10. ODA commitments;
11. Technical Cooperation Grant disbursements (included in 8);
12. Total OOF Net;
13. ODF Commitments by Purpose (per cent);
14. Grant element of ODA (per cent);
15. Other Aggregates (including Private).

12. In each block within a table, flows from individual DAC Members and multilateral agencies are shown separately along with sub-totals for DAC Members and multilateral agencies, for Arab donors combined, and for the European Economic Community and its Members combined. The data for Arab donors are treated as comparable with the figures for DAC Members and multilateral agencies, although there are some differences in coverage and quality. Omitted from the total reached in this way are financial flows from the IMF, other than concessional loans by the IMF Trust Fund SAF and ESAF, Central and Eastern European Countries (for which commitments and gross disbursements data are however shown separately in the lower right hand blocks: see "Other Aggregates" below), other developing countries, and grants by private voluntary agencies.

Loans by banks resident in each DAC Member country are included indistinguishably in the "Total Receipts Net" block. The amount thus included for DAC Members combined falls short of the memorandum figure under "Other Aggregates" shown for "bank sector loans" by the amount of lending out of "financial centres" and certain other adjustments (see Annex, paragraph A17).

13. In section B, data on commitments are shown in four separate panels: ODA commitments (grants plus loans), the "grant element" of ODA loans, ODF commitments, by purpose, and under "other aggregates", total commitments: all sources. The dollar values of data shown in the first panel are drawn from Member countries' replies to the DAC questionnaire. The percentage data in the two following panels are derived from the Creditor Reporting System.

14. A separate panel shows, the sectoral distribution of Official Development Financing (ODF) commitments from all sources to each developing country. The list of sectors refers to the economic sector of destination (i.e. the specific area of the recipient's economic or social structure whose development is, or is intended to be, fostered by the aid) rather than to the type of goods or services received. The contents of the headings are as follows:

Education: This sector includes educational infrastructure, services and investment in all areas. Specialised education in particular fields such as agriculture or energy is reported against the sector concerned. Educational activities involving the supply of human resources (teachers, volunteers, experts) figure in the line for Technical Co-operation.

Health: This sector covers assistance to hospitals and clinics, including specialised institutions such as those for tuberculosis, maternal and child care; other medical and dental services, including disease and epidemic control, vaccination programmes, nursing, provision of drugs, health demonstration, etc.; public health administration and medical insurance programmes.

Other Social Infrastructure: This sector covers assistance to: housing, both urban and rural, community development and community facilities.

Water Supply, Sanitation and Sewage: This sector groups all assistance given for water supply, use and sanitation, but excludes irrigation systems for agriculture.

Energy: This heading covers both the production and distribution of energy, including peaceful use of nuclear energy.

Telecommunications: Included here are amounts for communications and telecommunications, including radio and television but not the press or cinema.

Transportation: Covers essentially equipment or infrastructure for road, rail, water and air transport.

Agriculture: Includes crop and livestock development, provision of production requisites such as farm machinery and fertiliser, irrigation, pest control, veterinary services; services to the agricultural sector, fishing and forestry (including tree crops); conservation and extension, land reclamation; land and soil surveys, land and water use; agricultural construction; storage and transport facilities; agricultural development banks are included under this heading.

Extractive industries: Assistance to extractive industries, including development of natural resources, geology, prospecting, geological surveys and petroleum and natural gas is reported under this heading.

Manufacturing: This sector includes assistance to manufacturing industries of all kinds, including refining of petroleum and ores, processing of food and other agricultural products, assistance to manufacture of fertilisers and farm machinery, cottage industry and handicrafts and non-agricultural storage and warehousing.

Trade, Banking and Tourism: This sector covers: export promotion, trade, commerce and distribution; banking (including industrial development banks) and hotel and other tourist facilities.

Technical Co-operation: Activities whose primary purpose is to augment the level of knowledge, skills, technical know-how or productive aptitudes of the population of developing countries, i.e., increasing their stock of human intellectual capital, or their capacity for more effective use of their existing factor endowment. Accordingly, consists mainly of activities involving the supply of human resources (teachers, volunteers, experts) and action targeted on human resources (education, training, advice).

Multisector: Support for projects, other than river development schemes, which straddle several sectors, with a concentration on production facilities.

Programme Assistance: All general developmental contributions other than debt re-organisation, made available with no pre-imposed sector allocation, e.g., balance of payments and budget support and funds made available for capital projects at the recipient's choice, but not subject to agreement by the donor. This item includes in particular, sector-unallocated structural adjustment assistance.

Debt Reorganisation: Debt forgiveness, rescheduling, refinancing, etc.

Food Aid: Supplies of food under bilateral programmes, including food aid for emergency needs.

Emergency Assistance (other than Food aid): Emergency and distress relief in cash or in kind, other than food aid, but including aid to refugees.

Unspecified: Aid which cannot be assigned to another part of the table, and in the case of project or sector assistance, commitments for which the sectoral destination had not been specified at date of report.

Other Aggregates

15. Further data for each recipient country are shown for a number of resource flow aggregates, for which detailed information by source is not given in the other blocks of the table. The aggregates have been chosen so as to complete the picture for the country concerned, in terms of the analytical and policy uses of the figures. The additional data cover the main classes of private sector transactions of DAC Member country residents, the commitments by the official sector of (ODA + OOF), the terms of ODA commitments from DAC Members combined and from all sources, and gross disbursements and commitments by CEEC countries as a group.

Section C: Economic Indicators

16. Data are given for two indicators:

– GNP per capita, World Bank Atlas Basis;
– Population;

for use in conjunction with the financial flow statistics in Sections A and B. These data cover the years 1984 to 1989 or the latest year available. The format is identical to that of Section A.

17. The indicators are as defined by IBRD, the source of the figures (see paragraph 4 above), and to whose publications the reader is referred.

Concepts and Interpretation of Data

18. A note on the main concepts used in this report and remarks on specific particularities of the data will be found at the end of the volume.

Timing of Reporting

19. National data were supplied by Members up to 17th January 1992.

NOTES AND REFERENCES

16. Additional aggregate data can be found in the annual report of the Chairman of the DAC "Development Co-operation Efforts and Policies of Members of the Development Assistance Committee, 1990 Review".

17. All DAC countries, except Australia, New Zealand, Spain, and a number of financial centres reporting to BIS.

18. See Annex: Definition of Concepts used in this Report.

19. Approximately 35 to 40 per cent of Arab bilateral aid is geographically unallocated, depending on the year.

20. The reader will find in Section A the main aggregates including countries not shown individually in Section B. Other data of Section B are available on request.

21. A French translation of certain terms is given in the fold-out at rear.

N.B.   It is recalled that the DAC list of developing countries and territories is designed for statistical purposes, not as guidance for eligibility for aid or other preferential treatment. The names or geographical classification of countries or territories shown in the publication should be construed as having strictly geographical or functional meaning and do not have political implications or imply any expression of view regarding juridical status. The designation "developing countries" is used as a generic term in its own right covering both "countries" and "territories" and does not carry any special meaning as to the political or legal classification of the recipients concerned.

INTRODUCTION

1. Le présent rapport, douzième d'une série consacrée au volume et à l'origine des ressources financières extérieures reçues par les pays et territoires en développement, fournit des données détaillées sur la répartition géographique :

- Des versements bruts et nets.
- Des engagements.
- Des conditions de financement ainsi que
- La ventilation par secteur/objet des engagements de Financement public du développement (FPD).

pour chacun des 133 pays et territoires en développement en 1987, 1988, 1989 et 1990. Ces statistiques sont complétées par des données sur le revenu par tête et sur la population permettant d'interpréter les informations sur les apports de ressources à chaque pays dans une perspective plus large. L'objet du rapport est de dépeindre, par le biais d'une présentation synthétique en deux pages, un tableau aussi complet que possible du financement externe de chacun des pays considérés.

2. Les données indiquent les opérations entreprises avec chaque pays bénéficiaire par :

i) Les pays Membres du CAD (séparément ou en tant que groupe)[1].

ii) Les organismes multilatéraux (séparément ou en tant que groupe).

iii) Les pays arabes membres de l'OPEP en tant que groupe, et pour les engagements et versements bruts les pays de l'Europe centrale et orientale (PECO), également en tant que groupe.

Les pays Membres du Comité d'aide au développement de l'OCDE pour lesquels des données sont présentées sont : l'Allemagne, l'Australie, l'Autriche, la Belgique, le Canada, le Danemark, les Etats-Unis, la Finlande, la France, l'Irlande, l'Italie, le Japon, la Norvège, la Nouvelle-Zélande, les Pays-Bas, le Royaume-Uni, la Suède et la Suisse. Les données relatives à la Commission des communautés européennes, qui est aussi Membre du CAD, sont comprises sous la rubrique « organismes multilatéraux ». Par ailleurs, une ligne supplémentaire (CEE + Membres) présente des données sur les apports en provenance de la CEE elle-même et de ses pays membres faisant aussi partie du CAD. Les données de l'Espagne et du Portugal ne sont pas présentées même si ces pays sont devenus Membres du CAD en décembre 1991. Les données relatives aux apports financiers en provenance de sources multilatérales se rapportent aux organismes suivants : BAfD, BAsD, Banque mondiale, BID, CARIBBANK, FAfD, FIDA, IDA, SFI et le programme de prêts sociaux du Fonds de réétablissement européen. Les apports des organismes multilatéraux financés par les pays arabes membres de l'OPEP couvrent les organismes et programmes suivants : BADEA, Banque islamique de développement, FADES, FODI. Les organismes d'assistance technique et de secours des Nations Unies comprennent

essentiellement les programmes ou organismes suivants : ATNU, FISE, FNUAP, HCR, PAM, PNUD et UNRWA. Les apports de ressources financières des pays arabes membres de l'OPEP sont indiqués globalement pour les pays suivants : l'Algérie, l'Arabie saoudite, les Emirats arabes unis, l'Irak, le Koweït, la Libye, et le Qatar. Les apports en provenance des PECO sont indiqués globalement pour la Bulgarie, la Hongrie, la Pologne, la Roumanie, la Tchécoslovaquie et l'ancienne URSS.

3. Les chiffres relatifs à la variation des créances du secteur bancaire, indiqués pour information concernent les pays faisant des déclarations à la Banque des règlements internationaux[2] ainsi que les sociétés affiliées, établies dans des centres financiers de banques dont le siège se trouve aux Etats-Unis. Ils correspondent aux chiffres présentés dans les rapports publiés par la BRI, où les effets des variations des taux de change en fin de trimestres ont été éliminés. Dans le présent rapport, les chiffres trimestriels ainsi ajustés ont été additionnés afin d'élaborer des estimations portant sur des années entières (voir annexe, paragraphe A17).

Sources des données

4. Les chiffres concernant les apports bilatéraux du CAD sont fondés sur les réponses fournies par les pays Membres aux questionnaires établis par le Secrétariat de l'OCDE. Les données sur les apports multilatéraux sont extraites des rapports publiés par les organismes intéressés et complétées par des informations supplémentaires communiquées directement par ces organismes. Les chiffres relatifs à l'aide bilatérale des pays arabes membres de l'OPEP sont fondés sur les renseignements fournis par les ministères des finances du Koweït, de l'Arabie saoudite, des Emirats arabes unis ainsi que par le Fonds d'Abu Dhabi pour le développement économique arabe, le Fonds du Koweït pour le développement économique arabe, le Fonds saoudien pour le développement, et l'Administration générale pour l'Arabie du Sud et le Golfe. Les autres chiffres ont été établis à partir de sources secondaires et d'estimations du Secrétariat de l'OCDE. Les données présentées pour les pays arabes membres de l'OPEP et du PECO ont été, dans la mesure du possible, classées et traitées conformément aux normes et définitions du CAD[3].

Les données présentées pour le PNB par tête et pour la population figurant dans la Section C ont été communiquées par la BIRD.

Couverture des données

5. Les données sur les apports de ressources sont tirées de séries qui recouvrent la quasi-totalité des opérations dans chacune des catégories présentées. Les omissions sont essentiellement les suivantes :

i) Apports en provenance de pays qui ne sont ni des pays en développement ni des Membres du CAD (par exemple, Luxembourg et Afrique du Sud).

ii) Apports en provenance des PECO (à l'exception des engagements APD et des versements bruts). La distribution géographique pour 1990 n'était pas disponible au moment de la mise sous presse.

iii) Apports privés en provenance des pays arabes membres de l'OPEP.

iv) Seules quelques données fragmentaires sont disponibles sur les flux de ressources entre pays en développement.

6.   Pour l'ensemble des pays en développement, les deux dernières catégories *iii)* et *iv)* s'annulent au niveau de la balance des paiements, puisque le montant des apports à un pays correspond à des sorties pour le pays partenaire. S'agissant du point *iv)*, aucun chiffre n'est indiqué pour un pays bénéficiaire donné car, les renseignements disponibles étant incomplets, ce chiffre, s'il était présenté, risquerait d'être retenu comme correspondant au vrai total. La décision a donc été prise d'omettre tous les apports de ressources en provenance d'autres pays en développement, à l'exception de l'APD et des AASP en provenance des pays arabes membres de l'OPEP, jusqu'à ce qu'un niveau satisfaisant de couverture ait été atteint.

Montants non ventilés

7.   Un total notifié par une source peut, d'une manière usuelle, comprendre une composante parfois importante d'apports « non ventilés sur le plan géographique ». La quasi-totalité des dépenses administratives interviennent, par exemple, sur le territoire du pays donneur. Ces dépenses sont exclues des données par pays bénéficiaire de la section B où, toutefois, elles sont englobées dans les pages « unallocated » présentées pour « l'ensemble des bénéficiaires » et dans les totaux de la Section A. Pour plus de précisions sur le montant des dépenses administratives, on peut consulter un des rapports annuels récents du Président du CAD. Une autre partie des montants notifiés au CAD sous la rubrique « non ventilés sur le plan géographique » appartient effectivement à cette catégorie. C'est le cas, notamment, des dépenses encourues dans le pays donneur au titre de la recherche effectuée au profit d'un ensemble de pays en développement (maladies tropicales, par exemple). Une autre partie tient à des méthodes de collecte défectueuses, ou à des règles en matière de confidentialité qui empêchent de révéler le nom du pays partenaire. Pour l'APD et les autres opérations entreprises par le secteur public des pays du CAD et par les organismes multilatéraux, les montants qui ne font pas l'objet d'une répartition géographique sont trop peu importants dans l'ensemble pour entraîner une sous-estimation significative du chiffre relatif à un pays bénéficiaire donné. Toutefois, les montants importants non ventilés d'APD des pays arabes membres de l'OPEP[4] et la couverture variable des apports bilatéraux de ressources assorties de conditions non libérales en provenance de pays donneurs arabes peuvent se traduire par une distorsion importante pour certains pays bénéficiaires. Pour certaines catégories d'apports du secteur privé, en particulier l'investissement privé, la sous-estimation de l'apport net reçu par un pays donné peut être assez importante. C'est surtout le cas :

a) Des pays où des investissements sont effectués dans le secteur pétrolier ;

b) Des pays pour lesquels une partie importante des apports reçus sous forme d'investissements provient de pays dont les notifications comprennent d'importants montants non ventilés par pays. Dans cette dernière catégorie se trouvent en particulier le Canada, le Danemark, la Finlande, la Nouvelle-Zélande, la Suède et la Suisse.

c) Des pays pour lesquels les investissements des pays Membres du CAD ont été acheminés par l'intermédiaire d'un centre financier qui ne notifie pas au CAD, bien que la transaction avec le centre concerné ait fait l'objet d'une déclaration.

PRÉSENTATION

8.   Le rapport comprend trois sections :

Section A

9.   Cette section contient huit tableaux couvrant la période 1984 à 1990. Ces tableaux indiquent pour chaque pays ou territoire en développement, y compris ceux qui ne font pas l'objet d'une page à part dans la section B :

i) L'aide publique au développement : versements nets.

ii) L'aide publique au développement : engagements.

iii) Les apports totaux de ressources : versements nets.

en provenance, d'une part, de l'ensemble des pays du CAD, et d'autre part de l'ensemble des sources.

Deux tableaux présentent, pour chaque bénéficiaire, le montant en provenance des organismes multilatéraux des versements nets d'aide à des conditions libérales (« APD multilatérale ») et des versements nets totaux.

Chaque tableau de cette section présente un état récapitulatif des ressources reçues par différents groupes de pays en développement (voir l'annexe, paragraphe A21). Ces données font aussi l'objet d'une présentation graphique.

Section B

10.   Les tableaux de cette section concernent *chacun un seul pays en développement*[6] et indiquent les ressources qu'il a reçues, ventilées par types et par donneurs, avec des sous-totaux pour les Membres du CAD, les organismes multilatéraux et les donneurs arabes : les données pour l'ensemble des versements des PECO sont indiquées sous la rubrique « autres agrégats ». Les tableaux par pays sont complétés par des tableaux de même format présentant les mêmes informations pour des *groupes de pays en développement* (voir l'annexe, paragraphe A21).

Couverture

Tableaux détaillés présentant pour les différents pays bénéficiaires les ressources reçues, ventilées par origine

11.   La présentation des tableaux dans la section B est normalisée. Deux pages sont utilisées pour chaque pays. Elles contiennent chacune trois panneaux dans lesquels sont ventilées les catégories suivantes d'apports par origine[6] :

1. Apports totaux nets (4 + 12 + Privé) ;
2. Prêts APD bruts ;
3. Apports totaux bruts du secteur public (7 + 9) ;

4. APD, total net (5 + 8);
5. Prêts APD nets;
6. Apports totaux nets du secteur public (4 + 12);
7. APD, total brut;
8. Dons (11 compris);
9. Autres apports bruts du secteur public;
10. Engagements de l'APD;
11. Dons au titre de la coopération technique (inclus en 8);
12. Autres apports nets du secteur public;
13. Engagements du FPD ventilés par secteur;
14. Elément de libéralité des engagements de l'APD;
15. Autres agrégats (y compris le secteur privé);

12. Dans chacun des pavés d'un tableau, les apports des différents Membres du CAD et des institutions multilatérales sont indiqués séparément, avec des sous-totaux concernant respectivement l'ensemble des Membres du CAD, l'ensemble des organismes multilatéraux, l'ensemble des pays arabes membres de l'OPEP, et la Communauté économique européenne et ses membres en tant que groupe. On a considéré que les données relatives aux donneurs arabes sont comparables à celles concernant les Membres du CAD et les organismes multilatéraux, bien que leur couverture et leur qualité soient quelque peu différentes. Le montant total obtenu de cette façon ne comprend ni les apports financiers en provenance du FMI (à part les prêts du Fonds fiduciaire, FAS et FASR), ni ceux des Pays de l'Europe centrale et orientale (pour lesquels, toutefois, les données relatives aux engagements et versements bruts sont présentées dans le pavé du bas à droite : voir « Autres agrégats » ci-dessous), ni les apports d'autres pays en développement, ni les dons des organismes privés bénévoles. Les prêts consentis par les banques ayant leur siège dans chaque pays Membre du CAD sont inclus indistinctement dans les données du pavé « Recettes totales, nettes ». Le montant ainsi inclus pour l'ensemble des Membres du CAD est inférieur aux chiffres présentés pour mémoire dans le pavé « Autres agrégats », concernant les prêts du secteur bancaire; la différence correspond aux prêts bancaires consentis à partir des centres financiers et à certains autres ajustements (voir l'Annexe paragraphe A17).

13. Dans la section B, les données relatives aux engagements sont présentées dans quatre pavés : engagements d'APD (dons plus prêts), élément de libéralité (« élément-don ») des prêts d'APD, engagements de FPD ventilés par objet et, sous l'entête « autres agrégats », engagements totaux, toutes sources. Les chiffres en dollars dans le premier pavé proviennent des réponses aux questionnaires du CAD. Les pourcentages présentés dans les deux pavés suivants sont tirés des déclarations reçues dans le cadre du Système de notification des pays créanciers (SNPC).

14. Un bloc à part pour chaque bénéficiaire, toutes sources confondues, présente la ventilation sectorielle des engagements de Financement public du développement (FPD). La liste des secteurs se rapporte au secteur économique de destination (c'est-à-dire au secteur spécifique de l'économie ou de la structure sociale du pays bénéficiaire dont l'aide favorise ou est destinée à favoriser le développement), et non pas au type des biens ou services reçus par le bénéficiaire. Le contenu détaillé de chaque rubrique est présenté ci-après :

Education : Ce secteur couvre l'infrastructure, les services et les investissements dans l'éducation. La formation portant sur un domaine particulier, comme l'agriculture ou la tech-nologie industrielle, sera classée en regard du secteur intéressé. Les activités de formation qui font référence aux apports des ressources humaines (enseignants, volontaires, experts) figurent dans la Coopération technique.

Santé : Ce secteur couvre l'aide fournie pour les objets suivants : les hôpitaux et dispensaires, y compris les établissements spécialisés comme les sanatoriums pour tuberculeux; la protection maternelle et infantile; les autres services médicaux et dentaires, y compris la lutte contre les maladies et les épidémies, les programmes de vaccination, les soins infirmiers, la fourniture de médicaments, les services de démonstration relatifs à la santé, etc.; l'administration de la santé publique et les programmes d'assurance-maladie.

Infrastructure et services sociaux : Est classée dans ce secteur l'aide fournie pour la construction de logements, urbains et ruraux, le développement communautaire et les équipements collectifs.

Energie : Cette rubrique recouvre à la fois la production et la distribution d'énergie, y compris les utilisations pacifiques de l'énergie nucléaire.

Distribution d'eau et assainissement : Ce secteur regroupe toute l'aide fournie pour la distribution d'eau, son utilisation et l'assainissement, mais à l'exclusion des systèmes d'irrigation pour l'agriculture.

Télécommunications : Sont notifiés ici les montants affectés aux communications et télécommunications, y compris la radio et la télévision, mais à l'exclusion de la presse et du cinéma.

Transports (et navigation) : Groupent les engagements portant sur la fourniture de matériel ou la création d'infrastructures pour les transports par route, par rail, par eau et par air.

Agriculture : Comprend les concours accordés pour le développement de la culture et de l'élevage, la fourniture de moyens de production tels que matériel agricole et engrais, les concours fournis pour l'irrigation, la lutte contre les ennemis des cultures, les services vétérinaires; services agricoles, exploitation forestière (y compris arboriculture) et pêche; conservation du sol et extension des terres cultivables; construction de bâtiments agricoles, stockage et moyens de transport pour l'agriculture; études géodésiques et pédologiques, utilisation des sols et des ressources en eau; les banques de développement agricole sont incluses ici.

Industries extractives : L'aide aux industries extractives, y compris la mise en valeur des ressources naturelles, géologie, prospection, études géologiques, le pétrole et le gaz naturel est regroupée dans cette rubrique.

Industries manufacturières : Ce secteur comprend les industries manufacturières de toutes sortes, y compris raffinage du pétrole et des minerais, transformation des produits alimentaires et autres produits agricoles, fabrication d'engrais et de matériel agricole; l'artisanat et le stockage et entreposage de produits non agricoles.

Commerce, banque et tourisme : Ce secteur regroupe : la promotion des exportations, le commerce et la distribution; banque (y compris les banques de développement industriel) et les hôtels et autres installations touristiques.

Coopération technique : Activités financées par un pays donneur ayant pour but essentiel d'élever le niveau des connaissances, des qualifications, du savoir-faire technique ou des aptitudes productives de la population des pays en développement, c'est-à-dire d'accroître le stock de capital intellectuel de ces pays, ou leur aptitude à utiliser plus efficacement leur dotation de facteurs. En conséquence, la coopération technique concerne principalement les activités comportant l'apport de ressources humaines (enseignants, volontaires, experts) ou des actions ciblées sur les ressources humaines (enseignement, formation, conseils).

Destination plurisectorielle : Cette rubrique comprend l'aide à des projets, autres que les plans d'aménagement de bassins hydrographiques, qui chevauchent plusieurs secteurs et visent essentiellement des installations de production.

Aide aux programmes : Cette rubrique englobe toutes les contributions, autres que le réaménagement de la dette, mises à la disposition du bénéficiaire sans affectation préalable à un secteur, par exemple pour le soutien de la balance des paiements ou du budget, les fonds accordés pouvant être consacrés à des projets d'équipement que le bénéficiaire choisit sans solliciter l'accord du donneur. L'aide à l'ajustement structurel non affecté à un secteur est également incluse dans cette rubrique.

Réaménagements de dette : Toutes les opérations d'effacement, de rééchelonnement ou de refinancement de dettes.

Aide alimentaire : La fourniture d'aliments dans le cadre de programmes bilatéraux, y compris l'aide alimentaire d'urgence.

Aide d'urgence (sauf aide alimentaire) : Les secours d'urgence, en espèces ou en nature, à l'exception de l'aide alimentaire, mais y compris l'aide aux réfugiés.

Non spécifié : Toutes formes d'aide qui ne peuvent pas être portées dans une autre partie du tableau ainsi que, dans le cas de l'aide à des projets ou de l'aide sectorielle, les engagements dont le secteur de destination reste à préciser au moment de la déclaration.

Autres agrégats

15. Sous cette rubrique figurent, pour chaque pays étudié, des renseignements supplémentaires sur certaines catégories d'apports de ressources qui ne sont pas ventilées en détail dans les autres pavés. Les agrégats ont été choisis de manière à compléter les renseignements relatifs aux différents pays, dans la perspective de l'utilisation des données à des fins analytiques ou ayant trait aux mesures à envisager. Les données supplémentaires concernent les principaux types d'opérations entreprises par des résidents des pays Membres du CAD relevant du secteur privé ; les engagements (APD + AASP) souscrits par le secteur public ; les conditions dont sont assortis les engagements d'APD souscrits soit par l'ensemble des Membres du CAD, soit par l'ensemble des sources d'aide, et les versements bruts et engagements des PECO en tant que groupe.

Section C : Indicateurs économiques

16. Des données sont indiquées pour deux indicateurs :
  - PNB par habitant, méthode de l'Atlas de la Banque mondiale ;
  - Population.

Elles peuvent être rapprochées des statistiques sur les apports financiers figurant dans les sections A et B. Elles portent sur les années 1984 à 1989, ou la dernière année disponible. La présentation est identique à celle de la section A.

17. Les indicateurs sont calculés conformément aux définitions de la BIRD, qui est la source des données (voir paragraphe 4 ci-dessus), et aux publications de laquelle le lecteur pourra utilement se référer.

Concepts et interprétation des données

18. On trouvera en fin de volume une note récapitulant les principaux concepts utilisés, ainsi que des remarques portant sur des aspects particuliers des données contenues dans le rapport.

Date de notification

19. Les données nationales ont été fournies par les Membres jusqu'au 17 janvier 1992.

NOTES ET RÉFÉRENCES

16. On trouvera d'autres données agrégées dans le rapport annuel du Président du CAD « Coopération pour le développement – Efforts et politiques poursuivis par les Membres du Comité d'aide au développement, Examen 1990 ».

17. Tous les pays du CAD à l'exception de l'Australie, de l'Espagne et de la Nouvelle-Zélande, et certains centres financiers effectuant des déclarations à la BRI.

18. Voir annexe : Définition des concepts utilisés dans ce rapport.

19. Entre 35 et 40 pour cent de l'aide bilatérale arabe est « non ventilée » géographiquement, selon les années.

20. Le lecteur trouvera dans la section A les principaux agrégats concernant des pays qui ne font pas l'objet d'une page à part dans la section B. Les autres données, indiquées dans la Section B pour les pays qui ne figurent pas, sont disponibles sur demande.

21. Une traduction française de certains termes est donnée sur le dépliant à la fin du rapport.

ABBREVIATIONS

AfDB	=	African Development Bank
AfDF	=	African Development Fund
AFESD	=	Arab Fund for Economic and Social Development
AsDB	=	Asian Development Bank
BADEA	=	Arab Bank for Economic Development in Africa
BIS	=	Bank for International Settlements
CarDB	=	Caribbean Development Bank
CEECs	=	Central Eastern European Countries
DAC	=	Development Assistance Committee
EEC	=	European Economic Commission
ESAF	=	Enhanced Structural Adjustment Facility (IMF)
FTC	=	Free-standing Technical Co-operation
IBRD	=	International Bank for Reconstruction and Development
IDA	=	International Development Association
IDB	=	Inter-American Development Bank
IFAD	=	International Fund for Agricultural Development
IMF	=	International Monetary Fund
IFC	=	International Finance Corporation
IRTC	=	Investment-related Technical Co-operation
LDCs	=	Developing Countries
LICs	=	Low-income countries
LLDCs	=	Least Developed Countries
LMICs	=	Lower Middle-Income Countries
ODA	=	Official Development Assistance
ODF	=	Official Development Finance
OFID	=	OPEC Fund for International Development
OOF	=	Other Official Flows
OPEC	=	Organisation of Petrol Exporting Countries
SAF	=	Structural Adjustment Facility (IMF)
TC	=	Technical Co-operation
UMICs	=	Upper Middle-Income countries
UNDP	=	United Nations Development Programme
UNFPA	=	United Nations Fund for Population Assistance
UNHCR	=	United Nations High Commissioner for Refugees
UNICEF	=	United Nations Children's Fund
UNRWA	=	United Nations Relief and Works Agency
UNTA	=	United Nations Regular Programme of Technical Assistance
WFP	=	World Food Programme

ABRÉVIATIONS

AASP   = Autres apports du secteur public
APD   = Aide publique au développement
ATNU   = Programme régulier d'assistance technique de l'Organisation des Nations Unies
AASP   = Autres apports du secteur public
BADEA   = Banque arabe pour le développement économique en Afrique
BAfd   = Banque africaine de développement
BAsD   = Banque asiatique de développement
BID   = Banque interaméricaine de développement
BIRD   = Banque mondiale
BRI   = Banque de règlements internationaux
CAD   = Comité d'aide au développement
CARIBANK   = Banque de développement des Caraïbes
CEE   = Commission des communautés européennes
CT   = Coopération technique
CTP   = Coopération technique pure
CTAPE   = Coopération technique associée à un projet d'équipement
FADES   = Fonds arabe pour le développement économique et social
FAfD   = Fonds africain de développement
FAS   = Facilité d'ajustement structurel (FMI)
FASR   = Facilité d'ajustement structurel renforcée (FMI)
FIDA   = Fonds international de développement agricole
FISE   = Fonds des Nations Unies pour l'enfance
FPD   = Financement public du développement
FNUAP   = Fonds des Nations Unies pour la population
FODI   = Fonds de l'OPEP pour le développement international
HCR   = Haut commissariat des nations pour les réfugiés
IDA   = Association internationale du développement
OPEP   = Organisation des pays exportateurs de pétrole
PAN   = Programme alimentaire mondial
PECO   = Pays de l'Europe centrale et orientale
PFR   = Pays à faible revenu
PMA   = Pays les moins avancés
PNUD   = Programme des Nations Unies pour le développement
PRITI   = Pays à revenu intermédiaire, tranche inférieure
PRITS   = Pays à revenu intermédiaire, tranche supérieure
SFI   = Société financière internationale
UNRWA   = Office de secours et de travaux des Nations Unies pour les réfugiés de Palestine dans le Proche-Orient

EDITOR'S NOTE

1.   For data on outstanding debt, the reader is referred to the annual OECD report on "External Debt Statistics: Debt and Other External Liabilities of Developing, CEEC and Certain Other Countries and Territories", issued in November and for detailed data on debt and debt service, "Financing and External Debt of Developing Countries", issued toward the middle of the following year. Claims held by banks and non-bank trade creditors, including short term debt, are published jointly by the OECD and the Bank for International Settlements semiannually with a lag of 6-7 months.

2.   The following is drawn to the attention of users:

   – The disbursements data for CEEC countries have been revised, in some cases by significant amounts.

   – Reporting of 1990 data on commitments and private flows was incomplete for Austria, Belgium, Germany, New Zealand and the Netherlands.

   – Commitments by Sweden to certain countries are significantly understated.

   – ODA net disbursement data for 1990 include forgiveness of non-ODA debt whose eligibility for inclusion was under review when this report went to press.

3.   The deflators below (division factors) *for DAC countries combined* will enable the reader to make a rough adjustment of the dollar values shown in this report to correct them for, respectively, exchange rate changes against the dollar, and the combined effect of exchange rate and price changes.

	1987	1988	1989	1990
a) to correct for exchange rate changes only	100.8	104.8	100.0	104.2
b) to correct for exchange rate and price changes (i.e. to convert to real terms)	94.3	101.3	100.0	111.2

4.   The category "Least developed countries" (LLDCs) defined by the United Nations comprises 42 countries. The data shown for the group are for all 42 countries, irrespective of the date at which they were included in the category; the historical record has been modified to include countries which were classified as LLDCs after the year concerned.

NOTE DE L'ÉDITEUR

1.   Pour des données détaillées sur l'Endettement extérieur et le service de la dette, le lecteur consultera utilement le rapport annuel de l'OCDE « Statistiques de la dette extérieure, endettement et autres engagements des pays et territoires en développement, des PECO et de certains autres pays et territoires », qui paraît en décembre, ainsi que, pour des données détaillées sur l'endettement et le service de la dette « le financement de l'endettement externe des pays en développement » qui paraît vers le milieu de l'année suivante. Les données sur les créances détenues par les banques et les créanciers non bancaires relatives à leurs opérations commerciales, ainsi que sur la dette à court terme, sont publiées conjointement par l'OCDE et la Banque des règlements internationaux semestriellement, avec un décalage de six à sept mois par rapport à la date à laquelle se réfèrent les données.

2.   L'attention du lecteur est attirée sur les points suivants :

   – Les données concernant les versements et les engagements des PECO ont été révisées, dans certains cas dans des proportions importantes.

   – Les déclarations relatives à 1990 sur les engagements et sur les apports du secteur privé de l'Allemagne, l'Autriche, de la Belgique, de la Nouvelle-Zélande et des Pays-Bas sont incomplètes.

   – Les données relatives aux engagements de la Suède envers certains bénéficiaires sous-estiment de manière importante les montants réellement consentis.

   – Les versements nets d'APD en 1990 comprennent l'annulation de dettes non APD. L'inclusion de ces données est encore en considération par le CAD.

3.   Les déflateurs suivants (facteurs de division) concernant l'ensemble des pays du CAD permettront au lecteur d'ajuster approximativement les valeurs en dollars présentées dans ce rapport, pour tenir compte des variations des taux de change par rapport au dollar, et dans l'effet combiné, des variations des taux de change et des prix.

		1987	1988	1989	1990
a)	pour tenir compte des seules variations des taux de change	100.8	104.8	100.0	104.2
b)	pour tenir compte des variations des taux de change et des prix (et obtenir ainsi les données en termes réels)	94.3	101.3	100.0	111.9

4.   La catégorie « Les pays les moins avancés » (PMA) définie par les Nations Unies comprend désormais 42 pays ; Les données présentées dans ce rapport pour ce groupe recouvrent l'ensemble de ces 42 pays, c'est-à-dire que la série chronologique pour ce groupe a été modifiée afin d'y inclure des pays qui n'ont été classés comme PMA qu'après l'année à laquelle se réfèrent les données.

BASIC SUMMARY TABLES

TABLEAUX RESUMES DE BASE

	1984	1985	1986	1987	1988	1989	1990
EUROPE							
Albania	–	–	–	–	3.4	7.3	9.0
Cyprus	4.1	20.7	23.5	23.0	18.5	20.5	18.4
Gibraltar	11.0	28.9	20.8	14.6	16.2	0.5	0.6
Greece	8.1	6.9	15.2	30.7	32.4	27.4	32.9
Malta	4.3	5.6	0.9	0.3	-0.7	-3.7	0.9
Turkey	188.7	136.7	234.7	385.5	302.6	189.2	598.2
Yugoslavia	-1.4	6.8	14.4	29.9	36.2	36.5	39.5
Other Europe	80.8	98.9	120.9	30.6	65.8	64.6	54.4
Europe Unallocated	6.5	7.5	0.4	4.0	2.6	16.4	29.6
TOTAL	**302.0**	**312.0**	**430.9**	**518.4**	**477.1**	**358.7**	**783.5**
NORTH OF SAHARA							
Algeria	112.1	142.0	119.4	137.4	120.0	89.4	185.7
Egypt	1650.6	1680.8	1566.2	1574.8	1432.8	1408.9	3169.8
Libya	2.2	3.2	8.4	2.5	1.9	6.9	7.6
Morocco	247.7	317.8	292.1	350.0	402.2	389.1	562.1
Tunisia	140.7	121.7	147.1	200.9	235.8	177.7	213.1
North of Sahara Unall.	2.7	13.4	-0.2	21.0	13.2	18.8	4.0
TOTAL	**2156.0**	**2278.9**	**2132.9**	**2286.6**	**2205.9**	**2090.8**	**4142.3**
SOUTH OF SAHARA							
Angola	59.6	59.6	93.8	97.8	106.1	87.9	142.6
Benin	39.7	47.7	72.5	77.0	93.2	149.4	125.6
Botswana	64.9	59.1	82.0	124.3	125.4	120.0	121.2
Burkina Faso	122.2	122.2	175.3	195.6	218.8	199.0	238.3
Burundi	70.4	77.2	89.8	87.5	83.3	89.5	156.8
Cameroon	154.7	126.3	176.5	180.1	240.0	300.6	321.7
Cape Verde	39.3	40.8	76.3	62.6	59.4	48.5	54.2
Central African Rep.	68.3	61.6	84.9	108.8	107.4	99.3	99.9
Chad	58.9	95.8	102.2	119.6	146.0	128.1	178.1
Comoros	18.2	18.0	20.8	33.1	34.5	31.8	30.6
Congo	67.3	46.9	100.7	131.3	76.6	79.1	197.7
Cote d'Ivoire	114.2	110.5	137.9	221.3	226.3	260.1	530.2
Djibouti	48.5	46.4	64.6	59.5	71.2	63.9	88.3
Equatorial Guinea	8.0	6.9	10.5	21.7	23.8	19.6	20.2
Ethiopia	187.2	416.3	396.9	312.8	559.9	377.8	503.1
Gabon	67.4	51.9	58.7	70.5	98.7	121.0	126.8
Gambia	32.3	31.2	59.1	50.8	54.7	56.1	56.1
Ghana	95.3	95.9	120.6	130.6	235.8	350.4	261.7
Guinea	42.2	59.8	97.6	119.7	159.5	191.7	138.9
Guinea-Bissau	30.6	24.3	40.6	47.8	47.7	53.4	62.1
Kenya	294.4	328.9	382.8	444.1	609.9	620.6	735.2
Lesotho	66.0	51.5	56.0	62.5	70.1	68.8	85.1
Liberia	107.5	64.3	69.1	51.7	48.3	38.5	42.2
Madagascar	97.5	99.4	176.2	181.3	213.5	175.4	268.2
Malawi	51.7	52.9	85.0	170.2	181.4	181.7	216.0
Mali	223.7	251.3	203.8	222.4	260.0	300.6	312.2
Mauritania	68.7	100.3	105.1	97.5	111.0	160.3	106.1
Mauritius	24.4	22.2	47.8	49.6	44.9	50.0	75.5
Mayotte	13.8	19.8	26.1	37.7	43.5	43.3	58.5
Mozambique	190.1	216.9	319.2	534.7	731.1	546.1	690.6
Namibia	–	2.8	6.6	15.7	17.2	36.1	39.4
Niger	101.9	206.4	183.8	215.0	241.9	199.7	254.3
Nigeria	14.7	15.9	39.1	51.0	97.0	309.8	172.6
Reunion	328.9	351.9	441.1	543.4	570.9	678.4	920.7
Rwanda	96.0	103.2	123.7	137.8	137.2	131.6	182.2
St. Helena	10.0	12.1	13.5	20.1	27.0	47.2	23.3
Sao Tome & Principe	4.0	3.0	7.0	4.3	8.0	11.0	15.0
Senegal	245.7	196.5	315.7	358.8	367.8	536.4	581.7
Seychelles	13.6	12.2	20.7	18.8	17.8	15.1	31.6
Sierra Leone	22.6	30.3	51.3	43.8	52.5	72.2	39.9
Somalia	193.1	163.2	353.9	398.5	311.3	266.9	259.8
Sudan	309.0	647.2	468.7	442.9	500.6	434.3	418.7
Swaziland	17.6	18.2	24.8	29.7	22.6	11.6	36.1
Tanzania	409.8	372.6	513.9	719.3	785.6	687.6	837.5
Togo	53.1	53.3	91.7	85.9	128.2	108.0	154.9
Uganda	47.2	42.3	77.3	86.8	188.0	158.9	243.4
Zaire	209.4	209.6	296.1	338.5	400.3	432.9	628.5
Zambia	181.8	215.4	349.1	346.3	407.4	314.2	408.9
Zimbabwe	243.6	214.2	191.3	265.3	233.1	227.5	295.8
East African Community	2.5	10.8	1.8	1.2	0.8	–	–
DOM/TOM Unallocated	–	–	–	–	–	–	–
EAMA Unallocated	59.4	–	–	–	–	–	–
South of Sahara Unall.	125.5	262.1	371.4	498.5	526.7	528.9	558.1
TOTAL	**5216.1**	**5949.1**	**7474.5**	**8725.5**	**10123.5**	**10220.7**	**12146.3**
Africa Unspecified	143.8	187.2	162.1	200.9	202.7	342.5	273.3
AFRICA TOTAL	**7515.9**	**8415.3**	**9769.5**	**11213.0**	**12532.1**	**12654.0**	**16561.9**
N.& C. AMERICA							
Aruba	–	12.0	40.4	20.8	19.3	24.2	28.9
Bahamas	8.0	0.1	0.2	0.1	0.1	0.2	0.4

	1984	1985
Barbados	4.7	5.0
Belize	12.5	20.3
Bermuda	0.0	0.0
Costa Rica	185.7	238.9
Cuba	6.4	2.5
Dominican Republic	142.3	162.1
El Salvador	227.6	306.4
Guadeloupe	118.1	147.6
Guatemala	40.5	62.4
Haiti	71.0	102.6
Honduras	170.9	207.7
Jamaica	156.0	158.2
Martinique	231.8	268.6
Mexico	75.3	122.6
Netherlands Antilles	55.9	62.3
Nicaragua	71.7	67.2
Panama	56.8	44.5
St. Pierre & Miquelon	17.6	17.1
Trinidad & Tobago	1.5	0.8
Anguilla	1.5	1.5
Antigua and Barbuda	1.5	2.1
Cayman Islands	0.0	-0.1
Dominica	11.1	9.3
Grenada	22.8	30.6
Montserrat	1.8	1.7
St. Kitts-Nevis	1.6	2.3
St. Lucia	2.9	2.4
St. Vincent and Gr.	1.1	1.7
Turks & Caicos Isl.	5.3	4.7
Virgin Islands	1.1	1.5
West Indies Unall.	8.8	9.0
DOM/TOM Unallocated	–	–
N.& C. America Unall.	61.5	114.1
TOTAL	**1775.3**	**2190.0**
SOUTH AMERICA		
Argentina	25.6	31.0
Bolivia	109.6	126.4
Brazil	140.0	64.2
Chile	9.7	45.8
Colombia	41.6	36.7
Ecuador	61.4	70.8
Falkland Islands	8.0	13.8
Guiana	65.9	76.0
Guyana	6.4	6.0
Paraguay	33.1	28.3
Peru	241.6	285.7
Suriname	1.5	3.0
Uruguay	4.2	5.8
Venezuela	15.0	13.4
South America Unall.	10.9	28.5
TOTAL	**774.5**	**835.4**
America Unspecified	75.9	91.9
AMERICA TOTAL	**2625.6**	**3117.2**
MIDDLE EAST		
Bahrain	0.6	0.8
Iran	2.0	1.0
Iraq	-0.4	20.6
Israel	1255.9	1978.3
Jordan	63.8	70.5
Kuwait	3.4	3.2
Lebanon	54.9	44.7
Oman	6.5	14.7
Qatar	0.5	0.6
Saudi Arabia	26.6	17.2
Syria	15.2	13.1
United Arab Emirates	2.4	1.8
Yemen	87.5	94.8
Middle East Unall.	18.1	40.8
TOTAL	**1537.1**	**2302.0**
SOUTH ASIA		
Afghanistan	-1.0	6.9
Bangladesh	674.5	621.9
Bhutan	4.8	6.6
India	633.8	515.9
Maldives	3.4	6.9
Myanmar (Burma)	148.8	253.2
Nepal	98.4	123.5
Pakistan	302.7	427.9
Sri Lanka	318.7	334.1

1986	1987	1988	1989	1990
2.8	4.3	2.3	0.5	1.4
22.4	21.5	16.6	18.4	18.8
0.0	0.1	0.0	0.1	42.1
164.8	208.2	163.7	205.6	203.8
3.7	6.7	2.9	10.6	16.1
62.9	101.9	99.3	120.8	71.5
316.9	404.9	380.9	365.5	308.7
153.6	174.4	253.1	219.4	310.5
111.3	214.2	193.0	209.6	149.2
126.4	149.9	101.4	138.6	116.4
239.8	222.5	252.1	201.7	377.5
161.1	146.4	173.0	225.9	251.9
341.2	391.0	447.8	606.9	841.6
247.2	150.3	140.1	77.2	125.2
56.3	61.9	51.0	57.0	53.0
104.6	111.1	166.6	182.8	273.7
28.2	26.7	19.2	14.2	90.1
21.1	28.2	35.6	32.9	30.5
16.4	32.8	2.7	1.6	6.1
2.6	2.9	3.0	3.4	2.4
4.4	4.8	5.3	3.4	2.9
-0.1	1.2	11.5	-0.1	2.1
7.0	5.1	9.1	11.5	10.8
16.9	10.1	7.6	4.8	5.0
3.3	2.3	4.2	6.8	7.8
1.8	4.0	10.4	10.7	5.0
1.9	6.0	7.2	11.8	6.2
8.4	5.3	6.2	6.4	5.2
8.0	9.1	7.7	8.7	8.9
1.3	1.0	1.0	3.7	3.0
23.2	67.6	54.2	53.9	53.5
–	–	–	–	–
76.7	41.6	49.4	26.6	41.7
2376.2	2638.9	2697.3	2865.0	3471.8
57.8	62.2	113.6	179.3	153.7
196.6	213.0	227.8	302.6	344.8
132.6	256.3	192.2	193.3	141.4
-0.4	23.4	46.1	50.3	76.9
36.7	67.8	60.3	49.0	78.8
85.6	154.1	99.9	125.9	114.6
15.0	13.3	7.6	6.0	1.8
106.1	138.3	130.4	110.3	113.2
9.1	14.9	15.6	26.8	35.8
45.6	54.4	63.0	88.4	46.6
250.5	261.3	244.1	263.4	343.9
3.3	8.6	14.7	45.0	51.2
25.3	12.1	29.8	25.7	34.9
17.2	19.4	17.6	20.0	75.3
18.1	10.0	8.9	31.9	19.0
999.1	1309.1	1271.6	1518.0	1631.9
109.0	172.7	170.0	216.0	208.4
3484.3	4120.7	4138.9	4599.0	5312.0
1.5	1.1	1.1	3.2	1.9
13.4	46.9	52.1	60.0	34.3
20.9	79.3	-0.6	-5.3	-8.6
1937.0	1249.5	1239.4	1188.0	1370.6
109.5	171.5	122.9	130.5	431.2
3.7	2.1	4.4	2.1	2.2
38.5	65.4	99.1	83.2	71.6
29.4	15.2	13.9	16.9	11.3
1.5	1.7	1.1	3.0	1.3
19.7	10.8	12.8	9.2	12.8
41.4	88.9	168.3	108.8	69.4
32.7	113.2	-13.4	-7.3	2.8
116.7	162.4	168.6	195.1	168.8
7.1	35.2	44.2	19.6	30.8
2372.9	2043.1	1913.9	1806.9	2200.5
-1.7	37.7	66.8	82.4	100.1
760.9	926.7	930.9	972.3	1103.0
13.9	11.6	18.7	19.6	20.1
1014.9	950.0	949.5	1133.7	727.0
11.4	12.3	21.6	23.7	11.6
307.7	240.7	332.7	89.9	83.1
170.2	189.6	224.9	248.9	238.8
610.4	440.7	1003.7	682.2	653.5
388.2	326.1	436.0	397.3	403.8

	1984	1985	1986	1987	1988	1989	1990
South Asia Unall.	0.2	3.6	2.4	2.2	6.3	8.7	2.3
TOTAL	*2184.2*	*2300.5*	*3278.3*	*3137.6*	*3991.2*	*3658.7*	*3343.3*
FAR EAST ASIA							
Brunei	0.8	1.3	2.5	3.2	4.5	4.5	3.7
China	502.3	573.7	660.7	862.6	1196.2	1494.9	1416.4
Hong Kong	9.3	16.7	14.1	15.0	13.6	11.7	19.4
Indonesia	548.7	502.7	604.9	1122.5	1497.9	1703.7	1517.9
Kampuchea	8.4	5.6	5.7	8.9	9.8	17.8	28.3
Korea	-34.9	-8.1	-23.5	1.6	9.3	48.9	54.7
Korea, Dem.	–	0.4	1.1	10.2	4.5	3.3	0.9
Laos	13.8	15.5	19.2	30.4	36.2	42.9	51.2
Macao	0.1	0.1	0.1	0.1	0.2	0.2	0.1
Malaysia	299.3	202.6	174.5	352.2	96.7	132.0	458.6
Mongolia	0.1	0.4	0.6	0.6	0.7	1.6	6.3
Philippines	355.8	437.6	886.8	703.1	789.3	757.3	1100.3
Singapore	38.7	21.8	27.4	22.2	20.7	93.7	-3.2
Taiwan	-1.4	-2.1	-0.5	1.2	1.9	2.1	6.3
Thailand	357.1	385.5	390.8	435.8	514.1	657.4	731.5
Viet Nam	80.7	54.2	90.0	61.6	84.0	64.7	107.7
Far East Asia Unall.	26.3	21.7	30.8	27.0	47.1	49.5	95.1
TOTAL	*2205.2*	*2229.4*	*2885.1*	*3658.1*	*4326.4*	*5086.1*	*5595.4*
Asia Unspecified	53.3	57.2	80.8	62.4	114.1	74.8	102.6
ASIA TOTAL	*5979.7*	*6889.1*	*8617.1*	*8901.1*	*10345.6*	*10626.5*	*11241.7*
OCEANIA							
Cook Islands	7.4	8.8	25.5	9.7	10.9	11.1	10.1
Fiji	23.5	26.3	32.4	32.2	47.4	36.5	43.5
Kiribati	10.4	10.9	11.9	14.6	12.1	15.1	17.7
Nauru	0.0	0.1	0.0	0.1	0.2	0.1	0.2
New Caledonia	129.6	145.2	205.5	281.7	260.9	280.9	300.2
Niue	3.1	3.5	3.9	6.6	5.1	5.5	7.0
Pacif. Isl.(Fed. Sts.)	184.7	158.2	230.8	184.4	151.5	157.9	61.9
Papua New Guinea	294.9	240.6	242.9	254.8	307.4	314.3	320.0
Polynesia, French	171.6	170.5	247.2	293.4	326.6	286.0	258.0
Solomon Islands	13.7	13.5	19.4	22.1	34.8	37.9	31.1
Tokelau	1.7	1.6	1.8	1.6	3.4	4.3	4.4
Tonga	12.4	10.6	11.6	15.2	13.6	19.7	24.2
Tuvalu	5.2	3.2	3.8	24.9	13.3	5.7	4.8
Vanuatu	22.2	18.9	20.8	32.5	29.0	31.8	42.1
Wallis & Futuna	0.5	0.0	0.0	0.9	0.0	0.0	0.0
Western Samoa	11.0	13.2	18.1	21.8	22.0	20.5	27.7
TOM Unallocated	–	–	–	–	–	–	–
Oceania Unallocated	20.7	26.2	23.3	54.7	53.0	46.4	61.9
TOTAL	*912.4*	*851.0*	*1098.7*	*1251.0*	*1291.3*	*1273.6*	*1214.7*
LDCS Unspecified	2358.1	2333.0	2813.9	4011.7	4370.9	4716.5	5111.9
TOTAL,ALL LDCS	*19693.8*	*21917.6*	*26214.4*	*30015.9*	*33155.9*	*34228.1*	*40225.7*
INCOME GROUPS							
LLDCS	3924.8	4743.9	5661.6	6549.0	7518.1	6880.8	7716.7
OTHER LICS	6068.6	6212.8	8161.6	8682.8	10585.4	11356.2	13387.4
LMICS	2934.1	3028.8	3399.2	4168.0	4286.4	4408.3	5511.5
UMICS	3792.1	4725.1	5271.2	5405.6	5102.0	5432.4	7017.9
UNALLOCATED	2974.2	3206.9	3720.7	5210.5	5664.0	6150.4	6592.1

Legend:
- ⊕—⊕—⊕ LLDCS
- – · – · OTHER LICS
- ——— LMICS
- – – – UMICS

	1984	1985	1986	1987	1988	1989	1990
EUROPE							
Albania	–	–	–	–	5.6	10.4	11.0
Cyprus	17.4	37.3	35.3	41.4	44.1	40.6	36.7
Gibraltar	11.0	28.9	20.8	14.6	16.2	0.5	0.6
Greece	12.5	13.4	20.5	34.3	37.4	31.4	35.1
Malta	11.4	18.4	6.9	-1.4	-2.7	-5.2	4.5
Turkey	241.7	180.9	340.2	378.8	268.9	141.9	1264.7
Yugoslavia	2.9	10.6	18.6	35.1	43.9	42.9	47.7
Other Europe	97.5	102.4	139.1	63.6	106.5	77.9	66.6
Europe Unallocated	20.3	21.8	15.8	4.0	2.6	16.4	29.6
TOTAL	**414.7**	**413.5**	**597.1**	**570.4**	**522.6**	**356.7**	**1496.5**
NORTH OF SAHARA							
Algeria	121.8	173.0	165.1	214.4	171.4	152.4	226.8
Egypt	1775.3	1759.9	1716.0	1773.6	1537.3	1567.7	5604.2
Libya	5.0	5.4	10.9	6.6	5.6	16.9	20.2
Morocco	341.3	766.1	402.7	447.2	480.7	450.3	969.9
Tunisia	178.2	162.7	222.4	274.4	316.3	233.8	315.6
North of Sahara Unall.	2.7	13.4	-0.2	21.1	15.9	24.7	9.9
TOTAL	**2424.3**	**2880.5**	**2516.8**	**2737.3**	**2527.2**	**2445.9**	**7146.4**
SOUTH OF SAHARA							
Angola	95.0	91.5	131.1	135.0	158.9	148.2	211.7
Benin	76.5	94.7	138.1	137.7	161.6	262.8	261.5
Botswana	102.7	96.5	102.3	155.9	150.8	159.8	148.1
Burkina Faso	187.4	195.3	283.9	280.5	297.6	271.6	314.4
Burundi	139.8	139.4	187.6	202.2	187.9	195.7	264.9
Cameroon	183.5	153.0	224.8	212.5	284.5	458.3	483.1
Cape Verde	63.9	69.7	109.4	87.9	86.6	75.8	82.7
Central African Rep.	132.0	104.3	138.6	175.7	196.3	191.4	231.7
Chad	114.1	180.6	165.0	198.2	264.4	241.5	315.0
Comoros	41.0	47.6	46.3	54.3	51.9	44.7	42.4
Congo	96.7	69.1	110.2	151.8	88.8	91.3	209.4
Cote d'Ivoire	123.4	117.6	186.6	253.8	438.9	402.9	689.5
Djibouti	102.1	81.5	115.1	105.5	93.0	75.2	122.8
Equatorial Guinea	15.1	17.2	21.7	42.8	43.3	41.9	39.0
Ethiopia	361.4	710.2	635.5	633.5	969.9	751.8	888.2
Gabon	75.5	61.1	78.9	82.5	106.1	132.7	139.9
Gambia	53.0	49.6	101.0	100.1	82.1	92.4	95.1
Ghana	214.8	195.9	371.5	372.6	474.4	551.7	499.4
Guinea	121.2	115.2	174.9	213.4	261.9	346.3	292.0
Guinea-Bissau	55.2	57.7	71.0	110.9	98.8	101.7	122.3
Kenya	406.4	429.7	455.5	572.0	808.6	967.0	1083.7
Lesotho	100.2	93.3	87.8	107.5	108.0	127.2	137.8
Liberia	130.8	90.6	97.3	78.4	64.8	58.7	115.2
Madagascar	151.0	185.6	316.4	321.5	304.3	320.2	400.4
Malawi	182.0	113.0	198.4	280.5	366.0	411.6	478.7
Mali	319.0	376.2	372.2	366.0	427.4	453.9	473.8
Mauritania	173.7	206.7	224.7	184.6	184.4	242.1	210.6
Mauritius	33.7	26.8	56.2	65.0	59.3	58.3	89.0
Mayotte	14.0	20.8	28.3	38.8	43.5	43.3	58.5
Mozambique	259.1	300.1	421.3	650.8	892.9	771.7	946.1
Namibia	–	6.0	15.6	16.5	22.5	58.9	57.0
Niger	159.9	303.4	307.1	353.1	371.2	296.4	358.1
Nigeria	33.0	32.3	59.2	69.3	120.1	345.4	234.4
Reunion	346.3	383.5	505.7	574.3	608.1	698.6	940.9
Rwanda	164.7	179.6	210.7	244.8	251.9	232.6	287.0
St. Helena	10.0	12.2	13.5	20.1	27.1	47.2	23.4
Sao Tome & Principe	11.3	12.6	12.4	17.3	24.0	32.9	38.4
Senegal	365.1	288.7	566.9	641.6	568.6	649.6	788.4
Seychelles	15.1	22.2	28.6	24.2	20.7	19.8	35.1
Sierra Leone	58.7	64.9	87.1	68.4	104.4	100.3	70.1
Somalia	350.1	353.3	511.4	580.1	433.2	426.9	427.6
Sudan	618.7	1128.6	944.9	898.1	936.9	771.7	792.1
Swaziland	29.7	24.7	34.6	45.4	38.2	29.5	55.1
Tanzania	554.3	484.1	680.6	882.3	981.8	919.7	1154.9
Togo	108.8	111.5	174.3	125.3	199.4	182.8	210.2
Uganda	162.6	180.1	197.5	280.2	363.3	402.6	557.5
Zaire	302.6	305.9	448.1	627.0	575.7	634.3	822.9
Zambia	238.5	322.2	464.5	429.6	478.2	391.9	491.6
Zimbabwe	297.8	237.1	224.9	293.9	272.7	264.9	343.2
East African Community	2.5	10.8	1.8	1.2	0.8	–	–
DOM/TOM Unallocated	–	–	–	–	–	–	–
EAMA Unallocated	59.4	–	–	–	–	–	–
South of Sahara Unall.	197.7	471.4	392.3	513.2	648.3	706.8	745.0
TOTAL	**8211.1**	**9425.4**	**11533.2**	**13077.5**	**14801.6**	**15304.3**	**17879.4**
Africa Unspecified	739.9	389.1	383.1	453.9	365.2	536.0	486.1
AFRICA TOTAL	**11375.2**	**12695.0**	**14433.1**	**16268.7**	**17694.0**	**18286.2**	**25512.0**
N.& C. AMERICA							
Aruba	–	12.0	40.4	20.9	19.3	24.3	29.0
Bahamas	10.9	0.9	5.8	0.8	4.2	4.0	4.5

	1984	1985
Barbados	8.3	7.3
Belize	14.0	22.0
Bermuda	0.1	0.9
Costa Rica	217.6	280.1
Cuba	12.0	18.2
Dominican Republic	188.2	207.3
El Salvador	261.1	345.1
Guadeloupe	131.2	164.9
Guatemala	65.4	82.8
Haiti	133.0	149.7
Honduras	285.7	270.6
Jamaica	170.3	169.2
Martinique	247.3	293.4
Mexico	83.4	144.6
Netherlands Antilles	63.0	64.8
Nicaragua	113.7	102.4
Panama	72.1	69.2
St. Pierre & Miquelon	17.6	17.1
Trinidad & Tobago	4.6	6.6
Anguilla	1.7	2.7
Antigua and Barbuda	2.4	3.0
Cayman Islands	0.4	0.1
Dominica	16.6	16.9
Grenada	27.5	34.4
Montserrat	1.8	2.2
St. Kitts-Nevis	3.6	4.5
St. Lucia	5.7	7.0
St. Vincent and Gr.	4.0	5.5
Turks & Caicos Isl.	6.9	5.6
Virgin Islands	1.9	2.1
West Indies Unall.	8.8	9.1
DOM/TOM Unallocated	–	–
N.& C. America Unall.	67.7	121.4
TOTAL	**2248.4**	**2643.5**
SOUTH AMERICA		
Argentina	49.2	39.4
Bolivia	168.8	197.1
Brazil	160.8	122.8
Chile	2.5	40.4
Colombia	88.1	61.7
Ecuador	136.2	135.8
Falkland Islands	8.1	13.8
Guiana	70.4	89.9
Guyana	23.1	27.0
Paraguay	50.4	50.1
Peru	310.1	316.4
Suriname	5.1	11.0
Uruguay	3.9	4.9
Venezuela	14.1	11.2
South America Unall.	10.9	29.0
TOTAL	**1101.6**	**1150.4**
America Unspecified	151.8	181.1
AMERICA TOTAL	**3501.7**	**3975.0**
MIDDLE EAST		
Bahrain	199.3	72.4
Iran	12.9	16.5
Iraq	4.0	26.0
Israel	1255.9	1978.4
Jordan	687.0	537.7
Kuwait	4.5	4.2
Lebanon	77.4	83.2
Oman	66.7	78.0
Qatar	1.3	1.9
Saudi Arabia	35.7	28.8
Syria	640.9	609.8
United Arab Emirates	3.4	4.2
Yemen	425.8	391.6
Middle East Unall.	41.5	66.6
TOTAL	**3456.2**	**3899.2**
SOUTH ASIA		
Afghanistan	6.7	16.8
Bangladesh	1189.8	1130.8
Bhutan	17.9	24.1
India	1672.3	1592.0
Maldives	5.6	9.3
Myanmar (Burma)	269.0	345.7
Nepal	196.9	234.0
Pakistan	729.4	769.6
Sri Lanka	456.9	468.3

1986	1987	1988	1989	1990
3.8	6.4	3.2	2.2	3.0
24.1	23.6	25.1	28.6	28.8
0.1	0.2	0.0	0.1	42.1
195.7	228.5	186.8	225.6	227.5
18.0	29.7	19.5	23.7	33.4
92.6	129.5	117.7	142.4	93.1
340.7	426.1	419.5	443.5	346.6
205.6	181.4	266.2	232.0	323.0
134.8	240.8	235.0	260.6	198.8
175.3	218.0	146.7	199.9	183.2
283.5	258.0	321.5	242.5	448.2
177.8	167.7	192.6	262.2	280.2
380.4	398.6	461.4	618.6	853.3
251.6	155.5	172.9	86.1	139.8
57.5	64.5	53.4	61.3	57.4
150.3	140.8	213.1	225.0	323.8
52.2	40.5	21.9	17.5	92.4
21.1	28.3	35.6	32.9	30.5
19.1	34.4	8.6	6.0	10.3
3.0	4.1	3.9	6.5	5.6
5.1	5.6	8.5	4.4	4.1
2.0	2.2	12.1	1.3	3.5
11.0	14.4	17.0	23.2	19.8
24.5	19.7	20.5	15.1	13.9
3.8	3.4	5.7	7.1	8.5
5.5	7.5	14.0	13.2	7.7
11.7	10.9	17.6	18.3	12.6
12.4	13.4	16.6	15.0	13.7
8.9	9.6	8.0	8.8	10.1
1.5	2.3	2.0	5.8	5.1
31.5	105.0	78.1	77.6	77.3
–	–	–	–	–
83.1	45.3	85.3	45.2	60.3
2834.2	3037.3	3213.6	3380.4	3991.1
87.6	99.1	151.8	210.8	171.9
321.4	318.6	393.9	440.1	490.7
178.4	288.8	210.3	206.1	164.2
-5.1	21.4	44.0	61.1	94.2
63.5	77.9	61.6	67.1	87.0
146.5	203.5	136.4	159.6	153.7
15.0	13.3	7.6	6.0	1.8
137.1	147.0	145.3	118.9	121.9
30.7	28.7	27.1	44.2	108.9
66.4	80.9	75.4	92.2	56.5
271.5	292.2	272.2	304.9	392.3
13.6	22.3	21.4	50.9	57.5
26.7	17.8	40.8	38.4	46.6
16.0	18.7	17.7	20.8	79.0
22.9	22.7	34.0	64.6	51.7
1392.2	1652.7	1639.4	1885.6	2078.0
168.3	277.9	266.6	341.9	330.3
4394.7	4968.0	5119.7	5607.9	6399.4
99.6	0.3	-2.6	-2.7	101.0
26.9	71.1	81.5	96.3	68.5
33.3	91.4	9.6	11.2	51.8
1937.1	1250.8	1241.1	1191.6	1374.3
563.6	577.3	416.7	273.0	891.3
5.0	3.4	5.9	3.7	3.4
62.2	101.1	140.7	119.1	134.3
84.0	16.0	0.6	18.2	68.8
2.3	3.1	1.8	3.9	2.1
31.3	22.4	19.3	36.1	43.6
728.4	683.8	191.1	127.2	649.9
34.2	114.7	-12.0	-5.9	5.2
328.6	422.1	303.1	358.1	392.0
36.0	48.1	44.8	75.7	332.1
3972.5	3405.5	2441.5	2305.4	4118.2
2.3	45.0	72.4	167.0	143.1
1455.7	1635.7	1591.7	1800.8	2103.1
40.0	42.1	41.5	41.7	47.1
2119.5	1838.8	2097.3	1895.0	1586.0
16.3	18.6	27.5	28.2	22.1
415.7	367.3	450.9	183.9	170.5
300.9	346.8	399.0	493.6	428.8
970.3	879.4	1408.1	1129.5	1152.3
570.3	501.7	598.3	546.8	664.9

	1984	1985	1986	1987	1988	1989	1990
South Asia Unall.	0.2	103.6	128.6	14.8	32.3	23.2	16.8
TOTAL	4544.7	4694.2	6019.6	5690.7	6718.9	6309.8	6334.6

FAR EAST ASIA

	1984	1985	1986	1987	1988	1989	1990
Brunei	0.8	1.4	2.5	3.3	4.5	4.6	3.8
China	798.2	940.0	1133.9	1461.7	1988.9	2153.5	2076.2
Hong Kong	13.8	20.5	18.5	19.4	22.1	40.6	37.6
Indonesia	672.7	603.2	710.9	1245.9	1631.8	1839.2	1724.4
Kampuchea	16.9	12.9	13.2	14.2	18.5	30.3	41.6
Korea	-36.6	-8.6	-17.3	11.2	9.7	51.5	52.2
Korea, Dem.	–	5.7	5.6	16.9	10.3	8.6	8.4
Laos	34.1	37.0	48.2	58.3	77.0	139.3	151.7
Macao	0.5	0.4	0.4	0.1	0.4	0.3	0.2
Malaysia	326.6	229.2	192.0	363.4	103.7	140.2	469.6
Mongolia	0.1	3.3	4.6	3.0	3.1	6.4	13.1
Philippines	381.8	460.4	955.8	770.2	854.3	844.5	1276.7
Singapore	41.0	23.9	29.4	23.3	21.9	94.8	-3.0
Taiwan	5.4	-9.7	-10.1	-8.5	-6.9	2.1	36.3
Thailand	462.0	458.6	496.0	503.6	563.2	739.2	805.4
Viet Nam	108.6	114.0	146.5	111.0	147.8	129.0	190.3
Far East Asia Unall.	26.3	21.8	38.4	39.4	70.8	67.8	113.4
TOTAL	2852.4	2913.9	3768.3	4636.3	5520.9	6292.2	6997.9
Asia Unspecified	795.6	142.1	1701.4	1357.0	255.1	156.5	362.6
ASIA TOTAL	11648.8	11649.3	15461.8	15089.5	14936.4	15063.9	17813.4

OCEANIA

	1984	1985	1986	1987	1988	1989	1990
Cook Islands	8.1	9.7	26.4	11.0	12.0	12.6	12.3
Fiji	31.3	31.9	42.5	35.9	54.3	43.1	49.2
Kiribati	11.9	12.0	13.4	18.4	16.3	17.5	20.5
Nauru	0.0	0.1	0.0	0.1	0.2	0.1	0.2
New Caledonia	130.5	145.4	206.6	282.6	261.1	281.6	300.9
Niue	3.2	3.5	4.2	6.7	5.3	5.6	7.2
Pacif. Isl.(Fed. Sts.)	185.5	159.3	232.2	185.8	152.4	159.0	63.0
Papua New Guinea	320.1	257.2	263.4	322.7	379.6	339.3	376.3
Polynesia, French	172.0	172.0	247.6	294.5	331.2	288.6	260.6
Solomon Islands	19.4	20.8	30.1	57.1	58.3	49.2	44.2
Tokelau	1.8	1.8	2.0	1.8	3.7	4.6	4.8
Tonga	15.7	13.6	15.1	21.3	18.8	24.5	31.2
Tuvalu	5.5	3.3	4.4	25.7	14.0	6.9	5.0
Vanuatu	24.5	21.8	24.4	51.0	39.3	39.8	48.8
Wallis & Futuna	1.6	0.2	0.1	1.2	1.1	0.1	0.1
Western Samoa	20.0	19.1	23.3	35.2	30.7	31.3	50.7
TOM Unallocated	–	–	–	–	–	–	–
Oceania Unallocated	20.7	26.2	23.4	61.3	58.4	57.9	73.4
TOTAL	971.7	897.9	1159.0	1412.1	1436.4	1361.6	1348.5
LDCS Unspecified	3072.8	3432.5	3495.4	4748.8	6661.1	6604.8	7258.5
TOTAL,ALL LDCS	30984.9	33063.2	39541.3	43057.5	46370.1	47281.1	59828.2

INCOME GROUPS

	1984	1985	1986	1987	1988	1989	1990
LLDCS	7260.0	8352.5	9666.3	10900.2	11863.1	11791.6	13244.5
OTHER LICS	9065.3	9189.5	11948.7	12662.9	14806.8	15258.0	20241.9
LMICS	4410.4	4669.9	4930.5	5465.0	5159.8	5327.8	8139.0
UMICS	5030.6	5811.3	6473.8	6315.7	5921.2	6104.7	8255.9
UNALLOCATED	5218.7	5040.0	6522.0	7713.6	8619.2	8799.1	9946.9

Legend: LLDCS, OTHER LICS, LMICS, UMICS (years 1984–90, vertical axis 4000–22000)

	1984	1985	1986	1987	1988	1989	1990
EUROPE							
Albania	–	–	–	–	2.2	3.1	2.0
Cyprus	11.1	13.5	11.1	14.2	20.1	15.6	18.3
Gibraltar	–	–	–	–	–	–	–
Greece	4.5	6.5	5.3	3.7	5.0	4.0	2.2
Malta	1.4	0.3	1.6	0.7	1.6	2.2	1.7
Turkey	21.7	12.4	80.3	19.2	9.1	-4.8	-3.1
Yugoslavia	4.3	3.8	4.2	5.2	7.4	6.4	8.2
Other Europe	16.8	3.4	18.2	33.0	40.7	13.3	12.2
Europe Unallocated	13.8	14.3	15.4	–	–	–	–
TOTAL	*73.4*	*54.2*	*135.9*	*76.0*	*86.0*	*39.7*	*41.5*
NORTH OF SAHARA							
Algeria	9.7	22.0	17.8	25.3	24.1	40.7	36.1
Egypt	149.3	103.8	96.3	124.9	121.3	174.0	110.6
Libya	2.8	2.2	2.5	4.1	3.7	10.0	12.6
Morocco	20.1	44.4	41.1	35.8	57.2	63.6	49.1
Tunisia	29.0	35.7	36.5	46.4	77.1	60.8	51.1
North of Sahara Unall.	–	–	–	0.1	2.7	5.9	5.9
TOTAL	*211.0*	*208.0*	*194.1*	*236.6*	*286.1*	*355.0*	*265.4*
SOUTH OF SAHARA							
Angola	34.3	31.9	36.5	35.7	50.3	57.8	69.1
Benin	37.0	44.1	62.9	60.0	67.4	108.4	135.9
Botswana	27.6	34.2	21.5	31.9	24.7	42.1	27.9
Burkina Faso	53.2	69.5	98.0	78.4	76.4	72.4	73.3
Burundi	56.2	55.9	89.4	102.6	102.1	105.2	109.4
Cameroon	21.2	23.9	45.2	32.3	48.5	157.8	163.2
Cape Verde	23.3	27.1	31.4	24.1	26.0	26.8	28.4
Central African Rep.	63.4	42.3	50.4	58.6	86.5	92.7	131.3
Chad	54.9	84.8	62.8	78.5	118.4	113.4	134.7
Comoros	18.3	25.2	23.1	21.2	17.3	12.6	11.8
Congo	19.0	23.2	10.3	20.5	12.2	12.1	11.7
Cote d'Ivoire	9.2	7.1	48.7	32.6	212.7	142.9	159.3
Djibouti	20.2	22.8	21.5	22.4	18.4	10.2	20.1
Equatorial Guinea	7.1	10.3	11.1	20.9	19.5	22.2	18.8
Ethiopia	173.4	284.0	240.0	322.7	411.3	375.8	385.1
Gabon	5.7	9.4	6.2	7.1	8.9	12.6	13.1
Gambia	19.8	17.6	42.8	49.3	29.5	37.6	37.2
Ghana	124.1	105.9	247.5	246.9	225.3	199.1	234.4
Guinea	49.3	53.3	73.0	81.7	88.7	136.6	147.8
Guinea-Bissau	22.4	30.5	26.8	54.1	45.0	45.6	60.2
Kenya	80.8	79.4	68.0	123.8	195.3	346.8	344.0
Lesotho	31.1	38.7	32.2	45.5	38.5	58.8	53.1
Liberia	23.2	26.3	28.1	26.7	16.5	20.1	73.0
Madagascar	61.8	90.9	141.7	142.4	92.2	147.0	132.8
Malawi	130.3	60.0	113.2	110.1	184.6	230.0	262.7
Mali	86.0	98.2	128.5	136.1	162.0	150.6	146.2
Mauritania	55.5	46.4	56.8	72.7	77.0	86.3	104.2
Mauritius	6.2	2.5	6.7	12.0	11.2	9.5	12.6
Mayotte	0.2	1.0	2.2	1.1	0.0	–	–
Mozambique	66.1	76.9	95.4	113.1	158.8	222.3	255.5
Namibia	–	3.2	9.1	0.9	5.4	22.8	17.6
Niger	50.9	95.1	117.9	129.6	123.6	94.3	100.9
Nigeria	18.3	16.3	20.0	18.3	23.0	35.6	61.8
Reunion	17.5	31.6	64.6	30.8	37.2	20.2	20.2
Rwanda	62.8	71.2	80.9	101.2	112.0	95.0	98.9
St. Helena	0.0	0.0	0.0	0.0	0.1	0.0	0.0
Sao Tome & Principe	7.4	9.5	5.4	13.0	16.0	21.8	23.4
Senegal	60.7	54.5	218.2	252.4	176.8	101.7	203.3
Seychelles	1.5	8.6	6.5	4.7	2.5	4.8	3.5
Sierra Leone	22.6	34.4	30.0	21.0	39.8	27.8	30.3
Somalia	150.1	153.8	166.8	180.5	117.9	159.2	137.3
Sudan	192.5	267.2	285.5	247.6	332.8	312.2	371.6
Swaziland	12.1	6.5	9.8	15.7	15.6	17.8	19.0
Tanzania	136.9	101.5	161.5	163.0	195.9	231.1	313.8
Togo	53.7	49.1	74.7	36.9	72.6	75.5	55.1
Uganda	118.1	137.6	117.1	188.5	175.4	212.5	311.8
Zaire	93.2	96.4	152.0	288.4	175.4	201.5	194.4
Zambia	56.7	106.8	115.4	83.3	70.8	77.7	82.7
Zimbabwe	53.3	25.5	35.6	28.2	42.8	38.9	45.7
East African Community	–	–	–	–	–	–	–
DOM/TOM Unallocated	–	–	–	–	–	–	–
EAMA Unallocated	–	–	–	–	–	–	–
South of Sahara Unall.	18.1	83.8	20.9	14.7	121.7	177.8	178.3
TOTAL	*2506.7*	*2876.0*	*3614.0*	*3983.6*	*4482.4*	*4983.5*	*5626.1*
Africa Unspecified	105.7	201.9	211.9	232.5	156.1	190.3	212.8
AFRICA TOTAL	*2823.3*	*3285.9*	*4020.0*	*4452.7*	*4924.6*	*5528.8*	*6104.2*
N. & C. AMERICA							
Aruba	–	–	–	0.1	0.0	0.2	0.1
Bahamas	2.8	0.8	5.6	0.7	4.1	3.9	4.1

	1984	1985
Barbados	3.7	2.3
Belize	1.4	1.7
Bermuda	0.1	0.9
Costa Rica	31.9	41.2
Cuba	5.6	15.7
Dominican Republic	46.0	45.2
El Salvador	33.5	38.7
Guadeloupe	13.1	17.2
Guatemala	24.9	20.4
Haiti	62.0	47.1
Honduras	114.8	62.8
Jamaica	14.3	11.0
Martinique	15.6	24.8
Mexico	8.1	22.0
Netherlands Antilles	7.1	2.6
Nicaragua	42.0	35.2
Panama	15.2	24.7
St. Pierre & Miquelon	–	–
Trinidad & Tobago	3.1	5.8
Anguilla	0.3	1.2
Antigua and Barbuda	0.9	0.8
Cayman Islands	0.4	0.1
Dominica	5.5	7.6
Grenada	4.7	3.9
Montserrat	0.1	0.5
St. Kitts-Nevis	2.0	2.2
St. Lucia	2.8	4.5
St. Vincent and Gr.	2.9	3.9
Turks & Caicos Isl.	1.6	0.8
Virgin Islands	0.8	0.6
West Indies Unall.	–	0.1
DOM/TOM Unallocated	–	–
N.& C. America Unall.	6.2	7.3
TOTAL	*473.2*	*453.6*
SOUTH AMERICA		
Argentina	23.6	8.4
Bolivia	59.2	70.7
Brazil	23.4	60.3
Chile	-7.2	-5.4
Colombia	46.5	24.9
Ecuador	74.8	65.1
Falkland Islands	0.0	–
Guiana	4.5	13.9
Guyana	16.7	21.0
Paraguay	17.3	21.8
Peru	68.5	30.7
Suriname	3.6	3.1
Uruguay	-0.3	-0.9
Venezuela	-0.9	-2.3
South America Unall.	–	0.6
TOTAL	*329.6*	*311.7*
America Unspecified	75.9	89.2
AMERICA TOTAL	*878.6*	*854.5*
MIDDLE EAST		
Bahrain	0.6	0.0
Iran	10.9	15.4
Iraq	6.3	5.7
Israel	–	0.1
Jordan	21.2	16.0
Kuwait	1.1	1.0
Lebanon	22.4	26.3
Oman	6.2	3.9
Qatar	0.8	1.3
Saudi Arabia	9.1	11.6
Syria	24.1	37.0
United Arab Emirates	0.9	1.3
Yemen	106.8	112.2
Middle East Unall.	23.3	25.8
TOTAL	*233.7*	*257.6*
SOUTH ASIA		
Afghanistan	8.3	11.4
Bangladesh	501.4	499.2
Bhutan	12.8	14.7
India	1015.9	1047.9
Maldives	2.8	3.6
Myanmar (Burma)	120.2	92.5
Nepal	99.4	112.1
Pakistan	414.8	357.9
Sri Lanka	134.8	128.7

1986	1987	1988	1989	1990
1.0	2.1	0.9	1.7	1.5
1.7	2.1	8.6	10.2	10.0
0.1	0.1	–	0.0	–
30.8	20.3	23.1	19.9	23.8
14.3	23.0	16.6	13.2	17.3
29.7	27.6	18.4	21.7	21.6
24.4	21.2	38.6	78.0	38.0
52.0	7.1	13.2	12.5	12.5
23.5	26.6	42.0	51.0	49.6
48.8	68.1	45.3	61.3	66.8
43.7	35.5	69.4	40.9	70.7
16.5	20.7	19.2	35.4	28.5
39.2	7.6	13.7	11.7	11.7
4.4	5.2	32.8	8.9	14.7
1.2	2.6	2.5	4.3	4.4
45.8	29.7	46.6	42.2	50.1
24.0	13.8	2.8	3.4	2.4
–	0.0	0.0	–	–
2.7	1.6	5.9	4.4	4.1
0.4	1.2	1.0	3.1	3.2
0.7	0.7	3.2	1.0	1.2
2.0	1.0	0.6	1.4	1.4
4.0	9.2	7.8	11.7	9.0
7.5	9.6	12.9	10.2	8.8
0.5	1.1	1.4	0.4	0.7
3.7	3.5	3.6	2.5	2.7
9.8	4.9	10.5	6.5	6.4
4.1	8.1	10.5	8.6	8.5
0.9	0.6	0.3	0.1	1.3
0.2	1.3	0.9	2.1	2.0
8.4	37.4	23.9	23.8	23.8
–	–	–	–	–
6.5	3.7	35.9	18.6	18.6
457.9	*397.9*	*515.9*	*514.5*	*519.6*
29.8	36.8	38.2	31.5	18.2
124.8	105.6	166.1	137.6	145.9
47.3	35.9	18.4	13.5	22.8
-4.7	-2.0	-2.1	10.8	17.4
26.7	10.1	1.3	18.1	8.2
60.9	49.4	36.5	33.7	39.0
–	0.0	0.0	0.0	0.0
31.0	8.7	14.9	8.6	8.7
21.6	13.8	11.5	17.4	73.1
20.8	26.5	12.4	3.8	9.9
21.1	31.0	28.0	41.5	48.4
2.3	5.7	6.6	5.9	6.4
1.4	5.7	11.0	12.7	11.8
-1.1	-0.7	0.1	0.8	3.7
4.8	12.7	25.1	32.7	32.7
386.5	*339.1*	*368.1*	*368.3*	*446.2*
59.3	105.2	96.6	125.9	121.9
903.6	*842.2*	*980.7*	*1008.7*	*1087.6*
-0.1	0.0	0.9	2.7	0.7
13.5	24.1	29.4	36.3	34.2
12.3	2.1	1.1	16.5	5.1
0.1	1.3	1.7	3.7	3.7
20.7	24.5	10.8	17.3	23.9
1.3	1.3	1.6	1.5	1.2
21.1	17.5	30.4	32.3	28.7
1.9	2.3	1.5	6.1	6.4
0.9	1.4	0.8	0.9	0.8
11.6	11.6	6.5	26.9	30.8
55.2	19.8	36.4	33.3	30.3
1.5	1.5	1.4	1.5	2.4
104.9	107.7	109.9	129.1	91.0
28.8	12.9	0.5	56.1	301.2
273.6	*228.1*	*232.8*	*364.0*	*560.2*
7.3	8.6	6.2	86.3	43.4
613.5	682.7	674.5	843.7	1004.6
17.8	23.5	19.7	22.6	27.0
1087.4	911.9	1168.1	760.2	851.7
5.1	8.2	6.6	6.0	10.8
108.0	127.0	118.2	94.0	87.4
126.7	153.6	169.9	242.4	187.6
413.2	468.2	422.5	471.7	512.1
160.6	173.1	156.0	152.3	265.3

	1984	1985	1986	1987	1988	1989	1990
South Asia Unall.	–	–	–	12.7	26.0	14.5	14.5
TOTAL	*2310.3*	*2267.9*	*2539.5*	*2569.4*	*2767.5*	*2693.7*	*3004.4*
FAR EAST ASIA							
Brunei	–	0.1	0.1	0.1	0.1	0.1	0.0
China	246.5	344.3	450.5	588.3	783.9	656.3	659.8
Hong Kong	4.5	3.8	4.4	4.4	8.5	29.0	18.2
Indonesia	108.1	99.3	85.6	112.2	124.8	133.6	186.4
Kampuchea	8.5	7.3	7.5	5.4	8.7	12.5	13.3
Korea	2.9	4.0	4.4	3.9	2.3	3.7	3.3
Korea, Dem.	–	5.2	4.4	6.7	5.9	5.3	7.5
Laos	20.4	21.5	29.0	27.8	40.7	96.4	100.5
Macao	0.4	0.3	0.3	0.0	0.2	0.2	0.1
Malaysia	13.3	11.9	8.8	11.1	12.2	14.1	13.9
Mongolia	–	2.9	3.9	2.4	2.4	4.9	6.8
Philippines	26.4	23.4	69.3	67.4	65.1	86.9	176.4
Singapore	2.2	2.1	1.9	1.1	1.2	1.1	0.2
Taiwan	-0.5	-0.5	-0.5	-0.5	–	–	–
Thailand	87.0	61.8	97.1	72.3	55.9	88.7	76.9
Viet Nam	28.1	44.4	52.5	49.9	64.4	57.1	82.6
Far East Asia Unall.	–	0.2	7.6	12.4	23.7	18.3	18.3
TOTAL	*547.8*	*632.1*	*826.7*	*964.9*	*1200.0*	*1208.1*	*1364.2*
Asia Unspecified	71.5	84.9	96.4	132.4	140.7	81.7	155.2
ASIA TOTAL	**3163.3**	**3242.5**	**3736.1**	**3894.9**	**4341.0**	**4347.5**	**5084.1**
OCEANIA							
Cook Islands	0.7	1.0	0.9	1.4	1.1	1.4	2.2
Fiji	7.8	5.6	10.1	3.7	6.9	6.6	5.7
Kiribati	1.6	1.2	1.5	3.8	4.1	2.4	2.8
Nauru	–	–	–	–	–	–	–
New Caledonia	0.9	0.2	1.1	0.9	0.2	0.8	0.7
Niue	0.1	0.0	0.3	0.1	0.2	0.1	0.2
Pacif. Isl.(Fed. Sts.)	0.8	1.1	1.4	1.5	0.9	1.1	1.1
Papua New Guinea	25.4	16.9	20.8	68.2	72.4	25.3	56.4
Polynesia, French	0.5	1.5	0.4	1.1	4.6	2.7	2.6
Solomon Islands	5.5	6.1	8.4	33.8	23.4	11.7	13.1
Tokelau	0.1	0.2	0.2	0.2	0.3	0.3	0.4
Tonga	3.3	3.0	3.5	6.1	5.2	4.8	7.0
Tuvalu	0.3	0.2	0.6	0.8	0.7	1.2	0.2
Vanuatu	2.3	2.9	3.6	18.5	10.3	8.0	6.8
Wallis & Futuna	1.2	0.2	0.1	0.3	1.1	0.1	0.1
Western Samoa	9.1	5.6	4.5	11.3	8.2	10.0	22.8
TOM Unallocated	–	–	–	–	–	–	–
Oceania Unallocated	–	–	0.1	6.6	5.4	11.5	11.5
TOTAL	**59.3**	**45.5**	**57.5**	**158.1**	**144.9**	**87.8**	**133.5**
LDCS Unspecified	639.1	688.1	618.4	686.4	849.8	723.8	996.1
TOTAL,ALL LDCS	**7637.0**	**8170.6**	**9471.9**	**10110.2**	**11326.9**	**11736.3**	**13447.1**
INCOME GROUPS							
LLDCS	2760.1	2991.7	3420.0	3833.5	4168.8	4802.4	5311.2
OTHER LICS	2839.0	2898.5	3660.4	3904.6	4214.4	3919.5	4508.4
LMICS	725.7	627.5	755.4	663.3	915.6	990.1	1002.8
UMICS	358.8	456.5	557.4	439.2	520.0	543.3	533.7
UNALLOCATED	953.5	1196.2	1078.7	1269.7	1508.1	1481.0	2090.9

	1984	1985	1986	1987	1988	1989	1990
EUROPE							
Albania	–	–	–	–	2.2	3.1	2.0
Cyprus	18.6	81.0	97.8	125.2	54.0	33.3	26.3
Gibraltar	–	–	–	–	–	–	–
Greece	28.5	63.3	1.3	34.9	78.4	83.7	-13.4
Malta	1.0	-0.1	2.2	10.8	4.1	13.6	9.1
Turkey	505.4	636.2	668.1	751.1	619.1	67.1	291.9
Yugoslavia	276.1	216.3	90.4	-55.3	-310.9	-168.4	-43.7
Other Europe	36.8	125.5	34.0	8.6	9.2	-253.4	-52.6
Europe Unallocated	13.8	14.3	15.4	–	–	–	–
TOTAL	*880.2*	*1136.5*	*909.3*	*875.5*	*456.1*	*-221.0*	*219.6*
NORTH OF SAHARA							
Algeria	56.5	235.4	67.9	29.3	70.7	200.5	331.1
Egypt	337.3	256.2	232.1	235.0	147.9	220.0	45.8
Libya	1.8	30.6	-2.4	14.2	26.7	7.9	12.6
Morocco	231.7	371.2	404.5	341.7	407.2	432.3	557.9
Tunisia	107.1	145.0	135.3	183.4	222.7	315.1	287.4
North of Sahara Unall.	–	–	–	0.1	2.7	5.9	5.9
TOTAL	*734.3*	*1038.4*	*837.4*	*803.6*	*877.8*	*1181.7*	*1240.7*
SOUTH OF SAHARA							
Angola	34.3	34.7	42.0	42.5	57.0	58.2	71.0
Benin	36.3	43.6	63.3	64.5	65.5	101.3	134.4
Botswana	50.4	74.1	30.9	68.4	29.2	51.4	46.9
Burkina Faso	52.8	71.3	103.8	86.1	79.9	75.1	73.5
Burundi	66.7	62.0	94.5	107.2	103.8	103.1	105.6
Cameroon	61.3	70.1	125.5	107.2	87.7	237.7	259.0
Cape Verde	24.0	28.3	31.4	23.0	25.0	26.3	27.3
Central African Rep.	65.0	45.8	57.0	60.4	86.5	91.5	130.2
Chad	54.9	84.8	62.8	78.5	118.4	113.4	134.7
Comoros	20.1	28.5	23.8	21.2	17.3	12.6	11.8
Congo	37.4	44.3	26.5	54.3	98.2	9.5	8.4
Cote d'Ivoire	203.0	29.8	121.9	372.1	302.9	218.3	462.1
Djibouti	20.2	22.8	21.5	22.4	18.4	10.2	20.1
Equatorial Guinea	7.4	10.0	11.3	20.2	19.5	22.3	18.8
Ethiopia	171.5	280.9	237.6	317.6	402.1	388.5	385.3
Gabon	11.9	11.2	20.4	26.1	32.5	154.4	70.5
Gambia	22.9	19.2	42.8	47.6	28.0	37.2	36.7
Ghana	116.3	110.6	255.1	268.0	233.2	226.1	360.4
Guinea	60.6	53.5	67.1	70.6	80.0	127.3	136.9
Guinea-Bissau	25.8	33.5	27.5	53.1	44.4	44.0	58.9
Kenya	190.7	180.7	77.5	93.5	141.2	359.6	290.8
Lesotho	35.7	49.4	31.6	46.2	40.1	58.4	55.1
Liberia	41.2	47.1	27.9	27.0	22.9	18.7	38.4
Madagascar	61.4	94.4	159.4	159.6	106.7	146.9	136.5
Malawi	131.7	64.3	114.6	116.3	185.8	219.0	254.4
Mali	88.8	97.3	127.2	135.4	162.8	152.0	145.6
Mauritania	54.4	50.6	48.3	75.1	73.9	71.1	92.7
Mauritius	28.6	26.7	9.0	25.0	50.8	6.7	13.0
Mayotte	0.2	1.0	2.2	1.1	0.0	–	–
Mozambique	68.3	85.3	104.7	117.2	162.5	224.7	255.2
Namibia	–	3.2	9.1	0.9	5.4	22.8	17.6
Niger	48.0	95.1	118.4	127.6	117.5	90.6	99.8
Nigeria	249.9	255.6	474.3	296.3	78.9	447.7	367.1
Reunion	17.5	31.6	64.6	30.8	37.2	20.2	20.2
Rwanda	62.5	70.9	80.8	101.0	111.2	94.7	98.0
St. Helena	0.0	0.0	0.0	0.0	0.1	0.0	0.0
Sao Tome & Principe	7.4	9.5	5.4	14.0	16.0	21.9	23.4
Senegal	66.8	58.2	222.7	242.1	168.9	89.9	190.4
Seychelles	2.2	13.1	10.2	10.3	3.4	5.2	2.6
Sierra Leone	19.0	33.7	27.1	20.9	35.7	27.8	29.4
Somalia	150.8	146.2	161.6	180.2	118.3	158.4	136.9
Sudan	176.4	262.4	257.5	216.6	318.6	316.4	366.4
Swaziland	11.8	3.2	16.8	12.9	0.5	10.9	-2.6
Tanzania	144.4	135.6	140.6	140.9	173.3	203.7	285.3
Togo	52.6	48.0	72.3	33.5	67.7	70.3	49.1
Uganda	123.3	188.0	121.2	202.1	179.3	203.7	302.1
Zaire	89.1	120.4	196.9	324.0	238.3	257.3	327.1
Zambia	75.7	172.4	142.6	90.7	105.1	93.9	101.9
Zimbabwe	106.2	76.0	73.9	69.3	82.9	76.4	137.2
East African Community	–	–	–	–	–	–	–
DOM/TOM Unallocated	–	–	–	–	–	–	–
EAMA Unallocated	–	–	–	–	–	–	–
South of Sahara Unall.	2.6	-59.0	14.3	3.9	113.2	168.4	167.9
TOTAL	*3249.8*	*3519.5*	*4379.7*	*4825.3*	*4847.6*	*5745.6*	*6553.9*
Africa Unspecified	108.1	211.6	220.5	233.5	166.1	194.7	227.7
AFRICA TOTAL	*4092.3*	*4769.4*	*5437.6*	*5862.5*	*5891.4*	*7122.0*	*8022.4*
N.& C. AMERICA							
Aruba	–	–	–	0.1	0.0	0.2	0.1
Bahamas	3.3	0.0	13.8	2.9	9.4	21.1	42.7

	1984	1985
Barbados	14.2	9.1
Belize	3.5	5.5
Bermuda	0.1	0.9
Costa Rica	70.0	140.1
Cuba	5.6	15.7
Dominican Republic	70.9	90.3
El Salvador	69.0	73.4
Guadeloupe	13.1	17.2
Guatemala	59.7	111.7
Haiti	62.0	47.1
Honduras	227.1	136.8
Jamaica	62.7	106.4
Martinique	15.6	24.8
Mexico	776.3	689.7
Netherlands Antilles	7.1	2.6
Nicaragua	64.4	39.8
Panama	118.2	79.9
St. Pierre & Miquelon	–	–
Trinidad & Tobago	-0.1	1.0
Anguilla	0.3	1.2
Antigua and Barbuda	2.1	1.1
Cayman Islands	5.1	0.9
Dominica	5.5	7.7
Grenada	5.2	3.7
Montserrat	0.1	0.5
St. Kitts-Nevis	2.0	2.2
St. Lucia	3.7	4.8
St. Vincent and Gr.	3.1	4.1
Turks & Caicos Isl.	2.6	1.1
Virgin Islands	1.0	0.6
West Indies Unall.	–	0.1
DOM/TOM Unallocated	–	–
N.& C. America Unall.	6.2	10.2
TOTAL	*1679.5*	*1630.3*
SOUTH AMERICA		
Argentina	200.6	219.4
Bolivia	60.5	76.1
Brazil	1183.6	647.5
Chile	344.3	451.6
Colombia	484.6	600.5
Ecuador	110.3	115.8
Falkland Islands	0.0	–
Guiana	4.5	13.9
Guyana	24.5	28.1
Paraguay	71.7	51.4
Peru	222.4	152.1
Suriname	3.6	3.1
Uruguay	55.9	26.9
Venezuela	-19.4	-28.0
South America Unall.	–	0.6
TOTAL	*2747.1*	*2359.0*
America Unspecified	111.9	118.5
AMERICA TOTAL	*4538.4*	*4107.8*
MIDDLE EAST		
Bahrain	10.5	-1.1
Iran	-37.7	-34.0
Iraq	63.2	-24.3
Israel	0.2	-14.1
Jordan	45.4	76.7
Kuwait	1.1	1.0
Lebanon	19.8	26.7
Oman	31.2	21.8
Qatar	0.8	1.3
Saudi Arabia	9.1	11.6
Syria	63.9	91.2
United Arab Emirates	1.0	1.3
Yemen	115.8	123.2
Middle East Unall.	23.3	25.8
TOTAL	*347.5*	*307.1*
SOUTH ASIA		
Afghanistan	8.3	11.4
Bangladesh	485.6	490.6
Bhutan	12.8	14.7
India	1262.2	1233.7
Maldives	2.8	2.8
Myanmar (Burma)	120.0	92.3
Nepal	101.8	114.6
Pakistan	514.9	480.0
Sri Lanka	149.3	129.8

1986	1987	1988	1989	1990
8.1	15.3	11.2	4.0	10.1
2.4	3.5	9.2	14.4	13.2
0.1	0.1	—	0.0	—
95.5	10.8	16.5	44.9	13.6
14.3	23.0	16.6	13.2	17.3
56.2	44.0	28.4	49.8	55.0
32.4	25.3	31.4	56.7	-0.1
52.0	7.1	13.2	12.5	12.5
45.1	-1.4	48.4	51.3	63.5
48.7	68.0	45.3	61.2	66.4
67.9	34.4	106.2	55.8	56.2
40.5	81.3	44.5	78.4	48.5
39.2	7.6	13.7	11.7	11.7
888.9	405.2	851.5	762.7	2852.6
1.2	2.8	9.1	5.3	5.4
60.7	48.1	58.4	44.5	49.0
100.5	-6.7	4.8	3.7	-38.5
—	0.0	0.0	—	—
101.8	41.8	28.2	6.4	26.2
0.6	1.6	1.0	3.2	3.3
0.8	0.5	3.2	1.0	1.2
2.0	6.2	3.2	7.9	7.9
4.1	9.3	7.8	12.2	9.1
11.3	9.8	12.7	10.5	9.1
0.9	1.4	1.6	0.3	0.6
3.7	3.5	3.7	2.6	2.8
10.0	5.1	10.5	6.6	6.5
4.1	8.1	10.5	8.6	8.5
0.9	0.6	0.3	0.2	1.3
0.2	1.3	0.9	4.3	4.3
8.1	37.1	23.6	23.5	23.5
—	—	—	—	—
7.8	1.5	35.9	18.6	18.6
1723.4	*899.2*	*1460.8*	*1397.0*	*3402.1*
391.5	783.7	521.9	327.5	341.4
133.3	138.3	232.2	180.6	166.3
1092.3	133.2	173.1	76.1	-311.7
443.3	475.4	409.2	281.5	493.2
450.2	240.9	303.1	213.2	11.4
283.9	246.9	233.6	122.5	119.7
—	0.0	0.0	0.0	0.0
31.0	8.7	14.9	8.6	8.7
32.6	25.0	19.8	29.0	54.7
50.2	31.0	-7.4	-16.9	-19.4
120.3	166.0	72.1	43.8	51.7
2.3	6.5	7.7	7.7	10.4
45.1	88.0	80.8	85.6	44.8
-15.5	50.9	137.8	329.4	1056.6
4.8	12.7	25.1	32.7	32.7
3065.4	*2407.1*	*2223.8*	*1721.0*	*2060.3*
66.1	167.8	76.3	333.6	261.2
4854.8	*3474.1*	*3761.0*	*3451.6*	*5723.5*
-1.2	-1.3	6.0	8.4	0.7
-40.9	-44.3	-63.6	-30.7	-32.8
35.3	-58.7	1.0	30.4	-1.9
-0.7	-21.2	-28.3	-23.8	14.2
78.3	91.7	8.1	28.4	111.1
1.3	1.3	1.6	1.5	1.2
13.4	9.5	17.7	24.9	17.4
18.2	-0.7	1.6	1.0	-0.6
0.9	1.4	0.8	0.9	0.8
11.6	11.6	6.5	26.9	30.8
71.4	51.5	74.0	49.4	29.7
1.5	1.5	1.4	1.5	2.4
117.7	98.6	89.7	117.6	91.0
28.8	12.9	0.5	56.1	301.2
335.5	*153.9*	*117.0*	*292.4*	*565.1*
7.3	8.6	6.2	86.3	43.4
591.7	656.1	660.2	839.5	1002.5
17.8	23.5	19.7	22.6	27.0
1473.3	1590.6	2480.4	1976.9	2100.1
4.5	7.6	5.9	5.3	10.8
107.7	126.7	117.9	93.6	87.1
126.5	153.6	169.9	243.3	192.4
443.4	676.4	743.2	1019.8	986.8
157.7	172.2	142.3	156.2	256.8

	1984	1985	1986	1987	1988	1989	1990
South Asia Unall.	—	—	—	12.7	26.0	14.5	14.5
TOTAL	*2657.6*	*2569.7*	*2929.9*	*3427.9*	*4371.7*	*4458.1*	*4721.2*

FAR EAST ASIA

	1984	1985	1986	1987	1988	1989	1990
Brunei	—	0.1	0.1	0.1	0.1	0.1	0.0
China	315.2	693.3	771.3	792.1	1325.7	1260.9	1088.0
Hong Kong	1.4	-1.9	-2.0	-35.1	8.5	29.0	18.2
Indonesia	918.0	845.3	826.8	1395.5	1765.9	1510.6	1215.7
Kampuchea	8.5	7.3	7.5	5.4	8.7	12.5	13.3
Korea	447.9	165.9	-79.1	-389.5	-881.5	-565.8	-377.1
Korea, Dem.	—	5.2	4.4	6.7	5.9	5.3	7.5
Laos	20.4	21.5	29.0	27.8	40.7	96.4	100.5
Macao	0.4	0.3	0.3	0.0	0.2	0.2	0.1
Malaysia	78.2	32.3	-15.1	44.8	10.1	23.1	90.2
Mongolia	—	2.9	3.9	2.4	2.4	4.9	6.8
Philippines	354.9	223.7	158.4	178.1	106.2	301.3	671.0
Singapore	-8.7	-16.0	-22.7	-30.5	-22.8	-17.3	-37.9
Taiwan	-17.6	-17.4	-21.3	-131.4	-6.7	-7.1	-8.6
Thailand	418.5	357.8	248.7	35.1	-396.2	-98.3	-27.6
Viet Nam	28.0	44.3	52.4	49.7	64.4	57.0	82.5
Far East Asia Unall.	—	0.2	7.6	12.4	23.7	18.3	18.3
TOTAL	*2565.0*	*2364.8*	*1970.1*	*1963.5*	*2055.2*	*2630.9*	*2861.0*
Asia Unspecified	72.2	84.9	96.4	132.4	140.7	81.7	155.2
ASIA TOTAL	*5642.3*	*5326.6*	*5331.9*	*5677.8*	*6684.5*	*7463.2*	*8302.5*

OCEANIA

	1984	1985	1986	1987	1988	1989	1990
Cook Islands	0.7	1.0	0.9	1.4	1.1	1.4	2.2
Fiji	16.1	0.4	13.3	4.7	23.6	-1.2	-7.1
Kiribati	1.6	1.2	1.5	3.8	4.1	2.4	2.8
Nauru	—	—	—	—	—	—	—
New Caledonia	0.9	0.2	0.0	-0.2	-0.7	0.2	0.2
Niue	0.1	0.0	0.3	0.1	0.2	0.1	0.2
Pacif. Isl.(Fed. Sts.)	0.8	1.1	1.4	1.5	0.9	1.1	1.1
Papua New Guinea	35.9	30.6	57.8	102.1	111.3	52.3	129.2
Polynesia, French	—	1.5	0.4	3.3	7.0	2.4	2.3
Solomon Islands	5.5	6.1	8.4	33.8	23.4	11.7	13.1
Tokelau	0.1	0.2	0.2	0.2	0.3	0.3	0.4
Tonga	3.3	3.0	3.5	6.1	5.2	4.8	7.0
Tuvalu	0.3	0.2	0.6	0.8	0.7	1.2	0.2
Vanuatu	2.3	2.9	3.6	18.5	10.3	8.0	6.8
Wallis & Futuna	1.2	0.2	0.1	0.3	1.1	0.1	0.1
Western Samoa	9.1	5.6	4.5	11.3	8.2	10.0	22.8
TOM Unallocated	—	—	—	—	—	—	—
Oceania Unallocated	—	—	0.1	6.6	5.4	11.5	11.5
TOTAL	*77.7*	*54.0*	*96.5*	*194.2*	*202.0*	*106.1*	*192.8*
LDCS Unspecified	639.1	688.1	627.1	696.6	849.8	747.7	1174.5
TOTAL,ALL LDCS	*15870.0*	*16082.3*	*17257.5*	*16780.5*	*17844.9*	*18669.6*	*23635.3*

INCOME GROUPS

	1984	1985	1986	1987	1988	1989	1990
LLDCS	2825.7	3169.3	3375.7	3799.6	4082.4	4722.9	5206.3
OTHER LICS	5033.7	5167.7	6004.5	6927.2	8330.7	8537.1	8725.5
LMICS	3071.8	3256.1	3066.8	2932.3	2440.5	2017.5	2456.7
UMICS	3961.7	3393.4	3713.2	1791.2	1502.3	1685.0	4834.0
UNALLOCATED	977.2	1095.3	1097.3	1330.2	1489.1	1707.2	2412.8

Chart legend: ⊙—⊙—⊙ LLDCS; —·—·— OTHER LICS; ——— LMICS; — — — UMICS

Y-axis: 9000, 8500, 8000, 7500, 7000, 6500, 6000, 5500, 5000, 4500, 4000, 3500, 3000, 2500, 2000, 1500, 1000

X-axis: 1984, 85, 86, 87, 88, 89, 90

	1984	1985	1986	1987	1988	1989	1990			1984	1985
EUROPE									Barbados	-15.9	18.9
Albania	–	–	–	–	3.4	7.3	39.6		Belize	23.0	23.6
Cyprus	2.4	94.4	79.1	-33.1	136.5	208.4	300.6		Bermuda	328.8	766.4
Gibraltar	19.8	23.3	12.4	45.2	93.0	92.4	36.2		Costa Rica	221.2	257.1
Greece	586.2	89.3	-144.8	337.9	360.9	995.1	515.5		Cuba	50.3	24.6
Malta	4.1	8.3	8.6	14.0	8.3	33.3	86.1		Dominican Republic	149.7	174.8
Turkey	520.6	363.0	1142.5	1687.3	4262.7	1419.1	1145.2		El Salvador	224.7	301.8
Yugoslavia	314.5	34.0	-117.1	-165.2	-175.2	-167.0	-494.0		Guadeloupe	158.6	229.2
Other Europe	492.6	333.0	-499.8	223.5	620.7	1470.9	791.1		Guatemala	101.8	225.6
Europe Unallocated	292.7	289.6	-234.3	307.3	-590.1	-139.6	28.6		Haiti	71.2	94.7
TOTAL	**2232.8**	**1234.9**	**246.6**	**2416.8**	**4720.1**	**3919.8**	**2448.8**		Honduras	149.6	237.5
									Jamaica	300.8	119.5
NORTH OF SAHARA									Martinique	265.7	332.5
Algeria	500.1	595.3	-219.1	-1341.7	-74.4	-173.6	41.8		Mexico	13066.1	-2333.6
Egypt	2742.7	2653.2	2266.6	1726.9	3619.1	1889.8	1113.1		Netherlands Antilles	-1736.9	-1248.7
Libya	133.3	16.3	81.7	89.4	336.0	-67.5	-57.5		Nicaragua	81.3	76.7
Morocco	910.4	653.9	594.5	327.3	554.2	811.9	573.0		Panama	1112.6	1588.8
Tunisia	271.9	150.7	173.2	17.8	97.1	119.3	184.4		St. Pierre & Miquelon	18.9	17.9
North of Sahara Unall.	-58.7	35.3	-173.8	26.0	-100.5	39.6	-131.7		Trinidad & Tobago	146.4	-318.8
TOTAL	**4499.7**	**4104.7**	**2723.0**	**845.8**	**4431.5**	**2619.5**	**1723.1**		Anguilla	1.5	1.5
									Antigua and Barbuda	-6.1	21.6
SOUTH OF SAHARA									Cayman Islands	805.6	810.2
Angola	166.3	223.7	233.3	207.0	31.3	145.3	-76.4		Dominica	23.5	28.2
Benin	72.9	50.6	30.3	27.3	4.8	173.0	92.6		Grenada	25.3	29.5
Botswana	121.6	81.3	126.5	151.0	71.5	100.2	112.0		Montserrat	1.8	1.7
Burkina Faso	120.8	114.0	168.8	186.5	222.1	207.4	254.0		St. Kitts-Nevis	-4.6	2.5
Burundi	75.4	85.9	83.0	79.3	78.8	61.8	151.5		St. Lucia	1.7	2.4
Cameroon	212.0	153.0	103.4	203.1	376.3	402.9	415.7		St. Vincent and Gr.	1.2	3.7
Cape Verde	39.3	40.5	79.3	64.1	58.9	48.6	54.4		Turks & Caicos Isl.	-7.0	4.7
Central African Rep.	68.1	65.7	81.8	112.7	108.4	103.2	107.2		Virgin Islands	4.9	13.7
Chad	56.9	96.5	99.9	119.8	146.3	125.9	179.2		West Indies Unall.	-7.7	464.3
Comoros	18.1	18.0	21.0	33.3	36.8	31.8	29.9		DOM/TOM Unallocated	–	-5.9
Congo	65.6	15.5	310.2	200.2	25.2	-100.8	53.8		N.& C. America Unall.	864.0	184.4
Cote d'Ivoire	197.8	203.8	313.4	-45.0	73.1	-220.8	358.2		**TOTAL**	**16315.5**	**2683.8**
Djibouti	77.1	68.1	28.5	55.7	74.6	62.0	86.1				
Equatorial Guinea	10.4	7.7	20.0	25.7	31.7	41.3	21.0		**SOUTH AMERICA**		
Ethiopia	248.1	488.6	446.7	331.4	586.9	331.4	483.7		Argentina	901.9	1856.4
Gabon	56.3	202.3	275.2	419.2	586.6	360.8	156.9		Bolivia	100.4	125.8
Gambia	23.9	28.5	58.6	53.3	36.0	180.1	65.9		Brazil	6603.2	701.0
Ghana	95.6	88.2	141.2	196.9	257.8	521.0	267.7		Chile	1898.5	-328.3
Guinea	26.1	52.5	95.2	142.4	185.6	199.0	141.2		Colombia	686.5	-277.1
Guinea-Bissau	33.6	26.8	40.8	44.0	78.1	58.9	69.8		Ecuador	909.6	-90.2
Kenya	316.4	323.7	605.8	602.3	783.7	1007.3	1005.8		Falkland Islands	8.0	13.8
Lesotho	56.9	66.0	60.9	55.0	81.7	65.7	85.8		Guiana	70.9	89.5
Liberia	-287.3	-334.6	-285.0	-316.2	509.1	255.0	556.5		Guyana	-1.1	7.2
Madagascar	243.5	120.4	162.5	199.2	195.5	157.9	296.3		Paraguay	78.6	31.7
Malawi	79.9	53.3	106.6	208.2	218.2	170.6	216.9		Peru	423.8	-217.1
Mali	217.5	253.2	197.4	215.8	254.5	292.2	305.2		Suriname	-1.7	6.4
Mauritania	76.3	113.3	102.3	90.7	98.4	137.5	98.6		Uruguay	217.0	-150.8
Mauritius	26.5	-0.3	44.0	85.6	74.9	108.9	136.1		Venezuela	-310.7	-913.0
Mayotte	13.8	19.8	26.1	37.7	43.5	43.3	58.5		South America Unall.	68.1	1031.5
Mozambique	131.0	239.2	247.1	432.6	643.4	391.2	727.8		**TOTAL**	**11652.9**	**1886.8**
Namibia	–	21.8	-92.1	-21.9	-183.0	-121.9	-187.4		America Unspecified	1873.8	-9.8
Niger	79.6	190.7	170.0	270.0	194.5	178.1	241.3		**AMERICA TOTAL**	**29842.2**	**4560.9**
Nigeria	286.5	-97.3	652.9	1405.7	-100.4	1822.8	-301.4		**MIDDLE EAST**		
Reunion	430.5	482.8	552.1	636.8	752.4	813.2	1186.3		Bahrain	78.8	181.1
Rwanda	93.8	108.1	130.5	148.0	140.1	135.1	177.8		Iran	-328.1	-325.9
St. Helena	10.0	12.1	13.5	20.1	27.0	47.4	24.5		Iraq	1899.3	849.1
Sao Tome & Principe	4.0	3.0	7.0	4.6	24.3	10.4	14.4		Israel	1985.1	2562.6
Senegal	321.6	201.6	382.5	382.4	280.9	506.9	545.5		Jordan	182.3	-202.0
Seychelles	22.7	14.4	23.4	13.2	6.6	9.3	36.7		Kuwait	-26.9	-186.3
Sierra Leone	38.4	22.2	54.0	73.2	67.9	79.9	43.2		Lebanon	75.3	19.4
Somalia	204.0	187.5	448.5	433.3	280.6	239.7	254.6		Oman	189.3	116.7
Sudan	373.6	640.1	389.6	350.9	510.1	412.0	371.3		Qatar	-96.8	-12.6
Swaziland	36.5	28.0	25.0	28.6	24.4	3.9	32.4		Saudi Arabia	-308.5	151.6
Tanzania	445.1	390.1	485.6	794.4	776.1	655.6	806.9		Syria	70.6	38.0
Togo	61.0	38.6	53.3	69.6	142.3	78.3	157.4		United Arab Emirates	82.0	-303.0
Uganda	43.9	31.5	72.8	97.7	199.7	175.0	238.2		Yemen	66.8	88.9
Zaire	667.6	350.8	436.9	423.8	659.4	449.8	973.9		Middle East Unall.	319.3	-28.7
Zambia	321.5	350.3	523.7	269.4	379.3	493.1	449.9		**TOTAL**	**4188.6**	**2948.9**
Zimbabwe	325.2	240.6	205.1	377.3	314.2	291.0	286.1		**SOUTH ASIA**		
East African Community	2.5	10.8	1.8	1.2	0.8	–	–		Afghanistan	-2.0	-15.8
DOM/TOM Unallocated	–	-1.2	–	–	–	–	–		Bangladesh	725.1	598.9
EAMA Unallocated	59.4	–	–	–	–	–	–		Bhutan	4.8	6.6
South of Sahara Unall.	227.7	352.3	11.4	611.7	442.1	1599.8	842.8		India	908.7	1245.0
TOTAL	**6715.3**	**6544.0**	**8572.3**	**10608.3**	**10912.6**	**13341.8**	**12706.5**		Maldives	3.3	6.8
Africa Unspecified	-29.6	-295.4	-276.1	-1063.7	854.1	406.7	71.7		Myanmar (Burma)	158.2	218.5
AFRICA TOTAL	**11185.4**	**10353.3**	**11019.2**	**10390.3**	**16198.3**	**16368.0**	**14501.3**		Nepal	99.2	131.0
N.& C. AMERICA									Pakistan	179.5	398.0
Aruba	–	12.0	40.2	20.8	23.0	31.9	73.8		Sri Lanka	483.6	432.4
Bahamas	-106.4	521.1	860.6	1061.3	1335.0	932.7	163.0				

1986	1987	1988	1989	1990
31.5	-30.6	47.6	10.3	-9.8
16.7	20.2	24.4	19.6	19.9
1048.9	3584.9	1274.3	-806.4	1239.3
236.2	232.0	144.8	183.9	133.2
-53.5	-169.7	-53.0	42.5	121.8
284.9	136.2	81.9	119.2	96.2
298.4	396.8	381.6	371.5	340.5
253.6	294.5	372.2	284.7	353.5
80.9	162.0	210.7	154.9	144.7
124.2	143.8	97.4	138.0	114.7
230.1	209.2	270.2	186.6	368.9
37.9	166.3	314.1	346.7	280.5
385.9	451.4	526.1	690.0	879.0
394.6	1471.4	-4057.1	3107.0	-3967.5
-1444.5	284.5	1817.5	889.6	1173.4
111.2	128.3	184.0	137.2	260.8
1690.3	2282.4	1149.1	2603.3	1132.4
21.7	30.9	37.5	33.5	30.4
-92.3	15.5	-48.3	67.4	-116.3
2.6	1.6	1.0	2.2	2.4
44.8	27.5	6.8	32.2	4.7
1006.2	2233.8	3158.4	2254.3	2628.9
35.4	27.9	-3.6	32.9	22.0
17.1	12.2	9.4	-2.5	11.9
3.3	3.1	4.2	6.8	7.8
1.6	7.3	5.1	23.4	4.2
1.8	10.2	14.8	23.5	7.1
8.4	5.2	5.6	7.0	4.5
8.0	-0.7	7.9	8.8	7.7
-0.1	87.7	256.7	-73.8	179.9
323.5	270.3	59.0	40.5	53.2
–	–	–	–	–
9.3	135.8	958.9	1096.1	-1191.9
6019.2	13714.2	8617.1	12995.1	4574.8
4588.2	115.7	849.5	-1860.3	-1054.4
171.1	269.9	212.3	320.7	335.8
-93.0	-890.3	3271.5	3761.4	-1817.4
-315.7	-858.1	115.7	-298.3	475.3
673.9	-121.8	-1074.7	-537.7	192.9
680.5	98.3	-49.2	53.8	81.4
14.7	13.4	10.3	-0.5	-7.0
132.0	164.6	150.7	145.3	176.8
-5.4	16.9	17.0	30.0	109.5
67.1	72.4	63.3	77.0	24.6
-86.6	-50.6	-51.2	-10.2	-175.8
73.5	-46.5	-25.7	26.9	113.7
17.8	166.2	-347.3	310.4	-104.4
2812.3	2110.8	-193.9	125.1	-4852.0
103.6	-22.7	17.0	226.0	-127.1
8834.4	1038.1	2965.1	2369.7	-6627.9
-509.2	415.3	3109.2	2158.7	3525.7
14344.4	15167.6	14691.4	17523.4	1472.6
-20.4	-20.5	6.3	93.4	-16.0
-292.2	32.4	678.6	1539.8	603.8
-95.9	-85.2	10.3	348.5	-1054.6
2297.0	2113.4	6291.5	2029.6	1385.7
114.9	401.2	545.3	606.1	564.7
52.8	64.4	-130.4	-198.6	-134.0
108.5	66.2	138.8	84.1	10.7
235.4	61.4	-95.0	-327.5	59.4
-71.6	-24.7	-4.0	15.1	24.5
-372.9	286.3	-172.6	-26.7	552.0
108.7	95.3	359.2	204.5	141.8
-109.1	193.1	50.6	-136.5	-169.5
87.2	188.9	123.6	127.3	164.9
839.3	-455.5	-56.5	-128.0	-318.4
2881.5	2916.8	7745.6	4231.2	1815.1
-1.4	38.4	69.3	80.1	98.3
753.6	926.6	945.2	984.3	1168.6
14.0	11.6	36.7	18.5	23.1
2327.2	1931.4	1663.2	3194.4	2184.5
12.2	18.1	19.9	55.3	28.3
264.8	225.1	354.6	-7.0	27.9
200 3	216.3	254.2	250.4	232.3
614.1	328.2	1152.0	1349.9	747.6
334.9	369.4	431.9	591.5	420.2

	1984	1985	1986	1987	1988	1989	1990
South Asia Unall.	2.4	5.3	6.0	3.3	12.1	19.7	42.0
TOTAL	2562.8	3026.8	4525.5	4068.2	4939.1	6537.0	4972.6

FAR EAST ASIA

	1984	1985	1986	1987	1988	1989	1990
Brunei	-2.5	-3.6	-4.3	2.3	5.0	5.4	-7.1
China	573.5	1573.7	2684.8	3560.5	3932.4	4423.8	3729.9
Hong Kong	1253.1	-1204.5	-1383.3	4199.6	2597.7	1238.1	3935.6
Indonesia	2375.0	969.4	704.6	1734.8	1459.8	3321.0	2289.0
Kampuchea	6.4	5.6	6.0	8.9	9.8	4.8	28.4
Korea	1510.1	1433.0	464.7	-2047.7	-1022.7	-240.5	1458.8
Korea, Dem.	–	-11.3	-88.2	-38.4	4.3	-108.7	-41.5
Laos	14.8	42.6	19.4	30.5	36.5	43.5	51.2
Macao	6.8	-7.8	-3.7	46.6	-22.0	32.0	-13.2
Malaysia	1326.3	185.4	60.6	344.8	622.9	499.3	1244.2
Mongolia	0.1	0.4	0.8	0.4	0.7	3.5	5.1
Philippines	576.2	385.2	933.7	670.4	1204.5	914.3	1427.2
Singapore	1322.7	-251.3	-86.5	943.2	1680.7	2980.5	2795.8
Taiwan	-63.3	-493.4	-445.6	-164.3	-63.7	739.2	302.9
Thailand	1023.6	487.7	318.6	887.8	748.0	2399.8	2763.2
Viet Nam	75.6	33.6	66.3	34.4	97.3	83.3	105.1
Far East Asia Unall.	125.2	78.2	327.4	262.8	103.4	301.6	113.4
TOTAL	10123.7	3222.7	3575.3	10476.5	11394.6	16640.8	20188.0
Asia Unspecified	1390.5	461.2	1390.1	-440.2	-46.2	1091.1	983.6
ASIA TOTAL	18265.7	9659.6	12372.4	17021.2	24033.1	28500.2	27959.3

OCEANIA

	1984	1985	1986	1987	1988	1989	1990
Cook Islands	7.0	9.6	26.4	9.7	13.1	18.8	13.7
Fiji	15.8	22.1	33.5	17.5	33.0	57.5	77.5
Kiribati	9.8	10.8	12.3	14.5	12.1	15.2	17.7
Nauru	-0.2	2.3	45.7	0.8	26.8	-8.9	1.2
New Caledonia	131.7	161.5	218.5	268.2	327.9	304.2	355.6
Niue	3.1	3.5	3.9	6.6	5.1	5.5	9.2
Pacif. Isl.(Fed. Sts.)	206.9	154.1	373.3	199.5	252.6	156.9	176.9
Papua New Guinea	483.6	299.8	140.7	203.7	335.1	689.4	432.9
Polynesia, French	175.0	212.8	262.7	335.6	401.4	393.3	325.5
Solomon Islands	19.8	14.6	19.2	35.4	41.7	38.6	43.5
Tokelau	1.7	1.6	1.8	1.6	3.4	4.3	4.4
Tonga	12.4	10.6	11.6	30.5	0.8	26.9	24.0
Tuvalu	5.2	3.2	3.8	24.9	13.3	5.7	4.8
Vanuatu	43.0	35.6	-32.0	16.7	28.3	71.2	141.0
Wallis & Futuna	0.5	0.8	0.0	0.9	0.0	0.0	3.0
Western Samoa	4.3	14.2	17.7	21.3	22.1	19.8	33.9
TOM Unallocated	–	–	–	–	–	–	–
Oceania Unallocated	28.8	21.9	16.9	176.4	411.8	270.1	679.2
TOTAL	1148.4	978.9	1155.8	1363.8	1928.7	2068.3	2344.0
LDCS Unspecified	-1044.8	1360.0	11711.9	1746.9	3167.9	-1295.7	-2532.1
TOTAL,ALL LDCS	61629.6	28142.2	50850.2	48106.6	64739.4	67083.9	46188.4

INCOME GROUPS

	1984	1985	1986	1987	1988	1989	1990
LLDCS	3813.7	4462.8	5097.1	6230.6	7874.5	6802.9	8251.0
OTHER LICS	10889.4	9754.4	13617.7	14937.0	16897.0	21784.6	16325.2
LMICS	7092.2	3121.9	5696.0	4693.7	7058.8	6538.9	7628.7
UMICS	35720.6	6854.7	12891.7	20270.6	24566.3	26271.0	11950.0
UNALLOCATED	4113.7	3948.4	13547.7	1974.8	8342.9	5686.4	2033.5

Chart (y-axis: 0 to 40000; x-axis: 1984, 85, 86, 87, 88, 89, 90)

Legend:
- LLDCS
- OTHER LICS
- LMICS
- UMICS

	1984	1985	1986	1987	1988	1989	1990
EUROPE							
Albania	–	–	–	–	5.5	10.4	41.6
Cyprus	23.2	178.4	177.5	96.4	196.0	246.2	326.9
Gibraltar	19.8	23.3	12.4	45.2	93.0	92.4	36.2
Greece	614.8	141.6	-145.2	325.7	382.7	1078.8	502.1
Malta	11.3	20.8	19.1	22.6	8.8	43.2	97.2
Turkey	1232.3	1132.9	1863.0	2415.3	4688.3	1447.2	2106.7
Yugoslavia	589.5	67.6	-54.1	-250.2	-492.1	-335.4	-537.8
Other Europe	529.4	458.5	-465.8	232.1	629.9	1217.5	738.4
Europe Unallocated	306.4	303.9	-218.9	307.3	-590.1	-139.6	28.6
TOTAL	**3326.6**	**2326.9**	**1187.9**	**3194.4**	**4922.0**	**3660.6**	**3339.9**
NORTH OF SAHARA							
Algeria	502.6	775.3	-102.5	-1263.4	28.4	68.3	377.9
Egypt	3060.8	2890.2	2558.2	2035.4	3751.2	2096.9	3482.7
Libya	135.1	46.9	77.9	103.7	362.7	-59.7	-44.9
Morocco	1219.0	1437.5	1078.4	736.4	983.2	1252.4	1489.6
Tunisia	420.6	300.8	341.6	204.1	318.6	414.9	523.1
North of Sahara Unall.	-58.7	35.3	-173.8	26.1	-97.8	45.5	-125.8
TOTAL	**5279.3**	**5485.9**	**3779.7**	**1842.2**	**5346.4**	**3818.4**	**5702.5**
SOUTH OF SAHARA							
Angola	201.7	258.5	276.2	251.0	90.9	206.0	-5.3
Benin	109.1	97.0	96.3	92.5	71.3	279.3	226.9
Botswana	182.2	158.6	156.2	219.1	101.5	149.4	157.8
Burkina Faso	186.5	189.7	283.2	279.2	304.4	282.6	330.3
Burundi	155.3	154.2	185.9	198.6	185.1	165.9	255.8
Cameroon	280.7	225.8	232.0	310.3	460.0	640.5	672.9
Cape Verde	64.6	70.6	112.4	88.3	85.0	75.3	81.7
Central African Rep.	133.4	111.9	142.0	181.4	197.2	194.0	237.8
Chad	110.6	179.4	162.7	198.3	264.7	239.4	316.1
Comoros	42.8	50.8	47.1	54.4	54.2	44.7	41.7
Congo	111.9	58.6	335.9	254.4	123.4	-91.3	62.2
Cote d'Ivoire	400.8	233.7	435.3	327.1	376.1	-2.5	820.3
Djibouti	130.8	103.2	78.9	101.7	96.4	73.3	120.6
Equatorial Guinea	17.8	17.7	31.4	46.0	51.3	63.8	39.8
Ethiopia	414.3	779.5	682.9	647.0	987.8	718.2	869.0
Gabon	60.7	203.3	309.5	450.0	617.3	514.4	227.3
Gambia	47.7	48.4	100.5	100.9	62.0	215.9	104.5
Ghana	207.3	192.9	399.7	460.1	504.2	749.3	631.5
Guinea	116.5	108.1	166.6	225.0	279.2	344.3	283.5
Guinea-Bissau	61.6	63.3	71.9	105.9	128.5	105.6	128.7
Kenya	538.4	525.7	688.1	699.9	928.3	1366.5	1301.0
Lesotho	95.8	118.4	92.1	100.7	121.1	123.7	140.5
Liberia	-246.0	-287.5	-257.0	-289.3	532.0	273.7	594.9
Madagascar	281.3	207.2	320.4	360.0	294.3	302.6	432.2
Malawi	211.6	117.6	221.4	324.7	404.0	389.7	471.3
Mali	320.7	377.2	365.5	359.8	422.7	446.9	466.2
Mauritania	185.5	235.3	210.4	179.0	168.8	198.6	191.5
Mauritius	58.2	28.4	54.7	114.0	128.8	114.4	149.9
Mayotte	14.0	20.8	28.3	38.8	43.5	43.3	58.5
Mozambique	202.2	330.8	358.6	552.8	808.9	619.2	983.0
Namibia	–	25.0	-83.1	-21.1	-177.6	-99.1	-169.7
Niger	134.6	287.2	295.6	406.1	318.3	271.1	343.9
Nigeria	536.5	-241.6	1127.3	1702.1	-21.4	2270.4	65.7
Reunion	448.0	514.4	616.6	667.7	789.6	833.5	1206.5
Rwanda	162.1	184.2	217.4	254.8	263.7	235.8	281.7
St. Helena	10.0	12.2	13.5	20.1	27.1	47.4	24.6
Sao Tome & Principe	11.3	12.6	12.4	18.6	40.3	32.3	37.8
Senegal	455.8	306.1	638.8	659.9	467.4	606.0	739.3
Seychelles	24.6	28.1	34.6	22.8	10.1	14.4	39.2
Sierra Leone	70.9	56.1	86.9	97.8	113.7	108.0	72.5
Somalia	361.6	370.0	600.9	614.6	402.9	398.9	421.9
Sudan	672.5	1117.0	841.2	774.7	928.0	753.6	739.5
Swaziland	48.2	31.2	41.8	41.5	24.8	14.8	29.8
Tanzania	598.3	556.2	645.2	935.3	949.7	860.2	1095.9
Togo	115.7	95.6	133.6	105.6	208.4	147.9	206.7
Uganda	164.6	219.6	197.2	304.8	378.8	409.8	542.5
Zaire	747.7	461.5	613.1	736.2	885.1	707.1	1301.1
Zambia	397.2	522.7	666.3	360.1	484.4	586.9	551.8
Zimbabwe	432.3	314.1	277.0	447.0	393.8	365.8	425.1
East African Community	2.5	10.8	1.8	1.2	0.8	–	–
DOM/TOM Unallocated	–	-1.2	–	–	–	–	–
EAMA Unallocated	59.4	–	–	–	–	–	–
South of Sahara Unall.	286.3	419.6	25.7	615.6	555.3	1768.2	1019.3
TOTAL	**10437.7**	**10280.4**	**13392.8**	**15796.6**	**15936.4**	**19179.6**	**19367.4**
Africa Unspecified	568.9	-83.8	-46.5	-809.7	1026.6	604.7	299.5
AFRICA TOTAL	**16286.0**	**15682.5**	**17126.0**	**16829.2**	**22309.5**	**23602.6**	**25369.3**
N.& C. AMERICA							
Aruba	–	12.0	40.2	20.9	23.0	32.1	73.9
Bahamas	-103.1	521.1	874.4	1064.2	1344.4	953.8	205.7

	1984	1985
Barbados	-1.7	28.0
Belize	26.5	29.1
Bermuda	328.9	767.3
Costa Rica	291.2	397.2
Cuba	55.9	40.3
Dominican Republic	220.7	265.1
El Salvador	293.7	375.2
Guadeloupe	171.7	246.4
Guatemala	161.5	337.3
Haiti	133.2	141.8
Honduras	376.7	374.3
Jamaica	354.0	219.3
Martinique	281.3	357.3
Mexico	13834.1	-1687.8
Netherlands Antilles	-1729.8	-1246.1
Nicaragua	160.7	116.5
Panama	1230.9	1668.6
St. Pierre & Miquelon	18.9	17.9
Trinidad & Tobago	146.3	-317.8
Anguilla	1.7	2.7
Antigua and Barbuda	-3.9	22.7
Cayman Islands	810.7	811.1
Dominica	29.0	35.9
Grenada	30.5	33.1
Montserrat	1.8	2.2
St. Kitts-Nevis	-2.6	4.7
St. Lucia	5.4	7.1
St. Vincent and Gr.	4.2	7.8
Turks & Caicos Isl.	-4.4	5.8
Virgin Islands	5.9	14.2
West Indies Unall.	-7.7	464.4
DOM/TOM Unallocated	–	-5.9
N.& C. America Unall.	870.2	194.7
TOTAL	**17992.3**	**4263.5**
SOUTH AMERICA		
Argentina	1102.5	2075.8
Bolivia	160.9	201.9
Brazil	7794.4	1321.6
Chile	2242.8	123.4
Colombia	1171.1	323.4
Ecuador	1019.8	25.6
Falkland Islands	8.0	13.8
Guiana	75.4	103.3
Guyana	23.4	35.4
Paraguay	150.3	83.2
Peru	646.2	-65.0
Suriname	1.9	14.4
Uruguay	273.0	-123.9
Venezuela	-330.1	-941.0
South America Unall.	68.1	1032.1
TOTAL	**14407.5**	**4223.9**
America Unspecified	1985.7	108.7
AMERICA TOTAL	**34385.6**	**8596.2**
MIDDLE EAST		
Bahrain	326.8	301.6
Iran	-365.9	-359.7
Iraq	1960.7	924.5
Israel	1985.3	2548.5
Jordan	855.9	320.7
Kuwait	-25.8	-185.3
Lebanon	95.2	58.3
Oman	262.4	182.9
Qatar	-96.0	-11.3
Saudi Arabia	-299.4	163.1
Syria	736.0	688.9
United Arab Emirates	83.0	-293.7
Yemen	414.2	396.8
Middle East Unall.	342.7	-2.9
TOTAL	**6275.1**	**4732.3**
SOUTH ASIA		
Afghanistan	5.6	-5.9
Bangladesh	1239.7	1099.2
Bhutan	17.9	24.1
India	2193.6	2506.8
Maldives	5.5	9.9
Myanmar (Burma)	278.1	310.8
Nepal	200.1	244.0
Pakistan	708.6	897.0
Sri Lanka	632.7	567.7

1986	1987	1988	1989	1990
39.6	-15.3	58.8	14.2	0.3
19.1	23.6	33.6	33.9	33.0
1048.9	3585.1	1274.3	-806.4	1239.3
331.7	242.7	161.3	228.7	146.8
-39.2	-146.8	-36.3	55.6	139.1
341.1	180.3	110.3	169.0	151.2
330.8	422.2	412.9	428.3	340.4
305.5	301.6	385.3	297.2	366.1
126.0	160.6	259.2	206.3	208.2
173.0	211.8	142.6	199.2	181.1
297.9	243.6	376.4	242.4	425.1
69.2	239.7	353.9	426.1	328.8
425.2	459.0	539.7	701.7	890.7
1281.9	1879.4	-3205.6	3869.6	-1114.9
-1443.3	287.4	1826.6	895.0	1178.8
171.9	176.4	242.4	181.7	309.8
1790.8	2275.7	1153.9	2606.9	1093.9
21.7	30.9	37.5	33.5	30.4
9.4	57.3	-20.1	73.8	-90.1
3.2	3.2	2.0	5.3	5.7
45.5	28.1	9.9	33.2	5.9
1008.2	2240.0	3161.6	2262.1	2636.8
39.5	37.2	4.2	45.1	31.1
28.3	22.0	22.1	8.0	21.0
4.2	4.5	5.8	7.1	8.4
5.3	10.9	8.8	25.9	7.0
11.8	15.3	25.3	30.0	13.6
12.5	13.4	16.1	15.6	13.0
8.9	-0.1	8.2	9.0	9.0
0.1	89.0	257.6	-69.4	184.2
331.6	307.5	82.6	64.0	76.6
–	–	–	–	–
17.1	137.3	994.8	1114.7	-1173.2
7731.9	14608.3	10073.3	14393.0	7976.6
4979.8	899.5	1371.4	-1532.8	-713.0
304.4	408.1	444.5	501.3	502.1
998.1	-787.8	3433.8	3836.8	-2129.1
127.6	-377.7	524.9	-16.8	968.6
1124.2	119.0	-771.6	-324.5	204.2
964.4	345.1	184.3	176.3	201.0
14.7	13.3	10.3	-0.5	-7.0
163.4	173.3	165.5	153.9	185.5
27.2	41.9	36.8	59.1	164.2
117.3	103.5	55.8	60.1	5.2
33.7	115.3	21.0	33.5	-124.1
83.8	-31.9	-18.0	34.6	124.1
62.9	254.2	-266.6	396.0	-59.6
2796.8	2161.6	-56.1	454.5	-3795.4
108.4	-10.0	42.1	258.7	-94.5
11907.0	3427.4	5178.2	4090.0	-4567.6
-443.1	583.1	3185.5	2492.3	3786.9
19195.8	18618.9	18437.0	20975.2	7195.9
119.9	-22.9	13.2	93.3	83.1
-333.2	-11.9	615.1	1509.1	571.0
-61.9	-133.9	17.5	378.9	-1001.2
2296.3	2092.2	6263.2	2005.8	1399.9
651.4	869.6	837.9	759.7	1111.4
54.1	65.7	-128.9	-197.0	-132.8
124.6	94.0	167.6	112.8	62.1
291.3	42.4	-124.2	-338.9	109.9
-70.7	-23.2	-3.3	16.0	25.3
-361.3	298.0	-166.1	0.2	582.8
812.8	727.7	424.7	242.4	721.8
-100.7	201.8	51.1	-135.0	-167.1
312.0	439.4	237.9	278.8	388.0
868.1	-442.6	-55.9	-72.0	-17.1
4602.6	4196.1	8149.8	4654.0	3737.1
2.5	45.7	74.9	164.7	141.3
1428.5	1609.0	1591.6	1811.6	2166.4
40.1	42.1	59.5	40.6	50.1
3817.7	3499.0	4123.2	5172.4	4291.9
16.2	23.7	25.1	59.1	38.8
372.5	351.8	472.5	86.6	115.0
330.8	373.5	428.4	496.0	426.9
1004.6	974.6	1875.6	2345.3	1721.1
514.2	544.0	580.6	744.9	672.8

	1984	1985	1986	1987	1988	1989	1990
South Asia Unall.	2.4	105.3	132.2	15.9	38.1	34.2	56.5
TOTAL	5284.2	5758.8	7659.3	7479.3	9269.5	10955.5	9680.7
FAR EAST ASIA							
Brunei	-2.5	-3.5	-4.2	2.4	5.1	5.5	-7.1
China	938.1	2297.2	3478.8	4363.4	5266.9	5687.1	4817.9
Hong Kong	1254.4	-1206.4	-1385.3	4164.5	2606.3	1267.0	3953.8
Indonesia	3308.9	1815.9	1551.7	3141.5	3234.7	4833.5	3524.8
Kampuchea	14.8	12.9	13.5	14.2	18.5	17.3	41.6
Korea	1916.2	1592.3	385.4	-2437.7	-1906.0	-807.4	1076.1
Korea, Dem.	–	-6.0	-83.7	-31.7	10.2	-103.4	-34.0
Laos	35.2	64.1	48.4	58.3	77.3	139.9	151.7
Macao	7.2	-7.5	-3.4	46.6	-21.8	32.1	-13.0
Malaysia	1418.5	232.4	54.3	389.7	627.8	516.6	1331.5
Mongolia	0.1	3.3	4.7	2.8	3.1	8.4	11.9
Philippines	930.7	588.6	1091.8	848.0	1310.5	1215.8	2098.2
Singapore	1314.1	-267.3	-109.1	912.7	1657.9	2963.2	2757.9
Taiwan	-73.7	-518.0	-476.0	-305.0	-79.2	732.1	324.3
Thailand	1460.0	856.7	575.4	918.4	345.0	2294.7	2732.5
Viet Nam	103.7	93.3	122.8	83.7	161.0	147.4	187.6
Far East Asia Unall.	125.2	78.4	335.0	275.1	127.1	320.0	131.7
TOTAL	12751.0	5626.2	5600.0	12447.1	13444.3	19269.8	23087.3
Asia Unspecified	2133.5	546.1	3010.7	854.4	94.8	1172.8	1243.6
ASIA TOTAL	26443.8	16663.4	20872.6	24976.9	30958.4	36052.1	37748.7
OCEANIA							
Cook Islands	7.6	10.6	27.3	11.0	14.2	20.3	15.9
Fiji	31.9	22.5	46.7	22.2	56.6	56.2	70.4
Kiribati	11.4	12.0	13.8	18.3	16.3	17.5	20.5
Nauru	-0.2	2.3	45.7	0.8	26.8	-8.9	1.2
New Caledonia	132.6	161.7	218.5	268.0	327.3	304.4	355.8
Niue	3.2	3.5	4.2	6.7	5.3	5.6	9.4
Pacif. Isl.(Fed. Sts.)	207.7	155.2	374.7	201.0	253.5	157.9	178.0
Papua New Guinea	519.3	330.2	198.3	305.6	446.2	741.5	562.1
Polynesia, French	175.0	214.3	263.1	338.9	408.4	395.7	327.9
Solomon Islands	25.5	22.0	29.9	70.4	65.1	49.9	56.6
Tokelau	1.8	1.8	2.0	1.8	3.7	4.6	4.8
Tonga	15.7	13.6	15.1	36.6	5.9	31.7	31.0
Tuvalu	5.5	3.3	4.4	25.7	14.0	6.9	5.0
Vanuatu	45.3	38.5	-28.4	35.2	38.6	79.2	147.7
Wallis & Futuna	1.6	1.0	0.1	1.2	1.1	0.1	3.1
Western Samoa	13.4	20.1	22.9	34.7	30.8	30.6	56.9
TOM Unallocated	–	–	–	–	–	–	–
Oceania Unallocated	28.8	21.9	16.9	183.0	417.2	281.6	690.7
TOTAL	1226.1	1034.2	1255.1	1561.1	2131.0	2174.7	2537.0
LDCS Unspecified	-330.1	2459.5	12402.1	2494.2	5458.0	616.5	-207.0
TOTAL,ALL LDCS	81338.0	46757.4	72039.8	67674.7	84215.8	87081.6	75978.4
INCOME GROUPS							
LLDCS	7239.4	8281.3	9076.0	10547.2	12139.4	11631.7	13673.9
OTHER LICS	16084.3	14625.3	19735.3	21935.7	25208.6	30303.9	27396.8
LMICS	11115.1	7495.3	9561.5	8241.3	9302.4	8488.2	11710.2
UMICS	40515.6	10674.0	17299.5	22412.0	26286.1	28096.5	17487.4
UNALLOCATED	6383.7	5681.4	16367.6	4538.5	11279.1	8561.3	5710.2

Legend: LLDCS, OTHER LICS, LMICS, UMICS. Y-axis: 5000–45000. X-axis: 1984, 85, 86, 87, 88, 89, 90.

	1984	1985	1986	1987	1988	1989	1990
EUROPE							
Albania	–	–	–	–	5.9	11.7	13.8
Cyprus	25.2	21.7	17.4	22.0	15.9	25.3	13.4
Gibraltar	8.5	5.8	13.2	11.5	16.4	0.7	0.2
Greece	18.5	17.8	25.1	47.6	44.5	39.8	45.8
Malta	8.9	8.5	5.6	3.0	2.5	2.9	3.1
Turkey	529.0	295.7	360.1	769.8	419.9	734.1	492.8
Yugoslavia	38.3	10.3	83.6	24.0	105.1	31.7	92.3
Other Europe	140.5	96.5	134.2	49.5	98.5	68.6	112.9
Europe Unallocated	4.4	4.8	5.2	2.8	2.2	11.5	28.5
TOTAL	**773.2**	**461.1**	**644.4**	**930.1**	**710.8**	**926.3**	**802.9**
NORTH OF SAHARA							
Algeria	58.1	75.1	94.5	139.2	247.0	428.7	360.4
Egypt	1735.6	1853.5	1588.4	1331.6	2059.2	1532.9	13328.6
Libya	2.4	3.4	3.5	2.8	2.2	6.8	7.8
Morocco	449.7	301.2	415.6	447.1	584.5	455.0	831.7
Tunisia	160.9	202.5	415.1	293.8	366.8	356.7	416.0
North of Sahara Unall.	5.3	13.4	0.4	21.1	15.8	61.8	5.2
TOTAL	**2412.1**	**2449.1**	**2517.6**	**2235.6**	**3275.5**	**2841.9**	**14949.6**
SOUTH OF SAHARA							
Angola	67.6	76.4	92.5	96.8	106.2	102.0	184.0
Benin	74.4	41.7	73.0	70.4	137.3	182.5	170.2
Botswana	88.1	68.5	117.1	73.9	154.5	74.2	94.4
Burkina Faso	159.1	127.4	211.0	282.0	218.1	192.9	262.9
Burundi	73.6	77.3	77.2	105.6	109.2	101.9	135.8
Cameroon	260.0	141.3	217.8	288.8	284.2	331.2	405.3
Cape Verde	47.6	42.5	61.2	67.5	52.0	52.7	66.5
Central African Rep.	77.3	75.0	102.5	103.1	98.2	93.9	123.3
Chad	76.7	133.7	135.3	153.3	131.1	174.3	176.6
Comoros	24.6	12.7	23.2	35.5	34.9	29.0	25.4
Congo	65.2	47.8	145.0	150.0	65.0	91.8	288.6
Cote d'Ivoire	156.1	106.0	275.5	197.4	254.3	235.4	750.5
Djibouti	54.4	44.7	89.9	82.0	64.6	72.2	74.9
Equatorial Guinea	9.0	7.2	15.9	40.8	13.6	15.1	18.2
Ethiopia	285.4	372.5	454.3	466.8	533.6	315.0	473.0
Gabon	85.1	60.9	66.5	80.9	111.7	124.4	45.1
Gambia	44.6	23.4	51.0	48.0	80.0	50.7	51.5
Ghana	79.1	149.3	151.6	313.2	391.9	450.2	388.6
Guinea	62.7	108.4	120.0	129.6	182.1	209.6	204.3
Guinea-Bissau	30.2	32.4	41.8	75.9	44.1	56.3	69.8
Kenya	479.5	315.5	431.6	523.9	728.4	780.5	985.5
Lesotho	60.2	53.3	76.2	60.8	70.6	80.9	66.2
Liberia	92.4	60.1	90.0	61.1	50.2	47.9	23.4
Madagascar	135.8	140.8	184.8	220.4	308.0	204.9	211.8
Malawi	71.3	67.8	192.2	159.0	259.2	206.7	230.9
Mali	296.7	242.2	219.5	221.0	278.0	407.5	245.4
Mauritania	106.6	90.9	106.0	111.9	95.8	153.0	133.4
Mauritius	28.0	24.5	51.9	36.8	85.4	84.1	93.5
Mayotte	10.0	19.9	20.7	37.9	36.5	43.3	59.0
Mozambique	224.7	239.1	460.4	560.5	783.6	631.2	620.8
Namibia	–	10.2	7.4	8.1	15.3	29.4	81.3
Niger	196.6	169.4	263.1	234.0	250.3	192.6	226.0
Nigeria	30.9	28.8	47.5	59.6	125.6	493.6	214.6
Reunion	492.1	356.7	316.2	554.0	556.9	683.4	927.4
Rwanda	110.2	110.0	122.5	187.9	133.4	170.7	202.8
St. Helena	10.0	12.1	13.5	48.0	16.0	13.7	15.2
Sao Tome & Principe	4.3	1.9	7.7	5.6	17.9	13.1	10.9
Senegal	258.8	246.4	393.0	496.8	452.6	452.3	480.9
Seychelles	12.7	11.4	24.0	15.8	14.6	17.8	33.2
Sierra Leone	27.6	90.9	58.9	67.6	56.0	147.9	36.6
Somalia	185.9	207.9	572.5	468.7	379.4	226.1	169.3
Sudan	396.3	636.9	533.2	427.0	493.5	349.2	239.7
Swaziland	22.7	24.2	44.3	17.3	39.9	38.5	19.5
Tanzania	384.3	367.9	640.7	883.7	669.6	597.3	846.9
Togo	75.7	159.0	111.2	81.2	166.8	100.7	135.8
Uganda	88.4	48.6	122.2	138.9	218.3	170.2	333.0
Zaire	236.0	189.1	324.7	423.8	483.2	638.2	482.6
Zambia	252.7	265.8	318.5	373.1	321.0	278.4	438.8
Zimbabwe	269.0	145.8	245.0	241.0	330.5	273.1	236.2
East African Community	6.7	11.6	2.8	1.3	0.9	2.4	–
DOM/TOM Unallocated	–	–	–	–	–	–	–
EAMA Unallocated	73.6	–	–	–	–	–	–
South of Sahara Unall.	127.6	277.0	378.4	531.0	604.4	648.7	685.2
TOTAL	**6587.9**	**6374.7**	**8902.4**	**10119.1**	**11107.8**	**11132.3**	**12494.4**
Africa Unspecified	144.5	254.8	182.1	223.7	253.5	261.1	179.4
AFRICA TOTAL	**9144.5**	**9078.5**	**11602.1**	**12578.5**	**14636.8**	**14235.3**	**27623.3**
N.& C. AMERICA							
Aruba	–	30.1	16.2	20.8	31.6	18.9	29.8
Bahamas	0.1	0.1	0.1	0.1	0.1	0.2	2.1

	1984	1985
Barbados	8.9	5.8
Belize	14.7	34.6
Bermuda	0.0	0.0
Costa Rica	229.4	316.7
Cuba	6.4	3.6
Dominican Republic	179.6	173.1
El Salvador	336.7	389.6
Guadeloupe	142.6	151.1
Guatemala	94.4	114.1
Haiti	100.3	110.6
Honduras	120.1	312.7
Jamaica	247.9	163.9
Martinique	482.2	271.9
Mexico	130.5	218.7
Netherlands Antilles	61.5	67.7
Nicaragua	69.4	120.2
Panama	52.6	53.8
St. Pierre & Miquelon	12.8	18.8
Trinidad & Tobago	1.7	13.1
Anguilla	2.8	1.5
Antigua and Barbuda	2.8	2.7
Cayman Islands	–	–
Dominica	3.8	2.0
Grenada	57.0	18.8
Montserrat	3.3	1.7
St. Kitts-Nevis	5.4	0.6
St. Lucia	7.2	4.9
St. Vincent and Gr.	18.4	0.9
Turks & Caicos Isl.	6.9	4.7
Virgin Islands	1.1	1.6
West Indies Unall.	48.6	55.6
DOM/TOM Unallocated	–	–
N.& C. America Unall.	51.4	198.9
TOTAL	**2500.4**	**2864.0**
SOUTH AMERICA		
Argentina	28.4	35.7
Bolivia	129.7	108.9
Brazil	182.5	368.8
Chile	48.3	54.7
Colombia	113.3	61.4
Ecuador	63.9	130.9
Falkland Islands	3.8	13.2
Guiana	63.9	86.6
Guyana	10.7	5.7
Paraguay	33.9	77.1
Peru	269.2	207.3
Suriname	0.8	2.2
Uruguay	16.5	9.3
Venezuela	17.7	12.6
South America Unall.	9.8	9.4
TOTAL	**992.3**	**1183.6**
America Unspecified	68.1	58.7
AMERICA TOTAL	**3560.8**	**4106.3**
MIDDLE EAST		
Bahrain	0.6	0.8
Iran	17.3	16.0
Iraq	28.5	66.9
Israel	1317.9	2035.9
Jordan	85.9	150.4
Kuwait	3.4	3.3
Lebanon	61.1	38.2
Oman	17.7	23.8
Qatar	0.5	0.6
Saudi Arabia	25.9	15.3
Syria	17.2	14.9
United Arab Emirates	2.5	45.9
Yemen	99.7	106.9
Middle East Unall.	24.4	64.1
TOTAL	**1702.5**	**2582.8**
SOUTH ASIA		
Afghanistan	4.7	7.6
Bangladesh	782.7	698.6
Bhutan	3.8	15.4
India	1772.6	721.3
Maldives	7.6	6.2
Myanmar (Burma)	384.3	275.5
Nepal	106.0	198.1
Pakistan	659.2	807.4
Sri Lanka	374.8	294.3

1986	1987	1988	1989	1990
5.4	3.5	2.7	1.2	2.4
12.6	16.0	11.9	26.0	11.6
0.0	0.1	0.0	0.3	42.1
196.6	223.4	195.4	274.8	164.6
4.7	7.2	9.2	17.4	5.6
160.8	79.8	96.1	160.9	59.8
367.6	474.0	450.0	336.4	310.4
170.3	232.0	269.8	225.2	316.9
153.0	228.6	222.5	209.0	254.1
147.9	157.4	107.0	155.7	140.2
188.0	262.4	270.2	203.1	296.7
154.2	196.9	289.1	215.2	200.5
173.6	327.0	264.9	609.2	845.6
157.1	141.4	84.5	140.4	647.6
64.3	74.6	74.0	74.1	60.4
73.3	102.8	209.4	198.7	454.7
44.3	34.6	7.9	6.7	406.9
19.5	32.1	39.0	33.2	31.3
27.2	2.5	6.6	30.1	4.4
2.4	2.6	2.9	3.3	1.0
0.8	1.9	0.9	5.0	2.3
0.1	12.6	0.0	0.0	2.1
8.4	17.8	6.4	7.3	4.2
2.3	3.9	6.0	3.3	6.4
3.1	2.3	7.2	6.9	4.0
1.4	11.7	11.1	10.0	1.8
2.0	2.4	25.0	1.8	20.1
4.0	16.9	5.1	4.8	1.4
8.0	9.1	7.7	8.7	4.0
1.3	1.0	0.9	3.8	1.4
51.0	56.5	12.9	11.0	46.4
–	–	–	–	–
93.7	114.1	136.0	117.4	117.8
2315.3	*2870.1*	*2864.2*	*3119.8*	*4500.6*
88.2	143.2	271.6	208.9	145.2
190.1	261.8	414.2	355.5	386.3
167.0	207.2	194.1	210.0	202.2
58.0	72.9	77.2	93.8	151.8
225.1	79.3	150.3	167.6	188.7
110.5	142.7	246.9	184.0	264.4
18.5	13.2	7.1	6.1	0.8
102.1	158.4	151.6	110.9	125.4
4.8	14.7	21.8	86.0	57.8
51.0	135.1	55.5	47.9	116.2
199.6	255.3	342.9	374.0	288.0
4.5	7.9	42.3	36.9	33.9
30.3	29.6	30.9	118.6	29.5
19.2	28.8	17.8	65.2	34.6
2.7	31.4	15.9	48.6	22.5
1271.6	*1581.4*	*2040.2*	*2113.9*	*2047.3*
82.8	112.2	99.5	170.5	152.2
3669.7	*4563.7*	*5003.9*	*5404.2*	*6700.1*
1.5	1.1	1.1	4.2	1.9
20.4	54.2	63.3	62.7	97.2
7.9	11.9	13.3	12.6	12.6
2008.9	1368.4	1544.8	1443.5	1401.0
133.0	224.9	82.3	199.8	652.9
3.7	2.8	4.6	2.0	2.2
52.0	66.4	110.4	73.3	77.0
22.9	21.4	18.2	23.6	37.0
1.5	1.8	1.1	3.1	1.3
20.0	12.1	13.3	9.0	12.4
27.7	277.1	166.5	27.9	46.3
3.4	76.4	3.7	2.9	3.0
119.7	157.8	365.1	145.4	173.5
5.4	41.1	41.3	26.8	32.9
2428.1	*2317.2*	*2428.8*	*2036.6*	*2551.2*
8.2	52.9	99.5	104.7	126.4
866.3	973.9	1022.4	1184.8	1041.8
14.7	15.2	26.2	29.6	35.0
1455.0	2061.2	2447.0	1494.4	1503.0
8.7	14.1	25.9	18.1	10.4
371.8	399.6	117.0	17.2	32.5
161.9	288.0	240.1	244.9	218.2
605.4	1188.3	1207.6	1219.8	887.9
527.5	360.0	698.4	285.3	472.2

	1984	1985	1986	1987	1988	1989	1990
South Asia Unall.	2.0	18.7	21.1	2.4	15.6	26.9	13.9
TOTAL	*4097.5*	*3043.1*	*4040.6*	*5355.6*	*5899.5*	*4625.6*	*4341.3*
FAR EAST ASIA							
Brunei	0.9	1.3	2.7	3.5	4.7	4.8	3.5
China	503.4	549.2	949.4	1340.8	2611.6	1872.5	970.2
Hong Kong	15.7	14.1	13.6	15.3	11.7	13.6	19.7
Indonesia	998.6	1153.8	589.0	1915.3	2591.2	2533.9	2714.0
Kampuchea	8.4	3.2	3.8	10.1	9.8	18.8	18.7
Korea	249.7	272.3	49.9	389.1	283.8	135.4	787.6
Korea, Dem.	–	0.3	1.2	4.5	2.2	3.6	1.1
Laos	18.5	10.6	31.3	27.7	58.9	57.1	54.2
Macao	0.1	0.1	0.1	0.2	0.2	0.2	0.1
Malaysia	333.4	190.9	317.5	104.9	743.8	125.1	662.7
Mongolia	0.1	0.4	0.7	0.7	1.8	1.5	8.9
Philippines	423.3	338.7	1008.5	1024.2	1658.8	1403.8	1861.4
Singapore	46.1	28.4	25.3	31.0	110.9	24.5	24.9
Taiwan	7.6	2.4	3.7	6.6	6.6	8.6	9.9
Thailand	468.8	491.2	459.5	612.5	1054.1	508.3	1256.3
Viet Nam	55.6	64.6	85.8	52.7	85.7	72.5	98.3
Far East Asia Unall.	66.8	25.7	45.3	33.7	72.7	71.6	105.6
TOTAL	*3197.0*	*3147.2*	*3587.1*	*5572.7*	*9308.4*	*6855.8*	*8597.0*
Asia Unspecified	38.2	34.7	63.4	57.8	59.7	68.5	96.3
ASIA TOTAL	*9035.2*	*8807.8*	*10119.2*	*13303.2*	*17696.3*	*13586.5*	*15585.8*
OCEANIA							
Cook Islands	7.5	7.3	10.2	12.9	11.5	1.6	10.8
Fiji	30.1	27.2	47.3	26.8	52.9	30.8	28.5
Kiribati	8.7	10.8	6.4	8.6	13.8	15.8	12.3
Nauru	0.1	0.1	0.0	0.1	0.1	0.1	0.1
New Caledonia	111.5	155.9	159.8	282.4	282.7	284.0	338.3
Niue	3.4	3.6	2.5	5.1	4.1	0.3	5.9
Pacif. Isl.(Fed. Sts.)	162.4	119.2	215.6	10.2	392.1	200.9	173.5
Papua New Guinea	300.5	246.7	231.7	337.7	639.8	64.6	91.0
Polynesia, French	135.9	178.3	198.2	292.5	345.5	327.7	295.1
Solomon Islands	12.8	7.9	24.2	25.0	36.5	38.1	29.5
Tokelau	1.7	1.3	1.7	2.4	2.9	0.0	2.9
Tonga	10.3	7.6	15.2	11.9	19.3	18.1	21.7
Tuvalu	3.8	3.1	12.5	13.7	12.4	5.2	3.1
Vanuatu	21.7	21.2	20.2	29.0	23.6	47.9	30.0
Wallis & Futuna	8.1	11.4	–	–	0.0	–	0.0
Western Samoa	15.2	21.6	12.4	16.6	30.4	16.7	24.8
TOM Unallocated	77.2	–	–	–	–	–	–
Oceania Unallocated	47.1	22.0	22.9	18.4	45.4	45.5	50.7
TOTAL	*958.1*	*845.1*	*980.8*	*1093.1*	*1912.9*	*1097.0*	*1118.0*
LDCS Unspecified	2842.2	2510.5	3563.2	3570.0	4734.0	4618.3	6062.7
TOTAL,ALL LDCS	*26313.9*	*25809.3*	*30579.6*	*36038.6*	*44694.7*	*39873.9*	*57892.8*
INCOME GROUPS							
LLDCS	4985.6	5199.4	6931.5	7557.9	7917.9	7158.0	7370.0
OTHER LICS	8583.2	7618.6	9328.3	12522.9	17351.0	14842.2	26479.8
LMICS	4113.9	3669.9	4473.4	5332.0	6474.2	5042.4	6902.6
UMICS	4993.4	5761.7	5325.9	5808.5	6842.1	6634.4	9541.1
UNALLOCATED	3637.9	3559.8	4520.5	4817.4	6109.6	6196.8	7599.3

Legend: LLDCS · OTHER LICS · LMICS · UMICS

(Chart: y-axis 2000 to 28000; x-axis years 1984, 85, 86, 87, 88, 89, 90)

	1984	1985	1986	1987	1988	1989	1990
EUROPE							
Albania	–	–	–	–	8.1	14.8	15.8
Cyprus	48.4	35.3	43.0	30.9	59.5	43.0	33.4
Gibraltar	8.5	5.8	13.2	11.5	16.4	0.7	0.2
Greece	20.8	22.8	29.6	50.3	54.0	44.9	48.8
Malta	9.1	8.9	9.0	22.1	16.5	3.9	3.6
Turkey	567.9	364.2	419.0	840.5	458.8	772.8	2087.7
Yugoslavia	43.8	13.9	87.8	29.3	110.2	38.8	101.2
Other Europe	150.6	107.5	178.7	50.8	104.8	70.3	113.9
Europe Unallocated	18.1	24.3	20.6	2.8	2.2	11.5	28.5
TOTAL	**867.1**	**582.7**	**801.0**	**1038.1**	**830.5**	**1000.6**	**2433.2**
NORTH OF SAHARA							
Algeria	213.4	153.8	122.0	180.5	348.1	540.3	427.5
Egypt	1840.4	1949.3	1746.0	1595.7	2216.7	2050.9	16301.1
Libya	5.2	5.6	6.0	6.9	5.8	16.8	20.5
Morocco	539.6	860.1	703.8	527.5	674.8	766.8	1193.0
Tunisia	290.2	296.1	640.2	352.0	659.7	517.9	564.3
North of Sahara Unall.	5.3	13.4	0.4	22.5	16.0	70.0	13.4
TOTAL	**2894.1**	**3278.3**	**3218.4**	**2685.1**	**3921.1**	**3962.8**	**18519.7**
SOUTH OF SAHARA							
Angola	104.3	113.9	138.2	193.0	165.7	170.7	290.1
Benin	165.1	95.5	127.0	204.1	290.8	301.6	278.0
Botswana	110.1	113.1	144.1	148.3	209.7	128.4	166.3
Burkina Faso	246.2	249.5	263.1	331.0	366.8	453.3	351.3
Burundi	123.5	199.7	159.2	202.7	367.8	217.6	333.7
Cameroon	304.3	167.3	270.5	336.1	472.8	455.6	503.2
Cape Verde	94.1	61.6	89.8	108.5	116.9	78.5	131.8
Central African Rep.	96.8	117.5	173.9	201.7	210.0	196.7	296.0
Chad	144.5	210.0	254.8	331.3	309.7	397.5	324.4
Comoros	50.5	26.3	34.6	61.0	54.5	57.4	45.9
Congo	71.2	58.1	165.2	167.9	134.8	99.2	308.9
Cote d'Ivoire	169.4	115.7	338.7	251.2	463.3	402.1	932.5
Djibouti	111.0	76.1	152.8	117.1	109.2	124.9	88.8
Equatorial Guinea	26.9	41.0	41.9	59.2	44.4	28.9	46.9
Ethiopia	603.6	626.8	808.3	818.3	1152.3	862.9	856.9
Gabon	92.1	67.0	68.0	104.2	150.9	139.4	53.4
Gambia	82.1	33.2	113.6	89.0	137.0	120.1	109.3
Ghana	287.2	419.6	361.6	726.5	702.2	781.6	799.4
Guinea	237.2	176.7	209.2	372.5	466.7	390.0	463.5
Guinea-Bissau	76.1	62.1	62.8	188.5	90.8	193.8	104.8
Kenya	659.8	399.3	623.2	687.0	1087.6	1246.0	1389.2
Lesotho	125.2	91.9	139.6	108.5	188.4	135.3	140.3
Liberia	145.2	86.3	100.3	160.0	57.7	65.1	57.2
Madagascar	235.0	263.2	341.5	468.7	626.2	315.0	416.0
Malawi	143.9	222.0	265.0	316.7	495.6	481.5	511.2
Mali	411.4	438.1	361.5	356.7	568.3	642.1	517.1
Mauritania	191.5	250.2	200.9	260.3	261.0	288.4	257.7
Mauritius	40.9	30.0	59.3	70.8	104.1	89.8	99.6
Mayotte	13.5	19.9	20.7	38.0	36.5	48.5	64.3
Mozambique	308.1	357.1	541.6	866.7	1122.9	1076.4	862.2
Namibia	–	13.7	11.3	8.7	20.7	54.1	100.9
Niger	346.0	261.0	457.3	446.4	471.2	270.7	293.0
Nigeria	55.3	59.4	66.2	86.2	385.4	686.7	632.6
Reunion	529.3	387.1	353.5	592.5	596.4	716.5	960.4
Rwanda	161.0	199.1	229.5	351.9	203.4	296.2	369.0
St. Helena	10.0	12.2	13.5	48.2	16.1	13.8	15.3
Sao Tome & Principe	15.2	13.9	40.9	46.9	63.1	25.9	67.4
Senegal	445.8	312.9	637.8	935.2	643.0	624.1	741.3
Seychelles	14.0	23.1	25.2	18.4	66.2	27.4	41.4
Sierra Leone	84.9	110.9	90.7	130.3	80.0	183.5	111.8
Somalia	417.2	389.5	786.0	700.5	502.0	505.7	447.3
Sudan	720.4	1301.9	1303.4	1017.6	1024.8	756.9	518.2
Swaziland	39.3	28.0	53.8	50.7	70.7	57.6	33.0
Tanzania	516.7	464.9	887.2	1222.0	983.0	779.3	1567.4
Togo	125.8	234.2	177.4	157.6	301.5	196.5	308.2
Uganda	308.8	150.3	216.0	440.2	458.5	484.4	844.2
Zaire	376.1	386.6	600.3	834.0	650.3	944.1	614.0
Zambia	343.3	450.4	463.2	505.2	403.2	339.6	497.7
Zimbabwe	315.0	161.5	279.2	282.8	387.6	348.0	324.5
East African Community	7.1	11.6	2.8	1.3	0.9	2.4	–
DOM/TOM Unallocated	–	–	–	–	–	–	–
EAMA Unallocated	73.6	–	–	–	–	–	–
South of Sahara Unall.	399.7	352.1	383.5	552.5	863.9	930.2	974.0
TOTAL	**10774.9**	**10512.9**	**13709.6**	**16774.5**	**18756.4**	**18231.7**	**20261.2**
Africa Unspecified	888.7	358.9	428.6	680.8	457.2	471.3	408.7
AFRICA TOTAL	**14557.7**	**14150.1**	**17356.6**	**20140.5**	**23134.6**	**22665.8**	**39189.7**
N.& C. AMERICA							
Aruba	–	30.1	16.2	20.9	32.8	19.2	30.0
Bahamas	1.2	1.4	3.6	0.7	6.3	0.8	3.1

	1984	1985
Barbados	13.3	15.8
Belize	15.5	38.9
Bermuda	0.1	0.1
Costa Rica	268.9	338.6
Cuba	10.3	18.1
Dominican Republic	206.8	177.3
El Salvador	352.2	429.2
Guadeloupe	156.9	160.9
Guatemala	107.7	128.3
Haiti	135.1	155.0
Honduras	177.1	377.9
Jamaica	263.2	194.4
Martinique	501.8	293.6
Mexico	150.8	257.4
Netherlands Antilles	64.1	69.5
Nicaragua	92.5	141.7
Panama	64.8	83.1
St. Pierre & Miquelon	12.8	18.8
Trinidad & Tobago	6.5	18.9
Anguilla	3.3	3.2
Antigua and Barbuda	3.5	4.6
Cayman Islands	1.9	0.6
Dominica	7.1	9.5
Grenada	61.8	33.7
Montserrat	3.4	2.4
St. Kitts-Nevis	10.7	3.9
St. Lucia	25.4	6.6
St. Vincent and Gr.	32.5	3.0
Turks & Caicos Isl.	7.5	5.0
Virgin Islands	1.2	1.7
West Indies Unall.	48.6	55.7
DOM/TOM Unallocated	–	–
N.& C. America Unall.	95.3	199.3
TOTAL	**2903.6**	**3278.0**
SOUTH AMERICA		
Argentina	103.2	44.1
Bolivia	188.9	138.9
Brazil	226.9	434.7
Chile	51.4	60.0
Colombia	136.8	83.5
Ecuador	126.7	178.3
Falkland Islands	3.8	13.3
Guiana	77.9	102.5
Guyana	18.7	38.2
Paraguay	47.1	81.7
Peru	293.3	226.5
Suriname	7.3	41.2
Uruguay	55.5	18.7
Venezuela	20.2	15.6
South America Unall.	15.3	9.4
TOTAL	**1372.9**	**1486.8**
America Unspecified	133.4	125.2
AMERICA TOTAL	**4410.0**	**4890.1**
MIDDLE EAST		
Bahrain	148.4	59.2
Iran	28.1	31.5
Iraq	40.0	68.6
Israel	1317.9	2035.9
Jordan	690.5	617.8
Kuwait	4.5	4.2
Lebanon	86.3	93.7
Oman	73.9	84.6
Qatar	1.3	1.9
Saudi Arabia	34.9	26.8
Syria	700.7	708.6
United Arab Emirates	3.4	48.2
Yemen	633.7	507.8
Middle East Unall.	48.3	89.8
TOTAL	**3812.1**	**4378.1**
SOUTH ASIA		
Afghanistan	13.8	19.4
Bangladesh	1655.8	1530.4
Bhutan	35.3	54.1
India	2810.7	2015.4
Maldives	18.9	9.7
Myanmar (Burma)	434.8	343.0
Nepal	418.7	372.8
Pakistan	1403.0	1393.7
Sri Lanka	541.5	452.5

1986	1987	1988	1989	1990
6.1	5.1	3.6	5.0	6.3
23.3	19.0	29.4	38.7	24.7
0.1	0.2	0.0	0.3	42.1
216.4	235.4	211.9	289.8	179.9
18.2	28.7	25.6	30.7	22.0
164.8	93.1	101.0	229.2	66.0
402.9	679.2	468.0	356.2	418.1
197.7	273.6	285.0	236.8	328.5
177.2	291.6	260.1	243.1	317.4
222.9	234.9	124.7	264.5	272.7
314.1	317.4	330.7	229.9	415.6
176.1	219.9	347.9	243.6	222.7
195.1	338.2	276.5	622.4	858.9
196.3	164.3	121.1	174.5	721.8
64.5	75.2	91.3	77.7	64.1
107.9	137.3	261.9	242.3	503.0
49.6	39.1	11.2	10.0	409.9
19.5	32.2	39.0	33.2	31.3
38.9	4.8	17.7	52.6	26.6
4.7	2.8	5.3	3.6	1.4
3.4	2.2	2.0	7.2	4.6
1.0	12.7	2.1	1.2	3.3
17.3	36.7	14.7	14.1	8.8
7.1	16.9	13.4	10.0	11.6
3.7	4.2	8.5	8.6	6.1
4.8	16.0	17.4	17.0	9.0
10.8	11.7	35.4	8.0	33.2
16.0	23.5	22.8	11.7	7.1
8.7	9.6	8.1	13.7	10.2
4.8	2.1	2.3	10.6	8.2
52.0	106.5	52.0	47.5	82.9
–	–	–	–	–
99.9	120.5	198.7	200.4	200.8
2845.3	3576.2	3428.5	3754.0	5351.8
106.5	166.7	308.6	230.5	165.5
308.8	416.9	587.7	614.0	665.5
201.2	290.5	226.2	258.5	275.8
63.7	80.3	84.3	116.0	179.2
249.8	101.2	170.1	191.2	209.8
173.1	232.8	268.1	254.1	388.2
18.8	13.2	7.2	6.1	0.8
124.3	171.7	167.7	121.5	136.2
23.3	26.9	110.8	142.4	182.5
54.9	153.2	106.8	72.0	152.7
243.6	286.2	400.3	410.3	324.9
5.4	24.9	44.4	53.4	51.0
33.1	35.7	35.5	123.5	34.5
22.7	33.3	32.3	69.9	41.2
13.3	50.4	54.9	81.6	55.6
1642.6	2083.7	2604.8	2745.1	2863.2
156.3	209.6	177.4	254.8	229.5
4644.2	5869.5	6210.6	6753.9	8444.6
103.3	12.6	29.3	9.7	19.9
33.9	78.3	92.7	99.0	131.4
13.1	25.4	54.6	84.9	100.2
2009.6	1370.0	1547.4	1450.2	1407.8
784.9	672.7	485.7	492.9	1043.7
5.0	4.0	6.1	3.6	3.3
77.1	119.6	149.2	114.4	211.7
67.3	23.2	20.2	46.3	64.8
2.4	3.3	1.9	3.9	2.2
31.6	22.5	19.7	35.9	43.2
898.0	842.4	200.5	74.3	679.1
4.8	77.9	5.1	4.4	5.3
475.4	487.9	644.9	322.8	381.8
34.1	51.7	41.8	82.1	333.4
4540.6	3791.4	3299.1	2824.3	4427.7
17.7	63.6	116.4	187.2	165.9
1539.3	1930.9	1723.4	2200.2	2178.7
41.1	34.6	54.7	44.5	61.5
2061.3	3182.3	3362.4	2585.2	2579.5
13.5	35.0	37.8	35.1	22.1
476.3	510.5	138.5	37.0	66.8
307.3	574.5	453.8	633.6	442.4
1303.2	2099.8	1916.6	2044.3	1708.9
797.1	620.9	1057.0	518.0	973.8

	1984	1985	1986	1987	1988	1989	1990
South Asia Unall.	2.0	118.7	152.3	13.7	42.7	185.3	172.3
TOTAL	*7334.4*	*6309.8*	*6708.8*	*9065.9*	*8903.2*	*8470.4*	*8371.8*
FAR EAST ASIA							
Brunei	0.9	1.4	2.8	3.5	4.8	4.9	3.5
China	897.9	1210.1	1527.2	2106.1	3513.0	2590.3	2100.5
Hong Kong	20.1	17.8	18.0	19.7	20.2	45.8	41.1
Indonesia	1060.9	1249.3	681.7	2204.9	2740.8	2696.5	2925.5
Kampuchea	17.1	10.3	11.4	15.3	18.5	30.6	31.2
Korea	303.4	277.6	56.2	395.0	288.0	141.4	793.2
Korea, Dem.	–	5.4	5.6	11.2	8.1	8.8	8.6
Laos	40.8	25.4	61.0	141.9	110.5	208.3	134.3
Macao	0.5	0.4	0.4	0.2	0.3	0.3	0.2
Malaysia	361.1	210.5	330.0	115.0	755.2	138.2	675.2
Mongolia	0.1	3.3	4.6	3.1	4.2	6.4	15.8
Philippines	458.9	365.9	1103.1	1074.1	1870.7	1611.2	2176.2
Singapore	48.6	33.4	27.3	31.9	112.3	25.8	26.4
Taiwan	85.5	2.4	3.7	6.6	6.6	8.6	9.9
Thailand	519.3	562.0	498.0	678.8	1114.7	648.9	1380.7
Viet Nam	98.7	101.2	132.5	117.6	151.2	133.5	184.9
Far East Asia Unall.	66.8	26.0	52.1	50.7	96.0	88.0	122.0
TOTAL	*3980.5*	*4102.3*	*4515.5*	*6975.6*	*10815.1*	*8387.7*	*10629.1*
Asia Unspecified	732.1	111.2	1848.4	1349.2	200.5	150.2	251.6
ASIA TOTAL	*15859.0*	*14902.0*	*17613.3*	*21182.1*	*23218.0*	*19832.6*	*23680.2*
OCEANIA							
Cook Islands	8.1	7.9	10.9	16.8	12.4	2.6	16.7
Fiji	34.5	42.4	53.5	32.0	61.2	40.4	39.1
Kiribati	9.9	13.7	7.6	11.8	16.8	17.0	14.6
Nauru	0.1	0.1	0.0	0.1	0.1	0.1	0.1
New Caledonia	111.6	155.9	161.0	282.1	283.3	292.0	346.4
Niue	3.5	3.6	2.7	5.2	4.3	0.4	6.1
Pacif. Isl.(Fed. Sts.)	163.2	120.3	217.1	11.7	393.0	202.0	174.0
Papua New Guinea	320.9	269.4	275.4	430.9	722.8	144.8	127.3
Polynesia, French	137.1	178.5	198.7	296.4	353.7	331.3	298.6
Solomon Islands	25.9	11.8	44.0	67.8	55.4	40.4	36.2
Tokelau	1.8	1.5	1.9	2.6	3.2	0.3	3.3
Tonga	15.2	9.1	19.8	18.9	26.2	26.2	30.4
Tuvalu	4.5	3.3	12.7	15.1	12.9	6.2	3.1
Vanuatu	22.7	29.0	23.3	53.9	42.3	52.9	34.6
Wallis & Futuna	8.1	11.4	0.1	–	0.0	1.5	1.5
Western Samoa	26.1	30.9	29.4	29.8	48.7	51.2	46.0
TOM Unallocated	77.2	–	–	–	–	–	–
Oceania Unallocated	47.9	22.0	22.9	29.8	57.1	63.2	68.5
TOTAL	*1018.2*	*910.6*	*1080.8*	*1304.9*	*2093.3*	*1272.5*	*1246.4*
LDCS Unspecified	3546.6	3527.9	4280.1	4314.1	7135.6	6510.5	8030.5
TOTAL,ALL LDCS	*40258.7*	*38963.3*	*45776.2*	*53849.2*	*62622.7*	*58042.1*	*83024.5*
INCOME GROUPS							
LLDCS	9638.9	9754.8	11659.4	13939.9	14233.4	13800.0	14294.1
OTHER LICS	12300.3	11677.3	13392.6	18470.3	22966.5	20817.9	36152.9
LMICS	5483.5	5508.5	6538.3	6990.2	7963.5	6545.6	10732.6
UMICS	6630.0	6977.3	6638.3	6892.7	8062.3	7723.2	10873.2
UNALLOCATED	6206.1	5045.4	7547.7	7556.0	9397.0	9155.4	10971.7

SECTION B

INDIVIDUAL COUNTRY TABLES

TABLEAUX PAR PAYS

1. TOTAL RECEIPTS NET / 4. TOTAL ODA NET / 7. TOTAL ODA GROSS

	1987	1988	1989	1990	1987	1988	1989	1990	1987
	1. TOTAL RECEIPTS NET				**4. TOTAL ODA NET**				**7. TOTAL ODA GROSS**
DAC COUNTRIES									
Australia	0.0	0.0	0.4	1.2	0.0	0.0	0.4	1.2	0.0
Austria	0.1	0.1	1.4	1.5	0.1	0.1	1.4	1.5	0.1
Belgium	–	–	0.0	0.0	–	–	0.0	0.0	–
Canada	–	2.2	1.0	2.7	–	2.2	1.0	2.7	–
Denmark	-0.1	-0.2	1.6	1.6	-0.1	-0.2	1.6	1.6	0.0
Finland	–	0.5	1.1	0.2	–	0.5	1.1	0.2	–
France	0.9	2.8	-0.2	2.2	0.9	0.7	1.9	1.9	0.9
Germany	0.7	8.2	8.6	8.3	0.4	7.9	8.6	8.1	4.9
Ireland	–	0.1	–	0.1	–	0.1	–	0.1	–
Italy	0.4	1.1	–	–	–	1.1	–	–	–
Japan	0.0	–	0.0	0.0	0.0	–	0.0	0.0	–
Netherlands	0.9	3.5	3.0	0.7	0.9	3.5	2.6	3.1	0.9
New Zealand	–	–	–	–	–	–	–	–	–
Norway	0.2	–	1.2	3.4	0.2	–	1.2	3.4	0.2
Sweden	5.4	14.7	16.1	16.1	5.4	14.7	16.7	16.1	5.4
Switzerland	–	4.8	1.8	2.0	–	4.8	1.8	2.0	–
United Kingdom	1.0	2.3	4.1	2.4	1.0	2.3	4.1	2.4	1.0
United States	29.0	29.0	40.0	56.0	29.0	29.0	40.0	56.0	31.0
TOTAL	*38.4*	*69.3*	*80.1*	*98.3*	*37.7*	*66.8*	*82.4*	*100.1*	*44.5*
MULTILATERAL									
AF.D.F.	–	–	–	–	–	–	–	–	–
AF.D.B.	–	–	–	–	–	–	–	–	–
AS.D.B	-1.2	-1.1	-1.0	-1.0	-1.2	-1.1	-1.0	-1.0	–
CAR.D.B.	–	–	–	–	–	–	–	–	–
E.E.C.	1.6	0.3	7.7	7.7	1.6	0.3	7.7	7.7	1.6
IBRD	–	–	–	–	–	–	–	–	–
IDA	-1.1	-1.0	-1.0	-1.0	-1.1	-1.0	-1.0	-1.0	–
I.D.B.	–	–	–	–	–	–	–	–	–
IFAD	–	–	–	–	–	–	–	–	–
I.F.C.	–	–	–	–	–	–	–	–	–
IMF TRUST FUND	–	–	–	–	–	–	–	–	–
U.N. AGENCIES	–	–	–	–	–	–	–	–	–
UNDP	5.4	5.2	6.9	13.2	5.4	5.2	6.9	13.2	5.4
UNTA	2.6	1.2	2.2	1.3	2.6	1.2	2.2	1.3	2.6
UNICEF	1.0	0.8	0.8	0.0	1.0	0.8	0.8	0.0	1.0
UNRWA	–	–	–	–	–	–	–	–	–
WFP	0.0	0.0	48.0	13.0	0.0	0.0	48.0	13.0	0.0
UNHCR	–	0.1	3.9	0.9	–	0.1	3.9	0.9	–
Other Multilateral	0.5	0.9	18.9	9.3	0.5	0.9	18.9	9.3	0.5
Arab Agencies	-0.2	-0.2	-0.2	–	-0.2	-0.2	-0.2	–	–
TOTAL	*8.6*	*6.2*	*86.3*	*43.4*	*8.6*	*6.2*	*86.3*	*43.4*	*11.1*
ARAB COUNTRIES	*-1.3*	*-0.6*	*-1.7*	*-0.5*	*-1.3*	*-0.6*	*-1.7*	*-0.5*	*1.0*
E.E.C.+ MEMBERS	*5.2*	*18.2*	*24.9*	*23.0*	*4.6*	*15.7*	*26.5*	*24.8*	*9.3*
TOTAL	*45.7*	*74.9*	*164.7*	*141.3*	*45.1*	*72.4*	*166.9*	*143.1*	*56.6*

2. ODA LOANS GROSS / 5. ODA LOANS NET / 8. GRANTS

	1987	1988	1989	1990	1987	1988	1989	1990	1987
	2. ODA LOANS GROSS				**5. ODA LOANS NET**				**8. GRANTS**
DAC COUNTRIES									
Australia	–	–	–	–	–	–	–	–	0.0
Austria	–	–	–	–	–	–	–	–	0.1
Belgium	–	–	–	–	–	–	–	–	–
Canada	–	–	–	–	–	–	–	–	–
Denmark	–	–	–	–	-0.2	-0.2	-0.1	-0.2	0.0
Finland	–	–	–	–	–	–	–	–	–
France	–	–	–	–	–	–	–	–	0.9
Germany	–	–	–	–	-4.5	-4.4	-4.1	-4.6	4.9
Ireland	–	–	–	–	–	–	–	–	–
Italy	–	–	–	–	–	–	–	–	–
Japan	–	–	–	–	0.0	–	–	–	–
Netherlands	–	–	–	–	–	–	–	–	0.9
New Zealand	–	–	–	–	–	–	–	–	–
Norway	–	–	–	–	–	–	–	–	0.2
Sweden	–	–	–	–	–	–	–	–	5.4
Switzerland	–	–	–	–	–	–	–	–	–
United Kingdom	–	–	–	–	-0.1	-0.1	-0.1	-0.1	1.0
United States	–	–	–	–	-2.0	-3.0	-3.0	-4.0	31.0
TOTAL	–	–	–	–	*-6.8*	*-7.6*	*-7.3*	*-8.9*	*44.5*
MULTILATERAL	–	–	–	–	*-2.5*	*-2.3*	*-2.2*	*-2.2*	*11.1*
ARAB COUNTRIES	*0.0*	*1.6*	–	–	*-2.3*	*-0.7*	*-2.3*	*-0.5*	*1.0*
E.E.C.+ MEMBERS	–	–	–	–	*-4.7*	*-4.6*	*-4.3*	*-4.9*	*9.3*
TOTAL	*0.0*	*1.6*	–	–	*-11.6*	*-10.6*	*-11.7*	*-11.6*	*56.6*

3. TOTAL OFFICIAL GROSS / 6. TOTAL OFFICIAL NET / 9. TOTAL OOF GROSS

	1987	1988	1989	1990	1987	1988	1989	1990	1987
	3. TOTAL OFFICIAL GROSS				**6. TOTAL OFFICIAL NET**				**9. TOTAL OOF GROSS**
DAC COUNTRIES									
Australia	0.0	0.0	0.4	1.2	0.0	0.0	0.4	1.2	–
Austria	0.1	0.1	1.4	1.5	0.1	0.1	1.4	1.5	–
Belgium	–	–	0.0	0.0	–	–	0.0	0.0	–
Canada	–	2.2	1.0	2.7	–	2.2	1.0	2.7	–
Denmark	0.0	–	1.7	1.8	-0.1	-0.2	1.6	1.6	–
Finland	–	0.5	1.1	0.2	–	0.5	1.1	0.2	–
France	0.9	0.7	1.9	1.9	0.9	0.7	1.9	1.9	–
Germany	4.9	12.3	12.7	12.7	0.4	7.9	8.6	8.1	–
Ireland	–	0.1	–	0.1	–	0.1	–	0.1	–
Italy	–	1.1	–	–	–	1.1	–	–	–
Japan	–	–	0.0	0.0	0.0	–	0.0	0.0	–
Netherlands	0.9	3.5	2.6	3.1	0.9	3.5	2.6	3.1	–
New Zealand	–	–	–	–	–	–	–	–	–
Norway	0.2	–	1.2	3.4	0.2	–	1.2	3.4	–
Sweden	5.4	14.7	16.7	16.1	5.4	14.7	16.7	16.1	–
Switzerland	–	4.8	1.8	2.0	–	4.8	1.8	2.0	–
United Kingdom	1.0	2.4	4.2	2.5	1.0	2.3	4.1	2.4	–
United States	31.0	32.0	43.0	60.0	29.0	29.0	40.0	56.0	–
TOTAL	*44.5*	*74.4*	*89.6*	*109.0*	*37.7*	*66.8*	*82.4*	*100.1*	–
MULTILATERAL	*11.1*	*8.5*	*88.5*	*45.4*	*8.6*	*6.2*	*86.3*	*43.4*	–
ARAB COUNTRIES	*1.0*	*1.7*	*0.6*	–	*-1.3*	*-0.6*	*-1.7*	*-0.5*	–
E.E.C.+ MEMBERS	*9.3*	*20.3*	*30.8*	*29.7*	*4.6*	*15.7*	*26.5*	*24.8*	–
TOTAL	*56.6*	*84.6*	*178.7*	*154.4*	*45.1*	*72.4*	*166.9*	*143.1*	–

10. ODA COMMITMENTS

1988	1989	1990	1987	1988	1989	1990
0.0	0.4	1.2	0.1	0.0	0.6	0.6
0.1	1.4	1.5	0.1	0.1	1.4	3.4
–	0.0	0.0	1.0	–	0.0	0.0
2.2	1.0	2.7	0.2	2.9	0.8	2.8
–	1.7	1.8	–	2.8	–	2.2
0.5	1.1	0.2	–	–	1.2	2.3
0.7	1.9	1.9	0.9	0.7	1.9	19.5
12.3	12.7	12.7	5.0	12.4	14.6	15.3
0.1	–	0.1	–	0.1	–	0.1
1.1	–	–	–	1.1	–	–
–	0.0	0.0	–	–	0.0	0.0
3.5	2.6	3.1	0.4	2.8	2.6	3.3
–	–	–	–	–	–	–
–	1.2	3.4	0.0	–	–	–
14.7	16.7	16.1	5.4	14.7	16.7	–
4.8	1.8	2.0	–	4.7	1.8	1.9
2.4	4.2	2.5	1.0	2.4	4.2	2.5
32.0	43.0	60.0	38.9	54.8	58.8	72.6
74.4	89.6	109.0	52.9	99.5	104.7	126.4
–	–	–	–	–	–	–
–	–	–	–	–	–	–
–	–	–	–	–	–	–
0.3	7.7	7.7	0.2	8.7	1.8	1.8
–	–	–	–	–	–	–
–	–	–	–	–	–	–
–	–	–	–	–	–	–
–	–	–	–	–	–	–
–	–	–	9.5	8.2	80.7	37.7
5.2	6.9	13.2	–	–	–	–
1.2	2.2	1.3	–	–	–	–
0.8	0.8	0.0	–	–	–	–
–	–	–	–	–	–	–
0.0	48.0	13.0	–	–	–	–
0.1	3.9	0.9	–	–	–	–
0.9	18.9	9.3	–	–	–	–
–	–	–	–	–	–	–
8.5	88.5	45.4	9.7	16.9	82.5	39.5
1.7	0.6	–	1.0	–	–	–
20.3	30.8	29.7	8.4	30.9	25.1	44.6
84.6	178.7	154.4	63.6	116.4	187.2	165.9

11. TECH. COOP. GRANTS

1988	1989	1990	1987	1988	1989	1990
0.0	0.4	1.2	–	–	–	–
0.1	1.4	1.5	0.1	0.1	0.1	0.6
–	0.0	0.0	–	–	–	–
2.2	1.0	2.7	–	–	–	–
–	1.7	1.8	0.0	–	–	–
0.5	1.1	0.2	–	–	–	–
0.7	1.9	1.9	0.9	0.7	1.9	1.9
12.3	12.7	12.7	4.6	5.4	6.0	–
0.1	–	0.1	–	–	–	0.1
1.1	–	–	–	–	–	–
–	0.0	0.0	–	–	0.0	0.0
3.5	2.6	3.1	–	–	–	–
–	–	–	–	–	–	–
–	1.2	3.4	0.0	–	–	0.0
14.7	16.7	16.1	–	–	–	–
4.8	1.8	2.0	–	0.0	–	–
2.4	4.2	2.5	0.4	0.4	0.4	0.8
32.0	43.0	60.0	14.0	32.0	42.0	40.0
74.4	89.6	109.0	19.9	38.5	50.4	43.3
8.5	88.5	45.4	9.5	8.2	32.7	24.7
0.0	0.6	–	–	–	–	–
20.3	30.8	29.7	5.8	6.4	8.3	2.7
83.0	178.7	154.4	29.4	46.7	83.1	68.0

12. TOTAL OOF NET

1988	1989	1990	1987	1988	1989	1990
–	–	–	–	–	–	–
–	–	–	–	–	–	–
–	–	–	–	–	–	–
–	–	–	–	–	–	–
–	–	–	–	–	–	–
–	–	–	–	–	–	–
–	–	–	–	–	–	–
–	–	–	–	–	–	–
–	–	–	–	–	–	–
–	–	–	–	–	–	–
–	–	–	–	–	–	–
–	–	–	–	–	–	–
–	–	–	–	–	–	–
–	–	–	–	–	–	–
–	–	–	–	–	–	–
–	–	–	–	–	–	–
–	–	–	–	–	–	–
–	–	–	–	–	–	–
–	–	–	–	–	–	–
–	–	–	–	–	–	–
–	–	–	–	–	–	–

13. ODF COMMITMENTS: BY PURPOSE %

	1987	1988	1989	1990
Education	4	4	4	–
Health	2	8	9	–
Other Social Infrastr.	1	2	4	–
Water Sanitat. Sewage	–	–	–	–
Energy	3	1	–	–
Telecommunications	0	0	–	–
Transportation	–	–	1	–
Agriculture	1	3	13	–
Extractive Industries	6	–	–	–
Manufacturing	22	6	–	–
Trade Banking Tourism	0	–	2	–
Technical Cooperation	12	39	39	–
Multisector Aid	0	–	4	–
Programme	45	9	9	–
Debt Reorganisation	0	0	–	–
Food Aid	1	–	–	–
Emergency Aid	2	27	14	–
Unspecified	–	–	–	–
TOTAL	100	100	100	–

14. GRANT ELEMENT OF ODA %

DAC COUNTRIES

	1987	1988	1989	1990
Australia	100.0	100.0	100.0	–
Austria	100.0	100.0	100.0	–
Belgium	100.0	–	100.0	–
Canada	100.0	100.0	100.0	–
Denmark	–	100.0	–	–
Finland	–	–	100.0	–
France	100.0	100.0	100.0	–
Germany	100.0	100.0	100.0	–
Ireland	–	100.0	–	–
Italy	–	100.0	–	–
Japan	–	–	100.0	–
Netherlands	100.0	100.0	100.0	–
New Zealand	–	–	–	–
Norway	100.0	–	–	–
Sweden	100.0	100.0	100.0	–
Switzerland	–	100.0	100.0	–
United Kingdom	100.0	100.0	100.0	–
United States	100.0	100.0	100.0	–
TOTAL	100.0	100.0	100.0	–
MULTILATERAL	100.0	100.0	100.0	–
ARAB COUNTRIES	100.0	–	–	–
E.E.C.+ MEMBERS	100.0	100.0	100.0	–
TOTAL	100.0	100.0	100.0	–

15. OTHER AGGREGATES

	1987	1988	1989	1990
OFFICIAL COMMITMENTS:				
TOTAL BILATERAL	379.8	130.1	111.5	126.4
of which:				
Arab Countries	1.0	–	–	–
C.E.E.C.	326.0	30.6	6.8	–
TOTAL MULTILATERAL	9.7	16.9	82.5	39.5
TOTAL BIL.& MULTIL.	389.5	147.0	194.0	165.9
of which:				
ODA Grants	261.8	136.3	187.2	148.2
ODA Loans	127.8	10.7	6.8	17.7
DISBURSEMENTS:				
DAC COUNTRIES COMBINED				
OFFICIAL & PRIVATE GROSS:				
Contractual Lending	-0.2	–	–	0.0
Export Credits, Total	-0.2	–	–	0.0
Export Credits, Priv.	-0.2	–	–	0.0
NET:				
Contractual Lending	-6.9	-7.6	-7.8	-8.8
Export Credits Total	-0.2	–	-0.6	0.0
PRIVATE SECTOR NET	0.6	2.5	-2.2	-1.8
Direct Investment	0.4	–	–	–
Portfolio Investment	0.4	2.5	-1.7	-1.8
Export Credits	-0.2	–	-0.6	0.0
MARKET BORROWING:				
CHANGE IN CLAIMS				
Banks	-3.0	8.0	13.0	4.0
MEMORANDUM ITEM:				
C.E.E.C. (Gross)	221.9	196.7	107.1	–

	1987	1988	1989	1990		1987	1988	1989	1990		1987
1. TOTAL RECEIPTS NET					**4. TOTAL ODA NET**					**7. TOTAL ODA GROSS**	
DAC COUNTRIES											
Australia	–	–	–	–		–	–	–	–	Australia	–
Austria	77.9	-30.1	-28.6	-27.0		61.6	36.7	20.8	23.1	Austria	70.1
Belgium	-156.5	46.8	-29.1	-82.2		2.0	2.0	1.1	2.3	Belgium	2.0
Canada	-59.0	-44.7	40.3	-19.9		1.8	1.4	3.4	1.1	Canada	3.0
Denmark	-122.5	-151.0	-141.7	-178.6		-0.1	-0.2	-0.1	-0.3	Denmark	0.0
Finland	–	-0.2	21.0	9.0		–	–	0.0	0.1	Finland	–
France	-75.0	-157.2	-169.5	348.6		58.3	55.7	55.2	122.2	France	70.1
Germany	-134.2	257.8	226.0	359.9		-1.3	11.0	2.6	5.4	Germany	8.3
Ireland	–	–	–	–		–	–	–	–	Ireland	–
Italy	-367.7	-16.3	-243.2	-108.8		2.0	1.4	3.0	9.3	Italy	2.0
Japan	-329.6	-0.4	-75.0	-179.7		-3.8	-3.4	-2.7	0.3	Japan	0.4
Netherlands	-69.4	-85.2	-63.8	-128.3		–	–	0.0	1.9	Netherlands	–
New Zealand	–	–	–	–		–	–	–	–	New Zealand	–
Norway	0.1	0.0	4.6	-5.0		0.1	0.0	–	0.1	Norway	0.1
Sweden	-0.7	14.2	37.0	-14.3		16.3	14.2	4.6	19.2	Sweden	16.3
Switzerland	0.3	0.3	0.7	0.5		0.3	0.3	0.7	0.5	Switzerland	0.3
United Kingdom	-8.5	149.6	324.9	10.7		0.3	0.8	0.8	0.7	United Kingdom	0.3
United States	-97.0	-58.0	-77.0	57.0		–	–	–	–	United States	–
TOTAL	-1341.7	-74.4	-173.6	41.8		137.4	120.0	89.4	185.7	TOTAL	172.9
MULTILATERAL											
AF.D.F.	–	–	–	–		–	–	–	–	AF.D.F.	–
AF.D.B.	-2.1	6.6	6.6	87.0		–	–	–	–	AF.D.B.	–
AS.D.B	–	–	–	–		–	–	–	–	AS.D.B	–
CAR.D.B.	–	–	–	–		–	–	–	–	CAR.D.B.	–
E.E.C.	31.0	12.3	59.2	59.2		7.5	5.4	21.2	21.2	E.E.C.	7.5
IBRD	49.9	58.0	92.0	170.0		–	–	–	–	IBRD	–
IDA	–	–	–	–		–	–	–	–	IDA	–
I.D.B.	–	–	–	–		–	–	–	–	I.D.B.	–
IFAD	–	0.6	0.9	0.3		–	0.6	0.9	0.3	IFAD	–
I.F.C.	–	–	–	–		–	–	–	–	I.F.C.	–
IMF TRUST FUND	–	–	–	–		–	–	–	–	IMF TRUST FUND	–
U.N. AGENCIES	–	–	–	–		–	–	–	–	U.N. AGENCIES	–
UNDP	5.0	3.6	3.7	4.0		5.0	3.6	3.7	4.0	UNDP	5.0
UNTA	0.8	1.0	1.1	1.5		0.8	1.0	1.1	1.5	UNTA	0.8
UNICEF	0.4	0.3	0.6	0.5		0.4	0.3	0.6	0.5	UNICEF	0.4
UNRWA	–	–	–	–		–	–	–	–	UNRWA	–
WFP	0.9	2.8	3.6	2.3		0.9	2.8	3.6	2.3	WFP	0.9
UNHCR	6.9	4.5	3.2	5.6		6.9	4.5	3.2	5.6	UNHCR	6.9
Other Multilateral	0.2	0.2	0.8	0.8		0.2	0.2	0.8	0.8	Other Multilateral	0.2
Arab Agencies	-63.5	-19.2	28.9	–		3.8	5.8	5.7	–	Arab Agencies	5.4
TOTAL	29.3	70.7	200.5	331.1		25.3	24.1	40.7	36.1	TOTAL	26.9
ARAB COUNTRIES	*49.0*	*32.2*	*41.4*	*4.9*		*51.6*	*27.2*	*22.2*	*4.9*	*ARAB COUNTRIES*	*51.6*
E.E.C.+ MEMBERS	*-902.7*	*56.9*	*-37.3*	*280.3*		*68.6*	*76.1*	*83.9*	*162.5*	*E.E.C.+ MEMBERS*	*90.2*
TOTAL	**-1263.4**	**28.4**	**68.3**	**377.9**		**214.4**	**171.4**	**152.4**	**226.8**	**TOTAL**	**251.5**
2. ODA LOANS GROSS					**5. ODA LOANS NET**					**8. GRANTS**	
DAC COUNTRIES											
Australia	–	–	–	–		–	–	–	–	Australia	–
Austria	69.9	38.7	27.5	32.6		61.4	36.5	20.6	22.6	Austria	0.2
Belgium	–	–	–	–		–	–	–	–	Belgium	2.0
Canada	0.5	–	–	0.0		-0.8	-1.4	-0.7	-2.1	Canada	2.6
Denmark	–	–	–	–		-0.2	-0.2	-0.1	-0.3	Denmark	0.0
Finland	–	–	–	–		–	–	–	–	Finland	–
France	3.1	–	3.9	59.4		-8.7	-10.3	-4.7	50.4	France	67.0
Germany	–	10.7	4.3	0.5		-9.7	4.5	-4.9	-9.6	Germany	8.3
Ireland	–	–	–	–		–	–	–	–	Ireland	–
Italy	–	–	–	4.5		–	–	–	4.5	Italy	2.0
Japan	–	–	–	–		-4.1	-4.7	-4.4	-4.3	Japan	0.4
Netherlands	–	–	–	–		–	–	–	–	Netherlands	–
New Zealand	–	–	–	–		–	–	–	–	New Zealand	–
Norway	–	–	–	–		–	–	–	–	Norway	0.1
Sweden	–	–	–	–		–	–	–	–	Sweden	16.3
Switzerland	–	–	–	–		–	–	–	–	Switzerland	0.3
United Kingdom	–	–	–	–		–	–	–	–	United Kingdom	0.3
United States	–	–	–	–		–	–	–	–	United States	–
TOTAL	73.4	49.4	35.7	97.1		37.9	24.5	5.7	61.2	TOTAL	99.5
MULTILATERAL	5.4	9.1	7.4	1.1		3.8	6.3	5.6	-1.0	MULTILATERAL	21.5
ARAB COUNTRIES	*16.3*	*16.8*	*13.3*	*8.0*		*16.3*	*16.8*	*10.1*	*2.0*	*ARAB COUNTRIES*	*35.3*
E.E.C.+ MEMBERS	*3.1*	*10.7*	*8.2*	*64.4*		*-18.6*	*-5.9*	*-9.7*	*45.1*	*E.E.C.+ MEMBERS*	*87.1*
TOTAL	**95.1**	**75.2**	**56.3**	**106.2**		**58.0**	**47.6**	**21.5**	**62.2**	**TOTAL**	**156.4**
3. TOTAL OFFICIAL GROSS					**6. TOTAL OFFICIAL NET**					**9. TOTAL OOF GROSS**	
DAC COUNTRIES											
Australia	–	–	–	–		–	–	–	–	Australia	–
Austria	70.1	38.9	27.7	33.2		61.5	36.6	20.5	23.1	Austria	–
Belgium	16.5	2.0	10.5	10.8		16.5	2.0	10.5	10.8	Belgium	14.6
Canada	15.8	21.8	131.3	104.7		-55.0	-65.1	28.7	-55.9	Canada	12.8
Denmark	7.1	7.2	4.5	–		-26.5	-82.6	-65.2	-0.3	Denmark	7.1
Finland	–	–	0.0	0.1		–	–	0.0	0.1	Finland	–
France	70.1	66.0	63.8	134.7		58.3	55.7	55.2	122.7	France	–
Germany	28.5	50.6	40.0	108.9		-32.7	4.0	-10.7	67.6	Germany	20.1
Ireland	–	–	–	–		–	–	–	–	Ireland	–
Italy	2.0	5.5	24.9	136.8		-13.9	-12.8	20.7	96.2	Italy	–
Japan	29.4	61.1	111.5	178.8		-236.4	-246.9	-176.4	-44.7	Japan	29.1
Netherlands	–	–	0.0	1.9		–	–	0.0	1.9	Netherlands	–
New Zealand	–	–	–	–		–	–	–	–	New Zealand	–
Norway	0.1	0.0	–	0.1		0.1	0.0	–	0.1	Norway	–
Sweden	16.3	14.2	4.6	19.2		16.3	14.2	4.6	19.2	Sweden	–
Switzerland	0.3	0.3	0.7	0.5		0.3	0.3	0.7	0.5	Switzerland	–
United Kingdom	0.3	0.8	0.8	0.7		0.3	0.8	0.8	0.7	United Kingdom	–
United States	–	17.0	10.0	159.0		-98.0	-58.0	-77.0	58.0	United States	–
TOTAL	256.5	285.3	430.2	889.3		-309.3	-351.8	-187.5	300.0	TOTAL	83.6
MULTILATERAL	281.5	485.0	476.7	580.7		29.3	70.7	200.5	331.1	MULTILATERAL	254.6
ARAB COUNTRIES	*57.0*	*41.2*	*45.8*	*11.0*		*49.0*	*32.2*	*41.4*	*4.9*	*ARAB COUNTRIES*	*5.4*
E.E.C.+ MEMBERS	*156.9*	*146.0*	*205.3*	*454.5*		*33.0*	*-20.6*	*70.6*	*358.8*	*E.E.C.+ MEMBERS*	*66.7*
TOTAL	**595.0**	**811.5**	**952.7**	**1480.9**		**-231.0**	**-248.9**	**54.4**	**636.0**	**TOTAL**	**343.6**

ALGERIA

1988	1989	1990

10. ODA COMMITMENTS

1987	1988	1989	1990

1988	1989	1990		1987	1988	1989	1990
—	—	—		—	—	—	—
38.9	27.7	33.2		25.8	126.0	102.3	6.9
2.0	1.1	2.3		1.6	5.6	1.1	2.3
2.8	4.1	3.3		7.1	12.6	9.9	3.8
—	—	—		—	—	—	—
—	0.0	0.1		—	0.0	0.0	0.5
66.0	63.8	131.2		67.0	66.0	222.9	266.8
17.2	11.8	15.4		17.2	16.5	16.1	25.3
—	—	—		—	—	—	—
1.4	3.0	9.3		2.2	1.5	69.1	32.5
1.3	1.7	4.6		0.4	1.4	2.2	4.3
—	0.0	1.9		0.0	—	0.0	—
—	—	—		—	—	—	—
0.0	—	0.1		—	—	—	—
14.2	4.6	19.2		17.2	16.2	3.5	17.0
0.3	0.7	0.5		0.3	0.3	0.7	0.5
0.8	0.8	0.7		0.3	0.8	0.8	0.7
—	—	—		—	—	—	—
144.9	*119.4*	*221.6*		*139.2*	*247.0*	*428.7*	*360.4*
—	—	—		—	—	0.8	—
—	—	—		—	—	—	—
—	—	—		—	—	—	—
5.4	21.2	21.2		27.3	13.1	40.4	40.4
—	—	—		—	—	—	—
—	—	—		—	—	—	—
0.6	0.9	1.1		—	14.6	—	11.5
—	—	—		—	—	—	—
—	—	—		14.1	12.4	13.0	14.7
3.6	3.7	4.0		—	—	—	—
1.0	1.1	1.5		—	—	—	—
0.3	0.6	0.5		—	—	—	—
—	—	—		—	—	—	—
2.8	3.6	2.3		—	—	—	—
4.5	3.2	5.6		—	—	—	—
0.2	0.8	0.8		—	—	—	—
8.5	7.5	0.0		—	61.0	—	0.5
26.9	*42.5*	*36.9*		*41.3*	*101.1*	*54.2*	*67.1*
27.2	*25.4*	*11.0*		—	—	*57.3*	—
92.8	*101.7*	*181.9*		*115.6*	*103.5*	*350.5*	*367.9*
199.0	*187.3*	*269.5*		*180.5*	*348.1*	*540.3*	*427.5*

11. TECH. COOP. GRANTS

1988	1989	1990		1987	1988	1989	1990
—	—	—		—	—	—	—
0.2	0.2	0.6		0.2	0.2	0.2	0.3
2.0	1.1	2.3		1.8	1.5	0.8	1.7
2.8	4.1	3.2		—	1.4	1.6	1.1
—	—	—		0.0	—	—	—
—	0.0	0.1		—	—	0.0	—
66.0	59.9	71.8		45.0	44.1	39.8	71.6
6.5	7.5	15.0		7.6	6.1	6.6	12.6
—	—	—		—	—	—	—
1.4	3.0	4.7		1.0	0.7	0.9	1.9
1.3	1.7	4.6		0.4	1.3	1.7	4.2
—	0.0	1.9		—	—	—	—
—	—	—		—	—	—	—
0.0	—	0.1		—	—	—	—
14.2	4.6	19.2		0.7	0.6	1.1	0.4
0.3	0.7	0.5		0.0	—	—	—
0.8	0.8	0.7		0.2	0.6	0.8	0.7
—	—	—		—	—	—	—
95.5	*83.7*	*124.5*		*57.0*	*56.4*	*53.4*	*94.3*
17.8	*35.1*	*35.8*		*14.9*	*12.4*	*9.4*	*12.4*
10.5	*12.1*	*2.9*		—	—	—	—
82.1	*93.6*	*117.4*		*57.4*	*55.7*	*48.9*	*88.4*
123.8	*130.9*	*163.3*		*71.9*	*68.8*	*62.8*	*106.7*

12. TOTAL OOF NET

1988	1989	1990		1987	1988	1989	1990
—	—	—		-0.1	-0.1	-0.2	—
—	9.4	8.5		14.6	—	9.4	8.5
19.0	127.2	101.5		-56.8	-66.5	25.3	-57.0
7.2	4.5	—		-26.3	-82.4	-65.1	—
—	—	3.5		—	—	—	0.6
33.3	28.2	93.4		-31.4	-7.0	-13.2	62.3
—	—	—		—	—	—	—
4.1	21.9	127.6		-15.8	-14.3	17.6	86.9
59.8	109.8	174.2		-232.7	-243.5	-173.7	-45.0
—	—	—		—	—	—	—
—	—	—		—	—	—	—
—	—	—		—	—	—	—
—	—	—		—	—	—	—
17.0	10.0	159.0		-98.0	-58.0	-77.0	58.0
140.4	*310.9*	*667.7*		*-446.7*	*-471.8*	*-276.9*	*114.2*
458.1	*434.1*	*543.8*		*3.9*	*46.6*	*159.8*	*295.0*
14.0	*20.4*	—		*-2.6*	*4.9*	*19.1*	—
53.2	*103.6*	*272.7*		*-35.5*	*-96.7*	*-13.3*	*196.2*
612.4	*765.4*	*1211.4*		*-445.3*	*-420.3*	*-98.0*	*409.3*

13. ODF COMMITMENTS: BY PURPOSE %

	1987	1988	1989	1990
Education	1	0	3	—
Health	—	—	0	—
Other Social Infrastr.	—	1	15	—
Water Sanitat. Sewage	36	.18	3	—
Energy	—	0	13	—
Telecommunications	1	1	1	—
Transportation	17	40	15	—
Agriculture	26	6	22	—
Extractive Industries	—	—	0	—
Manufacturing	1	10	3	—
Trade Banking Tourism	2	—	13	—
Technical Cooperation	12	24	3	—
Multisector Aid	0	0	5	—
Programme	—	—	3	—
Debt Reorganisation	—	—	—	—
Food Aid	0	—	—	—
Emergency Aid	0	0	0	—
Unspecified	4	—	—	—
TOTAL	100	100	100	—

14. GRANT ELEMENT OF ODA %

DAC COUNTRIES

	1987	1988	1989	1990
Australia	—	—	—	—
Austria	29.2	29.8	30.2	—
Belgium	100.0	100.0	100.0	—
Canada	100.0	66.7	100.0	—
Denmark	—	—	—	—
Finland	—	100.0	100.0	—
France	100.0	100.0	76.1	—
Germany	100.0	100.0	100.0	—
Ireland	—	—	—	—
Italy	100.0	100.0	59.0	—
Japan	100.0	100.0	100.0	—
Netherlands	100.0	—	100.0	—
New Zealand	—	—	—	—
Norway	—	—	—	—
Sweden	100.0	100.0	100.0	—
Switzerland	100.0	100.0	100.0	—
United Kingdom	100.0	100.0	100.0	—
United States	—	—	—	—
TOTAL	*86.9*	*62.4*	*64.6*	—
MULTILATERAL	*100.0*	*56.4*	*100.0*	—
ARAB COUNTRIES	—	—	*47.5*	—
E.E.C.+ MEMBERS	*100.0*	*100.0*	*76.7*	—
TOTAL	*89.9*	*60.8*	*66.3*	—

15. OTHER AGGREGATES

	1987	1988	1989	1990
OFFICIAL COMMITMENTS:				
TOTAL BILATERAL	377.2	1056.0	1568.4	573.4
of which:				
Arab Countries	2.0	68.6	57.3	—
C.E.E.C.	—	—	—	—
TOTAL MULTILATERAL	816.3	742.3	1038.5	583.9
TOTAL BIL.& MULTIL.	1193.5	1798.2	2606.9	1157.4
of which:				
ODA Grants	154.9	138.0	151.4	184.2
ODA Loans	25.7	210.1	388.9	243.3
DISBURSEMENTS:				
DAC COUNTRIES COMBINED				
OFFICIAL & PRIVATE				
GROSS:				
Contractual Lending	842.4	1554.1	2315.9	3012.3
Export Credits, Total	759.1	1504.2	2265.8	2892.4
Export Credits, Priv.	700.0	1364.3	1978.8	2256.0
NET:				
Contractual Lending	-1325.6	-313.0	112.1	607.2
Export Credits Total	-1370.6	-337.1	94.1	526.7
PRIVATE SECTOR NET	-1032.5	277.3	13.9	-258.1
Direct Investment	19.7	15.1	-2.5	6.1
Portfolio Investment	-149.8	128.0	-376.3	-704.5
Export Credits	-902.3	134.3	392.7	440.3
MARKET BORROWING:				
CHANGE IN CLAIMS				
Banks	283.0	103.0	-223.0	67.0
MEMORANDUM ITEM:				
C.E.E.C. (Gross)	—	0.7	—	—

1. TOTAL RECEIPTS NET

DAC COUNTRIES

	1987	1988	1989	1990
Australia	0.0	0.0	—	1.3
Austria	1.4	0.7	0.7	0.6
Belgium	-0.1	18.0	87.1	-53.2
Canada	0.5	6.5	6.7	15.9
Denmark	11.5	-2.1	-2.8	-3.7
Finland	2.8	1.8	5.8	1.1
France	41.0	-51.9	23.1	-170.7
Germany	3.3	6.6	22.2	20.7
Ireland	—	—	—	0.1
Italy	49.0	14.0	-2.1	83.4
Japan	10.5	-2.0	-0.1	-1.3
Netherlands	36.2	2.3	-4.0	10.4
New Zealand	—	—	—	—
Norway	1.0	3.8	4.3	7.0
Sweden	29.9	32.7	25.2	22.7
Switzerland	0.8	1.7	2.3	4.2
United Kingdom	-4.8	-2.6	-10.2	1.2
United States	24.0	2.0	-13.0	-16.0
TOTAL	207.0	31.3	145.2	-76.4

MULTILATERAL

	1987	1988	1989	1990
AF.D.F.	0.9	5.1	4.4	16.0
AF.D.B.	6.7	6.7	-0.5	1.9
AS.D.B	—	—	—	—
CAR.D.B.	—	—	—	—
E.E.C.	8.3	21.4	19.6	19.6
IBRD	—	—	—	—
IDA	—	—	—	—
I.D.B.	—	—	—	—
IFAD	—	—	—	—
I.F.C.	—	—	—	—
IMF TRUST FUND	—	—	—	—
U.N. AGENCIES	—	—	—	—
UNDP	6.9	5.1	6.7	8.5
UNTA	1.3	0.8	1.1	1.3
UNICEF	6.9	6.1	8.3	7.3
UNRWA	—	—	—	—
WFP	9.8	7.8	7.6	10.2
UNHCR	1.6	3.4	7.5	3.2
Other Multilateral	2.0	2.5	4.0	3.2
Arab Agencies	-2.0	-1.9	-0.5	—
TOTAL	42.5	57.0	58.2	71.0
ARAB COUNTRIES	1.5	2.6	2.5	—
E.E.C.+ MEMBERS	144.5	5.7	132.9	-92.2
TOTAL	251.0	90.9	205.9	-5.3

2. ODA LOANS GROSS

DAC COUNTRIES

	1987	1988	1989	1990
Australia	—	—	—	—
Austria	1.0	—	—	—
Belgium	—	—	0.8	3.8
Canada	—	—	—	—
Denmark	5.7	4.0	—	—
Finland	—	—	—	—
France	1.9	3.9	5.1	9.2
Germany	—	—	—	—
Ireland	—	—	—	—
Italy	17.5	1.1	0.8	23.3
Japan	1.3	0.1	—	—
Netherlands	10.8	5.5	0.0	0.1
New Zealand	—	—	—	—
Norway	—	—	—	—
Sweden	—	—	—	—
Switzerland	—	—	—	—
United Kingdom	—	—	—	—
United States	—	—	—	—
TOTAL	38.2	14.5	6.7	36.3
MULTILATERAL	0.9	5.1	4.9	16.4
ARAB COUNTRIES	1.5	2.6	2.5	—
E.E.C.+ MEMBERS	35.9	14.5	6.7	36.3
TOTAL	40.6	22.2	14.2	52.8

3. TOTAL OFFICIAL GROSS

DAC COUNTRIES

	1987	1988	1989	1990
Australia	0.0	0.0	—	1.3
Austria	1.4	0.7	0.7	0.6
Belgium	3.6	1.9	6.8	7.5
Canada	0.5	6.5	6.2	16.4
Denmark	6.0	4.3	0.1	0.1
Finland	2.8	1.3	0.7	1.1
France	3.7	5.8	7.4	12.2
Germany	6.0	7.2	5.3	10.1
Ireland	—	—	—	0.1
Italy	54.6	24.5	21.6	143.4
Japan	1.4	0.1	—	0.0
Netherlands	15.6	12.4	4.9	16.8
New Zealand	—	—	—	—
Norway	0.9	4.5	4.2	7.3
Sweden	23.8	32.7	36.5	38.3
Switzerland	0.8	1.7	2.3	4.2
United Kingdom	0.4	0.9	2.2	2.2
United States	43.0	23.0	1.0	8.0
TOTAL	164.4	127.4	99.9	269.4
MULTILATERAL	44.5	60.5	61.6	73.9
ARAB COUNTRIES	1.5	2.6	2.5	—
E.E.C.+ MEMBERS	98.3	78.4	67.9	211.9
TOTAL	210.4	190.5	164.0	343.3

4. TOTAL ODA NET

	1987	1988	1989	1990
Australia	0.0	0.0	—	1.3
Austria	1.4	0.7	0.7	0.6
Belgium	0.1	0.4	0.9	4.1
Canada	0.5	6.0	3.2	11.2
Denmark	6.0	4.3	0.1	0.1
Finland	2.8	1.3	0.7	1.1
France	3.7	5.8	7.4	11.1
Germany	6.0	7.2	5.3	10.0
Ireland	—	—	—	0.1
Italy	28.4	24.3	18.5	37.7
Japan	1.4	-2.0	—	—
Netherlands	15.6	12.4	4.9	12.6
New Zealand	—	—	—	—
Norway	0.9	4.5	4.2	7.3
Sweden	23.8	32.7	36.5	38.3
Switzerland	0.8	1.7	2.3	4.2
United Kingdom	0.4	0.9	2.2	2.2
United States	6.0	6.0	1.0	1.0
TOTAL	97.8	106.1	87.9	142.6

	1987	1988	1989	1990
AF.D.F.	0.9	5.1	4.4	16.0
AF.D.B.	—	—	—	—
AS.D.B	—	—	—	—
CAR.D.B.	—	—	—	—
E.E.C.	8.3	21.4	19.6	19.6
IBRD	—	—	—	—
IDA	—	—	—	—
I.D.B.	—	—	—	—
IFAD	—	—	—	—
I.F.C.	—	—	—	—
IMF TRUST FUND	—	—	—	—
U.N. AGENCIES	—	—	—	—
UNDP	6.9	5.1	6.7	8.5
UNTA	1.3	0.8	1.1	1.3
UNICEF	6.9	6.1	8.3	7.3
UNRWA	—	—	—	—
WFP	9.8	7.8	7.6	10.2
UNHCR	1.6	3.4	7.5	3.2
Other Multilateral	2.0	2.5	4.0	3.2
Arab Agencies	-2.0	-1.9	-1.4	—
TOTAL	35.7	50.3	57.8	69.1
ARAB COUNTRIES	1.5	2.6	2.5	—
E.E.C.+ MEMBERS	68.6	76.7	58.8	97.3
TOTAL	135.0	158.9	148.2	211.7

5. ODA LOANS NET

	1987	1988	1989	1990
Australia	—	—	—	—
Austria	1.0	—	—	—
Belgium	—	—	0.8	3.8
Canada	—	—	—	—
Denmark	5.7	4.0	—	—
Finland	—	—	—	—
France	1.9	3.9	5.1	8.1
Germany	—	—	—	—
Ireland	—	—	—	—
Italy	14.6	1.0	-2.3	14.6
Japan	1.3	-2.1	—	0.0
Netherlands	10.8	5.5	0.0	-4.2
New Zealand	—	—	—	—
Norway	—	—	—	—
Sweden	—	—	—	—
Switzerland	—	—	—	—
United Kingdom	—	—	—	—
United States	—	—	—	—
TOTAL	35.3	12.3	3.6	22.4
MULTILATERAL	-1.1	3.2	3.0	15.8
ARAB COUNTRIES	1.5	2.6	2.5	—
E.E.C.+ MEMBERS	33.0	14.4	3.6	22.4
TOTAL	35.7	18.2	9.2	38.2

6. TOTAL OFFICIAL NET

	1987	1988	1989	1990
Australia	0.0	0.0	—	1.3
Austria	1.4	0.7	0.7	0.6
Belgium	3.6	1.9	6.8	7.3
Canada	0.5	6.5	6.2	15.9
Denmark	2.7	-0.8	-2.8	0.1
Finland	2.8	1.3	0.7	1.1
France	3.7	5.8	7.4	11.1
Germany	6.0	7.2	5.3	10.0
Ireland	—	—	—	0.1
Italy	49.0	24.5	18.5	91.5
Japan	1.4	-2.0	—	—
Netherlands	15.6	12.4	4.9	12.6
New Zealand	—	—	—	—
Norway	0.9	4.5	4.2	7.3
Sweden	23.8	32.7	36.5	38.3
Switzerland	0.8	1.7	2.3	4.2
United Kingdom	0.4	0.9	2.2	2.2
United States	24.0	2.0	-13.0	-16.0
TOTAL	136.5	99.2	79.9	187.4
MULTILATERAL	42.5	57.0	58.2	71.0
ARAB COUNTRIES	1.5	2.6	2.5	—
E.E.C.+ MEMBERS	89.3	73.3	61.9	154.4
TOTAL	180.5	158.8	140.6	258.4

7. TOTAL ODA GROSS

	1987
Australia	0.0
Austria	1.4
Belgium	0.1
Canada	0.5
Denmark	6.0
Finland	2.8
France	3.7
Germany	6.0
Ireland	—
Italy	31.3
Japan	1.4
Netherlands	15.6
New Zealand	—
Norway	0.9
Sweden	23.8
Switzerland	0.8
United Kingdom	0.4
United States	6.0
TOTAL	100.6
AF.D.F.	0.9
AF.D.B.	—
AS.D.B	—
CAR.D.B.	—
E.E.C.	8.3
IBRD	—
IDA	—
I.D.B.	—
IFAD	—
I.F.C.	—
IMF TRUST FUND	—
U.N. AGENCIES	—
UNDP	6.9
UNTA	1.3
UNICEF	6.9
UNRWA	—
WFP	9.8
UNHCR	1.6
Other Multilateral	2.0
Arab Agencies	—
TOTAL	37.8
ARAB COUNTRIES	1.5
E.E.C.+ MEMBERS	71.5
TOTAL	139.9

8. GRANTS

	1987
Australia	0.0
Austria	0.5
Belgium	0.1
Canada	0.5
Denmark	0.3
Finland	2.8
France	1.8
Germany	6.0
Ireland	—
Italy	13.8
Japan	0.0
Netherlands	4.8
New Zealand	—
Norway	0.9
Sweden	23.8
Switzerland	0.8
United Kingdom	0.4
United States	6.0
TOTAL	62.4
MULTILATERAL	36.8
ARAB COUNTRIES	—
E.E.C.+ MEMBERS	35.6
TOTAL	99.3

9. TOTAL OOF GROSS

	1987
Australia	—
Austria	—
Belgium	3.5
Canada	—
Denmark	—
Finland	—
France	—
Germany	—
Ireland	—
Italy	23.3
Japan	—
Netherlands	—
New Zealand	—
Norway	—
Sweden	—
Switzerland	—
United Kingdom	—
United States	37.0
TOTAL	63.8
MULTILATERAL	6.8
ARAB COUNTRIES	—
E.E.C.+ MEMBERS	26.8
TOTAL	70.5

10. ODA COMMITMENTS

1988	1989	1990	1987	1988	1989	1990
0.0	–	1.3	–	1.2	0.0	1.4
0.7	0.7	0.6	0.9	0.8	0.8	0.7
0.4	0.9	4.1	0.5	1.2	0.9	4.1
6.0	3.2	11.2	0.1	5.6	2.7	10.9
4.3	0.1	0.1	–	–	–	–
1.3	0.7	1.1	–	–	0.6	2.5
5.8	7.4	12.2	16.7	9.5	10.8	35.0
7.2	5.3	10.0	6.5	7.1	6.9	10.7
–	–	0.1	–	–	–	0.1
24.4	21.6	46.4	20.8	33.8	31.3	63.4
0.1	–	0.0	0.0	0.1	–	0.0
12.4	4.9	16.8	18.5	6.5	4.9	14.8
–	–	–	–	–	–	–
4.5	4.2	7.3	3.1	–	–	–
32.7	36.5	38.3	24.0	32.7	36.5	31.3
1.7	2.3	4.2	0.7	1.7	2.2	4.1
0.9	2.2	2.2	0.4	0.9	2.2	2.2
6.0	1.0	1.0	4.5	5.1	2.2	2.9
108.3	*91.0*	*156.5*	*96.8*	*106.2*	*102.0*	*183.9*
5.1	4.4	16.0	–	–	4.7	52.2
–	–	–	–	–	–	–
–	–	–	–	–	–	–
–	–	–	–	–	–	–
21.4	19.6	19.6	67.7	32.8	17.3	17.3
–	–	–	–	–	–	–
–	–	–	–	–	–	–
–	–	–	–	–	7.6	–
–	–	–	–	–	–	–
–	–	–	28.5	25.7	35.2	33.6
5.1	6.7	8.5	–	–	–	–
0.8	1.1	1.3	–	–	–	–
6.1	8.3	7.3	–	–	–	–
–	–	–	–	–	–	–
7.8	7.6	10.2	–	–	–	–
3.4	7.5	3.2	–	–	–	–
2.5	4.0	3.2	–	–	–	–
–	0.5	0.5	–	1.0	4.0	3.1
52.1	*59.7*	*69.6*	*96.2*	*59.5*	*68.8*	*106.1*
2.6	2.5	–	–	–	–	–
76.7	61.9	111.3	131.2	91.9	74.2	147.5
163.0	*153.2*	*226.1*	*193.0*	*165.7*	*170.7*	*290.1*

11. TECH. COOP. GRANTS

1988	1989	1990	1987	1988	1989	1990
0.0	–	1.3	–	0.0	–	0.2
0.7	0.7	0.6	0.4	0.1	–	0.3
0.4	0.1	0.2	0.0	–	–	0.0
6.0	3.2	11.2	–	0.1	0.1	0.5
0.2	0.1	0.1	3.1	4.0	0.1	–
1.3	0.7	1.1	0.1	0.1	–	–
1.9	2.4	3.0	1.6	1.9	1.1	2.5
7.2	5.3	10.0	1.5	1.5	1.2	1.7
–	–	0.1	–	–	–	0.1
23.3	20.8	23.1	3.3	3.7	3.7	3.7
0.1	–	0.0	0.0	0.1	–	0.0
6.9	4.9	16.8	1.4	2.2	2.1	2.7
–	–	–	–	–	–	–
4.5	4.2	7.3	0.3	0.9	0.0	0.1
32.7	36.5	38.3	3.4	6.2	11.5	0.3
1.7	2.3	4.2	0.1	0.1	–	–
0.9	2.2	2.2	0.4	0.9	2.1	1.1
6.0	1.0	1.0	–	–	–	–
93.7	*84.2*	*120.2*	*15.5*	*21.8*	*22.0*	*13.0*
47.1	54.8	53.2	19.0	21.8	27.6	23.4
–	–	–	–	–	–	–
62.3	55.2	74.9	11.5	18.2	10.4	11.7
140.8	*139.0*	*173.4*	*34.5*	*43.6*	*49.6*	*36.4*

12. TOTAL OOF NET

1988	1989	1990	1987	1988	1989	1990
–	–	–	–	–	–	–
1.6	5.9	3.4	3.5	1.6	5.9	3.3
0.5	3.0	5.2	–	0.5	3.0	4.7
–	–	–	-3.4	-5.1	-2.9	–
–	–	–	–	–	–	–
–	–	0.1	–	0.0	–	–
–	–	–	–	–	–	–
0.1	–	97.1	20.6	0.1	–	53.8
–	–	–	–	–	–	–
–	–	–	–	–	–	–
–	–	–	–	–	–	–
–	–	–	–	–	–	–
–	–	–	–	–	–	–
17.0	–	7.0	18.0	-4.0	-14.0	-17.0
19.2	*8.9*	*112.8*	*38.7*	*-6.9*	*-8.0*	*44.8*
8.3	*1.9*	*4.4*	*6.8*	*6.7*	*0.4*	*1.9*
–	–	–	–	–	–	–
1.7	5.9	100.6	20.7	-3.4	3.0	57.1
27.5	*10.8*	*117.2*	*45.5*	*-0.2*	*-7.6*	*46.7*

13. ODF COMMITMENTS: BY PURPOSE %

	1987	1988	1989	1990
Education	1	1	1	–
Health	2	5	7	–
Other Social Infrastr.	7	1	7	–
Water Sanitat. Sewage	2	–	–	–
Energy	2	–	3	–
Telecommunications	0	0	1	–
Transportation	6	–	1	–
Agriculture	3	26	10	–
Extractive Industries	–	–	–	–
Manufacturing	1	2	7	–
Trade Banking Tourism	0	4	0	–
Technical Cooperation	15	31	37	–
Multisector Aid	0	2	2	–
Programme	51	11	12	–
Debt Reorganisation	2	–	–	–
Food Aid	4	8	5	–
Emergency Aid	3	8	7	–
Unspecified	–	–	–	–
TOTAL	100	100	100	–

14. GRANT ELEMENT OF ODA %

DAC COUNTRIES	1987	1988	1989	1990
Australia	–	100.0	100.0	–
Austria	100.0	100.0	100.0	–
Belgium	100.0	100.0	100.0	–
Canada	100.0	100.0	100.0	–
Denmark	–	–	–	–
Finland	–	–	100.0	–
France	40.0	47.4	58.5	–
Germany	100.0	100.0	100.0	–
Ireland	–	–	–	–
Italy	91.5	97.7	90.2	–
Japan	100.0	68.3	–	–
Netherlands	70.5	100.0	100.0	–
New Zealand	–	–	–	–
Norway	100.0	–	–	–
Sweden	100.0	100.0	100.0	–
Switzerland	100.0	100.0	100.0	–
United Kingdom	100.0	100.0	100.0	–
United States	100.0	100.0	100.0	–
TOTAL	*82.2*	*94.5*	*92.6*	*–*
MULTILATERAL	*100.0*	*98.9*	*94.9*	*–*
ARAB COUNTRIES	*–*	*–*	*–*	*–*
E.E.C.+ MEMBERS	*86.4*	*93.7*	*89.8*	*–*
TOTAL	*90.8*	*96.1*	*93.4*	*–*

15. OTHER AGGREGATES

OFFICIAL COMMITMENTS:	1987	1988	1989	1990
TOTAL BILATERAL	270.8	108.2	194.8	282.5
of which:				
Arab Countries	–	–	–	–
C.E.E.C.	122.8	–	2.5	–
TOTAL MULTILATERAL	96.2	59.5	68.8	170.1
TOTAL BIL.& MULTIL.	367.0	167.7	263.6	452.6
of which:				
ODA Grants	177.6	154.8	140.7	186.7
ODA Loans	138.1	10.8	32.5	103.3

DISBURSEMENTS:				
DAC COUNTRIES COMBINED				
OFFICIAL & PRIVATE				
GROSS:				
Contractual Lending	217.4	91.8	137.5	115.2
Export Credits, Total	156.0	75.7	125.2	-19.2
Export Credits, Priv.	116.0	58.1	122.2	-33.5
NET:				
Contractual Lending	141.3	-32.6	16.6	-55.2
Export Credits Total	85.4	-46.5	7.4	-143.9
PRIVATE SECTOR NET	70.5	-67.8	65.4	-263.8
Direct Investment	-30.3	-54.1	-69.0	-137.7
Portfolio Investment	33.0	24.3	113.0	-4.2
Export Credits	67.8	-38.1	21.3	-121.9

MARKET BORROWING:				
CHANGE IN CLAIMS				
Banks	-34.0	12.0	292.0	94.0

MEMORANDUM ITEM:				
C.E.E.C. (Gross)	23.9	10.7	13.3	–

DISBURSEMENTS, UNLESS OTHERWISE STATE[D]

1. TOTAL RECEIPTS NET

DAC COUNTRIES	1987	1988	1989	1990
Australia	–	–	–	–
Austria	–	–	–	–
Belgium	–	–	–	–
Canada	-0.6	0.1	-1.0	0.1
Denmark	–	–	–	–
Finland	–	–	–	–
France	1.2	-2.0	–	–
Germany	–	–	–	0.0
Ireland	–	–	–	–
Italy	–	–	–	–
Japan	–	–	–	–
Netherlands	–	–	-0.1	–
New Zealand	–	–	–	–
Norway	–	–	–	–
Sweden	–	–	–	–
Switzerland	–	–	–	–
United Kingdom	1.0	2.9	3.3	2.3
United States	–	–	–	–
TOTAL	1.6	1.0	2.2	2.4
MULTILATERAL				
AF.D.F.	–	–	–	–
AF.D.B.	–	–	–	–
AS.D.B	–	–	–	–
CAR.D.B.	1.4	0.9	1.2	1.2
E.E.C.	–	–	1.8	1.8
IBRD	–	–	–	–
IDA	–	–	–	–
I.D.B.	–	–	–	–
IFAD	–	–	–	–
I.F.C.	–	–	–	–
IMF TRUST FUND	–	–	–	–
U.N. AGENCIES	–	–	–	–
UNDP	0.2	0.2	0.2	0.2
UNTA	–	–	–	–
UNICEF	–	–	–	–
UNRWA	–	–	–	–
WFP	–	–	–	–
UNHCR	–	–	–	–
Other Multilateral	0.0	–	0.0	0.1
Arab Agencies	–	–	–	–
TOTAL	1.6	1.0	3.2	3.3
ARAB COUNTRIES	–	–	–	–
E.E.C.+ MEMBERS	2.2	0.9	4.9	4.1
TOTAL	3.2	2.0	5.3	5.7

2. ODA LOANS GROSS

DAC COUNTRIES	1987	1988	1989	1990
Australia	–	–	–	–
Austria	–	–	–	–
Belgium	–	–	–	–
Canada	–	–	–	–
Denmark	–	–	–	–
Finland	–	–	–	–
France	–	–	–	–
Germany	–	–	–	–
Ireland	–	–	–	–
Italy	–	–	–	–
Japan	–	–	–	–
Netherlands	–	–	–	–
New Zealand	–	–	–	–
Norway	–	–	–	–
Sweden	–	–	–	–
Switzerland	–	–	–	–
United Kingdom	–	–	–	–
United States	–	–	–	–
TOTAL	–	–	–	–
MULTILATERAL	1.0	0.8	2.8	2.8
ARAB COUNTRIES	–	–	–	–
E.E.C.+ MEMBERS	–	–	1.7	1.7
TOTAL	1.0	0.8	2.8	2.8

3. TOTAL OFFICIAL GROSS

DAC COUNTRIES	1987	1988	1989	1990
Australia	–	–	–	–
Austria	–	–	–	–
Belgium	–	–	–	–
Canada	0.6	0.1	0.1	0.1
Denmark	–	–	–	–
Finland	–	–	–	–
France	–	–	–	–
Germany	–	–	–	–
Ireland	–	–	–	–
Italy	–	–	–	–
Japan	–	–	–	–
Netherlands	–	–	–	–
New Zealand	–	–	–	–
Norway	–	–	–	–
Sweden	–	–	–	–
Switzerland	–	–	–	–
United Kingdom	2.5	2.9	3.3	2.3
United States	–	–	–	–
TOTAL	3.1	3.0	3.4	2.4
MULTILATERAL	1.6	1.0	3.2	3.3
ARAB COUNTRIES	–	–	–	–
E.E.C.+ MEMBERS	2.5	2.9	5.0	4.1
TOTAL	4.7	4.0	6.6	5.7

4. TOTAL ODA NET

DAC COUNTRIES	1987	1988	1989	1990
Australia	–	–	–	–
Austria	–	–	–	–
Belgium	–	–	–	–
Canada	0.4	0.1	0.1	0.1
Denmark	–	–	–	–
Finland	–	–	–	–
France	–	–	–	–
Germany	–	–	–	–
Ireland	–	–	–	–
Italy	–	–	–	–
Japan	–	–	–	–
Netherlands	–	–	–	–
New Zealand	–	–	–	–
Norway	–	–	–	–
Sweden	–	–	–	–
Switzerland	–	–	–	–
United Kingdom	2.5	2.9	3.3	2.3
United States	–	–	–	–
TOTAL	2.9	3.0	3.4	2.4
MULTILATERAL				
AF.D.F.	–	–	–	–
AF.D.B.	–	–	–	–
AS.D.B	–	–	–	–
CAR.D.B.	1.0	0.8	1.1	1.1
E.E.C.	–	–	1.8	1.8
IBRD	–	–	–	–
IDA	–	–	–	–
I.D.B.	–	–	–	–
IFAD	–	–	–	–
I.F.C.	–	–	–	–
IMF TRUST FUND	–	–	–	–
U.N. AGENCIES	–	–	–	–
UNDP	0.2	0.2	0.2	0.2
UNTA	–	–	–	–
UNICEF	–	–	–	–
UNRWA	–	–	–	–
WFP	–	–	–	–
UNHCR	–	–	–	–
Other Multilateral	0.0	–	0.0	0.1
Arab Agencies	–	–	–	–
TOTAL	1.2	1.0	3.1	3.2
ARAB COUNTRIES	–	–	–	–
E.E.C.+ MEMBERS	2.5	2.9	5.0	4.1
TOTAL	4.1	3.9	6.5	5.6

5. ODA LOANS NET

DAC COUNTRIES	1987	1988	1989	1990
Australia	–	–	–	–
Austria	–	–	–	–
Belgium	–	–	–	–
Canada	–	–	–	–
Denmark	–	–	–	–
Finland	–	–	–	–
France	–	–	–	–
Germany	–	–	–	–
Ireland	–	–	–	–
Italy	–	–	–	–
Japan	–	–	–	–
Netherlands	–	–	–	–
New Zealand	–	–	–	–
Norway	–	–	–	–
Sweden	–	–	–	–
Switzerland	–	–	–	–
United Kingdom	–	–	–	–
United States	–	–	–	–
TOTAL	–	–	–	–
MULTILATERAL	1.0	0.8	2.8	2.8
ARAB COUNTRIES	–	–	–	–
E.E.C.+ MEMBERS	–	–	1.7	1.7
TOTAL	1.0	0.8	2.8	2.8

6. TOTAL OFFICIAL NET

DAC COUNTRIES	1987	1988	1989	1990
Australia	–	–	–	–
Austria	–	–	–	–
Belgium	–	–	–	–
Canada	-0.6	0.1	-1.0	0.1
Denmark	–	–	–	–
Finland	–	–	–	–
France	–	–	–	–
Germany	–	–	–	–
Ireland	–	–	–	–
Italy	–	–	–	–
Japan	–	–	–	–
Netherlands	–	–	–	–
New Zealand	–	–	–	–
Norway	–	–	–	–
Sweden	–	–	–	–
Switzerland	–	–	–	–
United Kingdom	2.5	2.9	3.3	2.3
United States	–	–	–	–
TOTAL	2.0	3.0	2.3	2.4
MULTILATERAL	1.6	1.0	3.2	3.3
ARAB COUNTRIES	–	–	–	–
E.E.C.+ MEMBERS	2.5	2.9	5.0	4.1
TOTAL	3.6	4.0	5.4	5.7

7. TOTAL ODA GROSS

	1987
Australia	–
Austria	–
Belgium	–
Canada	0.4
Denmark	–
Finland	–
France	–
Germany	–
Ireland	–
Italy	–
Japan	–
Netherlands	–
New Zealand	–
Norway	–
Sweden	–
Switzerland	–
United Kingdom	2.5
United States	–
TOTAL	2.9
AF.D.F.	–
AF.D.B.	–
AS.D.B	–
CAR.D.B.	1.0
E.E.C.	–
IBRD	–
IDA	–
I.D.B.	–
IFAD	–
I.F.C.	–
IMF TRUST FUND	–
U.N. AGENCIES	–
UNDP	0.2
UNTA	–
UNICEF	–
UNRWA	–
WFP	–
UNHCR	–
Other Multilateral	0.0
Arab Agencies	–
TOTAL	1.2
ARAB COUNTRIES	–
E.E.C.+ MEMBERS	2.5
TOTAL	4.1

8. GRANTS

	1987
Australia	–
Austria	–
Belgium	–
Canada	0.4
Denmark	–
Finland	–
France	–
Germany	–
Ireland	–
Italy	–
Japan	–
Netherlands	–
New Zealand	–
Norway	–
Sweden	–
Switzerland	–
United Kingdom	2.5
United States	–
TOTAL	2.9
MULTILATERAL	0.2
ARAB COUNTRIES	–
E.E.C.+ MEMBERS	2.5
TOTAL	3.1

9. TOTAL OOF GROSS

	1987
Australia	–
Austria	–
Belgium	–
Canada	0.2
Denmark	–
Finland	–
France	–
Germany	–
Ireland	–
Italy	–
Japan	–
Netherlands	–
New Zealand	–
Norway	–
Sweden	–
Switzerland	–
United Kingdom	–
United States	–
TOTAL	0.2
MULTILATERAL	0.4
ARAB COUNTRIES	–
E.E.C.+ MEMBERS	–
TOTAL	0.6

1988	1989	1990		1987	1988	1989	1990

10. ODA COMMITMENTS

1988	1989	1990		1987	1988	1989	1990
–	–	–		–	–	–	–
–	–	–		–	–	–	–
0.1	0.1	0.1		0.1	0.1	0.0	0.1
–	–	–		–	–	–	–
–	–	–		–	–	–	–
–	–	–		–	–	–	–
–	–	–		–	–	–	–
–	–	–		–	–	–	–
–	–	–		–	–	–	–
–	–	–		–	–	–	–
–	–	–		–	–	–	–
–	–	–		–	–	–	–
–	–	–		–	–	–	–
–	–	–		–	–	–	–
2.9	3.3	2.3		2.5	2.9	3.3	1.0
–	–	–		–	–	–	–
3.0	3.4	2.4		2.6	2.9	3.3	1.0
–	–	–		–	–	–	–
–	–	–		–	–	–	–
0.8	1.1	1.1		–	0.3	0.0	0.0
–	1.8	1.8		–	1.9	0.0	0.0
–	–	–		–	–	–	–
–	–	–		–	–	–	–
–	–	–		–	–	–	–
–	–	–		–	–	–	–
–	–	–		0.2	0.2	0.2	0.3
0.2	0.2	0.2		–	–	–	–
–	–	–		–	–	–	–
–	–	–		–	–	–	–
–	–	–		–	–	–	–
–	–	–		–	–	–	–
–	0.0	0.1		–	–	–	–
–	–	–		–	–	–	–
1.0	3.1	3.2		0.2	2.4	0.3	0.4
–	–	–		–	–	–	–
2.9	5.0	4.1		2.5	4.8	3.3	1.0
3.9	6.5	5.6		2.8	5.3	3.6	1.4

11. TECH. COOP. GRANTS

1988	1989	1990		1987	1988	1989	1990
–	–	–		–	–	–	–
–	–	–		–	–	–	–
0.1	0.1	0.1		–	0.3	0.1	0.1
–	–	–		–	–	–	–
–	–	–		–	–	–	–
–	–	–		–	–	–	–
–	–	–		–	–	–	–
–	–	–		–	–	–	–
–	–	–		–	–	–	–
–	–	–		–	–	–	–
–	–	–		–	–	–	–
–	–	–		–	–	–	–
2.9	3.3	2.3		1.0	0.8	0.8	1.0
–	–	–		–	–	–	–
3.0	3.4	2.4		1.0	1.1	0.9	1.1
0.2	0.3	0.4		0.2	0.2	0.2	0.3
–	–	–		–	–	–	–
2.9	3.4	2.4		1.0	0.8	0.8	1.0
3.2	3.7	2.8		1.1	1.3	1.1	1.4

12. TOTAL OOF NET

1988	1989	1990		1987	1988	1989	1990
–	–	–		–	–	–	–
–	–	–		–	–	–	–
–	–	–		-0.9	–	-1.1	–
–	–	–		–	–	–	–
–	–	–		–	–	–	–
–	–	–		–	–	–	–
–	–	–		–	–	–	–
–	–	–		–	–	–	–
–	–	–		–	–	–	–
–	–	–		–	–	–	–
–	–	–		–	–	–	–
–	–	–		–	–	–	–
–	–	–		–	–	–	–
–	–	–		–	–	–	–
–	–	–		–	–	–	–
–	–	–		-0.9	–	-1.1	–
0.1	0.1	0.1		0.4	0.1	0.1	0.1
–	–	–		–	–	–	–
–	–	–		–	–	–	–
0.1	0.1	0.1		-0.5	0.1	-1.0	0.1

13. ODF COMMITMENTS: BY PURPOSE %

	1987	1988	1989	1990
Education	–	–	–	–
Health	–	–	–	–
Other Social Infrastr.	–	–	–	–
Water Sanitat. Sewage	36	–	–	–
Energy	–	–	–	–
Telecommunications	–	–	–	–
Transportation	–	–	–	–
Agriculture	–	–	–	–
Extractive Industries	–	–	–	–
Manufacturing	–	–	–	–
Trade Banking Tourism	–	–	–	–
Technical Cooperation	27	35	100	–
Multisector Aid	37	65	–	–
Programme	–	–	–	–
Debt Reorganisation	–	–	–	–
Food Aid	–	–	–	–
Emergency Aid	–	–	–	–
Unspecified	–	–	–	–
TOTAL	100	100	100	–

14. GRANT ELEMENT OF ODA %

DAC COUNTRIES

	1987	1988	1989	1990
Australia	–	–	–	–
Austria	–	–	–	–
Belgium	–	–	–	–
Canada	100.0	100.0	100.0	–
Denmark	–	–	–	–
Finland	–	–	–	–
France	–	–	–	–
Germany	–	–	–	–
Ireland	–	–	–	–
Italy	–	–	–	–
Japan	–	–	–	–
Netherlands	–	–	–	–
New Zealand	–	–	–	–
Norway	–	–	–	–
Sweden	–	–	–	–
Switzerland	–	–	–	–
United Kingdom	100.0	100.0	100.0	–
United States	–	–	–	–
TOTAL	100.0	100.0	100.0	–
MULTILATERAL	100.0	100.0	100.0	–
ARAB COUNTRIES	–	–	–	–
E.E.C.+ MEMBERS	100.0	100.0	100.0	–
TOTAL	100.0	100.0	100.0	–

15. OTHER AGGREGATES

OFFICIAL COMMITMENTS:

	1987	1988	1989	1990
TOTAL BILATERAL	2.6	2.9	3.3	3.6
of which:				
Arab Countries	–	–	–	–
C.E.E.C.	–	–	–	–
TOTAL MULTILATERAL	0.2	2.4	0.3	0.4
TOTAL BIL.& MULTIL.	2.8	5.3	3.6	4.0
of which:				
ODA Grants	2.8	3.5	3.6	1.4
ODA Loans	–	1.8	–	–

DISBURSEMENTS:

DAC COUNTRIES COMBINED

OFFICIAL & PRIVATE

	1987	1988	1989	1990
GROSS:				
Contractual Lending	0.9	-1.2	–	–
Export Credits, Total	0.9	-1.2	–	–
Export Credits, Priv.	0.7	-1.2	–	–
NET:				
Contractual Lending	-2.1	-1.2	-1.1	–
Export Credits Total	-2.1	-1.2	-1.1	–
PRIVATE SECTOR NET	-0.4	-2.0	-0.1	0.0
Direct Investment	–	–	-0.1	–
Portfolio Investment	0.8	-0.8	–	0.0
Export Credits	-1.2	-1.2	–	–

MARKET BORROWING:

CHANGE IN CLAIMS

	1987	1988	1989	1990
Banks	–	–	–	–

MEMORANDUM ITEM:

	1987	1988	1989	1990
C.E.E.C. (Gross)	–	–	–	–

DISBURSEMENTS, UNLESS OTHERWISE STATED

	1987	1988	1989	1990		1987	1988	1989	1990		1987
1. TOTAL RECEIPTS NET					**4. TOTAL ODA NET**					**7. TOTAL ODA GROSS**	
DAC COUNTRIES											
Australia	–	–	0.0	–		–	–	0.0	–	Australia	–
Austria	–	–	–	–		–	–	–	–	Austria	–
Belgium	–	–	–	–		–	–	–	–	Belgium	–
Canada	1.2	1.5	1.9	0.6		1.2	2.5	1.9	1.2	Canada	1.3
Denmark	–	–	–	–		–	–	–	–	Denmark	–
Finland	–	–	0.0	–		–	–	0.0	–	Finland	–
France	1.3	1.7	1.1	-3.3		–	–	–	–	France	–
Germany	0.4	2.6	7.2	12.6		0.0	0.0	0.2	0.1	Germany	0.0
Ireland	–	–	–	–		–	–	–	–	Ireland	–
Italy	3.0	6.7	7.5	-5.5		–	–	–	–	Italy	–
Japan	0.1	0.0	0.1	–		0.1	0.0	0.1	–	Japan	0.1
Netherlands	–	–	4.4	-1.0		–	–	–	–	Netherlands	–
New Zealand	–	–	–	–		–	–	–	–	New Zealand	–
Norway	–	–	–	–		–	–	–	–	Norway	–
Sweden	–	–	–	–		–	–	–	–	Sweden	–
Switzerland	–	–	–	–		–	–	–	–	Switzerland	–
United Kingdom	19.5	-8.7	8.9	1.4		1.5	1.7	1.2	1.7	United Kingdom	1.6
United States	2.0	3.0	1.0	–		2.0	1.0	–	–	United States	2.0
TOTAL	27.5	6.8	32.2	4.7		4.8	5.3	3.4	2.9	TOTAL	5.0
MULTILATERAL											
AF.D.F.	–	–	–	–		–	–	–	–	AF.D.F.	–
AF.D.B.	–	–	–	–		–	–	–	–	AF.D.B.	–
AS.D.B	–	–	–	–		–	–	–	–	AS.D.B	–
CAR.D.B.	0.4	0.7	0.2	0.2		0.4	0.7	0.2	0.2	CAR.D.B.	0.4
E.E.C.	–	2.1	0.4	0.4		–	2.1	0.4	0.4	E.E.C.	–
IBRD	–	–	–	–		–	–	–	–	IBRD	–
IDA	–	–	–	–		–	–	–	–	IDA	–
I.D.B.	–	–	–	–		–	–	–	–	I.D.B.	–
IFAD	–	–	–	–		–	–	–	–	IFAD	–
I.F.C.	–	–	–	–		–	–	–	–	I.F.C.	–
IMF TRUST FUND	–	–	–	–		–	–	–	–	IMF TRUST FUND	–
U.N. AGENCIES	–	–	–	–		–	–	–	–	U.N. AGENCIES	–
UNDP	0.3	0.2	0.3	0.3		0.3	0.2	0.3	0.3	UNDP	0.3
UNTA	0.0	0.1	0.1	0.2		0.0	0.1	0.1	0.2	UNTA	0.0
UNICEF	0.0	–	–	–		0.0	–	–	–	UNICEF	0.0
UNRWA	–	–	–	–		–	–	–	–	UNRWA	–
WFP	0.1	–	–	–		0.1	–	–	–	WFP	0.1
UNHCR	–	–	–	–		–	–	–	–	UNHCR	–
Other Multilateral	0.0	0.1	0.1	0.1		0.0	0.1	0.1	0.1	Other Multilateral	0.0
Arab Agencies	-0.2	0.0	–	–		–	–	–	–	Arab Agencies	–
TOTAL	0.5	3.2	1.0	1.2		0.7	3.2	1.0	1.2	TOTAL	0.7
ARAB COUNTRIES	–	–	–	–		–	–	–	–	ARAB COUNTRIES	–
E.E.C.+ MEMBERS	24.2	4.3	29.6	4.6		1.5	3.9	1.8	2.2	E.E.C.+ MEMBERS	1.6
TOTAL	28.1	9.9	33.2	5.8		5.6	8.5	4.4	4.1	TOTAL	5.7
2. ODA LOANS GROSS					**5. ODA LOANS NET**					**8. GRANTS**	
DAC COUNTRIES											
Australia	–	–	–	–		–	–	–	–	Australia	–
Austria	–	–	–	–		–	–	–	–	Austria	–
Belgium	–	–	–	–		–	–	–	–	Belgium	–
Canada	–	–	–	–		-0.1	-0.2	-0.1	-0.1	Canada	1.3
Denmark	–	–	–	–		–	–	–	–	Denmark	–
Finland	–	–	–	–		–	–	–	–	Finland	–
France	–	–	–	–		–	–	–	–	France	–
Germany	–	–	–	–		–	–	–	–	Germany	0.0
Ireland	–	–	–	–		–	–	–	–	Ireland	–
Italy	–	–	–	–		–	–	–	–	Italy	–
Japan	–	–	–	–		–	–	–	–	Japan	0.1
Netherlands	–	–	–	–		–	–	–	–	Netherlands	–
New Zealand	–	–	–	–		–	–	–	–	New Zealand	–
Norway	–	–	–	–		–	–	–	–	Norway	–
Sweden	–	–	–	–		–	–	–	–	Sweden	–
Switzerland	–	–	–	–		–	–	–	–	Switzerland	–
United Kingdom	–	–	–	–		-0.1	-0.3	-0.1	-0.1	United Kingdom	1.6
United States	2.0	1.0	–	–		2.0	1.0	–	–	United States	–
TOTAL	2.0	1.0	–	–		1.8	0.5	-0.2	-0.1	TOTAL	3.0
MULTILATERAL	0.4	0.7	0.2	0.2		0.4	0.7	0.2	0.2	MULTILATERAL	0.4
ARAB COUNTRIES	–	–	–	–		–	–	–	–	ARAB COUNTRIES	–
E.E.C.+ MEMBERS	–	–	–	–		-0.1	-0.3	-0.1	-0.1	E.E.C.+ MEMBERS	1.6
TOTAL	2.4	1.7	0.2	0.2		2.2	1.2	-0.1	0.0	TOTAL	3.4
3. TOTAL OFFICIAL GROSS					**6. TOTAL OFFICIAL NET**					**9. TOTAL OOF GROSS**	
DAC COUNTRIES											
Australia	–	–	0.0	–		–	–	0.0	–	Australia	–
Austria	–	–	–	–		–	–	–	–	Austria	–
Belgium	–	–	–	–		–	–	–	–	Belgium	–
Canada	1.3	2.7	2.1	1.2		1.2	1.4	1.9	0.6	Canada	–
Denmark	–	–	–	–		–	–	–	–	Denmark	–
Finland	–	–	0.0	–		–	–	0.0	–	Finland	–
France	–	–	–	–		–	–	–	–	France	–
Germany	0.0	0.0	0.2	0.1		0.0	0.0	0.2	0.1	Germany	–
Ireland	–	–	–	–		–	–	–	–	Ireland	–
Italy	3.0	1.8	1.3	14.5		3.0	1.8	-0.9	-6.7	Italy	3.0
Japan	0.1	0.0	0.1	–		0.1	0.0	0.1	–	Japan	–
Netherlands	–	–	–	–		–	–	–	–	Netherlands	–
New Zealand	–	–	–	–		–	–	–	–	New Zealand	–
Norway	–	–	–	–		–	–	–	–	Norway	–
Sweden	–	–	–	–		–	–	–	–	Sweden	–
Switzerland	–	–	–	–		–	–	–	–	Switzerland	–
United Kingdom	1.6	2.1	1.2	1.8		1.4	1.7	1.1	1.7	United Kingdom	–
United States	2.0	3.0	1.0	1.0		2.0	3.0	1.0	–	United States	–
TOTAL	8.0	9.6	5.9	18.6		7.7	8.0	3.5	-4.3	TOTAL	3.0
MULTILATERAL	0.7	3.2	1.0	1.2		0.5	3.2	1.0	1.2	MULTILATERAL	–
ARAB COUNTRIES	–	–	–	–		–	–	–	–	ARAB COUNTRIES	–
E.E.C.+ MEMBERS	4.6	6.0	3.1	16.8		4.4	5.7	0.9	-4.5	E.E.C.+ MEMBERS	3.0
TOTAL	8.7	12.8	6.9	19.7		8.3	11.1	4.5	-3.2	TOTAL	3.0

10. ODA COMMITMENTS

1988	1989	1990	1987	1988	1989	1990
–	0.0	–	–	–	–	–
–	–	–	–	–	–	–
2.7	2.1	1.2	0.2	0.4	4.3	0.2
–	–	–	–	–	–	–
–	0.0	–	–	–	0.0	–
–	–	–	–	–	–	–
0.0	0.2	0.1	0.0	0.0	0.2	0.1
–	–	–	–	–	–	–
0.0	0.1	–	0.1	0.0	0.1	–
–	–	–	–	–	–	–
–	–	–	–	–	–	–
–	–	–	–	–	–	–
2.1	1.2	1.8	1.6	0.4	0.4	2.0
1.0	–	–	–	–	–	–
5.8	3.6	3.1	1.9	0.9	5.0	2.3
–	–	–	–	–	–	–
–	–	–	–	–	–	–
–	–	–	–	–	–	–
0.7	0.2	0.2	–	0.3	–	–
2.1	0.4	0.4	-0.1	0.5	1.8	1.8
–	–	–	–	–	–	–
–	–	–	–	–	–	–
–	–	–	–	–	–	–
–	–	–	–	–	–	–
–	–	–	0.4	0.4	0.4	0.6
0.2	0.3	0.3	–	–	–	–
0.1	0.1	0.2	–	–	–	–
–	–	–	–	–	–	–
–	–	–	–	–	–	–
0.1	0.1	0.1	–	–	–	–
–	–	–	–	–	–	–
3.2	1.0	1.2	0.2	1.2	2.2	2.4
–	–	–	–	–	–	–
4.2	1.8	2.3	1.5	1.0	2.4	3.8
9.0	4.6	4.3	2.2	2.0	7.2	4.6

11. TECH. COOP. GRANTS

1988	1989	1990	1987	1988	1989	1990
–	0.0	–	–	–	–	–
–	–	–	–	–	–	–
2.7	2.1	1.2	–	0.6	0.7	0.5
–	–	–	–	–	–	–
–	0.0	–	–	–	–	–
–	–	–	–	–	–	–
0.0	0.2	0.1	0.0	0.0	0.0	0.1
–	–	–	–	–	–	–
0.0	0.1	–	0.1	0.0	0.1	–
–	–	–	–	–	–	–
–	–	–	–	–	–	–
–	–	–	–	–	–	–
2.1	1.2	1.8	0.6	0.4	0.3	0.6
–	–	–	–	–	–	–
4.8	3.6	3.1	0.7	1.1	1.1	1.2
2.5	0.8	1.0	0.3	0.5	0.4	0.6
–	–	–	–	–	–	–
4.2	1.8	2.3	0.6	0.6	0.3	0.7
7.3	4.4	4.1	1.0	1.6	1.5	1.8

12. TOTAL OOF NET

1988	1989	1990	1987	1988	1989	1990
–	–	–	–	–	–	–
–	–	–	–	–	–	–
–	–	–	–	-1.1	–	-0.6
–	–	–	–	–	–	–
–	–	–	–	–	–	–
–	–	–	–	–	–	–
1.8	1.3	14.5	3.0	1.8	-0.9	-6.7
–	–	–	–	–	–	–
–	–	–	–	–	–	–
–	–	–	–	–	–	–
–	–	–	-0.1	0.0	0.0	0.0
2.0	1.0	1.0	–	2.0	1.0	–
3.8	2.3	15.5	2.9	2.7	0.1	-7.3
–	–	–	-0.2	0.0	–	–
–	–	–	–	–	–	–
1.8	1.3	14.5	2.9	1.8	-0.9	-6.7
3.8	2.3	15.5	2.7	2.6	0.1	-7.3

13. ODF COMMITMENTS: BY PURPOSE %

	1987	1988	1989	1990
Education	–	–	–	–
Health	–	–	–	–
Other Social Infrastr.	–	–	–	–
Water Sanitat. Sewage	–	–	–	–
Energy	–	–	–	–
Telecommunications	–	–	–	–
Transportation	47	46	2	–
Agriculture	2	14	–	–
Extractive Industries	–	–	–	–
Manufacturing	–	–	–	–
Trade Banking Tourism	–	2	82	–
Technical Cooperation	51	38	15	–
Multisector Aid	–	–	–	–
Programme	–	–	–	–
Debt Reorganisation	–	–	–	–
Food Aid	–	–	–	–
Emergency Aid	–	–	1	–
Unspecified	–	–	–	–
TOTAL	100	100	100	–

14. GRANT ELEMENT OF ODA %

DAC COUNTRIES

	1987	1988	1989	1990
Australia	–	–	–	–
Austria	–	–	–	–
Belgium	–	–	–	–
Canada	100.0	100.0	100.0	–
Denmark	–	–	–	–
Finland	–	–	100.0	–
France	–	–	–	–
Germany	100.0	100.0	100.0	–
Ireland	–	–	–	–
Italy	–	–	–	–
Japan	100.0	100.0	100.0	–
Netherlands	–	–	–	–
New Zealand	–	–	–	–
Norway	–	–	–	–
Sweden	–	–	–	–
Switzerland	–	–	–	–
United Kingdom	100.0	100.0	100.0	–
United States	–	–	–	–
TOTAL	100.0	100.0	100.0	–
MULTILATERAL	100.0	100.0	100.0	–
ARAB COUNTRIES	–	–	–	–
E.E.C.+ MEMBERS	100.0	100.0	100.0	–
TOTAL	100.0	100.0	100.0	–

15. OTHER AGGREGATES

	1987	1988	1989	1990
OFFICIAL COMMITMENTS:				
TOTAL BILATERAL	4.0	4.4	7.1	2.3
of which:				
Arab Countries	–	–	–	–
C.E.E.C.	–	–	–	–
TOTAL MULTILATERAL	0.2	1.2	2.2	2.4
TOTAL BIL.& MULTIL.	4.2	5.5	9.2	4.6
of which:				
ODA Grants	2.2	2.0	5.5	3.0
ODA Loans	–	–	1.7	1.7
DISBURSEMENTS:				
DAC COUNTRIES COMBINED				
OFFICIAL & PRIVATE				
GROSS:				
Contractual Lending	7.0	5.2	2.6	13.1
Export Credits, Total	5.0	2.2	1.6	12.1
Export Credits, Priv.	2.0	0.4	0.3	-2.4
NET:				
Contractual Lending	5.8	2.2	-2.1	-10.6
Export Credits Total	4.1	-0.3	-2.8	-10.4
PRIVATE SECTOR NET	19.8	-1.2	28.7	9.0
Direct Investment	19.4	-9.0	11.1	1.7
Portfolio Investment	-0.7	8.8	19.6	10.5
Export Credits	1.1	-1.0	-2.0	-3.2
MARKET BORROWING:				
CHANGE IN CLAIMS				
Banks	–	–	–	–
MEMORANDUM ITEM:				
C.E.E.C. (Gross)	–	–	–	–

1. TOTAL RECEIPTS NET

DAC COUNTRIES	1987	1988	1989	1990
Australia	2.0	-0.4	–	–
Austria	-0.7	-2.2	-2.5	-2.9
Belgium	-147.4	-5.5	-210.7	-170.9
Canada	73.9	-3.0	33.9	-2.9
Denmark	0.2	0.0	-0.3	0.0
Finland	0.5	-1.1	-0.2	0.1
France	31.9	140.6	-274.5	-170.9
Germany	429.5	511.6	316.2	542.6
Ireland	–	–	–	–
Italy	204.9	38.0	65.5	132.4
Japan	200.6	229.7	-97.9	22.7
Netherlands	-4.3	-74.6	-80.2	-210.2
New Zealand	–	0.0	–	0.1
Norway	0.1	0.7	0.0	3.3
Sweden	6.0	0.5	3.0	7.7
Switzerland	0.2	0.2	0.3	0.2
United Kingdom	43.6	66.9	4.2	-5.7
United States	-725.0	-52.0	-1617.0	-1200.0
TOTAL	115.8	849.5	-1860.3	-1054.4
MULTILATERAL				
AF.D.F.	–	–	–	–
AF.D.B.	–	–	–	–
AS.D.B	–	–	–	–
CAR.D.B.	–	–	–	–
E.E.C.	1.3	3.8	2.6	2.6
IBRD	661.7	299.0	95.0	170.0
IDA	–	–	–	–
I.D.B.	35.0	87.7	130.6	66.6
IFAD	–	–	–	–
I.F.C.	66.2	107.2	79.5	83.7
IMF TRUST FUND	–	–	–	–
U.N. AGENCIES	–	–	–	–
UNDP	16.0	21.4	16.3	15.0
UNTA	0.9	0.6	0.7	0.7
UNICEF	0.6	0.4	0.5	0.6
UNRWA	–	–	–	–
WFP	–	–	–	–
UNHCR	1.1	1.0	0.7	0.9
Other Multilateral	1.0	0.9	1.5	1.2
Arab Agencies	–	–	–	–
TOTAL	783.7	521.9	327.5	341.4
ARAB COUNTRIES	–	–	–	–
E.E.C.+ MEMBERS	559.5	680.8	-177.2	120.0
TOTAL	899.5	1371.4	-1532.8	-713.0

2. ODA LOANS GROSS

DAC COUNTRIES	1987	1988	1989	1990
Australia	–	–	–	–
Austria	–	–	–	–
Belgium	–	–	–	–
Canada	–	–	–	–
Denmark	–	–	–	–
Finland	–	–	–	–
France	–	–	–	–
Germany	–	9.3	0.0	13.6
Ireland	–	–	–	–
Italy	–	29.9	66.2	58.9
Japan	6.5	3.7	5.6	3.2
Netherlands	–	–	–	–
New Zealand	–	–	–	–
Norway	–	–	–	–
Sweden	–	–	–	–
Switzerland	–	–	–	–
United Kingdom	–	–	–	–
United States	–	–	–	–
TOTAL	6.5	42.9	71.9	75.7
MULTILATERAL	29.4	28.1	25.3	11.2
ARAB COUNTRIES	–	–	–	–
E.E.C.+ MEMBERS	–	39.2	66.2	72.5
TOTAL	35.9	71.0	97.2	86.9

3. TOTAL OFFICIAL GROSS

DAC COUNTRIES	1987	1988	1989	1990
Australia	–	–	–	–
Austria	0.1	0.1	0.2	0.2
Belgium	19.5	7.6	0.2	0.8
Canada	86.5	2.2	37.7	2.2
Denmark	0.2	0.0	0.1	0.0
Finland	0.0	0.0	0.1	0.1
France	22.6	9.0	54.1	41.9
Germany	223.6	473.1	264.8	369.5
Ireland	–	–	–	–
Italy	226.4	57.9	119.0	81.9
Japan	60.5	156.3	125.1	74.0
Netherlands	1.0	2.9	3.0	3.9
New Zealand	–	0.0	–	0.1
Norway	0.1	0.1	–	–
Sweden	0.5	0.5	0.7	1.9
Switzerland	0.2	0.2	0.3	0.2
United Kingdom	–	–	–	0.0
United States	43.0	29.0	1.0	149.0
TOTAL	684.2	739.0	606.2	725.5
MULTILATERAL	1041.3	907.7	721.0	812.5
ARAB COUNTRIES	0.2	–	–	–
E.E.C.+ MEMBERS	494.6	554.4	443.9	500.6
TOTAL	1725.7	1646.7	1327.2	1538.0

4. TOTAL ODA NET

DAC COUNTRIES	1987	1988	1989	1990
Australia	–	–	–	–
Austria	0.1	0.1	0.2	0.2
Belgium	0.6	0.5	0.2	0.8
Canada	1.8	2.2	2.6	2.2
Denmark	–	–	–	–
Finland	0.0	0.0	0.1	0.1
France	5.7	5.0	4.6	5.6
Germany	22.3	29.3	21.3	40.6
Ireland	–	–	–	–
Italy	9.7	46.8	114.6	81.9
Japan	20.2	26.0	31.9	16.4
Netherlands	1.0	2.9	3.0	3.9
New Zealand	–	0.0	–	0.1
Norway	0.1	0.1	–	–
Sweden	0.5	0.5	0.7	1.9
Switzerland	0.2	0.2	0.3	0.2
United Kingdom	–	–	–	0.0
United States	–	–	–	–
TOTAL	62.2	113.6	179.3	153.7
MULTILATERAL				
AF.D.F.	–	–	–	–
AF.D.B.	–	–	–	–
AS.D.B	–	–	–	–
CAR.D.B.	–	–	–	–
E.E.C.	1.3	3.8	2.6	2.6
IBRD	–	–	–	–
IDA	–	–	–	–
I.D.B.	15.9	10.1	9.1	-2.9
IFAD	–	–	–	–
I.F.C.	–	–	–	–
IMF TRUST FUND	–	–	–	–
U.N. AGENCIES	–	–	–	–
UNDP	16.0	21.4	16.3	15.0
UNTA	0.9	0.6	0.7	0.7
UNICEF	0.6	0.4	0.5	0.6
UNRWA	–	–	–	–
WFP	–	–	–	–
UNHCR	1.1	1.0	0.7	0.9
Other Multilateral	1.0	0.9	1.5	1.2
Arab Agencies	–	–	–	–
TOTAL	36.8	38.2	31.5	18.2
ARAB COUNTRIES	–	–	–	–
E.E.C.+ MEMBERS	40.7	88.3	146.3	135.4
TOTAL	99.1	151.8	210.8	171.9

5. ODA LOANS NET

DAC COUNTRIES	1987	1988	1989	1990
Australia	–	–	–	–
Austria	–	–	–	–
Belgium	–	–	–	–
Canada	0.0	0.0	0.0	0.0
Denmark	–	–	–	–
Finland	–	–	–	–
France	–	–	–	–
Germany	-1.2	8.6	0.0	12.6
Ireland	–	–	–	–
Italy	–	29.9	66.2	58.9
Japan	5.8	2.2	3.0	0.1
Netherlands	–	–	–	–
New Zealand	–	–	–	–
Norway	–	–	–	–
Sweden	–	–	–	–
Switzerland	–	–	–	–
United Kingdom	–	–	–	–
United States	–	–	–	–
TOTAL	4.5	40.6	69.2	71.6
MULTILATERAL	15.9	9.8	9.1	-3.4
ARAB COUNTRIES	–	–	–	–
E.E.C.+ MEMBERS	-1.2	38.4	66.2	71.5
TOTAL	20.5	50.4	78.3	68.2

6. TOTAL OFFICIAL NET

DAC COUNTRIES	1987	1988	1989	1990
Australia	–	–	–	–
Austria	0.1	0.1	0.2	0.2
Belgium	15.9	7.0	-0.1	0.8
Canada	73.8	-3.2	34.1	-2.8
Denmark	0.2	0.0	-0.3	0.0
Finland	0.0	0.0	0.1	0.1
France	12.3	2.6	54.1	41.9
Germany	196.2	271.8	124.8	320.5
Ireland	–	–	–	–
Italy	183.5	57.9	118.5	75.7
Japan	45.6	130.9	98.5	58.3
Netherlands	1.0	2.9	3.0	3.9
New Zealand	–	0.0	–	0.1
Norway	0.1	0.1	–	–
Sweden	0.5	0.5	0.7	1.9
Switzerland	0.2	0.2	0.3	0.2
United Kingdom	–	–	–	0.0
United States	31.0	19.0	-6.0	65.0
TOTAL	560.3	489.8	427.7	565.6
MULTILATERAL	783.7	521.9	327.5	341.4
ARAB COUNTRIES	–	–	–	–
E.E.C.+ MEMBERS	410.3	346.0	302.6	445.4
TOTAL	1344.0	1011.8	755.2	907.0

7. TOTAL ODA GROSS

	1987
Australia	–
Austria	0.1
Belgium	0.6
Canada	1.8
Denmark	–
Finland	0.0
France	5.7
Germany	23.6
Ireland	–
Italy	9.7
Japan	20.9
Netherlands	1.0
New Zealand	–
Norway	0.1
Sweden	0.5
Switzerland	0.2
United Kingdom	–
United States	–
TOTAL	64.2
AF.D.F.	–
AF.D.B.	–
AS.D.B	–
CAR.D.B.	–
E.E.C.	1.3
IBRD	–
IDA	–
I.D.B.	29.4
IFAD	–
I.F.C.	–
IMF TRUST FUND	–
U.N. AGENCIES	–
UNDP	16.0
UNTA	0.9
UNICEF	0.6
UNRWA	–
WFP	–
UNHCR	1.1
Other Multilateral	1.0
Arab Agencies	–
TOTAL	50.2
ARAB COUNTRIES	–
E.E.C.+ MEMBERS	41.9
TOTAL	114.5

8. GRANTS

	1987
Australia	–
Austria	0.1
Belgium	0.6
Canada	1.8
Denmark	–
Finland	0.0
France	5.7
Germany	23.6
Ireland	–
Italy	9.7
Japan	14.4
Netherlands	1.0
New Zealand	–
Norway	0.1
Sweden	0.5
Switzerland	0.2
United Kingdom	–
United States	–
TOTAL	57.7
MULTILATERAL	20.9
ARAB COUNTRIES	–
E.E.C.+ MEMBERS	41.9
TOTAL	78.6

9. TOTAL OOF GROSS

	1987
Australia	–
Austria	–
Belgium	18.9
Canada	84.7
Denmark	0.2
Finland	–
France	16.9
Germany	200.1
Ireland	–
Italy	216.7
Japan	39.6
Netherlands	–
New Zealand	–
Norway	–
Sweden	–
Switzerland	–
United Kingdom	–
United States	43.0
TOTAL	620.0
MULTILATERAL	991.0
ARAB COUNTRIES	0.2
E.E.C.+ MEMBERS	452.7
TOTAL	1611.3

10. ODA COMMITMENTS

1988	1989	1990	1987	1988	1989	1990
–	–	–	–	–	–	–
0.1	0.2	0.2	0.1	0.1	0.2	0.2
0.5	0.2	0.8	0.5	0.4	0.2	0.8
2.2	2.6	2.2	1.6	2.5	2.8	2.9
–	–	–	–	–	–	–
0.0	0.1	0.1	–	0.1	0.0	0.1
5.0	4.6	5.6	5.7	5.0	4.6	5.6
30.0	21.3	41.6	29.5	38.7	30.3	47.8
–	–	–	–	–	–	–
46.8	114.6	81.9	70.9	189.4	144.4	64.6
27.5	34.6	19.5	33.3	31.8	22.5	19.0
2.9	3.0	3.9	1.0	2.9	3.0	3.9
0.0	–	0.1	0.0	0.0	–	–
0.1	–	–	0.1	–	–	–
0.5	0.7	1.9	0.3	0.7	0.8	0.2
0.2	0.3	0.2	0.0	–	0.0	–
–	–	0.0	–	–	–	0.0
–	–	–	–	–	0.2	0.2
115.9	*182.0*	*157.8*	*143.2*	*271.6*	*208.9*	*145.2*
–	–	–	–	–	–	–
–	–	–	–	–	–	–
–	–	–	–	–	–	–
–	–	–	–	–	–	–
3.8	2.6	2.6	3.9	1.7	1.9	1.9
–	–	–	–	–	–	–
28.4	25.3	11.7	–	–	–	–
–	–	–	–	11.0	–	–
–	–	–	–	–	–	–
–	–	–	19.6	24.3	19.7	18.5
21.4	16.3	15.0	–	–	–	–
0.6	0.7	0.7	–	–	–	–
0.4	0.5	0.6	–	–	–	–
–	–	–	–	–	–	–
1.0	0.7	0.9	–	–	–	–
0.9	1.5	1.2	–	–	–	–
–	–	–	–	–	–	–
56.5	*47.7*	*32.8*	*23.5*	*37.1*	*21.6*	*20.3*
–	–	–	–	–	–	–
89.0	*146.3*	*136.4*	*111.6*	*238.1*	*184.4*	*124.5*
172.4	*229.7*	*190.6*	*166.7*	*308.6*	*230.5*	*165.5*

11. TECH. COOP. GRANTS

1988	1989	1990	1987	1988	1989	1990
–	–	–	–	–	–	–
0.1	0.2	0.2	0.1	0.1	0.1	0.2
0.5	0.2	0.8	0.2	0.1	–	–
2.2	2.6	2.2	–	0.0	0.1	0.3
–	–	–	–	–	–	–
0.0	0.1	0.1	0.0	0.0	–	0.1
5.0	4.6	5.6	5.7	5.0	4.6	5.6
20.7	21.3	28.0	23.6	20.7	18.9	25.1
–	–	–	–	–	–	–
16.9	48.4	23.0	9.7	9.0	18.3	13.2
23.8	28.9	16.3	14.1	18.6	15.0	15.6
2.9	3.0	3.9	1.0	2.9	3.0	3.9
0.0	–	0.1	–	0.0	–	0.1
0.1	–	–	0.1	–	–	–
0.5	0.7	1.9	0.5	0.5	0.7	1.7
0.2	0.3	0.2	0.1	0.2	–	–
–	–	0.0	–	–	–	0.0
–	–	–	–	–	–	–
73.0	*110.1*	*82.1*	*55.0*	*57.1*	*60.6*	*65.7*
28.4	*22.4*	*21.6*	*19.9*	*25.0*	*19.7*	*18.5*
–	–	–	–	–	–	–
49.8	*80.1*	*63.9*	*40.4*	*38.4*	*44.7*	*47.8*
101.4	*132.5*	*103.7*	*74.9*	*82.1*	*80.3*	*84.2*

12. TOTAL OOF NET

1988	1989	1990	1987	1988	1989	1990
–	–	–	–	–	–	–
–	–	–	–	–	–	–
7.1	–	–	15.3	6.5	-0.3	–
–	35.1	–	72.0	-5.4	31.5	-5.0
0.0	0.1	0.0	0.2	0.0	-0.3	0.0
–	–	–	–	–	–	–
4.0	49.5	36.3	6.5	-2.4	49.5	36.3
443.1	243.5	327.9	173.9	242.5	103.5	279.9
–	–	–	–	–	–	–
11.1	4.4	–	173.7	11.1	4.0	-6.3
128.7	90.5	54.5	25.5	104.9	66.6	41.9
–	–	–	–	–	–	–
–	–	–	–	–	–	–
–	–	–	–	–	–	–
–	–	–	–	–	–	–
29.0	1.0	149.0	31.0	19.0	-6.0	65.0
623.1	*424.2*	*567.7*	*498.1*	*376.2*	*248.4*	*411.9*
851.2	*673.4*	*779.7*	*746.9*	*483.7*	*296.0*	*323.2*
–	–	–	–	–	–	–
465.4	*297.6*	*364.2*	*369.6*	*257.7*	*156.3*	*310.0*
1474.3	*1097.5*	*1347.4*	*1245.0*	*860.0*	*544.4*	*735.1*

13. ODF COMMITMENTS: BY PURPOSE %

	1987	1988	1989	1990
Education	0	0	1	–
Health	0	5	6	–
Other Social Infrastr.	12	17	13	–
Water Sanitat. Sewage	–	3	0	–
Energy	1	26	–	–
Telecommunications	–	–	1	–
Transportation	–	–	–	–
Agriculture	10	10	4	–
Extractive Industries	–	0	–	–
Manufacturing	–	–	–	–
Trade Banking Tourism	68	9	24	–
Technical Cooperation	9	4	32	–
Multisector Aid	–	–	19	–
Programme	–	12	–	–
Debt Reorganisation	–	14	–	–
Food Aid	–	–	–	–
Emergency Aid	–	–	–	–
Unspecified	–	–	–	–
TOTAL	100	100	100	–

14. GRANT ELEMENT OF ODA %

DAC COUNTRIES

	1987	1988	1989	1990
Australia	–	–	–	–
Austria	100.0	100.0	100.0	–
Belgium	100.0	100.0	100.0	–
Canada	100.0	100.0	100.0	–
Denmark	–	–	–	–
Finland	–	100.0	100.0	–
France	100.0	100.0	100.0	–
Germany	100.0	58.9	100.0	–
Ireland	–	–	–	–
Italy	64.4	65.7	67.4	–
Japan	86.6	92.4	82.6	–
Netherlands	100.0	100.0	100.0	–
New Zealand	100.0	100.0	–	–
Norway	100.0	–	–	–
Sweden	100.0	100.0	100.0	–
Switzerland	100.0	–	100.0	–
United Kingdom	–	–	–	–
United States	–	–	100.0	–
TOTAL	*79.4*	*68.6*	*75.2*	*–*
MULTILATERAL	*100.0*	*100.0*	*100.0*	*–*
ARAB COUNTRIES	–	–	–	–
E.E.C.+ MEMBERS	77.5	65.5	74.0	–
TOTAL	*82.3*	*71.2*	*77.4*	*–*

15. OTHER AGGREGATES

OFFICIAL COMMITMENTS:

	1987	1988	1989	1990
TOTAL BILATERAL	560.6	1170.9	391.6	919.9
of which:				
Arab Countries	–	–	–	–
C.E.E.C.	–	–	–	–
TOTAL MULTILATERAL	1223.0	1870.8	59.4	378.1
TOTAL BIL.& MULTIL.	1783.6	3041.7	451.0	1298.0
of which:				
ODA Grants	101.4	134.2	118.5	148.6
ODA Loans	65.3	174.4	112.0	16.9

DISBURSEMENTS:

DAC COUNTRIES COMBINED

	1987	1988	1989	1990
OFFICIAL & PRIVATE				
GROSS:				
Contractual Lending	863.8	1112.8	666.9	781.2
Export Credits, Total	581.9	615.6	464.9	345.6
Export Credits, Priv.	237.4	450.1	171.8	137.9
NET:				
Contractual Lending	5.5	486.8	276.0	446.3
Export Credits Total	-222.7	195.3	78.6	62.7
PRIVATE SECTOR NET	-444.6	359.7	-2288.0	-1620.0
Direct Investment	216.5	-39.2	161.5	292.9
Portfolio Investment	-164.1	325.6	-2409.0	-1875.7
Export Credits	-497.0	73.3	-40.6	-37.2

MARKET BORROWING:

CHANGE IN CLAIMS

	1987	1988	1989	1990
Banks	1547.0	2982.0	-5100.0	-2773.0

MEMORANDUM ITEM:

	1987	1988	1989	1990
C.E.E.C. (Gross)	–	–	–	–

DISBURSEMENTS, UNLESS OTHERWISE STATED

	1987	1988	1989	1990	1987	1988	1989	1990	1987

1. TOTAL RECEIPTS NET (cols 1-4) / 4. TOTAL ODA NET (cols 5-8) / 7. TOTAL ODA GROSS (col 9)

DAC COUNTRIES

Country	1987	1988	1989	1990	1987	1988	1989	1990		1987
Australia	–	–	–	–	–	–	–	–	Australia	–
Austria	–	–	–	–	–	–	–	–	Austria	–
Belgium	–	–	–	–	–	–	–	–	Belgium	–
Canada	–	–	–	–	–	–	–	–	Canada	–
Denmark	–	–	–	–	–	–	–	–	Denmark	–
Finland	–	–	–	–	–	–	–	–	Finland	–
France	–	1.9	-1.7	–	–	–	–	–	France	–
Germany	0.0	–	0.0	0.1	–	–	–	–	Germany	–
Ireland	–	–	–	–	–	–	–	–	Ireland	–
Italy	–	1.9	–	0.0	–	–	–	–	Italy	–
Japan	–	–	–	–	–	–	–	–	Japan	–
Netherlands	20.8	19.3	33.6	73.7	20.8	19.3	24.2	28.9	Netherlands	20.8
New Zealand	–	–	–	–	–	–	–	–	New Zealand	–
Norway	–	–	–	–	–	–	–	–	Norway	–
Sweden	–	–	–	–	–	–	–	–	Sweden	–
Switzerland	–	–	–	–	–	–	–	–	Switzerland	–
United Kingdom	–	–	–	–	–	–	–	–	United Kingdom	–
United States	–	–	–	–	–	–	–	–	United States	–
TOTAL	20.8	23.0	31.9	73.8	20.8	19.3	24.2	28.9	**TOTAL**	20.8

MULTILATERAL

Agency	1987	1988	1989	1990	1987	1988	1989	1990		1987
AF.D.F.	–	–	–	–	–	–	–	–	AF.D.F.	–
AF.D.B.	–	–	–	–	–	–	–	–	AF.D.B.	–
AS.D.B	–	–	–	–	–	–	–	–	AS.D.B	–
CAR.D.B.	–	–	–	–	–	–	–	–	CAR.D.B.	–
E.E.C.	–	0.0	0.0	0.0	–	0.0	0.0	0.0	E.E.C.	–
IBRD	–	–	–	–	–	–	–	–	IBRD	–
IDA	–	–	–	–	–	–	–	–	IDA	–
I.D.B.	–	–	–	–	–	–	–	–	I.D.B.	–
IFAD	–	–	–	–	–	–	–	–	IFAD	–
I.F.C.	–	–	–	–	–	–	–	–	I.F.C.	–
IMF TRUST FUND	–	–	–	–	–	–	–	–	IMF TRUST FUND	–
U.N. AGENCIES	–	–	–	–	–	–	–	–	U.N. AGENCIES	–
UNDP	0.1	–	0.1	0.1	0.1	–	0.1	0.1	UNDP	0.1
UNTA	–	–	0.0	0.0	–	–	0.0	0.0	UNTA	–
UNICEF	–	–	–	–	–	–	–	–	UNICEF	–
UNRWA	–	–	–	–	–	–	–	–	UNRWA	–
WFP	–	–	–	–	–	–	–	–	WFP	–
UNHCR	–	–	0.0	0.0	–	–	0.0	0.0	UNHCR	–
Other Multilateral	–	–	0.0	0.0	–	–	0.0	0.0	Other Multilateral	–
Arab Agencies	–	–	–	–	–	–	–	–	Arab Agencies	–
TOTAL	0.1	0.0	0.2	0.1	0.1	0.0	0.2	0.1	**TOTAL**	0.1
ARAB COUNTRIES	–	–	–	–	–	–	–	–	**ARAB COUNTRIES**	–
E.E.C.+ MEMBERS	20.8	23.0	31.9	73.8	20.8	19.3	24.2	29.0	E.E.C.+ MEMBERS	20.8
TOTAL	20.9	23.0	32.1	73.9	20.9	19.3	24.3	29.0	**TOTAL**	20.9

2. ODA LOANS GROSS (cols 1-4) / 5. ODA LOANS NET (cols 5-8) / 8. GRANTS (col 9)

DAC COUNTRIES

Country	1987	1988	1989	1990	1987	1988	1989	1990		1987
Australia	–	–	–	–	–	–	–	–	Australia	–
Austria	–	–	–	–	–	–	–	–	Austria	–
Belgium	–	–	–	–	–	–	–	–	Belgium	–
Canada	–	–	–	–	–	–	–	–	Canada	–
Denmark	–	–	–	–	–	–	–	–	Denmark	–
Finland	–	–	–	–	–	–	–	–	Finland	–
France	–	–	–	–	–	–	–	–	France	–
Germany	–	–	–	–	–	–	–	–	Germany	–
Ireland	–	–	–	–	–	–	–	–	Ireland	–
Italy	–	–	–	–	–	–	–	–	Italy	–
Japan	–	–	–	–	–	–	–	–	Japan	–
Netherlands	7.4	7.6	7.1	13.0	7.4	7.6	7.1	13.0	Netherlands	13.4
New Zealand	–	–	–	–	–	–	–	–	New Zealand	–
Norway	–	–	–	–	–	–	–	–	Norway	–
Sweden	–	–	–	–	–	–	–	–	Sweden	–
Switzerland	–	–	–	–	–	–	–	–	Switzerland	–
United Kingdom	–	–	–	–	–	–	–	–	United Kingdom	–
United States	–	–	–	–	–	–	–	–	United States	–
TOTAL	7.4	7.6	7.1	13.0	7.4	7.6	7.1	13.0	**TOTAL**	13.4
MULTILATERAL	–	–	–	–	–	–	–	–	**MULTILATERAL**	0.1
ARAB COUNTRIES	–	–	–	–	–	–	–	–	**ARAB COUNTRIES**	–
E.E.C.+ MEMBERS	7.4	7.6	7.1	13.0	7.4	7.6	7.1	13.0	E.E.C.+ MEMBERS	13.4
TOTAL	7.4	7.6	7.1	13.0	7.4	7.6	7.1	13.0	**TOTAL**	13.5

3. TOTAL OFFICIAL GROSS (cols 1-4) / 6. TOTAL OFFICIAL NET (cols 5-8) / 9. TOTAL OOF GROSS (col 9)

DAC COUNTRIES

Country	1987	1988	1989	1990	1987	1988	1989	1990		1987
Australia	–	–	–	–	–	–	–	–	Australia	–
Austria	–	–	–	–	–	–	–	–	Austria	–
Belgium	–	–	–	–	–	–	–	–	Belgium	–
Canada	–	–	–	–	–	–	–	–	Canada	–
Denmark	–	–	–	–	–	–	–	–	Denmark	–
Finland	–	–	–	–	–	–	–	–	Finland	–
France	–	–	–	–	–	–	–	–	France	–
Germany	–	–	0.0	–	–	–	0.0	0.0	Germany	–
Ireland	–	–	–	–	–	–	–	–	Ireland	–
Italy	–	–	–	–	–	–	–	–	Italy	–
Japan	–	–	–	–	–	–	–	–	Japan	–
Netherlands	20.8	19.3	24.2	28.9	20.8	19.3	24.2	28.9	Netherlands	–
New Zealand	–	–	–	–	–	–	–	–	New Zealand	–
Norway	–	–	–	–	–	–	–	–	Norway	–
Sweden	–	–	–	–	–	–	–	–	Sweden	–
Switzerland	–	–	–	–	–	–	–	–	Switzerland	–
United Kingdom	–	–	–	–	–	–	–	–	United Kingdom	–
United States	–	–	–	–	–	–	–	–	United States	–
TOTAL	20.8	19.3	24.2	28.9	20.8	19.3	24.2	28.9	**TOTAL**	–
MULTILATERAL	0.1	0.0	0.2	0.1	0.1	0.0	0.2	0.1	**MULTILATERAL**	–
ARAB COUNTRIES	–	–	–	–	–	–	–	–	**ARAB COUNTRIES**	–
E.E.C.+ MEMBERS	20.8	19.3	24.2	29.0	20.8	19.3	24.2	28.9	E.E.C.+ MEMBERS	–
TOTAL	20.9	19.3	24.4	29.0	20.9	19.3	24.4	29.0	**TOTAL**	–

1988	1989	1990		1987	1988	1989	1990

10. ODA COMMITMENTS

1988	1989	1990		1987	1988	1989	1990
–	–	–		–	–	–	–
–	–	–		–	–	–	–
–	–	–		–	–	–	–
–	–	–		–	–	–	–
–	–	–		–	–	–	–
–	–	–		–	–	–	–
–	–	–		–	–	–	–
–	–	–		–	–	–	–
–	–	–		–	–	–	–
19.3	24.2	28.9		20.8	31.6	18.9	29.8
–	–	–		–	–	–	–
–	–	–		–	–	–	–
–	–	–		–	–	–	–
–	–	–		–	–	–	–
–	–	–		–	–	–	–
19.3	24.2	28.9		20.8	31.6	18.9	29.8
–	–	–		–	–	–	–
–	–	–		–	–	–	–
–	–	–		–	–	–	–
0.0	0.0	0.0		–	1.2	0.1	0.1
–	–	–		–	–	–	–
–	–	–		–	–	–	–
–	–	–		–	–	–	–
–	–	–		–	–	–	–
–	–	–		–	–	–	–
–	–	–		0.1	–	0.1	0.1
–	0.1	0.1		–	–	–	–
–	0.0	0.0		–	–	–	–
–	–	–		–	–	–	–
–	–	–		–	–	–	–
–	0.0	0.0		–	–	–	–
–	–	–		–	–	–	–
0.0	0.2	0.1		0.1	1.2	0.3	0.2
–	–	–		–	–	–	–
19.3	24.2	29.0		20.8	32.8	19.0	30.0
19.3	24.3	29.0		20.9	32.8	19.2	30.0

11. TECH. COOP. GRANTS

1988	1989	1990		1987	1988	1989	1990
–	–	–		–	–	–	–
–	–	–		–	–	–	–
–	–	–		–	–	–	–
–	–	–		–	–	–	–
–	–	–		–	–	–	–
–	–	–		–	–	–	–
–	–	–		–	–	–	–
–	–	–		–	–	–	–
11.7	17.1	15.9		3.6	4.3	1.8	2.2
–	–	–		–	–	–	–
–	–	–		–	–	–	–
–	–	–		–	–	–	–
–	–	–		–	–	–	–
11.7	17.1	15.9		3.6	4.3	1.8	2.2
0.0	0.2	0.1		0.1	0.0	0.1	0.1
–	–	–		–	–	–	–
11.7	17.2	15.9		3.6	4.4	1.8	2.2
11.7	17.3	16.0		3.7	4.4	2.0	2.2

12. TOTAL OOF NET

1988	1989	1990		1987	1988	1989	1990
–	–	–		–	–	–	–
–	–	–		–	–	–	–
–	–	–		–	–	–	–
–	–	–		–	–	–	–
–	0.0	–		–	–	0.0	0.0
–	–	–		–	–	–	–
–	–	–		–	–	–	–
–	–	–		–	–	–	–
–	–	–		–	–	–	–
–	–	–		–	–	–	–
–	–	–		–	–	–	–
–	0.0	–		–	–	0.0	0.0
–	–	–		–	–	–	–
–	–	–		–	–	–	–
–	0.0	–		–	–	0.0	0.0
–	0.0	–		–	–	0.0	0.0

13. ODF COMMITMENTS: BY PURPOSE %

	1987	1988	1989	1990
Education	1	1	1	–
Health	0	0	0	–
Other Social Infrastr.	22	22	23	–
Water Sanitat. Sewage	2	2	2	–
Energy	2	2	2	–
Telecommunications	1	1	1	–
Transportation	11	11	12	–
Agriculture	0	0	0	–
Extractive Industries	–	–	–	–
Manufacturing	–	–	–	–
Trade Banking Tourism	8	8	8	–
Technical Cooperation	18	17	12	–
Multisector Aid	35	35	37	–
Programme	–	–	–	–
Debt Reorganisation	–	–	–	–
Food Aid	0	0	0	–
Emergency Aid	–	–	–	–
Unspecified	–	–	–	–
TOTAL	100	100	100	–

14. GRANT ELEMENT OF ODA %

DAC COUNTRIES

	1987	1988	1989	1990
Australia	–	–	–	–
Austria	–	–	–	–
Belgium	–	–	–	–
Canada	–	–	–	–
Denmark	–	–	–	–
Finland	–	–	–	–
France	–	–	–	–
Germany	–	–	–	–
Ireland	–	–	–	–
Italy	–	–	–	–
Japan	–	–	–	–
Netherlands	85.8	90.4	85.1	–
New Zealand	–	–	–	–
Norway	–	–	–	–
Sweden	–	–	–	–
Switzerland	–	–	–	–
United Kingdom	–	–	–	–
United States	–	–	–	–
TOTAL	85.8	90.4	85.1	–
MULTILATERAL	100.0	100.0	100.0	–
ARAB COUNTRIES	–	–	–	–
E.E.C.+ MEMBERS	85.8	90.5	85.2	–
TOTAL	85.9	90.5	85.3	–

15. OTHER AGGREGATES

OFFICIAL COMMITMENTS:

	1987	1988	1989	1990
TOTAL BILATERAL	20.8	31.6	18.9	29.8
of which:				
Arab Countries	–	–	–	–
C.E.E.C.	–	–	–	–
TOTAL MULTILATERAL	0.1	1.2	0.3	0.2
TOTAL BIL.& MULTIL.	20.9	32.8	19.2	30.0
of which:				
ODA Grants	13.5	24.0	12.1	13.6
ODA Loans	7.4	8.8	7.1	16.5

DISBURSEMENTS:

DAC COUNTRIES COMBINED

OFFICIAL & PRIVATE

	1987	1988	1989	1990
GROSS:				
Contractual Lending	15.7	7.6	12.1	63.7
Export Credits, Total	8.3	–	5.0	50.6
Export Credits, Priv.	8.3	–	5.0	50.6
NET:				
Contractual Lending	15.7	7.6	12.1	60.8
Export Credits Total	8.3	–	5.0	47.8
PRIVATE SECTOR NET	0.0	3.7	7.7	44.9
Direct Investment	–	–	1.3	–
Portfolio Investment	-8.3	3.7	1.4	-2.9
Export Credits	8.3	–	5.0	47.8

MARKET BORROWING:

CHANGE IN CLAIMS

	1987	1988	1989	1990
Banks	–	–	–	–

MEMORANDUM ITEM:

	1987	1988	1989	1990
C.E.E.C. (Gross)	–	–	–	–

DISBURSEMENTS, UNLESS OTHERWISE STATED

1. TOTAL RECEIPTS NET

DAC COUNTRIES	1987	1988	1989	1990
Australia	–	–	–	–
Austria	–	–	–	0.0
Belgium	28.9	495.6	1.2	-160.1
Canada	-0.1	-0.1	-0.1	-0.5
Denmark	–	–	–	8.6
Finland	1.6	0.2	0.7	–
France	-21.9	92.3	98.6	-48.7
Germany	-15.5	21.5	11.1	3.5
Ireland	–	–	–	–
Italy	0.6	–	16.9	20.9
Japan	1336.1	518.8	533.0	228.3
Netherlands	5.3	-0.6	15.8	5.4
New Zealand	–	–	–	–
Norway	–	–	–	–
Sweden	-96.0	–	1.2	0.1
Switzerland	–	–	–	–
United Kingdom	21.4	57.5	117.2	-0.4
United States	-199.0	150.0	137.0	106.0
TOTAL	1061.3	1335.0	932.7	163.0
MULTILATERAL				
AF.D.F.	–	–	–	–
AF.D.B.	–	–	–	–
AS.D.B	–	–	–	–
CAR.D.B.	0.1	5.4	6.9	6.9
E.E.C.	0.2	1.8	13.0	13.0
IBRD	2.4	-1.0	–	-1.0
IDA	–	–	–	–
I.D.B.	-0.2	2.6	0.5	22.9
IFAD	–	–	–	–
I.F.C.	–	–	–	–
IMF TRUST FUND	–	–	–	–
U.N. AGENCIES	–	–	–	–
UNDP	0.1	0.2	0.3	0.4
UNTA	0.3	0.2	0.2	0.3
UNICEF	–	–	–	–
UNRWA	–	–	–	–
WFP	–	–	–	–
UNHCR	–	–	–	–
Other Multilateral	0.1	0.2	0.1	0.3
Arab Agencies	–	–	–	–
TOTAL	2.9	9.4	21.1	42.7
ARAB COUNTRIES	–	–	–	–
E.E.C.+ MEMBERS	18.9	668.1	273.8	-157.9
TOTAL	1064.2	1344.4	953.8	205.7

2. ODA LOANS GROSS

DAC COUNTRIES	1987	1988	1989	1990
Australia	–	–	–	–
Austria	–	–	–	–
Belgium	–	–	–	–
Canada	–	–	–	–
Denmark	–	–	–	–
Finland	–	–	–	–
France	–	–	–	–
Germany	–	–	–	–
Ireland	–	–	–	–
Italy	–	–	–	–
Japan	–	–	–	–
Netherlands	–	–	–	–
New Zealand	–	–	–	–
Norway	–	–	–	–
Sweden	–	–	–	–
Switzerland	–	–	–	–
United Kingdom	–	–	–	–
United States	–	–	–	–
TOTAL	–	–	–	–
MULTILATERAL	–	0.3	0.8	0.8
ARAB COUNTRIES	–	–	–	–
E.E.C.+ MEMBERS	–	–	–	–
TOTAL	–	0.3	0.8	0.8

3. TOTAL OFFICIAL GROSS

DAC COUNTRIES	1987	1988	1989	1990
Australia	–	–	–	–
Austria	–	–	–	0.0
Belgium	0.0	–	–	–
Canada	–	–	–	–
Denmark	–	–	–	–
Finland	–	–	–	–
France	0.0	–	–	–
Germany	0.0	–	–	–
Ireland	–	–	–	–
Italy	–	–	–	–
Japan	0.0	0.0	0.0	–
Netherlands	0.1	0.1	0.1	0.2
New Zealand	–	–	–	–
Norway	–	–	–	–
Sweden	–	–	–	–
Switzerland	–	–	–	–
United Kingdom	0.0	0.0	0.0	0.1
United States	–	–	–	–
TOTAL	0.2	0.1	0.2	0.4
MULTILATERAL	4.7	11.6	23.2	45.8
ARAB COUNTRIES	–	–	–	–
E.E.C.+ MEMBERS	0.3	1.9	13.1	13.4
TOTAL	4.9	11.7	23.3	46.2

4. TOTAL ODA NET

DAC COUNTRIES	1987	1988	1989	1990
Australia	–	–	–	–
Austria	–	–	–	0.0
Belgium	–	–	–	–
Canada	–	–	–	–
Denmark	–	–	–	–
Finland	–	–	–	–
France	0.0	–	–	–
Germany	0.0	–	–	–
Ireland	–	–	–	–
Italy	–	–	–	–
Japan	0.0	0.0	0.0	–
Netherlands	0.1	0.1	0.1	0.2
New Zealand	–	–	–	–
Norway	–	–	–	–
Sweden	–	–	–	–
Switzerland	–	–	–	–
United Kingdom	0.0	0.0	0.0	0.1
United States	–	–	–	–
TOTAL	0.1	0.1	0.2	0.4
MULTILATERAL				
AF.D.F.	–	–	–	–
AF.D.B.	–	–	–	–
AS.D.B	–	–	–	–
CAR.D.B.	–	0.3	0.8	0.8
E.E.C.	0.2	0.4	2.5	2.5
IBRD	–	–	–	–
IDA	–	–	–	–
I.D.B.	0.0	2.8	–	–
IFAD	–	–	–	–
I.F.C.	–	–	–	–
IMF TRUST FUND	–	–	–	–
U.N. AGENCIES	–	–	–	–
UNDP	0.1	0.2	0.3	0.4
UNTA	0.3	0.2	0.2	0.3
UNICEF	–	–	–	–
UNRWA	–	–	–	–
WFP	–	–	–	–
UNHCR	–	–	–	–
Other Multilateral	0.1	0.2	0.1	0.3
Arab Agencies	–	–	–	–
TOTAL	0.7	4.1	3.9	4.1
ARAB COUNTRIES	–	–	–	–
E.E.C.+ MEMBERS	0.3	0.5	2.6	2.8
TOTAL	0.8	4.2	4.0	4.5

5. ODA LOANS NET

DAC COUNTRIES	1987	1988	1989	1990
Australia	–	–	–	–
Austria	–	–	–	–
Belgium	–	–	–	–
Canada	–	–	–	–
Denmark	–	–	–	–
Finland	–	–	–	–
France	–	–	–	–
Germany	–	–	–	–
Ireland	–	–	–	–
Italy	–	–	–	–
Japan	–	–	–	–
Netherlands	–	–	–	–
New Zealand	–	–	–	–
Norway	–	–	–	–
Sweden	–	–	–	–
Switzerland	–	–	–	–
United Kingdom	–	–	–	–
United States	–	–	–	–
TOTAL	–	–	–	–
MULTILATERAL	–	0.3	0.8	0.8
ARAB COUNTRIES	–	–	–	–
E.E.C.+ MEMBERS	–	–	–	–
TOTAL	–	0.3	0.8	0.8

6. TOTAL OFFICIAL NET

DAC COUNTRIES	1987	1988	1989	1990
Australia	–	–	–	–
Austria	–	–	–	0.0
Belgium	–	–	–	–
Canada	-0.1	-0.1	-0.1	-0.5
Denmark	–	–	–	–
Finland	–	–	–	–
France	0.0	–	–	–
Germany	0.0	–	–	–
Ireland	–	–	–	–
Italy	–	–	–	–
Japan	0.0	0.0	0.0	–
Netherlands	0.1	0.1	0.1	0.2
New Zealand	–	–	–	–
Norway	–	–	–	–
Sweden	–	–	–	–
Switzerland	–	–	–	–
United Kingdom	0.0	0.0	0.0	0.1
United States	–	-2.0	-2.0	–
TOTAL	0.0	-2.0	-1.9	-0.2
MULTILATERAL	2.9	9.4	21.1	42.7
ARAB COUNTRIES	–	–	–	–
E.E.C.+ MEMBERS	0.3	1.9	13.1	13.4
TOTAL	2.9	7.3	19.2	42.6

7. TOTAL ODA GROSS

	1987
Australia	–
Austria	–
Belgium	–
Canada	–
Denmark	–
Finland	–
France	0.0
Germany	0.0
Ireland	–
Italy	–
Japan	0.0
Netherlands	0.1
New Zealand	–
Norway	–
Sweden	–
Switzerland	–
United Kingdom	0.0
United States	–
TOTAL	0.1
AF.D.F.	–
AF.D.B.	–
AS.D.B	–
CAR.D.B.	–
E.E.C.	0.2
IBRD	–
IDA	–
I.D.B.	0.0
IFAD	–
I.F.C.	–
IMF TRUST FUND	–
U.N. AGENCIES	–
UNDP	0.1
UNTA	0.3
UNICEF	–
UNRWA	–
WFP	–
UNHCR	–
Other Multilateral	0.1
Arab Agencies	–
TOTAL	0.7
ARAB COUNTRIES	–
E.E.C.+ MEMBERS	0.3
TOTAL	0.8

8. GRANTS

	1987
Australia	–
Austria	–
Belgium	–
Canada	–
Denmark	–
Finland	–
France	0.0
Germany	0.0
Ireland	–
Italy	–
Japan	0.0
Netherlands	0.1
New Zealand	–
Norway	–
Sweden	–
Switzerland	–
United Kingdom	0.0
United States	–
TOTAL	0.1
MULTILATERAL	0.7
ARAB COUNTRIES	–
E.E.C.+ MEMBERS	0.3
TOTAL	0.8

9. TOTAL OOF GROSS

	1987
Australia	–
Austria	–
Belgium	0.0
Canada	–
Denmark	–
Finland	–
France	–
Germany	–
Ireland	–
Italy	–
Japan	–
Netherlands	–
New Zealand	–
Norway	–
Sweden	–
Switzerland	–
United Kingdom	–
United States	–
TOTAL	0.0
MULTILATERAL	4.0
ARAB COUNTRIES	–
E.E.C.+ MEMBERS	0.0
TOTAL	4.1

1988	1989	1990
–	–	–
–	–	0.0
–	–	–
–	–	–
–	–	–
–	–	–
–	–	–
0.0	0.0	–
0.1	0.1	0.2
–	–	–
–	–	–
–	–	–
0.0	0.0	0.1
–	–	–
0.1	0.2	0.4
–	–	–
–	–	–
0.3	0.8	0.8
0.4	2.5	2.5
–	–	–
–	–	–
2.8	–	–
–	–	–
–	–	–
0.2	0.3	0.4
0.2	0.2	0.3
–	–	–
–	–	–
0.2	0.1	0.3
–	–	–
4.1	3.9	4.1
–	–	–
0.5	2.6	2.8
4.2	4.0	4.5
–	–	0.0
–	–	–
–	–	–
–	–	–
–	–	–
–	–	–
0.0	0.0	–
0.1	0.1	0.2
–	–	–
–	–	–
0.0	0.0	0.1
–	–	–
0.1	0.2	0.4
3.8	3.1	3.4
–	–	–
0.5	2.6	2.8
3.9	3.3	3.8
–	–	–
–	–	–
–	–	–
–	–	–
–	–	–
–	–	–
–	–	–
–	–	–
–	–	–
–	–	–
–	–	–
–	–	–
–	–	–
–	–	–
7.5	19.3	41.7
–	–	–
1.4	10.6	10.6
7.5	19.3	41.7

10. ODA COMMITMENTS

1987	1988	1989	1990
–	–	–	–
–	–	–	0.0
–	–	–	–
–	–	–	–
–	–	–	–
–	–	–	–
0.0	–	–	–
–	–	–	–
0.0	0.0	0.0	0.3
0.1	0.1	0.1	0.2
–	–	–	–
–	–	–	–
–	–	–	–
0.0	0.0	0.0	0.1
–	–	–	1.5
0.1	0.1	0.2	2.1
–	–	–	–
–	–	–	–
–	1.0	–	–
0.2	4.7	–	–
–	–	–	–
–	–	–	–
–	–	–	–
–	–	–	–
–	–	–	–
0.4	0.5	0.7	0.9
–	–	–	–
–	–	–	–
–	–	–	–
–	–	–	–
–	–	–	–
0.6	6.2	0.7	0.9
–	–	–	–
0.3	4.8	0.1	0.4
0.7	6.3	0.8	3.1

11. TECH. COOP. GRANTS

1987	1988	1989	1990
–	–	–	0.0
–	0.1	–	–
–	–	–	–
0.0	–	–	–
0.0	–	–	–
–	–	–	–
0.0	0.0	0.0	–
0.1	0.1	0.1	0.2
–	–	–	–
–	–	–	–
0.0	0.0	0.0	0.1
–	–	–	–
0.1	0.2	0.2	0.4
0.5	0.8	0.7	0.9
–	–	–	–
0.2	0.4	0.1	0.4
0.6	1.0	0.8	1.3

12. TOTAL OOF NET

1987	1988	1989	1990
–	–	–	–
0.0	–	–	–
-0.1	-0.1	-0.1	-0.5
–	–	–	–
–	–	–	–
–	–	–	–
–	–	–	–
–	–	–	–
–	–	–	–
–	–	–	–
–	–	–	–
–	–	–	–
–	–	–	–
–	–	–	–
–	–	–	–
–	-2.0	-2.0	–
-0.1	-2.1	-2.1	-0.5
2.2	5.3	17.2	38.6
–	–	–	–
0.0	1.4	10.6	10.6
2.1	3.1	15.1	38.1

13. ODF COMMITMENTS: BY PURPOSE %

	1987	1988	1989	1990
Education	–	–	59	–
Health	–	–	–	–
Other Social Infrastr.	–	–	–	–
Water Sanitat. Sewage	95	–	–	–
Energy	–	–	–	–
Telecommunications	–	–	–	–
Transportation	–	–	–	–
Agriculture	–	–	36	–
Extractive Industries	–	–	–	–
Manufacturing	–	–	–	–
Trade Banking Tourism	–	–	–	–
Technical Cooperation	5	100	5	–
Multisector Aid	–	–	–	–
Programme	–	–	–	–
Debt Reorganisation	–	–	–	–
Food Aid	–	–	–	–
Emergency Aid	–	–	–	–
Unspecified	–	–	–	–
TOTAL	100	100	100	–

14. GRANT ELEMENT OF ODA %

DAC COUNTRIES	1987	1988	1989	1990
Australia	–	–	–	–
Austria	–	–	–	–
Belgium	–	–	–	–
Canada	–	–	–	–
Denmark	–	–	–	–
Finland	–	–	–	–
France	–	–	–	–
Germany	100.0	–	–	–
Ireland	–	–	–	–
Italy	–	–	–	–
Japan	100.0	100.0	100.0	–
Netherlands	100.0	100.0	100.0	–
New Zealand	–	–	–	–
Norway	–	–	–	–
Sweden	–	–	–	–
Switzerland	–	–	–	–
United Kingdom	100.0	100.0	100.0	–
United States	–	–	–	–
TOTAL	*100.0*	*100.0*	*100.0*	–
MULTILATERAL	*100.0*	*100.0*	*100.0*	–
ARAB COUNTRIES	–	–	–	–
E.E.C.+ MEMBERS	*100.0*	*100.0*	*100.0*	–
TOTAL	*100.0*	*100.0*	*100.0*	–

15. OTHER AGGREGATES

	1987	1988	1989	1990
OFFICIAL COMMITMENTS:				
TOTAL BILATERAL	0.1	0.1	0.2	56.3
of which:				
Arab Countries	–	–	–	–
C.E.E.C.	–	–	–	–
TOTAL MULTILATERAL	11.1	137.3	4.0	4.2
TOTAL BIL.& MULTIL.	11.3	137.4	4.2	60.5
of which:				
ODA Grants	0.7	5.3	0.8	3.1
ODA Loans	–	1.0	–	–
DISBURSEMENTS:				
DAC COUNTRIES COMBINED				
OFFICIAL & PRIVATE				
GROSS:				
Contractual Lending	35.8	2.4	-2.1	-8.3
Export Credits, Total	35.8	2.4	-2.1	-8.3
Export Credits, Priv.	35.8	2.4	-2.1	-8.3
NET:				
Contractual Lending	-84.2	-4.5	-12.8	-16.5
Export Credits Total	-84.2	-4.5	-12.8	-16.5
PRIVATE SECTOR NET	1061.2	1337.1	934.6	163.2
Direct Investment	684.1	1153.3	956.9	319.1
Portfolio Investment	461.2	186.1	-11.6	-140.0
Export Credits	-84.0	-2.4	-10.7	-16.0
MARKET BORROWING:				
CHANGE IN CLAIMS				
Banks	–	–	–	–
MEMORANDUM ITEM:				
C.E.E.C. (Gross)	–	–	–	–

1. TOTAL RECEIPTS NET

DAC COUNTRIES	1987	1988	1989	1990
Australia	0.0	-0.4	-0.4	0.0
Austria	–	–	–	–
Belgium	-46.0	-10.1	30.3	11.7
Canada	–	–	-3.7	-3.7
Denmark	–	0.0	0.1	–
Finland	–	–	–	–
France	67.0	3.7	23.3	24.1
Germany	32.2	0.5	18.4	-35.3
Ireland	–	–	–	–
Italy	-21.9	1.3	–	2.9
Japan	-39.0	30.9	24.6	-33.9
Netherlands	-0.2	-22.8	10.1	18.4
New Zealand	–	–	–	–
Norway	–	–	–	–
Sweden	0.2	–	0.2	–
Switzerland	–	–	–	–
United Kingdom	-12.7	3.3	-9.4	-0.2
United States	–	–	–	–
TOTAL	*-20.5*	*6.2*	*93.4*	*-16.0*
MULTILATERAL				
AF.D.F.	–	–	–	–
AF.D.B.	–	–	–	–
AS.D.B	–	–	–	–
CAR.D.B.	–	–	–	–
E.E.C.	–	–	–	–
IBRD	–	–	–	–
IDA	–	–	–	–
I.D.B.	–	–	–	–
IFAD	–	–	–	–
I.F.C.	–	–	–	–
IMF TRUST FUND	–	–	–	–
U.N. AGENCIES	–	–	–	–
UNDP	0.6	0.7	0.2	0.1
UNTA	0.1	0.1	0.1	0.1
UNICEF	0.0	0.0	–	0.1
UNRWA	–	–	–	–
WFP	–	–	–	–
UNHCR	–	–	–	0.3
Other Multilateral	0.1	0.1	0.1	0.1
Arab Agencies	-2.1	5.1	8.1	–
TOTAL	*-1.3*	*6.0*	*8.4*	*0.6*
ARAB COUNTRIES	***-1.2***	***1.0***	***-8.6***	***98.5***
E.E.C.+ MEMBERS	*18.3*	*-24.2*	*72.8*	*21.5*
TOTAL	***-22.9***	***13.2***	***93.3***	***83.1***

2. ODA LOANS GROSS

DAC COUNTRIES	1987	1988	1989	1990
Australia	–	–	–	–
Austria	–	–	–	–
Belgium	–	–	–	–
Canada	–	–	–	–
Denmark	–	–	–	–
Finland	–	–	–	–
France	–	–	–	–
Germany	–	–	–	–
Ireland	–	–	–	–
Italy	–	–	–	–
Japan	–	–	–	–
Netherlands	–	–	–	–
New Zealand	–	–	–	–
Norway	–	–	–	–
Sweden	–	–	–	–
Switzerland	–	–	–	–
United Kingdom	–	–	–	–
United States	–	–	–	–
TOTAL	*–*	*–*	*–*	*–*
MULTILATERAL	*–*	*0.9*	*2.3*	*0.3*
ARAB COUNTRIES	***0.5***	***1.4***	***–***	***–***
E.E.C.+ MEMBERS	*–*	*–*	*–*	*–*
TOTAL	***0.5***	***2.3***	***2.3***	***0.3***

3. TOTAL OFFICIAL GROSS

DAC COUNTRIES	1987	1988	1989	1990
Australia	0.0	–	0.0	0.0
Austria	–	–	–	–
Belgium	–	–	–	–
Canada	–	–	–	–
Denmark	–	0.0	0.1	–
Finland	–	–	–	–
France	0.5	0.5	0.4	0.4
Germany	0.0	0.1	0.1	0.1
Ireland	–	–	–	–
Italy	–	–	–	5.8
Japan	0.5	0.5	2.7	1.3
Netherlands	0.0	0.0	0.0	0.1
New Zealand	–	–	–	–
Norway	–	–	–	–
Sweden	–	–	–	–
Switzerland	–	–	–	–
United Kingdom	–	–	–	–
United States	–	–	–	–
TOTAL	*1.1*	*1.1*	*3.3*	*7.6*
MULTILATERAL	*0.9*	*7.0*	*8.4*	*1.0*
ARAB COUNTRIES	***15.8***	***17.8***	***5.2***	***105.6***
E.E.C.+ MEMBERS	*0.5*	*0.6*	*0.6*	*6.3*
TOTAL	***17.8***	***25.8***	***16.9***	***114.2***

4. TOTAL ODA NET

	1987	1988	1989	1990
Australia	0.0	–	0.0	0.0
Austria	–	–	–	–
Belgium	–	–	–	–
Canada	–	–	–	–
Denmark	–	0.0	0.1	–
Finland	–	–	–	–
France	0.5	0.5	0.4	0.4
Germany	0.0	0.1	0.1	0.1
Ireland	–	–	–	–
Italy	–	–	–	–
Japan	0.5	0.5	2.7	1.3
Netherlands	0.0	0.0	0.0	0.1
New Zealand	–	–	–	–
Norway	–	–	–	–
Sweden	–	–	–	–
Switzerland	–	–	–	–
United Kingdom	–	–	–	–
United States	–	–	–	–
TOTAL	*1.1*	*1.1*	*3.2*	*1.9*
MULTILATERAL				
AF.D.F.	–	–	–	–
AF.D.B.	–	–	–	–
AS.D.B	–	–	–	–
CAR.D.B.	–	–	–	–
E.E.C.	–	–	–	–
IBRD	–	–	–	–
IDA	–	–	–	–
I.D.B.	–	–	–	–
IFAD	–	–	–	–
I.F.C.	–	–	–	–
IMF TRUST FUND	–	–	–	–
U.N. AGENCIES	–	–	–	–
UNDP	0.6	0.7	0.2	0.1
UNTA	0.1	0.1	0.1	0.1
UNICEF	0.0	0.0	–	0.1
UNRWA	–	–	–	–
WFP	–	–	–	–
UNHCR	–	–	–	0.3
Other Multilateral	0.1	0.1	0.1	0.1
Arab Agencies	-0.8	0.1	2.3	–
TOTAL	*0.0*	*0.9*	*2.7*	*0.6*
ARAB COUNTRIES	***-0.8***	***-4.6***	***-8.6***	***98.5***
E.E.C.+ MEMBERS	*0.5*	*0.6*	*0.6*	*0.6*
TOTAL	***0.3***	***-2.6***	***-2.7***	***101.0***

5. ODA LOANS NET

	1987	1988	1989	1990
Australia	–	–	–	–
Austria	–	–	–	–
Belgium	–	–	–	–
Canada	–	–	–	–
Denmark	–	–	–	–
Finland	–	–	–	–
France	–	–	–	–
Germany	–	–	–	–
Ireland	–	–	–	–
Italy	–	–	–	–
Japan	–	–	–	–
Netherlands	–	–	–	–
New Zealand	–	–	–	–
Norway	–	–	–	–
Sweden	–	–	–	–
Switzerland	–	–	–	–
United Kingdom	–	–	–	–
United States	–	–	–	–
TOTAL	*–*	*–*	*–*	*–*
MULTILATERAL	*-0.9*	*-0.1*	*2.3*	*-0.3*
ARAB COUNTRIES	***-11.3***	***-12.7***	***-13.8***	***-7.1***
E.E.C.+ MEMBERS	*–*	*–*	*–*	*–*
TOTAL	***-12.3***	***-12.8***	***-11.5***	***-7.4***

6. TOTAL OFFICIAL NET

	1987	1988	1989	1990
Australia	0.0	–	0.0	0.0
Austria	–	–	–	–
Belgium	–	–	–	–
Canada	–	–	-3.7	-3.7
Denmark	–	0.0	0.1	–
Finland	–	–	–	–
France	0.5	0.5	0.4	0.4
Germany	0.0	0.1	0.0	0.1
Ireland	–	–	–	–
Italy	–	–	–	2.9
Japan	0.5	0.5	2.7	1.3
Netherlands	0.0	0.0	0.0	0.1
New Zealand	–	–	–	–
Norway	–	–	–	–
Sweden	–	–	–	–
Switzerland	–	–	–	–
United Kingdom	–	–	–	–
United States	–	–	–	–
TOTAL	*1.1*	*1.1*	*-0.4*	*1.0*
MULTILATERAL	*-1.3*	*6.0*	*8.4*	*0.6*
ARAB COUNTRIES	***-1.2***	***1.0***	***-8.6***	***98.5***
E.E.C.+ MEMBERS	*0.5*	*0.6*	*0.5*	*3.4*
TOTAL	***-1.4***	***8.0***	***-0.6***	***100.2***

7. TOTAL ODA GROSS

	1987
Australia	0.0
Austria	–
Belgium	–
Canada	–
Denmark	–
Finland	–
France	0.5
Germany	0.0
Ireland	–
Italy	–
Japan	0.5
Netherlands	0.0
New Zealand	–
Norway	–
Sweden	–
Switzerland	–
United Kingdom	–
United States	–
TOTAL	*1.1*
AF.D.F.	–
AF.D.B.	–
AS.D.B	–
CAR.D.B.	–
E.E.C.	–
IBRD	–
IDA	–
I.D.B.	–
IFAD	–
I.F.C.	–
IMF TRUST FUND	–
U.N. AGENCIES	–
UNDP	0.6
UNTA	0.1
UNICEF	0.0
UNRWA	–
WFP	–
UNHCR	–
Other Multilateral	0.1
Arab Agencies	0.1
TOTAL	*0.9*
ARAB COUNTRIES	***11.1***
E.E.C.+ MEMBERS	*0.5*
TOTAL	***13.1***

8. GRANTS

	1987
Australia	0.0
Austria	–
Belgium	–
Canada	–
Denmark	–
Finland	–
France	0.5
Germany	0.0
Ireland	–
Italy	–
Japan	0.5
Netherlands	0.0
New Zealand	–
Norway	–
Sweden	–
Switzerland	–
United Kingdom	–
United States	–
TOTAL	*1.1*
MULTILATERAL	*0.9*
ARAB COUNTRIES	***10.6***
E.E.C.+ MEMBERS	*0.5*
TOTAL	***12.5***

9. TOTAL OOF GROSS

	1987
Australia	–
Austria	–
Belgium	–
Canada	–
Denmark	–
Finland	–
France	–
Germany	0.0
Ireland	–
Italy	–
Japan	–
Netherlands	–
New Zealand	–
Norway	–
Sweden	–
Switzerland	–
United Kingdom	–
United States	–
TOTAL	*0.0*
MULTILATERAL	*–*
ARAB COUNTRIES	***4.8***
E.E.C.+ MEMBERS	*0.0*
TOTAL	***4.8***

1988	1989	1990	1987	1988	1989	1990

10. ODA COMMITMENTS

1988	1989	1990	1987	1988	1989	1990
–	0.0	0.0	0.0	–	0.0	–
–	–	–	–	–	–	–
–	–	–	–	–	–	–
0.0	0.1	–	–	–	–	–
–	–	–	–	–	–	–
0.5	0.4	0.4	0.5	0.5	0.4	0.4
0.1	0.1	0.1	0.0	0.1	0.1	0.1
–	–	–	–	–	–	–
0.5	2.7	1.3	0.6	0.6	3.7	1.3
0.0	0.0	0.1	0.0	0.0	0.0	0.1
–	–	–	–	–	–	–
–	–	–	–	–	–	–
–	–	–	–	–	–	–
–	–	–	–	–	–	–
1.1	3.2	1.9	1.1	1.1	4.2	1.9
–	–	–	–	–	–	–
–	–	–	–	–	–	–
–	–	–	–	–	–	–
–	–	–	–	–	–	–
–	–	–	–	–	–	–
–	–	–	–	–	–	–
–	–	–	–	–	–	–
–	–	–	–	–	–	–
–	–	–	0.8	0.9	0.4	0.7
0.7	0.2	0.1	–	–	–	–
0.1	0.1	0.1	–	–	–	–
0.0	–	0.1	–	–	–	–
–	–	–	–	–	–	–
–	–	0.3	–	–	–	–
0.1	0.1	0.1	–	–	–	–
1.0	2.3	0.4	–	19.7	–	–
1.9	2.7	1.0	0.8	20.6	0.4	0.7
9.5	5.2	105.6	10.6	7.7	5.1	17.4
0.6	0.6	0.6	0.5	0.5	0.5	0.6
12.5	11.1	108.5	12.6	29.3	9.7	19.9

11. TECH. COOP. GRANTS

1988	1989	1990	1987	1988	1989	1990
–	0.0	0.0	0.0	–	0.0	0.0
–	–	–	–	–	–	–
–	–	–	–	–	–	–
0.0	0.1	–	–	0.0	–	–
–	–	–	–	–	–	–
0.5	0.4	0.4	0.5	0.5	0.4	0.4
0.1	0.1	0.1	0.0	0.1	0.1	0.1
–	–	–	–	–	–	–
0.5	2.7	1.3	0.5	0.5	2.2	1.3
0.0	0.0	0.1	0.0	0.0	0.0	0.1
–	–	–	–	–	–	–
–	–	–	–	–	–	–
–	–	–	–	–	–	–
–	–	–	–	–	–	–
1.1	3.2	1.9	1.1	1.1	2.8	1.9
1.0	0.4	0.8	0.8	0.9	0.4	0.6
8.1	5.2	105.6	–	–	–	–
0.6	0.6	0.6	0.5	0.6	0.5	0.6
10.2	8.8	108.2	1.9	1.9	3.1	2.5

12. TOTAL OOF NET

1988	1989	1990	1987	1988	1989	1990
–	–	–	–	–	–	–
–	–	–	–	–	–	–
–	–	–	–	–	-3.7	-3.7
–	–	–	–	–	–	–
–	–	–	–	–	–	–
–	0.0	–	0.0	–	0.0	0.0
–	–	–	–	–	–	–
–	–	5.8	–	–	–	2.9
–	–	–	–	–	–	–
–	–	–	–	–	–	–
–	–	–	–	–	–	–
–	–	–	–	–	–	–
–	–	–	–	–	–	–
–	–	–	–	–	–	–
–	0.0	5.8	0.0	–	-3.7	-0.8
5.1	5.7	–	-1.3	5.1	5.7	–
8.2	–	–	-0.4	5.5	–	–
–	0.0	5.8	0.0	–	0.0	2.9
13.3	5.8	5.8	-1.7	10.6	2.1	-0.8

13. ODF COMMITMENTS: BY PURPOSE %

	1987	1988	1989	1990
Education	84	26	58	–
Health	–	–	–	–
Other Social Infrastr.	–	–	–	–
Water Sanitat. Sewage	–	–	–	–
Energy	–	–	–	–
Telecommunications	–	–	–	–
Transportation	–	66	–	–
Agriculture	–	–	–	–
Extractive Industries	–	–	–	–
Manufacturing	–	2	–	–
Trade Banking Tourism	–	–	–	–
Technical Cooperation	16	7	37	–
Multisector Aid	–	–	–	–
Programme	–	–	–	–
Debt Reorganisation	–	–	–	–
Food Aid	–	–	–	–
Emergency Aid	–	–	5	–
Unspecified	–	–	–	–
TOTAL	100	100	100	–

14. GRANT ELEMENT OF ODA %

DAC COUNTRIES

	1987	1988	1989	1990
Australia	100.0	–	100.0	–
Austria	–	–	–	–
Belgium	–	–	–	–
Canada	–	–	–	–
Denmark	–	–	–	–
Finland	–	–	–	–
France	100.0	100.0	100.0	–
Germany	100.0	100.0	100.0	–
Ireland	–	–	–	–
Italy	–	–	–	–
Japan	100.0	100.0	100.0	–
Netherlands	100.0	100.0	100.0	–
New Zealand	–	–	–	–
Norway	–	–	–	–
Sweden	–	–	–	–
Switzerland	–	–	–	–
United Kingdom	–	–	–	–
United States	–	–	–	–
TOTAL	*100.0*	*100.0*	*100.0*	*–*
MULTILATERAL	*100.0*	*28.9*	*100.0*	*–*
ARAB COUNTRIES	**100.0**	**100.0**	**100.0**	**–**
E.E.C.+ MEMBERS	100.0	100.0	100.0	–
TOTAL	**100.0**	**50.1**	**100.0**	**–**

15. OTHER AGGREGATES

	1987	1988	1989	1990
OFFICIAL COMMITMENTS:				
TOTAL BILATERAL	87.2	8.8	9.3	19.2
of which:				
Arab Countries	86.0	7.7	5.1	17.4
C.E.E.C.	–	–	–	–
TOTAL MULTILATERAL	0.8	20.6	0.4	0.7
TOTAL BIL.& MULTIL.	88.0	29.3	9.7	19.9
of which:				
ODA Grants	12.6	9.6	9.7	2.5
ODA Loans	–	19.7	–	17.4
DISBURSEMENTS:				
DAC COUNTRIES COMBINED				
OFFICIAL & PRIVATE				
GROSS:				
Contractual Lending	5.4	9.5	42.2	14.5
Export Credits, Total	5.4	9.5	42.2	14.5
Export Credits, Priv.	5.4	9.5	42.2	8.8
NET:				
Contractual Lending	-84.7	3.8	-11.6	-19.3
Export Credits Total	-84.7	3.8	-11.5	-19.3
PRIVATE SECTOR NET	-21.5	5.2	93.9	-17.0
Direct Investment	16.0	34.8	45.9	27.1
Portfolio Investment	47.2	-33.4	55.9	-25.6
Export Credits	-84.7	3.8	-7.9	-18.5
MARKET BORROWING:				
CHANGE IN CLAIMS				
Banks	–	–	–	–
MEMORANDUM ITEM:				
C.E.E.C. (Gross)	–	–	–	–

DISBURSEMENTS, UNLESS OTHERWISE STATED

	1987	1988	1989	1990

1. TOTAL RECEIPTS NET

DAC COUNTRIES

	1987	1988	1989	1990
Australia	5.8	10.2	39.6	20.0
Austria	0.2	0.7	0.8	1.4
Belgium	5.4	3.6	0.2	9.9
Canada	102.0	117.0	73.2	102.3
Denmark	27.6	33.9	38.7	62.1
Finland	2.7	18.1	14.6	12.4
France	33.2	18.4	17.6	41.3
Germany	65.4	57.5	62.5	78.1
Ireland	0.2	0.4	0.2	0.1
Italy	4.1	0.2	2.0	1.4
Japan	328.5	338.2	371.7	414.2
Netherlands	72.8	71.4	71.4	79.5
New Zealand	0.1	0.1	0.1	0.0
Norway	33.2	36.2	33.6	43.9
Sweden	42.6	17.3	23.3	26.4
Switzerland	2.3	6.6	10.4	9.5
United Kingdom	58.7	95.5	86.3	97.1
United States	142.0	120.0	138.0	169.0
TOTAL	926.6	945.2	984.3	1168.6

MULTILATERAL

	1987	1988	1989	1990
AF.D.F.	–	–	–	–
AF.D.B.	–	–	–	–
AS.D.B	173.0	221.6	316.6	303.7
CAR.D.B.	–	–	–	–
E.E.C.	39.7	54.1	105.4	105.4
IBRD	-1.2	-1.0	-2.0	-2.0
IDA	327.9	287.0	288.0	449.0
I.D.B.	–	–	–	–
IFAD	21.2	7.6	10.3	21.3
I.F.C.	0.3	1.3	-1.0	–
IMF TRUST FUND	–	–	–	–
U.N. AGENCIES	–	–	–	–
UNDP	35.2	29.7	33.9	29.4
UNTA	4.8	2.5	4.8	3.7
UNICEF	20.3	23.2	23.8	33.8
UNRWA	–	–	–	–
WFP	59.4	53.1	58.4	51.2
UNHCR	–	0.2	0.2	0.1
Other Multilateral	3.3	4.7	10.4	6.8
Arab Agencies	-27.8	-23.6	-9.2	–
TOTAL	656.1	660.2	839.5	1002.4
ARAB COUNTRIES	26.3	-13.7	-12.2	-4.6
E.E.C.+ MEMBERS	307.1	334.9	384.3	474.9
TOTAL	1609.0	1591.6	1811.6	2166.4

2. ODA LOANS GROSS

DAC COUNTRIES

	1987	1988	1989	1990
Australia	–	–	–	–
Austria	–	–	–	–
Belgium	–	–	–	1.8
Canada	–	–	–	–
Denmark	0.0	–	–	–
Finland	–	–	–	–
France	14.7	8.1	2.0	25.9
Germany	–	–	–	–
Ireland	–	–	–	–
Italy	–	–	–	–
Japan	221.6	243.1	258.7	271.0
Netherlands	1.3	–	3.9	3.1
New Zealand	–	–	–	–
Norway	–	–	–	–
Sweden	–	–	–	–
Switzerland	–	–	–	–
United Kingdom	–	0.4	0.9	3.5
United States	16.0	38.0	12.0	35.0
TOTAL	253.6	289.7	277.5	340.3
MULTILATERAL	544.7	534.6	637.2	800.4
ARAB COUNTRIES	35.0	9.5	12.1	11.9
E.E.C.+ MEMBERS	16.0	8.6	6.8	34.3
TOTAL	833.3	833.8	926.8	1152.6

3. TOTAL OFFICIAL GROSS

DAC COUNTRIES

	1987	1988	1989	1990
Australia	8.4	11.2	39.6	20.8
Austria	0.2	0.7	0.8	1.4
Belgium	5.2	4.8	1.0	9.9
Canada	102.0	117.0	73.2	102.3
Denmark	27.5	33.9	38.7	57.6
Finland	2.7	18.1	14.6	12.4
France	30.2	21.5	24.3	41.6
Germany	66.1	57.4	62.3	78.9
Ireland	0.2	0.4	0.2	0.1
Italy	4.1	0.2	2.0	1.4
Japan	357.4	376.8	411.0	422.7
Netherlands	70.6	73.4	69.6	78.9
New Zealand	0.1	0.1	0.1	0.0
Norway	33.2	36.2	33.6	43.9
Sweden	41.8	17.3	23.3	26.4
Switzerland	2.3	6.6	10.4	9.5
United Kingdom	57.1	74.8	89.8	99.1
United States	147.0	122.0	145.0	174.0
TOTAL	956.1	972.3	1039.5	1180.9
MULTILATERAL	755.9	714.2	887.2	1040.2
ARAB COUNTRIES	47.5	9.7	16.0	11.9
E.E.C.+ MEMBERS	300.8	320.3	393.2	472.9
TOTAL	1759.4	1696.1	1942.7	2233.0

4. TOTAL ODA NET

DAC COUNTRIES

	1987	1988	1989	1990
Australia	8.4	11.2	29.0	11.6
Austria	0.2	0.7	0.8	1.4
Belgium	5.2	3.5	0.1	9.9
Canada	102.0	117.0	73.2	102.3
Denmark	27.5	33.8	38.7	54.1
Finland	2.7	18.1	14.6	12.4
France	30.2	21.5	24.2	41.5
Germany	66.1	57.4	62.3	77.3
Ireland	0.2	0.4	0.2	0.1
Italy	4.1	0.2	2.0	1.4
Japan	334.2	342.0	370.6	373.6
Netherlands	67.0	71.8	65.9	71.5
New Zealand	0.1	0.1	0.1	0.0
Norway	33.2	36.2	33.6	43.9
Sweden	41.8	17.3	23.3	26.2
Switzerland	2.3	6.6	10.4	9.5
United Kingdom	55.7	73.2	85.2	97.3
United States	146.0	120.0	138.0	169.0
TOTAL	926.7	930.9	972.3	1103.0

MULTILATERAL

	1987	1988	1989	1990
AF.D.F.	–	–	–	–
AF.D.B.	–	–	–	–
AS.D.B	173.6	221.8	316.8	303.9
CAR.D.B.	–	–	–	–
E.E.C.	39.7	54.1	105.4	105.4
IBRD	–	–	–	–
IDA	327.9	287.0	288.0	449.0
I.D.B.	–	–	–	–
IFAD	21.2	7.6	10.3	21.3
I.F.C.	–	–	–	–
IMF TRUST FUND	–	–	–	–
U.N. AGENCIES	–	–	–	–
UNDP	35.2	29.7	33.9	29.4
UNTA	4.8	2.5	4.8	3.7
UNICEF	20.3	23.2	23.8	33.8
UNRWA	–	–	–	–
WFP	59.4	53.1	58.4	51.2
UNHCR	–	0.2	0.2	0.1
Other Multilateral	3.3	4.7	10.4	6.8
Arab Agencies	-2.7	-9.2	-8.2	–
TOTAL	682.7	674.5	843.7	1004.6
ARAB COUNTRIES	26.3	-13.7	-15.2	-4.6
E.E.C.+ MEMBERS	295.6	315.9	384.1	458.5
TOTAL	1635.7	1591.7	1800.8	2103.1

5. ODA LOANS NET

DAC COUNTRIES

	1987	1988	1989	1990
Australia	–	–	–	–
Austria	–	–	–	–
Belgium	–	-1.2	-0.9	1.8
Canada	–	–	–	–
Denmark	0.0	–	–	–
Finland	–	–	–	–
France	14.7	8.1	2.0	25.8
Germany	–	–	–	–
Ireland	–	–	–	–
Italy	–	–	–	–
Japan	198.3	208.2	218.3	221.9
Netherlands	1.3	–	3.9	3.1
New Zealand	–	–	–	–
Norway	–	–	–	–
Sweden	–	–	–	–
Switzerland	–	–	–	–
United Kingdom	-1.4	-1.2	-0.6	1.9
United States	15.0	36.0	5.0	30.0
TOTAL	227.9	250.0	227.7	284.6
MULTILATERAL	519.2	505.2	603.1	762.9
ARAB COUNTRIES	13.9	-13.9	-16.1	-4.6
E.E.C.+ MEMBERS	14.6	5.8	4.4	32.6
TOTAL	761.0	741.3	814.8	1042.9

6. TOTAL OFFICIAL NET

DAC COUNTRIES

	1987	1988	1989	1990
Australia	8.4	11.2	39.6	20.8
Austria	0.2	0.7	0.8	1.4
Belgium	5.2	3.5	0.1	9.9
Canada	102.0	117.0	73.2	102.3
Denmark	27.6	33.9	38.7	57.6
Finland	2.7	18.1	14.6	12.4
France	30.2	21.5	24.2	41.5
Germany	66.1	57.4	62.3	78.9
Ireland	0.2	0.4	0.2	0.1
Italy	4.1	0.2	2.0	1.4
Japan	334.2	342.0	370.6	373.6
Netherlands	70.6	73.3	69.2	78.6
New Zealand	0.1	0.1	0.1	0.0
Norway	33.2	36.2	33.6	43.9
Sweden	41.8	17.3	23.3	26.4
Switzerland	2.3	6.6	10.4	9.5
United Kingdom	55.7	73.2	88.4	97.6
United States	141.0	120.0	138.0	169.0
TOTAL	925.4	932.5	989.4	1124.9
MULTILATERAL	656.1	660.2	839.5	1002.4
ARAB COUNTRIES	26.3	-13.7	-12.2	-4.6
E.E.C.+ MEMBERS	299.3	317.4	390.6	470.9
TOTAL	1607.8	1578.9	1816.7	2122.8

7. TOTAL ODA GROSS

	1987
Australia	8.4
Austria	0.2
Belgium	5.2
Canada	102.0
Denmark	27.5
Finland	2.7
France	30.2
Germany	66.1
Ireland	0.2
Italy	4.1
Japan	357.4
Netherlands	67.0
New Zealand	0.1
Norway	33.2
Sweden	41.8
Switzerland	2.3
United Kingdom	57.1
United States	147.0
TOTAL	952.4
AF.D.F.	–
AF.D.B.	–
AS.D.B	177.5
CAR.D.B.	–
E.E.C.	39.7
IBRD	–
IDA	335.9
I.D.B.	–
IFAD	22.1
I.F.C.	–
IMF TRUST FUND	–
U.N. AGENCIES	–
UNDP	35.2
UNTA	4.8
UNICEF	20.3
UNRWA	–
WFP	59.4
UNHCR	–
Other Multilateral	3.3
Arab Agencies	9.9
TOTAL	708.3
ARAB COUNTRIES	47.5
E.E.C.+ MEMBERS	297.1
TOTAL	1708.1

8. GRANTS

	1987
Australia	8.4
Austria	0.2
Belgium	5.2
Canada	102.0
Denmark	27.5
Finland	2.7
France	15.5
Germany	66.1
Ireland	0.2
Italy	4.1
Japan	135.9
Netherlands	65.7
New Zealand	0.1
Norway	33.2
Sweden	41.8
Switzerland	2.3
United Kingdom	57.1
United States	131.0
TOTAL	698.8
MULTILATERAL	163.6
ARAB COUNTRIES	12.4
E.E.C.+ MEMBERS	281.1
TOTAL	874.8

9. TOTAL OOF GROSS

	1987
Australia	–
Austria	–
Belgium	–
Canada	–
Denmark	0.1
Finland	–
France	–
Germany	–
Ireland	–
Italy	–
Japan	–
Netherlands	3.7
New Zealand	–
Norway	–
Sweden	–
Switzerland	–
United Kingdom	–
United States	–
TOTAL	3.7
MULTILATERAL	47.6
ARAB COUNTRIES	–
E.E.C.+ MEMBERS	3.7
TOTAL	51.3

1988	1989	1990	1987	1988	1989	1990

10. ODA COMMITMENTS

1988	1989	1990	1987	1988	1989	1990
11.2	29.0	11.6	9.6	18.7	24.0	21.4
0.7	0.8	1.4	0.2	0.7	0.8	1.4
4.8	1.0	9.9	6.2	10.5	1.0	9.9
117.0	73.2	102.3	89.6	97.6	74.1	66.6
33.8	38.7	54.1	17.9	32.0	94.3	18.4
18.1	14.6	12.4	28.2	15.1	11.8	8.3
21.5	24.3	41.6	38.9	13.5	70.5	13.6
57.4	62.3	77.3	66.7	47.7	149.9	91.2
0.4	0.2	0.1	0.2	0.4	0.2	0.1
0.2	2.0	1.4	3.8	0.2	1.9	2.8
376.8	411.0	422.7	290.3	449.2	324.5	336.4
71.8	65.9	71.5	92.7	49.8	68.2	160.4
0.1	0.1	0.0	0.1	0.1	–	–
36.2	33.6	43.9	18.6	7.1	25.4	44.4
17.3	23.3	26.2	41.8	17.3	23.3	23.7
6.6	10.4	9.5	9.5	24.1	7.2	8.0
74.8	86.7	98.9	70.3	71.2	159.0	43.9
122.0	145.0	174.0	189.5	167.2	148.9	191.3
970.6	*1022.1*	*1158.7*	*973.9*	*1022.4*	*1184.8*	*1041.8*
–	–	–	–	–	–	–
–	–	–	–	–	–	–
227.8	325.6	314.1	426.2	266.9	351.9	364.3
–	–	–	–	–	–	–
54.1	105.4	105.4	65.0	84.8	78.6	78.6
–	–	–	–	–	–	–
296.0	299.0	462.0	312.0	228.0	425.0	541.0
–	–	–	–	–	–	–
7.6	10.9	23.3	0.3	7.5	8.2	0.7
–	–	–	–	–	–	–
–	–	–	–	–	–	–
–	–	–	123.0	113.3	131.4	125.0
29.7	33.9	29.4	–	–	–	–
2.5	4.8	3.7	–	–	–	–
23.2	23.8	33.8	–	–	–	–
–	–	–	–	–	–	–
53.1	58.4	51.2	–	–	–	–
0.2	0.2	0.1	–	–	–	–
4.7	10.4	6.8	–	–	–	–
5.2	5.5	9.2	18.8	0.1	7.0	10.0
703.9	*877.7*	*1039.0*	*945.2*	*700.6*	*1002.1*	*1119.6*
9.7	*13.0*	*11.9*	*11.9*	*0.4*	*13.4*	*17.3*
318.7	*386.4*	*460.1*	*361.7*	*310.1*	*623.4*	*418.9*
1684.2	*1912.9*	*2209.6*	*1930.9*	*1723.4*	*2200.2*	*2178.7*

11. TECH. COOP. GRANTS

1988	1989	1990	1987	1988	1989	1990
11.2	29.0	11.6	0.8	1.1	1.0	1.2
0.7	0.8	1.4	0.1	0.2	0.2	0.4
4.8	1.0	8.1	0.7	0.9	0.5	0.2
117.0	73.2	102.3	–	5.3	3.8	7.3
33.8	38.7	54.1	10.5	9.6	9.5	6.8
18.1	14.6	12.4	0.1	0.8	1.3	3.6
13.3	22.2	15.7	0.7	0.9	0.9	1.1
57.4	62.3	77.3	16.2	12.9	12.9	14.3
0.4	0.2	0.1	0.2	0.2	0.2	0.1
0.2	2.0	1.4	0.3	–	0.1	–
133.7	152.3	151.6	11.3	15.0	16.7	20.0
71.8	62.0	68.4	8.6	11.6	13.2	17.1
0.1	0.1	0.0	0.1	0.1	–	0.0
36.2	33.6	43.9	0.6	1.0	1.4	1.6
17.3	23.3	26.2	4.1	1.1	5.1	0.9
6.6	10.4	9.5	0.6	0.7	–	–
74.3	85.8	95.4	17.2	24.3	25.9	32.9
84.0	133.0	139.0	29.0	35.0	48.0	58.0
681.0	*744.6*	*818.5*	*100.9*	*120.7*	*140.6*	*165.2*
169.3	*240.5*	*238.6*	*64.2*	*78.7*	*73.0*	*73.8*
0.2	*0.9*	–	–	–	–	–
310.1	*379.7*	*425.9*	*54.9*	*78.9*	*63.1*	*72.4*
850.4	*986.1*	*1057.1*	*165.0*	*199.4*	*213.6*	*239.0*

12. TOTAL OOF NET

1988	1989	1990	1987	1988	1989	1990
–	10.6	9.3	–	–	10.6	9.3
–	–	–	–	–	–	–
–	–	–	–	–	–	–
0.1	–	3.5	0.1	0.1	–	3.5
–	–	–	–	–	–	–
–	–	–	–	–	–	–
–	–	1.6	–	–	–	1.6
–	–	–	–	–	–	–
–	–	–	–	–	–	–
–	–	–	–	–	–	–
1.6	3.7	7.4	3.7	1.5	3.3	7.1
–	–	–	–	–	–	–
–	–	0.1	–	–	–	0.1
–	3.1	0.3	–	–	3.1	0.3
–	–	–	–5.0	–	–	–
1.7	*17.4*	*22.2*	*–1.3*	*1.6*	*17.1*	*21.9*
10.3	*9.5*	*1.2*	*–26.7*	*–14.3*	*–4.2*	*–2.2*
–	*3.0*	–	–	–	*3.0*	–
1.7	*6.8*	*12.8*	*3.7*	*1.6*	*6.5*	*12.5*
11.9	*29.9*	*23.4*	*–28.0*	*–12.7*	*15.9*	*19.7*

13. ODF COMMITMENTS: BY PURPOSE %

	1987	1988	1989	1990
Education	0	0	1	–
Health	4	3	2	–
Other Social Infrastr.	2	11	5	–
Water Sanitat. Sewage	2	2	2	–
Energy	11	2	30	–
Telecommunications	1	0	1	–
Transportation	17	10	12	–
Agriculture	13	15	12	–
Extractive Industries	0	0	0	–
Manufacturing	6	14	6	–
Trade Banking Tourism	10	4	1	–
Technical Cooperation	11	13	11	–
Multisector Aid	1	0	1	–
Programme	9	11	6	–
Debt Reorganisation	2	5	4	–
Food Aid	8	8	4	–
Emergency Aid	1	1	0	–
Unspecified	1	0	0	–
TOTAL	100	100	100	–

14. GRANT ELEMENT OF ODA %

DAC COUNTRIES

	1987	1988	1989	1990
Australia	100.0	100.0	100.0	–
Austria	100.0	100.0	100.0	–
Belgium	100.0	100.0	100.0	–
Canada	100.0	100.0	100.0	–
Denmark	100.0	100.0	100.0	–
Finland	100.0	100.0	100.0	–
France	82.6	100.0	76.4	–
Germany	100.0	100.0	100.0	–
Ireland	100.0	100.0	100.0	–
Italy	100.0	100.0	100.0	–
Japan	81.7	81.0	85.0	–
Netherlands	100.0	100.0	100.0	–
New Zealand	100.0	100.0	–	–
Norway	100.0	100.0	100.0	–
Sweden	100.0	100.0	100.0	–
Switzerland	100.0	100.0	100.0	–
United Kingdom	100.0	100.0	100.0	–
United States	97.6	92.7	98.6	–
TOTAL	*93.4*	*90.4*	*94.3*	–
MULTILATERAL	*84.2*	*85.7*	*83.5*	–
ARAB COUNTRIES	*100.0*	*100.0*	*55.6*	–
E.E.C.+ MEMBERS	*98.1*	*100.0*	*97.3*	–
TOTAL	*88.8*	*88.6*	*89.1*	–

15. OTHER AGGREGATES

OFFICIAL COMMITMENTS:

	1987	1988	1989	1990
TOTAL BILATERAL	995.3	1026.2	1236.2	1252.0
of which:				
Arab Countries	11.9	0.4	20.9	17.3
C.E.E.C.	1.7	–	–	–
TOTAL MULTILATERAL	951.6	719.6	1017.7	1119.6
TOTAL BIL.& MULTIL.	1947.0	1745.8	2253.9	2371.5
of which:				
ODA Grants	960.0	868.5	1157.5	1008.6
ODA Loans	972.6	854.9	1042.8	1170.1

DISBURSEMENTS:

DAC COUNTRIES COMBINED

OFFICIAL & PRIVATE

GROSS:	1987	1988	1989	1990
Contractual Lending	341.5	339.5	430.4	375.2
Export Credits, Total	84.2	48.2	146.1	22.0
Export Credits, Priv.	84.2	48.2	135.5	12.7
NET:				
Contractual Lending	236.5	249.4	311.7	283.1
Export Credits Total	4.9	–2.1	77.6	–14.0
PRIVATE SECTOR NET	1.2	12.7	–5.1	43.7
Direct Investment	–4.9	9.1	6.0	48.9
Portfolio Investment	–3.8	5.7	–78.1	18.1
Export Credits	9.9	–2.1	67.0	–23.3

MARKET BORROWING:

CHANGE IN CLAIMS

	1987	1988	1989	1990
Banks	64.0	8.0	56.0	1.0

MEMORANDUM ITEM:

	1987	1988	1989	1990
C.E.E.C. (Gross)	21.1	49.2	–	–

1. TOTAL RECEIPTS NET

DAC COUNTRIES	1987	1988	1989	1990
Australia	0.0	–	–	–
Austria	–	0.0	0.0	0.0
Belgium	-0.2	0.2	2.7	-0.5
Canada	3.0	-0.5	-3.7	4.8
Denmark	–	–	–	6.6
Finland	–	1.0	4.9	0.0
France	0.9	0.0	0.8	-4.0
Germany	0.9	0.3	0.1	0.4
Ireland	–	–	–	–
Italy	0.0	–	–	2.3
Japan	-0.4	39.1	0.1	-35.1
Netherlands	0.7	1.4	0.6	21.9
New Zealand	–	–	–	–
Norway	0.0	0.0	0.0	–
Sweden	-3.3	–	–	-9.5
Switzerland	–	–	–	–
United Kingdom	-28.3	6.3	5.8	4.2
United States	-4.0	–	-1.0	-1.0
TOTAL	*-30.6*	*47.6*	*10.3*	*-9.8*
MULTILATERAL				
AF.D.F.	–	–	–	–
AF.D.B.	–	–	–	–
AS.D.B	–	–	–	–
CAR.D.B.	5.0	6.6	0.8	0.8
E.E.C.	1.3	-1.1	-1.0	-1.0
IBRD	-1.2	-3.0	-4.0	-2.0
IDA	–	–	–	–
I.D.B.	9.1	8.3	8.3	11.8
IFAD	–	–	–	–
I.F.C.	0.8	0.5	0.0	-0.2
IMF TRUST FUND	–	–	–	–
U.N. AGENCIES	–	–	–	–
UNDP	0.4	0.1	0.2	0.3
UNTA	0.3	0.1	0.2	0.1
UNICEF	–	–	–	–
UNRWA	–	–	–	–
WFP	–	–	–	–
UNHCR	–	–	–	–
Other Multilateral	0.2	0.3	0.2	0.3
Arab Agencies	-0.6	-0.6	-0.7	–
TOTAL	*15.3*	*11.2*	*4.0*	*10.1*
ARAB COUNTRIES	–	–	–	–
E.E.C.+ MEMBERS	*-24.7*	*7.0*	*9.0*	*30.0*
TOTAL	**-15.3**	**58.8**	**14.2**	**0.3**

2. ODA LOANS GROSS

DAC COUNTRIES	1987	1988	1989	1990
Australia	–	–	–	–
Austria	–	–	–	–
Belgium	–	–	–	–
Canada	0.0	–	–	–
Denmark	–	–	–	–
Finland	–	0.5	0.0	–
France	–	–	–	–
Germany	–	–	–	–
Ireland	–	–	–	–
Italy	–	–	–	–
Japan	–	–	–	–
Netherlands	–	–	–	–
New Zealand	–	–	–	–
Norway	–	–	–	–
Sweden	–	–	–	–
Switzerland	–	–	–	–
United Kingdom	0.4	–	–	–
United States	–	–	–	–
TOTAL	*0.4*	*0.5*	*0.0*	*–*
MULTILATERAL	*2.3*	*1.8*	*2.4*	*1.7*
ARAB COUNTRIES	–	–	–	–
E.E.C.+ MEMBERS	*0.4*	*–*	*–*	*–*
TOTAL	**2.7**	**2.3**	**2.4**	**1.7**

3. TOTAL OFFICIAL GROSS

DAC COUNTRIES	1987	1988	1989	1990
Australia	0.0	–	–	–
Austria	–	0.0	0.0	0.0
Belgium	0.1	0.1	–	–
Canada	4.5	3.1	1.2	8.0
Denmark	–	–	–	–
Finland	–	0.5	0.0	0.0
France	0.0	0.0	0.0	0.0
Germany	0.5	0.3	0.2	0.4
Ireland	–	–	–	–
Italy	0.0	–	–	–
Japan	0.1	19.6	0.1	0.3
Netherlands	0.7	0.8	0.6	0.9
New Zealand	–	–	–	–
Norway	0.0	0.0	0.0	–
Sweden	–	–	–	–
Switzerland	–	–	–	–
United Kingdom	0.9	0.9	0.4	7.8
United States	–	–	–	–
TOTAL	*6.8*	*25.3*	*2.5*	*17.3*
MULTILATERAL	*24.6*	*22.4*	*14.6*	*21.5*
ARAB COUNTRIES	–	–	–	–
E.E.C.+ MEMBERS	*4.5*	*2.0*	*1.6*	*9.4*
TOTAL	**31.5**	**47.7**	**17.1**	**38.8**

4. TOTAL ODA NET

DAC COUNTRIES	1987	1988	1989	1990
Australia	0.0	–	–	–
Austria	–	0.0	0.0	0.0
Belgium	0.1	0.1	–	–
Canada	2.3	2.0	0.3	0.7
Denmark	–	–	–	–
Finland	–	0.5	0.0	0.0
France	0.0	0.0	0.0	0.0
Germany	0.5	0.3	0.2	0.4
Ireland	–	–	–	–
Italy	0.0	–	–	–
Japan	0.1	0.1	0.1	0.3
Netherlands	0.7	0.8	0.6	0.9
New Zealand	–	–	–	–
Norway	0.0	0.0	0.0	–
Sweden	–	–	–	–
Switzerland	–	–	–	–
United Kingdom	0.5	-1.4	0.3	0.3
United States	–	–	-1.0	-1.0
TOTAL	*4.3*	*2.3*	*0.5*	*1.4*
MULTILATERAL				
AF.D.F.	–	–	–	–
AF.D.B.	–	–	–	–
AS.D.B	–	–	–	–
CAR.D.B.	0.1	0.1	0.2	0.2
E.E.C.	0.1	-0.4	0.3	0.3
IBRD	–	–	–	–
IDA	–	–	–	–
I.D.B.	1.4	1.1	1.0	0.4
IFAD	–	–	–	–
I.F.C.	–	–	–	–
IMF TRUST FUND	–	–	–	–
U.N. AGENCIES	–	–	–	–
UNDP	0.4	0.1	0.2	0.3
UNTA	0.3	0.1	0.2	0.1
UNICEF	–	–	–	–
UNRWA	–	–	–	–
WFP	–	–	–	–
UNHCR	–	–	–	–
Other Multilateral	0.2	0.3	0.2	0.3
Arab Agencies	-0.3	-0.4	-0.5	–
TOTAL	*2.1*	*0.9*	*1.7*	*1.5*
ARAB COUNTRIES	–	–	–	–
E.E.C.+ MEMBERS	*1.9*	*-0.7*	*1.4*	*1.8*
TOTAL	**6.4**	**3.2**	**2.2**	**3.0**

5. ODA LOANS NET

DAC COUNTRIES	1987	1988	1989	1990
Australia	–	–	–	–
Austria	–	–	–	–
Belgium	–	–	–	–
Canada	-0.5	-0.7	-0.9	–
Denmark	–	–	–	–
Finland	–	0.5	0.0	–
France	–	–	–	–
Germany	–	–	–	–
Ireland	–	–	–	–
Italy	–	–	–	–
Japan	–	–	–	–
Netherlands	–	–	–	–
New Zealand	–	–	–	–
Norway	–	–	–	–
Sweden	–	–	–	–
Switzerland	–	–	–	–
United Kingdom	0.0	-2.4	-0.1	-0.2
United States	–	–	-1.0	-1.0
TOTAL	*-0.6*	*-2.6*	*-2.0*	*-1.2*
MULTILATERAL	*1.0*	*0.3*	*0.7*	*0.4*
ARAB COUNTRIES	–	–	–	–
E.E.C.+ MEMBERS	*0.0*	*-2.4*	*-0.1*	*-0.2*
TOTAL	**0.5**	**-2.2**	**-1.2**	**-0.8**

6. TOTAL OFFICIAL NET

DAC COUNTRIES	1987	1988	1989	1990
Australia	0.0	–	–	–
Austria	–	0.0	0.0	0.0
Belgium	0.1	0.1	–	–
Canada	0.9	-0.3	-1.7	4.8
Denmark	–	–	–	–
Finland	–	0.5	0.0	0.0
France	0.0	0.0	0.0	0.0
Germany	0.5	0.3	0.2	0.4
Ireland	–	–	–	–
Italy	0.0	–	–	–
Japan	0.1	19.6	0.1	0.3
Netherlands	0.7	0.8	0.6	0.9
New Zealand	–	–	–	–
Norway	0.0	0.0	0.0	–
Sweden	–	–	–	–
Switzerland	–	–	–	–
United Kingdom	-0.3	-2.2	-0.4	6.8
United States	-4.0	–	-1.0	-1.0
TOTAL	*-2.0*	*18.7*	*-2.2*	*12.1*
MULTILATERAL	*15.3*	*11.2*	*4.0*	*10.1*
ARAB COUNTRIES	–	–	–	–
E.E.C.+ MEMBERS	*2.4*	*-2.2*	*-0.6*	*7.1*
TOTAL	**13.4**	**29.9**	**1.7**	**22.2**

7. TOTAL ODA GROSS

	1987
Australia	0.0
Austria	–
Belgium	0.1
Canada	2.9
Denmark	–
Finland	–
France	0.0
Germany	0.5
Ireland	–
Italy	0.0
Japan	0.1
Netherlands	0.7
New Zealand	–
Norway	0.0
Sweden	–
Switzerland	–
United Kingdom	0.9
United States	–
TOTAL	*5.2*
AF.D.F.	–
AF.D.B.	–
AS.D.B	–
CAR.D.B.	0.1
E.E.C.	0.1
IBRD	–
IDA	–
I.D.B.	2.3
IFAD	–
I.F.C.	–
IMF TRUST FUND	–
U.N. AGENCIES	–
UNDP	0.4
UNTA	0.3
UNICEF	–
UNRWA	–
WFP	–
UNHCR	–
Other Multilateral	0.2
Arab Agencies	–
TOTAL	*3.4*
ARAB COUNTRIES	–
E.E.C.+ MEMBERS	*2.3*
TOTAL	**8.6**

8. GRANTS

	1987
Australia	0.0
Austria	–
Belgium	0.1
Canada	2.9
Denmark	–
Finland	–
France	0.0
Germany	0.5
Ireland	–
Italy	0.0
Japan	0.1
Netherlands	0.7
New Zealand	–
Norway	0.0
Sweden	–
Switzerland	–
United Kingdom	0.5
United States	–
TOTAL	*4.8*
MULTILATERAL	*1.1*
ARAB COUNTRIES	–
E.E.C.+ MEMBERS	*1.9*
TOTAL	**5.9**

9. TOTAL OOF GROSS

	1987
Australia	–
Austria	–
Belgium	–
Canada	1.6
Denmark	–
Finland	–
France	–
Germany	–
Ireland	–
Italy	–
Japan	–
Netherlands	–
New Zealand	–
Norway	–
Sweden	–
Switzerland	–
United Kingdom	–
United States	–
TOTAL	*1.6*
MULTILATERAL	*21.2*
ARAB COUNTRIES	–
E.E.C.+ MEMBERS	*2.2*
TOTAL	**22.9**

10. ODA COMMITMENTS

1988	1989	1990	1987	1988	1989	1990
–	–	–	–	–	–	–
0.0	0.0	0.0	–	0.0	0.0	0.0
0.1	–	–	–	0.1	–	–
2.7	1.2	0.7	0.7	0.8	0.3	0.4
–	–	–	–	–	–	–
0.5	0.0	0.0	0.5	–	–	–
0.0	0.0	0.0	0.0	0.0	0.0	0.0
0.3	0.2	0.4	0.7	0.1	0.1	0.7
–	–	–	–	–	–	–
0.1	0.1	0.3	0.1	0.1	0.1	–
0.8	0.6	0.9	0.7	0.8	–	0.9
–	–	–	–	–	–	–
0.0	0.0	–	–	–	–	–
–	–	–	–	–	–	–
0.9	0.4	0.4	0.9	0.9	0.5	0.4
–	–	–	–	0.0	0.3	–
5.3	*2.5*	*2.6*	*3.5*	*2.7*	*1.2*	*2.4*
–	–	–	–	–	–	–
–	–	–	–	–	–	–
0.1	0.2	0.2	–	–	2.0	2.0
-0.4	0.3	0.3	0.6	0.5	1.2	1.2
–	–	–	–	–	–	–
2.2	2.2	1.5	–	–	–	–
–	–	–	–	–	–	–
–	–	–	0.9	0.5	0.6	0.7
0.1	0.2	0.3	–	–	–	–
0.1	0.2	0.1	–	–	–	–
–	–	–	–	–	–	–
0.3	0.2	0.3	–	–	–	–
–	–	–	–	–	–	–
2.4	*3.3*	*2.7*	*1.6*	*0.9*	*3.9*	*3.9*
–	–	–	–	–	–	–
1.6	*1.6*	*2.0*	*2.9*	*2.3*	*1.8*	*3.2*
7.7	*5.8*	*5.3*	*5.1*	*3.6*	*5.0*	*6.3*

11. TECH. COOP. GRANTS

1988	1989	1990	1987	1988	1989	1990
–	–	–	0.0	–	–	–
0.0	0.0	0.0	–	0.0	0.0	0.0
0.1	–	–	0.1	–	–	–
2.7	1.2	0.7	–	0.3	0.2	0.1
–	–	–	–	–	–	–
–	–	0.0	–	–	–	–
0.0	0.0	0.0	0.0	0.0	0.0	0.0
0.3	0.2	0.4	0.5	0.3	0.1	0.1
–	–	–	–	–	–	–
0.1	0.1	0.3	0.0	–	–	–
0.8	0.6	0.9	0.1	0.1	0.1	0.3
0.0	0.0	–	0.7	0.8	0.6	0.9
–	–	–	–	–	–	–
0.9	0.4	0.4	–	0.0	–	–
–	–	–	–	–	–	–
4.8	*2.5*	*2.6*	0.5	0.6	0.4	0.4
0.6	1.0	1.0	–	–	–	–
–	–	–	*1.9*	*2.0*	*1.4*	*1.7*
1.6	*1.6*	*2.0*	*1.0*	*0.5*	*0.6*	*0.7*
5.4	*3.5*	*3.6*	*1.9*	*1.7*	*1.0*	*1.3*
			2.9	*2.5*	*2.0*	*2.4*

12. TOTAL OOF NET

1988	1989	1990	1987	1988	1989	1990
–	–	–	–	–	–	–
–	–	–	–	–	–	–
0.4	–	7.3	-1.5	-2.3	-2.0	4.1
–	–	–	–	–	–	–
–	–	–	–	–	–	–
–	–	–	–	–	–	–
–	–	–	–	–	–	–
19.5	–	–	–	19.5	–	–
–	–	–	–	–	–	–
–	–	7.4	-0.7	-0.8	-0.7	6.6
–	–	–	-4.0	–	–	–
19.9	–	*14.7*	*-6.2*	*16.4*	*-2.7*	*10.7*
20.0	*11.3*	*18.8*	*13.2*	*10.4*	*2.3*	*8.6*
–	–	–	–	–	–	–
0.4	–	*7.4*	*0.5*	*-1.4*	*-2.0*	*5.3*
40.0	*11.3*	*33.5*	*7.0*	*26.7*	*-0.5*	*19.2*

13. ODF COMMITMENTS: BY PURPOSE %

	1987	1988	1989	1990
Education	71	–	–	–
Health	–	–	–	–
Other Social Infrastr.	–	–	–	–
Water Sanitat. Sewage	–	–	–	–
Energy	–	–	90	–
Telecommunications	0	–	–	–
Transportation	–	–	–	–
Agriculture	15	–	–	–
Extractive Industries	–	–	–	–
Manufacturing	2	–	–	–
Trade Banking Tourism	–	–	–	–
Technical Cooperation	12	10	10	–
Multisector Aid	–	90	–	–
Programme	–	–	–	–
Debt Reorganisation	–	–	–	–
Food Aid	–	–	–	–
Emergency Aid	–	–	–	–
Unspecified	–	–	–	–
TOTAL	100	100	100	–

14. GRANT ELEMENT OF ODA %

DAC COUNTRIES	1987	1988	1989	1990
Australia	–	–	–	–
Austria	–	100.0	100.0	–
Belgium	–	100.0	–	–
Canada	100.0	100.0	100.0	–
Denmark	–	–	–	–
Finland	25.0	–	–	–
France	100.0	100.0	100.0	–
Germany	100.0	100.0	100.0	–
Ireland	–	–	–	–
Italy	–	–	–	–
Japan	100.0	100.0	100.0	–
Netherlands	100.0	100.0	–	–
New Zealand	–	–	–	–
Norway	–	–	–	–
Sweden	–	–	–	–
Switzerland	–	–	–	–
United Kingdom	100.0	100.0	100.0	–
United States	–	100.0	100.0	–
TOTAL	*88.0*	*100.0*	*100.0*	–
MULTILATERAL	*100.0*	*100.0*	*100.0*	–
ARAB COUNTRIES	–	–	–	–
E.E.C.+ MEMBERS	*100.0*	*100.0*	*100.0*	–
TOTAL	*92.0*	*100.0*	*100.0*	–

15. OTHER AGGREGATES

	1987	1988	1989	1990
OFFICIAL COMMITMENTS:				
TOTAL BILATERAL	4.8	22.2	32.6	2.4
of which:				
Arab Countries	–	–	–	–
C.E.E.C.	–	–	–	–
TOTAL MULTILATERAL	8.7	0.9	15.9	6.5
TOTAL BIL.& MULTIL.	13.5	23.1	48.4	8.9
of which:				
ODA Grants	4.2	3.5	1.9	3.2
ODA Loans	0.9	0.1	3.1	3.1
DISBURSEMENTS:				
DAC COUNTRIES COMBINED				
OFFICIAL & PRIVATE				
GROSS:				
Contractual Lending	4.8	21.2	0.5	39.0
Export Credits, Total	4.4	1.1	0.5	31.6
Export Credits, Priv.	2.8	0.7	0.5	24.3
NET:				
Contractual Lending	-9.6	9.8	-10.5	29.6
Export Credits Total	-8.3	-6.4	-7.7	24.2
PRIVATE SECTOR NET	-28.7	28.9	12.5	-21.9
Direct Investment	-27.8	14.6	15.5	-7.4
Portfolio Investment	1.9	18.3	2.7	-34.6
Export Credits	-2.8	-4.0	-5.7	20.1
MARKET BORROWING:				
CHANGE IN CLAIMS				
Banks	–	–	–	–
MEMORANDUM ITEM:				
C.E.E.C. (Gross)	–	–	–	–

	1987	1988	1989	1990		1987	1988	1989	1990		1987
1. TOTAL RECEIPTS NET					**4. TOTAL ODA NET**					**7. TOTAL ODA GROSS**	
DAC COUNTRIES											
Australia	0.0	0.0	–	–		0.0	0.0	–	–	Australia	0.0
Austria	–	–	–	–		–	–	–	–	Austria	–
Belgium	–	0.0	0.0	–		–	0.0	0.0	–	Belgium	–
Canada	5.2	9.4	-1.5	6.7		5.2	1.3	0.4	1.1	Canada	5.5
Denmark	–	–	–	–		–	–	–	–	Denmark	–
Finland	–	–	–	–		–	–	–	–	Finland	–
France	–	–	–	1.1		–	–	–	–	France	–
Germany	0.1	0.1	0.1	0.0		0.1	0.1	0.1	0.0	Germany	0.1
Ireland	–	–	–	–		–	–	–	–	Ireland	–
Italy	0.0	–	–	–		0.0	–	–	–	Italy	0.0
Japan	0.0	0.1	0.1	-9.6		0.0	0.1	0.1	0.0	Japan	0.0
Netherlands	0.0	0.3	0.3	0.3		0.0	0.3	0.2	0.3	Netherlands	0.0
New Zealand	–	–	–	–		–	–	–	–	New Zealand	–
Norway	0.0	–	–	0.0		0.0	–	–	0.0	Norway	0.0
Sweden	–	–	–	–		–	–	–	–	Sweden	–
Switzerland	–	–	–	–		–	–	–	–	Switzerland	–
United Kingdom	1.8	4.7	4.5	7.3		3.2	4.9	3.6	5.3	United Kingdom	3.4
United States	13.0	10.0	16.0	14.0		13.0	10.0	14.0	12.0	United States	13.0
TOTAL	20.2	24.4	19.6	19.9		21.5	16.6	18.4	18.8	TOTAL	22.0
MULTILATERAL											
AF.D.F.	–	–	–	–		–	–	–	–	AF.D.F.	–
AF.D.B.	–	–	–	–		–	–	–	–	AF.D.B.	–
AS.D.B	–	–	–	–		–	–	–	–	AS.D.B	–
CAR.D.B.	1.6	4.0	7.7	7.7		1.0	3.5	7.4	7.4	CAR.D.B.	1.0
E.E.C.	0.2	4.0	0.8	0.8		0.1	3.8	1.0	1.0	E.E.C.	0.1
IBRD	0.7	–	4.0	2.0		–	–	–	–	IBRD	–
IDA	–	–	–	–		–	–	–	–	IDA	–
I.D.B.	–	–	–	–		–	–	–	–	I.D.B.	–
IFAD	–	0.4	0.1	0.3		–	0.4	0.1	0.3	IFAD	–
I.F.C.	–	–	–	1.0		–	–	–	–	I.F.C.	–
IMF TRUST FUND	–	–	–	–		–	–	–	–	IMF TRUST FUND	–
U.N. AGENCIES	–	–	–	–		–	–	–	–	U.N. AGENCIES	–
UNDP	0.4	0.3	0.4	0.4		0.4	0.3	0.4	0.4	UNDP	0.4
UNTA	0.3	0.3	0.2	0.2		0.3	0.3	0.2	0.2	UNTA	0.3
UNICEF	0.2	0.1	0.1	0.1		0.2	0.1	0.1	0.1	UNICEF	0.2
UNRWA	–	–	–	–		–	–	–	–	UNRWA	–
WFP	–	–	–	–		–	–	–	–	WFP	–
UNHCR	–	–	0.2	0.5		–	–	0.2	0.5	UNHCR	–
Other Multilateral	0.1	0.1	0.1	0.1		0.1	0.1	0.1	0.1	Other Multilateral	0.1
Arab Agencies	–	–	0.7	–		–	–	0.7	–	Arab Agencies	–
TOTAL	3.5	9.2	14.4	13.2		2.1	8.5	10.2	10.0	TOTAL	2.1
ARAB COUNTRIES	–	–	–	–		–	–	–	–	ARAB COUNTRIES	–
E.E.C.+ MEMBERS	2.2	9.0	5.8	9.6		3.4	9.0	4.9	6.6	E.E.C.+ MEMBERS	3.6
TOTAL	23.6	33.6	33.9	33.0		23.6	25.1	28.6	28.8	TOTAL	24.1
2. ODA LOANS GROSS					**5. ODA LOANS NET**					**8. GRANTS**	
DAC COUNTRIES											
Australia	–	–	–	–		–	–	–	–	Australia	0.0
Austria	–	–	–	–		–	–	–	–	Austria	–
Belgium	–	–	–	–		–	–	–	–	Belgium	–
Canada	–	–	–	–		-0.3	-0.2	-0.3	-0.1	Canada	5.5
Denmark	–	–	–	–		–	–	–	–	Denmark	–
Finland	–	–	–	–		–	–	–	–	Finland	–
France	–	–	–	–		–	–	–	–	France	–
Germany	–	–	–	–		–	–	–	–	Germany	0.1
Ireland	–	–	–	–		–	–	–	–	Ireland	–
Italy	–	–	–	–		–	–	–	–	Italy	0.0
Japan	–	–	–	–		–	–	–	–	Japan	0.0
Netherlands	–	–	–	–		–	–	–	–	Netherlands	0.0
New Zealand	–	–	–	–		–	–	–	–	New Zealand	–
Norway	–	–	–	–		–	–	–	–	Norway	0.0
Sweden	–	–	–	–		–	–	–	–	Sweden	–
Switzerland	–	–	–	–		–	–	–	–	Switzerland	–
United Kingdom	2.0	2.5	1.9	4.2		1.8	2.3	1.7	3.0	United Kingdom	1.4
United States	3.0	–	2.0	2.0		3.0	–	2.0	2.0	United States	10.0
TOTAL	5.0	2.5	3.9	6.2		4.5	2.1	3.4	4.9	TOTAL	17.0
MULTILATERAL	1.0	3.9	8.2	8.0		1.0	3.9	8.2	8.0	MULTILATERAL	1.1
ARAB COUNTRIES	–	–	–	–		–	–	–	–	ARAB COUNTRIES	–
E.E.C.+ MEMBERS	2.0	2.5	1.9	4.2		1.8	2.3	1.7	3.0	E.E.C.+ MEMBERS	1.6
TOTAL	6.0	6.4	12.1	14.2		5.5	6.0	11.6	13.0	TOTAL	18.1
3. TOTAL OFFICIAL GROSS					**6. TOTAL OFFICIAL NET**					**9. TOTAL OOF GROSS**	
DAC COUNTRIES											
Australia	0.0	0.0	–	–		0.0	0.0	–	–	Australia	–
Austria	–	–	–	–		–	–	–	–	Austria	–
Belgium	–	0.0	0.0	–		–	0.0	0.0	–	Belgium	–
Canada	5.5	1.6	0.7	1.3		5.2	1.3	0.4	1.1	Canada	–
Denmark	–	–	–	–		–	–	–	–	Denmark	–
Finland	–	–	–	–		–	–	–	–	Finland	–
France	–	–	–	–		–	–	–	–	France	–
Germany	0.1	0.1	0.1	0.0		0.1	0.1	0.1	0.0	Germany	–
Ireland	–	–	–	–		–	–	–	–	Ireland	–
Italy	0.0	–	–	–		0.0	–	–	–	Italy	–
Japan	0.0	0.1	0.1	0.0		0.0	0.1	0.1	0.0	Japan	–
Netherlands	0.0	0.3	0.2	0.3		0.0	0.3	0.2	0.3	Netherlands	–
New Zealand	–	–	–	–		–	–	–	–	New Zealand	–
Norway	0.0	–	–	0.0		0.0	–	–	0.0	Norway	–
Sweden	–	–	–	–		–	–	–	–	Sweden	–
Switzerland	–	–	–	–		–	–	–	–	Switzerland	–
United Kingdom	3.4	5.7	6.2	9.7		2.0	4.1	4.7	7.4	United Kingdom	–
United States	13.0	10.0	15.0	14.0		13.0	10.0	15.0	14.0	United States	–
TOTAL	22.0	17.6	22.3	25.4		20.3	15.8	20.6	22.9	TOTAL	–
MULTILATERAL	3.8	10.3	15.5	14.7		3.5	9.2	14.4	13.2	MULTILATERAL	1.7
ARAB COUNTRIES	–	–	–	–		–	–	–	–	ARAB COUNTRIES	–
E.E.C.+ MEMBERS	3.7	10.1	7.5	11.0		2.3	8.4	5.8	8.5	E.E.C.+ MEMBERS	0.1
TOTAL	25.8	27.9	37.9	40.0		23.7	25.0	34.9	36.1	TOTAL	1.7

10. ODA COMMITMENTS

1988	1989	1990	1987	1988	1989	1990
0.0	–	–	–	0.0	0.0	0.0
–	–	–	–	–	–	–
0.0	0.0	–	–	0.0	0.0	–
1.6	0.7	1.3	0.2	0.4	0.1	0.3
–	–	–	–	–	–	–
0.1	0.1	0.0	0.1	0.1	0.1	0.0
–	–	–	–	–	–	–
–	–	–	0.0	–	–	–
0.1	0.1	0.0	0.0	0.1	0.2	0.0
0.3	0.2	0.3	0.0	0.3	0.6	0.3
–	–	0.0	0.0	–	–	–
–	–	–	–	–	–	–
5.1	3.8	6.4	1.3	2.2	14.2	3.9
10.0	14.0	12.0	14.3	8.9	10.8	7.1
17.0	*18.9*	*20.0*	*16.0*	*11.9*	*26.0*	*11.6*
–	–	–	–	–	–	–
–	–	–	–	–	–	–
3.5	7.4	7.4	0.3	7.5	1.0	1.0
3.8	1.0	1.0	1.8	8.0	10.7	10.7
–	–	–	–	–	–	–
0.4	0.1	0.3	–	–	–	–
–	–	–	–	–	–	–
–	–	–	1.0	0.8	1.0	1.3
0.3	0.4	0.4	–	–	–	–
0.3	0.2	0.2	–	–	–	–
0.1	0.1	0.1	–	–	–	–
–	–	–	–	–	–	–
–	0.2	0.5	–	–	–	–
0.1	0.1	0.1	–	–	–	–
–	0.7	0.3	–	1.2	–	–
8.5	10.2	10.3	3.0	17.5	12.7	13.1
–	–	–	–	–	–	–
9.2	5.1	7.7	3.2	10.5	25.6	15.0
25.5	*29.1*	*30.4*	*19.0*	*29.4*	*38.7*	*24.7*

11. TECH. COOP. GRANTS

1988	1989	1990	1987	1988	1989	1990
0.0	–	–	0.0	0.0	–	–
–	–	–	–	–	–	–
0.0	0.0	–	–	–	–	–
1.6	0.7	1.3	–	0.1	0.1	0.3
–	–	–	–	–	–	–
–	–	–	–	–	–	–
0.1	0.1	0.0	0.1	0.1	0.1	0.0
–	–	–	0.0	–	–	–
0.1	0.1	0.0	0.0	0.1	0.1	0.0
0.3	0.2	0.3	0.0	0.3	0.2	0.3
–	–	0.0	0.0	–	–	–
–	–	–	–	–	–	–
2.6	1.9	2.2	1.1	1.9	1.6	2.1
10.0	12.0	10.0	8.0	9.0	10.0	9.0
14.5	15.0	13.9	9.2	11.4	12.1	11.7
4.6	2.0	2.3	1.1	1.5	1.0	1.3
–	–	–	–	–	–	–
6.7	3.2	3.6	1.3	3.0	1.9	2.4
19.1	*17.0*	*16.2*	*10.3*	*13.0*	*13.1*	*13.0*

12. TOTAL OOF NET

1988	1989	1990	1987	1988	1989	1990
–	–	–	–	–	–	–
–	–	–	–	–	–	–
–	–	–	–	–	–	–
–	–	–	–	–	–	–
–	–	–	–	–	–	–
–	–	–	–	–	–	–
–	–	–	–	–	–	–
–	–	–	–	–	–	–
–	–	–	–	–	–	–
–	–	–	–	–	–	–
–	–	–	–	–	–	–
–	–	–	–	–	–	–
–	–	–	–	–	–	–
0.6	2.4	3.3	-1.3	-0.8	1.1	2.1
–	1.0	2.0	–	–	1.0	2.0
0.6	*3.4*	*5.3*	*-1.3*	*-0.8*	*2.1*	*4.1*
1.8	*5.4*	*4.4*	*1.4*	*0.6*	*4.2*	*3.2*
–	–	–	–	–	–	–
0.9	*2.4*	*3.3*	*-1.1*	*-0.6*	*1.0*	*1.9*
2.4	*8.8*	*9.7*	*0.1*	*-0.1*	*6.3*	*7.3*

13. ODF COMMITMENTS: BY PURPOSE %

	1987	1988	1989	1990
Education	6	3	5	–
Health	10	3	4	–
Other Social Infrastr.	1	2	1	–
Water Sanitat. Sewage	–	0	–	–
Energy	6	–	–	–
Telecommunications	–	–	–	–
Transportation	7	19	10	–
Agriculture	16	38	5	–
Extractive Industries	–	–	–	–
Manufacturing	–	–	2	–
Trade Banking Tourism	5	6	2	–
Technical Cooperation	45	29	33	–
Multisector Aid	2	–	33	–
Programme	4	–	–	–
Debt Reorganisation	–	–	–	–
Food Aid	–	0	6	–
Emergency Aid	–	–	–	–
Unspecified	–	–	–	–
TOTAL	100	100	100	–

14. GRANT ELEMENT OF ODA %

DAC COUNTRIES

	1987	1988	1989	1990
Australia	–	100.0	100.0	–
Austria	–	–	–	–
Belgium	–	100.0	100.0	–
Canada	100.0	100.0	100.0	–
Denmark	–	–	–	–
Finland	–	–	–	–
France	–	–	–	–
Germany	100.0	100.0	100.0	–
Ireland	–	–	–	–
Italy	100.0	–	–	–
Japan	100.0	100.0	100.0	–
Netherlands	100.0	100.0	100.0	–
New Zealand	–	–	–	–
Norway	100.0	–	–	–
Sweden	–	–	–	–
Switzerland	–	–	–	–
United Kingdom	100.0	100.0	70.1	–
United States	93.6	100.0	100.0	–
TOTAL	*94.3*	*100.0*	*83.6*	–
MULTILATERAL	*60.2*	*92.2*	*100.0*	–
ARAB COUNTRIES	–	–	–	–
E.E.C.+ MEMBERS	*100.0*	*100.0*	*83.4*	–
TOTAL	*86.6*	*96.3*	*88.7*	–

15. OTHER AGGREGATES

OFFICIAL COMMITMENTS:

	1987	1988	1989	1990
TOTAL BILATERAL	18.0	25.0	29.0	11.6
of which:				
Arab Countries	–	–	–	–
C.E.C.				
TOTAL MULTILATERAL	6.9	30.5	13.5	14.9
TOTAL BIL.& MULTIL.	24.8	55.4	42.5	26.5
of which:				
ODA Grants	15.0	21.6	25.4	22.0
ODA Loans	4.0	7.8	13.3	2.7

DISBURSEMENTS:

DAC COUNTRIES COMBINED

	1987	1988	1989	1990
OFFICIAL & PRIVATE				
GROSS:				
Contractual Lending	5.0	13.9	9.4	17.0
Export Credits, Total	–	10.8	2.1	5.6
Export Credits, Priv.	–	10.8	2.1	5.6
NET:				
Contractual Lending	3.1	12.0	4.5	4.9
Export Credits Total	-0.1	10.7	-1.0	-4.1
PRIVATE SECTOR NET	-0.1	8.6	-1.0	-3.0
Direct Investment	–	0.0	–	0.2
Portfolio Investment	–	-2.0	0.0	0.9
Export Credits	-0.1	10.7	-1.0	-4.1

MARKET BORROWING:

CHANGE IN CLAIMS

	1987	1988	1989	1990
Banks	-32.0	-7.0	58.0	-39.0

MEMORANDUM ITEM:

	1987	1988	1989	1990
C.E.E.C. (Gross)	–	–	–	–

DISBURSEMENTS, UNLESS OTHERWISE STATED

1. TOTAL RECEIPTS NET

DAC COUNTRIES	1987	1988	1989	1990
Australia	–	–	–	–
Austria	0.0	0.0	0.0	0.0
Belgium	1.5	-31.6	7.8	-20.2
Canada	2.6	2.0	1.0	1.4
Denmark	0.3	0.3	0.1	0.1
Finland	–	–	–	–
France	6.8	22.8	66.4	55.5
Germany	30.5	29.0	29.8	27.3
Ireland	–	–	–	–
Italy	2.7	14.7	3.4	12.3
Japan	3.8	6.5	11.8	2.9
Netherlands	2.5	5.8	2.9	6.8
New Zealand	–	–	–	–
Norway	-16.3	-46.7	-4.1	-6.6
Sweden	–	–	–	–
Switzerland	2.0	2.2	9.2	9.6
United Kingdom	-11.9	-4.2	38.7	-1.5
United States	3.0	4.0	6.0	5.0
TOTAL	27.3	4.8	173.0	92.5
MULTILATERAL				
AF.D.F.	7.8	5.1	6.4	22.4
AF.D.B.	-1.1	-0.8	-2.8	-1.4
AS.D.B	–	–	–	–
CAR.D.B.	–	–	–	–
E.E.C.	11.8	28.3	36.6	36.6
IBRD	–	–	–	–
IDA	21.0	21.0	46.0	55.0
I.D.B.	–	–	–	–
IFAD	6.6	1.0	3.5	5.4
I.F.C.	–	–	–	–
IMF TRUST FUND	–	–	–	–
U.N. AGENCIES	–	–	–	–
UNDP	6.0	5.9	6.3	6.7
UNTA	1.1	0.9	1.1	0.9
UNICEF	1.6	1.1	2.4	2.2
UNRWA	–	–	–	–
WFP	1.7	3.4	1.6	4.1
UNHCR	–	0.3	0.3	0.2
Other Multilateral	1.3	1.0	2.5	2.2
Arab Agencies	7.0	-1.7	-2.6	–
TOTAL	64.5	65.5	101.3	134.4
ARAB COUNTRIES	0.7	1.0	5.0	–
E.E.C.+ MEMBERS	44.0	65.0	185.7	116.9
TOTAL	92.5	71.3	279.3	226.9

2. ODA LOANS GROSS

DAC COUNTRIES	1987	1988	1989	1990
Australia	–	–	–	–
Austria	–	–	–	–
Belgium	–	–	1.1	–
Canada	–	–	–	–
Denmark	0.3	0.2	–	0.0
Finland	–	–	–	–
France	12.6	13.0	41.4	28.0
Germany	–	–	–	2.4
Ireland	–	–	–	–
Italy	–	–	–	–
Japan	–	–	–	–
Netherlands	–	–	–	–
New Zealand	–	–	–	–
Norway	–	–	–	1.6
Sweden	–	–	–	–
Switzerland	–	–	–	–
United Kingdom	–	–	–	–
United States	–	–	–	–
TOTAL	12.9	13.2	42.5	32.0
MULTILATERAL	39.4	32.8	61.4	89.6
ARAB COUNTRIES	1.0	1.4	5.0	–
E.E.C.+ MEMBERS	12.9	16.5	44.8	32.7
TOTAL	53.3	47.3	108.9	121.6

3. TOTAL OFFICIAL GROSS

DAC COUNTRIES	1987	1988	1989	1990
Australia	–	–	–	–
Austria	0.0	0.0	0.0	0.0
Belgium	3.2	78.3	47.0	1.6
Canada	2.7	2.1	1.1	1.4
Denmark	17.7	0.3	0.1	0.1
Finland	–	–	–	–
France	25.8	41.2	88.0	75.1
Germany	31.2	28.8	29.9	32.9
Ireland	–	–	–	–
Italy	2.7	2.8	3.4	25.4
Japan	3.8	6.5	11.8	2.9
Netherlands	5.4	5.7	5.6	7.1
New Zealand	–	–	–	–
Norway	0.2	0.1	–	1.6
Sweden	–	–	–	–
Switzerland	2.0	2.2	9.2	9.6
United Kingdom	0.2	0.6	0.5	0.6
United States	3.0	4.0	9.0	5.0
TOTAL	97.8	172.6	205.5	163.3
MULTILATERAL	69.5	75.6	111.6	145.6
ARAB COUNTRIES	1.0	1.4	5.0	–
E.E.C.+ MEMBERS	98.2	186.2	211.2	179.6
TOTAL	168.3	249.6	322.1	308.9

4. TOTAL ODA NET

	1987	1988	1989	1990
Australia	–	–	–	–
Austria	0.0	0.0	0.0	0.0
Belgium	2.1	1.0	1.8	1.3
Canada	2.7	2.1	1.1	1.1
Denmark	0.3	0.3	0.1	0.1
Finland	–	–	–	–
France	23.9	39.6	83.7	66.7
Germany	30.9	28.3	29.2	27.8
Ireland	–	–	–	–
Italy	2.7	2.8	3.4	2.1
Japan	3.8	6.5	11.8	2.9
Netherlands	5.4	5.7	5.6	6.8
New Zealand	–	–	–	–
Norway	0.2	0.1	–	1.6
Sweden	–	–	–	–
Switzerland	2.0	2.2	9.2	9.6
United Kingdom	0.2	0.6	0.5	0.6
United States	3.0	4.0	3.0	5.0
TOTAL	77.0	93.2	149.4	125.6
MULTILATERAL				
AF.D.F.	7.8	5.1	6.4	22.4
AF.D.B.	–	–	–	–
AS.D.B	–	–	–	–
CAR.D.B.	–	–	–	–
E.E.C.	11.8	28.3	36.6	36.6
IBRD	–	–	–	–
IDA	21.0	21.0	46.0	55.0
I.D.B.	–	–	–	–
IFAD	6.6	1.0	3.5	5.4
I.F.C.	–	–	–	–
IMF TRUST FUND	–	–	–	–
U.N. AGENCIES	–	–	–	–
UNDP	6.0	5.9	6.3	6.7
UNTA	1.1	0.9	1.1	0.9
UNICEF	1.6	1.1	2.4	2.2
UNRWA	–	–	–	–
WFP	1.7	3.4	1.6	4.1
UNHCR	–	0.3	0.3	0.2
Other Multilateral	1.3	1.0	2.5	2.2
Arab Agencies	1.3	-0.6	1.8	–
TOTAL	60.0	67.4	108.4	135.9
ARAB COUNTRIES	0.7	1.0	5.0	–
E.E.C.+ MEMBERS	77.2	106.6	160.9	142.0
TOTAL	137.7	161.6	262.8	261.5

5. ODA LOANS NET

DAC COUNTRIES	1987	1988	1989	1990
Australia	–	–	–	–
Austria	–	–	–	–
Belgium	–	–	1.1	–
Canada	–	–	–	–
Denmark	-17.1	0.2	–	0.0
Finland	–	–	–	–
France	10.7	11.4	37.1	22.7
Germany	–	–	–	2.2
Ireland	–	–	–	–
Italy	–	–	–	–
Japan	–	–	–	–
Netherlands	–	–	–	-0.3
New Zealand	–	–	–	–
Norway	–	–	–	1.6
Sweden	–	–	–	–
Switzerland	–	–	–	–
United Kingdom	–	–	–	–
United States	–	–	-3.0	–
TOTAL	-6.4	11.6	35.2	26.3
MULTILATERAL	36.5	29.7	59.1	82.9
ARAB COUNTRIES	0.7	1.0	5.0	–
E.E.C.+ MEMBERS	-6.6	14.8	40.4	26.8
TOTAL	30.8	42.3	99.3	109.1

6. TOTAL OFFICIAL NET

	1987	1988	1989	1990
Australia	–	–	–	–
Austria	0.0	0.0	0.0	0.0
Belgium	3.2	78.3	47.0	1.6
Canada	2.6	2.0	1.0	1.4
Denmark	0.3	0.3	0.1	0.1
Finland	–	–	–	–
France	23.9	39.6	83.7	69.9
Germany	30.5	28.8	29.9	27.0
Ireland	–	–	–	–
Italy	2.7	2.8	3.4	18.9
Japan	3.8	6.5	11.8	2.9
Netherlands	5.4	5.7	5.6	6.8
New Zealand	–	–	–	–
Norway	0.2	0.1	–	1.6
Sweden	–	–	–	–
Switzerland	2.0	2.2	9.2	9.6
United Kingdom	0.2	0.6	0.5	0.6
United States	3.0	4.0	6.0	5.0
TOTAL	77.6	170.9	198.1	145.3
MULTILATERAL	64.5	65.5	101.3	134.4
ARAB COUNTRIES	0.7	1.0	5.0	–
E.E.C.+ MEMBERS	77.9	184.4	206.8	161.4
TOTAL	142.9	237.5	304.4	279.7

7. TOTAL ODA GROSS

	1987
Australia	–
Austria	0.0
Belgium	2.1
Canada	2.7
Denmark	17.7
Finland	–
France	25.8
Germany	30.9
Ireland	–
Italy	2.7
Japan	3.8
Netherlands	5.4
New Zealand	–
Norway	0.2
Sweden	–
Switzerland	2.0
United Kingdom	0.2
United States	3.0
TOTAL	96.3
AF.D.F.	7.9
AF.D.B.	–
AS.D.B	–
CAR.D.B.	–
E.E.C.	12.0
IBRD	–
IDA	21.5
I.D.B.	–
IFAD	6.6
I.F.C.	–
IMF TRUST FUND	–
U.N. AGENCIES	–
UNDP	6.0
UNTA	1.1
UNICEF	1.6
UNRWA	–
WFP	1.7
UNHCR	–
Other Multilateral	1.3
Arab Agencies	3.5
TOTAL	63.0
ARAB COUNTRIES	1.0
E.E.C.+ MEMBERS	96.7
TOTAL	160.2

8. GRANTS

	1987
Australia	–
Austria	0.0
Belgium	2.1
Canada	2.7
Denmark	17.4
Finland	–
France	13.2
Germany	30.9
Ireland	–
Italy	2.7
Japan	3.8
Netherlands	5.4
New Zealand	–
Norway	0.2
Sweden	–
Switzerland	2.0
United Kingdom	0.2
United States	3.0
TOTAL	83.4
MULTILATERAL	23.5
ARAB COUNTRIES	–
E.E.C.+ MEMBERS	83.8
TOTAL	106.9

9. TOTAL OOF GROSS

	1987
Australia	–
Austria	–
Belgium	1.1
Canada	–
Denmark	–
Finland	–
France	–
Germany	0.4
Ireland	–
Italy	–
Japan	–
Netherlands	–
New Zealand	–
Norway	–
Sweden	–
Switzerland	–
United Kingdom	–
United States	–
TOTAL	1.5
MULTILATERAL	6.5
ARAB COUNTRIES	–
E.E.C.+ MEMBERS	1.5
TOTAL	8.0

10. ODA COMMITMENTS

1988	1989	1990	1987	1988	1989	1990
–	–	–	–	–	4.8	–
0.0	0.0	0.0	0.0	0.0	0.0	0.0
1.0	1.8	1.3	2.1	2.3	1.8	1.3
2.1	1.1	1.1	0.1	–	1.6	1.7
0.3	0.1	0.1	17.4	–	–	16.3
–	–	–	–	–	–	–
41.2	88.0	72.0	18.2	61.6	79.1	70.1
28.3	29.2	27.9	14.9	47.9	16.4	56.5
–	–	–	–	–	–	–
2.8	3.4	2.1	4.3	5.3	2.5	0.6
6.5	11.8	2.9	6.4	11.2	6.2	4.3
5.7	5.6	7.1	4.5	4.5	4.9	9.9
–	–	–	–	–	–	–
0.1	–	1.6	0.2	–	2.9	1.6
–	–	–	–	–	–	–
2.2	9.2	9.6	0.5	0.8	24.7	2.0
0.6	0.5	0.6	0.2	0.6	1.3	0.3
4.0	6.0	5.0	1.8	3.1	36.3	5.4
94.8	*156.7*	*131.3*	*70.4*	*137.3*	*182.5*	*170.2*
5.2	7.0	23.1	44.8	16.1	–	53.0
–	–	–	–	–	–	–
–	–	–	–	–	–	–
28.5	36.8	36.8	42.6	78.9	17.1	17.1
–	–	–	–	–	–	–
22.0	47.0	56.0	19.5	37.0	64.0	3.0
–	–	–	–	–	–	–
1.0	3.5	5.4	10.2	–	–	–
–	–	–	–	–	–	–
–	–	–	–	–	–	–
–	–	–	11.5	12.6	14.1	16.4
5.9	6.3	6.7	–	–	–	–
0.9	1.1	0.9	–	–	–	–
1.1	2.4	2.2	–	–	–	–
–	–	–	–	–	–	–
3.4	1.6	4.1	–	–	–	–
0.3	0.3	0.2	–	–	–	–
1.0	2.5	2.2	–	–	–	–
1.2	2.2	3.0	–	–	13.9	18.4
70.5	*110.7*	*140.7*	*128.6*	*144.6*	*109.1*	*107.8*
1.4	*5.0*	–	*5.0*	*9.0*	*10.0*	–
108.4	*165.4*	*147.9*	*104.1*	*201.1*	*123.1*	*172.2*
166.6	*272.4*	*272.0*	*204.1*	*290.8*	*301.6*	*278.0*

11. TECH. COOP. GRANTS

1988	1989	1990	1987	1988	1989	1990
–	–	–	–	–	–	–
0.0	0.0	0.0	0.0	0.0	0.0	–
1.0	0.7	1.3	1.0	0.6	0.5	0.5
2.1	1.1	1.1	–	0.7	1.0	0.8
0.1	0.1	0.1	–	0.1	–	0.0
–	–	–	–	–	–	–
28.2	46.6	44.0	96.9	10.1	9.7	13.1
28.3	29.2	25.6	16.3	13.0	14.7	14.9
–	–	–	–	–	–	–
2.8	3.4	2.1	2.6	1.5	0.9	0.9
6.5	11.8	2.9	0.3	0.2	0.4	0.2
5.7	5.6	7.1	4.2	4.2	4.5	4.4
–	–	–	–	–	–	–
0.1	–	–	0.2	–	–	–
–	–	–	–	–	–	–
2.2	9.2	9.6	1.7	1.4	–	–
0.6	0.5	0.6	0.2	0.5	0.4	0.1
4.0	6.0	5.0	2.0	3.0	3.0	3.0
81.6	*114.2*	*99.4*	*125.3*	*35.3*	*35.1*	*37.8*
37.7	*49.3*	*51.0*	*10.6*	*10.9*	*12.6*	*12.3*
–	–	–	–	–	–	–
91.8	*120.6*	*115.2*	*121.9*	*31.6*	*30.8*	*33.9*
119.3	*163.5*	*150.4*	*135.9*	*46.1*	*47.6*	*50.0*

12. TOTAL OOF NET

1988	1989	1990	1987	1988	1989	1990
–	–	–	–	–	–	–
–	–	–	–	–	–	–
77.3	45.2	0.3	1.1	77.3	45.2	0.3
–	–	0.3	-0.1	-0.1	-0.1	0.3
–	–	–	–	–	–	–
–	–	3.2	–	–	–	3.2
0.5	0.7	5.0	-0.4	0.5	0.7	-0.8
–	–	–	–	–	–	–
–	–	23.3	–	–	–	16.7
–	–	–	–	–	–	–
–	–	–	–	–	–	–
–	–	–	–	–	–	–
–	–	–	–	–	–	–
–	–	–	–	–	–	–
–	3.0	–	–	–	3.0	–
77.8	*48.8*	*32.0*	*0.7*	*77.7*	*48.7*	*19.6*
5.1	*1.0*	*5.0*	*4.5*	*-1.9*	*-7.2*	*-1.4*
–	–	–	–	–	–	–
77.8	*45.8*	*31.7*	*0.8*	*77.8*	*45.8*	*19.4*
82.9	*49.8*	*36.9*	*5.2*	*75.8*	*41.5*	*18.2*

13. ODF COMMITMENTS: BY PURPOSE %

	1987	1988	1989	1990
Education	0	0	2	–
Health	0	–	15	–
Other Social Infrastr.	2	27	7	–
Water Sanitat. Sewage	7	22	3	–
Energy	2	–	2	–
Telecommunications	1	9	6	–
Transportation	18	7	10	–
Agriculture	14	6	1	–
Extractive Industries	–	–	–	–
Manufacturing	–	–	–	–
Trade Banking Tourism	9	–	–	–
Technical Cooperation	24	28	15	–
Multisector Aid	1	–	0	–
Programme	1	–	38	–
Debt Reorganisation	11	–	0	–
Food Aid	2	0	1	–
Emergency Aid	0	0	–	–
Unspecified	8	0	0	–
TOTAL	100	100	100	–

14. GRANT ELEMENT OF ODA %

DAC COUNTRIES

	1987	1988	1989	1990
Australia	–	–	100.0	–
Austria	100.0	100.0	100.0	–
Belgium	100.0	100.0	100.0	–
Canada	100.0	–	100.0	–
Denmark	100.0	–	–	–
Finland	–	–	–	–
France	89.3	73.3	82.0	–
Germany	100.0	100.0	100.0	–
Ireland	–	–	–	–
Italy	100.0	100.0	100.0	–
Japan	100.0	100.0	100.0	–
Netherlands	100.0	100.0	100.0	–
New Zealand	–	–	–	–
Norway	100.0	–	100.0	–
Sweden	–	–	–	–
Switzerland	100.0	100.0	100.0	–
United Kingdom	100.0	100.0	100.0	–
United States	100.0	100.0	100.0	–
TOTAL	*97.2*	*88.0*	*92.4*	–
MULTILATERAL	*90.3*	*93.1*	*81.0*	–
ARAB COUNTRIES	*48.8*	*61.4*	*51.9*	–
E.E.C.+ MEMBERS	*98.0*	*91.8*	*87.7*	–
TOTAL	*91.8*	*89.8*	*86.4*	–

15. OTHER AGGREGATES

OFFICIAL COMMITMENTS:	1987	1988	1989	1990
TOTAL BILATERAL	83.7	146.3	292.6	198.7
of which:				
Arab Countries	5.0	9.0	10.0	–
C.E.E.C.	8.2	–	–	–
TOTAL MULTILATERAL	134.0	149.5	113.9	107.8
TOTAL BIL.& MULTIL.	217.7	295.8	406.4	306.5
of which:				
ODA Grants	114.2	194.5	156.4	175.0
ODA Loans	98.1	96.3	145.3	103.0

DISBURSEMENTS:

DAC COUNTRIES COMBINED

OFFICIAL & PRIVATE	1987	1988	1989	1990
GROSS:				
Contractual Lending	-1.4	87.4	120.7	51.5
Export Credits, Total	-14.6	-3.6	30.5	-9.4
Export Credits, Priv.	-14.6	-3.6	29.9	-12.1
NET:				
Contractual Lending	-56.2	-74.2	72.3	0.1
Export Credits Total	-49.9	-163.5	-10.6	-46.7
PRIVATE SECTOR NET	-50.4	-166.1	-25.1	-52.7
Direct Investment	0.1	0.0	0.5	0.7
Portfolio Investment	-1.1	-2.7	-14.5	-7.9
Export Credits	-49.3	-163.4	-11.1	-45.5

MARKET BORROWING:

CHANGE IN CLAIMS	1987	1988	1989	1990
Banks	-31.0	-33.0	-38.0	-21.0

MEMORANDUM ITEM:	1987	1988	1989	1990
C.E.E.C. (Gross)	0.0	–	–	–

DISBURSEMENTS, UNLESS OTHERWISE STATE[D]

1. TOTAL RECEIPTS NET

DAC COUNTRIES	1987	1988	1989	1990
Australia	-0.4	-0.5	12.6	7.2
Austria	–	–	–	–
Belgium	59.2	67.2	105.1	-52.1
Canada	-18.2	-49.0	-1.9	1.6
Denmark	-5.3	-1.1	–	–
Finland	–	–	7.9	–
France	143.7	71.0	25.7	87.2
Germany	-31.4	92.1	-78.4	-29.5
Ireland	–	–	–	–
Italy	–	–	5.1	-36.1
Japan	-21.2	229.6	244.6	351.7
Netherlands	-0.1	–	–	33.8
New Zealand	–	–	–	–
Norway	–	–	0.0	–
Sweden	-5.7	–	2.3	89.6
Switzerland	–	–	–	–
United Kingdom	0.4	3.8	-3.6	5.9
United States	3464.0	861.0	-1126.0	780.0
TOTAL	*3584.9*	*1274.3*	*-806.4*	*1239.3*
MULTILATERAL				
AF.D.F.	–	–	–	–
AF.D.B.	–	–	–	–
AS.D.B	–	–	–	–
CAR.D.B.	–	–	–	–
E.E.C.	–	–	–	–
IBRD	–	–	–	–
IDA	–	–	–	–
I.D.B.	–	–	–	–
IFAD	–	–	–	–
I.F.C.	–	–	–	–
IMF TRUST FUND	–	–	–	–
U.N. AGENCIES	–	–	–	–
UNDP	0.1	–	0.0	–
UNTA	0.0	–	–	–
UNICEF	–	–	–	–
UNRWA	–	–	–	–
WFP	–	–	–	–
UNHCR	–	–	–	–
Other Multilateral	–	–	–	–
Arab Agencies	–	–	–	–
TOTAL	*0.1*	*–*	*0.0*	*–*
ARAB COUNTRIES	–	–	–	–
E.E.C.+ MEMBERS	166.4	233.1	54.0	9.2
TOTAL	*3585.1*	*1274.3*	*-806.4*	*1239.3*

2. ODA LOANS GROSS

DAC COUNTRIES	1987	1988	1989	1990
Australia	–	–	–	–
Austria	–	–	–	–
Belgium	–	–	–	–
Canada	–	–	–	–
Denmark	–	–	–	–
Finland	–	–	–	–
France	–	–	–	–
Germany	–	–	–	42.1
Ireland	–	–	–	–
Italy	–	–	–	–
Japan	–	–	–	–
Netherlands	–	–	–	–
New Zealand	–	–	–	–
Norway	–	–	–	–
Sweden	–	–	–	–
Switzerland	–	–	–	–
United Kingdom	–	–	–	–
United States	–	–	–	–
TOTAL	–	–	–	*42.1*
MULTILATERAL	–	–	–	–
ARAB COUNTRIES	–	–	–	–
E.E.C.+ MEMBERS	–	–	–	42.1
TOTAL	*–*	*–*	*–*	*42.1*

3. TOTAL OFFICIAL GROSS

DAC COUNTRIES	1987	1988	1989	1990
Australia	–	–	13.1	7.7
Austria	–	–	–	–
Belgium	0.0	–	–	–
Canada	–	–	1.6	2.0
Denmark	–	–	–	–
Finland	–	–	–	–
France	–	–	–	–
Germany	–	–	–	42.1
Ireland	–	–	–	–
Italy	–	–	–	–
Japan	–	–	–	–
Netherlands	–	–	–	–
New Zealand	–	–	–	–
Norway	–	–	0.0	–
Sweden	–	–	–	–
Switzerland	–	–	–	–
United Kingdom	0.1	0.0	0.1	0.0
United States	–	–	–	–
TOTAL	*0.1*	*0.0*	*14.8*	*51.7*
MULTILATERAL	*0.1*	*–*	*0.0*	*–*
ARAB COUNTRIES	–	–	–	–
E.E.C.+ MEMBERS	0.1	0.0	0.1	42.1
TOTAL	*0.2*	*0.0*	*14.8*	*51.7*

4. TOTAL ODA NET

	1987	1988	1989	1990
Australia	–	–	–	–
Austria	–	–	–	–
Belgium	–	–	–	–
Canada	–	–	–	–
Denmark	–	–	–	–
Finland	–	–	–	–
France	–	–	–	–
Germany	–	–	–	42.1
Ireland	–	–	–	–
Italy	–	–	–	–
Japan	–	–	–	–
Netherlands	–	–	–	–
New Zealand	–	–	–	–
Norway	–	–	0.0	–
Sweden	–	–	–	–
Switzerland	–	–	–	–
United Kingdom	0.1	0.0	0.1	0.0
United States	–	–	–	–
TOTAL	*0.1*	*0.0*	*0.1*	*42.1*
AF.D.F.	–	–	–	–
AF.D.B.	–	–	–	–
AS.D.B	–	–	–	–
CAR.D.B.	–	–	–	–
E.E.C.	–	–	–	–
IBRD	–	–	–	–
IDA	–	–	–	–
I.D.B.	–	–	–	–
IFAD	–	–	–	–
I.F.C.	–	–	–	–
IMF TRUST FUND	–	–	–	–
U.N. AGENCIES	–	–	–	–
UNDP	0.1	–	0.0	–
UNTA	0.0	–	–	–
UNICEF	–	–	–	–
UNRWA	–	–	–	–
WFP	–	–	–	–
UNHCR	–	–	–	–
Other Multilateral	–	–	–	–
Arab Agencies	–	–	–	–
TOTAL	*0.1*	*–*	*0.0*	*–*
ARAB COUNTRIES	–	–	–	–
E.E.C.+ MEMBERS	0.1	0.0	0.1	42.1
TOTAL	*0.2*	*0.0*	*0.1*	*42.1*

5. ODA LOANS NET

	1987	1988	1989	1990
Australia	–	–	–	–
Austria	–	–	–	–
Belgium	–	–	–	–
Canada	–	–	–	–
Denmark	–	–	–	–
Finland	–	–	–	–
France	–	–	–	–
Germany	–	–	–	42.1
Ireland	–	–	–	–
Italy	–	–	–	–
Japan	–	–	–	–
Netherlands	–	–	–	–
New Zealand	–	–	–	–
Norway	–	–	–	–
Sweden	–	–	–	–
Switzerland	–	–	–	–
United Kingdom	–	–	–	–
United States	–	–	–	–
TOTAL	–	–	–	*42.1*
MULTILATERAL	–	–	–	–
ARAB COUNTRIES	–	–	–	–
E.E.C.+ MEMBERS	–	–	–	42.1
TOTAL	*–*	*–*	*–*	*42.1*

6. TOTAL OFFICIAL NET

	1987	1988	1989	1990
Australia	-0.4	-0.5	12.6	7.2
Austria	–	–	–	–
Belgium	0.0	–	–	–
Canada	-18.2	-49.0	-1.9	1.6
Denmark	-4.0	–	–	–
Finland	–	–	–	–
France	–	–	–	–
Germany	–	–	–	42.1
Ireland	–	–	–	–
Italy	–	–	–	–
Japan	–	–	–	–
Netherlands	–	–	–	–
New Zealand	–	–	–	–
Norway	–	–	0.0	–
Sweden	–	–	–	–
Switzerland	–	–	–	–
United Kingdom	0.1	0.0	0.1	0.0
United States	–	–	–	–
TOTAL	*-22.5*	*-49.4*	*10.8*	*50.9*
MULTILATERAL	*0.1*	*–*	*0.0*	*–*
ARAB COUNTRIES	–	–	–	–
E.E.C.+ MEMBERS	-3.9	0.0	0.1	42.1
TOTAL	*-22.4*	*-49.4*	*10.8*	*50.9*

7. TOTAL ODA GROSS

	1987
Australia	–
Austria	–
Belgium	–
Canada	–
Denmark	–
Finland	–
France	–
Germany	–
Ireland	–
Italy	–
Japan	–
Netherlands	–
New Zealand	–
Norway	–
Sweden	–
Switzerland	–
United Kingdom	0.1
United States	–
TOTAL	*0.1*
AF.D.F.	–
AF.D.B.	–
AS.D.B	–
CAR.D.B.	–
E.E.C.	–
IBRD	–
IDA	–
I.D.B.	–
IFAD	–
I.F.C.	–
IMF TRUST FUND	–
U.N. AGENCIES	–
UNDP	0.1
UNTA	0.0
UNICEF	–
UNRWA	–
WFP	–
UNHCR	–
Other Multilateral	–
Arab Agencies	–
TOTAL	*0.1*
ARAB COUNTRIES	–
E.E.C.+ MEMBERS	0.1
TOTAL	*0.2*

8. GRANTS

	1987
Australia	–
Austria	–
Belgium	–
Canada	–
Denmark	–
Finland	–
France	–
Germany	–
Ireland	–
Italy	–
Japan	–
Netherlands	–
New Zealand	–
Norway	–
Sweden	–
Switzerland	–
United Kingdom	0.1
United States	–
TOTAL	*0.1*
MULTILATERAL	*0.1*
ARAB COUNTRIES	–
E.E.C.+ MEMBERS	0.1
TOTAL	*0.2*

9. TOTAL OOF GROSS

	1987
Australia	–
Austria	–
Belgium	0.0
Canada	–
Denmark	–
Finland	–
France	–
Germany	–
Ireland	–
Italy	–
Japan	–
Netherlands	–
New Zealand	–
Norway	–
Sweden	–
Switzerland	–
United Kingdom	–
United States	–
TOTAL	*0.0*
MULTILATERAL	*–*
ARAB COUNTRIES	–
E.E.C.+ MEMBERS	0.0
TOTAL	*0.0*

MILLION US DOLLARS, UNLESS OTHERWISE STATED

10. ODA COMMITMENTS

1988	1989	1990	1987	1988	1989	1990
–	–	–	–	–	–	–
–	–	–	–	–	–	–
–	–	–	–	–	–	–
–	–	–	–	–	–	–
–	–	–	–	–	–	–
–	–	42.1	–	–	–	42.1
–	–	–	–	–	–	–
–	–	–	0.0	–	–	–
–	–	–	–	–	0.2	–
–	–	–	–	–	–	–
–	0.0	–	–	–	–	–
–	–	–	–	–	–	–
0.0	0.1	0.0	0.1	0.0	0.1	0.0
–	–	–	–	–	–	–
0.0	0.1	42.1	0.1	0.0	0.3	42.1

1988	1989	1990	1987	1988	1989	1990
–	–	–	–	–	–	–
–	–	–	–	–	–	–
–	–	–	–	–	–	–
–	–	–	–	–	–	–
–	–	–	–	–	–	–
–	–	–	–	–	–	–
–	–	–	0.1	–	0.0	–
–	0.0	–	–	–	–	–
–	–	–	–	–	–	–
–	–	–	–	–	–	–
–	–	–	–	–	–	–
–	–	–	–	–	–	–
–	0.0	–	0.1	–	0.0	–
–	–	–	–	–	–	–
0.0	0.1	42.1	0.1	0.0	0.3	42.1
0.0	0.1	42.1	0.2	0.0	0.3	42.1

11. TECH. COOP. GRANTS

1988	1989	1990	1987	1988	1989	1990
–	–	–	–	–	–	–
–	–	–	–	–	–	–
–	–	–	–	–	–	–
–	–	–	–	–	–	–
–	–	–	–	–	–	–
–	–	–	–	–	–	–
–	–	–	–	–	–	–
–	–	–	–	–	–	–
–	0.0	–	–	–	0.0	–
–	–	–	–	–	–	–
–	–	–	–	–	–	–
0.0	0.1	0.0	0.1	0.0	0.1	0.0
–	–	–	–	–	–	–
0.0	0.1	0.0	0.1	0.0	0.1	0.0
–	0.0	–	0.1	–	0.0	–
–	–	–	–	–	–	–
0.0	0.1	0.0	0.1	0.0	0.1	0.0
0.0	0.1	0.0	0.2	0.0	0.1	0.0

12. TOTAL OOF NET

1988	1989	1990	1987	1988	1989	1990
–	13.1	7.7	-0.4	-0.5	12.6	7.2
–	–	–	–	–	–	–
–	–	–	0.0	–	–	–
–	1.6	2.0	-18.2	-49.0	-1.9	1.6
–	–	–	-4.0	–	–	–
–	–	–	–	–	–	–
–	–	–	–	–	–	–
–	–	–	–	–	–	–
–	–	–	–	–	–	–
–	–	–	–	–	–	–
–	–	–	–	–	–	–
–	–	–	–	–	–	–
–	14.7	9.6	-22.6	-49.4	10.7	8.8
–	–	–	–	–	–	–
–	–	–	-4.0	–	–	–
–	14.7	9.6	-22.6	-49.4	10.7	8.8

13. ODF COMMITMENTS: BY PURPOSE %

	1987	1988	1989	1990
Education	–	–	–	–
Health	–	–	–	–
Other Social Infrastr.	–	–	–	–
Water Sanitat. Sewage	–	–	–	–
Energy	–	–	–	–
Telecommunications	–	–	–	–
Transportation	–	–	–	–
Agriculture	–	–	–	–
Extractive Industries	–	–	–	–
Manufacturing	–	–	–	–
Trade Banking Tourism	–	–	–	–
Technical Cooperation	73	96	100	–
Multisector Aid	–	–	–	–
Programme	–	–	–	–
Debt Reorganisation	–	–	–	–
Food Aid	–	–	–	–
Emergency Aid	27	4	–	–
Unspecified	–	–	–	–
TOTAL	100	100	100	–

14. GRANT ELEMENT OF ODA %

DAC COUNTRIES

	1987	1988	1989	1990
Australia	–	–	–	–
Austria	–	–	–	–
Belgium	–	–	–	–
Canada	–	–	–	–
Denmark	–	–	–	–
Finland	–	–	–	–
France	–	–	–	–
Germany	–	–	–	–
Ireland	–	–	–	–
Italy	–	–	–	–
Japan	100.0	–	–	–
Netherlands	–	–	100.0	–
New Zealand	–	–	–	–
Norway	–	–	–	–
Sweden	–	–	–	–
Switzerland	–	–	–	–
United Kingdom	100.0	100.0	100.0	–
United States	–	–	–	–
TOTAL	100.0	100.0	100.0	–
MULTILATERAL	100.0	–	100.0	–
ARAB COUNTRIES	–	–	–	–
E.E.C.+ MEMBERS	100.0	100.0	100.0	–
TOTAL	100.0	100.0	100.0	–

15. OTHER AGGREGATES

OFFICIAL COMMITMENTS:

	1987	1988	1989	1990
TOTAL BILATERAL	0.1	0.0	20.8	56.4
of which:				
Arab Countries	–	–	–	–
C.E.E.C.	–	–	–	–
TOTAL MULTILATERAL	0.1	–	0.0	–
TOTAL BIL.& MULTIL.	0.2	0.0	20.8	56.4
of which:				
ODA Grants	0.2	0.0	0.3	0.0
ODA Loans	–	–	–	42.1

DISBURSEMENTS:

DAC COUNTRIES COMBINED

OFFICIAL & PRIVATE	1987	1988	1989	1990
GROSS:				
Contractual Lending	-1.2	11.4	40.7	69.8
Export Credits, Total	-1.2	11.4	40.7	27.7
Export Credits, Priv.	-1.2	11.4	26.0	18.1
NET:				
Contractual Lending	-44.6	-55.4	12.3	31.2
Export Credits Total	-44.6	-55.4	12.3	-10.8
PRIVATE SECTOR NET	3607.4	1323.7	-817.3	1188.4
Direct Investment	3465.5	1272.2	-768.9	1138.8
Portfolio Investment	164.0	57.5	-49.9	69.3
Export Credits	-22.0	-5.9	1.5	-19.6

MARKET BORROWING:

CHANGE IN CLAIMS

	1987	1988	1989	1990
Banks	–	–	–	–

MEMORANDUM ITEM:

	1987	1988	1989	1990
C.E.E.C. (Gross)	–	–	–	–

1. TOTAL RECEIPTS NET

	1987	1988	1989	1990
DAC COUNTRIES				
Australia	–	0.0	–	–
Austria	0.1	0.2	0.1	0.1
Belgium	5.3	-14.0	11.0	3.6
Canada	26.7	4.1	4.8	8.8
Denmark	2.3	2.4	1.4	1.6
Finland	0.0	0.1	0.0	0.1
France	-3.8	7.5	1.2	7.2
Germany	45.3	34.1	55.6	59.8
Ireland	0.0	0.0	0.0	–
Italy	7.0	28.3	14.3	17.1
Japan	51.0	34.7	92.9	93.5
Netherlands	17.8	19.5	39.2	31.2
New Zealand	–	–	–	0.0
Norway	2.2	2.4	1.7	2.5
Sweden	0.1	2.1	4.1	2.5
Switzerland	16.2	19.4	14.4	15.7
United Kingdom	-3.5	4.4	-24.0	6.3
United States	103.0	67.0	104.0	86.0
TOTAL	*269.9*	*212.3*	*320.7*	*335.8*
MULTILATERAL				
AF.D.F.	–	–	–	–
AF.D.B.	–	–	–	–
AS.D.B	–	–	–	–
CAR.D.B.	–	–	–	–
E.E.C.	15.5	18.8	10.6	10.6
IBRD	-16.6	-23.0	-19.0	-21.0
IDA	38.9	110.0	77.0	47.0
I.D.B.	75.6	94.3	72.6	97.8
IFAD	3.2	2.3	3.5	3.1
I.F.C.	-0.1	5.5	1.4	4.0
IMF TRUST FUND	–	–	–	–
U.N. AGENCIES	–	–	–	–
UNDP	9.4	10.1	13.3	9.6
UNTA	1.2	0.8	1.3	1.4
UNICEF	3.0	2.1	3.1	4.1
UNRWA	–	–	–	–
WFP	7.4	7.8	11.8	6.6
UNHCR	–	–	–	0.1
Other Multilateral	1.1	2.0	3.0	3.1
Arab Agencies	-0.2	1.4	2.1	–
TOTAL	*138.3*	*232.1*	*180.6*	*166.3*
ARAB COUNTRIES	–	–	–	–
E.E.C.+ MEMBERS	*85.9*	*101.1*	*109.3*	*137.3*
TOTAL	**408.1**	**444.5**	**501.3**	**502.1**

2. ODA LOANS GROSS

	1987	1988	1989	1990
DAC COUNTRIES				
Australia	–	–	–	–
Austria	–	–	–	–
Belgium	–	–	–	–
Canada	–	–	–	–
Denmark	1.0	0.8	0.3	–
Finland	–	–	–	–
France	0.1	0.7	0.9	0.1
Germany	13.1	8.2	28.0	28.8
Ireland	–	–	–	–
Italy	–	14.2	1.4	5.3
Japan	35.9	6.9	52.6	73.2
Netherlands	–	–	–	–
New Zealand	–	–	–	–
Norway	–	–	–	–
Sweden	–	–	–	–
Switzerland	–	–	–	–
United Kingdom	–	–	–	–
United States	16.0	4.0	12.0	7.0
TOTAL	*66.1*	*34.9*	*95.0*	*114.4*
MULTILATERAL	*74.6*	*133.0*	*107.4*	*129.1*
ARAB COUNTRIES	–	–	–	–
E.E.C.+ MEMBERS	*14.2*	*24.0*	*30.4*	*34.2*
TOTAL	**140.6**	**167.9**	**202.4**	**243.5**

3. TOTAL OFFICIAL GROSS

	1987	1988	1989	1990
DAC COUNTRIES				
Australia	–	0.0	–	–
Austria	0.1	0.2	0.1	0.1
Belgium	62.7	2.8	32.6	11.1
Canada	33.8	4.2	4.9	8.8
Denmark	2.3	2.4	1.4	1.6
Finland	0.0	0.1	0.0	0.1
France	2.4	3.7	4.3	11.2
Germany	59.2	35.2	70.3	61.8
Ireland	0.0	0.0	0.0	–
Italy	7.0	28.3	14.4	22.3
Japan	62.3	36.3	94.5	111.0
Netherlands	13.7	22.4	36.4	30.9
New Zealand	–	–	–	0.0
Norway	2.2	2.4	1.7	2.5
Sweden	0.2	2.1	4.1	2.5
Switzerland	16.2	19.4	14.4	15.7
United Kingdom	2.9	5.3	6.5	7.2
United States	131.0	75.0	121.0	87.0
TOTAL	*396.1*	*239.7*	*406.6*	*373.7*
MULTILATERAL	*171.9*	*271.4*	*222.4*	*221.7*
ARAB COUNTRIES	–	–	–	–
E.E.C.+ MEMBERS	*165.6*	*118.9*	*176.5*	*156.6*
TOTAL	**568.0**	**511.1**	**629.0**	**595.4**

4. TOTAL ODA NET

	1987	1988	1989	1990
DAC COUNTRIES				
Australia	–	0.0	–	–
Austria	0.1	0.2	0.1	0.1
Belgium	2.0	2.8	4.5	6.2
Canada	2.1	4.1	4.8	8.8
Denmark	2.3	2.3	1.4	1.0
Finland	0.0	0.1	0.0	0.1
France	2.4	3.3	3.8	11.2
Germany	31.1	29.7	48.6	57.4
Ireland	0.0	0.0	0.0	–
Italy	7.0	28.3	14.4	22.3
Japan	53.8	35.3	92.9	95.2
Netherlands	13.7	22.4	36.4	30.9
New Zealand	–	–	–	0.0
Norway	2.2	2.4	1.7	2.5
Sweden	0.2	2.1	4.1	2.5
Switzerland	16.2	19.4	14.4	15.7
United Kingdom	2.8	5.3	6.5	7.0
United States	77.0	70.0	69.0	84.0
TOTAL	*213.0*	*227.8*	*302.6*	*344.8*
AF.D.F.	–	–	–	–
AF.D.B.	–	–	–	–
AS.D.B	–	–	–	–
CAR.D.B.	–	–	–	–
E.E.C.	15.5	18.8	10.6	10.6
IBRD	–	–	–	–
IDA	38.9	110.0	77.0	47.0
I.D.B.	26.2	10.8	12.0	60.4
IFAD	3.2	2.3	3.5	3.1
I.F.C.	–	–	–	–
IMF TRUST FUND	–	–	–	–
U.N. AGENCIES	–	–	–	–
UNDP	9.4	10.1	13.3	9.6
UNTA	1.2	0.8	1.3	1.4
UNICEF	3.0	2.1	3.1	4.1
UNRWA	–	–	–	–
WFP	7.4	7.8	11.8	6.6
UNHCR	–	–	–	0.1
Other Multilateral	1.1	2.0	3.0	3.1
Arab Agencies	-0.2	1.4	2.1	–
TOTAL	*105.6*	*166.1*	*137.6*	*145.9*
ARAB COUNTRIES	–	–	–	–
E.E.C.+ MEMBERS	*76.7*	*112.9*	*126.1*	*146.5*
TOTAL	**318.6**	**393.9**	**440.1**	**490.7**

5. ODA LOANS NET

	1987	1988	1989	1990
Australia	–	–	–	–
Austria	–	–	–	-0.3
Belgium	–	–	–	0.0
Canada	0.0	0.0	0.0	–
Denmark	1.0	0.8	0.3	–
Finland	–	–	–	–
France	0.1	0.3	0.5	0.0
Germany	6.6	8.2	23.3	27.6
Ireland	–	–	–	–
Italy	–	14.2	1.4	5.3
Japan	27.4	6.0	50.9	57.4
Netherlands	–	–	–	–
New Zealand	–	–	–	–
Norway	–	–	–	–
Sweden	–	–	–	–
Switzerland	–	–	–	–
United Kingdom	-0.1	–	–	-0.2
United States	5.0	1.0	2.0	7.0
TOTAL	*40.0*	*30.5*	*78.3*	*96.8*
MULTILATERAL	*65.3*	*122.3*	*93.0*	*110.9*
ARAB COUNTRIES	–	–	–	–
E.E.C.+ MEMBERS	*7.6*	*23.5*	*25.4*	*32.5*
TOTAL	**105.3**	**152.8**	**171.3**	**207.8**

6. TOTAL OFFICIAL NET

	1987	1988	1989	1990
Australia	–	0.0	–	–
Austria	0.1	0.2	0.1	0.1
Belgium	62.7	2.8	32.6	10.8
Canada	26.7	4.1	4.8	8.8
Denmark	2.3	2.4	1.4	1.6
Finland	0.0	0.1	0.0	0.1
France	2.4	3.3	3.9	11.2
Germany	49.4	35.1	53.2	60.6
Ireland	0.0	0.0	0.0	–
Italy	7.0	28.3	14.4	22.3
Japan	53.8	35.3	92.9	95.2
Netherlands	13.7	22.4	36.4	30.9
New Zealand	–	–	–	0.0
Norway	2.2	2.4	1.7	2.5
Sweden	0.2	2.1	4.1	2.5
Switzerland	16.2	19.4	14.4	15.7
United Kingdom	2.8	5.3	6.5	7.0
United States	103.0	67.0	104.0	86.0
TOTAL	*342.5*	*230.3*	*370.3*	*355.2*
MULTILATERAL	*138.3*	*232.1*	*180.6*	*166.3*
ARAB COUNTRIES	–	–	–	–
E.E.C.+ MEMBERS	*155.6*	*118.4*	*158.9*	*154.9*
TOTAL	**480.8**	**462.5**	**550.9**	**521.5**

7. TOTAL ODA GROSS

	1987
Australia	–
Austria	0.1
Belgium	2.0
Canada	2.1
Denmark	2.3
Finland	0.0
France	2.4
Germany	37.5
Ireland	0.0
Italy	7.0
Japan	62.3
Netherlands	13.7
New Zealand	–
Norway	2.2
Sweden	0.2
Switzerland	16.2
United Kingdom	2.9
United States	88.0
TOTAL	*239.0*
AF.D.F.	–
AF.D.B.	–
AS.D.B	–
CAR.D.B.	–
E.E.C.	15.5
IBRD	–
IDA	39.9
I.D.B.	33.3
IFAD	4.1
I.F.C.	–
IMF TRUST FUND	–
U.N. AGENCIES	–
UNDP	9.4
UNTA	1.2
UNICEF	3.0
UNRWA	–
WFP	7.4
UNHCR	–
Other Multilateral	1.1
Arab Agencies	0.2
TOTAL	*114.8*
ARAB COUNTRIES	–
E.E.C.+ MEMBERS	*83.2*
TOTAL	**353.9**

8. GRANTS

	1987
Australia	–
Austria	0.1
Belgium	2.0
Canada	2.1
Denmark	1.3
Finland	0.0
France	2.3
Germany	24.4
Ireland	0.0
Italy	7.0
Japan	26.4
Netherlands	13.7
New Zealand	–
Norway	2.2
Sweden	0.2
Switzerland	16.2
United Kingdom	2.9
United States	72.0
TOTAL	*173.0*
MULTILATERAL	*40.3*
ARAB COUNTRIES	–
E.E.C.+ MEMBERS	*69.0*
TOTAL	**213.2**

9. TOTAL OOF GROSS

	1987
Australia	–
Austria	–
Belgium	60.6
Canada	31.7
Denmark	–
Finland	–
France	21.7
Germany	–
Ireland	–
Italy	–
Japan	–
Netherlands	–
New Zealand	–
Norway	–
Sweden	–
Switzerland	–
United Kingdom	–
United States	43.0
TOTAL	*157.0*
MULTILATERAL	*57.1*
ARAB COUNTRIES	–
E.E.C.+ MEMBERS	*82.4*
TOTAL	**214.1**

10. ODA COMMITMENTS

1988	1989	1990	1987	1988	1989	1990
0.0	–	–	0.0	0.0	–	–
0.2	0.1	0.1	0.1	0.2	0.1	8.9
2.8	4.5	6.5	5.0	8.2	4.5	6.5
4.2	4.9	8.8	1.6	7.2	10.5	12.2
2.3	1.4	1.0	2.6	1.8	2.6	–
0.1	0.0	0.1	–	–	0.0	0.2
3.7	4.2	11.2	3.0	5.8	3.3	20.9
29.7	53.2	58.6	61.3	70.5	78.0	32.1
0.0	0.0	–	0.0	0.0	0.0	–
28.3	14.4	22.3	31.9	29.0	11.2	57.5
36.3	94.5	111.0	41.7	126.7	107.7	61.5
22.4	36.4	30.9	2.9	28.5	34.1	41.6
–	–	0.0	–	–	–	–
2.4	1.7	2.5	0.7	–	–	–
2.1	4.1	2.5	0.1	0.4	8.7	5.3
19.4	14.4	15.7	16.0	23.8	20.8	12.3
5.3	6.5	7.2	11.0	7.1	2.3	9.5
73.0	79.0	84.0	83.8	105.0	71.7	118.0
232.2	*319.3*	*362.3*	*261.8*	*414.2*	*355.5*	*386.3*
–	–	–	–	–	–	–
–	–	–	–	–	–	–
–	–	–	–	–	–	–
–	–	–	–	–	–	–
18.8	10.6	10.6	33.6	17.8	30.1	30.1
–	–	–	–	–	–	–
111.0	78.0	49.0	90.4	107.0	92.0	141.0
18.7	23.5	74.1	3.7	20.7	103.9	70.9
3.6	4.7	4.7	5.4	–	–	12.4
–	–	–	–	–	–	–
–	–	–	22.0	22.8	32.5	24.9
10.1	13.3	9.6	–	–	–	–
0.8	1.3	1.4	–	–	–	–
2.1	3.1	4.1	–	–	–	–
–	–	–	–	–	–	–
7.8	11.8	6.6	–	–	–	–
–	–	0.1	–	–	–	–
2.0	3.0	3.1	–	–	–	–
1.9	2.7	1.3	–	5.2	–	–
176.8	*152.0*	*164.5*	*155.1*	*173.5*	*258.5*	*279.2*
–	–	–	–	–	–	–
113.3	131.2	148.2	151.3	168.8	166.0	198.1
409.0	**471.3**	**526.9**	**416.9**	**587.7**	**614.0**	**665.5**

11. TECH. COOP. GRANTS

1988	1989	1990	1987	1988	1989	1990
0.0	–	–	–	–	–	–
0.2	0.1	0.1	0.1	0.1	0.1	0.1
2.8	4.5	6.5	1.2	0.6	0.4	0.5
4.2	4.9	8.8	–	0.4	0.2	0.1
1.5	1.2	1.0	0.1	0.0	–	0.0
0.1	0.0	0.1	0.0	0.0	–	–
3.0	3.4	11.2	2.3	2.5	2.4	5.4
21.5	25.3	29.8	23.3	20.1	19.7	23.5
0.0	0.0	–	0.0	0.0	0.0	–
14.1	13.0	17.0	5.9	5.3	2.6	2.0
29.4	41.9	37.8	11.2	12.6	12.3	15.2
22.4	36.4	30.9	2.4	13.9	16.5	22.0
–	–	0.0	–	–	–	0.0
2.4	1.7	2.5	0.1	0.2	0.1	0.1
2.1	4.1	2.5	0.1	0.2	0.1	1.3
19.4	14.4	15.7	1.9	2.9	–	–
5.3	6.5	7.2	2.8	3.1	2.1	4.0
69.0	67.0	77.0	12.0	4.0	16.0	22.0
197.3	*224.3*	*248.0*	*63.4*	*65.9*	*72.5*	*96.3*
43.8	*44.6*	*35.5*	*16.6*	*19.2*	*20.7*	*18.3*
–	–	–	–	–	–	–
89.4	100.7	114.1	*40.0*	*49.7*	*43.6*	*57.5*
241.1	**268.9**	**283.4**	**80.1**	**85.1**	**93.1**	**114.6**

12. TOTAL OOF NET

1988	1989	1990	1987	1988	1989	1990
–	–	–	–	–	–	–
–	–	–	–	–	–	–
–	28.1	4.6	60.6	–	28.1	4.6
–	–	–	24.6	–	–	–
0.1	–	0.6	0.0	0.1	0.0	0.6
–	–	–	–	–	–	–
–	0.0	0.0	–	–	0.0	0.0
5.5	17.1	3.2	18.3	5.5	4.7	3.2
–	–	–	–	–	–	–
–	–	–	–	–	–	–
–	–	–	–	–	–	–
–	–	–	–	–	–	–
–	–	–	–	–	–	–
–	–	–	–	–	–	–
2.0	42.0	3.0	26.0	-3.0	35.0	2.0
7.5	*87.3*	*11.4*	*129.5*	*2.5*	*67.8*	*10.4*
94.6	*70.5*	*57.1*	*32.7*	*66.0*	*43.0*	*20.4*
–	–	–	–	–	–	–
5.5	45.3	8.4	*78.9*	*5.5*	*32.8*	*8.4*
102.1	**157.8**	**68.5**	**162.2**	**68.6**	**110.8**	**30.8**

13. ODF COMMITMENTS: BY PURPOSE %

	1987	1988	1989	1990
Education	0	0	1	–
Health	2	1	2	–
Other Social Infrastr.	5	10	11	–
Water Sanitat. Sewage	0	4	2	–
Energy	3	3	0	–
Telecommunications	–	0	1	–
Transportation	13	15	12	–
Agriculture	22	11	4	–
Extractive Industries	0	7	6	–
Manufacturing	0	1	1	–
Trade Banking Tourism	3	11	15	–
Technical Cooperation	19	19	20	–
Multisector Aid	0	0	7	–
Programme	15	13	3	–
Debt Reorganisation	9	–	4	–
Food Aid	8	4	6	–
Emergency Aid	0	1	3	–
Unspecified	0	0	3	–
TOTAL	100	100	100	–

14. GRANT ELEMENT OF ODA %

DAC COUNTRIES	1987	1988	1989	1990
Australia	100.0	100.0	–	–
Austria	100.0	100.0	100.0	–
Belgium	100.0	100.0	100.0	–
Canada	100.0	100.0	100.0	–
Denmark	100.0	100.0	100.0	–
Finland	–	–	100.0	–
France	100.0	100.0	100.0	–
Germany	79.1	86.6	81.1	–
Ireland	100.0	100.0	100.0	–
Italy	79.2	100.0	100.0	–
Japan	67.3	77.1	74.7	–
Netherlands	100.0	100.0	100.0	–
New Zealand	–	–	–	–
Norway	100.0	–	–	–
Sweden	100.0	100.0	100.0	–
Switzerland	100.0	100.0	100.0	–
United Kingdom	99.6	100.0	100.0	–
United States	100.0	98.4	100.0	–
TOTAL	*87.1*	*90.2*	*88.0*	–
MULTILATERAL	*88.4*	*83.3*	*84.0*	–
ARAB COUNTRIES	–	–	–	–
E.E.C.+ MEMBERS	*86.6*	*94.3*	*90.3*	–
TOTAL	*87.6*	*88.2*	*86.6*	–

15. OTHER AGGREGATES

	1987	1988	1989	1990
OFFICIAL COMMITMENTS:				
TOTAL BILATERAL	430.4	418.3	453.5	421.2
of which:				
Arab Countries	–	–	–	–
C.E.E.C.	–	–	–	–
TOTAL MULTILATERAL	243.3	271.8	325.4	399.2
TOTAL BIL.& MULTIL.	673.7	690.1	778.9	820.4
of which:				
ODA Grants	251.7	344.4	317.7	346.9
ODA Loans	165.2	243.3	296.3	318.6
DISBURSEMENTS:				
DAC COUNTRIES COMBINED				
OFFICIAL & PRIVATE				
GROSS:				
Contractual Lending	218.0	45.7	157.3	123.5
Export Credits, Total	27.0	3.3	-19.8	-0.5
Export Credits, Priv.	-4.6	3.3	-24.7	-2.0
NET:				
Contractual Lending	106.2	29.1	92.6	90.7
Export Credits Total	-58.6	-3.9	-59.0	-14.7
PRIVATE SECTOR NET	-72.7	-18.0	-49.6	-19.4
Direct Investment	–	-2.9	0.3	0.0
Portfolio Investment	-9.8	-11.1	3.3	-3.1
Export Credits	-62.8	-3.9	-53.2	-16.3
MARKET BORROWING:				
CHANGE IN CLAIMS				
Banks	-58.0	-148.0	-228.0	-68.0
MEMORANDUM ITEM:				
C.E.E.C. (Gross)	–	–	–	–

1. TOTAL RECEIPTS NET

DAC COUNTRIES	1987	1988	1989	1990
Australia	0.5	1.7	6.1	1.6
Austria	0.0	0.0	0.0	0.0
Belgium	1.8	0.6	0.8	-0.2
Canada	9.0	4.5	14.0	10.2
Denmark	18.5	7.0	6.7	6.0
Finland	0.2	0.4	1.2	1.8
France	5.1	2.2	0.8	1.8
Germany	39.2	0.5	-33.1	27.3
Ireland	0.1	–	–	–
Italy	0.1	-7.0	30.0	0.4
Japan	0.2	20.5	11.2	0.7
Netherlands	4.2	4.3	4.9	4.8
New Zealand	0.2	0.1	0.1	0.1
Norway	17.0	18.0	18.7	21.9
Sweden	15.5	21.1	16.5	24.2
Switzerland	0.0	–	–	–
United Kingdom	18.5	-18.4	6.4	-4.5
United States	21.0	16.0	16.0	16.0
TOTAL	151.0	71.5	100.2	112.0
MULTILATERAL				
AF.D.F.	10.9	0.5	20.6	9.2
AF.D.B.	31.9	5.0	6.5	24.3
AS.D.B.	–	–	–	–
CAR.D.B.	–	–	–	–
E.E.C.	10.9	8.5	15.8	15.8
IBRD	-2.0	-1.0	-3.0	-12.0
IDA	-0.2	–	–	–
I.D.B.	–	–	–	–
IFAD	0.7	-0.4	–	–
I.F.C.	–	–	–	–
IMF TRUST FUND	–	–	–	–
U.N. AGENCIES	–	–	–	–
UNDP	3.0	5.2	6.1	4.4
UNTA	0.8	0.6	0.6	0.7
UNICEF	1.0	0.8	1.2	0.8
UNRWA	–	–	–	–
WFP	9.0	6.3	3.0	1.0
UNHCR	1.1	1.5	0.6	0.5
Other Multilateral	1.2	1.2	2.1	2.1
Arab Agencies	0.1	1.0	-2.0	-1.1
TOTAL	68.4	29.2	51.4	46.9
ARAB COUNTRIES	-0.3	0.8	-2.2	-1.1
E.E.C.+ MEMBERS	98.3	-2.4	32.3	51.4
TOTAL	219.1	101.5	149.4	157.8

2. ODA LOANS GROSS

DAC COUNTRIES	1987	1988	1989	1990
Australia	–	–	–	–
Austria	–	–	–	–
Belgium	1.4	–	–	–
Canada	–	–	–	–
Denmark	–	–	–	–
Finland	–	–	–	–
France	2.3	0.5	–	0.5
Germany	–	–	–	–
Ireland	–	–	–	–
Italy	–	–	–	–
Japan	0.1	20.4	11.2	0.1
Netherlands	0.3	0.5	0.7	0.5
New Zealand	–	–	–	–
Norway	–	–	–	1.8
Sweden	–	–	–	–
Switzerland	–	–	–	–
United Kingdom	–	1.3	–	0.5
United States	–	–	–	–
TOTAL	4.1	22.6	11.9	3.3
MULTILATERAL	13.6	3.5	23.0	14.1
ARAB COUNTRIES	0.7	3.4	0.0	–
E.E.C.+ MEMBERS	4.0	2.8	2.0	2.8
TOTAL	18.4	29.5	34.9	17.5

3. TOTAL OFFICIAL GROSS

DAC COUNTRIES	1987	1988	1989	1990
Australia	0.5	1.7	6.1	2.8
Austria	0.0	0.0	0.0	0.0
Belgium	1.5	0.1	0.0	0.1
Canada	10.6	6.2	15.6	11.9
Denmark	23.0	7.0	6.7	6.0
Finland	0.2	0.4	1.2	1.8
France	2.8	1.3	0.7	2.2
Germany	39.5	26.1	14.2	27.2
Ireland	0.1	–	–	–
Italy	0.1	1.9	0.3	0.4
Japan	0.1	20.5	11.3	0.7
Netherlands	5.4	4.3	4.5	4.4
New Zealand	0.2	0.1	0.1	0.1
Norway	17.0	18.0	18.7	21.8
Sweden	14.2	21.1	17.4	25.1
Switzerland	0.0	–	–	–
United Kingdom	19.5	14.7	12.8	14.8
United States	21.0	17.0	16.0	17.0
TOTAL	155.6	140.4	125.5	136.0
MULTILATERAL	89.9	54.1	76.3	78.7
ARAB COUNTRIES	1.8	3.4	0.0	–
E.E.C.+ MEMBERS	103.9	66.3	57.3	73.2
TOTAL	247.4	197.9	201.9	214.7

4. TOTAL ODA NET

DAC COUNTRIES	1987	1988	1989	1990
Australia	0.5	1.5	4.1	2.6
Austria	0.0	0.0	0.0	0.0
Belgium	1.5	0.1	0.0	0.1
Canada	10.6	6.2	15.6	11.9
Denmark	18.6	7.0	6.7	6.0
Finland	0.2	0.4	1.2	1.8
France	2.8	1.3	0.7	2.2
Germany	21.3	14.3	14.2	19.2
Ireland	0.1	–	–	–
Italy	0.1	1.9	0.3	0.4
Japan	0.1	20.5	11.3	0.7
Netherlands	5.4	4.3	3.9	4.4
New Zealand	0.2	0.1	0.1	0.1
Norway	17.0	18.0	18.7	21.8
Sweden	14.2	21.1	17.4	25.1
Switzerland	0.0	–	–	–
United Kingdom	10.7	12.6	10.9	10.3
United States	21.0	16.0	15.0	15.0
TOTAL	124.3	125.4	120.0	121.2
MULTILATERAL				
AF.D.F.	10.9	0.5	20.6	9.2
AF.D.B.	–	–	–	–
AS.D.B.	–	–	–	–
CAR.D.B.	–	–	–	–
E.E.C.	5.0	8.7	9.2	9.2
IBRD	–	–	–	–
IDA	-0.2	–	–	–
I.D.B.	–	–	–	–
IFAD	0.7	-0.4	–	–
I.F.C.	–	–	–	–
IMF TRUST FUND	–	–	–	–
U.N. AGENCIES	–	–	–	–
UNDP	3.0	5.2	6.1	4.4
UNTA	0.8	0.6	0.6	0.7
UNICEF	1.0	0.8	1.2	0.8
UNRWA	–	–	–	–
WFP	9.0	6.3	3.0	1.0
UNHCR	1.1	1.5	0.6	0.5
Other Multilateral	1.2	1.2	2.1	2.1
Arab Agencies	-0.7	0.3	-1.3	–
TOTAL	31.9	24.7	42.1	27.9
ARAB COUNTRIES	-0.3	0.8	-2.2	-1.1
E.E.C.+ MEMBERS	65.4	50.3	45.8	51.6
TOTAL	155.9	150.8	159.8	148.1

5. ODA LOANS NET

DAC COUNTRIES	1987	1988	1989	1990
Australia	–	–	–	–
Austria	–	–	–	–
Belgium	1.4	–	–	–
Canada	–	–	–	–
Denmark	-4.4	–	–	–
Finland	–	–	–	–
France	2.3	0.5	–	0.5
Germany	–	–	–	–
Ireland	–	–	–	–
Italy	–	–	–	–
Japan	0.1	20.4	11.2	0.1
Netherlands	0.3	0.5	0.7	0.5
New Zealand	–	–	–	–
Norway	–	–	–	1.8
Sweden	–	–	–	–
Switzerland	–	–	–	–
United Kingdom	-1.9	-0.8	-1.9	-1.5
United States	–	-1.0	–	-1.0
TOTAL	-2.2	19.5	10.0	0.3
MULTILATERAL	10.5	0.9	20.3	12.1
ARAB COUNTRIES	-1.4	0.8	-2.2	-1.1
E.E.C.+ MEMBERS	-2.4	0.5	0.0	0.6
TOTAL	6.9	21.2	28.1	11.4

6. TOTAL OFFICIAL NET

DAC COUNTRIES	1987	1988	1989	1990
Australia	0.5	1.7	6.1	1.6
Austria	0.0	0.0	0.0	0.0
Belgium	1.5	0.1	0.0	0.1
Canada	9.0	4.5	14.0	10.2
Denmark	18.5	7.0	6.7	6.0
Finland	0.2	0.4	1.2	1.8
France	2.0	1.3	0.7	2.2
Germany	39.4	0.4	-33.2	27.1
Ireland	0.1	–	–	–
Italy	0.1	1.9	0.3	0.4
Japan	0.1	20.5	11.3	0.7
Netherlands	4.2	4.3	4.0	4.3
New Zealand	0.2	0.1	0.1	0.1
Norway	17.0	18.0	18.7	21.8
Sweden	14.2	21.1	17.4	25.1
Switzerland	0.0	–	–	–
United Kingdom	16.5	10.4	8.7	8.7
United States	21.0	16.0	16.0	16.0
TOTAL	144.5	107.9	71.9	125.8
MULTILATERAL	68.4	29.2	51.4	46.9
ARAB COUNTRIES	-0.3	0.8	-2.2	-1.1
E.E.C.+ MEMBERS	93.1	34.0	3.0	64.6
TOTAL	212.6	137.8	121.1	171.6

7. TOTAL ODA GROSS

	1987
Australia	0.5
Austria	0.0
Belgium	1.5
Canada	10.6
Denmark	23.0
Finland	0.2
France	2.8
Germany	21.3
Ireland	0.1
Italy	0.1
Japan	0.1
Netherlands	5.4
New Zealand	0.2
Norway	17.0
Sweden	14.2
Switzerland	0.0
United Kingdom	12.5
United States	21.0
TOTAL	130.6
AF.D.F.	11.0
AF.D.B.	–
AS.D.B.	–
CAR.D.B.	–
E.E.C.	5.2
IBRD	–
IDA	–
I.D.B.	–
IFAD	1.4
I.F.C.	–
IMF TRUST FUND	–
U.N. AGENCIES	–
UNDP	3.0
UNTA	0.8
UNICEF	1.0
UNRWA	–
WFP	9.0
UNHCR	1.1
Other Multilateral	1.2
Arab Agencies	1.3
TOTAL	35.0
ARAB COUNTRIES	1.8
E.E.C.+ MEMBERS	71.8
TOTAL	167.4

8. GRANTS

	1987
Australia	0.5
Austria	0.0
Belgium	0.1
Canada	10.6
Denmark	23.0
Finland	0.2
France	0.5
Germany	21.3
Ireland	0.1
Italy	0.1
Japan	0.0
Netherlands	5.1
New Zealand	0.2
Norway	17.0
Sweden	14.2
Switzerland	0.0
United Kingdom	12.5
United States	21.0
TOTAL	126.6
MULTILATERAL	21.3
ARAB COUNTRIES	1.1
E.E.C.+ MEMBERS	67.8
TOTAL	149.0

9. TOTAL OOF GROSS

	1987
Australia	–
Austria	–
Belgium	–
Canada	–
Denmark	–
Finland	–
France	–
Germany	18.1
Ireland	–
Italy	–
Japan	–
Netherlands	–
New Zealand	–
Norway	–
Sweden	–
Switzerland	–
United Kingdom	6.9
United States	–
TOTAL	25.1
MULTILATERAL	55.0
ARAB COUNTRIES	–
E.E.C.+ MEMBERS	32.1
TOTAL	80.0

10. ODA COMMITMENTS

1988	1989	1990	1987	1988	1989	1990
1.5	4.1	2.6	0.3	1.7	–	2.7
0.0	0.0	0.0	0.0	0.0	0.0	0.0
0.1	0.0	0.1	0.0	0.7	0.0	0.1
6.2	15.6	11.9	2.2	12.5	0.5	6.5
7.0	6.7	6.0	8.2	–	–	5.0
0.4	1.2	1.8	0.0	–	0.2	0.3
1.3	0.7	2.2	0.5	0.9	0.7	3.5
14.3	14.2	19.2	5.0	31.5	21.8	19.8
–	–	–	0.1	–	–	–
1.9	0.3	0.4	0.1	1.8	0.3	0.4
20.5	11.3	0.7	0.0	22.1	0.1	0.6
4.3	3.9	4.4	5.7	3.8	4.0	3.5
0.1	0.1	0.1	0.2	0.1	–	–
18.0	18.7	21.8	6.3	23.5	8.5	12.3
21.1	17.4	25.1	14.2	21.1	17.8	16.5
–	–	–	0.0	–	–	–
14.7	12.8	12.3	11.8	14.7	12.8	12.3
17.0	15.0	16.0	19.1	20.2	7.5	10.9
128.4	*121.9*	*124.2*	*73.9*	*154.5*	*74.2*	*94.4*
0.7	21.0	9.5	36.4	9.5	6.1	9.3
–	–	–	–	–	–	–
–	–	–	–	–	–	–
8.9	9.3	9.3	14.6	14.7	33.1	33.1
–	–	–	–	–	–	–
–	–	–	–	–	–	–
0.2	0.5	0.4	–	–	–	–
–	–	–	–	–	–	–
–	–	–	16.2	15.5	13.6	9.6
5.2	6.1	4.4	–	–	–	–
0.6	0.6	0.7	–	–	–	–
0.8	1.2	0.8	–	–	–	–
–	–	–	–	–	–	–
6.3	3.0	1.0	–	–	–	–
1.5	0.6	0.5	–	–	–	–
1.2	2.1	2.1	–	–	–	–
2.0	0.3	3.1	6.1	3.0	1.5	16.6
27.3	*44.8*	*31.9*	*73.2*	*42.7*	*54.3*	*68.5*
3.4	0.0	–	1.1	12.5	–	3.4
52.5	47.8	53.7	46.0	68.1	72.6	77.7
159.1	*166.7*	*156.1*	*148.3*	*209.7*	*128.4*	*166.3*

11. TECH. COOP. GRANTS

1988	1989	1990	1987	1988	1989	1990
1.5	4.1	2.6	0.4	0.7	0.6	1.0
0.0	0.0	0.0	0.0	0.0	0.0	0.0
0.1	0.0	0.1	0.1	0.0	–	0.1
6.2	15.6	11.9	–	0.8	0.4	1.1
7.0	6.7	6.0	1.0	2.5	0.9	1.9
0.4	1.2	1.8	0.0	0.2	–	–
0.9	0.7	1.7	0.5	0.9	0.7	0.8
14.3	14.2	19.2	10.5	11.9	10.2	12.4
–	–	–	0.1	–	–	–
1.9	0.3	0.4	0.1	–	0.3	0.4
0.2	0.1	0.6	0.0	0.2	0.0	0.1
3.9	3.1	3.9	2.9	3.0	3.0	3.3
0.1	0.1	0.1	0.0	0.0	–	0.1
18.0	18.7	20.0	6.0	5.0	4.9	5.9
21.1	17.4	25.1	4.5	6.6	6.4	0.6
–	–	–	–	–	–	–
13.4	12.8	11.8	9.4	10.7	10.5	9.5
17.0	15.0	16.0	6.0	12.0	10.0	15.0
105.9	*110.0*	*120.9*	*41.5*	*54.5*	*47.9*	*52.2*
23.8	21.8	17.8	8.3	10.9	10.6	8.5
–	–	–	–	–	–	–
49.7	45.8	51.0	25.6	30.7	25.5	28.4
129.6	*131.8*	*138.7*	*49.8*	*65.4*	*58.5*	*60.7*

12. TOTAL OOF NET

1988	1989	1990	1987	1988	1989	1990
0.2	2.0	0.2	–	0.2	2.0	-1.0
–	–	–	–	–	–	–
–	–	–	-1.7	-1.6	-1.7	-1.7
–	–	–	0.0	–	–	–
–	–	–	–	–	–	–
–	–	–	-0.8	–	–	–
11.7	–	8.0	18.1	-13.9	-47.4	7.9
–	–	–	–	–	–	–
–	–	–	–	–	–	–
–	0.6	–	-1.2	–	0.1	-0.1
–	–	–	–	–	–	–
–	–	–	–	–	–	–
–	–	2.5	–	–	–	–
–	1.0	1.0	5.9	-2.2	-2.2	-1.6
12.0	3.6	11.8	20.2	-17.5	-48.1	4.6
26.9	*31.5*	*46.8*	*36.6*	*4.5*	*9.4*	*19.0*
–	–	–	–	–	–	–
13.8	9.5	19.5	27.7	-16.3	-42.8	13.0
38.8	*35.2*	*58.6*	*56.7*	*-13.0*	*-38.7*	*23.6*

13. ODF COMMITMENTS: BY PURPOSE %

	1987	1988	1989	1990
Education	7	28	31	–
Health	0	4	1	–
Other Social Infrastr.	2	4	2	–
Water Sanitat. Sewage	3	6	8	–
Energy	–	–	–	–
Telecommunications	–	–	4	–
Transportation	32	17	21	–
Agriculture	0	3	0	–
Extractive Industries	–	3	–	–
Manufacturing	0	–	1	–
Trade Banking Tourism	2	0	–	–
Technical Cooperation	34	26	27	–
Multisector Aid	8	0	2	–
Programme	–	0	1	–
Debt Reorganisation	5	1	–	–
Food Aid	6	7	–	–
Emergency Aid	0	–	1	–
Unspecified	0	–	–	–
TOTAL	100	100	100	–

14. GRANT ELEMENT OF ODA %

DAC COUNTRIES

	1987	1988	1989	1990
Australia	100.0	100.0	–	–
Austria	100.0	100.0	100.0	–
Belgium	100.0	100.0	100.0	–
Canada	100.0	100.0	100.0	–
Denmark	100.0	–	–	–
Finland	100.0	–	100.0	–
France	100.0	100.0	100.0	–
Germany	100.0	100.0	100.0	–
Ireland	100.0	–	–	–
Italy	100.0	100.0	100.0	–
Japan	100.0	70.3	100.0	–
Netherlands	100.0	100.0	100.0	–
New Zealand	100.0	100.0	–	–
Norway	100.0	100.0	100.0	–
Sweden	100.0	100.0	100.0	–
Switzerland	100.0	–	–	–
United Kingdom	100.0	100.0	100.0	–
United States	100.0	100.0	100.0	–
TOTAL	*100.0*	*95.7*	*100.0*	*–*
MULTILATERAL	*85.3*	*86.8*	*95.6*	*–*
ARAB COUNTRIES	*100.0*	*42.0*	*–*	*–*
E.E.C.+ MEMBERS	*100.0*	*100.0*	*100.0*	*–*
TOTAL	*94.8*	*90.3*	*98.0*	*–*

15. OTHER AGGREGATES

OFFICIAL COMMITMENTS:

	1987	1988	1989	1990
TOTAL BILATERAL	88.1	181.5	80.4	98.2
of which:				
Arab Countries	1.1	12.5	–	3.4
C.E.E.C.	–	0.3	–	–
TOTAL MULTILATERAL	137.2	73.9	87.2	100.3
TOTAL BIL.& MULTIL.	225.4	255.4	167.6	198.5
of which:				
ODA Grants	99.4	161.4	120.1	133.6
ODA Loans	48.9	48.6	8.3	32.7

DISBURSEMENTS:

DAC COUNTRIES COMBINED

OFFICIAL & PRIVATE

	1987	1988	1989	1990
GROSS:				
Contractual Lending	37.4	38.7	52.0	14.4
Export Credits, Total	8.3	4.4	38.5	-0.5
Export Credits, Priv.	8.3	4.2	36.5	-0.7
NET:				
Contractual Lending	22.8	-34.0	-19.9	-10.7
Export Credits Total	3.2	-37.5	18.5	-18.4
PRIVATE SECTOR NET	6.5	-36.4	28.3	-13.8
Direct Investment	1.4	-0.6	9.1	1.0
Portfolio Investment	0.2	0.2	1.0	0.9
Export Credits	4.9	-36.0	18.2	-15.6

MARKET BORROWING:

CHANGE IN CLAIMS

	1987	1988	1989	1990
Banks	3.0	-4.0	-6.0	-13.0

MEMORANDUM ITEM:

	1987	1988	1989	1990
C.E.E.C. (Gross)	–	–	–	–

1. TOTAL RECEIPTS NET

DAC COUNTRIES	1987	1988	1989	1990
Australia	-0.1	0.0	0.0	-0.1
Austria	-1.2	0.0	0.6	29.6
Belgium	-335.3	28.6	-194.5	-39.6
Canada	4.1	-7.5	55.0	24.7
Denmark	-0.9	0.8	-3.1	1.5
Finland	5.9	2.8	20.3	15.1
France	93.2	-551.7	-20.5	-752.9
Germany	587.3	446.9	513.8	536.6
Ireland	0.0	0.0	0.0	0.0
Italy	296.5	118.3	113.1	-89.7
Japan	-329.0	403.8	-85.6	1250.7
Netherlands	40.2	32.0	74.7	319.0
New Zealand	–	–	–	0.0
Norway	-1.5	1.2	0.4	0.3
Sweden	15.5	0.2	-50.0	-42.3
Switzerland	1.4	1.6	1.4	2.1
United Kingdom	438.7	391.5	614.8	-113.5
United States	-1705.0	2403.0	2721.0	-2959.0
TOTAL	-890.3	3271.5	3761.4	-1817.4
MULTILATERAL				
AF.D.F.	–	–	–	–
AF.D.B.	–	–	–	–
AS.D.B	–	–	–	–
CAR.D.B.	–	–	–	–
E.E.C.	2.1	4.7	2.5	2.5
IBRD	25.0	20.0	-62.0	-476.0
IDA	–	–	–	–
I.D.B.	73.6	91.6	26.1	-36.1
IFAD	2.5	-1.4	-1.5	-0.6
I.F.C.	-6.3	33.4	68.1	154.3
IMF TRUST FUND	–	–	–	–
U.N. AGENCIES	–	–	–	–
UNDP	7.6	12.7	13.2	16.8
UNTA	2.3	1.6	2.2	2.0
UNICEF	3.4	2.2	5.8	6.6
UNRWA	–	–	–	–
WFP	20.0	3.9	13.7	12.6
UNHCR	–	–	–	0.2
Other Multilateral	3.0	4.4	8.0	6.1
Arab Agencies	–	–	–	–
TOTAL	133.2	173.1	76.1	-311.7
ARAB COUNTRIES	-30.7	-10.8	-0.7	–
E.E.C.+ MEMBERS	1121.7	471.0	1100.8	-135.9
TOTAL	-787.9	3433.8	3836.8	-2129.1

2. ODA LOANS GROSS

DAC COUNTRIES	1987	1988	1989	1990
Australia	–	–	–	–
Austria	–	–	–	–
Belgium	–	–	–	–
Canada	–	–	–	–
Denmark	–	–	–	–
Finland	–	–	–	–
France	18.3	2.3	15.6	6.0
Germany	111.9	7.5	11.6	5.0
Ireland	–	–	–	–
Italy	–	–	–	–
Japan	65.3	48.7	98.2	43.6
Netherlands	0.0	0.2	–	–
New Zealand	–	–	–	–
Norway	–	–	–	–
Sweden	–	–	–	–
Switzerland	–	–	–	–
United Kingdom	–	–	0.1	–
United States	–	–	–	–
TOTAL	195.5	58.7	125.6	54.6
MULTILATERAL	46.1	36.9	15.8	22.9
ARAB COUNTRIES	–	–	–	–
E.E.C.+ MEMBERS	130.2	10.0	27.4	11.0
TOTAL	241.6	95.6	141.4	77.4

3. TOTAL OFFICIAL GROSS

DAC COUNTRIES	1987	1988	1989	1990
Australia	0.0	0.1	0.0	0.0
Austria	0.9	0.8	0.9	1.2
Belgium	22.3	2.2	10.9	7.1
Canada	4.0	4.7	71.4	40.9
Denmark	0.8	1.0	–	0.7
Finland	0.3	0.4	0.2	0.2
France	574.5	36.0	783.4	196.1
Germany	929.8	276.9	905.7	611.3
Ireland	0.0	0.0	0.0	0.0
Italy	389.5	40.0	18.7	15.2
Japan	146.5	116.6	142.6	98.5
Netherlands	6.7	10.4	10.3	11.4
New Zealand	–	–	–	0.0
Norway	0.1	0.6	0.5	0.6
Sweden	–	0.2	0.4	0.6
Switzerland	1.4	1.6	1.4	2.1
United Kingdom	1.3	2.6	2.3	2.5
United States	106.0	24.0	34.0	473.0
TOTAL	2184.1	517.8	1982.8	1461.5
MULTILATERAL	1312.7	1474.1	1233.1	1279.7
ARAB COUNTRIES	1.4	–	–	–
E.E.C.+ MEMBERS	1927.0	373.5	1733.9	846.9
TOTAL	3498.2	1992.0	3215.9	2741.2

4. TOTAL ODA NET

DAC COUNTRIES	1987	1988	1989	1990
Australia	0.0	0.1	0.0	0.0
Austria	0.6	0.4	0.8	1.1
Belgium	1.7	2.2	1.3	2.9
Canada	3.6	4.0	3.9	2.9
Denmark	–	0.4	–	–
Finland	0.3	0.4	0.2	0.2
France	20.9	11.9	11.6	18.9
Germany	146.4	54.6	33.2	31.5
Ireland	0.0	0.0	0.0	0.0
Italy	8.8	30.5	18.5	14.8
Japan	82.1	66.4	124.2	64.7
Netherlands	6.2	10.4	9.9	11.0
New Zealand	–	–	–	0.0
Norway	0.1	0.6	0.5	0.6
Sweden	–	0.2	0.4	0.3
Switzerland	1.4	1.6	1.4	2.1
United Kingdom	1.3	2.6	2.3	2.5
United States	-17.0	6.0	-15.0	-12.0
TOTAL	256.3	192.2	193.3	141.4
MULTILATERAL				
AF.D.F.	–	–	–	–
AF.D.B.	–	–	–	–
AS.D.B	–	–	–	–
CAR.D.B.	–	–	–	–
E.E.C.	2.1	4.7	2.5	2.5
IBRD	–	–	–	–
IDA	–	–	–	–
I.D.B.	-4.9	-9.8	-30.4	-23.3
IFAD	2.5	-1.4	-1.5	-0.6
I.F.C.	–	–	–	–
IMF TRUST FUND	–	–	–	–
U.N. AGENCIES	–	–	–	–
UNDP	7.6	12.7	13.2	16.8
UNTA	2.3	1.6	2.2	2.0
UNICEF	3.4	2.2	5.8	6.6
UNRWA	–	–	–	–
WFP	20.0	3.9	13.7	12.6
UNHCR	–	–	–	0.2
Other Multilateral	3.0	4.4	8.0	6.1
Arab Agencies	–	–	–	–
TOTAL	35.9	18.4	13.5	22.8
ARAB COUNTRIES	-3.4	-0.3	-0.7	–
E.E.C.+ MEMBERS	187.4	117.2	79.3	84.1
TOTAL	288.8	210.3	206.1	164.2

5. ODA LOANS NET

DAC COUNTRIES	1987	1988	1989	1990
Australia	–	–	–	–
Austria	-0.3	-0.4	-0.1	0.0
Belgium	–	–	–	–
Canada	-0.5	-0.5	-0.5	-0.5
Denmark	–	–	–	–
Finland	–	–	–	–
France	8.7	0.0	1.1	-1.6
Germany	98.5	6.5	-12.6	-18.1
Ireland	–	–	–	–
Italy	–	–	–	–
Japan	55.0	31.5	87.0	26.7
Netherlands	0.0	0.2	–	0.0
New Zealand	–	–	–	–
Norway	–	–	–	–
Sweden	–	–	–	–
Switzerland	–	–	–	–
United Kingdom	–	–	0.1	–
United States	-23.0	-1.0	-18.0	-13.0
TOTAL	138.3	36.4	57.1	-6.5
MULTILATERAL	-2.5	-11.9	-32.8	-23.9
ARAB COUNTRIES	-3.4	-0.3	-0.7	–
E.E.C.+ MEMBERS	107.1	6.7	-11.3	-19.7
TOTAL	132.4	24.2	23.6	-30.5

6. TOTAL OFFICIAL NET

DAC COUNTRIES	1987	1988	1989	1990
Australia	-0.1	0.0	0.0	-0.1
Austria	0.6	0.4	0.8	1.1
Belgium	21.9	1.0	7.4	7.1
Canada	3.6	-7.7	55.2	24.9
Denmark	-0.8	0.9	-0.2	0.4
Finland	0.3	0.4	0.2	0.2
France	552.4	33.6	677.3	188.6
Germany	688.3	215.4	218.0	320.4
Ireland	0.0	0.0	0.0	0.0
Italy	330.8	35.2	13.3	5.8
Japan	113.8	69.5	59.1	49.7
Netherlands	6.5	10.3	10.3	11.3
New Zealand	–	–	–	0.0
Norway	0.1	0.6	0.5	0.6
Sweden	–	0.2	0.4	0.6
Switzerland	1.4	1.6	1.4	2.1
United Kingdom	1.2	2.6	2.0	2.5
United States	29.0	-15.0	-200.0	242.0
TOTAL	1748.9	348.8	845.9	857.1
MULTILATERAL	133.1	173.1	76.1	-311.7
ARAB COUNTRIES	-30.7	-10.8	-0.7	–
E.E.C.+ MEMBERS	1602.4	303.5	930.7	538.6
TOTAL	1851.3	511.2	921.3	545.4

7. TOTAL ODA GROSS

	1987
Australia	0.0
Austria	0.9
Belgium	1.7
Canada	4.0
Denmark	–
Finland	0.3
France	30.5
Germany	159.8
Ireland	0.0
Italy	8.8
Japan	92.4
Netherlands	6.2
New Zealand	–
Norway	0.1
Sweden	–
Switzerland	1.4
United Kingdom	1.3
United States	6.0
TOTAL	313.5
AF.D.F.	–
AF.D.B.	–
AS.D.B	–
CAR.D.B.	–
E.E.C.	2.1
IBRD	–
IDA	–
I.D.B.	41.0
IFAD	5.2
I.F.C.	–
IMF TRUST FUND	–
U.N. AGENCIES	–
UNDP	7.6
UNTA	2.3
UNICEF	3.4
UNRWA	–
WFP	20.0
UNHCR	–
Other Multilateral	3.0
Arab Agencies	–
TOTAL	84.5
ARAB COUNTRIES	–
E.E.C.+ MEMBERS	210.5
TOTAL	398.0

8. GRANTS

	1987
Australia	0.0
Austria	0.9
Belgium	1.7
Canada	4.0
Denmark	–
Finland	0.3
France	12.2
Germany	47.9
Ireland	0.0
Italy	8.8
Japan	27.1
Netherlands	6.2
New Zealand	–
Norway	0.1
Sweden	–
Switzerland	1.4
United Kingdom	1.3
United States	6.0
TOTAL	118.0
MULTILATERAL	38.4
ARAB COUNTRIES	–
E.E.C.+ MEMBERS	80.3
TOTAL	156.4

9. TOTAL OOF GROSS

	1987
Australia	–
Austria	–
Belgium	20.6
Canada	–
Denmark	0.8
Finland	–
France	544.0
Germany	770.0
Ireland	–
Italy	380.7
Japan	54.1
Netherlands	0.5
New Zealand	–
Norway	–
Sweden	–
Switzerland	–
United Kingdom	–
United States	100.0
TOTAL	1870.6
MULTILATERAL	1228.2
ARAB COUNTRIES	1.4
E.E.C.+ MEMBERS	1716.5
TOTAL	3100.2

10. ODA COMMITMENTS

1988	1989	1990	1987	1988	1989	1990
0.1	0.0	0.0	0.1	0.1	0.0	0.0
0.8	0.9	1.2	0.9	0.8	0.9	1.1
2.2	1.3	2.9	2.0	1.2	1.3	2.9
4.5	4.4	3.4	2.7	3.8	2.7	16.3
0.4	–	–	–	–	–	–
0.4	0.2	0.2	0.1	0.3	0.2	0.7
14.2	26.1	26.4	28.1	11.9	33.7	20.5
55.7	57.4	54.6	95.3	60.4	65.5	73.0
0.0	0.0	0.0	0.0	0.0	0.0	0.0
30.5	18.5	14.8	11.8	35.0	16.9	18.2
83.5	135.4	81.6	52.7	61.9	72.9	50.2
10.4	9.9	11.0	5.5	10.4	9.9	11.0
–	–	0.0	–	–	–	–
0.6	0.5	0.6	0.0	–	–	–
0.2	0.4	0.3	–	0.2	0.4	–
1.6	1.4	2.1	1.1	1.5	1.2	1.5
2.6	2.3	2.5	1.3	2.6	2.3	2.5
7.0	3.0	1.0	5.7	4.0	2.0	4.4
214.5	*261.8*	*202.5*	*207.2*	*194.1*	*210.0*	*202.2*
–	–	–	–	–	–	–
–	–	–	–	–	–	–
–	–	–	–	–	–	–
4.7	2.5	2.5	2.0	7.2	5.6	5.6
–	–	–	–	–	–	–
–	–	–	–	–	–	–
37.6	16.7	21.5	45.0	–	–	–
–	–	1.4	–	–	–	23.9
–	–	–	–	–	–	–
–	–	–	36.2	24.9	42.9	44.2
12.7	13.2	16.8	–	–	–	–
1.6	2.2	2.0	–	–	–	–
2.2	5.8	6.6	–	–	–	–
–	–	–	–	–	–	–
3.9	13.7	12.6	–	–	–	–
–	–	0.2	–	–	–	–
4.4	8.0	6.1	–	–	–	–
–	–	–	–	–	–	–
67.1	*62.1*	*69.6*	*83.2*	*32.1*	*48.5*	*73.7*
–	–	–	–	–	–	–
120.5	*118.0*	*114.7*	*146.1*	*128.7*	*135.2*	*133.6*
281.6	*323.9*	*272.1*	*290.5*	*226.2*	*258.5*	*275.8*

11. TECH. COOP. GRANTS

1988	1989	1990	1987	1988	1989	1990
0.1	0.0	0.0	–	–	–	–
0.8	0.9	1.2	0.7	0.6	0.7	1.0
2.2	1.3	2.9	0.8	0.2	–	0.6
4.5	4.4	3.4	–	0.9	1.0	0.8
0.4	–	–	–	0.4	0.0	–
0.4	0.2	0.2	0.0	0.1	0.2	0.1
11.9	10.5	20.5	12.2	11.9	10.5	20.5
48.2	45.8	49.6	47.9	48.0	37.3	39.4
0.0	0.0	0.0	0.0	0.0	0.0	0.0
30.5	18.5	14.8	8.8	8.0	9.9	10.4
34.8	37.2	38.0	27.1	34.6	37.2	38.0
10.2	9.9	11.0	5.3	9.2	8.8	11.0
–	–	0.0	–	–	–	0.0
0.6	0.5	0.6	–	0.1	0.2	0.2
0.2	0.4	0.3	–	–	–	–
1.6	1.4	2.1	0.2	0.2	–	–
2.6	2.2	2.5	1.3	2.5	2.1	2.5
7.0	3.0	1.0	–	1.0	2.0	1.0
155.8	136.2	147.9	104.2	117.7	110.0	125.2
30.2	46.3	46.7	17.0	22.5	29.2	31.6
–	–	–	–	–	–	–
110.5	90.6	103.8	76.9	81.7	68.7	84.2
186.0	*182.5*	*194.6*	*121.2*	*140.2*	*139.2*	*156.8*

12. TOTAL OOF NET

1988	1989	1990	1987	1988	1989	1990
–	–	–	-0.1	-0.1	–	-0.1
–	–	–	–	–	–	–
–	9.6	4.2	20.1	-1.2	6.1	4.2
0.2	67.0	37.5	–	-11.7	51.3	22.0
0.6	–	0.7	-0.8	0.5	-0.2	0.4
–	–	–	–	–	–	–
21.8	757.3	169.7	531.5	21.7	665.7	169.7
221.2	848.3	556.8	541.9	160.7	184.8	289.0
–	–	–	–	–	–	–
9.5	0.2	0.4	322.0	4.7	-5.1	-9.0
33.1	7.2	17.0	31.7	3.1	-65.0	-15.0
–	0.4	0.4	0.3	-0.1	0.4	0.4
–	–	–	–	–	–	–
–	–	0.3	–	–	–	0.3
–	–	–	–	–	–	–
–	–	–	0.0	–	-0.2	–
17.0	31.0	472.0	46.0	-21.0	-185.0	254.0
303.4	*1721.0*	*1259.0*	*1492.6*	*156.6*	*652.6*	*715.7*
1407.0	*1170.9*	*1210.2*	*97.2*	*154.8*	*62.6*	*-334.5*
–	–	–	*-27.3*	*-10.5*	–	–
253.0	*1615.8*	*732.2*	*1415.0*	*186.3*	*851.4*	*454.6*
1710.4	*2892.0*	*2469.1*	*1562.5*	*300.9*	*715.2*	*381.2*

13. ODF COMMITMENTS: BY PURPOSE %

	1987	1988	1989	1990
Education	3	6	0	–
Health	–	12	9	–
Other Social Infrastr.	24	0	5	–
Water Sanitat. Sewage	6	7	1	–
Energy	5	–	2	–
Telecommunications	–	–	–	–
Transportation	19	11	1	–
Agriculture	10	38	32	–
Extractive Industries	1	1	1	–
Manufacturing	2	1	1	–
Trade Banking Tourism	0	9	0	–
Technical Cooperation	5	14	7	–
Multisector Aid	–	1	0	–
Programme	–	–	–	–
Debt Reorganisation	25	–	41	–
Food Aid	0	–	–	–
Emergency Aid	0	0	0	–
Unspecified	–	–	–	–
TOTAL	100	100	100	–

14. GRANT ELEMENT OF ODA %

DAC COUNTRIES

	1987	1988	1989	1990
Australia	100.0	100.0	100.0	–
Austria	100.0	100.0	100.0	–
Belgium	100.0	100.0	100.0	–
Canada	100.0	100.0	100.0	–
Denmark	–	–	–	–
Finland	100.0	100.0	100.0	–
France	100.0	82.1	100.0	–
Germany	56.5	100.0	68.4	–
Ireland	100.0	100.0	100.0	–
Italy	100.0	100.0	100.0	–
Japan	99.0	95.2	98.2	–
Netherlands	100.0	100.0	100.0	–
New Zealand	–	–	–	–
Norway	100.0	–	–	–
Sweden	–	100.0	100.0	–
Switzerland	100.0	100.0	100.0	–
United Kingdom	100.0	100.0	59.7	–
United States	100.0	100.0	100.0	–
TOTAL	*72.0*	*96.4*	*81.4*	–
MULTILATERAL	*83.1*	*74.6*	*71.3*	–
ARAB COUNTRIES	–	–	–	–
E.E.C.+ MEMBERS	*65.5*	*96.6*	*76.8*	–
TOTAL	*74.4*	*91.3*	*78.1*	–

15. OTHER AGGREGATES

OFFICIAL COMMITMENTS:

	1987	1988	1989	1990
TOTAL BILATERAL	2159.3	301.3	2704.9	1022.3
of which:				
Arab Countries	–	–	–	–
C.E.E.C.	60.0	–	45.0	–
TOTAL MULTILATERAL	1625.2	1440.7	1721.9	2083.8
TOTAL BIL.& MULTIL.	3784.5	1742.0	4426.8	3106.1
of which:				
ODA Grants	168.6	202.0	202.4	230.9
ODA Loans	181.9	24.3	101.1	44.9

DISBURSEMENTS:

DAC COUNTRIES COMBINED

OFFICIAL & PRIVATE

	1987	1988	1989	1990
GROSS:				
Contractual Lending	2972.3	741.2	2752.2	1578.0
Export Credits, Total	1228.1	536.7	1385.1	812.0
Export Credits, Priv.	911.3	384.9	910.7	270.0
NET:				
Contractual Lending	1633.9	-32.9	719.5	278.0
Export Credits	73.6	-163.4	-183.7	-346.9
PRIVATE SECTOR NET	-2639.2	2922.6	2915.5	-2674.5
Direct Investment	1380.3	2736.3	3286.8	1782.7
Portfolio Investment	-4027.5	406.6	-386.2	-4031.5
Export Credits	8.1	-220.2	14.9	-425.6

MARKET BORROWING:

CHANGE IN CLAIMS

	1987	1988	1989	1990
Banks	-2776.0	-3839.0	-4971.0	-5758.0

MEMORANDUM ITEM:

	1987	1988	1989	1990
C.E.E.C. (Gross)	–	–	–	–

1. TOTAL RECEIPTS NET / 4. TOTAL ODA NET / 7. TOTAL ODA GROSS

	1. TOTAL RECEIPTS NET				4. TOTAL ODA NET				7. TOTAL ODA GROSS
	1987	1988	1989	1990	1987	1988	1989	1990	1987
DAC COUNTRIES									
Australia	–	0.1	0.0	0.0	–	0.1	0.0	0.0	–
Austria	-0.2	-0.2	4.7	1.2	0.4	0.4	5.2	1.9	0.4
Belgium	2.9	2.0	1.1	2.8	3.0	1.8	1.2	2.9	3.0
Canada	10.7	29.4	11.4	11.9	12.0	29.4	11.4	10.1	12.0
Denmark	1.2	0.5	7.8	10.3	1.2	0.5	7.8	10.3	10.7
Finland	–	–	–	–	–	–	–	–	–
France	58.3	50.1	67.1	88.9	64.6	52.1	70.1	85.3	66.8
Germany	36.2	43.0	33.5	45.1	36.3	43.2	33.3	45.2	36.3
Ireland	–	–	–	–	–	–	–	–	–
Italy	20.6	40.0	28.8	40.9	20.6	31.7	16.1	29.8	20.6
Japan	7.7	7.9	3.2	1.7	7.7	7.9	3.2	1.7	7.7
Netherlands	26.9	25.9	30.5	34.6	27.6	28.2	31.3	34.5	27.6
New Zealand	–	–	–	–	–	–	–	–	–
Norway	–	1.4	0.4	–	–	1.4	0.4	–	–
Sweden	–	0.5	–	0.1	–	0.5	–	0.1	–
Switzerland	3.1	4.1	4.5	5.0	3.1	4.1	4.5	5.0	3.1
United Kingdom	0.3	0.6	0.5	0.5	0.3	0.6	0.5	0.5	0.3
United States	19.0	17.0	14.0	11.0	19.0	17.0	14.0	11.0	19.0
TOTAL	*186.5*	*222.1*	*207.4*	*254.0*	*195.6*	*218.8*	*199.0*	*238.3*	*207.3*
MULTILATERAL									
AF.D.F.	4.5	7.7	8.6	9.5	4.5	7.7	8.6	9.5	4.7
AF.D.B.	8.4	3.3	3.6	1.1	–	–	–	–	–
AS.D.B	–	–	–	–	–	–	–	–	–
CAR.D.B.	–	–	–	–	–	–	–	–	–
E.E.C.	14.5	22.9	13.2	13.2	15.2	23.7	14.0	14.0	17.0
IBRD	–	–	–	–	–	–	–	–	–
IDA	21.1	19.0	24.0	14.0	21.1	19.0	24.0	14.0	21.6
I.D.B.	–	–	–	–	–	–	–	–	–
IFAD	5.8	1.4	0.9	1.7	5.8	1.4	0.9	1.7	5.8
I.F.C.	–	-0.1	–	0.0	–	–	–	–	–
IMF TRUST FUND	–	–	–	–	–	–	–	–	–
U.N. AGENCIES	–	–	–	–	–	–	–	–	–
UNDP	11.8	11.8	12.5	14.4	11.8	11.8	12.5	14.4	11.8
UNTA	2.3	1.4	1.4	1.3	2.3	1.4	1.4	1.3	2.3
UNICEF	4.3	3.3	4.5	5.4	4.3	3.3	4.5	5.4	4.3
UNRWA	–	–	–	–	–	–	–	–	–
WFP	0.8	3.4	2.6	7.3	0.8	3.4	2.6	7.3	0.8
UNHCR	–	0.3	0.3	0.3	–	0.3	0.3	0.3	–
Other Multilateral	9.9	8.5	5.2	5.6	9.9	8.5	5.2	5.6	9.9
Arab Agencies	2.8	-2.8	-1.4	–	2.8	-4.0	-1.4	–	7.0
TOTAL	*86.1*	*79.9*	*75.1*	*73.5*	*78.4*	*76.4*	*72.4*	*73.3*	*85.0*
ARAB COUNTRIES	*6.6*	*2.4*	*0.1*	*2.8*	*6.6*	*2.4*	*0.1*	*2.8*	*7.3*
E.E.C.+ MEMBERS	*160.8*	*184.9*	*182.4*	*236.2*	*168.7*	*181.8*	*174.3*	*222.5*	*182.1*
TOTAL	***279.2***	***304.4***	***282.6***	***330.3***	***280.6***	***297.6***	***271.6***	***314.4***	***299.6***

2. ODA LOANS GROSS / 5. ODA LOANS NET / 8. GRANTS

	2. ODA LOANS GROSS				5. ODA LOANS NET				8. GRANTS
	1987	1988	1989	1990	1987	1988	1989	1990	1987
DAC COUNTRIES									
Australia	–	–	–	–	–	–	–	–	–
Austria	–	–	4.8	–	–	–	4.8	–	0.4
Belgium	–	–	–	–	–	–	–	–	3.0
Canada	–	–	–	–	–	–	–	–	12.0
Denmark	–	–	–	–	-9.5	–	–	–	10.7
Finland	–	–	–	–	–	–	–	–	–
France	42.5	31.7	35.7	27.0	40.4	29.6	25.6	18.5	24.3
Germany	–	–	–	–	–	–	–	–	36.3
Ireland	–	–	–	–	–	–	–	–	–
Italy	–	–	–	–	–	–	–	–	20.6
Japan	–	–	–	–	–	–	–	–	7.7
Netherlands	–	–	–	–	–	–	–	–	27.6
New Zealand	–	–	–	–	–	–	–	–	–
Norway	–	–	–	–	–	–	–	–	–
Sweden	–	–	–	–	–	–	–	–	–
Switzerland	–	–	–	–	–	–	–	–	3.1
United Kingdom	–	–	–	–	–	–	–	–	0.3
United States	–	–	–	–	–	–	–	–	19.0
TOTAL	*42.5*	*31.7*	*40.5*	*27.0*	*30.9*	*29.6*	*30.4*	*18.5*	*164.8*
MULTILATERAL	*42.2*	*35.6*	*40.3*	*39.7*	*35.6*	*24.9*	*32.1*	*29.7*	*42.8*
ARAB COUNTRIES	*5.1*	*2.3*	*1.0*	*2.8*	*4.3*	*1.3*	*-1.0*	*2.8*	*2.2*
E.E.C.+ MEMBERS	*45.8*	*35.6*	*38.1*	*29.4*	*32.4*	*31.2*	*26.7*	*19.6*	*136.2*
TOTAL	***89.8***	***69.6***	***81.7***	***69.4***	***70.8***	***55.7***	***61.4***	***50.9***	***209.8***

3. TOTAL OFFICIAL GROSS / 6. TOTAL OFFICIAL NET / 9. TOTAL OOF GROSS

	3. TOTAL OFFICIAL GROSS				6. TOTAL OFFICIAL NET				9. TOTAL OOF GROSS
	1987	1988	1989	1990	1987	1988	1989	1990	1987
DAC COUNTRIES									
Australia	–	0.1	0.0	0.0	–	0.1	0.0	0.0	–
Austria	0.4	0.4	5.2	1.9	0.4	0.4	5.2	1.9	–
Belgium	3.0	1.8	1.2	2.9	3.0	1.8	1.2	2.9	–
Canada	17.0	29.4	11.4	10.1	10.7	29.4	11.4	10.1	5.1
Denmark	10.7	0.5	7.8	10.3	1.2	0.5	7.8	10.3	–
Finland	–	–	–	–	–	–	–	–	–
France	66.8	54.2	80.2	95.4	64.6	50.4	69.3	86.7	–
Germany	36.3	43.2	33.3	45.2	36.3	43.2	33.3	45.2	–
Ireland	–	–	–	–	–	–	–	–	–
Italy	20.6	31.7	16.1	29.8	20.6	31.7	16.1	29.8	–
Japan	7.7	7.9	3.2	1.7	7.7	7.9	3.2	1.7	–
Netherlands	28.0	28.2	31.4	34.5	28.0	28.2	31.2	34.4	0.4
New Zealand	–	–	–	–	–	–	–	–	–
Norway	–	1.4	0.4	–	–	1.4	0.4	–	–
Sweden	–	0.5	–	0.1	–	0.5	–	0.1	–
Switzerland	3.1	4.1	4.5	5.0	3.1	4.1	4.5	5.0	–
United Kingdom	0.3	0.6	0.5	0.5	0.3	0.6	0.5	0.5	–
United States	19.0	17.0	14.0	11.0	19.0	17.0	14.0	11.0	–
TOTAL	*212.7*	*220.9*	*209.2*	*248.5*	*194.7*	*217.1*	*198.1*	*239.6*	*5.5*
MULTILATERAL	*93.6*	*91.7*	*84.5*	*88.8*	*86.1*	*79.9*	*75.1*	*73.5*	*8.6*
ARAB COUNTRIES	*7.3*	*3.4*	*2.1*	*2.8*	*6.6*	*2.4*	*0.1*	*2.8*	*–*
E.E.C.+ MEMBERS	*182.5*	*186.1*	*185.8*	*233.9*	*168.4*	*179.3*	*172.6*	*222.9*	*0.4*
TOTAL	***313.6***	***316.1***	***295.7***	***340.0***	***287.4***	***299.4***	***273.3***	***315.9***	***14.0***

10. ODA COMMITMENTS

1988	1989	1990	1987	1988	1989	1990
0.1	0.0	0.0	0.1	0.1	0.0	0.0
0.4	5.2	1.9	0.3	0.4	5.3	2.0
1.8	1.2	2.9	1.6	2.6	1.2	2.9
29.4	11.4	10.1	24.8	42.8	15.9	5.4
0.5	7.8	10.3	9.5	20.1	–	11.7
–	–	–	–	–	–	–
54.2	80.2	93.8	77.7	48.0	62.5	92.6
43.2	33.3	45.2	54.0	19.8	45.0	52.3
–	–	–	–	–	–	–
31.7	16.1	29.8	50.0	18.8	6.7	25.3
7.9	3.2	1.7	3.3	7.1	2.3	2.6
28.2	31.3	34.5	34.8	42.1	33.1	42.2
–	–	–	–	–	–	–
1.4	0.4	–	4.5	–	–	–
0.5	–	0.1	–	0.5	–	–
4.1	4.5	5.0	2.1	1.5	7.0	13.6
0.6	0.5	0.5	0.3	0.6	0.5	0.5
17.0	14.0	11.0	18.9	13.9	13.5	11.8
220.9	*209.1*	*246.8*	*282.0*	*218.1*	*192.9*	*262.9*
7.8	8.9	10.1	–	19.1	44.6	4.1
–	–	–	–	–	–	–
–	–	–	–	–	–	–
–	–	–	–	–	–	–
26.0	15.3	15.3	9.6	73.1	50.0	50.0
–	–	–	–	–	–	–
20.0	25.0	15.0	–	18.0	64.0	–
–	–	–	–	–	–	–
1.4	0.9	1.7	10.1	0.2	–	–
–	–	–	–	–	–	–
–	–	–	–	–	–	–
–	–	–	29.0	28.6	26.4	34.2
11.8	12.5	14.4	–	–	–	–
1.4	1.4	1.3	–	–	–	–
3.3	4.5	5.4	–	–	–	–
–	–	–	–	–	–	–
3.4	2.6	7.3	–	–	–	–
0.3	0.3	0.3	–	–	–	–
8.5	5.2	5.6	–	–	–	–
3.3	4.2	10.7	0.5	9.6	33.6	0.2
87.1	*80.6*	*86.9*	*49.1*	*148.6*	*218.6*	*88.4*
3.4	*2.1*	*2.8*	*–*	*0.1*	*41.7*	*–*
186.1	*185.8*	*232.3*	*237.5*	*225.0*	*198.8*	*277.4*
311.4	*291.8*	*336.5*	*331.0*	*366.8*	*453.3*	*351.3*

11. TECH. COOP. GRANTS

1988	1989	1990	1987	1988	1989	1990
0.1	0.0	0.0	–	–	–	–
0.4	0.5	1.9	0.3	0.4	0.1	0.9
1.8	1.2	2.9	1.1	0.5	0.5	0.9
29.4	11.4	10.1	–	1.3	1.7	2.5
0.5	7.8	10.3	0.7	0.5	0.3	1.0
–	–	–	–	–	–	–
22.6	44.5	66.8	17.0	17.9	19.6	26.0
43.2	33.3	45.2	15.3	16.6	14.3	18.9
–	–	–	–	–	–	–
31.7	16.1	29.8	3.7	0.8	0.9	2.2
7.9	3.2	1.7	0.5	0.2	0.1	0.2
28.2	31.3	34.5	20.9	24.6	29.0	31.7
–	–	–	–	–	–	–
1.4	0.4	–	–	–	–	–
0.5	–	0.1	–	–	–	0.1
4.1	4.5	5.0	1.5	2.8	–	–
0.6	0.5	0.5	0.2	0.5	0.5	0.2
17.0	14.0	11.0	9.0	7.0	4.0	5.0
189.2	*168.7*	*219.8*	*70.2*	*73.1*	*70.8*	*89.6*
51.5	*40.3*	*47.2*	*29.7*	*27.1*	*23.8*	*26.9*
1.1	*1.1*	*–*	*–*	*–*	*–*	*–*
150.6	*147.7*	*202.9*	*60.5*	*63.3*	*65.0*	*81.0*
241.9	*210.1*	*267.1*	*99.9*	*100.1*	*94.6*	*116.5*

12. TOTAL OOF NET

1988	1989	1990	1987	1988	1989	1990
–	–	–	–	–	–	–
–	–	–	–	–	–	–
–	–	–	-1.3	–	–	–
–	–	–	–	–	–	–
–	–	1.6	–	-1.7	-0.8	1.4
–	–	0.0	–	–	–	0.0
–	–	–	–	–	–	–
–	–	–	–	–	–	–
0.0	0.0	–	0.4	0.0	-0.1	-0.1
–	–	–	–	–	–	–
–	–	–	–	–	–	–
–	–	–	–	–	–	–
–	–	–	–	–	–	–
0.0	*0.0*	*1.6*	*-0.9*	*-1.7*	*-0.9*	*1.3*
4.7	*3.9*	*1.9*	*7.7*	*3.5*	*2.7*	*0.2*
–	*–*	*–*	*–*	*–*	*–*	*–*
0.0	*0.0*	*1.6*	*-0.3*	*-2.5*	*-1.8*	*0.4*
4.7	*3.9*	*3.6*	*6.8*	*1.9*	*1.8*	*1.5*

13. ODF COMMITMENTS: BY PURPOSE %

	1987	1988	1989	1990
Education	1	0	1	–
Health	1	1	2	–
Other Social Infrastr.	8	14	9	–
Water Sanitat. Sewage	7	1	25	–
Energy	1	6	5	–
Telecommunications	–	0	1	–
Transportation	4	7	5	–
Agriculture	17	12	14	–
Extractive Industries	–	–	0	–
Manufacturing	9	5	4	–
Trade Banking Tourism	4	0	–	–
Technical Cooperation	35	26	27	–
Multisector Aid	2	0	0	–
Programme	6	3	3	–
Debt Reorganisation	3	–	–	–
Food Aid	4	23	2	–
Emergency Aid	0	0	–	–
Unspecified	0	1	2	–
TOTAL	100	100	100	–

14. GRANT ELEMENT OF ODA %

DAC COUNTRIES	1987	1988	1989	1990
Australia	100.0	100.0	100.0	–
Austria	100.0	100.0	92.5	–
Belgium	100.0	100.0	100.0	–
Canada	100.0	100.0	100.0	–
Denmark	100.0	100.0	–	–
Finland	–	–	–	–
France	70.0	83.3	82.3	–
Germany	100.0	100.0	100.0	–
Ireland	–	–	–	–
Italy	100.0	100.0	100.0	–
Japan	100.0	100.0	100.0	–
Netherlands	100.0	100.0	100.0	–
New Zealand	–	–	–	–
Norway	100.0	–	–	–
Sweden	–	100.0	–	–
Switzerland	100.0	100.0	100.0	–
United Kingdom	100.0	100.0	100.0	–
United States	100.0	100.0	100.0	–
TOTAL	*91.7*	*96.3*	*94.1*	*–*
MULTILATERAL	*96.1*	*90.6*	*81.1*	*–*
ARAB COUNTRIES	*–*	*100.0*	*57.0*	*–*
E.E.C.+ MEMBERS	*90.2*	*96.3*	*94.2*	*–*
TOTAL	*92.4*	*93.9*	*84.5*	*–*

15. OTHER AGGREGATES

	1987	1988	1989	1990
OFFICIAL COMMITMENTS:				
TOTAL BILATERAL	282.0	235.5	241.9	262.9
of which:				
Arab Countries	–	0.1	41.7	–
C.E.E.C.	–	17.3	–	–
TOTAL MULTILATERAL	49.1	148.6	218.6	88.4
TOTAL BIL.& MULTIL.	331.0	384.1	460.5	351.3
of which:				
ODA Grants	267.2	290.8	229.1	281.7
ODA Loans	63.9	93.3	224.2	69.6
DISBURSEMENTS:				
DAC COUNTRIES COMBINED				
OFFICIAL & PRIVATE				
GROSS:				
Contractual Lending	44.1	38.5	60.4	49.9
Export Credits, Total	1.2	6.8	19.9	21.4
Export Credits, Priv.	-3.8	6.8	19.9	21.3
NET:				
Contractual Lending	24.1	30.7	38.0	36.5
Export Credits Total	-7.1	2.8	8.6	16.7
PRIVATE SECTOR NET	-8.2	5.0	9.3	14.4
Direct Investment	0.3	0.8	1.3	0.5
Portfolio Investment	-2.7	1.4	-0.5	-2.8
Export Credits	-5.8	2.8	8.6	16.7
MARKET BORROWING:				
CHANGE IN CLAIMS				
Banks	-3.0	-11.0	–	-5.0
MEMORANDUM ITEM:				
C.E.E.C. (Gross)	–	–	–	–

1. TOTAL RECEIPTS NET / 4. TOTAL ODA NET / 7. TOTAL ODA GROSS

	1. TOTAL RECEIPTS NET 1987	1988	1989	1990	4. TOTAL ODA NET 1987	1988	1989	1990	7. TOTAL ODA GROSS 1987
DAC COUNTRIES									
Australia	–	0.0	–	–	–	0.0	–	–	–
Austria	0.5	3.7	2.9	9.7	0.5	3.7	2.9	9.7	0.5
Belgium	18.2	17.0	16.3	38.1	19.7	17.3	17.2	39.5	19.7
Canada	1.0	0.7	1.0	0.4	1.0	0.7	1.0	0.4	1.0
Denmark	0.1	0.3	0.3	0.2	–	0.3	0.3	0.0	–
Finland	0.0	–	–	–	0.0	–	–	–	0.0
France	17.1	20.7	24.3	33.6	24.2	25.7	27.9	37.7	25.4
Germany	15.5	14.5	20.5	30.4	16.2	14.4	20.7	30.4	16.2
Ireland	0.2	0.1	0.2	0.1	0.2	0.1	0.2	0.1	0.2
Italy	5.3	4.8	1.5	7.3	5.1	5.0	1.5	7.3	5.1
Japan	11.0	9.6	10.9	10.0	11.0	9.6	10.9	10.0	11.0
Netherlands	2.4	2.1	1.5	1.3	1.6	1.2	1.2	1.3	1.6
New Zealand	–	–	–	–	–	–	–	–	–
Norway	1.2	–	–	–	1.2	–	–	–	1.2
Sweden	–	–	–	–	–	–	–	–	–
Switzerland	2.7	2.2	2.4	2.1	2.7	2.2	2.4	2.1	2.7
United Kingdom	0.2	0.2	-23.1	0.3	0.2	0.2	0.3	0.3	0.2
United States	4.0	3.0	3.0	18.0	4.0	3.0	3.0	18.0	4.0
TOTAL	*79.3*	*78.8*	*61.8*	*151.5*	*87.5*	*83.3*	*89.5*	*156.8*	*88.6*
MULTILATERAL									
AF.D.F.	19.9	13.4	8.9	4.2	19.9	13.4	8.9	4.2	20.2
AF.D.B.	5.7	1.7	-2.9	-3.8	–	–	–	–	–
AS.D.B	–	–	–	–	–	–	–	–	–
CAR.D.B.	–	–	–	–	–	–	–	–	–
E.E.C.	10.2	27.3	35.5	35.5	10.2	27.3	35.5	35.5	10.4
IBRD	–	–	–	–	–	–	–	–	–
IDA	40.5	44.0	45.0	48.0	40.5	44.0	45.0	48.0	42.2
I.D.B.	–	–	–	–	–	–	–	–	–
IFAD	3.4	0.4	0.5	1.6	3.4	0.4	0.5	1.6	3.5
I.F.C.	-3.7	–	0.0	–	–	–	–	–	–
IMF TRUST FUND	–	–	–	–	–	–	–	–	–
U.N. AGENCIES	–	–	–	–	–	–	–	–	–
UNDP	5.0	5.5	6.2	9.6	5.0	5.5	6.2	9.6	5.0
UNTA	1.0	0.9	1.1	1.0	1.0	0.9	1.1	1.0	1.0
UNICEF	2.4	2.0	2.7	3.3	2.4	2.0	2.7	3.3	2.4
UNRWA	–	–	–	–	–	–	–	–	–
WFP	2.0	3.2	2.7	3.0	2.0	3.2	2.7	3.0	2.0
UNHCR	0.5	1.7	1.3	0.6	0.5	1.7	1.3	0.6	0.5
Other Multilateral	1.5	2.1	1.9	2.8	1.5	2.1	1.9	2.8	1.5
Arab Agencies	18.7	1.8	0.2	–	16.2	1.8	-0.5	–	17.6
TOTAL	*107.2*	*103.7*	*103.1*	*105.6*	*102.6*	*102.1*	*105.2*	*109.4*	*106.4*
ARAB COUNTRIES	***12.1***	***2.5***	***1.0***	***-1.3***	***12.1***	***2.5***	***1.0***	***-1.3***	***13.4***
E.E.C.+ MEMBERS	*69.2*	*87.0*	*77.1*	*146.8*	*77.4*	*91.5*	*104.8*	*152.1*	*78.7*
TOTAL	***198.6***	***185.1***	***165.9***	***255.8***	***202.2***	***187.9***	***195.7***	***264.9***	***208.4***

2. ODA LOANS GROSS / 5. ODA LOANS NET / 8. GRANTS

	2. ODA LOANS GROSS 1987	1988	1989	1990	5. ODA LOANS NET 1987	1988	1989	1990	8. GRANTS 1987
DAC COUNTRIES									
Australia	–	–	–	–	–	–	–	–	–
Austria	–	3.2	2.3	8.8	–	3.2	2.3	8.8	0.5
Belgium	2.9	–	–	0.8	2.9	–	–	0.8	16.7
Canada	–	–	–	–	–	–	–	–	1.0
Denmark	–	–	–	–	–	–	–	–	–
Finland	–	–	–	–	–	–	–	–	0.0
France	14.1	13.7	16.2	15.9	13.0	11.5	11.8	10.6	11.3
Germany	–	–	–	–	–	–	–	–	16.2
Ireland	–	–	–	–	–	–	–	–	0.2
Italy	0.6	–	0.1	1.0	0.6	–	0.1	1.0	4.5
Japan	5.5	6.2	2.6	2.6	5.5	6.2	2.6	2.6	5.4
Netherlands	0.8	0.1	–	0.1	0.8	0.1	–	-4.9	0.8
New Zealand	–	–	–	–	–	–	–	–	–
Norway	–	–	–	–	–	–	–	–	1.2
Sweden	–	–	–	–	–	–	–	–	–
Switzerland	–	–	–	–	–	–	–	–	2.7
United Kingdom	–	–	–	–	–	–	–	–	0.2
United States	–	–	–	–	–	–	–	–	4.0
TOTAL	*24.0*	*23.3*	*21.2*	*29.1*	*22.9*	*21.1*	*16.7*	*18.8*	*64.6*
MULTILATERAL	*84.8*	*64.6*	*60.5*	*60.5*	*81.0*	*61.5*	*55.6*	*54.4*	*21.6*
ARAB COUNTRIES	***13.4***	***3.2***	***3.6***	***0.5***	***12.1***	***1.5***	***0.7***	***-1.3***	***0.0***
E.E.C.+ MEMBERS	*19.7*	*15.9*	*18.6*	*20.1*	*18.4*	*13.5*	*13.8*	*9.4*	*59.0*
TOTAL	***122.1***	***91.1***	***85.3***	***90.0***	***116.0***	***84.1***	***73.0***	***71.9***	***86.2***

3. TOTAL OFFICIAL GROSS / 6. TOTAL OFFICIAL NET / 9. TOTAL OOF GROSS

	3. TOTAL OFFICIAL GROSS 1987	1988	1989	1990	6. TOTAL OFFICIAL NET 1987	1988	1989	1990	9. TOTAL OOF GROSS 1987
DAC COUNTRIES									
Australia	–	0.0	–	–	–	0.0	–	–	–
Austria	0.5	3.7	2.9	9.7	0.5	3.7	2.9	9.7	–
Belgium	19.9	17.3	17.3	39.6	19.9	17.3	17.3	39.6	0.3
Canada	1.0	0.7	1.0	0.4	1.0	0.7	1.0	0.4	–
Denmark	0.1	0.3	0.3	0.2	0.1	0.3	0.3	0.2	0.1
Finland	0.0	–	–	–	0.0	–	–	–	–
France	25.4	27.9	32.3	43.0	24.2	25.7	27.9	37.7	–
Germany	16.2	14.4	20.7	30.4	16.2	14.4	20.7	30.4	–
Ireland	0.2	0.1	0.2	0.1	0.2	0.1	0.2	0.1	–
Italy	5.1	5.0	1.5	7.3	5.1	5.0	1.5	7.3	–
Japan	11.0	9.6	10.9	10.0	11.0	9.6	10.9	10.0	–
Netherlands	1.6	1.2	1.2	6.9	1.6	1.2	1.2	2.0	–
New Zealand	–	–	–	–	–	–	–	–	–
Norway	1.2	–	–	–	1.2	–	–	–	–
Sweden	–	–	–	–	–	–	–	–	–
Switzerland	2.7	2.2	2.4	2.1	2.7	2.2	2.4	2.1	–
United Kingdom	0.2	0.2	0.3	0.3	0.2	0.2	0.3	0.3	–
United States	4.0	3.0	3.0	18.0	4.0	3.0	3.0	18.0	–
TOTAL	*89.0*	*85.5*	*94.1*	*168.0*	*87.9*	*83.3*	*89.6*	*157.7*	*0.4*
MULTILATERAL	*116.3*	*109.2*	*110.7*	*115.4*	*107.2*	*103.7*	*103.1*	*105.6*	*9.9*
ARAB COUNTRIES	***13.4***	***4.2***	***3.9***	***0.5***	***12.1***	***2.5***	***1.0***	***-1.3***	***–***
E.E.C.+ MEMBERS	*79.1*	*93.9*	*109.8*	*163.8*	*77.8*	*91.5*	*104.9*	*153.0*	*0.4*
TOTAL	***218.7***	***198.9***	***208.7***	***283.8***	***207.1***	***189.6***	***193.7***	***262.0***	***10.3***

10. ODA COMMITMENTS

1988	1989	1990	1987	1988	1989	1990
0.0	–	–	–	0.0	–	–
3.7	2.9	9.7	0.5	5.8	2.7	9.8
17.3	17.2	39.5	19.2	19.8	17.2	39.5
0.7	1.0	0.4	1.0	0.6	3.7	0.7
0.3	0.3	0.0	–	–	0.6	–
–	–	–	–	–	–	0.1
27.9	32.3	43.0	25.7	32.4	28.2	22.7
14.4	20.7	30.4	32.6	27.6	18.2	13.4
0.1	0.2	0.1	0.2	0.1	0.2	0.1
5.0	1.5	7.3	7.8	4.5	1.8	5.7
9.6	10.9	10.0	13.1	8.2	19.5	9.8
1.2	1.2	6.2	0.8	1.5	0.9	12.4
–	–	–	–	–	–	–
–	–	–	–	–	–	–
2.2	2.4	2.1	2.0	2.5	6.2	0.9
0.2	0.3	0.3	0.2	0.2	0.3	0.3
3.0	3.0	18.0	2.6	6.0	2.7	20.5
85.5	*93.9*	*167.0*	*105.6*	*109.2*	*101.9*	*135.8*
13.6	9.3	5.0	–	11.0	11.1	41.4
–	–	–	–	–	–	–
–	–	–	–	–	–	–
27.5	35.9	35.9	45.2	69.9	55.7	55.7
–	–	–	–	–	–	–
44.0	46.0	49.0	36.3	151.0	33.0	71.0
–	–	–	–	–	–	–
0.4	0.5	2.3	0.2	9.3	–	–
–	–	–	–	–	–	–
–	–	–	12.5	15.3	15.8	20.1
5.5	6.2	9.6	–	–	–	–
0.9	1.1	1.0	–	–	–	–
2.0	2.7	3.3	–	–	–	–
3.2	2.7	3.0	–	–	–	–
1.7	1.3	0.6	–	–	–	–
2.1	1.9	2.8	–	–	–	–
4.5	2.5	2.0	–	2.1	–	–
105.2	*110.1*	*114.3*	*94.1*	*258.6*	*115.7*	*188.2*
4.2	*3.9*	*0.5*	*2.9*	–	–	*9.6*
93.9	*109.6*	*162.8*	*131.6*	*156.0*	*122.9*	*149.8*
194.9	*208.0*	*281.8*	*202.7*	*367.8*	*217.6*	*333.7*

11. TECH. COOP. GRANTS

1988	1989	1990	1987	1988	1989	1990
0.0	–	–	–	–	–	–
0.4	0.7	0.9	0.4	0.3	0.0	0.2
17.3	17.2	38.8	14.9	14.5	14.4	15.0
0.7	1.0	0.4	–	0.0	–	0.0
0.3	0.3	0.0	–	0.1	–	–
–	–	–	0.0	–	–	–
14.2	16.1	27.1	9.0	9.7	9.5	11.3
14.4	20.7	30.4	8.9	7.9	9.5	11.4
0.1	0.2	0.1	0.2	0.1	0.2	0.1
5.0	1.4	6.3	4.3	3.0	0.2	1.0
3.4	8.3	7.4	0.3	0.3	0.7	0.5
1.1	1.2	6.1	0.4	0.9	0.9	1.1
–	–	–	–	–	–	–
–	–	–	–	–	–	–
2.2	2.4	2.1	1.3	0.8	–	–
0.2	0.3	0.3	0.2	0.2	0.2	0.3
3.0	3.0	18.0	3.0	3.0	3.0	3.0
62.2	*72.8*	*138.0*	*42.8*	*40.9*	*38.6*	*43.9*
40.6	*49.6*	*53.9*	*11.5*	*13.7*	*13.1*	*17.2*
1.0	*0.4*	–	–	–	–	–
78.0	*91.0*	*142.7*	*38.8*	*38.0*	*34.9*	*40.1*
103.9	*122.7*	*191.8*	*54.3*	*54.6*	*51.7*	*61.1*

12. TOTAL OOF NET

1988	1989	1990	1987	1988	1989	1990
–	–	–	–	–	–	–
–	0.1	0.1	0.3	–	0.1	0.1
–	–	0.1	–	–	–	–
–	–	0.1	0.1	–	–	0.1
–	–	–	–	–	–	–
–	–	–	–	–	–	–
–	–	–	–	–	–	–
–	–	–	–	–	–	–
–	–	0.7	–	–	–	0.7
–	–	–	–	–	–	–
–	–	–	–	–	–	–
–	–	–	–	–	–	–
–	0.1	1.0	0.4	–	0.1	1.0
4.0	*0.6*	*1.1*	*4.6*	*1.7*	*-2.1*	*-3.8*
–	–	–	–	–	–	–
–	0.1	1.0	0.4	–	0.1	1.0
4.0	*0.7*	*2.0*	*4.9*	*1.7*	*-2.0*	*-2.9*

13. ODF COMMITMENTS: BY PURPOSE %

	1987	1988	1989	1990
Education	0	12	0	–
Health	2	7	1	–
Other Social Infrastr.	17	2	16	–
Water Sanitat. Sewage	–	3	0	–
Energy	0	4	5	–
Telecommunications	4	–	3	–
Transportation	6	8	3	–
Agriculture	12	5	26	–
Extractive Industries	0	–	–	–
Manufacturing	1	2	–	–
Trade Banking Tourism	–	3	–	–
Technical Cooperation	43	18	26	–
Multisector Aid	–	0	2	–
Programme	15	35	7	–
Debt Reorganisation	–	–	0	–
Food Aid	–	–	–	–
Emergency Aid	–	0	0	–
Unspecified	–	–	10	–
TOTAL	100	100	100	–

14. GRANT ELEMENT OF ODA %

DAC COUNTRIES

	1987	1988	1989	1990
Australia	–	100.0	–	–
Austria	100.0	92.6	92.4	–
Belgium	97.8	100.0	100.0	–
Canada	100.0	100.0	100.0	–
Denmark	–	–	100.0	–
Finland	–	–	–	–
France	79.3	73.2	81.0	–
Germany	100.0	100.0	100.0	–
Ireland	100.0	100.0	100.0	–
Italy	100.0	100.0	100.0	–
Japan	76.5	100.0	82.3	–
Netherlands	100.0	100.0	100.0	–
New Zealand	–	–	–	–
Norway	–	–	–	–
Sweden	–	–	–	–
Switzerland	100.0	100.0	100.0	–
United Kingdom	100.0	100.0	100.0	–
United States	100.0	100.0	100.0	–
TOTAL	*91.6*	*90.9*	*91.2*	–
MULTILATERAL	*94.4*	*87.0*	*90.4*	–
ARAB COUNTRIES	*80.9*	–	–	–
E.E.C.+ MEMBERS	*95.6*	*94.0*	*95.4*	–
TOTAL	*92.7*	*88.2*	*90.8*	–

15. OTHER AGGREGATES

OFFICIAL COMMITMENTS:

	1987	1988	1989	1990
TOTAL BILATERAL	108.7	109.2	102.0	146.3
of which:				
Arab Countries	2.9	–	–	9.6
C.E.E.C.	–	–	–	–
TOTAL MULTILATERAL	94.3	260.8	115.7	194.2
TOTAL BIL.& MULTIL.	203.0	370.0	217.7	340.4
of which:				
ODA Grants	136.6	159.1	138.9	186.2
ODA Loans	66.1	208.7	78.6	147.5

DISBURSEMENTS:

DAC COUNTRIES COMBINED

OFFICIAL & PRIVATE

	1987	1988	1989	1990
GROSS:				
Contractual Lending	19.0	18.5	19.5	25.5
Export Credits, Total	-5.1	-4.8	-1.7	-4.4
Export Credits, Priv.	-5.1	-4.8	-1.7	-4.4
NET:				
Contractual Lending	16.8	15.0	-11.2	13.9
Export Credits Total	-6.2	-6.1	-28.0	-5.7
PRIVATE SECTOR NET	-8.6	-4.5	-27.8	-6.2
Direct Investment	-0.5	1.8	0.5	0.1
Portfolio Investment	-1.9	-0.2	-0.3	-0.6
Export Credits	-6.2	-6.1	-28.0	-5.7

MARKET BORROWING:

CHANGE IN CLAIMS

	1987	1988	1989	1990
Banks	-5.0	-16.0	-2.0	21.0

MEMORANDUM ITEM:

	1987	1988	1989	1990
C.E.E.C. (Gross)	0.1	–	–	–

1. TOTAL RECEIPTS NET

DAC COUNTRIES	1987	1988	1989	1990
Australia	–	–	–	–
Austria	0.0	36.9	0.0	0.1
Belgium	3.9	5.7	34.6	22.5
Canada	13.3	62.5	93.1	49.9
Denmark	33.9	18.7	3.7	-1.7
Finland	0.0	0.0	0.0	0.0
France	69.5	48.0	-12.4	111.0
Germany	71.3	136.9	129.8	165.1
Ireland	0.0	0.0	–	0.0
Italy	3.9	29.2	77.5	8.1
Japan	12.5	-3.7	4.1	4.7
Netherlands	-0.3	28.9	11.4	9.6
New Zealand	–	–	–	–
Norway	0.3	0.2	0.1	0.0
Sweden	-0.2	–	0.5	-0.1
Switzerland	5.8	5.9	4.3	4.6
United Kingdom	-21.8	-13.9	39.2	-1.1
United States	11.0	21.0	17.0	43.0
TOTAL	203.0	376.3	402.9	415.7
MULTILATERAL				
AF.D.F.	1.4	0.7	0.0	0.3
AF.D.B.	24.2	16.8	5.2	61.4
AS.D.B	–	–	–	–
CAR.D.B.	–	–	–	–
E.E.C.	14.2	36.9	147.1	147.1
IBRD	47.2	12.0	72.0	33.0
IDA	4.7	2.0	-1.0	-3.0
I.D.B.	–	–	–	–
IFAD	5.5	2.3	0.9	7.2
I.F.C.	–	4.0	1.3	–
IMF TRUST FUND	–	–	–	–
U.N. AGENCIES	–	–	–	–
UNDP	4.8	6.4	5.4	5.8
UNTA	1.0	0.9	1.3	1.1
UNICEF	0.8	1.4	0.8	1.1
UNRWA	–	–	–	–
WFP	3.5	1.8	1.7	1.6
UNHCR	2.8	1.6	1.2	1.1
Other Multilateral	1.0	1.1	1.6	2.3
Arab Agencies	-4.0	-0.1	0.2	–
TOTAL	107.2	87.7	237.7	259.0
ARAB COUNTRIES	0.1	-4.0	-0.1	-1.9
E.E.C.+ MEMBERS	174.6	290.4	431.0	460.7
TOTAL	310.3	460.0	640.5	672.9

2. ODA LOANS GROSS

DAC COUNTRIES	1987	1988	1989	1990
Australia	–	–	–	–
Austria	–	–	–	–
Belgium	2.7	3.3	1.9	–
Canada	1.3	–	–	1.6
Denmark	0.6	–	–	–
Finland	–	–	–	–
France	28.4	93.0	57.1	142.7
Germany	36.4	13.9	23.6	22.0
Ireland	–	–	–	–
Italy	–	–	35.1	2.4
Japan	11.7	0.2	–	0.5
Netherlands	–	12.1	8.5	5.7
New Zealand	–	–	–	–
Norway	–	–	–	–
Sweden	–	–	–	–
Switzerland	1.1	2.6	1.9	1.2
United Kingdom	–	–	–	0.4
United States	1.0	–	6.0	9.0
TOTAL	83.1	125.0	134.0	185.4
MULTILATERAL	12.9	8.3	3.3	8.2
ARAB COUNTRIES	2.9	0.2	–	–
E.E.C.+ MEMBERS	68.0	122.3	126.2	173.1
TOTAL	99.0	133.5	137.4	193.6

3. TOTAL OFFICIAL GROSS

DAC COUNTRIES	1987	1988	1989	1990
Australia	–	–	–	–
Austria	0.0	0.0	0.0	0.1
Belgium	9.2	11.1	10.2	6.3
Canada	12.5	54.4	99.4	177.8
Denmark	14.4	8.6	7.0	–
Finland	0.0	0.0	0.0	0.0
France	90.3	158.2	109.5	249.3
Germany	78.4	39.2	72.4	157.4
Ireland	0.0	0.0	–	0.0
Italy	2.8	7.3	68.2	6.2
Japan	12.5	0.9	2.2	4.7
Netherlands	4.7	17.4	13.1	18.1
New Zealand	–	–	–	–
Norway	0.3	0.2	0.1	0.0
Sweden	–	–	0.1	–
Switzerland	6.0	6.1	4.3	4.6
United Kingdom	11.2	9.6	8.3	5.1
United States	21.0	23.0	29.0	83.0
TOTAL	263.3	336.2	423.7	712.5
MULTILATERAL	156.3	145.5	293.8	324.6
ARAB COUNTRIES	2.9	0.2	–	–
E.E.C.+ MEMBERS	235.1	298.6	445.9	599.6
TOTAL	422.6	481.9	717.4	1037.1

4. TOTAL ODA NET

DAC COUNTRIES	1987	1988	1989	1990
Australia	–	–	–	–
Austria	0.0	0.0	0.0	0.1
Belgium	7.5	11.1	9.2	4.3
Canada	11.9	15.0	32.9	28.9
Denmark	0.4	-0.1	-0.1	–
Finland	0.0	0.0	0.0	0.0
France	59.9	128.1	95.6	171.8
Germany	50.0	27.3	44.7	43.6
Ireland	0.0	0.0	–	0.0
Italy	2.8	7.2	66.7	6.0
Japan	12.5	0.9	2.2	4.7
Netherlands	4.7	17.4	13.1	15.0
New Zealand	–	–	–	–
Norway	0.3	0.2	0.1	0.0
Sweden	–	–	0.1	–
Switzerland	5.8	5.9	4.3	4.6
United Kingdom	4.4	3.9	3.6	3.7
United States	20.0	23.0	28.0	39.0
TOTAL	180.1	240.0	300.6	321.7
AF.D.F.	1.4	0.7	0.0	0.3
AF.D.B.	–	–	–	–
AS.D.B	–	–	–	–
CAR.D.B.	–	–	–	–
E.E.C.	8.7	30.5	145.8	145.8
IBRD	–	–	–	–
IDA	4.7	2.0	-1.0	-3.0
I.D.B.	–	–	–	–
IFAD	5.5	2.3	0.9	7.2
I.F.C.	–	–	–	–
IMF TRUST FUND	–	–	–	–
U.N. AGENCIES	–	–	–	–
UNDP	4.8	6.4	5.4	5.8
UNTA	1.0	0.9	1.3	1.1
UNICEF	0.8	1.4	0.8	1.1
UNRWA	–	–	–	–
WFP	3.5	1.8	1.7	1.6
UNHCR	2.8	1.6	1.2	1.1
Other Multilateral	1.0	1.1	1.6	2.3
Arab Agencies	-1.9	-0.1	0.2	–
TOTAL	32.3	48.5	157.8	163.2
ARAB COUNTRIES	0.1	-4.0	-0.1	-1.9
E.E.C.+ MEMBERS	138.3	225.4	378.7	390.2
TOTAL	212.5	284.5	458.3	483.1

5. ODA LOANS NET

DAC COUNTRIES	1987	1988	1989	1990
Australia	–	–	–	–
Austria	-0.1	–	–	–
Belgium	2.7	3.3	1.9	–
Canada	0.7	–	-0.3	-121.2
Denmark	0.4	-0.1	-0.1	–
Finland	–	–	–	–
France	15.0	83.5	55.2	101.4
Germany	33.1	7.4	23.4	16.8
Ireland	–	–	–	–
Italy	-0.1	-0.1	33.6	2.2
Japan	11.7	0.2	–	0.5
Netherlands	–	12.1	8.5	5.7
New Zealand	–	–	–	–
Norway	–	–	–	–
Sweden	–	–	–	–
Switzerland	0.9	2.4	1.9	1.2
United Kingdom	-1.6	-2.2	-1.1	0.4
United States	–	–	5.0	-16.0
TOTAL	62.7	106.4	128.0	-8.9
MULTILATERAL	7.5	2.7	-1.8	1.9
ARAB COUNTRIES	0.1	-4.0	-0.1	-1.9
E.E.C.+ MEMBERS	47.3	101.5	119.5	124.7
TOTAL	70.3	105.1	126.0	-8.9

6. TOTAL OFFICIAL NET

DAC COUNTRIES	1987	1988	1989	1990
Australia	–	–	–	–
Austria	0.0	0.0	0.0	0.1
Belgium	9.2	11.1	10.2	6.3
Canada	11.9	47.9	98.0	52.4
Denmark	13.3	6.4	3.7	-0.4
Finland	0.0	0.0	0.0	0.0
France	66.5	135.6	104.3	164.5
Germany	70.0	23.8	71.7	92.5
Ireland	0.0	0.0	–	0.0
Italy	2.6	7.2	66.7	6.0
Japan	12.5	0.9	2.2	4.7
Netherlands	4.7	17.4	13.1	18.1
New Zealand	–	–	–	–
Norway	0.3	0.2	0.1	0.0
Sweden	–	–	0.1	–
Switzerland	5.8	5.9	4.3	4.6
United Kingdom	9.6	7.2	7.1	5.1
United States	12.0	21.0	18.0	43.0
TOTAL	218.3	284.6	399.6	396.8
MULTILATERAL	107.2	87.7	237.7	259.0
ARAB COUNTRIES	0.1	-4.0	-0.1	-1.9
E.E.C.+ MEMBERS	190.0	245.6	424.0	439.2
TOTAL	325.6	368.3	637.1	653.9

7. TOTAL ODA GROSS

	1987
Australia	–
Austria	0.0
Belgium	7.5
Canada	12.5
Denmark	0.6
Finland	0.0
France	73.3
Germany	53.3
Ireland	0.0
Italy	2.8
Japan	12.5
Netherlands	4.7
New Zealand	–
Norway	0.3
Sweden	–
Switzerland	6.0
United Kingdom	6.0
United States	21.0
TOTAL	200.5
AF.D.F.	1.4
AF.D.B.	–
AS.D.B	–
CAR.D.B.	–
E.E.C.	10.9
IBRD	–
IDA	6.0
I.D.B.	–
IFAD	5.5
I.F.C.	–
IMF TRUST FUND	–
U.N. AGENCIES	–
UNDP	4.8
UNTA	1.0
UNICEF	0.8
UNRWA	–
WFP	3.5
UNHCR	2.8
Other Multilateral	1.0
Arab Agencies	–
TOTAL	37.7
ARAB COUNTRIES	2.9
E.E.C.+ MEMBERS	159.1
TOTAL	241.2

8. GRANTS

	1987
Australia	–
Austria	0.0
Belgium	4.8
Canada	11.2
Denmark	–
Finland	0.0
France	44.9
Germany	16.9
Ireland	0.0
Italy	2.8
Japan	0.8
Netherlands	4.7
New Zealand	–
Norway	0.3
Sweden	–
Switzerland	4.9
United Kingdom	6.0
United States	20.0
TOTAL	117.4
MULTILATERAL	24.8
ARAB COUNTRIES	–
E.E.C.+ MEMBERS	91.1
TOTAL	142.2

9. TOTAL OOF GROSS

	1987
Australia	–
Austria	–
Belgium	1.7
Canada	–
Denmark	13.8
Finland	–
France	17.0
Germany	25.1
Ireland	–
Italy	–
Japan	–
Netherlands	–
New Zealand	–
Norway	–
Sweden	–
Switzerland	–
United Kingdom	5.1
United States	–
TOTAL	62.8
MULTILATERAL	118.6
ARAB COUNTRIES	–
E.E.C.+ MEMBERS	75.9
TOTAL	181.4

1988	1989	1990	1987	1988	1989	1990

10. ODA COMMITMENTS

1988	1989	1990	1987	1988	1989	1990
–	–	–	–	–	–	–
0.0	0.0	0.1	0.0	0.0	0.0	0.1
11.1	9.2	4.3	9.1	5.1	9.2	4.3
15.0	33.2	151.7	7.0	16.7	34.2	31.2
–	–	–	–	–	–	–
0.0	0.0	0.0	0.0	7.2	0.0	0.2
137.6	97.5	213.0	62.6	116.5	163.9	158.5
33.8	44.9	48.8	97.7	63.6	20.4	76.6
0.0	–	0.0	0.0	0.0	0.0	0.0
7.3	68.2	6.2	4.5	20.5	55.2	11.9
0.9	2.2	4.7	41.9	5.6	0.8	7.4
17.4	13.1	15.0	15.7	19.4	5.5	12.0
–	–	–	–	–	–	–
0.2	0.1	0.0	0.3	–	–	–
–	0.1	–	–	0.1	–	–
6.1	4.3	4.6	11.6	0.1	1.3	0.6
6.1	4.7	3.7	6.1	7.3	4.8	3.7
23.0	29.0	64.0	32.2	22.0	35.8	98.7
258.6	*306.7*	*516.1*	*288.8*	*284.2*	*331.2*	*405.3*
0.7	0.1	0.3	0.6	9.1	13.9	4.2
–	–	–	–	–	–	–
–	–	–	–	–	–	–
32.8	147.6	147.6	32.8	154.5	80.8	80.8
–	–	–	–	–	–	–
4.0	1.0	–	–	–	–	–
2.3	1.5	7.9	–	11.2	17.8	–
–	–	–	–	–	–	–
–	–	–	–	–	–	–
–	–	–	13.9	13.1	12.0	13.0
6.4	5.4	5.8	–	–	–	–
0.9	1.3	1.1	–	–	–	–
1.4	0.8	1.1	–	–	–	–
–	–	–	–	–	–	–
1.8	1.7	1.6	–	–	–	–
1.6	1.2	1.1	–	–	–	–
1.1	1.6	2.3	–	–	–	–
1.2	0.8	–	–	0.8	–	–
54.1	*163.0*	*168.8*	*47.3*	*188.6*	*124.4*	*97.9*
0.2	–	–	–	–	–	–
246.1	*385.4*	*438.7*	*228.4*	*387.0*	*339.9*	*347.9*
312.9	**469.7**	**684.9**	**336.1**	**472.8**	**455.6**	**503.2**

11. TECH. COOP. GRANTS

1988	1989	1990	1987	1988	1989	1990
–	–	–	–	–	–	–
0.0	0.0	0.1	0.0	0.0	0.0	0.1
7.9	7.3	4.3	2.8	1.5	1.5	1.0
15.0	33.2	150.1	–	6.1	7.0	11.7
–	–	–	1.1	–	–	–
0.0	0.0	0.0	0.0	0.0	0.0	0.0
44.6	40.5	70.4	40.5	39.6	37.2	52.0
19.9	21.3	26.8	16.9	19.7	19.7	21.0
0.0	–	0.0	0.0	0.0	–	0.0
7.3	33.1	3.8	–	7.2	2.8	2.6
0.7	2.2	4.2	0.4	0.7	0.5	1.2
5.3	4.6	9.3	4.5	4.7	4.3	5.4
–	–	–	–	–	–	–
0.2	0.1	0.0	0.0	–	0.1	0.0
–	0.1	–	–	–	0.1	–
3.5	2.5	3.4	1.1	2.0	–	–
6.1	4.7	3.3	3.0	5.7	4.3	3.2
23.0	23.0	55.0	11.0	18.0	19.0	18.0
133.6	*172.6*	*330.7*	*81.4*	*105.2*	*96.4*	*116.3*
45.8	*159.7*	*160.6*	*11.2*	*12.7*	*10.4*	*11.4*
–	–	–	–	–	–	–
123.9	*259.2*	*265.6*	*69.7*	*79.9*	*69.7*	*85.3*
179.4	**332.3**	**491.3**	**92.6**	**118.0**	**106.8**	**127.7**

12. TOTAL OOF NET

1988	1989	1990	1987	1988	1989	1990
–	–	–	–	–	–	–
–	0.9	1.9	1.7	–	0.9	1.9
39.4	66.2	26.2	–	32.8	65.1	23.5
8.6	7.0	–	12.9	6.5	3.8	-0.4
–	–	–	–	–	–	–
20.6	12.0	36.2	6.6	7.5	8.7	-7.3
5.4	27.4	108.6	20.1	-3.5	26.9	48.9
–	–	–	–	–	–	–
–	–	3.1	-0.2	–	–	–
–	–	–	–	–	–	3.1
–	–	–	–	–	–	–
–	–	–	–	–	–	–
3.5	3.5	1.3	5.1	3.3	3.5	1.3
–	–	19.0	-8.0	-2.0	-10.0	4.0
77.6	*117.0*	*196.4*	*38.2*	*44.6*	*99.0*	*75.1*
91.4	*130.8*	*155.8*	*74.8*	*39.2*	*79.9*	*95.8*
–	–	–	–	–	–	–
52.5	*60.6*	*160.9*	*51.7*	*20.2*	*45.2*	*48.9*
169.0	**247.8**	**352.2**	**113.0**	**83.9**	**178.8**	**170.9**

13. ODF COMMITMENTS: BY PURPOSE %

	1987	1988	1989	1990
Education	1	2	3	–
Health	1	4	1	–
Other Social Infrastr.	12	7	18	–
Water Sanitat. Sewage	0	4	2	–
Energy	1	7	2	–
Telecommunications	4	5	–	–
Transportation	48	2	5	–
Agriculture	8	27	15	–
Extractive Industries	–	0	–	–
Manufacturing	1	0	1	–
Trade Banking Tourism	0	1	1	–
Technical Cooperation	23	25	11	–
Multisector Aid	0	5	1	–
Programme	0	9	35	–
Debt Reorganisation	–	–	6	–
Food Aid	–	–	–	–
Emergency Aid	0	0	–	–
Unspecified	0	–	–	–
TOTAL	100	100	100	–

14. GRANT ELEMENT OF ODA %

DAC COUNTRIES

	1987	1988	1989	1990
Australia	–	–	–	–
Austria	100.0	100.0	100.0	–
Belgium	100.0	100.0	100.0	–
Canada	100.0	100.0	100.0	–
Denmark	–	–	–	–
Finland	100.0	69.8	100.0	–
France	80.5	55.9	58.5	–
Germany	56.7	71.2	73.8	–
Ireland	100.0	100.0	–	–
Italy	100.0	73.1	85.8	–
Japan	39.3	100.0	100.0	–
Netherlands	64.0	67.9	100.0	–
New Zealand	–	–	–	–
Norway	100.0	–	–	–
Sweden	–	100.0	–	–
Switzerland	100.0	100.0	100.0	–
United Kingdom	100.0	100.0	100.0	–
United States	97.0	100.0	100.0	–
TOTAL	*69.0*	*70.3*	*78.4*	–
MULTILATERAL	*94.8*	*99.8*	*98.5*	–
ARAB COUNTRIES	–	–	–	–
E.E.C.+ MEMBERS	*73.4*	*78.8*	*79.0*	–
TOTAL	**74.1**	**81.3**	**83.6**	–

15. OTHER AGGREGATES

	1987	1988	1989	1990
OFFICIAL COMMITMENTS:				
TOTAL BILATERAL	379.6	445.5	574.1	465.4
of which:				
Arab Countries	–	–	–	–
C.E.E.C.	–	–	–	–
TOTAL MULTILATERAL	70.7	451.4	479.8	154.4
TOTAL BIL.& MULTIL.	450.4	896.9	1053.9	619.7
of which:				
ODA Grants	166.9	306.3	271.1	334.9
ODA Loans	169.2	166.5	184.5	168.4
DISBURSEMENTS:				
DAC COUNTRIES COMBINED				
OFFICIAL & PRIVATE				
GROSS:				
Contractual Lending	131.7	368.5	368.4	434.3
Export Credits, Total	22.3	215.1	215.5	154.2
Export Credits, Priv.	-12.5	165.9	118.5	54.6
NET:				
Contractual Lending	32.3	223.6	283.9	76.0
Export Credits Total	-46.3	102.3	140.8	46.3
PRIVATE SECTOR NET	-15.2	91.7	3.3	18.9
Direct Investment	11.2	26.8	4.7	8.6
Portfolio Investment	40.5	-7.7	-59.5	-1.6
Export Credits	-67.0	72.6	58.1	12.0
MARKET BORROWING:				
CHANGE IN CLAIMS				
Banks	-50.0	169.0	-184.0	93.0
MEMORANDUM ITEM:				
C.E.E.C. (Gross)	–	–	–	–

1. TOTAL RECEIPTS NET

DAC COUNTRIES

	1987	1988	1989	1990
Australia	–	–	–	–
Austria	2.3	1.6	2.9	3.5
Belgium	4.1	2.2	1.8	3.6
Canada	0.4	0.0	0.5	0.5
Denmark	1.5	0.1	0.2	-0.7
Finland	1.6	1.0	–	–
France	4.9	4.2	4.0	7.4
Germany	13.2	7.1	4.4	6.1
Ireland	–	–	–	–
Italy	8.6	8.3	12.6	6.3
Japan	2.3	6.4	1.2	0.9
Netherlands	8.2	9.5	7.1	9.8
New Zealand	–	–	–	–
Norway	1.4	0.9	0.8	1.0
Sweden	8.1	11.5	8.2	8.8
Switzerland	1.6	2.1	1.8	2.1
United Kingdom	0.1	0.1	0.1	0.1
United States	6.0	4.0	3.0	5.0
TOTAL	64.1	58.9	48.6	54.4

MULTILATERAL

	1987	1988	1989	1990
AF.D.F.	2.6	2.9	3.3	3.6
AF.D.B.	-1.0	-1.1	-1.0	-1.1
AS.D.B	–	–	–	–
CAR.D.B.	–	–	–	–
E.E.C.	6.1	6.2	4.1	4.1
IBRD	–	–	–	–
IDA	0.9	1.0	3.0	2.0
I.D.B.	–	–	–	–
IFAD	–	–	–	–
I.F.C.	–	–	–	–
IMF TRUST FUND	–	–	–	–
U.N. AGENCIES	–	–	–	–
UNDP	4.3	4.3	3.0	3.9
UNTA	0.8	0.6	0.9	0.9
UNICEF	1.5	1.5	1.1	0.9
UNRWA	–	–	–	–
WFP	3.9	4.1	5.4	9.6
UNHCR	–	–	–	–
Other Multilateral	4.6	5.8	5.9	3.4
Arab Agencies	-0.6	-0.3	0.6	–
TOTAL	23.1	25.0	26.3	27.3
ARAB COUNTRIES	1.2	1.2	0.5	–
E.E.C.+ MEMBERS	46.6	37.6	34.3	36.7
TOTAL	88.3	85.0	75.3	81.7

2. ODA LOANS GROSS

DAC COUNTRIES

	1987	1988	1989	1990
Australia	–	–	–	–
Austria	–	–	–	–
Belgium	–	–	–	–
Canada	–	–	–	–
Denmark	–	–	–	–
Finland	–	–	–	–
France	0.7	–	–	–
Germany	–	–	–	–
Ireland	–	–	–	–
Italy	–	–	–	–
Japan	–	–	–	–
Netherlands	–	–	–	–
New Zealand	–	–	–	–
Norway	–	–	–	–
Sweden	–	–	–	–
Switzerland	–	–	–	–
United Kingdom	–	–	–	–
United States	–	–	–	–
TOTAL	0.7	–	–	–
MULTILATERAL	3.6	3.9	8.7	5.9
ARAB COUNTRIES	0.8	0.5	–	–
E.E.C.+ MEMBERS	0.7	–	–	–
TOTAL	5.2	4.4	8.7	5.9

3. TOTAL OFFICIAL GROSS

DAC COUNTRIES

	1987	1988	1989	1990
Australia	–	–	–	–
Austria	2.3	1.6	2.9	3.5
Belgium	4.1	2.3	1.8	3.6
Canada	0.4	0.0	0.5	0.5
Denmark	1.7	0.7	0.1	0.1
Finland	1.6	1.0	–	–
France	4.8	4.0	4.0	6.8
Germany	13.2	7.1	4.4	6.1
Ireland	–	–	–	–
Italy	8.6	8.3	12.6	6.3
Japan	2.3	6.4	1.2	0.9
Netherlands	8.2	9.5	7.1	9.8
New Zealand	–	–	–	–
Norway	1.4	0.9	0.8	1.0
Sweden	7.9	11.5	8.3	8.9
Switzerland	1.6	2.1	1.8	2.1
United Kingdom	0.1	0.1	0.1	0.1
United States	6.0	4.0	3.0	5.0
TOTAL	64.2	59.4	48.6	54.6
MULTILATERAL	25.1	26.7	30.1	29.2
ARAB COUNTRIES	1.2	1.9	0.6	–
E.E.C.+ MEMBERS	47.0	38.5	34.6	37.1
TOTAL	90.5	87.9	79.2	83.7

4. TOTAL ODA NET

	1987	1988	1989	1990
Australia	–	–	–	–
Austria	2.3	1.6	2.9	3.5
Belgium	4.1	2.3	1.8	3.6
Canada	0.4	0.0	0.5	0.5
Denmark	0.2	0.7	0.1	0.1
Finland	1.6	1.0	–	–
France	4.9	4.0	4.0	6.4
Germany	13.2	7.1	4.4	6.1
Ireland	–	–	–	–
Italy	8.6	8.3	12.6	6.3
Japan	2.3	6.4	1.2	0.9
Netherlands	8.2	9.5	7.1	9.8
New Zealand	–	–	–	–
Norway	1.4	0.9	0.8	1.0
Sweden	7.9	11.5	8.3	8.9
Switzerland	1.6	2.1	1.8	2.1
United Kingdom	0.1	0.1	0.1	0.1
United States	6.0	4.0	3.0	5.0
TOTAL	62.6	59.4	48.5	54.2
AF.D.F.	2.6	2.9	3.3	3.6
AF.D.B.	–	–	–	–
AS.D.B	–	–	–	–
CAR.D.B.	–	–	–	–
E.E.C.	6.1	6.2	4.1	4.1
IBRD	–	–	–	–
IDA	0.9	1.0	3.0	2.0
I.D.B.	–	–	–	–
IFAD	–	–	–	–
I.F.C.	–	–	–	–
IMF TRUST FUND	–	–	–	–
U.N. AGENCIES	–	–	–	–
UNDP	4.3	4.3	3.0	3.9
UNTA	0.8	0.6	0.9	0.9
UNICEF	1.5	1.5	1.1	0.9
UNRWA	–	–	–	–
WFP	3.9	4.1	5.4	9.6
UNHCR	–	–	–	–
Other Multilateral	4.6	5.8	5.9	3.4
Arab Agencies	-0.6	-0.3	0.1	–
TOTAL	24.1	26.0	26.8	28.4
ARAB COUNTRIES	1.2	1.2	0.5	–
E.E.C.+ MEMBERS	45.3	38.1	34.2	36.5
TOTAL	87.9	86.6	75.8	82.7

5. ODA LOANS NET

	1987	1988	1989	1990
Australia	–	–	–	–
Austria	–	–	–	–
Belgium	–	–	–	–
Canada	–	–	–	–
Denmark	–	–	–	–
Finland	–	–	–	–
France	0.7	–	0.0	-0.3
Germany	–	–	–	–
Ireland	–	–	–	–
Italy	–	–	–	–
Japan	–	–	–	–
Netherlands	–	–	–	–
New Zealand	–	–	–	–
Norway	–	–	–	–
Sweden	–	–	–	–
Switzerland	–	–	–	–
United Kingdom	–	–	–	–
United States	–	–	–	–
TOTAL	0.7	–	0.0	-0.3
MULTILATERAL	2.6	3.3	6.0	5.0
ARAB COUNTRIES	0.8	-0.2	-0.1	–
E.E.C.+ MEMBERS	0.5	-0.3	-0.3	-0.6
TOTAL	4.2	3.0	5.8	4.6

6. TOTAL OFFICIAL NET

	1987	1988	1989	1990
Australia	–	–	–	–
Austria	2.3	1.6	2.9	3.5
Belgium	4.1	2.3	1.8	3.6
Canada	0.4	0.0	0.5	0.5
Denmark	1.7	0.7	0.1	-0.1
Finland	1.6	1.0	–	–
France	4.9	4.0	4.0	6.4
Germany	13.2	7.1	4.4	6.1
Ireland	–	–	–	–
Italy	8.6	8.3	12.6	6.3
Japan	2.3	6.4	1.2	0.9
Netherlands	8.2	9.5	7.1	9.8
New Zealand	–	–	–	–
Norway	1.4	0.9	0.8	1.0
Sweden	7.9	11.5	8.3	8.9
Switzerland	1.6	2.1	1.8	2.1
United Kingdom	0.1	0.1	0.1	0.1
United States	6.0	4.0	3.0	5.0
TOTAL	64.2	59.4	48.5	54.0
MULTILATERAL	23.1	25.0	26.3	27.3
ARAB COUNTRIES	1.2	1.2	0.5	–
E.E.C.+ MEMBERS	46.9	38.1	34.2	36.2
TOTAL	88.4	85.5	75.3	81.3

7. TOTAL ODA GROSS

	1987
Australia	–
Austria	2.3
Belgium	4.1
Canada	0.4
Denmark	0.2
Finland	1.6
France	4.8
Germany	13.2
Ireland	–
Italy	8.6
Japan	2.3
Netherlands	8.2
New Zealand	–
Norway	1.4
Sweden	7.9
Switzerland	1.6
United Kingdom	0.1
United States	6.0
TOTAL	62.6
AF.D.F.	2.6
AF.D.B.	–
AS.D.B	–
CAR.D.B.	–
E.E.C.	6.3
IBRD	–
IDA	0.9
I.D.B.	–
IFAD	–
I.F.C.	–
IMF TRUST FUND	–
U.N. AGENCIES	–
UNDP	4.3
UNTA	0.8
UNICEF	1.5
UNRWA	–
WFP	3.9
UNHCR	–
Other Multilateral	4.6
Arab Agencies	0.2
TOTAL	25.1
ARAB COUNTRIES	1.2
E.E.C.+ MEMBERS	45.5
TOTAL	88.9

8. GRANTS

	1987
Australia	–
Austria	2.3
Belgium	4.1
Canada	0.4
Denmark	0.2
Finland	1.6
France	4.1
Germany	13.2
Ireland	–
Italy	8.6
Japan	2.3
Netherlands	8.2
New Zealand	–
Norway	1.4
Sweden	7.9
Switzerland	1.6
United Kingdom	0.1
United States	6.0
TOTAL	61.9
MULTILATERAL	21.5
ARAB COUNTRIES	0.3
E.E.C.+ MEMBERS	44.8
TOTAL	83.7

9. TOTAL OOF GROSS

	1987
Australia	–
Austria	–
Belgium	–
Canada	–
Denmark	1.6
Finland	–
France	–
Germany	–
Ireland	–
Italy	–
Japan	–
Netherlands	–
New Zealand	–
Norway	–
Sweden	–
Switzerland	–
United Kingdom	–
United States	–
TOTAL	1.6
MULTILATERAL	–
ARAB COUNTRIES	–
E.E.C.+ MEMBERS	1.6
TOTAL	1.6

10. ODA COMMITMENTS

1988	1989	1990	1987	1988	1989	1990
–	–	–	–	–	–	–
1.6	2.9	3.5	3.3	1.9	2.7	4.9
2.3	1.8	3.6	7.0	2.6	1.8	3.6
0.0	0.5	0.5	0.3	0.3	0.2	0.4
0.7	0.1	0.1	–	–	–	8.6
1.0	–	–	–	1.0	–	–
4.0	4.0	6.8	4.5	2.8	4.8	4.6
7.1	4.4	6.1	13.1	6.2	8.1	5.8
–	–	–	–	–	–	–
8.3	12.6	6.3	15.6	13.7	8.3	5.5
6.4	1.2	0.9	4.5	1.0	0.2	2.7
9.5	7.1	9.8	5.6	4.9	10.9	10.4
–	–	–	–	–	–	–
0.9	0.8	1.0	0.5	–	0.0	–
11.5	8.3	8.9	7.9	11.5	8.3	11.5
2.1	1.8	2.1	1.5	1.9	2.4	2.2
0.1	0.1	0.1	0.1	0.1	0.1	0.1
4.0	3.0	5.0	3.7	4.1	5.0	6.3
59.4	48.6	54.6	67.5	52.0	52.7	66.5
2.9	3.5	3.9	10.2	13.8	0.3	33.1
–	–	–	–	–	–	–
–	–	–	–	–	–	–
6.6	4.4	4.4	5.9	30.0	7.4	7.4
–	–	–	–	–	–	–
1.0	3.0	2.0	4.2	5.0	–	–
–	–	–	–	–	–	–
–	–	–	5.6	–	0.3	6.0
–	–	–	–	–	–	–
–	–	–	15.2	16.2	16.3	18.7
4.3	3.0	3.9	–	–	–	–
0.6	0.9	0.9	–	–	–	–
1.5	1.1	0.9	–	–	–	–
–	–	–	–	–	–	–
4.1	5.4	9.6	–	–	–	–
–	–	–	–	–	–	–
5.8	5.9	3.4	–	–	–	–
–	2.4	0.2	–	–	1.5	–
26.7	29.6	29.2	41.0	64.9	25.8	65.3
1.9	0.6	–	–	–	–	–
38.5	34.6	37.1	51.7	60.3	41.4	46.0
87.9	78.7	83.7	108.5	116.9	78.5	131.8

11. TECH. COOP. GRANTS

1988	1989	1990	1987	1988	1989	1990
–	–	–	–	–	–	–
1.6	2.9	3.5	1.1	1.3	0.1	0.5
2.3	1.8	3.6	0.4	0.2	0.1	0.1
0.0	0.5	0.5	–	0.0	–	–
0.7	0.1	0.1	0.1	0.0	–	–
1.0	–	–	–	–	–	–
4.0	4.0	6.8	1.6	1.4	1.6	2.2
7.1	4.4	6.1	4.0	3.5	2.1	2.7
–	–	–	–	–	–	–
8.3	12.6	6.3	3.6	0.5	0.7	0.9
6.4	1.2	0.9	0.2	0.2	0.2	0.7
9.5	7.1	9.8	1.5	1.6	1.5	1.5
–	–	–	–	–	–	–
0.9	0.8	1.0	0.5	–	–	–
11.5	8.3	8.9	0.2	0.9	0.3	0.6
2.1	1.8	2.1	0.7	0.6	–	–
0.1	0.1	0.1	0.1	0.1	0.1	0.1
4.0	3.0	5.0	3.0	2.0	1.0	2.0
59.4	48.6	54.6	16.7	12.3	7.7	11.3
22.8	20.8	23.3	11.7	13.2	10.9	9.2
1.4	0.6	–	–	–	–	–
38.5	34.6	37.1	11.6	8.5	6.2	7.5
83.5	70.0	77.9	28.4	25.5	18.6	20.4

12. TOTAL OOF NET

1988	1989	1990	1987	1988	1989	1990
–	–	–	–	–	–	–
–	–	–	–	–	–	–
–	–	–	–	–	–	–
–	–	–	1.6	–	–	-0.2
–	–	–	–	–	–	–
–	–	–	–	–	–	–
–	–	–	–	–	–	–
–	–	–	–	–	–	–
–	–	–	–	–	–	–
–	–	–	–	–	–	–
–	–	–	–	–	–	–
–	–	–	–	–	–	–
–	–	–	–	–	–	–
–	–	–	–	–	–	–
–	–	–	1.6	–	–	-0.2
–	0.5	–	-1.0	-1.1	-0.5	-1.1
–	–	–	–	–	–	–
–	–	–	1.6	–	–	-0.2
–	0.5	–	0.5	-1.1	-0.5	-1.3

13. ODF COMMITMENTS: BY PURPOSE %

	1987	1988	1989	1990
Education	6	–	22	–
Health	0	–	0	–
Other Social Infrastr.	0	2	1	–
Water Sanitat. Sewage	1	3	1	–
Energy	1	–	1	–
Telecommunications	1	–	–	–
Transportation	2	15	6	–
Agriculture	31	18	7	–
Extractive Industries	–	–	–	–
Manufacturing	2	–	3	–
Trade Banking Tourism	–	–	3	–
Technical Cooperation	38	33	32	–
Multisector Aid	0	2	1	–
Programme	11	15	17	–
Debt Reorganisation	–	–	–	–
Food Aid	8	11	5	–
Emergency Aid	–	–	0	–
Unspecified	–	–	0	–
TOTAL	100	100	100	–

14. GRANT ELEMENT OF ODA %

DAC COUNTRIES	1987	1988	1989	1990
Australia	–	–	–	–
Austria	100.0	100.0	100.0	–
Belgium	100.0	100.0	100.0	–
Canada	100.0	100.0	100.0	–
Denmark	–	–	–	–
Finland	–	100.0	–	–
France	100.0	100.0	100.0	–
Germany	100.0	100.0	100.0	–
Ireland	–	–	–	–
Italy	100.0	100.0	100.0	–
Japan	100.0	100.0	100.0	–
Netherlands	100.0	100.0	100.0	–
New Zealand	–	–	–	–
Norway	100.0	–	100.0	–
Sweden	100.0	100.0	100.0	–
Switzerland	100.0	100.0	100.0	–
United Kingdom	100.0	100.0	100.0	–
United States	100.0	100.0	100.0	–
TOTAL	100.0	100.0	100.0	–
MULTILATERAL	91.3	96.2	91.4	–
ARAB COUNTRIES	–	–	–	–
E.E.C.+ MEMBERS	100.0	100.0	100.0	–
TOTAL	96.7	98.1	96.4	–

15. OTHER AGGREGATES

	1987	1988	1989	1990
OFFICIAL COMMITMENTS:				
TOTAL BILATERAL	67.5	63.4	52.7	66.5
of which:				
Arab Countries	–	–	–	–
C.E.E.C.	–	–	–	–
TOTAL MULTILATERAL	42.0	64.9	25.8	65.3
TOTAL BIL.& MULTIL.	109.5	128.3	78.5	131.8
of which:				
ODA Grants	88.6	94.6	76.6	92.8
ODA Loans	19.9	22.3	1.8	39.0
DISBURSEMENTS:				
DAC COUNTRIES COMBINED				
OFFICIAL & PRIVATE				
GROSS:				
Contractual Lending	2.5	–	0.5	–
Export Credits, Total	0.2	–	0.5	–
Export Credits, Priv.	0.2	–	0.5	–
NET:				
Contractual Lending	2.2	-0.6	-0.1	-1.2
Export Credits Total	-0.1	-0.6	0.0	-0.6
PRIVATE SECTOR NET	-0.1	-0.5	0.0	0.4
Direct Investment	–	0.0	0.0	0.1
Portfolio Investment	0.0	0.1	0.0	1.0
Export Credits	-0.1	-0.6	0.0	-0.6
MARKET BORROWING:				
CHANGE IN CLAIMS				
Banks	3.0	-2.0	1.0	1.0
MEMORANDUM ITEM:				
C.E.E.C. (Gross)	–	1.2	–	–

1. TOTAL RECEIPTS NET

DAC COUNTRIES	1987	1988	1989	1990
Australia	–	–	–	–
Austria	–	–	–	–
Belgium	165.3	120.7	71.2	371.0
Canada	0.0	0.0	–	–
Denmark	–	–	–	–
Finland	1.4	2.2	32.9	–
France	7.7	431.3	-31.0	677.2
Germany	422.5	398.9	243.5	256.6
Ireland	–	–	–	–
Italy	–	7.7	47.6	-32.8
Japan	1626.8	2117.5	1889.8	1353.0
Netherlands	4.3	77.6	–	–
New Zealand	–	–	–	–
Norway	-0.8	–	–	-0.4
Sweden	10.4	–	0.2	–
Switzerland	–	–	–	–
United Kingdom	-0.8	3.6	0.1	4.3
United States	-3.0	-1.0	–	–
TOTAL	2233.8	3158.4	2254.2	2628.9
MULTILATERAL				
AF.D.F.	–	–	–	–
AF.D.B.	–	–	–	–
AS.D.B	–	–	–	–
CAR.D.B.	6.2	3.2	7.4	7.4
E.E.C.	-0.2	-0.2	0.3	0.3
IBRD	–	–	–	–
IDA	–	–	–	–
I.D.B.	–	–	–	–
IFAD	–	–	–	–
I.F.C.	–	–	–	–
IMF TRUST FUND	–	–	–	–
U.N. AGENCIES	–	–	–	–
UNDP	0.1	0.2	0.1	0.2
UNTA	–	–	–	–
UNICEF	–	–	–	–
UNRWA	–	–	–	–
WFP	–	–	–	–
UNHCR	–	–	–	–
Other Multilateral	–	0.0	0.0	–
Arab Agencies	–	–	–	–
TOTAL	6.2	3.2	7.9	7.9
ARAB COUNTRIES	–	–	–	–
E.E.C.+ MEMBERS	598.8	1039.5	331.7	1276.7
TOTAL	2240.0	3161.6	2262.1	2636.8

2. ODA LOANS GROSS

DAC COUNTRIES	1987	1988	1989	1990
Australia	–	–	–	–
Austria	–	–	–	–
Belgium	–	–	–	–
Canada	–	–	–	–
Denmark	–	–	–	–
Finland	–	–	–	–
France	–	–	–	–
Germany	1.3	11.6	–	–
Ireland	–	–	–	–
Italy	–	–	–	–
Japan	–	–	–	–
Netherlands	–	–	–	–
New Zealand	–	–	–	–
Norway	–	–	–	–
Sweden	–	–	–	–
Switzerland	–	–	–	–
United Kingdom	–	–	–	2.3
United States	–	–	–	–
TOTAL	1.3	11.6	–	2.3
MULTILATERAL	0.9	0.3	0.7	0.7
ARAB COUNTRIES	–	–	–	–
E.E.C.+ MEMBERS	1.3	11.6	–	2.3
TOTAL	2.1	11.9	0.7	3.0

3. TOTAL OFFICIAL GROSS

DAC COUNTRIES	1987	1988	1989	1990
Australia	–	–	–	–
Austria	–	–	–	–
Belgium	–	–	–	–
Canada	0.0	0.0	–	–
Denmark	–	–	–	–
Finland	–	–	–	–
France	–	–	–	–
Germany	1.3	11.6	–	–
Ireland	–	–	–	–
Italy	–	–	–	–
Japan	–	–	–	–
Netherlands	–	–	–	–
New Zealand	–	–	–	–
Norway	–	–	–	–
Sweden	–	–	–	–
Switzerland	–	–	–	–
United Kingdom	–	2.9	2.1	5.5
United States	–	–	–	–
TOTAL	1.3	14.5	2.1	5.5
MULTILATERAL	6.4	3.4	8.1	8.1
ARAB COUNTRIES	–	–	–	–
E.E.C.+ MEMBERS	1.3	14.4	2.7	6.0
TOTAL	7.6	17.9	10.2	13.6

4. TOTAL ODA NET

	1987	1988	1989	1990
Australia	–	–	–	–
Austria	–	–	–	–
Belgium	–	–	–	–
Canada	0.0	0.0	–	–
Denmark	–	–	–	–
Finland	–	–	–	–
France	–	–	–	–
Germany	1.3	11.6	–	–
Ireland	–	–	–	–
Italy	–	–	–	–
Japan	–	–	–	–
Netherlands	–	–	–	–
New Zealand	–	–	–	–
Norway	–	–	–	–
Sweden	–	–	–	–
Switzerland	–	–	–	–
United Kingdom	-0.1	-0.1	-0.1	2.1
United States	–	–	–	–
TOTAL	1.2	11.5	-0.1	2.1
AF.D.F.	–	–	–	–
AF.D.B.	–	–	–	–
AS.D.B	–	–	–	–
CAR.D.B.	0.9	0.3	0.7	0.7
E.E.C.	–	–	0.5	0.5
IBRD	–	–	–	–
IDA	–	–	–	–
I.D.B.	–	–	–	–
IFAD	–	–	–	–
I.F.C.	–	–	–	–
IMF TRUST FUND	–	–	–	–
U.N. AGENCIES	–	–	–	–
UNDP	0.1	0.2	0.1	0.2
UNTA	–	–	–	–
UNICEF	–	–	–	–
UNRWA	–	–	–	–
WFP	–	–	–	–
UNHCR	–	0.0	0.0	–
Other Multilateral	–	0.0	0.0	–
Arab Agencies	–	–	–	–
TOTAL	1.0	0.6	1.4	1.4
ARAB COUNTRIES	–	–	–	–
E.E.C.+ MEMBERS	1.1	11.5	0.4	2.7
TOTAL	2.2	12.1	1.3	3.5

5. ODA LOANS NET

	1987	1988	1989	1990
Australia	–	–	–	–
Austria	–	–	–	–
Belgium	–	–	–	–
Canada	–	–	–	–
Denmark	–	–	–	–
Finland	–	–	–	–
France	–	–	–	–
Germany	1.3	11.6	–	–
Ireland	–	–	–	–
Italy	–	–	–	–
Japan	–	–	–	–
Netherlands	–	–	–	–
New Zealand	–	–	–	–
Norway	–	–	–	–
Sweden	–	–	–	–
Switzerland	–	–	–	–
United Kingdom	-0.1	-0.1	-0.1	2.1
United States	–	–	–	–
TOTAL	1.1	11.5	-0.1	2.1
MULTILATERAL	0.9	0.3	0.7	0.7
ARAB COUNTRIES	–	–	–	–
E.E.C.+ MEMBERS	1.1	11.5	-0.1	2.1
TOTAL	2.0	11.8	0.6	2.8

6. TOTAL OFFICIAL NET

	1987	1988	1989	1990
Australia	–	–	–	–
Austria	–	–	–	–
Belgium	–	–	–	–
Canada	0.0	0.0	–	–
Denmark	–	–	–	–
Finland	–	–	–	–
France	–	–	–	–
Germany	1.3	11.6	–	–
Ireland	–	–	–	–
Italy	–	–	–	–
Japan	–	–	–	–
Netherlands	–	–	–	–
New Zealand	–	–	–	–
Norway	–	–	–	–
Sweden	–	–	–	–
Switzerland	–	–	–	–
United Kingdom	-0.1	2.4	1.3	4.6
United States	-3.0	-1.0	–	–
TOTAL	-1.9	13.0	1.3	4.6
MULTILATERAL	6.2	3.2	7.9	7.9
ARAB COUNTRIES	–	–	–	–
E.E.C.+ MEMBERS	0.9	13.8	1.6	4.9
TOTAL	4.3	16.2	9.1	12.4

7. TOTAL ODA GROSS

	1987
Australia	–
Austria	–
Belgium	–
Canada	0.0
Denmark	–
Finland	–
France	–
Germany	1.3
Ireland	–
Italy	–
Japan	–
Netherlands	–
New Zealand	–
Norway	–
Sweden	–
Switzerland	–
United Kingdom	–
United States	–
TOTAL	1.3
AF.D.F.	–
AF.D.B.	–
AS.D.B	–
CAR.D.B.	0.9
E.E.C.	–
IBRD	–
IDA	–
I.D.B.	–
IFAD	–
I.F.C.	–
IMF TRUST FUND	–
U.N. AGENCIES	–
UNDP	0.1
UNTA	–
UNICEF	–
UNRWA	–
WFP	–
UNHCR	–
Other Multilateral	–
Arab Agencies	–
TOTAL	1.0
ARAB COUNTRIES	–
E.E.C.+ MEMBERS	1.3
TOTAL	2.3

8. GRANTS

	1987
Australia	–
Austria	–
Belgium	–
Canada	0.0
Denmark	–
Finland	–
France	–
Germany	–
Ireland	–
Italy	–
Japan	–
Netherlands	–
New Zealand	–
Norway	–
Sweden	–
Switzerland	–
United Kingdom	–
United States	–
TOTAL	0.0
MULTILATERAL	0.1
ARAB COUNTRIES	–
E.E.C.+ MEMBERS	–
TOTAL	0.2

9. TOTAL OOF GROSS

	1987
Australia	–
Austria	–
Belgium	–
Canada	–
Denmark	–
Finland	–
France	–
Germany	–
Ireland	–
Italy	–
Japan	–
Netherlands	–
New Zealand	–
Norway	–
Sweden	–
Switzerland	–
United Kingdom	–
United States	–
TOTAL	–
MULTILATERAL	5.3
ARAB COUNTRIES	–
E.E.C.+ MEMBERS	–
TOTAL	5.3

1988	1989	1990		1987	1988	1989	1990

10. ODA COMMITMENTS

1988	1989	1990		1987	1988	1989	1990
–	–	–		–	–	–	–
–	–	–		–	–	–	–
0.0	–	–		0.0	0.0	–	–
–	–	–		–	–	–	–
–	–	–		–	–	–	–
–	–	–		–	–	–	–
11.6	–	–		12.6	–	–	–
–	–	–		–	–	–	–
–	–	–		–	–	–	–
–	–	–		–	–	–	–
–	–	–		–	–	–	–
–	–	–		–	–	–	–
–	–	–		–	–	–	–
–	0.0	2.3		–	–	0.0	2.1
–	–	–		–	–	–	–
11.6	0.0	2.3		12.6	0.0	0.0	2.1
–	–	–		–	–	–	–
–	–	–		–	–	–	–
0.3	0.7	0.7		–	–	1.0	1.0
–	0.5	0.5		–	1.8	–	–
–	–	–		–	–	–	–
–	–	–		–	–	–	–
–	–	–		–	–	–	–
–	–	–		0.1	0.3	0.2	0.2
0.2	0.1	0.2		–	–	–	–
–	–	–		–	–	–	–
–	–	–		–	–	–	–
–	–	–		–	–	–	–
0.0	0.0	–		–	–	–	–
–	–	–		–	–	–	–
0.6	1.4	1.4		0.1	2.0	1.2	1.2
–	–	–		–	–	–	–
11.6	0.5	2.8		12.6	1.8	0.0	2.1
12.2	1.4	3.7		12.7	2.1	1.2	3.3

11. TECH. COOP. GRANTS

1988	1989	1990		1987	1988	1989	1990
–	–	–		–	–	–	–
–	–	–		–	–	–	–
0.0	–	–		–	–	–	–
–	–	–		–	–	–	–
–	–	–		–	–	–	–
–	–	–		–	–	–	–
–	–	–		–	–	–	–
–	–	–		–	–	–	–
–	–	–		–	–	–	–
–	–	–		–	–	–	–
–	–	–		–	–	–	–
–	–	–		–	–	–	–
–	–	–		–	–	–	–
–	0.0	–		–	–	0.0	-0.1
–	–	–		–	–	–	–
0.0	0.0	–		–	–	0.0	-0.1
0.3	0.7	0.7		0.1	0.3	0.2	0.2
–	–	–		–	–	–	–
–	0.5	0.5		–	–	0.0	-0.1
0.3	0.7	0.7		0.1	0.3	0.2	0.1

12. TOTAL OOF NET

1988	1989	1990		1987	1988	1989	1990
–	–	–		–	–	–	–
–	–	–		–	–	–	–
–	–	–		–	–	–	–
–	–	–		–	–	–	–
–	–	–		–	–	–	–
–	–	–		–	–	–	–
–	–	–		–	–	–	–
–	–	–		–	–	–	–
–	–	–		–	–	–	–
–	–	–		–	–	–	–
–	–	–		–	–	–	–
–	–	–		–	–	–	–
–	–	–		–	–	–	–
2.9	2.1	3.2		0.0	2.5	1.4	2.4
–	–	–		-3.0	-1.0	–	–
2.9	2.1	3.2		-3.0	1.5	1.4	2.4
2.8	6.7	6.7		5.2	2.6	6.5	6.5
–	–	–		–	–	–	–
2.9	2.1	3.2		-0.2	2.3	1.2	2.2
5.7	8.8	9.9		2.1	4.1	7.9	8.9

13. ODF COMMITMENTS: BY PURPOSE %

	1987	1988	1989	1990
Education	–	–	–	–
Health	–	–	–	–
Other Social Infrastr.	–	–	–	–
Water Sanitat. Sewage	–	–	–	–
Energy	–	–	–	–
Telecommunications	–	–	–	–
Transportation	–	–	–	–
Agriculture	–	–	–	–
Extractive Industries	–	–	–	–
Manufacturing	99	–	–	–
Trade Banking Tourism	–	–	–	–
Technical Cooperation	1	100	100	–
Multisector Aid	–	–	–	–
Programme	–	–	–	–
Debt Reorganisation	–	–	–	–
Food Aid	–	–	–	–
Emergency Aid	–	–	–	–
Unspecified	–	–	–	–
TOTAL	100	100	100	–

14. GRANT ELEMENT OF ODA %

DAC COUNTRIES

	1987	1988	1989	1990
Australia	–	–	–	–
Austria	–	–	–	–
Belgium	–	–	–	–
Canada	100.0	100.0	–	–
Denmark	–	–	–	–
Finland	–	–	–	–
France	–	–	–	–
Germany	35.6	–	–	–
Ireland	–	–	–	–
Italy	–	–	–	–
Japan	–	–	–	–
Netherlands	–	–	–	–
New Zealand	–	–	–	–
Norway	–	–	–	–
Sweden	–	–	–	–
Switzerland	–	–	–	–
United Kingdom	–	–	100.0	–
United States	–	–	–	–
TOTAL	35.8	100.0	100.0	–
MULTILATERAL	100.0	100.0	100.0	–
ARAB COUNTRIES	–	–	–	–
E.E.C.+ MEMBERS	35.6	100.0	100.0	–
TOTAL	36.4	100.0	100.0	–

15. OTHER AGGREGATES

OFFICIAL COMMITMENTS:

	1987	1988	1989	1990
TOTAL BILATERAL	12.6	0.0	10.2	2.1
of which:				
Arab Countries	–	–	–	–
C.E.E.C.	–	–	–	–
TOTAL MULTILATERAL	4.1	2.0	8.7	8.7
TOTAL BIL.& MULTIL.	16.7	2.1	19.0	10.8
of which:				
ODA Grants	0.2	2.1	0.2	0.0
ODA Loans	12.6	–	1.0	3.3

DISBURSEMENTS:

DAC COUNTRIES COMBINED

	1987	1988	1989	1990
OFFICIAL & PRIVATE				
GROSS:				
Contractual Lending	28.5	1.1	-0.4	-11.0
Export Credits, Total	27.3	-13.3	-2.5	-16.5
Export Credits, Priv.	27.3	-13.3	-2.5	-16.5
NET:				
Contractual Lending	20.9	-12.6	-2.5	-12.6
Export Credits Total	19.8	-26.6	-3.7	-17.2
PRIVATE SECTOR NET	2235.7	3145.4	2253.0	2624.4
Direct Investment	1660.5	2075.0	1884.0	935.1
Portfolio Investment	552.4	1096.0	372.7	1706.5
Export Credits	22.8	-25.6	-3.7	-17.2

MARKET BORROWING:

CHANGE IN CLAIMS

	1987	1988	1989	1990
Banks	–	–	–	–

MEMORANDUM ITEM:

	1987	1988	1989	1990
C.E.E.C. (Gross)	–	–	–	–

1. TOTAL RECEIPTS NET

DAC COUNTRIES	1987	1988	1989	1990
Australia	–	–	–	–
Austria	0.1	0.1	0.1	0.1
Belgium	0.3	0.3	1.0	5.4
Canada	0.3	0.3	0.5	0.3
Denmark	2.9	7.1	2.8	0.7
Finland	–	–	–	–
France	87.1	68.0	62.5	70.5
Germany	15.6	14.6	13.4	14.9
Ireland	–	–	–	–
Italy	0.4	0.4	1.0	0.7
Japan	1.4	13.5	11.4	8.7
Netherlands	0.4	1.0	4.2	-0.4
New Zealand	–	–	–	–
Norway	–	–	–	–
Sweden	–	–	–	–
Switzerland	0.1	0.1	1.3	0.1
United Kingdom	–	0.1	0.1	0.1
United States	4.0	3.0	5.0	6.0
TOTAL	112.7	108.4	103.2	107.2
MULTILATERAL				
A.F.D.F.	3.2	4.8	31.5	17.1
A.F.D.B.	1.8	0.0	-1.2	-1.1
AS.D.B	–	–	–	–
CAR.D.B.	–	–	–	–
E.E.C.	6.4	29.4	22.8	22.8
IBRD	–	–	–	–
IDA	27.9	39.0	22.0	72.0
I.D.B.	–	–	–	–
IFAD	2.0	1.5	1.3	1.8
I.F.C.	–	–	–	–
IMF TRUST FUND	–	–	–	–
U.N. AGENCIES	–	–	–	–
UNDP	6.7	7.5	7.1	7.1
UNTA	1.0	0.9	1.0	1.4
UNICEF	1.2	1.4	2.1	2.9
UNRWA	–	–	–	–
WFP	1.1	–	3.0	3.8
UNHCR	1.9	0.7	0.4	0.4
Other Multilateral	1.0	1.4	1.2	2.0
Arab Agencies	6.4	0.0	0.3	–
TOTAL	60.4	86.5	91.5	130.2
ARAB COUNTRIES	8.3	2.3	-0.6	0.5
E.E.C.+ MEMBERS	113.2	120.9	107.7	114.7
TOTAL	181.5	197.2	194.0	237.8

2. ODA LOANS GROSS

DAC COUNTRIES	1987	1988	1989	1990
Australia	–	–	–	–
Austria	–	–	–	–
Belgium	–	–	–	–
Canada	–	–	–	–
Denmark	–	–	–	–
Finland	–	–	–	–
France	38.0	15.3	12.8	8.7
Germany	–	–	–	–
Ireland	–	–	–	–
Italy	–	–	–	1.2
Japan	–	2.0	1.8	0.7
Netherlands	–	–	–	–
New Zealand	–	–	–	–
Norway	–	–	–	–
Sweden	–	–	–	–
Switzerland	–	–	–	–
United Kingdom	–	–	–	–
United States	–	–	–	–
TOTAL	38.0	17.3	14.6	10.5
MULTILATERAL	40.3	46.2	56.1	91.7
ARAB COUNTRIES	8.8	2.5	–	0.6
E.E.C.+ MEMBERS	38.0	15.3	12.8	9.8
TOTAL	87.2	65.9	70.8	102.9

3. TOTAL OFFICIAL GROSS

DAC COUNTRIES	1987	1988	1989	1990
Australia	–	–	–	–
Austria	0.1	0.1	0.1	0.1
Belgium	0.2	0.1	0.1	0.1
Canada	0.3	0.3	0.5	0.3
Denmark	2.9	7.1	2.8	0.7
Finland	–	–	–	–
France	85.9	69.4	68.9	74.6
Germany	16.1	14.7	13.0	14.7
Ireland	–	–	–	–
Italy	0.4	0.4	1.0	1.6
Japan	1.4	13.5	11.4	8.7
Netherlands	0.4	0.2	0.2	0.3
New Zealand	–	–	–	–
Norway	–	–	–	–
Sweden	–	–	–	–
Switzerland	0.1	0.1	1.3	0.1
United Kingdom	–	0.1	0.1	0.1
United States	4.0	3.0	5.0	10.0
TOTAL	111.9	109.0	104.3	111.3
MULTILATERAL	61.6	88.4	94.2	132.4
ARAB COUNTRIES	9.0	2.6	0.0	0.6
E.E.C.+ MEMBERS	112.4	121.9	108.9	114.9
TOTAL	182.5	200.0	198.6	244.3

4. TOTAL ODA NET

DAC COUNTRIES	1987	1988	1989	1990
Australia	–	–	–	–
Austria	0.1	0.1	0.1	0.1
Belgium	0.2	0.1	0.1	0.1
Canada	0.3	0.3	0.5	0.3
Denmark	1.2	6.7	2.8	0.7
Finland	–	–	–	–
France	84.7	68.3	63.9	71.0
Germany	16.0	14.6	13.0	13.8
Ireland	–	–	–	–
Italy	0.4	0.4	1.0	1.6
Japan	1.4	13.5	11.4	8.7
Netherlands	0.4	0.2	0.2	0.3
New Zealand	–	–	–	–
Norway	–	–	–	–
Sweden	–	–	–	–
Switzerland	0.1	0.1	1.3	0.1
United Kingdom	–	0.1	0.1	0.1
United States	4.0	3.0	5.0	3.0
TOTAL	108.8	107.4	99.3	99.9
MULTILATERAL				
A.F.D.F.	3.2	4.8	31.5	17.1
A.F.D.B.	–	–	–	–
AS.D.B	–	–	–	–
CAR.D.B.	–	–	–	–
E.E.C.	6.4	29.4	22.8	22.8
IBRD	–	–	–	–
IDA	27.9	39.0	22.0	72.0
I.D.B.	–	–	–	–
IFAD	2.0	1.5	1.3	1.8
I.F.C.	–	–	–	–
IMF TRUST FUND	–	–	–	–
U.N. AGENCIES	–	–	–	–
UNDP	6.7	7.5	7.1	7.1
UNTA	1.0	0.9	1.0	1.4
UNICEF	1.2	1.4	2.1	2.9
UNRWA	–	–	–	–
WFP	1.1	–	3.0	3.8
UNHCR	1.9	0.7	0.4	0.4
Other Multilateral	1.0	1.4	1.2	2.0
Arab Agencies	6.4	0.0	0.3	–
TOTAL	58.6	86.5	92.7	131.3
ARAB COUNTRIES	8.3	2.3	-0.6	0.5
E.E.C.+ MEMBERS	109.3	119.8	103.9	110.5
TOTAL	175.7	196.3	191.4	231.7

5. ODA LOANS NET

DAC COUNTRIES	1987	1988	1989	1990
Australia	–	–	–	–
Austria	–	–	–	–
Belgium	–	–	–	–
Canada	–	–	–	–
Denmark	–	–	–	–
Finland	–	–	–	–
France	36.8	14.2	8.4	5.5
Germany	-0.1	-0.1	–	–
Ireland	–	–	–	–
Italy	–	–	–	1.2
Japan	–	2.0	1.8	0.7
Netherlands	–	–	–	–
New Zealand	–	–	–	–
Norway	–	–	–	–
Sweden	–	–	–	–
Switzerland	–	–	–	–
United Kingdom	–	–	–	–
United States	–	–	–	–
TOTAL	36.7	16.1	10.3	7.4
MULTILATERAL	39.3	44.9	54.9	91.0
ARAB COUNTRIES	8.2	2.2	-0.6	0.5
E.E.C.+ MEMBERS	36.7	13.7	8.4	6.7
TOTAL	84.3	63.2	64.5	98.9

6. TOTAL OFFICIAL NET

DAC COUNTRIES	1987	1988	1989	1990
Australia	–	–	–	–
Austria	0.1	0.1	0.1	0.1
Belgium	0.2	0.1	0.1	0.1
Canada	0.3	0.3	0.5	0.3
Denmark	2.9	7.1	2.8	0.7
Finland	–	–	–	–
France	84.6	68.3	63.4	71.0
Germany	15.6	14.6	13.0	14.7
Ireland	–	–	–	–
Italy	0.4	0.4	1.0	0.7
Japan	1.4	13.5	11.4	8.7
Netherlands	0.4	0.2	0.2	0.3
New Zealand	–	–	–	–
Norway	–	–	–	–
Sweden	–	–	–	–
Switzerland	0.1	0.1	1.3	0.1
United Kingdom	–	0.1	0.1	0.1
United States	4.0	3.0	5.0	6.0
TOTAL	110.0	107.8	98.9	102.9
MULTILATERAL	60.4	86.5	91.5	130.2
ARAB COUNTRIES	8.3	2.3	-0.6	0.5
E.E.C.+ MEMBERS	110.5	120.2	103.4	110.4
TOTAL	178.8	196.6	189.7	233.5

7. TOTAL ODA GROSS

	1987
Australia	–
Austria	0.1
Belgium	0.2
Canada	0.3
Denmark	1.2
Finland	–
France	85.9
Germany	16.1
Ireland	–
Italy	0.4
Japan	1.4
Netherlands	0.4
New Zealand	–
Norway	–
Sweden	–
Switzerland	0.1
United Kingdom	–
United States	4.0
TOTAL	110.2
AF.D.F.	3.3
AF.D.B.	–
AS.D.B	–
CAR.D.B.	–
E.E.C.	6.4
IBRD	–
IDA	28.0
I.D.B.	–
IFAD	2.0
I.F.C.	–
IMF TRUST FUND	–
U.N. AGENCIES	–
UNDP	6.7
UNTA	1.0
UNICEF	1.2
UNRWA	–
WFP	1.1
UNHCR	1.9
Other Multilateral	1.0
Arab Agencies	7.1
TOTAL	59.6
ARAB COUNTRIES	9.0
E.E.C.+ MEMBERS	110.6
TOTAL	178.7

8. GRANTS

	1987
Australia	–
Austria	0.1
Belgium	0.2
Canada	0.3
Denmark	1.2
Finland	–
France	47.9
Germany	16.1
Ireland	–
Italy	0.4
Japan	1.4
Netherlands	0.4
New Zealand	–
Norway	–
Sweden	–
Switzerland	0.1
United Kingdom	–
United States	4.0
TOTAL	72.1
MULTILATERAL	19.2
ARAB COUNTRIES	0.1
E.E.C.+ MEMBERS	72.6
TOTAL	91.5

9. TOTAL OOF GROSS

	1987
Australia	–
Austria	–
Belgium	–
Canada	–
Denmark	1.8
Finland	–
France	–
Germany	–
Ireland	–
Italy	–
Japan	–
Netherlands	–
New Zealand	–
Norway	–
Sweden	–
Switzerland	–
United Kingdom	–
United States	–
TOTAL	1.8
MULTILATERAL	2.0
ARAB COUNTRIES	–
E.E.C.+ MEMBERS	1.8
TOTAL	3.8

10. ODA COMMITMENTS

1988	1989	1990	1987	1988	1989	1990
–	–	–	–	–	–	–
0.1	0.1	0.1	0.1	0.1	0.1	0.5
0.1	0.1	0.1	0.0	0.1	0.1	0.1
0.3	0.5	0.3	0.3	0.4	0.4	0.6
6.7	2.8	0.7	–	–	–	1.0
–	–	–	–	–	–	–
69.4	68.3	74.1	74.5	61.1	70.9	82.2
14.7	13.0	13.8	17.5	12.1	11.8	20.5
–	–	–	–	–	–	–
0.4	1.0	1.6	0.5	0.3	1.1	1.8
13.5	11.4	8.7	7.1	20.2	5.3	12.1
0.2	0.2	0.3	0.4	0.2	0.2	0.3
–	–	–	–	–	–	–
–	–	–	–	–	–	–
0.1	1.3	0.1	–	–	–	–
0.1	0.1	0.1	–	0.1	0.1	0.2
3.0	5.0	3.0	2.6	3.7	4.0	4.0
108.6	103.7	103.0	103.1	98.2	93.9	123.3
5.1	31.7	17.5	6.5	1.8	24.2	–
–	–	–	–	–	–	–
–	–	–	–	–	–	–
29.9	22.8	22.8	43.8	45.1	28.9	28.9
–	–	–	–	–	–	–
39.0	22.0	72.0	33.0	53.0	18.0	126.0
–	–	–	–	–	–	–
1.5	1.3	1.8	–	0.2	10.1	0.2
–	–	–	–	–	–	–
–	–	–	–	–	–	–
–	–	–	12.8	11.8	14.8	17.6
7.5	7.1	7.1	–	–	–	–
0.9	1.0	1.4	–	–	–	–
1.4	2.1	2.9	–	–	–	–
–	–	–	–	–	–	–
–	3.0	3.8	–	–	–	–
0.7	0.4	0.4	–	–	–	–
1.4	1.2	2.0	–	–	–	–
0.6	1.4	0.6	–	–	–	–
87.8	93.9	132.3	96.1	111.8	96.0	172.7
2.6	0.0	0.6	2.4	–	6.8	–
121.5	108.3	113.6	136.8	118.9	113.1	135.0
199.0	197.7	236.0	201.7	210.0	196.7	296.0

11. TECH. COOP. GRANTS

1988	1989	1990	1987	1988	1989	1990
–	–	–	–	–	–	–
0.1	0.1	0.1	0.1	0.1	0.1	0.1
0.1	0.1	0.1	0.1	0.1	–	–
0.3	0.5	0.3	–	–	–	–
6.7	2.8	0.7	–	0.1	0.0	0.0
–	–	–	–	–	–	–
54.1	55.5	65.5	27.0	28.4	25.7	31.5
14.7	13.0	13.8	6.1	7.3	5.6	6.9
–	–	–	–	–	–	–
0.4	1.0	0.4	0.4	0.4	0.2	0.4
11.5	9.6	8.0	0.7	0.8	0.8	0.7
0.2	0.2	0.3	0.4	0.2	0.2	0.3
–	–	–	–	–	–	–
–	–	–	–	–	–	–
0.1	1.3	0.1	0.1	0.1	–	–
0.1	0.1	0.1	–	0.1	0.1	0.1
3.0	5.0	3.0	2.0	3.0	5.0	3.0
91.3	89.1	92.5	36.8	40.5	37.6	43.0
41.6	37.8	40.6	12.6	12.7	11.8	13.9
0.1	0.0	–	–	–	–	–
106.2	95.5	103.8	34.8	37.5	31.8	39.2
133.1	126.9	133.1	49.4	53.2	49.4	56.9

12. TOTAL OOF NET

1988	1989	1990	1987	1988	1989	1990
–	–	–	–	–	–	–
–	–	–	–	–	–	–
–	–	–	–	–	–	–
0.4	–	–	1.8	0.4	–	–
–	–	–	–	–	–	–
–	0.6	0.4	-0.1	–	-0.5	0.0
–	–	0.9	-0.4	–	–	0.9
–	–	–	–	–	–	–
–	–	–	–	–	–	-0.9
–	–	–	–	–	–	–
–	–	–	–	–	–	–
–	–	–	–	–	–	–
–	–	–	–	–	–	–
–	–	7.0	–	–	–	3.0
0.4	0.6	8.3	1.2	0.4	-0.5	3.0
0.6	0.3	0.1	1.9	-0.1	-1.2	-1.1
–	–	–	–	–	–	–
0.4	0.6	1.3	1.2	0.4	-0.5	0.0
1.0	0.9	8.4	3.1	0.3	-1.7	1.9

13. ODF COMMITMENTS: BY PURPOSE %

	1987	1988	1989	1990
Education	1	12	–	–
Health	4	–	1	–
Other Social Infrastr.	1	1	1	–
Water Sanitat. Sewage	–	–	–	–
Energy	3	–	30	–
Telecommunications	–	0	–	–
Transportation	19	9	7	–
Agriculture	18	12	0	–
Extractive Industries	0	–	–	–
Manufacturing	9	3	0	–
Trade Banking Tourism	–	–	–	–
Technical Cooperation	42	37	26	–
Multisector Aid	–	0	0	–
Programme	2	25	25	–
Debt Reorganisation	–	–	0	–
Food Aid	1	–	–	–
Emergency Aid	0	–	–	–
Unspecified	–	–	9	–
TOTAL	100	100	100	–

14. GRANT ELEMENT OF ODA %

DAC COUNTRIES

	1987	1988	1989	1990
Australia	–	–	–	–
Austria	100.0	100.0	100.0	–
Belgium	100.0	100.0	100.0	–
Canada	100.0	100.0	100.0	–
Denmark	–	–	–	–
Finland	–	–	–	–
France	85.7	96.5	91.5	–
Germany	100.0	100.0	100.0	–
Ireland	–	–	–	–
Italy	100.0	100.0	100.0	–
Japan	100.0	93.5	100.0	–
Netherlands	100.0	100.0	100.0	–
New Zealand	–	–	–	–
Norway	–	–	–	–
Sweden	–	–	–	–
Switzerland	–	–	–	–
United Kingdom	–	100.0	100.0	–
United States	100.0	100.0	100.0	–
TOTAL	89.9	96.5	93.8	–
MULTILATERAL	95.9	88.8	87.7	–
ARAB COUNTRIES	81.0	–	47.8	–
E.E.C.+ MEMBERS	92.5	98.2	94.3	–
TOTAL	92.3	92.2	89.0	–

15. OTHER AGGREGATES

OFFICIAL COMMITMENTS:

	1987	1988	1989	1990
TOTAL BILATERAL	107.2	99.8	102.5	131.8
of which:				
Arab Countries	2.4	–	6.8	–
C.E.E.C.	–	–	–	–
TOTAL MULTILATERAL	96.1	111.8	96.0	172.7
TOTAL BIL.& MULTIL.	203.3	211.6	198.6	304.5
of which:				
ODA Grants	133.5	144.8	105.8	133.2
ODA Loans	68.2	65.2	90.9	162.8

DISBURSEMENTS:

DAC COUNTRIES COMBINED

OFFICIAL & PRIVATE

	1987	1988	1989	1990
GROSS:				
Contractual Lending	34.5	17.3	14.3	19.2
Export Credits, Total	-5.3	-0.4	-0.9	0.3
Export Credits, Priv.	-5.3	-0.4	-0.9	0.3
NET:				
Contractual Lending	32.6	16.1	8.1	9.7
Export Credits Total	-5.3	-0.4	-1.6	-4.7
PRIVATE SECTOR NET	2.6	0.6	4.3	4.3
Direct Investment	0.5	0.7	0.7	6.3
Portfolio Investment	7.5	0.3	5.3	-1.3
Export Credits	-5.3	-0.4	-1.6	-0.7

MARKET BORROWING:

CHANGE IN CLAIMS

	1987	1988	1989	1990
Banks	1.0	12.0	-7.0	–

MEMORANDUM ITEM:

	1987	1988	1989	1990
C.E.E.C. (Gross)	–	–	–	–

1. TOTAL RECEIPTS NET

DAC COUNTRIES	1987	1988	1989	1990
Australia	0.0	–	–	–
Austria	–	–	–	0.0
Belgium	0.3	0.8	0.4	0.4
Canada	0.8	0.7	0.4	0.3
Denmark	–	–	0.0	–
Finland	0.3	0.2	0.0	0.4
France	74.1	75.2	77.8	126.5
Germany	6.8	12.8	12.3	13.1
Ireland	–	–	–	–
Italy	7.3	25.1	12.3	8.9
Japan	0.1	0.0	0.0	0.0
Netherlands	8.8	2.6	6.6	5.6
New Zealand	–	–	–	–
Norway	0.1	0.0	0.1	0.5
Sweden	0.3	–	0.0	0.1
Switzerland	4.6	8.4	6.6	5.2
United Kingdom	0.3	0.5	0.4	0.3
United States	16.0	20.0	9.0	18.0
TOTAL	119.8	146.3	125.9	179.2
MULTILATERAL				
AF.D.F.	2.2	2.4	23.2	23.9
AF.D.B.	–	–	–	–
AS.D.B	–	–	–	–
CAR.D.B.	–	–	–	–
E.E.C.	36.2	49.8	33.2	33.2
IBRD	–	–	–	–
IDA	12.2	34.0	23.0	44.0
I.D.B.	–	–	–	–
IFAD	–	–	–	–
I.F.C.	–	–	–	–
IMF TRUST FUND	–	–	–	–
U.N. AGENCIES				
UNDP	16.5	15.5	12.6	14.0
UNTA	1.3	0.8	1.3	1.3
UNICEF	2.5	2.6	2.7	4.3
UNRWA	–	–	–	–
WFP	2.9	9.2	12.0	10.5
UNHCR	–	–	–	–
Other Multilateral	3.0	2.7	5.4	3.7
Arab Agencies	1.7	1.3	0.1	–
TOTAL	78.5	118.4	113.4	134.7
ARAB COUNTRIES	0.0	0.0	–	2.3
E.E.C.+ MEMBERS	133.8	166.7	142.9	187.8
TOTAL	198.3	264.7	239.4	316.1

2. ODA LOANS GROSS

DAC COUNTRIES	1987	1988	1989	1990
Australia	–	–	–	–
Austria	–	–	–	–
Belgium	–	–	–	–
Canada	–	–	–	–
Denmark	–	–	–	–
Finland	–	–	–	–
France	24.7	21.2	14.2	22.1
Germany	–	–	1.7	–
Ireland	–	–	–	–
Italy	–	–	–	5.8
Japan	–	–	–	–
Netherlands	–	–	–	–
New Zealand	–	–	–	–
Norway	–	–	–	–
Sweden	–	–	–	–
Switzerland	–	–	–	–
United Kingdom	–	–	–	–
United States	–	–	–	–
TOTAL	24.7	21.2	15.9	27.9
MULTILATERAL	17.3	38.4	49.9	70.6
ARAB COUNTRIES	–	–	–	2.3
E.E.C.+ MEMBERS	25.2	21.9	17.3	29.3
TOTAL	42.0	59.7	65.8	100.8

3. TOTAL OFFICIAL GROSS

DAC COUNTRIES	1987	1988	1989	1990
Australia	0.0	–	–	–
Austria	–	–	–	0.0
Belgium	0.3	0.8	0.4	0.4
Canada	0.8	0.7	0.4	0.3
Denmark	–	–	0.0	–
Finland	0.3	0.2	0.0	0.4
France	74.3	74.9	78.6	127.3
Germany	6.8	13.1	13.9	13.4
Ireland	–	–	–	–
Italy	7.3	25.1	12.4	8.9
Japan	0.1	0.0	0.0	0.0
Netherlands	8.8	2.3	6.7	5.6
New Zealand	–	–	–	–
Norway	0.1	0.0	0.1	0.5
Sweden	0.3	–	0.0	0.1
Switzerland	4.6	8.4	6.6	5.2
United Kingdom	0.3	0.5	0.4	0.3
United States	16.0	20.0	9.0	18.0
TOTAL	120.0	146.0	128.6	180.4
MULTILATERAL	80.5	119.9	115.9	136.1
ARAB COUNTRIES	0.0	0.0	–	2.3
E.E.C.+ MEMBERS	134.8	166.5	145.6	189.1
TOTAL	200.5	265.9	244.5	318.7

4. TOTAL ODA NET

DAC COUNTRIES	1987	1988	1989	1990
Australia	0.0	–	–	–
Austria	–	–	–	0.0
Belgium	0.3	0.8	0.4	0.4
Canada	0.8	0.7	0.4	0.3
Denmark	–	–	–	–
Finland	0.3	0.2	0.0	0.4
France	73.9	74.9	78.1	125.0
Germany	6.8	13.1	13.9	13.4
Ireland	–	–	–	–
Italy	7.3	25.1	12.4	8.9
Japan	0.1	0.0	0.0	0.0
Netherlands	8.8	2.3	6.7	5.6
New Zealand	–	–	–	–
Norway	0.1	0.0	0.1	0.5
Sweden	0.3	–	0.0	0.1
Switzerland	4.6	8.4	6.6	5.2
United Kingdom	0.3	0.5	0.4	0.3
United States	16.0	20.0	9.0	18.0
TOTAL	119.6	146.0	128.1	178.1
AF.D.F.	2.2	2.4	23.2	23.9
AF.D.B.	–	–	–	–
AS.D.B	–	–	–	–
CAR.D.B.	–	–	–	–
E.E.C.	36.2	49.8	33.2	33.2
IBRD	–	–	–	–
IDA	12.2	34.0	23.0	44.0
I.D.B.	–	–	–	–
IFAD	–	–	–	–
I.F.C.	–	–	–	–
IMF TRUST FUND	–	–	–	–
U.N. AGENCIES				
UNDP	16.5	15.5	12.6	14.0
UNTA	1.3	0.8	1.3	1.3
UNICEF	2.5	2.6	2.7	4.3
UNRWA	–	–	–	–
WFP	2.9	9.2	12.0	10.5
UNHCR	–	–	–	–
Other Multilateral	3.0	2.7	5.4	3.7
Arab Agencies	1.7	1.3	0.1	–
TOTAL	78.5	118.4	113.4	134.7
ARAB COUNTRIES	0.0	0.0	–	2.3
E.E.C.+ MEMBERS	133.7	166.4	145.1	186.7
TOTAL	198.2	264.4	241.5	315.0

5. ODA LOANS NET

DAC COUNTRIES	1987	1988	1989	1990
Australia	–	–	–	–
Austria	–	–	–	–
Belgium	–	–	–	–
Canada	–	–	–	–
Denmark	–	–	–	–
Finland	–	–	–	–
France	24.3	21.2	13.7	20.0
Germany	–	–	1.7	–
Ireland	–	–	–	–
Italy	–	–	–	5.8
Japan	–	–	–	–
Netherlands	–	–	–	–
New Zealand	–	–	–	–
Norway	–	–	–	–
Sweden	–	–	–	–
Switzerland	–	–	–	–
United Kingdom	–	–	–	–
United States	–	–	–	–
TOTAL	24.3	21.2	15.4	25.8
MULTILATERAL	15.3	36.9	47.5	68.4
ARAB COUNTRIES	–	–	–	2.3
E.E.C.+ MEMBERS	24.1	21.9	16.7	27.1
TOTAL	39.6	58.1	62.8	96.4

6. TOTAL OFFICIAL NET

DAC COUNTRIES	1987	1988	1989	1990
Australia	0.0	–	–	–
Austria	–	–	–	0.0
Belgium	0.3	0.8	0.4	0.4
Canada	0.8	0.7	0.4	0.3
Denmark	–	–	0.0	–
Finland	0.3	0.2	0.0	0.4
France	73.9	74.9	78.1	125.0
Germany	6.6	12.9	13.4	13.3
Ireland	–	–	–	–
Italy	7.3	25.1	12.4	8.9
Japan	0.1	0.0	0.0	0.0
Netherlands	8.8	2.3	6.7	5.6
New Zealand	–	–	–	–
Norway	0.1	0.0	0.1	0.5
Sweden	0.3	–	0.0	0.1
Switzerland	4.6	8.4	6.6	5.2
United Kingdom	0.3	0.5	0.4	0.3
United States	16.0	20.0	9.0	18.0
TOTAL	119.4	145.7	127.6	177.9
MULTILATERAL	78.5	118.4	113.4	134.7
ARAB COUNTRIES	0.0	0.0	–	2.3
E.E.C.+ MEMBERS	133.4	166.1	144.6	186.6
TOTAL	197.9	264.1	241.0	314.9

7. TOTAL ODA GROSS

	1987
Australia	0.0
Austria	–
Belgium	0.3
Canada	0.8
Denmark	–
Finland	0.3
France	74.3
Germany	6.8
Ireland	–
Italy	7.3
Japan	0.1
Netherlands	8.8
New Zealand	–
Norway	0.1
Sweden	0.3
Switzerland	4.6
United Kingdom	0.3
United States	16.0
TOTAL	120.0
AF.D.F.	2.4
AF.D.B.	–
AS.D.B	–
CAR.D.B.	–
E.E.C.	37.0
IBRD	–
IDA	13.0
I.D.B.	–
IFAD	–
I.F.C.	–
IMF TRUST FUND	–
U.N. AGENCIES	–
UNDP	16.5
UNTA	1.3
UNICEF	2.5
UNRWA	–
WFP	2.9
UNHCR	–
Other Multilateral	3.0
Arab Agencies	1.9
TOTAL	80.5
ARAB COUNTRIES	0.0
E.E.C.+ MEMBERS	134.8
TOTAL	200.5

8. GRANTS

	1987
Australia	0.0
Austria	–
Belgium	0.3
Canada	0.8
Denmark	–
Finland	0.3
France	49.6
Germany	6.8
Ireland	–
Italy	7.3
Japan	0.1
Netherlands	8.8
New Zealand	–
Norway	0.1
Sweden	0.3
Switzerland	4.6
United Kingdom	0.3
United States	16.0
TOTAL	95.3
MULTILATERAL	63.2
ARAB COUNTRIES	0.0
E.E.C.+ MEMBERS	109.6
TOTAL	158.5

9. TOTAL OOF GROSS

	1987
Australia	–
Austria	–
Belgium	–
Canada	–
Denmark	–
Finland	–
France	–
Germany	–
Ireland	–
Italy	–
Japan	–
Netherlands	–
New Zealand	–
Norway	–
Sweden	–
Switzerland	–
United Kingdom	–
United States	–
TOTAL	–
MULTILATERAL	–
ARAB COUNTRIES	–
E.E.C.+ MEMBERS	–
TOTAL	–

1988	1989	1990		1987	1988	1989	1990

10. ODA COMMITMENTS

1988	1989	1990	1987	1988	1989	1990
–	–	–	0.0	–	–	–
–	–	0.0	–	–	–	0.0
0.8	0.4	0.4	0.6	1.9	0.4	0.4
0.7	0.4	0.3	0.9	0.7	0.2	0.4
–	–	–	–	–	–	–
0.2	0.0	0.4	–	–	–	0.0
74.9	78.6	127.1	72.3	67.8	105.8	117.5
13.1	13.9	13.4	15.1	27.2	29.2	15.6
–	–	–	–	–	–	–
25.1	12.4	8.9	34.8	6.4	7.4	8.9
0.0	0.0	0.0	0.1	0.0	0.0	0.0
2.3	6.7	5.6	7.3	3.2	7.2	7.4
–	–	–	–	–	–	–
0.0	0.1	0.5	–	–	–	–
–	0.0	0.1	0.3	–	0.0	–
8.4	6.6	5.2	8.9	5.1	5.7	14.3
0.5	0.4	0.3	0.3	0.5	0.4	0.3
20.0	9.0	18.0	12.9	18.3	18.1	11.9
146.0	*128.6*	*180.2*	*153.3*	*131.1*	*174.3*	*176.6*
2.7	23.5	24.2	42.7	–	51.3	13.8
–	–	–	–	–	–	–
–	–	–	–	–	–	–
–	–	–	–	–	–	–
49.9	33.2	33.2	79.9	30.7	64.1	64.1
–	–	–	–	–	–	–
35.0	25.0	45.0	17.4	117.0	60.0	24.0
–	–	–	–	–	–	–
–	–	–	–	–	–	0.3
–	–	–	–	–	–	–
–	–	–	–	–	–	–
–	–	–	26.3	30.9	33.9	33.7
15.5	12.6	14.0	–	–	–	–
0.8	1.3	1.3	–	–	–	–
2.6	2.7	4.3	–	–	–	–
–	–	–	–	–	–	–
9.2	12.0	10.5	–	–	–	–
–	–	–	–	–	–	–
2.7	5.4	3.7	–	–	–	–
1.5	0.3	–	11.8	–	9.3	12.0
119.9	*115.9*	*136.1*	*178.0*	*178.5*	*218.6*	*147.8*
0.0	–	*2.3*	–	*0.0*	*4.5*	–
166.5	*145.6*	*188.9*	*210.2*	*137.6*	*214.3*	*214.1*
265.9	*244.4*	*318.5*	*331.3*	*309.7*	*397.5*	*324.4*

11. TECH. COOP. GRANTS

1988	1989	1990	1987	1988	1989	1990
–	–	–	–	–	–	–
–	–	0.0	–	–	–	–
0.8	0.4	0.4	0.2	0.0	–	–
0.7	0.4	0.3	–	0.1	0.0	0.0
–	–	–	–	–	–	–
0.2	0.0	0.4	–	–	–	–
53.6	64.5	105.1	12.3	12.8	14.7	18.9
13.1	12.2	13.4	3.1	4.9	4.8	7.3
–	–	–	–	–	–	–
25.1	12.4	3.1	1.2	1.1	1.4	1.2
0.0	0.0	0.0	0.1	0.0	0.0	0.0
2.3	6.7	5.6	2.1	1.2	1.7	2.1
–	–	–	–	–	–	–
0.0	0.1	0.5	–	–	–	–
–	0.0	0.1	–	–	–	–
8.4	6.6	5.2	2.3	1.4	–	–
0.5	0.4	0.3	0.2	0.2	0.2	0.2
20.0	9.0	18.0	6.0	10.0	7.0	8.0
124.7	*112.7*	*152.3*	*27.4*	*31.7*	*29.8*	*37.8*
81.5	*66.0*	*65.5*	*24.6*	*23.1*	*21.9*	*23.2*
0.0	–	–	–	–	–	–
144.5	*128.3*	*159.6*	*20.3*	*21.7*	*22.7*	*29.7*
206.3	*178.7*	*217.7*	*52.0*	*54.8*	*51.7*	*61.0*

12. TOTAL OOF NET

1988	1989	1990	1987	1988	1989	1990
–	–	–	–	–	–	–
–	–	–	–	–	–	–
–	–	–	–	–	–	–
–	0.0	–	–	–	0.0	–
–	–	0.2	–	–	–	0.0
–	–	–	-0.2	-0.2	-0.5	-0.1
–	–	–	–	–	–	–
–	–	–	–	–	–	–
–	–	–	–	–	–	–
–	–	–	–	–	–	–
–	–	–	–	–	–	–
–	–	–	–	–	–	–
–	–	–	–	–	–	–
–	0.0	0.2	-0.2	-0.2	-0.5	-0.1
–	–	–	–	–	–	–
–	–	–	–	–	–	–
–	0.0	0.2	-0.2	-0.2	-0.5	-0.1
–	*0.0*	*0.2*	*-0.2*	*-0.2*	*-0.5*	*-0.1*

13. ODF COMMITMENTS: BY PURPOSE %

	1987	1988	1989	1990
Education	3	8	9	–
Health	4	1	3	–
Other Social Infrastr.	14	8	4	–
Water Sanitat. Sewage	0	1	6	–
Energy	0	2	–	–
Telecommunications	11	1	3	–
Transportation	3	25	27	–
Agriculture	21	11	15	–
Extractive Industries	–	0	–	–
Manufacturing	–	3	0	–
Trade Banking Tourism	4	9	0	–
Technical Cooperation	27	21	18	–
Multisector Aid	11	0	1	–
Programme	1	8	13	–
Debt Reorganisation	–	–	–	–
Food Aid	1	1	0	–
Emergency Aid	1	0	–	–
Unspecified	0	1	0	–
TOTAL	100	100	100	–

14. GRANT ELEMENT OF ODA %

DAC COUNTRIES

	1987	1988	1989	1990
Australia	100.0	–	–	–
Austria	–	–	–	–
Belgium	100.0	100.0	100.0	–
Canada	100.0	100.0	100.0	–
Denmark	–	–	–	–
Finland	–	–	100.0	–
France	88.3	92.9	89.2	–
Germany	100.0	100.0	100.0	–
Ireland	–	–	–	–
Italy	100.0	100.0	100.0	–
Japan	100.0	100.0	100.0	–
Netherlands	100.0	100.0	100.0	–
New Zealand	–	–	–	–
Norway	–	–	–	–
Sweden	100.0	–	100.0	–
Switzerland	100.0	100.0	100.0	–
United Kingdom	100.0	100.0	100.0	–
United States	100.0	100.0	100.0	–
TOTAL	*94.5*	*96.3*	*93.5*	–
MULTILATERAL	*91.6*	*86.3*	*87.9*	–
ARAB COUNTRIES	–	*100.0*	*80.9*	–
E.E.C.+ MEMBERS	*96.0*	*96.4*	*94.5*	–
TOTAL	*92.9*	*90.0*	*90.2*	–

15. OTHER AGGREGATES

OFFICIAL COMMITMENTS:

	1987	1988	1989	1990
TOTAL BILATERAL	153.3	132.7	182.8	205.4
of which:				
Arab Countries	–	0.0	4.5	–
C.E.E.C.	–	–	–	–
TOTAL MULTILATERAL	178.0	178.5	218.6	147.8
TOTAL BIL.& MULTIL.	331.3	311.2	401.4	353.2
of which:				
ODA Grants	239.8	177.6	237.3	239.1
ODA Loans	91.5	132.1	160.2	85.3

DISBURSEMENTS:

DAC COUNTRIES COMBINED

	1987	1988	1989	1990
OFFICIAL & PRIVATE				
GROSS:				
Contractual Lending	23.9	21.0	16.4	28.4
Export Credits, Total	-0.8	-0.2	0.5	0.4
Export Credits, Priv.	-0.8	-0.2	0.5	0.4
NET:				
Contractual Lending	23.0	20.5	15.1	25.7
Export Credits Total	-1.1	-0.5	0.2	0.1
PRIVATE SECTOR NET	0.4	0.6	-1.7	1.3
Direct Investment	0.8	0.3	-1.7	–
Portfolio Investment	0.7	0.8	-0.1	1.2
Export Credits	-1.1	-0.5	0.2	0.1

MARKET BORROWING:

CHANGE IN CLAIMS

	1987	1988	1989	1990
Banks	3.0	8.0	-2.0	3.0

MEMORANDUM ITEM:

	1987	1988	1989	1990
C.E.E.C. (Gross)	–	–	–	–

DISBURSEMENTS, UNLESS OTHERWISE STATED

	1987	1988	1989	1990

1. TOTAL RECEIPTS NET

DAC COUNTRIES

	1987	1988	1989	1990
Australia	-0.1	0.0	0.0	0.0
Austria	-2.0	-2.0	-1.7	0.6
Belgium	-53.1	32.4	-56.9	-27.5
Canada	14.1	14.1	2.7	70.6
Denmark	-0.7	-0.3	-0.1	4.9
Finland	4.0	0.6	0.6	10.1
France	-163.2	-5.1	10.6	41.2
Germany	26.4	-1.7	54.6	154.1
Ireland	–	–	–	0.0
Italy	1.3	6.5	37.6	5.7
Japan	153.5	255.4	-100.7	335.0
Netherlands	17.6	8.6	16.0	62.8
New Zealand	–	0.0	0.0	0.0
Norway	1.2	2.8	2.5	6.2
Sweden	2.5	0.0	5.5	33.1
Switzerland	1.7	1.8	2.4	1.7
United Kingdom	68.1	114.7	60.7	5.8
United States	-929.0	-312.0	-332.0	-229.0
TOTAL	*-858.1*	*115.7*	*-298.3*	*475.3*

MULTILATERAL

	1987	1988	1989	1990
AF.D.F.	–	–	–	–
AF.D.B.	–	–	–	–
AS.D.B	–	–	–	–
CAR.D.B.	–	–	–	–
E.E.C.	2.3	1.7	12.7	12.7
IBRD	270.6	211.0	98.0	132.0
IDA	-0.7	-1.0	-1.0	-1.0
I.D.B.	148.2	188.7	155.0	171.3
IFAD	–	–	–	–
I.F.C.	51.0	4.0	10.6	167.0
IMF TRUST FUND	–	–	–	–
U.N. AGENCIES	–	–	–	–
UNDP	2.6	3.2	3.8	9.0
UNTA	1.1	0.8	1.4	1.4
UNICEF	0.2	0.4	0.5	0.5
UNRWA	–	–	–	–
WFP	–	–	–	–
UNHCR	–	–	–	0.0
Other Multilateral	0.1	0.4	0.5	0.4
Arab Agencies	–	–	–	–
TOTAL	*475.4*	*409.2*	*281.5*	*493.2*
ARAB COUNTRIES	*5.0*	*–*	*–*	*–*
E.E.C.+ MEMBERS	*-101.4*	*156.8*	*135.1*	*259.7*
TOTAL	*-377.7*	*524.9*	*-16.8*	*968.6*

2. ODA LOANS GROSS

DAC COUNTRIES

	1987	1988	1989	1990
Australia	–	–	–	–
Austria	–	–	–	–
Belgium	–	–	–	–
Canada	–	–	–	–
Denmark	–	–	–	–
Finland	–	–	–	4.8
France	0.9	0.9	0.4	–
Germany	–	–	–	–
Ireland	–	–	–	–
Italy	–	–	–	–
Japan	–	2.0	12.2	–
Netherlands	–	–	–	–
New Zealand	–	–	–	–
Norway	–	–	–	–
Sweden	–	–	–	–
Switzerland	–	–	–	–
United Kingdom	–	–	–	–
United States	–	–	–	–
TOTAL	*0.9*	*2.9*	*12.5*	*4.8*
MULTILATERAL	*–*	*–*	*–*	*–*
ARAB COUNTRIES	*–*	*–*	*–*	*–*
E.E.C.+ MEMBERS	*0.9*	*0.9*	*0.4*	*–*
TOTAL	*0.9*	*2.9*	*12.5*	*4.8*

3. TOTAL OFFICIAL GROSS

DAC COUNTRIES

	1987	1988	1989	1990
Australia	0.0	0.0	0.0	0.0
Austria	0.1	0.1	0.3	0.6
Belgium	1.8	1.8	1.8	3.2
Canada	16.7	20.7	11.7	63.1
Denmark	0.1	0.0	0.2	5.0
Finland	0.1	0.1	0.3	5.6
France	14.4	19.1	8.0	6.7
Germany	26.6	31.2	84.2	68.6
Ireland	–	–	–	0.0
Italy	3.4	10.7	19.8	10.5
Japan	10.7	233.3	66.2	143.6
Netherlands	7.7	9.2	9.5	14.5
New Zealand	–	0.0	0.0	0.0
Norway	0.4	0.9	2.5	6.1
Sweden	–	–	0.0	8.9
Switzerland	1.7	1.8	2.4	1.7
United Kingdom	0.4	0.5	0.4	0.7
United States	67.0	42.0	–	17.0
TOTAL	*151.1*	*371.5*	*207.2*	*355.8*
MULTILATERAL	*575.0*	*536.0*	*559.6*	*764.8*
ARAB COUNTRIES	*5.0*	*–*	*–*	*–*
E.E.C.+ MEMBERS	*56.7*	*74.2*	*136.5*	*121.9*
TOTAL	*731.1*	*907.5*	*766.8*	*1120.6*

4. TOTAL ODA NET

DAC COUNTRIES

	1987	1988	1989	1990
Australia	0.0	0.0	0.0	0.0
Austria	0.1	0.1	0.3	0.6
Belgium	1.8	1.8	1.8	3.2
Canada	2.6	3.2	4.2	3.3
Denmark	0.1	0.0	0.2	5.0
Finland	0.1	0.1	0.3	5.6
France	4.1	4.1	3.4	6.2
Germany	26.1	18.2	16.8	20.4
Ireland	–	–	–	0.0
Italy	3.4	10.7	19.8	10.5
Japan	9.7	15.0	18.3	18.7
Netherlands	7.0	8.6	8.9	14.1
New Zealand	–	0.0	0.0	0.0
Norway	0.4	0.9	2.5	6.1
Sweden	0.0	0.0	–	8.9
Switzerland	1.7	1.8	2.4	1.7
United Kingdom	0.4	0.5	0.4	0.7
United States	-34.0	-19.0	-29.0	-28.0
TOTAL	*23.4*	*46.1*	*50.3*	*76.9*

MULTILATERAL

	1987	1988	1989	1990
AF.D.F.	–	–	–	–
AF.D.B.	–	–	–	–
AS.D.B	–	–	–	–
CAR.D.B.	–	–	–	–
E.E.C.	2.3	1.7	12.7	12.7
IBRD	–	–	–	–
IDA	-0.7	-1.0	-1.0	-1.0
I.D.B.	-7.6	-7.6	-7.0	-5.6
IFAD	–	–	–	–
I.F.C.	–	–	–	–
IMF TRUST FUND	–	–	–	–
U.N. AGENCIES	–	–	–	–
UNDP	2.6	3.2	3.8	9.0
UNTA	1.1	0.8	1.4	1.4
UNICEF	0.2	0.4	0.5	0.5
UNRWA	–	–	–	–
WFP	–	–	–	–
UNHCR	–	–	–	0.0
Other Multilateral	0.1	0.4	0.5	0.4
Arab Agencies	–	–	–	–
TOTAL	*-2.0*	*-2.1*	*10.8*	*17.4*
ARAB COUNTRIES	*–*	*–*	*–*	*–*
E.E.C.+ MEMBERS	*45.3*	*45.6*	*64.0*	*72.7*
TOTAL	*21.4*	*44.0*	*61.0*	*94.2*

5. ODA LOANS NET

DAC COUNTRIES

	1987	1988	1989	1990
Australia	–	–	–	–
Austria	–	–	–	–
Belgium	–	–	–	–
Canada	-0.2	-0.2	-0.2	-0.2
Denmark	–	–	–	–
Finland	–	–	–	4.8
France	-0.3	0.0	-0.5	-0.5
Germany	-0.1	-0.1	-2.2	-2.8
Ireland	–	–	–	–
Italy	–	–	–	–
Japan	-1.0	-1.0	10.8	-0.9
Netherlands	-0.7	-0.6	-0.6	-0.4
New Zealand	–	–	–	–
Norway	–	–	–	–
Sweden	0.0	0.0	0.0	–
Switzerland	–	–	–	–
United Kingdom	–	–	–	–
United States	-37.0	-23.0	-29.0	-29.0
TOTAL	*-39.4*	*-25.1*	*-21.8*	*-29.1*
MULTILATERAL	*-8.3*	*-8.6*	*-8.0*	*-6.6*
ARAB COUNTRIES	*–*	*–*	*–*	*–*
E.E.C.+ MEMBERS	*-1.1*	*-0.8*	*-3.3*	*-3.7*
TOTAL	*-47.7*	*-33.7*	*-29.8*	*-35.7*

6. TOTAL OFFICIAL NET

DAC COUNTRIES

	1987	1988	1989	1990
Australia	-0.1	0.0	0.0	0.0
Austria	0.1	0.1	0.3	0.6
Belgium	1.8	1.8	1.8	3.2
Canada	12.6	14.5	3.1	54.3
Denmark	0.1	0.0	0.2	5.0
Finland	0.1	0.1	0.3	5.6
France	13.2	18.1	2.7	2.1
Germany	26.4	30.6	81.3	61.4
Ireland	–	–	–	0.0
Italy	3.4	10.2	19.8	10.5
Japan	9.7	230.3	64.8	142.7
Netherlands	7.0	8.6	8.9	14.1
New Zealand	–	0.0	0.0	0.0
Norway	0.4	0.9	2.5	6.1
Sweden	0.0	0.0	–	8.9
Switzerland	1.7	1.8	2.4	1.7
United Kingdom	0.4	0.5	0.4	0.7
United States	25.0	11.0	-46.0	-32.0
TOTAL	*101.6*	*328.6*	*142.4*	*284.7*
MULTILATERAL	*475.4*	*409.2*	*281.5*	*493.2*
ARAB COUNTRIES	*5.0*	*–*	*–*	*–*
E.E.C.+ MEMBERS	*54.6*	*71.5*	*127.7*	*109.6*
TOTAL	*582.0*	*737.8*	*423.8*	*777.9*

7. TOTAL ODA GROSS

	1987
Australia	0.0
Austria	0.1
Belgium	1.8
Canada	2.8
Denmark	0.1
Finland	0.1
France	5.3
Germany	26.3
Ireland	–
Italy	3.4
Japan	10.7
Netherlands	7.7
New Zealand	–
Norway	0.4
Sweden	–
Switzerland	1.7
United Kingdom	0.4
United States	3.0
TOTAL	*63.7*

	1987
AF.D.F.	–
AF.D.B.	–
AS.D.B	–
CAR.D.B.	–
E.E.C.	2.3
IBRD	–
IDA	–
I.D.B.	0.0
IFAD	–
I.F.C.	–
IMF TRUST FUND	–
U.N. AGENCIES	–
UNDP	2.6
UNTA	1.1
UNICEF	0.2
UNRWA	–
WFP	–
UNHCR	–
Other Multilateral	0.1
Arab Agencies	–
TOTAL	*6.3*
ARAB COUNTRIES	*–*
E.E.C.+ MEMBERS	*47.3*
TOTAL	*70.0*

8. GRANTS

	1987
Australia	0.0
Austria	0.1
Belgium	1.8
Canada	2.8
Denmark	0.1
Finland	0.1
France	4.4
Germany	26.3
Ireland	–
Italy	3.4
Japan	10.7
Netherlands	7.7
New Zealand	–
Norway	0.4
Sweden	–
Switzerland	1.7
United Kingdom	0.4
United States	3.0
TOTAL	*62.8*
MULTILATERAL	*6.3*
ARAB COUNTRIES	*–*
E.E.C.+ MEMBERS	*46.4*
TOTAL	*69.1*

9. TOTAL OOF GROSS

	1987
Australia	–
Austria	–
Belgium	–
Canada	13.9
Denmark	–
Finland	–
France	9.1
Germany	0.3
Ireland	–
Italy	–
Japan	–
Netherlands	–
New Zealand	–
Norway	–
Sweden	–
Switzerland	–
United Kingdom	–
United States	64.0
TOTAL	*87.4*
MULTILATERAL	*568.8*
ARAB COUNTRIES	*5.0*
E.E.C.+ MEMBERS	*9.4*
TOTAL	*661.1*

10. ODA COMMITMENTS

1988	1989	1990	1987	1988	1989	1990
0.0	0.0	0.0	0.0	0.0	0.0	0.0
0.1	0.3	0.6	0.1	0.1	0.4	0.6
1.8	1.8	3.2	1.0	2.7	1.8	3.2
3.4	4.4	3.5	3.2	3.4	5.2	2.1
0.0	0.2	5.0	0.5	–	–	10.4
0.1	0.3	5.6	–	–	0.3	5.9
5.1	4.3	6.7	6.2	4.2	4.0	14.4
18.3	19.0	23.2	28.9	21.7	18.8	37.5
–	–	0.0	–	–	–	0.0
10.7	19.8	10.5	3.9	13.5	21.1	15.8
18.0	19.6	19.6	17.5	12.0	29.2	13.4
9.2	9.5	14.5	6.6	10.3	9.3	15.0
0.0	0.0	0.0	0.0	0.0	–	–
0.9	2.5	6.1	0.4	–	–	–
–	0.0	8.9	–	–	0.0	0.0
1.8	2.4	1.7	2.3	1.7	1.6	31.7
0.5	0.4	0.7	0.4	0.5	0.4	0.7
4.0	–	1.0	1.8	7.1	1.6	1.0
74.1	*84.6*	*110.7*	*72.9*	*77.2*	*93.8*	*151.8*
–	–	–	–	–	–	–
–	–	–	–	–	–	–
–	–	–	–	–	–	–
1.7	12.7	12.7	3.5	2.2	16.0	16.0
–	–	–	–	–	–	–
–	–	–	–	–	–	–
–	–	–	–	–	–	–
–	–	–	–	–	–	–
–	–	–	3.9	4.8	6.2	11.3
3.2	3.8	9.0	–	–	–	–
0.8	1.4	1.4	–	–	–	–
0.4	0.5	0.5	–	–	–	–
–	–	–	–	–	–	–
–	–	0.0	–	–	–	–
0.4	0.5	0.4	–	–	–	–
–	–	–	–	–	–	–
6.5	*18.8*	*24.0*	*7.5*	*7.0*	*22.2*	*27.4*
–	–	–	–	–	–	–
47.3	*67.7*	*76.5*	*51.0*	*55.1*	*71.5*	*113.1*
80.6	*103.4*	*134.7*	*80.3*	*84.3*	*116.0*	*179.2*

11. TECH. COOP. GRANTS

1988	1989	1990	1987	1988	1989	1990
0.0	0.0	0.0	–	–	–	–
0.1	0.3	0.6	0.1	0.1	0.1	0.2
1.8	1.8	3.2	0.6	0.3	0.1	0.1
3.4	4.4	3.5	–	–	–	0.0
0.0	0.2	5.0	–	0.0	–	0.5
0.1	0.3	0.8	–	0.1	–	0.0
4.2	4.0	6.7	4.4	4.2	4.0	6.0
18.3	19.0	23.2	26.1	18.3	14.8	17.2
–	–	0.0	–	–	–	0.0
10.7	19.8	10.5	3.0	8.1	11.1	6.2
16.0	7.5	19.6	6.7	8.9	7.5	13.0
9.2	9.5	14.5	5.1	5.9	5.8	13.8
0.0	0.0	0.0	–	0.0	–	0.0
0.9	2.5	6.1	0.1	0.1	0.5	0.3
–	0.0	8.9	–	–	–	0.7
1.8	2.4	1.7	0.1	0.1	–	–
0.5	0.4	0.7	0.4	0.5	0.4	0.6
4.0	–	1.0	–	–	–	1.0
71.2	*72.0*	*105.9*	*46.5*	*46.5*	*44.2*	*59.6*
6.5	18.8	24.0	4.4	5.5	6.2	11.3
–	–	–	–	–	–	–
46.5	67.4	76.5	40.1	38.0	36.2	44.5
77.7	*90.9*	*129.9*	*50.9*	*52.0*	*50.4*	*70.9*

12. TOTAL OOF NET

1988	1989	1990	1987	1988	1989	1990
–	–	–	-0.2	–	-0.1	–
–	–	–	–	–	–	–
–	–	–	–	–	–	–
17.3	7.3	59.7	10.0	11.4	-1.0	51.0
–	–	–	–	–	–	–
14.0	3.7	–	9.1	14.0	-0.8	-4.1
12.9	65.2	45.4	0.3	12.4	64.4	41.0
–	–	–	–	–	–	–
–	–	–	–	-0.5	–	–
215.3	46.5	124.0	–	215.3	46.5	124.0
–	–	–	–	–	–	–
–	–	–	–	–	–	–
–	–	–	–	–	–	–
–	–	–	–	–	–	–
38.0	–	16.0	59.0	30.0	-17.0	-4.0
297.5	*122.6*	*245.1*	*78.2*	*282.6*	*92.1*	*207.9*
529.5	*540.8*	*740.8*	*477.4*	*411.3*	*270.7*	*475.8*
–	–	–	*5.0*	–	–	–
26.8	*68.8*	*45.4*	*9.3*	*25.9*	*63.7*	*36.9*
827.0	*663.4*	*985.9*	*560.6*	*693.8*	*362.8*	*683.7*

13. ODF COMMITMENTS: BY PURPOSE %

	1987	1988	1989	1990
Education	0	0	1	–
Health	0	1	0	–
Other Social Infrastr.	5	0	27	–
Water Sanitat. Sewage	0	8	1	–
Energy	55	21	–	–
Telecommunications	–	–	0	–
Transportation	–	–	50	–
Agriculture	1	0	3	–
Extractive Industries	–	30	–	–
Manufacturing	–	–	0	–
Trade Banking Tourism	–	–	10	–
Technical Cooperation	7	8	7	–
Multisector Aid	0	–	1	–
Programme	31	31	–	–
Debt Reorganisation	0	–	–	–
Food Aid	0	1	0	–
Emergency Aid	0	0	0	–
Unspecified	–	–	–	–
TOTAL	100	100	100	–

14. GRANT ELEMENT OF ODA %

DAC COUNTRIES

	1987	1988	1989	1990
Australia	100.0	100.0	100.0	–
Austria	100.0	100.0	100.0	–
Belgium	100.0	100.0	100.0	–
Canada	100.0	100.0	100.0	–
Denmark	100.0	–	–	–
Finland	–	–	100.0	–
France	100.0	100.0	100.0	–
Germany	100.0	100.0	100.0	–
Ireland	–	–	–	–
Italy	100.0	100.0	100.0	–
Japan	100.0	100.0	76.5	–
Netherlands	100.0	100.0	100.0	–
New Zealand	100.0	100.0	–	–
Norway	100.0	–	–	–
Sweden	–	–	100.0	–
Switzerland	100.0	100.0	100.0	–
United Kingdom	100.0	100.0	100.0	–
United States	100.0	100.0	100.0	–
TOTAL	*100.0*	*100.0*	*92.7*	–
MULTILATERAL	*100.0*	*100.0*	*100.0*	–
ARAB COUNTRIES	–	–	–	–
E.E.C.+ MEMBERS	*100.0*	*100.0*	*100.0*	–
TOTAL	*100.0*	*100.0*	*94.1*	–

15. OTHER AGGREGATES

OFFICIAL COMMITMENTS:

	1987	1988	1989	1990
TOTAL BILATERAL	206.4	621.8	325.8	289.1
of which:				
Arab Countries	–	–	–	–
C.E.E.C.				
TOTAL MULTILATERAL	386.4	228.7	1520.5	420.3
TOTAL BIL.& MULTIL.	592.7	850.5	1846.3	709.4
of which:				
ODA Grants	78.5	82.3	103.8	174.2
ODA Loans	1.8	2.0	12.2	5.0

DISBURSEMENTS:

DAC COUNTRIES COMBINED

OFFICIAL & PRIVATE	1987	1988	1989	1990
GROSS:				
Contractual Lending	140.5	414.6	320.5	498.0
Export Credits, Total	66.5	146.3	257.7	356.9
Export Credits, Priv.	52.6	116.4	186.1	248.6
NET:				
Contractual Lending	-25.1	290.3	131.0	326.7
Export Credits Total	-55.8	50.1	107.2	223.6
PRIVATE SECTOR NET	-959.7	-212.9	-440.7	190.6
Direct Investment	69.7	461.9	425.7	411.0
Portfolio Investment	-965.7	-709.9	-927.8	-368.7
Export Credits	-63.6	35.1	61.5	148.3

MARKET BORROWING:

CHANGE IN CLAIMS

	1987	1988	1989	1990
Banks	-1600.0	-1790.0	-1772.0	-616.0

MEMORANDUM ITEM:

	1987	1988	1989	1990
C.E.E.C. (Gross)	–	0.6	0.5	–

1. TOTAL RECEIPTS NET

DAC COUNTRIES	1987	1988	1989	1990
Australia	15.7	9.5	35.2	66.7
Austria	2.4	18.7	50.2	183.0
Belgium	16.5	-0.4	2.7	3.9
Canada	149.2	93.9	69.9	266.8
Denmark	25.6	18.1	1.5	-9.2
Finland	6.1	35.4	34.3	16.1
France	185.4	473.3	712.5	672.7
Germany	217.0	344.3	350.0	376.3
Ireland	0.1	0.0	0.0	–
Italy	73.3	131.2	103.7	69.7
Japan	2438.4	2455.5	2401.5	1368.1
Netherlands	18.4	36.8	75.3	66.5
New Zealand	0.2	0.2	0.4	1.1
Norway	12.4	10.9	10.4	19.2
Sweden	8.3	21.5	103.0	74.6
Switzerland	5.6	11.3	7.9	8.4
United Kingdom	152.1	365.3	345.3	628.2
United States	234.0	-93.0	120.0	-82.0
TOTAL	3560.5	3932.4	4423.8	3729.9
MULTILATERAL				
AF.D.F.	–	–	–	–
AF.D.B.	–	–	–	–
AS.D.B	-4.6	5.7	55.6	55.0
CAR.D.B.	–	–	–	–
E.E.C.	6.7	45.8	41.2	41.2
IBRD	206.1	514.0	542.0	375.0
IDA	393.6	552.0	505.0	505.0
I.D.B.	–	–	–	–
IFAD	33.0	10.7	6.7	17.5
I.F.C.	3.0	25.0	10.6	–
IMF TRUST FUND	–	–	–	–
U.N. AGENCIES	–	–	–	–
UNDP	27.7	31.2	30.6	48.5
UNTA	5.4	2.6	5.5	6.6
UNICEF	17.0	14.5	16.7	14.6
UNRWA	–	–	–	–
WFP	86.5	101.5	23.9	8.7
UNHCR	4.6	4.0	4.1	4.1
Other Multilateral	13.3	17.4	18.9	11.8
Arab Agencies	–	1.3	–	–
TOTAL	792.1	1325.7	1260.9	1088.0
ARAB COUNTRIES	10.8	8.8	2.3	–
E.E.C.+ MEMBERS	695.0	1414.3	1632.3	1849.2
TOTAL	4363.4	5266.9	5687.1	4817.9

2. ODA LOANS GROSS

DAC COUNTRIES	1987	1988	1989	1990
Australia	–	–	–	–
Austria	1.4	16.5	48.8	100.2
Belgium	21.6	10.9	–	–
Canada	–	3.9	5.6	34.8
Denmark	20.6	15.4	4.4	1.5
Finland	1.5	0.4	–	8.7
France	35.7	123.2	169.2	71.1
Germany	1.4	14.4	82.0	187.1
Ireland	–	–	–	–
Italy	72.1	86.2	111.0	36.2
Japan	422.8	519.9	669.2	538.5
Netherlands	1.3	33.6	37.6	15.7
New Zealand	–	–	–	–
Norway	–	–	–	–
Sweden	–	–	–	–
Switzerland	5.3	10.5	6.4	2.8
United Kingdom	–	–	–	–
United States	–	–	–	–
TOTAL	583.7	835.1	1134.1	996.5
MULTILATERAL	426.5	562.7	511.7	522.5
ARAB COUNTRIES	18.8	19.0	22.7	–
E.E.C.+ MEMBERS	152.8	283.7	404.1	311.5
TOTAL	1029.1	1416.8	1668.5	1518.9

3. TOTAL OFFICIAL GROSS

DAC COUNTRIES	1987	1988	1989	1990
Australia	14.8	21.6	33.2	67.9
Austria	2.4	17.5	50.2	183.0
Belgium	28.1	15.1	2.7	6.4
Canada	151.3	93.0	90.4	280.7
Denmark	30.1	20.5	11.9	12.1
Finland	2.1	0.7	3.7	16.1
France	46.9	134.0	179.9	88.0
Germany	82.5	100.5	159.7	285.0
Ireland	0.1	0.0	0.0	–
Italy	108.8	117.4	127.1	56.0
Japan	866.0	1144.1	1650.2	1705.9
Netherlands	3.2	36.8	40.2	17.0
New Zealand	0.2	0.2	0.4	1.1
Norway	8.3	10.1	6.3	5.8
Sweden	5.0	21.5	42.5	32.1
Switzerland	5.6	11.3	7.9	8.4
United Kingdom	6.6	50.6	27.9	33.3
United States	20.0	61.0	49.0	83.0
TOTAL	1381.9	1855.8	2483.0	2881.6
MULTILATERAL	894.2	1364.7	1323.3	1308.9
ARAB COUNTRIES	18.8	19.0	22.7	–
E.E.C.+ MEMBERS	312.8	520.6	590.6	539.0
TOTAL	2294.9	3239.5	3829.0	4190.6

4. TOTAL ODA NET

DAC COUNTRIES	1987	1988	1989	1990
Australia	14.3	20.6	24.6	31.5
Austria	2.4	17.5	50.2	102.8
Belgium	25.3	15.1	1.3	4.5
Canada	32.2	35.6	37.4	67.7
Denmark	23.2	19.5	11.0	11.0
Finland	2.1	0.6	3.6	16.1
France	46.9	134.0	179.9	88.0
Germany	29.3	45.6	111.9	228.9
Ireland	0.0	0.0	0.0	–
Italy	106.7	111.5	118.8	45.3
Japan	553.1	673.7	832.2	723.0
Netherlands	3.2	36.8	40.2	17.0
New Zealand	0.2	0.2	0.4	1.1
Norway	8.3	10.1	6.3	5.8
Sweden	5.0	21.5	42.5	31.9
Switzerland	5.6	11.3	7.9	8.4
United Kingdom	4.8	42.5	26.8	33.3
United States	–	–	–	–
TOTAL	862.6	1196.2	1494.9	1416.4
MULTILATERAL				
AF.D.F.	–	–	–	–
AF.D.B.	–	–	–	–
AS.D.B	0.7	2.9	3.6	1.8
CAR.D.B.	–	–	–	–
E.E.C.	6.7	45.8	41.2	41.2
IBRD	–	–	–	–
IDA	393.6	552.0	505.0	505.0
I.D.B.	–	–	–	–
IFAD	33.0	10.7	6.7	17.5
I.F.C.	–	–	–	–
IMF TRUST FUND	–	–	–	–
U.N. AGENCIES	–	–	–	–
UNDP	27.7	31.2	30.6	48.5
UNTA	5.4	2.6	5.5	6.6
UNICEF	17.0	14.5	16.7	14.6
UNRWA	–	–	–	–
WFP	86.5	101.5	23.9	8.7
UNHCR	4.6	4.0	4.1	4.1
Other Multilateral	13.3	17.4	18.9	11.8
Arab Agencies	–	1.3	–	–
TOTAL	588.3	783.9	656.3	659.8
ARAB COUNTRIES	10.8	8.8	2.3	–
E.E.C.+ MEMBERS	246.1	450.9	531.1	469.3
TOTAL	1461.7	1988.9	2153.5	2076.2

5. ODA LOANS NET

DAC COUNTRIES	1987	1988	1989	1990
Australia	–	–	–	–
Austria	1.4	16.5	48.8	100.2
Belgium	21.6	10.9	–	–
Canada	–	3.9	5.6	34.8
Denmark	20.6	15.4	3.4	0.4
Finland	1.5	0.3	-0.1	8.7
France	35.7	123.2	169.2	71.1
Germany	-46.5	-34.6	36.2	133.7
Ireland	–	–	–	–
Italy	71.7	85.4	106.7	33.7
Japan	422.8	519.0	668.1	521.7
Netherlands	1.3	33.6	37.6	15.7
New Zealand	–	–	–	–
Norway	–	–	–	–
Sweden	–	–	–	–
Switzerland	5.3	10.5	6.4	2.8
United Kingdom	–	–	–	–
United States	–	–	–	–
TOTAL	535.3	784.1	1081.8	922.7
MULTILATERAL	426.5	562.7	511.7	522.5
ARAB COUNTRIES	10.8	8.8	2.3	–
E.E.C.+ MEMBERS	104.3	233.8	353.1	254.5
TOTAL	972.6	1355.6	1595.8	1445.2

6. TOTAL OFFICIAL NET

DAC COUNTRIES	1987	1988	1989	1990
Australia	14.5	20.9	29.7	64.2
Austria	2.4	17.5	50.2	183.0
Belgium	28.1	15.1	2.7	6.4
Canada	148.8	86.4	75.4	267.9
Denmark	24.4	17.3	5.6	10.2
Finland	2.1	0.6	3.6	16.1
France	46.9	134.0	179.9	88.0
Germany	-6.6	51.4	113.8	231.6
Ireland	0.1	0.0	0.0	–
Italy	99.7	112.0	113.7	52.9
Japan	-415.8	987.0	1521.4	1158.5
Netherlands	3.2	36.8	40.2	17.0
New Zealand	0.2	0.2	0.4	1.1
Norway	8.3	10.1	6.3	5.8
Sweden	5.0	21.5	42.5	32.1
Switzerland	5.6	11.3	7.9	8.4
United Kingdom	6.6	50.6	27.9	33.3
United States	8.0	48.0	34.0	71.0
TOTAL	-18.7	1620.7	2255.1	2247.3
MULTILATERAL	792.1	1325.7	1260.9	1088.0
ARAB COUNTRIES	10.8	8.8	2.3	–
E.E.C.+ MEMBERS	209.0	463.0	525.0	480.6
TOTAL	784.2	2955.2	3518.3	3335.3

7. TOTAL ODA GROSS

	1987
Australia	14.3
Austria	2.4
Belgium	25.3
Canada	32.2
Denmark	23.2
Finland	2.1
France	46.9
Germany	77.3
Ireland	0.1
Italy	107.2
Japan	553.1
Netherlands	3.2
New Zealand	0.2
Norway	8.3
Sweden	5.0
Switzerland	5.6
United Kingdom	4.8
United States	–
TOTAL	911.0
AF.D.F.	–
AF.D.B.	–
AS.D.B	0.7
CAR.D.B.	–
E.E.C.	6.7
IBRD	–
IDA	393.6
I.D.B.	–
IFAD	33.0
I.F.C.	–
IMF TRUST FUND	–
U.N. AGENCIES	–
UNDP	27.7
UNTA	5.4
UNICEF	17.0
UNRWA	–
WFP	86.5
UNHCR	4.6
Other Multilateral	13.3
Arab Agencies	–
TOTAL	588.3
ARAB COUNTRIES	18.8
E.E.C.+ MEMBERS	294.5
TOTAL	1518.1

8. GRANTS

	1987
Australia	14.3
Austria	0.9
Belgium	3.7
Canada	32.2
Denmark	2.6
Finland	0.6
France	11.2
Germany	75.8
Ireland	0.1
Italy	35.0
Japan	130.3
Netherlands	1.8
New Zealand	0.2
Norway	8.3
Sweden	5.0
Switzerland	0.4
United Kingdom	4.8
United States	–
TOTAL	327.3
MULTILATERAL	161.8
ARAB COUNTRIES	–
E.E.C.+ MEMBERS	141.8
TOTAL	489.1

9. TOTAL OOF GROSS

	1987
Australia	0.6
Austria	–
Belgium	2.8
Canada	119.1
Denmark	6.9
Finland	–
France	–
Germany	5.2
Ireland	–
Italy	1.6
Japan	312.9
Netherlands	–
New Zealand	–
Norway	–
Sweden	–
Switzerland	–
United Kingdom	1.8
United States	20.0
TOTAL	470.9
MULTILATERAL	305.9
ARAB COUNTRIES	–
E.E.C.+ MEMBERS	18.3
TOTAL	776.8

10. ODA COMMITMENTS

1988	1989	1990	1987	1988	1989	1990
20.6	24.6	31.5	16.8	24.3	30.4	44.2
17.5	50.2	102.8	18.1	75.6	147.4	30.0
15.1	1.3	4.5	11.5	19.1	1.3	4.5
35.6	37.4	67.7	64.7	73.9	84.7	62.9
19.5	11.9	12.1	–	25.4	–	–
0.7	3.7	16.1	0.2	6.5	30.8	53.0
134.0	179.9	88.0	73.2	285.6	177.7	22.6
94.6	157.7	282.3	130.6	290.1	402.8	234.5
0.0	0.0	–	0.1	0.0	0.0	–
112.4	123.1	47.8	224.6	71.6	67.3	7.8
674.6	833.3	739.8	710.9	1468.2	861.9	443.0
36.8	40.2	17.0	14.1	82.9	11.7	1.2
0.2	0.4	1.1	0.2	0.2	–	–
10.1	6.3	5.8	7.3	6.5	4.9	4.5
21.5	42.5	31.9	8.5	29.3	39.4	34.1
11.3	7.9	8.4	26.9	0.9	0.9	0.1
42.5	26.8	33.3	33.3	151.5	11.3	27.8
–	–	–	–	–	–	–
1247.1	1547.2	1490.1	1340.8	2611.6	1872.5	970.2
–	–	–	–	–	–	–
–	–	–	–	–	–	–
2.9	3.6	1.8	–	–	–	–
–	–	–	–	–	–	–
45.8	41.2	41.2	43.3	68.6	60.6	60.6
–	–	–	–	–	–	–
552.0	505.0	505.0	541.2	615.0	515.0	918.0
–	–	–	–	–	–	–
10.7	6.7	17.5	–	18.0	22.1	0.2
–	–	–	–	–	–	–
–	–	–	–	–	–	–
–	–	–	154.5	171.2	99.7	94.3
31.2	30.6	48.5	–	–	–	–
2.6	5.5	6.6	–	–	–	–
14.5	16.7	14.6	–	–	–	–
–	–	–	–	–	–	–
101.5	23.9	8.7	–	–	–	–
4.0	4.1	4.1	–	–	–	–
17.4	18.9	11.8	–	–	–	–
1.3	–	–	4.0	–	–	–
783.9	656.3	659.8	743.0	872.8	697.4	1073.1
19.0	22.7	–	22.3	28.7	20.4	57.3
500.8	582.2	526.2	530.6	994.8	732.8	359.0
2050.1	2226.2	2149.9	2106.1	3513.0	2590.3	2100.5

11. TECH. COOP. GRANTS

1988	1989	1990	1987	1988	1989	1990
20.6	24.6	31.5	13.9	19.2	16.1	15.3
1.0	1.4	2.7	0.8	0.9	1.3	2.7
4.3	1.3	4.5	3.3	3.1	0.9	1.3
31.7	31.8	32.9	–	12.9	10.9	10.1
4.1	7.6	10.6	6.6	7.0	3.4	0.4
0.3	3.7	7.4	0.4	0.2	1.6	9.0
10.8	10.7	16.9	11.2	10.7	9.5	12.1
80.2	75.7	95.2	55.4	63.8	64.1	73.8
0.0	0.0	–	0.1	0.0	0.0	–
26.2	12.1	11.6	31.9	13.3	5.2	3.3
154.7	164.1	201.3	76.0	102.7	106.2	163.5
3.2	2.6	1.3	1.6	2.7	2.6	1.2
0.2	0.4	1.1	0.1	0.2	–	1.1
10.1	6.3	5.8	2.1	1.5	0.7	1.0
21.5	42.5	31.9	1.6	3.3	5.0	2.4
0.8	1.5	5.6	0.3	0.3	–	–
42.5	26.8	33.3	4.4	9.7	11.1	8.5
–	–	–	–	–	–	–
412.1	413.1	493.6	209.5	251.4	238.4	305.6
221.2	144.6	137.3	69.9	77.8	75.8	85.7
–	–	–	–	–	–	–
217.0	178.0	214.7	116.3	118.3	96.7	100.6
633.3	557.6	631.0	279.4	329.2	314.2	391.2

12. TOTAL OOF NET

1988	1989	1990	1987	1988	1989	1990
0.9	8.5	36.4	0.2	0.3	5.0	32.7
–	–	80.2	–	–	–	80.2
–	1.4	1.9	2.8	–	1.4	1.9
57.4	53.0	213.0	116.6	50.8	38.0	200.2
1.0	–	–	1.2	-2.1	-5.4	-0.8
–	–	–	–	–	–	–
5.8	2.0	2.7	-35.9	5.8	2.0	2.6
5.0	4.0	8.2	-7.0	0.4	-5.1	7.6
469.5	816.8	966.1	-969.0	313.3	689.2	435.4
–	–	–	–	–	–	–
–	–	–	–	–	–	–
–	–	0.2	–	–	–	0.2
8.0	1.1	–	1.8	8.0	1.1	–
61.0	49.0	83.0	8.0	48.0	34.0	71.0
608.7	935.8	1391.5	-881.3	424.5	760.2	830.9
580.7	667.0	649.2	203.8	541.7	604.6	428.2
–	–	–	–	–	–	–
19.9	8.4	12.8	-37.1	12.1	-6.1	11.3
1189.4	1602.8	2040.7	-677.4	966.2	1364.8	1259.1

13. ODF COMMITMENTS: BY PURPOSE %

	1987	1988	1989	1990
Education	2	2	0	–
Health	3	0	2	–
Other Social Infrastr.	8	8	6	–
Water Sanitat. Sewage	5	5	4	–
Energy	13	17	7	–
Telecommunications	2	4	1	–
Transportation	21	17	25	–
Agriculture	3	11	7	–
Extractive Industries	0	1	15	–
Manufacturing	11	15	15	–
Trade Banking Tourism	15	13	12	–
Technical Cooperation	12	8	7	–
Multisector Aid	1	0	0	–
Programme	1	–	–	–
Debt Reorganisation	–	–	–	–
Food Aid	1	0	–	–
Emergency Aid	0	0	0	–
Unspecified	1	0	–	–
TOTAL	100	100	100	–

14. GRANT ELEMENT OF ODA %

DAC COUNTRIES

	1987	1988	1989	1990
Australia	100.0	100.0	100.0	–
Austria	31.7	42.4	41.6	–
Belgium	100.0	100.0	100.0	–
Canada	100.0	94.4	100.0	–
Denmark	–	100.0	–	–
Finland	100.0	100.0	100.0	–
France	92.7	68.9	69.5	–
Germany	92.4	65.7	79.2	–
Ireland	100.0	100.0	100.0	–
Italy	69.9	81.9	69.8	–
Japan	64.6	66.2	68.4	–
Netherlands	65.4	54.5	72.0	–
New Zealand	100.0	100.0	–	–
Norway	100.0	100.0	100.0	–
Sweden	100.0	100.0	100.0	–
Switzerland	100.0	100.0	100.0	–
United Kingdom	100.0	100.0	100.0	–
United States	–	–	–	–
TOTAL	*72.7*	*69.9*	*72.3*	*–*
MULTILATERAL	*86.4*	*84.9*	*83.1*	*–*
ARAB COUNTRIES	*27.8*	*36.8*	*26.4*	*–*
E.E.C.+ MEMBERS	*81.9*	*75.8*	*78.0*	*–*
TOTAL	**77.4**	**73.2**	**74.9**	**–**

15. OTHER AGGREGATES

	1987	1988	1989	1990
OFFICIAL COMMITMENTS:				
TOTAL BILATERAL	2616.4	3459.2	3450.4	2186.6
of which:				
Arab Countries	22.3	28.7	20.4	57.3
C.E.E.C.	–	84.0	125.0	–
TOTAL MULTILATERAL	1815.0	2273.8	1461.1	1248.1
TOTAL BIL.& MULTIL.	4431.4	5733.0	4911.6	3434.7
of which:				
ODA Grants	630.3	868.9	645.1	716.0
ODA Loans	1475.8	2644.1	2070.3	1384.5
DISBURSEMENTS:				
DAC COUNTRIES COMBINED				
OFFICIAL & PRIVATE				
GROSS:				
Contractual Lending	2187.6	2826.6	4069.3	4098.3
Export Credits, Total	1292.2	1553.5	2161.4	2135.2
Export Credits, Priv.	1142.8	1396.4	2001.9	1712.2
NET:				
Contractual Lending	73.5	2259.3	2945.5	2858.5
Export Credits Total	506.3	1191.6	1216.5	1498.4
PRIVATE SECTOR NET	3579.1	2311.7	2168.8	1482.7
Direct Investment	1271.1	-34.3	368.5	364.4
Portfolio Investment	1878.8	1281.8	694.2	11.5
Export Credits	429.3	1064.2	1106.1	1106.7
MARKET BORROWING:				
CHANGE IN CLAIMS				
Banks	4960.0	7212.0	-439.0	7539.0
MEMORANDUM ITEM:				
C.E.E.C. (Gross)	–	–	–	–

DISBURSEMENTS, UNLESS OTHERWISE STATE[D]

1. TOTAL RECEIPTS NET

DAC COUNTRIES	1987	1988	1989	1990
Australia	0.0	0.0	–	–
Austria	0.5	0.5	0.5	0.6
Belgium	-12.6	-4.9	1.7	-6.1
Canada	11.7	31.4	27.9	4.9
Denmark	-5.9	-5.8	-6.4	-7.2
Finland	2.5	-0.6	-0.6	0.1
France	-276.7	12.0	-39.4	65.3
Germany	65.8	96.1	75.1	120.6
Ireland	–	–	–	0.0
Italy	13.3	-5.7	-28.2	-65.2
Japan	28.2	15.9	-109.9	235.8
Netherlands	49.4	-3.8	13.1	24.6
New Zealand	0.0	0.0	0.0	0.0
Norway	2.1	7.9	0.1	-4.3
Sweden	19.2	0.5	-4.0	-6.2
Switzerland	1.9	1.6	1.9	2.9
United Kingdom	-36.2	-5.9	58.4	3.9
United States	15.0	-1214.0	-528.0	-177.0
TOTAL	-121.8	-1074.7	-537.7	192.9
MULTILATERAL				
AF.D.F.	–	–	–	–
AF.D.B.	–	–	–	–
AS.D.B	–	–	–	–
CAR.D.B.	–	–	–	–
E.E.C.	1.1	3.4	4.0	4.0
IBRD	65.6	146.0	29.0	-221.0
IDA	-0.7	-1.0	-1.0	-1.0
I.D.B.	151.4	139.3	164.5	150.3
IFAD	2.1	0.6	2.6	–
I.F.C.	9.4	-0.8	-6.2	61.3
IMF TRUST FUND	–	–	–	–
U.N. AGENCIES	–	–	–	–
UNDP	7.1	9.5	11.6	10.1
UNTA	1.3	0.7	0.6	1.4
UNICEF	3.0	1.9	1.9	2.9
UNRWA	–	–	–	–
WFP	–	2.8	4.6	2.0
UNHCR	–	–	–	0.0
Other Multilateral	0.6	0.8	1.6	1.4
Arab Agencies	–	–	–	–
TOTAL	240.9	303.2	213.2	11.4
ARAB COUNTRIES	–	–	–	–
E.E.C.+ MEMBERS	-201.8	85.5	78.3	139.9
TOTAL	119.0	-771.6	-324.5	204.2

2. ODA LOANS GROSS

DAC COUNTRIES	1987	1988	1989	1990
Australia	–	–	–	–
Austria	–	–	–	–
Belgium	–	–	–	–
Canada	–	–	–	–
Denmark	–	–	–	–
Finland	–	–	–	–
France	18.2	–	4.0	9.2
Germany	7.9	8.9	5.9	3.1
Ireland	–	–	–	–
Italy	0.5	1.7	0.2	9.1
Japan	–	–	3.2	2.9
Netherlands	1.7	–	1.4	1.1
New Zealand	–	–	–	–
Norway	–	–	–	–
Sweden	–	–	–	–
Switzerland	0.4	–	0.8	1.9
United Kingdom	–	–	–	–
United States	–	–	–	–
TOTAL	28.6	10.6	15.5	27.2
MULTILATERAL	15.3	13.3	20.6	13.5
ARAB COUNTRIES	–	–	–	–
E.E.C.+ MEMBERS	28.2	10.6	11.6	22.4
TOTAL	43.9	23.9	36.2	40.6

3. TOTAL OFFICIAL GROSS

DAC COUNTRIES	1987	1988	1989	1990
Australia	0.0	0.0	–	–
Austria	0.5	0.5	0.5	0.6
Belgium	1.5	1.7	1.7	1.9
Canada	15.6	45.7	42.4	21.9
Denmark	0.1	0.0	0.1	–
Finland	0.0	0.1	0.1	0.1
France	23.4	6.4	10.4	19.4
Germany	58.3	72.9	51.9	33.9
Ireland	–	–	–	0.0
Italy	15.0	11.9	7.7	17.6
Japan	85.4	56.7	33.3	32.3
Netherlands	15.1	13.5	15.1	13.0
New Zealand	0.0	0.0	0.0	0.0
Norway	0.1	0.2	0.1	0.4
Sweden	0.1	0.5	0.2	0.0
Switzerland	1.9	1.6	1.9	2.9
United Kingdom	1.3	3.2	1.8	3.6
United States	49.0	19.0	24.0	8.0
TOTAL	267.3	234.1	191.2	155.6
MULTILATERAL	604.5	747.3	661.5	556.8
ARAB COUNTRIES	–	–	–	–
E.E.C.+ MEMBERS	115.7	113.0	92.6	93.3
TOTAL	871.8	981.3	852.7	712.4

4. TOTAL ODA NET

DAC COUNTRIES	1987	1988	1989	1990
Australia	0.0	0.0	–	–
Austria	0.5	0.5	0.5	0.6
Belgium	0.7	1.1	1.1	1.6
Canada	4.9	14.7	10.8	7.1
Denmark	-0.1	-0.1	-0.1	-0.1
Finland	0.0	0.1	0.1	0.1
France	22.1	5.3	9.5	17.9
Germany	22.8	22.6	18.0	24.6
Ireland	–	–	–	0.0
Italy	14.2	11.9	6.8	16.3
Japan	4.5	6.7	10.2	11.8
Netherlands	13.4	12.0	13.4	11.3
New Zealand	0.0	0.0	0.0	0.0
Norway	0.1	0.2	0.1	0.4
Sweden	0.1	0.5	0.2	0.0
Switzerland	1.9	1.6	1.9	2.9
United Kingdom	0.8	2.0	1.5	3.0
United States	-18.0	-19.0	-25.0	-19.0
TOTAL	67.8	60.3	49.0	78.8
MULTILATERAL				
AF.D.F.	–	–	–	–
AF.D.B.	–	–	–	–
AS.D.B	–	–	–	–
CAR.D.B.	–	–	–	–
E.E.C.	1.1	3.4	4.0	4.0
IBRD	–	–	–	–
IDA	-0.7	-1.0	-1.0	-1.0
I.D.B.	-4.4	-17.4	-7.8	-12.5
IFAD	2.1	0.6	2.6	–
I.F.C.	–	–	–	–
IMF TRUST FUND	–	–	–	–
U.N. AGENCIES	–	–	–	–
UNDP	7.1	9.5	11.6	10.1
UNTA	1.3	0.7	0.6	1.4
UNICEF	3.0	1.9	1.9	2.9
UNRWA	–	–	–	–
WFP	–	2.8	4.6	2.0
UNHCR	–	–	–	0.0
Other Multilateral	0.6	0.8	1.6	1.4
Arab Agencies	–	–	–	–
TOTAL	10.1	1.3	18.1	8.2
ARAB COUNTRIES	–	–	–	–
E.E.C.+ MEMBERS	74.9	58.3	54.2	78.7
TOTAL	77.9	61.6	67.1	87.0

5. ODA LOANS NET

DAC COUNTRIES	1987	1988	1989	1990
Australia	–	–	–	–
Austria	–	–	–	–
Belgium	-0.5	-0.6	-0.4	–
Canada	-1.1	-1.4	-1.6	-1.3
Denmark	-0.1	-0.1	-0.1	-0.1
Finland	–	–	–	–
France	16.9	-1.1	3.1	7.7
Germany	-1.0	0.9	-2.6	-4.1
Ireland	–	–	–	–
Italy	0.5	1.7	-0.6	8.4
Japan	-6.3	-3.6	-6.7	-3.4
Netherlands	0.0	-1.4	-0.3	-0.6
New Zealand	–	–	–	–
Norway	–	–	–	–
Sweden	–	–	–	–
Switzerland	0.4	–	0.8	1.9
United Kingdom	-0.4	-0.5	-0.4	-0.5
United States	-24.0	-24.0	-27.0	-24.0
TOTAL	-15.7	-30.1	-35.8	-16.1
MULTILATERAL	-3.2	-18.7	-7.0	-14.0
ARAB COUNTRIES	–	–	–	–
E.E.C.+ MEMBERS	15.3	-1.1	-1.3	10.8
TOTAL	-18.8	-48.8	-42.8	-30.1

6. TOTAL OFFICIAL NET

DAC COUNTRIES	1987	1988	1989	1990
Australia	0.0	0.0	–	–
Austria	0.5	0.5	0.5	0.6
Belgium	1.1	1.1	1.3	1.9
Canada	11.7	31.4	27.9	4.9
Denmark	0.0	-0.2	-0.1	-0.2
Finland	0.0	0.1	0.1	0.1
France	22.1	5.3	9.5	17.9
Germany	36.8	48.1	30.8	20.2
Ireland	–	–	–	0.0
Italy	14.7	11.9	6.8	16.9
Japan	7.1	-5.3	-68.5	-28.1
Netherlands	13.1	11.7	13.1	11.0
New Zealand	0.0	0.0	0.0	0.0
Norway	0.1	0.2	0.1	0.4
Sweden	0.1	0.5	0.2	0.0
Switzerland	1.9	1.6	1.9	2.9
United Kingdom	0.8	2.8	1.5	3.0
United States	14.0	-21.0	-48.0	-66.0
TOTAL	124.1	88.8	-23.0	-14.3
MULTILATERAL	240.9	303.2	213.2	11.4
ARAB COUNTRIES	–	–	–	–
E.E.C.+ MEMBERS	89.7	84.1	66.8	74.7
TOTAL	365.0	392.0	190.2	-3.0

7. TOTAL ODA GROSS

	1987
Australia	0.0
Austria	0.5
Belgium	1.2
Canada	5.9
Denmark	0.0
Finland	0.0
France	23.4
Germany	31.7
Ireland	–
Italy	14.1
Japan	10.8
Netherlands	15.1
New Zealand	0.0
Norway	0.1
Sweden	0.1
Switzerland	1.9
United Kingdom	1.3
United States	6.0
TOTAL	112.1
AF.D.F.	–
AF.D.B.	–
AS.D.B	–
CAR.D.B.	–
E.E.C.	1.1
IBRD	–
IDA	–
I.D.B.	13.0
IFAD	2.4
I.F.C.	–
IMF TRUST FUND	–
U.N. AGENCIES	–
UNDP	7.1
UNTA	1.3
UNICEF	3.0
UNRWA	–
WFP	–
UNHCR	–
Other Multilateral	0.6
Arab Agencies	–
TOTAL	28.5
ARAB COUNTRIES	–
E.E.C.+ MEMBERS	87.8
TOTAL	140.6

8. GRANTS

	1987
Australia	0.0
Austria	0.5
Belgium	1.2
Canada	5.9
Denmark	0.0
Finland	0.0
France	5.3
Germany	23.8
Ireland	–
Italy	13.7
Japan	10.8
Netherlands	13.4
New Zealand	0.0
Norway	0.1
Sweden	0.1
Switzerland	1.5
United Kingdom	1.3
United States	6.0
TOTAL	83.5
MULTILATERAL	13.2
ARAB COUNTRIES	–
E.E.C.+ MEMBERS	59.6
TOTAL	96.7

9. TOTAL OOF GROSS

	1987
Australia	–
Austria	–
Belgium	0.4
Canada	9.7
Denmark	0.1
Finland	–
France	–
Germany	26.5
Ireland	–
Italy	0.8
Japan	74.6
Netherlands	–
New Zealand	–
Norway	–
Sweden	–
Switzerland	–
United Kingdom	–
United States	43.0
TOTAL	155.1
MULTILATERAL	576.0
ARAB COUNTRIES	–
E.E.C.+ MEMBERS	27.8
TOTAL	731.1

10. ODA COMMITMENTS

1988	1989	1990		1987	1988	1989	1990
0.0	–	–		–	0.0	0.0	0.0
0.5	0.5	0.6		0.5	0.5	0.5	0.6
1.7	1.6	1.6		2.2	1.9	1.6	1.6
16.2	12.4	8.5		2.5	17.8	10.1	3.4
0.0	–	–		–	–	–	–
0.1	0.1	0.1		–	0.2	–	0.3
6.4	10.4	19.4		5.3	20.8	61.9	13.9
30.6	26.5	31.8		16.1	26.9	25.6	32.2
–	–	0.0		–	–	–	0.0
11.9	7.7	17.0		12.5	14.9	17.2	55.6
10.3	20.1	18.1		10.2	16.9	14.9	14.7
13.5	15.1	13.0		12.8	13.0	18.2	11.9
0.0	0.0	0.0		0.0	0.0	–	–
0.2	0.1	0.4		0.1	–	–	–
0.5	0.2	0.0		0.2	0.5	0.0	–
1.6	1.9	2.9		2.0	1.5	0.3	21.8
2.5	1.8	3.6		1.3	10.7	3.2	9.3
5.0	2.0	5.0		13.8	24.8	14.1	23.5
101.0	*100.4*	*122.1*		*79.3*	*150.3*	*167.6*	*188.7*
–	–	–		–	–	–	–
–	–	–		–	–	–	–
–	–	–		–	–	–	–
3.4	4.0	4.0		0.7	4.1	3.3	3.3
–	–	–		–	–	–	–
–	–	–		–	–	–	–
13.1	18.3	13.3		–	–	–	–
1.2	3.2	0.7		9.3	–	–	–
–	–	–		–	–	–	–
–	–	–		12.0	15.7	20.3	17.7
9.5	11.6	10.1		–	–	–	–
0.7	0.6	1.4		–	–	–	–
1.9	1.9	2.9		–	–	–	–
–	–	–		–	–	–	–
2.8	4.6	2.0		–	–	–	–
–	–	0.0		–	–	–	–
0.8	1.6	1.4		–	–	–	–
–	–	–		–	–	–	–
33.4	*45.7*	*35.7*		*21.9*	*19.8*	*23.6*	*21.1*
–	–	–		–	–	–	–
70.0	67.0	90.4		50.8	92.3	131.0	127.8
134.3	*146.1*	*157.7*		*101.2*	*170.1*	*191.2*	*209.8*

11. TECH. COOP. GRANTS

1988	1989	1990		1987	1988	1989	1990
0.0	–	–		0.0	–	–	–
0.5	0.5	0.6		0.5	0.5	0.5	0.6
1.7	1.6	1.6		0.4	0.3	0.1	0.1
16.2	12.4	8.5		–	0.6	0.8	0.2
0.0	–	–		–	0.0	–	–
0.1	0.1	0.1		0.0	0.1	–	–
6.4	6.4	10.2		5.3	5.9	6.4	9.4
21.7	20.6	28.7		23.8	21.7	17.4	24.7
–	–	0.0		–	–	–	0.0
10.2	7.4	8.0		12.8	7.8	4.9	2.3
10.3	16.9	15.3		8.7	9.5	10.9	13.1
13.5	13.7	11.8		12.4	11.7	12.3	11.6
0.0	0.0	0.0		0.0	0.0	–	0.0
0.2	0.1	0.4		0.1	0.0	0.0	0.0
0.5	0.2	0.0		0.1	0.2	0.2	–
1.6	1.1	1.0		0.9	0.4	–	–
2.5	1.8	3.6		1.2	2.5	1.8	3.2
5.0	2.0	5.0		1.0	1.0	2.0	4.0
90.3	*84.8*	*94.9*		*67.1*	*62.2*	*57.1*	*69.2*
20.1	25.1	22.2		12.2	13.9	15.7	15.8
–	–	–		–	–	–	–
59.3	55.4	68.0		56.1	50.9	42.8	51.2
110.4	*109.9*	*117.1*		*79.3*	*76.1*	*72.8*	*85.0*

12. TOTAL OOF NET

1988	1989	1990		1987	1988	1989	1990
–	–	–		–	–	–	–
–	0.1	0.2		0.4	–	0.1	0.2
29.5	30.0	13.4		6.8	16.7	17.1	-2.3
–	0.1	–		0.1	-0.1	0.0	-0.1
–	–	–		–	–	–	–
42.3	25.4	2.1		14.0	25.5	12.8	-4.4
–	–	0.6		0.6	–	–	0.6
46.5	13.2	14.2		2.7	-12.0	-78.7	-39.9
–	–	–		-0.3	-0.3	-0.3	-0.3
–	–	–		–	–	–	–
–	–	–		–	–	–	–
–	–	–		–	–	–	–
0.8	–	–		–	0.8	–	–
14.0	22.0	3.0		32.0	-2.0	-23.0	-47.0
133.1	*90.8*	*33.5*		*56.3*	*28.5*	*-72.0*	*-93.2*
713.9	615.8	521.1		230.8	301.9	195.1	3.2
–	–	–		–	–	–	–
43.1	25.6	3.0		14.8	25.9	12.6	-4.0
847.0	*706.6*	*554.7*		*287.1*	*330.4*	*123.1*	*-90.0*

13. ODF COMMITMENTS: BY PURPOSE %

	1987	1988	1989	1990
Education	0	0	9	–
Health	0	0	0	–
Other Social Infrastr.	0	2	1	–
Water Sanitat. Sewage	0	0	24	–
Energy	–	70	29	–
Telecommunications	1	4	3	–
Transportation	69	–	–	–
Agriculture	1	13	1	–
Extractive Industries	–	0	–	–
Manufacturing	0	0	–	–
Trade Banking Tourism	3	–	26	–
Technical Cooperation	26	9	7	–
Multisector Aid	–	0	0	–
Programme	–	–	–	–
Debt Reorganisation	–	–	–	–
Food Aid	–	1	–	–
Emergency Aid	0	0	0	–
Unspecified	–	0	–	–
TOTAL	100	100	100	–

14. GRANT ELEMENT OF ODA %

DAC COUNTRIES

	1987	1988	1989	1990
Australia	–	100.0	100.0	–
Austria	100.0	100.0	100.0	–
Belgium	100.0	100.0	100.0	–
Canada	100.0	100.0	100.0	–
Denmark	–	–	–	–
Finland	–	100.0	–	–
France	100.0	53.6	73.4	–
Germany	100.0	100.0	100.0	–
Ireland	–	–	–	–
Italy	95.7	88.6	67.2	–
Japan	100.0	100.0	100.0	–
Netherlands	100.0	100.0	100.0	–
New Zealand	100.0	100.0	–	–
Norway	100.0	–	–	–
Sweden	100.0	100.0	100.0	–
Switzerland	100.0	100.0	100.0	–
United Kingdom	100.0	100.0	100.0	–
United States	100.0	100.0	100.0	–
TOTAL	*99.3*	*89.6*	*89.3*	–
MULTILATERAL	*87.0*	*100.0*	*81.0*	–
ARAB COUNTRIES	–	–	–	–
E.E.C.+ MEMBERS	*98.9*	*83.9*	*85.6*	–
TOTAL	**96.9**	**90.8**	**87.2**	–

15. OTHER AGGREGATES

	1987	1988	1989	1990
OFFICIAL COMMITMENTS:				
TOTAL BILATERAL	276.5	180.0	510.0	208.8
of which:				
Arab Countries	–	–	–	–
C.E.E.C.	–	–	–	–
TOTAL MULTILATERAL	1048.8	463.0	267.3	981.6
TOTAL BIL.& MULTIL.	1325.3	643.0	777.3	1190.4
of which:				
ODA Grants	90.5	151.3	122.5	169.1
ODA Loans	10.8	18.7	68.6	40.7
DISBURSEMENTS:				
DAC COUNTRIES COMBINED				
OFFICIAL & PRIVATE				
GROSS:				
Contractual Lending	416.3	306.8	510.4	703.7
Export Credits, Total	327.7	296.1	494.2	664.9
Export Credits, Priv.	233.8	165.3	404.6	651.1
NET:				
Contractual Lending	91.8	-52.1	41.2	247.2
Export Credits Total	47.9	-21.6	76.7	252.0
PRIVATE SECTOR NET	-245.9	-1163.5	-514.7	207.2
Direct Investment	-30.8	-1361.4	-188.2	222.6
Portfolio Investment	-267.6	246.3	-476.1	-380.0
Export Credits	52.5	-48.4	149.6	364.6
MARKET BORROWING:				
CHANGE IN CLAIMS				
Banks	-215.0	526.0	-409.0	-59.0
MEMORANDUM ITEM:				
C.E.E.C. (Gross)	–	–	–	–

1. TOTAL RECEIPTS NET

	1987	1988	1989	1990
DAC COUNTRIES				
Australia	0.4	–	0.1	–
Austria	–	–	–	–
Belgium	2.4	1.6	3.4	0.1
Canada	–	0.1	0.1	0.0
Denmark	–	–	–	–
Finland	–	–	–	–
France	22.8	32.4	22.3	23.4
Germany	3.0	0.3	0.8	0.5
Ireland	–	–	–	–
Italy	0.1	0.0	0.0	–
Japan	3.3	2.2	3.8	4.3
Netherlands	0.2	0.3	0.3	0.6
New Zealand	–	–	–	–
Norway	–	–	–	–
Sweden	–	–	–	–
Switzerland	0.0	0.0	0.0	0.1
United Kingdom	–	–	0.0	–
United States	1.0	–	1.0	1.0
TOTAL	*33.3*	*36.8*	*31.8*	*29.9*
MULTILATERAL				
AF.D.F.	1.1	–	0.2	–
AF.D.B.	–	–	–	–
AS.D.B	–	–	–	–
CAR.D.B.	–	–	–	–
E.E.C.	6.2	9.0	3.6	3.6
IBRD	–	–	–	–
IDA	4.4	2.0	1.0	1.0
I.D.B.	–	–	–	–
IFAD	0.9	0.1	0.1	0.4
I.F.C.	–	–	–	–
IMF TRUST FUND	–	–	–	–
U.N. AGENCIES	–	–	–	–
UNDP	2.6	2.6	3.1	3.1
UNTA	1.1	1.1	1.5	0.8
UNICEF	0.4	0.6	0.5	0.5
UNRWA	–	–	–	–
WFP	3.2	1.0	1.5	1.2
UNHCR	–	–	–	–
Other Multilateral	0.5	0.9	1.0	1.3
Arab Agencies	0.7	0.0	0.1	–
TOTAL	*21.2*	*17.3*	*12.6*	*11.8*
ARAB COUNTRIES	*0.0*	*0.1*	*0.2*	*–*
E.E.C.+ MEMBERS	*34.8*	*43.5*	*30.4*	*28.1*
TOTAL	*54.4*	*54.2*	*44.7*	*41.7*

2. ODA LOANS GROSS

	1987	1988	1989	1990
DAC COUNTRIES				
Australia	–	–	–	–
Austria	–	–	–	–
Belgium	0.3	–	2.0	–
Canada	–	–	–	–
Denmark	–	–	–	–
Finland	–	–	–	–
France	5.6	6.0	4.4	1.5
Germany	–	–	–	–
Ireland	–	–	–	–
Italy	–	–	–	–
Japan	–	–	–	–
Netherlands	–	–	–	–
New Zealand	–	–	–	–
Norway	–	–	–	–
Sweden	–	–	–	–
Switzerland	–	–	–	–
United Kingdom	–	–	–	–
United States	–	–	–	–
TOTAL	*5.9*	*6.0*	*6.4*	*1.5*
MULTILATERAL	*8.0*	*2.6*	*1.9*	*2.0*
ARAB COUNTRIES	*0.0*	*–*	*–*	*–*
E.E.C.+ MEMBERS	*6.4*	*6.4*	*7.1*	*2.2*
TOTAL	*13.9*	*8.5*	*8.4*	*3.5*

3. TOTAL OFFICIAL GROSS

	1987	1988	1989	1990
DAC COUNTRIES				
Australia	0.4	–	0.1	–
Austria	–	–	–	–
Belgium	2.4	1.6	3.4	0.1
Canada	–	0.1	0.1	0.0
Denmark	–	–	–	–
Finland	–	–	–	–
France	22.6	30.1	22.6	25.0
Germany	3.0	0.3	0.8	0.5
Ireland	–	–	–	–
Italy	0.1	0.0	0.0	–
Japan	3.3	2.2	3.8	4.3
Netherlands	0.2	0.3	0.3	0.6
New Zealand	–	–	–	–
Norway	–	–	–	–
Sweden	–	–	–	–
Switzerland	0.0	0.0	0.0	0.1
United Kingdom	–	–	0.0	–
United States	1.0	–	1.0	1.0
TOTAL	*33.1*	*34.5*	*32.1*	*31.6*
MULTILATERAL	*21.6*	*17.4*	*12.7*	*11.9*
ARAB COUNTRIES	*0.1*	*0.1*	*0.2*	*–*
E.E.C.+ MEMBERS	*34.6*	*41.2*	*30.7*	*29.7*
TOTAL	*54.8*	*52.0*	*45.0*	*43.5*

4. TOTAL ODA NET

	1987	1988	1989	1990
Australia	0.4	–	0.1	–
Austria	–	–	–	–
Belgium	2.4	1.6	3.4	0.1
Canada	–	0.1	0.1	0.0
Denmark	–	–	–	–
Finland	–	–	–	–
France	22.6	30.1	22.3	24.1
Germany	3.0	0.3	0.8	0.5
Ireland	–	–	–	–
Italy	0.1	0.0	0.0	–
Japan	3.3	2.2	3.8	4.3
Netherlands	0.2	0.3	0.3	0.6
New Zealand	–	–	–	–
Norway	–	–	–	–
Sweden	–	–	–	–
Switzerland	0.0	0.0	0.0	0.1
United Kingdom	–	–	0.0	–
United States	1.0	–	1.0	1.0
TOTAL	*33.1*	*34.5*	*31.8*	*30.6*
MULTILATERAL				
AF.D.F.	1.1	–	0.2	–
AF.D.B.	–	–	–	–
AS.D.B	–	–	–	–
CAR.D.B.	–	–	–	–
E.E.C.	6.2	9.0	3.6	3.6
IBRD	–	–	–	–
IDA	4.4	2.0	1.0	1.0
I.D.B.	–	–	–	–
IFAD	0.9	0.1	0.1	0.4
I.F.C.	–	–	–	–
IMF TRUST FUND	–	–	–	–
U.N. AGENCIES	–	–	–	–
UNDP	2.6	2.6	3.1	3.1
UNTA	1.1	1.1	1.5	0.8
UNICEF	0.4	0.6	0.5	0.5
UNRWA	–	–	–	–
WFP	3.2	1.0	1.5	1.2
UNHCR	–	–	–	–
Other Multilateral	0.5	0.9	1.0	1.3
Arab Agencies	0.7	0.0	0.1	–
TOTAL	*21.2*	*17.3*	*12.6*	*11.8*
ARAB COUNTRIES	*0.0*	*0.1*	*0.2*	*–*
E.E.C.+ MEMBERS	*34.6*	*41.2*	*30.4*	*28.8*
TOTAL	*54.3*	*51.9*	*44.7*	*42.4*

5. ODA LOANS NET

	1987	1988	1989	1990
Australia	–	–	–	–
Austria	–	–	–	–
Belgium	0.3	–	2.0	–
Canada	–	–	–	–
Denmark	–	–	–	–
Finland	–	–	–	–
France	5.5	6.0	4.2	0.6
Germany	–	–	–	–
Ireland	–	–	–	–
Italy	–	–	–	–
Japan	–	–	–	–
Netherlands	–	–	–	–
New Zealand	–	–	–	–
Norway	–	–	–	–
Sweden	–	–	–	–
Switzerland	–	–	–	–
United Kingdom	–	–	–	–
United States	–	–	–	–
TOTAL	*5.8*	*6.0*	*6.2*	*0.6*
MULTILATERAL	*7.6*	*2.5*	*1.9*	*2.0*
ARAB COUNTRIES	*-0.1*	*–*	*–*	*–*
E.E.C.+ MEMBERS	*6.4*	*6.4*	*6.8*	*1.3*
TOTAL	*13.3*	*8.4*	*8.1*	*2.6*

6. TOTAL OFFICIAL NET

	1987	1988	1989	1990
Australia	0.4	–	0.1	–
Austria	–	–	–	–
Belgium	2.4	1.6	3.4	0.1
Canada	–	0.1	0.1	0.0
Denmark	–	–	–	–
Finland	–	–	–	–
France	22.6	30.1	22.3	24.1
Germany	3.0	0.3	0.8	0.5
Ireland	–	–	–	–
Italy	0.1	0.0	0.0	–
Japan	3.3	2.2	3.8	4.3
Netherlands	0.2	0.3	0.3	0.6
New Zealand	–	–	–	–
Norway	–	–	–	–
Sweden	–	–	–	–
Switzerland	0.0	0.0	0.0	0.1
United Kingdom	–	–	0.0	–
United States	1.0	–	1.0	1.0
TOTAL	*33.1*	*34.5*	*31.8*	*30.7*
MULTILATERAL	*21.2*	*17.3*	*12.6*	*11.8*
ARAB COUNTRIES	*0.0*	*0.1*	*0.2*	*–*
E.E.C.+ MEMBERS	*34.6*	*41.2*	*30.4*	*28.8*
TOTAL	*54.3*	*51.9*	*44.7*	*42.4*

7. TOTAL ODA GROSS

	1987
Australia	0.4
Austria	–
Belgium	2.4
Canada	–
Denmark	–
Finland	–
France	22.6
Germany	3.0
Ireland	–
Italy	0.1
Japan	3.3
Netherlands	0.2
New Zealand	–
Norway	–
Sweden	–
Switzerland	0.0
United Kingdom	–
United States	1.0
TOTAL	*33.1*
AF.D.F.	1.1
AF.D.B.	–
AS.D.B	–
CAR.D.B.	–
E.E.C.	6.2
IBRD	–
IDA	4.4
I.D.B.	–
IFAD	0.9
I.F.C.	–
IMF TRUST FUND	–
U.N. AGENCIES	–
UNDP	2.6
UNTA	1.1
UNICEF	0.4
UNRWA	–
WFP	3.2
UNHCR	–
Other Multilateral	0.5
Arab Agencies	1.1
TOTAL	*21.6*
ARAB COUNTRIES	*0.1*
E.E.C.+ MEMBERS	*34.6*
TOTAL	*54.8*

8. GRANTS

	1987
Australia	0.4
Austria	–
Belgium	2.1
Canada	–
Denmark	–
Finland	–
France	17.1
Germany	3.0
Ireland	–
Italy	0.1
Japan	3.3
Netherlands	0.2
New Zealand	–
Norway	–
Sweden	–
Switzerland	0.0
United Kingdom	–
United States	1.0
TOTAL	*27.2*
MULTILATERAL	*13.6*
ARAB COUNTRIES	*0.1*
E.E.C.+ MEMBERS	*28.2*
TOTAL	*40.9*

9. TOTAL OOF GROSS

	1987
Australia	–
Austria	–
Belgium	–
Canada	–
Denmark	–
Finland	–
France	–
Germany	–
Ireland	–
Italy	–
Japan	–
Netherlands	–
New Zealand	–
Norway	–
Sweden	–
Switzerland	–
United Kingdom	–
United States	–
TOTAL	*–*
MULTILATERAL	*–*
ARAB COUNTRIES	*–*
E.E.C.+ MEMBERS	*–*
TOTAL	*–*

10. ODA COMMITMENTS

1988	1989	1990	1987	1988	1989	1990
–	0.1	–	0.0	0.5	–	–
–	–	–	–	–	–	–
1.6	3.4	0.1	2.0	1.3	3.4	0.1
0.1	0.1	0.0	0.1	0.1	0.0	0.1
–	–	–	–	–	–	–
–	–	–	–	–	–	0.0
30.1	22.6	25.0	27.4	25.4	18.5	19.6
0.3	0.8	0.5	3.0	1.4	0.3	0.2
–	–	–	–	–	–	–
0.0	0.0	–	0.1	0.0	0.0	–
2.2	3.8	4.3	1.9	5.0	5.5	3.7
0.3	0.3	0.6	0.2	0.3	0.3	0.6
–	–	–	–	–	–	–
–	–	–	–	–	–	–
–	–	–	–	–	–	–
0.0	0.0	0.1	0.0	–	–	–
–	0.0	–	–	–	0.0	–
–	1.0	1.0	0.7	1.0	1.0	1.2
34.5	*32.1*	*31.5*	*35.5*	*34.9*	*29.0*	*25.4*

1988	1989	1990	1987	1988	1989	1990
–	0.2	–	–	–	–	–
–	–	–	–	–	–	–
–	–	–	–	–	–	–
9.0	3.6	3.6	8.7	12.1	13.4	13.4
–	–	–	7.9	–	–	–
2.0	1.0	1.0	–	–	–	–
–	–	–	–	–	–	0.2
0.1	0.1	0.4	–	–	–	–
–	–	–	7.8	6.2	7.6	6.8
–	–	–	–	–	–	–
2.6	3.1	3.1	–	–	–	–
1.1	1.5	0.8	–	–	–	–
0.6	0.5	0.5	–	–	–	–
–	–	–	–	–	–	–
1.0	1.5	1.2	–	–	–	–
–	–	–	–	–	–	–
0.9	1.0	1.3	–	–	–	–
0.1	0.2	0.2	1.0	1.3	–	–
17.4	*12.7*	*11.9*	*25.5*	*19.5*	*21.0*	*20.4*
0.1	*0.2*	–	–	*0.1*	*7.5*	–
41.2	*30.7*	*29.7*	*41.6*	*40.4*	*35.9*	*33.9*
52.0	*45.0*	*43.4*	*61.0*	*54.5*	*57.4*	*45.9*

11. TECH. COOP. GRANTS

1988	1989	1990	1987	1988	1989	1990
–	0.1	–	–	–	0.1	–
–	–	–	–	–	–	–
1.6	1.4	0.1	2.1	1.5	1.4	0.1
0.1	0.1	0.0	–	–	–	–
–	–	–	–	–	–	–
24.1	18.2	23.4	8.2	8.9	7.5	9.2
0.3	0.8	0.5	3.0	0.3	0.2	0.2
–	–	–	–	–	–	–
0.0	0.0	–	0.0	–	0.0	–
2.2	3.8	4.3	0.6	0.5	0.5	0.3
0.3	0.3	0.6	0.2	0.3	0.3	0.6
–	–	–	–	–	–	–
0.0	0.0	0.1	0.0	0.0	–	–
–	0.0	–	–	–	0.0	–
–	1.0	1.0	1.0	–	1.0	1.0
28.5	*25.6*	*30.0*	*15.2*	*11.5*	*11.0*	*11.2*
14.9	*10.7*	*9.9*	*5.1*	*5.9*	*6.1*	*5.6*
0.1	*0.2*	–	–	–	–	–
34.8	*23.6*	*27.5*	*14.2*	*11.6*	*9.4*	*10.0*
43.5	*36.6*	*39.9*	*20.4*	*17.3*	*17.1*	*16.8*

12. TOTAL OOF NET

1988	1989	1990	1987	1988	1989	1990
–	–	–	–	–	–	–
–	–	–	–	–	–	–
–	–	–	–	–	–	–
–	–	–	–	–	–	–
–	–	0.1	–	–	–	0.1
–	–	–	–	–	–	–
–	–	–	–	–	–	–
–	–	–	–	–	–	–
–	–	–	–	–	–	–
–	–	–	–	–	–	–
–	–	–	–	–	–	–
–	–	–	–	–	–	–
–	–	–	–	–	–	–
–	–	–	–	–	–	–
–	–	0.1	–	–	–	0.1
–	–	–	–	–	–	–
–	–	–	–	–	–	–
–	–	0.1	–	–	–	0.1
–	–	0.1	–	–	–	0.1

13. ODF COMMITMENTS: BY PURPOSE %

	1987	1988	1989	1990
Education	19	0	1	–
Health	0	2	1	–
Other Social Infrastr.	1	6	2	–
Water Sanitat. Sewage	–	–	22	–
Energy	22	4	–	–
Telecommunications	4	5	12	–
Transportation	4	1	3	–
Agriculture	1	15	5	–
Extractive Industries	–	–	–	–
Manufacturing	2	–	–	–
Trade Banking Tourism	–	0	1	–
Technical Cooperation	44	58	48	–
Multisector Aid	–	1	1	–
Programme	1	4	–	–
Debt Reorganisation	–	–	–	–
Food Aid	3	3	2	–
Emergency Aid	0	–	–	–
Unspecified	–	–	–	–
TOTAL	100	100	100	–

14. GRANT ELEMENT OF ODA %

DAC COUNTRIES

	1987	1988	1989	1990
Australia	100.0	100.0	–	–
Austria	–	–	–	–
Belgium	97.7	100.0	100.0	–
Canada	100.0	100.0	100.0	–
Denmark	–	–	–	–
Finland	–	–	–	–
France	89.3	96.5	100.0	–
Germany	100.0	100.0	100.0	–
Ireland	–	–	–	–
Italy	100.0	100.0	100.0	–
Japan	100.0	100.0	100.0	–
Netherlands	100.0	100.0	100.0	–
New Zealand	–	–	–	–
Norway	–	–	–	–
Sweden	–	–	–	–
Switzerland	100.0	–	–	–
United Kingdom	–	–	100.0	–
United States	100.0	100.0	100.0	–
TOTAL	*91.6*	*97.4*	*100.0*	–
MULTILATERAL	*91.7*	*96.7*	*100.0*	–
ARAB COUNTRIES	–	*100.0*	*68.8*	–
E.E.C.+ MEMBERS	*92.4*	*97.8*	*100.0*	–
TOTAL	*91.6*	*97.2*	*95.8*	–

15. OTHER AGGREGATES

OFFICIAL COMMITMENTS:

	1987	1988	1989	1990
TOTAL BILATERAL	35.5	34.9	37.5	25.4
of which:				
Arab Countries	–	0.1	7.5	–
C.E.E.C.	–	–	–	–
TOTAL MULTILATERAL	25.5	19.5	21.0	20.4
TOTAL BIL.& MULTIL.	61.0	54.5	58.5	45.9
of which:				
ODA Grants	39.8	50.2	48.6	45.0
ODA Loans	21.2	4.2	8.8	0.9

DISBURSEMENTS:

DAC COUNTRIES COMBINED

	1987	1988	1989	1990
OFFICIAL & PRIVATE				
GROSS:				
Contractual Lending	5.9	6.0	6.4	1.6
Export Credits, Total	–	–	–	–
Export Credits, Priv.	–	–	–	–
NET:				
Contractual Lending	5.8	6.0	6.2	0.7
Export Credits Total	–	–	–	–
PRIVATE SECTOR NET	0.2	2.3	–	-0.7
Direct Investment	0.2	0.2	–	–
Portfolio Investment	–	2.2	–	-0.7
Export Credits	–	–	–	–

MARKET BORROWING:

CHANGE IN CLAIMS

	1987	1988	1989	1990
Banks	2.0	–	1.0	-2.0

MEMORANDUM ITEM:

	1987	1988	1989	1990
C.E.E.C. (Gross)	–	–	–	–

1. TOTAL RECEIPTS NET

	1987	1988	1989	1990
DAC COUNTRIES				
Australia	0.0	—	0.0	—
Austria	—	0.0	0.0	0.0
Belgium	1.5	15.9	-3.6	1.4
Canada	6.6	3.2	0.3	0.2
Denmark	-0.1	-0.1	-0.1	-0.1
Finland	—	—	0.0	—
France	168.9	24.9	-111.9	65.4
Germany	-10.0	1.7	28.1	-16.7
Ireland	—	—	—	—
Italy	19.2	-7.3	-15.0	8.6
Japan	-0.1	0.1	0.1	0.4
Netherlands	5.3	3.9	6.5	5.1
New Zealand	—	—	—	—
Norway	0.0	5.0	0.1	0.0
Sweden	—	—	—	0.1
Switzerland	0.2	0.1	0.1	0.2
United Kingdom	-0.4	-26.3	-5.5	-13.9
United States	9.0	4.0	—	3.0
TOTAL	*200.2*	*25.2*	*-100.8*	*53.8*
MULTILATERAL				
AF.D.F.	0.6	0.6	0.2	0.2
AF.D.B.	10.9	36.3	-8.6	0.9
AS.D.B	—	—	—	—
CAR.D.B.	—	—	—	—
E.E.C.	3.8	5.3	4.2	4.2
IBRD	16.8	47.0	6.0	-4.0
IDA	1.1	1.0	1.0	—
I.D.B.	—	—	—	—
IFAD	2.3	0.9	0.7	0.5
I.F.C.	2.1	—	0.2	—
IMF TRUST FUND	—	—	—	—
U.N. AGENCIES	—	—	—	—
UNDP	3.2	2.3	1.3	1.6
UNTA	1.0	1.5	1.1	0.7
UNICEF	0.3	0.4	0.6	1.1
UNRWA	—	—	—	—
WFP	0.7	1.9	0.9	1.0
UNHCR	—	0.7	0.7	0.6
Other Multilateral	11.3	0.6	1.1	1.7
Arab Agencies	0.1	-0.3	—	—
TOTAL	*54.3*	*98.2*	*9.5*	*8.4*
ARAB COUNTRIES	—	—	—	—
E.E.C.+ MEMBERS	*188.3*	*18.0*	*-97.3*	*54.0*
TOTAL	**254.4**	**123.4**	**-91.3**	**62.2**

2. ODA LOANS GROSS

	1987	1988	1989	1990
DAC COUNTRIES				
Australia	—	—	—	—
Austria	—	—	—	—
Belgium	2.7	—	—	—
Canada	—	—	—	—
Denmark	—	—	—	—
Finland	—	—	—	—
France	87.4	21.4	19.0	111.7
Germany	2.3	4.1	1.6	0.8
Ireland	—	—	—	—
Italy	7.7	4.8	1.5	11.2
Japan	—	—	—	—
Netherlands	—	—	—	—
New Zealand	—	—	—	—
Norway	—	—	—	—
Sweden	—	—	—	—
Switzerland	—	—	—	—
United Kingdom	—	—	—	—
United States	—	—	—	2.0
TOTAL	*100.0*	*30.3*	*22.1*	*125.8*
MULTILATERAL	*4.3*	*2.7*	*7.1*	*6.4*
ARAB COUNTRIES	—	—	—	—
E.E.C.+ MEMBERS	*100.1*	*30.3*	*27.1*	*128.8*
TOTAL	**104.3**	**32.9**	**29.2**	**132.1**

3. TOTAL OFFICIAL GROSS

	1987	1988	1989	1990
DAC COUNTRIES				
Australia	0.0	—	0.0	—
Austria	—	0.0	0.0	0.0
Belgium	9.4	3.8	0.8	0.9
Canada	6.8	3.4	0.5	19.6
Denmark	—	—	—	—
Finland	—	—	0.0	—
France	249.1	98.8	73.7	175.7
Germany	12.5	9.5	21.0	14.2
Ireland	—	—	—	—
Italy	12.6	6.1	2.7	16.4
Japan	0.1	0.1	0.1	0.4
Netherlands	0.3	3.0	0.4	0.4
New Zealand	—	—	—	—
Norway	0.0	0.2	0.1	0.0
Sweden	—	—	—	0.1
Switzerland	0.2	0.1	0.1	0.2
United Kingdom	0.3	0.5	0.4	0.4
United States	12.0	4.0	—	3.0
TOTAL	*303.2*	*129.4*	*99.9*	*231.3*
MULTILATERAL	*63.3*	*111.8*	*26.5*	*20.0*
ARAB COUNTRIES	—	—	—	—
E.E.C.+ MEMBERS	*288.6*	*128.2*	*104.1*	*213.2*
TOTAL	**366.5**	**241.3**	**126.4**	**251.2**

4. TOTAL ODA NET

	1987	1988	1989	1990
DAC COUNTRIES				
Australia	0.0	—	0.0	—
Austria	—	0.0	0.0	0.0
Belgium	3.1	0.2	0.0	0.8
Canada	0.5	0.2	0.5	0.2
Denmark	—	—	—	—
Finland	—	—	0.0	—
France	113.0	55.7	67.7	169.3
Germany	6.0	8.5	7.6	6.8
Ireland	—	—	—	—
Italy	6.9	5.1	2.1	16.0
Japan	0.1	0.1	0.1	0.4
Netherlands	0.3	3.0	0.4	0.4
New Zealand	—	—	—	—
Norway	0.0	0.2	0.1	0.0
Sweden	—	—	—	0.1
Switzerland	0.2	0.1	0.1	0.2
United Kingdom	0.3	0.5	0.4	0.4
United States	1.0	3.0	—	3.0
TOTAL	*131.3*	*76.6*	*79.1*	*197.7*
MULTILATERAL				
AF.D.F.	0.6	0.6	0.2	0.2
AF.D.B.	—	—	—	—
AS.D.B	—	—	—	—
CAR.D.B.	—	—	—	—
E.E.C.	-0.1	2.3	4.4	4.4
IBRD	—	—	—	—
IDA	1.1	1.0	1.0	—
I.D.B.	—	—	—	—
IFAD	2.3	0.9	0.7	0.5
I.F.C.	—	—	—	—
IMF TRUST FUND	—	—	—	—
U.N. AGENCIES	—	—	—	—
UNDP	3.2	2.3	1.3	1.6
UNTA	1.0	1.5	1.1	0.7
UNICEF	0.3	0.4	0.6	1.1
UNRWA	—	—	—	—
WFP	0.7	1.9	0.9	1.0
UNHCR	—	0.7	0.7	0.6
Other Multilateral	11.3	0.6	1.1	1.7
Arab Agencies	—	—	—	—
TOTAL	*20.5*	*12.2*	*12.1*	*11.7*
ARAB COUNTRIES	—	—	—	—
E.E.C.+ MEMBERS	*129.4*	*75.3*	*82.6*	*198.2*
TOTAL	**151.8**	**88.8**	**91.3**	**209.4**

5. ODA LOANS NET

	1987	1988	1989	1990
DAC COUNTRIES				
Australia	—	—	—	—
Austria	—	—	—	—
Belgium	2.7	—	—	—
Canada	—	—	—	-19.4
Denmark	—	—	—	—
Finland	—	—	—	—
France	82.7	20.6	18.2	111.7
Germany	2.0	4.0	1.4	0.8
Ireland	—	—	—	—
Italy	6.3	4.7	1.0	10.9
Japan	—	—	—	—
Netherlands	—	—	—	—
New Zealand	—	—	—	—
Norway	—	—	—	—
Sweden	—	—	—	—
Switzerland	—	—	—	—
United Kingdom	—	—	—	—
United States	—	—	—	2.0
TOTAL	*93.7*	*29.3*	*20.6*	*106.0*
MULTILATERAL	*3.5*	*1.8*	*6.3*	*5.2*
ARAB COUNTRIES	—	—	—	—
E.E.C.+ MEMBERS	*93.2*	*28.6*	*25.0*	*127.8*
TOTAL	**97.2**	**31.1**	**26.9**	**111.2**

6. TOTAL OFFICIAL NET

	1987	1988	1989	1990
DAC COUNTRIES				
Australia	0.0	—	0.0	—
Austria	—	0.0	0.0	0.0
Belgium	9.4	2.9	0.8	0.9
Canada	6.6	3.2	0.3	0.2
Denmark	—	—	—	—
Finland	—	—	0.0	—
France	244.4	97.6	72.6	175.1
Germany	10.6	8.8	20.8	14.2
Ireland	—	—	—	—
Italy	8.3	6.0	2.1	16.0
Japan	0.1	0.1	0.1	0.4
Netherlands	0.3	1.0	0.4	0.4
New Zealand	—	—	—	—
Norway	0.0	0.2	0.1	0.0
Sweden	—	—	—	0.1
Switzerland	0.2	0.1	0.1	0.2
United Kingdom	0.3	0.5	0.4	0.4
United States	9.0	4.0	—	3.0
TOTAL	*289.1*	*124.4*	*97.8*	*210.9*
MULTILATERAL	*54.3*	*98.2*	*9.5*	*8.4*
ARAB COUNTRIES	—	—	—	—
E.E.C.+ MEMBERS	*277.1*	*122.1*	*101.2*	*211.1*
TOTAL	**343.3**	**222.6**	**107.2**	**219.3**

7. TOTAL ODA GROSS

	1987
Australia	0.0
Austria	—
Belgium	3.1
Canada	0.5
Denmark	—
Finland	—
France	117.6
Germany	6.2
Ireland	—
Italy	8.3
Japan	0.1
Netherlands	0.3
New Zealand	—
Norway	0.0
Sweden	—
Switzerland	0.2
United Kingdom	0.3
United States	1.0
TOTAL	*137.5*
AF.D.F.	0.6
AF.D.B.	—
AS.D.B	—
CAR.D.B.	—
E.E.C.	0.5
IBRD	—
IDA	1.3
I.D.B.	—
IFAD	2.3
I.F.C.	—
IMF TRUST FUND	—
U.N. AGENCIES	—
UNDP	3.2
UNTA	1.0
UNICEF	0.3
UNRWA	—
WFP	0.7
UNHCR	—
Other Multilateral	11.3
Arab Agencies	—
TOTAL	*21.3*
ARAB COUNTRIES	—
E.E.C.+ MEMBERS	*136.3*
TOTAL	**158.8**

8. GRANTS

	1987
Australia	0.0
Austria	—
Belgium	0.5
Canada	0.5
Denmark	—
Finland	—
France	30.3
Germany	4.0
Ireland	—
Italy	0.6
Japan	0.1
Netherlands	0.3
New Zealand	—
Norway	0.0
Sweden	—
Switzerland	0.2
United Kingdom	0.3
United States	1.0
TOTAL	*37.6*
MULTILATERAL	*16.9*
ARAB COUNTRIES	—
E.E.C.+ MEMBERS	*36.2*
TOTAL	**54.5**

9. TOTAL OOF GROSS

	1987
Australia	—
Austria	—
Belgium	6.3
Canada	6.4
Denmark	—
Finland	—
France	131.5
Germany	6.2
Ireland	—
Italy	4.3
Japan	—
Netherlands	—
New Zealand	—
Norway	—
Sweden	—
Switzerland	—
United Kingdom	—
United States	11.0
TOTAL	*165.7*
MULTILATERAL	*42.0*
ARAB COUNTRIES	—
E.E.C.+ MEMBERS	*152.3*
TOTAL	**207.7**

10. ODA COMMITMENTS

1988	1989	1990	1987	1988	1989	1990
–	0.0	–	–	–	–	–
0.0	0.0	0.0	–	0.0	0.0	0.0
0.2	0.0	0.8	2.7	1.4	0.0	0.8
0.2	0.5	19.6	0.6	0.4	0.4	0.6
–	–	–	–	–	–	–
–	0.0	–	–	–	0.0	–
56.4	68.5	169.3	140.8	41.0	73.8	251.9
8.6	7.7	6.8	1.8	10.9	1.9	26.1
–	–	–	–	–	–	–
5.2	2.7	16.4	2.6	6.9	14.0	5.2
0.1	0.1	0.4	0.1	0.1	0.1	0.4
3.0	0.4	0.4	0.2	3.0	0.4	0.4
–	–	–	–	–	–	–
0.2	0.1	0.0	0.0	–	–	–
–	–	0.1	–	–	–	–
0.1	0.1	0.2	0.1	0.1	0.1	0.1
0.5	0.4	0.4	0.3	0.5	0.4	0.4
3.0	–	3.0	0.8	0.7	0.7	2.8
77.5	*80.6*	*217.4*	*150.0*	*65.0*	*91.8*	*288.6*
0.6	0.2	0.2	–	–	–	3.5
–	–	–	–	–	–	–
–	–	–	–	–	–	–
3.1	5.0	5.0	0.9	62.2	1.6	1.6
–	–	–	–	–	–	–
1.0	1.0	–	–	–	–	–
–	–	–	–	–	–	–
1.1	0.9	1.1	–	0.3	–	8.7
–	–	–	–	–	–	–
–	–	–	–	–	–	–
–	–	–	16.5	7.4	5.8	6.6
2.3	1.3	1.6	–	–	–	–
1.5	1.1	0.7	–	–	–	–
0.4	0.6	1.1	–	–	–	–
–	–	–	–	–	–	–
1.9	0.9	1.0	–	–	–	–
0.7	0.7	0.6	–	–	–	–
0.6	1.1	1.7	–	–	–	–
–	–	–	0.5	–	–	–
13.1	*12.9*	*13.0*	*17.9*	*69.8*	*7.4*	*20.3*
–	–	–	–	–	–	–
77.0	*84.7*	*199.1*	*149.3*	*125.9*	*92.1*	*286.4*
90.6	**93.5**	**230.3**	**167.9**	**134.8**	**99.2**	**308.9**

11. TECH. COOP. GRANTS

1988	1989	1990	1987	1988	1989	1990
–	0.0	–	–	–	0.0	–
0.0	0.0	0.0	–	0.0	0.0	0.0
0.2	0.0	0.8	0.5	0.1	–	0.1
0.2	0.5	19.6	–	–	–	–
–	–	–	–	–	–	–
–	0.0	–	–	–	–	–
35.0	49.5	57.6	26.3	26.8	25.0	36.2
4.5	6.2	5.9	3.8	4.2	5.9	5.9
–	–	–	–	–	–	–
0.4	1.1	5.2	0.3	0.4	0.4	1.3
0.1	0.1	0.4	0.1	0.1	0.1	0.4
3.0	0.4	0.4	0.3	0.3	0.4	0.4
–	–	–	–	–	–	–
0.2	0.1	0.0	0.0	0.1	0.0	0.0
–	–	0.1	–	–	–	–
0.1	0.1	0.2	0.1	0.1	–	–
0.5	0.4	0.4	0.3	0.5	0.4	0.4
3.0	–	1.0	1.0	–	–	1.0
47.3	*58.5*	*91.6*	*32.6*	*32.6*	*32.3*	*45.8*
10.4	*5.8*	*6.6*	*16.0*	*6.0*	*4.9*	*5.6*
–	–	–	–	–	–	–
46.7	*57.6*	*70.3*	*31.7*	*32.9*	*32.1*	*44.3*
57.7	**64.4**	**98.2**	**48.6**	**38.7**	**37.2**	**51.3**

12. TOTAL OOF NET

1988	1989	1990	1987	1988	1989	1990
–	–	–	–	–	–	–
3.6	0.8	0.1	6.3	2.7	0.8	0.1
3.2	–	–	6.1	3.0	-0.3	–
–	–	–	–	–	–	–
42.4	5.3	6.4	131.5	41.9	4.9	5.7
0.9	13.2	7.4	4.6	0.3	13.2	7.4
–	–	–	–	–	–	–
0.9	–	–	1.4	0.9	–	–
–	–	–	–	-2.0	–	–
–	–	–	–	–	–	–
–	–	–	–	–	–	–
–	–	–	–	–	–	–
–	–	–	–	–	–	–
–	–	–	–	–	–	–
1.0	–	–	8.0	1.0	–	–
51.9	*19.3*	*13.9*	*157.8*	*47.8*	*18.6*	*13.2*
98.7	*13.6*	*7.0*	*33.8*	*86.0*	*-2.7*	*-3.3*
–	–	–	–	–	–	–
51.2	*19.4*	*14.1*	*147.7*	*46.8*	*18.6*	*12.9*
150.7	**32.9**	**20.9**	**191.6**	**133.8**	**15.9**	**9.9**

13. ODF COMMITMENTS: BY PURPOSE %

	1987	1988	1989	1990
Education	1	1	1	–
Health	0	1	1	–
Other Social Infrastr.	8	2	3	–
Water Sanitat. Sewage	–	4	16	–
Energy	–	–	14	–
Telecommunications	–	–	9	–
Transportation	1	8	9	–
Agriculture	3	19	3	–
Extractive Industries	–	–	–	–
Manufacturing	8	13	12	–
Trade Banking Tourism	0	0	–	–
Technical Cooperation	17	52	32	–
Multisector Aid	–	0	–	–
Programme	61	–	–	–
Debt Reorganisation	1	0	–	–
Food Aid	–	–	–	–
Emergency Aid	0	–	–	–
Unspecified	0	–	–	–
TOTAL	100	100	100	–

14. GRANT ELEMENT OF ODA %

DAC COUNTRIES	1987	1988	1989	1990
Australia	–	–	–	–
Austria	–	100.0	100.0	–
Belgium	100.0	100.0	100.0	–
Canada	100.0	100.0	100.0	–
Denmark	–	–	–	–
Finland	–	–	100.0	–
France	51.8	97.4	78.2	–
Germany	100.0	86.9	80.2	–
Ireland	–	–	–	–
Italy	43.8	58.3	59.9	–
Japan	100.0	100.0	100.0	–
Netherlands	100.0	100.0	100.0	–
New Zealand	–	–	–	–
Norway	100.0	–	–	–
Sweden	–	–	–	–
Switzerland	100.0	100.0	100.0	–
United Kingdom	100.0	100.0	100.0	–
United States	100.0	99.3	100.0	–
TOTAL	*53.4*	*91.7*	*75.5*	–
MULTILATERAL	*100.0*	*100.0*	*98.0*	–
ARAB COUNTRIES	–	–	–	–
E.E.C.+ MEMBERS	*53.2*	*95.0*	*75.6*	–
TOTAL	**60.2**	**95.4**	**77.5**	–

15. OTHER AGGREGATES

	1987	1988	1989	1990
OFFICIAL COMMITMENTS:				
TOTAL BILATERAL	164.0	78.1	112.9	847.6
of which:				
Arab Countries	–	–	–	–
C.E.E.C.	–	–	–	–
TOTAL MULTILATERAL	166.3	78.6	50.7	47.7
TOTAL BIL.& MULTIL.	330.3	156.7	163.6	895.3
of which:				
ODA Grants	55.1	105.4	59.1	67.3
ODA Loans	112.8	29.4	40.1	241.5
DISBURSEMENTS:				
DAC COUNTRIES COMBINED				
OFFICIAL & PRIVATE				
GROSS:				
Contractual Lending	234.2	14.9	-59.3	73.0
Export Credits, Total	-19.4	-63.0	-87.4	-59.2
Export Credits, Priv.	-31.2	-67.3	-100.6	-66.6
NET:				
Contractual Lending	181.5	-43.3	-101.5	28.7
Export Credits Total	-66.0	-116.7	-127.7	-83.1
PRIVATE SECTOR NET	-88.9	-99.2	-198.5	-157.1
Direct Investment	8.0	7.4	3.3	6.7
Portfolio Investment	-27.2	13.9	-61.1	-73.3
Export Credits	-69.8	-120.4	-140.6	-90.5
MARKET BORROWING:				
CHANGE IN CLAIMS				
Banks	-133.0	-154.0	-167.0	-138.0
MEMORANDUM ITEM:				
C.E.E.C. (Gross)	0.8	0.3	1.0	–

DISBURSEMENTS, UNLESS OTHERWISE STATE

	1987	1988	1989	1990		1987	1988	1989	1990			1987
1. TOTAL RECEIPTS NET						**4. TOTAL ODA NET**					**7. TOTAL ODA GROSS**	
DAC COUNTRIES												
Australia	0.8	1.7	1.0	1.3		0.8	1.7	1.0	1.3		Australia	0.8
Austria	–	–	–	–		–	–	–	–		Austria	–
Belgium	–	–	–	–		–	–	–	–		Belgium	–
Canada	0.0	0.0	–	–		0.0	0.0	–	–		Canada	0.0
Denmark	–	–	–	–		–	–	–	–		Denmark	–
Finland	–	–	–	–		–	–	–	–		Finland	–
France	–	–	0.0	10.9		–	–	0.0	0.0		France	–
Germany	0.1	0.0	0.0	0.1		0.1	0.0	0.0	0.1		Germany	0.1
Ireland	–	–	–	–		–	–	–	–		Ireland	–
Italy	–	–	0.2	-5.0		–	–	–	–		Italy	–
Japan	0.3	2.4	7.7	-1.9		0.3	0.2	0.2	0.3		Japan	0.3
Netherlands	0.1	0.0	0.0	–		0.1	0.0	0.0	–		Netherlands	0.1
New Zealand	8.3	8.8	9.9	8.4		8.3	8.8	9.9	8.4		New Zealand	8.3
Norway	–	–	–	–		–	–	–	–		Norway	–
Sweden	–	–	–	–		–	–	–	–		Sweden	–
Switzerland	–	–	–	–		–	–	–	–		Switzerland	–
United Kingdom	0.1	0.2	–	0.0		0.1	0.2	–	0.0		United Kingdom	0.1
United States	–	–	–	–		–	–	–	–		United States	–
TOTAL	9.7	13.1	18.8	13.7		9.7	10.9	11.1	10.1		TOTAL	9.7
MULTILATERAL												
AF.D.F.	–	–	–	–		–	–	–	–		AF.D.F.	–
AF.D.B.	–	–	–	–		–	–	–	–		AF.D.B.	–
AS.D.B	0.5	0.2	0.4	1.3		0.5	0.2	0.4	1.3		AS.D.B	0.4
CAR.D.B.	–	–	–	–		–	–	–	–		CAR.D.B.	–
E.E.C.	–	–	–	–		–	–	–	–		E.E.C.	–
IBRD	–	–	–	–		–	–	–	–		IBRD	–
IDA	–	–	–	–		–	–	–	–		IDA	–
I.D.B.	–	–	–	–		–	–	–	–		I.D.B.	–
IFAD	–	–	–	–		–	–	–	–		IFAD	–
I.F.C.	–	–	–	–		–	–	–	–		I.F.C.	–
IMF TRUST FUND	–	–	–	–		–	–	–	–		IMF TRUST FUND	–
U.N. AGENCIES	–	–	–	–		–	–	–	–		U.N. AGENCIES	–
UNDP	0.6	0.6	0.6	0.4		0.6	0.6	0.6	0.4		UNDP	0.6
UNTA	0.3	0.2	0.4	0.4		0.3	0.2	0.4	0.4		UNTA	0.3
UNICEF	–	–	–	–		–	–	–	–		UNICEF	–
UNRWA	–	–	–	–		–	–	–	–		UNRWA	–
WFP	–	–	–	–		–	–	–	–		WFP	–
UNHCR	–	–	–	–		–	–	–	–		UNHCR	–
Other Multilateral	0.1	0.1	0.1	0.1		0.1	0.1	0.1	0.1		Other Multilateral	0.1
Arab Agencies	–	–	–	–		–	–	–	–		Arab Agencies	–
TOTAL	1.4	1.1	1.4	2.2		1.4	1.1	1.4	2.2		TOTAL	1.4
ARAB COUNTRIES	–	–	–	–		–	–	–	–		ARAB COUNTRIES	–
E.E.C.+ MEMBERS	0.3	0.2	0.3	5.9		0.3	0.2	0.1	0.1		E.E.C.+ MEMBERS	0.3
TOTAL	11.1	14.2	20.3	15.9		11.1	12.0	12.6	12.3		TOTAL	11.1
2. ODA LOANS GROSS						**5. ODA LOANS NET**					**8. GRANTS**	
DAC COUNTRIES												
Australia	–	–	–	–		–	–	–	–		Australia	0.8
Austria	–	–	–	–		–	–	–	–		Austria	–
Belgium	–	–	–	–		–	–	–	–		Belgium	–
Canada	–	–	–	–		–	–	–	–		Canada	0.0
Denmark	–	–	–	–		–	–	–	–		Denmark	–
Finland	–	–	–	–		–	–	–	–		Finland	–
France	–	–	–	–		–	–	–	–		France	–
Germany	–	–	–	–		–	–	–	–		Germany	0.1
Ireland	–	–	–	–		–	–	–	–		Ireland	–
Italy	–	–	–	–		–	–	–	–		Italy	–
Japan	–	–	–	–		–	–	–	–		Japan	0.3
Netherlands	–	–	–	–		–	–	–	–		Netherlands	0.1
New Zealand	–	–	–	–		–	–	–	–		New Zealand	8.3
Norway	–	–	–	–		–	–	–	–		Norway	–
Sweden	–	–	–	–		–	–	–	–		Sweden	–
Switzerland	–	–	–	–		–	–	–	–		Switzerland	–
United Kingdom	–	–	–	–		–	–	–	–		United Kingdom	0.1
United States	–	–	–	–		–	–	–	–		United States	–
TOTAL	–	–	–	–		–	–	–	–		TOTAL	9.7
MULTILATERAL	0.2	0.0	0.3	0.8		0.2	0.0	0.3	0.8		MULTILATERAL	1.2
ARAB COUNTRIES	–	–	–	–		–	–	–	–		ARAB COUNTRIES	–
E.E.C.+ MEMBERS	–	–	–	–		–	–	–	–		E.E.C.+ MEMBERS	0.3
TOTAL	0.2	0.0	0.3	0.8		0.2	0.0	0.3	0.8		TOTAL	10.9
3. TOTAL OFFICIAL GROSS						**6. TOTAL OFFICIAL NET**					**9. TOTAL OOF GROSS**	
DAC COUNTRIES												
Australia	0.8	1.7	1.0	1.3		0.8	1.7	1.0	1.3		Australia	–
Austria	–	–	–	–		–	–	–	–		Austria	–
Belgium	–	–	–	–		–	–	–	–		Belgium	–
Canada	0.0	0.0	–	–		0.0	0.0	–	–		Canada	–
Denmark	–	–	–	–		–	–	–	–		Denmark	–
Finland	–	–	–	–		–	–	–	–		Finland	–
France	–	–	0.0	4.3		–	–	0.0	4.3		France	–
Germany	0.1	0.0	0.0	0.1		0.1	0.0	0.0	0.1		Germany	–
Ireland	–	–	–	–		–	–	–	–		Ireland	–
Italy	–	–	0.3	26.4		–	–	0.2	-5.0		Italy	–
Japan	0.3	0.2	0.2	0.3		0.3	0.2	0.2	0.3		Japan	–
Netherlands	0.1	0.0	0.0	–		0.1	0.0	0.0	–		Netherlands	–
New Zealand	8.3	8.8	9.9	8.4		8.3	8.8	9.9	8.4		New Zealand	–
Norway	–	–	–	–		–	–	–	–		Norway	–
Sweden	–	–	–	–		–	–	–	–		Sweden	–
Switzerland	–	–	–	–		–	–	–	–		Switzerland	–
United Kingdom	0.1	0.2	–	0.0		0.1	0.2	–	0.0		United Kingdom	–
United States	–	–	–	–		–	–	–	–		United States	–
TOTAL	9.7	10.9	11.4	40.7		9.7	10.9	11.3	9.3		TOTAL	–
MULTILATERAL	1.4	1.1	1.4	2.2		1.4	1.1	1.4	2.2		MULTILATERAL	–
ARAB COUNTRIES	–	–	–	–		–	–	–	–		ARAB COUNTRIES	–
E.E.C.+ MEMBERS	0.3	0.2	0.4	30.7		0.3	0.2	0.3	-0.7		E.E.C.+ MEMBERS	–
TOTAL	11.1	12.0	12.9	42.9		11.1	12.0	12.8	11.5		TOTAL	–

COOK ISLANDS

1988	1989	1990		1987	1988	1989	1990		1987	1988	1989	1990

10. ODA COMMITMENTS

1988	1989	1990	1987	1988	1989	1990
1.7	1.0	1.3	0.6	1.1	1.3	1.2
–	–	–	–	–	–	–
0.0	–	–	0.2	0.0	–	0.0
–	–	–	–	–	–	–
–	0.0	0.0	3.3	–	0.0	0.0
0.0	0.0	0.1	0.1	0.0	0.0	0.1
–	–	–	–	–	–	–
0.2	0.2	0.3	0.4	0.2	0.2	0.3
0.0	0.0	–	0.1	0.1	0.0	–
8.8	9.9	8.4	8.0	9.8	–	9.2
–	–	–	–	–	–	–
–	–	–	–	–	–	–
0.2	–	0.0	0.1	0.2	–	0.0
–	–	–	0.0	0.2	0.0	0.1
10.9	11.1	10.1	12.9	11.5	1.5	10.8
–	–	–	–	–	–	–
0.2	0.4	1.3	3.1	–	–	5.1
–	–	–	–	–	–	–
–	–	–	–	–	–	–
–	–	–	–	–	–	–
–	–	–	–	–	–	–
–	–	–	–	–	–	–
–	–	–	0.9	0.9	1.0	0.8
0.6	0.6	0.4	–	–	–	–
0.2	0.4	0.4	–	–	–	–
–	–	–	–	–	–	–
–	–	–	–	–	–	–
0.1	0.1	0.1	–	–	–	–
–	–	–	–	–	–	–
1.1	1.4	2.2	4.0	0.9	1.0	5.9
–	–	–	–	–	–	–
0.2	0.1	0.1	3.7	0.3	0.1	0.1
12.0	12.6	12.3	16.8	12.4	2.6	16.7

11. TECH. COOP. GRANTS

1988	1989	1990	1987	1988	1989	1990
1.7	1.0	1.3	0.3	0.7	0.8	0.8
–	–	–	–	–	–	–
0.0	–	–	–	–	–	–
–	–	–	–	–	–	–
–	0.0	0.0	–	–	0.0	0.0
0.0	0.0	0.1	0.1	0.0	0.0	0.1
–	–	–	–	–	–	–
0.2	0.2	0.3	0.2	0.2	0.2	0.3
0.0	0.0	–	0.1	0.0	0.0	–
8.8	9.9	8.4	0.6	1.2	–	0.5
–	–	–	–	–	–	–
–	–	–	–	–	–	–
0.2	–	0.0	–	–	–	0.0
–	–	–	–	–	–	–
10.9	11.1	10.1	1.4	2.1	1.1	1.7
1.0	1.1	1.4	0.9	0.9	1.0	0.8
–	–	–	–	–	–	–
0.2	0.1	0.1	0.2	0.0	0.1	0.1
11.9	12.2	11.5	2.3	3.0	2.1	2.5

12. TOTAL OOF NET

1988	1989	1990	1987	1988	1989	1990
–	–	–	–	–	–	–
–	–	–	–	–	–	–
–	–	–	–	–	–	–
–	–	–	–	–	–	–
–	–	4.3	–	–	–	4.3
–	–	–	–	–	–	–
–	0.3	26.4	–	–	0.2	-5.0
–	–	–	–	–	–	–
–	–	–	–	–	–	–
–	–	–	–	–	–	–
–	–	–	–	–	–	–
–	–	–	–	–	–	–
–	0.3	30.6	–	–	0.2	-0.8
–	–	–	–	–	–	–
–	0.3	30.6	–	–	0.2	-0.8
–	0.3	30.6	–	–	0.2	-0.8

13. ODF COMMITMENTS: BY PURPOSE %

	1987	1988	1989	1990
Education	–	–	–	–
Health	–	–	–	–
Other Social Infrastr.	32	–	–	–
Water Sanitat. Sewage	–	–	–	–
Energy	–	–	–	–
Telecommunications	–	–	–	–
Transportation	1	0	2	–
Agriculture	30	–	–	–
Extractive Industries	–	–	–	–
Manufacturing	–	–	–	–
Trade Banking Tourism	–	–	–	–
Technical Cooperation	36	82	92	–
Multisector Aid	–	1	3	–
Programme	–	14	4	–
Debt Reorganisation	–	–	–	–
Food Aid	–	–	–	–
Emergency Aid	1	3	–	–
Unspecified	–	–	–	–
TOTAL	100	100	100	–

14. GRANT ELEMENT OF ODA %

DAC COUNTRIES

	1987	1988	1989	1990
Australia	100.0	100.0	100.0	–
Austria	–	–	–	–
Belgium	–	–	–	–
Canada	100.0	100.0	–	–
Denmark	–	–	–	–
Finland	–	–	–	–
France	67.1	–	100.0	–
Germany	100.0	100.0	100.0	–
Ireland	–	–	–	–
Italy	–	–	–	–
Japan	100.0	100.0	100.0	–
Netherlands	100.0	100.0	100.0	–
New Zealand	100.0	100.0	–	–
Norway	–	–	–	–
Sweden	–	–	–	–
Switzerland	–	–	–	–
United Kingdom	100.0	100.0	–	–
United States	100.0	100.0	100.0	–
TOTAL	91.5	100.0	100.0	–
MULTILATERAL	83.3	100.0	100.0	–
ARAB COUNTRIES	–	–	–	–
E.E.C.+ MEMBERS	70.0	100.0	100.0	–
TOTAL	89.5	100.0	100.0	–

15. OTHER AGGREGATES

	1987	1988	1989	1990
OFFICIAL COMMITMENTS:				
TOTAL BILATERAL	12.9	11.5	1.6	10.8
of which:				
Arab Countries	–	–	–	–
C.E.E.C.	–	–	–	–
TOTAL MULTILATERAL	4.0	0.9	1.0	5.9
TOTAL BIL.& MULTIL.	16.8	12.4	2.6	16.7
of which:				
ODA Grants	10.5	12.4	2.6	11.6
ODA Loans	6.4	–	–	5.1
DISBURSEMENTS:				
DAC COUNTRIES COMBINED				
OFFICIAL & PRIVATE				
GROSS:				
Contractual Lending	–	–	0.3	30.6
Export Credits, Total	–	–	0.3	26.4
Export Credits, Priv.	–	–	–	–
NET:				
Contractual Lending	–	–	0.2	-0.8
Export Credits Total	–	–	0.2	-5.0
PRIVATE SECTOR NET	–	2.2	7.5	4.4
Direct Investment	–	2.2	7.5	4.4
Portfolio Investment	–	–	–	–
Export Credits	–	–	–	–
MARKET BORROWING:				
CHANGE IN CLAIMS				
Banks	–	–	–	–
MEMORANDUM ITEM:				
C.E.E.C. (Gross)	–	–	–	–

	1987	1988	1989	1990		1987	1988	1989	1990			1987
1. TOTAL RECEIPTS NET					**4. TOTAL ODA NET**					**7. TOTAL ODA GROSS**		
DAC COUNTRIES												
Australia	0.0	0.0	–	–		0.0	0.0	–	–	Australia		0.0
Austria	-0.5	-0.5	1.9	0.7		0.1	0.1	1.9	0.7	Austria		0.1
Belgium	2.4	-1.7	-2.6	-10.5		0.2	0.3	0.1	0.2	Belgium		0.2
Canada	15.5	13.4	6.3	16.0		15.5	13.1	6.4	13.4	Canada		15.5
Denmark	–	0.1	0.1	0.4		–	0.1	0.1	0.4	Denmark		–
Finland	0.0	0.0	0.1	–		0.0	0.0	0.1	–	Finland		0.0
France	7.0	-21.8	-11.0	-19.3		5.1	3.7	2.8	3.5	France		5.1
Germany	9.3	17.2	15.5	46.1		11.1	12.3	13.2	24.7	Germany		11.2
Ireland	0.0	–	–	–		0.0	–	–	–	Ireland		0.0
Italy	2.1	10.5	7.4	1.4		2.1	3.6	5.8	2.1	Italy		2.1
Japan	10.1	8.4	6.3	-32.9		4.8	6.3	8.4	40.1	Japan		5.0
Netherlands	18.1	9.7	2.9	14.1		6.5	9.9	10.1	13.6	Netherlands		6.5
New Zealand	–	–	–	–		–	–	–	–	New Zealand		–
Norway	0.2	0.3	0.5	-0.4		0.2	0.3	0.5	0.2	Norway		0.2
Sweden	1.3	3.6	5.1	7.9		0.8	3.6	5.1	7.6	Sweden		0.8
Switzerland	1.1	1.0	1.4	1.6		1.1	1.0	1.4	1.6	Switzerland		1.1
United Kingdom	4.2	-0.4	5.9	5.3		0.7	2.3	5.7	2.7	United Kingdom		0.7
United States	161.0	105.0	144.0	103.0		160.0	107.0	144.0	93.0	United States		162.0
TOTAL	232.0	144.8	183.9	133.2		208.2	163.7	205.6	203.8	TOTAL		210.5
MULTILATERAL												
AF.D.F.	–	–	–	–		–	–	–	–	AF.D.F.		–
AF.D.B.	–	–	–	–		–	–	–	–	AF.D.B.		–
AS.D.B	–	–	–	–		–	–	–	–	AS.D.B		–
CAR.D.B.	–	–	–	–		–	–	–	–	CAR.D.B.		–
E.E.C.	4.4	6.9	5.6	5.6		4.4	6.9	5.6	5.6	E.E.C.		4.4
IBRD	-18.5	-32.0	9.0	-40.0		–	–	–	–	IBRD		–
IDA	-0.1	–	–	–		-0.1	–	–	–	IDA		–
I.D.B.	10.9	31.3	17.2	34.4		3.3	5.3	0.8	4.5	I.D.B.		10.3
IFAD	1.0	-0.7	-0.2	-0.3		1.0	-0.7	-0.2	-0.3	IFAD		1.0
I.F.C.	1.3	-0.2	-0.3	–		–	–	–	–	I.F.C.		–
IMF TRUST FUND	–	–	–	–		–	–	–	–	IMF TRUST FUND		–
U.N. AGENCIES	–	–	–	–		–	–	–	–	U.N. AGENCIES		–
UNDP	1.6	2.4	4.0	2.6		1.6	2.4	4.0	2.6	UNDP		1.6
UNTA	1.0	0.7	0.8	0.8		1.0	0.7	0.8	0.8	UNTA		1.0
UNICEF	0.2	0.2	0.1	0.2		0.2	0.2	0.1	0.2	UNICEF		0.2
UNRWA	–	–	–	–		–	–	–	–	UNRWA		–
WFP	1.4	1.3	0.4	2.4		1.4	1.3	0.4	2.4	WFP		1.4
UNHCR	6.9	5.8	6.3	5.0		6.9	5.8	6.3	5.0	UNHCR		6.9
Other Multilateral	0.8	1.3	2.2	2.9		0.8	1.3	2.2	2.9	Other Multilateral		0.8
Arab Agencies	–	-0.4	-0.2	–		–	–	–	–	Arab Agencies		–
TOTAL	10.8	16.5	44.9	13.6		20.3	23.1	19.9	23.8	TOTAL		27.4
ARAB COUNTRIES	–	–	–	–		–	–	–	–	ARAB COUNTRIES		–
E.E.C.+ MEMBERS	47.6	20.5	23.8	43.1		30.1	39.1	43.5	52.8	E.E.C.+ MEMBERS		30.1
TOTAL	242.7	161.3	228.7	146.8		228.5	186.8	225.5	227.5	TOTAL		237.9
2. ODA LOANS GROSS					**5. ODA LOANS NET**					**8. GRANTS**		
DAC COUNTRIES												
Australia	–	–	–	–		–	–	–	–	Australia		0.0
Austria	–	–	–	–		–	–	–	–	Austria		0.1
Belgium	–	–	–	–		–	–	–	–	Belgium		0.2
Canada	1.0	–	–	–		1.0	–	–	–	Canada		14.6
Denmark	–	–	–	–		–	–	–	–	Denmark		–
Finland	–	–	–	–		–	–	–	–	Finland		0.0
France	3.3	1.5	–	–		3.3	1.5	–	–	France		1.9
Germany	1.0	0.0	–	7.9		0.9	0.0	0.0	7.8	Germany		10.2
Ireland	–	–	–	–		–	–	–	–	Ireland		0.0
Italy	–	–	3.4	0.2		–	–	3.4	0.2	Italy		2.1
Japan	0.3	0.2	0.8	34.5		0.1	0.0	0.6	33.0	Japan		4.7
Netherlands	1.3	–	1.8	–		1.3	–	1.8	–	Netherlands		5.2
New Zealand	–	–	–	–		–	–	–	–	New Zealand		–
Norway	–	–	–	–		–	–	–	–	Norway		0.2
Sweden	–	–	–	–		–	–	–	–	Sweden		0.8
Switzerland	–	–	–	–		–	–	–	–	Switzerland		1.1
United Kingdom	0.1	1.0	4.6	1.8		0.1	1.0	4.6	1.8	United Kingdom		0.6
United States	23.0	15.0	17.0	5.0		21.0	11.0	11.0	–	United States		139.0
TOTAL	29.9	17.7	27.5	49.5		27.6	13.5	21.3	42.8	TOTAL		180.6
MULTILATERAL	10.3	14.7	9.4	15.6		3.2	2.4	0.1	2.7	MULTILATERAL		17.0
ARAB COUNTRIES	–	–	–	–		–	–	–	–	ARAB COUNTRIES		–
E.E.C.+ MEMBERS	5.7	2.5	9.8	9.9		5.6	2.5	9.7	9.8	E.E.C.+ MEMBERS		24.5
TOTAL	40.2	32.4	36.9	65.0		30.9	15.8	21.4	45.4	TOTAL		197.6
3. TOTAL OFFICIAL GROSS					**6. TOTAL OFFICIAL NET**					**9. TOTAL OOF GROSS**		
DAC COUNTRIES												
Australia	0.0	0.0	–	–		0.0	0.0	–	–	Australia		–
Austria	0.1	0.1	1.9	0.7		0.1	0.1	1.9	0.7	Austria		–
Belgium	0.2	0.3	0.1	0.2		0.2	0.3	0.1	0.2	Belgium		–
Canada	15.5	13.4	6.4	16.0		15.5	13.4	6.3	16.0	Canada		–
Denmark	–	0.1	0.1	0.4		–	0.1	0.1	0.4	Denmark		–
Finland	0.0	0.0	0.1	–		0.0	0.0	0.1	–	Finland		–
France	5.1	3.7	2.8	3.5		5.1	3.7	2.8	3.5	France		–
Germany	11.2	12.4	13.4	29.8		11.1	12.3	13.3	29.6	Germany		–
Ireland	0.0	–	–	–		0.0	–	–	–	Ireland		–
Italy	2.1	3.6	5.8	2.1		2.1	3.6	5.8	2.1	Italy		–
Japan	5.0	6.5	8.6	41.7		4.8	6.3	8.4	40.1	Japan		–
Netherlands	6.5	10.2	10.3	14.3		6.5	10.2	10.2	14.3	Netherlands		–
New Zealand	–	–	–	–		–	–	–	–	New Zealand		–
Norway	0.2	0.3	0.5	0.2		0.2	0.3	0.5	0.2	Norway		–
Sweden	0.8	3.6	5.1	7.9		0.8	3.6	5.1	7.9	Sweden		–
Switzerland	1.1	1.0	1.4	1.6		1.1	1.0	1.4	1.6	Switzerland		–
United Kingdom	4.2	2.8	9.5	8.8		4.2	-0.4	5.9	5.3	United Kingdom		3.5
United States	163.0	110.0	150.0	124.0		161.0	105.0	144.0	103.0	United States		1.0
TOTAL	215.0	168.1	216.0	251.1		212.8	159.6	206.0	224.8	TOTAL		4.5
MULTILATERAL	55.7	80.0	102.3	89.6		10.8	16.5	44.9	13.6	MULTILATERAL		28.3
ARAB COUNTRIES	–	–	–	–		–	–	–	–	ARAB COUNTRIES		–
E.E.C.+ MEMBERS	33.7	40.0	47.6	64.7		33.6	36.8	43.9	61.0	E.E.C.+ MEMBERS		3.5
TOTAL	270.7	248.0	318.3	340.7		223.5	176.1	250.9	238.5	TOTAL		32.9

COSTA RICA

1988	1989	1990	1987	1988	1989	1990

10. ODA COMMITMENTS

1988	1989	1990	1987	1988	1989	1990
0.0	–	–	–	0.0	0.0	0.0
0.1	1.9	0.7	0.1	0.2	2.8	0.3
0.3	0.1	0.2	0.2	0.3	0.1	0.2
13.1	6.4	13.4	13.1	11.3	8.6	7.0
0.1	0.1	0.4	–	–	3.4	0.1
0.0	0.1	–	–	7.2	0.1	0.1
3.7	2.8	3.5	1.9	2.2	2.8	3.5
12.3	13.3	24.8	8.6	20.1	10.6	30.1
–	–	–	0.0	–	–	–
3.6	5.8	2.1	1.8	5.9	2.4	2.5
6.5	8.6	41.7	5.6	7.4	98.7	7.1
9.9	10.1	13.6	7.1	10.4	11.5	14.9
–	–	–	–	–	–	–
0.3	0.5	0.2	0.2	–	0.2	–
3.6	5.1	7.6	5.2	5.6	6.4	2.7
1.0	1.4	1.6	0.8	0.5	0.4	0.7
2.3	5.7	2.7	0.7	2.3	5.7	2.7
111.0	150.0	98.0	178.2	122.0	121.2	92.9
167.9	211.8	210.4	223.4	195.4	274.8	164.6
–	–	–	–	–	–	–
–	–	–	–	–	–	–
–	–	–	–	–	–	–
6.9	5.6	5.6	0.3	0.2	1.3	1.3
–	–	–	–	–	–	–
–	–	–	–	–	–	–
17.0	9.9	16.6	–	–	–	–
–	–	0.5	–	4.7	–	–
–	–	–	–	–	–	–
–	–	–	11.7	11.6	13.7	14.0
2.4	4.0	2.6	–	–	–	–
0.7	0.8	0.8	–	–	–	–
0.2	0.1	0.2	–	–	–	–
–	–	–	–	–	–	–
1.3	0.4	2.4	–	–	–	–
5.8	6.3	5.0	–	–	–	–
1.3	2.2	2.9	–	–	–	–
–	–	–	–	–	–	–
35.5	29.2	36.7	12.0	16.5	15.0	15.3
–	–	–	–	–	–	–
39.1	43.5	52.9	20.6	41.4	37.8	55.2
203.4	241.1	247.1	235.4	211.9	289.8	179.9

11. TECH. COOP. GRANTS

1988	1989	1990	1987	1988	1989	1990
0.0	–	–	0.0	–	–	–
0.1	1.9	0.7	0.1	0.1	0.0	0.1
0.3	0.1	0.2	0.2	0.1	0.1	0.0
13.1	6.4	13.4	–	0.3	0.8	0.7
0.1	0.1	0.4	–	0.1	0.1	0.0
0.0	0.1	–	0.0	–	–	–
2.2	2.8	3.5	1.9	2.2	2.8	3.5
12.3	13.3	16.9	9.7	11.3	12.5	16.5
–	–	–	0.0	–	–	–
3.6	2.4	1.9	2.1	0.9	0.6	0.7
6.3	7.8	7.2	4.4	6.2	6.1	6.8
9.9	8.4	13.6	4.8	8.0	7.8	7.2
–	–	–	–	–	–	–
0.3	0.5	0.2	0.2	0.2	0.3	0.2
3.6	5.1	7.6	0.8	2.9	1.8	4.9
1.0	1.4	1.6	0.2	0.1	–	–
1.3	1.0	0.9	0.6	1.3	1.0	0.8
96.0	133.0	93.0	12.0	14.0	19.0	21.0
150.2	184.3	161.0	36.9	47.5	52.9	62.4
20.8	19.8	21.1	11.2	10.4	13.3	11.6
–	–	–	–	–	–	–
36.6	33.7	43.0	20.0	23.8	24.9	28.8
171.0	204.1	182.1	48.1	57.9	66.3	73.9

12. TOTAL OOF NET

1988	1989	1990	1987	1988	1989	1990
–	–	–	–	–	–	–
–	–	–	–	–	–	–
0.3	–	2.6	–	0.3	0.0	2.6
–	–	–	–	–	–	–
–	–	–	–	–	–	–
0.1	0.1	5.1	–	0.1	0.1	5.0
–	–	–	–	–	–	–
–	–	–	–	–	–	–
0.4	0.2	0.7	–	0.3	0.1	0.7
–	–	–	–	–	–	–
–	–	0.3	–	–	–	0.3
–	–	–	–	–	–	–
0.5	3.9	6.1	3.5	-2.7	0.3	2.6
-1.0	–	26.0	1.0	-2.0	–	10.0
0.1	4.1	40.7	4.5	-4.0	0.4	21.1
44.5	73.1	53.0	-9.5	-6.6	24.9	-10.1
–	–	–	–	–	–	–
0.9	4.1	11.8	3.5	-2.3	0.4	8.2
44.7	77.2	93.6	-5.0	-10.7	25.3	10.9

13. ODF COMMITMENTS: BY PURPOSE %

	1987	1988	1989	1990
Education	5	1	1	–
Health	1	1	1	–
Other Social Infrastr.	2	6	1	–
Water Sanitat. Sewage	–	–	0	–
Energy	0	18	0	–
Telecommunications	–	0	–	–
Transportation	–	8	1	–
Agriculture	20	4	7	–
Extractive Industries	4	1	–	–
Manufacturing	–	–	1	–
Trade Banking Tourism	2	1	–	–
Technical Cooperation	20	14	27	–
Multisector Aid	2	6	0	–
Programme	38	37	59	–
Debt Reorganisation	–	1	–	–
Food Aid	5	3	1	–
Emergency Aid	0	0	1	–
Unspecified	–	–	0	–
TOTAL	100	100	100	–

14. GRANT ELEMENT OF ODA %

DAC COUNTRIES

	1987	1988	1989	1990
Australia	–	100.0	100.0	–
Austria	100.0	100.0	100.0	–
Belgium	100.0	100.0	100.0	–
Canada	100.0	100.0	100.0	–
Denmark	–	–	100.0	–
Finland	–	–	100.0	–
France	100.0	100.0	100.0	–
Germany	100.0	100.0	100.0	–
Ireland	100.0	–	–	–
Italy	100.0	100.0	100.0	–
Japan	97.6	100.0	56.8	–
Netherlands	100.0	100.0	91.8	–
New Zealand	–	–	–	–
Norway	100.0	–	100.0	–
Sweden	100.0	100.0	100.0	–
Switzerland	100.0	100.0	100.0	–
United Kingdom	100.0	100.0	100.0	–
United States	94.3	94.5	100.0	–
TOTAL	95.4	96.4	83.9	–
MULTILATERAL	100.0	100.0	100.0	–
ARAB COUNTRIES	–	–	–	–
E.E.C.+ MEMBERS	100.0	100.0	97.2	–
TOTAL	95.6	96.6	84.7	–

15. OTHER AGGREGATES

OFFICIAL COMMITMENTS:

	1987	1988	1989	1990
TOTAL BILATERAL	227.3	197.3	281.2	233.3
of which:				
Arab Countries	–	–	–	–
C.E.E.C.	–	–	–	–
TOTAL MULTILATERAL	118.8	168.6	203.8	120.8
TOTAL BIL.& MULTIL.	346.1	365.9	485.0	354.1
of which:				
ODA Grants	208.4	185.9	192.9	149.8
ODA Loans	27.0	26.0	96.9	30.1

DISBURSEMENTS:

DAC COUNTRIES COMBINED

OFFICIAL & PRIVATE	1987	1988	1989	1990
GROSS:				
Contractual Lending	34.6	18.1	30.4	87.4
Export Credits, Total	0.1	-0.5	-1.2	-0.1
Export Credits, Priv.	0.1	0.3	-1.2	-2.7
NET:				
Contractual Lending	25.2	8.4	20.4	59.6
Export Credits Total	-7.0	-1.8	-1.3	-17.6
PRIVATE SECTOR NET	19.2	-14.8	-22.2	-91.6
Direct Investment	3.0	2.8	7.4	0.3
Portfolio Investment	23.2	-16.6	-28.3	-87.7
Export Credits	-7.0	-1.0	-1.2	-4.2

MARKET BORROWING:

CHANGE IN CLAIMS

	1987	1988	1989	1990
Banks	-20.0	-101.0	-166.0	-330.0

MEMORANDUM ITEM:

	1987	1988	1989	1990
C.E.E.C. (Gross)	–	–	–	–

1. TOTAL RECEIPTS NET

DAC COUNTRIES

	1987	1988	1989	1990
Australia	–	–	–	–
Austria	-6.0	-6.2	-5.7	-6.7
Belgium	-19.2	22.4	-17.2	24.7
Canada	9.3	23.9	15.9	39.7
Denmark	0.0	0.0	0.2	0.4
Finland	–	0.1	–	0.1
France	-35.5	-52.2	-272.1	194.6
Germany	6.6	16.1	18.8	21.4
Ireland	–	–	–	–
Italy	-15.0	11.7	-1.2	8.9
Japan	6.7	25.5	27.0	53.7
Netherlands	6.0	-23.4	-11.8	-5.1
New Zealand	–	–	–	–
Norway	0.3	0.2	-20.5	-10.9
Sweden	–	–	–	–
Switzerland	0.5	0.4	0.4	1.3
United Kingdom	4.3	26.6	44.7	10.3
United States	-3.0	28.0	1.0	26.0
TOTAL	-45.0	73.2	-220.8	358.2

MULTILATERAL

	1987	1988	1989	1990
AF.D.F.	–	–	-0.1	2.1
AF.D.B.	25.6	104.7	66.8	166.9
AS.D.B	–	–	–	–
CAR.D.B.	–	–	–	–
E.E.C.	39.7	208.7	126.9	126.9
IBRD	291.4	-17.0	11.0	138.0
IDA	-0.1	–	–	–
I.D.B.	–	–	–	–
IFAD	0.6	0.6	1.0	0.5
I.F.C.	8.6	–	3.4	3.6
IMF TRUST FUND	–	–	–	–
U.N. AGENCIES	–	–	–	–
UNDP	3.5	3.9	4.0	6.9
UNTA	1.1	0.8	1.2	1.4
UNICEF	1.1	0.2	0.8	1.6
UNRWA	–	–	–	–
WFP	0.1	0.1	1.9	6.6
UNHCR	–	0.3	0.3	6.0
Other Multilateral	0.6	0.8	1.3	1.6
Arab Agencies	–	–	–	–
TOTAL	372.1	302.9	218.3	462.1
ARAB COUNTRIES	–	–	–	–
E.E.C.+ MEMBERS	-13.1	209.9	-111.8	382.0
TOTAL	327.1	376.1	-2.5	820.3

2. ODA LOANS GROSS

DAC COUNTRIES

	1987	1988	1989	1990
Australia	–	–	–	–
Austria	–	–	–	–
Belgium	0.1	0.1	–	–
Canada	2.4	–	–	–
Denmark	–	–	–	–
Finland	–	–	–	–
France	135.3	150.9	127.3	377.2
Germany	5.7	12.8	4.2	9.5
Ireland	–	–	–	–
Italy	–	–	–	–
Japan	0.2	10.4	3.9	35.2
Netherlands	0.5	0.2	–	–
New Zealand	–	–	–	–
Norway	–	–	–	–
Sweden	–	–	–	–
Switzerland	–	–	–	–
United Kingdom	1.3	3.0	1.3	0.5
United States	–	–	5.0	15.0
TOTAL	145.5	177.2	141.7	437.5
MULTILATERAL	0.6	0.6	1.1	3.7
ARAB COUNTRIES	–	–	–	–
E.E.C.+ MEMBERS	142.8	166.8	132.9	387.3
TOTAL	146.0	177.8	142.9	441.1

3. TOTAL OFFICIAL GROSS

DAC COUNTRIES

	1987	1988	1989	1990
Australia	–	–	–	–
Austria	0.1	0.1	0.1	0.1
Belgium	19.4	47.1	13.6	44.4
Canada	21.4	24.5	16.1	108.2
Denmark	0.2	0.2	0.2	0.7
Finland	–	0.1	–	0.1
France	243.0	209.3	220.2	562.2
Germany	21.2	43.2	29.3	55.2
Ireland	–	–	–	–
Italy	2.9	35.8	22.9	33.8
Japan	2.8	18.4	25.8	55.2
Netherlands	5.9	0.8	1.9	1.2
New Zealand	–	–	–	–
Norway	0.3	0.2	0.1	0.3
Sweden	–	–	–	–
Switzerland	0.5	0.4	0.4	1.3
United Kingdom	7.5	12.8	14.4	18.8
United States	11.0	38.0	18.0	31.0
TOTAL	336.0	430.8	362.9	912.5
MULTILATERAL	463.6	452.5	348.6	612.3
ARAB COUNTRIES	–	–	–	–
E.E.C.+ MEMBERS	353.6	572.1	442.7	856.6
TOTAL	799.6	883.3	711.5	1524.8

4. TOTAL ODA NET

DAC COUNTRIES

	1987	1988	1989	1990
Australia	–	–	–	–
Austria	0.1	0.1	0.1	0.1
Belgium	4.6	4.8	3.7	3.4
Canada	8.8	11.4	10.1	11.9
Denmark	0.1	0.1	0.2	0.7
Finland	–	0.1	–	0.1
France	183.4	162.8	196.5	416.3
Germany	14.4	19.4	13.5	19.2
Ireland	–	–	–	–
Italy	2.9	2.2	1.1	2.0
Japan	2.8	18.4	25.8	55.1
Netherlands	1.0	0.7	0.5	1.2
New Zealand	–	–	–	–
Norway	0.3	0.2	0.1	0.3
Sweden	–	–	–	–
Switzerland	0.5	0.4	0.4	1.3
United Kingdom	1.6	2.9	2.1	1.7
United States	1.0	3.0	6.0	17.0
TOTAL	221.3	226.3	260.1	530.2

MULTILATERAL

	1987	1988	1989	1990
AF.D.F.	–	–	-0.1	2.1
AF.D.B.	–	–	–	–
AS.D.B	–	–	–	–
CAR.D.B.	–	–	–	–
E.E.C.	25.7	206.1	132.6	132.6
IBRD	–	–	–	–
IDA	-0.1	–	–	–
I.D.B.	–	–	–	–
IFAD	0.6	0.6	1.0	0.5
I.F.C.	–	–	–	–
IMF TRUST FUND	–	–	–	–
U.N. AGENCIES	–	–	–	–
UNDP	3.5	3.9	4.0	6.9
UNTA	1.1	0.8	1.2	1.4
UNICEF	1.1	0.2	0.8	1.6
UNRWA	–	–	–	–
WFP	0.1	0.1	1.9	6.6
UNHCR	–	0.3	0.3	6.0
Other Multilateral	0.6	0.8	1.3	1.6
Arab Agencies	–	–	–	–
TOTAL	32.6	212.7	142.9	159.3
ARAB COUNTRIES	–	–	–	–
E.E.C.+ MEMBERS	233.6	398.8	350.3	577.1
TOTAL	253.8	438.9	402.9	689.5

5. ODA LOANS NET

DAC COUNTRIES

	1987	1988	1989	1990
Australia	–	–	–	–
Austria	–	–	–	–
Belgium	–	–	–	-1.1
Canada	2.4	0.0	–	-68.5
Denmark	-0.1	-0.1	–	–
Finland	–	–	–	–
France	128.0	122.1	115.1	292.1
Germany	4.1	8.8	3.1	6.2
Ireland	–	–	–	–
Italy	–	–	–	–
Japan	0.2	10.4	3.9	35.1
Netherlands	0.5	0.2	–	–
New Zealand	–	–	–	–
Norway	–	–	–	–
Sweden	–	–	–	–
Switzerland	–	–	–	–
United Kingdom	1.0	1.9	0.9	0.5
United States	–	–	5.0	10.0
TOTAL	136.2	143.2	128.0	274.3
MULTILATERAL	-1.6	-1.1	-0.5	1.2
ARAB COUNTRIES	–	–	–	–
E.E.C.+ MEMBERS	131.5	131.1	117.7	296.3
TOTAL	134.6	142.1	127.5	275.5

6. TOTAL OFFICIAL NET

DAC COUNTRIES

	1987	1988	1989	1990
Australia	–	–	–	–
Austria	0.1	0.1	0.1	0.1
Belgium	19.3	46.8	13.6	43.3
Canada	9.3	23.9	15.9	39.7
Denmark	0.0	0.0	0.2	0.4
Finland	–	0.1	–	0.1
France	234.9	139.5	181.2	419.9
Germany	16.3	27.9	24.3	25.8
Ireland	–	–	–	–
Italy	2.8	33.9	21.5	17.5
Japan	2.8	18.4	25.8	55.1
Netherlands	5.7	0.2	1.5	1.2
New Zealand	–	–	–	–
Norway	0.3	0.2	0.1	0.3
Sweden	–	–	–	–
Switzerland	0.5	0.4	0.4	1.3
United Kingdom	6.1	11.3	13.1	18.3
United States	-3.0	28.0	1.0	26.0
TOTAL	295.0	330.6	298.6	648.9
MULTILATERAL	372.1	302.9	218.3	462.1
ARAB COUNTRIES	–	–	–	–
E.E.C.+ MEMBERS	324.8	468.2	382.3	653.3
TOTAL	667.1	633.5	516.8	1111.0

7. TOTAL ODA GROSS

	1987
Australia	–
Austria	0.1
Belgium	4.7
Canada	8.8
Denmark	0.2
Finland	–
France	190.6
Germany	16.0
Ireland	–
Italy	2.9
Japan	2.8
Netherlands	1.0
New Zealand	–
Norway	0.3
Sweden	–
Switzerland	0.5
United Kingdom	1.9
United States	1.0
TOTAL	230.5
AF.D.F.	–
AF.D.B.	–
AS.D.B	–
CAR.D.B.	–
E.E.C.	27.8
IBRD	–
IDA	–
I.D.B.	–
IFAD	0.6
I.F.C.	–
IMF TRUST FUND	–
U.N. AGENCIES	–
UNDP	3.5
UNTA	1.1
UNICEF	1.1
UNRWA	–
WFP	0.1
UNHCR	–
Other Multilateral	0.6
Arab Agencies	–
TOTAL	34.7
ARAB COUNTRIES	–
E.E.C.+ MEMBERS	244.9
TOTAL	265.3

8. GRANTS

	1987
Australia	–
Austria	0.1
Belgium	4.6
Canada	6.4
Denmark	0.2
Finland	–
France	55.3
Germany	10.3
Ireland	–
Italy	2.9
Japan	2.6
Netherlands	0.5
New Zealand	–
Norway	0.3
Sweden	–
Switzerland	0.5
United Kingdom	0.6
United States	1.0
TOTAL	85.1
MULTILATERAL	34.2
ARAB COUNTRIES	–
E.E.C.+ MEMBERS	102.1
TOTAL	119.3

9. TOTAL OOF GROSS

	1987
Australia	–
Austria	–
Belgium	14.8
Canada	12.6
Denmark	0.0
Finland	–
France	52.4
Germany	5.3
Ireland	–
Italy	–
Japan	–
Netherlands	4.9
New Zealand	–
Norway	–
Sweden	–
Switzerland	–
United Kingdom	5.6
United States	10.0
TOTAL	105.5
MULTILATERAL	428.8
ARAB COUNTRIES	–
E.E.C.+ MEMBERS	108.7
TOTAL	534.4

1988	1989	1990
–	–	–
0.1	0.1	0.1
4.8	3.7	4.5
11.4	10.1	80.4
0.2	0.2	0.7
0.1	–	0.1
191.6	208.8	501.4
23.4	14.6	22.5
–	–	–
2.2	1.1	2.0
18.4	25.8	55.2
0.7	0.5	1.2
–	–	–
0.2	0.1	0.3
–	–	–
0.4	0.4	1.3
3.9	2.5	1.7
3.0	6.0	22.0
260.3	273.8	693.4
–	–	2.4
–	–	–
–	–	–
–	–	–
207.8	134.0	134.0
–	–	–
–	–	–
0.6	1.1	1.3
–	–	–
–	–	–
–	–	–
3.9	4.0	6.9
0.8	1.2	1.4
0.2	0.8	1.6
–	–	–
0.1	1.9	6.6
0.3	0.3	6.0
0.8	1.3	1.6
–	–	–
214.4	144.5	161.7
–	–	–
434.5	365.4	668.1
474.7	418.3	855.1

1987	1988	1989	1990

10. ODA COMMITMENTS

1987	1988	1989	1990
–	–	–	–
0.1	0.1	0.1	0.1
2.5	2.1	3.7	4.5
4.5	11.2	7.3	22.6
–	–	–	5.2
–	–	–	0.2
167.5	201.1	181.2	559.8
10.1	21.7	11.9	48.7
–	–	–	–
2.8	2.3	2.0	3.0
6.9	10.2	20.0	71.7
1.0	1.2	1.6	0.7
–	–	–	–
0.3	–	–	–
–	–	–	–
0.3	0.3	0.3	1.0
0.6	1.0	1.2	1.2
0.8	3.3	6.2	31.9
197.4	254.3	235.4	750.5
–	–	9.9	10.5
–	–	–	–
–	–	–	–
–	–	–	–
47.4	203.1	147.5	147.5
–	–	–	–
–	–	–	–
–	–	–	–
6.4	6.0	9.4	24.1
–	–	–	–
–	–	–	–
–	–	–	–
–	–	–	–
–	–	–	–
–	–	–	–
–	–	–	–
–	–	–	–
–	–	–	–
–	–	–	–
53.8	209.1	166.7	182.0
–	–	–	–
231.9	432.3	349.1	770.5
251.2	463.3	402.1	932.5

11. TECH. COOP. GRANTS

Left block (1988, 1989, 1990):

1988	1989	1990
–	–	–
0.1	0.1	0.1
4.8	3.7	4.5
11.4	10.1	80.4
0.2	0.2	0.7
0.1	–	0.1
40.7	81.5	124.2
10.6	10.4	13.0
–	–	–
2.2	1.1	2.0
8.0	21.9	20.0
0.5	0.5	1.2
–	–	–
0.2	0.1	0.3
–	–	–
0.4	0.4	1.3
1.0	1.1	1.2
3.0	1.0	7.0
83.1	132.1	255.9
213.8	143.4	158.1
–	–	–
267.7	232.6	280.8
296.9	275.5	414.0

Middle block (1987, 1988, 1989, 1990):

1987	1988	1989	1990
–	–	–	–
0.1	0.1	0.1	0.1
3.9	3.5	2.7	3.3
–	1.3	0.8	–
0.2	0.2	–	0.0
–	–	–	–
52.2	36.8	75.8	93.0
9.3	10.0	7.5	9.2
–	–	–	–
2.6	1.4	1.0	1.8
1.4	2.1	1.7	2.9
0.5	0.5	0.5	0.7
–	–	–	–
0.3	0.2	0.1	0.3
–	–	–	–
0.1	0.1	–	–
0.6	1.0	1.1	1.2
1.0	1.0	1.0	1.0
72.1	58.2	92.2	113.5
7.3	6.6	7.5	17.5
–	–	–	–
70.2	54.0	88.6	109.2
79.3	64.7	99.7	131.0

12. TOTAL OOF NET

Left block (1988, 1989, 1990):

1988	1989	1990
–	–	–
42.3	9.9	39.9
13.1	6.0	27.8
–	–	–
17.7	11.4	60.8
19.8	14.7	32.7
–	–	–
33.7	21.8	31.7
–	–	–
0.2	1.4	–
–	–	–
–	–	–
8.8	11.9	17.1
35.0	12.0	9.0
170.6	89.1	219.1
238.1	204.1	450.6
–	–	–
137.6	77.3	188.5
408.6	293.2	669.7

Middle block (1987, 1988, 1989, 1990):

1987	1988	1989	1990
–	–	–	–
14.8	42.0	9.9	39.9
0.6	12.5	5.8	27.8
-0.1	-0.1	–	-0.3
–	–	–	–
51.5	-23.2	-15.4	3.7
1.9	8.4	10.8	6.6
–	–	–	–
-0.1	31.7	20.4	15.5
–	–	–	–
4.7	-0.4	1.0	–
–	–	–	–
–	–	–	–
4.5	8.4	11.0	16.6
-4.0	25.0	-5.0	9.0
73.7	104.3	38.5	118.7
339.6	90.3	75.4	302.8
–	–	–	–
91.2	69.4	32.0	76.2
413.3	194.6	113.9	421.5

13. ODF COMMITMENTS: BY PURPOSE %

	1987	1988	1989	1990
Education	0	1	0	–
Health	1	0	1	–
Other Social Infrastr.	33	0	10	–
Water Sanitat. Sewage	0	–	0	–
Energy	0	28	15	–
Telecommunications	0	–	0	–
Transportation	11	27	1	–
Agriculture	10	23	35	–
Extractive Industries	–	–	–	–
Manufacturing	10	2	1	–
Trade Banking Tourism	0	0	0	–
Technical Cooperation	18	11	14	–
Multisector Aid	0	0	0	–
Programme	15	–	16	–
Debt Reorganisation	–	7	7	–
Food Aid	–	0	1	–
Emergency Aid	–	–	–	–
Unspecified	–	–	–	–
TOTAL	100	100	100	–

14. GRANT ELEMENT OF ODA %

DAC COUNTRIES	1987	1988	1989	1990
Australia	–	–	–	–
Austria	100.0	100.0	100.0	–
Belgium	100.0	100.0	100.0	–
Canada	100.0	100.0	100.0	–
Denmark	–	–	–	–
Finland	–	–	–	–
France	52.9	55.0	65.1	–
Germany	97.9	68.4	94.5	–
Ireland	–	–	–	–
Italy	100.0	100.0	100.0	–
Japan	100.0	100.0	100.0	–
Netherlands	100.0	100.0	100.0	–
New Zealand	–	–	–	–
Norway	100.0	–	–	–
Sweden	–	–	–	–
Switzerland	100.0	100.0	100.0	–
United Kingdom	100.0	100.0	21.4	–
United States	100.0	100.0	59.4	–
TOTAL	59.8	64.7	62.6	–
MULTILATERAL	100.0	100.0	99.0	–
ARAB COUNTRIES	–	–	–	–
E.E.C.+ MEMBERS	65.8	82.0	73.9	–
TOTAL	68.5	83.5	76.0	–

15. OTHER AGGREGATES

OFFICIAL COMMITMENTS:	1987	1988	1989	1990
TOTAL BILATERAL	306.4	746.1	278.5	1259.1
of which:				
Arab Countries	–	–	–	–
C.E.E.C.	–	–	–	–
TOTAL MULTILATERAL	294.0	531.1	552.4	538.6
TOTAL BIL.& MULTIL.	600.4	1277.1	830.9	1797.7
of which:				
ODA Grants	139.4	299.9	286.1	359.1
ODA Loans	111.8	163.5	116.0	573.4

DISBURSEMENTS:

DAC COUNTRIES COMBINED

OFFICIAL & PRIVATE	1987	1988	1989	1990
GROSS:				
Contractual Lending	234.9	351.8	216.7	587.1
Export Credits, Total	-2.3	17.1	7.2	-22.9
Export Credits, Priv.	-14.9	4.0	-13.5	-68.9
NET:				
Contractual Lending	118.7	157.8	53.0	281.5
Export Credits Total	-102.8	-90.8	-99.7	-80.3
PRIVATE SECTOR NET	-340.1	-257.4	-519.4	-290.7
Direct Investment	5.6	13.2	2.4	13.4
Portfolio Investment	-255.5	-180.9	-408.8	-193.1
Export Credits	-90.2	-89.8	-112.9	-111.0

MARKET BORROWING:

CHANGE IN CLAIMS	1987	1988	1989	1990
Banks	-205.0	-16.0	-163.0	-452.0

MEMORANDUM ITEM:	1987	1988	1989	1990
C.E.E.C. (Gross)	0.1	–	–	–

DISBURSEMENTS, UNLESS OTHERWISE STATE[D]

	1987	1988	1989	1990	1987	1988	1989	1990	1987
1. TOTAL RECEIPTS NET					**4. TOTAL ODA NET**				**7. TOTAL ODA GROSS**
DAC COUNTRIES									
Australia	-2.1	-2.3	–	-1.2	0.0	–	–	–	Australia 0.0
Austria	-1.0	-3.2	-1.9	0.1	–	-0.1	-0.1	0.1	Austria –
Belgium	0.8	-3.3	6.0	-1.7	0.0	0.0	–	–	Belgium 0.0
Canada	2.0	0.1	-0.6	-1.3	0.1	0.2	0.2	0.2	Canada 0.1
Denmark	-1.4	–	–	–	–	–	–	–	Denmark –
Finland	0.2	2.4	-1.3	0.1	0.0	-0.3	0.1	0.1	Finland 0.0
France	-108.2	-40.1	-48.3	37.7	1.0	1.7	0.8	0.8	France 1.0
Germany	0.8	4.0	6.6	27.3	0.2	0.2	0.2	1.1	Germany 0.2
Ireland	–	–	–	–	–	–	–	–	Ireland –
Italy	-50.2	-14.1	46.0	17.5	0.1	0.1	5.4	10.5	Italy 0.1
Japan	-26.5	-0.6	-1.8	43.1	0.2	0.5	0.4	0.6	Japan 0.2
Netherlands	7.1	3.1	1.0	0.8	0.7	0.1	0.0	0.0	Netherlands 1.6
New Zealand	–	–	–	–	–	–	–	–	New Zealand –
Norway	0.5	–	0.0	0.1	0.5	–	0.0	0.1	Norway 0.5
Sweden	5.7	0.6	1.3	2.9	3.9	0.6	3.5	2.6	Sweden 4.0
Switzerland	0.0	0.0	0.0	0.0	0.0	0.0	0.0	0.0	Switzerland 0.0
United Kingdom	2.6	0.4	35.4	-3.4	–	–	–	0.0	United Kingdom –
United States	–	–	–	–	–	–	–	–	United States –
TOTAL	*-169.7*	*-53.0*	*42.5*	*121.8*	*6.7*	*2.9*	*10.6*	*16.1*	*TOTAL* 7.7
MULTILATERAL									
AF.D.F.	–	–	–	–	–	–	–	–	AF.D.F. –
AF.D.B.	–	–	–	–	–	–	–	–	AF.D.B. –
AS.D.B	–	–	–	–	–	–	–	–	AS.D.B –
CAR.D.B.	–	–	–	–	–	–	–	–	CAR.D.B. –
E.E.C.	–	–	–	–	–	–	–	–	E.E.C. –
IBRD	–	–	–	–	–	–	–	–	IBRD –
IDA	–	–	–	–	–	–	–	–	IDA –
I.D.B.	–	–	–	–	–	–	–	–	I.D.B. –
IFAD	1.4	0.2	-0.1	0.9	1.4	0.2	-0.1	0.9	IFAD 2.5
I.F.C.	–	–	–	–	–	–	–	–	I.F.C. –
IMF TRUST FUND	–	–	–	–	–	–	–	–	IMF TRUST FUND –
U.N. AGENCIES	–	–	–	–	–	–	–	–	U.N. AGENCIES –
UNDP	2.7	3.2	2.2	1.3	2.7	3.2	2.2	1.3	UNDP 2.7
UNTA	1.2	1.3	1.4	1.3	1.2	1.3	1.4	1.3	UNTA 1.2
UNICEF	0.0	0.1	0.2	0.2	0.0	0.1	0.2	0.2	UNICEF 0.0
UNRWA	–	–	–	–	–	–	–	–	UNRWA –
WFP	17.5	11.0	9.0	13.2	17.5	11.0	9.0	13.2	WFP 17.5
UNHCR	–	–	–	–	–	–	–	–	UNHCR –
Other Multilateral	0.2	0.8	0.5	0.4	0.2	0.8	0.5	0.4	Other Multilateral 0.2
Arab Agencies	–	–	–	–	–	–	–	–	Arab Agencies –
TOTAL	*23.0*	*16.6*	*13.2*	*17.3*	*23.0*	*16.6*	*13.2*	*17.3*	*TOTAL* 24.1
ARAB COUNTRIES	–	–	–	–	–	–	–	–	**ARAB COUNTRIES** –
E.E.C.+ MEMBERS	*-148.5*	*-50.0*	*46.6*	*78.2*	*1.9*	*2.0*	*6.4*	*12.5*	*E.E.C.+ MEMBERS* 2.8
TOTAL	*-146.7*	*-36.3*	*55.6*	*139.1*	*29.7*	*19.5*	*23.7*	*33.4*	*TOTAL* 31.8
2. ODA LOANS GROSS					**5. ODA LOANS NET**				**8. GRANTS**
DAC COUNTRIES									
Australia	–	–	–	–	–	–	–	–	Australia 0.0
Austria	–	–	–	–	–	-0.1	-0.1	–	Austria –
Belgium	–	–	–	–	–	–	–	–	Belgium 0.0
Canada	–	–	–	–	–	–	–	–	Canada 0.1
Denmark	–	–	–	–	–	–	–	–	Denmark –
Finland	–	–	–	–	–	-0.3	–	–	Finland 0.0
France	–	–	–	–	–	–	–	–	France 1.0
Germany	–	–	–	–	–	–	–	–	Germany 0.2
Ireland	–	–	–	–	–	–	–	–	Ireland –
Italy	–	–	2.3	10.5	–	–	2.3	10.5	Italy 0.1
Japan	–	–	–	–	–	–	–	–	Japan 0.2
Netherlands	1.5	–	–	–	0.5	–	–	–	Netherlands 0.2
New Zealand	–	–	–	–	–	–	–	–	New Zealand –
Norway	–	–	–	–	–	–	–	–	Norway 0.5
Sweden	–	–	–	–	0.0	-0.1	-0.1	–	Sweden 4.0
Switzerland	–	–	–	–	–	–	–	–	Switzerland 0.0
United Kingdom	–	–	–	–	–	–	–	–	United Kingdom –
United States	–	–	–	–	–	–	–	–	United States –
TOTAL	*1.5*	*–*	*2.3*	*10.5*	*0.5*	*-0.5*	*2.1*	*10.5*	*TOTAL* 6.2
MULTILATERAL	*2.5*	*1.1*	*0.3*	*1.1*	*1.4*	*0.2*	*-0.1*	*0.9*	*MULTILATERAL* 21.6
ARAB COUNTRIES	–	–	–	–	–	–	–	–	**ARAB COUNTRIES** –
E.E.C.+ MEMBERS	*1.5*	*–*	*2.3*	*10.5*	*0.5*	*–*	*2.3*	*10.5*	*E.E.C.+ MEMBERS* 1.3
TOTAL	*4.0*	*1.1*	*2.6*	*11.6*	*1.9*	*-0.3*	*2.0*	*11.4*	*TOTAL* 27.8
3. TOTAL OFFICIAL GROSS					**6. TOTAL OFFICIAL NET**				**9. TOTAL OOF GROSS**
DAC COUNTRIES									
Australia	0.0	–	–	–	-2.1	-2.3	–	-1.2	Australia –
Austria	–	0.0	0.0	0.1	-1.0	-3.2	-1.9	0.1	Austria –
Belgium	9.5	2.2	–	–	9.4	2.2	–	–	Belgium 9.5
Canada	2.4	0.5	0.2	0.2	2.0	0.1	-1.0	-1.3	Canada 2.3
Denmark	–	–	–	–	–	–	–	–	Denmark –
Finland	0.0	0.0	0.1	0.1	0.0	-0.3	0.1	0.1	Finland –
France	1.0	1.7	0.8	0.8	0.8	1.7	0.8	0.8	France –
Germany	1.7	13.2	0.3	7.0	1.7	2.5	0.3	7.0	Germany 1.5
Ireland	–	–	–	–	–	–	–	–	Ireland –
Italy	14.0	0.1	5.4	18.7	12.2	0.1	5.4	15.7	Italy 14.0
Japan	0.2	0.5	0.4	0.6	0.2	0.5	0.4	0.6	Japan –
Netherlands	1.6	0.1	0.0	0.0	0.7	0.1	0.0	0.0	Netherlands –
New Zealand	–	–	–	–	–	–	–	–	New Zealand –
Norway	0.5	–	0.0	0.1	0.5	–	0.0	0.1	Norway –
Sweden	4.0	0.7	3.6	2.6	3.9	0.6	3.5	2.6	Sweden –
Switzerland	0.0	0.0	0.0	0.0	0.0	0.0	0.0	0.0	Switzerland –
United Kingdom	–	–	–	0.0	–	–	–	0.0	United Kingdom –
United States	–	–	–	–	–	–	–	–	United States –
TOTAL	*35.0*	*18.9*	*10.8*	*30.2*	*28.3*	*1.9*	*7.6*	*24.4*	*TOTAL* 27.3
MULTILATERAL	*24.1*	*17.5*	*13.6*	*17.5*	*23.0*	*16.6*	*13.2*	*17.3*	*MULTILATERAL* –
ARAB COUNTRIES	–	–	–	–	–	–	–	–	**ARAB COUNTRIES** –
E.E.C.+ MEMBERS	*27.8*	*17.2*	*6.5*	*26.6*	*24.7*	*6.5*	*6.5*	*23.6*	*E.E.C.+ MEMBERS* 25.0
TOTAL	*59.1*	*36.5*	*24.4*	*47.7*	*51.3*	*18.5*	*20.8*	*41.7*	*TOTAL* 27.3

10. ODA COMMITMENTS

1988	1989	1990	1987	1988	1989	1990
–	–	–	–	–	–	–
0.0	0.0	0.1	–	0.0	0.0	0.1
0.0	–	–	–	0.7	–	–
0.2	0.2	0.2	0.0	0.6	0.2	0.0
–	–	–	–	–	–	–
0.0	0.1	0.1	–	–	–	0.1
1.7	0.8	0.8	1.0	1.7	0.8	0.8
0.2	0.2	1.1	0.2	0.2	0.2	1.0
–	–	–	–	–	–	–
0.1	5.4	10.5	0.0	1.5	13.1	–
0.5	0.4	0.6	0.2	0.5	0.4	0.6
0.1	0.0	0.0	1.6	0.1	0.0	0.0
–	–	–	–	–	–	–
–	0.0	0.1	0.1	–	–	–
0.7	3.6	2.6	4.1	4.0	2.7	3.0
0.0	0.0	0.0	–	–	–	–
–	–	0.0	–	–	–	0.0
–	–	–	–	–	–	–
3.5	10.7	16.1	7.2	9.2	17.4	5.5
–	–	–	–	–	–	–
–	–	–	–	–	–	–
–	–	–	–	0.0	–	–
–	–	–	–	–	–	–
–	–	–	–	–	–	–
1.1	0.3	1.1	–	–	–	–
–	–	–	–	–	–	–
–	–	–	21.6	16.4	13.3	16.4
3.2	2.2	1.3	–	–	–	–
1.3	1.4	1.3	–	–	–	–
0.1	0.2	0.2	–	–	–	–
–	–	–	–	–	–	–
11.0	9.0	13.2	–	–	–	–
–	–	–	–	–	–	–
0.8	0.5	0.4	–	–	–	–
–	–	–	–	–	–	–
17.5	13.6	17.5	21.6	16.4	13.3	16.4
–	–	–	–	–	–	–
2.0	6.4	12.5	2.8	4.1	14.1	1.8
21.0	24.3	33.7	28.7	25.6	30.7	22.0

11. TECH. COOP. GRANTS

1988	1989	1990	1987	1988	1989	1990
–	–	–	0.0	–	–	–
0.0	0.0	0.1	–	0.0	0.0	0.0
0.0	–	–	0.0	0.0	–	–
0.2	0.2	0.2	–	–	–	–
–	–	–	–	–	–	–
0.0	0.1	0.1	0.0	0.0	0.1	0.1
1.7	0.8	0.8	1.0	1.7	0.8	0.8
0.2	0.2	1.1	0.2	0.2	0.2	1.1
–	–	–	–	–	–	–
0.1	3.1	–	0.1	0.1	–	–
0.5	0.4	0.6	0.2	0.5	0.4	0.6
0.1	0.0	0.0	0.2	0.1	0.0	0.0
–	–	–	–	–	–	–
–	0.0	0.1	0.0	–	0.0	0.0
0.7	3.6	2.6	4.0	0.7	3.6	2.6
0.0	0.0	0.0	0.0	0.0	–	–
–	–	0.0	–	–	–	0.0
–	–	–	–	–	–	–
3.5	8.5	5.6	5.6	3.2	5.1	5.2
16.4	13.3	16.4	4.1	5.4	4.2	3.2
–	–	–	–	–	–	–
2.0	4.1	2.0	1.3	2.0	1.0	2.0
19.8	21.7	22.0	9.7	8.6	9.3	8.5

12. TOTAL OOF NET

1988	1989	1990	1987	1988	1989	1990
–	–	–	-2.1	-2.3	–	-1.2
–	–	–	-1.0	-3.1	-1.8	–
2.2	–	–	9.4	2.2	–	–
0.3	–	–	1.9	-0.1	-1.1	-1.5
–	–	–	–	–	–	–
–	–	–	–	–	–	–
–	–	–	-0.2	–	–	–
13.0	0.0	5.9	1.5	2.3	0.0	5.9
–	–	8.2	12.1	–	–	5.2
–	–	–	–	–	–	–
–	–	–	–	–	–	–
–	–	–	–	–	–	–
–	–	–	–	–	–	–
–	–	–	–	–	–	–
–	–	–	–	–	–	–
15.5	0.0	14.1	21.6	-1.0	-2.9	8.3
–	–	–	–	–	–	–
–	–	–	–	–	–	–
15.1	0.0	14.1	22.9	4.4	0.0	11.1
15.5	0.0	14.1	21.6	-1.0	-2.9	8.3

13. ODF COMMITMENTS: BY PURPOSE %

	1987	1988	1989	1990
Education	0	–	–	–
Health	0	–	9	–
Other Social Infrastr.	1	0	–	–
Water Sanitat. Sewage	–	–	–	–
Energy	–	–	–	–
Telecommunications	–	–	–	–
Transportation	–	–	–	–
Agriculture	–	1	0	–
Extractive Industries	–	–	7	–
Manufacturing	–	–	49	–
Trade Banking Tourism	–	–	–	–
Technical Cooperation	5	6	35	–
Multisector Aid	94	87	–	–
Programme	–	–	–	–
Debt Reorganisation	1	6	–	–
Food Aid	–	–	–	–
Emergency Aid	–	–	–	–
Unspecified	–	–	–	–
TOTAL	100	100	100	–

14. GRANT ELEMENT OF ODA %

DAC COUNTRIES

	1987	1988	1989	1990
Australia	–	–	–	–
Austria	–	100.0	100.0	–
Belgium	–	100.0	–	–
Canada	100.0	100.0	100.0	–
Denmark	–	–	–	–
Finland	–	–	–	–
France	100.0	100.0	100.0	–
Germany	100.0	100.0	100.0	–
Ireland	–	–	–	–
Italy	100.0	100.0	69.7	–
Japan	100.0	100.0	100.0	–
Netherlands	64.0	100.0	100.0	–
New Zealand	–	–	–	–
Norway	100.0	–	–	–
Sweden	100.0	100.0	100.0	–
Switzerland	–	–	–	–
United Kingdom	–	–	–	–
United States	–	–	–	–
TOTAL	91.9	100.0	77.1	–
MULTILATERAL	100.0	100.0	100.0	–
ARAB COUNTRIES	–	–	–	–
E.E.C.+ MEMBERS	78.9	100.0	71.8	–
TOTAL	98.0	100.0	87.0	–

15. OTHER AGGREGATES

	1987	1988	1989	1990
OFFICIAL COMMITMENTS:				
TOTAL BILATERAL	250.0	243.0	19.3	5.6
of which:				
Arab Countries	–	–	–	–
C.E.E.C.	185.0	221.3	1.9	–
TOTAL MULTILATERAL	21.6	16.4	13.3	16.4
TOTAL BIL.& MULTIL.	271.6	259.4	32.6	22.0
of which:				
ODA Grants	27.3	25.6	21.2	22.0
ODA Loans	186.5	185.0	11.4	–
DISBURSEMENTS:				
DAC COUNTRIES COMBINED				
OFFICIAL & PRIVATE				
GROSS:				
Contractual Lending	16.3	-13.4	74.1	9.6
Export Credits, Total	-10.0	-28.6	71.8	-0.9
Export Credits, Priv.	-12.3	-28.9	71.7	-15.1
NET:				
Contractual Lending	-105.5	-51.3	47.5	-18.0
Export Credits Total	-128.7	-55.2	45.4	-28.5
PRIVATE SECTOR NET	-198.0	-54.8	34.9	97.4
Direct Investment	0.1	0.1	0.2	1.2
Portfolio Investment	-70.7	-5.2	-13.7	133.1
Export Credits	-127.5	-49.7	48.4	-36.8
MARKET BORROWING:				
CHANGE IN CLAIMS				
Banks	-50.0	-222.0	-7.0	761.0
MEMORANDUM ITEM:				
C.E.E.C. (Gross)	838.1	844.6	722.1	–

1. TOTAL RECEIPTS NET

DAC COUNTRIES	1987	1988	1989	1990
Australia	-0.2	-0.1	0.0	0.0
Austria	-1.0	-1.0	-0.9	-1.0
Belgium	4.9	-2.5	-0.5	13.6
Canada	–	–	0.0	–
Denmark	–	–	–	–
Finland	3.9	0.2	1.4	–
France	-58.4	115.1	91.9	65.9
Germany	5.2	2.7	115.3	134.3
Ireland	–	–	–	–
Italy	0.0	0.5	5.7	2.8
Japan	2.1	-2.8	6.3	12.4
Netherlands	5.1	5.2	-19.4	19.2
New Zealand	–	–	–	–
Norway	1.0	–	0.6	0.1
Sweden	–	–	0.2	–
Switzerland	0.1	0.1	0.1	0.2
United Kingdom	-4.8	5.1	-11.3	37.2
United States	9.0	14.0	19.0	16.0
TOTAL	*-33.1*	*136.5*	*208.4*	*300.6*
MULTILATERAL				
AF.D.F.	–	–	–	–
AF.D.B.	–	–	–	–
AS.D.B	–	–	–	–
CAR.D.B.	–	–	–	–
E.E.C.	19.1	8.5	7.2	7.2
IBRD	1.4	-19.0	-60.0	4.0
IDA	–	–	–	–
I.D.B.	–	–	–	–
IFAD	–	-0.1	–	–
I.F.C.	-0.2	-0.2	-1.0	–
IMF TRUST FUND	–	–	–	–
U.N. AGENCIES	–	–	–	–
UNDP	0.7	0.6	0.3	0.6
UNTA	0.5	0.4	0.5	0.8
UNICEF	–	–	–	–
UNRWA	–	–	–	–
WFP	0.5	0.3	0.0	–
UNHCR	5.7	15.2	10.1	12.4
Other Multilateral	97.5	48.3	76.2	1.3
Arab Agencies	–	–	–	–
TOTAL	*125.2*	*54.0*	*33.3*	*26.3*
ARAB COUNTRIES	*4.3*	*5.5*	*4.5*	*–*
E.E.C.+ MEMBERS	*-28.9*	*134.6*	*189.0*	*280.1*
TOTAL	*96.4*	*196.0*	*246.2*	*326.9*

2. ODA LOANS GROSS

DAC COUNTRIES	1987	1988	1989	1990
Australia	–	–	–	–
Austria	–	–	–	–
Belgium	–	–	–	–
Canada	–	–	–	–
Denmark	–	–	–	–
Finland	–	–	–	–
France	3.3	1.3	0.1	0.0
Germany	–	–	–	–
Ireland	–	–	–	–
Italy	–	–	–	–
Japan	–	–	–	–
Netherlands	–	–	–	–
New Zealand	–	–	–	–
Norway	–	–	–	–
Sweden	–	–	–	–
Switzerland	–	–	–	–
United Kingdom	–	–	–	–
United States	–	–	–	–
TOTAL	*3.3*	*1.3*	*0.1*	*0.0*
MULTILATERAL	*2.2*	*4.1*	*3.1*	*2.4*
ARAB COUNTRIES	*6.1*	*7.2*	*6.2*	*–*
E.E.C.+ MEMBERS	*5.5*	*2.8*	*1.3*	*1.2*
TOTAL	*11.5*	*12.6*	*9.4*	*2.4*

3. TOTAL OFFICIAL GROSS

DAC COUNTRIES	1987	1988	1989	1990
Australia	–	–	0.0	0.0
Austria	0.6	0.6	0.6	0.8
Belgium	–	–	–	–
Canada	0.0	0.0	0.0	–
Denmark	–	–	–	–
Finland	–	–	–	–
France	4.2	2.0	0.8	0.8
Germany	3.8	3.7	21.9	11.0
Ireland	–	–	–	–
Italy	0.0	–	0.0	0.0
Japan	0.0	0.1	0.1	0.1
Netherlands	0.0	–	–	–
New Zealand	–	–	–	–
Norway	–	–	–	–
Sweden	–	–	–	–
Switzerland	0.1	0.1	0.1	0.2
United Kingdom	1.5	1.3	1.1	2.1
United States	17.0	15.0	19.0	16.0
TOTAL	*27.3*	*22.9*	*43.7*	*31.0*
MULTILATERAL	*151.4*	*112.4*	*136.0*	*59.9*
ARAB COUNTRIES	*6.1*	*7.2*	*6.2*	*–*
E.E.C.+ MEMBERS	*29.8*	*16.9*	*33.1*	*23.2*
TOTAL	*184.7*	*142.5*	*185.8*	*90.9*

4. TOTAL ODA NET

	1987	1988	1989	1990
Australia	–	–	0.0	0.0
Austria	-1.0	-1.0	-0.9	-1.0
Belgium	–	–	–	–
Canada	0.0	0.0	0.0	–
Denmark	–	–	–	–
Finland	–	–	–	–
France	4.0	1.9	0.6	0.5
Germany	1.3	1.1	0.5	0.6
Ireland	–	–	–	–
Italy	0.0	–	0.0	0.0
Japan	0.0	0.1	0.1	0.1
Netherlands	0.0	–	–	–
New Zealand	–	–	–	–
Norway	–	–	–	–
Sweden	–	–	–	–
Switzerland	0.1	0.1	0.1	0.2
United Kingdom	1.5	1.3	1.1	2.0
United States	17.0	15.0	19.0	16.0
TOTAL	*23.0*	*18.5*	*20.5*	*18.4*
MULTILATERAL				
AF.D.F.	–	–	–	–
AF.D.B.	–	–	–	–
AS.D.B	–	–	–	–
CAR.D.B.	–	–	–	–
E.E.C.	7.0	1.6	3.4	3.4
IBRD	–	–	–	–
IDA	–	–	–	–
I.D.B.	–	–	–	–
IFAD	–	-0.1	–	–
I.F.C.	–	–	–	–
IMF TRUST FUND	–	–	–	–
U.N. AGENCIES	–	–	–	–
UNDP	0.7	0.6	0.3	0.6
UNTA	0.5	0.4	0.5	0.8
UNICEF	–	–	–	–
UNRWA	–	–	–	–
WFP	0.5	0.3	0.0	–
UNHCR	5.7	15.2	10.1	12.4
Other Multilateral	-0.2	2.1	1.3	1.1
Arab Agencies	–	–	–	–
TOTAL	*14.2*	*20.1*	*15.6*	*18.3*
ARAB COUNTRIES	*4.3*	*5.5*	*4.5*	*–*
E.E.C.+ MEMBERS	*13.8*	*5.9*	*5.6*	*6.5*
TOTAL	*41.4*	*44.1*	*40.6*	*36.7*

5. ODA LOANS NET

DAC COUNTRIES	1987	1988	1989	1990
Australia	–	–	–	–
Austria	-1.6	-1.6	-1.5	-1.8
Belgium	–	–	–	–
Canada	–	–	–	–
Denmark	–	–	–	–
Finland	–	–	–	–
France	3.2	1.2	-0.1	-0.3
Germany	-2.5	-2.6	-2.4	-2.8
Ireland	–	–	–	–
Italy	–	–	–	–
Japan	–	–	–	–
Netherlands	–	–	–	–
New Zealand	–	–	–	–
Norway	–	–	–	–
Sweden	–	–	–	–
Switzerland	–	–	–	–
United Kingdom	0.0	0.0	0.0	0.0
United States	–	–	–	–
TOTAL	*-1.0*	*-3.1*	*-4.1*	*-4.9*
MULTILATERAL	*1.8*	*3.4*	*2.3*	*2.0*
ARAB COUNTRIES	*4.3*	*5.5*	*4.5*	*–*
E.E.C.+ MEMBERS	*2.8*	*0.1*	*-1.4*	*-1.9*
TOTAL	*5.0*	*5.8*	*2.7*	*-2.9*

6. TOTAL OFFICIAL NET

DAC COUNTRIES	1987	1988	1989	1990
Australia	-0.2	-0.1	0.0	0.0
Austria	-1.0	-1.0	-0.9	-1.0
Belgium	–	–	–	–
Canada	–	–	0.0	–
Denmark	–	–	–	–
Finland	–	–	–	–
France	4.0	1.9	0.6	0.5
Germany	-0.9	-1.1	16.7	3.7
Ireland	–	–	–	–
Italy	0.0	–	0.0	0.0
Japan	0.0	0.1	0.1	0.1
Netherlands	0.0	–	–	–
New Zealand	–	–	–	–
Norway	–	–	–	–
Sweden	–	–	–	–
Switzerland	0.1	0.1	0.1	0.2
United Kingdom	1.5	1.3	1.1	2.0
United States	16.0	14.0	19.0	16.0
TOTAL	*19.6*	*15.2*	*36.7*	*21.5*
MULTILATERAL	*125.2*	*54.0*	*33.3*	*26.3*
ARAB COUNTRIES	*4.3*	*5.5*	*4.5*	*–*
E.E.C.+ MEMBERS	*23.7*	*10.6*	*25.6*	*13.4*
TOTAL	*149.1*	*74.6*	*74.5*	*47.8*

7. TOTAL ODA GROSS

	1987
Australia	–
Austria	0.6
Belgium	–
Canada	0.0
Denmark	–
Finland	–
France	4.2
Germany	3.8
Ireland	–
Italy	0.0
Japan	0.0
Netherlands	0.0
New Zealand	–
Norway	–
Sweden	–
Switzerland	0.1
United Kingdom	1.5
United States	17.0
TOTAL	*27.3*
AF.D.F.	–
AF.D.B.	–
AS.D.B	–
CAR.D.B.	–
E.E.C.	7.0
IBRD	–
IDA	–
I.D.B.	–
IFAD	–
I.F.C.	–
IMF TRUST FUND	–
U.N. AGENCIES	–
UNDP	0.7
UNTA	0.5
UNICEF	–
UNRWA	–
WFP	0.5
UNHCR	5.7
Other Multilateral	0.2
Arab Agencies	–
TOTAL	*14.6*
ARAB COUNTRIES	*6.1*
E.E.C.+ MEMBERS	*16.5*
TOTAL	*47.9*

8. GRANTS

	1987
Australia	–
Austria	0.6
Belgium	–
Canada	0.0
Denmark	–
Finland	–
France	0.9
Germany	3.8
Ireland	–
Italy	0.0
Japan	0.0
Netherlands	0.0
New Zealand	–
Norway	–
Sweden	–
Switzerland	0.1
United Kingdom	1.5
United States	17.0
TOTAL	*24.0*
MULTILATERAL	*12.4*
ARAB COUNTRIES	*–*
E.E.C.+ MEMBERS	*11.0*
TOTAL	*36.4*

9. TOTAL OOF GROSS

	1987
Australia	–
Austria	–
Belgium	–
Canada	–
Denmark	–
Finland	–
France	–
Germany	–
Ireland	–
Italy	–
Japan	–
Netherlands	–
New Zealand	–
Norway	–
Sweden	–
Switzerland	–
United Kingdom	–
United States	–
TOTAL	*–*
MULTILATERAL	*136.8*
ARAB COUNTRIES	*–*
E.E.C.+ MEMBERS	*13.3*
TOTAL	*136.8*

10. ODA COMMITMENTS

1988	1989	1990	1987	1988	1989	1990
–	0.0	0.0	–	–	–	0.0
0.6	0.6	0.8	0.6	0.6	0.6	0.8
–	–	–	–	–	–	–
0.0	0.0	–	–	0.0	–	–
–	–	–	–	–	–	–
2.0	0.8	0.8	0.9	0.8	0.7	0.8
3.7	2.9	3.4	3.4	3.3	2.8	3.3
–	–	–	–	–	–	–
–	0.0	0.0	–	–	0.0	0.0
0.1	0.1	0.1	0.0	0.1	0.1	0.1
–	–	–	0.0	–	–	–
–	–	–	–	–	–	–
–	–	–	–	–	–	–
0.1	0.1	0.2	–	–	–	–
1.3	1.1	2.1	2.1	1.1	1.0	3.5
15.0	19.0	16.0	15.0	10.0	20.0	5.0
22.9	24.7	23.4	22.0	15.9	25.3	13.4
–	–	–	–	–	–	–
–	–	–	–	–	–	–
–	–	–	–	–	–	–
1.6	3.4	3.4	1.3	0.0	4.7	4.7
–	–	–	–	–	–	–
–	–	–	–	–	–	–
–	–	–	–	–	–	–
–	–	–	–	–	–	–
–	–	–	–	–	–	–
–	–	–	7.6	16.7	11.1	14.2
0.6	0.3	0.6	–	–	–	–
0.4	0.5	0.8	–	–	–	–
–	–	–	–	–	–	–
0.3	0.0	–	–	–	–	–
15.2	10.1	12.4	–	–	–	–
2.8	2.1	1.5	–	2.5	1.9	1.1
–	–	–	–	–	–	–
20.8	16.4	18.7	8.9	19.3	17.6	20.0
7.2	6.2	–	–	24.4	–	–
8.6	8.2	9.7	7.6	5.2	9.2	12.2
50.9	47.3	42.0	30.9	59.5	43.0	33.4

11. TECH. COOP. GRANTS

1988	1989	1990	1987	1988	1989	1990
–	0.0	0.0	–	–	0.0	0.0
0.6	0.6	0.8	0.6	0.6	0.6	0.8
0.0	0.0	–	–	–	–	–
–	–	–	–	–	–	–
0.8	0.7	0.8	0.9	0.8	0.7	0.8
3.7	2.9	3.4	3.8	3.7	2.9	3.4
–	–	–	–	–	–	–
–	0.0	0.0	0.0	–	0.0	0.0
0.1	0.1	0.1	0.0	0.1	0.1	0.1
–	–	–	–	–	–	–
–	–	–	–	–	–	–
0.1	0.1	0.2	0.1	0.1	–	–
1.3	1.1	2.1	0.6	1.1	0.9	0.8
15.0	19.0	16.0	–	–	–	–
21.6	24.6	23.3	6.0	6.3	5.3	5.9
16.7	13.3	16.3	7.8	16.4	11.1	14.2
–	–	–	–	–	–	–
5.8	7.0	8.4	6.0	5.5	4.6	5.0
38.3	37.9	39.7	13.9	22.7	16.4	20.1

12. TOTAL OOF NET

1988	1989	1990	1987	1988	1989	1990
–	–	–	-0.2	-0.1	–	–
–	–	–	–	–	–	–
–	–	–	0.0	0.0	–	–
–	–	–	–	–	–	–
–	19.0	7.6	-2.2	-2.2	16.2	3.1
–	–	–	–	–	–	–
–	–	–	-1.0	-1.0	–	–
–	19.0	7.6	-3.4	-3.4	16.2	3.1
91.6	119.6	41.3	111.1	33.9	17.7	8.0
–	–	–	–	–	–	–
8.3	24.9	13.5	9.9	4.7	20.0	6.9
91.6	138.6	48.9	107.6	30.5	33.9	11.0

13. ODF COMMITMENTS: BY PURPOSE %

	1987	1988	1989	1990
Education	17	8	28	–
Health	–	–	–	–
Other Social Infrastr.	–	–	–	–
Water Sanitat. Sewage	5	13	–	–
Energy	–	–	–	–
Telecommunications	–	–	–	–
Transportation	–	36	–	–
Agriculture	–	24	–	–
Extractive Industries	–	–	–	–
Manufacturing	–	–	–	–
Trade Banking Tourism	–	–	–	–
Technical Cooperation	44	19	44	–
Multisector Aid	–	–	–	–
Programme	–	–	–	–
Debt Reorganisation	–	–	–	–
Food Aid	–	–	–	–
Emergency Aid	34	–	28	–
Unspecified	–	–	–	–
TOTAL	100	100	100	–

14. GRANT ELEMENT OF ODA %

DAC COUNTRIES

	1987	1988	1989	1990
Australia	–	–	–	–
Austria	100.0	100.0	100.0	–
Belgium	–	–	–	–
Canada	–	100.0	–	–
Denmark	–	–	–	–
Finland	–	–	–	–
France	100.0	100.0	100.0	–
Germany	100.0	100.0	100.0	–
Ireland	–	–	–	–
Italy	–	–	100.0	–
Japan	100.0	100.0	100.0	–
Netherlands	100.0	–	–	–
New Zealand	–	–	–	–
Norway	–	–	–	–
Sweden	–	–	–	–
Switzerland	–	–	–	–
United Kingdom	100.0	100.0	100.0	–
United States	100.0	100.0	100.0	–
TOTAL	100.0	100.0	100.0	–
MULTILATERAL	100.0	100.0	100.0	–
ARAB COUNTRIES	–	26.7	–	–
E.E.C.+ MEMBERS	100.0	100.0	100.0	–
TOTAL .	100.0	68.6	100.0	–

15. OTHER AGGREGATES

OFFICIAL COMMITMENTS:

	1987	1988	1989	1990
TOTAL BILATERAL	22.0	40.2	25.9	13.4
of which:				
Arab Countries	–	24.4	–	–
C.E.E.C.	–	–	–	–
TOTAL MULTILATERAL	116.4	151.5	123.3	74.1
TOTAL BIL.& MULTIL.	138.4	191.8	149.2	87.5
of which:				
ODA Grants	29.6	32.6	41.1	32.3
ODA Loans	1.3	26.9	1.9	1.1

DISBURSEMENTS:

DAC COUNTRIES COMBINED

	1987	1988	1989	1990
OFFICIAL & PRIVATE				
GROSS:				
Contractual Lending	-53.9	87.1	193.2	106.7
Export Credits, Total	-57.2	85.9	193.1	106.6
Export Credits, Priv.	-57.2	85.9	176.2	103.5
NET:				
Contractual Lending	-86.6	53.7	120.1	65.8
Export Credits Total	-85.6	56.8	124.3	70.7
PRIVATE SECTOR NET	-52.7	121.4	171.7	279.1
Direct Investment	3.4	-10.6	11.1	27.5
Portfolio Investment	26.1	71.9	50.5	179.6
Export Credits	-82.2	60.1	110.1	72.1

MARKET BORROWING:

CHANGE IN CLAIMS

	1987	1988	1989	1990
Banks	193.0	356.0	298.0	538.0

MEMORANDUM ITEM:

	1987	1988	1989	1990
C.E.E.C. (Gross)	–	–	–	–

	1987	1988	1989	1990		1987	1988	1989	1990		1987

1. TOTAL RECEIPTS NET | 4. TOTAL ODA NET | 7. TOTAL ODA GROSS

DAC COUNTRIES

	1987	1988	1989	1990	1987	1988	1989	1990		1987
Australia	–	–	–	–	–	–	–	–	Australia	–
Austria	0.0	0.1	–	–	0.0	0.1	–	–	Austria	0.0
Belgium	0.2	0.0	–	1.2	0.1	0.1	0.0	0.0	Belgium	0.1
Canada	0.1	0.1	0.4	0.0	0.1	0.1	0.4	0.0	Canada	0.1
Denmark	0.0	0.1	0.1	0.0	0.0	0.1	0.1	0.0	Denmark	0.0
Finland	–	–	–	0.0	–	–	–	0.0	Finland	–
France	43.4	47.3	37.7	54.8	46.1	41.2	39.4	55.8	France	46.5
Germany	2.8	4.0	2.9	2.0	2.0	4.2	3.0	2.1	Germany	2.0
Ireland	–	–	–	–	–	–	–	–	Ireland	–
Italy	6.2	17.3	13.0	18.3	6.2	17.3	13.0	18.3	Italy	6.2
Japan	1.4	3.6	3.8	5.8	1.4	3.6	3.8	5.8	Japan	1.4
Netherlands	0.2	–	–	–	–	–	–	–	Netherlands	–
New Zealand	–	–	–	–	–	–	–	–	New Zealand	–
Norway	–	–	–	–	–	–	–	–	Norway	–
Sweden	–	–	–	–	–	–	–	–	Sweden	–
Switzerland	0.2	0.3	0.1	0.1	0.2	0.3	0.1	0.1	Switzerland	0.2
United Kingdom	-1.9	-2.1	0.1	-2.2	0.3	0.2	0.1	0.1	United Kingdom	0.3
United States	3.0	4.0	4.0	6.0	3.0	4.0	4.0	6.0	United States	3.0
TOTAL	*55.7*	*74.6*	*62.0*	*86.1*	*59.5*	*71.2*	*63.9*	*88.3*	*TOTAL*	*59.8*

MULTILATERAL

	1987	1988	1989	1990	1987	1988	1989	1990		1987
AF.D.F.	5.4	4.7	1.4	6.0	5.4	4.7	1.4	6.0	AF.D.F.	5.4
AF.D.B.	–	–	–	–	–	–	–	–	AF.D.B.	–
AS.D.B	–	–	–	–	–	–	–	–	AS.D.B	–
CAR.D.B.	–	–	–	–	–	–	–	–	CAR.D.B.	–
E.E.C.	1.5	2.4	4.3	4.3	1.5	2.4	4.3	4.3	E.E.C.	1.6
IBRD	–	–	–	–	–	–	–	–	IBRD	–
IDA	6.8	5.0	2.0	3.0	6.8	5.0	2.0	3.0	IDA	6.8
I.D.B.	–	–	–	–	–	–	–	–	I.D.B.	–
IFAD	0.2	–	0.3	0.2	0.2	–	0.3	0.2	IFAD	0.2
I.F.C.	–	–	–	–	–	–	–	–	I.F.C.	–
IMF TRUST FUND	–	–	–	–	–	–	–	–	IMF TRUST FUND	–
U.N. AGENCIES	–	–	–	–	–	–	–	–	U.N. AGENCIES	–
UNDP	1.4	2.4	1.4	2.2	1.4	2.4	1.4	2.2	UNDP	1.4
UNTA	0.8	0.5	0.6	0.6	0.8	0.5	0.6	0.6	UNTA	0.8
UNICEF	0.3	0.1	0.3	1.0	0.3	0.1	0.3	1.0	UNICEF	0.3
UNRWA	–	–	–	–	–	–	–	–	UNRWA	–
WFP	1.4	2.1	0.3	2.0	1.4	2.1	0.3	2.0	WFP	1.4
UNHCR	2.5	1.7	1.0	0.6	2.5	1.7	1.0	0.6	UNHCR	2.5
Other Multilateral	0.2	0.4	0.2	0.2	0.2	0.4	0.2	0.2	Other Multilateral	0.2
Arab Agencies	2.0	-0.9	-1.4	–	2.0	-0.9	-1.4	–	Arab Agencies	4.9
TOTAL	*22.4*	*18.4*	*10.2*	*20.1*	*22.4*	*18.4*	*10.2*	*20.1*	*TOTAL*	*25.4*
ARAB COUNTRIES	***23.6***	***3.4***	***1.1***	***14.4***	***23.6***	***3.4***	***1.1***	***14.4***	***ARAB COUNTRIES***	***26.3***
E.E.C.+ MEMBERS	*52.4*	*69.0*	*58.1*	*78.4*	*56.2*	*65.6*	*60.0*	*80.6*	*E.E.C.+ MEMBERS*	*56.6*
TOTAL	***101.7***	***96.4***	***73.3***	***120.6***	***105.5***	***93.0***	***75.2***	***122.8***	***TOTAL***	***111.5***

2. ODA LOANS GROSS | 5. ODA LOANS NET | 8. GRANTS

DAC COUNTRIES

	1987	1988	1989	1990	1987	1988	1989	1990		1987
Australia	–	–	–	–	–	–	–	–	Australia	–
Austria	–	–	–	–	–	–	–	–	Austria	0.0
Belgium	–	–	–	–	–	–	–	–	Belgium	0.1
Canada	–	–	–	–	–	–	–	–	Canada	0.1
Denmark	–	–	–	–	–	–	–	–	Denmark	0.0
Finland	–	–	–	–	–	–	–	–	Finland	–
France	2.4	2.4	4.3	3.7	2.0	2.0	3.3	1.1	France	44.1
Germany	–	–	–	–	–	–	–	–	Germany	2.0
Ireland	–	–	–	–	–	–	–	–	Ireland	–
Italy	–	–	3.6	12.2	–	–	3.6	12.2	Italy	6.2
Japan	–	–	–	–	–	–	–	–	Japan	1.4
Netherlands	–	–	–	–	–	–	–	–	Netherlands	–
New Zealand	–	–	–	–	–	–	–	–	New Zealand	–
Norway	–	–	–	–	–	–	–	–	Norway	–
Sweden	–	–	–	–	–	–	–	–	Sweden	–
Switzerland	–	–	–	–	–	–	–	–	Switzerland	0.2
United Kingdom	–	–	–	–	–	–	–	–	United Kingdom	0.3
United States	–	–	–	–	–	–	–	–	United States	3.0
TOTAL	*2.4*	*2.4*	*7.9*	*16.0*	*2.0*	*2.0*	*6.8*	*13.3*	*TOTAL*	*57.4*
MULTILATERAL	*16.6*	*12.5*	*5.1*	*9.7*	*13.6*	*8.7*	*1.7*	*7.7*	*MULTILATERAL*	*8.8*
ARAB COUNTRIES	***8.1***	***7.6***	***3.4***	***2.1***	***5.3***	***3.4***	***0.8***	***-0.7***	***ARAB COUNTRIES***	***18.2***
E.E.C.+ MEMBERS	*2.4*	*2.4*	*7.9*	*16.0*	*1.9*	*1.9*	*6.7*	*13.1*	*E.E.C.+ MEMBERS*	*54.3*
TOTAL	***27.0***	***22.5***	***16.4***	***27.8***	***21.0***	***14.1***	***9.3***	***20.2***	***TOTAL***	***84.5***

3. TOTAL OFFICIAL GROSS | 6. TOTAL OFFICIAL NET | 9. TOTAL OOF GROSS

DAC COUNTRIES

	1987	1988	1989	1990	1987	1988	1989	1990		1987
Australia	–	–	–	–	–	–	–	–	Australia	–
Austria	0.0	0.1	–	–	0.0	0.1	–	–	Austria	–
Belgium	0.1	0.1	0.0	0.0	0.1	0.1	0.0	0.0	Belgium	–
Canada	0.1	0.1	0.4	0.0	0.1	0.1	0.4	0.0	Canada	–
Denmark	0.0	0.1	0.1	0.0	0.0	0.1	0.1	0.0	Denmark	–
Finland	–	–	–	0.0	–	–	–	0.0	Finland	–
France	46.5	41.6	40.5	58.4	46.1	41.2	39.4	55.7	France	0.0
Germany	2.0	4.2	3.0	2.1	2.0	4.2	3.0	2.1	Germany	–
Ireland	–	–	–	–	–	–	–	–	Ireland	–
Italy	6.2	17.3	13.0	18.3	6.2	17.3	13.0	18.3	Italy	–
Japan	1.4	3.6	3.8	5.8	1.4	3.6	3.8	5.8	Japan	–
Netherlands	–	–	–	–	–	–	–	–	Netherlands	–
New Zealand	–	–	–	–	–	–	–	–	New Zealand	–
Norway	–	–	–	–	–	–	–	–	Norway	–
Sweden	–	–	–	–	–	–	–	–	Sweden	–
Switzerland	0.2	0.3	0.1	0.1	0.2	0.3	0.1	0.1	Switzerland	–
United Kingdom	0.3	0.2	0.1	0.1	0.3	0.2	0.1	0.1	United Kingdom	–
United States	3.0	4.0	4.0	6.0	3.0	4.0	4.0	6.0	United States	–
TOTAL	*59.8*	*71.6*	*64.9*	*91.0*	*59.5*	*71.2*	*63.9*	*88.3*	*TOTAL*	–
MULTILATERAL	*25.4*	*22.2*	*13.7*	*20.8*	*22.4*	*18.4*	*10.2*	*20.1*	*MULTILATERAL*	–
ARAB COUNTRIES	***26.3***	***7.6***	***3.7***	***17.3***	***23.6***	***3.4***	***1.1***	***14.4***	***ARAB COUNTRIES***	–
E.E.C.+ MEMBERS	*56.6*	*66.0*	*61.2*	*83.5*	*56.2*	*65.6*	*60.0*	*80.6*	*E.E.C.+ MEMBERS*	–
TOTAL	***111.5***	***101.4***	***82.3***	***129.1***	***105.5***	***93.0***	***75.2***	***122.8***	***TOTAL***	–

10. ODA COMMITMENTS

1988	1989	1990		1987	1988	1989	1990
–	–	–		–	–	–	–
0.1	–	–		–	0.3	0.0	0.0
0.1	0.0	0.0		0.1	0.2	0.1	0.2
0.1	0.4	0.0		–	–	–	–
0.1	0.1	0.0		–	–	–	–
–	–	0.0		44.1	48.2	37.0	48.8
41.6	40.5	58.4		5.0	2.8	3.0	1.9
4.2	3.0	2.1		–	–	–	–
–	–	–		26.7	4.3	21.4	11.6
17.3	13.0	18.3		3.5	4.9	7.3	9.0
3.6	3.8	5.8		–	–	–	–
–	–	–		–	–	–	–
–	–	–		–	–	–	–
–	–	–		–	–	–	–
0.3	0.1	0.1		0.2	0.3	0.1	0.1
0.2	0.1	0.1		0.3	0.2	0.1	0.1
4.0	4.0	6.0		2.1	3.5	3.1	3.3
71.6	*64.9*	*91.0*		*82.0*	*64.6*	*72.2*	*74.9*
4.7	1.4	6.0		4.8	8.9	19.0	3.2
–	–	–		–	–	–	–
–	–	–		–	–	–	–
2.5	4.5	4.5		2.6	17.3	4.2	4.2
–	–	–		–	–	–	–
5.0	2.0	3.0		–	–	15.0	–
–	0.3	0.2		–	–	1.3	–
–	–	–		–	–	–	–
–	–	–		–	–	–	–
				6.5	7.1	3.6	6.6
2.4	1.4	2.2		–	–	–	–
0.5	0.6	0.6		–	–	–	–
0.1	0.3	1.0		–	–	–	–
–	–	–		–	–	–	–
2.1	0.3	2.0		–	–	–	–
1.7	1.0	0.6		–	–	–	–
0.4	0.2	0.2		–	–	–	–
2.8	1.9	0.5		0.2	2.0	0.1	–
22.2	*13.7*	*20.8*		*14.1*	*35.3*	*43.2*	*13.9*
7.6	*3.7*	*17.3*		*21.0*	*9.3*	*9.6*	–
66.0	*61.2*	*83.5*		*78.6*	*73.0*	*65.7*	*66.5*
101.4	*82.3*	*129.1*		*117.1*	*109.2*	*124.9*	*88.8*

11. TECH. COOP. GRANTS

1988	1989	1990		1987	1988	1989	1990
–	–	–		–	–	–	–
0.1	–	–		0.1	–	–	–
0.1	0.0	0.0		–	–	–	–
0.1	0.4	0.0		0.0	0.1	0.1	0.0
0.1	0.1	0.0		–	–	–	–
–	–	0.0		27.2	27.4	26.5	33.5
39.2	36.2	54.7		1.6	2.6	2.5	1.7
4.2	3.0	2.1		–	–	–	–
–	–	–		1.4	1.2	0.3	0.3
17.3	9.4	6.0		0.1	0.1	0.1	0.5
3.6	3.8	5.8		–	–	–	–
–	–	–		–	–	–	–
–	–	–		–	–	–	–
–	–	–		–	–	–	–
0.3	0.1	0.1		–	–	–	–
0.2	0.1	0.1		0.3	0.2	0.1	0.1
4.0	4.0	6.0		2.0	2.0	1.0	4.0
69.2	*57.1*	*75.1*		*32.5*	*33.6*	*30.6*	*40.0*
9.7	*8.5*	*11.1*		*5.3*	*5.8*	*3.4*	*4.6*
–	*0.3*	*15.2*		–	–	–	–
63.6	*53.3*	*67.5*		*30.7*	*32.3*	*29.5*	*35.5*
78.9	*65.9*	*101.3*		*37.9*	*39.4*	*34.0*	*44.6*

12. TOTAL OOF NET

1988	1989	1990		1987	1988	1989	1990
–	–	–		–	–	–	–
–	–	–		–	–	–	–
–	–	–		–	–	–	–
–	–	–		–	–	–	–
–	–	–		–	–	–	–
–	–	–		–	–	–	0.0
–	–	–		–	–	–	–
–	–	–		–	–	–	–
–	–	–		–	–	–	–
–	–	–		–	–	–	–
–	–	–		–	–	–	–
–	–	–		–	–	–	–
–	–	–		–	–	–	–
–	–	–		–	–	–	–
–	–	–		–	–	–	0.0
–	–	–		–	–	–	–
–	–	–		–	–	–	–
–	–	–		–	–	–	0.0
–	–	–		–	–	–	*0.0*

13. ODF COMMITMENTS: BY PURPOSE %

	1987	1988	1989	1990
Education	5	1	12	–
Health	0	1	–	–
Other Social Infrastr.	6	9	1	–
Water Sanitat. Sewage	15	5	–	–
Energy	0	2	9	–
Telecommunications	0	13	–	–
Transportation	2	16	35	–
Agriculture	0	2	8	–
Extractive Industries	1	–	–	–
Manufacturing	0	–	–	–
Trade Banking Tourism	4	–	–	–
Technical Cooperation	33	48	29	–
Multisector Aid	19	0	3	–
Programme	4	–	0	–
Debt Reorganisation	–	–	–	–
Food Aid	3	3	1	–
Emergency Aid	5	1	0	–
Unspecified	–	–	–	–
TOTAL	100	100	100	–

14. GRANT ELEMENT OF ODA %

DAC COUNTRIES

	1987	1988	1989	1990
Australia	–	–	–	–
Austria	–	–	–	–
Belgium	100.0	100.0	100.0	–
Canada	100.0	100.0	100.0	–
Denmark	–	–	–	–
Finland	–	–	–	–
France	100.0	91.4	99.0	–
Germany	100.0	100.0	100.0	–
Ireland	–	–	–	–
Italy	100.0	100.0	61.8	–
Japan	100.0	100.0	100.0	–
Netherlands	–	–	–	–
New Zealand	–	–	–	–
Norway	–	–	–	–
Sweden	–	–	–	–
Switzerland	100.0	100.0	100.0	–
United Kingdom	100.0	100.0	100.0	–
United States	100.0	100.0	100.0	–
TOTAL	*100.0*	*93.6*	*88.1*	–
MULTILATERAL	*84.8*	*96.0*	*85.4*	–
ARAB COUNTRIES	**100.0**	**50.6**	**54.7**	–
E.E.C.+ MEMBERS	*100.0*	*94.1*	*86.9*	–
TOTAL	**96.3**	**90.1**	**84.6**	–

15. OTHER AGGREGATES

	1987	1988	1989	1990
OFFICIAL COMMITMENTS:				
TOTAL BILATERAL	103.0	73.9	81.7	74.9
of which:				
Arab Countries	21.0	9.3	9.6	–
C.E.E.C.	–	–	–	–
TOTAL MULTILATERAL	14.1	35.3	43.2	13.9
TOTAL BIL.& MULTIL.	117.1	109.2	124.9	88.8
of which:				
ODA Grants	112.3	78.8	59.9	85.4
ODA Loans	4.8	30.4	65.0	3.4
DISBURSEMENTS:				
DAC COUNTRIES COMBINED				
OFFICIAL & PRIVATE				
GROSS:				
Contractual Lending	-0.3	8.5	5.7	14.7
Export Credits, Total	-2.7	6.1	-2.2	-1.3
Export Credits, Priv.	-2.7	6.1	-2.2	-1.3
NET:				
Contractual Lending	-2.8	5.2	4.6	9.6
Export Credits Total	-4.8	3.2	-2.2	-3.6
PRIVATE SECTOR NET	-3.8	3.4	-1.9	-2.2
Direct Investment	0.4	–	-0.1	0.1
Portfolio Investment	0.6	0.3	0.4	1.4
Export Credits	-4.8	3.2	-2.2	-3.6
MARKET BORROWING:				
CHANGE IN CLAIMS				
Banks	-2.0	-6.0	15.0	-27.0
MEMORANDUM ITEM:				
C.E.E.C. (Gross)	–	–	–	–

	1987	1988	1989	1990
1. TOTAL RECEIPTS NET				
DAC COUNTRIES				
Australia	–	–	0.0	–
Austria	0.0	0.0	0.0	0.0
Belgium	0.1	0.1	0.0	0.0
Canada	3.9	4.8	4.6	2.6
Denmark	–	–	–	–
Finland	–	–	–	–
France	1.1	-6.4	1.4	3.4
Germany	0.3	0.2	0.4	0.3
Ireland	–	–	–	–
Italy	–	0.1	–	–
Japan	0.2	0.2	0.3	13.6
Netherlands	0.0	0.0	0.0	0.0
New Zealand	–	–	–	–
Norway	–	–	–	–
Sweden	–	–	–	–
Switzerland	0.0	0.0	–	0.1
United Kingdom	22.3	-2.6	26.0	2.0
United States	–	–	–	–
TOTAL	*27.9*	*-3.6*	*32.9*	*22.0*
MULTILATERAL				
AF.D.F.	–	–	–	–
AF.D.B.	–	–	–	–
AS.D.B	–	–	–	–
CAR.D.B.	5.3	3.2	4.8	4.8
E.E.C.	2.2	3.3	1.8	1.8
IBRD	–	–	–	–
IDA	1.1	–	2.0	1.0
I.D.B.	–	–	–	–
IFAD	0.2	0.2	0.4	0.6
I.F.C.	–	–	0.5	–
IMF TRUST FUND	–	–	–	–
U.N. AGENCIES	–	–	–	–
UNDP	0.3	0.4	0.4	0.5
UNTA	0.3	0.3	0.4	0.4
UNICEF	–	–	–	–
UNRWA	–	–	–	–
WFP	–	0.7	2.2	–
UNHCR	–	–	–	–
Other Multilateral	0.1	0.1	0.1	0.1
Arab Agencies	-0.2	-0.3	-0.3	–
TOTAL	*9.3*	*7.8*	*12.2*	*9.1*
ARAB COUNTRIES	–	–	–	–
E.E.C.+ MEMBERS	25.9	-5.4	29.7	7.5
TOTAL	**37.2**	**4.2**	**45.1**	**31.1**
2. ODA LOANS GROSS				
DAC COUNTRIES				
Australia	–	–	–	–
Austria	–	–	–	–
Belgium	–	–	–	–
Canada	–	–	–	–
Denmark	–	–	–	–
Finland	–	–	–	–
France	1.1	0.2	2.0	3.2
Germany	–	–	–	–
Ireland	–	–	–	–
Italy	–	–	–	–
Japan	–	–	–	2.0
Netherlands	–	–	–	–
New Zealand	–	–	–	–
Norway	–	–	–	–
Sweden	–	–	–	–
Switzerland	–	–	–	–
United Kingdom	0.5	1.3	2.9	1.1
United States	–	–	–	–
TOTAL	*1.6*	*1.5*	*4.9*	*6.3*
MULTILATERAL	*6.6*	*3.4*	*8.0*	*7.3*
ARAB COUNTRIES	–	–	–	–
E.E.C.+ MEMBERS	1.6	1.5	5.9	5.3
TOTAL	**8.1**	**4.9**	**12.9**	**13.5**
3. TOTAL OFFICIAL GROSS				
DAC COUNTRIES				
Australia	–	–	0.0	–
Austria	0.0	0.0	0.0	0.0
Belgium	0.1	0.1	0.0	0.0
Canada	4.0	5.0	4.9	2.8
Denmark	–	–	–	–
Finland	–	–	–	–
France	1.1	0.2	2.1	3.2
Germany	0.4	0.2	0.3	0.3
Ireland	–	–	–	–
Italy	–	0.1	–	–
Japan	0.2	0.2	0.3	2.2
Netherlands	0.0	0.0	0.0	0.0
New Zealand	–	–	–	–
Norway	–	–	–	–
Sweden	–	–	–	–
Switzerland	0.0	0.0	–	0.1
United Kingdom	1.4	3.5	4.1	2.4
United States	–	–	–	–
TOTAL	*7.1*	*9.4*	*11.7*	*11.1*
MULTILATERAL	*9.6*	*8.1*	*12.6*	*9.2*
ARAB COUNTRIES	–	–	–	–
E.E.C.+ MEMBERS	5.1	7.4	8.3	7.8
TOTAL	**16.7**	**17.5**	**24.3**	**20.3**

	1987	1988	1989	1990
4. TOTAL ODA NET				
Australia	–	–	0.0	–
Austria	0.0	0.0	0.0	0.0
Belgium	0.1	0.1	0.0	0.0
Canada	2.1	4.9	4.9	2.8
Denmark	–	–	–	–
Finland	–	–	–	–
France	1.1	0.2	2.1	3.2
Germany	0.3	0.2	0.3	0.3
Ireland	–	–	–	–
Italy	–	0.1	–	–
Japan	0.2	0.2	0.3	2.2
Netherlands	0.0	0.0	0.0	0.0
New Zealand	–	–	–	–
Norway	–	–	–	–
Sweden	–	–	–	–
Switzerland	0.0	0.0	–	0.1
United Kingdom	1.3	3.4	4.0	2.1
United States	–	–	–	–
TOTAL	*5.1*	*9.1*	*11.5*	*10.8*
AF.D.F.	–	–	–	–
AF.D.B.	–	–	–	–
AS.D.B	–	–	–	–
CAR.D.B.	5.2	3.2	4.7	4.7
E.E.C.	2.2	3.3	1.8	1.8
IBRD	–	–	–	–
IDA	1.1	–	2.0	1.0
I.D.B.	–	–	–	–
IFAD	0.2	0.2	0.4	0.6
I.F.C.	–	–	–	–
IMF TRUST FUND	–	–	–	–
U.N. AGENCIES	–	–	–	–
UNDP	0.3	0.4	0.4	0.5
UNTA	0.3	0.3	0.4	0.4
UNICEF	–	–	–	–
UNRWA	–	–	–	–
WFP	–	0.7	2.2	–
UNHCR	–	–	–	–
Other Multilateral	0.1	0.1	0.1	0.1
Arab Agencies	-0.2	-0.3	-0.3	–
TOTAL	*9.2*	*7.8*	*11.7*	*9.0*
ARAB COUNTRIES	–	–	–	–
E.E.C.+ MEMBERS	5.0	7.3	8.2	7.5
TOTAL	**14.4**	**17.0**	**23.2**	**19.8**
5. ODA LOANS NET				
Australia	–	–	–	–
Austria	–	–	–	–
Belgium	–	–	–	–
Canada	0.0	-0.1	0.0	0.0
Denmark	–	–	–	–
Finland	–	–	–	–
France	1.1	0.2	2.0	3.2
Germany	-0.1	0.0	–	–
Ireland	–	–	–	–
Italy	–	–	–	–
Japan	–	–	–	2.0
Netherlands	–	–	–	–
New Zealand	–	–	–	–
Norway	–	–	–	–
Sweden	–	–	–	–
Switzerland	–	–	–	–
United Kingdom	0.4	1.3	2.8	0.8
United States	–	–	–	–
TOTAL	*1.4*	*1.3*	*4.8*	*6.0*
MULTILATERAL	*6.4*	*3.1*	*7.7*	*7.0*
ARAB COUNTRIES	–	–	–	–
E.E.C.+ MEMBERS	1.5	1.4	5.8	5.0
TOTAL	**7.8**	**4.5**	**12.5**	**13.0**
6. TOTAL OFFICIAL NET				
Australia	–	–	0.0	–
Austria	0.0	0.0	0.0	0.0
Belgium	0.1	0.1	0.0	0.0
Canada	3.9	4.8	4.6	2.6
Denmark	–	–	–	–
Finland	–	–	–	–
France	1.1	0.2	2.1	3.2
Germany	0.3	0.2	0.3	0.3
Ireland	–	–	–	–
Italy	–	0.1	–	–
Japan	0.2	0.2	0.3	2.2
Netherlands	0.0	0.0	0.0	0.0
New Zealand	–	–	–	–
Norway	–	–	–	–
Sweden	–	–	–	–
Switzerland	0.0	0.0	–	0.1
United Kingdom	1.3	3.4	4.0	2.0
United States	–	–	–	–
TOTAL	*6.9*	*9.0*	*11.3*	*10.4*
MULTILATERAL	*9.3*	*7.8*	*12.2*	*9.1*
ARAB COUNTRIES	–	–	–	–
E.E.C.+ MEMBERS	4.9	7.2	8.2	7.4
TOTAL	**16.2**	**16.8**	**23.6**	**19.5**

	1987
7. TOTAL ODA GROSS	
Australia	–
Austria	0.0
Belgium	0.1
Canada	2.1
Denmark	–
Finland	–
France	1.1
Germany	0.4
Ireland	–
Italy	–
Japan	0.2
Netherlands	0.0
New Zealand	–
Norway	–
Sweden	–
Switzerland	0.0
United Kingdom	1.4
United States	–
TOTAL	*5.3*
AF.D.F.	–
AF.D.B.	–
AS.D.B	–
CAR.D.B.	5.2
E.E.C.	2.2
IBRD	–
IDA	1.1
I.D.B.	–
IFAD	0.2
I.F.C.	–
IMF TRUST FUND	–
U.N. AGENCIES	–
UNDP	0.3
UNTA	0.3
UNICEF	–
UNRWA	–
WFP	–
UNHCR	–
Other Multilateral	0.1
Arab Agencies	0.1
TOTAL	*9.5*
ARAB COUNTRIES	–
E.E.C.+ MEMBERS	5.1
TOTAL	**14.7**
8. GRANTS	
Australia	–
Austria	0.0
Belgium	0.1
Canada	2.1
Denmark	–
Finland	–
France	0.0
Germany	0.4
Ireland	–
Italy	–
Japan	0.2
Netherlands	0.0
New Zealand	–
Norway	–
Sweden	–
Switzerland	0.0
United Kingdom	0.9
United States	–
TOTAL	*3.7*
MULTILATERAL	*2.9*
ARAB COUNTRIES	–
E.E.C.+ MEMBERS	3.5
TOTAL	**6.6**
9. TOTAL OOF GROSS	
Australia	–
Austria	–
Belgium	–
Canada	1.8
Denmark	–
Finland	–
France	–
Germany	–
Ireland	–
Italy	–
Japan	–
Netherlands	–
New Zealand	–
Norway	–
Sweden	–
Switzerland	–
United Kingdom	–
United States	–
TOTAL	*1.8*
MULTILATERAL	*0.1*
ARAB COUNTRIES	–
E.E.C.+ MEMBERS	–
TOTAL	**2.0**

1988	1989	1990	1987	1988	1989	1990

10. ODA COMMITMENTS

1988	1989	1990	1987	1988	1989	1990
–	0.0	–	–	–	–	–
0.0	0.0	0.0	0.0	0.0	0.0	0.0
0.1	0.0	0.0	0.1	0.0	0.0	0.0
4.9	4.9	2.8	4.4	2.9	0.2	0.9
–	–	–	–	–	–	–
0.2	2.1	3.2	3.5	1.9	4.7	1.9
0.2	0.3	0.3	0.2	0.1	0.9	0.1
–	–	–	–	–	–	–
0.1	–	–	–	0.1	–	–
0.2	0.3	2.2	0.5	0.3	0.3	0.1
0.0	0.0	0.0	0.0	0.0	0.0	0.0
–	–	–	–	–	–	–
–	–	–	–	–	–	–
0.0	–	0.1	–	–	–	–
3.5	4.1	2.4	9.0	1.0	1.2	1.2
–	–	–	0.2	0.1	–	–
9.3	11.7	11.1	17.8	6.4	7.3	4.2
–	–	–	–	–	–	–
–	–	–	–	–	–	–
3.2	4.7	4.7	6.6	6.7	1.7	1.7
3.3	1.8	1.8	4.9	0.1	2.0	2.0
–	–	–	–	–	–	–
–	2.0	1.0	6.0	–	–	–
–	–	–	–	–	–	–
0.2	0.4	0.6	–	–	–	–
–	–	–	–	–	–	–
–	–	–	0.7	1.5	3.1	1.0
0.4	0.4	0.5	–	–	–	–
0.3	0.4	0.4	–	–	–	–
–	–	–	–	–	–	–
0.7	2.2	–	–	–	–	–
0.1	0.1	0.1	–	–	–	–
–	–	0.0	0.5	–	–	–
8.1	11.9	9.0	18.8	8.3	6.7	4.6
–	–	–	–	–	–	–
7.4	8.3	7.8	17.7	3.2	8.8	5.2
17.4	23.6	20.1	36.7	14.7	14.1	8.8

11. TECH. COOP. GRANTS

1988	1989	1990	1987	1988	1989	1990
–	0.0	–	–	–	–	–
0.0	0.0	0.0	0.0	0.0	0.0	0.0
0.1	0.0	0.0	0.0	–	–	–
4.9	4.9	2.8	–	0.8	0.7	0.4
–	–	–	–	–	–	–
–	–	–	–	–	–	–
0.0	0.0	0.0	0.0	0.0	0.0	0.0
0.2	0.3	0.3	0.4	0.2	0.3	0.3
–	–	–	–	–	–	–
0.1	–	–	–	0.1	–	–
0.2	0.3	0.2	0.2	0.2	0.2	0.1
0.0	0.0	0.0	0.0	0.0	0.0	0.0
–	–	–	–	–	–	–
–	–	–	–	–	–	–
0.0	–	0.1	–	–	–	–
2.2	1.2	1.3	0.8	1.0	1.1	1.2
–	–	–	–	–	–	–
7.8	6.8	4.8	1.4	2.2	2.3	2.1
4.7	3.9	1.8	0.8	1.0	0.9	1.0
–	–	–	–	–	–	–
5.9	2.4	2.5	1.2	1.5	1.4	1.6
12.5	10.7	6.6	2.2	3.3	3.3	3.1

12. TOTAL OOF NET

1988	1989	1990	1987	1988	1989	1990
–	–	–	–	–	–	–
–	–	–	–	–	–	–
0.1	–	–	1.8	-0.1	-0.2	-0.2
–	–	–	–	–	–	–
–	–	–	–	–	–	–
–	–	–	–	–	–	–
–	–	–	–	–	–	–
–	–	–	–	–	–	–
–	–	–	–	–	–	–
–	–	–	–	–	–	–
–	–	–	–	–	–	–
–	–	–	-0.1	-0.1	–	-0.1
0.1	–	–	1.8	-0.2	-0.2	-0.4
0.0	0.7	0.1	0.0	0.0	0.6	0.1
–	–	–	–	–	–	–
–	–	–	-0.1	-0.1	–	-0.1
0.1	0.7	0.1	1.8	-0.2	0.4	-0.2

13. ODF COMMITMENTS: BY PURPOSE %

	1987	1988	1989	1990
Education	2	–	–	–
Health	–	16	46	–
Other Social Infrastr.	–	2	21	–
Water Sanitat. Sewage	–	–	–	–
Energy	34	–	–	–
Telecommunications	–	–	–	–
Transportation	–	27	0	–
Agriculture	10	31	0	–
Extractive Industries	–	–	–	–
Manufacturing	–	–	–	–
Trade Banking Tourism	–	–	11	–
Technical Cooperation	8	23	21	–
Multisector Aid	34	–	–	–
Programme	12	–	–	–
Debt Reorganisation	–	–	–	–
Food Aid	–	1	–	–
Emergency Aid	–	–	0	–
Unspecified	–	–	–	–
TOTAL	100	100	100	–

14. GRANT ELEMENT OF ODA %

DAC COUNTRIES	1987	1988	1989	1990
Australia	–	–	–	–
Austria	100.0	100.0	100.0	–
Belgium	100.0	100.0	100.0	–
Canada	100.0	100.0	100.0	–
Denmark	–	–	–	–
Finland	–	–	–	–
France	38.4	97.8	41.0	–
Germany	100.0	100.0	100.0	–
Ireland	–	–	–	–
Italy	–	100.0	–	–
Japan	100.0	100.0	100.0	–
Netherlands	100.0	100.0	100.0	–
New Zealand	–	–	–	–
Norway	–	–	–	–
Sweden	–	–	–	–
Switzerland	–	–	–	–
United Kingdom	73.0	100.0	100.0	–
United States	100.0	100.0	–	–
TOTAL	74.3	99.3	61.9	–
MULTILATERAL	82.7	100.0	100.0	–
ARAB COUNTRIES	–	–	–	–
E.E.C.+ MEMBERS	65.7	98.7	68.3	–
TOTAL	76.9	99.5	77.6	–

15. OTHER AGGREGATES

OFFICIAL COMMITMENTS:	1987	1988	1989	1990
TOTAL BILATERAL	17.8	6.4	7.3	4.2
of which:				
Arab Countries	–	–	–	–
C.E.E.C.	–	–	–	–
TOTAL MULTILATERAL	18.8	8.3	7.4	4.6
TOTAL BIL.& MULTIL.	36.7	14.7	14.8	8.8
of which:				
ODA Grants	7.5	8.5	7.8	5.3
ODA Loans	29.2	6.1	6.3	3.4

DISBURSEMENTS:

DAC COUNTRIES COMBINED

OFFICIAL & PRIVATE GROSS:	1987	1988	1989	1990
Contractual Lending	3.4	1.6	4.9	6.3
Export Credits, Total	1.8	0.1	–	–
Export Credits, Priv.	–	–	–	–
NET:				
Contractual Lending	3.2	1.2	4.5	5.6
Export Credits Total	1.8	-0.1	-0.2	-0.2
PRIVATE SECTOR NET	21.0	-12.6	21.5	11.6
Direct Investment	21.1	-6.0	22.0	0.0
Portfolio Investment	0.0	-6.6	-0.5	11.6
Export Credits	–	–	–	–

MARKET BORROWING:

CHANGE IN CLAIMS

Banks	–	-6.0	-5.0	–

MEMORANDUM ITEM:

C.E.E.C. (Gross)	–	–	–	–

1. TOTAL RECEIPTS NET

DAC COUNTRIES	1987	1988	1989	1990
Australia	–	–	–	–
Austria	0.0	0.0	–	0.0
Belgium	-2.2	0.8	-2.4	-0.5
Canada	0.2	0.4	0.8	0.6
Denmark	–	–	–	–
Finland	0.0	–	–	0.0
France	-1.6	-0.2	-0.1	-0.6
Germany	20.8	15.1	11.1	14.7
Ireland	–	–	–	–
Italy	13.0	-2.6	27.9	10.4
Japan	39.0	20.3	20.0	18.1
Netherlands	3.9	1.5	7.4	27.6
New Zealand	–	–	–	–
Norway	1.0	-6.1	-0.7	-0.4
Sweden	2.1	3.3	0.8	0.8
Switzerland	–	0.1	0.5	0.5
United Kingdom	0.1	0.2	0.0	0.0
United States	60.0	49.0	54.0	25.0
TOTAL	*136.3*	*81.9*	*119.2*	*96.2*
MULTILATERAL				
AF.D.F.	–	–	–	–
AF.D.B.	–	–	–	–
AS.D.B	–	–	–	–
CAR.D.B.	–	–	–	–
E.E.C.	4.5	5.7	3.0	3.0
IBRD	-1.8	-7.0	12.0	20.0
IDA	-0.1	–	–	–
I.D.B.	32.1	26.3	28.3	21.7
IFAD	5.2	-0.2	1.1	2.2
I.F.C.	0.7	-0.7	-0.3	2.4
IMF TRUST FUND	–	–	–	–
U.N. AGENCIES	–	–	–	–
UNDP	1.4	2.1	3.0	3.2
UNTA	0.8	0.7	0.6	0.7
UNICEF	0.4	0.6	0.6	1.0
UNRWA	–	–	–	–
WFP	0.2	–	0.7	0.2
UNHCR	–	–	–	–
Other Multilateral	0.7	0.9	0.8	0.6
Arab Agencies	–	–	–	–
TOTAL	*44.0*	*28.4*	*49.8*	*55.0*
ARAB COUNTRIES	*–*	*–*	*–*	*–*
E.E.C.+ MEMBERS	*38.4*	*20.5*	*46.9*	*54.6*
TOTAL	**180.3**	**110.3**	**169.0**	**151.2**

4. TOTAL ODA NET

	1987	1988	1989	1990
Australia	–	–	–	–
Austria	0.0	0.0	–	0.0
Belgium	0.1	0.2	0.3	0.2
Canada	0.5	0.4	0.8	0.6
Denmark	–	–	–	–
Finland	0.0	–	–	0.0
France	0.9	1.0	1.2	2.4
Germany	16.3	15.1	10.7	12.4
Ireland	–	–	–	–
Italy	4.8	3.8	27.4	9.2
Japan	17.7	22.9	22.6	17.5
Netherlands	1.3	2.2	2.4	2.6
New Zealand	–	–	–	–
Norway	0.9	0.2	0.2	0.3
Sweden	0.3	3.3	0.8	0.8
Switzerland	–	0.1	0.5	0.5
United Kingdom	0.1	0.2	0.0	0.0
United States	59.0	50.0	54.0	25.0
TOTAL	*101.9*	*99.3*	*120.8*	*71.5*
AF.D.F.	–	–	–	–
AF.D.B.	–	–	–	–
AS.D.B	–	–	–	–
CAR.D.B.	–	–	–	–
E.E.C.	4.5	5.7	3.0	3.0
IBRD	–	–	–	–
IDA	-0.1	–	–	–
I.D.B.	14.6	8.6	11.8	10.8
IFAD	5.2	-0.2	1.1	2.2
I.F.C.	–	–	–	–
IMF TRUST FUND	–	–	–	–
U.N. AGENCIES	–	–	–	–
UNDP	1.4	2.1	3.0	3.2
UNTA	0.8	0.7	0.6	0.7
UNICEF	0.4	0.6	0.6	1.0
UNRWA	–	–	–	–
WFP	0.2	–	0.7	0.2
UNHCR	–	–	–	–
Other Multilateral	0.7	0.9	0.8	0.6
Arab Agencies	–	–	–	–
TOTAL	*27.6*	*18.4*	*21.7*	*21.6*
ARAB COUNTRIES	*–*	*–*	*–*	*–*
E.E.C.+ MEMBERS	*28.0*	*28.2*	*45.0*	*29.8*
TOTAL	**129.5**	**117.7**	**142.4**	**93.1**

7. TOTAL ODA GROSS

	1987
Australia	–
Austria	0.0
Belgium	0.1
Canada	0.6
Denmark	–
Finland	0.0
France	0.9
Germany	16.5
Ireland	–
Italy	4.8
Japan	17.7
Netherlands	1.3
New Zealand	–
Norway	0.9
Sweden	0.3
Switzerland	–
United Kingdom	0.1
United States	65.0
TOTAL	*108.3*
AF.D.F.	–
AF.D.B.	–
AS.D.B	–
CAR.D.B.	–
E.E.C.	4.5
IBRD	–
IDA	–
I.D.B.	20.5
IFAD	5.7
I.F.C.	–
IMF TRUST FUND	–
U.N. AGENCIES	–
UNDP	1.4
UNTA	0.8
UNICEF	0.4
UNRWA	–
WFP	0.2
UNHCR	–
Other Multilateral	0.7
Arab Agencies	–
TOTAL	*34.1*
ARAB COUNTRIES	*–*
E.E.C.+ MEMBERS	*28.2*
TOTAL	**142.4**

2. ODA LOANS GROSS

DAC COUNTRIES	1987	1988	1989	1990
Australia	–	–	–	–
Austria	–	–	–	–
Belgium	–	–	–	–
Canada	–	–	–	–
Denmark	–	–	–	–
Finland	–	–	–	–
France	–	–	–	–
Germany	7.2	6.6	1.4	1.1
Ireland	–	–	–	–
Italy	–	–	24.1	6.8
Japan	12.1	16.4	14.3	0.5
Netherlands	–	–	–	–
New Zealand	–	–	–	–
Norway	–	–	–	–
Sweden	–	–	–	–
Switzerland	–	–	–	–
United Kingdom				
United States	20.0	7.0	30.0	11.0
TOTAL	*39.3*	*30.0*	*69.7*	*19.3*
MULTILATERAL	*25.5*	*18.0*	*21.9*	*23.1*
ARAB COUNTRIES	*–*	*–*	*–*	*–*
E.E.C.+ MEMBERS	*7.2*	*6.6*	*25.5*	*7.8*
TOTAL	**64.7**	**48.1**	**91.6**	**42.4**

5. ODA LOANS NET

	1987	1988	1989	1990
Australia	–	–	–	–
Austria	–	–	–	–
Belgium	–	–	–	–
Canada	-0.1	-0.1	-0.3	-0.2
Denmark	–	–	–	–
Finland	–	–	–	–
France	–	–	–	–
Germany	7.0	6.4	1.4	1.1
Ireland	–	–	–	–
Italy	–	–	24.1	6.8
Japan	12.0	16.3	14.0	0.1
Netherlands	–	–	–	–
New Zealand	–	–	–	–
Norway	–	–	–	–
Sweden	–	–	–	–
Switzerland	–	–	–	–
United Kingdom				
United States	14.0	-6.0	21.0	7.0
TOTAL	*32.9*	*16.5*	*60.2*	*14.8*
MULTILATERAL	*18.9*	*7.9*	*13.0*	*13.0*
ARAB COUNTRIES	*–*	*–*	*–*	*–*
E.E.C.+ MEMBERS	*7.0*	*6.4*	*25.5*	*7.8*
TOTAL	**51.8**	**24.4**	**73.1**	**27.7**

8. GRANTS

	1987
Australia	–
Austria	0.0
Belgium	0.1
Canada	0.6
Denmark	–
Finland	0.0
France	0.9
Germany	9.3
Ireland	–
Italy	4.8
Japan	5.6
Netherlands	1.3
New Zealand	–
Norway	0.9
Sweden	0.3
Switzerland	–
United Kingdom	0.1
United States	45.0
TOTAL	*69.1*
MULTILATERAL	*8.6*
ARAB COUNTRIES	*–*
E.E.C.+ MEMBERS	*21.0*
TOTAL	**77.7**

3. TOTAL OFFICIAL GROSS

DAC COUNTRIES	1987	1988	1989	1990
Australia	–	–	–	–
Austria	0.0	0.0	–	0.0
Belgium	0.1	0.2	0.3	0.2
Canada	0.6	0.6	1.1	0.8
Denmark	–	–	–	–
Finland	0.0	–	–	0.0
France	2.4	1.0	1.2	2.4
Germany	20.8	18.7	12.9	14.0
Ireland	–	–	–	–
Italy	4.8	3.8	27.4	9.2
Japan	17.7	23.0	22.8	17.8
Netherlands	2.3	2.2	2.4	2.6
New Zealand	–	–	–	–
Norway	0.9	0.2	0.2	0.3
Sweden	0.3	3.3	0.8	0.8
Switzerland	–	0.1	0.5	0.5
United Kingdom	0.1	0.2	0.0	0.0
United States	69.0	63.0	64.0	30.0
TOTAL	*119.1*	*116.1*	*133.5*	*78.6*
MULTILATERAL	*72.7*	*62.7*	*91.5*	*97.1*
ARAB COUNTRIES	*–*	*–*	*–*	*–*
E.E.C.+ MEMBERS	*34.9*	*31.7*	*47.2*	*31.4*
TOTAL	**191.8**	**178.8**	**225.0**	**175.7**

6. TOTAL OFFICIAL NET

	1987	1988	1989	1990
Australia	–	–	–	–
Austria	0.0	0.0	–	0.0
Belgium	0.1	0.2	0.3	0.2
Canada	0.2	0.4	0.8	0.6
Denmark	–	–	–	–
Finland	0.0	–	–	0.0
France	2.4	1.0	1.2	2.4
Germany	20.5	18.4	12.9	14.0
Ireland	–	–	–	–
Italy	4.8	3.8	27.4	9.2
Japan	17.7	22.9	22.6	17.5
Netherlands	-0.6	1.7	2.3	2.4
New Zealand	–	–	–	–
Norway	0.9	0.2	0.2	0.3
Sweden	0.3	3.3	0.8	0.8
Switzerland	–	0.1	0.5	0.5
United Kingdom	0.1	0.2	0.0	0.0
United States	60.0	49.0	54.0	25.0
TOTAL	*106.4*	*101.2*	*122.8*	*72.9*
MULTILATERAL	*44.0*	*28.4*	*49.8*	*55.0*
ARAB COUNTRIES	*–*	*–*	*–*	*–*
E.E.C.+ MEMBERS	*31.8*	*31.0*	*47.0*	*31.2*
TOTAL	**150.4**	**129.6**	**172.6**	**127.9**

9. TOTAL OOF GROSS

	1987
Australia	–
Austria	–
Belgium	–
Canada	–
Denmark	–
Finland	–
France	1.4
Germany	4.3
Ireland	–
Italy	–
Japan	–
Netherlands	1.0
New Zealand	–
Norway	–
Sweden	–
Switzerland	–
United Kingdom	–
United States	4.0
TOTAL	*10.7*
MULTILATERAL	*38.6*
ARAB COUNTRIES	*–*
E.E.C.+ MEMBERS	*6.7*
TOTAL	**49.3**

10. ODA COMMITMENTS

1988	1989	1990	1987	1988	1989	1990
—	—	—	—	—	—	—
0.0	—	0.0	0.0	0.0	—	0.0
0.2	0.3	0.2	0.2	0.2	0.3	0.2
0.6	1.1	0.8	0.7	0.6	1.1	0.8
—	—	—	—	—	—	—
—	—	0.0	—	—	—	0.0
1.0	1.2	2.4	0.9	1.0	1.2	2.4
15.4	10.7	12.4	13.0	6.4	15.7	11.2
—	—	—	—	—	—	—
3.8	27.4	9.2	4.5	3.3	45.7	9.5
23.0	22.8	17.8	4.4	12.1	15.6	13.0
2.2	2.4	2.6	1.2	2.2	2.4	2.6
—	—	—	1.8	—	—	—
0.2	0.2	0.3	—	—	—	—
3.3	0.8	0.8	0.5	1.1	0.3	0.6
0.1	0.5	0.5	—	—	—	—
0.2	0.0	0.0	0.1	0.2	0.0	0.0
63.0	63.0	29.0	52.7	69.0	78.6	19.4
112.8	*130.3*	*76.0*	*79.8*	*96.1*	*160.9*	*59.8*
—	—	—	—	—	—	—
—	—	—	—	—	—	—
—	—	—	—	—	—	—
5.7	3.0	3.0	2.0	0.6	0.6	0.6
—	—	—	—	—	—	—
17.4	19.9	19.7	—	—	62.0	—
1.1	2.0	3.4	7.8	—	—	—
—	—	—	—	—	—	—
—	—	—	3.4	4.3	5.7	5.7
2.1	3.0	3.2	—	—	—	—
0.7	0.6	0.7	—	—	—	—
0.6	0.6	1.0	—	—	—	—
—	—	—	—	—	—	—
—	0.7	0.2	—	—	—	—
—	—	—	—	—	—	—
0.9	0.8	0.6	—	—	—	—
—	—	—	—	—	—	—
28.6	*30.6*	*31.8*	*13.3*	*4.9*	*68.3*	*6.3*
—	—	—	—	—	—	—
28.4	*45.0*	*29.8*	*21.8*	*13.8*	*65.9*	*26.6*
141.4	*160.9*	*107.8*	*93.1*	*100.9*	*229.2*	*66.0*

11. TECH. COOP. GRANTS

1988	1989	1990	1987	1988	1989	1990
—	—	—	—	—	—	—
0.0	—	0.0	0.0	0.0	—	0.0
0.2	0.3	0.2	0.1	—	—	0.0
0.6	1.1	0.8	—	0.0	—	0.0
—	—	—	—	—	—	—
—	—	0.0	0.0	—	—	—
1.0	1.2	2.4	0.9	1.0	1.2	2.4
8.7	9.3	11.3	8.6	8.5	8.5	10.9
—	—	—	—	—	—	—
3.8	3.4	2.4	1.3	1.0	—	—
6.6	8.5	17.3	3.5	4.9	4.9	6.5
2.2	2.4	2.6	1.2	2.1	2.2	2.6
—	—	—	—	—	—	—
0.2	0.2	0.3	0.9	—	—	—
3.3	0.8	0.8	0.3	3.3	0.7	0.6
0.1	0.5	0.5	—	—	—	—
0.2	0.0	0.0	0.1	0.2	0.0	0.0
56.0	33.0	18.0	7.0	11.0	14.0	14.0
82.8	*60.6*	*56.7*	*23.9*	*31.8*	*31.6*	*37.0*
10.5	*8.7*	*8.7*	*4.1*	*4.3*	*5.0*	*5.5*
—	—	—	—	—	—	—
21.8	*19.6*	*22.0*	*13.0*	*12.7*	*12.0*	*15.8*
93.3	*69.3*	*65.4*	*28.0*	*36.1*	*36.6*	*42.5*

12. TOTAL OOF NET

1988	1989	1990	1987	1988	1989	1990
—	—	—	—	—	—	—
—	—	—	—	—	—	—
—	—	—	-0.3	—	—	—
—	—	—	—	—	—	—
—	—	—	1.4	—	—	—
3.3	2.2	1.6	4.2	3.3	2.1	1.6
—	—	—	—	—	—	—
—	—	—	—	—	—	—
—	—	—	-1.9	-0.5	-0.1	-0.2
—	—	—	—	—	—	—
—	—	—	—	—	—	—
—	—	—	—	—	—	—
—	1.0	1.0	1.0	-1.0	—	—
3.3	*3.2*	*2.6*	*4.5*	*1.8*	*2.0*	*1.4*
34.1	*60.9*	*65.4*	*16.4*	*10.0*	*28.2*	*33.3*
—	—	—	—	—	—	—
3.3	*2.2*	*1.6*	*3.8*	*2.8*	*2.0*	*1.4*
37.4	*64.1*	*68.0*	*20.9*	*11.8*	*30.2*	*34.7*

13. ODF COMMITMENTS: BY PURPOSE %

	1987	1988	1989	1990
Education	1	2	4	—
Health	3	2	1	—
Other Social Infrastr.	1	0	0	—
Water Sanitat. Sewage	—	0	—	—
Energy	—	49	21	—
Telecommunications	—	—	—	—
Transportation	—	—	—	—
Agriculture	42	5	6	—
Extractive Industries	—	—	—	—
Manufacturing	—	—	—	—
Trade Banking Tourism	21	7	16	—
Technical Cooperation	18	17	28	—
Multisector Aid	0	—	—	—
Programme	—	—	—	—
Debt Reorganisation	0	0	—	—
Food Aid	13	16	24	—
Emergency Aid	0	0	—	—
Unspecified	—	1	—	—
TOTAL	100	100	100	—

14. GRANT ELEMENT OF ODA %

DAC COUNTRIES

	1987	1988	1989	1990
Australia	—	—	—	—
Austria	100.0	100.0	—	—
Belgium	100.0	100.0	100.0	—
Canada	100.0	100.0	100.0	—
Denmark	—	—	—	—
Finland	—	—	—	—
France	100.0	100.0	100.0	—
Germany	100.0	100.0	100.0	—
Ireland	—	—	—	—
Italy	100.0	100.0	66.6	—
Japan	95.7	96.7	98.8	—
Netherlands	100.0	100.0	100.0	—
New Zealand	—	—	—	—
Norway	100.0	—	—	—
Sweden	100.0	100.0	100.0	—
Switzerland	—	—	—	—
United Kingdom	100.0	100.0	100.0	—
United States	97.4	96.8	87.3	—
TOTAL	*98.0*	*97.3*	*84.2*	—
MULTILATERAL	*100.0*	*100.0*	*100.0*	—
ARAB COUNTRIES	—	—	—	—
E.E.C.+ MEMBERS	*100.0*	*100.0*	*76.9*	—
TOTAL	*98.2*	*97.4*	*84.8*	—

15. OTHER AGGREGATES

	1987	1988	1989	1990
OFFICIAL COMMITMENTS:				
TOTAL BILATERAL	86.0	96.1	166.9	63.6
of which:				
Arab Countries	—	—	—	—
C.E.E.C.	—	—	—	—
TOTAL MULTILATERAL	13.3	110.5	205.2	12.3
TOTAL BIL.& MULTIL.	99.3	206.6	372.0	75.8
of which:				
ODA Grants	81.5	95.2	103.1	58.2
ODA Loans	11.6	5.8	126.1	7.9
DISBURSEMENTS:				
DAC COUNTRIES COMBINED				
OFFICIAL & PRIVATE				
GROSS:				
Contractual Lending	84.0	33.6	72.2	45.7
Export Credits, Total	34.0	0.2	1.5	25.4
Export Credits, Priv.	34.0	0.2	-0.7	23.8
NET:				
Contractual Lending	47.2	-0.7	56.5	33.1
Export Credits Total	6.6	-19.1	-3.5	18.6
PRIVATE SECTOR NET	29.9	-19.3	-3.6	23.4
Direct Investment	2.5	1.3	0.9	2.9
Portfolio Investment	17.5	-1.5	1.3	3.5
Export Credits	9.9	-19.1	-5.7	17.0
MARKET BORROWING:				
CHANGE IN CLAIMS				
Banks	-12.0	-190.0	137.0	-139.0
MEMORANDUM ITEM:				
C.E.E.C. (Gross)	—	—	—	—

1. TOTAL RECEIPTS NET

DAC COUNTRIES	1987	1988	1989	1990
Australia	–	0.1	0.1	0.0
Austria	0.3	0.3	0.3	0.4
Belgium	-23.4	9.9	6.4	-7.5
Canada	2.5	10.5	1.3	6.4
Denmark	-1.7	-0.4	0.1	-0.1
Finland	0.5	0.5	0.3	0.4
France	42.1	-11.3	33.8	13.9
Germany	22.8	39.3	60.3	65.6
Ireland	0.0	–	–	–
Italy	15.0	26.3	131.7	56.2
Japan	46.6	31.0	166.7	24.1
Netherlands	89.7	20.3	15.4	3.2
New Zealand	0.1	0.1	0.1	0.0
Norway	-0.3	-5.8	-4.7	-3.9
Sweden	-5.0	0.6	-2.1	-1.0
Switzerland	3.2	2.7	3.1	3.9
United Kingdom	2.9	12.8	-1.8	9.8
United States	-97.0	-186.0	-357.0	-90.0
TOTAL	98.3	-49.2	53.8	81.4
MULTILATERAL				
AF.D.F.	–	–	–	–
AF.D.B.	–	–	–	–
AS.D.B	–	–	–	–
CAR.D.B.	–	–	–	–
E.E.C.	2.3	2.8	5.1	5.1
IBRD	94.9	124.0	29.0	6.0
IDA	-0.6	-1.0	-1.0	-1.0
I.D.B.	140.5	95.0	78.8	89.3
IFAD	1.1	0.4	-0.5	0.9
I.F.C.	-2.4	–	2.5	–
IMF TRUST FUND	–	–	–	–
U.N. AGENCIES	–	–	–	–
UNDP	6.1	5.3	2.4	6.2
UNTA	1.5	1.4	1.3	1.5
UNICEF	0.5	0.7	1.0	1.6
UNRWA	–	–	–	–
WFP	1.9	3.7	2.7	7.5
UNHCR	–	–	–	0.1
Other Multilateral	1.1	1.4	1.1	2.4
Arab Agencies	–	–	–	–
TOTAL	246.9	233.6	122.5	119.7
ARAB COUNTRIES	-0.1	–	–	–
E.E.C.+ MEMBERS	149.8	99.6	250.9	146.1
TOTAL	345.1	184.3	176.3	201.0

2. ODA LOANS GROSS

DAC COUNTRIES	1987	1988	1989	1990
Australia	–	–	–	–
Austria	–	–	–	–
Belgium	–	–	–	–
Canada	–	–	–	–
Denmark	–	–	–	–
Finland	0.1	0.0	0.0	–
France	4.1	4.0	5.0	9.9
Germany	1.1	4.4	2.1	3.5
Ireland	–	–	–	–
Italy	8.2	3.7	25.9	2.9
Japan	47.4	14.0	23.5	16.9
Netherlands	0.2	–	–	–
New Zealand	–	–	–	–
Norway	–	–	–	–
Sweden	–	–	–	–
Switzerland	–	–	–	–
United Kingdom	0.2	–	–	–
United States	7.0	6.0	3.0	4.0
TOTAL	68.2	32.2	59.6	37.1
MULTILATERAL	43.8	30.4	30.9	26.1
ARAB COUNTRIES	–	–	–	–
E.E.C.+ MEMBERS	13.7	12.1	33.0	16.2
TOTAL	112.0	62.6	90.5	63.2

3. TOTAL OFFICIAL GROSS

DAC COUNTRIES	1987	1988	1989	1990
Australia	–	0.1	0.1	0.0
Austria	0.3	0.3	0.3	0.4
Belgium	5.4	3.8	4.1	4.3
Canada	3.8	13.2	6.2	10.4
Denmark	1.3	0.1	0.1	0.2
Finland	0.2	0.5	0.3	0.4
France	14.7	19.5	23.3	40.4
Germany	22.0	36.0	42.6	39.3
Ireland	0.0	–	–	–
Italy	21.3	12.3	175.9	90.2
Japan	52.0	17.6	145.5	24.5
Netherlands	6.2	6.0	6.4	8.2
New Zealand	0.1	0.1	0.1	0.0
Norway	1.1	0.3	0.2	0.6
Sweden	0.7	0.6	0.5	0.8
Switzerland	3.2	2.7	3.1	3.9
United Kingdom	4.2	2.7	1.9	9.9
United States	53.0	57.0	27.0	59.0
TOTAL	189.4	172.6	437.4	292.6
MULTILATERAL	330.9	325.5	206.7	221.8
ARAB COUNTRIES	0.0	–	–	–
E.E.C.+ MEMBERS	77.3	83.1	259.3	197.7
TOTAL	520.3	498.1	644.1	514.4

4. TOTAL ODA NET

	1987	1988	1989	1990
	–	0.1	0.1	0.0
	0.3	0.3	0.3	0.4
	3.3	3.8	3.4	3.5
	0.8	0.6	0.9	4.3
	–	0.0	0.1	0.0
	0.2	0.5	0.3	0.4
	6.3	5.8	10.1	15.0
	18.4	19.0	16.7	20.9
	0.0	–	–	–
	21.3	12.3	42.4	12.3
	46.1	16.1	24.4	15.1
	6.2	5.7	6.4	8.2
	0.1	0.1	0.1	0.0
	1.1	0.3	0.2	0.6
	0.7	0.6	0.5	0.8
	3.2	2.7	3.1	3.9
	3.1	2.1	1.9	2.3
	43.0	30.0	15.0	27.0
TOTAL	154.1	99.9	125.9	114.6
	–	–	–	–
	–	–	–	–
	–	–	–	–
	–	–	–	–
	2.3	2.8	5.1	5.1
	–	–	–	–
	-0.6	-1.0	-1.0	-1.0
	35.5	21.9	21.6	14.6
	1.1	0.4	-0.5	0.9
	–	–	–	–
	–	–	–	–
	–	–	–	–
	6.1	5.3	2.4	6.2
	1.5	1.4	1.3	1.5
	0.5	0.7	1.0	1.6
	–	–	–	–
	1.9	3.7	2.7	7.5
	–	–	–	0.1
	1.1	1.4	1.1	2.4
	–	–	–	–
TOTAL	49.4	36.5	33.7	39.0
	–	–	–	–
	61.0	51.4	86.2	67.3
	203.5	136.4	159.6	153.7

5. ODA LOANS NET

	1987	1988	1989	1990
	–	–	–	–
	–	–	–	–
	–	–	–	–
	-0.2	-0.2	-0.3	-0.3
	–	-0.1	–	-0.3
	0.1	0.0	0.0	–
	4.1	4.0	5.0	9.9
	1.0	4.4	2.1	3.1
	–	–	–	–
	8.2	3.7	25.9	2.9
	43.4	12.5	14.5	7.4
	0.2	0.0	–	0.0
	–	–	–	–
	–	–	–	–
	–	–	–	–
	–	–	–	–
	0.2	–	–	–
	6.0	1.0	-4.0	1.0
TOTAL	62.9	25.3	43.2	23.6
MULTILATERAL	35.6	21.3	19.8	13.6
ARAB COUNTRIES	–	–	–	–
E.E.C.+ MEMBERS	13.6	12.0	33.0	15.5
TOTAL	98.6	46.6	63.1	37.2

6. TOTAL OFFICIAL NET

	1987	1988	1989	1990
	–	0.1	0.1	0.0
	0.3	0.3	0.3	0.4
	5.4	3.8	3.9	4.2
	2.4	10.8	1.8	6.5
	-1.7	-0.4	0.1	-0.1
	0.2	0.5	0.3	0.4
	14.7	15.7	18.9	23.5
	20.8	27.4	30.4	24.2
	0.0	–	–	–
	20.8	12.3	165.4	78.3
	48.0	14.2	127.4	12.1
	6.0	5.7	6.0	7.6
	0.1	0.1	0.1	0.0
	1.1	0.3	0.2	0.6
	0.7	0.6	0.5	0.8
	3.2	2.7	3.1	3.9
	4.2	1.8	1.5	9.9
	51.0	47.0	17.0	46.0
TOTAL	177.1	142.8	376.9	218.2
MULTILATERAL	246.9	233.6	122.5	119.7
ARAB COUNTRIES	-0.1	–	–	–
E.E.C.+ MEMBERS	72.5	69.2	231.2	152.7
TOTAL	423.9	376.4	499.3	337.9

7. TOTAL ODA GROSS

	1987
Australia	–
Austria	0.3
Belgium	3.3
Canada	1.1
Denmark	–
Finland	0.2
France	6.3
Germany	18.5
Ireland	0.0
Italy	21.3
Japan	50.1
Netherlands	6.2
New Zealand	0.1
Norway	1.1
Sweden	0.7
Switzerland	3.2
United Kingdom	3.1
United States	44.0
TOTAL	159.4
AF.D.F.	–
AF.D.B.	–
AS.D.B	–
CAR.D.B.	–
E.E.C.	2.3
IBRD	–
IDA	–
I.D.B.	43.0
IFAD	1.1
I.F.C.	–
IMF TRUST FUND	–
U.N. AGENCIES	–
UNDP	6.1
UNTA	1.5
UNICEF	0.5
UNRWA	–
WFP	1.9
UNHCR	–
Other Multilateral	1.1
Arab Agencies	–
TOTAL	57.5
ARAB COUNTRIES	–
E.E.C.+ MEMBERS	61.1
TOTAL	217.0

8. GRANTS

	1987
Australia	–
Austria	0.3
Belgium	3.3
Canada	1.1
Denmark	–
Finland	0.1
France	2.2
Germany	17.4
Ireland	0.0
Italy	13.1
Japan	2.7
Netherlands	6.1
New Zealand	0.1
Norway	1.1
Sweden	0.7
Switzerland	3.2
United Kingdom	3.0
United States	37.0
TOTAL	91.2
MULTILATERAL	13.7
ARAB COUNTRIES	–
E.E.C.+ MEMBERS	47.4
TOTAL	104.9

9. TOTAL OOF GROSS

	1987
Australia	–
Austria	–
Belgium	2.0
Canada	2.8
Denmark	1.3
Finland	–
France	8.4
Germany	3.5
Ireland	–
Italy	–
Japan	2.0
Netherlands	–
New Zealand	–
Norway	–
Sweden	–
Switzerland	–
United Kingdom	1.1
United States	9.0
TOTAL	30.0
MULTILATERAL	273.4
ARAB COUNTRIES	0.0
E.E.C.+ MEMBERS	16.2
TOTAL	303.4

10. ODA COMMITMENTS

1988	1989	1990	1987	1988	1989	1990
0.1	0.1	0.0	0.1	0.1	0.1	0.1
0.3	0.3	0.4	0.3	0.3	0.3	0.5
3.8	3.4	3.5	4.6	–	3.4	3.5
0.9	1.2	4.6	1.5	4.2	1.0	18.6
0.1	0.1	0.2	–	–	–	–
0.5	0.3	0.4	–	0.3	0.3	0.2
5.8	10.1	15.0	10.3	10.6	20.5	94.2
19.0	16.7	21.3	21.1	26.0	37.6	20.2
–	–	–	0.0	–	–	–
12.3	42.4	12.3	43.6	34.1	35.2	10.0
17.6	33.4	24.5	2.9	137.1	27.3	78.2
5.8	6.4	8.2	6.7	5.7	9.9	8.5
0.1	0.1	0.0	0.0	0.0	–	–
0.3	0.2	0.6	0.8	–	–	–
0.6	0.5	0.8	0.8	1.0	0.9	1.2
2.7	3.1	3.9	2.3	2.1	7.5	2.4
2.1	1.9	2.3	3.1	2.1	1.9	2.3
35.0	22.0	30.0	44.4	23.6	38.2	24.5
106.8	*142.2*	*128.1*	*142.7*	*246.9*	*184.0*	*264.4*
–	–	–	–	–	–	–
–	–	–	–	–	–	–
–	–	–	–	–	–	–
2.8	5.1	5.1	15.5	8.8	5.4	5.4
–	–	–	–	–	–	–
30.0	31.2	25.6	63.5	–	56.2	92.2
0.4	–	1.5	–	–	–	6.9
–	–	–	–	–	–	–
–	–	–	11.0	12.4	8.5	19.4
5.3	2.4	6.2	–	–	–	–
1.4	1.3	1.5	–	–	–	–
0.7	1.0	1.6	–	–	–	–
–	–	–	–	–	–	–
3.7	2.7	7.5	–	–	–	–
–	–	0.1	–	–	–	–
1.4	1.1	2.4	–	–	–	–
–	–	–	–	–	–	–
45.6	*44.8*	*51.5*	*90.1*	*21.2*	*70.1*	*123.8*
–	–	–	–	–	–	–
51.6	*86.2*	*68.1*	*105.0*	*87.3*	*113.8*	*144.1*
152.4	*187.0*	*179.6*	*232.8*	*268.1*	*254.1*	*388.2*

11. TECH. COOP. GRANTS

1988	1989	1990	1987	1988	1989	1990
0.1	0.1	0.0	–	–	–	–
0.3	0.3	0.4	0.2	0.3	0.3	0.4
3.8	3.4	3.5	2.7	2.4	1.8	1.5
0.9	1.2	4.6	–	–	–	0.1
0.1	0.1	0.2	–	0.1	0.0	–
0.5	0.3	0.4	0.1	–	–	–
1.7	5.1	5.1	2.2	1.7	2.2	5.1
14.6	14.6	17.8	17.1	14.6	13.6	16.8
–	–	–	0.0	–	–	–
8.6	16.6	9.5	12.6	4.3	6.3	3.3
3.6	9.9	7.7	2.3	3.6	3.8	3.1
5.8	6.4	8.2	4.6	5.2	5.8	6.5
0.1	0.1	0.0	0.0	0.1	–	0.0
0.3	0.2	0.6	0.0	0.0	–	–
0.6	0.5	0.8	0.4	0.3	0.5	0.7
2.7	3.1	3.9	0.7	0.7	–	–
2.1	1.9	2.3	1.8	2.1	1.9	2.3
29.0	19.0	26.0	13.0	15.0	16.0	15.0
74.6	*82.6*	*91.0*	*57.8*	*50.2*	*52.1*	*54.9*
15.2	13.9	25.5	9.8	10.1	5.9	11.8
–	–	–	–	–	–	–
39.5	*53.2*	*51.8*	*41.7*	*31.7*	*31.6*	*35.6*
89.8	*96.6*	*116.5*	*67.6*	*60.4*	*58.0*	*66.7*

12. TOTAL OOF NET

1988	1989	1990	1987	1988	1989	1990
–	–	–	–	–	–	–
–	0.7	0.8	2.0	–	0.5	0.7
12.3	5.0	5.9	1.6	10.2	0.9	2.2
0.0	–	–	-1.7	-0.3	–	0.0
–	–	–	–	–	–	–
13.7	13.1	25.4	8.4	9.9	8.8	8.5
17.0	25.8	18.0	2.4	8.4	13.6	3.3
–	–	–	–	–	–	–
–	133.5	77.9	-0.5	–	123.0	66.0
–	112.1	–	2.0	-1.9	103.0	-3.0
0.2	–	–	-0.2	0.0	-0.4	-0.6
–	–	–	–	–	–	–
–	–	–	–	–	–	–
0.6	–	7.6	1.1	-0.3	-0.5	7.6
22.0	5.0	29.0	8.0	17.0	2.0	19.0
65.9	*295.2*	*164.5*	*23.0*	*43.0*	*251.0*	*103.6*
279.9	*161.9*	*170.3*	*197.5*	*197.1*	*88.7*	*80.6*
–	–	–	*-0.1*	–	–	–
31.5	*173.2*	*129.6*	*11.4*	*17.7*	*145.1*	*85.4*
345.8	*457.1*	*334.8*	*220.4*	*240.0*	*339.7*	*184.2*

13. ODF COMMITMENTS: BY PURPOSE %

	1987	1988	1989	1990
Education	0	2	1	–
Health	1	1	2	–
Other Social Infrastr.	0	18	1	–
Water Sanitat. Sewage	6	–	6	–
Energy	6	–	–	–
Telecommunications	0	22	21	–
Transportation	13	–	–	–
Agriculture	23	26	14	–
Extractive Industries	–	1	0	–
Manufacturing	0	0	–	–
Trade Banking Tourism	25	–	2	–
Technical Cooperation	11	20	16	–
Multisector Aid	0	–	–	–
Programme	3	2	31	–
Debt Reorganisation	0	8	4	–
Food Aid	1	2	2	–
Emergency Aid	11	0	–	–
Unspecified	0	–	0	–
TOTAL	100	100	100	–

14. GRANT ELEMENT OF ODA %

DAC COUNTRIES

	1987	1988	1989	1990
Australia	100.0	100.0	100.0	–
Austria	100.0	100.0	100.0	–
Belgium	100.0	–	100.0	–
Canada	100.0	100.0	100.0	–
Denmark	–	–	–	–
Finland	–	–	100.0	–
France	77.4	73.3	68.9	–
Germany	100.0	68.2	64.2	–
Ireland	100.0	–	–	–
Italy	71.6	87.7	71.0	–
Japan	100.0	54.9	53.2	–
Netherlands	100.0	100.0	100.0	–
New Zealand	100.0	100.0	–	–
Norway	100.0	–	–	–
Sweden	100.0	100.0	100.0	–
Switzerland	100.0	100.0	100.0	–
United Kingdom	100.0	100.0	100.0	–
United States	99.1	100.0	100.0	–
TOTAL	*89.7*	*68.8*	*77.3*	–
MULTILATERAL	*83.6*	*94.5*	*83.9*	–
ARAB COUNTRIES	–	–	–	–
E.E.C.+ MEMBERS	*86.3*	*81.3*	*73.5*	–
TOTAL	*87.4*	*71.3*	*78.1*	–

15. OTHER AGGREGATES

	1987	1988	1989	1990
OFFICIAL COMMITMENTS:				
TOTAL BILATERAL	190.3	345.8	453.7	423.0
of which:				
Arab Countries	–	–	–	–
C.E.E.C.				
TOTAL MULTILATERAL	483.5	85.3	117.4	414.8
TOTAL BIL.& MULTIL.	673.7	431.1	571.1	837.9
of which:				
ODA Grants	128.7	114.3	120.2	126.0
ODA Loans	104.1	153.8	133.9	262.2
DISBURSEMENTS:				
DAC COUNTRIES COMBINED				
OFFICIAL & PRIVATE				
GROSS:				
Contractual Lending	243.1	233.3	473.8	299.1
Export Credits, Total	149.6	149.7	152.4	121.8
Export Credits, Priv.	144.9	135.4	119.0	97.5
NET:				
Contractual Lending	54.2	120.8	268.1	81.9
Export Credits Total	-30.7	60.0	-8.8	-46.1
PRIVATE SECTOR NET	-78.8	-192.1	-323.0	-136.8
Direct Investment	38.2	-0.4	9.0	-2.1
Portfolio Investment	-85.3	-244.4	-306.0	-89.4
Export Credits	-31.7	52.7	-26.0	-45.3
MARKET BORROWING:				
CHANGE IN CLAIMS				
Banks	-410.0	-127.0	-276.0	-601.0
MEMORANDUM ITEM:				
C.E.E.C. (Gross)	–	–	–	–

	1987	1988	1989	1990		1987	1988	1989	1990		1987
1. TOTAL RECEIPTS NET					**4. TOTAL ODA NET**					**7. TOTAL ODA GROSS**	
DAC COUNTRIES											
Australia	38.5	-7.6	-75.1	-183.0		8.4	1.5	9.9	17.3	Australia	8.4
Austria	27.6	37.1	-6.2	8.3		26.9	1.3	-5.5	-13.1	Austria	30.6
Belgium	-31.9	-4.3	-33.6	-11.8		3.5	1.6	0.1	6.9	Belgium	3.5
Canada	36.8	62.0	21.2	51.6		20.5	32.4	21.2	32.0	Canada	21.4
Denmark	78.5	-0.6	9.1	23.8		38.1	3.7	2.4	19.7	Denmark	38.1
Finland	12.9	22.7	24.4	24.8		6.7	23.7	28.5	24.8	Finland	6.7
France	271.1	-104.5	-161.5	1.3		102.8	66.9	61.2	139.7	France	109.5
Germany	723.6	372.6	264.3	427.4		157.4	157.7	203.3	347.1	Germany	174.7
Ireland	–	–	–	–		–	–	–	–	Ireland	–
Italy	-478.3	270.7	101.6	32.7		33.3	116.6	56.1	86.6	Italy	33.6
Japan	98.9	158.1	143.0	43.7		93.9	172.9	78.7	98.9	Japan	111.5
Netherlands	17.8	14.3	44.7	53.9		24.2	21.0	29.2	44.4	Netherlands	27.5
New Zealand	–	–	–	0.0		–	–	–	0.0	New Zealand	–
Norway	-7.1	0.2	-8.5	2.8		0.2	0.6	0.9	2.6	Norway	0.3
Sweden	12.8	0.9	-5.7	-15.6		2.1	0.9	0.5	0.6	Sweden	2.1
Switzerland	10.2	1.6	1.0	2.6		10.2	1.6	1.0	2.6	Switzerland	10.1
United Kingdom	92.4	107.1	638.0	62.7		11.6	31.8	16.5	13.9	United Kingdom	12.9
United States	823.0	2689.0	933.0	588.0		1035.0	799.0	905.0	2346.0	United States	1046.0
TOTAL	1726.9	3619.1	1889.8	1113.1		1574.8	1432.8	1408.9	3169.8	TOTAL	1636.9
MULTILATERAL											
AF.D.F.	1.5	1.9	0.3	2.7		1.5	1.9	0.3	2.7	AF.D.F.	1.5
AF.D.B.	43.2	48.7	81.5	20.0		–	–	–	–	AF.D.B.	–
AS.D.B	–	–	–	–		–	–	–	–	AS.D.B	–
CAR.D.B.	–	–	–	–		–	–	–	–	CAR.D.B.	–
E.E.C.	109.2	88.1	63.6	63.6		69.6	77.2	65.3	65.3	E.E.C.	69.6
IBRD	14.0	-28.0	-33.0	-84.0		–	–	–	–	IBRD	–
IDA	24.5	17.0	8.0	1.0		24.5	17.0	8.0	1.0	IDA	27.6
I.D.B.	–	–	–	–		–	–	–	–	I.D.B.	–
IFAD	6.1	2.6	7.1	9.8		6.1	2.6	7.1	9.8	IFAD	6.1
I.F.C.	12.1	-20.1	-12.2	1.0		–	–	–	–	I.F.C.	–
IMF TRUST FUND	–	–	–	–		–	–	–	–	IMF TRUST FUND	–
U.N. AGENCIES	–	–	–	–		–	–	–	–	U.N. AGENCIES	–
UNDP	6.2	8.7	8.3	9.7		6.2	8.7	8.3	9.7	UNDP	6.2
UNTA	2.5	1.5	2.4	1.7		2.5	1.5	2.4	1.7	UNTA	2.5
UNICEF	4.6	3.8	3.3	4.0		4.6	3.8	3.3	4.0	UNICEF	4.6
UNRWA	–	–	–	–		–	–	–	–	UNRWA	–
WFP	15.6	13.3	4.8	10.1		15.6	13.3	4.8	10.1	WFP	15.6
UNHCR	1.0	0.7	0.7	0.7		1.0	0.7	0.7	0.7	UNHCR	1.0
Other Multilateral	3.4	3.8	7.5	5.5		3.4	3.8	7.5	5.5	Other Multilateral	3.4
Arab Agencies	-8.8	6.0	77.5	–		-10.0	-9.2	66.2	–	Arab Agencies	–
TOTAL	235.0	147.9	220.0	45.8		124.9	121.3	174.0	110.6	TOTAL	138.0
ARAB COUNTRIES	73.6	-15.8	-12.8	2323.8		73.9	-16.8	-15.1	2323.8	ARAB COUNTRIES	104.0
E.E.C.+ MEMBERS	782.5	743.3	926.2	653.5		440.5	476.4	434.2	723.5	E.E.C.+ MEMBERS	469.4
TOTAL	2035.4	3751.2	2096.9	3482.7		1773.6	1537.4	1567.7	5604.2	TOTAL	1878.8
2. ODA LOANS GROSS					**5. ODA LOANS NET**					**8. GRANTS**	
DAC COUNTRIES											
Australia	–	–	–	–		–	–	–	–	Australia	8.4
Austria	27.4	8.6	1.4	–		23.7	-0.1	-8.1	-16.4	Austria	3.2
Belgium	3.1	–	–	–		3.1	–	-0.2	–	Belgium	0.5
Canada	–	5.2	2.5	0.1		-0.8	5.2	2.5	0.1	Canada	21.4
Denmark	37.9	3.0	0.9	2.0		37.9	3.0	0.9	2.0	Denmark	0.2
Finland	2.9	15.4	14.3	7.0		2.9	15.4	14.3	7.0	Finland	3.9
France	94.4	32.7	25.2	124.1		87.6	26.4	17.7	114.2	France	15.1
Germany	143.3	184.3	180.9	187.5		126.0	123.9	166.1	183.3	Germany	31.4
Ireland	–	–	–	–		–	–	–	–	Ireland	–
Italy	10.9	54.6	34.3	40.4		10.6	50.8	29.2	36.5	Italy	22.7
Japan	81.8	125.8	56.7	105.4		64.3	112.0	27.1	34.4	Japan	29.6
Netherlands	1.2	5.3	7.0	3.8		-2.0	3.5	7.0	3.8	Netherlands	26.2
New Zealand	–	–	–	–		–	–	–	–	New Zealand	–
Norway	–	–	–	–		-0.1	–	–	-0.1	Norway	0.3
Sweden	–	–	–	–		–	–	–	–	Sweden	2.1
Switzerland	10.1	0.8	0.6	2.5		10.1	0.8	0.6	2.5	Switzerland	0.1
United Kingdom	0.5	0.2	0.6	–		-0.8	-1.3	-0.7	-1.5	United Kingdom	12.4
United States	197.0	226.0	144.0	204.0		186.0	163.0	80.0	73.0	United States	849.0
TOTAL	610.5	661.6	468.2	676.7		548.5	502.5	336.1	438.9	TOTAL	1026.3
MULTILATERAL	35.2	26.4	97.5	24.2		22.1	13.2	82.4	9.6	MULTILATERAL	102.8
ARAB COUNTRIES	3.6	10.2	12.3	0.1		-26.5	-16.9	-18.1	-19.5	ARAB COUNTRIES	100.4
E.E.C.+ MEMBERS	291.4	280.9	249.8	358.7		262.4	207.2	220.9	339.2	E.E.C.+ MEMBERS	178.0
TOTAL	649.3	698.3	578.0	701.0		544.1	498.8	400.4	428.9	TOTAL	1229.5
3. TOTAL OFFICIAL GROSS					**6. TOTAL OFFICIAL NET**					**9. TOTAL OOF GROSS**	
DAC COUNTRIES											
Australia	8.4	1.5	9.9	17.3		8.3	1.5	9.9	17.3	Australia	–
Austria	30.6	10.0	4.1	3.3		26.3	0.4	-6.1	-13.6	Austria	–
Belgium	9.7	50.2	10.5	10.3		9.7	50.2	10.3	10.3	Belgium	6.2
Canada	26.0	75.8	33.2	57.0		18.1	71.2	27.4	51.6	Canada	4.7
Denmark	38.1	9.9	14.5	19.7		29.9	1.7	9.1	19.7	Denmark	–
Finland	6.7	23.7	28.5	24.8		6.7	23.7	28.5	24.8	Finland	–
France	109.5	73.1	68.8	149.7		102.8	66.9	61.2	139.7	France	–
Germany	268.4	701.0	323.6	525.9		221.7	512.1	299.1	515.3	Germany	93.7
Ireland	–	–	–	–		–	–	–	–	Ireland	–
Italy	35.3	297.0	68.8	94.2		34.6	282.0	53.2	85.3	Italy	1.8
Japan	111.5	186.7	145.1	193.4		93.9	172.9	115.5	122.5	Japan	–
Netherlands	27.5	22.8	29.2	44.4		24.2	21.0	29.2	43.3	Netherlands	–
New Zealand	–	–	–	0.0		–	–	–	0.0	New Zealand	–
Norway	0.3	0.6	0.9	2.6		0.2	0.6	0.9	2.6	Norway	–
Sweden	2.1	0.9	0.5	0.6		2.1	0.9	0.5	0.6	Sweden	–
Switzerland	10.1	1.6	1.0	2.6		10.2	1.6	1.0	2.6	Switzerland	–
United Kingdom	12.9	33.2	17.9	15.3		11.6	31.8	16.5	13.9	United Kingdom	–
United States	1046.0	2707.0	975.0	2477.0		1013.0	2615.0	890.0	900.0	United States	–
TOTAL	1743.2	4195.1	1731.3	3638.2		1613.3	3853.4	1546.1	1935.9	TOTAL	106.3
MULTILATERAL	400.9	363.1	444.4	302.6		234.9	147.9	220.0	45.8	MULTILATERAL	262.9
ARAB COUNTRIES	104.0	11.7	17.6	2343.4		73.6	-15.8	-12.8	2323.8	ARAB COUNTRIES	–
E.E.C.+ MEMBERS	622.3	1290.7	612.2	938.4		543.7	1053.8	542.2	891.0	E.E.C.+ MEMBERS	152.9
TOTAL	2248.1	4569.9	2193.2	6284.2		1921.8	3985.6	1753.3	4305.4	TOTAL	369.2

10. ODA COMMITMENTS

1988	1989	1990		1987	1988	1989	1990
1.5	9.9	17.3		6.3	8.4	9.6	8.6
10.0	4.1	3.3		3.2	1.4	1.5	2.3
1.6	0.3	6.9		0.8	0.1	0.3	6.9
32.4	21.2	32.0		32.0	15.3	49.5	15.2
3.7	2.4	19.7		–	0.9	34.5	26.7
23.7	28.5	24.8		8.7	9.0	20.6	23.0
73.1	68.8	149.7		52.8	130.6	168.1	16.7
218.0	218.0	351.2		226.6	301.0	118.0	437.8
–	–	–		–	–	–	–
120.4	61.1	90.6		53.5	189.7	129.6	58.1
186.7	108.3	169.8		40.0	337.8	63.6	336.0
22.8	29.2	44.4		28.9	45.6	21.2	35.9
–	–	0.0		–	–	–	–
0.6	0.9	2.6		0.4	–	–	–
0.9	0.5	0.6		3.1	1.6	0.5	1.3
1.6	1.0	2.6		0.4	0.5	0.0	–
33.2	17.9	15.3		26.5	16.1	12.5	13.4
862.0	969.0	2477.0		848.6	1001.1	903.4	12346.7
1592.0	*1541.0*	*3407.7*		*1331.6*	*2059.2*	*1532.9*	*13328.6*
1.9	0.4	2.9		–	–	38.1	–
–	–	–		–	–	–	–
–	–	–		–	–	–	–
–	–	–		–	–	–	–
77.2	65.3	65.3		105.8	88.5	80.6	80.6
–	–	–		–	–	–	–
21.0	13.0	8.0		–	–	–	–
–	–	–		–	–	–	–
2.6	7.1	10.8		–	–	–	–
–	–	–		–	–	–	–
–	–	–		33.2	31.8	27.1	31.8
8.7	8.3	9.7		–	–	–	–
1.5	2.4	1.7		–	–	–	–
3.8	3.3	4.0		–	–	–	–
–	–	–		–	–	–	–
13.3	4.8	10.1		–	–	–	–
0.7	0.7	0.7		–	–	–	–
3.8	7.5	5.5		–	–	–	–
–	76.2	1.5		–	1.2	261.3	1.7
134.5	*189.0*	*120.2*		*138.9*	*121.4*	*407.0*	*114.0*
10.4	*15.3*	*2343.4*		*125.1*	*36.0*	*111.0*	*2858.4*
550.1	*463.1*	*743.0*		*494.8*	*772.4*	*564.7*	*676.1*
1736.9	*1745.3*	*5871.3*		*1595.7*	*2216.7*	*2050.9*	*16301.1*

11. TECH. COOP. GRANTS

1988	1989	1990		1987	1988	1989	1990
1.5	9.9	17.3		0.6	-0.3	0.1	0.2
1.4	2.6	3.3		1.4	1.4	1.3	1.9
1.6	0.3	6.9		0.2	0.1	–	–
27.2	18.7	31.9		–	1.2	5.5	3.2
0.7	1.6	17.7		0.2	1.6	0.2	0.1
8.3	14.2	17.8		0.0	0.1	1.5	9.1
40.5	43.5	25.6		150.0	13.2	11.3	16.7
33.7	37.2	163.8		29.0	28.7	28.8	32.6
–	–	–		–	–	–	–
65.8	26.9	50.1		12.4	8.4	7.9	4.9
60.9	51.6	64.4		13.8	17.1	18.6	19.1
17.6	22.3	40.6		10.7	8.5	13.1	11.5
–	–	0.0		–	–	–	–
0.6	0.9	2.6		0.2	0.3	0.7	0.4
0.9	0.5	0.6		0.8	0.9	0.5	0.6
0.7	0.4	0.1		0.1	0.1	–	–
33.1	17.2	15.3		8.5	12.1	10.8	11.5
636.0	825.0	2273.0		419.0	481.0	590.0	679.0
930.4	*1072.8*	*2731.0*		*646.7*	*574.3*	*690.2*	*790.7*
108.0	*91.6*	*96.1*		*22.9*	*22.6*	*22.3*	*21.6*
0.1	*3.0*	*2343.3*		–	–	–	–
269.1	*213.3*	*384.3*		*216.1*	*76.8*	*72.1*	*77.3*
1038.6	*1167.3*	*5170.4*		*669.6*	*596.8*	*712.5*	*812.3*

12. TOTAL OOF NET

1988	1989	1990		1987	1988	1989	1990
–	–	–		-0.2	–	–	–
–	–	–		-0.6	-0.9	-0.5	-0.5
48.7	10.1	3.4		6.2	48.7	10.1	3.4
43.5	12.0	25.0		-2.4	38.8	6.2	19.6
6.2	12.1	–		-8.2	-1.9	6.7	–
–	–	–		–	–	–	–
–	–	–		–	–	–	–
483.0	105.5	174.7		64.3	354.5	95.8	168.2
–	–	–		–	–	–	–
176.7	7.7	3.7		1.4	165.4	-2.9	-1.3
–	36.8	23.7		–	–	36.8	23.7
–	–	–		–	–	–	-1.1
–	–	–		–	–	–	–
–	–	–		–	–	–	–
–	–	–		–	–	–	–
–	–	–		–	–	–	–
1845.0	6.0	–		-22.0	1816.0	-15.0	-1446.0
2603.1	*190.3*	*230.5*		*38.4*	*2420.6*	*137.2*	*-1234.0*
228.7	*255.3*	*182.4*		*110.1*	*26.6*	*46.0*	*-64.8*
1.3	*2.3*	–		*-0.3*	*1.0*	*2.3*	–
740.7	*149.1*	*195.5*		*103.2*	*577.4*	*108.1*	*167.5*
2833.0	*448.0*	*412.8*		*148.2*	*2448.2*	*185.5*	*-1298.7*

13. ODF COMMITMENTS: BY PURPOSE %

	1987	1988	1989	1990
Education	2	2	4	–
Health	2	4	2	–
Other Social Infrastr.	3	4	3	–
Water Sanitat. Sewage	7	4	5	–
Energy	12	17	27	–
Telecommunications	–	2	2	–
Transportation	0	0	3	–
Agriculture	8	9	5	–
Extractive Industries	–	–	1	–
Manufacturing	5	12	1	–
Trade Banking Tourism	–	4	–	–
Technical Cooperation	29	24	28	–
Multisector Aid	0	2	1	–
Programme	13	4	12	–
Debt Reorganisation	18	1	2	–
Food Aid	1	9	3	–
Emergency Aid	–	0	–	–
Unspecified	0	–	–	–
TOTAL	100	100	100	–

14. GRANT ELEMENT OF ODA %

DAC COUNTRIES

	1987	1988	1989	1990
Australia	100.0	100.0	100.0	–
Austria	100.0	100.0	100.0	–
Belgium	100.0	100.0	100.0	–
Canada	100.0	94.3	100.0	–
Denmark	–	100.0	100.0	–
Finland	100.0	100.0	100.0	–
France	100.0	79.7	69.3	–
Germany	74.1	76.3	63.2	–
Ireland	–	–	–	–
Italy	91.2	85.1	70.5	–
Japan	100.0	59.5	100.0	–
Netherlands	100.0	97.5	100.0	–
New Zealand	–	–	–	–
Norway	100.0	–	–	–
Sweden	100.0	100.0	100.0	–
Switzerland	100.0	100.0	100.0	–
United Kingdom	100.0	100.0	100.0	–
United States	98.9	91.0	96.9	–
TOTAL	*94.4*	*82.8*	*88.8*	–
MULTILATERAL	*100.0*	*100.0*	*66.8*	–
ARAB COUNTRIES	**88.3**	**38.7**	**52.2**	–
E.E.C.+ MEMBERS	*86.4*	*83.5*	*75.4*	–
TOTAL	**94.4**	**83.0**	**82.6**	–

15. OTHER AGGREGATES

OFFICIAL COMMITMENTS:

	1987	1988	1989	1990
TOTAL BILATERAL	4200.1	4602.9	2123.4	16520.0
of which:				
Arab Countries	179.1	44.1	115.7	3158.4
C.E.E.C.	528.3	197.0	458.1	–
TOTAL MULTILATERAL	180.4	469.6	901.2	646.3
TOTAL BIL.& MULTIL.	4380.4	5072.5	3024.6	17166.2
of which:				
ODA Grants	1321.3	1216.5	1250.9	15404.8
ODA Loans	315.0	1000.2	941.0	896.3

DISBURSEMENTS:

DAC COUNTRIES COMBINED

OFFICIAL & PRIVATE

	1987	1988	1989	1990
GROSS:				
Contractual Lending	2458.8	3834.3	2218.5	1394.5
Export Credits, Total	1769.5	659.3	1738.1	715.9
Export Credits, Priv.	1754.5	577.5	1568.5	493.7
NET:				
Contractual Lending	968.9	2592.8	1020.8	-1485.5
Export Credits Total	359.0	-322.8	673.6	-492.6
PRIVATE SECTOR NET	113.6	-234.3	343.7	-822.7
Direct Investment	-213.5	40.5	115.7	-170.9
Portfolio Investment	-67.5	47.6	-328.0	32.2
Export Credits	394.6	-322.4	556.0	-684.1

MARKET BORROWING:

CHANGE IN CLAIMS

	1987	1988	1989	1990
Banks	-675.0	-383.0	-199.0	-656.0

MEMORANDUM ITEM:

	1987	1988	1989	1990
C.E.E.C. (Gross)	5.1	12.9	25.3	–

	1987	1988	1989	1990		1987	1988	1989	1990		1987

1. TOTAL RECEIPTS NET

DAC COUNTRIES

						4. TOTAL ODA NET					7. TOTAL ODA GROSS	
Australia	0.1	0.0	0.1	–		0.1	0.0	0.1	–		Australia	0.1
Austria	0.1	0.1	0.2	0.1		0.1	0.1	0.2	0.1		Austria	0.1
Belgium	3.6	0.7	0.2	4.9		3.6	0.7	0.2	0.9		Belgium	3.6
Canada	3.6	3.9	0.7	0.6		3.6	3.9	0.7	0.6		Canada	3.8
Denmark	0.1	–	0.7	0.1		0.1	–	0.7	0.1		Denmark	0.1
Finland	0.2	0.0	0.2	0.1		0.2	0.0	0.2	0.1		Finland	0.2
France	0.5	12.9	8.3	1.2		4.8	8.9	2.8	1.2		France	5.3
Germany	9.9	17.9	28.4	29.1		12.5	20.6	27.8	27.3		Germany	12.9
Ireland	–	–	–	–		–	–	–	–		Ireland	–
Italy	13.0	16.5	5.3	10.9		13.0	16.5	5.3	10.5		Italy	13.0
Japan	2.4	2.4	3.5	7.4		3.4	2.1	3.5	8.2		Japan	6.6
Netherlands	4.0	7.6	8.9	36.8		4.0	7.7	8.9	9.3		Netherlands	4.0
New Zealand	–	–	–	–		–	–	–	–		New Zealand	–
Norway	1.6	0.9	2.6	2.0		1.6	0.9	2.6	2.0		Norway	1.6
Sweden	0.3	0.4	0.6	1.1		0.3	0.4	0.6	1.1		Sweden	0.3
Switzerland	0.9	1.0	1.7	0.1		0.9	1.0	1.7	0.1		Switzerland	0.9
United Kingdom	0.7	0.3	0.2	0.2		0.7	0.3	0.2	0.2		United Kingdom	0.7
United States	356.0	317.0	310.0	246.0		356.0	318.0	310.0	247.0		United States	360.0
TOTAL	*396.8*	*381.6*	*371.5*	*340.5*		*404.9*	*380.9*	*365.5*	*308.7*		*TOTAL*	*413.0*

MULTILATERAL

A.F.D.F.	–	–	–	–		–	–	–	–		A.F.D.F.	–
A.F.D.B.	–	–	–	–		–	–	–	–		A.F.D.B.	–
A.S.D.B	–	–	–	–		–	–	–	–		A.S.D.B	–
CAR.D.B.	–	–	–	–		–	–	–	–		CAR.D.B.	–
E.E.C.	4.5	3.4	3.7	3.7		4.5	3.4	3.7	3.7		E.E.C.	4.5
IBRD	-4.7	2.0	-8.0	-13.0		–	–	–	–		IBRD	–
IDA	-0.5	–	–	-1.0		-0.5	–	–	-1.0		IDA	–
I.D.B.	8.3	8.7	46.1	-6.3		-0.5	18.0	59.4	18.8		I.D.B.	4.5
IFAD	0.7	0.4	–	1.4		0.7	0.4	–	1.4		IFAD	0.7
I.F.C.	–	–	–	–		–	–	–	–		I.F.C.	–
IMF TRUST FUND	–	–	–	–		–	–	–	–		IMF TRUST FUND	–
U.N. AGENCIES	–	–	–	–		–	–	–	–		U.N. AGENCIES	–
UNDP	2.0	2.7	2.8	2.5		2.0	2.7	2.8	2.5		UNDP	2.0
UNTA	0.9	0.5	1.0	0.8		0.9	0.5	1.0	0.8		UNTA	0.9
UNICEF	0.6	0.6	1.1	2.0		0.6	0.6	1.1	2.0		UNICEF	0.6
UNRWA	–	–	–	–		–	–	–	–		UNRWA	–
WFP	12.8	12.0	7.7	8.1		12.8	12.0	7.7	8.1		WFP	12.8
UNHCR	–	0.4	1.0	0.8		–	0.4	1.0	0.8		UNHCR	–
Other Multilateral	0.7	0.7	1.3	0.9		0.7	0.7	1.3	0.9		Other Multilateral	0.7
Arab Agencies	-0.1	-0.1	0.0	–		-0.1	-0.1	0.0	–		Arab Agencies	–
TOTAL	*25.3*	*31.4*	*56.7*	*-0.1*		*21.2*	*38.6*	*78.0*	*38.0*		*TOTAL*	*26.8*
ARAB COUNTRIES	*–*	*–*	*–*	*–*		*–*	*–*	*–*	*–*		*ARAB COUNTRIES*	*–*
E.E.C.+ MEMBERS	*36.2*	*59.2*	*55.7*	*86.9*		*43.2*	*57.9*	*49.6*	*53.2*		*E.E.C.+ MEMBERS*	*44.0*
TOTAL	*422.2*	*412.9*	*428.3*	*340.4*		*426.1*	*419.5*	*443.5*	*346.6*		*TOTAL*	*439.8*

2. ODA LOANS GROSS / 5. ODA LOANS NET / 8. GRANTS

DAC COUNTRIES

						5. ODA LOANS NET					8. GRANTS	
Australia	–	–	–	–		–	–	–	–		Australia	0.1
Austria	–	–	–	–		–	–	–	–		Austria	0.1
Belgium	2.4	–	–	–		2.4	–	–	–		Belgium	1.2
Canada	–	–	–	–		-0.1	-0.1	-1.4	-0.4		Canada	3.8
Denmark	–	–	–	–		–	–	–	–		Denmark	0.1
Finland	–	–	–	–		–	–	–	–		Finland	0.2
France	1.8	6.2	1.8	0.1		1.4	5.9	1.6	0.1		France	3.4
Germany	2.3	9.5	11.2	7.5		1.9	9.3	11.2	7.5		Germany	10.6
Ireland	–	–	–	–		–	–	–	–		Ireland	–
Italy	–	–	–	–		–	–	–	–		Italy	13.0
Japan	–	–	–	–		-3.2	-3.4	–	–		Japan	6.6
Netherlands	–	–	–	–		–	–	–	–		Netherlands	4.0
New Zealand	–	–	–	–		–	–	–	–		New Zealand	–
Norway	–	–	–	–		–	–	–	–		Norway	1.6
Sweden	–	–	–	–		–	–	–	–		Sweden	0.3
Switzerland	–	–	–	–		–	–	–	–		Switzerland	0.9
United Kingdom	–	–	–	–		–	–	–	–		United Kingdom	0.7
United States	45.0	41.0	43.0	42.0		41.0	38.0	38.0	39.0		United States	315.0
TOTAL	*51.5*	*56.7*	*56.0*	*49.6*		*43.4*	*49.6*	*49.4*	*46.2*		*TOTAL*	*361.5*
MULTILATERAL	*4.9*	*21.6*	*63.8*	*31.3*		*-0.7*	*16.4*	*58.9*	*19.1*		*MULTILATERAL*	*21.9*
ARAB COUNTRIES	*–*	*–*	*–*	*–*		*–*	*–*	*–*	*–*		*ARAB COUNTRIES*	*–*
E.E.C.+ MEMBERS	*6.5*	*15.7*	*13.0*	*7.6*		*5.7*	*15.2*	*12.8*	*7.6*		*E.E.C.+ MEMBERS*	*37.5*
TOTAL	*56.4*	*78.3*	*119.8*	*80.9*		*42.7*	*66.0*	*108.3*	*65.3*		*TOTAL*	*383.4*

3. TOTAL OFFICIAL GROSS / 6. TOTAL OFFICIAL NET / 9. TOTAL OOF GROSS

DAC COUNTRIES

						6. TOTAL OFFICIAL NET					9. TOTAL OOF GROSS	
Australia	0.1	0.0	0.1	–		0.1	0.0	0.1	–		Australia	–
Austria	0.1	0.1	0.2	0.1		0.1	0.1	0.2	0.1		Austria	–
Belgium	3.6	0.7	0.2	1.0		3.6	0.7	0.2	1.0		Belgium	–
Canada	3.8	4.1	2.1	1.1		3.6	3.9	0.7	0.6		Canada	–
Denmark	0.1	–	0.7	0.1		0.1	–	0.7	0.1		Denmark	–
Finland	0.2	0.0	0.2	0.1		0.2	0.0	0.2	0.1		Finland	–
France	5.3	9.2	3.0	1.2		4.8	8.9	2.8	1.2		France	–
Germany	12.9	20.7	27.8	27.3		12.5	20.6	27.8	27.3		Germany	–
Ireland	–	–	–	–		–	–	–	–		Ireland	–
Italy	13.0	16.5	5.3	10.5		13.0	16.5	5.3	10.5		Italy	–
Japan	6.6	5.5	3.5	8.2		3.4	2.1	3.5	8.2		Japan	–
Netherlands	4.0	7.7	8.9	9.3		4.0	7.7	8.9	9.3		Netherlands	–
New Zealand	–	–	–	–		–	–	–	–		New Zealand	–
Norway	1.6	0.9	2.6	2.0		1.6	0.9	2.6	2.0		Norway	–
Sweden	0.3	0.4	0.6	1.1		0.3	0.4	0.6	1.1		Sweden	–
Switzerland	0.9	1.0	1.7	0.1		0.9	1.0	1.7	0.1		Switzerland	–
United Kingdom	0.7	0.3	0.2	0.2		0.7	0.3	0.2	0.2		United Kingdom	–
United States	360.0	321.0	315.0	250.0		356.0	317.0	310.0	246.0		United States	–
TOTAL	*413.0*	*388.0*	*372.0*	*312.2*		*404.9*	*379.9*	*365.5*	*307.7*		*TOTAL*	*–*
MULTILATERAL	*52.1*	*58.0*	*87.0*	*54.1*		*25.3*	*31.4*	*56.7*	*-0.1*		*MULTILATERAL*	*25.2*
ARAB COUNTRIES	*–*	*–*	*–*	*–*		*–*	*–*	*–*	*–*		*ARAB COUNTRIES*	*–*
E.E.C.+ MEMBERS	*44.0*	*58.4*	*49.8*	*53.2*		*43.2*	*57.9*	*49.6*	*53.2*		*E.E.C.+ MEMBERS*	*–*
TOTAL	*465.0*	*446.0*	*459.0*	*366.3*		*430.2*	*411.3*	*422.2*	*307.6*		*TOTAL*	*25.2*

EL SALVADOR

10. ODA COMMITMENTS

1988	1989	1990	1987	1988	1989	1990
0.0	0.1	–		0.0	0.0	0.0
0.1	0.2	0.1	0.1	0.0	0.2	0.1
0.7	0.2	0.9	4.4	0.5	0.2	0.9
4.1	2.1	1.1	3.8	3.1	1.6	3.0
–	0.7	0.1	–	–	0.7	–
0.0	0.2	0.1	–	–	0.2	0.4
9.2	3.0	1.2	14.3	1.2	1.1	1.1
20.7	27.8	27.3	18.8	47.9	45.8	4.6
–	–	–	–	–	–	–
16.5	5.3	10.5	15.9	31.8	4.6	2.7
5.5	3.5	8.2	4.5	11.0	4.1	6.2
7.7	8.9	9.3	3.0	7.7	9.8	9.9
–	–	–	–	–	–	–
0.9	2.6	2.0	0.3	–	–	–
0.4	0.6	1.1	0.3	0.4	0.6	–
1.0	1.7	0.1	0.9	1.6	1.3	0.1
0.3	0.2	0.2	0.7	0.3	0.2	0.2
321.0	315.0	250.0	407.1	344.6	266.0	281.3
388.0	*372.0*	*312.1*	*474.0*	*450.0*	*336.4*	*310.4*
–	–	–	–	–	–	–
–	–	–	–	–	–	–
–	–	–	–	–	–	–
3.4	3.7	3.7	22.1	1.0	4.9	4.9
–	–	–	–	–	–	–
–	–	–	–	–	–	–
23.1	64.3	29.7	166.0	–	–	78.4
0.4	–	1.6	–	–	–	9.3
–	–	–	–	–	–	–
–	–	–	17.0	17.0	15.0	15.1
2.7	2.8	2.5	–	–	–	–
0.5	1.0	0.8	–	–	–	–
0.6	1.1	2.0	–	–	–	–
12.0	7.7	8.1	–	–	–	–
0.4	1.0	0.8	–	–	–	–
0.7	1.3	0.9	–	–	–	–
–	–	–	–	–	–	–
43.8	*83.0*	*50.1*	*205.2*	*18.0*	*19.9*	*107.7*
–	–	–	–	–	–	–
58.4	*49.8*	*53.2*	*79.2*	*90.3*	*67.3*	*24.2*
431.8	*455.0*	*362.2*	*679.2*	*468.0*	*356.2*	*418.1*

11. TECH. COOP. GRANTS

1988	1989	1990	1987	1988	1989	1990
0.0	0.1	–	–	–	–	–
0.1	0.2	0.1	0.0	0.0	0.0	0.0
0.7	0.2	0.9	0.1	0.0	–	0.0
4.1	2.1	1.1	–	–	0.0	0.0
–	0.7	0.1	–	–	–	–
0.0	0.2	0.1	0.0	0.0	–	0.0
3.0	1.2	1.1	0.7	0.9	1.1	1.1
11.3	16.7	19.8	8.6	8.9	7.0	8.7
–	–	–	–	–	–	–
16.5	5.3	10.5	2.7	0.4	0.3	0.0
5.5	3.5	8.2	0.2	0.3	0.2	0.3
7.7	8.9	9.3	2.2	6.9	7.2	8.0
–	–	–	–	–	–	–
0.9	2.6	2.0	0.1	0.1	0.2	0.1
0.4	0.6	1.1	–	–	–	–
1.0	1.7	0.1	–	0.0	–	–
0.3	0.2	0.2	0.1	0.0	0.0	0.0
280.0	272.0	208.0	70.0	85.0	115.0	102.0
331.3	*316.1*	*262.5*	*84.7*	*102.7*	*131.0*	*120.3*
22.2	*19.2*	*18.8*	*4.6*	*5.4*	*7.2*	*7.0*
–	–	–	–	–	–	–
42.7	*36.8*	*45.5*	*14.7*	*17.7*	*15.6*	*17.8*
353.5	*335.2*	*281.3*	*89.3*	*108.1*	*138.2*	*127.3*

12. TOTAL OOF NET

1988	1989	1990	1987	1988	1989	1990
–	–	–	–	–	–	–
–	0.0	0.1	–	–	0.0	0.1
–	–	–	–	–	–	–
–	–	–	–	–	–	–
–	–	–	–	–	–	–
–	–	–	–	–	–	–
–	–	–	–	–	–	–
–	–	–	–	–	–	–
–	–	–	–	–	–	–
–	–	–	–	–	–	–
–	–	–	–	–	–	–
–	–	–	–	–	–	–
–	–	–	–	–1.0	–	–1.0
–	0.0	0.1	–	–1.0	0.0	–0.9
14.2	*4.0*	*4.0*	*4.1*	*–7.2*	*–21.3*	*–38.1*
–	–	–	–	–	–	–
–	0.0	0.1	–	–	0.0	0.1
14.2	*4.0*	*4.1*	*4.1*	*–8.2*	*–21.3*	*–39.0*

13. ODF COMMITMENTS: BY PURPOSE %

	1987	1988	1989	1990
Education	3	2	3	–
Health	4	3	10	–
Other Social Infrastr.	12	3	5	–
Water Sanitat. Sewage	1	23	2	–
Energy	1	1	2	–
Telecommunications	–	1	0	–
Transportation	–	1	–	–
Agriculture	7	4	6	–
Extractive Industries	–	–	–	–
Manufacturing	0	–	–	–
Trade Banking Tourism	2	1	5	–
Technical Cooperation	29	19	27	–
Multisector Aid	0	0	–	–
Programme	20	24	36	–
Debt Reorganisation	–	–	–	–
Food Aid	5	11	3	–
Emergency Aid	16	7	1	–
Unspecified	–	–	–	–
TOTAL	100	100	100	–

14. GRANT ELEMENT OF ODA %

DAC COUNTRIES

	1987	1988	1989	1990
Australia	–	100.0	100.0	–
Austria	100.0	100.0	100.0	–
Belgium	91.5	100.0	100.0	–
Canada	100.0	100.0	100.0	–
Denmark	–	–	100.0	–
Finland	–	–	100.0	–
France	76.7	100.0	100.0	–
Germany	100.0	89.5	97.2	–
Ireland	–	–	–	–
Italy	100.0	100.0	100.0	–
Japan	100.0	100.0	100.0	–
Netherlands	100.0	100.0	100.0	–
New Zealand	–	–	–	–
Norway	100.0	–	–	–
Sweden	100.0	100.0	100.0	–
Switzerland	100.0	100.0	100.0	–
United Kingdom	100.0	100.0	100.0	–
United States	97.0	93.5	99.4	–
TOTAL	*96.6*	*93.9*	*99.1*	–
MULTILATERAL	*92.6*	*78.3*	*100.0*	–
ARAB COUNTRIES	–	–	–	–
E.E.C.+ MEMBERS	95.3	94.4	98.1	–
TOTAL	*96.2*	*89.3*	*99.2*	–

15. OTHER AGGREGATES

OFFICIAL COMMITMENTS:

	1987	1988	1989	1990
TOTAL BILATERAL	474.0	450.0	336.4	310.5
of which:				
Arab Countries	–	–	–	–
C.E.E.C.	–	–	–	–
TOTAL MULTILATERAL	270.2	18.0	19.9	147.7
TOTAL BIL.& MULTIL.	744.2	468.0	356.2	458.2
of which:				
ODA Grants	462.8	367.2	343.4	255.2
ODA Loans	216.4	100.8	12.9	162.9

DISBURSEMENTS:

DAC COUNTRIES COMBINED

	1987	1988	1989	1990
OFFICIAL & PRIVATE				
GROSS:				
Contractual Lending	57.3	82.2	97.5	68.7
Export Credits, Total	5.8	25.6	41.5	19.1
Export Credits, Priv.	5.8	25.6	41.5	19.1
NET:				
Contractual Lending	33.5	60.7	69.9	41.5
Export Credits Total	–9.9	12.1	20.5	–3.7
PRIVATE SECTOR NET	–8.0	1.7	6.1	32.8
Direct Investment	–3.1	–2.6	0.2	–0.2
Portfolio Investment	5.0	–7.8	–14.6	36.6
Export Credits	–9.9	12.1	20.5	–3.7

MARKET BORROWING:

CHANGE IN CLAIMS

	1987	1988	1989	1990
Banks	10.0	–109.0	76.0	12.0

MEMORANDUM ITEM:

	1987	1988	1989	1990
C.E.E.C. (Gross)	–	0.3	0.2	–

	1987	1988	1989	1990		1987	1988	1989	1990		1987
1. TOTAL RECEIPTS NET					**4. TOTAL ODA NET**					**7. TOTAL ODA GROSS**	
DAC COUNTRIES											
Australia	–	–	–	–		–	0.0	0.0	0.0	Australia	–
Austria	–	0.0	0.0	0.0		–	0.1	0.0	0.1	Austria	–
Belgium	1.8	0.1	22.5	-0.1		0.1	0.1	0.0	0.1	Belgium	0.1
Canada	0.1	0.1	0.1	0.1		0.1	0.1	0.1	0.1	Canada	0.1
Denmark	–	–	–	–		–	–	–	–	Denmark	–
Finland	–	–	–	–		–	–	–	–	Finland	–
France	14.4	18.6	14.0	17.0		14.1	18.0	15.0	16.1	France	14.1
Germany	0.4	0.8	1.6	2.1		0.5	1.4	1.6	2.0	Germany	0.5
Ireland	–	–	–	–		–	–	–	–	Ireland	–
Italy	3.6	10.2	1.9	0.1		3.6	2.3	1.8	0.1	Italy	3.6
Japan	0.6	0.8	0.0	0.7		0.6	0.8	0.0	0.7	Japan	0.6
Netherlands	2.1	0.0	0.0	0.0		0.1	0.0	0.0	0.0	Netherlands	0.1
New Zealand	–	–	–	–		–	–	–	–	New Zealand	–
Norway	–	–	–	–		–	–	–	–	Norway	–
Sweden	–	–	–	–		–	–	–	–	Sweden	–
Switzerland	0.2	0.0	–	–		0.2	0.0	–	–	Switzerland	0.2
United Kingdom	0.3	0.0	0.1	0.1		0.3	0.0	0.1	0.1	United Kingdom	0.3
United States	2.0	1.0	1.0	1.0		2.0	1.0	1.0	1.0	United States	2.0
TOTAL	25.7	31.7	41.3	21.0		21.7	23.8	19.6	20.2	TOTAL	21.7
MULTILATERAL											
AF.D.F.	1.6	1.2	0.7	0.2		1.6	1.2	0.7	0.2	AF.D.F.	1.6
AF.D.B.	-0.7	-0.2	0.1	0.1		–	–	–	–	AF.D.B.	–
AS.D.B	–	–	–	–		–	–	–	–	AS.D.B	–
CAR.D.B.	–	–	–	–		–	–	–	–	CAR.D.B.	–
E.E.C.	5.7	6.7	7.1	7.1		5.7	6.7	7.1	7.1	E.E.C.	5.7
IBRD	–	–	–	–		–	–	–	–	IBRD	–
IDA	10.4	6.0	8.0	2.0		10.4	6.0	8.0	2.0	IDA	10.4
I.D.B.	–	–	–	–		–	–	–	–	I.D.B.	–
IFAD	0.3	0.3	0.3	0.3		0.3	0.3	0.3	0.3	IFAD	0.3
I.F.C.	–	–	–	–		–	–	–	–	I.F.C.	–
IMF TRUST FUND	–	–	–	–		–	–	–	–	IMF TRUST FUND	–
U.N. AGENCIES	–	–	–	–		–	–	–	–	U.N. AGENCIES	–
UNDP	1.8	1.9	2.7	4.0		1.8	1.9	2.7	4.0	UNDP	1.8
UNTA	0.5	0.7	0.7	0.6		0.5	0.7	0.7	0.6	UNTA	0.5
UNICEF	0.2	0.2	0.4	0.8		0.2	0.2	0.4	0.8	UNICEF	0.2
UNRWA	–	–	–	–		–	–	–	–	UNRWA	–
WFP	0.1	2.0	1.1	2.6		0.1	2.0	1.1	2.6	WFP	0.1
UNHCR	–	–	–	–		–	–	–	–	UNHCR	–
Other Multilateral	0.4	0.8	1.2	1.1		0.4	0.8	1.2	1.1	Other Multilateral	0.4
Arab Agencies	0.1	–	0.1	–		0.1	-0.2	0.1	–	Arab Agencies	0.5
TOTAL	20.2	19.5	22.3	18.8		20.9	19.5	22.2	18.7	TOTAL	21.4
ARAB COUNTRIES	0.1	–	0.2	–		0.1	–	0.2	–	ARAB COUNTRIES	0.1
E.E.C.+ MEMBERS	28.4	36.6	47.3	26.3		24.5	28.6	25.6	25.5	E.E.C.+ MEMBERS	24.5
TOTAL	46.0	51.3	63.8	39.8		42.8	43.3	41.9	38.9	TOTAL	43.2
2. ODA LOANS GROSS					**5. ODA LOANS NET**					**8. GRANTS**	
DAC COUNTRIES											
Australia	–	–	–	–		–	–	–	–	Australia	–
Austria	–	–	–	–		–	–	–	–	Austria	–
Belgium	–	–	–	–		–	–	–	–	Belgium	0.1
Canada	–	–	–	–		–	–	–	–	Canada	0.1
Denmark	–	–	–	–		–	–	–	–	Denmark	–
Finland	–	–	–	–		–	–	–	–	Finland	–
France	7.4	10.0	5.7	3.4		7.4	10.0	5.7	3.4	France	6.7
Germany	–	–	–	–		–	–	–	–	Germany	0.5
Ireland	–	–	–	–		–	–	–	–	Ireland	–
Italy	–	–	–	–		–	–	–	–	Italy	3.6
Japan	–	–	–	–		–	–	–	–	Japan	0.6
Netherlands	–	–	–	–		–	–	–	–	Netherlands	0.1
New Zealand	–	–	–	–		–	–	–	–	New Zealand	–
Norway	–	–	–	–		–	–	–	–	Norway	–
Sweden	–	–	–	–		–	–	–	–	Sweden	–
Switzerland	–	–	–	–		–	–	–	–	Switzerland	0.2
United Kingdom	–	–	–	–		–	–	–	–	United Kingdom	0.3
United States	–	–	–	–		–	–	–	–	United States	2.0
TOTAL	7.4	10.0	5.7	3.4		7.4	10.0	5.7	3.4	TOTAL	14.4
MULTILATERAL	13.5	8.9	12.5	6.3		13.0	8.5	12.5	5.8	MULTILATERAL	7.9
ARAB COUNTRIES	–	–	–	–		–	–	–	–	ARAB COUNTRIES	0.1
E.E.C.+ MEMBERS	8.0	11.2	9.3	6.9		8.0	11.2	9.3	6.9	E.E.C.+ MEMBERS	16.5
TOTAL	20.8	18.9	18.2	9.7		20.4	18.5	18.2	9.2	TOTAL	22.4
3. TOTAL OFFICIAL GROSS					**6. TOTAL OFFICIAL NET**					**9. TOTAL OOF GROSS**	
DAC COUNTRIES											
Australia	–	–	–	–		–	–	–	–	Australia	–
Austria	–	0.0	0.0	0.0		–	0.0	0.0	0.0	Austria	–
Belgium	0.1	0.1	0.0	0.1		0.1	0.1	0.0	0.1	Belgium	–
Canada	0.1	0.1	0.1	0.1		0.1	0.1	0.1	0.1	Canada	–
Denmark	–	–	–	–		–	–	–	–	Denmark	–
Finland	–	–	–	–		–	–	–	–	Finland	–
France	14.1	18.0	15.0	16.1		14.1	18.0	15.0	16.1	France	–
Germany	0.5	1.4	1.6	2.0		0.5	1.4	1.6	2.0	Germany	–
Ireland	–	–	–	–		–	–	–	–	Ireland	–
Italy	3.6	2.3	5.8	0.1		3.6	2.3	5.8	0.1	Italy	–
Japan	0.6	0.8	0.0	0.7		0.6	0.8	0.0	0.7	Japan	–
Netherlands	0.1	0.0	0.0	0.0		0.1	0.0	0.0	0.0	Netherlands	–
New Zealand	–	–	–	–		–	–	–	–	New Zealand	–
Norway	–	–	–	–		–	–	–	–	Norway	–
Sweden	–	–	–	–		–	–	–	–	Sweden	–
Switzerland	0.2	0.0	–	–		0.2	0.0	–	–	Switzerland	–
United Kingdom	0.3	0.0	0.1	0.1		0.3	0.0	0.1	0.1	United Kingdom	–
United States	2.0	1.0	1.0	1.0		2.0	1.0	1.0	1.0	United States	–
TOTAL	21.7	23.8	23.6	20.2		21.7	23.8	23.6	20.2	TOTAL	–
MULTILATERAL	21.5	20.2	22.2	19.5		20.2	19.5	22.3	18.8	MULTILATERAL	0.2
ARAB COUNTRIES	0.1	–	0.2	–		0.1	–	0.2	–	ARAB COUNTRIES	–
E.E.C.+ MEMBERS	24.5	28.6	29.7	25.5		24.5	28.6	29.7	25.5	E.E.C.+ MEMBERS	–
TOTAL	43.4	44.0	46.0	39.7		42.0	43.3	46.1	39.0	TOTAL	0.2

1988	1989	1990		1987	1988	1989	1990
				10. ODA COMMITMENTS			
0.0	0.0	0.0		–	0.0	0.0	0.0
0.1	0.0	0.1		0.0	0.0	0.0	0.1
0.1	0.1	0.1		0.1	0.1	0.1	0.2
–	–	–		–	–	–	–
–	–	–		–	–	–	–
18.0	15.0	16.1		31.4	8.2	12.5	14.6
1.4	1.6	2.0		0.1	2.4	0.1	0.3
–	–	–		–	–	–	–
2.3	1.8	0.1		7.1	1.4	0.2	0.6
0.8	0.0	0.7		0.6	0.1	0.8	0.7
0.0	0.0	0.0		0.1	0.0	0.0	0.0
–	–	–		–	–	–	–
–	–	–		–	–	–	–
0.0	–	–		0.2	0.0	–	–
0.0	0.1	0.1		0.3	0.0	0.1	0.1
1.0	1.0	1.0		0.8	1.3	1.3	1.5
23.8	*19.6*	*20.2*		*40.8*	*13.6*	*15.1*	*18.2*
1.2	0.7	0.2		8.8	17.2	–	0.6
–	–	–		–	–	–	–
–	–	–		–	–	–	–
6.7	7.1	7.1		1.5	4.2	7.7	7.7
6.0	8.0	2.0		5.1	–	–	6.0
–	–	–		–	–	–	–
0.3	0.3	0.3		–	–	–	5.3
–	–	–		–	–	–	–
–	–	–		2.9	5.5	6.1	9.1
1.9	2.7	4.0		–	–	–	–
0.7	0.7	0.6		–	–	–	–
0.2	0.4	0.8		–	–	–	–
2.0	1.1	2.6		–	–	–	–
0.8	1.2	1.1		–	–	–	–
0.2	0.1	0.2		0.1	–	–	–
19.9	22.2	19.0		18.4	26.9	13.8	28.7
–	0.2	–		–	3.9	–	–
28.6	25.6	25.5		40.6	16.2	20.7	23.5
43.7	*41.9*	*39.2*		*59.2*	*44.4*	*28.9*	*46.9*
				11. TECH. COOP. GRANTS			
–	–	–		–	–	–	–
0.0	0.0	0.0		–	0.0	0.0	0.0
0.1	0.0	0.1		0.0	0.1	–	–
0.1	0.1	0.1		–	–	–	–
–	–	–		–	–	–	–
–	–	–		–	–	–	–
8.0	9.2	12.7		1.5	3.2	3.8	4.8
1.4	1.6	2.0		0.5	1.4	1.5	1.7
–	–	–		–	–	–	–
2.3	1.8	0.1		0.4	0.6	1.1	0.1
0.8	0.0	0.7		0.1	0.1	0.0	0.0
0.0	0.0	0.0		0.1	0.0	0.0	0.0
–	–	–		–	–	–	–
0.0	–	–		–	–	–	–
0.0	0.1	0.1		–	0.0	0.0	–
1.0	1.0	1.0		1.0	1.0	1.0	1.0
13.8	13.8	16.8		3.7	6.5	7.4	7.5
11.0	9.7	12.7		2.9	3.7	4.9	6.4
–	0.2	–		–	–	–	–
17.4	16.3	18.6		2.7	5.5	6.3	6.5
24.8	*23.7*	*29.5*		*6.6*	*10.2*	*12.3*	*14.0*
				12. TOTAL OOF NET			
–	–	–		–	–	–	–
–	–	–		–	–	–	–
–	–	–		–	–	–	–
–	–	–		–	–	–	–
–	–	–		–	–	–	–
–	–	–		–	–	–	–
–	–	–		–	–	–	–
–	0.0	–		–	–	0.0	–
–	4.0	–		–	–	4.0	–
–	–	–		–	–	–	–
–	–	–		–	–	–	–
–	–	–		–	–	–	–
–	–	–		–	–	–	–
–	–	–		–	–	–	–
–	4.1	–		–	–	4.1	–
0.3	0.1	0.6		-0.7	0.0	0.1	0.1
–	–	–		–	–	–	–
–	4.1	–		–	–	4.1	–
0.3	*4.1*	*0.6*		*-0.7*	*0.0*	*4.2*	*0.1*

13. ODF COMMITMENTS: BY PURPOSE %

	1987	1988	1989	1990
Education	9	1	–	–
Health	–	–	4	–
Other Social Infrastr.	1	5	9	–
Water Sanitat. Sewage	0	–	–	–
Energy	32	2	15	–
Telecommunications	5	–	–	–
Transportation	13	23	–	–
Agriculture	24	6	5	–
Extractive Industries	–	–	–	–
Manufacturing	–	–	–	–
Trade Banking Tourism	2	0	–	–
Technical Cooperation	13	62	60	–
Multisector Aid	–	–	3	–
Programme	–	–	–	–
Debt Reorganisation	–	–	–	–
Food Aid	–	–	4	–
Emergency Aid	1	–	–	–
Unspecified	–	–	–	–
TOTAL	100	100	100	–

14. GRANT ELEMENT OF ODA %

DAC COUNTRIES

	1987	1988	1989	1990
Australia	–	–	–	–
Austria	–	100.0	100.0	–
Belgium	100.0	100.0	100.0	–
Canada	100.0	100.0	100.0	–
Denmark	–	–	–	–
Finland	–	–	–	–
France	68.0	100.0	90.3	–
Germany	100.0	100.0	100.0	–
Ireland	–	–	–	–
Italy	100.0	100.0	100.0	–
Japan	100.0	100.0	100.0	–
Netherlands	100.0	100.0	100.0	–
New Zealand	–	–	–	–
Norway	–	–	–	–
Sweden	–	–	–	–
Switzerland	100.0	100.0	–	–
United Kingdom	100.0	100.0	100.0	–
United States	100.0	100.0	100.0	–
TOTAL	*75.3*	*100.0*	*92.0*	–
MULTILATERAL	*86.2*	*100.0*	*100.0*	–
ARAB COUNTRIES	–	*51.5*	–	–
E.E.C.+ MEMBERS	*75.2*	*100.0*	*94.1*	–
TOTAL	**79.4**	**93.0**	**95.8**	–

15. OTHER AGGREGATES

OFFICIAL COMMITMENTS:

	1987	1988	1989	1990
TOTAL BILATERAL	40.8	17.5	19.1	18.2
of which:				
Arab Countries	–	3.9	–	–
C.E.E.C.	–	–	–	–
TOTAL MULTILATERAL	18.4	27.9	13.8	28.7
TOTAL BIL.& MULTIL.	59.2	45.4	32.9	46.9
of which:				
ODA Grants	20.0	23.2	27.1	31.0
ODA Loans	39.2	21.1	1.8	15.8

DISBURSEMENTS:

DAC COUNTRIES COMBINED

OFFICIAL & PRIVATE

	1987	1988	1989	1990
GROSS:				
Contractual Lending	7.1	17.4	12.7	3.4
Export Credits, Total	-0.3	7.4	2.9	0.1
Export Credits, Priv.	-0.3	7.4	2.9	0.1
NET:				
Contractual Lending	7.1	17.4	5.9	3.4
Export Credits Total	-0.3	7.4	-3.9	0.1
PRIVATE SECTOR NET	3.9	7.9	17.7	0.8
Direct Investment	1.7	0.5	0.8	1.1
Portfolio Investment	2.6	0.1	20.8	-0.4
Export Credits	-0.3	7.4	-3.9	0.1

MARKET BORROWING:

CHANGE IN CLAIMS

	1987	1988	1989	1990
Banks	-12.0	-1.0	-1.0	14.0

MEMORANDUM ITEM:

	1987	1988	1989	1990
C.E.E.C. (Gross)	0.2	–	–	–

DISBURSEMENTS, UNLESS OTHERWISE STATE

1. TOTAL RECEIPTS NET

DAC COUNTRIES	1987	1988	1989	1990
Australia	7.7	-3.2	5.6	13.5
Austria	1.3	13.3	1.5	1.2
Belgium	6.1	28.9	6.5	13.6
Canada	25.1	24.0	16.4	26.9
Denmark	0.7	5.1	4.3	0.9
Finland	12.9	10.3	16.2	21.2
France	7.5	8.4	11.4	4.6
Germany	26.9	43.2	54.3	56.9
Ireland	0.1	0.1	0.1	0.9
Italy	136.6	246.6	101.9	144.9
Japan	23.2	12.3	9.0	8.7
Netherlands	6.8	22.8	10.9	31.3
New Zealand	–	–	–	0.0
Norway	11.7	16.9	21.1	25.5
Sweden	51.7	53.2	27.0	41.0
Switzerland	7.6	8.8	5.5	7.5
United Kingdom	4.6	34.2	19.7	36.1
United States	1.0	62.0	20.0	49.0
TOTAL	331.4	587.0	331.4	483.7
MULTILATERAL				
AF.D.F.	23.4	17.0	27.5	42.5
AF.D.B.	4.3	0.8	22.2	7.3
AS.D.B	–	–	–	–
CAR.D.B.	–	–	–	–
E.E.C.	95.9	153.4	53.8	53.8
IBRD	-9.4	-10.0	-10.0	-7.0
IDA	81.8	72.0	66.0	69.0
I.D.B.	–	–	–	–
IFAD	11.9	3.8	4.4	5.1
I.F.C.	–	–	0.5	–
IMF TRUST FUND	–	–	–	–
U.N. AGENCIES	–	–	–	–
UNDP	28.8	22.6	19.0	18.2
UNTA	3.1	2.1	2.4	2.6
UNICEF	15.1	19.4	18.9	22.4
UNRWA	–	–	–	–
WFP	31.1	40.1	66.0	88.5
UNHCR	27.9	73.7	88.2	74.3
Other Multilateral	4.5	6.3	24.5	8.8
Arab Agencies	-0.7	1.0	5.1	–
TOTAL	317.6	402.1	388.5	385.3
ARAB COUNTRIES	*-2.0*	*-1.3*	*-1.8*	*–*
E.E.C.+ MEMBERS	285.3	542.7	263.0	342.9
TOTAL	**647.0**	**987.8**	**718.2**	**869.0**

4. TOTAL ODA NET

	1987	1988	1989	1990
Australia	15.7	7.2	9.7	12.5
Austria	1.3	13.3	1.5	1.2
Belgium	2.3	6.6	3.9	4.6
Canada	25.9	25.7	18.9	28.3
Denmark	0.7	5.1	4.3	0.9
Finland	11.6	10.5	16.5	21.2
France	7.2	9.4	11.5	15.4
Germany	26.7	36.3	49.6	46.7
Ireland	0.1	0.1	0.1	0.9
Italy	127.8	232.0	138.4	169.1
Japan	13.7	12.3	11.2	10.3
Netherlands	6.8	22.6	10.7	24.9
New Zealand	–	–	–	0.0
Norway	11.7	16.9	21.1	25.5
Sweden	35.1	53.2	32.3	48.9
Switzerland	7.6	8.8	5.5	7.5
United Kingdom	13.7	33.8	19.7	35.2
United States	5.0	66.0	23.0	50.0
TOTAL	312.8	559.9	377.8	503.1
AF.D.F.	23.4	17.0	27.5	42.5
AF.D.B.	–	–	–	–
AS.D.B	–	–	–	–
CAR.D.B.	–	–	–	–
E.E.C.	95.9	153.4	53.8	53.8
IBRD	–	–	–	–
IDA	81.8	72.0	66.0	69.0
I.D.B.	–	–	–	–
IFAD	11.9	3.8	4.4	5.1
I.F.C.	–	–	–	–
IMF TRUST FUND	–	–	–	–
U.N. AGENCIES	–	–	–	–
UNDP	28.8	22.6	19.0	18.2
UNTA	3.1	2.1	2.4	2.6
UNICEF	15.1	19.4	18.9	22.4
UNRWA	–	–	–	–
WFP	31.1	40.1	66.0	88.5
UNHCR	27.9	73.7	88.2	74.3
Other Multilateral	4.5	6.3	24.5	8.8
Arab Agencies	-0.7	1.0	5.1	–
TOTAL	322.7	411.3	375.8	385.1
ARAB COUNTRIES	*-2.0*	*-1.3*	*-1.8*	*–*
E.E.C.+ MEMBERS	281.2	499.2	292.1	351.5
TOTAL	**633.5**	**969.9**	**751.8**	**888.2**

7. TOTAL ODA GROSS

	1987
Australia	15.7
Austria	1.3
Belgium	2.3
Canada	25.9
Denmark	0.7
Finland	11.6
France	7.2
Germany	27.9
Ireland	0.1
Italy	128.9
Japan	15.6
Netherlands	6.8
New Zealand	–
Norway	11.7
Sweden	35.1
Switzerland	7.6
United Kingdom	14.0
United States	8.0
TOTAL	320.4
AF.D.F.	23.5
AF.D.B.	–
AS.D.B	–
CAR.D.B.	–
E.E.C.	96.0
IBRD	–
IDA	85.1
I.D.B.	–
IFAD	11.9
I.F.C.	–
IMF TRUST FUND	–
U.N. AGENCIES	–
UNDP	28.8
UNTA	3.1
UNICEF	15.1
UNRWA	–
WFP	31.1
UNHCR	27.9
Other Multilateral	4.5
Arab Agencies	0.5
TOTAL	327.4
ARAB COUNTRIES	*–*
E.E.C.+ MEMBERS	284.0
TOTAL	**647.8**

2. ODA LOANS GROSS

DAC COUNTRIES	1987	1988	1989	1990
Australia	–	–	–	–
Austria	–	10.5	–	–
Belgium	–	5.8	3.2	–
Canada	–	–	–	–
Denmark	–	–	–	–
Finland	–	–	–	–
France	–	–	–	–
Germany	1.1	0.6	11.8	0.3
Ireland	–	–	–	–
Italy	30.6	75.3	30.8	42.6
Japan	–	–	–	–
Netherlands	–	–	–	–
New Zealand	–	–	–	–
Norway	–	–	–	–
Sweden	–	–	–	–
Switzerland	–	–	–	–
United Kingdom	–	–	–	–
United States	–	–	–	–
TOTAL	31.7	92.2	45.7	43.0
MULTILATERAL	123.6	119.2	117.7	135.2
ARAB COUNTRIES	*–*	*–*	*–*	*–*
E.E.C.+ MEMBERS	34.4	101.4	54.6	51.9
TOTAL	**155.3**	**211.4**	**163.4**	**178.2**

5. ODA LOANS NET

DAC COUNTRIES	1987	1988	1989	1990
Australia	–	–	–	–
Austria	–	10.5	–	–
Belgium	–	5.8	3.2	–
Canada	–	–	–	–
Denmark	–	–	–	–
Finland	–	–	–	–
France	–	–	–	–
Germany	-0.2	-1.9	9.0	0.3
Ireland	–	–	–	–
Italy	29.4	74.0	19.8	38.0
Japan	-1.9	-2.1	-2.0	-0.9
Netherlands	–	–	–	–
New Zealand	–	–	–	–
Norway	–	–	–	–
Sweden	–	–	–	–
Switzerland	–	–	–	–
United Kingdom	-0.3	-0.4	-0.3	-0.4
United States	-3.0	-3.0	-3.0	-3.0
TOTAL	24.0	82.9	26.7	34.0
MULTILATERAL	118.9	113.4	111.5	128.0
ARAB COUNTRIES	*-2.0*	*-1.3*	*-1.9*	*–*
E.E.C.+ MEMBERS	31.6	97.1	40.4	46.7
TOTAL	**140.9**	**195.0**	**136.3**	**162.1**

8. GRANTS

	1987
Australia	15.7
Austria	1.3
Belgium	2.3
Canada	25.9
Denmark	0.7
Finland	11.6
France	7.2
Germany	26.8
Ireland	0.1
Italy	98.4
Japan	15.6
Netherlands	6.8
New Zealand	–
Norway	11.7
Sweden	35.1
Switzerland	7.6
United Kingdom	14.0
United States	8.0
TOTAL	288.8
MULTILATERAL	203.8
ARAB COUNTRIES	*–*
E.E.C.+ MEMBERS	249.6
TOTAL	**492.5**

3. TOTAL OFFICIAL GROSS

DAC COUNTRIES	1987	1988	1989	1990
Australia	15.7	7.2	9.7	12.5
Austria	1.3	13.3	1.5	1.2
Belgium	2.5	6.6	4.0	4.6
Canada	28.5	27.2	18.9	29.6
Denmark	0.7	5.1	4.3	0.9
Finland	11.6	10.5	16.5	21.2
France	7.2	9.4	11.5	15.4
Germany	27.9	38.9	52.4	46.7
Ireland	0.1	0.1	0.1	0.9
Italy	128.9	233.3	149.3	173.7
Japan	15.6	14.4	13.1	11.2
Netherlands	6.8	22.6	10.7	24.9
New Zealand	–	–	–	0.0
Norway	11.7	16.9	21.1	25.5
Sweden	35.1	53.2	32.3	48.9
Switzerland	7.6	8.8	5.5	7.5
United Kingdom	14.0	34.2	20.1	35.6
United States	8.0	69.0	26.0	53.0
TOTAL	323.1	570.7	396.8	513.4
MULTILATERAL	332.4	420.4	406.2	404.9
ARAB COUNTRIES	*–*	*–*	*0.1*	*–*
E.E.C.+ MEMBERS	284.2	503.6	306.4	356.7
TOTAL	**655.6**	**991.0**	**803.2**	**918.3**

6. TOTAL OFFICIAL NET

	1987	1988	1989	1990
Australia	15.6	7.2	9.7	12.5
Austria	1.3	13.3	1.5	1.2
Belgium	2.5	6.6	4.0	4.6
Canada	25.1	24.0	16.4	26.9
Denmark	0.7	5.1	4.3	0.9
Finland	11.6	10.5	16.5	21.2
France	7.2	9.4	11.5	15.4
Germany	26.7	36.3	49.6	46.7
Ireland	0.1	0.1	0.1	0.9
Italy	127.8	232.0	138.4	169.1
Japan	13.7	12.3	11.2	10.3
Netherlands	6.8	22.6	10.7	24.9
New Zealand	–	–	–	0.0
Norway	11.7	16.9	21.1	25.5
Sweden	35.1	53.2	32.3	48.9
Switzerland	7.6	8.8	5.5	7.5
United Kingdom	13.7	33.8	19.7	35.2
United States	1.0	62.0	19.0	49.0
TOTAL	308.1	554.1	371.3	500.8
MULTILATERAL	317.6	402.1	388.5	385.3
ARAB COUNTRIES	*-2.0*	*-1.3*	*-1.8*	*–*
E.E.C.+ MEMBERS	281.3	499.2	292.2	351.6
TOTAL	**623.7**	**954.9**	**758.1**	**886.2**

9. TOTAL OOF GROSS

	1987
Australia	–
Austria	–
Belgium	0.1
Canada	2.6
Denmark	0.0
Finland	–
France	–
Germany	–
Ireland	–
Italy	–
Japan	–
Netherlands	–
New Zealand	–
Norway	–
Sweden	–
Switzerland	–
United Kingdom	–
United States	–
TOTAL	2.7
MULTILATERAL	5.1
ARAB COUNTRIES	*–*
E.E.C.+ MEMBERS	0.1
TOTAL	**7.8**

1988	1989	1990		1987	1988	1989	1990			1987	1988	1989	1990

10. ODA COMMITMENTS

13. ODF COMMITMENTS: BY PURPOSE %

1988	1989	1990	1987	1988	1989	1990	Purpose	1987	1988	1989	1990
7.2	9.7	12.5	18.2	2.1	3.5	9.3	Education	1	10	1	–
13.3	1.5	1.2	5.0	16.6	1.0	0.9	Health	2	7	1	–
6.6	3.9	4.6	2.4	14.7	3.9	4.6	Other Social Infrastr.	19	1	0	–
25.7	18.9	28.3	27.8	21.6	16.2	33.5	Water Sanitat. Sewage	2	2	0	–
5.1	4.3	0.9	–	1.7	1.6	1.2	Energy	8	9	1	–
10.5	16.5	21.2	12.9	5.9	30.0	10.1	Telecommunications	0	–	–	–
9.4	11.5	15.4	7.8	9.3	11.2	12.1	Transportation	0	3	19	–
38.9	52.4	46.7	37.7	55.6	46.9	59.2	Agriculture	22	15	44	–
0.1	0.1	0.9	0.1	0.1	0.1	0.9	Extractive Industries	3	–	–	–
233.3	149.3	173.7	256.1	222.8	97.4	128.7	Manufacturing	5	0	6	–
14.4	13.1	11.2	15.5	20.2	9.1	22.7	Trade Banking Tourism	–	–	–	–
22.6	10.7	24.9	7.4	22.7	10.8	24.4	Technical Cooperation	22	24	20	–
–	–	0.0	–	–	–	–	Multisector Aid	1	0	0	–
16.9	21.1	25.5	5.5	2.8	0.3	0.5	Programme	3	6	–	–
53.2	32.3	48.9	35.1	53.2	32.1	24.5	Debt Reorganisation	0	0	0	–
8.8	5.5	7.5	9.9	7.5	4.6	9.8	Food Aid	9	14	4	–
34.2	20.1	35.6	14.0	34.2	19.2	35.6	Emergency Aid	3	7	2	–
69.0	26.0	53.0	11.4	42.8	27.3	95.1	Unspecified	0	–	–	–
569.2	396.8	512.0	466.8	533.6	315.0	473.0	TOTAL	100	100	100	

14. GRANT ELEMENT OF ODA %

DAC COUNTRIES

1988	1989	1990	1987	1988	1989	1990	Country	1987	1988	1989	1990
17.5	28.4	43.7	24.2	19.5	166.6	4.0	Australia	100.0	100.0	100.0	–
–	–	–	–	–	–	–	Austria	100.0	94.6	100.0	–
–	–	–	–	–	–	–	Belgium	100.0	100.0	100.0	–
153.4	54.0	54.0	154.9	241.0	90.3	90.3	Canada	100.0	100.0	100.0	–
–	–	–	–	–	–	–	Denmark	–	100.0	100.0	–
76.0	70.0	73.0	46.0	188.0	72.0	75.0	Finland	100.0	100.0	100.0	–
–	–	–	–	–	–	–	France	100.0	100.0	100.0	–
3.8	4.4	5.3	5.8	–	–	–	Germany	100.0	86.5	100.0	–
–	–	–	–	–	–	–	Ireland	100.0	100.0	100.0	–
–	–	–	110.5	164.2	219.1	214.7	Italy	94.9	91.9	79.5	–
22.6	19.0	18.2	–	–	–	–	Japan	100.0	100.0	100.0	–
2.1	2.4	2.6	–	–	–	–	Netherlands	100.0	100.0	100.0	–
19.4	18.9	22.4	–	–	–	–	New Zealand	–	–	–	–
–	–	–	–	–	–	–	Norway	100.0	100.0	100.0	–
40.1	66.0	88.5	–	–	–	–	Sweden	100.0	100.0	100.0	–
73.7	88.2	74.3	–	–	–	–	Switzerland	100.0	100.0	100.0	–
6.3	24.5	8.8	–	–	–	–	United Kingdom	100.0	100.0	100.0	–
2.2	6.2	4.5	10.1	6.0	–	–	United States	100.0	100.0	100.0	–
417.1	382.1	395.1	351.5	618.7	547.9	383.9	TOTAL	97.2	95.0	93.3	–
–	0.1	–	–	–	–	–	MULTILATERAL	92.1	93.1	89.2	–
503.6	306.4	356.7	480.6	602.1	281.3	356.9	ARAB COUNTRIES	–	–	–	–
986.3	779.0	907.2	818.3	1152.3	862.9	856.9	E.E.C.+ MEMBERS	97.1	95.6	92.6	–
							TOTAL	94.8	94.0	90.4	–

11. TECH. COOP. GRANTS

15. OTHER AGGREGATES

1988	1989	1990	1987	1988	1989	1990		1987	1988	1989	1990
7.2	9.7	12.5	0.2	0.5	0.3	0.6					
2.8	1.5	1.2	0.4	0.5	0.3	0.4					
0.8	0.8	4.6	0.2	0.2	0.0	–	**OFFICIAL COMMITMENTS:**				
25.7	18.9	28.3	–	1.9	1.9	–	TOTAL BILATERAL	500.9	587.4	320.1	473.0
5.1	4.3	0.9	0.3	0.5	0.3	0.2	of which:				
10.5	16.5	21.2	0.5	0.7	1.9	1.3	Arab Countries	–	–	–	–
9.4	11.5	15.4	7.0	6.2	7.8	10.0	C.E.E.C.	34.1	50.0	5.1	–
38.3	40.7	46.4	11.4	16.8	9.3	15.1	TOTAL MULTILATERAL	375.7	726.3	555.7	424.0
0.1	0.1	0.9	0.1	0.1	0.1	0.5	TOTAL BIL.& MULTIL.	876.6	1313.7	875.9	897.0
158.0	118.6	131.1	26.7	17.4	38.2	83.0	of which:				
14.4	13.1	11.2	2.4	3.2	2.2	1.9	ODA Grants	694.7	897.3	567.3	777.9
22.6	10.7	24.9	2.5	5.6	5.6	6.9	ODA Loans	157.6	305.0	300.7	79.0
–	–	0.0	–	–	–	0.0					
16.9	21.1	25.5	0.4	1.0	1.2	1.6	**DISBURSEMENTS:**				
53.2	32.3	48.9	9.8	7.4	8.4	3.0					
8.8	5.5	7.5	0.1	0.9	–	–	DAC COUNTRIES COMBINED				
34.2	20.1	35.6	3.6	8.0	3.6	3.4	OFFICIAL & PRIVATE				
69.0	26.0	53.0	–	–	–	–	GROSS:				
477.0	351.1	469.1	65.5	70.8	81.0	127.8	Contractual Lending	135.6	163.6	104.2	90.9
297.9	264.3	259.9	81.3	125.8	153.0	126.2	Export Credits, Total	104.0	71.4	58.5	47.9
–	0.1	–	–	–	–	–	Export Credits, Priv.	101.4	70.0	58.5	46.6
402.2	251.7	304.8	53.8	56.5	64.9	119.1	NET:				
774.9	615.5	729.0	146.9	196.6	234.0	254.0	Contractual Lending	41.9	96.5	-1.2	-3.3
							Export Credits Total	17.8	13.7	-27.9	-37.3

12. TOTAL OOF NET

1988	1989	1990	1987	1988	1989	1990		1987	1988	1989	1990
							PRIVATE SECTOR NET	23.3	32.9	-39.8	-17.2
–	–	–	0.0	–	–	–	Direct Investment	-2.6	1.7	–	11.6
–	–	–	–	–	–	–	Portfolio Investment	3.3	11.7	-18.4	6.2
–	0.0	0.0	0.1	–	0.0	0.0	Export Credits	22.6	19.4	-21.4	-35.0
1.4	–	1.3	-0.8	-1.8	-2.5	-1.3					
–	–	–	0.0	–	–	–	**MARKET BORROWING:**				
–	–	–	–	–	–	–					
–	–	–	–	–	–	–	**CHANGE IN CLAIMS**				
–	–	–	–	–	–	–					
–	–	–	–	–	–	–	Banks	25.0	9.0	-11.0	81.0
–	–	–	–	–	–	–					
–	–	–	–	–	–	–	**MEMORANDUM ITEM:**				
–	–	–	–	–	–	–					
–	–	–	-4.0	-4.0	-4.0	-1.0	C.E.E.C. (Gross)	101.2	76.7	46.0	–
1.4	0.0	1.4	-4.7	-5.8	-6.5	-2.3					
3.3	24.1	9.8	-5.1	-9.2	12.7	0.3					
–	–	–	–	–	–	–					
–	0.0	0.0	0.1	–	0.0	0.0					
4.7	24.2	11.1	-9.8	-15.0	6.2	-2.0					

	1987	1988	1989	1990		1987	1988	1989	1990		1987

1. TOTAL RECEIPTS NET

DAC COUNTRIES

	1987	1988	1989	1990
Australia	5.9	-9.0	25.6	31.8
Austria	–	–	–	–
Belgium	0.1	0.1	0.0	0.4
Canada	0.2	0.2	0.1	0.1
Denmark	–	–	–	–
Finland	0.2	0.3	0.3	0.4
France	1.9	10.2	2.8	4.2
Germany	1.8	2.1	1.8	1.9
Ireland	–	–	–	–
Italy	–	–	–	–
Japan	7.1	26.9	21.9	27.4
Netherlands	-0.2	0.4	0.5	0.9
New Zealand	3.8	1.8	2.7	6.2
Norway	0.1	0.1	–	–
Sweden	–	–	–	–
Switzerland	–	–	–	–
United Kingdom	-3.3	-2.1	2.7	3.3
United States	–	2.0	-1.0	1.0
TOTAL	17.5	33.0	57.5	77.5

MULTILATERAL

	1987	1988	1989	1990
AF.D.F.	–	–	–	–
AF.D.B.	–	–	–	–
AS.D.B	0.8	20.0	0.2	-6.3
CAR.D.B.	–	–	–	–
E.E.C.	8.6	0.0	-0.4	-0.4
IBRD	-6.4	-1.0	-3.0	-4.0
IDA	–	–	–	–
I.D.B.	–	–	–	–
IFAD	–	–	–	–
I.F.C.	-0.6	2.0	-0.7	–
IMF TRUST FUND	–	–	–	–
U.N. AGENCIES	–	–	–	–
UNDP	0.6	1.5	1.1	1.4
UNTA	0.9	0.5	1.0	1.2
UNICEF	–	–	–	–
UNRWA	–	–	–	–
WFP	0.0	–	–	–
UNHCR	–	–	–	–
Other Multilateral	0.7	0.6	0.7	1.1
Arab Agencies	–	–	–	–
TOTAL	4.7	23.6	-1.2	-7.1
ARAB COUNTRIES	–	–	–	–
E.E.C.+ MEMBERS	8.9	10.7	7.3	10.2
TOTAL	22.2	56.6	56.2	70.4

2. ODA LOANS GROSS

DAC COUNTRIES

	1987	1988	1989	1990
Australia	–	–	–	–
Austria	–	–	–	–
Belgium	–	–	–	–
Canada	–	–	–	–
Denmark	–	–	–	–
Finland	–	–	–	–
France	–	–	0.4	1.2
Germany	–	–	–	–
Ireland	–	–	–	–
Italy	–	–	–	–
Japan	–	–	–	–
Netherlands	–	–	–	–
New Zealand	–	–	–	–
Norway	–	–	–	–
Sweden	–	–	–	–
Switzerland	–	–	–	–
United Kingdom	–	–	–	–
United States	–	–	–	–
TOTAL	–	–	0.4	1.2
MULTILATERAL	–	–	1.1	1.1
ARAB COUNTRIES	–	–	–	–
E.E.C.+ MEMBERS	–	–	1.5	2.3
TOTAL	–	–	1.5	2.3

3. TOTAL OFFICIAL GROSS

DAC COUNTRIES

	1987	1988	1989	1990
Australia	11.3	19.8	19.1	20.7
Austria	–	–	–	–
Belgium	0.1	0.1	–	–
Canada	0.2	0.2	0.1	0.1
Denmark	–	–	–	–
Finland	0.2	0.3	0.3	0.4
France	1.9	10.2	2.2	2.6
Germany	1.8	2.1	1.8	1.9
Ireland	–	–	–	–
Italy	–	–	–	–
Japan	10.3	9.1	7.5	9.0
Netherlands	0.6	0.4	0.5	0.9
New Zealand	3.8	1.8	2.7	6.2
Norway	0.1	0.1	–	–
Sweden	–	–	–	–
Switzerland	–	–	–	–
United Kingdom	2.7	2.2	7.6	7.9
United States	1.0	3.0	1.0	1.0
TOTAL	34.0	49.1	42.7	50.6
MULTILATERAL	22.0	38.7	15.7	19.1
ARAB COUNTRIES	–	–	–	–
E.E.C.+ MEMBERS	19.1	18.7	15.4	16.7
TOTAL	56.1	87.8	58.4	69.6

4. TOTAL ODA NET

	1987	1988	1989	1990
Australia	11.3	19.8	18.7	19.4
Austria	0.1	0.1	–	–
Belgium	0.1	0.1	–	–
Canada	0.2	0.2	0.1	0.1
Denmark	–	–	–	–
Finland	0.2	0.3	0.3	0.4
France	1.9	10.2	2.2	2.6
Germany	1.8	2.1	1.8	1.9
Ireland	–	–	–	–
Italy	–	–	–	–
Japan	10.3	9.1	7.5	9.0
Netherlands	0.6	0.4	0.5	0.9
New Zealand	3.8	1.8	2.7	6.2
Norway	0.1	0.1	–	–
Sweden	–	–	–	–
Switzerland	–	–	–	–
United Kingdom	0.9	0.5	1.8	2.1
United States	1.0	3.0	1.0	1.0
TOTAL	32.2	47.4	36.5	43.5

(MULTILATERAL)

	1987	1988	1989	1990
AF.D.F.	–	–	–	–
AF.D.B.	–	–	–	–
AS.D.B	–	1.5	2.2	0.4
CAR.D.B.	–	–	–	–
E.E.C.	1.4	2.7	1.7	1.7
IBRD	–	–	–	–
IDA	–	–	–	–
I.D.B.	–	–	–	–
IFAD	–	–	–	–
I.F.C.	–	–	–	–
IMF TRUST FUND	–	–	–	–
U.N. AGENCIES	–	–	–	–
UNDP	0.6	1.5	1.1	1.4
UNTA	0.9	0.5	1.0	1.2
UNICEF	–	–	–	–
UNRWA	–	–	–	–
WFP	0.0	–	–	–
UNHCR	–	–	–	–
Other Multilateral	0.7	0.6	0.7	1.1
Arab Agencies	–	–	–	–
TOTAL	3.7	6.9	6.6	5.7
ARAB COUNTRIES	–	–	–	–
E.E.C.+ MEMBERS	6.7	16.0	7.9	9.2
TOTAL	35.9	54.3	43.1	49.2

5. ODA LOANS NET

	1987	1988	1989	1990
Australia	–	–	–	–
Austria	–	–	–	–
Belgium	–	–	–	–
Canada	–	–	–	–
Denmark	–	–	–	–
Finland	–	–	–	–
France	–	–	0.4	1.2
Germany	–	–	–	–
Ireland	–	–	–	–
Italy	–	–	–	–
Japan	–	–	–	–
Netherlands	–	–	–	–
New Zealand	–	–	–	–
Norway	–	–	–	–
Sweden	–	–	–	–
Switzerland	–	–	–	–
United Kingdom	-1.8	-1.7	-1.5	-1.6
United States	–	–	–	–
TOTAL	-1.8	-1.7	-1.1	-0.4
MULTILATERAL	–	–	1.1	1.1
ARAB COUNTRIES	–	–	–	–
E.E.C.+ MEMBERS	-1.8	-1.7	0.0	0.7
TOTAL	-1.8	-1.7	0.0	0.7

6. TOTAL OFFICIAL NET

	1987	1988	1989	1990
Australia	8.7	16.9	16.1	17.8
Austria	–	–	–	–
Belgium	0.1	0.1	–	–
Canada	0.2	0.2	0.1	0.1
Denmark	–	–	–	–
Finland	0.2	0.3	0.3	0.4
France	1.9	10.2	2.2	2.6
Germany	1.8	2.1	1.8	1.9
Ireland	–	–	–	–
Italy	–	–	–	–
Japan	10.3	9.1	7.5	9.0
Netherlands	0.6	0.4	0.5	0.9
New Zealand	3.8	1.8	2.7	6.2
Norway	0.1	0.1	–	–
Sweden	–	–	–	–
Switzerland	–	–	–	–
United Kingdom	-2.5	-2.3	3.4	3.3
United States	–	2.0	-1.0	1.0
TOTAL	25.2	40.8	33.6	43.1
MULTILATERAL	4.7	23.6	-1.2	-7.1
ARAB COUNTRIES	–	–	–	–
E.E.C.+ MEMBERS	10.5	10.5	7.4	8.2
TOTAL	29.9	64.4	32.4	36.0

7. TOTAL ODA GROSS

	1987
Australia	11.3
Austria	–
Belgium	0.1
Canada	0.2
Denmark	–
Finland	0.2
France	1.9
Germany	1.8
Ireland	–
Italy	–
Japan	10.3
Netherlands	0.6
New Zealand	3.8
Norway	0.1
Sweden	–
Switzerland	–
United Kingdom	2.7
United States	1.0
TOTAL	34.0
AF.D.F.	–
AF.D.B.	–
AS.D.B	–
CAR.D.B.	–
E.E.C.	1.4
IBRD	–
IDA	–
I.D.B.	–
IFAD	–
I.F.C.	–
IMF TRUST FUND	–
U.N. AGENCIES	–
UNDP	0.6
UNTA	0.9
UNICEF	–
UNRWA	–
WFP	0.0
UNHCR	–
Other Multilateral	0.7
Arab Agencies	–
TOTAL	3.7
ARAB COUNTRIES	–
E.E.C.+ MEMBERS	8.5
TOTAL	37.7

8. GRANTS

	1987
Australia	11.3
Austria	–
Belgium	0.1
Canada	0.2
Denmark	–
Finland	0.2
France	1.9
Germany	1.8
Ireland	–
Italy	–
Japan	10.3
Netherlands	0.6
New Zealand	3.8
Norway	0.1
Sweden	–
Switzerland	–
United Kingdom	2.7
United States	1.0
TOTAL	34.0
MULTILATERAL	3.7
ARAB COUNTRIES	–
E.E.C.+ MEMBERS	8.5
TOTAL	37.7

9. TOTAL OOF GROSS

	1987
Australia	–
Austria	–
Belgium	–
Canada	–
Denmark	–
Finland	–
France	–
Germany	–
Ireland	–
Italy	–
Japan	–
Netherlands	–
New Zealand	–
Norway	–
Sweden	–
Switzerland	–
United Kingdom	–
United States	–
TOTAL	–
MULTILATERAL	18.4
ARAB COUNTRIES	–
E.E.C.+ MEMBERS	10.6
TOTAL	18.4

10. ODA COMMITMENTS

1988	1989	1990	1987	1988	1989	1990
19.8	18.7	19.4	12.5	20.2	10.9	11.1
–	–	–	–	–	–	–
0.1	–	–	–	0.1	–	–
0.2	0.1	0.1	0.4	0.2	0.1	0.0
–	–	–	–	–	–	–
0.3	0.3	0.4	–	–	0.9	0.0
10.2	2.2	2.6	1.9	13.8	1.7	1.4
2.1	1.8	1.9	1.1	3.7	3.3	0.7
–	–	–	–	–	–	–
–	–	–	–	–	–	–
9.1	7.5	9.0	3.8	8.5	8.7	7.1
0.4	0.5	0.9	0.6	0.4	0.5	0.9
1.8	2.7	6.2	3.0	3.1	–	2.7
0.1	–	–	–	–	–	–
–	–	–	–	–	–	–
–	–	–	–	–	–	–
2.2	3.3	3.7	2.7	2.1	3.2	3.7
3.0	1.0	1.0	0.9	0.9	1.5	0.9
49.1	38.0	45.1	26.8	52.9	30.8	28.5
–	–	–	–	–	–	–
–	–	–	–	–	–	–
1.5	2.2	0.4	–	–	–	–
–	–	–	–	–	–	–
2.7	1.7	1.7	1.6	5.6	6.9	6.9
–	–	–	–	–	–	–
–	–	–	–	–	–	–
–	–	–	–	–	–	–
–	–	–	–	–	–	–
–	–	–	2.3	2.7	2.7	3.7
1.5	1.1	1.4	–	–	–	–
0.5	1.0	1.2	–	–	–	–
–	–	–	–	–	–	–
–	–	–	–	–	–	–
0.6	0.7	1.1	–	–	–	–
–	–	–	1.3	–	–	–
6.9	6.6	5.7	5.2	8.2	9.6	10.6
–	–	–	–	–	–	–
17.7	9.4	10.8	7.9	25.7	15.6	13.6
56.0	44.6	50.8	32.0	61.2	40.4	39.1

11. TECH. COOP. GRANTS

1988	1989	1990	1987	1988	1989	1990
19.8	18.7	19.4	6.3	11.3	13.2	12.1
–	–	–	–	–	–	–
0.1	–	–	0.1	–	–	–
0.2	0.1	0.1	–	0.1	0.0	–
–	–	–	–	–	–	–
0.3	0.3	0.4	0.2	–	–	–
10.2	1.7	1.4	1.9	10.2	1.7	1.4
2.1	1.8	1.9	1.8	2.1	1.7	1.8
–	–	–	–	–	–	–
–	–	–	–	–	–	–
9.1	7.5	9.0	3.4	6.0	5.7	7.0
0.4	0.5	0.9	0.5	0.4	0.5	0.9
1.8	2.7	6.2	1.1	0.8	–	6.1
0.1	–	–	–	0.0	–	–
–	–	–	–	–	–	–
–	–	–	–	–	–	–
2.2	3.3	3.7	2.2	1.8	2.2	2.8
3.0	1.0	1.0	1.0	1.0	1.0	1.0
49.1	37.6	43.9	18.4	33.7	26.0	32.9
6.9	5.5	4.6	2.5	2.8	2.7	3.7
–	–	–	–	–	–	–
17.7	7.8	8.5	6.7	14.7	6.1	6.9
56.0	43.1	48.6	20.9	36.6	28.7	36.6

12. TOTAL OOF NET

1988	1989	1990	1987	1988	1989	1990
–	0.4	1.3	-2.6	-2.9	-2.5	-1.6
–	–	–	–	–	–	–
–	–	–	–	–	–	–
–	–	–	–	–	–	–
–	–	–	–	–	–	–
–	–	–	–	–	–	–
–	–	–	–	–	–	–
–	–	–	–	–	–	–
–	–	–	–	–	–	–
–	–	–	–	–	–	–
–	–	–	–	–	–	–
–	–	–	–	–	–	–
–	–	–	–	–	–	–
–	4.3	4.2	-3.4	-2.8	1.7	1.2
–	–	–	-1.0	-1.0	-2.0	–
–	4.7	5.5	-7.0	-6.6	-2.9	-0.4
31.8	9.1	13.4	1.1	16.7	-7.8	-12.8
–	–	–	–	–	–	–
1.0	6.1	5.9	3.9	-5.5	-0.5	-1.0
31.8	13.8	18.8	-5.9	10.1	-10.7	-13.2

13. ODF COMMITMENTS: BY PURPOSE %

	1987	1988	1989	1990
Education	–	–	2	–
Health	3	2	–	–
Other Social Infrastr.	0	0	–	–
Water Sanitat. Sewage	1	0	–	–
Energy	10	–	–	–
Telecommunications	–	0	21	–
Transportation	–	33	–	–
Agriculture	4	19	6	–
Extractive Industries	–	–	–	–
Manufacturing	27	2	–	–
Trade Banking Tourism	–	–	0	–
Technical Cooperation	47	34	68	–
Multisector Aid	1	2	1	–
Programme	5	8	0	–
Debt Reorganisation	–	–	–	–
Food Aid	–	–	1	–
Emergency Aid	1	–	0	–
Unspecified	–	–	–	–
TOTAL	100	100	100	–

14. GRANT ELEMENT OF ODA %

DAC COUNTRIES

	1987	1988	1989	1990
Australia	100.0	100.0	100.0	–
Austria	–	–	–	–
Belgium	–	100.0	–	–
Canada	100.0	100.0	100.0	–
Denmark	–	–	–	–
Finland	–	–	100.0	–
France	100.0	89.0	100.0	–
Germany	100.0	100.0	100.0	–
Ireland	–	–	–	–
Italy	–	–	–	–
Japan	100.0	100.0	100.0	–
Netherlands	100.0	100.0	100.0	–
New Zealand	100.0	100.0	–	–
Norway	–	–	–	–
Sweden	–	–	–	–
Switzerland	–	–	–	–
United Kingdom	100.0	100.0	100.0	–
United States	100.0	100.0	100.0	–
TOTAL	100.0	97.1	100.0	–
MULTILATERAL	100.0	100.0	100.0	–
ARAB COUNTRIES	–	–	–	–
E.E.C.+ MEMBERS	100.0	94.1	100.0	–
TOTAL	100.0	97.5	100.0	–

15. OTHER AGGREGATES

	1987	1988	1989	1990
OFFICIAL COMMITMENTS:				
TOTAL BILATERAL	26.7	52.9	41.9	35.2
of which:				
Arab Countries	–	–	–	–
C.E.E.C.	–	–	–	–
TOTAL MULTILATERAL	28.6	41.2	48.2	47.5
TOTAL BIL.& MULTIL.	55.3	94.2	90.1	82.7
of which:				
ODA Grants	32.0	57.5	40.4	39.1
ODA Loans	–	3.6	–	–
DISBURSEMENTS:				
DAC COUNTRIES COMBINED				
OFFICIAL & PRIVATE				
GROSS:				
Contractual Lending	0.4	2.2	5.3	7.9
Export Credits, Total	0.4	2.2	0.6	2.6
Export Credits, Priv.	0.4	2.2	0.2	1.3
NET:				
Contractual Lending	-10.8	-9.1	-5.4	-0.6
Export Credits Total	-5.5	-4.5	-5.9	-1.2
PRIVATE SECTOR NET	-7.7	-7.8	23.9	34.4
Direct Investment	-4.8	-19.6	25.3	29.2
Portfolio Investment	-0.8	12.6	0.0	5.1
Export Credits	-2.0	-0.7	-1.5	0.2
MARKET BORROWING:				
CHANGE IN CLAIMS				
Banks	-73.0	-5.0	-7.0	-16.0
MEMORANDUM ITEM:				
C.E.E.C. (Gross)	–	–	–	–

1. TOTAL RECEIPTS NET

DAC COUNTRIES	1987	1988	1989	1990
Australia	–	–	–	–
Austria	–	–	–	–
Belgium	13.0	-9.3	-10.0	15.0
Canada	7.1	9.8	18.7	17.4
Denmark	–	–	–	–
Finland	1.5	-0.2	-0.2	-0.2
France	298.1	529.5	265.1	125.6
Germany	39.2	31.2	21.8	-26.1
Ireland	–	–	–	–
Italy	18.5	14.3	10.4	27.6
Japan	-14.3	-4.4	5.1	0.2
Netherlands	9.0	5.6	3.9	-0.7
New Zealand	–	–	–	–
Norway	–	–	–	–
Sweden	–	–	–	0.0
Switzerland	0.6	0.1	0.1	0.0
United Kingdom	40.6	-2.0	33.1	-15.1
United States	6.0	12.0	13.0	13.0
TOTAL	*419.2*	*586.6*	*360.8*	*156.9*
MULTILATERAL				
AF.D.F.	–	–	–	–
AF.D.B.	17.7	5.5	42.1	40.6
AS.D.B	–	–	–	–
CAR.D.B.	–	–	–	–
E.E.C.	4.1	4.1	7.7	7.7
IBRD	-1.3	8.0	37.0	9.0
IDA	–	–	–	–
I.D.B.	–	–	–	–
IFAD	–	–	–	–
I.F.C.	–	12.0	65.0	10.0
IMF TRUST FUND	–	–	–	–
U.N. AGENCIES	–	–	–	–
UNDP	2.4	2.0	1.0	1.0
UNTA	0.6	0.7	0.7	0.6
UNICEF	0.1	–	–	–
UNRWA	–	–	–	–
WFP	–	–	–	–
UNHCR	–	0.1	0.1	0.1
Other Multilateral	0.4	0.5	1.0	1.4
Arab Agencies	2.1	-0.4	-0.1	–
TOTAL	*26.1*	*32.5*	*154.4*	*70.5*
ARAB COUNTRIES	***4.7***	***-1.7***	***-0.9***	***–***
E.E.C.+ MEMBERS	*422.4*	*573.4*	*331.9*	*134.0*
TOTAL	***450.0***	***617.3***	***514.4***	***227.3***

2. ODA LOANS GROSS

DAC COUNTRIES	1987	1988	1989	1990
Australia	–	–	–	–
Austria	–	–	–	–
Belgium	–	–	–	–
Canada	0.3	–	–	–
Denmark	–	–	–	–
Finland	0.6	–	–	–
France	31.1	50.5	62.5	97.3
Germany	0.7	0.5	1.0	0.9
Ireland	–	–	–	–
Italy	–	–	–	–
Japan	–	–	4.6	–
Netherlands	–	–	–	–
New Zealand	–	–	–	–
Norway	–	–	–	–
Sweden	–	–	–	–
Switzerland	–	–	–	–
United Kingdom	–	–	–	–
United States	–	–	–	–
TOTAL	*32.6*	*51.0*	*68.1*	*98.2*
MULTILATERAL	*2.2*	*0.1*	*–*	*–*
ARAB COUNTRIES	***7.0***	***–***	***0.7***	***–***
E.E.C.+ MEMBERS	*31.8*	*51.1*	*63.5*	*98.2*
TOTAL	***41.8***	***51.1***	***68.9***	***98.2***

3. TOTAL OFFICIAL GROSS

DAC COUNTRIES	1987	1988	1989	1990
Australia	–	–	–	–
Austria	–	–	–	–
Belgium	14.2	23.6	16.3	32.6
Canada	7.1	9.8	18.7	22.7
Denmark	–	–	–	–
Finland	0.6	–	–	–
France	280.4	321.6	206.5	191.4
Germany	28.4	33.0	16.0	67.7
Ireland	–	–	–	–
Italy	21.3	16.4	0.8	29.3
Japan	0.1	0.3	5.1	0.1
Netherlands	3.2	0.3	0.4	0.4
New Zealand	–	–	–	–
Norway	–	–	–	–
Sweden	–	–	–	0.0
Switzerland	0.6	0.1	0.1	0.0
United Kingdom	0.0	0.0	0.1	0.1
United States	6.0	15.0	15.0	16.0
TOTAL	*361.9*	*420.0*	*278.7*	*360.3*
MULTILATERAL	*33.4*	*42.3*	*272.4*	*98.2*
ARAB COUNTRIES	***7.0***	***–***	***0.7***	***–***
E.E.C.+ MEMBERS	*354.0*	*401.3*	*250.2*	*331.8*
TOTAL	***402.3***	***462.3***	***551.8***	***458.5***

4. TOTAL ODA NET

DAC COUNTRIES	1987	1988	1989	1990
Australia	–	–	–	–
Austria	–	–	–	–
Belgium	3.1	2.9	2.7	1.9
Canada	2.7	3.7	5.0	7.3
Denmark	–	–	–	–
Finland	0.6	–	–	–
France	60.9	89.4	104.2	113.4
Germany	1.3	1.2	1.8	1.7
Ireland	–	–	–	–
Italy	0.1	–	0.8	0.0
Japan	0.1	0.3	5.1	0.1
Netherlands	0.1	0.2	0.4	0.3
New Zealand	–	–	–	–
Norway	–	–	–	–
Sweden	–	–	–	0.0
Switzerland	0.6	0.1	0.1	0.0
United Kingdom	0.0	0.0	0.1	0.1
United States	1.0	1.0	1.0	2.0
TOTAL	*70.5*	*98.7*	*121.0*	*126.8*
MULTILATERAL				
AF.D.F.	–	–	–	–
AF.D.B.	–	–	–	–
AS.D.B	–	–	–	–
CAR.D.B.	–	–	–	–
E.E.C.	1.5	6.0	9.9	9.9
IBRD	–	–	–	–
IDA	–	–	–	–
I.D.B.	–	–	–	–
IFAD	–	–	–	–
I.F.C.	–	–	–	–
IMF TRUST FUND	–	–	–	–
U.N. AGENCIES	–	–	–	–
UNDP	2.4	2.0	1.0	1.0
UNTA	0.6	0.7	0.7	0.6
UNICEF	0.1	–	–	–
UNRWA	–	–	–	–
WFP	–	–	–	–
UNHCR	–	0.1	0.1	0.1
Other Multilateral	0.4	0.5	1.0	1.4
Arab Agencies	2.1	-0.4	-0.1	–
TOTAL	*7.1*	*8.9*	*12.6*	*13.1*
ARAB COUNTRIES	***4.9***	***-1.6***	***-0.9***	***–***
E.E.C.+ MEMBERS	*67.1*	*99.7*	*119.7*	*127.2*
TOTAL	***82.5***	***106.1***	***132.7***	***139.9***

5. ODA LOANS NET

DAC COUNTRIES	1987	1988	1989	1990
Australia	–	–	–	–
Austria	–	–	–	–
Belgium	–	–	–	–
Canada	0.3	–	–	-6.5
Denmark	–	–	–	–
Finland	0.6	–	–	–
France	25.0	46.5	61.7	72.8
Germany	0.7	0.4	1.0	0.9
Ireland	–	–	–	–
Italy	–	–	–	–
Japan	–	–	4.6	–
Netherlands	0.0	-0.1	–	-0.1
New Zealand	–	–	–	–
Norway	–	–	–	–
Sweden	–	–	–	–
Switzerland	–	–	–	–
United Kingdom	–	–	–	–
United States	–	–	–	–
TOTAL	*26.5*	*46.8*	*67.3*	*67.1*
MULTILATERAL	*1.6*	*-0.8*	*-0.8*	*-0.4*
ARAB COUNTRIES	***4.9***	***-1.6***	***-0.9***	***–***
E.E.C.+ MEMBERS	*25.2*	*46.4*	*62.3*	*73.2*
TOTAL	***33.1***	***44.4***	***65.7***	***66.7***

6. TOTAL OFFICIAL NET

DAC COUNTRIES	1987	1988	1989	1990
Australia	–	–	–	–
Austria	–	–	–	–
Belgium	14.2	23.5	16.3	32.6
Canada	7.1	9.8	18.7	16.0
Denmark	–	–	–	–
Finland	0.6	–	–	–
France	261.2	304.8	205.3	126.3
Germany	24.9	28.6	13.8	38.7
Ireland	–	–	–	–
Italy	18.5	15.0	0.8	27.6
Japan	0.1	0.3	5.1	0.1
Netherlands	3.1	-0.1	0.4	0.3
New Zealand	–	–	–	–
Norway	–	–	–	–
Sweden	–	–	–	0.0
Switzerland	0.6	0.1	0.1	0.0
United Kingdom	0.0	0.0	0.1	0.1
United States	6.0	12.0	13.0	13.0
TOTAL	*336.2*	*393.9*	*273.4*	*254.9*
MULTILATERAL	*26.1*	*32.5*	*154.4*	*70.5*
ARAB COUNTRIES	***4.7***	***-1.7***	***-0.9***	***–***
E.E.C.+ MEMBERS	*325.9*	*375.9*	*244.3*	*233.4*
TOTAL	***367.0***	***424.7***	***427.0***	***325.3***

7. TOTAL ODA GROSS

	1987
Australia	–
Austria	–
Belgium	3.1
Canada	2.7
Denmark	–
Finland	0.6
France	67.0
Germany	1.3
Ireland	–
Italy	0.1
Japan	0.1
Netherlands	0.1
New Zealand	–
Norway	–
Sweden	–
Switzerland	0.6
United Kingdom	0.0
United States	1.0
TOTAL	*76.6*
AF.D.F.	–
AF.D.B.	–
AS.D.B	–
CAR.D.B.	–
E.E.C.	2.0
IBRD	–
IDA	–
I.D.B.	–
IFAD	–
I.F.C.	–
IMF TRUST FUND	–
U.N. AGENCIES	–
UNDP	2.4
UNTA	0.6
UNICEF	0.1
UNRWA	–
WFP	–
UNHCR	–
Other Multilateral	0.4
Arab Agencies	2.2
TOTAL	*7.7*
ARAB COUNTRIES	***7.0***
E.E.C.+ MEMBERS	*73.7*
TOTAL	***91.3***

8. GRANTS

	1987
Australia	–
Austria	–
Belgium	3.1
Canada	2.4
Denmark	–
Finland	–
France	35.9
Germany	0.6
Ireland	–
Italy	0.1
Japan	0.1
Netherlands	0.1
New Zealand	–
Norway	–
Sweden	–
Switzerland	0.6
United Kingdom	0.0
United States	1.0
TOTAL	*44.0*
MULTILATERAL	*5.5*
ARAB COUNTRIES	***–***
E.E.C.+ MEMBERS	*41.9*
TOTAL	***49.5***

9. TOTAL OOF GROSS

	1987
Australia	–
Austria	–
Belgium	11.0
Canada	4.4
Denmark	–
Finland	–
France	213.4
Germany	27.1
Ireland	–
Italy	21.2
Japan	–
Netherlands	3.2
New Zealand	–
Norway	–
Sweden	–
Switzerland	–
United Kingdom	–
United States	5.0
TOTAL	*285.3*
MULTILATERAL	*25.7*
ARAB COUNTRIES	***–***
E.E.C.+ MEMBERS	*280.3*
TOTAL	***311.0***

10. ODA COMMITMENTS

1988	1989	1990	1987	1988	1989	1990
–	–	–	–	–	–	–
–	–	–	–	–	–	–
2.9	2.7	1.9	1.2	4.0	2.7	1.9
3.7	5.0	13.8	4.0	13.8	0.8	1.1
–	–	–	–	–	–	–
–	–	–	1.3	–	–	–
93.4	105.1	137.8	70.9	87.8	112.4	35.0
1.3	1.8	1.7	1.6	4.0	0.6	4.6
–	–	–	–	–	–	–
–	0.8	0.0	0.0	–	0.7	0.0
0.3	5.1	0.1	0.1	0.3	5.1	0.1
0.3	0.4	0.4	0.1	0.3	0.4	0.4
–	–	–	–	–	–	–
–	–	–	–	–	–	–
–	–	0.0	–	–	–	–
0.1	0.1	0.0	0.5	0.0	–	–
0.0	0.1	0.1	0.0	0.0	0.1	0.1
1.0	1.0	2.0	1.1	1.5	1.6	1.9
103.0	*121.8*	*157.8*	*80.9*	*111.7*	*124.4*	*45.0*
–	–	–	–	31.4	–	2.2
–	–	–	–	–	–	–
–	–	–	–	–	–	–
6.4	10.3	10.3	19.8	4.5	3.0	3.0
–	–	–	–	–	–	–
–	–	–	–	–	–	–
–	–	–	–	–	9.3	–
–	–	–	–	–	–	–
–	–	–	–	–	–	–
–	–	–	3.5	3.4	2.7	3.2
2.0	1.0	1.0	–	–	–	–
0.7	0.7	0.6	–	–	–	–
–	–	–	–	–	–	–
–	–	–	–	–	–	–
0.1	0.1	0.1	–	–	–	–
0.5	1.0	1.4	–	–	–	–
–	–	0.3	–	–	–	–
9.8	*13.4*	*13.5*	*23.3*	*39.3*	*15.0*	*8.4*
–	0.7	–	–	–	–	–
104.3	*121.0*	*152.2*	*93.6*	*100.6*	*119.8*	*44.9*
112.7	**135.9**	**171.3**	**104.2**	**150.9**	**139.4**	**53.4**

11. TECH. COOP. GRANTS

1988	1989	1990	1987	1988	1989	1990
–	–	–	–	–	–	–
–	–	–	–	–	–	–
2.9	2.7	1.9	2.6	2.0	1.6	0.9
3.7	5.0	13.8	–	2.3	2.4	1.5
–	–	–	–	–	–	–
42.9	42.6	40.5	32.0	27.4	22.6	26.8
0.8	0.7	0.8	0.6	0.8	0.7	0.8
–	–	–	–	–	–	–
–	0.8	0.0	0.1	–	0.0	0.0
0.3	0.4	0.1	0.1	0.3	0.4	0.1
0.3	0.4	0.4	0.1	0.3	0.4	0.4
–	–	–	–	–	–	–
–	–	0.0	–	–	–	–
0.1	0.1	0.0	0.1	0.1	–	–
0.0	0.1	0.1	0.0	0.0	0.1	0.1
1.0	1.0	2.0	1.0	1.0	1.0	2.0
52.0	53.7	59.7	36.6	34.2	29.2	32.6
9.6	13.4	13.5	3.7	4.3	2.7	3.2
–	–	–	–	–	–	–
53.2	*57.5*	*54.0*	*35.5*	*31.4*	*25.4*	*29.0*
61.6	**67.0**	**73.1**	**40.3**	**38.5**	**32.0**	**35.8**

12. TOTAL OOF NET

1988	1989	1990	1987	1988	1989	1990
–	–	–	–	–	–	–
–	–	–	–	–	–	–
20.8	13.6	30.7	11.0	20.6	13.6	30.7
6.1	13.7	8.9	4.4	6.1	13.7	8.8
–	–	–	–	–	–	–
228.1	101.4	53.6	200.3	215.5	101.0	13.0
31.7	14.2	66.0	23.5	27.4	12.1	37.0
–	–	–	–	–	–	–
16.4	–	29.3	18.4	15.0	–	27.6
–	–	–	3.0	-0.4	–	–
–	–	–	–	–	–	–
–	–	–	–	–	–	–
–	–	–	–	–	–	–
–	–	–	–	–	–	–
14.0	14.0	14.0	5.0	11.0	12.0	11.0
317.1	*156.9*	*202.5*	*265.7*	*295.2*	*152.4*	*128.1*
32.5	*259.0*	*84.8*	*19.0*	*23.6*	*141.9*	*57.4*
–	–	–	*-0.2*	*-0.1*	–	–
296.9	*129.2*	*179.6*	*258.8*	*276.2*	*124.5*	*106.2*
349.6	**415.9**	**287.2**	**284.5**	**318.6**	**294.3**	**185.5**

13. ODF COMMITMENTS: BY PURPOSE %

	1987	1988	1989	1990
Education	1	1	–	–
Health	0	1	1	–
Other Social Infrastr.	1	0	3	–
Water Sanitat. Sewage	–	–	–	–
Energy	0	0	–	–
Telecommunications	10	1	0	–
Transportation	3	9	38	–
Agriculture	9	2	1	–
Extractive Industries	0	14	14	–
Manufacturing	5	0	–	–
Trade Banking Tourism	–	3	–	–
Technical Cooperation	27	11	16	–
Multisector Aid	–	5	0	–
Programme	13	44	26	–
Debt Reorganisation	26	8	–	–
Food Aid	–	–	–	–
Emergency Aid	–	0	–	–
Unspecified	4	–	–	–
TOTAL	100	100	100	–

14. GRANT ELEMENT OF ODA %

DAC COUNTRIES

	1987	1988	1989	1990
Australia	–	–	–	–
Austria	–	–	–	–
Belgium	100.0	100.0	100.0	–
Canada	100.0	100.0	100.0	–
Denmark	–	–	–	–
Finland	–	–	–	–
France	83.1	69.6	62.8	–
Germany	54.4	65.8	100.0	–
Ireland	–	–	–	–
Italy	100.0	–	100.0	–
Japan	100.0	100.0	100.0	–
Netherlands	100.0	100.0	100.0	–
New Zealand	–	–	–	–
Norway	–	–	–	–
Sweden	–	–	–	–
Switzerland	100.0	100.0	–	–
United Kingdom	100.0	100.0	100.0	–
United States	100.0	100.0	100.0	–
TOTAL	*83.8*	*75.5*	*65.5*	–
MULTILATERAL	*100.0*	*100.0*	*100.0*	–
ARAB COUNTRIES	–	–	–	–
E.E.C.+ MEMBERS	*86.7*	*72.5*	*65.5*	–
TOTAL	**88.1**	**77.3**	**67.3**	–

15. OTHER AGGREGATES

	1987	1988	1989	1990
OFFICIAL COMMITMENTS:				
TOTAL BILATERAL	462.6	486.7	452.5	198.3
of which:				
Arab Countries	–	–	–	–
C.E.E.C.	–	–	–	–
TOTAL MULTILATERAL	39.8	345.8	118.1	8.4
TOTAL BIL.& MULTIL.	502.4	832.5	570.6	206.6
of which:				
ODA Grants	72.7	73.8	60.1	45.7
ODA Loans	31.5	77.2	79.4	7.7
DISBURSEMENTS:				
DAC COUNTRIES COMBINED				
OFFICIAL & PRIVATE				
GROSS:				
Contractual Lending	314.3	312.4	197.9	202.7
Export Credits, Total	12.3	-44.7	-7.0	-62.1
Export Credits, Priv.	-1.4	-55.6	-25.6	-96.6
NET:				
Contractual Lending	257.3	231.5	143.4	27.1
Export Credits Total	-22.4	-106.6	-60.3	-150.0
PRIVATE SECTOR NET	83.0	192.6	87.5	-98.0
Direct Investment	105.3	82.7	168.7	80.7
Portfolio Investment	10.3	220.5	-6.5	-11.9
Export Credits	-32.6	-110.5	-74.8	-166.8
MARKET BORROWING:				
CHANGE IN CLAIMS				
Banks	-33.0	111.0	-5.0	-170.0
MEMORANDUM ITEM:				
C.E.E.C. (Gross)	–	–	–	–

1. TOTAL RECEIPTS NET

DAC COUNTRIES	1987	1988	1989	1990
Australia	0.0	0.0	0.0	0.0
Austria	0.0	0.0	0.1	3.2
Belgium	0.1	-0.1	0.1	-0.2
Canada	1.2	0.3	0.7	0.2
Denmark	0.1	4.0	10.4	3.3
Finland	–	–	–	0.0
France	5.6	0.9	3.0	5.1
Germany	8.5	6.3	5.1	7.6
Ireland	0.1	0.0	0.0	0.0
Italy	9.2	8.2	6.0	0.9
Japan	4.5	3.8	2.0	6.4
Netherlands	1.9	9.0	3.7	14.4
New Zealand	–	–	–	–
Norway	1.4	4.4	4.3	0.0
Sweden	0.1	0.4	0.2	0.4
Switzerland	–	–	4.2	0.0
United Kingdom	10.7	-12.4	130.4	12.4
United States	10.0	11.0	10.0	12.0
TOTAL	53.3	36.0	180.1	65.9
MULTILATERAL				
AF.D.F.	17.6	6.4	5.9	8.0
AF.D.B.	-0.8	-1.2	0.3	-0.5
AS.D.B	–	–	–	–
CAR.D.B.	–	–	–	–
E.E.C.	7.6	8.3	6.9	6.9
IBRD	–	–	–	–
IDA	13.6	5.0	15.0	10.0
I.D.B.	–	–	–	–
IFAD	1.8	0.8	0.9	1.5
I.F.C.	–	–	0.2	–
IMF TRUST FUND	–	–	–	–
U.N. AGENCIES	–	–	–	–
UNDP	4.2	5.0	4.2	4.2
UNTA	1.0	0.5	0.6	0.9
UNICEF	0.2	0.3	0.5	0.6
UNRWA	–	–	–	–
WFP	5.1	4.1	3.9	2.8
UNHCR	–	–	–	–
Other Multilateral	1.7	2.0	1.7	2.4
Arab Agencies	-4.6	-3.2	-2.8	–
TOTAL	47.6	28.0	37.2	36.7
ARAB COUNTRIES	0.0	-2.0	-1.3	1.9
E.E.C.+ MEMBERS	43.7	24.3	165.5	50.5
TOTAL	100.9	62.0	215.9	104.5

2. ODA LOANS GROSS

DAC COUNTRIES	1987	1988	1989	1990
Australia	–	–	–	–
Austria	–	–	–	3.1
Belgium	–	–	–	–
Canada	–	–	–	–
Denmark	–	–	–	–
Finland	–	–	–	–
France	4.1	0.6	2.7	3.6
Germany	–	–	–	–
Ireland	–	–	–	–
Italy	–	–	–	–
Japan	–	–	–	–
Netherlands	–	0.6	–	0.0
New Zealand	–	–	–	–
Norway	–	2.2	2.2	–
Sweden	–	–	–	–
Switzerland	–	–	–	–
United Kingdom	–	–	–	–
United States	–	–	–	–
TOTAL	4.1	3.4	4.9	6.8
MULTILATERAL	33.8	12.5	22.4	19.8
ARAB COUNTRIES	0.6	0.4	3.8	4.2
E.E.C.+ MEMBERS	4.1	1.2	2.7	3.6
TOTAL	38.4	16.3	31.0	30.8

3. TOTAL OFFICIAL GROSS

DAC COUNTRIES	1987	1988	1989	1990
Australia	0.0	0.0	0.0	0.0
Austria	0.0	0.0	0.1	3.2
Belgium	0.1	0.0	–	0.3
Canada	1.2	0.3	0.7	0.2
Denmark	0.1	7.0	10.4	3.3
Finland	–	–	–	0.0
France	4.6	1.1	4.2	8.0
Germany	9.5	6.6	5.4	8.4
Ireland	0.1	0.0	0.0	0.0
Italy	9.2	8.2	6.0	0.9
Japan	4.5	3.8	2.0	6.4
Netherlands	1.9	6.7	3.7	9.2
New Zealand	–	–	–	–
Norway	1.4	3.8	3.0	2.3
Sweden	0.3	0.4	0.3	0.5
Switzerland	–	–	4.2	0.0
United Kingdom	11.8	11.6	8.3	13.0
United States	10.0	11.0	10.0	12.0
TOTAL	54.6	60.7	58.3	67.8
MULTILATERAL	54.0	32.9	43.6	39.1
ARAB COUNTRIES	0.6	0.4	3.8	4.2
E.E.C.+ MEMBERS	45.0	49.7	45.0	50.2
TOTAL	109.1	94.0	105.7	111.1

4. TOTAL ODA NET

DAC COUNTRIES	1987	1988	1989	1990
Australia	0.0	0.0	0.0	0.0
Austria	0.0	0.0	0.1	3.2
Belgium	0.1	0.0	–	0.3
Canada	1.2	0.3	0.7	0.2
Denmark	0.1	4.0	10.4	3.3
Finland	–	–	–	0.0
France	4.6	1.1	3.5	6.0
Germany	6.5	6.1	5.2	3.7
Ireland	0.1	0.0	0.0	0.0
Italy	9.2	8.2	6.0	0.9
Japan	4.5	3.8	2.0	6.4
Netherlands	1.9	5.1	3.7	4.7
New Zealand	–	–	–	–
Norway	1.4	3.8	3.0	2.3
Sweden	0.3	0.4	0.3	0.5
Switzerland	–	–	4.2	0.0
United Kingdom	10.9	10.7	7.1	12.4
United States	10.0	11.0	10.0	12.0
TOTAL	50.8	54.7	56.1	56.1
MULTILATERAL				
AF.D.F.	17.6	6.4	5.9	8.0
AF.D.B.	–	–	–	–
AS.D.B	–	–	–	–
CAR.D.B.	–	–	–	–
E.E.C.	7.6	8.3	6.9	6.9
IBRD	–	–	–	–
IDA	13.6	5.0	15.0	10.0
I.D.B.	–	–	–	–
IFAD	1.8	0.8	0.9	1.5
I.F.C.	–	–	–	–
IMF TRUST FUND	–	–	–	–
U.N. AGENCIES	–	–	–	–
UNDP	4.2	5.0	4.2	4.2
UNTA	1.0	0.5	0.6	0.9
UNICEF	0.2	0.3	0.5	0.6
UNRWA	–	–	–	–
WFP	5.1	4.1	3.9	2.8
UNHCR	–	–	–	–
Other Multilateral	1.7	2.0	1.7	2.4
Arab Agencies	-3.7	-3.0	-1.9	–
TOTAL	49.3	29.5	37.6	37.2
ARAB COUNTRIES	0.0	-2.0	-1.3	1.9
E.E.C.+ MEMBERS	41.0	43.5	42.7	38.3
TOTAL	100.1	82.1	92.4	95.1

5. ODA LOANS NET

DAC COUNTRIES	1987	1988	1989	1990
Australia	–	–	–	–
Austria	–	–	–	3.1
Belgium	–	–	–	–
Canada	–	–	–	–
Denmark	–	-3.0	–	–
Finland	–	–	–	–
France	4.1	0.6	2.0	1.7
Germany	-1.0	-0.5	-0.2	-0.6
Ireland	–	–	–	–
Italy	–	–	–	–
Japan	–	–	–	–
Netherlands	–	0.6	–	0.0
New Zealand	–	–	–	–
Norway	–	2.2	2.2	–
Sweden	–	–	–	–
Switzerland	–	–	–	–
United Kingdom	-0.8	-1.0	-1.2	-0.6
United States	–	–	–	–
TOTAL	2.3	-1.0	2.7	3.6
MULTILATERAL	29.2	9.1	19.5	17.5
ARAB COUNTRIES	0.0	-2.0	-1.3	1.9
E.E.C.+ MEMBERS	2.1	-3.4	0.4	0.3
TOTAL	31.5	6.0	20.8	23.0

6. TOTAL OFFICIAL NET

DAC COUNTRIES	1987	1988	1989	1990
Australia	0.0	0.0	0.0	0.0
Austria	0.0	0.0	0.1	3.2
Belgium	0.1	0.0	–	0.3
Canada	1.2	0.3	0.7	0.2
Denmark	0.1	4.0	10.4	3.3
Finland	–	–	–	0.0
France	4.6	1.1	3.5	6.0
Germany	8.2	6.1	5.2	7.7
Ireland	0.1	0.0	0.0	0.0
Italy	9.2	8.2	6.0	0.9
Japan	4.5	3.8	2.0	6.4
Netherlands	1.9	6.7	3.7	9.2
New Zealand	–	–	–	–
Norway	1.4	3.8	3.0	2.3
Sweden	0.3	0.4	0.3	0.5
Switzerland	–	–	4.2	0.0
United Kingdom	10.7	10.4	7.1	12.4
United States	10.0	11.0	10.0	12.0
TOTAL	52.3	56.0	56.1	64.6
MULTILATERAL	47.6	28.0	37.2	36.7
ARAB COUNTRIES	0.0	-2.0	-1.3	1.9
E.E.C.+ MEMBERS	42.5	44.9	42.7	46.8
TOTAL	99.9	82.0	92.0	103.2

7. TOTAL ODA GROSS

	1987
Australia	0.0
Austria	0.0
Belgium	0.1
Canada	1.2
Denmark	0.1
Finland	–
France	4.6
Germany	7.5
Ireland	0.1
Italy	9.2
Japan	4.5
Netherlands	1.9
New Zealand	–
Norway	1.4
Sweden	0.3
Switzerland	–
United Kingdom	11.8
United States	10.0
TOTAL	52.6
AF.D.F.	17.6
AF.D.B.	–
AS.D.B	–
CAR.D.B.	–
E.E.C.	7.8
IBRD	–
IDA	13.8
I.D.B.	–
IFAD	1.8
I.F.C.	–
IMF TRUST FUND	–
U.N. AGENCIES	–
UNDP	4.2
UNTA	1.0
UNICEF	0.2
UNRWA	–
WFP	5.1
UNHCR	–
Other Multilateral	1.7
Arab Agencies	0.6
TOTAL	53.9
ARAB COUNTRIES	0.6
E.E.C.+ MEMBERS	43.0
TOTAL	107.1

8. GRANTS

	1987
Australia	0.0
Austria	0.0
Belgium	0.1
Canada	1.2
Denmark	0.1
Finland	–
France	0.5
Germany	7.5
Ireland	0.1
Italy	9.2
Japan	4.5
Netherlands	1.9
New Zealand	–
Norway	1.4
Sweden	0.3
Switzerland	–
United Kingdom	11.8
United States	10.0
TOTAL	48.5
MULTILATERAL	20.1
ARAB COUNTRIES	–
E.E.C.+ MEMBERS	39.0
TOTAL	68.6

9. TOTAL OOF GROSS

	1987
Australia	–
Austria	–
Belgium	–
Canada	–
Denmark	–
Finland	–
France	–
Germany	2.0
Ireland	–
Italy	–
Japan	–
Netherlands	–
New Zealand	–
Norway	–
Sweden	–
Switzerland	–
United Kingdom	–
United States	–
TOTAL	2.0
MULTILATERAL	0.1
ARAB COUNTRIES	–
E.E.C.+ MEMBERS	2.0
TOTAL	2.1

10. ODA COMMITMENTS

1988	1989	1990	1987	1988	1989	1990
0.0	0.0	0.0	0.0	–	0.0	0.0
0.0	0.1	3.2	0.0	0.2	0.0	13.2
0.0	–	0.3	–	–	–	0.3
0.3	0.7	0.2	0.3	0.4	8.2	0.2
7.0	10.4	3.3	–	21.5	0.4	1.6
–	–	0.0	–	–	0.1	0.0
1.1	4.2	8.0	0.9	7.9	0.5	0.6
6.6	5.4	4.4	5.5	6.8	4.2	3.9
0.0	0.0	0.0	0.1	0.0	0.0	0.0
8.2	6.0	0.9	9.9	12.4	5.9	2.8
3.8	2.0	6.4	5.2	3.2	2.8	7.4
5.1	3.7	4.7	1.0	6.6	1.3	3.0
–	–	–	–	–	–	–
3.8	3.0	2.3	3.4	–	2.2	1.6
0.4	0.3	0.5	0.3	0.4	0.2	–
–	4.2	0.0	–	–	4.2	–
11.6	8.3	13.0	9.7	9.5	15.5	9.6
11.0	10.0	12.0	12.0	11.1	5.2	7.1
59.1	*58.3*	*59.2*	*48.0*	*80.0*	*50.7*	*51.5*
6.4	6.2	8.3	8.0	9.1	21.8	12.6
–	–	–	–	–	–	–
–	–	–	–	–	–	–
8.5	7.1	7.1	11.7	24.0	6.5	6.5
–	–	–	–	–	–	–
5.0	15.0	10.0	5.6	10.0	23.0	22.0
–	–	–	–	–	–	–
0.8	0.9	1.5	–	–	4.2	–
–	–	–	–	–	–	–
–	–	–	12.3	11.9	10.8	10.8
5.0	4.2	4.2	–	–	–	–
0.5	0.6	0.9	–	–	–	–
0.3	0.5	0.6	–	–	–	–
–	–	–	–	–	–	–
4.1	3.9	2.8	–	–	–	–
–	–	–	–	–	–	–
2.0	1.7	2.4	–	–	–	–
0.3	0.4	0.2	0.2	1.9	3.0	5.7
32.9	*40.5*	*37.9*	*37.7*	*57.0*	*69.4*	*57.6*
0.4	*3.8*	*4.2*	*3.2*	–	–	*0.2*
48.2	*45.0*	*41.6*	*38.7*	*88.9*	*34.3*	*28.4*
92.4	*102.5*	*101.3*	*89.0*	*137.0*	*120.1*	*109.3*

11. TECH. COOP. GRANTS

1988	1989	1990	1987	1988	1989	1990
0.0	0.0	0.0	0.0	0.0	0.0	0.0
0.0	0.1	0.0	0.0	0.0	0.0	0.0
0.0	–	0.3	0.1	0.0	–	–
0.3	0.7	0.2	–	–	–	0.2
7.0	10.4	3.3	0.1	0.9	0.3	0.3
–	–	0.0	–	–	–	–
0.5	1.5	4.4	0.5	0.5	0.5	0.6
6.6	5.4	4.4	2.6	2.9	2.8	2.6
0.0	0.0	0.0	0.1	0.0	0.0	0.0
8.2	6.0	0.9	1.5	0.2	0.2	–
3.8	2.0	6.4	0.5	0.8	0.8	0.7
4.5	3.7	4.7	1.0	1.4	1.3	1.6
–	–	–	–	–	–	–
1.6	0.9	2.3	0.8	0.1	0.0	0.2
0.4	0.3	0.5	–	0.0	0.0	–
–	4.2	0.0	–	–	–	–
11.6	9.3	13.0	3.7	5.0	4.9	4.8
11.0	10.0	12.0	3.0	7.0	6.0	6.0
55.7	*53.4*	*52.5*	*14.0*	*18.9*	*16.8*	*17.1*
20.4	*18.1*	*18.1*	*7.5*	*8.9*	*7.0*	*8.0*
–	–	–	–	–	–	–
47.0	*42.3*	*38.0*	*9.9*	*12.1*	*9.9*	*10.0*
76.1	*71.5*	*70.5*	*21.5*	*27.8*	*23.8*	*25.1*

12. TOTAL OOF NET

1988	1989	1990	1987	1988	1989	1990
–	–	–	–	–	–	–
–	–	–	–	–	–	–
–	–	–	–	–	–	–
–	–	–	–	–	–	–
–	–	–	–	–	–	–
–	–	–	–	–	–	–
–	–	4.1	1.7	–	–	4.0
–	–	–	–	–	–	–
–	–	–	–	–	–	–
1.6	–	4.5	–	1.6	0.0	4.5
–	–	–	–	–	–	–
–	–	–	–	–	–	–
–	–	–	–	–	–	–
–	–	–	-0.2	-0.2	–	–
–	–	–	–	–	–	–
1.6	–	*8.6*	*1.5*	*1.3*	*0.0*	*8.5*
–	*3.1*	*1.2*	*-1.7*	*-1.4*	*-0.4*	*-0.5*
–	–	–	–	–	–	–
1.6	–	*8.6*	*1.5*	*1.3*	*0.0*	*8.5*
1.6	*3.1*	*9.8*	*-0.3*	*-0.1*	*-0.4*	*8.0*

13. ODF COMMITMENTS: BY PURPOSE %

	1987	1988	1989	1990
Education	0	2	–	–
Health	25	5	5	–
Other Social Infrastr.	0	1	1	–
Water Sanitat. Sewage	2	7	–	–
Energy	9	16	2	–
Telecommunications	–	7	0	–
Transportation	8	1	24	–
Agriculture	6	17	1	–
Extractive Industries	–	0	–	–
Manufacturing	0	–	–	–
Trade Banking Tourism	–	–	12	–
Technical Cooperation	24	27	21	–
Multisector Aid	0	0	3	–
Programme	16	6	27	–
Debt Reorganisation	3	3	–	–
Food Aid	7	4	2	–
Emergency Aid	0	0	–	–
Unspecified	0	2	–	–
TOTAL	100	100	100	–

14. GRANT ELEMENT OF ODA %

DAC COUNTRIES

	1987	1988	1989	1990
Australia	100.0	–	100.0	–
Austria	100.0	100.0	100.0	–
Belgium	–	–	–	–
Canada	100.0	100.0	100.0	–
Denmark	–	100.0	100.0	–
Finland	–	–	100.0	–
France	100.0	55.3	100.0	–
Germany	100.0	100.0	100.0	–
Ireland	100.0	100.0	100.0	–
Italy	100.0	100.0	100.0	–
Japan	100.0	100.0	100.0	–
Netherlands	100.0	100.0	100.0	–
New Zealand	–	–	–	–
Norway	54.0	–	26.7	–
Sweden	100.0	100.0	100.0	–
Switzerland	–	–	100.0	–
United Kingdom	100.0	100.0	100.0	–
United States	100.0	100.0	100.0	–
TOTAL	*96.8*	*95.5*	*96.9*	–
MULTILATERAL	*93.9*	*92.9*	*83.9*	–
ARAB COUNTRIES	*81.0*	–	–	–
E.E.C.+ MEMBERS	*100.0*	*95.7*	*100.0*	–
TOTAL	*95.0*	*94.6*	*89.1*	–

15. OTHER AGGREGATES

	1987	1988	1989	1990
OFFICIAL COMMITMENTS:				
TOTAL BILATERAL	56.6	81.6	50.7	57.8
of which:				
Arab Countries	3.2	–	–	0.2
C.E.E.C.	–	–	–	–
TOTAL MULTILATERAL	37.7	58.5	69.4	57.6
TOTAL BIL.& MULTIL.	94.4	140.1	120.1	115.4
of which:				
ODA Grants	69.7	101.5	66.4	56.2
ODA Loans	19.3	35.6	53.7	53.0
DISBURSEMENTS:				
DAC COUNTRIES COMBINED				
OFFICIAL & PRIVATE				
GROSS:				
Contractual Lending	7.4	7.2	157.6	14.6
Export Credits, Total	1.4	2.2	152.7	-0.7
Export Credits, Priv.	1.4	2.2	152.7	-0.7
NET:				
Contractual Lending	3.6	-22.8	125.8	8.9
Export Credits Total	-0.1	-23.1	123.1	-3.1
PRIVATE SECTOR NET	1.1	-19.9	124.0	1.4
Direct Investment	0.7	1.2	0.8	0.8
Portfolio Investment	0.5	2.0	0.1	3.7
Export Credits	-0.1	-23.1	123.1	-3.2
MARKET BORROWING:				
CHANGE IN CLAIMS				
Banks	-1.0	-4.0	-5.0	7.0
MEMORANDUM ITEM:				
C.E.E.C. (Gross)	–	–	–	–

1. TOTAL RECEIPTS NET

DAC COUNTRIES	1987	1988	1989	1990
Australia	0.3	0.7	0.7	0.8
Austria	0.3	0.3	8.1	2.0
Belgium	0.2	0.1	0.6	0.1
Canada	17.9	20.1	38.6	27.0
Denmark	0.0	10.9	3.7	3.2
Finland	0.1	0.1	0.1	0.5
France	18.6	12.0	9.6	19.7
Germany	18.2	26.1	47.9	96.7
Ireland	0.1	0.0	0.0	0.0
Italy	10.4	16.0	9.9	-8.7
Japan	20.8	65.2	97.9	73.3
Netherlands	17.9	24.4	21.4	39.2
New Zealand	–	–	0.0	0.0
Norway	3.7	-1.5	-3.1	-9.7
Sweden	–	0.5	11.9	0.9
Switzerland	3.8	10.6	5.4	3.7
United Kingdom	71.8	75.2	241.3	5.9
United States	13.0	-3.0	27.0	13.0
TOTAL	*196.9*	*257.8*	*521.0*	*267.7*
MULTILATERAL				
AF.D.F.	15.5	14.9	2.0	2.9
AF.D.B.	18.3	6.4	28.0	36.2
AS.D.B	–	–	–	–
CAR.D.B.	–	–	–	–
E.E.C.	10.0	20.2	22.3	22.3
IBRD	-11.4	-11.0	-9.0	-10.0
IDA	189.7	165.0	146.0	184.0
I.D.B.	–	–	–	–
IFAD	4.2	3.2	0.2	1.4
I.F.C.	16.9	10.0	2.3	97.1
IMF TRUST FUND	–	–	–	–
U.N. AGENCIES	–	–	–	–
UNDP	4.9	7.2	8.7	8.3
UNTA	1.1	1.1	1.4	1.5
UNICEF	2.9	0.9	2.5	2.0
UNRWA	–	–	–	–
WFP	14.3	12.1	17.4	10.4
UNHCR	–	0.2	0.2	0.2
Other Multilateral	3.8	1.8	2.8	4.2
Arab Agencies	-2.2	1.2	1.5	–
TOTAL	*268.0*	*233.2*	*226.1*	*360.4*
ARAB COUNTRIES	***-4.9***	***13.3***	***2.2***	***3.4***
E.E.C.+ MEMBERS	*147.1*	*185.0*	*356.7*	*178.5*
TOTAL	***460.1***	***504.2***	***749.3***	***631.5***

4. TOTAL ODA NET

DAC COUNTRIES	1987	1988	1989	1990
Australia	0.3	0.7	0.7	0.8
Austria	0.3	0.3	8.1	2.0
Belgium	0.2	0.2	0.1	0.2
Canada	18.3	20.9	39.8	28.4
Denmark	-0.1	10.9	3.7	3.2
Finland	0.1	0.1	0.1	0.5
France	7.9	16.0	10.4	11.7
Germany	18.7	26.4	47.2	66.0
Ireland	0.1	0.0	0.0	0.0
Italy	10.4	8.5	14.5	10.5
Japan	20.8	63.2	97.9	71.9
Netherlands	13.3	20.7	20.7	24.8
New Zealand	–	–	0.0	0.0
Norway	4.1	0.9	0.5	0.6
Sweden	–	0.5	6.5	2.0
Switzerland	3.8	10.6	5.4	3.7
United Kingdom	27.7	49.9	71.9	22.3
United States	5.0	6.0	23.0	13.0
TOTAL	*130.6*	*235.8*	*350.4*	*261.7*
MULTILATERAL				
AF.D.F.	15.5	14.9	2.0	2.9
AF.D.B.	–	–	–	–
AS.D.B	–	–	–	–
CAR.D.B.	–	–	–	–
E.E.C.	11.8	20.4	19.6	19.6
IBRD	–	–	–	–
IDA	189.7	165.0	146.0	184.0
I.D.B.	–	–	–	–
IFAD	4.2	3.2	0.2	1.4
I.F.C.	–	–	–	–
IMF TRUST FUND	–	–	–	–
U.N. AGENCIES	–	–	–	–
UNDP	4.9	7.2	8.7	8.3
UNTA	1.1	1.1	1.4	1.5
UNICEF	2.9	0.9	2.5	2.0
UNRWA	–	–	–	–
WFP	14.3	12.1	17.4	10.4
UNHCR	–	0.2	0.2	0.2
Other Multilateral	3.8	1.8	2.8	4.2
Arab Agencies	-1.4	-1.5	-1.5	–
TOTAL	*246.9*	*225.3*	*199.1*	*234.4*
ARAB COUNTRIES	***-4.9***	***13.3***	***2.2***	***3.4***
E.E.C.+ MEMBERS	*89.9*	*153.0*	*188.0*	*158.2*
TOTAL	***372.6***	***474.4***	***551.7***	***499.4***

7. TOTAL ODA GROSS

	1987
Australia	0.3
Austria	0.3
Belgium	0.2
Canada	19.1
Denmark	0.3
Finland	0.1
France	8.1
Germany	27.5
Ireland	0.1
Italy	10.4
Japan	20.8
Netherlands	13.3
New Zealand	–
Norway	4.1
Sweden	–
Switzerland	3.8
United Kingdom	32.3
United States	12.0
TOTAL	*152.4*
AF.D.F.	16.6
AF.D.B.	–
AS.D.B	–
CAR.D.B.	–
E.E.C.	11.8
IBRD	–
IDA	191.0
I.D.B.	–
IFAD	4.2
I.F.C.	–
IMF TRUST FUND	–
U.N. AGENCIES	–
UNDP	4.9
UNTA	1.1
UNICEF	2.9
UNRWA	–
WFP	14.3
UNHCR	–
Other Multilateral	3.8
Arab Agencies	0.2
TOTAL	*250.8*
ARAB COUNTRIES	***0.0***
E.E.C.+ MEMBERS	*103.8*
TOTAL	***403.2***

2. ODA LOANS GROSS

DAC COUNTRIES	1987	1988	1989	1990
Australia	–	–	–	–
Austria	–	–	7.6	–
Belgium	–	–	–	–
Canada	0.0	–	–	–
Denmark	–	–	–	–
Finland	–	–	–	–
France	5.4	13.8	8.5	6.0
Germany	13.2	13.7	31.0	22.4
Ireland	–	–	–	–
Italy	9.7	7.9	13.5	8.6
Japan	0.7	24.9	69.8	42.1
Netherlands	5.6	4.8	8.8	11.5
New Zealand	–	–	–	–
Norway	–	–	–	–
Sweden	–	–	–	–
Switzerland	–	–	–	–
United Kingdom	0.0	0.7	1.8	2.6
United States	8.0	6.0	7.0	7.0
TOTAL	*42.6*	*71.8*	*147.9*	*100.2*
MULTILATERAL	*214.1*	*186.0*	*151.2*	*196.2*
ARAB COUNTRIES	***–***	***18.4***	***7.2***	***5.4***
E.E.C.+ MEMBERS	*35.9*	*42.2*	*64.5*	*52.0*
TOTAL	***256.6***	***276.2***	***306.2***	***301.7***

5. ODA LOANS NET

DAC COUNTRIES	1987	1988	1989	1990
Australia	–	–	–	–
Austria	–	–	7.6	–
Belgium	–	–	–	–
Canada	-0.7	–	–	-66.5
Denmark	-0.4	-0.4	-1.3	–
Finland	–	–	–	–
France	5.2	13.6	6.7	5.3
Germany	4.4	5.1	31.0	-209.4
Ireland	–	–	–	–
Italy	9.7	7.9	13.5	8.6
Japan	0.7	24.9	69.8	42.1
Netherlands	5.6	4.8	8.8	11.5
New Zealand	–	–	–	–
Norway	–	–	–	–
Sweden	–	–	–	–
Switzerland	–	–	–	–
United Kingdom	-4.6	-5.2	-3.9	-3.5
United States	1.0	-3.0	2.0	5.0
TOTAL	*20.8*	*47.7*	*134.2*	*-206.9*
MULTILATERAL	*210.1*	*182.9*	*146.4*	*190.2*
ARAB COUNTRIES	***-4.9***	***13.3***	***2.2***	***3.4***
E.E.C.+ MEMBERS	*21.9*	*27.1*	*55.8*	*-186.6*
TOTAL	***226.0***	***243.8***	***282.8***	***-13.3***

8. GRANTS

	1987
Australia	0.3
Austria	0.3
Belgium	0.2
Canada	19.0
Denmark	0.3
Finland	0.1
France	2.7
Germany	14.3
Ireland	0.1
Italy	0.7
Japan	20.2
Netherlands	7.7
New Zealand	–
Norway	4.1
Sweden	–
Switzerland	3.8
United Kingdom	32.2
United States	4.0
TOTAL	*109.8*
MULTILATERAL	*36.8*
ARAB COUNTRIES	***0.0***
E.E.C.+ MEMBERS	*67.9*
TOTAL	***146.6***

3. TOTAL OFFICIAL GROSS

DAC COUNTRIES	1987	1988	1989	1990
Australia	0.3	0.7	0.7	0.8
Austria	0.3	0.3	8.1	2.0
Belgium	0.2	0.2	0.1	0.2
Canada	19.1	20.9	40.0	94.9
Denmark	0.3	11.3	5.0	3.2
Finland	0.1	0.1	0.1	0.5
France	10.9	19.6	12.1	12.7
Germany	27.5	35.0	47.2	316.1
Ireland	0.1	0.0	0.0	0.0
Italy	10.4	8.5	14.5	10.5
Japan	20.8	63.2	97.9	71.9
Netherlands	13.7	21.3	20.8	28.0
New Zealand	–	–	0.0	0.0
Norway	4.1	0.9	0.5	0.6
Sweden	–	0.5	6.5	2.0
Switzerland	3.8	10.6	5.4	3.7
United Kingdom	32.9	58.5	82.3	35.3
United States	12.0	15.0	28.0	15.0
TOTAL	*156.3*	*266.6*	*369.1*	*597.6*
MULTILATERAL	*291.1*	*253.8*	*243.6*	*391.2*
ARAB COUNTRIES	***0.0***	***18.4***	***7.2***	***5.4***
E.E.C.+ MEMBERS	*107.7*	*176.6*	*206.3*	*430.4*
TOTAL	***447.4***	***538.8***	***619.9***	***994.2***

6. TOTAL OFFICIAL NET

DAC COUNTRIES	1987	1988	1989	1990
Australia	0.3	0.7	0.7	0.8
Austria	0.3	0.3	8.1	2.0
Belgium	0.2	0.2	0.1	0.2
Canada	17.9	20.1	38.6	27.0
Denmark	0.0	10.9	3.7	3.2
Finland	0.1	0.1	0.1	0.5
France	10.5	19.4	10.1	11.2
Germany	18.7	26.4	47.2	84.4
Ireland	0.1	0.0	0.0	0.0
Italy	10.4	8.5	14.5	10.5
Japan	20.8	63.2	97.9	71.9
Netherlands	13.7	21.2	20.8	27.8
New Zealand	–	–	0.0	0.0
Norway	4.1	0.9	0.5	0.6
Sweden	–	0.5	6.5	2.0
Switzerland	3.8	10.6	5.4	3.7
United Kingdom	27.9	52.2	76.7	29.2
United States	5.0	6.0	23.0	13.0
TOTAL	*133.6*	*241.2*	*353.7*	*288.1*
MULTILATERAL	*268.0*	*233.2*	*226.1*	*360.4*
ARAB COUNTRIES	***-4.9***	***13.3***	***2.2***	***3.4***
E.E.C.+ MEMBERS	*91.4*	*159.0*	*195.3*	*188.9*
TOTAL	***396.8***	***487.7***	***582.1***	***651.9***

9. TOTAL OOF GROSS

	1987
Australia	–
Austria	–
Belgium	–
Canada	0.0
Denmark	0.0
Finland	–
France	2.8
Germany	–
Ireland	–
Italy	–
Japan	–
Netherlands	0.4
New Zealand	–
Norway	–
Sweden	–
Switzerland	–
United Kingdom	0.6
United States	–
TOTAL	*3.9*
MULTILATERAL	*40.3*
ARAB COUNTRIES	***–***
E.E.C.+ MEMBERS	*3.9*
TOTAL	***44.2***

GHANA

1988	1989	1990	1987	1988	1989	1990

10. ODA COMMITMENTS

1988	1989	1990		1987	1988	1989	1990
0.7	0.7	0.8		0.3	0.3	0.2	0.9
0.3	8.1	2.0		0.2	0.3	8.1	2.2
0.2	0.1	0.2		0.0	0.1	0.1	0.2
20.9	39.8	94.9		35.2	44.7	50.4	13.1
11.3	5.0	3.2		14.9	—	8.2	1.1
0.1	0.1	0.5		—	—	0.0	0.2
16.1	12.1	12.4		10.0	2.6	5.2	52.5
35.0	47.2	297.8		32.5	56.7	25.1	100.3
0.0	0.0	0.0		0.1	0.0	0.0	0.0
8.5	14.5	10.5		14.8	47.3	0.7	1.9
63.2	97.9	71.9		100.5	129.6	127.4	114.2
20.7	20.7	24.8		22.9	24.4	18.4	21.4
—	0.0	0.0		—	0.0	—	—
0.9	0.5	0.6		7.9	0.1	—	—
0.5	6.5	2.0		0.0	0.4	6.8	0.5
10.6	5.4	3.7		3.7	18.0	1.1	1.9
55.9	77.5	28.4		45.4	49.9	60.5	48.0
15.0	28.0	15.0		24.9	17.5	138.2	30.0
260.0	364.1	568.8		313.2	391.9	450.2	388.6
15.5	2.8	3.9		26.4	17.6	—	58.6
—	—	—		—	—	—	—
—	—	—		—	—	—	—
20.4	19.6	19.6		57.0	25.3	24.2	24.2
—	—	—		—	—	—	—
166.0	147.0	186.0		289.6	209.0	247.0	288.0
—	—	—		—	—	—	—
3.2	0.2	1.7		0.2	—	17.4	13.2
—	—	—		—	—	—	—
—	—	—		—	—	—	—
—	—	—		27.1	23.3	32.9	26.5
7.2	8.7	8.3		—	—	—	—
1.1	1.4	1.5		—	—	—	—
0.9	2.5	2.0		—	—	—	—
—	—	—		—	—	—	—
12.1	17.4	10.4		—	—	—	—
0.2	0.2	0.2		—	—	—	—
1.8	2.8	4.2		—	—	—	—
—	0.2	3.6		4.4	6.4	10.0	0.3
228.4	202.6	241.3		404.6	281.5	331.4	410.8
18.4	7.2	5.4		8.7	28.8	—	—
168.2	196.7	396.8		197.4	206.3	142.2	249.7
506.8	573.9	815.4		726.5	702.2	781.6	799.4

11. TECH. COOP. GRANTS

1988	1989	1990		1987	1988	1989	1990
0.7	0.7	0.8		0.3	0.7	0.7	0.8
0.3	0.5	2.0		0.2	0.2	0.2	0.2
0.2	0.1	0.2		0.2	0.1	—	—
20.9	39.8	94.9		—	3.5	3.2	—
11.3	5.0	3.2		0.2	0.2	0.5	0.1
0.1	0.1	0.5		0.0	—	—	0.0
2.4	3.7	6.4		2.3	2.4	2.9	2.9
21.3	16.2	275.4		12.8	19.1	12.9	15.7
0.0	0.0	0.0		0.1	0.0	0.0	0.0
0.6	1.0	1.9		0.7	0.4	0.3	0.1
38.4	28.1	29.8		5.6	7.0	6.6	8.2
15.9	11.9	13.3		3.0	4.5	4.0	4.2
—	0.0	0.0		—	—	—	0.0
0.9	0.5	0.6		0.4	0.1	0.1	0.2
0.5	6.5	2.0		—	0.5	0.2	0.1
10.6	5.4	3.7		0.1	0.1	—	—
55.1	75.7	25.8		6.1	6.9	7.4	10.5
9.0	21.0	8.0		1.0	2.0	5.0	3.0
188.2	216.2	468.6		32.8	47.6	43.9	46.0
42.4	51.5	45.1		13.3	12.4	15.5	16.1
0.0	—	—		—	—	—	—
126.0	132.2	344.8		25.9	34.7	28.0	33.4
230.6	267.7	513.7		46.1	60.0	59.4	62.1

12. TOTAL OOF NET

1988	1989	1990		1987	1988	1989	1990
—	—	—		—	—	—	—
—	—	—		—	—	—	—
—	0.2	—		—	—	—	—
—	—	—		-0.4	-0.8	-1.2	-1.4
—	—	—		0.0	—	—	—
3.5	—	0.3		2.6	3.4	-0.3	-0.4
—	—	18.4		—	—	—	18.4
—	—	—		—	—	—	—
—	—	—		—	—	—	—
0.5	0.0	3.2		0.4	0.5	0.0	3.0
—	—	—		—	—	—	—
—	—	—		—	—	—	—
—	—	—		—	—	—	—
2.7	4.8	6.9		0.3	2.3	4.8	6.9
6.7	5.0	28.8		3.0	5.4	3.3	26.4
25.4	40.9	150.0		21.2	7.9	27.0	126.1
—	—	—		—	—	—	—
8.4	9.7	33.6		1.5	6.0	7.3	30.6
32.0	46.0	178.8		24.1	13.3	30.4	152.5

13. ODF COMMITMENTS: BY PURPOSE %

	1987	1988	1989	1990
Education	8	0	1	—
Health	1	1	0	—
Other Social Infrastr.	1	2	10	—
Water Sanitat. Sewage	2	4	8	—
Energy	9	2	6	—
Telecommunications	3	15	—	—
Transportation	14	16	1	—
Agriculture	13	10	16	—
Extractive Industries	—	6	1	—
Manufacturing	3	3	0	—
Trade Banking Tourism	0	15	23	—
Technical Cooperation	10	9	7	—
Multisector Aid	0	1	1	—
Programme	32	14	23	—
Debt Reorganisation	1	1	0	—
Food Aid	5	2	2	—
Emergency Aid	—	0	—	—
Unspecified	0	0	—	—
TOTAL	100	100	100	—

14. GRANT ELEMENT OF ODA %

DAC COUNTRIES

	1987	1988	1989	1990
Australia	100.0	100.0	100.0	—
Austria	100.0	100.0	93.5	—
Belgium	100.0	100.0	100.0	—
Canada	100.0	100.0	100.0	—
Denmark	100.0	—	100.0	—
Finland	—	—	100.0	—
France	49.4	92.9	72.2	—
Germany	95.3	90.0	85.9	—
Ireland	100.0	100.0	100.0	—
Italy	67.5	66.7	100.0	—
Japan	67.4	73.1	72.5	—
Netherlands	83.9	83.2	59.6	—
New Zealand	—	100.0	—	—
Norway	100.0	100.0	—	—
Sweden	100.0	100.0	100.0	—
Switzerland	100.0	100.0	100.0	—
United Kingdom	100.0	100.0	100.0	—
United States	82.2	93.3	99.1	—
TOTAL	83.3	84.2	89.1	—
MULTILATERAL	86.1	82.9	81.5	—
ARAB COUNTRIES	69.5	31.2	—	—
E.E.C.+ MEMBERS	92.0	87.6	90.3	—
TOTAL	84.6	81.6	85.8	—

15. OTHER AGGREGATES

	1987	1988	1989	1990
OFFICIAL COMMITMENTS:				
TOTAL BILATERAL	343.6	423.6	465.8	396.0
of which:				
Arab Countries	8.7	28.8	—	—
C.E.E.C.	0.5	0.0	—	—
TOTAL MULTILATERAL	405.1	424.3	382.6	527.8
TOTAL BIL.& MULTIL.	748.7	847.9	848.5	923.7
of which:				
ODA Grants	259.3	260.8	360.7	268.4
ODA Loans	467.7	441.4	421.0	530.9
DISBURSEMENTS:				
DAC COUNTRIES COMBINED				
OFFICIAL & PRIVATE				
GROSS:				
Contractual Lending	91.8	90.5	323.3	177.9
Export Credits, Total	45.4	12.1	170.5	49.0
Export Credits, Priv.	45.4	12.1	170.4	49.0
NET:				
Contractual Lending	50.0	53.1	277.9	-203.1
Export Credits Total	25.8	-0.8	139.2	-24.1
PRIVATE SECTOR NET	63.3	16.5	167.2	-20.4
Direct Investment	25.9	20.7	23.8	0.1
Portfolio Investment	11.2	-4.2	3.1	2.2
Export Credits	26.2	0.0	140.4	-22.7
MARKET BORROWING:				
CHANGE IN CLAIMS				
Banks	-40.0	-12.0	-108.0	64.0
MEMORANDUM ITEM:				
C.E.E.C. (Gross)	—	0.0	—	—

	1987	1988	1989	1990		1987	1988	1989	1990		1987
1. TOTAL RECEIPTS NET					**4. TOTAL ODA NET**					**7. TOTAL ODA GROSS**	
DAC COUNTRIES											
Australia	0.1	3.2	2.4	5.2		0.1	0.1	0.0	0.1	Australia	0.1
Austria	4.4	1.8	2.0	3.3		2.9	2.8	2.7	3.1	Austria	3.0
Belgium	-37.6	58.2	225.6	-270.6		–	–	–	–	Belgium	–
Canada	-1.0	-1.0	-1.0	-0.7		–	–	–	–	Canada	–
Denmark	-2.3	–	-1.6	-2.6		–	–	–	–	Denmark	–
Finland	–	–	–	0.0		–	–	–	0.0	Finland	–
France	82.9	-60.1	-19.0	150.4		5.6	4.2	3.0	4.0	France	6.6
Germany	278.9	280.5	304.8	167.0		26.0	25.5	22.2	27.1	Germany	36.4
Ireland	–	–	–	–		–	–	–	–	Ireland	–
Italy	-19.8	4.7	11.7	-49.1		1.5	2.1	3.3	3.8	Italy	1.5
Japan	105.4	238.8	410.9	563.2		0.5	1.0	1.3	0.9	Japan	0.5
Netherlands	-7.4	-71.1	-81.5	-27.0		-0.1	-0.1	-0.1	-0.1	Netherlands	–
New Zealand	–	–	–	–		–	–	–	–	New Zealand	–
Norway	0.2	0.6	0.3	-1.6		0.0	–	–	–	Norway	0.0
Sweden	2.1	–	9.8	-5.8		–	–	–	–	Sweden	–
Switzerland	0.2	0.1	0.0	0.0		0.2	0.1	0.0	0.0	Switzerland	0.2
United Kingdom	-20.3	-49.7	133.6	-33.1		0.1	–	–	0.0	United Kingdom	0.1
United States	-48.0	-45.0	-3.0	17.0		-6.0	-3.0	-5.0	-6.0	United States	-3.0
TOTAL	*337.9*	*360.9*	*995.1*	*515.5*		*30.6*	*32.4*	*27.4*	*32.9*	*TOTAL*	*45.3*
MULTILATERAL											
AF.D.F.	–	–	–	–		–	–	–	–	AF.D.F.	–
AF.D.B.	–	–	–	–		–	–	–	–	AF.D.B.	–
AS.D.B	–	–	–	–		–	–	–	–	AS.D.B	–
CAR.D.B.	–	–	–	–		–	–	–	–	CAR.D.B.	–
E.E.C.	-24.8	-27.4	-27.9	-27.9		1.1	0.3	0.5	0.5	E.E.C.	1.1
IBRD	-33.2	-36.0	-36.0	-42.0		–	–	–	–	IBRD	–
IDA	–	–	–	–		–	–	–	–	IDA	–
I.D.B.	–	–	–	–		–	–	–	–	I.D.B.	–
IFAD	–	–	–	–		–	–	–	–	IFAD	–
I.F.C.	-5.3	–	-0.5	–		–	–	–	–	I.F.C.	–
IMF TRUST FUND	–	–	–	–		–	–	–	–	IMF TRUST FUND	–
U.N. AGENCIES	–	–	–	–		–	–	–	–	U.N. AGENCIES	–
UNDP	1.0	0.1	0.1	–		1.0	0.1	0.1	–	UNDP	1.0
UNTA	0.2	0.3	0.4	0.2		0.2	0.3	0.4	0.2	UNTA	0.2
UNICEF	–	–	–	–		–	–	–	–	UNICEF	–
UNRWA	–	–	–	–		–	–	–	–	UNRWA	–
WFP	–	–	–	–		–	–	–	–	WFP	–
UNHCR	1.5	2.3	1.7	1.5		1.5	2.3	1.7	1.5	UNHCR	1.5
Other Multilateral	95.5	139.1	146.0	54.8		-0.1	2.0	1.4	0.0	Other Multilateral	0.0
Arab Agencies	–	–	–	–		–	–	–	–	Arab Agencies	–
TOTAL	*34.9*	*78.4*	*83.7*	*-13.4*		*3.7*	*5.0*	*4.0*	*2.2*	*TOTAL*	*3.9*
ARAB COUNTRIES	***-47.1***	***-56.6***	***–***	***–***		***–***	***–***	***–***	***–***	***ARAB COUNTRIES***	***–***
E.E.C.+ MEMBERS	*249.6*	*135.0*	*545.7*	*-93.0*		*34.1*	*31.9*	*28.8*	*35.3*	*E.E.C.+ MEMBERS*	*45.7*
TOTAL	**325.7**	**382.7**	**1078.8**	**502.1**		**34.3**	**37.4**	**31.4**	**35.1**	**TOTAL**	**49.2**
2. ODA LOANS GROSS					**5. ODA LOANS NET**					**8. GRANTS**	
DAC COUNTRIES											
Australia	–	–	–	–		–	–	–	–	Australia	0.1
Austria	–	–	–	–		-0.1	0.0	0.0	–	Austria	3.0
Belgium	–	–	–	–		–	–	–	–	Belgium	–
Canada	–	–	–	–		–	–	–	–	Canada	–
Denmark	–	–	–	–		–	–	–	–	Denmark	–
Finland	–	–	–	–		–	–	–	–	Finland	–
France	–	–	–	–		-1.0	-0.5	-1.0	-1.0	France	6.6
Germany	–	–	–	–		-10.4	-8.1	-6.7	-5.5	Germany	36.4
Ireland	–	–	–	–		–	–	–	–	Ireland	–
Italy	–	–	–	–		–	–	–	–	Italy	1.5
Japan	–	–	–	–		–	–	–	–	Japan	0.5
Netherlands	–	–	–	–		-0.1	-0.1	-0.1	-0.1	Netherlands	–
New Zealand	–	–	–	–		–	–	–	–	New Zealand	–
Norway	–	–	–	–		–	–	–	–	Norway	0.0
Sweden	–	–	–	–		–	–	–	–	Sweden	–
Switzerland	–	–	–	–		–	–	–	–	Switzerland	0.2
United Kingdom	–	–	–	–		–	–	–	–	United Kingdom	0.1
United States	–	–	–	–		-3.0	-2.0	-3.0	-4.0	United States	-3.0
TOTAL	*–*	*–*	*–*	*–*		*-14.7*	*-10.7*	*-10.8*	*-10.7*	*TOTAL*	*45.3*
MULTILATERAL	*–*	*2.0*	*1.6*	*–*		*-0.2*	*1.5*	*0.9*	*-0.5*	*MULTILATERAL*	*3.9*
ARAB COUNTRIES	***–***	***–***	***–***	***–***		***–***	***–***	***–***	***–***	***ARAB COUNTRIES***	***–***
E.E.C.+ MEMBERS	*–*	*–*	*–*	*–*		*-11.6*	*-9.0*	*-8.2*	*-7.0*	*E.E.C.+ MEMBERS*	*45.7*
TOTAL	**–**	**2.0**	**1.6**	**–**		**-14.9**	**-9.2**	**-9.9**	**-11.2**	**TOTAL**	**49.2**
3. TOTAL OFFICIAL GROSS					**6. TOTAL OFFICIAL NET**					**9. TOTAL OOF GROSS**	
DAC COUNTRIES											
Australia	0.1	0.1	4.8	0.1		0.1	0.1	4.8	-0.3	Australia	–
Austria	3.0	2.8	2.8	3.1		2.9	2.8	2.7	3.1	Austria	–
Belgium	–	–	–	–		–	–	–	–	Belgium	–
Canada	–	–	–	–		-1.0	-1.0	-1.0	-0.7	Canada	–
Denmark	–	–	–	–		–	–	–	–	Denmark	–
Finland	–	–	–	0.0		–	–	–	0.0	Finland	–
France	6.6	4.6	3.9	5.1		5.6	4.2	3.0	4.0	France	–
Germany	38.0	34.9	28.9	32.6		6.5	-48.2	18.5	24.6	Germany	1.6
Ireland	–	–	–	–		–	–	–	–	Ireland	–
Italy	1.5	2.1	3.3	37.2		1.5	2.1	3.3	23.4	Italy	–
Japan	0.5	1.0	1.3	0.9		0.5	1.0	1.3	0.9	Japan	–
Netherlands	–	–	–	–		-0.1	-0.1	-0.1	-0.1	Netherlands	–
New Zealand	–	–	–	–		–	–	–	–	New Zealand	–
Norway	0.0	–	–	–		0.0	–	–	–	Norway	–
Sweden	–	–	–	–		–	–	–	–	Sweden	–
Switzerland	0.2	0.1	0.0	0.0		0.2	0.1	0.0	0.0	Switzerland	–
United Kingdom	0.1	–	–	0.0		0.1	–	–	0.0	United Kingdom	–
United States	-3.0	-1.0	-2.0	-2.0		-15.0	-11.0	-14.0	-16.0	United States	–
TOTAL	*46.9*	*44.5*	*43.0*	*76.9*		*1.3*	*-50.2*	*18.5*	*38.9*	*TOTAL*	*1.6*
MULTILATERAL	*109.6*	*154.1*	*162.6*	*65.7*		*34.9*	*78.4*	*83.7*	*-13.4*	*MULTILATERAL*	*105.8*
ARAB COUNTRIES	***–***	***–***	***–***	***–***		***-47.1***	***-56.6***	***–***	***–***	***ARAB COUNTRIES***	***–***
E.E.C.+ MEMBERS	*47.2*	*42.3*	*37.0*	*75.7*		*-11.2*	*-69.4*	*-3.2*	*24.0*	*E.E.C.+ MEMBERS*	*1.6*
TOTAL	**156.5**	**198.6**	**205.7**	**142.6**		**-10.8**	**-28.4**	**102.2**	**25.5**	**TOTAL**	**107.3**

1988	1989	1990		1987	1988	1989	1990

10. ODA COMMITMENTS

1988	1989	1990		1987	1988	1989	1990
0.1	0.0	0.1		0.1	0.1	0.1	0.1
2.8	2.8	3.1		3.1	2.8	2.8	3.1
–	–	–		–	–	–	–
–	–	–		–	–	–	–
–	–	0.0		–	–	–	–
4.6	3.9	5.1		6.6	4.6	3.9	5.1
33.5	28.9	32.6		35.5	33.9	28.4	32.8
–	–	–		–	–	–	–
2.1	3.3	3.8		1.5	2.1	3.3	3.8
1.0	1.3	0.9		0.6	1.0	1.4	0.9
–	–	–		–	–	–	–
–	–	–		–	–	–	–
–	–	–		–	–	–	–
0.1	0.0	0.0		0.2	–	–	–
–	–	0.0		0.1	–	–	0.0
-1.0	-2.0	-2.0		–	–	–	–
43.1	38.3	43.6		47.6	44.5	39.8	45.8
–	–	–		–	–	–	–
–	–	–		–	–	–	–
–	–	–		–	–	–	–
0.7	0.8	0.8		–	4.6	1.2	1.2
–	–	–		–	–	–	–
–	–	–		–	–	–	–
–	–	–		–	–	–	–
–	–	–		–	–	–	–
–	–	–		2.7	2.8	2.3	1.9
0.1	0.1	–		–	–	–	–
0.3	0.4	0.2		–	–	–	–
–	–	–		–	–	–	–
2.3	1.7	1.5		–	–	–	–
2.1	1.8	0.2		–	2.0	1.6	–
–	–	–		–	–	–	–
5.5	4.7	2.7		2.7	9.5	5.1	3.1
–	–	–		–	–	–	–
40.9	37.0	42.3		43.7	45.3	36.8	42.9
48.6	43.0	46.3		50.3	54.0	44.9	48.8

11. TECH. COOP. GRANTS

1988	1989	1990		1987	1988	1989	1990
0.1	0.0	0.1		0.1	0.1	0.0	0.1
2.8	2.8	3.1		3.0	2.8	2.8	3.1
–	–	–		–	–	–	–
–	–	–		–	–	–	–
–	–	0.0		–	–	–	0.0
4.6	3.9	5.1		6.6	4.6	3.9	5.1
33.5	28.9	32.6		36.3	33.5	28.9	32.6
–	–	–		–	–	–	–
2.1	3.3	3.8		1.5	2.1	3.3	3.8
1.0	1.3	0.9		0.5	1.0	1.3	0.9
–	–	–		0.0	–	–	–
–	–	–		–	–	–	–
–	–	–		–	–	–	–
0.1	0.0	0.0		0.0	0.1	–	–
–	–	0.0		–	–	–	0.0
-1.0	-2.0	-2.0		–	–	–	–
43.1	38.3	43.6		48.0	44.1	40.2	45.5
3.5	3.1	2.7		2.7	3.3	2.2	1.9
–	–	–		–	–	–	–
40.9	37.0	42.3		44.4	40.7	36.2	41.5
46.6	41.4	46.3		50.7	47.4	42.5	47.4

12. TOTAL OOF NET

1988	1989	1990		1987	1988	1989	1990
–	4.8	–		–	–	4.8	-0.4
–	–	–		–	–	–	–
–	–	–		-1.0	-1.0	-1.0	-0.7
–	–	–		–	–	–	–
–	–	–		–	–	–	–
1.4	–	–		-19.4	-73.6	-3.7	-2.5
–	–	–		–	–	–	–
–	–	33.4		–	–	–	19.6
–	–	–		–	–	–	–
–	–	–		–	–	–	–
–	–	–		–	–	–	–
–	–	–		–	–	–	–
–	–	–		–	–	–	–
–	–	–		-9.0	-8.0	-9.0	-10.0
1.4	4.8	33.4		-29.4	-82.6	-8.9	6.0
148.6	157.9	63.0		31.3	73.4	79.7	-15.6
–	–	–		-47.1	-56.6	–	–
1.4	–	33.4		-45.3	-101.3	-32.1	-11.3
150.0	162.7	96.3		-45.2	-65.8	70.8	-9.6

13. ODF COMMITMENTS: BY PURPOSE %

	1987	1988	1989	1990
Education	–	–	–	–
Health	–	–	–	–
Other Social Infrastr.	–	–	–	–
Water Sanitat. Sewage	–	–	–	–
Energy	–	–	–	–
Telecommunications	–	–	–	–
Transportation	–	–	–	–
Agriculture	–	–	–	–
Extractive Industries	–	–	–	–
Manufacturing	–	–	–	–
Trade Banking Tourism	–	–	–	–
Technical Cooperation	100	100	100	–
Multisector Aid	–	–	–	–
Programme	–	–	–	–
Debt Reorganisation	–	–	–	–
Food Aid	–	–	–	–
Emergency Aid	0	0	–	–
Unspecified	–	–	–	–
TOTAL	100	100	100	–

14. GRANT ELEMENT OF ODA %

DAC COUNTRIES

	1987	1988	1989	1990
Australia	100.0	100.0	100.0	–
Austria	100.0	100.0	100.0	–
Belgium	–	–	–	–
Canada	–	–	–	–
Denmark	–	–	–	–
Finland	–	–	–	–
France	100.0	100.0	100.0	–
Germany	100.0	100.0	100.0	–
Ireland	–	–	–	–
Italy	100.0	100.0	100.0	–
Japan	100.0	100.0	100.0	–
Netherlands	–	–	–	–
New Zealand	–	–	–	–
Norway	–	–	–	–
Sweden	–	–	–	–
Switzerland	100.0	–	–	–
United Kingdom	100.0	–	–	–
United States	–	–	–	–
TOTAL	100.0	100.0	100.0	–
MULTILATERAL	100.0	100.0	100.0	–
ARAB COUNTRIES	–	–	–	–
E.E.C.+ MEMBERS	100.0	100.0	100.0	–
TOTAL	100.0	100.0	100.0	–

15. OTHER AGGREGATES

	1987	1988	1989	1990
OFFICIAL COMMITMENTS:				
TOTAL BILATERAL	47.6	44.5	51.8	45.8
of which:				
Arab Countries	–	–	–	–
C.E.E.C.	–	–	–	–
TOTAL MULTILATERAL	108.5	158.1	163.0	66.0
TOTAL BIL.& MULTIL.	156.1	202.6	214.7	111.8
of which:				
ODA Grants	50.3	51.9	43.2	48.8
ODA Loans	–	2.0	1.6	–
DISBURSEMENTS:				
DAC COUNTRIES COMBINED				
OFFICIAL & PRIVATE				
GROSS:				
Contractual Lending	62.1	47.4	140.8	22.7
Export Credits, Total	62.1	47.4	140.8	22.7
Export Credits, Priv.	62.0	47.4	136.0	-10.7
NET:				
Contractual Lending	-275.2	-244.9	-112.7	-241.4
Export Credits Total	-260.5	-234.3	-100.9	-230.7
PRIVATE SECTOR NET	336.6	411.1	976.6	476.6
Direct Investment	152.6	109.2	233.5	267.1
Portfolio Investment	413.6	452.1	836.0	446.2
Export Credits	-229.6	-150.3	-92.9	-236.7
MARKET BORROWING:				
CHANGE IN CLAIMS				
Banks	-906.0	507.0	1160.0	-92.0
MEMORANDUM ITEM:				
C.E.E.C. (Gross)	–	–	–	–

1. TOTAL RECEIPTS NET

DAC COUNTRIES	1987	1988	1989	1990
Australia	–	–	–	–
Austria	–	–	–	–
Belgium	-0.5	0.1	0.1	0.0
Canada	8.2	6.3	2.9	0.2
Denmark	–	–	–	–
Finland	–	-0.2	-0.1	–
France	0.2	-0.2	0.2	–
Germany	0.4	0.3	0.2	9.1
Ireland	–	–	–	–
Italy	–	–	–	–
Japan	0.1	0.2	0.3	1.8
Netherlands	0.1	0.1	-5.8	-0.2
New Zealand	–	–	–	–
Norway	0.0	0.0	0.0	0.0
Sweden	–	–	–	–
Switzerland	–	–	–	–
United Kingdom	0.7	2.7	-0.2	0.9
United States	3.0	–	–	–
TOTAL	*12.2*	*9.4*	*-2.5*	*11.9*
MULTILATERAL				
AF.D.F.	–	–	–	–
AF.D.B.	–	–	–	–
AS.D.B	–	–	–	–
CAR.D.B.	7.7	5.7	4.8	4.8
E.E.C.	1.2	6.3	2.7	2.7
IBRD	–	–	–	–
IDA	0.7	1.0	1.0	1.0
I.D.B.	–	–	–	–
IFAD	0.3	0.0	–	0.2
I.F.C.	0.5	–	–	–
IMF TRUST FUND	–	–	–	–
U.N. AGENCIES	–	–	–	–
UNDP	0.3	0.3	0.3	0.2
UNTA	0.2	0.2	0.1	0.1
UNICEF	–	–	–	–
UNRWA	–	–	–	–
WFP	–	0.1	1.4	–
UNHCR	–	–	–	–
Other Multilateral	0.1	0.1	0.1	0.1
Arab Agencies	-1.2	-0.9	–	–
TOTAL	*9.8*	*12.7*	*10.5*	*9.1*
ARAB COUNTRIES	–	–	–	–
E.E.C.+ MEMBERS	*2.2*	*9.3*	*-2.8*	*12.6*
TOTAL	*22.0*	*22.1*	*8.0*	*21.0*

2. ODA LOANS GROSS

DAC COUNTRIES	1987	1988	1989	1990
Australia	–	–	–	–
Austria	–	–	–	–
Belgium	–	–	–	–
Canada	–	–	–	–
Denmark	–	–	–	–
Finland	–	–	–	–
France	–	–	–	–
Germany	–	–	–	–
Ireland	–	–	–	–
Italy	–	–	–	–
Japan	–	–	–	–
Netherlands	–	–	–	–
New Zealand	–	–	–	–
Norway	–	–	–	–
Sweden	–	–	–	–
Switzerland	–	–	–	–
United Kingdom	0.4	1.1	1.2	0.7
United States	–	–	–	–
TOTAL	*0.4*	*1.1*	*1.2*	*0.7*
MULTILATERAL	*8.7*	*8.1*	*6.0*	*6.1*
ARAB COUNTRIES	–	–	–	–
E.E.C.+ MEMBERS	*0.4*	*2.7*	*1.6*	*1.1*
TOTAL	*9.1*	*9.2*	*7.2*	*6.8*

3. TOTAL OFFICIAL GROSS

DAC COUNTRIES	1987	1988	1989	1990
Australia	–	–	–	–
Austria	0.0	–	0.0	–
Belgium	0.0	0.0	0.0	–
Canada	8.2	6.6	3.2	1.3
Denmark	–	–	–	–
Finland	–	–	–	–
France	0.2	–	–	–
Germany	0.4	0.3	0.2	0.3
Ireland	–	–	–	–
Italy	–	–	–	–
Japan	0.1	0.2	0.3	1.8
Netherlands	0.1	0.1	0.1	0.2
New Zealand	–	–	–	–
Norway	0.0	0.0	0.0	0.0
Sweden	–	–	–	–
Switzerland	–	–	–	–
United Kingdom	1.2	2.2	2.2	2.0
United States	5.0	–	–	–
TOTAL	*15.2*	*9.5*	*6.0*	*5.6*
MULTILATERAL	*11.2*	*13.8*	*10.6*	*9.5*
ARAB COUNTRIES	–	–	–	–
E.E.C.+ MEMBERS	*3.2*	*9.1*	*5.4*	*5.4*
TOTAL	*26.4*	*23.2*	*16.6*	*15.1*

4. TOTAL ODA NET

DAC COUNTRIES	1987	1988	1989	1990
Australia	–	–	–	–
Austria	–	–	–	–
Belgium	0.0	0.0	0.0	–
Canada	5.2	4.9	2.1	1.3
Denmark	–	–	–	–
Finland	–	–	–	–
France	0.2	–	–	–
Germany	0.4	0.3	0.2	0.3
Ireland	–	–	–	–
Italy	–	–	–	–
Japan	0.1	0.2	0.3	1.8
Netherlands	0.1	0.1	0.1	0.2
New Zealand	–	–	–	–
Norway	0.0	0.0	0.0	0.0
Sweden	–	–	–	–
Switzerland	–	–	–	–
United Kingdom	1.0	2.1	2.2	1.4
United States	3.0	–	–	–
TOTAL	*10.1*	*7.6*	*4.8*	*5.0*
MULTILATERAL				
AF.D.F.	–	–	–	–
AF.D.B.	–	–	–	–
AS.D.B	–	–	–	–
CAR.D.B.	7.6	5.5	4.6	4.6
E.E.C.	1.2	6.3	2.7	2.7
IBRD	–	–	–	–
IDA	0.7	1.0	1.0	1.0
I.D.B.	–	–	–	–
IFAD	0.3	0.0	–	0.2
I.F.C.	–	–	–	–
IMF TRUST FUND	–	–	–	–
U.N. AGENCIES	–	–	–	–
UNDP	0.3	0.3	0.3	0.2
UNTA	0.2	0.2	0.1	0.1
UNICEF	–	–	–	–
UNRWA	–	–	–	–
WFP	–	0.1	1.4	–
UNHCR	–	–	–	–
Other Multilateral	0.1	0.1	0.1	0.1
Arab Agencies	-0.8	-0.5	–	–
TOTAL	*9.6*	*12.9*	*10.2*	*8.8*
ARAB COUNTRIES	–	–	–	–
E.E.C.+ MEMBERS	*3.0*	*8.8*	*5.2*	*4.7*
TOTAL	*19.7*	*20.5*	*15.1*	*13.9*

5. ODA LOANS NET

DAC COUNTRIES	1987	1988	1989	1990
Australia	–	–	–	–
Austria	–	–	–	–
Belgium	0.0	0.0	0.0	–
Canada	0.0	0.0	0.0	–
Denmark	–	–	–	–
Finland	–	–	–	–
France	–	–	–	–
Germany	–	–	–	–
Ireland	–	–	–	–
Italy	–	–	–	–
Japan	–	–	–	–
Netherlands	–	–	–	–
New Zealand	–	–	–	–
Norway	–	–	–	–
Sweden	–	–	–	–
Switzerland	–	–	–	–
United Kingdom	0.2	1.0	1.2	0.1
United States	-2.0	–	–	–
TOTAL	*-1.8*	*1.0*	*1.1*	*0.1*
MULTILATERAL	*7.8*	*7.4*	*5.8*	*6.0*
ARAB COUNTRIES	–	–	–	–
E.E.C.+ MEMBERS	*0.2*	*2.5*	*1.4*	*0.4*
TOTAL	*6.0*	*8.4*	*7.0*	*6.1*

6. TOTAL OFFICIAL NET

DAC COUNTRIES	1987	1988	1989	1990
Australia	–	–	–	–
Austria	–	–	–	–
Belgium	0.0	0.0	0.0	–
Canada	8.2	6.3	2.9	0.2
Denmark	–	–	–	–
Finland	–	–	–	–
France	0.2	–	–	–
Germany	0.4	0.3	0.2	0.3
Ireland	–	–	–	–
Italy	–	–	–	–
Japan	0.1	0.2	0.3	1.8
Netherlands	0.1	0.1	0.1	0.2
New Zealand	–	–	–	–
Norway	0.0	0.0	0.0	0.0
Sweden	–	–	–	–
Switzerland	–	–	–	–
United Kingdom	1.0	2.0	2.1	1.3
United States	3.0	–	–	–
TOTAL	*13.0*	*9.0*	*5.6*	*3.9*
MULTILATERAL	*9.8*	*12.7*	*10.5*	*9.1*
ARAB COUNTRIES	–	–	–	–
E.E.C.+ MEMBERS	*3.0*	*8.8*	*5.1*	*4.6*
TOTAL	*22.8*	*21.7*	*16.1*	*13.0*

7. TOTAL ODA GROSS

	1987
Australia	–
Austria	–
Belgium	0.0
Canada	5.2
Denmark	–
Finland	–
France	0.2
Germany	0.4
Ireland	–
Italy	–
Japan	0.1
Netherlands	0.1
New Zealand	–
Norway	0.0
Sweden	–
Switzerland	–
United Kingdom	1.2
United States	5.0
TOTAL	*12.2*
AF.D.F.	–
AF.D.B.	–
AS.D.B	–
CAR.D.B.	7.6
E.E.C.	1.2
IBRD	–
IDA	0.7
I.D.B.	–
IFAD	0.5
I.F.C.	–
IMF TRUST FUND	–
U.N. AGENCIES	–
UNDP	0.3
UNTA	0.2
UNICEF	–
UNRWA	–
WFP	–
UNHCR	–
Other Multilateral	0.1
Arab Agencies	–
TOTAL	*10.6*
ARAB COUNTRIES	–
E.E.C.+ MEMBERS	*3.2*
TOTAL	*22.8*

8. GRANTS

	1987
Australia	–
Austria	–
Belgium	0.0
Canada	5.2
Denmark	–
Finland	–
France	0.2
Germany	0.4
Ireland	–
Italy	–
Japan	0.1
Netherlands	0.1
New Zealand	–
Norway	0.0
Sweden	–
Switzerland	–
United Kingdom	0.8
United States	5.0
TOTAL	*11.8*
MULTILATERAL	*1.8*
ARAB COUNTRIES	–
E.E.C.+ MEMBERS	*2.8*
TOTAL	*13.7*

9. TOTAL OOF GROSS

	1987
Australia	–
Austria	–
Belgium	–
Canada	3.0
Denmark	–
Finland	–
France	–
Germany	–
Ireland	–
Italy	–
Japan	–
Netherlands	–
New Zealand	–
Norway	–
Sweden	–
Switzerland	–
United Kingdom	–
United States	–
TOTAL	*3.0*
MULTILATERAL	*0.6*
ARAB COUNTRIES	–
E.E.C.+ MEMBERS	–
TOTAL	*3.6*

1988	1989	1990
–	–	–
0.0	0.0	–
4.9	2.1	1.3
–	–	–
–	–	–
0.3	0.2	0.3
–	–	–
–	–	–
0.2	0.3	1.8
0.1	0.1	0.2
–	–	–
0.0	0.0	0.0
–	–	–
–	–	–
2.2	2.2	2.0
–	–	–
7.8	*4.9*	*5.6*

10. ODA COMMITMENTS

1987	1988	1989	1990
–	–	–	–
–	–	–	–
0.0	0.0	0.0	–
1.3	4.6	0.3	0.6
–	–	–	–
–	–	–	–
0.7	0.1	0.2	0.3
–	–	–	–
–	–	–	–
0.1	0.2	1.7	3.4
0.1	0.1	0.1	0.2
–	–	–	–
0.1	–	–	–
–	–	–	–
–	–	–	–
1.7	1.0	1.0	1.9
–	–	–	–
3.9	*6.0*	*3.3*	*6.4*

1988	1989	1990
–	–	–
–	–	–
5.5	4.6	4.6
6.4	2.9	2.9
–	–	–
1.0	1.0	1.0
–	–	0.2
–	–	–
–	–	–
–	–	–
0.3	0.3	0.2
0.2	0.1	0.1
–	–	–
0.1	1.4	–
–	–	–
0.1	0.1	0.1
–	–	–
13.6	*10.4*	*9.0*
–	–	–
9.1	*5.4*	*5.4*
21.4	*15.3*	*14.6*

1987	1988	1989	1990
–	–	–	–
–	–	–	–
6.9	4.9	2.6	2.6
4.9	1.7	2.1	2.1
–	–	–	–
–	–	–	–
–	–	–	–
–	–	–	–
0.6	0.7	1.9	0.4
–	–	–	–
–	–	–	–
–	–	–	–
–	–	–	–
–	–	–	–
–	–	–	–
–	–	–	–
0.5	–	–	0.1
13.0	*7.3*	*6.7*	*5.2*
–	–	–	–
7.4	*2.9*	*3.4*	*4.5*
16.9	*13.4*	*10.0*	*11.6*

11. TECH. COOP. GRANTS

1988	1989	1990
–	–	–
–	–	–
0.0	0.0	–
4.9	2.1	1.3
–	–	–
–	–	–
0.3	0.2	0.3
–	–	–
0.2	0.3	1.8
0.1	0.1	0.2
–	–	–
0.0	0.0	0.0
–	–	–
–	–	–
1.1	1.0	1.3
–	–	–
6.7	*3.7*	*4.9*
5.5	*4.4*	*2.9*
–	–	–
6.4	*3.8*	*4.3*
12.2	*8.1*	*7.8*

1987	1988	1989	1990
–	–	–	–
–	–	–	–
0.0	–	–	–
–	0.9	0.6	0.7
–	–	–	–
0.0	–	–	–
0.4	0.3	0.2	0.2
–	–	–	–
0.1	0.2	0.2	0.2
0.1	0.1	0.1	0.2
–	–	–	–
0.0	–	–	0.0
–	–	–	–
–	–	–	–
0.8	1.0	1.0	1.1
4.0	–	–	–
5.3	*2.5*	*2.0*	*2.5*
0.6	*0.7*	*0.5*	*0.4*
–	–	–	–
1.3	*1.6*	*1.2*	*1.5*
5.9	*3.2*	*2.5*	*2.9*

12. TOTAL OOF NET

1988	1989	1990
–	–	–
–	–	–
1.7	1.1	–
–	–	–
–	–	–
–	–	–
–	–	–
–	–	–
–	–	–
–	–	–
–	–	–
–	–	–
–	–	–
1.7	*1.1*	–
0.2	*0.3*	*0.5*
–	–	–
–	–	–
1.9	*1.3*	*0.5*

1987	1988	1989	1990
–	–	–	–
–	–	–	–
3.0	1.5	0.8	-1.0
–	–	–	–
–	–	–	–
–	–	–	–
–	–	–	–
–	–	–	–
–	–	–	–
–	–	–	–
0.0	0.0	0.0	0.0
–	–	–	–
2.9	*1.4*	*0.8*	*-1.1*
0.2	*-0.2*	*0.3*	*0.3*
–	–	–	–
0.0	0.0	0.0	0.0
3.1	*1.2*	*1.0*	*-0.8*

	1987	1988	1989	1990
13. ODF COMMITMENTS: BY PURPOSE %				
Education	11	–	–	–
Health	–	–	6	–
Other Social Infrastr.	–	–	–	–
Water Sanitat. Sewage	6	9	4	–
Energy	–	–	–	–
Telecommunications	–	–	–	–
Transportation	36	–	–	–
Agriculture	–	59	41	–
Extractive Industries	–	–	–	–
Manufacturing	–	–	–	–
Trade Banking Tourism	–	–	–	–
Technical Cooperation	47	32	49	–
Multisector Aid	1	–	–	–
Programme	–	–	–	–
Debt Reorganisation	–	–	–	–
Food Aid	–	–	–	–
Emergency Aid	–	–	–	–
Unspecified	–	–	–	–
TOTAL	100	100	100	–

	1987	1988	1989	1990
14. GRANT ELEMENT OF ODA %				
DAC COUNTRIES				
Australia	–	–	–	–
Austria	–	–	–	–
Belgium	100.0	100.0	100.0	–
Canada	100.0	100.0	100.0	–
Denmark	–	–	–	–
Finland	–	–	–	–
France	–	–	–	–
Germany	100.0	100.0	100.0	–
Ireland	–	–	–	–
Italy	–	–	–	–
Japan	100.0	100.0	100.0	–
Netherlands	100.0	100.0	100.0	–
New Zealand	–	–	–	–
Norway	100.0	–	–	–
Sweden	–	–	–	–
Switzerland	–	–	–	–
United Kingdom	100.0	100.0	100.0	–
United States	–	–	–	–
TOTAL	*100.0*	*100.0*	*100.0*	–
MULTILATERAL	*91.4*	*100.0*	*100.0*	–
ARAB COUNTRIES	–	–	–	–
E.E.C.+ MEMBERS	*100.0*	*100.0*	*100.0*	–
TOTAL	*95.7*	*100.0*	*100.0*	–

15. OTHER AGGREGATES

	1987	1988	1989	1990
OFFICIAL COMMITMENTS:				
TOTAL BILATERAL	3.9	6.0	3.3	8.2
of which:				
Arab Countries	–	–	–	–
C.E.E.C.	–	–	–	–
TOTAL MULTILATERAL	13.0	8.1	6.7	5.2
TOTAL BIL.& MULTIL.	16.9	14.1	10.0	13.4
of which:				
ODA Grants	7.3	9.0	6.2	7.9
ODA Loans	9.5	4.4	3.7	3.7
DISBURSEMENTS:				
DAC COUNTRIES COMBINED				
OFFICIAL & PRIVATE				
GROSS:				
Contractual Lending	3.8	6.2	3.1	1.6
Export Credits, Total	3.4	5.1	1.9	0.9
Export Credits, Priv.	0.5	3.4	0.8	0.9
NET:				
Contractual Lending	0.8	2.9	-0.6	-1.4
Export Credits Total	2.6	2.0	-1.6	-1.5
PRIVATE SECTOR NET	-0.8	0.4	-8.1	8.0
Direct Investment	-0.4	–	0.2	–
Portfolio Investment	0.0	-0.1	-5.8	8.4
Export Credits	-0.3	0.5	-2.5	-0.4
MARKET BORROWING:				
CHANGE IN CLAIMS				
Banks	–	–	7.0	-3.0
MEMORANDUM ITEM:				
C.E.E.C. (Gross)	–	–	–	–

1. TOTAL RECEIPTS NET

DAC COUNTRIES	1987	1988	1989	1990
Australia	–	0.0	0.0	–
Austria	1.9	2.0	2.0	3.5
Belgium	0.4	0.8	1.1	19.2
Canada	1.1	0.4	1.0	0.8
Denmark	–	–	–	0.1
Finland	0.0	0.0	–	0.0
France	19.1	22.1	-24.6	-4.2
Germany	-9.3	16.0	13.9	20.7
Ireland	–	–	–	–
Italy	8.2	16.9	23.7	5.7
Japan	3.0	6.9	2.7	1.8
Netherlands	4.3	6.4	5.5	11.0
New Zealand	–	–	–	–
Norway	1.0	1.2	1.9	2.6
Sweden	0.2	–	0.1	0.2
Switzerland	0.3	0.6	0.8	1.1
United Kingdom	-1.0	-0.5	-9.0	0.3
United States	133.0	138.0	136.0	82.0
TOTAL	162.0	210.8	154.9	144.7
MULTILATERAL				
AF.D.F.	–	–	–	–
AF.D.B.	–	–	–	–
AS.D.B	–	–	–	–
CAR.D.B.	–	–	–	–
E.E.C.	5.8	3.9	7.2	7.2
IBRD	-10.6	-22.0	-13.0	11.0
IDA	–	–	–	–
I.D.B.	-15.4	52.5	37.1	18.4
IFAD	0.6	0.5	0.3	0.2
I.F.C.	–	–	–	–
IMF TRUST FUND	–	–	–	–
U.N. AGENCIES	–	–	–	–
UNDP	2.8	3.1	4.5	3.4
UNTA	0.7	0.6	0.8	0.5
UNICEF	1.2	0.6	1.5	2.7
UNRWA	–	–	–	–
WFP	13.0	7.7	10.3	18.1
UNHCR	–	1.0	1.2	0.9
Other Multilateral	0.6	0.7	1.0	1.1
Arab Agencies	-0.1	-0.1	0.5	–
TOTAL	-1.4	48.4	51.3	63.5
ARAB COUNTRIES	–	–	–	–
E.E.C.+ MEMBERS	27.4	65.7	17.8	60.1
TOTAL	160.6	259.2	206.3	208.2

2. ODA LOANS GROSS

DAC COUNTRIES	1987	1988	1989	1990
Australia	–	–	–	–
Austria	–	–	–	–
Belgium	–	–	–	–
Canada	–	–	–	–
Denmark	–	–	–	–
Finland	–	–	–	–
France	4.4	1.8	0.3	0.0
Germany	14.5	7.9	0.3	1.1
Ireland	–	–	–	–
Italy	3.5	11.6	16.6	5.2
Japan	–	–	–	–
Netherlands	–	–	–	–
New Zealand	–	–	–	–
Norway	–	–	–	–
Sweden	–	–	–	–
Switzerland	–	–	–	–
United Kingdom	–	–	–	–
United States	28.0	20.0	30.0	26.0
TOTAL	50.4	41.3	47.2	32.3
MULTILATERAL	10.4	32.3	34.2	23.1
ARAB COUNTRIES	–	–	–	–
E.E.C.+ MEMBERS	22.4	21.3	17.2	6.3
TOTAL	60.8	73.6	81.4	55.4

3. TOTAL OFFICIAL GROSS

DAC COUNTRIES	1987	1988	1989	1990
Australia	–	0.0	0.0	–
Austria	1.9	2.0	2.0	3.5
Belgium	0.3	0.7	1.7	1.3
Canada	1.1	1.4	1.0	0.8
Denmark	–	–	–	0.1
Finland	0.0	0.0	–	0.0
France	12.1	3.1	1.9	2.0
Germany	33.3	22.9	20.1	24.6
Ireland	–	–	–	–
Italy	7.2	16.9	28.9	15.2
Japan	2.5	4.4	3.9	5.3
Netherlands	2.6	6.7	7.3	11.1
New Zealand	–	–	–	–
Norway	1.2	1.3	1.9	2.6
Sweden	0.2	–	0.1	0.2
Switzerland	0.3	0.6	0.8	1.1
United Kingdom	–	0.0	0.0	0.2
United States	156.0	137.0	150.0	93.0
TOTAL	218.7	197.0	219.5	160.9
MULTILATERAL	50.3	112.3	112.1	87.9
ARAB COUNTRIES	–	–	–	–
E.E.C.+ MEMBERS	61.4	54.3	67.1	61.7
TOTAL	269.0	309.3	331.6	248.8

4. TOTAL ODA NET

DAC COUNTRIES	1987	1988	1989	1990
Australia	–	0.0	0.0	–
Austria	1.9	2.0	2.0	3.5
Belgium	0.3	0.7	1.7	1.3
Canada	1.1	1.3	1.0	0.8
Denmark	–	–	–	0.1
Finland	0.0	0.0	–	0.0
France	12.1	3.1	1.9	2.0
Germany	29.8	22.0	14.2	18.0
Ireland	–	–	–	–
Italy	7.2	16.9	28.8	15.2
Japan	2.5	4.4	3.9	5.3
Netherlands	2.6	6.7	7.3	11.1
New Zealand	–	–	–	–
Norway	1.2	1.3	1.9	2.6
Sweden	0.2	–	0.1	0.2
Switzerland	0.3	0.6	0.8	1.1
United Kingdom	–	0.0	0.0	0.2
United States	155.0	134.0	146.0	88.0
TOTAL	214.2	193.0	209.6	149.2
AF.D.F.	–	–	–	–
AF.D.B.	–	–	–	–
AS.D.B	–	–	–	–
CAR.D.B.	–	–	–	–
E.E.C.	5.8	3.9	7.2	7.2
IBRD	–	–	–	–
IDA	–	–	–	–
I.D.B.	2.1	24.0	23.8	15.5
IFAD	0.6	0.5	0.3	0.2
I.F.C.	–	–	–	–
IMF TRUST FUND	–	–	–	–
U.N. AGENCIES	–	–	–	–
UNDP	2.8	3.1	4.5	3.4
UNTA	0.7	0.6	0.8	0.5
UNICEF	1.2	0.6	1.5	2.7
UNRWA	–	–	–	–
WFP	13.0	7.7	10.3	18.1
UNHCR	–	1.0	1.2	0.9
Other Multilateral	0.6	0.7	1.0	1.1
Arab Agencies	-0.1	-0.1	0.5	–
TOTAL	26.6	42.0	51.0	49.6
ARAB COUNTRIES	–	–	–	–
E.E.C.+ MEMBERS	57.8	53.5	61.2	55.1
TOTAL	240.8	235.0	260.6	198.8

5. ODA LOANS NET

DAC COUNTRIES	1987	1988	1989	1990
Australia	–	–	–	–
Austria	–	–	–	–
Belgium	–	–	–	–
Canada	0.0	-0.1	–	0.0
Denmark	–	–	–	–
Finland	–	–	–	–
France	4.4	1.8	0.3	0.0
Germany	14.5	7.7	0.1	1.0
Ireland	–	–	–	–
Italy	3.5	11.6	16.6	5.1
Japan	–	–	–	–
Netherlands	–	–	–	–
New Zealand	–	–	–	–
Norway	–	–	–	–
Sweden	–	–	–	–
Switzerland	–	–	–	–
United Kingdom	–	–	–	–
United States	27.0	17.0	27.0	22.0
TOTAL	49.4	38.0	44.0	28.1
MULTILATERAL	2.3	23.5	23.5	16.7
ARAB COUNTRIES	–	–	–	–
E.E.C.+ MEMBERS	22.4	21.1	17.0	6.1
TOTAL	51.7	61.4	67.5	44.7

6. TOTAL OFFICIAL NET

DAC COUNTRIES	1987	1988	1989	1990
Australia	–	0.0	0.0	–
Austria	1.9	2.0	2.0	3.5
Belgium	0.3	0.7	1.7	1.3
Canada	1.1	0.4	1.0	0.8
Denmark	–	–	–	0.1
Finland	0.0	0.0	–	0.0
France	12.1	3.1	1.9	2.0
Germany	9.1	14.0	11.0	24.2
Ireland	–	–	–	–
Italy	7.2	16.9	28.8	15.2
Japan	2.5	4.4	3.9	5.3
Netherlands	2.6	6.7	7.3	11.1
New Zealand	–	–	–	–
Norway	1.2	1.3	1.9	2.6
Sweden	0.2	–	0.1	0.2
Switzerland	0.3	0.6	0.8	1.1
United Kingdom	–	0.0	0.0	0.2
United States	152.0	133.0	147.0	88.0
TOTAL	190.4	183.2	207.3	155.4
MULTILATERAL	-1.4	48.4	51.3	63.5
ARAB COUNTRIES	–	–	–	–
E.E.C.+ MEMBERS	37.1	45.5	57.9	61.3
TOTAL	189.0	231.6	258.7	218.9

7. TOTAL ODA GROSS

DAC COUNTRIES	1987
Australia	–
Austria	1.9
Belgium	0.3
Canada	1.1
Denmark	–
Finland	0.0
France	12.1
Germany	29.8
Ireland	–
Italy	7.2
Japan	2.5
Netherlands	2.6
New Zealand	–
Norway	1.2
Sweden	0.2
Switzerland	0.3
United Kingdom	–
United States	156.0
TOTAL	215.2
AF.D.F.	–
AF.D.B.	–
AS.D.B	–
CAR.D.B.	–
E.E.C.	5.8
IBRD	–
IDA	–
I.D.B.	10.2
IFAD	0.6
I.F.C.	–
IMF TRUST FUND	–
U.N. AGENCIES	–
UNDP	2.8
UNTA	0.7
UNICEF	1.2
UNRWA	–
WFP	13.0
UNHCR	–
Other Multilateral	0.6
Arab Agencies	–
TOTAL	34.8
ARAB COUNTRIES	–
E.E.C.+ MEMBERS	57.8
TOTAL	249.9

8. GRANTS

DAC COUNTRIES	1987
Australia	–
Austria	1.9
Belgium	0.3
Canada	1.1
Denmark	–
Finland	0.0
France	7.7
Germany	15.3
Ireland	–
Italy	3.7
Japan	2.5
Netherlands	2.6
New Zealand	–
Norway	1.2
Sweden	0.2
Switzerland	0.3
United Kingdom	–
United States	128.0
TOTAL	164.8
MULTILATERAL	24.4
ARAB COUNTRIES	–
E.E.C.+ MEMBERS	35.4
TOTAL	189.2

9. TOTAL OOF GROSS

DAC COUNTRIES	1987
Australia	–
Austria	–
Belgium	–
Canada	–
Denmark	–
Finland	–
France	–
Germany	3.5
Ireland	–
Italy	–
Japan	–
Netherlands	–
New Zealand	–
Norway	–
Sweden	–
Switzerland	–
United Kingdom	–
United States	–
TOTAL	3.5
MULTILATERAL	15.5
ARAB COUNTRIES	–
E.E.C.+ MEMBERS	3.5
TOTAL	19.0

10. ODA COMMITMENTS

1988	1989	1990	1987	1988	1989	1990
0.0	0.0	–	0.0	0.0	0.0	0.0
2.0	2.0	3.5	1.9	2.0	2.0	4.6
0.7	1.7	1.3	1.9	0.5	1.7	1.3
1.4	1.0	0.8	1.5	1.7	0.3	9.3
–	–	0.1	–	–	–	0.4
0.0	–	0.0	–	–	–	0.0
3.1	1.9	2.0	1.6	1.3	15.7	2.0
22.2	14.4	18.2	29.3	38.4	22.2	25.3
–	–	–	–	–	–	–
16.9	28.9	15.2	1.0	6.5	14.1	19.4
4.4	3.9	5.3	3.1	4.4	4.2	52.8
6.7	7.3	11.1	2.4	6.8	18.0	21.1
–	–	–	–	–	–	–
1.3	1.9	2.6	1.0	–	–	–
–	0.1	0.2	0.2	–	0.1	–
0.6	0.8	1.1	0.0	0.1	8.7	0.6
0.0	0.0	0.2	–	0.0	0.0	0.2
137.0	149.0	92.0	184.8	160.7	121.9	117.3
196.3	*212.8*	*153.4*	*228.6*	*222.5*	*209.0*	*254.1*
–	–	–	–	–	–	–
–	–	–	–	–	–	–
–	–	–	–	–	–	–
3.9	7.2	7.2	1.0	13.3	3.9	3.9
–	–	–	–	–	–	–
32.8	34.4	21.5	43.8	10.6	–	32.8
0.5	0.3	0.5	–	–	7.0	–
–	–	–	–	–	–	–
–	–	–	18.2	13.7	19.2	26.7
3.1	4.5	3.4	–	–	–	–
0.6	0.8	0.5	–	–	–	–
0.6	1.5	2.7	–	–	–	–
–	–	–	–	–	–	–
7.7	10.3	18.1	–	–	–	–
1.0	1.2	0.9	–	–	–	–
0.7	1.0	1.1	–	–	–	–
–	0.5	1.1	–	–	4.0	–
50.9	*61.7*	*57.0*	*63.0*	*37.6*	*34.1*	*63.4*
–	–	–	–	–	–	–
53.6	*61.4*	*55.3*	*37.2*	*67.0*	*75.6*	*73.4*
247.1	*274.5*	*210.4*	*291.6*	*260.1*	*243.1*	*317.4*

11. TECH. COOP. GRANTS

1988	1989	1990	1987	1988	1989	1990
0.0	0.0	–	–	–	–	–
2.0	2.0	3.5	1.9	2.0	1.9	2.8
0.7	1.7	1.3	0.1	0.0	–	0.0
1.4	1.0	0.8	–	–	0.0	0.1
–	–	0.1	–	–	–	–
0.0	–	0.0	0.0	–	–	–
1.3	1.6	2.0	1.4	1.3	1.6	2.0
14.3	14.1	17.0	9.3	7.5	8.6	11.4
–	–	–	–	–	–	–
5.4	12.2	10.1	1.0	0.8	0.4	8.9
4.4	3.9	5.3	2.2	4.0	3.6	4.9
6.7	7.3	11.1	2.2	5.9	5.7	8.3
–	–	–	–	–	–	–
1.3	1.9	2.6	0.0	–	0.0	0.3
–	0.1	0.2	–	–	–	0.0
0.6	0.8	1.1	0.1	0.0	–	–
0.0	0.0	0.2	–	0.0	0.0	0.2
117.0	119.0	66.0	19.0	26.0	37.0	42.0
155.0	*165.6*	*121.1*	*37.1*	*47.6*	*58.9*	*80.9*
18.6	*27.5*	*33.9*	*5.6*	*7.4*	*9.0*	*8.6*
–	–	–	–	–	–	–
32.4	*44.2*	*49.0*	*14.4*	*17.0*	*16.3*	*30.8*
173.6	*193.1*	*155.0*	*42.7*	*54.9*	*67.9*	*89.5*

12. TOTAL OOF NET

1988	1989	1990	1987	1988	1989	1990
–	–	–	–	–	–	–
–	–	–	–	–	–	–
–	–	–	–	-0.8	–	–
–	–	–	–	–	–	–
–	–	–	–	–	–	–
0.7	5.7	6.4	-20.7	-8.0	-3.2	6.2
–	–	–	–	–	–	–
–	–	–	–	–	–	–
–	–	–	–	–	–	–
–	–	–	–	–	–	–
–	–	–	–	–	–	–
–	–	–	–	–	–	–
–	1.0	1.0	-3.0	-1.0	1.0	–
0.7	*6.7*	*7.4*	*-23.7*	*-9.8*	*-2.2*	*6.2*
61.4	*50.4*	*30.9*	*-28.1*	*6.4*	*0.3*	*13.9*
–	–	–	–	–	–	–
0.7	*5.7*	*6.4*	*-20.7*	*-8.0*	*-3.2*	*6.2*
62.1	*57.1*	*38.3*	*-51.8*	*-3.4*	*-2.0*	*20.1*

13. ODF COMMITMENTS: BY PURPOSE %

	1987	1988	1989	1990
Education	6	1	5	–
Health	3	2	3	–
Other Social Infrastr.	14	3	15	–
Water Sanitat. Sewage	–	8	0	–
Energy	–	21	4	–
Telecommunications	0	–	–	–
Transportation	10	5	4	–
Agriculture	2	13	10	–
Extractive Industries	–	–	–	–
Manufacturing	0	–	–	–
Trade Banking Tourism	–	–	–	–
Technical Cooperation	23	17	30	–
Multisector Aid	0	0	0	–
Programme	29	20	24	–
Debt Reorganisation	–	1	–	–
Food Aid	11	10	3	–
Emergency Aid	0	1	0	–
Unspecified	0	–	–	–
TOTAL	100	100	100	–

14. GRANT ELEMENT OF ODA %

DAC COUNTRIES

	1987	1988	1989	1990
Australia	100.0	100.0	100.0	–
Austria	100.0	100.0	100.0	–
Belgium	100.0	100.0	100.0	–
Canada	100.0	100.0	100.0	–
Denmark	–	–	–	–
Finland	–	–	–	–
France	100.0	100.0	70.8	–
Germany	93.6	93.5	100.0	–
Ireland	–	–	–	–
Italy	100.0	100.0	100.0	–
Japan	100.0	100.0	100.0	–
Netherlands	100.0	100.0	100.0	–
New Zealand	–	–	–	–
Norway	100.0	–	–	–
Sweden	100.0	–	100.0	–
Switzerland	100.0	100.0	100.0	–
United Kingdom	–	100.0	100.0	–
United States	92.3	89.3	99.9	–
TOTAL	*93.0*	*91.2*	*97.7*	*–*
MULTILATERAL	*82.0*	*100.0*	*82.5*	*–*
ARAB COUNTRIES	*–*	*–*	*–*	*–*
E.E.C.+ MEMBERS	*95.0*	*96.3*	*94.0*	*–*
TOTAL	*90.2*	*92.1*	*95.4*	*–*

15. OTHER AGGREGATES

OFFICIAL COMMITMENTS:

	1987	1988	1989	1990
TOTAL BILATERAL	231.6	222.5	210.5	258.1
of which:				
Arab Countries	–	–	–	–
C.E.E.C.	–	–	–	–
TOTAL MULTILATERAL	63.0	128.6	34.1	63.4
TOTAL BIL.& MULTIL.	294.6	351.1	244.6	321.4
of which:				
ODA Grants	208.6	200.3	217.6	205.8
ODA Loans	83.0	59.8	25.5	111.7

DISBURSEMENTS:

DAC COUNTRIES COMBINED

OFFICIAL & PRIVATE

	1987	1988	1989	1990
GROSS:				
Contractual Lending	50.5	63.6	62.0	40.2
Export Credits, Total	-0.3	22.3	13.8	6.8
Export Credits, Priv.	-0.3	22.3	8.1	0.5
NET:				
Contractual Lending	-3.8	36.1	25.8	17.6
Export Credits Total	-37.9	2.5	-14.5	-10.2
PRIVATE SECTOR NET	-28.4	27.6	-52.4	-10.7
Direct Investment	-14.6	0.3	2.6	-4.7
Portfolio Investment	12.5	18.6	-39.1	10.6
Export Credits	-26.3	8.6	-15.9	-16.6

MARKET BORROWING:

CHANGE IN CLAIMS

	1987	1988	1989	1990
Banks	-37.0	44.0	-18.0	-75.0

MEMORANDUM ITEM:

	1987	1988	1989	1990
C.E.E.C. (Gross)	–	–	–	–

1. TOTAL RECEIPTS NET

DAC COUNTRIES	1987	1988	1989	1990
Australia	–	–	–	–
Austria	–	–	–	–
Belgium	0.3	–	0.1	–
Canada	–	–	–	-0.1
Denmark	–	–	–	–
Finland	–	–	–	–
France	165.1	150.0	149.4	174.6
Germany	-0.5	–	–	3.2
Ireland	–	–	–	–
Italy	–	–	0.5	–
Japan	-0.3	-0.1	-0.8	-0.9
Netherlands	0.1	0.8	0.4	–
New Zealand	–	–	–	–
Norway	–	–	–	–
Sweden	–	–	–	–
Switzerland	–	–	0.2	–
United Kingdom	–	–	-4.4	–
United States	–	–	–	–
TOTAL	164.6	150.7	145.3	176.8
MULTILATERAL				
AF.D.F.	–	–	–	–
AF.D.B.	–	–	–	–
AS.D.B	–	–	–	–
CAR.D.B.	–	–	–	–
E.E.C.	8.7	14.8	8.4	8.4
IBRD	–	–	–	–
IDA	–	–	–	–
I.D.B.	–	–	–	–
IFAD	–	–	–	–
I.F.C.	–	–	–	–
IMF TRUST FUND	–	–	–	–
U.N. AGENCIES	–	–	–	–
UNDP	–	–	–	–
UNTA	–	0.0	0.0	0.0
UNICEF	–	–	–	–
UNRWA	–	–	–	–
WFP	–	–	–	–
UNHCR	–	–	0.1	0.3
Other Multilateral	–	–	–	–
Arab Agencies	–	–	–	–
TOTAL	8.7	14.9	8.6	8.7
ARAB COUNTRIES	–	–	–	–
E.E.C.+ MEMBERS	173.6	165.6	154.4	186.2
TOTAL	173.3	165.5	153.9	185.5

2. ODA LOANS GROSS

DAC COUNTRIES	1987	1988	1989	1990
Australia	–	–	–	–
Austria	–	–	–	–
Belgium	–	–	–	–
Canada	–	–	–	–
Denmark	–	–	–	–
Finland	–	–	–	–
France	–	–	–	–
Germany	–	–	–	–
Ireland	–	–	–	–
Italy	–	–	–	–
Japan	–	–	–	–
Netherlands	–	–	–	–
New Zealand	–	–	–	–
Norway	–	–	–	–
Sweden	–	–	–	–
Switzerland	–	–	–	–
United Kingdom	–	–	–	–
United States	–	–	–	–
TOTAL	–	–	–	–
MULTILATERAL	–	–	–	–
ARAB COUNTRIES	–	–	–	–
E.E.C.+ MEMBERS	–	–	–	–
TOTAL	–	–	–	–

3. TOTAL OFFICIAL GROSS

DAC COUNTRIES	1987	1988	1989	1990
Australia	–	–	–	–
Austria	–	–	–	–
Belgium	–	–	–	–
Canada	–	–	–	–
Denmark	–	–	–	–
Finland	–	–	–	–
France	171.3	157.6	157.5	226.5
Germany	–	–	–	–
Ireland	–	–	–	–
Italy	–	–	–	–
Japan	–	–	–	–
Netherlands	–	–	–	–
New Zealand	–	–	–	–
Norway	–	–	–	–
Sweden	–	–	–	–
Switzerland	–	–	0.2	–
United Kingdom	–	–	–	–
United States	–	–	–	–
TOTAL	171.3	157.6	157.6	226.5
MULTILATERAL	8.7	14.9	8.6	8.8
ARAB COUNTRIES	–	–	–	–
E.E.C.+ MEMBERS	180.0	172.4	165.9	234.9
TOTAL	180.0	172.4	166.2	235.3

4. TOTAL ODA NET

DAC COUNTRIES	1987	1988	1989	1990
Australia	–	–	–	–
Austria	–	–	–	–
Belgium	–	–	–	–
Canada	–	–	–	–
Denmark	–	–	–	–
Finland	–	–	–	–
France	138.3	130.5	110.2	113.2
Germany	–	–	–	–
Ireland	–	–	–	–
Italy	–	–	–	–
Japan	–	0.0	0.0	0.0
Netherlands	–	–	–	–
New Zealand	–	–	–	–
Norway	–	–	–	–
Sweden	–	–	–	–
Switzerland	–	–	0.2	–
United Kingdom	–	–	–	–
United States	–	–	–	–
TOTAL	138.3	130.4	110.3	113.2
MULTILATERAL				
AF.D.F.	–	–	–	–
AF.D.B.	–	–	–	–
AS.D.B	–	–	–	–
CAR.D.B.	–	–	–	–
E.E.C.	8.7	14.8	8.4	8.4
IBRD	–	–	–	–
IDA	–	–	–	–
I.D.B.	–	–	–	–
IFAD	–	–	–	–
I.F.C.	–	–	–	–
IMF TRUST FUND	–	–	–	–
U.N. AGENCIES	–	–	–	–
UNDP	–	–	–	–
UNTA	–	0.0	0.0	0.0
UNICEF	–	–	–	–
UNRWA	–	–	–	–
WFP	–	–	–	–
UNHCR	–	–	0.1	0.3
Other Multilateral	–	–	–	–
Arab Agencies	–	–	–	–
TOTAL	8.7	14.9	8.6	8.7
ARAB COUNTRIES	–	–	–	–
E.E.C.+ MEMBERS	147.0	145.3	118.6	121.6
TOTAL	147.0	145.3	118.9	121.9

5. ODA LOANS NET

DAC COUNTRIES	1987	1988	1989	1990
Australia	–	–	–	–
Austria	–	–	–	–
Belgium	–	–	–	–
Canada	–	–	–	–
Denmark	–	–	–	–
Finland	–	–	–	–
France	-1.2	-0.8	-0.7	-0.8
Germany	–	–	–	–
Ireland	–	–	–	–
Italy	–	–	–	–
Japan	–	0.0	0.0	0.0
Netherlands	–	–	–	–
New Zealand	–	–	–	–
Norway	–	–	–	–
Sweden	–	–	–	–
Switzerland	–	–	–	–
United Kingdom	–	–	–	–
United States	–	–	–	–
TOTAL	-1.2	-0.8	-0.8	-0.8
MULTILATERAL	0.0	0.0	0.0	0.0
ARAB COUNTRIES	–	–	–	–
E.E.C.+ MEMBERS	-1.2	-0.8	-0.8	-0.8
TOTAL	-1.2	-0.8	-0.8	-0.8

6. TOTAL OFFICIAL NET

DAC COUNTRIES	1987	1988	1989	1990
Australia	–	–	–	–
Austria	–	–	–	–
Belgium	–	–	–	–
Canada	–	–	–	–
Denmark	–	–	–	–
Finland	–	–	–	–
France	165.1	150.0	149.4	174.6
Germany	–	–	–	–
Ireland	–	–	–	–
Italy	–	–	–	–
Japan	–	0.0	0.0	0.0
Netherlands	–	–	–	–
New Zealand	–	–	–	–
Norway	–	–	–	–
Sweden	–	–	–	–
Switzerland	–	–	0.2	–
United Kingdom	–	–	–	–
United States	–	–	–	–
TOTAL	165.1	150.0	149.5	174.6
MULTILATERAL	8.7	14.9	8.6	8.7
ARAB COUNTRIES	–	–	–	–
E.E.C.+ MEMBERS	173.8	164.8	157.8	183.0
TOTAL	173.8	164.8	158.0	183.3

7. TOTAL ODA GROSS

DAC COUNTRIES	1987
Australia	–
Austria	–
Belgium	–
Canada	–
Denmark	–
Finland	–
France	139.4
Germany	–
Ireland	–
Italy	–
Japan	–
Netherlands	–
New Zealand	–
Norway	–
Sweden	–
Switzerland	–
United Kingdom	–
United States	–
TOTAL	139.4
AF.D.F.	–
AF.D.B.	–
AS.D.B	–
CAR.D.B.	–
E.E.C.	8.7
IBRD	–
IDA	–
I.D.B.	–
IFAD	–
I.F.C.	–
IMF TRUST FUND	–
U.N. AGENCIES	–
UNDP	–
UNTA	–
UNICEF	–
UNRWA	–
WFP	–
UNHCR	–
Other Multilateral	–
Arab Agencies	–
TOTAL	8.7
ARAB COUNTRIES	–
E.E.C.+ MEMBERS	148.2
TOTAL	148.2

8. GRANTS

	1987
Australia	–
Austria	–
Belgium	–
Canada	–
Denmark	–
Finland	–
France	139.4
Germany	–
Ireland	–
Italy	–
Japan	–
Netherlands	–
New Zealand	–
Norway	–
Sweden	–
Switzerland	–
United Kingdom	–
United States	–
TOTAL	139.4
MULTILATERAL	8.7
ARAB COUNTRIES	–
E.E.C.+ MEMBERS	148.2
TOTAL	148.2

9. TOTAL OOF GROSS

	1987
Australia	–
Austria	–
Belgium	–
Canada	–
Denmark	–
Finland	–
France	31.9
Germany	–
Ireland	–
Italy	–
Japan	–
Netherlands	–
New Zealand	–
Norway	–
Sweden	–
Switzerland	–
United Kingdom	–
United States	–
TOTAL	31.9
MULTILATERAL	–
ARAB COUNTRIES	–
E.E.C.+ MEMBERS	31.9
TOTAL	31.9

10. ODA COMMITMENTS

1988	1989	1990	1987	1988	1989	1990
–	–	–	–	–	–	–
–	–	–	–	–	–	–
–	–	–	–	–	–	–
–	–	–	–	–	–	–
–	–	–	–	–	–	–
131.3	110.9	114.0	158.4	151.6	110.9	114.3
–	–	–	–	–	–	11.1
–	–	–	–	–	–	–
–	–	–	–	–	–	–
–	–	–	–	–	–	–
–	–	–	–	–	–	–
–	–	–	–	–	–	–
–	–	–	–	–	–	–
–	0.2	–	–	–	–	–
–	–	–	–	–	–	–
–	–	–	–	–	–	–
131.3	111.1	114.0	158.4	151.6	110.9	125.4
–	–	–	–	–	–	–
–	–	–	–	–	–	–
–	–	–	–	–	–	–
14.9	8.4	8.4	13.3	16.0	10.5	10.5
–	–	–	–	–	–	–
–	–	–	–	–	–	–
–	–	–	–	–	–	–
–	–	–	–	–	–	–
–	–	–	–	0.0	0.1	0.3
0.0	0.0	0.0	–	–	–	–
–	–	–	–	–	–	–
–	0.1	0.3	–	–	–	–
–	–	–	–	–	–	–
–	–	–	–	–	–	–
14.9	8.6	8.8	13.3	16.0	10.6	10.8
–	–	–	–	–	–	–
146.1	119.4	122.4	171.7	167.6	121.4	135.9
146.1	119.7	122.7	171.7	167.7	121.5	136.2

11. TECH. COOP. GRANTS

1988	1989	1990	1987	1988	1989	1990
–	–	–	–	–	–	–
–	–	–	–	–	–	–
–	–	–	–	–	–	–
–	–	–	–	–	–	–
–	–	–	–	–	–	–
131.3	110.9	114.0	52.9	48.7	18.7	26.9
–	–	–	–	–	–	–
–	–	–	–	–	–	–
–	–	–	–	–	–	–
–	–	–	–	–	–	–
–	–	–	–	–	–	–
–	–	–	–	–	–	–
–	0.2	–	–	–	–	–
–	–	–	–	–	–	–
–	–	–	–	–	–	–
131.3	111.1	114.0	52.9	48.7	18.7	26.9
14.9	8.6	8.8	–	1.6	0.1	0.3
–	–	–	–	–	–	–
146.1	119.4	122.4	52.9	50.3	18.7	26.9
146.1	119.7	122.7	52.9	50.4	18.8	27.2

12. TOTAL OOF NET

1988	1989	1990	1987	1988	1989	1990
–	–	–	–	–	–	–
–	–	–	–	–	–	–
–	–	–	–	–	–	–
–	–	–	–	–	–	–
26.3	46.6	112.5	26.8	19.5	39.2	61.4
–	–	–	–	–	–	–
–	–	–	–	–	–	–
–	–	–	–	–	–	–
–	–	–	–	–	–	–
–	–	–	–	–	–	–
–	–	–	–	–	–	–
–	–	–	–	–	–	–
–	–	–	–	–	–	–
26.3	46.6	112.5	26.8	19.5	39.2	61.4
–	–	–	–	–	–	–
–	–	–	–	–	–	–
26.3	46.6	112.5	26.8	19.5	39.2	61.4
26.3	46.6	112.5	26.8	19.5	39.2	61.4

13. ODF COMMITMENTS: BY PURPOSE %

	1987	1988	1989	1990
Education	–	–	–	–
Health	–	–	–	–
Other Social Infrastr.	–	–	–	–
Water Sanitat. Sewage	–	–	–	–
Energy	–	–	–	–
Telecommunications	–	–	–	–
Transportation	–	–	–	–
Agriculture	–	–	–	–
Extractive Industries	–	–	–	–
Manufacturing	–	–	–	–
Trade Banking Tourism	–	–	–	–
Technical Cooperation	100	100	100	–
Multisector Aid	–	–	–	–
Programme	–	–	–	–
Debt Reorganisation	–	–	–	–
Food Aid	–	–	–	–
Emergency Aid	–	–	–	–
Unspecified	–	–	–	–
TOTAL	100	100	100	–

14. GRANT ELEMENT OF ODA %

DAC COUNTRIES

	1987	1988	1989	1990
Australia	–	–	–	–
Austria	–	–	–	–
Belgium	–	–	–	–
Canada	–	–	–	–
Denmark	–	–	–	–
Finland	–	–	–	–
France	100.0	100.0	100.0	–
Germany	–	–	–	–
Ireland	–	–	–	–
Italy	–	–	–	–
Japan	–	–	–	–
Netherlands	–	–	–	–
New Zealand	–	–	–	–
Norway	–	–	–	–
Sweden	–	–	–	–
Switzerland	–	–	–	–
United Kingdom	–	–	–	–
United States	–	–	–	–
TOTAL	*100.0*	*100.0*	*100.0*	–
MULTILATERAL	*100.0*	*100.0*	*100.0*	–
ARAB COUNTRIES	–	–	–	–
E.E.C.+ MEMBERS	*100.0*	*100.0*	*100.0*	–
TOTAL	*100.0*	*100.0*	*100.0*	–

15. OTHER AGGREGATES

OFFICIAL COMMITMENTS:

	1987	1988	1989	1990
TOTAL BILATERAL	189.7	181.4	157.9	241.9
of which:				
Arab Countries	–	–	–	–
C.E.E.C.				
TOTAL MULTILATERAL	13.3	16.0	10.6	10.8
TOTAL BIL.& MULTIL.	203.1	197.4	168.5	252.7
of which:				
ODA Grants	171.7	167.7	121.5	125.1
ODA Loans	–	–	–	11.1

DISBURSEMENTS:

DAC COUNTRIES COMBINED

	1987	1988	1989	1990
OFFICIAL & PRIVATE				
GROSS:				
Contractual Lending	31.9	26.3	46.6	112.5
Export Credits, Total	–	–	–	–
Export Credits, Priv.	–	–	–	–
NET:				
Contractual Lending	25.6	18.7	34.0	60.5
Export Credits Total	0.0	–	-4.4	-0.1
PRIVATE SECTOR NET	-0.5	0.7	-4.2	2.2
Direct Investment	-0.4	0.6	0.3	2.4
Portfolio Investment	–	0.1	–	0.0
Export Credits	0.0	–	-4.4	-0.1

MARKET BORROWING:

CHANGE IN CLAIMS

	1987	1988	1989	1990
Banks	6.0	2.0	6.0	-4.0

MEMORANDUM ITEM:

	1987	1988	1989	1990
C.E.E.C. (Gross)	–	–	–	–

1. TOTAL RECEIPTS NET

DAC COUNTRIES	1987	1988	1989	1990
Australia	–	–	0.0	–
Austria	0.0	0.1	0.0	0.1
Belgium	2.7	3.7	3.2	-2.0
Canada	4.8	6.6	7.9	7.4
Denmark	2.9	1.1	2.2	1.0
Finland	0.0	0.1	0.0	0.0
France	51.0	86.8	101.1	88.6
Germany	24.8	11.4	49.2	20.4
Ireland	–	–	–	–
Italy	7.6	31.4	21.5	13.2
Japan	22.5	26.6	7.8	8.9
Netherlands	0.4	0.6	0.6	1.2
New Zealand	–	–	–	–
Norway	1.5	2.5	0.0	-15.7
Sweden	–	0.2	–	0.3
Switzerland	0.4	0.6	0.6	1.0
United Kingdom	0.7	1.2	0.8	0.8
United States	23.0	13.0	4.0	16.0
TOTAL	*142.4*	*185.6*	*199.0*	*141.2*
MULTILATERAL				
AF.D.F.	13.6	9.5	19.4	27.8
AF.D.B.	0.4	-1.1	2.5	2.8
AS.D.B	–	–	–	–
CAR.D.B.	–	–	–	–
E.E.C.	13.3	10.7	29.2	29.2
IBRD	-10.0	-12.0	-11.0	-12.0
IDA	38.2	43.0	63.0	51.0
I.D.B.	–	–	–	–
IFAD	2.8	–	–	1.5
I.F.C.	-1.7	4.5	-2.6	–
IMF TRUST FUND	–	–	–	–
U.N. AGENCIES	–	–	–	–
UNDP	6.9	10.9	13.0	12.5
UNTA	1.2	1.0	1.3	1.1
UNICEF	1.6	1.5	2.2	2.8
UNRWA	–	–	–	–
WFP	2.0	2.5	1.3	8.6
UNHCR	–	–	–	9.9
Other Multilateral	2.0	2.5	2.3	1.8
Arab Agencies	0.5	7.1	6.7	–
TOTAL	*70.6*	*80.0*	*127.3*	*136.9*
ARAB COUNTRIES	***12.0***	***13.6***	***18.0***	***5.3***
E.E.C.+ MEMBERS	*103.5*	*146.8*	*207.7*	*152.4*
TOTAL	**225.0**	**279.2**	**344.3**	**283.5**

2. ODA LOANS GROSS

DAC COUNTRIES	1987	1988	1989	1990
Australia	–	–	–	–
Austria	–	–	–	–
Belgium	–	–	–	–
Canada	–	–	–	–
Denmark	–	–	0.9	–
Finland	–	–	–	–
France	30.8	68.3	62.9	54.9
Germany	1.2	–	0.2	–
Ireland	–	–	–	–
Italy	–	–	12.5	3.0
Japan	13.8	23.4	1.5	1.7
Netherlands	–	–	–	–
New Zealand	–	–	–	–
Norway	–	–	–	–
Sweden	–	–	–	–
Switzerland	–	–	–	–
United Kingdom	–	–	–	–
United States	8.0	–	–	–
TOTAL	*53.8*	*91.8*	*77.9*	*59.6*
MULTILATERAL	*59.3*	*61.9*	*92.6*	*86.1*
ARAB COUNTRIES	***13.6***	***11.0***	***23.2***	***10.0***
E.E.C.+ MEMBERS	*33.3*	*68.3*	*79.7*	*61.2*
TOTAL	**126.6**	**164.6**	**193.6**	**155.8**

3. TOTAL OFFICIAL GROSS

DAC COUNTRIES	1987	1988	1989	1990
Australia	–	–	0.0	–
Austria	0.0	0.1	0.0	0.1
Belgium	0.5	0.4	2.4	0.5
Canada	4.8	6.6	6.7	3.9
Denmark	2.9	1.1	7.6	1.0
Finland	0.0	0.1	0.0	0.0
France	52.7	83.6	100.4	100.5
Germany	29.1	15.5	51.1	20.3
Ireland	–	–	–	–
Italy	5.2	44.8	21.2	13.2
Japan	22.8	26.8	8.8	9.4
Netherlands	0.4	0.6	0.6	1.2
New Zealand	–	–	–	–
Norway	1.2	0.5	0.0	0.8
Sweden	–	0.2	–	0.3
Switzerland	0.4	0.6	0.6	1.0
United Kingdom	0.7	1.2	0.8	0.8
United States	30.0	15.0	5.0	23.0
TOTAL	*150.8*	*196.8*	*205.4*	*176.1*
MULTILATERAL	*90.2*	*102.7*	*147.2*	*159.6*
ARAB COUNTRIES	***13.6***	***15.0***	***23.2***	***10.0***
E.E.C.+ MEMBERS	*106.3*	*159.3*	*215.0*	*168.4*
TOTAL	**254.5**	**314.4**	**375.9**	**345.7**

4. TOTAL ODA NET

	1987	1988	1989	1990
Australia	–	–	0.0	–
Austria	0.0	0.1	0.0	0.1
Belgium	0.5	0.4	0.6	0.5
Canada	4.8	6.6	6.7	3.9
Denmark	2.9	1.1	2.2	1.0
Finland	0.0	0.1	0.0	0.0
France	49.1	81.9	96.1	86.5
Germany	22.9	14.2	51.0	20.3
Ireland	–	–	–	–
Italy	5.2	12.8	21.2	13.2
Japan	22.5	26.5	8.0	9.2
Netherlands	0.4	0.6	0.6	1.2
New Zealand	–	–	–	–
Norway	1.2	0.5	0.0	0.8
Sweden	–	0.2	–	0.3
Switzerland	0.4	0.6	0.6	1.0
United Kingdom	0.7	1.2	0.8	0.8
United States	9.0	13.0	4.0	–
TOTAL	*119.7*	*159.5*	*191.7*	*138.9*
AF.D.F.	13.6	9.5	19.4	27.8
AF.D.B.	–	–	–	–
AS.D.B	–	–	–	–
CAR.D.B.	–	–	–	–
E.E.C.	13.1	12.3	30.8	30.8
IBRD	–	–	–	–
IDA	38.2	43.0	63.0	51.0
I.D.B.	–	–	–	–
IFAD	2.8	–	–	1.5
I.F.C.	–	–	–	–
IMF TRUST FUND	–	–	–	–
U.N. AGENCIES	–	–	–	–
UNDP	6.9	10.9	13.0	12.5
UNTA	1.2	1.0	1.3	1.1
UNICEF	1.6	1.5	2.2	2.8
UNRWA	–	–	–	–
WFP	2.0	2.5	1.3	8.6
UNHCR	–	–	–	9.9
Other Multilateral	2.0	2.5	2.3	1.8
Arab Agencies	0.4	5.7	3.4	–
TOTAL	*81.7*	*88.7*	*136.6*	*147.8*
ARAB COUNTRIES	***12.0***	***13.6***	***18.0***	***5.3***
E.E.C.+ MEMBERS	*94.8*	*124.4*	*203.1*	*154.4*
TOTAL	**213.4**	**261.9**	**346.3**	**292.0**

5. ODA LOANS NET

	1987	1988	1989	1990
Australia	–	–	–	–
Austria	–	–	–	–
Belgium	–	–	–	–
Canada	–	–	–	–
Denmark	–	–	-4.6	–
Finland	–	–	–	–
France	29.1	66.7	58.5	47.9
Germany	-0.1	-1.3	0.2	0.0
Ireland	–	–	–	–
Italy	–	–	12.5	3.0
Japan	13.6	23.1	0.6	1.5
Netherlands	–	–	–	–
New Zealand	–	–	–	–
Norway	–	–	–	–
Sweden	–	–	–	–
Switzerland	–	–	–	–
United Kingdom	–	–	–	–
United States	1.0	-2.0	-1.0	-7.0
TOTAL	*43.6*	*86.5*	*66.1*	*45.3*
MULTILATERAL	*56.3*	*58.0*	*88.9*	*82.3*
ARAB COUNTRIES	***12.0***	***9.6***	***18.0***	***5.3***
E.E.C.+ MEMBERS	*30.4*	*65.4*	*69.9*	*54.2*
TOTAL	**111.9**	**154.1**	**173.0**	**133.0**

6. TOTAL OFFICIAL NET

	1987	1988	1989	1990
Australia	–	–	0.0	–
Austria	0.0	0.1	0.0	0.1
Belgium	-0.9	0.4	2.1	-0.9
Canada	4.8	6.6	6.7	3.9
Denmark	2.9	1.1	2.2	1.0
Finland	0.0	0.1	0.0	0.0
France	50.2	80.1	94.4	91.5
Germany	25.8	12.1	49.8	20.3
Ireland	–	–	–	–
Italy	5.2	30.6	21.2	13.2
Japan	22.5	26.5	8.0	9.2
Netherlands	0.4	0.6	0.6	1.2
New Zealand	–	–	–	–
Norway	1.2	0.5	0.0	0.8
Sweden	–	0.2	–	0.3
Switzerland	0.4	0.6	0.6	1.0
United Kingdom	0.7	1.2	0.8	0.8
United States	23.0	13.0	4.0	16.0
TOTAL	*136.3*	*173.4*	*190.5*	*158.5*
MULTILATERAL	*70.6*	*80.0*	*127.3*	*136.9*
ARAB COUNTRIES	***12.0***	***13.6***	***18.0***	***5.3***
E.E.C.+ MEMBERS	*97.6*	*136.7*	*200.3*	*156.4*
TOTAL	**218.8**	**267.1**	**335.8**	**300.7**

7. TOTAL ODA GROSS

	1987
Australia	–
Austria	0.0
Belgium	0.5
Canada	4.8
Denmark	2.9
Finland	0.0
France	50.8
Germany	24.2
Ireland	–
Italy	5.2
Japan	22.8
Netherlands	0.4
New Zealand	–
Norway	1.2
Sweden	–
Switzerland	0.4
United Kingdom	0.7
United States	16.0
TOTAL	*129.9*
AF.D.F.	13.9
AF.D.B.	–
AS.D.B	–
CAR.D.B.	–
E.E.C.	13.1
IBRD	–
IDA	38.4
I.D.B.	–
IFAD	2.8
I.F.C.	–
IMF TRUST FUND	–
U.N. AGENCIES	–
UNDP	6.9
UNTA	1.2
UNICEF	1.6
UNRWA	–
WFP	2.0
UNHCR	–
Other Multilateral	2.0
Arab Agencies	2.9
TOTAL	*84.7*
ARAB COUNTRIES	***13.6***
E.E.C.+ MEMBERS	*97.8*
TOTAL	**228.1**

8. GRANTS

	1987
Australia	–
Austria	0.0
Belgium	0.5
Canada	4.8
Denmark	2.9
Finland	0.0
France	20.0
Germany	23.0
Ireland	–
Italy	5.2
Japan	8.9
Netherlands	0.4
New Zealand	–
Norway	1.2
Sweden	–
Switzerland	0.4
United Kingdom	0.7
United States	8.0
TOTAL	*76.1*
MULTILATERAL	*25.4*
ARAB COUNTRIES	***–***
E.E.C.+ MEMBERS	*64.5*
TOTAL	**101.5**

9. TOTAL OOF GROSS

	1987
Australia	–
Austria	–
Belgium	–
Canada	–
Denmark	–
Finland	–
France	2.0
Germany	4.9
Ireland	–
Italy	–
Japan	–
Netherlands	–
New Zealand	–
Norway	–
Sweden	–
Switzerland	–
United Kingdom	–
United States	14.0
TOTAL	*20.9*
MULTILATERAL	*5.5*
ARAB COUNTRIES	***–***
E.E.C.+ MEMBERS	*8.5*
TOTAL	**26.4**

Left / Middle blocks

1988	1989	1990		1987	1988	1989	1990
			10. ODA COMMITMENTS				
–	0.0	–		0.0	–	0.0	0.0
0.1	0.0	0.1		0.0	0.1	0.0	0.8
0.4	0.6	0.5		0.8	1.7	0.6	0.5
6.6	6.7	3.9		3.7	12.1	5.1	11.6
1.1	7.6	1.0		–	–	1.4	12.1
0.1	0.0	0.0		–	–	0.0	0.2
83.6	100.4	93.6		58.2	80.7	97.2	75.1
15.5	51.0	20.3		28.9	20.3	42.7	32.8
–	–	–		–	–	–	–
12.8	21.2	13.2		10.0	26.4	20.2	7.6
26.8	8.8	9.4		9.5	10.7	11.8	45.0
0.6	0.6	1.2		0.4	0.6	0.6	1.2
–	–	–		–	–	–	–
0.5	0.0	0.8		0.3	–	–	–
0.2	–	0.3		–	0.2	–	–
0.6	0.6	1.0		0.1	0.8	0.6	0.2
1.2	0.8	0.8		0.7	1.2	0.8	0.8
15.0	5.0	7.0		17.0	27.6	28.6	16.2
164.7	*203.4*	*153.2*		*129.6*	*182.1*	*209.6*	*204.2*
9.7	19.7	28.5		27.2	1.6	72.1	10.0
–	–	–		–	–	–	–
–	–	–		–	–	–	–
12.3	30.8	30.8		98.8	92.1	16.5	16.5
–	–	–		–	–	–	–
43.0	63.0	52.0		88.2	153.0	57.0	167.0
–	–	1.5		0.2	15.5	–	0.2
–	–	–		–	–	–	–
–	–	–		–	–	–	–
–	–	–		13.7	18.4	20.1	36.7
10.9	13.0	12.5		–	–	–	–
1.0	1.3	1.1		–	–	–	–
1.5	2.2	2.8		–	–	–	–
–	–	–		–	–	–	–
2.5	1.3	8.6		–	–	–	–
–	–	9.9		–	–	–	–
2.5	2.3	1.8		–	–	–	–
9.3	6.8	1.1		9.2	–	14.8	9.8
92.7	*140.3*	*150.5*		*237.2*	*280.5*	*180.4*	*240.1*
15.0	*23.2*	*10.0*		*5.6*	*4.0*	–	*19.2*
127.3	*212.9*	*161.4*		*197.8*	*222.8*	*179.8*	*146.7*
272.4	*367.0*	*313.7*		*372.5*	*466.7*	*390.0*	*463.5*
			11. TECH. COOP. GRANTS				
–	0.0	–		–	–	–	–
0.1	0.0	0.1		0.0	0.1	0.0	0.0
0.4	0.6	0.5		0.3	0.1	–	0.1
6.6	6.7	3.9		–	0.1	0.8	3.4
1.1	6.7	1.0		0.3	0.0	0.0	–
0.1	0.0	0.0		–	–	–	–
15.2	37.6	38.6		6.8	8.4	9.1	14.0
15.5	50.8	20.3		7.2	6.8	7.2	9.3
–	–	–		–	–	–	–
12.8	8.8	10.2		3.9	3.7	2.4	2.1
3.4	7.4	7.7		0.9	0.5	0.7	1.2
0.6	0.6	1.2		0.4	0.6	0.6	1.2
–	–	–		–	–	–	–
0.5	0.0	0.8		0.3	0.1	–	0.2
0.2	–	0.3		–	–	–	–
0.6	0.6	1.0		0.3	0.5	–	–
1.2	0.8	0.8		0.7	1.0	0.5	0.6
15.0	5.0	7.0		2.0	2.0	3.0	3.0
73.0	*125.6*	*93.6*		*23.0*	*23.8*	*24.4*	*35.2*
30.8	*47.8*	*64.4*		*12.8*	*18.4*	*18.8*	*28.1*
4.0	–	–		–	–	–	–
59.0	*133.2*	*100.2*		*20.7*	*23.1*	*19.9*	*27.3*
107.8	*173.3*	*157.9*		*35.8*	*42.2*	*43.2*	*63.3*
			12. TOTAL OOF NET				
–	–	–		–	–	–	–
–	–	–		–	–	–	–
–	1.8	–		-1.4	–	1.6	-1.4
–	–	–		–	–	–	–
–	–	–		0.0	–	–	–
–	–	7.0		1.1	-1.8	-1.7	5.0
–	0.2	–		2.9	-2.1	-1.1	0.0
–	–	–		–	–	–	–
32.0	–	–		–	17.8	–	–
–	–	–		–	–	–	–
–	–	–		–	–	–	–
–	–	–		–	–	–	–
–	–	–		–	–	–	–
–	–	–		–	–	–	–
–	–	16.0		14.0	–	–	16.0
32.0	*2.0*	*23.0*		*16.5*	*13.9*	*-1.2*	*19.6*
10.0	*6.9*	*9.1*		*-11.1*	*-8.7*	*-9.3*	*-10.8*
–	–	–		–	–	–	–
32.0	*2.0*	*7.0*		*2.8*	*12.4*	*-2.8*	*2.0*
42.1	*8.9*	*32.0*		*5.5*	*5.2*	*-10.5*	*8.8*

13. ODF COMMITMENTS: BY PURPOSE %

	1987	1988	1989	1990
Education	6	0	3	–
Health	12	0	3	–
Other Social Infrastr.	4	10	9	–
Water Sanitat. Sewage	5	4	21	–
Energy	3	2	5	–
Telecommunications	–	0	0	–
Transportation	34	21	18	–
Agriculture	6	17	7	–
Extractive Industries	0	4	–	–
Manufacturing	0	2	0	–
Trade Banking Tourism	2	0	–	–
Technical Cooperation	12	15	15	–
Multisector Aid	2	2	1	–
Programme	5	17	12	–
Debt Reorganisation	4	–	2	–
Food Aid	5	2	2	–
Emergency Aid	–	–	–	–
Unspecified	–	3	–	–
TOTAL	100	100	100	–

14. GRANT ELEMENT OF ODA %

DAC COUNTRIES

	1987	1988	1989	1990
Australia	100.0	–	100.0	–
Austria	100.0	100.0	100.0	–
Belgium	100.0	100.0	100.0	–
Canada	100.0	100.0	100.0	–
Denmark	–	–	100.0	–
Finland	–	–	100.0	–
France	73.2	66.9	73.9	–
Germany	87.9	100.0	97.7	–
Ireland	–	–	–	–
Italy	100.0	100.0	74.2	–
Japan	100.0	100.0	82.8	–
Netherlands	100.0	100.0	100.0	–
New Zealand	–	–	–	–
Norway	100.0	–	–	–
Sweden	–	100.0	–	–
Switzerland	100.0	100.0	100.0	–
United Kingdom	100.0	100.0	100.0	–
United States	80.2	100.0	100.0	–
TOTAL	*82.7*	*85.3*	*84.1*	–
MULTILATERAL	*89.6*	*87.3*	*82.2*	–
ARAB COUNTRIES	*81.4*	*100.0*	–	–
E.E.C.+ MEMBERS	*90.1*	*86.9*	*81.9*	–
TOTAL	*87.0*	*86.6*	*83.3*	–

15. OTHER AGGREGATES

OFFICIAL COMMITMENTS:

	1987	1988	1989	1990
TOTAL BILATERAL	160.3	234.7	269.9	239.4
of which:				
Arab Countries	5.6	4.0	–	19.2
C.E.E.C.	4.0	16.5	–	–
TOTAL MULTILATERAL	272.0	288.0	197.8	368.3
TOTAL BIL.& MULTIL.	432.3	522.7	467.7	607.7
of which:				
ODA Grants	203.2	232.4	145.6	169.5
ODA Loans	173.2	250.8	244.4	294.1

DISBURSEMENTS:

DAC COUNTRIES COMBINED

OFFICIAL & PRIVATE

GROSS:	1987	1988	1989	1990
Contractual Lending	67.7	120.5	82.0	87.0
Export Credits, Total	-7.0	-3.3	2.2	4.4
Export Credits, Priv.	-7.0	-3.3	2.2	4.4
NET:				
Contractual Lending	51.4	95.5	65.9	49.9
Export Credits Total	-9.6	-5.4	1.0	-15.0
PRIVATE SECTOR NET	6.2	12.2	8.5	-17.2
Direct Investment	6.1	7.0	3.6	0.3
Portfolio Investment	8.9	10.1	4.0	-2.5
Export Credits	-8.7	-5.0	1.0	-15.0

MARKET BORROWING:

CHANGE IN CLAIMS

	1987	1988	1989	1990
Banks	7.0	–	-8.0	22.0

MEMORANDUM ITEM:

	1987	1988	1989	1990
C.E.E.C. (Gross)	42.8	40.5	4.0	–

	1987	1988	1989	1990	1987	1988	1989	1990		1987
1. TOTAL RECEIPTS NET					**4. TOTAL ODA NET**				**7. TOTAL ODA GROSS**	
DAC COUNTRIES										
Australia	–	–	–	–	–	–	–	–	Australia	–
Austria	0.2	0.2	0.5	0.2	0.2	0.2	0.5	0.2	Austria	0.2
Belgium	0.7	-0.3	0.7	1.8	0.7	0.5	0.2	0.1	Belgium	0.7
Canada	0.3	0.3	0.4	0.1	0.3	0.3	0.4	0.1	Canada	0.3
Denmark	1.4	1.1	1.0	1.8	1.4	1.1	1.0	1.8	Denmark	1.4
Finland	–	–	–	–	–	–	–	–	Finland	–
France	-2.8	6.9	9.5	15.6	4.9	5.6	8.0	9.3	France	5.1
Germany	2.0	2.4	1.6	2.7	1.6	2.4	1.7	2.7	Germany	1.6
Ireland	–	–	–	–	–	–	–	–	Ireland	–
Italy	10.6	35.7	20.3	15.9	7.2	6.1	16.5	16.1	Italy	7.2
Japan	1.2	2.1	1.2	3.1	1.2	2.0	1.3	3.1	Japan	1.2
Netherlands	9.5	8.7	8.3	6.3	9.6	8.7	8.3	6.3	Netherlands	9.6
New Zealand	–	–	–	–	–	–	–	–	New Zealand	–
Norway	–	0.0	0.0	–	–	0.0	0.0	–	Norway	–
Sweden	12.7	14.8	10.4	13.2	12.7	14.8	10.7	13.2	Sweden	12.7
Switzerland	4.0	4.1	1.9	2.1	4.0	4.1	1.9	2.1	Switzerland	4.0
United Kingdom	0.1	0.1	0.1	0.1	0.1	0.1	0.1	0.1	United Kingdom	0.1
United States	4.0	2.0	3.0	7.0	4.0	2.0	3.0	7.0	United States	4.0
TOTAL	44.0	78.1	58.9	69.8	47.8	47.7	53.4	62.1	TOTAL	48.0
MULTILATERAL										
AF.D.F.	13.2	9.2	2.9	18.5	13.2	9.2	2.9	18.5	AF.D.F.	13.3
AF.D.B.	-1.5	-0.4	-0.8	-1.3	–	–	–	–	AF.D.B.	–
AS.D.B	–	–	–	–	–	–	–	–	AS.D.B	–
CAR.D.B.	–	–	–	–	–	–	–	–	CAR.D.B.	–
E.E.C.	11.1	6.9	11.0	11.0	11.1	6.9	11.0	11.0	E.E.C.	11.1
IBRD	–	–	–	–	–	–	–	–	IBRD	–
IDA	18.6	16.0	19.0	15.0	18.6	16.0	19.0	15.0	IDA	18.6
I.D.B.	–	–	–	–	–	–	–	–	I.D.B.	–
IFAD	0.8	1.4	0.9	1.7	0.8	1.4	0.9	1.7	IFAD	0.8
I.F.C.	–	–	–	–	–	–	–	–	I.F.C.	–
IMF TRUST FUND	–	–	–	–	–	–	–	–	IMF TRUST FUND	–
U.N. AGENCIES									U.N. AGENCIES	–
UNDP	4.2	5.4	6.0	5.2	4.2	5.4	6.0	5.2	UNDP	4.2
UNTA	1.0	0.7	0.9	0.9	1.0	0.7	0.9	0.9	UNTA	1.0
UNICEF	0.7	0.7	1.0	1.7	0.7	0.7	1.0	1.7	UNICEF	0.7
UNRWA	–	–	–	–	–	–	–	–	UNRWA	–
WFP	2.3	2.9	1.0	3.7	2.3	2.9	1.0	3.7	WFP	2.3
UNHCR	–	–	–	–	–	–	–	–	UNHCR	–
Other Multilateral	1.9	1.9	2.3	2.7	1.9	1.9	2.3	2.7	Other Multilateral	1.9
Arab Agencies	0.8	-0.2	-0.1	–	0.3	–	0.6	–	Arab Agencies	0.4
TOTAL	53.1	44.4	44.0	58.9	54.1	45.0	45.6	60.2	TOTAL	54.2
ARAB COUNTRIES	8.8	6.0	2.7	0.0	9.0	6.0	2.7	0.0	ARAB COUNTRIES	10.5
E.E.C.+ MEMBERS	32.6	61.5	52.5	55.1	36.5	31.3	46.6	47.4	E.E.C.+ MEMBERS	36.6
TOTAL	105.9	128.5	105.6	128.7	110.9	98.8	101.7	122.3	TOTAL	112.7
2. ODA LOANS GROSS					**5. ODA LOANS NET**				**8. GRANTS**	
DAC COUNTRIES										
Australia	–	–	–	–	–	–	–	–	Australia	–
Austria	–	–	–	–	–	–	–	–	Austria	0.2
Belgium	–	–	–	–	–	–	–	–	Belgium	0.7
Canada	–	–	–	–	–	–	–	–	Canada	0.3
Denmark	–	–	–	–	–	–	–	–	Denmark	1.4
Finland	–	–	–	–	–	–	–	–	Finland	–
France	–	–	0.6	–	-0.2	-0.3	0.2	-0.1	France	5.1
Germany	–	–	–	–	–	0.0	0.0	–	Germany	1.6
Ireland	–	–	–	–	–	–	–	–	Ireland	–
Italy	–	–	–	12.0	–	–	–	12.0	Italy	7.2
Japan	–	–	–	–	–	–	–	–	Japan	1.2
Netherlands	–	–	0.2	–	–	–	–	–	Netherlands	9.6
New Zealand	–	–	–	–	–	–	–	–	New Zealand	–
Norway	–	–	–	–	–	–	–	–	Norway	–
Sweden	–	–	–	–	–	–	–	–	Sweden	12.7
Switzerland	–	–	–	–	–	–	–	–	Switzerland	4.0
United Kingdom	–	–	–	–	–	–	–	–	United Kingdom	0.1
United States	–	–	–	–	–	–	–	–	United States	4.0
TOTAL	–	–	0.7	12.0	-0.2	-0.3	0.2	11.9	TOTAL	48.0
MULTILATERAL	34.5	26.9	25.2	36.2	34.4	26.7	23.5	35.7	MULTILATERAL	19.8
ARAB COUNTRIES	8.5	5.9	3.5	–	6.9	5.3	1.7	0.0	ARAB COUNTRIES	2.0
E.E.C.+ MEMBERS	1.8	0.2	1.3	12.6	1.6	-0.2	0.8	12.5	E.E.C.+ MEMBERS	34.8
TOTAL	43.0	32.8	29.5	48.2	41.1	31.7	25.4	47.6	TOTAL	69.8
3. TOTAL OFFICIAL GROSS					**6. TOTAL OFFICIAL NET**				**9. TOTAL OOF GROSS**	
DAC COUNTRIES										
Australia	–	–	–	–	–	–	–	–	Australia	–
Austria	0.2	0.2	0.5	0.2	0.2	0.2	0.5	0.2	Austria	–
Belgium	0.7	0.5	2.8	0.1	0.7	0.5	2.8	0.1	Belgium	–
Canada	0.3	0.3	0.4	0.1	0.3	0.3	0.4	0.1	Canada	–
Denmark	1.4	1.1	1.0	1.8	1.4	1.1	1.0	1.8	Denmark	–
Finland	–	–	–	–	–	–	–	–	Finland	–
France	5.1	5.9	8.3	9.5	4.9	5.6	8.0	9.3	France	–
Germany	1.6	2.4	1.7	2.7	1.6	2.4	1.6	2.7	Germany	–
Ireland	–	–	–	–	–	–	–	–	Ireland	–
Italy	7.2	6.1	21.4	17.9	7.2	6.1	21.4	15.9	Italy	–
Japan	1.2	2.0	1.3	3.1	1.2	2.0	1.3	3.1	Japan	–
Netherlands	9.6	8.7	8.4	6.3	9.6	8.7	8.3	6.3	Netherlands	–
New Zealand	–	–	–	–	–	–	–	–	New Zealand	–
Norway	–	0.0	0.0	–	–	0.0	0.0	–	Norway	–
Sweden	12.7	14.8	10.7	13.2	12.7	14.8	10.7	13.2	Sweden	–
Switzerland	4.0	4.1	1.9	2.1	4.0	4.1	1.9	2.1	Switzerland	–
United Kingdom	0.1	0.1	0.1	0.1	0.1	0.1	0.1	0.1	United Kingdom	–
United States	4.0	2.0	3.0	7.0	4.0	2.0	3.0	7.0	United States	–
TOTAL	48.0	48.0	61.4	64.0	47.8	47.7	60.8	61.8	TOTAL	–
MULTILATERAL	54.7	45.3	47.3	60.9	53.1	44.4	44.0	58.9	MULTILATERAL	0.5
ARAB COUNTRIES	10.5	6.6	4.6	–	8.8	6.0	2.7	0.0	ARAB COUNTRIES	–
E.E.C.+ MEMBERS	36.6	31.6	54.6	49.3	36.5	31.3	54.1	47.1	E.E.C.+ MEMBERS	–
TOTAL	113.2	99.9	113.2	124.8	109.7	98.2	107.5	120.7	TOTAL	0.5

10. ODA COMMITMENTS

1988	1989	1990	1987	1988	1989	1990
–	–	–	–	–	–	–
0.2	0.5	0.2	0.2	0.0	0.8	0.4
0.5	0.2	0.1	0.7	0.4	0.2	0.1
0.3	0.4	0.1	0.4	0.3	0.2	0.0
1.1	1.0	1.8	5.4	–	–	–
–	–	–	–	–	–	–
5.9	8.3	9.5	4.7	8.5	8.8	9.4
2.4	1.7	2.7	2.7	1.8	5.7	12.4
–	–	–	–	–	–	–
6.1	16.5	16.1	23.4	6.7	17.1	17.0
2.0	1.3	3.1	2.2	3.2	0.1	4.9
8.7	8.4	6.3	11.5	4.9	9.5	3.8
–	–	–	–	–	–	–
0.0	0.0	–	–	–	–	–
14.8	10.7	13.2	14.5	14.8	10.7	14.4
4.1	1.9	2.1	8.3	1.6	0.1	2.4
0.1	0.1	0.1	0.1	0.1	0.1	0.1
2.0	3.0	7.0	1.8	1.8	2.9	5.1
48.0	*53.9*	*62.2*	*75.9*	*44.1*	*56.3*	*69.8*
9.4	3.3	19.0	33.8	9.1	53.4	15.2
–	–	–	–	–	–	–
–	–	–	–	–	–	–
–	–	–	–	–	–	–
6.9	11.0	11.0	32.3	12.1	5.8	5.8
–	–	–	–	–	–	–
16.0	19.0	15.0	22.9	14.0	52.0	–
–	–	–	–	–	–	–
1.4	0.9	1.7	5.5	–	–	–
–	–	–	–	–	–	–
–	–	–	10.1	11.6	11.2	14.1
5.4	6.0	5.2	–	–	–	–
0.7	0.9	0.9	–	–	–	–
0.7	1.0	1.7	–	–	–	–
–	–	–	–	–	–	–
2.9	1.0	3.7	–	–	–	–
–	–	–	–	–	–	–
1.9	2.3	2.7	–	–	–	–
–	2.0	0.2	–	–	5.3	–
45.2	*47.3*	*60.9*	*104.7*	*46.8*	*127.6*	*35.1*
6.6	*4.6*	–	*8.0*	–	*9.9*	–
31.6	*47.1*	*47.5*	*80.7*	*34.5*	*47.2*	*48.4*
99.8	*105.7*	*123.1*	*188.5*	*90.8*	*193.8*	*104.8*

11. TECH. COOP. GRANTS

1988	1989	1990	1987	1988	1989	1990
–	–	–	–	–	–	–
0.2	0.5	0.2	0.2	0.2	0.0	0.1
0.5	0.2	0.1	0.1	–	–	–
0.3	0.4	0.1	–	0.0	–	0.1
1.1	1.0	1.8	–	0.5	–	–
–	–	–	–	–	–	–
5.9	7.7	9.5	2.0	2.2	2.7	3.7
2.4	1.7	2.7	1.5	1.7	0.8	1.8
–	–	–	–	–	–	–
6.1	16.5	4.1	1.7	1.5	0.1	0.6
2.0	1.3	3.1	0.1	0.0	0.1	0.1
8.7	8.3	6.3	3.3	3.3	2.9	3.1
–	–	–	–	–	–	–
0.0	0.0	–	–	0.0	0.0	–
14.8	10.7	13.2	4.9	7.8	6.5	0.5
4.1	1.9	2.1	1.1	1.3	–	–
0.1	0.1	0.1	0.1	0.1	0.1	0.1
2.0	3.0	7.0	3.0	2.0	2.0	2.0
48.0	*53.2*	*50.1*	*17.9*	*20.8*	*15.1*	*12.1*
18.3	*22.0*	*24.7*	*9.4*	*12.8*	*10.1*	*10.4*
0.7	*1.0*	–	–	–	–	–
31.4	*45.8*	*34.9*	*10.2*	*13.5*	*6.5*	*9.3*
67.0	*76.2*	*74.8*	*27.3*	*33.6*	*25.2*	*22.5*

12. TOTAL OOF NET

1988	1989	1990	1987	1988	1989	1990
–	–	–	–	–	–	–
–	2.6	–	–	–	2.6	–
–	–	–	–	–	–	–
–	–	–	–	–	–	–
–	–	–	–	–	–	–
–	–	–	–	–	–	0.0
–	–	–	–	–	0.0	–
–	4.9	1.8	–	–	4.9	-0.2
–	–	–	–	–	–	–
–	–	–	–	–	–	–
–	–	–	–	–	–	–
–	–	–	–	–	–	–
–	–	–	–	–	–	–
–	7.5	1.8	–	–	7.5	-0.2
0.1	–	–	-1.0	-0.6	-1.6	-1.3
–	–	–	-0.2	–	–	–
–	7.5	1.8	–	–	7.5	-0.2
0.1	*7.5*	*1.8*	*-1.2*	*-0.6*	*5.9*	*-1.5*

13. ODF COMMITMENTS: BY PURPOSE %

	1987	1988	1989	1990
Education	1	20	9	–
Health	10	1	2	–
Other Social Infrastr.	13	11	15	–
Water Sanitat. Sewage	–	1	4	–
Energy	0	2	3	–
Telecommunications	1	3	1	–
Transportation	9	1	16	–
Agriculture	15	8	2	–
Extractive Industries	–	–	–	–
Manufacturing	2	3	1	–
Trade Banking Tourism	2	1	1	–
Technical Cooperation	17	38	16	–
Multisector Aid	1	4	1	–
Programme	25	0	30	–
Debt Reorganisation	–	–	–	–
Food Aid	1	2	–	–
Emergency Aid	0	0	–	–
Unspecified	2	5	–	–
TOTAL	100	100	100	–

14. GRANT ELEMENT OF ODA %

DAC COUNTRIES

	1987	1988	1989	1990
Australia	–	–	–	–
Austria	100.0	100.0	100.0	–
Belgium	100.0	100.0	100.0	–
Canada	100.0	100.0	100.0	–
Denmark	100.0	–	–	–
Finland	–	–	–	–
France	100.0	100.0	100.0	–
Germany	100.0	100.0	100.0	–
Ireland	–	–	–	–
Italy	100.0	100.0	100.0	–
Japan	100.0	100.0	100.0	–
Netherlands	100.0	100.0	100.0	–
New Zealand	–	–	–	–
Norway	–	–	–	–
Sweden	100.0	100.0	100.0	–
Switzerland	100.0	100.0	100.0	–
United Kingdom	100.0	100.0	100.0	–
United States	100.0	100.0	100.0	–
TOTAL	*100.0*	*100.0*	*100.0*	–
MULTILATERAL	*89.0*	*92.7*	*82.3*	–
ARAB COUNTRIES	*69.3*	–	*53.9*	–
E.E.C.+ MEMBERS	*100.0*	*100.0*	*100.0*	–
TOTAL	*92.7*	*96.6*	*86.4*	–

15. OTHER AGGREGATES

OFFICIAL COMMITMENTS:

	1987	1988	1989	1990
TOTAL BILATERAL	91.8	47.6	73.7	73.8
of which:				
Arab Countries	8.0	–	9.9	–
C.E.E.C.	8.0	–	–	–
TOTAL MULTILATERAL	104.7	46.8	127.6	35.1
TOTAL BIL.& MULTIL.	196.5	94.3	201.3	108.8
of which:				
ODA Grants	120.4	66.7	69.5	61.7
ODA Loans	76.2	24.1	124.2	43.1

DISBURSEMENTS:

DAC COUNTRIES COMBINED

	1987	1988	1989	1990
OFFICIAL & PRIVATE				
GROSS:				
Contractual Lending	4.4	35.5	20.9	15.1
Export Credits, Total	4.4	35.5	12.7	3.1
Export Credits, Priv.	4.4	35.5	12.7	1.3
NET:				
Contractual Lending	3.2	28.7	4.1	11.6
Export Credits Total	3.4	29.0	-3.6	0.0
PRIVATE SECTOR NET	-3.8	30.3	-2.0	8.0
Direct Investment	0.1	0.7	0.5	2.0
Portfolio Investment	-7.3	0.7	1.1	6.0
Export Credits	3.4	29.0	-3.6	0.0

MARKET BORROWING:

CHANGE IN CLAIMS

	1987	1988	1989	1990
Banks	-9.0	3.0	5.0	17.0

MEMORANDUM ITEM:

	1987	1988	1989	1990
C.E.E.C. (Gross)	–	–	–	–

1. TOTAL RECEIPTS NET

DAC COUNTRIES	1987	1988	1989	1990
Australia	0.0	0.0	0.0	0.0
Austria	–	–	–	–
Belgium	0.1	–	–	-0.1
Canada	4.8	6.2	9.0	18.5
Denmark	0.0	0.9	–	0.2
Finland	0.0	–	–	–
France	–	0.0	0.2	9.5
Germany	0.6	1.0	1.2	10.4
Ireland	0.0	0.0	0.0	–
Italy	–	–	–	2.6
Japan	0.5	1.8	1.1	4.5
Netherlands	0.4	-0.5	0.1	-4.2
New Zealand	–	–	–	0.0
Norway	0.0	0.3	0.1	0.1
Sweden	–	–	1.0	–
Switzerland	0.0	0.0	–	–
United Kingdom	3.5	2.3	10.4	27.2
United States	7.0	5.0	7.0	41.0
TOTAL	16.9	17.0	30.0	109.5
MULTILATERAL				
AF.D.F.	–	–	–	–
AF.D.B.	–	–	–	–
AS.D.B	–	–	–	–
CAR.D.B.	0.0	–	–	–
E.E.C.	6.8	5.1	7.5	7.5
IBRD	0.0	–	-1.0	-31.0
IDA	0.4	-1.0	–	55.0
I.D.B.	15.2	12.5	18.4	16.1
IFAD	0.5	–	1.5	0.5
I.F.C.	–	–	-1.4	–
IMF TRUST FUND	–	–	–	–
U.N. AGENCIES	–	–	–	–
UNDP	1.2	2.3	2.8	3.7
UNTA	0.5	0.3	0.6	0.5
UNICEF	0.1	0.3	0.2	0.4
UNRWA	–	–	–	–
WFP	0.1	0.1	0.0	1.3
UNHCR	–	–	–	–
Other Multilateral	0.2	0.2	0.4	0.6
Arab Agencies	–	–	0.0	–
TOTAL	25.0	19.8	29.0	54.7
ARAB COUNTRIES	–	–	–	–
E.E.C.+ MEMBERS	11.4	8.8	19.4	53.0
TOTAL	41.9	36.8	59.1	164.2

4. TOTAL ODA NET

DAC COUNTRIES	1987	1988	1989	1990
Australia	0.0	0.0	0.0	0.0
Austria	–	–	–	–
Belgium	–	0.1	–	–
Canada	4.8	6.2	8.5	15.7
Denmark	–	–	–	–
Finland	0.0	–	–	–
France	–	0.0	0.2	1.2
Germany	0.1	0.1	0.0	11.2
Ireland	0.0	0.0	0.0	–
Italy	–	–	–	2.6
Japan	0.8	2.0	1.2	4.6
Netherlands	0.2	–	–	1.0
New Zealand	–	–	–	0.0
Norway	0.0	0.3	0.1	0.1
Sweden	–	–	1.0	–
Switzerland	0.0	0.0	–	–
United Kingdom	1.0	0.9	10.8	16.3
United States	8.0	6.0	5.0	-17.0
TOTAL	14.9	15.6	26.8	35.8
MULTILATERAL				
AF.D.F.	–	–	–	–
AF.D.B.	–	–	–	–
AS.D.B	–	–	–	–
CAR.D.B.	0.0	–	–	–
E.E.C.	6.8	5.1	7.5	7.5
IBRD	–	–	–	–
IDA	0.4	-1.0	–	55.0
I.D.B.	4.0	4.2	4.4	3.5
IFAD	0.5	–	1.5	0.5
I.F.C.	–	–	–	–
IMF TRUST FUND	–	–	–	–
U.N. AGENCIES	–	–	–	–.
UNDP	1.2	2.3	2.8	3.7
UNTA	0.5	0.3	0.6	0.5
UNICEF	0.1	0.3	0.2	0.4
UNRWA	–	–	–	–
WFP	0.1	0.1	0.0	1.3
UNHCR	–	–	–	–
Other Multilateral	0.2	0.2	0.4	0.6
Arab Agencies	–	–	0.0	–
TOTAL	13.8	11.5	17.4	73.1
ARAB COUNTRIES	–	–	–	–
E.E.C.+ MEMBERS	8.1	6.2	18.5	39.9
TOTAL	28.7	27.1	44.2	108.9

7. TOTAL ODA GROSS

	1987
Australia	0.0
Austria	–
Belgium	–
Canada	4.8
Denmark	–
Finland	0.0
France	–
Germany	0.1
Ireland	0.0
Italy	–
Japan	0.8
Netherlands	0.2
New Zealand	–
Norway	0.0
Sweden	–
Switzerland	0.0
United Kingdom	1.0
United States	8.0
TOTAL	15.0
AF.D.F.	–
AF.D.B.	–
AS.D.B	–
CAR.D.B.	0.0
E.E.C.	7.1
IBRD	–
IDA	0.6
I.D.B.	4.0
IFAD	0.5
I.F.C.	–
IMF TRUST FUND	–
U.N. AGENCIES	–
UNDP	1.2
UNTA	0.5
UNICEF	0.1
UNRWA	–
WFP	0.1
UNHCR	–
Other Multilateral	0.2
Arab Agencies	–
TOTAL	14.2
ARAB COUNTRIES	–
E.E.C.+ MEMBERS	8.3
TOTAL	29.1

2. ODA LOANS GROSS

DAC COUNTRIES	1987	1988	1989	1990
Australia	–	–	–	–
Austria	–	–	–	–
Belgium	–	–	–	–
Canada	0.7	–	–	–
Denmark	–	–	–	–
Finland	–	–	–	–
France	–	–	–	–
Germany	–	–	–	11.1
Ireland	–	–	–	–
Italy	–	–	–	–
Japan	–	–	–	–
Netherlands	–	–	–	–
New Zealand	–	–	–	–
Norway	–	–	–	–
Sweden	–	–	–	–
Switzerland	–	–	–	–
United Kingdom	–	–	–	–
United States	6.0	6.0	7.0	6.0
TOTAL	6.7	6.0	7.0	17.1
MULTILATERAL	5.5	3.6	7.8	61.1
ARAB COUNTRIES	–	–	–	–
E.E.C.+ MEMBERS	1.9	1.3	–	11.1
TOTAL	12.1	9.6	14.8	78.2

5. ODA LOANS NET

DAC COUNTRIES	1987	1988	1989	1990
Australia	–	–	–	–
Austria	–	–	–	–
Belgium	–	–	–	–
Canada	0.7	–	–	–
Denmark	–	–	–	–
Finland	–	–	–	–
France	–	–	–	–
Germany	–	–	–	11.1
Ireland	–	–	–	–
Italy	–	–	–	–
Japan	0.0	0.0	0.0	0.0
Netherlands	–	–	–	-4.0
New Zealand	–	–	–	–
Norway	–	–	–	–
Sweden	–	–	–	–
Switzerland	–	–	–	–
United Kingdom	–	–	–	–
United States	6.0	6.0	5.0	-18.0
TOTAL	6.6	6.0	5.0	-10.9
MULTILATERAL	5.1	1.5	5.7	58.8
ARAB COUNTRIES	–	–	–	–
E.E.C.+ MEMBERS	1.6	1.1	-0.2	6.9
TOTAL	11.7	7.5	10.6	47.9

8. GRANTS

	1987
Australia	0.0
Austria	–
Belgium	–
Canada	4.2
Denmark	–
Finland	0.0
France	–
Germany	0.1
Ireland	0.0
Italy	–
Japan	0.8
Netherlands	0.2
New Zealand	–
Norway	0.0
Sweden	–
Switzerland	0.0
United Kingdom	1.0
United States	2.0
TOTAL	8.3
MULTILATERAL	8.7
ARAB COUNTRIES	–
E.E.C.+ MEMBERS	6.5
TOTAL	17.0

3. TOTAL OFFICIAL GROSS

DAC COUNTRIES	1987	1988	1989	1990
Australia	0.0	0.0	0.0	0.0
Austria	–	–	–	–
Belgium	–	0.1	–	–
Canada	4.8	6.2	8.5	18.5
Denmark	0.1	1.3	–	0.2
Finland	0.0	–	–	–
France	–	0.0	0.2	1.2
Germany	0.1	0.1	0.0	12.6
Ireland	0.0	0.0	0.0	–
Italy	–	–	–	2.6
Japan	0.8	2.1	1.3	4.7
Netherlands	0.2	–	–	5.0
New Zealand	–	–	–	0.0
Norway	0.0	0.3	0.1	0.1
Sweden	–	–	1.0	–
Switzerland	0.0	0.0	–	–
United Kingdom	1.0	0.9	10.8	27.2
United States	8.0	6.0	9.0	68.0
TOTAL	15.1	16.9	30.9	140.1
MULTILATERAL	26.1	22.6	34.2	88.7
ARAB COUNTRIES	–	–	–	–
E.E.C.+ MEMBERS	8.4	7.7	18.7	56.6
TOTAL	41.2	39.5	65.1	228.7

6. TOTAL OFFICIAL NET

DAC COUNTRIES	1987	1988	1989	1990
Australia	0.0	0.0	0.0	0.0
Austria	–	–	–	–
Belgium	–	0.1	–	–
Canada	4.8	6.2	8.5	18.5
Denmark	0.1	1.2	–	0.2
Finland	0.0	–	–	–
France	–	0.0	0.2	1.2
Germany	0.1	0.1	0.0	11.4
Ireland	0.0	0.0	0.0	–
Italy	–	–	–	2.6
Japan	0.8	2.0	1.2	4.6
Netherlands	0.2	–	–	1.0
New Zealand	–	–	–	0.0
Norway	0.0	0.3	0.1	0.1
Sweden	–	–	1.0	–
Switzerland	0.0	0.0	–	–
United Kingdom	1.0	0.9	10.8	27.2
United States	7.0	5.0	7.0	41.0
TOTAL	14.0	15.8	28.8	107.8
MULTILATERAL	25.0	19.8	29.0	54.7
ARAB COUNTRIES	–	–	–	–
E.E.C.+ MEMBERS	8.2	7.4	18.5	51.2
TOTAL	39.1	35.6	57.9	162.5

9. TOTAL OOF GROSS

	1987
Australia	–
Austria	–
Belgium	–
Canada	–
Denmark	0.1
Finland	–
France	–
Germany	0.0
Ireland	–
Italy	–
Japan	–
Netherlands	–
New Zealand	–
Norway	–
Sweden	–
Switzerland	–
United Kingdom	–
United States	–
TOTAL	0.1
MULTILATERAL	12.0
ARAB COUNTRIES	–
E.E.C.+ MEMBERS	0.1
TOTAL	12.1

1988	1989	1990		1987	1988	1989	1990

10. ODA COMMITMENTS

1988	1989	1990	1987	1988	1989	1990
0.0	0.0	0.0	0.0	0.0	0.0	0.0
–	–	–	–	–	–	–
0.1	–	–	–	–	–	–
6.2	8.5	15.7	0.8	8.2	42.9	17.6
–	–	–	–	–	–	–
0.0	0.2	1.2	–	0.0	1.0	0.0
0.1	0.0	11.2	0.1	0.1	2.2	1.3
0.0	0.0	–	0.0	0.0	0.0	–
–	–	2.6	–	–	1.9	2.7
2.1	1.3	4.7	1.9	0.6	6.1	6.0
–	–	5.0	0.2	–	–	6.3
–	–	0.0	–	–	–	–
0.3	0.1	0.1	0.0	–	–	–
–	1.0	–	–	–	1.0	–
0.0	–	–	–	–	–	–
0.9	10.8	16.3	1.0	0.9	23.8	9.1
6.0	7.0	7.0	10.7	12.1	7.1	14.8
15.7	*28.9*	*63.9*	*14.7*	*21.8*	*86.0*	*57.8*
–	–	–	–	–	–	–
–	–	–	–	–	–	–
–	–	–	–	0.2	–	–
5.4	7.7	7.7	3.3	57.7	6.1	6.1
–	–	–	–	–	–	–
–	–	55.0	–	–	–	85.0
5.0	6.3	5.6	6.8	27.9	46.4	27.0
–	1.5	0.5	–	–	–	–
–	–	–	–	–	–	–
–	–	–	2.0	3.2	4.0	6.6
2.3	2.8	3.7	–	–	–	–
0.3	0.6	0.5	–	–	–	–
0.3	0.2	0.4	–	–	–	–
–	–	–	–	–	–	–
0.1	0.0	1.3	–	–	–	–
–	–	–	–	–	–	–
0.2	0.4	0.6	–	–	–	–
–	0.0	–	–	–	–	–
13.6	*19.5*	*75.4*	*12.1*	*89.0*	*56.5*	*124.7*
–	–	–	–	–	–	–
6.5	*18.7*	*44.2*	*4.6*	*58.7*	*35.0*	*25.5*
29.3	*48.4*	*139.3*	*26.9*	*110.8*	*142.4*	*182.5*

11. TECH. COOP. GRANTS

1988	1989	1990	1987	1988	1989	1990
0.0	0.0	0.0	0.0	0.0	0.0	0.0
–	–	–	–	–	–	–
0.1	–	–	–	–	–	–
6.2	8.5	15.7	–	0.2	1.0	0.7
–	–	–	–	–	–	–
0.0	0.2	1.2	–	0.0	0.0	0.0
0.1	0.0	0.1	0.1	0.1	0.0	0.1
0.0	0.0	–	0.0	0.0	0.0	–
–	–	2.6	–	–	–	–
2.1	1.3	4.7	0.1	0.5	0.8	0.2
–	–	5.0	0.2	–	–	–
–	–	0.0	–	–	–	–
0.3	0.1	0.1	0.0	0.1	–	–
–	1.0	–	–	–	–	–
0.0	–	–	0.0	0.0	–	–
0.9	10.8	16.3	1.0	0.9	1.3	2.9
–	–	1.0	–	–	–	–
9.7	*21.9*	*46.8*	*1.3*	*1.9*	*3.2*	*3.9*
10.0	11.7	14.3	2.7	4.0	3.9	5.3
–	–	–	–	–	–	–
5.2	18.7	33.0	1.9	2.0	1.4	3.0
19.7	*33.6*	*61.1*	*4.0*	*5.9*	*7.2*	*9.2*

12. TOTAL OOF NET

1988	1989	1990	1987	1988	1989	1990
–	–	–	–	–	–	–
–	–	–	–	–	–	–
–	–	2.8	–	–	–	2.8
1.3	–	0.2	0.1	1.2	–	0.2
–	–	–	–	–	–	–
–	–	–	–	–	–	–
–	–	1.3	0.0	–	–	0.2
–	–	–	–	–	–	–
–	–	–	–	–	–	–
–	–	–	–	–	–	–
–	–	–	–	–	–	–
–	–	–	–	–	–	–
–	–	–	–	–	–	–
–	–	10.9	–	–	–	10.9
–	2.0	61.0	-1.0	-1.0	2.0	58.0
1.3	*2.0*	*76.2*	*-0.9*	*0.2*	*2.0*	*72.0*
9.0	14.7	13.3	11.3	8.3	11.6	-18.4
–	–	–	–	–	–	–
1.3	–	12.4	0.1	1.2	–	11.3
10.3	*16.7*	*89.5*	*10.4*	*8.5*	*13.6*	*53.6*

13. ODF COMMITMENTS: BY PURPOSE %

	1987	1988	1989	1990
Education	0	–	3	–
Health	–	–	–	–
Other Social Infrastr.	1	–	–	–
Water Sanitat. Sewage	–	–	–	–
Energy	–	–	5	–
Telecommunications	..	–	–	–
Transportation	–	–	–	–
Agriculture	51	30	32	–
Extractive Industries	–	–	–	–
Manufacturing	0	1	0	–
Trade Banking Tourism	0	–	–	–
Technical Cooperation	12	21	9	–
Multisector Aid	–	–	1	–
Programme	–	–	34	–
Debt Reorganisation	–	–	9	–
Food Aid	36	48	7	–
Emergency Aid	–	–	–	–
Unspecified	–	–	–	–
TOTAL	100	100	100	

14. GRANT ELEMENT OF ODA %

DAC COUNTRIES	1987	1988	1989	1990
Australia	100.0	100.0	100.0	–
Austria	–	–	–	–
Belgium	–	–	–	–
Canada	100.0	100.0	100.0	–
Denmark	–	–	–	–
Finland	–	–	–	–
France	–	100.0	100.0	–
Germany	100.0	100.0	100.0	–
Ireland	100.0	100.0	100.0	–
Italy	–	–	100.0	–
Japan	100.0	100.0	100.0	–
Netherlands	100.0	–	–	–
New Zealand	–	–	–	–
Norway	100.0	–	–	–
Sweden	–	–	100.0	–
Switzerland	–	–	–	–
United Kingdom	100.0	100.0	100.0	–
United States	64.8	89.8	59.4	–
TOTAL	*74.4*	*94.4*	*96.7*	*–*
MULTILATERAL	*86.6*	*100.0*	*100.0*	*–*
ARAB COUNTRIES	*–*	*–*	*–*	*–*
E.E.C.+ MEMBERS	*100.0*	*100.0*	*100.0*	*–*
TOTAL	*79.9*	*98.5*	*96.9*	*–*

15. OTHER AGGREGATES

	1987	1988	1989	1990
OFFICIAL COMMITMENTS:				
TOTAL BILATERAL	16.1	21.8	110.1	65.9
of which:				
Arab Countries	–	–	–	–
C.E.E.C.	–	–	–	–
TOTAL MULTILATERAL	12.1	89.0	56.5	124.7
TOTAL BIL.& MULTIL.	28.3	110.8	166.6	190.6
of which:				
ODA Grants	10.7	79.9	84.6	53.0
ODA Loans	16.2	30.9	57.9	129.5
DISBURSEMENTS:				
DAC COUNTRIES COMBINED				
OFFICIAL & PRIVATE				
GROSS:				
Contractual Lending	7.0	7.3	14.8	95.9
Export Credits, Total	0.2	–	5.8	5.4
Export Credits, Priv.	0.2	–	5.8	2.6
NET:				
Contractual Lending	4.1	4.6	10.1	54.4
Export Credits Total	-1.6	-1.5	3.2	-6.8
PRIVATE SECTOR NET	2.9	1.2	1.2	1.7
Direct Investment	4.0	1.9	-2.1	7.8
Portfolio Investment	0.5	0.8	0.1	0.6
Export Credits	-1.6	-1.5	3.2	-6.6
MARKET BORROWING:				
CHANGE IN CLAIMS				
Banks	7.0	-22.0	–	82.0
MEMORANDUM ITEM:				
C.E.E.C. (Gross)	–	–	–	–

	1987	1988	1989	1990		1987	1988	1989	1990		1987
1. TOTAL RECEIPTS NET					**4. TOTAL ODA NET**					**7. TOTAL ODA GROSS**	
DAC COUNTRIES											
Australia	0.1	–	–	–		0.1	–	–	–	Australia	0.1
Austria	-0.6	-0.3	0.0	0.0		0.0	0.0	0.0	0.0	Austria	0.0
Belgium	-0.9	-0.3	0.8	1.8		2.3	1.9	0.9	2.1	Belgium	2.3
Canada	8.9	5.9	9.1	10.4		8.9	5.9	9.1	10.4	Canada	8.9
Denmark	–	1.2	–	–		–	1.2	–	–	Denmark	–
Finland	–	–	–	–		–	–	–	–	Finland	–
France	19.3	20.2	27.3	32.1		19.8	20.5	27.5	31.8	France	20.0
Germany	10.7	11.8	14.4	12.8		11.3	11.6	14.4	13.4	Germany	12.2
Ireland	–	–	–	–		–	–	–	–	Ireland	–
Italy	0.1	–	2.0	-0.4		0.1	–	2.0	0.5	Italy	0.1
Japan	10.1	15.0	11.2	2.8		10.1	15.0	11.2	2.8	Japan	10.1
Netherlands	0.3	1.1	1.1	1.2		0.6	1.4	1.4	1.4	Netherlands	0.6
New Zealand	–	–	–	–		–	–	–	–	New Zealand	–
Norway	0.1	0.5	0.1	0.2		0.1	0.5	0.1	0.2	Norway	0.1
Sweden	0.2	0.3	0.4	0.1		0.2	0.3	0.4	0.1	Sweden	0.2
Switzerland	3.5	2.2	3.7	3.7		3.5	2.2	3.7	3.7	Switzerland	3.5
United Kingdom	0.0	0.0	–	–		0.0	0.0	–	–	United Kingdom	0.0
United States	92.0	40.0	68.0	50.0		93.0	41.0	68.0	50.0	United States	93.0
TOTAL	143.8	97.4	138.0	114.7		149.9	101.4	138.6	116.4	TOTAL	151.1
MULTILATERAL											
AF.D.F.	–	–	–	–		–	–	–	–	AF.D.F.	–
AF.D.B.	–	–	–	–		–	–	–	–	AF.D.B.	–
AS.D.B	–	–	–	–		–	–	–	–	AS.D.B	–
CAR.D.B.	–	–	–	–		–	–	–	–	CAR.D.B.	–
E.E.C.	4.5	3.9	20.8	20.8		4.5	3.9	20.8	20.8	E.E.C.	4.5
IBRD	–	–	–	–		–	–	–	–	IBRD	–
IDA	45.6	19.0	10.0	12.0		45.6	19.0	10.0	12.0	IDA	46.2
I.D.B.	2.4	5.8	9.9	11.7		2.4	5.8	9.9	11.7	I.D.B.	5.0
IFAD	4.2	2.1	2.9	3.9		4.2	2.1	2.9	3.9	IFAD	4.2
I.F.C.	-0.1	–	-0.1	-0.4		–	–	–	–	I.F.C.	–
IMF TRUST FUND	–	–	–	–		–	–	–	–	IMF TRUST FUND	–
U.N. AGENCIES	–	–	–	–		–	–	–	–	U.N. AGENCIES	–
UNDP	5.8	8.0	8.6	11.9		5.8	8.0	8.6	11.9	UNDP	5.8
UNTA	1.0	0.4	0.6	0.5		1.0	0.4	0.6	0.5	UNTA	1.0
UNICEF	1.5	2.2	3.0	2.2		1.5	2.2	3.0	2.2	UNICEF	1.5
UNRWA	–	–	–	–		–	–	–	–	UNRWA	–
WFP	2.8	2.8	3.9	1.7		2.8	2.8	3.9	1.7	WFP	2.8
UNHCR	–	0.2	0.2	0.1		–	0.2	0.2	0.1	UNHCR	–
Other Multilateral	0.8	1.2	2.1	2.0		0.8	1.2	2.1	2.0	Other Multilateral	0.8
Arab Agencies	-0.5	-0.2	-0.6	–		-0.5	-0.2	-0.6	–	Arab Agencies	0.5
TOTAL	68.0	45.3	61.2	66.4		68.1	45.3	61.3	66.8	TOTAL	72.3
ARAB COUNTRIES	–	–	–	–		–	–	–	–	ARAB COUNTRIES	–
E.E.C.+ MEMBERS	34.0	37.8	66.4	68.3		38.5	40.5	67.0	70.0	E.E.C.+ MEMBERS	39.7
TOTAL	211.8	142.6	199.2	181.1		218.0	146.7	199.9	183.2	TOTAL	223.4
2. ODA LOANS GROSS					**5. ODA LOANS NET**					**8. GRANTS**	
DAC COUNTRIES											
Australia	–	–	–	–		–	–	–	–	Australia	0.1
Austria	–	–	–	–		–	–	–	–	Austria	0.0
Belgium	–	–	–	–		–	–	–	–	Belgium	2.3
Canada	–	–	–	–		–	–	–	–	Canada	8.9
Denmark	–	–	–	–		–	–	–	–	Denmark	–
Finland	–	–	–	–		–	–	–	–	Finland	–
France	11.5	10.0	10.9	13.0		11.2	10.0	10.6	12.0	France	8.5
Germany	–	–	–	–		-0.9	0.0	–	–	Germany	12.2
Ireland	–	–	–	–		–	–	–	–	Ireland	–
Italy	–	–	–	–		–	–	–	–	Italy	0.1
Japan	–	–	–	–		–	–	–	–	Japan	10.1
Netherlands	–	–	–	–		–	–	–	–	Netherlands	0.6
New Zealand	–	–	–	–		–	–	–	–	New Zealand	–
Norway	–	–	–	–		–	–	–	–	Norway	0.1
Sweden	–	–	–	–		–	–	–	–	Sweden	0.2
Switzerland	–	–	–	–		–	–	–	–	Switzerland	3.5
United Kingdom	–	–	–	–		–	–	–	–	United Kingdom	0.0
United States	–	–	–	–		–	–	–	–	United States	93.0
TOTAL	11.5	10.0	10.9	13.0		10.4	10.0	10.6	12.0	TOTAL	139.6
MULTILATERAL	55.8	32.0	27.5	32.0		51.6	26.5	21.0	26.5	MULTILATERAL	16.5
ARAB COUNTRIES	–	–	–	–		–	–	–	–	ARAB COUNTRIES	–
E.E.C.+ MEMBERS	11.5	10.0	10.9	13.0		10.4	10.0	10.6	12.0	E.E.C.+ MEMBERS	28.2
TOTAL	67.3	42.0	38.4	45.0		62.0	36.4	31.6	38.5	TOTAL	156.0
3. TOTAL OFFICIAL GROSS					**6. TOTAL OFFICIAL NET**					**9. TOTAL OOF GROSS**	
DAC COUNTRIES											
Australia	0.1	–	–	–		0.1	–	–	–	Australia	–
Austria	0.0	0.0	0.0	0.0		0.0	0.0	0.0	0.0	Austria	–
Belgium	2.3	1.9	0.9	2.1		2.3	1.9	0.9	2.1	Belgium	–
Canada	8.9	5.9	9.1	10.4		8.9	5.9	9.1	10.4	Canada	–
Denmark	–	1.2	–	–		–	1.2	–	–	Denmark	–
Finland	–	–	–	–		–	–	–	–	Finland	–
France	20.0	20.5	27.8	32.7		19.8	20.5	27.5	31.8	France	–
Germany	12.2	11.6	14.4	13.4		11.3	11.6	14.4	13.4	Germany	–
Ireland	–	–	–	–		–	–	–	–	Ireland	–
Italy	0.1	–	2.0	0.5		0.1	–	2.0	0.5	Italy	–
Japan	10.1	15.0	11.2	2.8		10.1	15.0	11.2	2.8	Japan	–
Netherlands	0.6	1.4	1.4	1.4		0.6	1.4	1.4	1.4	Netherlands	–
New Zealand	–	–	–	–		–	–	–	–	New Zealand	–
Norway	0.1	0.5	0.1	0.2		0.1	0.5	0.1	0.2	Norway	–
Sweden	0.2	0.3	0.4	0.1		0.2	0.3	0.4	0.1	Sweden	–
Switzerland	3.5	2.2	3.7	3.7		3.5	2.2	3.7	3.7	Switzerland	–
United Kingdom	0.0	0.0	–	–		0.0	0.0	–	–	United Kingdom	–
United States	93.0	41.0	68.0	50.0		92.0	40.0	68.0	50.0	United States	–
TOTAL	151.1	101.5	138.9	117.3		148.9	100.4	138.6	116.4	TOTAL	–
MULTILATERAL	72.3	50.8	67.7	72.0		68.0	45.3	61.2	66.4	MULTILATERAL	–
ARAB COUNTRIES	–	–	–	–		–	–	–	–	ARAB COUNTRIES	–
E.E.C.+ MEMBERS	39.7	40.6	67.3	70.9		38.5	40.5	67.0	70.0	E.E.C.+ MEMBERS	–
TOTAL	223.4	152.3	206.6	189.3		216.9	145.7	199.8	182.8	TOTAL	–

10. ODA COMMITMENTS

1988	1989	1990	1987	1988	1989	1990
–	–	–	0.0	–	–	–
0.0	0.0	0.0	0.0	0.0	0.0	0.0
1.9	0.9	2.1	3.3	1.8	0.9	2.1
5.9	9.1	10.4	8.5	2.5	28.8	12.2
1.2	–	–	–	–	–	0.2
–	–	–	–	–	–	–
20.5	27.8	32.7	16.4	20.9	37.6	34.6
11.6	14.4	13.4	11.2	16.1	4.2	22.8
–	–	–	–	–	–	–
–	2.0	0.5	0.1	–	2.0	0.5
15.0	11.2	2.8	10.2	13.5	10.6	8.0
1.4	1.4	1.4	0.4	1.4	1.4	1.4
–	–	–	–	–	–	–
0.5	0.1	0.2	–	–	–	–
0.3	0.4	0.1	0.2	0.3	0.4	–
2.2	3.7	3.7	5.4	1.4	0.4	2.0
0.0	–	–	0.0	0.0	–	–
41.0	68.0	50.0	101.8	49.2	69.4	56.3
101.5	*138.9*	*117.3*	*157.4*	*107.0*	*155.7*	*140.2*
–	–	–	–	–	–	–
–	–	–	–	–	–	–
–	–	–	–	–	–	–
3.9	20.8	20.8	2.6	2.9	24.7	24.7
–	–	–	–	–	–	–
20.0	11.0	13.0	63.0	–	55.0	28.0
9.4	14.1	15.6	–	–	–	56.0
2.1	3.0	3.9	–	0.1	10.8	–
–	–	–	–	–	–	–
–	–	–	11.9	14.7	18.3	18.4
8.0	8.6	11.9	–	–	–	–
0.4	0.6	0.5	–	–	–	–
2.2	3.0	2.2	–	–	–	–
2.8	3.9	1.7	–	–	–	–
0.2	0.2	0.1	–	–	–	–
1.2	2.1	2.0	–	–	–	–
0.8	0.5	0.2	–	–	–	5.3
50.8	*67.7*	*71.9*	*77.5*	*17.7*	*108.8*	*132.5*
–	–	–	–	–	–	–
40.6	67.3	70.9	33.9	43.0	70.8	86.4
152.3	*206.6*	*189.2*	*234.9*	*124.7*	*264.5*	*272.7*

11. TECH. COOP. GRANTS

1988	1989	1990	1987	1988	1989	1990
–	–	–	0.1	–	–	–
0.0	0.0	0.0	0.0	0.0	0.0	0.0
1.9	0.9	2.1	1.0	0.4	–	–
5.9	9.1	10.4	–	1.8	2.2	1.4
1.2	–	–	–	–	–	–
–	–	–	–	–	–	–
10.5	16.9	19.8	7.9	6.7	7.2	9.5
11.6	14.4	13.4	6.2	7.1	5.9	7.3
–	–	–	–	–	–	–
–	2.0	0.5	0.1	–	0.0	–
15.0	11.2	2.8	0.2	0.2	0.2	0.3
1.4	1.4	1.4	0.4	1.1	1.2	1.4
–	–	–	–	–	–	–
0.5	0.1	0.2	–	0.0	–	–
0.3	0.4	0.1	–	–	–	0.1
2.2	3.7	3.7	1.9	0.4	–	–
0.0	–	–	0.0	0.0	–	–
41.0	68.0	50.0	20.0	28.0	35.0	33.0
91.5	*128.1*	*104.4*	*37.8*	*45.7*	*51.7*	*53.1*
18.8	40.2	39.9	9.8	12.6	14.4	16.7
–	–	–	–	–	–	–
30.6	56.4	58.0	16.3	15.9	14.3	18.3
110.3	*168.3*	*144.2*	*47.6*	*58.3*	*66.2*	*69.8*

12. TOTAL OOF NET

1988	1989	1990	1987	1988	1989	1990
–	–	–	–	–	–	–
–	–	–	–	–	–	–
–	–	–	–	–	–	–
–	–	–	–	–	–	–
–	–	–	–	–	–	–
–	–	0.0	–	–	–	0.0
–	–	–	–	–	–	–
–	–	–	–	–	–	–
–	–	–	–	–	–	–
–	–	–	–	–	–	–
–	–	–	–	–	–	–
–	–	–	–	–	–	–
–	–	–	-1.0	-1.0	–	–
–	–	0.0	-1.0	-1.0	–	0.0
–	–	0.1	-0.1	–	-0.1	-0.4
–	–	–	–	–	–	–
–	–	0.0	–	–	–	0.0
–	–	0.1	*-1.1*	*-1.0*	*-0.1*	*-0.4*

13. ODF COMMITMENTS: BY PURPOSE %

	1987	1988	1989	1990
Education	3	5	3	–
Health	5	5	8	–
Other Social Infrastr.	3	4	7	–
Water Sanitat. Sewage	17	2	14	–
Energy	1	6	11	–
Telecommunications	0	0	0	–
Transportation	7	2	0	–
Agriculture	6	11	14	–
Extractive Industries	–	–	–	–
Manufacturing	–	–	–	–
Trade Banking Tourism	2	2	4	–
Technical Cooperation	20	50	25	–
Multisector Aid	1	–	0	–
Programme	24	0	–	–
Debt Reorganisation	–	–	–	–
Food Aid	9	13	12	–
Emergency Aid	0	0	1	–
Unspecified	0	0	–	–
TOTAL	100	100	100	–

14. GRANT ELEMENT OF ODA %

DAC COUNTRIES

	1987	1988	1989	1990
Australia	100.0	–	–	–
Austria	100.0	100.0	100.0	–
Belgium	100.0	100.0	100.0	–
Canada	100.0	100.0	100.0	–
Denmark	–	–	–	–
Finland	–	–	–	–
France	100.0	78.8	80.3	–
Germany	100.0	100.0	100.0	–
Ireland	–	–	–	–
Italy	100.0	–	100.0	–
Japan	100.0	100.0	100.0	–
Netherlands	100.0	100.0	100.0	–
New Zealand	–	–	–	–
Norway	–	–	–	–
Sweden	100.0	100.0	100.0	–
Switzerland	100.0	100.0	100.0	–
United Kingdom	100.0	100.0	–	–
United States	100.0	100.0	100.0	–
TOTAL	*100.0*	*95.9*	*95.2*	–
MULTILATERAL	*81.9*	*100.0*	*90.0*	–
ARAB COUNTRIES	–	–	–	–
E.E.C.+ MEMBERS	*100.0*	*89.7*	*89.5*	–
TOTAL	*91.7*	*96.4*	*93.4*	–

15. OTHER AGGREGATES

	1987	1988	1989	1990
OFFICIAL COMMITMENTS:				
TOTAL BILATERAL	157.4	107.0	159.0	140.2
of which:				
Arab Countries	–	–	–	–
C.E.E.C.	–	–	–	–
TOTAL MULTILATERAL	77.5	17.7	108.8	132.5
TOTAL BIL.& MULTIL.	234.9	124.7	267.8	272.7
of which:				
ODA Grants	171.9	115.4	179.6	163.6
ODA Loans	63.0	9.3	84.9	109.1
DISBURSEMENTS:				
DAC COUNTRIES COMBINED				
OFFICIAL & PRIVATE				
GROSS:				
Contractual Lending	11.2	10.0	10.9	13.0
Export Credits, Total	-0.3	0.0	–	0.0
Export Credits, Priv.	-0.3	0.0	–	–
NET:				
Contractual Lending	8.5	8.6	10.5	11.1
Export Credits Total	-1.9	-1.4	0.0	-0.9
PRIVATE SECTOR NET	-5.1	-3.1	-0.6	-1.6
Direct Investment	0.9	0.0	0.3	-0.2
Portfolio Investment	-5.2	-2.6	-0.9	-0.6
Export Credits	-0.9	-0.4	0.0	-0.9
MARKET BORROWING:				
CHANGE IN CLAIMS				
Banks	-2.0	3.0	–	5.0
MEMORANDUM ITEM:				
C.E.E.C. (Gross)	–	–	–	–

1. TOTAL RECEIPTS NET

DAC COUNTRIES	1987	1988	1989	1990
Australia	0.0	0.0	0.0	0.1
Austria	0.0	0.1	0.0	0.0
Belgium	-3.3	0.4	0.8	1.5
Canada	2.9	8.3	9.3	7.2
Denmark	-1.2	-1.3	-1.7	0.3
Finland	0.0	0.1	0.0	–
France	2.2	1.2	3.8	-4.7
Germany	12.4	21.1	24.0	18.4
Ireland	–	–	–	–
Italy	2.2	24.7	-2.1	26.4
Japan	23.5	49.0	39.7	83.1
Netherlands	10.1	4.8	1.8	14.6
New Zealand	–	–	–	–
Norway	0.4	0.3	0.5	0.9
Sweden	–	–	–	0.0
Switzerland	7.2	4.7	7.5	3.7
United Kingdom	-0.2	0.8	1.0	1.5
United States	153.0	156.0	102.0	216.0
TOTAL	*209.2*	*270.2*	*186.6*	*368.9*
MULTILATERAL				
AF.D.F.	–	–	–	–
AF.D.B.	–	–	–	–
AS.D.B	–	–	–	–
CAR.D.B.	–	–	–	–
E.E.C.	4.2	6.1	8.9	8.9
IBRD	-0.4	17.0	2.0	-12.0
IDA	-0.7	-1.0	–	-2.0
I.D.B.	1.8	47.7	21.7	34.1
IFAD	2.7	0.3	–	1.1
I.F.C.	-0.9	–	–	0.8
IMF TRUST FUND	–	–	–	–
U.N. AGENCIES	–	–	–	–
UNDP	5.1	4.1	4.0	4.3
UNTA	0.5	0.4	0.7	0.4
UNICEF	0.8	0.3	1.3	1.5
UNRWA	–	–	–	–
WFP	5.3	15.7	1.6	6.2
UNHCR	15.1	14.0	13.5	11.4
Other Multilateral	1.3	1.5	2.1	1.6
Arab Agencies	-0.4	–	–	–
TOTAL	*34.4*	*106.2*	*55.8*	*56.2*
ARAB COUNTRIES	*–*	*–*	*–*	*–*
E.E.C.+ MEMBERS	*26.3*	*57.9*	*36.4*	*66.8*
TOTAL	*243.6*	*376.4*	*242.4*	*425.1*

2. ODA LOANS GROSS

DAC COUNTRIES	1987	1988	1989	1990
Australia	–	–	–	–
Austria	–	–	–	–
Belgium	–	–	–	–
Canada	0.0	–	–	–
Denmark	–	–	–	–
Finland	–	–	–	–
France	3.1	4.0	2.7	0.9
Germany	5.9	6.9	15.3	7.1
Ireland	–	–	–	–
Italy	–	6.7	3.6	20.4
Japan	17.6	22.7	15.0	55.3
Netherlands	0.5	–	–	6.5
New Zealand	–	–	–	–
Norway	–	–	–	–
Sweden	–	–	–	–
Switzerland	–	0.2	–	–
United Kingdom	0.4	1.1	0.1	–
United States	34.0	28.0	41.0	25.0
TOTAL	*61.4*	*69.7*	*77.7*	*115.3*
MULTILATERAL	*8.7*	*37.3*	*15.9*	*54.5*
ARAB COUNTRIES	*–*	*–*	*–*	*–*
E.E.C.+ MEMBERS	*9.8*	*18.7*	*21.7*	*35.0*
TOTAL	*70.2*	*107.0*	*93.5*	*169.8*

3. TOTAL OFFICIAL GROSS

DAC COUNTRIES	1987	1988	1989	1990
Australia	0.0	0.0	0.0	0.1
Austria	0.0	0.1	0.0	0.0
Belgium	0.5	0.5	0.9	1.0
Canada	3.4	9.4	9.3	7.2
Denmark	0.2	0.2	0.1	0.3
Finland	0.0	0.1	0.0	–
France	3.6	4.9	3.2	1.9
Germany	16.5	22.5	25.9	20.5
Ireland	–	–	–	–
Italy	2.2	7.5	7.3	26.4
Japan	35.0	48.1	40.0	86.4
Netherlands	6.0	6.0	7.0	20.8
New Zealand	–	–	–	–
Norway	0.4	0.3	0.5	0.9
Sweden	–	–	–	0.0
Switzerland	7.2	4.7	7.5	3.7
United Kingdom	1.3	2.2	1.2	1.5
United States	156.0	159.0	105.0	219.0
TOTAL	*232.6*	*265.6*	*208.0*	*389.8*
MULTILATERAL	*71.7*	*164.5*	*71.6*	*192.7*
ARAB COUNTRIES	*–*	*–*	*–*	*–*
E.E.C.+ MEMBERS	*34.6*	*50.0*	*54.4*	*81.3*
TOTAL	*304.3*	*430.1*	*279.6*	*582.5*

4. TOTAL ODA NET

DAC COUNTRIES	1987	1988	1989	1990
Australia	0.0	0.0	0.0	0.1
Austria	0.0	0.1	0.0	0.0
Belgium	0.5	0.5	0.9	1.0
Canada	3.4	3.3	9.3	7.2
Denmark	0.2	0.2	0.1	0.3
Finland	0.0	0.1	0.0	–
France	3.6	4.9	3.2	1.9
Germany	12.7	19.5	22.6	14.5
Ireland	–	–	–	–
Italy	2.2	7.5	7.3	26.4
Japan	35.0	48.1	40.0	85.1
Netherlands	3.5	5.7	7.0	19.8
New Zealand	–	–	–	–
Norway	0.4	0.3	0.5	0.9
Sweden	–	–	–	0.0
Switzerland	7.2	4.7	7.5	3.7
United Kingdom	0.7	2.2	1.2	1.5
United States	153.0	155.0	102.0	215.0
TOTAL	*222.5*	*252.1*	*201.7*	*377.5*
MULTILATERAL				
AF.D.F.	–	–	–	–
AF.D.B.	–	–	–	–
AS.D.B	–	–	–	–
CAR.D.B.	–	–	–	–
E.E.C.	4.2	6.1	8.9	8.9
IBRD	–	–	–	–
IDA	-0.7	-1.0	–	-2.0
I.D.B.	1.7	27.9	8.8	37.4
IFAD	2.7	0.3	–	1.1
I.F.C.	–	–	–	–
IMF TRUST FUND	–	–	–	–
U.N. AGENCIES	–	–	–	–
UNDP	5.1	4.1	4.0	4.3
UNTA	0.5	0.4	0.7	0.4
UNICEF	0.8	0.3	1.3	1.5
UNRWA	–	–	–	–
WFP	5.3	15.7	1.6	6.2
UNHCR	15.1	14.0	13.5	11.4
Other Multilateral	1.3	1.5	2.1	1.6
Arab Agencies	-0.4	–	–	–
TOTAL	*35.5*	*69.4*	*40.9*	*70.7*
ARAB COUNTRIES	*–*	*–*	*–*	*–*
E.E.C.+ MEMBERS	*27.6*	*46.7*	*51.1*	*74.3*
TOTAL	*258.0*	*321.5*	*242.5*	*448.2*

5. ODA LOANS NET

DAC COUNTRIES	1987	1988	1989	1990
Australia	–	–	–	–
Austria	–	–	–	–
Belgium	–	–	–	–
Canada	0.0	–	–	–
Denmark	–	–	–	–
Finland	–	–	–	–
France	3.1	4.0	2.7	0.9
Germany	5.6	6.9	15.3	6.9
Ireland	–	–	–	–
Italy	–	6.7	3.6	20.4
Japan	17.6	22.7	15.0	54.0
Netherlands	0.5	-0.3	–	5.5
New Zealand	–	–	–	–
Norway	–	–	–	–
Sweden	–	–	–	–
Switzerland	–	0.2	–	–
United Kingdom	-0.2	1.1	0.1	–
United States	32.0	25.0	38.0	22.0
TOTAL	*58.5*	*66.4*	*74.7*	*109.7*
MULTILATERAL	*3.0*	*25.5*	*8.8*	*36.5*
ARAB COUNTRIES	*–*	*–*	*–*	*–*
E.E.C.+ MEMBERS	*8.9*	*18.4*	*21.7*	*33.7*
TOTAL	*61.5*	*91.9*	*83.5*	*146.3*

6. TOTAL OFFICIAL NET

DAC COUNTRIES	1987	1988	1989	1990
Australia	0.0	0.0	0.0	0.1
Austria	0.0	0.1	0.0	0.0
Belgium	0.5	0.5	0.9	1.0
Canada	2.9	8.3	9.3	7.2
Denmark	0.2	0.2	0.1	0.3
Finland	0.0	0.1	0.0	–
France	3.6	4.9	3.2	1.9
Germany	16.2	20.3	25.7	19.8
Ireland	–	–	–	–
Italy	2.2	7.5	7.3	26.4
Japan	35.0	48.1	40.0	85.1
Netherlands	5.6	5.6	6.5	12.9
New Zealand	–	–	–	–
Norway	0.4	0.3	0.5	0.9
Sweden	–	–	–	0.0
Switzerland	7.2	4.7	7.5	3.7
United Kingdom	-0.2	0.8	1.2	1.5
United States	153.0	156.0	102.0	216.0
TOTAL	*226.7*	*257.4*	*204.3*	*376.8*
MULTILATERAL	*34.4*	*106.2*	*55.8*	*56.2*
ARAB COUNTRIES	*–*	*–*	*–*	*–*
E.E.C.+ MEMBERS	*32.3*	*46.0*	*53.7*	*72.7*
TOTAL	*261.1*	*363.6*	*260.1*	*433.0*

7. TOTAL ODA GROSS

	1987
Australia	0.0
Austria	0.0
Belgium	0.5
Canada	3.4
Denmark	0.2
Finland	0.0
France	3.6
Germany	13.0
Ireland	–
Italy	2.2
Japan	35.0
Netherlands	3.5
New Zealand	–
Norway	0.4
Sweden	–
Switzerland	7.2
United Kingdom	1.3
United States	155.0
TOTAL	*225.4*
AF.D.F.	–
AF.D.B.	–
AS.D.B	–
CAR.D.B.	–
E.E.C.	4.2
IBRD	–
IDA	–
I.D.B.	6.3
IFAD	2.7
I.F.C.	–
IMF TRUST FUND	–
U.N. AGENCIES	–
UNDP	5.1
UNTA	0.5
UNICEF	0.8
UNRWA	–
WFP	5.3
UNHCR	15.1
Other Multilateral	1.3
Arab Agencies	–
TOTAL	*41.2*
ARAB COUNTRIES	*–*
E.E.C.+ MEMBERS	*28.5*
TOTAL	*266.7*

8. GRANTS

	1987
Australia	0.0
Austria	0.0
Belgium	0.5
Canada	3.4
Denmark	0.2
Finland	0.0
France	0.5
Germany	7.1
Ireland	–
Italy	2.2
Japan	17.4
Netherlands	2.9
New Zealand	–
Norway	0.4
Sweden	–
Switzerland	7.2
United Kingdom	0.9
United States	121.0
TOTAL	*164.0*
MULTILATERAL	*32.5*
ARAB COUNTRIES	*–*
E.E.C.+ MEMBERS	*18.7*
TOTAL	*196.5*

9. TOTAL OOF GROSS

	1987
Australia	–
Austria	–
Belgium	–
Canada	–
Denmark	–
Finland	–
France	–
Germany	3.6
Ireland	–
Italy	–
Japan	–
Netherlands	2.6
New Zealand	–
Norway	–
Sweden	–
Switzerland	–
United Kingdom	–
United States	1.0
TOTAL	*7.2*
MULTILATERAL	*30.5*
ARAB COUNTRIES	*–*
E.E.C.+ MEMBERS	*6.1*
TOTAL	*37.7*

10. ODA COMMITMENTS

1988	1989	1990	1987	1988	1989	1990
0.0	0.0	0.1	0.0	0.1	0.0	0.0
0.1	0.0	0.0	0.0	0.1	0.0	0.0
0.5	0.9	1.0	0.1	0.2	0.9	1.0
3.3	9.3	7.2	18.9	14.6	18.6	1.9
0.2	0.1	0.3	0.5	–	–	2.0
0.1	0.0	–	–	–	0.0	0.2
4.9	3.2	1.9	3.1	6.1	0.5	3.5
19.5	22.6	14.8	18.6	17.9	37.6	4.7
–	–	–	–	–	–	–
7.5	7.3	26.4	2.4	34.7	7.9	1.8
48.1	40.0	86.4	10.7	41.5	31.1	72.6
6.0	7.0	20.8	3.2	5.7	18.3	16.9
–	–	–	–	–	–	–
0.3	0.5	0.9	0.6	–	–	–
–	–	0.0	–	–	–	–
4.7	7.5	3.7	1.9	5.8	2.3	2.4
2.2	1.2	1.5	0.9	1.1	1.1	1.5
158.0	105.0	218.0	201.4	142.7	84.8	188.2
255.4	*204.7*	*383.1*	*262.4*	*270.2*	*203.1*	*296.7*
–	–	–	–	–	–	–
–	–	–	–	–	–	–
–	–	–	–	–	–	–
6.1	8.9	8.9	17.2	11.6	3.6	3.6
–	–	–	–	–	–	–
–	–	–	–	–	–	–
38.4	14.7	53.3	–	12.9	–	90.0
0.5	1.2	1.2	6.3	–	–	–
–	–	–	–	–	–	–
–	–	–	28.0	36.1	23.2	25.3
4.1	4.0	4.3	–	–	–	–
0.4	0.7	0.4	–	–	–	–
0.3	1.3	1.5	–	–	–	–
–	–	–	–	–	–	–
15.7	1.6	6.2	–	–	–	–
14.0	13.5	11.4	–	–	–	–
1.5	2.1	1.6	–	–	–	–
–	–	–	3.5	–	–	–
81.1	*47.9*	*88.7*	*54.9*	*60.6*	*26.8*	*118.9*
–	–	–	–	–	–	–
47.0	*51.1*	*75.6*	*46.0*	*77.1*	*69.9*	*35.0*
336.6	*252.6*	*471.7*	*317.4*	*330.7*	*229.9*	*415.6*

11. TECH. COOP. GRANTS

1988	1989	1990	1987	1988	1989	1990
0.0	0.0	0.1	0.0	–	–	–
0.1	0.0	0.0	0.0	0.1	0.0	0.0
0.5	0.9	1.0	0.5	0.4	0.8	0.8
3.3	9.3	7.2	–	1.2	2.4	2.0
0.2	0.1	0.3	–	–	–	–
0.1	0.0	–	0.0	–	–	–
0.9	0.6	0.9	0.5	0.4	0.5	0.6
12.6	7.3	7.6	3.3	4.0	2.5	2.8
–	–	–	–	–	–	–
0.8	3.7	6.0	2.2	0.6	0.4	0.0
25.4	25.0	31.1	5.0	6.6	7.4	8.7
6.0	7.0	14.3	2.2	5.4	6.6	11.2
–	–	–	–	–	–	–
0.3	0.5	0.9	0.0	0.1	0.1	–
–	–	0.0	–	–	–	–
4.5	7.5	3.7	1.6	1.6	–	–
1.1	1.1	1.5	0.9	1.0	1.0	1.4
130.0	64.0	193.0	24.0	35.0	47.0	49.0
185.8	*127.0*	*267.8*	*40.3*	*56.4*	*68.6*	*76.5*
43.8	*32.1*	*34.2*	*23.3*	*22.1*	*21.6*	*19.1*
–	–	–	–	–	–	–
28.3	*29.5*	*40.6*	*10.3*	*13.6*	*11.7*	*16.8*
229.6	*159.1*	*301.9*	*63.6*	*78.6*	*90.3*	*95.6*

12. TOTAL OOF NET

1988	1989	1990	1987	1988	1989	1990
–	–	–	–	–	–	–
–	–	–	–	–	–	–
–	–	–	–	–	–	–
6.2	–	–	-0.6	5.0	–	–
–	–	–	–	–	–	–
–	–	–	–	–	–	–
3.0	3.3	5.8	3.6	0.8	3.1	5.2
–	–	–	–	–	–	–
–	–	–	–	–	–	–
–	–	–	2.1	-0.1	-0.5	-6.9
–	–	–	–	–	–	–
–	–	–	–	–	–	–
–	–	–	–	–	–	–
–	–	–	-0.9	-1.4	–	–
1.0	–	1.0	–	1.0	–	1.0
10.2	*3.3*	*6.8*	*4.2*	*5.3*	*2.6*	*-0.7*
83.3	*23.7*	*104.0*	*-1.1*	*36.8*	*15.0*	*-14.6*
–	–	–	–	–	–	–
3.0	*3.3*	*5.8*	*4.8*	*-0.7*	*2.6*	*-1.7*
93.5	*27.0*	*110.8*	*3.1*	*42.1*	*17.6*	*-15.2*

13. ODF COMMITMENTS: BY PURPOSE %

	1987	1988	1989	1990
Education	4	6	6	–
Health	9	5	5	–
Other Social Infrastr.	8	2	9	–
Water Sanitat. Sewage	13	11	6	–
Energy	2	–	5	–
Telecommunications	0	–	–	–
Transportation	3	–	–	–
Agriculture	9	17	8	–
Extractive Industries	–	–	1	–
Manufacturing	0	–	–	–
Trade Banking Tourism	1	2	1	–
Technical Cooperation	24	20	45	–
Multisector Aid	1	0	–	–
Programme	22	31	5	–
Debt Reorganisation	–	–	–	–
Food Aid	4	5	10	–
Emergency Aid	0	0	0	–
Unspecified	0	0	0	–
TOTAL	100	100	100	–

14. GRANT ELEMENT OF ODA %

DAC COUNTRIES	1987	1988	1989	1990
Australia	100.0	100.0	100.0	–
Austria	100.0	100.0	100.0	–
Belgium	100.0	100.0	100.0	–
Canada	100.0	100.0	100.0	–
Denmark	100.0	–	–	–
Finland	–	–	100.0	–
France	100.0	71.7	100.0	–
Germany	94.6	94.8	100.0	–
Ireland	–	–	–	–
Italy	100.0	66.9	100.0	–
Japan	100.0	100.0	100.0	–
Netherlands	100.0	100.0	80.6	–
New Zealand	–	–	–	–
Norway	100.0	–	–	–
Sweden	–	–	–	–
Switzerland	100.0	100.0	100.0	–
United Kingdom	100.0	100.0	100.0	–
United States	94.8	96.2	93.1	–
TOTAL	*95.6*	*92.8*	*95.0*	–
MULTILATERAL	*80.4*	*100.0*	*100.0*	–
ARAB COUNTRIES	–	–	–	–
E.E.C.+ MEMBERS	97.7	81.7	93.2	–
TOTAL	*90.0*	*93.9*	*95.6*	–

15. OTHER AGGREGATES

	1987	1988	1989	1990
OFFICIAL COMMITMENTS:				
TOTAL BILATERAL	266.2	276.4	204.4	338.2
of which:				
Arab Countries	–	–	–	–
C.E.E.C.				
TOTAL MULTILATERAL	59.3	173.6	26.8	223.7
TOTAL BIL.& MULTIL.	325.6	449.9	231.2	561.9
of which:				
ODA Grants	263.5	256.8	187.5	258.1
ODA Loans	53.9	74.0	42.4	157.5
DISBURSEMENTS:				
DAC COUNTRIES COMBINED				
OFFICIAL & PRIVATE				
GROSS:				
Contractual Lending	68.2	110.8	113.9	123.5
Export Credits, Total	-0.3	37.2	36.2	7.2
Export Credits, Priv.	-0.3	31.0	32.9	1.5
NET:				
Contractual Lending	45.0	94.6	77.6	90.8
Export Credits Total	-19.3	28.1	3.6	-12.5
PRIVATE SECTOR NET	-17.5	12.8	-17.7	-7.9
Direct Investment	0.8	0.8	0.2	6.3
Portfolio Investment	-0.6	-11.1	-18.2	4.0
Export Credits	-17.7	23.0	0.3	-18.2
MARKET BORROWING:				
CHANGE IN CLAIMS				
Banks	-8.0	-15.0	-94.0	-110.0
MEMORANDUM ITEM:				
C.E.E.C. (Gross)	–	–	–	–

	1987	1988	1989	1990	1987	1988	1989	1990	1987
1. TOTAL RECEIPTS NET					**4. TOTAL ODA NET**				**7. TOTAL ODA GROSS**
DAC COUNTRIES									
Australia	425.9	495.4	-568.3	661.2	6.9	5.4	3.2	4.3	Australia 6.9
Austria	0.1	0.6	0.9	1.9	0.0	0.3	0.1	-0.1	Austria 0.0
Belgium	12.6	-83.0	-27.8	140.5	0.1	0.0	0.1	0.1	Belgium 0.1
Canada	-0.2	-0.3	-0.2	0.4	0.1	0.0	0.0	–	Canada 0.1
Denmark	-13.4	-0.2	–	2.9	–	–	–	–	Denmark –
Finland	2.7	2.9	3.0	0.2	0.0	0.1	0.1	0.2	Finland 0.0
France	184.8	110.5	-93.2	-3.6	2.3	2.4	2.1	2.6	France 2.3
Germany	-31.6	125.9	42.7	18.4	2.4	1.7	1.5	2.2	Germany 2.4
Ireland	–	–	–	–	–	–	–	–	Ireland –
Italy	9.3	14.1	136.6	-1.0	0.1	–	–	–	Italy 0.1
Japan	1333.8	1589.9	2111.7	2271.0	2.6	2.9	4.0	9.2	Japan 2.6
Netherlands	266.0	-10.6	-48.5	209.9	0.2	0.1	0.1	0.2	Netherlands 0.2
New Zealand	–	–	–	0.2	–	–	–	0.2	New Zealand –
Norway	0.1	1.8	0.0	1.5	0.1	0.1	–	–	Norway 0.1
Sweden	-0.8	–	21.2	0.4	–	–	–	–	Sweden –
Switzerland	0.0	–	0.0	–	0.0	–	0.0	–	Switzerland 0.0
United Kingdom	557.4	-376.4	-702.2	210.9	0.4	0.5	0.4	0.5	United Kingdom 0.4
United States	1453.0	727.0	362.0	421.0	–	–	–	–	United States –
TOTAL	*4199.6*	*2597.7*	*1238.0*	*3935.6*	*15.0*	*13.6*	*11.7*	*19.4*	*TOTAL 15.0*
MULTILATERAL									
AF.D.F.	–	–	–	–	–	–	–	–	AF.D.F. –
AF.D.B.	–	–	–	–	–	–	–	–	AF.D.B. –
AS.D.B	-39.5	–	–	–	–	–	–	–	AS.D.B –
CAR.D.B.	–	–	–	–	–	–	–	–	CAR.D.B. –
E.E.C.	–	–	2.4	2.4	–	–	2.4	2.4	E.E.C. –
IBRD	–	–	–	–	–	–	–	–	IBRD –
IDA	–	–	–	–	–	–	–	–	IDA –
I.D.B.	–	–	–	–	–	–	–	–	I.D.B. –
IFAD	–	–	–	–	–	–	–	–	IFAD –
I.F.C.	–	–	–	–	–	–	–	–	I.F.C. –
IMF TRUST FUND	–	–	–	–	–	–	–	–	IMF TRUST FUND –
U.N. AGENCIES	–	–	–	–	–	–	–	–	U.N. AGENCIES –
UNDP	0.1	–	0.0	0.1	0.1	–	0.0	0.1	UNDP 0.1
UNTA	0.1	0.0	0.1	0.1	0.1	0.0	0.1	0.1	UNTA 0.1
UNICEF	–	–	–	–	–	–	–	–	UNICEF –
UNRWA	–	–	–	–	–	–	–	–	UNRWA –
WFP	–	–	–	–	–	–	–	–	WFP –
UNHCR	4.3	8.5	26.4	15.5	4.3	8.5	26.4	15.5	UNHCR 4.3
Other Multilateral	0.0	0.0	0.1	–	0.0	0.0	0.1	–	Other Multilateral 0.0
Arab Agencies	–	–	–	–	–	–	–	–	Arab Agencies –
TOTAL	*-35.1*	*8.5*	*29.0*	*18.2*	*4.4*	*8.5*	*29.0*	*18.2*	*TOTAL 4.4*
ARAB COUNTRIES	–	–	–	–	–	–	–	–	**ARAB COUNTRIES** –
E.E.C.+ MEMBERS	*985.0*	*-219.7*	*-689.9*	*580.3*	*5.4*	*4.8*	*6.6*	*8.0*	*E.E.C.+ MEMBERS 5.4*
TOTAL	*4164.5*	*2606.3*	*1267.0*	*3953.8*	*19.4*	*22.1*	*40.6*	*37.6*	*TOTAL 19.4*
2. ODA LOANS GROSS					**5. ODA LOANS NET**				**8. GRANTS**
DAC COUNTRIES									
Australia	–	–	–	–	–	–	–	–	Australia 6.9
Austria	–	0.3	0.1	0.1	–	0.3	0.1	-0.2	Austria 0.0
Belgium	–	–	–	–	–	–	–	–	Belgium 0.1
Canada	–	–	–	–	–	–	–	–	Canada 0.1
Denmark	–	–	–	–	–	–	–	–	Denmark –
Finland	–	–	–	–	–	–	–	–	Finland 0.0
France	–	–	–	–	–	–	–	–	France 2.3
Germany	–	–	–	–	–	–	–	–	Germany 2.4
Ireland	–	–	–	–	–	–	–	–	Ireland –
Italy	–	–	–	–	–	–	–	–	Italy 0.1
Japan	0.3	–	–	–	0.3	0.0	0.0	0.0	Japan 2.3
Netherlands	–	–	–	–	–	–	–	–	Netherlands 0.2
New Zealand	–	–	–	–	–	–	–	–	New Zealand –
Norway	–	–	–	–	–	–	–	–	Norway 0.1
Sweden	–	–	–	–	–	–	–	–	Sweden –
Switzerland	–	–	–	–	–	–	–	–	Switzerland 0.0
United Kingdom	–	–	–	–	–	–	–	–	United Kingdom 0.4
United States	–	–	–	–	–	–	–	–	United States –
TOTAL	*0.3*	*0.3*	*0.1*	*0.1*	*0.3*	*0.3*	*0.0*	*-0.2*	*TOTAL 14.7*
MULTILATERAL	–	–	–	–	–	–	–	–	*MULTILATERAL 4.4*
ARAB COUNTRIES	–	–	–	–	–	–	–	–	**ARAB COUNTRIES** –
E.E.C.+ MEMBERS	–	–	–	–	–	–	–	–	*E.E.C.+ MEMBERS 5.4*
TOTAL	*0.3*	*0.3*	*0.1*	*0.1*	*0.3*	*0.3*	*0.0*	*-0.2*	*TOTAL 19.1*
3. TOTAL OFFICIAL GROSS					**6. TOTAL OFFICIAL NET**				**9. TOTAL OOF GROSS**
DAC COUNTRIES									
Australia	6.9	5.4	3.2	4.3	6.9	5.4	3.2	4.3	Australia –
Austria	0.0	0.3	0.1	0.3	0.0	0.3	0.1	-0.1	Austria –
Belgium	1.0	0.0	0.6	0.5	1.0	0.0	0.6	0.5	Belgium 0.9
Canada	0.1	0.0	0.0	–	0.1	0.0	0.0	–	Canada –
Denmark	–	–	–	–	-0.4	-0.2	–	–	Denmark –
Finland	0.0	0.1	0.1	0.2	0.0	0.1	0.1	0.2	Finland –
France	2.3	2.4	2.1	2.6	2.3	2.4	2.1	2.6	France –
Germany	2.6	2.6	1.8	3.0	2.6	2.6	1.8	3.0	Germany 0.2
Ireland	–	–	–	–	–	–	–	–	Ireland –
Italy	0.1	–	–	–	0.1	–	–	–	Italy –
Japan	40.4	2.9	4.0	9.3	40.4	2.9	4.0	9.2	Japan 37.9
Netherlands	0.2	0.1	0.1	0.2	0.2	0.1	0.1	0.2	Netherlands –
New Zealand	–	–	–	0.2	–	–	–	0.2	New Zealand –
Norway	0.1	0.1	–	–	0.1	0.1	–	–	Norway –
Sweden	–	–	–	–	–	–	–	–	Sweden –
Switzerland	0.0	–	0.0	–	0.0	–	0.0	–	Switzerland –
United Kingdom	0.4	0.5	0.4	0.5	0.4	0.5	0.4	0.5	United Kingdom –
United States	–	–	–	–	-8.0	-8.0	-8.0	-8.0	United States –
TOTAL	*54.0*	*14.4*	*12.5*	*21.0*	*45.6*	*6.2*	*4.5*	*12.6*	*TOTAL 39.0*
MULTILATERAL	*4.4*	*8.5*	*29.0*	*18.2*	*-35.1*	*8.5*	*29.0*	*18.2*	*MULTILATERAL –*
ARAB COUNTRIES	–	–	–	–	–	–	–	–	**ARAB COUNTRIES** –
E.E.C.+ MEMBERS	*6.5*	*5.7*	*7.4*	*9.2*	*6.1*	*5.4*	*7.4*	*9.2*	*E.E.C.+ MEMBERS 1.1*
TOTAL	*58.4*	*23.0*	*41.5*	*39.2*	*10.5*	*14.7*	*33.4*	*30.8*	*TOTAL 39.0*

Left panel

1988	1989	1990		1987	1988	1989	1990

10. ODA COMMITMENTS

1988	1989	1990		1987	1988	1989	1990
5.4	3.2	4.3		6.7	2.8	4.8	4.2
0.3	0.1	0.3		0.0	0.6	0.0	0.1
0.0	0.1	0.1		0.0	0.1	0.1	0.1
0.0	0.0	–		0.1	0.0	0.0	–
–	–	–		–	–	–	–
0.1	0.1	0.2		–	–	–	0.4
2.4	2.1	2.6		2.3	2.4	2.1	2.6
1.7	1.5	2.2		2.4	2.2	1.4	2.6
–	–	–		–	–	–	–
–	–	–		0.1	–	–	–
2.9	4.0	9.3		3.1	2.8	4.7	9.1
0.1	0.1	0.2		0.2	0.1	0.1	0.2
–	–	0.2		–	–	–	–
0.1	–	–		–	–	–	–
–	–	–		–	–	–	–
–	0.0	–		0.0	–	–	–
0.5	0.4	0.5		0.4	0.5	0.4	0.5
–	–	–		0.1	0.2	–	–
13.6	*11.7*	*19.8*		*15.3*	*11.7*	*13.6*	*19.7*
–	–	–		–	–	–	–
–	–	–		–	–	–	–
–	–	–		–	–	–	–
–	2.4	2.4		–	–	5.6	5.6
–	–	–		–	–	–	–
–	–	–		–	–	–	–
–	–	–		–	–	–	–
–	–	–		–	–	–	–
–	–	–		4.4	8.5	26.6	15.8
–	0.0	0.1		–	–	–	–
0.0	0.1	0.1		–	–	–	–
–	–	–		–	–	–	–
–	–	–		–	–	–	–
–	–	–		–	–	–	–
8.5	26.4	15.5		–	–	–	–
0.0	0.1	–		–	–	–	–
–	–	–		–	–	–	–
8.5	*29.0*	*18.2*		*4.4*	*8.5*	*32.2*	*21.4*
–	–	–		–	–	–	–
4.8	*6.6*	*8.0*		*5.3*	*5.3*	*9.7*	*11.6*
22.1	*40.7*	*38.0*		*19.7*	*20.2*	*45.8*	*41.1*

11. TECH. COOP. GRANTS

1988	1989	1990		1987	1988	1989	1990
5.4	3.2	4.3		6.9	5.4	3.1	4.3
–	0.0	0.1		–	–	0.0	0.1
0.0	0.1	0.1		0.0	–	–	–
0.0	0.0	–		–	–	–	–
–	–	–		–	–	–	–
0.1	0.1	0.2		0.0	–	–	–
2.4	2.1	2.6		2.3	2.4	2.1	2.6
1.7	1.5	2.2		2.4	1.7	1.4	1.7
–	–	–		–	–	–	–
–	–	–		0.1	–	–	–
2.9	4.0	9.3		2.3	2.6	4.0	9.0
0.1	0.1	0.2		0.2	0.1	0.1	0.1
–	–	0.2		–	–	–	0.2
0.1	–	–		–	–	–	–
–	–	–		–	–	–	–
–	0.0	–		–	–	–	–
0.5	0.4	0.5		0.3	0.4	0.4	0.3
–	–	–		–	–	–	–
13.3	*11.6*	*19.7*		*14.5*	*12.6*	*11.2*	*18.3*
8.5	29.0	18.2		4.4	8.5	26.6	15.8
–	–	–		–	–	–	–
4.8	*6.6*	*8.0*		*5.3*	*4.7*	*4.0*	*4.7*
21.8	*40.6*	*37.9*		*18.9*	*21.1*	*37.8*	*34.1*

12. TOTAL OOF NET

1988	1989	1990		1987	1988	1989	1990
–	–	–		–	–	–	–
–	0.5	0.4		0.9	–	0.5	0.4
–	–	–		-0.4	-0.2	–	–
–	–	–		–	–	–	–
–	–	–		–	–	–	–
0.9	0.3	0.8		0.2	0.9	0.3	0.8
–	–	–		–	–	–	–
–	–	–		37.9	–	–	–
–	–	–		–	–	–	–
–	–	–		–	–	–	–
–	–	–		–	–	–	–
–	–	–		–	–	–	–
–	–	–		–	–	–	–
–	–	–		-8.0	-8.0	-8.0	-8.0
0.9	0.8	1.2		30.6	-7.4	-7.2	-6.8
–	–	–		-39.5	–	–	–
–	–	–		–	–	–	–
0.9	0.8	1.2		0.7	0.6	0.8	1.2
0.9	*0.8*	*1.2*		*-8.9*	*-7.4*	*-7.2*	*-6.8*

Right panel

13. ODF COMMITMENTS: BY PURPOSE %

	1987	1988	1989	1990
Education	1	–	1	–
Health	–	2	–	–
Other Social Infrastr.	–	–	–	–
Water Sanitat. Sewage	–	–	–	–
Energy	5	–	0	–
Telecommunications	–	–	–	–
Transportation	–	–	–	–
Agriculture	–	–	–	–
Extractive Industries	–	–	–	–
Manufacturing	1	1	–	–
Trade Banking Tourism	–	–	–	–
Technical Cooperation	92	97	99	–
Multisector Aid	–	–	–	–
Programme	–	–	–	–
Debt Reorganisation	–	–	–	–
Food Aid	–	–	–	–
Emergency Aid	0	0	–	–
Unspecified	–	–	–	–
TOTAL	100	100	100	–

14. GRANT ELEMENT OF ODA %

DAC COUNTRIES	1987	1988	1989	1990
Australia	100.0	100.0	100.0	–
Austria	100.0	35.2	100.0	–
Belgium	100.0	100.0	100.0	–
Canada	100.0	100.0	100.0	–
Denmark	–	–	–	–
Finland	–	–	–	–
France	100.0	100.0	100.0	–
Germany	100.0	100.0	100.0	–
Ireland	–	–	–	–
Italy	100.0	–	–	–
Japan	93.7	100.0	100.0	–
Netherlands	100.0	100.0	100.0	–
New Zealand	–	–	–	–
Norway	–	–	–	–
Sweden	–	–	–	–
Switzerland	100.0	–	–	–
United Kingdom	100.0	100.0	100.0	–
United States	100.0	100.0	–	–
TOTAL	*98.7*	*96.6*	*100.0*	–
MULTILATERAL	*100.0*	*100.0*	*100.0*	–
ARAB COUNTRIES	–	–	–	–
E.E.C.+ MEMBERS	*100.0*	*100.0*	*100.0*	–
TOTAL	*99.0*	*98.1*	*100.0*	–

15. OTHER AGGREGATES

	1987	1988	1989	1990
OFFICIAL COMMITMENTS:				
TOTAL BILATERAL	58.9	11.7	34.4	20.1
of which:				
Arab Countries	–	–	–	–
C.E.E.C.	–	–	–	–
TOTAL MULTILATERAL	4.4	8.5	32.2	21.4
TOTAL BIL.& MULTIL.	63.3	20.2	66.5	41.5
of which:				
ODA Grants	19.4	19.6	45.8	41.1
ODA Loans	0.3	0.6	–	–
DISBURSEMENTS:				
DAC COUNTRIES COMBINED				
OFFICIAL & PRIVATE				
GROSS:				
Contractual Lending	518.3	-349.5	542.8	436.9
Export Credits, Total	480.1	-349.8	542.8	436.7
Export Credits, Priv.	480.1	-349.8	542.9	436.7
NET:				
Contractual Lending	142.9	-587.1	-277.3	156.5
Export Credits Total	104.7	-587.4	-277.4	156.8
PRIVATE SECTOR NET	4154.0	2591.5	1233.6	3922.9
Direct Investment	3298.2	2627.3	1076.5	2172.8
Portfolio Investment	742.7	543.4	426.4	1585.4
Export Credits	113.2	-579.2	-269.2	164.7
MARKET BORROWING:				
CHANGE IN CLAIMS				
Banks	–	–	–	–
MEMORANDUM ITEM:				
C.E.E.C. (Gross)	–	–	–	–

1. TOTAL RECEIPTS NET

DAC COUNTRIES	1987	1988	1989	1990
Australia	1.3	0.1	8.7	48.2
Austria	-7.1	-6.2	7.9	-1.5
Belgium	26.9	8.3	78.7	-17.5
Canada	75.0	80.2	71.7	94.9
Denmark	41.6	33.2	70.2	37.9
Finland	2.1	1.4	0.8	3.5
France	72.2	-70.2	85.8	89.7
Germany	33.6	136.5	585.6	382.2
Ireland	0.1	0.0	0.0	0.0
Italy	31.6	64.8	60.9	24.1
Japan	649.3	1122.8	1096.9	514.4
Netherlands	124.9	134.5	91.2	172.3
New Zealand	0.1	0.1	0.1	0.2
Norway	35.0	24.4	17.3	18.9
Sweden	280.0	56.4	528.5	654.8
Switzerland	23.5	22.2	19.7	12.9
United Kingdom	415.3	-63.4	296.3	69.5
United States	126.0	118.0	174.0	80.0
TOTAL	1931.4	1663.2	3194.3	2184.5
MULTILATERAL				
AF.D.F.	–	–	–	–
AF.D.B.	–	–	–	–
AS.D.B	11.6	56.9	82.0	202.4
CAR.D.B.	–	–	–	–
E.E.C.	105.0	153.3	111.7	111.7
IBRD	708.1	1225.0	1114.0	970.0
IDA	656.2	820.0	473.0	540.0
I.D.B.	–	–	–	–
IFAD	37.9	9.4	10.2	19.2
I.F.C.	-41.0	31.0	24.0	79.9
IMF TRUST FUND	–	–	–	–
U.N. AGENCIES	–	–	–	–
UNDP	29.8	28.1	24.1	23.0
UNTA	5.7	2.6	6.6	2.2
UNICEF	42.5	56.9	72.5	79.2
UNRWA	–	–	–	–
WFP	23.4	60.0	39.0	44.1
UNHCR	–	3.8	3.6	4.5
Other Multilateral	13.1	16.9	18.7	24.1
Arab Agencies	-1.9	16.5	-2.5	–
TOTAL	1590.6	2480.4	1976.9	2100.1
ARAB COUNTRIES	-23.0	-20.3	1.1	7.3
E.E.C.+ MEMBERS	851.3	397.1	1380.3	869.8
TOTAL	3499.0	4123.2	5172.4	4291.9

2. ODA LOANS GROSS

DAC COUNTRIES	1987	1988	1989	1990
Australia	–	–	–	–
Austria	0.0	–	9.2	0.2
Belgium	–	–	–	7.5
Canada	7.1	–	–	–
Denmark	9.5	8.3	3.2	0.1
Finland	0.7	0.1	0.2	2.4
France	71.9	48.9	75.4	57.4
Germany	178.0	198.9	173.0	232.9
Ireland	–	–	–	–
Italy	40.8	52.8	63.1	11.7
Japan	362.4	237.7	318.5	149.6
Netherlands	56.5	59.2	40.1	91.0
New Zealand	–	–	–	–
Norway	3.1	–	–	–
Sweden	–	–	–	–
Switzerland	1.4	0.9	4.6	3.2
United Kingdom	–	–	1.8	5.2
United States	32.0	51.0	30.0	15.0
TOTAL	763.3	657.6	719.1	576.1
MULTILATERAL	768.2	933.5	585.3	677.4
ARAB COUNTRIES	9.1	4.8	25.0	17.3
E.E.C.+ MEMBERS	356.6	368.0	356.7	405.8
TOTAL	1540.5	1595.9	1329.4	1270.8

3. TOTAL OFFICIAL GROSS

DAC COUNTRIES	1987	1988	1989	1990
Australia	1.5	2.4	9.4	48.4
Austria	0.6	0.5	9.8	1.5
Belgium	1.3	1.5	1.6	9.1
Canada	76.1	97.0	83.2	106.1
Denmark	43.8	35.6	49.7	38.7
Finland	0.9	1.2	1.2	3.1
France	80.1	63.2	114.0	72.1
Germany	240.7	267.3	221.4	331.2
Ireland	0.1	0.0	0.0	0.0
Italy	43.8	58.1	75.7	17.3
Japan	415.5	564.7	588.0	304.0
Netherlands	132.8	148.4	127.8	188.0
New Zealand	0.1	0.1	0.1	0.2
Norway	30.4	27.8	24.9	25.6
Sweden	43.6	56.4	203.1	59.0
Switzerland	23.5	22.2	19.7	13.5
United Kingdom	128.5	180.0	163.1	156.0
United States	158.0	231.0	192.0	96.0
TOTAL	1421.3	1757.4	1884.6	1469.9
MULTILATERAL	2142.8	2874.6	2423.8	2655.3
ARAB COUNTRIES	9.2	5.0	25.8	17.3
E.E.C.+ MEMBERS	776.2	907.4	864.9	924.1
TOTAL	3573.3	4636.9	4334.1	4142.5

4. TOTAL ODA NET

DAC COUNTRIES	1987	1988	1989	1990
Australia	1.5	2.4	9.4	20.2
Austria	-1.4	-1.3	8.0	-1.2
Belgium	-1.9	-2.7	-2.7	4.3
Canada	38.5	49.2	24.3	22.6
Denmark	42.1	34.0	48.2	37.1
Finland	0.9	1.2	1.2	3.0
France	69.4	52.9	103.4	51.5
Germany	136.6	152.3	122.5	169.2
Ireland	0.1	0.0	0.0	0.0
Italy	43.0	56.7	71.0	14.3
Japan	303.9	179.5	257.2	87.3
Netherlands	104.0	115.2	92.4	148.5
New Zealand	0.1	0.1	0.1	0.2
Norway	30.4	27.8	24.9	25.0
Sweden	43.6	56.4	203.1	59.0
Switzerland	23.5	22.2	19.7	12.9
United Kingdom	76.6	112.6	81.9	97.1
United States	39.0	91.0	69.0	-24.0
TOTAL	950.0	949.5	1133.7	727.0
MULTILATERAL				
AF.D.F.	–	–	–	–
AF.D.B.	–	–	–	–
AS.D.B	–	0.6	3.3	3.9
CAR.D.B.	–	–	–	–
E.E.C.	105.0	153.3	111.7	111.7
IBRD	–	–	–	–
IDA	656.2	820.0	473.0	540.0
I.D.B.	–	–	–	–
IFAD	37.9	9.4	10.2	19.2
I.F.C.	–	–	–	–
IMF TRUST FUND	–	–	–	–
U.N. AGENCIES	–	–	–	–
UNDP	29.8	28.1	24.1	23.0
UNTA	5.7	2.6	6.6	2.2
UNICEF	42.5	56.9	72.5	79.2
UNRWA	–	–	–	–
WFP	23.4	60.0	39.0	44.1
UNHCR	–	3.8	3.6	4.5
Other Multilateral	13.1	16.9	18.7	24.1
Arab Agencies	-1.9	16.5	-2.5	–
TOTAL	911.9	1168.1	760.2	851.7
ARAB COUNTRIES	-23.0	-20.3	1.1	7.3
E.E.C.+ MEMBERS	575.0	674.4	628.4	633.7
TOTAL	1838.8	2097.3	1895.0	1586.0

5. ODA LOANS NET

DAC COUNTRIES	1987	1988	1989	1990
Australia	–	–	–	–
Austria	-2.0	-1.9	7.5	-2.6
Belgium	-3.0	-4.1	-4.2	2.7
Canada	-1.4	-9.7	-10.4	-11.2
Denmark	8.0	6.8	1.8	-1.6
Finland	0.7	0.1	0.1	2.3
France	61.1	38.5	64.8	36.8
Germany	83.8	97.9	74.2	113.0
Ireland	–	–	–	–
Italy	40.0	51.4	58.4	8.8
Japan	270.8	133.9	222.2	53.4
Netherlands	27.7	26.0	4.7	51.4
New Zealand	–	–	–	–
Norway	3.1	–	–	-0.6
Sweden	–	–	–	–
Switzerland	1.4	0.9	4.6	2.6
United Kingdom	-51.9	-46.6	-47.8	-41.8
United States	-70.0	-58.0	-73.0	-99.0
TOTAL	368.2	235.2	302.7	114.1
MULTILATERAL	691.8	845.3	480.7	555.6
ARAB COUNTRIES	-23.2	-20.5	0.4	7.3
E.E.C.+ MEMBERS	165.6	169.9	151.8	169.2
TOTAL	1036.8	1060.0	783.8	677.0

6. TOTAL OFFICIAL NET

DAC COUNTRIES	1987	1988	1989	1990
Australia	1.3	2.2	9.2	48.2
Austria	-6.3	-6.2	8.0	-1.2
Belgium	-1.8	-2.7	-2.7	4.3
Canada	67.5	87.3	72.2	93.1
Denmark	42.3	34.0	48.1	37.1
Finland	0.9	1.2	1.2	3.0
France	69.4	52.9	103.4	51.5
Germany	25.8	125.4	122.5	208.7
Ireland	0.1	0.0	0.0	0.0
Italy	43.0	56.7	71.0	14.3
Japan	321.6	459.3	491.4	207.9
Netherlands	104.0	113.6	91.2	147.6
New Zealand	0.1	0.1	0.1	0.2
Norway	30.4	27.8	24.9	25.0
Sweden	43.6	56.4	203.1	59.0
Switzerland	23.5	22.2	19.7	12.9
United Kingdom	76.6	133.4	113.5	109.0
United States	30.0	94.0	53.0	-38.0
TOTAL	872.2	1257.8	1429.9	982.5
MULTILATERAL	1590.6	2480.4	1976.9	2100.1
ARAB COUNTRIES	-23.0	-20.3	1.1	7.3
E.E.C.+ MEMBERS	464.5	666.7	658.8	684.2
TOTAL	2439.7	3717.8	3408.0	3089.9

7. TOTAL ODA GROSS

	1987
Australia	1.5
Austria	0.6
Belgium	1.2
Canada	47.0
Denmark	43.6
Finland	0.9
France	80.1
Germany	230.8
Ireland	0.1
Italy	43.8
Japan	395.5
Netherlands	132.8
New Zealand	0.1
Norway	30.4
Sweden	43.6
Switzerland	23.5
United Kingdom	128.5
United States	141.0
TOTAL	1345.1
AF.D.F.	–
AF.D.B.	–
AS.D.B	–
CAR.D.B.	–
E.E.C.	105.0
IBRD	–
IDA	725.0
I.D.B.	–
IFAD	37.9
I.F.C.	–
IMF TRUST FUND	–
U.N. AGENCIES	–
UNDP	29.8
UNTA	5.7
UNICEF	42.5
UNRWA	–
WFP	23.4
UNHCR	–
Other Multilateral	13.1
Arab Agencies	5.7
TOTAL	988.3
ARAB COUNTRIES	9.2
E.E.C.+ MEMBERS	766.0
TOTAL	2342.6

8. GRANTS

	1987
Australia	1.5
Austria	0.6
Belgium	1.2
Canada	39.9
Denmark	34.1
Finland	0.2
France	8.3
Germany	52.8
Ireland	0.1
Italy	3.0
Japan	33.2
Netherlands	76.3
New Zealand	0.1
Norway	27.3
Sweden	43.6
Switzerland	22.1
United Kingdom	128.5
United States	109.0
TOTAL	581.8
MULTILATERAL	220.1
ARAB COUNTRIES	0.2
E.E.C.+ MEMBERS	409.4
TOTAL	802.0

9. TOTAL OOF GROSS

	1987
Australia	–
Austria	–
Belgium	0.1
Canada	29.1
Denmark	0.2
Finland	–
France	–
Germany	9.9
Ireland	–
Italy	–
Japan	20.0
Netherlands	0.0
New Zealand	–
Norway	–
Sweden	–
Switzerland	–
United Kingdom	–
United States	17.0
TOTAL	76.3
MULTILATERAL	1154.5
ARAB COUNTRIES	–
E.E.C.+ MEMBERS	10.2
TOTAL	1230.8

10. ODA COMMITMENTS

1988	1989	1990	1987	1988	1989	1990
2.4	9.4	20.2	1.6	2.2	3.1	3.4
0.5	9.8	1.5	0.6	0.7	9.7	1.4
1.5	1.5	9.1	1.8	0.5	1.5	9.1
58.9	34.7	33.8	201.7	32.8	–	16.9
35.5	49.6	38.7	67.9	57.6	61.8	19.7
1.2	1.2	3.1	0.9	7.5	0.7	1.1
63.2	114.0	72.1	15.0	114.0	202.7	70.4
253.3	221.4	289.1	335.6	477.0	292.8	506.9
0.0	0.0	0.0	0.1	0.0	0.0	0.0
58.1	75.7	17.3	125.9	27.9	7.2	11.1
283.3	353.6	183.5	446.2	1247.9	80.3	261.0
148.4	127.8	188.0	269.3	145.5	217.6	163.5
0.1	0.1	0.2	0.1	0.1	–	–
27.8	24.9	25.6	77.7	7.5	14.3	9.2
56.4	203.1	59.0	43.6	56.4	203.1	65.9
22.2	19.7	13.5	37.1	14.9	35.6	31.4
159.1	131.5	144.2	268.1	75.6	169.6	214.3
200.0	172.0	90.0	168.1	178.8	194.6	117.9
1372.0	*1550.1*	*1189.0*	*2061.2*	*2447.0*	*1494.3*	*1503.0*
–	–	–	–	–	–	–
–	–	–	–	–	–	–
0.6	3.3	3.9	–	–	–	–
–	–	–	–	–	–	–
153.3	111.7	111.7	125.4	151.8	–	–
–	–	–	–	–	–	–
895.0	566.0	648.0	824.6	587.0	875.0	893.0
–	–	–	–	–	–	–
9.4	10.8	22.1	11.9	0.2	17.6	–
–	–	–	–	–	–	–
–	–	–	–	–	–	–
–	–	–	114.6	168.2	164.5	177.0
28.1	24.1	23.0	–	–	–	–
2.6	6.6	2.2	–	–	–	–
56.9	72.5	79.2	–	–	–	–
–	–	–	–	–	–	–
60.0	39.0	44.1	–	–	–	–
3.8	3.6	4.5	–	–	–	–
16.9	18.7	24.1	–	–	–	–
29.6	8.4	7.3	7.0	8.0	10.0	6.5
1256.2	*864.7*	*970.0*	*1083.5*	*915.2*	*1067.0*	*1076.5*
5.0	*25.8*	*17.3*	*37.7*	*0.2*	*23.8*	–
872.4	*833.2*	*870.3*	*1209.2*	*1049.9*	*953.2*	*995.0*
2633.1	*2440.6*	*2176.3*	*3182.3*	*3362.4*	*2585.2*	*2579.5*

11. TECH. COOP. GRANTS

1988	1989	1990	1987	1988	1989	1990
2.4	9.4	20.2	1.2	1.5	1.9	1.8
0.5	0.6	1.3	0.5	0.5	0.4	0.6
1.5	1.5	1.6	0.4	0.3	0.0	0.1
58.9	34.7	33.8	–	4.7	12.2	2.1
27.2	46.4	38.7	13.9	11.6	29.3	13.1
1.1	1.1	0.7	0.0	0.1	0.1	0.2
14.4	38.6	14.7	8.3	10.2	8.8	9.4
54.4	48.4	56.2	46.9	53.9	29.4	36.3
0.0	0.0	0.0	0.1	0.0	0.0	0.0
5.3	12.6	5.6	0.9	3.7	2.0	0.5
45.6	35.1	33.9	10.1	10.3	10.5	11.7
89.2	87.6	97.1	30.8	38.5	41.3	48.2
0.1	0.1	0.2	0.1	0.0	–	0.2
27.8	24.9	25.6	1.2	1.4	1.6	1.1
56.4	203.1	59.0	4.7	4.4	75.0	2.2
21.3	15.1	10.3	1.3	1.9	–	–
159.1	129.7	139.0	24.1	40.4	39.2	53.9
149.0	142.0	75.0	29.0	24.0	36.0	25.0
714.3	*830.9*	*612.9*	*173.5*	*207.4*	*287.7*	*206.6*
322.7	*279.5*	*292.6*	*97.1*	*130.2*	*125.5*	*132.9*
0.2	*0.8*	–	–	–	–	–
504.5	*476.6*	*464.5*	*131.3*	*180.6*	*150.0*	*161.6*
1037.3	*1111.1*	*905.4*	*270.6*	*337.6*	*413.1*	*339.5*

12. TOTAL OOF NET

1988	1989	1990	1987	1988	1989	1990
–	–	28.2	-0.2	-0.2	-0.2	27.9
–	–	–	-4.9	-4.9	–	–
–	0.0	0.0	0.1	–	0.0	0.0
38.1	48.5	72.3	29.0	38.1	47.9	70.5
0.0	0.0	–	0.2	0.0	-0.1	–
–	–	–	–	–	–	–
14.0	–	42.0	-110.8	-27.0	–	39.5
–	–	–	–	–	–	–
–	–	–	–	–	–	–
281.4	234.3	120.6	17.7	279.9	234.1	120.6
–	–	–	0.0	-1.5	-1.1	-0.8
–	–	–	–	–	–	–
–	–	–	–	–	–	–
–	–	–	–	–	–	–
20.9	31.6	11.8	–	20.9	31.6	11.8
31.0	20.0	6.0	-9.0	3.0	-16.0	-14.0
385.4	*334.5*	*280.9*	*-77.8*	*308.2*	*296.3*	*255.5*
1618.4	*1559.0*	*1685.3*	*678.7*	*1312.3*	*1216.7*	*1248.3*
–	–	–	–	–	–	–
34.9	*31.7*	*53.9*	*-110.5*	*-7.6*	*30.5*	*50.5*
2003.8	*1893.6*	*1966.2*	*600.9*	*1620.5*	*1513.0*	*1503.9*

13. ODF COMMITMENTS: BY PURPOSE %

	1987	1988	1989	1990
Education	0	0	5	–
Health	1	1	3	–
Other Social Infrastr.	2	5	2	–
Water Sanitat. Sewage	5	0	1	–
Energy	26	61	48	–
Telecommunications	5	1	2	–
Transportation	7	8	2	–
Agriculture	13	3	7	–
Extractive Industries	11	1	3	–
Manufacturing	15	6	8	–
Trade Banking Tourism	2	6	8	–
Technical Cooperation	4	3	8	–
Multisector Aid	1	0	0	–
Programme	1	2	1	–
Debt Reorganisation	0	0	0	–
Food Aid	2	1	2	–
Emergency Aid	3	0	0	–
Unspecified	0	0	0	–
TOTAL	100	100	100	–

14. GRANT ELEMENT OF ODA %

DAC COUNTRIES

	1987	1988	1989	1990
Australia	100.0	100.0	100.0	–
Austria	96.1	81.5	69.3	–
Belgium	100.0	100.0	100.0	–
Canada	100.0	100.0	–	–
Denmark	100.0	100.0	100.0	–
Finland	26.6	100.0	100.0	–
France	34.3	71.7	75.0	–
Germany	74.6	74.8	69.1	–
Ireland	100.0	100.0	100.0	–
Italy	65.9	100.0	100.0	–
Japan	54.2	62.1	80.5	–
Netherlands	81.4	84.3	90.6	–
New Zealand	100.0	100.0	–	–
Norway	97.1	100.0	100.0	–
Sweden	100.0	100.0	100.0	–
Switzerland	100.0	100.0	100.0	–
United Kingdom	100.0	100.0	100.0	–
United States	96.7	100.0	100.0	–
TOTAL	*77.9*	*73.4*	*87.8*	–
MULTILATERAL	*85.5*	*84.7*	*81.8*	–
ARAB COUNTRIES	*39.5*	*100.0*	*33.0*	–
E.E.C.+ MEMBERS	*79.7*	*83.3*	*82.9*	–
TOTAL	*80.0*	*76.9*	*85.0*	–

15. OTHER AGGREGATES

	1987	1988	1989	1990
OFFICIAL COMMITMENTS:				
TOTAL BILATERAL	3323.4	8574.8	3583.9	1637.0
of which:				
Arab Countries	37.7	0.2	23.8	–
C.E.E.C.	1100.0	5281.0	1574.1	–
TOTAL MULTILATERAL	3985.2	3487.2	3838.7	3145.1
TOTAL BIL.& MULTIL.	7308.5	12061.9	7422.6	4782.1
of which:				
ODA Grants	1354.8	993.8	1172.1	902.0
ODA Loans	2877.5	7649.6	2987.2	1677.5
DISBURSEMENTS:				
DAC COUNTRIES COMBINED				
OFFICIAL & PRIVATE				
GROSS:				
Contractual Lending	1684.2	1161.4	2014.4	1946.9
Export Credits, Total	900.7	201.5	1029.2	1236.6
Export Credits, Priv.	844.7	118.3	960.8	1091.6
NET:				
Contractual Lending	718.3	126.6	1416.8	1078.9
Export Credits Total	329.9	-409.3	849.3	831.6
PRIVATE SECTOR NET	1059.3	405.4	1764.4	1202.0
Direct Investment	212.3	91.3	252.1	161.7
Portfolio Investment	419.0	731.0	694.5	329.3
Export Credits	428.0	-416.8	817.8	710.9
MARKET BORROWING:				
CHANGE IN CLAIMS				
Banks	1050.0	1444.0	1157.0	1409.0
MEMORANDUM ITEM:				
C.E.E.C. (Gross)	276.2	285.8	310.0	–

1. TOTAL RECEIPTS NET

DAC COUNTRIES

	1987	1988	1989	1990
Australia	60.9	132.4	177.8	252.8
Austria	32.9	13.3	1.5	17.4
Belgium	14.7	-36.8	-20.2	43.6
Canada	43.9	21.2	30.4	69.8
Denmark	-18.7	-17.0	-8.1	-11.2
Finland	2.1	3.8	9.6	3.1
France	7.4	-35.9	87.8	62.5
Germany	17.3	126.8	34.0	33.5
Ireland	0.1	–	–	–
Italy	11.1	1.7	6.3	8.9
Japan	1825.9	998.5	1959.9	1521.8
Netherlands	155.1	146.5	117.3	269.3
New Zealand	2.3	2.9	2.2	3.1
Norway	-5.8	-3.0	-4.5	-6.2
Sweden	26.7	–	-3.1	-22.8
Switzerland	7.4	28.4	21.4	19.4
United Kingdom	11.6	39.0	125.8	-120.9
United States	-460.0	38.0	783.0	145.0
TOTAL	*1734.9*	*1459.8*	*3321.0*	*2289.0*

MULTILATERAL

	1987	1988	1989	1990
AF.D.F.	–	–	–	–
AF.D.B.	–	–	–	–
AS.D.B	312.3	476.8	645.8	713.9
CAR.D.B.	–	–	–	–
E.E.C.	6.3	8.3	13.9	13.9
IBRD	1004.1	1219.0	783.0	436.0
IDA	8.7	-5.0	-7.0	-11.0
I.D.B.	–	–	–	–
IFAD	15.6	10.8	10.1	8.6
I.F.C.	-0.8	10.2	10.7	2.6
IMF TRUST FUND	–	–	–	–
U.N. AGENCIES	–	–	–	–
UNDP	21.2	20.6	19.1	17.0
UNTA	5.1	3.7	5.2	4.3
UNICEF	10.5	11.9	11.3	10.0
UNRWA	–	–	–	–
WFP	5.2	2.7	7.6	8.0
UNHCR	2.9	1.7	2.0	4.0
Other Multilateral	5.3	6.7	10.0	8.4
Arab Agencies	-1.0	-1.4	-1.0	–
TOTAL	*1395.5*	*1765.9*	*1510.6*	*1215.7*
ARAB COUNTRIES	***11.2***	***9.1***	***1.9***	***20.0***
E.E.C.+ MEMBERS	*205.0*	*232.6*	*356.7*	*299.6*
TOTAL	*3141.5*	*3234.7*	*4833.5*	*3524.8*

2. ODA LOANS GROSS

DAC COUNTRIES

	1987	1988	1989	1990
Australia	–	–	–	
Austria	0.3	10.2	15.4	33.9
Belgium	–	9.5	8.1	–
Canada	2.4	–	–	–
Denmark	0.8	0.5	10.4	2.6
Finland	–	1.4	4.1	0.6
France	36.3	59.8	105.9	124.7
Germany	100.0	147.3	94.5	160.6
Ireland	–	–	–	–
Italy	14.8	–	15.9	7.4
Japan	804.6	1121.5	1260.6	964.8
Netherlands	91.5	98.5	96.3	122.1
New Zealand	–	–	–	–
Norway	–	–	–	–
Sweden	–	–	–	–
Switzerland	–	14.4	13.8	5.3
United Kingdom	1.1	0.7	0.4	–
United States	62.0	45.0	41.0	13.0
TOTAL	*1113.7*	*1508.8*	*1666.3*	*1434.9*
MULTILATERAL	*64.7*	*76.0*	*75.7*	*129.4*
ARAB COUNTRIES	***23.8***	***27.9***	***19.8***	***32.0***
E.E.C.+ MEMBERS	*244.5*	*316.4*	*331.5*	*417.3*
TOTAL	*1202.3*	*1612.7*	*1761.9*	*1596.3*

3. TOTAL OFFICIAL GROSS

DAC COUNTRIES

	1987	1988	1989	1990
Australia	52.6	134.2	162.5	204.0
Austria	36.5	21.9	17.4	35.9
Belgium	10.0	13.3	13.7	9.3
Canada	61.8	46.1	54.4	81.0
Denmark	0.8	1.1	11.6	5.7
Finland	1.8	3.3	5.8	2.7
France	43.5	67.6	115.3	136.0
Germany	232.8	236.6	179.6	262.6
Ireland	0.1	–	–	–
Italy	19.8	2.8	21.2	11.3
Japan	1834.1	1647.8	1892.3	1514.9
Netherlands	170.0	188.1	198.7	235.6
New Zealand	2.3	2.9	2.2	3.1
Norway	0.6	2.2	1.3	0.3
Sweden	–	–	–	0.1
Switzerland	7.4	28.4	21.4	19.4
United Kingdom	20.0	30.9	34.1	40.3
United States	133.0	140.0	161.0	217.0
TOTAL	*2626.8*	*2567.1*	*2892.2*	*2779.2*
MULTILATERAL	*1805.4*	*2265.9*	*2069.3*	*1867.1*
ARAB COUNTRIES	***24.4***	***27.9***	***20.5***	***32.0***
E.E.C.+ MEMBERS	*503.2*	*548.7*	*587.9*	*714.7*
TOTAL	*4456.7*	*4860.9*	*4982.0*	*4678.4*

4. TOTAL ODA NET

DAC COUNTRIES

	1987	1988	1989	1990
Australia	48.2	71.7	83.1	77.4
Austria	0.6	6.9	4.4	21.2
Belgium	5.8	6.2	10.7	-1.6
Canada	43.0	40.1	33.4	48.4
Denmark	0.3	0.6	11.1	4.9
Finland	1.8	3.3	5.8	2.7
France	37.3	57.1	108.9	122.4
Germany	61.8	97.6	52.4	99.0
Ireland	0.1	–	–	–
Italy	19.4	1.3	17.5	9.8
Japan	707.3	984.9	1145.3	867.8
Netherlands	140.3	156.2	161.5	190.1
New Zealand	2.1	2.3	2.2	3.1
Norway	0.6	2.0	0.5	-0.2
Sweden	–	–	–	0.1
Switzerland	7.4	28.4	21.4	19.4
United Kingdom	10.4	17.2	14.5	22.4
United States	36.0	22.0	31.0	31.0
TOTAL	*1122.5*	*1497.9*	*1703.7*	*1517.9*

MULTILATERAL

	1987	1988	1989	1990
AF.D.F.	–	–	–	–
AF.D.B.	–	–	–	–
AS.D.B	32.4	64.9	62.5	123.3
CAR.D.B.	–	–	–	–
E.E.C.	6.3	8.3	13.9	13.9
IBRD	–	–	–	–
IDA	8.7	-5.0	-7.0	-11.0
I.D.B.	–	–	–	–
IFAD	15.6	10.8	10.1	8.6
I.F.C.	–	–	–	–
IMF TRUST FUND	–	–	–	–
U.N. AGENCIES	–	–	–	–
UNDP	21.2	20.6	19.1	17.0
UNTA	5.1	3.7	5.2	4.3
UNICEF	10.5	11.9	11.3	10.0
UNRWA	–	–	–	–
WFP	5.2	2.7	7.6	8.0
UNHCR	2.9	1.7	2.0	4.0
Other Multilateral	5.3	6.7	10.0	8.4
Arab Agencies	-1.0	-1.4	-1.0	–
TOTAL	*112.2*	*124.8*	*133.6*	*186.4*
ARAB COUNTRIES	***11.2***	***9.1***	***1.9***	***20.0***
E.E.C.+ MEMBERS	*281.9*	*344.6*	*390.5*	*460.9*
TOTAL	*1245.9*	*1631.8*	*1839.2*	*1724.4*

5. ODA LOANS NET

DAC COUNTRIES

	1987	1988	1989	1990
Australia	–	–	–	–
Austria	0.3	6.5	4.1	20.8
Belgium	–	2.5	8.1	-8.1
Canada	0.0	-3.1	-4.9	-3.5
Denmark	0.3	0.0	10.0	1.8
Finland	–	1.4	4.1	0.6
France	30.1	49.3	99.6	111.1
Germany	21.3	54.7	8.0	48.2
Ireland	–	–	–	–
Italy	14.5	-1.5	12.2	5.9
Japan	570.7	841.7	998.8	700.7
Netherlands	66.7	68.2	66.8	83.8
New Zealand	–	–	–	–
Norway	–	-0.2	-0.7	-0.4
Sweden	–	–	–	–
Switzerland	–	14.4	13.8	5.3
United Kingdom	-2.9	-3.8	-3.3	-4.0
United States	2.0	-19.0	-25.0	-57.0
TOTAL	*703.1*	*1011.2*	*1191.6*	*905.2*
MULTILATERAL	*52.2*	*62.5*	*59.3*	*108.6*
ARAB COUNTRIES	***10.6***	***9.1***	***1.2***	***20.0***
E.E.C.+ MEMBERS	*130.1*	*169.6*	*201.4*	*238.7*
TOTAL	*765.9*	*1082.8*	*1252.1*	*1033.8*

6. TOTAL OFFICIAL NET

DAC COUNTRIES

	1987	1988	1989	1990
Australia	46.8	126.0	157.8	197.4
Austria	36.5	18.3	6.2	22.8
Belgium	10.0	6.2	13.7	1.2
Canada	39.7	22.2	33.9	65.4
Denmark	-10.2	-7.3	6.0	4.9
Finland	1.8	3.3	5.8	2.7
France	37.3	57.1	108.9	117.6
Germany	70.2	62.3	44.2	93.3
Ireland	0.1	–	–	–
Italy	19.4	1.3	17.5	9.8
Japan	1586.3	1352.3	1577.3	1214.7
Netherlands	143.9	156.8	168.0	193.4
New Zealand	2.3	2.9	2.2	3.1
Norway	0.6	1.8	0.4	-0.4
Sweden	–	–	–	0.1
Switzerland	7.4	28.4	21.4	19.4
United Kingdom	15.4	24.4	26.7	31.4
United States	3.0	2.0	21.0	63.0
TOTAL	*2010.5*	*1857.8*	*2210.9*	*2039.6*
MULTILATERAL	*1395.5*	*1765.9*	*1510.6*	*1215.7*
ARAB COUNTRIES	***11.2***	***9.1***	***1.9***	***20.0***
E.E.C.+ MEMBERS	*292.5*	*309.0*	*398.8*	*465.4*
TOTAL	*3417.2*	*3632.8*	*3723.4*	*3275.4*

7. TOTAL ODA GROSS

DAC COUNTRIES

	1987
Australia	48.2
Austria	0.6
Belgium	5.8
Canada	45.4
Denmark	0.8
Finland	1.8
France	43.5
Germany	140.4
Ireland	0.1
Italy	19.8
Japan	941.1
Netherlands	165.0
New Zealand	2.1
Norway	0.6
Sweden	–
Switzerland	7.4
United Kingdom	14.5
United States	96.0
TOTAL	*1533.1*

	1987
AF.D.F.	–
AF.D.B.	–
AS.D.B	36.7
CAR.D.B.	–
E.E.C.	6.3
IBRD	–
IDA	14.4
I.D.B.	–
IFAD	16.9
I.F.C.	–
IMF TRUST FUND	–
U.N. AGENCIES	–
UNDP	21.2
UNTA	5.1
UNICEF	10.5
UNRWA	–
WFP	5.2
UNHCR	2.9
Other Multilateral	5.3
Arab Agencies	0.2
TOTAL	*124.7*
ARAB COUNTRIES	***24.4***
E.E.C.+ MEMBERS	*396.2*
TOTAL	*1682.3*

8. GRANTS

	1987
Australia	48.2
Austria	0.3
Belgium	5.8
Canada	43.0
Denmark	–
Finland	1.8
France	7.2
Germany	40.5
Ireland	0.1
Italy	4.9
Japan	136.6
Netherlands	73.5
New Zealand	2.1
Norway	0.6
Sweden	–
Switzerland	7.4
United Kingdom	13.4
United States	34.0
TOTAL	*419.4*
MULTILATERAL	*60.0*
ARAB COUNTRIES	***0.6***
E.E.C.+ MEMBERS	*151.8*
TOTAL	*480.0*

9. TOTAL OOF GROSS

	1987
Australia	4.4
Austria	35.9
Belgium	4.2
Canada	16.3
Denmark	0.0
Finland	–
France	–
Germany	92.3
Ireland	–
Italy	–
Japan	892.9
Netherlands	4.9
New Zealand	0.2
Norway	–
Sweden	–
Switzerland	–
United Kingdom	5.5
United States	37.0
TOTAL	*1093.7*
MULTILATERAL	*1680.7*
ARAB COUNTRIES	***–***
E.E.C.+ MEMBERS	*107.0*
TOTAL	*2774.4*

1988	1989	1990	1987	1988	1989	1990

10. ODA COMMITMENTS

1988	1989	1990	1987	1988	1989	1990
71.7	83.1	77.4	32.2	84.0	106.2	62.8
10.5	15.7	34.3	17.6	19.2	20.7	26.8
13.3	10.7	6.5	7.1	11.9	10.7	6.5
43.3	38.4	51.9	37.6	88.9	81.7	37.6
1.1	11.5	5.7	–	–	3.4	0.6
3.3	5.8	2.7	1.7	8.9	0.6	3.9
67.6	115.3	136.0	46.7	137.2	288.9	209.7
190.2	138.8	211.4	139.0	151.4	179.4	268.2
–	–	–	0.1	–	–	–
2.8	21.2	11.3	3.9	8.1	48.4	0.5
1264.7	1407.1	1131.9	1336.3	1701.0	1455.2	1500.9
186.5	191.0	228.4	113.7	254.6	222.2	202.6
2.3	2.2	3.1	2.1	2.4	–	3.3
2.2	1.2	0.3	3.1	–	–	–
–	–	0.1	–	–	–	–
28.4	21.4	19.4	16.8	8.3	7.0	19.6
21.7	18.2	26.4	33.3	35.6	45.2	317.0
86.0	97.0	101.0	124.2	79.8	64.4	54.2
1995.5	2178.5	2047.7	1915.3	2591.2	2533.9	2714.0
–	–	–	–	–	–	–
69.3	67.5	128.9	146.1	79.4	106.2	136.7
–	–	–	–	–	–	–
8.3	13.9	13.9	37.2	2.9	1.2	1.2
–	–	–	–	–	–	–
1.0	1.0	–	–	–	–	–
–	–	–	–	–	–	–
12.2	12.6	12.8	13.7	0.3	–	21.9
–	–	–	–	–	–	–
–	–	–	50.2	47.2	55.2	51.6
20.6	19.1	17.0	–	–	–	–
3.7	5.2	4.3	–	–	–	–
11.9	11.3	10.0	–	–	–	–
–	–	–	–	–	–	–
2.7	7.6	8.0	–	–	–	–
1.7	2.0	4.0	–	–	–	–
6.7	10.0	8.4	–	–	–	–
0.3	–	–	–	–	–	–
138.3	150.1	207.2	247.2	129.9	162.6	211.5
27.9	20.5	32.0	42.4	19.7	–	–
491.5	520.6	639.5	380.9	601.6	799.5	1006.2
2161.7	2349.0	2286.9	2204.9	2740.8	2696.5	2925.5

11. TECH. COOP. GRANTS

1988	1989	1990	1987	1988	1989	1990
71.7	83.1	77.4	30.2	35.7	43.0	42.9
0.3	0.3	0.4	0.3	0.2	0.3	0.4
3.8	2.6	6.5	4.4	2.7	1.5	2.7
43.3	38.4	51.9	–	6.9	10.2	12.7
0.6	1.1	3.0	–	0.3	1.3	2.1
1.9	1.6	2.1	0.1	0.7	0.7	1.7
7.8	9.4	11.3	7.2	7.0	7.2	10.6
42.9	44.3	50.8	40.0	42.7	36.6	40.7
–	–	–	0.1	–	–	–
2.8	5.3	4.0	4.9	2.8	3.6	3.3
143.2	146.5	167.1	67.9	93.8	101.8	108.7
88.0	94.7	106.3	50.8	56.7	63.0	73.7
2.3	2.2	3.1	1.3	1.2	–	2.8
2.2	1.2	0.3	0.6	1.5	0.2	0.2
–	–	0.1	–	–	–	0.0
14.0	7.6	14.1	1.4	3.5	–	–
21.0	17.8	26.4	8.9	15.9	12.4	19.5
41.0	56.0	88.0	21.0	31.0	44.0	41.0
486.7	512.1	612.7	239.0	302.6	325.7	363.0
62.3	74.4	77.9	45.8	45.5	47.6	43.7
–	0.7	–	–	–	–	–
175.1	189.1	222.2	116.9	129.1	125.6	152.5
549.0	587.2	690.6	284.7	348.1	373.2	406.7

12. TOTAL OOF NET

1988	1989	1990	1987	1988	1989	1990
62.5	79.4	126.7	-1.5	54.3	74.7	120.1
11.4	1.8	1.7	35.9	11.4	1.8	1.6
–	2.9	2.8	4.2	–	2.9	2.8
2.8	16.0	29.0	-3.2	-17.9	0.5	17.0
–	0.1	–	-10.6	-7.9	-5.2	–
–	–	–	–	–	–	–
–	–	–	–	–	–	-4.9
46.4	40.8	51.2	8.4	-35.4	-8.2	-5.7
–	–	–	–	–	–	–
–	–	–	–	–	–	–
383.1	485.2	383.0	879.0	367.4	432.1	346.9
1.6	7.7	7.3	3.6	0.5	6.5	3.3
0.5	–	–	0.2	0.5	–	–
–	0.1	–	–	-0.2	-0.1	-0.2
–	–	–	–	–	–	–
9.2	15.8	13.9	5.0	7.2	12.2	9.0
54.0	64.0	116.0	-33.0	-20.0	-10.0	32.0
571.6	713.8	731.6	888.0	359.9	507.2	521.7
2127.6	1919.2	1659.9	1283.2	1641.1	1377.0	1029.3
–	–	–	–	–	–	–
57.2	67.3	75.2	10.6	-35.6	8.3	4.5
2699.1	2633.0	2391.5	2171.3	2001.0	1884.1	1551.0

13. ODF COMMITMENTS: BY PURPOSE %

	1987	1988	1989	1990
Education	1	8	5	–
Health	1	1	2	–
Other Social Infrastr.	5	8	3	–
Water Sanitat. Sewage	0	2	1	–
Energy	9	2	17	–
Telecommunications	3	3	1	–
Transportation	24	9	19	–
Agriculture	12	9	9	–
Extractive Industries	2	0	0	–
Manufacturing	0	1	1	–
Trade Banking Tourism	4	7	14	–
Technical Cooperation	6	8	6	–
Multisector Aid	1	17	8	–
Programme	29	23	15	–
Debt Reorganisation	0	0	0	–
Food Aid	1	1	0	–
Emergency Aid	0	0	0	–
Unspecified	2	0	0	–
TOTAL	100	100	100	–

14. GRANT ELEMENT OF ODA %

DAC COUNTRIES

	1987	1988	1989	1990
Australia	100.0	100.0	100.0	–
Austria	52.7	53.6	53.3	–
Belgium	100.0	100.0	100.0	–
Canada	100.0	100.0	100.0	–
Denmark	–	–	100.0	–
Finland	100.0	76.8	100.0	–
France	78.8	63.9	56.9	–
Germany	59.6	65.1	73.7	–
Ireland	100.0	–	–	–
Italy	100.0	100.0	71.0	–
Japan	58.9	63.5	65.7	–
Netherlands	78.7	75.6	71.8	–
New Zealand	100.0	100.0	–	–
Norway	100.0	–	–	–
Sweden	–	–	–	–
Switzerland	100.0	100.0	100.0	–
United Kingdom	100.0	100.0	100.0	–
United States	86.5	88.4	96.7	–
TOTAL	65.6	68.8	69.9	–
MULTILATERAL	85.4	81.0	88.6	–
ARAB COUNTRIES	37.0	37.8	–	–
E.E.C.+ MEMBERS	76.3	72.2	68.3	–
TOTAL	67.2	69.2	70.7	–

15. OTHER AGGREGATES

	1987	1988	1989	1990
OFFICIAL COMMITMENTS:				
TOTAL BILATERAL	3213.4	3706.1	3611.5	3835.7
of which:				
Arab Countries	42.4	19.7	–	–
C.E.E.C.	–	–	–	–
TOTAL MULTILATERAL	2131.0	1668.9	2877.4	2865.9
TOTAL BIL.& MULTIL.	5344.4	5375.0	6488.9	6701.6
of which:				
ODA Grants	553.5	694.7	684.2	910.4
ODA Loans	1651.5	2046.1	2012.3	2015.1
DISBURSEMENTS:				
DAC COUNTRIES COMBINED				
OFFICIAL & PRIVATE				
GROSS:				
Contractual Lending	2922.1	2349.2	2729.3	2469.1
Export Credits, Total	1035.3	483.9	604.3	639.1
Export Credits, Priv.	726.0	279.2	359.5	317.4
NET:				
Contractual Lending	1444.7	1037.8	1491.1	866.2
Export Credits Total	-16.1	-326.5	-123.0	-418.9
PRIVATE SECTOR NET	-275.7	-398.0	1110.1	249.4
Direct Investment	-570.2	-7.1	1418.0	600.0
Portfolio Investment	429.6	-68.0	-110.5	195.3
Export Credits	-135.0	-322.9	-197.3	-546.0
MARKET BORROWING:				
CHANGE IN CLAIMS				
Banks	757.0	1017.0	1626.0	7597.0
MEMORANDUM ITEM:				
C.E.E.C. (Gross)	–	–	–	–

1. TOTAL RECEIPTS NET

DAC COUNTRIES	1987	1988	1989	1990
Australia	18.8	54.4	-13.3	57.3
Austria	8.0	8.7	11.5	19.3
Belgium	-1.0	1.9	3.7	-7.5
Canada	-6.7	-9.2	1.5	0.9
Denmark	-0.2	-0.2	-0.2	-0.2
Finland	0.0	0.3	0.7	2.5
France	-31.1	-27.8	2.7	3.6
Germany	133.2	278.9	172.7	421.3
Ireland	0.0	–	–	0.2
Italy	186.7	372.8	1288.5	491.4
Japan	-295.3	-14.6	54.8	-420.3
Netherlands	–	0.8	0.3	32.7
New Zealand	–	0.0	–	–
Norway	0.0	0.2	8.3	-3.5
Sweden	0.5	1.8	1.9	3.5
Switzerland	1.0	1.0	1.9	2.3
United Kingdom	18.6	28.7	4.7	0.5
United States	–	-19.0	–	–
TOTAL	*32.4*	*678.6*	*1539.8*	*603.8*
MULTILATERAL				
AF.D.F.	–	–	–	–
AF.D.B.	–	–	–	–
AS.D.B	–	–	–	–
CAR.D.B.	–	–	–	–
E.E.C.	–	–	–	–
IBRD	-68.5	-93.0	-67.0	-67.0
IDA	–	–	–	–
I.D.B.	–	–	–	–
IFAD	–	–	–	–
I.F.C.	–	–	–	0.0
IMF TRUST FUND	–	–	–	–
U.N. AGENCIES	–	–	–	–
UNDP	4.4	3.7	3.9	5.3
UNTA	1.1	0.8	1.6	2.3
UNICEF	0.0	0.5	4.6	2.5
UNRWA	–	–	–	–
WFP	2.2	1.6	2.4	11.5
UNHCR	16.1	22.3	18.2	12.3
Other Multilateral	0.3	0.6	5.5	0.4
Arab Agencies	–	–	–	–
TOTAL	*-44.3*	*-63.6*	*-30.7*	*-32.8*
ARAB COUNTRIES	*0.1*	*–*	*0.0*	*–*
E.E.C.+ MEMBERS	*306.2*	*655.1*	*1472.5*	*942.0*
TOTAL	**-11.9**	**615.1**	**1509.1**	**571.0**

2. ODA LOANS GROSS

DAC COUNTRIES	1987	1988	1989	1990
Australia	–	–	–	–
Austria	–	–	–	–
Belgium	–	–	–	–
Canada	–	–	–	–
Denmark	–	–	–	–
Finland	–	–	–	–
France	–	–	–	–
Germany	–	–	–	–
Ireland	–	–	–	–
Italy	–	–	–	–
Japan	–	–	–	–
Netherlands	–	–	–	–
New Zealand	–	–	–	–
Norway	–	–	–	–
Sweden	–	–	–	–
Switzerland	–	–	–	–
United Kingdom	–	–	–	–
United States	–	–	–	–
TOTAL	*–*	*–*	*–*	*–*
MULTILATERAL	*–*	*–*	*–*	*–*
ARAB COUNTRIES	*–*	*–*	*–*	*–*
E.E.C.+ MEMBERS	*–*	*–*	*–*	*–*
TOTAL	**–**	**–**	**–**	**–**

3. TOTAL OFFICIAL GROSS

DAC COUNTRIES	1987	1988	1989	1990
Australia	–	0.1	0.1	2.0
Austria	8.0	8.7	11.5	19.3
Belgium	0.6	0.3	0.0	0.0
Canada	–	0.3	–	0.9
Denmark	–	–	–	–
Finland	0.0	0.3	0.7	2.5
France	5.0	4.8	4.4	6.2
Germany	41.1	39.6	39.0	59.3
Ireland	0.0	–	–	0.2
Italy	0.6	1.3	6.2	1.4
Japan	2.1	2.2	3.5	7.4
Netherlands	–	0.2	–	1.1
New Zealand	–	0.0	–	–
Norway	0.0	0.2	0.0	0.5
Sweden	0.8	1.8	1.5	3.4
Switzerland	1.0	1.0	1.9	2.3
United Kingdom	–	–	–	0.5
United States	–	–	–	–
TOTAL	*59.2*	*60.8*	*68.7*	*107.0*
MULTILATERAL	*24.1*	*29.4*	*36.3*	*34.3*
ARAB COUNTRIES	*0.1*	*–*	*0.0*	*–*
E.E.C.+ MEMBERS	*47.3*	*46.1*	*49.6*	*68.7*
TOTAL	**83.4**	**90.2**	**105.0**	**141.3**

4. TOTAL ODA NET

DAC COUNTRIES	1987	1988	1989	1990
Australia	–	0.1	0.1	2.0
Austria	8.0	8.7	11.5	19.3
Belgium	0.6	0.3	0.0	0.0
Canada	–	0.3	–	0.9
Denmark	-0.2	-0.2	-0.2	-0.2
Finland	0.0	0.3	0.7	2.5
France	3.1	3.9	3.6	6.1
Germany	30.9	35.9	36.5	53.1
Ireland	0.0	–	–	0.2
Italy	0.6	1.3	0.9	1.4
Japan	2.1	2.2	3.5	-58.9
Netherlands	–	0.2	–	1.1
New Zealand	–	0.0	–	–
Norway	0.0	0.2	0.0	0.5
Sweden	0.8	1.8	1.5	3.4
Switzerland	1.0	1.0	1.9	2.3
United Kingdom	–	–	–	0.5
United States	–	-4.0	–	–
TOTAL	*46.9*	*52.1*	*60.0*	*34.3*
AF.D.F.	–	–	–	–
AF.D.B.	–	–	–	–
AS.D.B	–	–	–	–
CAR.D.B.	–	–	–	–
E.E.C.	–	–	–	–
IBRD	–	–	–	–
IDA	–	–	–	–
I.D.B.	–	–	–	–
IFAD	–	–	–	–
I.F.C.	–	–	–	–
IMF TRUST FUND	–	–	–	–
U.N. AGENCIES	–	–	–	–
UNDP	4.4	3.7	3.9	5.3
UNTA	1.1	0.8	1.6	2.3
UNICEF	0.0	0.5	4.6	2.5
UNRWA	–	–	–	–
WFP	2.2	1.6	2.4	11.5
UNHCR	16.1	22.3	18.2	12.3
Other Multilateral	0.3	0.6	5.5	0.4
Arab Agencies	–	–	–	–
TOTAL	*24.1*	*29.4*	*36.3*	*34.2*
ARAB COUNTRIES	*0.1*	*–*	*0.0*	*–*
E.E.C.+ MEMBERS	*35.0*	*41.4*	*40.8*	*62.3*
TOTAL	**71.1**	**81.5**	**96.3**	**68.5**

5. ODA LOANS NET

DAC COUNTRIES	1987	1988	1989	1990
Australia	–	–	–	–
Austria	0.0	–	–	–
Belgium	–	–	–	–
Canada	–	–	–	–
Denmark	-0.2	-0.2	-0.2	-0.2
Finland	–	–	–	–
France	-1.8	-0.9	-0.8	-0.1
Germany	-5.7	-3.6	-1.2	-3.1
Ireland	–	–	–	–
Italy	–	–	–	–
Japan	–	–	–	-66.3
Netherlands	–	–	–	–
New Zealand	–	–	–	–
Norway	–	–	–	–
Sweden	–	–	–	–
Switzerland	–	–	–	–
United Kingdom	–	–	–	–
United States	–	-4.0	–	–
TOTAL	*-7.7*	*-8.7*	*-2.1*	*-69.7*
MULTILATERAL	*–*	*–*	*–*	*–*
ARAB COUNTRIES	*–*	*–*	*–*	*–*
E.E.C.+ MEMBERS	*-7.6*	*-4.7*	*-2.1*	*-3.4*
TOTAL	**-7.7**	**-8.7**	**-2.1**	**-69.7**

6. TOTAL OFFICIAL NET

DAC COUNTRIES	1987	1988	1989	1990
Australia	–	0.1	0.1	2.0
Austria	8.0	8.7	11.5	19.3
Belgium	0.6	0.3	0.0	0.0
Canada	-6.7	-9.2	–	0.9
Denmark	-0.2	-0.2	-0.2	-0.2
Finland	0.0	0.3	0.7	2.5
France	3.1	3.9	3.6	6.1
Germany	33.2	33.9	32.6	49.7
Ireland	0.0	–	–	0.2
Italy	0.6	1.3	3.3	1.4
Japan	2.1	2.2	3.5	-189.3
Netherlands	–	0.2	–	1.1
New Zealand	–	0.0	–	–
Norway	0.0	0.2	0.0	0.5
Sweden	0.8	1.8	1.5	3.4
Switzerland	1.0	1.0	1.9	2.3
United Kingdom	–	–	–	0.5
United States	–	-19.0	–	–
TOTAL	*42.5*	*25.5*	*58.5*	*-99.6*
MULTILATERAL	*-44.3*	*-63.6*	*-30.7*	*-32.8*
ARAB COUNTRIES	*0.1*	*–*	*0.0*	*–*
E.E.C.+ MEMBERS	*37.4*	*39.4*	*39.4*	*58.9*
TOTAL	**-1.8**	**-38.1**	**27.8**	**-132.4**

7. TOTAL ODA GROSS

	1987
Australia	–
Austria	8.0
Belgium	0.6
Canada	–
Denmark	–
Finland	0.0
France	5.0
Germany	36.5
Ireland	0.0
Italy	0.6
Japan	2.1
Netherlands	–
New Zealand	–
Norway	0.0
Sweden	0.8
Switzerland	1.0
United Kingdom	–
United States	–
TOTAL	*54.6*
AF.D.F.	–
AF.D.B.	–
AS.D.B	–
CAR.D.B.	–
E.E.C.	–
IBRD	–
IDA	–
I.D.B.	–
IFAD	–
I.F.C.	–
IMF TRUST FUND	–
U.N. AGENCIES	–
UNDP	4.4
UNTA	1.1
UNICEF	0.0
UNRWA	–
WFP	2.2
UNHCR	16.1
Other Multilateral	0.3
Arab Agencies	–
TOTAL	*24.1*
ARAB COUNTRIES	*0.1*
E.E.C.+ MEMBERS	*42.6*
TOTAL	**78.8**

8. GRANTS

	1987
Australia	–
Austria	8.0
Belgium	0.6
Canada	–
Denmark	–
Finland	0.0
France	5.0
Germany	36.5
Ireland	0.0
Italy	0.6
Japan	2.1
Netherlands	–
New Zealand	–
Norway	0.0
Sweden	0.8
Switzerland	1.0
United Kingdom	–
United States	–
TOTAL	*54.6*
MULTILATERAL	*24.1*
ARAB COUNTRIES	*0.1*
E.E.C.+ MEMBERS	*42.6*
TOTAL	**78.8**

9. TOTAL OOF GROSS

	1987
Australia	–
Austria	–
Belgium	–
Canada	–
Denmark	–
Finland	–
France	–
Germany	4.6
Ireland	–
Italy	–
Japan	–
Netherlands	–
New Zealand	–
Norway	–
Sweden	–
Switzerland	–
United Kingdom	–
United States	–
TOTAL	*4.6*
MULTILATERAL	*–*
ARAB COUNTRIES	*–*
E.E.C.+ MEMBERS	*4.6*
TOTAL	**4.6**

10. ODA COMMITMENTS

1988	1989	1990	1987	1988	1989	1990
0.1	0.1	2.0	–	0.1	0.1	0.0
8.7	11.5	19.3	8.0	8.7	11.5	19.3
0.3	0.0	0.0	–	0.3	0.0	0.0
0.3	–	0.9	–	0.3	–	0.9
–	–	–	–	–	–	–
0.3	0.7	2.5	–	–	0.7	1.7
4.8	4.4	6.2	5.0	4.8	4.4	6.2
39.6	37.7	56.3	36.9	42.4	37.6	56.2
–	–	0.2	0.0	–	–	0.2
1.3	0.9	1.4	0.6	1.3	0.9	1.4
2.2	3.5	7.4	2.0	2.4	4.2	8.1
0.2	–	1.1	–	0.2	–	0.3
0.0	–	–	–	0.0	–	–
0.2	0.0	0.5	–	–	–	–
1.8	1.5	3.4	0.8	1.8	1.5	–
1.0	1.9	2.3	1.0	1.0	1.8	2.3
–	–	0.5	–	–	–	0.5
–	–	–	–	–	–	–
60.8	*62.1*	*104.0*	*54.2*	*63.3*	*62.7*	*97.2*
–	–	–	–	–	–	–
–	–	–	–	–	–	–
–	–	–	–	–	–	–
–	–	–	–	–	–	–
–	–	–	–	–	–	–
–	–	–	–	–	–	–
–	–	–	–	–	–	–
–	–	–	–	–	–	–
–	–	–	24.1	29.4	36.3	34.2
3.7	3.9	5.3	–	–	–	–
0.8	1.6	2.3	–	–	–	–
0.5	4.6	2.5	–	–	–	–
–	–	–	–	–	–	–
1.6	2.4	11.5	–	–	–	–
22.3	18.2	12.3	–	–	–	–
0.6	5.5	0.4	–	–	–	–
–	–	0.1	–	–	–	0.0
29.4	*36.3*	*34.3*	*24.1*	*29.4*	*36.3*	*34.2*
–	*0.0*	–	–	–	–	–
46.1	*42.9*	*65.7*	*42.4*	*49.0*	*42.9*	*64.8*
90.2	**98.4**	**138.3**	**78.3**	**92.7**	**99.0**	**131.4**

11. TECH. COOP. GRANTS

1988	1989	1990	1987	1988	1989	1990
0.1	0.1	2.0	–	0.1	0.1	0.1
8.7	11.5	19.3	7.0	8.7	8.6	10.1
0.3	0.0	0.0	0.1	0.1	–	–
0.3	–	0.9	–	–	–	–
–	–	–	–	–	–	–
0.3	0.7	2.5	0.0	–	–	0.3
4.8	4.4	6.2	5.0	4.8	4.4	6.2
39.6	37.7	56.3	35.7	38.9	37.3	52.6
–	–	0.2	0.0	–	–	0.2
1.3	0.9	1.4	0.6	0.8	0.8	0.9
2.2	3.5	7.4	1.8	2.2	3.5	5.7
0.2	–	1.1	–	–	–	–
0.0	–	–	–	–	–	–
0.2	0.0	0.5	–	–	–	–
1.8	1.5	3.4	–	–	–	–
1.0	1.9	2.3	–	–	–	–
–	–	0.5	–	–	–	–
–	–	–	–	–	–	–
60.8	*62.1*	*104.0*	*50.2*	*55.6*	*54.7*	*76.0*
29.4	*36.3*	*34.3*	*22.0*	*27.8*	*33.9*	*22.7*
–	*0.0*	–	–	–	–	–
46.1	*42.9*	*65.7*	*41.4*	*44.6*	*42.5*	*59.9*
90.2	**98.4**	**138.3**	**72.2**	**83.4**	**88.6**	**98.7**

12. TOTAL OOF NET

1988	1989	1990	1987	1988	1989	1990
–	–	–	–	–	–	–
–	–	–	–	–	–	–
–	–	–	-6.7	-9.6	–	–
–	–	–	–	–	–	–
–	–	–	–	–	–	–
–	–	–	–	–	–	–
–	1.3	3.0	2.4	-2.0	-3.9	-3.4
–	–	–	–	–	–	–
–	5.3	–	–	–	2.4	–
–	–	–	–	–	–	-130.5
–	–	–	–	–	–	–
–	–	–	–	–	–	–
–	–	–	–	–	–	–
–	–	–	–	–	–	–
–	–	–	–	-15.0	–	–
–	6.7	3.0	-4.4	-26.6	-1.4	-133.9
–	–	0.0	-68.5	-93.0	-67.0	-67.0
–	–	–	–	–	–	–
–	6.7	3.0	2.4	-2.0	-1.4	-3.4
–	**6.7**	**3.0**	**-72.9**	**-119.6**	**-68.4**	**-200.9**

13. ODF COMMITMENTS: BY PURPOSE %

	1987	1988	1989	1990
Education	–	–	0	–
Health	–	–	–	–
Other Social Infrastr.	–	–	–	–
Water Sanitat. Sewage	–	–	–	–
Energy	–	–	96	–
Telecommunications	–	–	–	–
Transportation	–	–	–	–
Agriculture	–	–	–	–
Extractive Industries	–	–	–	–
Manufacturing	2	–	–	–
Trade Banking Tourism	–	–	–	–
Technical Cooperation	96	96	4	–
Multisector Aid	–	–	–	–
Programme	–	–	–	–
Debt Reorganisation	–	–	–	–
Food Aid	0	–	–	–
Emergency Aid	2	4	0	–
Unspecified	–	–	–	–
TOTAL	100	100	100	–

14. GRANT ELEMENT OF ODA %

DAC COUNTRIES

	1987	1988	1989	1990
Australia	–	100.0	100.0	–
Austria	100.0	100.0	100.0	–
Belgium	–	100.0	100.0	–
Canada	–	100.0	–	–
Denmark	–	–	–	–
Finland	–	–	100.0	–
France	100.0	100.0	100.0	–
Germany	100.0	100.0	100.0	–
Ireland	100.0	–	–	–
Italy	100.0	100.0	100.0	–
Japan	100.0	100.0	100.0	–
Netherlands	–	100.0	–	–
New Zealand	–	100.0	–	–
Norway	–	–	–	–
Sweden	100.0	100.0	100.0	–
Switzerland	100.0	100.0	100.0	–
United Kingdom	–	–	–	–
United States	–	–	–	–
TOTAL	*100.0*	*100.0*	*100.0*	–
MULTILATERAL	*100.0*	*100.0*	*100.0*	–
ARAB COUNTRIES	–	–	–	–
E.E.C.+ MEMBERS	*100.0*	*100.0*	*100.0*	–
TOTAL	*100.0*	*100.0*	*100.0*	–

15. OTHER AGGREGATES

OFFICIAL COMMITMENTS:

	1987	1988	1989	1990
TOTAL BILATERAL	54.2	63.3	2020.7	97.2
of which:				
Arab Countries	–	–	1958.0	–
C.E.E.C.	–	–	1958.0	–
TOTAL MULTILATERAL	24.1	29.4	36.3	34.2
TOTAL BIL.& MULTIL.	78.3	92.7	2057.0	131.4
of which:				
ODA Grants	78.3	92.7	99.0	131.4
ODA Loans	–	–	1908.0	–

DISBURSEMENTS:

DAC COUNTRIES COMBINED

OFFICIAL & PRIVATE

	1987	1988	1989	1990
GROSS:				
Contractual Lending	647.6	1066.6	2073.8	2131.4
Export Credits, Total	642.6	1066.6	2073.8	2131.4
Export Credits, Priv.	642.6	1066.6	2068.2	2121.1
NET:				
Contractual Lending	337.7	632.2	1464.5	805.6
Export Credits Total	342.7	642.9	1471.8	881.7
PRIVATE SECTOR NET	-10.1	653.2	1481.3	703.4
Direct Investment	-307.6	60.5	-19.4	-361.9
Portfolio Investment	-52.0	-74.9	31.6	63.5
Export Credits	349.5	667.5	1469.1	1001.9

MARKET BORROWING:

CHANGE IN CLAIMS

	1987	1988	1989	1990
Banks	-200.0	252.0	636.0	1249.0

MEMORANDUM ITEM:

	1987	1988	1989	1990
C.E.E.C. (Gross)	–	–	–	–

1. TOTAL RECEIPTS NET

DAC COUNTRIES	1987	1988	1989	1990
Australia	20.8	14.5	122.5	30.3
Austria	0.6	0.7	1.1	1.3
Belgium	31.1	2.7	10.3	-87.8
Canada	–	–	8.7	-5.9
Denmark	–	–	–	–
Finland	5.1	6.0	0.0	2.1
France	244.1	-156.7	-246.2	227.1
Germany	14.2	289.6	-128.9	-651.1
Ireland	–	–	–	–
Italy	-629.9	125.2	-390.6	-446.0
Japan	49.3	-175.5	-46.6	-70.2
Netherlands	8.9	-5.9	-10.5	10.5
New Zealand	–	–	–	–
Norway	5.2	-5.4	1.3	0.1
Sweden	-15.3	–	30.8	-28.6
Switzerland	0.9	–	0.6	–
United Kingdom	158.8	-112.9	1012.2	-29.3
United States	21.0	28.0	-16.0	-7.0
TOTAL	-85.2	10.3	348.5	-1054.6
MULTILATERAL				
AF.D.F.	–	–	–	–
AF.D.B.	–	–	–	–
AS.D.B	–	–	–	–
CAR.D.B.	–	–	–	–
E.E.C.	–	–	–	–
IBRD	-5.9	-9.0	-4.0	-7.0
IDA	–	–	–	–
I.D.B.	–	–	–	–
IFAD	–	–	–	–
I.F.C.	–	–	–	–
IMF TRUST FUND	–	–	–	–
U.N. AGENCIES	–	–	–	–
UNDP	1.7	2.1	3.7	2.0
UNTA	1.0	0.9	1.0	0.7
UNICEF	–	0.3	4.0	1.5
UNRWA	–	–	–	–
WFP	–	–	–	–
UNHCR	–	–	–	0.5
Other Multilateral	0.2	0.1	0.8	0.4
Arab Agencies	-55.5	6.6	24.9	–
TOTAL	-58.7	1.0	30.4	-1.9
ARAB COUNTRIES	10.0	6.2	0.0	55.3
E.E.C.+ MEMBERS	-172.9	141.9	246.3	-976.7
TOTAL	-133.9	17.5	378.9	-1001.2

2. ODA LOANS GROSS

DAC COUNTRIES	1987	1988	1989	1990
Australia	–	–	–	–
Austria	–	–	–	–
Belgium	–	–	–	–
Canada	–	–	–	–
Denmark	–	–	–	–
Finland	–	–	–	–
France	–	–	–	–
Germany	–	–	–	–
Ireland	–	–	–	–
Italy	–	–	–	–
Japan	70.8	1.8	–	–
Netherlands	–	–	–	–
New Zealand	–	–	–	–
Norway	–	–	–	–
Sweden	–	–	–	–
Switzerland	–	–	–	–
United Kingdom	–	–	–	–
United States	–	–	–	–
TOTAL	70.8	1.8	–	–
MULTILATERAL	0.1	–	6.2	12.5
ARAB COUNTRIES	–	–	–	–
E.E.C.+ MEMBERS	–	–	–	–
TOTAL	70.9	1.8	6.2	12.5

3. TOTAL OFFICIAL GROSS

DAC COUNTRIES	1987	1988	1989	1990
Australia	–	0.1	0.1	0.1
Austria	0.7	0.7	1.1	1.4
Belgium	0.2	0.2	0.0	0.0
Canada	–	–	–	–
Denmark	–	–	–	–
Finland	0.0	0.2	–	2.1
France	4.0	3.6	3.2	3.2
Germany	34.7	14.1	7.1	655.7
Ireland	–	–	–	–
Italy	212.9	2.5	1.7	0.5
Japan	73.0	4.1	3.7	4.0
Netherlands	0.1	–	–	–
New Zealand	–	–	–	–
Norway	–	–	–	0.1
Sweden	0.0	–	–	0.7
Switzerland	0.9	–	0.6	–
United Kingdom	–	–	–	–
United States	24.0	39.0	8.0	5.0
TOTAL	350.4	64.4	25.5	672.7
MULTILATERAL	89.5	176.6	75.1	19.3
ARAB COUNTRIES	10.0	9.1	0.0	55.3
E.E.C.+ MEMBERS	251.9	20.3	11.9	659.4
TOTAL	450.0	250.1	100.6	747.4

4. TOTAL ODA NET

DAC COUNTRIES	1987	1988	1989	1990
Australia	–	0.1	0.1	0.1
Austria	0.6	0.7	1.1	1.3
Belgium	0.2	0.2	0.0	0.0
Canada	–	–	–	–
Denmark	–	–	–	–
Finland	0.0	0.2	–	2.1
France	4.0	3.6	3.2	3.2
Germany	2.9	2.3	1.9	3.3
Ireland	–	–	–	–
Italy	0.4	2.5	1.7	0.5
Japan	70.2	-10.1	-13.8	-19.8
Netherlands	0.1	–	–	–
New Zealand	–	–	–	–
Norway	–	–	–	0.1
Sweden	0.0	–	–	0.7
Switzerland	0.9	–	0.6	–
United Kingdom	–	–	–	–
United States	–	–	–	–
TOTAL	79.3	-0.7	-5.3	-8.6
MULTILATERAL				
AF.D.F.	–	–	–	–
AF.D.B.	–	–	–	–
AS.D.B	–	–	–	–
CAR.D.B.	–	–	–	–
E.E.C.	–	–	–	–
IBRD	–	–	–	–
IDA	–	–	–	–
I.D.B.	–	–	–	–
IFAD	–	–	–	–
I.F.C.	–	–	–	–
IMF TRUST FUND	–	–	–	–
U.N. AGENCIES	–	–	–	–
UNDP	1.7	2.1	3.7	2.0
UNTA	1.0	0.9	1.0	0.7
UNICEF	–	0.3	4.0	1.5
UNRWA	–	–	–	–
WFP	–	–	–	–
UNHCR	–	–	–	0.5
Other Multilateral	0.2	0.1	0.8	0.4
Arab Agencies	-0.7	-2.3	7.0	–
TOTAL	2.1	1.1	16.5	5.1
ARAB COUNTRIES	10.0	9.1	0.0	55.3
E.E.C.+ MEMBERS	7.6	8.5	6.8	7.0
TOTAL	91.4	9.6	11.2	51.8

5. ODA LOANS NET

DAC COUNTRIES	1987	1988	1989	1990
Australia	–	–	–	–
Austria	0.0	0.0	0.0	-0.1
Belgium	–	–	–	–
Canada	–	–	–	–
Denmark	–	–	–	–
Finland	–	–	–	–
France	–	–	–	–
Germany	–	–	–	–
Ireland	–	–	–	–
Italy	–	–	–	–
Japan	68.0	-12.4	-17.6	-23.7
Netherlands	–	–	–	–
New Zealand	–	–	–	–
Norway	–	–	–	–
Sweden	–	–	–	–
Switzerland	–	–	–	–
United Kingdom	–	–	–	–
United States	–	–	–	–
TOTAL	68.0	-12.5	-17.6	-23.8
MULTILATERAL	-0.8	-3.0	5.7	12.5
ARAB COUNTRIES	–	–	–	–
E.E.C.+ MEMBERS	–	–	–	–
TOTAL	67.1	-15.4	-12.0	-11.3

6. TOTAL OFFICIAL NET

DAC COUNTRIES	1987	1988	1989	1990
Australia	–	0.1	0.1	0.1
Austria	0.6	0.7	1.1	1.3
Belgium	0.2	0.2	0.0	0.0
Canada	–	–	–	–
Denmark	–	–	–	–
Finland	0.0	0.2	–	2.1
France	4.0	3.6	3.2	3.2
Germany	28.3	-12.4	6.5	652.6
Ireland	–	–	–	–
Italy	184.8	2.5	1.7	0.5
Japan	70.2	-10.1	-13.8	-19.8
Netherlands	0.1	–	–	–
New Zealand	–	–	–	–
Norway	–	–	–	0.1
Sweden	0.0	–	–	0.7
Switzerland	0.9	–	0.6	–
United Kingdom	–	–	–	–
United States	21.0	29.0	-16.0	-7.0
TOTAL	310.2	13.7	-16.7	633.8
MULTILATERAL	-58.7	1.0	30.4	-1.9
ARAB COUNTRIES	10.0	6.2	0.0	55.3
E.E.C.+ MEMBERS	217.5	-6.2	11.4	656.3
TOTAL	261.5	20.8	13.7	687.2

7. TOTAL ODA GROSS

DAC COUNTRIES	1987
Australia	–
Austria	0.7
Belgium	0.2
Canada	–
Denmark	–
Finland	0.0
France	4.0
Germany	2.9
Ireland	–
Italy	0.4
Japan	73.0
Netherlands	0.1
New Zealand	–
Norway	–
Sweden	0.0
Switzerland	0.9
United Kingdom	–
United States	–
TOTAL	82.2
AF.D.F.	–
AF.D.B.	–
AS.D.B	–
CAR.D.B.	–
E.E.C.	–
IBRD	–
IDA	–
I.D.B.	–
IFAD	–
I.F.C.	–
IMF TRUST FUND	–
U.N. AGENCIES	–
UNDP	1.7
UNTA	1.0
UNICEF	–
UNRWA	–
WFP	–
UNHCR	–
Other Multilateral	0.2
Arab Agencies	0.2
TOTAL	3.0
ARAB COUNTRIES	10.0
E.E.C.+ MEMBERS	7.6
TOTAL	95.2

8. GRANTS

DAC COUNTRIES	1987
Australia	–
Austria	0.7
Belgium	0.2
Canada	–
Denmark	–
Finland	0.0
France	4.0
Germany	2.9
Ireland	–
Italy	0.4
Japan	2.2
Netherlands	0.1
New Zealand	–
Norway	–
Sweden	0.0
Switzerland	0.9
United Kingdom	–
United States	–
TOTAL	11.4
MULTILATERAL	2.9
ARAB COUNTRIES	10.0
E.E.C.+ MEMBERS	7.6
TOTAL	24.3

9. TOTAL OOF GROSS

	1987
Australia	–
Austria	–
Belgium	–
Canada	–
Denmark	–
Finland	–
France	–
Germany	31.8
Ireland	–
Italy	212.5
Japan	–
Netherlands	–
New Zealand	–
Norway	–
Sweden	–
Switzerland	–
United Kingdom	–
United States	24.0
TOTAL	268.3
MULTILATERAL	86.5
ARAB COUNTRIES	–
E.E.C.+ MEMBERS	244.3
TOTAL	354.8

1988	1989	1990		1987	1988	1989	1990

10. ODA COMMITMENTS

Left columns (1988, 1989, 1990):

1988	1989	1990
0.1	0.1	0.1
0.7	1.1	1.4
0.2	0.0	0.0
–	–	–
0.2	–	2.1
3.6	3.2	3.2
2.3	1.9	3.3
–	–	–
2.5	1.7	0.5
4.1	3.7	4.0
–	–	–
–	–	–
–	–	0.1
–	–	0.7
–	0.6	–
–	–	–
–	–	–
13.6	*12.3*	*15.3*

Middle columns (1987, 1988, 1989, 1990):

1987	1988	1989	1990
–	0.1	0.1	0.0
0.7	0.7	1.1	1.4
0.0	0.0	0.0	0.0
–	0.3	–	–
–	–	–	–
–	–	–	0.2
4.0	3.6	3.2	3.2
2.9	2.3	1.9	3.3
–	–	–	–
0.8	3.8	1.7	0.5
2.4	2.5	4.0	4.0
0.1	–	–	–
–	–	–	–
–	–	–	–
–	–	–	–
0.9	–	0.6	–
–	–	–	–
–	–	–	–
11.9	*13.3*	*12.6*	*12.6*

Continuation (net/total blocks):

1988	1989	1990		1987	1988	1989	1990
–	–	–		–	–	–	–
–	–	–		–	–	–	–
–	–	–		–	–	–	–
–	–	–		–	–	–	–
–	–	–		–	–	–	–
–	–	–		–	–	–	–
–	–	–		–	–	–	–
–	–	–		–	–	–	–
–	–	–		–	–	–	–
–	–	–		–	–	–	–
–	–	–		2.8	3.5	9.5	5.1
2.1	3.7	2.0		–	–	–	–
0.9	1.0	0.7		–	–	–	–
0.3	4.0	1.5		–	–	–	–
–	–	–		–	–	–	–
–	–	0.5		–	–	–	–
0.1	0.8	0.4		–	–	–	–
0.7	7.5	12.5		0.6	28.8	22.8	–
4.1	*17.0*	*17.6*		*3.5*	*32.2*	*32.3*	*5.1*
9.1	*0.0*	*55.3*		*10.0*	*9.1*	*40.1*	*82.5*
8.5	*6.8*	*7.0*		*7.9*	*9.7*	*6.8*	*7.0*
26.8	*29.3*	*88.2*		*25.4*	*54.6*	*84.9*	*100.2*

11. TECH. COOP. GRANTS

1988	1989	1990		1987	1988	1989	1990
0.1	0.1	0.1		–	0.1	0.1	0.1
0.7	1.1	1.4		0.7	0.7	0.7	0.7
0.2	0.0	0.0		0.2	0.2	–	–
–	–	–		–	–	–	–
0.2	–	2.1		0.0	–	–	0.1
3.6	3.2	3.2		4.0	3.6	3.2	3.2
2.3	1.9	3.3		2.5	2.2	1.9	2.6
–	–	–		–	–	–	–
2.5	1.7	0.5		0.2	2.4	0.4	0.5
2.3	3.7	4.0		2.2	2.3	3.7	4.0
–	–	–		0.1	–	–	–
–	–	–		–	–	–	–
–	–	0.1		0.0	–	–	–
–	–	0.7		–	–	–	–
–	0.6	–		–	–	–	–
–	–	–		–	–	–	–
–	–	–		–	–	–	–
11.8	*12.3*	*15.3*		*9.8*	*11.5*	*9.9*	*11.1*
4.1	*10.8*	*5.1*		*2.8*	*3.5*	*9.5*	*5.1*
9.1	*0.0*	*55.3*		–	–	–	–
8.5	*6.8*	*7.0*		*7.0*	*8.3*	*5.5*	*6.3*
25.0	*23.1*	*75.7*		*12.7*	*14.9*	*19.4*	*16.1*

12. TOTAL OOF NET

1988	1989	1990		1987	1988	1989	1990
–	–	–		–	–	–	–
–	–	0.0		–	–	–	0.0
–	–	–		–	–	–	–
–	–	–		–	–	–	–
–	–	–		–	–	–	–
11.8	5.2	652.4		25.4	-14.7	4.6	649.3
–	–	–		184.5	–	–	–
–	–	–		–	–	–	–
–	–	–		–	–	–	–
–	–	–		–	–	–	–
–	–	–		–	–	–	–
–	–	–		–	–	–	–
39.0	8.0	5.0		21.0	29.0	-16.0	-7.0
50.8	*13.2*	*657.4*		*230.9*	*14.3*	*-11.4*	*642.3*
172.5	*58.1*	*1.7*		*-60.8*	*-0.1*	*13.9*	*-7.0*
–	–	–		–	*-2.9*	–	–
11.8	*5.2*	*652.4*		*209.9*	*-14.7*	*4.6*	*649.3*
223.3	*71.3*	*659.2*		*170.1*	*11.3*	*2.5*	*635.3*

13. ODF COMMITMENTS: BY PURPOSE %

	1987	1988	1989	1990
Education	–	0	–	–
Health	0	–	49	–
Other Social Infrastr.	–	–	–	–
Water Sanitat. Sewage	–	–	–	–
Energy	4	–	–	–
Telecommunications	–	–	–	–
Transportation	–	–	–	–
Agriculture	–	–	2	–
Extractive Industries	2	–	–	–
Manufacturing	5	–	16	–
Trade Banking Tourism	–	–	–	–
Technical Cooperation	50	29	22	–
Multisector Aid	–	–	–	–
Programme	–	53	12	–
Debt Reorganisation	–	–	–	–
Food Aid	38	17	–	–
Emergency Aid	2	1	–	–
Unspecified	0	–	–	–
TOTAL	100	100	100	–

14. GRANT ELEMENT OF ODA %

DAC COUNTRIES

	1987	1988	1989	1990
Australia	–	100.0	100.0	–
Austria	100.0	100.0	100.0	–
Belgium	100.0	100.0	100.0	–
Canada	–	100.0	–	–
Denmark	–	–	–	–
Finland	–	–	–	–
France	100.0	100.0	100.0	–
Germany	100.0	100.0	100.0	–
Ireland	–	–	–	–
Italy	100.0	100.0	100.0	–
Japan	100.0	100.0	100.0	–
Netherlands	100.0	–	–	–
New Zealand	–	–	–	–
Norway	–	–	–	–
Sweden	–	–	–	–
Switzerland	100.0	–	100.0	–
United Kingdom	–	–	–	–
United States	–	–	–	–
TOTAL	*100.0*	*100.0*	*100.0*	–
MULTILATERAL	*100.0*	*43.7*	*56.3*	–
ARAB COUNTRIES	*100.0*	*100.0*	*51.7*	–
E.E.C.+ MEMBERS	*100.0*	*100.0*	*100.0*	–
TOTAL	*100.0*	*66.8*	*60.6*	–

15. OTHER AGGREGATES

	1987	1988	1989	1990
OFFICIAL COMMITMENTS:				
TOTAL BILATERAL	305.5	69.5	61.8	177.2
of which:				
Arab Countries	50.0	9.1	40.1	82.5
C.E.E.C.	–	–	–	–
TOTAL MULTILATERAL	44.6	112.6	71.6	5.1
TOTAL BIL.& MULTIL.	350.1	182.2	133.5	182.2
of which:				
ODA Grants	25.4	25.9	22.4	17.7
ODA Loans	–	28.7	62.5	82.5
DISBURSEMENTS:				
DAC COUNTRIES COMBINED				
OFFICIAL & PRIVATE				
GROSS:				
Contractual Lending	1912.0	1365.2	3307.0	2366.3
Export Credits, Total	1597.0	1351.6	3307.0	2366.3
Export Credits, Priv.	1573.0	1312.6	3293.8	1709.0
NET:				
Contractual Lending	-361.3	31.2	379.3	-219.3
Export Credits Total	-639.1	58.4	397.4	-192.4
PRIVATE SECTOR NET	-395.4	-3.4	365.2	-1688.4
Direct Investment	13.2	0.2	2.7	0.4
Portfolio Investment	251.5	-33.0	-45.7	-851.1
Export Credits	-660.1	29.4	408.3	-837.7
MARKET BORROWING:				
CHANGE IN CLAIMS				
Banks	-69.0	719.0	56.0	-1186.0
MEMORANDUM ITEM:				
C.E.E.C. (Gross)	78.1	85.5	63.0	–

1. TOTAL RECEIPTS NET / 4. TOTAL ODA NET / 7. TOTAL ODA GROSS

	1. TOTAL RECEIPTS NET 1987	1988	1989	1990	4. TOTAL ODA NET 1987	1988	1989	1990	7. TOTAL ODA GROSS 1987
DAC COUNTRIES									
Australia	0.0	6.6	10.3	-0.6	0.0	0.1	0.3	0.1	0.0
Austria	0.2	0.2	0.5	0.2	0.2	0.2	0.5	0.2	0.2
Belgium	65.0	53.6	-57.4	-78.7	0.1	0.1	0.1	0.1	0.1
Canada	-14.5	-13.5	-19.5	-12.1	0.3	0.3	0.5	1.8	0.3
Denmark	-3.0	-2.7	-2.1	-2.0	–	–	–	–	–
Finland	8.4	5.5	1.1	–	–	–	–	–	–
France	19.0	19.0	-60.5	-15.2	4.4	5.1	4.9	6.1	4.4
Germany	145.6	-3.2	-23.9	36.1	36.5	35.3	18.3	39.3	111.3
Ireland	–	–	–	–	–	–	–	–	–
Italy	7.4	-2.2	0.8	1.5	0.5	0.7	2.5	13.3	0.5
Japan	-1.4	0.2	4.2	3.1	0.4	0.4	0.4	0.5	0.4
Netherlands	-5.5	-9.9	2.9	0.0	5.7	5.0	5.4	7.0	5.7
New Zealand	–	–	–	0.0	–	–	–	0.0	–
Norway	-0.1	–	–	0.1	–	–	–	0.1	–
Sweden	16.1	–	-13.1	-13.7	–	–	0.4	4.6	–
Switzerland	0.6	1.2	2.7	1.5	0.6	1.2	2.7	1.5	0.6
United Kingdom	13.8	10.8	76.7	-13.5	–	0.0	0.0	0.0	–
United States	1862.0	6226.0	2107.0	1479.0	1201.0	1191.0	1152.0	1296.0	1225.0
TOTAL	*2113.4*	*6291.5*	*2029.6*	*1385.7*	*1249.5*	*1239.4*	*1188.0*	*1370.6*	*1348.3*
MULTILATERAL									
AF.D.F.	–	–	–	–	–	–	–	–	–
AF.D.B.	–	–	–	–	–	–	–	–	–
AS.D.B	–	–	–	–	–	–	–	–	–
CAR.D.B.	–	–	–	–	–	–	–	–	–
E.E.C.	-8.7	-11.4	14.2	14.2	1.3	1.6	3.7	3.7	1.3
IBRD	-12.1	-17.0	-38.0	–	–	–	–	–	–
IDA	–	–	–	–	–	–	–	–	–
I.D.B.	–	–	–	–	–	–	–	–	–
IFAD	–	–	–	–	–	–	–	–	–
I.F.C.	-0.4	–	–	–	–	–	–	–	–
IMF TRUST FUND	–	–	–	–	–	–	–	–	–
U.N. AGENCIES	–	–	–	–	–	–	–	–	–
UNDP	–	–	–	–	–	–	–	–	–
UNTA	–	0.1	–	–	–	0.1	–	–	–
UNICEF	–	–	–	–	–	–	–	–	–
UNRWA	–	–	–	–	–	–	–	–	–
WFP	–	–	–	–	–	–	–	–	–
UNHCR	–	–	–	–	–	–	–	–	–
Other Multilateral	–	–	–	–	–	–	–	–	–
Arab Agencies	–	–	–	–	–	–	–	–	–
TOTAL	*-21.2*	*-28.3*	*-23.8*	*14.2*	*1.3*	*1.7*	*3.7*	*3.7*	*1.3*
ARAB COUNTRIES	–	–	–	–	–	–	–	–	–
E.E.C.+ MEMBERS	*233.5*	*54.0*	*-49.5*	*-57.5*	*48.4*	*47.9*	*34.9*	*69.5*	*123.2*
TOTAL	*2092.2*	*6263.2*	*2005.8*	*1399.9*	*1250.8*	*1241.1*	*1191.6*	*1374.3*	*1349.6*

2. ODA LOANS GROSS / 5. ODA LOANS NET / 8. GRANTS

	2. ODA LOANS GROSS 1987	1988	1989	1990	5. ODA LOANS NET 1987	1988	1989	1990	8. GRANTS 1987
DAC COUNTRIES									
Australia	–	–	–	–	–	–	–	–	0.0
Austria	–	–	0.3	–	–	–	0.3	–	0.2
Belgium	–	–	–	–	–	–	–	–	0.1
Canada	–	–	–	–	–	–	–	–	0.3
Denmark	–	–	–	–	–	–	–	–	–
Finland	–	–	–	–	–	–	–	–	–
France	–	–	–	–	–	–	–	–	4.4
Germany	77.5	82.2	68.9	122.1	2.7	5.7	-5.0	26.6	33.9
Ireland	–	–	–	–	–	–	–	–	–
Italy	–	–	–	–	–	–	–	–	0.5
Japan	–	–	–	–	–	–	–	–	0.4
Netherlands	–	–	–	–	–	–	–	–	5.7
New Zealand	–	–	–	–	–	–	–	–	–
Norway	–	–	–	–	–	–	–	–	–
Sweden	–	–	–	–	–	–	–	–	–
Switzerland	–	–	–	–	–	–	–	–	0.6
United Kingdom	–	–	–	–	–	–	–	–	–
United States	–	–	–	–	-24.0	-34.0	-37.0	-44.0	1225.0
TOTAL	*77.5*	*82.2*	*69.2*	*122.1*	*-21.3*	*-28.3*	*-41.7*	*-17.4*	*1270.8*
MULTILATERAL	–	–	–	–	–	–	–	–	*1.3*
ARAB COUNTRIES	–	–	–	–	–	–	–	–	–
E.E.C.+ MEMBERS	*77.5*	*82.2*	*68.9*	*122.1*	*2.7*	*5.7*	*-5.0*	*26.6*	*45.7*
TOTAL	*77.5*	*82.2*	*69.2*	*122.1*	*-21.3*	*-28.3*	*-41.7*	*-17.4*	*1272.1*

3. TOTAL OFFICIAL GROSS / 6. TOTAL OFFICIAL NET / 9. TOTAL OOF GROSS

	3. TOTAL OFFICIAL GROSS 1987	1988	1989	1990	6. TOTAL OFFICIAL NET 1987	1988	1989	1990	9. TOTAL OOF GROSS 1987
DAC COUNTRIES									
Australia	0.0	0.1	10.3	0.1	0.0	0.1	10.3	-0.6	–
Austria	0.2	0.2	0.5	0.2	0.2	0.2	0.5	0.2	–
Belgium	0.6	0.1	0.2	0.3	0.6	0.1	0.2	0.3	0.5
Canada	2.8	4.1	1.7	2.6	-14.5	-13.5	-19.5	-12.1	2.6
Denmark	–	–	–	–	–	–	–	–	–
Finland	–	–	–	–	–	–	–	–	–
France	4.4	5.1	4.9	6.1	4.4	5.1	4.9	6.1	–
Germany	126.0	116.4	105.3	152.9	43.3	30.5	24.2	49.9	14.7
Ireland	–	–	–	–	–	–	–	–	–
Italy	35.3	10.7	7.6	22.0	7.8	-2.2	-1.3	2.1	34.8
Japan	0.4	0.4	0.4	0.5	0.4	0.4	0.4	0.5	–
Netherlands	5.7	5.0	5.4	7.0	5.7	5.0	5.4	7.0	–
New Zealand	–	–	–	0.0	–	–	–	0.0	–
Norway	–	–	–	0.1	–	–	–	0.1	–
Sweden	–	–	0.4	4.6	–	–	0.4	4.6	–
Switzerland	0.6	1.2	2.7	1.5	0.6	1.2	2.7	1.5	–
United Kingdom	–	0.0	0.0	0.0	–	0.0	0.0	0.0	–
United States	1236.0	1218.0	1189.0	1340.0	1164.0	1150.0	1121.0	1264.0	11.0
TOTAL	*1411.9*	*1361.2*	*1328.3*	*1538.0*	*1212.3*	*1176.8*	*1149.1*	*1323.6*	*63.6*
MULTILATERAL	*1.3*	*1.7*	*29.5*	*29.5*	*-21.2*	*-28.3*	*-23.8*	*14.2*	–
ARAB COUNTRIES	–	–	–	–	–	–	–	–	–
E.E.C.+ MEMBERS	*173.2*	*138.9*	*152.9*	*217.8*	*53.0*	*27.1*	*47.5*	*79.6*	*50.0*
TOTAL	*1413.2*	*1362.9*	*1357.8*	*1567.4*	*1191.1*	*1148.5*	*1125.3*	*1337.7*	*63.6*

1988	1989	1990	1987	1988	1989	1990

10. ODA COMMITMENTS

1988	1989	1990	1987	1988	1989	1990
0.1	0.3	0.1	0.1	0.0	0.1	0.1
0.2	0.5	0.2	0.2	0.2	0.5	0.2
0.1	0.1	0.1	0.0	0.1	0.1	0.1
0.3	0.5	1.8	0.3	0.5	0.4	1.6
–	–	–	–	–	–	–
–	–	–	–	–	–	–
5.1	4.9	6.1	4.4	5.1	4.9	6.1
111.8	92.2	134.9	131.1	301.3	267.5	100.3
–	–	–	–	–	–	–
0.7	2.5	13.3	0.6	6.1	2.9	13.0
0.4	0.4	0.5	0.4	0.4	0.4	0.5
5.0	5.4	7.0	5.7	5.0	5.5	5.8
–	–	0.0	–	–	–	–
–	–	0.1	–	–	–	–
–	0.4	4.6	–	–	0.4	–
1.2	2.7	1.5	0.5	1.2	2.6	1.5
0.0	0.0	0.0	–	0.0	0.0	0.0
1225.0	1189.0	1340.0	1225.3	1225.0	1158.2	1271.9
1349.9	1298.9	1510.1	1368.4	1544.8	1443.5	1401.0
–	–	–	–	–	–	–
–	–	–	–	–	–	–
–	–	–	–	–	–	–
1.6	3.7	3.7	1.6	2.5	6.7	6.7
–	–	–	–	–	–	–
–	–	–	–	–	–	–
–	–	–	–	–	–	–
–	–	–	–	0.1	–	–
–	–	–	–	–	–	–
0.1	–	–	–	–	–	–
–	–	–	–	–	–	–
–	–	–	–	–	–	–
–	–	–	–	–	–	–
1.7	3.7	3.7	1.6	2.6	6.7	6.7
–	–	–	–	–	–	–
124.4	108.8	165.0	143.3	320.0	287.6	132.0
1351.6	1302.5	1513.8	1370.0	1547.4	1450.2	1407.8

11. TECH. COOP. GRANTS

1988	1989	1990	1987	1988	1989	1990
0.1	0.3	0.1	0.0	0.0	0.0	0.0
0.2	0.2	0.2	0.2	0.2	0.2	0.2
0.1	0.1	0.1	0.1	0.1	–	–
0.3	0.5	1.8	–	–	–	–
–	–	–	–	–	–	–
5.1	4.9	6.1	4.4	5.1	4.9	6.1
29.7	23.4	12.7	33.9	29.7	23.4	12.3
–	–	–	–	–	–	–
0.7	2.5	13.3	0.5	0.7	1.0	6.4
0.4	0.4	0.5	0.4	0.4	0.4	0.5
5.0	5.4	7.0	5.7	5.0	4.8	5.1
–	–	0.0	–	–	–	0.0
–	–	0.1	–	–	–	–
–	0.4	4.6	–	–	–	0.1
1.2	2.7	1.5	0.0	0.1	–	–
0.0	0.0	0.0	–	0.0	0.0	–
1225.0	1189.0	1340.0	–	–	–	–
1267.7	1229.7	1388.0	45.0	41.1	34.7	30.7
1.7	3.7	3.7	0.4	0.8	–	–
–	–	–	–	–	–	–
42.2	39.9	42.8	44.8	41.2	34.1	29.9
1269.4	1233.3	1391.7	45.4	41.9	34.7	30.7

12. TOTAL OOF NET

1988	1989	1990	1987	1988	1989	1990
–	10.0	–	–	–	10.0	-0.7
–	–	–	–	–	–	–
–	0.1	0.2	0.5	–	0.1	0.2
3.8	1.2	0.8	-14.8	-13.8	-19.9	-13.9
–	–	–	–	–	–	–
–	–	–	–	–	–	–
4.6	13.0	18.0	6.8	-4.8	5.9	10.6
–	–	–	–	–	–	–
10.0	5.2	8.8	7.3	-2.9	-3.8	-11.1
–	–	–	–	–	–	–
–	–	–	–	–	–	–
–	–	–	–	–	–	–
–	–	–	–	–	–	–
–	–	–	–	–	–	–
-7.0	–	–	-37.0	-41.0	-31.0	-32.0
11.3	29.5	27.8	-37.2	-62.6	-38.8	-47.0
–	25.8	25.8	-22.5	-30.0	-27.5	10.5
–	–	–	–	–	–	–
14.6	44.1	52.8	4.6	-20.7	12.7	10.1
11.3	55.3	53.7	-59.7	-92.6	-66.3	-36.5

13. ODF COMMITMENTS: BY PURPOSE %

	1987	1988	1989	1990
Education	–	–	–	–
Health	–	–	0	–
Other Social Infrastr.	–	2	–	–
Water Sanitat. Sewage	4	–	–	–
Energy	1	2	2	–
Telecommunications	–	–	–	–
Transportation	–	14	14	–
Agriculture	–	–	0	–
Extractive Industries	–	–	–	–
Manufacturing	–	–	–	–
Trade Banking Tourism	3	–	0	–
Technical Cooperation	3	3	2	–
Multisector Aid	–	–	–	–
Programme	89	79	81	–
Debt Reorganisation	–	–	–	–
Food Aid	–	–	0	–
Emergency Aid	–	0	0	–
Unspecified	–	–	–	–
TOTAL	100	100	100	–

14. GRANT ELEMENT OF ODA %

DAC COUNTRIES

	1987	1988	1989	1990
Australia	100.0	100.0	100.0	–
Austria	100.0	100.0	58.0	–
Belgium	100.0	100.0	100.0	–
Canada	100.0	100.0	100.0	–
Denmark	–	–	–	–
Finland	–	–	–	–
France	100.0	100.0	100.0	–
Germany	52.9	39.9	49.2	–
Ireland	–	–	–	–
Italy	100.0	100.0	100.0	–
Japan	100.0	100.0	100.0	–
Netherlands	100.0	100.0	100.0	–
New Zealand	–	–	–	–
Norway	–	–	–	–
Sweden	–	–	100.0	–
Switzerland	100.0	100.0	100.0	–
United Kingdom	–	100.0	100.0	–
United States	100.0	100.0	100.0	–
TOTAL	95.5	88.3	90.6	–
MULTILATERAL	100.0	100.0	100.0	–
ARAB COUNTRIES	–	–	–	–
E.E.C.+ MEMBERS	56.9	43.4	52.7	–
TOTAL	95.5	88.3	90.6	–

15. OTHER AGGREGATES

OFFICIAL COMMITMENTS:

	1987	1988	1989	1990
TOTAL BILATERAL	1493.9	1595.4	1470.6	1434.4
of which:				
Arab Countries	–	–	–	–
C.E.E.C.	–	–	–	–
TOTAL MULTILATERAL	1.6	2.6	32.1	32.1
TOTAL BIL.& MULTIL.	1495.5	1597.9	1502.6	1466.5
of which:				
ODA Grants	1272.7	1275.1	1207.9	1321.1
ODA Loans	97.3	272.3	242.3	86.6

DISBURSEMENTS:

DAC COUNTRIES COMBINED
OFFICIAL & PRIVATE

	1987	1988	1989	1990
GROSS:				
Contractual Lending	425.8	371.0	269.0	257.8
Export Credits, Total	346.3	288.8	197.5	127.0
Export Credits, Priv.	285.2	277.6	177.2	110.7
NET:				
Contractual Lending	66.3	-6.5	-128.7	-169.3
Export Credits Total	85.6	21.9	-88.5	-159.3
PRIVATE SECTOR NET	901.1	5114.7	880.5	62.2
Direct Investment	202.5	93.8	88.4	89.5
Portfolio Investment	573.3	4936.5	833.3	74.6
Export Credits	125.3	84.5	-41.3	-102.0

MARKET BORROWING:

CHANGE IN CLAIMS

	1987	1988	1989	1990
Banks	-623.0	-595.0	-1155.0	103.0

MEMORANDUM ITEM:

	1987	1988	1989	1990
C.E.E.C. (Gross)	–	–	–	–

	1987	1988	1989	1990		1987	1988	1989	1990		1987

1. TOTAL RECEIPTS NET / 4. TOTAL ODA NET / 7. TOTAL ODA GROSS

DAC COUNTRIES	1987	1988	1989	1990	4. TOTAL ODA NET	1987	1988	1989	1990	7. TOTAL ODA GROSS	1987
Australia	0.1	0.2	0.1	0.1		0.1	0.2	0.1	0.1	Australia	0.1
Austria	0.0	0.0	0.0	0.0		0.0	0.0	0.0	0.0	Austria	0.0
Belgium	1.1	-0.5	-0.6	0.3		0.6	0.1	0.2	0.1	Belgium	0.6
Canada	27.0	54.2	51.9	65.8		24.4	43.2	39.6	28.0	Canada	24.6
Denmark	–	–	–	–		–	–	–	–	Denmark	–
Finland	6.0	-0.9	-1.0	–		0.0	0.1	0.0	–	Finland	0.0
France	-1.7	-0.9	-12.2	-5.2		0.4	0.3	1.2	0.8	France	0.5
Germany	15.1	54.5	43.5	15.4		10.4	28.7	42.4	15.5	Germany	10.4
Ireland	–	0.0	–	–		–	0.0	–	–	Ireland	–
Italy	10.8	17.7	12.6	-8.3		4.4	17.6	11.8	3.6	Italy	5.3
Japan	3.3	6.3	18.6	66.8		3.3	5.6	22.9	63.5	Japan	4.8
Netherlands	0.9	4.8	20.0	30.3		6.4	4.7	10.7	25.5	Netherlands	11.8
New Zealand	0.0	0.0	0.0	–		0.0	0.0	0.0	–	New Zealand	0.0
Norway	-1.5	7.7	0.4	-1.2		2.6	3.0	2.2	2.6	Norway	2.6
Sweden	-0.5	0.7	0.3	1.4		–	0.7	0.3	1.4	Sweden	–
Switzerland	0.1	0.2	0.1	0.1		0.1	0.2	0.1	0.1	Switzerland	0.1
United Kingdom	10.6	39.1	25.9	24.0		4.7	8.5	4.5	6.9	United Kingdom	6.8
United States	95.0	131.0	187.0	91.0		89.0	60.0	90.0	104.0	United States	91.0
TOTAL	*166.3*	*314.1*	*346.7*	*280.5*		*146.4*	*173.0*	*225.9*	*251.9*	*TOTAL*	*158.5*
MULTILATERAL											
AF.D.F.	–	–	–	–		–	–	–	–	AF.D.F.	–
AF.D.B.	–	–	–	–		–	–	–	–	AF.D.B.	–
AS.D.B	–	–	–	–		–	–	–	–	AS.D.B	–
CAR.D.B.	4.4	8.5	9.3	9.3		1.9	1.6	3.9	3.9	CAR.D.B.	1.9
E.E.C.	7.4	10.7	21.2	21.2		7.0	4.0	14.5	14.5	E.E.C.	7.0
IBRD	22.6	2.0	-2.0	-27.0		–	–	–	–	IBRD	–
IDA	–	–	–	–		–	–	–	–	IDA	–
I.D.B.	46.0	18.2	31.9	29.5		6.3	7.3	2.6	-1.0	I.D.B.	10.4
IFAD	2.6	0.3	0.3	0.2		2.6	0.3	0.3	0.2	IFAD	2.6
I.F.C.	-0.4	1.2	4.8	4.4		–	–	–	–	I.F.C.	–
IMF TRUST FUND	–	–	–	–		–	–	–	–	IMF TRUST FUND	–
U.N. AGENCIES	–	–	–	–		–	–	–	–	U.N. AGENCIES	–
UNDP	1.7	2.7	3.7	2.5		1.7	2.7	3.7	2.5	UNDP	1.7
UNTA	0.8	1.0	1.1	0.7		0.8	1.0	1.1	0.7	UNTA	0.8
UNICEF	0.3	0.4	0.6	0.7		0.3	0.4	0.6	0.7	UNICEF	0.3
UNRWA	–	–	–	–		–	–	–	–	UNRWA	–
WFP	0.8	2.0	5.7	6.4		0.8	2.0	5.7	6.4	WFP	0.8
UNHCR	–	–	–	–		–	–	–	–	UNHCR	–
Other Multilateral	0.9	0.8	1.1	0.6		0.9	0.8	1.1	0.6	Other Multilateral	0.9
Arab Agencies	-5.6	-3.2	0.8	–		-1.5	-0.8	2.0	–	Arab Agencies	–
TOTAL	*81.3*	*44.5*	*78.4*	*48.5*		*20.7*	*19.2*	*35.4*	*28.5*	*TOTAL*	*26.4*
ARAB COUNTRIES	***-7.8***	***-4.6***	***0.9***	***-0.2***		***0.6***	***0.4***	***0.9***	***-0.2***	***ARAB COUNTRIES***	***0.6***
E.E.C.+ MEMBERS	*44.3*	*125.4*	*110.5*	*77.7*		*33.9*	*64.0*	*85.1*	*66.8*	*E.E.C.+ MEMBERS*	*42.3*
TOTAL	***239.7***	***353.9***	***426.1***	***328.8***		***167.7***	***192.6***	***262.2***	***280.2***	***TOTAL***	***185.4***

2. ODA LOANS GROSS / 5. ODA LOANS NET / 8. GRANTS

DAC COUNTRIES	1987	1988	1989	1990	5. ODA LOANS NET	1987	1988	1989	1990	8. GRANTS	1987
Australia	–	–	–	–		–	–	–	–	Australia	0.1
Austria	–	–	–	–		–	–	–	–	Austria	0.0
Belgium	0.5	–	–	–		0.5	–	–	–	Belgium	0.1
Canada	–	–	–	3.0		-0.2	–	–	3.0	Canada	24.6
Denmark	–	–	–	–		–	–	–	–	Denmark	–
Finland	–	–	–	–		–	–	–	–	Finland	0.0
France	0.2	–	0.0	0.3		0.2	–	0.0	0.2	France	0.3
Germany	6.5	10.0	38.0	10.8		6.5	10.0	37.9	10.7	Germany	3.9
Ireland	–	–	–	–		–	–	–	–	Ireland	–
Italy	2.3	16.2	11.3	1.2		1.4	15.2	9.6	0.8	Italy	3.0
Japan	3.7	4.1	23.9	62.4		2.2	4.1	22.6	62.3	Japan	1.1
Netherlands	9.6	0.6	12.5	8.9		4.3	0.3	5.2	2.9	Netherlands	2.1
New Zealand	–	–	–	–		–	–	–	–	New Zealand	0.0
Norway	–	–	–	–		–	–	–	–	Norway	2.6
Sweden	–	–	–	–		–	–	–	–	Sweden	–
Switzerland	–	–	–	–		–	–	–	–	Switzerland	0.1
United Kingdom	5.3	6.1	1.8	1.7		3.3	5.0	0.3	1.7	United Kingdom	1.4
United States	35.0	46.0	34.0	40.0		33.0	29.0	17.0	37.0	United States	56.0
TOTAL	*63.2*	*83.0*	*121.5*	*128.4*		*51.0*	*63.6*	*92.5*	*118.5*	*TOTAL*	*95.4*
MULTILATERAL	*17.2*	*13.0*	*14.3*	*9.9*		*11.5*	*7.0*	*8.8*	*2.8*	*MULTILATERAL*	*9.2*
ARAB COUNTRIES	***0.6***	***0.4***	***0.9***	***0.1***		***0.6***	***0.4***	***0.9***	***-0.2***	***ARAB COUNTRIES***	***–***
E.E.C.+ MEMBERS	*27.9*	*32.9*	*63.6*	*23.0*		*19.5*	*30.5*	*53.0*	*16.2*	*E.E.C.+ MEMBERS*	*14.4*
TOTAL	***80.9***	***96.4***	***136.7***	***138.3***		***63.1***	***71.0***	***102.3***	***121.0***	***TOTAL***	***104.5***

3. TOTAL OFFICIAL GROSS / 6. TOTAL OFFICIAL NET / 9. TOTAL OOF GROSS

DAC COUNTRIES	1987	1988	1989	1990	6. TOTAL OFFICIAL NET	1987	1988	1989	1990	9. TOTAL OOF GROSS	1987
Australia	0.1	0.2	0.1	0.1		0.1	0.2	0.1	0.1	Australia	–
Austria	0.0	0.0	0.0	0.0		0.0	0.0	0.0	0.0	Austria	–
Belgium	0.7	0.1	0.2	0.1		0.7	0.1	0.2	0.1	Belgium	0.0
Canada	28.8	56.0	54.6	69.7		27.0	54.2	51.9	65.8	Canada	4.2
Denmark	–	–	–	–		–	–	–	–	Denmark	–
Finland	0.0	0.1	0.0	–		0.0	0.1	0.0	–	Finland	–
France	2.1	3.8	1.2	2.3		1.8	3.8	1.2	0.8	France	1.6
Germany	10.4	28.7	42.8	15.6		10.4	28.7	42.7	15.4	Germany	–
Ireland	–	0.0	–	–		–	0.0	–	–	Ireland	–
Italy	11.2	18.6	17.3	4.0		9.3	17.6	12.6	3.6	Italy	5.8
Japan	4.8	5.6	24.3	63.6		3.1	5.4	22.9	63.3	Japan	–
Netherlands	12.9	5.0	23.1	32.4		7.2	4.5	15.4	26.3	Netherlands	1.2
New Zealand	0.0	0.0	0.0	–		0.0	0.0	0.0	–	New Zealand	–
Norway	2.6	3.0	2.2	2.6		2.6	3.0	2.2	2.6	Norway	–
Sweden	–	0.7	0.3	1.4		–	0.7	0.3	1.4	Sweden	–
Switzerland	0.1	0.2	0.1	0.1		0.1	0.2	0.1	0.1	Switzerland	–
United Kingdom	10.9	34.5	33.3	26.2		4.2	32.5	29.7	24.2	United Kingdom	4.1
United States	91.0	127.0	155.0	110.0		87.0	92.0	120.0	104.0	United States	–
TOTAL	*175.4*	*283.6*	*354.5*	*328.1*		*153.4*	*243.1*	*299.4*	*307.7*	*TOTAL*	*16.9*
MULTILATERAL	*143.5*	*118.9*	*160.5*	*143.5*		*81.3*	*44.5*	*78.4*	*48.5*	*MULTILATERAL*	*117.1*
ARAB COUNTRIES	***0.6***	***0.4***	***0.9***	***0.1***		***-7.8***	***-4.6***	***0.9***	***-0.2***	***ARAB COUNTRIES***	***–***
E.E.C.+ MEMBERS	*55.5*	*101.6*	*139.3*	*102.1*		*41.0*	*97.9*	*123.1*	*91.7*	*E.E.C.+ MEMBERS*	*13.2*
TOTAL	***319.4***	***402.9***	***515.9***	***471.7***		***226.9***	***282.9***	***378.7***	***356.0***	***TOTAL***	***133.9***

1988	1989	1990

10. ODA COMMITMENTS

1987	1988	1989	1990

1988	1989	1990		1987	1988	1989	1990
0.2	0.1	0.1		0.0	0.2	0.2	0.2
0.0	0.0	0.0		0.0	0.0	0.0	0.0
0.1	0.2	0.1		0.6	0.1	0.2	0.1
43.2	39.6	28.0		17.7	29.9	20.1	29.8
–	–	–		–	–	–	–
0.1	0.0	–		–	–	–	–
0.3	1.2	0.9		0.6	0.3	1.5	6.2
28.7	42.5	15.6		16.7	24.3	38.7	18.6
0.0	–	–		–	0.0	–	–
18.6	13.5	4.0		21.7	20.1	2.1	4.2
5.6	24.3	63.6		2.4	108.8	21.6	26.0
5.0	17.9	31.5		11.9	4.0	17.6	26.2
0.0	0.0	–		0.0	–	–	–
3.0	2.2	2.6		0.6	0.8	1.4	5.3
0.7	0.3	1.4		0.7	2.2	0.2	1.8
0.2	0.1	0.1		0.0	0.2	0.1	0.1
9.6	5.9	6.9		16.0	4.8	4.2	3.8
77.0	107.0	107.0		108.1	93.3	107.4	78.3
192.4	254.9	261.8		196.9	289.1	215.2	200.5
–	–	–		–	–	–	–
–	–	–		–	–	–	–
1.6	3.9	3.9		–	21.0	5.4	5.4
4.0	14.5	14.5		10.0	31.0	5.9	5.9
–	–	–		–	–	–	–
11.7	7.2	3.7		2.0	–	–	–
1.1	0.7	1.6		6.6	–	–	–
–	–	–		–	–	–	–
–	–	–		4.5	6.8	12.1	10.9
2.7	3.7	2.5		–	–	–	–
1.0	1.1	0.7		–	–	–	–
0.4	0.6	0.7		–	–	–	–
–	–	–		–	–	–	–
2.0	5.7	6.4		–	–	–	–
–	–	–		–	–	–	–
0.8	1.1	0.6		–	–	5.0	–
–	2.5	0.7					
25.2	40.8	35.2		23.1	58.8	28.4	22.2
0.4	0.9	0.1		–	–	–	–
66.4	95.7	73.5		77.4	84.6	70.1	65.1
218.0	296.6	297.1		219.9	347.9	243.6	222.7

11. TECH. COOP. GRANTS

1988	1989	1990		1987	1988	1989	1990
0.2	0.1	0.1		0.1	0.0	0.0	0.0
0.0	0.0	0.0		0.0	0.0	0.0	0.0
0.1	0.2	0.1		0.1	–	–	–
43.2	39.6	25.0		–	0.6	1.0	1.0
–	–	–		–	–	–	–
0.1	0.0	–		–	0.0	–	–
0.3	1.2	0.6		0.3	0.3	0.3	0.5
18.7	4.5	4.8		3.7	4.3	4.4	4.5
0.0	–	–		–	0.0	–	–
2.4	2.2	2.8		0.9	0.6	–	–
1.5	0.4	1.2		1.1	0.6	0.4	0.6
4.4	5.4	22.6		1.0	1.0	1.0	1.1
0.0	0.0	–		0.0	0.0	–	–
3.0	2.2	2.6		0.1	0.2	0.2	0.2
0.7	0.3	1.4		–	0.4	0.3	1.4
0.2	0.1	0.1		–	0.0	–	–
3.5	4.2	5.2		1.4	2.7	3.6	3.1
31.0	73.0	67.0		20.0	18.0	20.0	18.0
109.4	133.4	133.5		28.7	28.8	31.2	30.4
12.2	26.5	25.3		4.5	6.3	6.4	4.5
–	–	–		–	–	–	–
33.5	32.1	50.6		8.3	10.3	9.3	9.1
121.6	159.9	158.8		33.2	35.1	37.6	34.9

12. TOTAL OOF NET

1988	1989	1990		1987	1988	1989	1990
–	–	–		–	–	–	–
–	–	–		–	–	–	–
–	0.0	–		0.0	–	0.0	–
12.8	15.0	41.7		2.6	11.0	12.3	37.8
–	–	–		–	–	–	–
3.5	–	1.4		1.4	3.4	–	0.0
–	0.3	0.0		–	–	0.3	0.0
–	3.8	–		4.9	–	0.9	–
–	–	–		-0.2	-0.2	–	-0.2
–	5.2	0.9		0.8	-0.2	4.8	0.9
–	–	–		–	–	–	–
–	–	–		–	–	–	–
–	–	–		–	–	–	–
24.9	27.4	19.3		-0.5	24.0	25.3	17.3
50.0	48.0	3.0		-2.0	32.0	30.0	–
91.1	99.7	66.3		7.0	70.0	73.5	55.8
93.7	119.7	108.3		60.6	25.3	43.0	20.0
–	–	–		-8.4	-5.0	–	–
35.2	43.6	28.6		7.0	33.9	37.9	25.0
184.8	219.3	174.6		59.2	90.3	116.5	75.8

13. ODF COMMITMENTS: BY PURPOSE %

	1987	1988	1989	1990
Education	2	3	2	–
Health	3	5	1	–
Other Social Infrastr.	14	9	3	–
Water Sanitat. Sewage	4	10	–	–
Energy	6	1	0	–
Telecommunications	0	28	–	–
Transportation	0	–	–	–
Agriculture	8	8	1	–
Extractive Industries	0	–	1	–
Manufacturing	13	1	5	–
Trade Banking Tourism	4	1	1	–
Technical Cooperation	9	11	11	–
Multisector Aid	0	0	9	–
Programme	12	5	22	–
Debt Reorganisation	8	0	6	–
Food Aid	17	.17	17	–
Emergency Aid	0	1	21	–
Unspecified	–	0	–	–
TOTAL	100	100	100	–

14. GRANT ELEMENT OF ODA %

DAC COUNTRIES	1987	1988	1989	1990
Australia	100.0	100.0	100.0	–
Austria	100.0	100.0	100.0	–
Belgium	81.3	100.0	100.0	–
Canada	100.0	100.0	100.0	–
Denmark	–	–	–	–
Finland	–	–	–	–
France	100.0	100.0	100.0	–
Germany	54.5	85.2	67.1	–
Ireland	–	100.0	–	–
Italy	61.0	68.9	77.7	–
Japan	70.4	51.7	51.9	–
Netherlands	63.6	100.0	76.1	–
New Zealand	100.0	–	–	–
Norway	100.0	100.0	100.0	–
Sweden	100.0	100.0	100.0	–
Switzerland	100.0	100.0	100.0	–
United Kingdom	24.8	100.0	100.0	–
United States	83.1	85.4	88.7	–
TOTAL	73.9	73.6	81.1	–
MULTILATERAL	100.0	89.8	85.3	–
ARAB COUNTRIES	–	–	–	–
E.E.C.+ MEMBERS	58.3	88.0	74.5	–
TOTAL	75.7	75.8	81.5	–

15. OTHER AGGREGATES

	1987	1988	1989	1990
OFFICIAL COMMITMENTS:				
TOTAL BILATERAL	230.9	380.6	331.2	265.6
of which:				
Arab Countries	–	–	–	–
C.E.E.C.	–	–	–	–
TOTAL MULTILATERAL	187.4	99.8	211.5	237.8
TOTAL BIL.& MULTIL.	418.4	480.3	542.7	503.4
of which:				
ODA Grants	107.5	160.9	136.8	125.4
ODA Loans	112.4	187.0	106.8	97.4
DISBURSEMENTS:				
DAC COUNTRIES COMBINED				
OFFICIAL & PRIVATE				
GROSS:				
Contractual Lending	89.8	201.9	272.8	200.0
Export Credits, Total	13.9	41.5	66.9	47.0
Export Credits, Priv.	9.8	27.7	51.7	5.3
NET:				
Contractual Lending	24.9	121.2	174.3	139.8
Export Credits Total	-32.8	-13.6	3.0	1.1
PRIVATE SECTOR NET	12.9	71.0	47.3	-27.3
Direct Investment	-5.0	44.1	49.1	66.2
Portfolio Investment	51.0	39.3	-10.0	-59.0
Export Credits	-33.1	-12.4	8.2	-34.5
MARKET BORROWING:				
CHANGE IN CLAIMS				
Banks	4.0	50.0	114.0	-76.0
MEMORANDUM ITEM:				
C.E.E.C. (Gross)	–	–	–	–

DISBURSEMENTS, UNLESS OTHERWISE STATED

1. TOTAL RECEIPTS NET

DAC COUNTRIES	1987	1988	1989	1990
Australia	0.6	0.6	0.7	1.0
Austria	-3.1	-4.2	-1.4	-5.6
Belgium	10.0	0.8	1.7	3.3
Canada	3.4	10.7	17.1	21.1
Denmark	-1.2	-1.4	-1.4	-1.6
Finland	0.1	5.1	-0.1	3.9
France	165.2	224.3	64.8	16.0
Germany	99.2	47.2	49.2	195.9
Ireland	0.1	0.1	0.0	0.3
Italy	7.5	-12.9	0.1	11.5
Japan	2.9	14.5	12.2	167.9
Netherlands	-1.6	5.2	-0.7	5.1
New Zealand	–	–	–	–
Norway	-0.6	-0.6	-0.6	0.8
Sweden	2.2	3.0	0.6	3.3
Switzerland	0.2	0.1	3.2	0.7
United Kingdom	57.4	98.9	333.7	29.2
United States	59.0	154.0	127.0	112.0
TOTAL	*401.2*	*545.3*	*606.1*	*564.7*
MULTILATERAL				
AF.D.F.	–	–	–	–
AF.D.B.	–	–	–	–
AS.D.B	–	–	–	–
CAR.D.B.	–	–	–	–
E.E.C.	4.8	6.9	20.2	20.2
IBRD	69.7	24.0	10.0	71.0
IDA	-1.0	-1.0	-1.0	-1.0
I.D.B.	–	–	–	–
IFAD	3.4	-1.8	-0.8	1.5
I.F.C.	-11.6	-13.7	-4.4	0.3
IMF TRUST FUND	–	–	–	–
U.N. AGENCIES	–	–	–	–
UNDP	2.0	2.3	2.9	3.1
UNTA	0.9	1.0	1.0	0.8
UNICEF	0.2	0.2	0.4	2.5
UNRWA	–	–	–	–
WFP	8.3	7.0	7.8	9.8
UNHCR	–	–	–	0.4
Other Multilateral	1.1	1.4	1.8	2.6
Arab Agencies	14.0	-18.2	-9.3	–
TOTAL	*91.7*	*8.1*	*28.4*	*111.1*
ARAB COUNTRIES	**376.7**	**284.5**	**125.2**	**435.6**
E.E.C.+ MEMBERS	*341.4*	*369.0*	*467.7*	*279.9*
TOTAL	**869.6**	**837.9**	**759.7**	**1111.4**

2. ODA LOANS GROSS

DAC COUNTRIES	1987	1988	1989	1990
Australia	–	–	–	–
Austria	–	–	–	–
Belgium	–	–	–	–
Canada	–	–	–	–
Denmark	–	–	–	–
Finland	–	–	–	–
France	0.0	2.6	0.8	5.3
Germany	17.0	8.9	13.6	32.9
Ireland	–	–	–	–
Italy	–	–	3.2	5.8
Japan	22.6	11.2	6.9	157.4
Netherlands	–	–	–	–
New Zealand	–	–	–	–
Norway	–	–	–	–
Sweden	–	–	–	–
Switzerland	–	–	3.0	–
United Kingdom	3.9	2.8	4.3	0.8
United States	11.0	5.0	7.0	5.0
TOTAL	*54.5*	*30.5*	*38.8*	*207.1*
MULTILATERAL	*16.7*	*4.9*	*6.3*	*7.1*
ARAB COUNTRIES	**19.0**	**23.6**	**14.9**	**10.5**
E.E.C.+ MEMBERS	*21.5*	*14.3*	*22.4*	*45.2*
TOTAL	**90.2**	**58.9**	**60.1**	**224.7**

3. TOTAL OFFICIAL GROSS

DAC COUNTRIES	1987	1988	1989	1990
Australia	0.5	0.6	0.7	1.0
Austria	0.2	0.2	0.3	1.5
Belgium	0.2	0.1	0.4	0.5
Canada	3.4	10.7	17.1	21.1
Denmark	–	0.8	–	–
Finland	0.1	–	0.5	3.9
France	3.3	6.0	3.8	10.6
Germany	33.8	32.5	51.4	199.9
Ireland	0.1	0.1	0.0	0.3
Italy	6.5	5.8	7.4	27.1
Japan	29.9	20.3	14.3	201.6
Netherlands	0.1	0.1	0.1	5.5
New Zealand	–	–	–	–
Norway	–	–	0.0	1.5
Sweden	2.4	3.0	0.1	5.4
Switzerland	0.2	0.1	3.2	0.7
United Kingdom	7.9	7.3	8.4	9.9
United States	110.0	76.0	139.0	143.0
TOTAL	*198.4*	*163.5*	*246.6*	*633.3*
MULTILATERAL	*242.3*	*179.4*	*156.8*	*180.7*
ARAB COUNTRIES	**428.7**	**340.1**	**174.6**	**450.5**
E.E.C.+ MEMBERS	*59.8*	*63.7*	*96.4*	*278.5*
TOTAL	**869.5**	**683.0**	**578.0**	**1264.5**

4. TOTAL ODA NET

DAC COUNTRIES	1987	1988	1989	1990
Australia	0.5	0.6	0.7	1.0
Austria	-3.1	-4.2	-1.8	-5.6
Belgium	0.1	0.1	0.1	0.1
Canada	3.4	10.7	10.1	18.0
Denmark	–	-0.6	–	–
Finland	0.1	–	0.5	3.9
France	2.7	5.7	3.8	6.8
Germany	27.2	21.5	29.0	174.0
Ireland	0.1	0.1	0.0	0.3
Italy	5.4	0.9	2.1	7.5
Japan	24.4	14.5	12.2	145.0
Netherlands	0.1	0.1	0.1	5.5
New Zealand	–	–	–	–
Norway	-0.6	-0.6	-0.6	0.8
Sweden	2.4	3.0	0.1	5.4
Switzerland	0.2	0.1	3.2	0.7
United Kingdom	2.7	2.0	7.9	9.9
United States	106.0	69.0	63.0	58.0
TOTAL	*171.5*	*122.9*	*130.5*	*431.2*
MULTILATERAL				
AF.D.F.	–	–	–	–
AF.D.B.	–	–	–	–
AS.D.B	–	–	–	–
CAR.D.B.	–	–	–	–
E.E.C.	3.1	3.6	4.2	4.2
IBRD	–	–	–	–
IDA	-1.0	-1.0	-1.0	-1.0
I.D.B.	–	–	–	–
IFAD	3.4	-1.8	-0.8	1.5
I.F.C.	–	–	–	–
IMF TRUST FUND	–	–	–	–
U.N. AGENCIES	–	–	–	–
UNDP	2.0	2.3	2.9	3.1
UNTA	0.9	1.0	1.0	0.8
UNICEF	0.2	0.2	0.4	2.5
UNRWA	–	–	–	–
WFP	8.3	7.0	7.8	9.8
UNHCR	–	–	–	0.4
Other Multilateral	1.1	1.4	1.8	2.6
Arab Agencies	6.6	-2.0	1.2	–
TOTAL	*24.5*	*10.8*	*17.3*	*23.9*
ARAB COUNTRIES	**381.3**	**283.0**	**125.2**	**436.2**
E.E.C.+ MEMBERS	*41.4*	*33.5*	*47.3*	*208.3*
TOTAL	**577.3**	**416.7**	**273.0**	**891.3**

5. ODA LOANS NET

DAC COUNTRIES	1987	1988	1989	1990
Australia	–	–	–	–
Austria	-3.4	-4.4	-2.0	-7.1
Belgium	–	–	–	–
Canada	–	–	–	–
Denmark	–	-0.6	–	–
Finland	–	–	–	–
France	-0.6	2.4	0.8	1.5
Germany	10.4	-2.0	13.2	32.2
Ireland	–	–	–	–
Italy	-1.1	-2.3	-0.9	0.8
Japan	17.1	5.4	4.9	136.5
Netherlands	–	–	–	–
New Zealand	–	–	–	–
Norway	-0.6	-0.6	-0.6	-0.7
Sweden	–	–	–	–
Switzerland	–	–	3.0	–
United Kingdom	-1.0	-2.4	3.8	0.8
United States	7.0	–	–	-3.0
TOTAL	*27.8*	*-4.6*	*22.1*	*161.0*
MULTILATERAL	*9.5*	*-4.8*	*-0.3*	*1.9*
ARAB COUNTRIES	**-19.7**	**-16.6**	**-34.5**	**-3.8**
E.E.C.+ MEMBERS	*8.3*	*-5.0*	*17.3*	*35.7*
TOTAL	**17.6**	**-26.0**	**-12.8**	**159.1**

6. TOTAL OFFICIAL NET

DAC COUNTRIES	1987	1988	1989	1990
Australia	0.5	0.6	0.7	1.0
Austria	-3.1	-4.2	-1.8	-5.6
Belgium	0.2	0.1	0.4	0.5
Canada	3.4	10.7	17.1	21.1
Denmark	-0.2	0.0	-0.1	-0.2
Finland	0.1	–	0.5	3.9
France	2.7	5.7	3.8	6.8
Germany	27.2	21.5	48.2	195.9
Ireland	0.1	0.1	0.0	0.3
Italy	5.4	2.5	0.1	11.0
Japan	24.4	14.5	12.2	180.7
Netherlands	0.1	0.1	0.1	5.5
New Zealand	–	–	–	–
Norway	-0.6	-0.6	-0.6	0.8
Sweden	2.4	3.0	0.1	5.4
Switzerland	0.2	0.1	3.2	0.7
United Kingdom	2.9	2.1	7.9	9.9
United States	59.0	-69.0	127.0	113.0
TOTAL	*124.6*	*-12.8*	*218.7*	*550.5*
MULTILATERAL	*91.7*	*8.1*	*28.4*	*111.1*
ARAB COUNTRIES	**376.7**	**284.5**	**125.2**	**435.6**
E.E.C.+ MEMBERS	*43.3*	*39.0*	*80.5*	*249.8*
TOTAL	**593.0**	**279.8**	**372.4**	**1097.2**

7. TOTAL ODA GROSS

	1987
Australia	0.5
Austria	0.2
Belgium	0.1
Canada	3.4
Denmark	–
Finland	0.1
France	3.3
Germany	33.7
Ireland	0.1
Italy	6.5
Japan	29.9
Netherlands	0.1
New Zealand	–
Norway	–
Sweden	2.4
Switzerland	0.2
United Kingdom	7.7
United States	110.0
TOTAL	*198.2*
AF.D.F.	–
AF.D.B.	–
AS.D.B	–
CAR.D.B.	–
E.E.C.	3.1
IBRD	–
IDA	–
I.D.B.	–
IFAD	4.2
I.F.C.	–
IMF TRUST FUND	–
U.N. AGENCIES	–
UNDP	2.0
UNTA	0.9
UNICEF	0.2
UNRWA	–
WFP	8.3
UNHCR	–
Other Multilateral	1.1
Arab Agencies	11.9
TOTAL	*31.7*
ARAB COUNTRIES	**420.0**
E.E.C.+ MEMBERS	*54.6*
TOTAL	**649.8**

8. GRANTS

	1987
Australia	0.5
Austria	0.2
Belgium	0.1
Canada	3.4
Denmark	–
Finland	0.1
France	3.2
Germany	16.8
Ireland	0.1
Italy	6.5
Japan	7.4
Netherlands	0.1
New Zealand	–
Norway	–
Sweden	2.4
Switzerland	0.2
United Kingdom	3.8
United States	99.0
TOTAL	*143.7*
MULTILATERAL	*15.0*
ARAB COUNTRIES	**400.9**
E.E.C.+ MEMBERS	*33.2*
TOTAL	**559.6**

9. TOTAL OOF GROSS

	1987
Australia	–
Austria	–
Belgium	0.1
Canada	–
Denmark	–
Finland	–
France	–
Germany	0.0
Ireland	–
Italy	–
Japan	–
Netherlands	–
New Zealand	–
Norway	–
Sweden	–
Switzerland	–
United Kingdom	0.2
United States	–
TOTAL	*0.3*
MULTILATERAL	*210.6*
ARAB COUNTRIES	**8.8**
E.E.C.+ MEMBERS	*5.2*
TOTAL	**219.7**

10. ODA COMMITMENTS

1988	1989	1990	1987	1988	1989	1990
0.6	0.7	1.0	0.1	1.3	0.2	0.2
0.2	0.3	1.5	0.2	0.2	0.3	1.5
0.1	0.1	0.1	0.0	0.3	0.1	0.1
10.7	10.1	18.0	22.3	1.7	0.9	32.4
0.0	–	–	–	–	–	–
–	0.5	3.9	–	2.3	0.0	4.0
6.0	3.8	10.6	3.2	3.4	2.6	10.9
32.5	29.5	174.7	42.2	17.6	27.1	204.7
0.1	0.0	0.3	0.1	0.1	0.0	0.3
3.2	6.2	12.4	7.7	10.7	1.0	10.9
20.3	14.3	165.9	7.9	10.2	134.9	301.3
0.1	0.1	5.5	0.1	0.1	0.1	2.9
–	–	–	–	–	–	–
–	0.0	1.5	0.1	–	–	–
3.0	0.1	5.4	2.5	3.0	1.0	0.2
0.1	3.2	0.7	0.1	–	0.3	0.5
7.2	8.4	9.9	27.5	12.7	3.3	9.1
74.0	70.0	66.0	110.8	18.8	28.0	74.0
158.0	*147.2*	*477.3*	*224.9*	*82.3*	*199.8*	*652.9*
–	–	–	–	–	–	–
–	–	–	–	–	–	–
–	–	–	–	–	–	–
3.6	4.2	4.2	0.9	19.9	9.1	9.1
–	–	–	–	–	–	–
–	0.5	3.3	–	–	–	–
–	–	–	–	–	–	–
–	–	–	–	–	–	–
–	–	–	12.4	12.0	13.7	19.2
2.3	2.9	3.1	–	–	–	–
1.0	1.0	0.8	–	–	–	–
0.2	0.4	2.5	–	–	–	–
–	–	–	–	–	–	–
7.0	7.8	9.8	–	–	–	–
–	–	0.4	–	–	–	–
1.4	1.8	2.6	–	–	–	–
4.9	5.6	3.5	–	1.4	63.4	0.3
20.5	24.0	30.2	13.4	33.2	86.2	28.6
323.1	*174.6*	*450.5*	*434.5*	*370.1*	*207.0*	*362.1*
52.8	*52.3*	*217.7*	*81.8*	*64.7*	*43.3*	*247.9*
501.6	*345.8*	*958.0*	*672.7*	*485.7*	*492.9*	*1043.7*

11. TECH. COOP. GRANTS

1988	1989	1990	1987	1988	1989	1990
0.6	0.7	1.0	0.5	0.6	0.4	0.8
0.2	0.3	1.5	0.2	0.2	0.2	0.3
0.1	0.1	0.1	0.0	0.0	–	–
10.7	10.1	18.0	–	–	0.1	0.2
0.0	–	–	–	–	–	–
–	0.5	3.9	–	–	–	–
3.4	3.0	5.3	3.2	3.4	2.6	4.8
23.6	15.9	141.8	16.8	23.6	15.3	17.6
0.1	0.0	0.3	0.1	0.1	0.0	0.3
3.2	3.0	6.7	3.7	2.6	2.1	2.0
9.1	7.4	8.5	7.1	8.8	6.8	6.3
0.1	0.1	5.5	0.1	0.1	0.1	0.1
–	–	–	–	–	–	–
–	0.0	1.5	–	–	0.0	0.0
3.0	0.1	5.4	0.2	0.1	0.1	0.2
0.1	0.2	0.7	0.1	0.1	–	–
4.4	4.1	9.2	2.2	2.6	2.6	2.9
69.0	63.0	61.0	17.0	32.0	34.0	23.0
127.5	*108.4*	*270.2*	*51.3*	*74.0*	*64.4*	*58.5*
15.6	*17.6*	*23.1*	*4.3*	*9.2*	*5.9*	*9.4*
299.6	*159.8*	*440.0*	–	–	–	–
38.4	*29.9*	*172.6*	*26.3*	*36.5*	*22.7*	*27.7*
442.7	*285.8*	*733.3*	*55.6*	*83.2*	*70.3*	*67.9*

12. TOTAL OOF NET

1988	1989	1990	1987	1988	1989	1990
–	–	–	–	–	–	–
–	–	–	–	–	–	–
–	0.3	0.3	0.1	–	0.3	0.3
–	7.0	3.1	–	–	7.0	3.1
0.8	–	–	-0.2	0.6	-0.1	-0.2
–	–	–	–	–	–	–
–	–	–	–	–	–	–
–	21.9	25.1	0.0	–	19.1	21.9
–	–	–	–	–	–	–
2.7	1.2	14.7	–	1.6	-2.1	3.5
–	–	35.7	–	–	–	35.7
–	–	–	–	–	–	–
–	–	–	–	–	–	–
–	–	–	–	–	–	–
–	–	–	–	–	–	–
0.1	–	–	0.2	0.1	–	–
2.0	69.0	77.0	-47.0	-138.0	64.0	55.0
5.5	*99.4*	*156.0*	*-46.9*	*-135.7*	*88.3*	*119.3*
158.9	*132.8*	*150.5*	*67.2*	*-2.7*	*11.1*	*87.2*
17.0	–	–	*-4.5*	*1.5*	–	*-0.6*
11.0	*44.0*	*60.8*	*1.8*	*5.5*	*33.3*	*41.5*
181.4	*232.2*	*306.5*	*15.8*	*-136.9*	*99.4*	*205.9*

13. ODF COMMITMENTS: BY PURPOSE %

	1987	1988	1989	1990
Education	3	7	12	–
Health	1	0	0	–
Other Social Infrastr.	4	1	7	–
Water Sanitat. Sewage	–	0	2	–
Energy	0	0	6	–
Telecommunications	–	1	–	–
Transportation	4	2	16	–
Agriculture	1	2	0	–
Extractive Industries	4	6	14	–
Manufacturing	0	–	1	–
Trade Banking Tourism	2	1	–	–
Technical Cooperation	12	11	10	–
Multisector Aid	3	2	0	–
Programme	66	67	22	–
Debt Reorganisation	–	–	7	–
Food Aid	–	0	2	–
Emergency Aid	–	–	–	–
Unspecified	–	–	–	–
TOTAL	100	100	100	–

14. GRANT ELEMENT OF ODA %

DAC COUNTRIES	1987	1988	1989	1990
Australia	100.0	100.0	100.0	–
Austria	100.0	100.0	100.0	–
Belgium	100.0	100.0	100.0	–
Canada	100.0	100.0	100.0	–
Denmark	–	–	–	–
Finland	–	100.0	100.0	–
France	100.0	100.0	100.0	–
Germany	77.5	100.0	63.3	–
Ireland	100.0	100.0	100.0	–
Italy	100.0	70.4	100.0	–
Japan	100.0	100.0	60.6	–
Netherlands	100.0	100.0	100.0	–
New Zealand	–	–	–	–
Norway	100.0	–	–	–
Sweden	100.0	100.0	100.0	–
Switzerland	100.0	–	100.0	–
United Kingdom	69.1	63.6	100.0	–
United States	99.0	99.5	100.0	–
TOTAL	*91.5*	*90.4*	*67.7*	–
MULTILATERAL	*100.0*	*99.2*	*54.5*	–
ARAB COUNTRIES	*95.6*	*98.5*	*77.2*	–
E.E.C.+ MEMBERS	*78.0*	*87.7*	*71.0*	–
TOTAL	*94.3*	*97.2*	*69.3*	–

15. OTHER AGGREGATES

	1987	1988	1989	1990
OFFICIAL COMMITMENTS:				
TOTAL BILATERAL	928.1	519.4	501.4	1262.5
of which:				
Arab Countries	690.3	395.1	207.0	362.1
C.E.E.C.	–	–	–	–
TOTAL MULTILATERAL	297.8	153.6	326.8	58.4
TOTAL BIL.& MULTIL.	1225.8	672.9	828.2	1320.9
of which:				
ODA Grants	605.2	456.9	226.7	671.5
ODA Loans	67.5	28.8	266.2	372.2
DISBURSEMENTS:				
DAC COUNTRIES COMBINED				
OFFICIAL & PRIVATE				
GROSS:				
Contractual Lending	404.6	366.7	742.1	619.7
Export Credits, Total	350.1	335.5	656.2	294.7
Export Credits, Priv.	350.1	330.8	604.2	257.3
NET:				
Contractual Lending	238.6	136.5	611.7	436.0
Export Credits Total	211.0	140.6	543.9	164.7
PRIVATE SECTOR NET	276.6	558.1	387.4	14.2
Direct Investment	-2.2	-4.3	0.5	-0.7
Portfolio Investment	20.8	285.5	-114.8	-141.4
Export Credits	258.0	276.9	501.6	156.3
MARKET BORROWING:				
CHANGE IN CLAIMS				
Banks	554.0	338.0	-58.0	-142.0
MEMORANDUM ITEM:				
C.E.E.C. (Gross)	1.4	2.0	–	–

1. TOTAL RECEIPTS NET / 4. TOTAL ODA NET / 7. TOTAL ODA GROSS

	1987	1988	1989	1990		1987	1988	1989	1990		1987
1. TOTAL RECEIPTS NET					**4. TOTAL ODA NET**					**7. TOTAL ODA GROSS**	
DAC COUNTRIES											
Australia	1.6	2.1	3.9	4.3		1.6	2.1	3.9	4.3	Australia	1.6
Austria	–	0.0	0.0	1.2		–	0.0	0.0	1.2	Austria	–
Belgium	0.3	0.0	0.0	0.3		0.3	0.0	0.0	0.3	Belgium	0.3
Canada	–	–	–	0.2		–	–	–	0.2	Canada	–
Denmark	–	–	–	0.5		–	–	–	0.5	Denmark	–
Finland	0.5	0.2	0.7	0.3		0.5	0.2	0.7	0.3	Finland	0.5
France	1.5	0.4	0.9	3.0		1.5	0.4	0.9	3.0	France	1.5
Germany	0.2	0.3	0.5	3.6		0.2	0.3	0.5	3.6	Germany	0.2
Ireland	–	–	–	–		–	–	–	–	Ireland	–
Italy	–	–	–	–		–	–	–	–	Italy	–
Japan	–	0.9	-11.0	0.2		–	0.9	2.0	0.2	Japan	–
Netherlands	0.2	0.5	0.8	4.1		0.2	0.5	0.8	4.1	Netherlands	0.2
New Zealand	–	–	–	0.0		–	–	–	0.0	New Zealand	–
Norway	0.4	–	0.3	2.0		0.4	–	0.3	2.0	Norway	0.4
Sweden	2.1	0.8	3.1	2.9		2.1	0.8	3.1	2.9	Sweden	2.1
Switzerland	0.1	0.3	0.2	0.6		0.1	0.3	0.2	0.6	Switzerland	0.1
United Kingdom	–	0.2	0.5	0.2		–	0.2	0.5	0.2	United Kingdom	0.0
United States	2.0	4.0	5.0	5.0		2.0	4.0	5.0	5.0	United States	2.0
TOTAL	*8.9*	*9.8*	*4.8*	*28.4*		*8.9*	*9.8*	*17.8*	*28.3*	*TOTAL*	*8.9*
MULTILATERAL											
AF.D.F.	–	–	–	–		–	–	–	–	AF.D.F.	–
AF.D.B.	–	–	–	–		–	–	–	–	AF.D.B.	–
AS.D.B	–	–	–	–		–	–	–	–	AS.D.B	–
CAR.D.B.	–	–	–	–		–	–	–	–	CAR.D.B.	–
E.E.C.	0.3	3.3	1.3	1.3		0.3	3.3	1.3	1.3	E.E.C.	0.3
IBRD	–	–	–	–		–	–	–	–	IBRD	–
IDA	–	–	–	–		–	–	–	–	IDA	–
I.D.B.	–	–	–	–		–	–	–	–	I.D.B.	–
IFAD	–	–	–	–		–	–	–	–	IFAD	–
I.F.C.	–	–	–	–		–	–	–	–	I.F.C.	–
IMF TRUST FUND	–	–	–	–		–	–	–	–	IMF TRUST FUND	–
U.N. AGENCIES	–	–	–	–		–	–	–	–	U.N. AGENCIES	–
UNDP	–	–	0.2	0.4		–	–	0.2	0.4	UNDP	–
UNTA	0.0	0.0	0.1	0.3		0.0	0.0	0.1	0.3	UNTA	0.0
UNICEF	4.3	4.7	4.5	5.3		4.3	4.7	4.5	5.3	UNICEF	4.3
UNRWA	–	–	–	–		–	–	–	–	UNRWA	–
WFP	–	–	–	4.8		–	–	–	4.8	WFP	–
UNHCR	–	0.4	0.6	1.0		–	0.4	0.6	1.0	UNHCR	–
Other Multilateral	0.7	0.2	6.0	0.3		0.7	0.2	6.0	0.3	Other Multilateral	0.7
Arab Agencies	–	0.0	–	–		–	0.0	–	–	Arab Agencies	–
TOTAL	*5.4*	*8.7*	*12.5*	*13.3*		*5.4*	*8.7*	*12.5*	*13.3*	*TOTAL*	*5.4*
ARAB COUNTRIES	–	–	–	–		–	–	–	–	**ARAB COUNTRIES**	–
E.E.C.+ MEMBERS	2.5	4.8	3.9	12.9		2.5	4.8	3.9	12.9	E.E.C.+ MEMBERS	2.6
TOTAL	*14.2*	*18.5*	*17.3*	*41.6*		*14.2*	*18.5*	*30.3*	*41.6*	*TOTAL*	*14.3*

2. ODA LOANS GROSS / 5. ODA LOANS NET / 8. GRANTS

	1987	1988	1989	1990		1987	1988	1989	1990		1987
2. ODA LOANS GROSS					**5. ODA LOANS NET**					**8. GRANTS**	
DAC COUNTRIES											
Australia	–	–	–	–		–	–	–	–	Australia	1.6
Austria	–	–	–	–		–	–	–	–	Austria	–
Belgium	–	–	–	–		–	–	–	–	Belgium	0.3
Canada	–	–	–	–		–	–	–	–	Canada	–
Denmark	–	–	–	–		–	–	–	–	Denmark	–
Finland	–	–	–	–		–	–	–	–	Finland	0.5
France	–	–	–	–		–	–	–	–	France	1.5
Germany	–	–	–	–		–	–	–	–	Germany	0.2
Ireland	–	–	–	–		–	–	–	–	Ireland	–
Italy	–	–	–	–		–	–	–	–	Italy	–
Japan	–	–	–	–		–	–	–	–	Japan	–
Netherlands	–	–	–	–		–	–	–	–	Netherlands	0.2
New Zealand	–	–	–	–		–	–	–	–	New Zealand	–
Norway	–	–	–	–		–	–	–	–	Norway	0.4
Sweden	–	–	–	–		–	–	–	–	Sweden	2.1
Switzerland	–	–	–	–		–	–	–	–	Switzerland	0.1
United Kingdom	–	–	–	–		0.0	0.0	0.0	–	United Kingdom	0.0
United States	–	–	–	–		–	–	–	–	United States	2.0
TOTAL	–	–	–	–		*0.0*	*0.0*	*0.0*	–	*TOTAL*	*8.9*
MULTILATERAL	–	–	–	–		–	–	–	–	*MULTILATERAL*	*5.4*
ARAB COUNTRIES	–	–	–	–		–	–	–	–	**ARAB COUNTRIES**	–
E.E.C.+ MEMBERS	–	–	–	–		0.0	0.0	0.0	–	E.E.C.+ MEMBERS	2.6
TOTAL	–	–	–	–		*0.0*	*0.0*	*0.0*	–	*TOTAL*	*14.3*

3. TOTAL OFFICIAL GROSS / 6. TOTAL OFFICIAL NET / 9. TOTAL OOF GROSS

	1987	1988	1989	1990		1987	1988	1989	1990		1987
3. TOTAL OFFICIAL GROSS					**6. TOTAL OFFICIAL NET**					**9. TOTAL OOF GROSS**	
DAC COUNTRIES											
Australia	1.6	2.1	3.9	4.3		1.6	2.1	3.9	4.3	Australia	–
Austria	–	0.0	0.0	1.2		–	0.0	0.0	1.2	Austria	–
Belgium	0.3	0.0	0.0	0.3		0.3	0.0	0.0	0.3	Belgium	–
Canada	–	–	–	0.2		–	–	–	0.2	Canada	–
Denmark	–	–	–	0.5		–	–	–	0.5	Denmark	–
Finland	0.5	0.2	0.7	0.3		0.5	0.2	0.7	0.3	Finland	–
France	1.5	0.4	0.9	3.0		1.5	0.4	0.9	3.0	France	–
Germany	0.2	0.3	0.5	3.6		0.2	0.3	0.5	3.6	Germany	–
Ireland	–	–	–	–		–	–	–	–	Ireland	–
Italy	–	–	–	–		–	–	–	–	Italy	–
Japan	–	0.9	2.0	0.2		–	0.9	2.0	0.2	Japan	–
Netherlands	0.2	0.5	0.8	4.1		0.2	0.5	0.8	4.1	Netherlands	–
New Zealand	–	–	–	0.0		–	–	–	0.0	New Zealand	–
Norway	0.4	–	0.3	2.0		0.4	–	0.3	2.0	Norway	–
Sweden	2.1	0.8	3.1	2.9		2.1	0.8	3.1	2.9	Sweden	–
Switzerland	0.1	0.3	0.2	0.6		0.1	0.3	0.2	0.6	Switzerland	–
United Kingdom	0.0	0.2	0.5	0.2		–	0.2	0.5	0.2	United Kingdom	–
United States	2.0	4.0	5.0	5.0		2.0	4.0	5.0	5.0	United States	–
TOTAL	*8.9*	*9.8*	*17.8*	*28.3*		*8.9*	*9.8*	*17.8*	*28.3*	*TOTAL*	–
MULTILATERAL	*5.4*	*8.7*	*12.5*	*13.3*		*5.4*	*8.7*	*12.5*	*13.3*	*MULTILATERAL*	–
ARAB COUNTRIES	–	–	–	–		–	–	–	–	**ARAB COUNTRIES**	
E.E.C.+ MEMBERS	2.6	4.8	3.9	12.9		2.5	4.8	3.9	12.9	E.E.C.+ MEMBERS	–
TOTAL	*14.3*	*18.5*	*30.4*	*41.6*		*14.2*	*18.5*	*30.3*	*41.6*	*TOTAL*	–

1988	1989	1990		1987	1988	1989	1990

10. ODA COMMITMENTS

1988	1989	1990		1987	1988	1989	1990
2.1	3.9	4.3		2.3	1.7	5.8	-2.1
0.0	0.0	1.2		–	0.0	0.0	1.2
0.0	0.0	0.3		0.1	0.1	0.0	0.3
–	–	0.2		0.0	–	0.1	0.5
–	–	0.5		–	–	–	0.5
0.2	0.7	0.3		–	–	0.7	0.6
0.4	0.9	3.0		1.3	0.4	0.9	3.0
0.3	0.5	3.6		0.0	0.8	0.6	2.9
–	–	–		–	–	–	–
–	–	–		–	–	–	–
0.9	2.0	0.2		–	0.9	0.2	0.2
0.5	0.8	4.1		0.2	0.5	1.0	3.2
–	–	0.0		–	–	–	–
–	0.3	2.0		0.1	–	–	–
0.8	3.1	2.9		2.1	0.8	3.1	–
0.3	0.2	0.6		0.1	0.3	0.2	0.6
0.2	0.5	0.2		0.0	0.2	0.5	0.2
4.0	5.0	5.0		3.9	4.0	5.7	7.6
9.8	*17.8*	*28.3*		*10.1*	*9.8*	*18.8*	*18.7*
–	–	–		–	–	–	–
–	–	–		–	–	–	–
–	–	–		–	–	–	–
–	–	–		–	–	–	–
3.3	1.3	1.3		0.2	3.4	0.5	0.5
–	–	–		–	–	–	–
–	–	–		–	–	–	–
–	–	–		–	–	–	–
–	–	–		–	–	–	–
–	–	–		5.0	5.4	11.3	12.0
–	0.2	0.4		–	–	–	–
0.0	0.1	0.3		–	–	–	–
4.7	4.5	5.3		–	–	–	–
–	–	–		–	–	–	–
–	–	4.8		–	–	–	–
0.4	0.6	1.0		–	–	–	–
0.2	6.0	0.3		–	–	–	–
0.0	–	–		–	–	–	–
8.7	*12.5*	*13.3*		*5.2*	*8.8*	*11.8*	*12.5*
–	–	–		–	–	–	–
4.8	3.9	12.9		1.9	5.4	3.6	10.6
18.5	*30.4*	*41.6*		*15.3*	*18.5*	*30.6*	*31.2*

11. TECH. COOP. GRANTS

2.1	3.9	4.3		0.2	0.0	0.0	0.0
0.0	0.0	1.2		–	–	–	0.0
0.0	0.0	0.3		0.0	–	–	–
–	–	0.2		–	–	–	–
–	–	0.5		–	–	–	–
0.2	0.7	0.3		–	–	–	0.1
0.4	0.9	3.0		0.9	0.4	0.9	3.0
0.3	0.5	3.6		0.2	0.1	0.2	2.7
–	–	–		–	–	–	–
–	–	–		–	–	–	–
0.9	2.0	0.2		–	0.9	0.2	0.2
0.5	0.8	4.1		0.2	0.5	0.5	0.8
–	–	0.0		–	–	–	–
–	0.3	2.0		–	–	–	–
0.8	3.1	2.9		–	–	0.0	0.0
0.3	0.2	0.6		–	–	–	–
0.2	0.5	0.2		–	0.2	0.4	–
4.0	5.0	5.0		2.0	–	4.0	5.0
9.8	*17.8*	*28.3*		*3.5*	*2.1*	*6.3*	*11.8*
8.7	*12.5*	*13.3*		*5.1*	*6.4*	*11.3*	*7.2*
–	–	–		–	–	–	–
4.8	3.9	12.9		1.4	2.3	2.1	6.5
18.5	*30.4*	*41.6*		*8.6*	*8.5*	*17.6*	*19.0*

12. TOTAL OOF NET

–	–	–		–	–	–	–
–	–	–		–	–	–	–
–	–	–		–	–	–	–
–	–	–		–	–	–	–
–	–	–		–	–	–	–
–	–	–		–	–	–	–
–	–	–		–	–	–	–
–	–	–		–	–	–	–
–	–	–		–	–	–	–
–	–	–		–	–	–	–
–	–	–		–	–	–	–
–	–	–		–	–	–	–
–	–	–		–	–	–	–
–	–	–		–	–	–	–
–	–	–		–	–	–	–
–	–	–		–	–	–	–
–	–	–		–	–	–	–
–	–	–		–	–	–	–

13. ODF COMMITMENTS: BY PURPOSE %

	1987	1988	1989	1990
Education	–	–	–	–
Health	–	–	–	–
Other Social Infrastr.	–	–	–	–
Water Sanitat. Sewage	–	–	–	–
Energy	–	–	–	–
Telecommunications	–	–	–	–
Transportation	–	–	–	–
Agriculture	–	–	–	–
Extractive Industries	–	–	–	–
Manufacturing	5	–	–	–
Trade Banking Tourism	–	–	–	–
Technical Cooperation	5	6	59	–
Multisector Aid	1	19	–	–
Programme	87	72	–	–
Debt Reorganisation	0	0	1	–
Food Aid	–	–	–	–
Emergency Aid	2	3	41	–
Unspecified	–	–	–	–
TOTAL	100	100	100	–

14. GRANT ELEMENT OF ODA %

DAC COUNTRIES

	1987	1988	1989	1990
Australia	100.0	100.0	100.0	–
Austria	–	100.0	100.0	–
Belgium	100.0	100.0	100.0	–
Canada	100.0	–	100.0	–
Denmark	–	–	–	–
Finland	–	–	100.0	–
France	100.0	100.0	100.0	–
Germany	100.0	100.0	100.0	–
Ireland	–	–	–	–
Italy	–	–	–	–
Japan	–	100.0	100.0	–
Netherlands	100.0	100.0	100.0	–
New Zealand	–	–	–	–
Norway	100.0	–	–	–
Sweden	100.0	100.0	100.0	–
Switzerland	100.0	100.0	100.0	–
United Kingdom	100.0	100.0	100.0	–
United States	99.7	97.8	99.1	–
TOTAL	*99.9*	*99.1*	*99.7*	–
MULTILATERAL	*100.0*	*100.0*	*100.0*	–
ARAB COUNTRIES	–	–	–	–
E.E.C.+ MEMBERS	100.0	100.0	100.0	–
TOTAL	*99.9*	*99.5*	*99.8*	–

15. OTHER AGGREGATES

OFFICIAL COMMITMENTS:

	1987	1988	1989	1990
TOTAL BILATERAL	193.2	201.8	18.8	18.7
of which:				
Arab Countries	–	–	–	–
C.E.E.C.	183.1	192.0	–	–
TOTAL MULTILATERAL	5.2	8.8	11.8	12.5
TOTAL BIL.& MULTIL.	198.4	210.5	30.6	31.2
of which:				
ODA Grants	68.4	68.3	30.4	31.1
ODA Loans	130.0	142.3	0.2	0.2

DISBURSEMENTS:

DAC COUNTRIES COMBINED

OFFICIAL & PRIVATE
GROSS:

	1987	1988	1989	1990
Contractual Lending	–	–	–	–
Export Credits, Total	–	–	–	–
Export Credits, Priv.	–	–	–	–
NET:				
Contractual Lending	0.0	0.0	0.0	–
Export Credits Total	–	–	–	–
PRIVATE SECTOR NET	–	–	-13.0	0.0
Direct Investment	–	–	–	–
Portfolio Investment	–	–	-13.0	0.0
Export Credits	–	–	–	–

MARKET BORROWING:

CHANGE IN CLAIMS

	1987	1988	1989	1990
Banks	5.0	1.0	4.0	15.0

MEMORANDUM ITEM:

	1987	1988	1989	1990
C.E.E.C. (Gross)	178.1	189.0	213.8	–

1. TOTAL RECEIPTS NET

DAC COUNTRIES	1987	1988	1989	1990
Australia	1.0	1.1	2.0	2.7
Austria	1.3	-6.3	-1.6	0.9
Belgium	-0.8	2.9	10.6	102.1
Canada	15.7	17.4	28.4	32.4
Denmark	24.3	34.8	33.7	36.3
Finland	14.7	27.4	30.1	30.2
France	92.1	144.6	104.4	89.3
Germany	37.8	42.5	57.2	131.2
Ireland	0.3	0.0	0.5	0.4
Italy	40.2	53.1	53.4	51.8
Japan	59.0	144.6	149.3	104.9
Netherlands	50.0	64.1	50.7	91.1
New Zealand	0.0	0.2	0.4	0.5
Norway	30.2	31.3	27.2	22.5
Sweden	34.5	27.3	29.2	28.9
Switzerland	3.9	5.2	4.9	4.0
United Kingdom	142.1	143.3	336.1	174.7
United States	56.0	50.0	91.0	102.0
TOTAL	602.3	783.7	1007.3	1005.8
MULTILATERAL				
AF.D.F.	7.9	5.4	27.8	12.0
AF.D.B.	3.3	7.2	48.2	0.3
AS.D.B	–	–	–	–
CAR.D.B.	–	–	–	–
E.E.C.	23.6	70.2	92.8	92.8
IBRD	-21.0	-53.0	-58.0	-92.0
IDA	69.9	95.0	223.0	230.0
I.D.B.	–	–	–	–
IFAD	1.6	0.5	3.4	3.5
I.F.C.	-8.7	-6.0	0.1	15.0
IMF TRUST FUND	–	–	–	–
U.N. AGENCIES	–	–	–	–
UNDP	5.9	5.6	4.6	12.6
UNTA	1.1	1.0	1.0	1.2
UNICEF	1.6	2.0	3.9	5.2
UNRWA	–	–	–	–
WFP	1.6	5.2	3.3	3.5
UNHCR	2.5	2.7	2.3	2.0
Other Multilateral	3.6	5.2	6.6	4.7
Arab Agencies	0.5	0.3	0.8	–
TOTAL	93.5	141.2	359.6	290.7
ARAB COUNTRIES	*4.1*	*3.4*	*-0.4*	*4.5*
E.E.C.+ MEMBERS	409.5	555.5	739.3	769.6
TOTAL	699.9	928.3	1366.5	1301.0

2. ODA LOANS GROSS

DAC COUNTRIES	1987	1988	1989	1990
Australia	–	–	–	–
Austria	7.9	–	–	–
Belgium	0.8	–	–	1.5
Canada	0.1	–	–	–
Denmark	6.6	5.2	2.0	3.2
Finland	0.8	–	–	–
France	26.1	25.4	26.6	51.2
Germany	22.6	31.0	24.4	21.9
Ireland	–	–	–	–
Italy	1.9	22.3	35.9	33.8
Japan	31.4	85.4	88.0	25.7
Netherlands	3.4	4.7	1.7	10.0
New Zealand	–	–	–	–
Norway	–	–	–	–
Sweden	–	–	–	–
Switzerland	0.3	0.9	–	–
United Kingdom	3.4	0.9	0.1	0.1
United States	13.0	10.0	9.0	7.0
TOTAL	118.4	185.8	187.5	154.4
MULTILATERAL	82.1	106.7	260.5	251.0
ARAB COUNTRIES	*6.8*	*6.2*	*3.8*	*8.7*
E.E.C.+ MEMBERS	64.8	91.3	90.5	121.7
TOTAL	207.2	298.7	451.7	414.0

3. TOTAL OFFICIAL GROSS

DAC COUNTRIES	1987	1988	1989	1990
Australia	1.0	1.1	2.0	2.7
Austria	8.4	0.5	1.1	2.1
Belgium	2.3	3.1	3.2	7.6
Canada	20.3	40.4	35.1	132.6
Denmark	28.0	36.3	34.8	40.0
Finland	14.5	27.7	25.2	30.2
France	29.8	32.6	31.2	59.3
Germany	58.3	61.5	70.6	522.8
Ireland	0.3	0.0	0.5	0.4
Italy	33.1	37.6	56.1	53.6
Japan	69.6	150.4	153.7	101.3
Netherlands	60.8	62.5	55.1	73.7
New Zealand	0.0	0.2	0.4	0.5
Norway	30.2	31.3	27.2	22.5
Sweden	26.8	27.3	29.5	31.2
Switzerland	3.9	5.2	4.9	4.0
United Kingdom	45.5	88.1	88.4	78.9
United States	59.0	55.0	76.0	147.0
TOTAL	491.8	660.7	694.8	1310.2
MULTILATERAL	186.3	243.9	463.7	415.8
ARAB COUNTRIES	*6.8*	*6.2*	*3.8*	*8.7*
E.E.C.+ MEMBERS	291.9	400.5	440.6	936.9
TOTAL	684.8	910.4	1162.3	1734.6

4. TOTAL ODA NET

DAC COUNTRIES	1987	1988	1989	1990
Australia	1.0	1.1	2.0	2.7
Austria	8.3	0.4	0.4	2.1
Belgium	2.3	3.0	3.2	7.6
Canada	19.6	24.0	22.1	19.5
Denmark	27.1	35.4	33.9	36.8
Finland	14.5	27.7	25.2	30.2
France	29.4	32.2	30.9	58.6
Germany	52.4	55.9	56.1	143.1
Ireland	0.3	0.0	0.5	0.4
Italy	33.1	37.6	56.0	53.5
Japan	63.7	144.7	147.8	93.2
Netherlands	56.5	56.7	49.0	67.0
New Zealand	0.0	0.2	0.4	0.5
Norway	30.2	31.3	27.2	22.5
Sweden	26.8	27.3	29.5	31.2
Switzerland	3.9	5.2	4.9	4.0
United Kingdom	32.2	75.1	72.6	67.3
United States	43.0	52.0	59.0	95.0
TOTAL	444.1	609.9	620.6	735.2
MULTILATERAL				
AF.D.F.	7.9	5.4	27.8	12.0
AF.D.B.	–	–	–	–
AS.D.B	–	–	–	–
CAR.D.B.	–	–	–	–
E.E.C.	29.2	73.5	69.3	69.3
IBRD	–	–	–	–
IDA	69.9	95.0	223.0	230.0
I.D.B.	–	–	–	–
IFAD	1.6	0.5	3.4	3.5
I.F.C.	–	–	–	–
IMF TRUST FUND	–	–	–	–
U.N. AGENCIES	–	–	–	–
UNDP	5.9	5.6	4.6	12.6
UNTA	1.1	1.0	1.0	1.2
UNICEF	1.6	2.0	3.9	5.2
UNRWA	–	–	–	–
WFP	1.6	5.2	3.3	3.5
UNHCR	2.5	2.7	2.3	2.0
Other Multilateral	3.6	5.2	6.6	4.7
Arab Agencies	-1.1	-0.8	1.7	–
TOTAL	123.8	195.3	346.8	344.0
ARAB COUNTRIES	*4.1*	*3.4*	*-0.4*	*4.5*
E.E.C.+ MEMBERS	262.4	369.5	371.5	503.6
TOTAL	572.0	808.6	967.0	1083.7

5. ODA LOANS NET

DAC COUNTRIES	1987	1988	1989	1990
Australia	–	–	–	–
Austria	7.9	-0.1	-0.8	–
Belgium	0.7	-0.1	-0.1	1.5
Canada	-0.3	-16.2	–	-93.2
Denmark	5.8	4.4	1.2	0.0
Finland	0.8	–	–	–
France	25.7	25.0	26.3	50.5
Germany	17.7	25.4	20.7	-351.4
Ireland	–	–	–	–
Italy	1.9	22.3	35.8	33.7
Japan	25.5	79.8	82.1	17.7
Netherlands	-0.7	-0.8	-4.2	3.3
New Zealand	–	–	–	–
Norway	–	–	–	–
Sweden	–	–	–	–
Switzerland	0.3	0.9	–	–
United Kingdom	-7.6	-11.0	-7.1	-7.6
United States	12.0	7.0	4.0	-36.0
TOTAL	89.7	136.5	158.0	-381.5
MULTILATERAL	78.1	101.6	255.9	244.5
ARAB COUNTRIES	*4.0*	*3.4*	*-0.4*	*4.5*
E.E.C.+ MEMBERS	43.5	66.8	72.7	-269.9
TOTAL	171.9	241.5	413.5	-132.5

6. TOTAL OFFICIAL NET

DAC COUNTRIES	1987	1988	1989	1990
Australia	1.0	1.1	2.0	2.7
Austria	8.3	0.4	0.4	2.1
Belgium	2.3	3.0	3.2	7.6
Canada	15.7	17.4	28.4	32.4
Denmark	27.2	35.4	33.9	36.8
Finland	14.5	27.7	25.2	30.2
France	29.4	32.2	30.9	58.6
Germany	48.8	49.4	60.9	139.2
Ireland	0.3	0.0	0.5	0.4
Italy	33.1	37.6	56.0	53.5
Japan	63.7	144.7	147.8	93.2
Netherlands	56.3	56.5	48.9	66.6
New Zealand	0.0	0.2	0.4	0.5
Norway	30.2	31.3	27.2	22.5
Sweden	26.8	27.3	29.5	31.2
Switzerland	3.9	5.2	4.9	4.0
United Kingdom	27.7	71.1	73.7	67.3
United States	56.0	50.0	69.0	102.0
TOTAL	445.1	590.7	642.5	750.6
MULTILATERAL	93.5	141.2	359.6	290.8
ARAB COUNTRIES	*4.1*	*3.4*	*-0.4*	*4.5*
E.E.C.+ MEMBERS	248.7	355.4	400.7	522.7
TOTAL	542.7	735.3	1001.8	1045.9

7. TOTAL ODA GROSS

	1987
Australia	1.0
Austria	8.4
Belgium	2.3
Canada	20.0
Denmark	27.9
Finland	14.5
France	29.8
Germany	57.2
Ireland	0.3
Italy	33.1
Japan	69.6
Netherlands	60.7
New Zealand	0.0
Norway	30.2
Sweden	26.8
Switzerland	3.9
United Kingdom	43.2
United States	44.0
TOTAL	472.7
AF.D.F.	7.9
AF.D.B.	–
AS.D.B	–
CAR.D.B.	–
E.E.C.	29.3
IBRD	–
IDA	72.1
I.D.B.	–
IFAD	1.6
I.F.C.	–
IMF TRUST FUND	–
U.N. AGENCIES	–
UNDP	5.9
UNTA	1.1
UNICEF	1.6
UNRWA	–
WFP	1.6
UNHCR	2.5
Other Multilateral	3.6
Arab Agencies	0.6
TOTAL	127.8
ARAB COUNTRIES	*6.8*
E.E.C.+ MEMBERS	283.7
TOTAL	607.3

8. GRANTS

	1987
Australia	1.0
Austria	0.5
Belgium	1.5
Canada	19.9
Denmark	21.2
Finland	13.7
France	3.7
Germany	34.6
Ireland	0.3
Italy	31.2
Japan	38.3
Netherlands	57.3
New Zealand	0.0
Norway	30.2
Sweden	26.8
Switzerland	3.6
United Kingdom	39.8
United States	31.0
TOTAL	354.4
MULTILATERAL	45.7
ARAB COUNTRIES	*0.1*
E.E.C.+ MEMBERS	218.8
TOTAL	400.1

9. TOTAL OOF GROSS

	1987
Australia	–
Austria	–
Belgium	–
Canada	0.4
Denmark	0.1
Finland	–
France	–
Germany	1.1
Ireland	–
Italy	–
Japan	–
Netherlands	0.2
New Zealand	–
Norway	–
Sweden	–
Switzerland	–
United Kingdom	2.3
United States	15.0
TOTAL	19.0
MULTILATERAL	58.5
ARAB COUNTRIES	–
E.E.C.+ MEMBERS	8.3
TOTAL	77.5

10. ODA COMMITMENTS

1988	1989	1990	1987	1988	1989	1990
1.1	2.0	2.7	0.4	0.5	1.2	1.9
0.5	1.1	2.1	0.4	2.5	0.4	2.5
3.1	3.2	7.6	5.2	6.8	3.2	7.6
40.2	22.1	112.8	39.7	41.6	7.0	14.7
36.2	34.7	40.0	34.4	32.2	28.2	13.8
27.7	25.2	30.2	10.7	28.7	62.9	48.2
32.6	31.2	59.3	35.8	3.4	35.4	38.6
61.5	59.7	516.4	34.0	70.1	58.7	162.1
0.0	0.5	0.4	0.3	0.0	0.5	0.4
37.6	56.1	53.6	67.0	106.3	15.2	11.8
150.4	153.7	101.3	67.3	157.6	294.3	270.8
62.2	54.8	73.7	77.0	50.6	68.1	62.8
0.2	0.4	0.5	0.0	1.3	–	0.2
31.3	27.2	22.5	21.2	17.7	8.0	51.1
27.3	29.5	31.2	26.8	27.3	29.5	24.5
5.2	4.9	4.0	6.8	9.4	5.6	1.3
87.1	79.8	75.1	50.0	111.8	101.7	58.3
55.0	64.0	138.0	47.0	60.8	60.8	215.0
659.2	650.1	1271.1	523.9	728.4	780.5	985.5
5.4	27.8	12.0	–	14.7	42.4	39.9
–	–	–	–	–	–	–
–	–	–	–	–	–	–
73.5	69.3	69.3	81.5	142.9	58.9	58.9
–	–	–	–	–	–	–
98.0	226.0	234.0	62.6	176.0	334.0	253.0
–	–	–	–	–	–	–
0.5	3.4	3.6	–	–	8.2	22.6
–	–	–	–	–	–	–
–	–	–	–	–	–	–
–	–	–	16.3	21.6	21.6	29.2
5.6	4.6	12.6	–	–	–	–
1.0	1.0	1.2	–	–	–	–
2.0	3.9	5.2	–	–	–	–
–	–	–	–	–	–	–
5.2	3.3	3.5	–	–	–	–
2.7	2.3	2.0	–	–	–	–
5.2	6.6	4.7	–	–	–	–
1.3	3.4	1.3	–	–	0.5	–
200.4	351.4	349.5	160.4	355.2	465.5	403.7
6.2	3.8	8.7	2.7	4.0	–	–
393.9	389.3	895.2	385.2	524.0	369.8	414.3
865.8	1005.2	1629.2	687.0	1087.6	1246.0	1389.2

11. TECH. COOP. GRANTS

1988	1989	1990	1987	1988	1989	1990
1.1	2.0	2.7	0.3	0.4	1.7	2.0
0.5	1.1	2.1	0.4	0.4	0.2	0.3
3.1	3.2	6.1	0.9	1.0	1.2	1.4
40.2	22.1	112.8	–	5.9	5.5	2.4
31.1	32.7	36.7	7.9	11.0	5.7	9.5
27.7	25.2	30.2	0.5	0.6	2.3	6.7
7.2	4.6	8.1	3.7	3.4	3.4	3.4
30.5	35.4	494.5	33.1	29.2	27.3	33.6
0.0	0.5	0.4	0.3	0.0	0.5	0.4
15.4	20.2	19.8	10.1	4.9	4.7	8.3
65.0	65.7	75.5	20.1	22.2	22.8	25.9
57.5	53.2	63.7	21.4	21.7	19.4	20.9
0.2	0.4	0.5	0.0	0.1	–	0.2
31.3	27.2	22.5	6.5	5.8	7.1	6.2
27.3	29.5	31.2	1.7	3.1	3.4	3.1
4.3	4.9	4.0	2.5	2.2	–	–
86.2	79.7	75.0	18.8	29.3	26.2	27.1
45.0	55.0	131.0	10.0	19.0	25.0	31.0
473.4	462.6	1116.7	138.0	160.0	156.4	182.3
93.7	90.9	98.5	16.5	18.4	18.3	25.7
–	–	–	–	–	–	–
302.6	298.8	773.5	97.8	102.2	88.4	104.5
567.1	553.5	1215.2	154.4	178.4	174.7	208.0

12. TOTAL OOF NET

1988	1989	1990	1987	1988	1989	1990
–	–	–	–	–	–	–
–	–	–	–	–	–	–
–	–	–	–	–	–	–
0.2	13.0	19.9	-3.9	-6.6	6.2	12.8
0.0	0.1	–	0.1	0.0	–	–
–	–	–	–	–	–	–
–	10.9	6.4	-3.5	-6.5	4.7	-3.9
–	–	–	–	–	–	–
–	–	–	–	–	–	–
–	–	–	–	–	–	–
0.3	0.2	–	-0.2	-0.1	-0.1	-0.4
–	–	–	–	–	–	–
–	–	–	–	–	–	–
1.0	8.6	3.8	-4.5	-4.0	1.1	-0.1
–	12.0	9.0	13.0	-2.0	10.0	7.0
1.5	44.8	39.0	1.0	-19.2	22.0	15.4
43.1	112.3	66.3	-30.3	-54.1	12.9	-53.2
–	–	–	–	–	–	–
6.6	51.2	41.7	-13.7	-14.0	29.2	19.1
44.6	157.1	105.4	-29.2	-73.3	34.8	-37.8

13. ODF COMMITMENTS: BY PURPOSE %

	1987	1988	1989	1990
Education	3	2	1	–
Health	2	7	4	–
Other Social Infrastr.	6	2	3	–
Water Sanitat. Sewage	7	8	15	–
Energy	2	2	5	–
Telecommunications	2	9	10	–
Transportation	9	2	7	–
Agriculture	27	19	8	–
Extractive Industries	0	0	–	–
Manufacturing	2	1	2	–
Trade Banking Tourism	0	11	26	–
Technical Cooperation	23	22	13	–
Multisector Aid	5	1	1	–
Programme	7	10	5	–
Debt Reorganisation	2	2	1	–
Food Aid	1	2	0	–
Emergency Aid	0	–	0	–
Unspecified	0	0	–	–
TOTAL	100	100	100	–

14. GRANT ELEMENT OF ODA %

DAC COUNTRIES

	1987	1988	1989	1990
Australia	100.0	100.0	100.0	–
Austria	100.0	100.0	100.0	–
Belgium	100.0	100.0	100.0	–
Canada	100.0	100.0	100.0	–
Denmark	100.0	100.0	100.0	–
Finland	100.0	100.0	100.0	–
France	67.8	100.0	51.2	–
Germany	95.8	95.1	89.0	–
Ireland	100.0	100.0	100.0	–
Italy	100.0	68.0	97.7	–
Japan	72.9	79.9	70.1	–
Netherlands	96.4	100.0	92.4	–
New Zealand	100.0	100.0	–	–
Norway	100.0	100.0	100.0	–
Sweden	100.0	100.0	100.0	–
Switzerland	100.0	100.0	100.0	–
United Kingdom	100.0	100.0	100.0	–
United States	94.5	92.4	99.6	–
TOTAL	93.0	89.9	84.9	–
MULTILATERAL	89.1	90.3	82.3	–
ARAB COUNTRIES	100.0	80.7	–	–
E.E.C.+ MEMBERS	95.8	92.8	92.1	–
TOTAL	91.8	90.0	83.9	–

15. OTHER AGGREGATES

	1987	1988	1989	1990
OFFICIAL COMMITMENTS:				
TOTAL BILATERAL	549.6	754.7	823.1	1172.9
of which:				
Arab Countries	2.7	4.0	–	–
C.E.E.C.	–	–	–	–
TOTAL MULTILATERAL	191.6	388.1	557.7	439.8
TOTAL BIL.& MULTIL.	741.2	1142.8	1380.7	1612.8
of which:				
ODA Grants	523.6	686.6	553.5	807.5
ODA Loans	163.3	401.0	692.5	581.8
DISBURSEMENTS:				
DAC COUNTRIES COMBINED				
OFFICIAL & PRIVATE				
GROSS:				
Contractual Lending	273.1	391.4	639.5	528.2
Export Credits, Total	152.1	204.3	432.1	365.8
Export Credits, Priv.	135.7	204.1	407.3	334.8
NET:				
Contractual Lending	148.1	247.5	468.6	-111.4
Export Credits Total	63.0	115.1	301.2	272.5
PRIVATE SECTOR NET	157.2	193.0	364.7	255.1
Direct Investment	82.3	36.3	55.9	3.8
Portfolio Investment	17.6	26.5	20.2	-3.3
Export Credits	57.3	130.2	288.7	254.7
MARKET BORROWING:				
CHANGE IN CLAIMS				
Banks	154.0	79.0	80.0	165.0
MEMORANDUM ITEM:				
C.E.E.C. (Gross)	–	–	–	–

1. TOTAL RECEIPTS NET

DAC COUNTRIES	1987	1988	1989	1990
Australia	2.5	1.8	5.4	3.7
Austria	–	–	–	–
Belgium	–	–	–	–
Canada	0.0	0.0	–	–
Denmark	–	–	–	–
Finland	–	–	–	–
France	–	–	–	–
Germany	0.2	0.0	0.1	0.0
Ireland	–	–	–	–
Italy	–	–	–	0.0
Japan	6.5	5.3	5.3	9.4
Netherlands	–	–	–	–
New Zealand	1.8	1.7	1.7	1.7
Norway	–	–	–	–
Sweden	–	–	–	–
Switzerland	–	–	–	–
United Kingdom	3.6	3.4	2.7	3.0
United States	–	–	–	–
TOTAL	14.5	12.1	15.2	17.7
MULTILATERAL				
AF.D.F.	–	–	–	–
AF.D.B.	–	–	–	–
AS.D.B	0.9	0.3	0.5	0.9
CAR.D.B.	–	–	–	–
E.E.C.	2.1	2.8	0.6	0.6
IBRD	–	–	–	–
IDA	–	–	–	–
I.D.B.	–	–	–	–
IFAD	–	–	–	–
I.F.C.	–	–	–	–
IMF TRUST FUND	–	–	–	–
U.N. AGENCIES	–	–	–	–
UNDP	0.6	0.7	0.9	1.0
UNTA	0.3	0.2	0.3	0.3
UNICEF	–	–	–	–
UNRWA	–	–	–	–
WFP	–	–	–	–
UNHCR	–	–	–	–
Other Multilateral	0.0	0.1	0.1	0.0
Arab Agencies	–	–	–	–
TOTAL	3.8	4.1	2.4	2.8
ARAB COUNTRIES	–	–	–	–
E.E.C.+ MEMBERS	5.8	6.2	3.4	3.5
TOTAL	18.3	16.3	17.5	20.5

4. TOTAL ODA NET

DAC COUNTRIES	1987	1988	1989	1990
Australia	2.5	1.8	5.4	3.7
Austria	–	–	–	–
Belgium	–	–	–	–
Canada	0.0	0.0	–	–
Denmark	–	–	–	–
Finland	–	–	–	–
France	–	–	–	–
Germany	0.0	0.0	0.0	–
Ireland	–	–	–	–
Italy	–	–	–	–
Japan	6.5	5.3	5.3	9.4
Netherlands	–	–	–	–
New Zealand	1.8	1.7	1.7	1.7
Norway	–	–	–	–
Sweden	–	–	–	–
Switzerland	–	–	–	–
United Kingdom	3.8	3.4	2.7	3.0
United States	–	–	–	–
TOTAL	14.6	12.1	15.1	17.7
MULTILATERAL				
AF.D.F.	–	–	–	–
AF.D.B.	–	–	–	–
AS.D.B	0.9	0.3	0.5	0.9
CAR.D.B.	–	–	–	–
E.E.C.	2.1	2.8	0.6	0.6
IBRD	–	–	–	–
IDA	–	–	–	–
I.D.B.	–	–	–	–
IFAD	–	–	–	–
I.F.C.	–	–	–	–
IMF TRUST FUND	–	–	–	–
U.N. AGENCIES	–	–	–	–
UNDP	0.6	0.7	0.9	1.0
UNTA	0.3	0.2	0.3	0.3
UNICEF	–	–	–	–
UNRWA	–	–	–	–
WFP	–	–	–	–
UNHCR	–	–	–	–
Other Multilateral	0.0	0.1	0.1	0.0
Arab Agencies	–	–	–	–
TOTAL	3.8	4.1	2.4	2.8
ARAB COUNTRIES	–	–	–	–
E.E.C.+ MEMBERS	5.9	6.2	3.4	3.5
TOTAL	18.4	16.3	17.5	20.5

7. TOTAL ODA GROSS

	1987
Australia	2.5
Austria	–
Belgium	–
Canada	0.0
Denmark	–
Finland	–
France	–
Germany	0.0
Ireland	–
Italy	–
Japan	6.5
Netherlands	–
New Zealand	1.8
Norway	–
Sweden	–
Switzerland	–
United Kingdom	3.8
United States	–
TOTAL	14.6
AF.D.F.	–
AF.D.B.	–
AS.D.B	0.9
CAR.D.B.	–
E.E.C.	2.1
IBRD	–
IDA	–
I.D.B.	–
IFAD	–
I.F.C.	–
IMF TRUST FUND	–
U.N. AGENCIES	–
UNDP	0.6
UNTA	0.3
UNICEF	–
UNRWA	–
WFP	–
UNHCR	–
Other Multilateral	0.0
Arab Agencies	–
TOTAL	3.8
ARAB COUNTRIES	–
E.E.C.+ MEMBERS	5.9
TOTAL	18.4

2. ODA LOANS GROSS

DAC COUNTRIES	1987	1988	1989	1990
Australia	–	–	–	–
Austria	–	–	–	–
Belgium	–	–	–	–
Canada	–	–	–	–
Denmark	–	–	–	–
Finland	–	–	–	–
France	–	–	–	–
Germany	–	–	–	–
Ireland	–	–	–	–
Italy	–	–	–	–
Japan	–	–	–	–
Netherlands	–	–	–	–
New Zealand	–	–	–	–
Norway	–	–	–	–
Sweden	–	–	–	–
Switzerland	–	–	–	–
United Kingdom	–	–	–	–
United States	–	–	–	–
TOTAL	–	–	–	–
MULTILATERAL	0.9	0.3	0.1	0.7
ARAB COUNTRIES	–	–	–	–
E.E.C.+ MEMBERS	–	–	–	–
TOTAL	0.9	0.3	0.1	0.7

5. ODA LOANS NET

	1987	1988	1989	1990
	–	–	–	–
	–	–	–	–
	–	–	–	–
	–	–	–	–
	–	–	–	–
	–	–	–	–
	–	–	–	–
	–	–	–	–
	–	–	–	–
	–	–	–	–
	–	–	–	–
	–	–	–	–
	–	–	–	–
	–	–	–	–
	–	–	–	–
	–	–	–	–
	–	–	–	–
	–	–	–	–
TOTAL	–	–	–	–
MULTILATERAL	0.9	0.3	0.0	0.7
ARAB COUNTRIES	–	–	–	–
E.E.C.+ MEMBERS	–	–	–	–
TOTAL	0.9	0.3	0.0	0.7

8. GRANTS

	1987
Australia	2.5
Austria	–
Belgium	–
Canada	0.0
Denmark	–
Finland	–
France	–
Germany	0.0
Ireland	–
Italy	–
Japan	6.5
Netherlands	–
New Zealand	1.8
Norway	–
Sweden	–
Switzerland	–
United Kingdom	3.8
United States	–
TOTAL	14.6
MULTILATERAL	2.9
ARAB COUNTRIES	–
E.E.C.+ MEMBERS	5.9
TOTAL	17.5

3. TOTAL OFFICIAL GROSS

DAC COUNTRIES	1987	1988	1989	1990
Australia	2.5	1.8	5.4	3.7
Austria	–	–	–	–
Belgium	–	–	–	–
Canada	0.0	0.0	–	–
Denmark	–	–	–	–
Finland	–	–	–	–
France	–	–	–	–
Germany	0.0	0.0	0.0	–
Ireland	–	–	–	–
Italy	–	–	–	–
Japan	6.5	5.3	5.3	9.4
Netherlands	–	–	–	–
New Zealand	1.8	1.7	1.7	1.7
Norway	–	–	–	–
Sweden	–	–	–	–
Switzerland	–	–	–	–
United Kingdom	3.8	3.4	2.7	3.0
United States	–	–	–	–
TOTAL	14.6	12.1	15.1	17.7
MULTILATERAL	3.8	4.1	2.4	2.8
ARAB COUNTRIES	–	–	–	–
E.E.C.+ MEMBERS	5.9	6.2	3.4	3.5
TOTAL	18.4	16.3	17.5	20.5

6. TOTAL OFFICIAL NET

DAC COUNTRIES	1987	1988	1989	1990
Australia	2.5	1.8	5.4	3.7
Austria	–	–	–	–
Belgium	–	–	–	–
Canada	0.0	0.0	–	–
Denmark	–	–	–	–
Finland	–	–	–	–
France	–	–	–	–
Germany	0.0	0.0	0.0	–
Ireland	–	–	–	–
Italy	–	–	–	–
Japan	6.5	5.3	5.3	9.4
Netherlands	–	–	–	–
New Zealand	1.8	1.7	1.7	1.7
Norway	–	–	–	–
Sweden	–	–	–	–
Switzerland	–	–	–	–
United Kingdom	3.8	3.4	2.7	3.0
United States	–	–	–	–
TOTAL	14.6	12.1	15.1	17.7
MULTILATERAL	3.8	4.1	2.4	2.8
ARAB COUNTRIES	–	–	–	–
E.E.C.+ MEMBERS	5.9	6.2	3.4	3.5
TOTAL	18.4	16.3	17.5	20.5

9. TOTAL OOF GROSS

	1987
Australia	–
Austria	–
Belgium	–
Canada	–
Denmark	–
Finland	–
France	–
Germany	–
Ireland	–
Italy	–
Japan	–
Netherlands	–
New Zealand	–
Norway	–
Sweden	–
Switzerland	–
United Kingdom	–
United States	–
TOTAL	–
MULTILATERAL	–
ARAB COUNTRIES	–
E.E.C.+ MEMBERS	–
TOTAL	–

Left panel (continued)

1988	1989	1990
1.8	5.4	3.7
–	–	–
–	–	–
0.0	–	–
–	–	–
–	–	–
0.0	0.0	–
–	–	–
–	–	–
5.3	5.3	9.4
–	–	–
1.7	1.7	1.7
–	–	–
–	–	–
–	–	–
3.4	2.7	3.0
–	–	–
12.1	15.1	17.7

1988	1989	1990
–	–	–
–	–	–
0.3	0.5	1.0
2.8	0.6	0.6
–	–	–
–	–	–
–	–	–
–	–	–
0.7	0.9	1.0
0.2	0.3	0.3
–	–	–
–	–	–
0.1	0.1	0.0
–	–	–
4.1	2.4	2.8
–	–	–
6.2	3.4	3.5
16.3	17.5	20.5

1988	1989	1990
1.8	5.4	3.7
–	–	–
0.0	–	–
–	–	–
–	–	–
0.0	0.0	–
–	–	–
5.3	5.3	9.4
–	–	–
1.7	1.7	1.7
–	–	–
–	–	–
3.4	2.7	3.0
–	–	–
12.1	15.1	17.7
3.8	2.3	2.1
–	–	–
6.2	3.4	3.5
16.0	17.4	19.8

1988	1989	1990
–	–	–
–	–	–
–	–	–
–	–	–
–	–	–
–	–	–
–	–	–
–	–	–
–	–	–
–	–	–
–	–	–
–	–	–
–	–	–
–	–	–
–	–	–
–	–	–
–	–	–
–	–	–

10. ODA COMMITMENTS

1987	1988	1989	1990
1.0	1.0	2.9	2.7
–	–	–	–
–	–	–	–
0.2	0.0	–	–
–	–	–	–
–	–	–	–
0.0	0.0	0.0	–
–	–	–	–
–	–	–	–
3.3	7.2	10.6	5.6
–	–	–	–
1.2	2.8	–	1.7
–	–	–	–
2.7	2.5	2.0	2.3
0.1	0.3	0.4	0.1
8.5	13.8	15.8	12.3

1987	1988	1989	1990
–	–	–	–
–	–	–	–
0.1	0.9	–	1.0
2.3	1.1	–	–
–	–	–	–
–	–	–	–
–	–	–	–
0.8	1.0	1.2	1.3
–	–	–	–
–	–	–	–
–	–	–	–
–	–	–	–
–	–	–	–
–	–	–	–
3.3	3.1	1.2	2.3
–	–	–	–
5.0	3.7	2.0	2.3
11.8	16.8	17.0	14.6

11. TECH. COOP. GRANTS

1987	1988	1989	1990
0.9	0.9	1.5	1.8
–	–	–	–
–	–	–	–
–	–	–	–
–	–	–	–
0.0	0.0	0.0	–
–	–	–	–
3.0	3.9	3.6	1.6
–	–	–	–
0.4	0.9	–	0.9
–	–	–	–
–	–	–	–
2.6	2.5	1.9	2.2
–	–	–	–
7.0	8.1	7.0	6.5
0.9	1.4	1.2	1.3
–	–	–	–
2.8	2.9	1.9	2.2
7.9	9.5	8.3	7.8

12. TOTAL OOF NET

1987	1988	1989	1990
–	–	–	–
–	–	–	–
–	–	–	–
–	–	–	–
–	–	–	–
–	–	–	–
–	–	–	–
–	–	–	–
–	–	–	–
–	–	–	–
–	–	–	–
–	–	–	–
–	–	–	–
–	–	–	–
–	–	–	–
–	–	–	–
–	–	–	–
–	–	–	–

13. ODF COMMITMENTS: BY PURPOSE %

	1987	1988	1989	1990
Education	–	–	–	–
Health	–	–	38	–
Other Social Infrastr.	–	–	–	–
Water Sanitat. Sewage	4	–	–	–
Energy	–	–	5	–
Telecommunications	–	–	–	–
Transportation	–	19	1	–
Agriculture	–	7	–	–
Extractive Industries	–	–	–	–
Manufacturing	–	–	–	–
Trade Banking Tourism	–	3	–	–
Technical Cooperation	96	65	49	–
Multisector Aid	1	2	3	–
Programme	–	5	4	–
Debt Reorganisation	–	–	–	–
Food Aid	–	–	–	–
Emergency Aid	–	–	–	–
Unspecified	–	–	–	–
TOTAL	100	100	100	–

14. GRANT ELEMENT OF ODA %

DAC COUNTRIES	1987	1988	1989	1990
Australia	100.0	100.0	100.0	–
Austria	–	–	–	–
Belgium	–	–	–	–
Canada	100.0	100.0	–	–
Denmark	–	–	–	–
Finland	–	–	–	–
France	–	–	–	–
Germany	100.0	100.0	100.0	–
Ireland	–	–	–	–
Italy	–	–	–	–
Japan	100.0	100.0	100.0	–
Netherlands	–	–	–	–
New Zealand	100.0	100.0	–	–
Norway	–	–	–	–
Sweden	–	–	–	–
Switzerland	–	–	–	–
United Kingdom	100.0	100.0	100.0	–
United States	100.0	100.0	100.0	–
TOTAL	100.0	100.0	100.0	–
MULTILATERAL	100.0	100.0	90.8	–
ARAB COUNTRIES	–	–	–	–
E.E.C.+ MEMBERS	100.0	100.0	100.0	–
TOTAL	100.0	100.0	98.9	–

15. OTHER AGGREGATES

	1987	1988	1989	1990
OFFICIAL COMMITMENTS:				
TOTAL BILATERAL	8.6	13.8	15.8	12.3
of which:				
Arab Countries	–	–	–	–
C.E.E.C.	–	–	–	–
TOTAL MULTILATERAL	3.3	3.1	1.2	2.3
TOTAL BIL.& MULTIL.	11.8	16.8	17.1	14.6
of which:				
ODA Grants	11.7	15.9	17.1	13.6
ODA Loans	0.1	0.9	–	1.0
DISBURSEMENTS:				
DAC COUNTRIES COMBINED				
OFFICIAL & PRIVATE				
GROSS:				
Contractual Lending	–	–	–	–
Export Credits, Total	–	–	–	–
Export Credits, Priv.	–	–	–	–
NET:				
Contractual Lending	-0.2	–	–	–
Export Credits Total	-0.2	–	–	–
PRIVATE SECTOR NET	-0.1	–	0.0	–
Direct Investment	–	–	–	0.0
Portfolio Investment	0.1	–	0.0	0.0
Export Credits	-0.2	–	–	–
MARKET BORROWING:				
CHANGE IN CLAIMS				
Banks	5.0	-5.0	–	–
MEMORANDUM ITEM:				
C.E.E.C. (Gross)	–	–	–	–

1. TOTAL RECEIPTS NET

DAC COUNTRIES	1987	1988	1989	1990
Australia	2.8	-25.2	136.0	-77.4
Austria	66.1	-42.0	-58.6	-18.8
Belgium	-193.7	-73.2	-1.4	-187.3
Canada	-25.1	0.2	-21.2	-38.4
Denmark	-0.5	-0.2	0.1	4.4
Finland	1.6	-0.9	2.7	1.1
France	-44.9	170.9	-81.5	36.5
Germany	79.8	-61.0	141.4	681.4
Ireland	–	–	–	–
Italy	-0.2	–	4.5	1.4
Japan	-159.6	-86.9	50.3	582.5
Netherlands	-41.9	-18.4	15.8	1.0
New Zealand	0.1	0.0	0.0	–
Norway	-1.1	-20.5	-1.3	0.3
Sweden	-53.3	–	-27.7	-6.8
Switzerland	–	0.0	–	0.0
United Kingdom	-14.7	39.5	-62.4	0.1
United States	-1663.0	-905.0	-337.0	479.0
TOTAL	-2047.7	-1022.7	-240.5	1458.8
MULTILATERAL				
AF.D.F.	–	–	–	–
AF.D.B.	–	–	–	–
AS.D.B	-115.5	-69.6	-378.2	21.4
CAR.D.B.	–	–	–	–
E.E.C.	–	–	–	–
IBRD	-279.7	-814.0	-216.0	-402.0
IDA	-1.6	-2.0	-2.0	-2.0
I.D.B.	–	–	–	–
IFAD	–	–	–	–
I.F.C.	1.9	-0.1	24.3	–
IMF TRUST FUND	–	–	–	–
U.N. AGENCIES	–	–	–	–
UNDP	2.7	2.1	3.4	2.7
UNTA	1.7	1.1	1.6	1.2
UNICEF	0.4	0.3	0.5	0.4
UNRWA	–	–	–	–
WFP	–	–	–	–
UNHCR	–	0.1	0.3	0.3
Other Multilateral	0.7	0.6	0.3	0.9
Arab Agencies	–	–	–	–
TOTAL	-389.5	-881.5	-565.8	-377.1
ARAB COUNTRIES	-0.4	-1.9	-1.1	-5.7
E.E.C.+ MEMBERS	-216.0	57.6	16.4	537.4
TOTAL	-2437.7	-1906.0	-807.4	1076.1

2. ODA LOANS GROSS

DAC COUNTRIES	1987	1988	1989	1990
Australia	–	–	–	–
Austria	–	–	–	–
Belgium	–	–	–	–
Canada	–	–	–	–
Denmark	–	–	–	–
Finland	–	–	–	–
France	–	–	–	–
Germany	4.1	0.7	18.6	0.1
Ireland	–	–	–	–
Italy	–	–	–	–
Japan	187.0	194.6	196.5	189.7
Netherlands	–	–	–	–
New Zealand	–	–	–	–
Norway	–	–	–	–
Sweden	–	–	–	–
Switzerland	–	–	–	–
United Kingdom	–	–	–	–
United States	6.0	4.0	4.0	4.0
TOTAL	197.1	199.3	219.1	193.7
MULTILATERAL	–	–	–	–
ARAB COUNTRIES	10.1	4.5	7.1	2.6
E.E.C.+ MEMBERS	4.1	0.7	18.6	0.1
TOTAL	207.2	203.8	226.2	196.3

3. TOTAL OFFICIAL GROSS

DAC COUNTRIES	1987	1988	1989	1990
Australia	0.7	0.7	0.4	0.6
Austria	42.1	7.1	2.3	3.1
Belgium	6.8	0.4	3.4	2.6
Canada	0.0	0.2	8.1	0.3
Denmark	0.0	0.2	0.1	1.4
Finland	0.0	–	0.1	0.3
France	1.2	1.9	1.4	6.2
Germany	111.1	78.3	83.9	38.5
Ireland	–	–	–	–
Italy	0.2	–	–	–
Japan	216.4	242.9	234.0	240.8
Netherlands	0.9	–	–	–
New Zealand	0.1	0.0	0.0	–
Norway	–	–	–	–
Sweden	–	–	–	–
Switzerland	–	0.0	–	0.0
United Kingdom	0.3	0.4	0.2	0.1
United States	40.0	5.0	4.0	4.0
TOTAL	419.8	336.9	337.9	297.8
MULTILATERAL	605.4	527.8	273.9	239.2
ARAB COUNTRIES	10.1	4.5	7.1	2.6
E.E.C.+ MEMBERS	120.6	81.0	88.9	48.7
TOTAL	1035.4	869.2	619.0	539.6

4. TOTAL ODA NET

DAC COUNTRIES	1987	1988	1989	1990
Australia	0.7	0.7	0.4	0.6
Austria	2.2	2.3	2.3	3.1
Belgium	0.4	0.4	0.1	0.1
Canada	0.0	0.2	0.1	0.1
Denmark	-0.1	-0.2	0.1	-0.2
Finland	0.0	–	0.1	0.3
France	1.2	1.9	1.4	6.2
Germany	11.3	17.0	37.3	24.9
Ireland	–	–	–	–
Italy	0.2	–	–	–
Japan	6.6	12.6	41.0	50.4
Netherlands	0.8	–	–	–
New Zealand	0.1	0.0	0.0	–
Norway	–	–	–	–
Sweden	–	–	–	–
Switzerland	–	0.0	–	0.0
United Kingdom	0.3	0.4	0.2	0.1
United States	-22.0	-26.0	-34.0	-31.0
TOTAL	1.6	9.3	48.9	54.7
MULTILATERAL				
AF.D.F.	–	–	–	–
AF.D.B.	–	–	–	–
AS.D.B	0.1	0.1	-0.3	-0.3
CAR.D.B.	–	–	–	–
E.E.C.	–	–	–	–
IBRD	–	–	–	–
IDA	-1.6	-2.0	-2.0	-2.0
I.D.B.	–	–	–	–
IFAD	–	–	–	–
I.F.C.	–	–	–	–
IMF TRUST FUND	–	–	–	–
U.N. AGENCIES	–	–	–	–
UNDP	2.7	2.1	3.4	2.7
UNTA	1.7	1.1	1.6	1.2
UNICEF	0.4	0.3	0.5	0.4
UNRWA	–	–	–	–
WFP	–	–	–	–
UNHCR	–	0.1	0.3	0.3
Other Multilateral	0.7	0.6	0.3	0.9
Arab Agencies	–	–	–	–
TOTAL	3.9	2.3	3.7	3.3
ARAB COUNTRIES	5.7	-1.9	-1.1	-5.7
E.E.C.+ MEMBERS	14.1	19.4	39.0	31.2
TOTAL	11.2	9.7	51.5	52.2

5. ODA LOANS NET

DAC COUNTRIES	1987	1988	1989	1990
Australia	–	–	–	–
Austria	–	–	–	–
Belgium	–	–	–	–
Canada	0.0	–	–	0.0
Denmark	-0.2	-0.2	–	-0.2
Finland	–	–	–	–
France	–	–	–	–
Germany	-15.6	-10.9	7.4	-13.1
Ireland	–	–	–	–
Italy	–	–	–	–
Japan	-22.8	-23.1	3.4	-0.6
Netherlands	-0.1	–	–	–
New Zealand	–	–	–	–
Norway	–	–	–	–
Sweden	–	–	–	–
Switzerland	–	–	–	–
United Kingdom	–	–	–	–
United States	-22.0	-26.0	-34.0	-31.0
TOTAL	-60.7	-60.1	-23.2	-44.9
MULTILATERAL	-1.9	-2.3	-2.3	-2.3
ARAB COUNTRIES	5.7	-1.9	-1.1	-5.7
E.E.C.+ MEMBERS	-15.8	-11.0	7.4	-13.3
TOTAL	-56.8	-64.2	-26.7	-52.9

6. TOTAL OFFICIAL NET

DAC COUNTRIES	1987	1988	1989	1990
Australia	0.7	0.7	0.4	0.6
Austria	42.1	-21.5	-40.8	1.2
Belgium	6.8	0.4	3.4	2.6
Canada	-25.1	0.2	-21.2	-38.4
Denmark	-0.1	-0.1	0.1	1.2
Finland	0.0	–	0.1	0.3
France	1.2	1.9	1.4	6.2
Germany	41.6	-25.8	47.9	0.5
Ireland	–	–	–	–
Italy	0.2	–	–	–
Japan	-8.8	25.2	41.0	48.6
Netherlands	0.8	–	–	–
New Zealand	0.1	0.0	0.0	–
Norway	–	–	–	–
Sweden	–	–	–	–
Switzerland	–	0.0	–	0.0
United Kingdom	0.3	0.4	0.2	0.1
United States	-1074.0	-154.0	-149.0	-131.0
TOTAL	-1014.3	-172.7	-116.6	-108.2
MULTILATERAL	-389.5	-881.5	-565.8	-377.1
ARAB COUNTRIES	-0.4	-1.9	-1.1	-5.7
E.E.C.+ MEMBERS	50.8	-23.3	52.9	10.5
TOTAL	-1404.3	-1056.1	-683.5	-490.9

7. TOTAL ODA GROSS

DAC COUNTRIES	1987
Australia	0.7
Austria	2.2
Belgium	0.4
Canada	0.0
Denmark	0.0
Finland	0.0
France	1.2
Germany	31.0
Ireland	–
Italy	0.2
Japan	216.4
Netherlands	0.9
New Zealand	0.1
Norway	–
Sweden	–
Switzerland	–
United Kingdom	0.3
United States	6.0
TOTAL	259.4
AF.D.F.	–
AF.D.B.	–
AS.D.B	0.4
CAR.D.B.	–
E.E.C.	–
IBRD	–
IDA	–
I.D.B.	–
IFAD	–
I.F.C.	–
IMF TRUST FUND	–
U.N. AGENCIES	–
UNDP	2.7
UNTA	1.7
UNICEF	0.4
UNRWA	–
WFP	–
UNHCR	–
Other Multilateral	0.7
Arab Agencies	–
TOTAL	5.8
ARAB COUNTRIES	10.1
E.E.C.+ MEMBERS	34.1
TOTAL	275.3

8. GRANTS

	1987
Australia	0.7
Austria	2.2
Belgium	0.4
Canada	0.0
Denmark	0.0
Finland	0.0
France	1.2
Germany	26.9
Ireland	–
Italy	0.2
Japan	29.4
Netherlands	0.9
New Zealand	0.1
Norway	–
Sweden	–
Switzerland	–
United Kingdom	0.3
United States	–
TOTAL	62.3
MULTILATERAL	5.8
ARAB COUNTRIES	–
E.E.C.+ MEMBERS	30.0
TOTAL	68.0

9. TOTAL OOF GROSS

	1987
Australia	–
Austria	39.9
Belgium	6.4
Canada	–
Denmark	–
Finland	–
France	–
Germany	80.1
Ireland	–
Italy	–
Japan	–
Netherlands	–
New Zealand	–
Norway	–
Sweden	–
Switzerland	–
United Kingdom	–
United States	34.0
TOTAL	160.5
MULTILATERAL	599.7
ARAB COUNTRIES	–
E.E.C.+ MEMBERS	86.5
TOTAL	760.1

10. ODA COMMITMENTS

1988	1989	1990	1987	1988	1989	1990
0.7	0.4	0.6	0.6	0.5	0.7	0.6
2.3	2.3	3.1	2.2	2.3	2.3	3.1
0.4	0.1	0.1	0.1	0.1	0.1	0.1
0.2	0.1	0.2	–	0.2	0.1	0.3
–	0.1	–	–	–	–	–
–	0.1	0.3	–	0.1	0.2	0.6
1.9	1.4	6.2	1.2	3.6	1.1	6.1
28.6	48.5	38.1	36.7	20.7	31.0	33.4
–	–	–	–	–	–	–
–	–	–	0.2	–	–	–
230.3	234.0	240.6	341.5	251.9	96.1	739.4
–	–	–	–	–	–	–
0.0	0.0	–	0.0	–	–	–
–	–	–	–	–	–	–
–	–	–	–	–	–	–
0.0	–	0.0	–	–	–	–
0.4	0.2	0.1	0.3	0.4	0.2	–
4.0	4.0	4.0	6.3	4.1	3.5	4.0
268.7	*291.2*	*293.3*	*389.1*	*283.8*	*135.4*	*787.6*
–	–	–	–	–	–	–
–	–	–	–	–	–	–
0.4	–	–	–	–	–	–
–	–	–	0.0	–	–	–
–	–	–	–	–	–	–
–	–	–	–	–	–	–
–	–	–	–	–	–	–
–	–	–	–	–	–	–
–	–	–	–	–	–	–
–	–	–	5.4	4.2	6.0	5.6
2.1	3.4	2.7	–	–	–	–
1.1	1.6	1.2	–	–	–	–
0.3	0.5	0.4	–	–	–	–
–	–	–	–	–	–	–
0.1	0.3	0.3	–	–	–	–
0.6	0.3	0.9	–	–	–	–
–	–	–	0.5	–	–	–
4.5	*6.0*	*5.6*	*5.9*	*4.2*	*6.0*	*5.6*
4.5	*7.1*	*2.6*	*–*	*–*	*–*	*–*
31.2	*50.3*	*44.5*	*38.5*	*24.7*	*32.4*	*39.6*
277.7	*304.4*	*301.4*	*395.0*	*288.0*	*141.4*	*793.2*

11. TECH. COOP. GRANTS

1988	1989	1990	1987	1988	1989	1990
0.7	0.4	0.6	0.6	0.6	0.3	0.6
2.3	2.3	3.1	2.2	2.3	2.3	3.1
0.4	0.1	0.1	0.3	0.1	0.0	0.0
0.2	0.1	0.2	–	–	–	–
–	0.1	–	0.0	–	0.1	–
–	0.1	0.3	0.0	–	0.1	0.3
1.9	1.4	6.2	1.2	1.2	1.1	6.1
27.9	30.0	38.0	26.9	27.9	26.8	34.6
–	–	–	–	–	–	–
–	–	–	0.2	–	–	–
35.6	37.6	50.9	29.2	35.6	37.4	50.8
–	–	–	0.8	–	–	–
0.0	0.0	–	0.0	0.0	–	–
–	–	–	–	–	–	–
–	–	–	–	–	–	–
0.0	–	0.0	–	0.0	–	–
0.4	0.2	0.1	0.2	0.4	0.2	0.1
–	–	–	–	–	–	–
69.4	*72.2*	*99.6*	*61.6*	*68.1*	*68.3*	*95.6*
4.5	*6.0*	*5.6*	*5.4*	*4.2*	*6.0*	*5.6*
–	–	–	–	–	–	–
30.5	*31.7*	*44.5*	*29.6*	*29.5*	*28.2*	*40.8*
73.9	*78.2*	*105.1*	*67.0*	*72.3*	*74.3*	*101.1*

12. TOTAL OOF NET

1988	1989	1990	1987	1988	1989	1990
–	–	–	–	–	–	–
4.7	–	–	39.9	-23.8	-43.1	-2.0
–	3.4	2.5	6.4	–	3.4	2.5
–	8.0	0.1	-25.1	–	-21.3	-38.5
0.2	–	1.4	–	0.1	–	1.4
–	–	–	–	–	–	–
–	–	–	–	–	–	–
49.7	35.3	0.4	30.3	-42.8	10.6	-24.4
–	–	–	–	–	–	–
12.6	–	0.2	-15.4	12.6	–	-1.7
–	–	–	–	–	–	–
–	–	–	–	–	–	–
–	–	–	–	–	–	–
–	–	–	–	–	–	–
–	–	–	–	–	–	–
1.0	–	–	-1052.0	-128.0	-115.0	-100.0
68.2	46.7	4.5	-1015.9	-182.0	-165.5	-162.9
523.3	267.9	233.7	-393.4	-883.8	-569.6	-380.3
–	–	–	*-6.1*	–	–	–
49.9	38.7	4.2	36.7	-42.7	13.9	-20.6
591.5	*314.6*	*238.2*	*-1415.5*	*-1065.8*	*-735.1*	*-543.2*

13. ODF COMMITMENTS: BY PURPOSE %

	1987	1988	1989	1990
Education	15	8	4	–
Health	–	7	0	–
Other Social Infrastr.	33	3	–	–
Water Sanitat. Sewage	0	9	5	–
Energy	1	–	–	–
Telecommunications	–	–	–	–
Transportation	–	46	65	–
Agriculture	18	6	–	–
Extractive Industries	–	–	–	–
Manufacturing	4	0	0	–
Trade Banking Tourism	9	8	10	–
Technical Cooperation	13	11	16	–
Multisector Aid	–	–	–	–
Programme	5	–	–	–
Debt Reorganisation	1	1	1	–
Food Aid	–	–	–	–
Emergency Aid	0	–	0	–
Unspecified	–	–	–	–
TOTAL	100	100	100	–

14. GRANT ELEMENT OF ODA %

DAC COUNTRIES	1987	1988	1989	1990
Australia	100.0	100.0	100.0	–
Austria	100.0	100.0	100.0	–
Belgium	100.0	100.0	100.0	–
Canada	–	100.0	100.0	–
Denmark	–	–	–	–
Finland	–	100.0	100.0	–
France	100.0	100.0	100.0	–
Germany	100.0	100.0	100.0	–
Ireland	–	–	–	–
Italy	100.0	–	–	–
Japan	49.3	51.4	66.5	–
Netherlands	–	–	–	–
New Zealand	100.0	–	–	–
Norway	–	–	–	–
Sweden	–	–	–	–
Switzerland	–	–	–	–
United Kingdom	100.0	100.0	100.0	–
United States	67.1	67.1	67.1	–
TOTAL	*56.4*	*56.4*	*75.4*	*–*
MULTILATERAL	*100.0*	*100.0*	*100.0*	*–*
ARAB COUNTRIES	*–*	*–*	*–*	*–*
E.E.C.+ MEMBERS	*100.0*	*100.0*	*100.0*	*–*
TOTAL	*57.2*	*57.0*	*76.4*	*–*

15. OTHER AGGREGATES

	1987	1988	1989	1990
OFFICIAL COMMITMENTS:				
TOTAL BILATERAL	418.1	300.1	138.7	791.4
of which:				
Arab Countries	–	–	–	–
C.E.E.C.	–	–	–	–
TOTAL MULTILATERAL	343.2	346.8	246.8	119.9
TOTAL BIL. & MULTIL.	761.4	646.9	385.5	911.4
of which:				
ODA Grants	80.0	70.8	82.3	101.4
ODA Loans	315.0	217.2	59.1	691.8
DISBURSEMENTS:				
DAC COUNTRIES COMBINED				
OFFICIAL & PRIVATE				
GROSS:				
Contractual Lending	929.2	810.7	497.7	242.9
Export Credits, Total	732.1	598.7	260.5	47.6
Export Credits, Priv.	580.3	544.2	235.3	47.5
NET:				
Contractual Lending	-1274.0	-141.2	-639.1	-636.7
Export Credits Total	-1213.3	-92.8	-632.2	-591.4
PRIVATE SECTOR NET	-1033.4	-850.0	-123.9	1567.0
Direct Investment	828.0	753.6	382.8	556.9
Portfolio Investment	-1672.7	-1705.5	-59.7	1436.2
Export Credits	-188.8	101.8	-447.0	-426.1
MARKET BORROWING:				
CHANGE IN CLAIMS				
Banks	-5781.0	-1965.0	1205.0	4154.0
MEMORANDUM ITEM:				
C.E.E.C. (Gross)	–	–	–	–

1. TOTAL RECEIPTS NET

DAC COUNTRIES	1987	1988	1989	1990
Australia	4.2	4.3	6.8	6.0
Austria	–	–	0.0	–
Belgium	0.0	0.1	–	0.2
Canada	0.0	0.0	0.0	0.1
Denmark	–	–	–	–
Finland	–	–	0.1	–
France	1.0	1.4	2.1	4.0
Germany	-1.8	-1.2	0.4	3.1
Ireland	–	–	–	–
Italy	–	–	–	–
Japan	14.0	11.3	19.7	16.9
Netherlands	0.4	0.1	0.0	0.1
New Zealand	0.0	0.0	0.0	0.0
Norway	0.1	0.2	0.2	1.2
Sweden	12.5	20.0	11.2	17.1
Switzerland	–	0.1	3.0	2.5
United Kingdom	0.1	0.2	0.0	0.0
United States	–	–	–	–
TOTAL	*30.5*	*36.5*	*43.5*	*51.2*
MULTILATERAL				
AF.D.F.	–	–	–	–
AF.D.B.	–	–	–	–
AS.D.B	3.2	5.7	36.0	44.3
CAR.D.B.	–	–	–	–
E.E.C.	1.5	0.5	1.3	1.3
IBRD	–	–	–	–
IDA	5.0	10.0	35.0	33.0
I.D.B.	–	–	–	–
IFAD	2.2	1.6	2.6	3.8
I.F.C.	–	–	–	–
IMF TRUST FUND	–	–	–	–
U.N. AGENCIES	–	–	–	–
UNDP	13.7	10.5	12.2	12.2
UNTA	1.1	1.0	1.7	1.5
UNICEF	0.9	1.5	1.5	1.9
UNRWA	–	–	–	–
WFP	0.3	9.5	1.9	–
UNHCR	0.5	0.8	0.6	0.8
Other Multilateral	0.2	0.3	4.2	1.7
Arab Agencies	-0.6	-0.4	-0.4	–
TOTAL	*27.8*	*40.7*	*96.4*	*100.5*
ARAB COUNTRIES	–	–	–	–
E.E.C.+ MEMBERS	*1.2*	*1.0*	*3.7*	*8.7*
TOTAL	*58.3*	*77.2*	*139.9*	*151.7*

2. ODA LOANS GROSS

DAC COUNTRIES	1987	1988	1989	1990
Australia	–	–	–	–
Austria	–	–	–	–
Belgium	–	–	–	–
Canada	–	–	–	–
Denmark	–	–	–	–
Finland	–	–	–	–
France	–	–	–	–
Germany	–	–	–	–
Ireland	–	–	–	–
Italy	–	–	–	–
Japan	–	–	–	–
Netherlands	–	–	–	–
New Zealand	–	–	–	–
Norway	–	–	–	–
Sweden	–	–	–	–
Switzerland	–	–	–	–
United Kingdom	–	–	–	–
United States	–	–	–	–
TOTAL	–	–	–	–
MULTILATERAL	*10.7*	*18.1*	*69.7*	*78.2*
ARAB COUNTRIES	–	–	–	–
E.E.C.+ MEMBERS	–	–	–	–
TOTAL	*10.7*	*18.1*	*69.7*	*78.2*

3. TOTAL OFFICIAL GROSS

DAC COUNTRIES	1987	1988	1989	1990
Australia	4.2	4.3	6.8	6.0
Austria	–	–	0.0	–
Belgium	0.0	0.1	–	0.2
Canada	0.0	0.0	0.0	0.1
Denmark	–	–	–	–
Finland	–	–	0.1	–
France	1.0	1.2	1.9	4.0
Germany	0.1	0.2	0.8	3.7
Ireland	–	–	–	–
Italy	–	–	–	–
Japan	15.3	13.7	21.2	19.1
Netherlands	0.4	0.1	0.0	0.1
New Zealand	0.0	0.0	0.0	0.0
Norway	0.1	0.2	0.2	1.2
Sweden	12.5	20.0	11.2	17.1
Switzerland	–	0.1	3.0	2.5
United Kingdom	0.1	0.2	0.0	0.0
United States	–	–	–	–
TOTAL	*33.7*	*40.2*	*45.2*	*54.0*
MULTILATERAL	*29.4*	*42.3*	*98.2*	*101.6*
ARAB COUNTRIES	–	–	–	–
E.E.C.+ MEMBERS	*3.1*	*2.2*	*4.0*	*9.3*
TOTAL	*63.0*	*82.5*	*143.4*	*155.6*

4. TOTAL ODA NET

DAC COUNTRIES	1987	1988	1989	1990
Australia	4.2	4.3	6.8	6.0
Austria	–	–	0.0	–
Belgium	0.0	0.1	–	0.2
Canada	0.0	0.0	0.0	0.1
Denmark	–	–	–	–
Finland	–	–	0.1	–
France	1.0	1.2	1.9	4.0
Germany	-1.9	-1.2	0.4	2.6
Ireland	–	–	–	–
Italy	–	–	–	–
Japan	14.0	11.2	19.4	17.4
Netherlands	0.4	0.1	0.0	0.1
New Zealand	0.0	0.0	0.0	0.0
Norway	0.1	0.2	0.2	1.2
Sweden	12.5	20.0	11.2	17.1
Switzerland	–	0.1	3.0	2.5
United Kingdom	0.1	0.2	0.0	0.0
United States	–	–	–	–
TOTAL	*30.4*	*36.2*	*42.9*	*51.2*
MULTILATERAL				
AF.D.F.	–	–	–	–
AF.D.B.	–	–	–	–
AS.D.B	3.2	5.7	36.0	44.3
CAR.D.B.	–	–	–	–
E.E.C.	1.5	0.5	1.3	1.3
IBRD	–	–	–	–
IDA	5.0	10.0	35.0	33.0
I.D.B.	–	–	–	–
IFAD	2.2	1.6	2.6	3.8
I.F.C.	–	–	–	–
IMF TRUST FUND	–	–	–	–
U.N. AGENCIES	–	–	–	–
UNDP	13.7	10.5	12.2	12.2
UNTA	1.1	1.0	1.7	1.5
UNICEF	0.9	1.5	1.5	1.9
UNRWA	–	–	–	–
WFP	0.3	9.5	1.9	–
UNHCR	0.5	0.8	0.6	0.8
Other Multilateral	0.2	0.3	4.2	1.7
Arab Agencies	-0.6	-0.4	-0.4	–
TOTAL	*27.8*	*40.7*	*96.4*	*100.5*
ARAB COUNTRIES	–	–	–	–
E.E.C.+ MEMBERS	*1.1*	*0.9*	*3.5*	*8.2*
TOTAL	*58.3*	*77.0*	*139.3*	*151.7*

5. ODA LOANS NET

DAC COUNTRIES	1987	1988	1989	1990
Australia	–	–	–	–
Austria	–	–	–	–
Belgium	–	–	–	–
Canada	–	–	–	–
Denmark	–	–	–	–
Finland	–	–	–	–
France	–	–	–	–
Germany	-2.0	-1.4	-0.5	-1.1
Ireland	–	–	–	–
Italy	–	–	–	–
Japan	-1.2	-2.6	-1.8	-1.7
Netherlands	–	–	–	–
New Zealand	–	–	–	–
Norway	–	–	–	–
Sweden	–	–	–	–
Switzerland	–	–	–	–
United Kingdom	–	0.0	–	–
United States	–	–	–	–
TOTAL	*-3.2*	*-3.9*	*-2.3*	*-2.8*
MULTILATERAL	*9.1*	*16.5*	*67.9*	*76.2*
ARAB COUNTRIES	–	–	–	–
E.E.C.+ MEMBERS	*-2.0*	*-1.4*	*-0.5*	*-1.1*
TOTAL	*5.9*	*12.6*	*65.6*	*73.4*

6. TOTAL OFFICIAL NET

DAC COUNTRIES	1987	1988	1989	1990
Australia	4.2	4.3	6.8	6.0
Austria	–	–	0.0	–
Belgium	0.0	0.1	–	0.2
Canada	0.0	0.0	0.0	0.1
Denmark	–	–	–	–
Finland	–	–	0.1	–
France	1.0	1.2	1.9	4.0
Germany	-1.9	-1.2	0.4	2.6
Ireland	–	–	–	–
Italy	–	–	–	–
Japan	14.0	11.2	19.4	17.4
Netherlands	0.4	0.1	0.0	0.1
New Zealand	0.0	0.0	0.0	0.0
Norway	0.1	0.2	0.2	1.2
Sweden	12.5	20.0	11.2	17.1
Switzerland	–	0.1	3.0	2.5
United Kingdom	0.1	0.2	0.0	0.0
United States	–	–	–	–
TOTAL	*30.4*	*36.2*	*42.9*	*51.2*
MULTILATERAL	*27.8*	*40.7*	*96.4*	*100.5*
ARAB COUNTRIES	–	–	–	–
E.E.C.+ MEMBERS	*1.1*	*0.9*	*3.5*	*8.2*
TOTAL	*58.3*	*77.0*	*139.3*	*151.7*

7. TOTAL ODA GROSS

	1987
Australia	4.2
Austria	–
Belgium	0.0
Canada	0.0
Denmark	–
Finland	–
France	1.0
Germany	0.1
Ireland	–
Italy	–
Japan	15.3
Netherlands	0.4
New Zealand	0.0
Norway	0.1
Sweden	12.5
Switzerland	–
United Kingdom	0.1
United States	–
TOTAL	*33.7*
AF.D.F.	–
AF.D.B.	–
AS.D.B	3.7
CAR.D.B.	–
E.E.C.	1.5
IBRD	–
IDA	5.0
I.D.B.	–
IFAD	2.2
I.F.C.	–
IMF TRUST FUND	–
U.N. AGENCIES	–
UNDP	13.7
UNTA	1.1
UNICEF	0.9
UNRWA	–
WFP	0.3
UNHCR	0.5
Other Multilateral	0.2
Arab Agencies	0.4
TOTAL	*29.3*
ARAB COUNTRIES	–
E.E.C.+ MEMBERS	*3.1*
TOTAL	*63.0*

8. GRANTS

	1987
Australia	4.2
Austria	–
Belgium	0.0
Canada	0.0
Denmark	–
Finland	–
France	1.0
Germany	0.1
Ireland	–
Italy	–
Japan	15.3
Netherlands	0.4
New Zealand	0.0
Norway	0.1
Sweden	12.5
Switzerland	–
United Kingdom	0.1
United States	–
TOTAL	*33.7*
MULTILATERAL	*18.7*
ARAB COUNTRIES	–
E.E.C.+ MEMBERS	*3.1*
TOTAL	*52.4*

9. TOTAL OOF GROSS

	1987
Australia	–
Austria	–
Belgium	–
Canada	–
Denmark	–
Finland	–
France	–
Germany	–
Ireland	–
Italy	–
Japan	–
Netherlands	–
New Zealand	–
Norway	–
Sweden	–
Switzerland	–
United Kingdom	–
United States	–
TOTAL	–
MULTILATERAL	–
ARAB COUNTRIES	–
E.E.C.+ MEMBERS	–
TOTAL	–

10. ODA COMMITMENTS

1988	1989	1990	1987	1988	1989	1990
4.3	6.8	6.0	1.7	13.3	8.2	3.5
–	0.0	–	–	–	0.0	–
0.1	–	0.2	0.1	–	–	0.2
0.0	0.0	0.1	0.1	–	0.0	0.4
–	–	–	–	–	–	–
–	0.1	–	–	–	0.1	–
1.2	1.9	4.0	1.0	1.2	2.8	3.4
0.2	0.8	3.7	0.2	0.2	0.8	5.0
–	–	–	–	–	–	–
–	–	–	–	1.8	–	0.0
13.7	21.2	19.1	11.2	22.0	19.9	20.8
0.1	0.0	0.1	0.3	0.1	0.0	0.1
0.0	0.0	0.0	0.0	–	–	–
0.2	0.2	1.2	–	–	–	1.0
20.0	11.2	17.1	13.1	20.0	11.2	15.6
0.1	3.0	2.5	–	0.1	14.0	3.5
0.2	0.0	0.0	0.1	0.2	0.0	0.0
–	–	–	–	–	–	0.6
40.2	*45.2*	*54.0*	*27.7*	*58.9*	*57.1*	*54.2*
–	–	–	–	–	–	–
6.2	36.5	45.0	42.7	11.2	61.7	27.9
–	–	–	–	–	–	–
0.5	1.3	1.3	10.4	7.1	3.2	3.2
–	–	–	–	–	–	–
10.0	35.0	33.0	39.9	10.0	64.0	25.0
–	–	–	–	–	–	–
1.6	2.6	3.8	4.5	–	0.2	5.8
–	–	–	–	–	–	–
–	–	–	16.6	23.4	22.0	18.1
10.5	12.2	12.2	–	–	–	–
1.0	1.7	1.5	–	–	–	–
1.5	1.5	1.9	–	–	–	–
9.5	1.9	–	–	–	–	–
0.8	0.6	0.8	–	–	–	–
0.3	4.2	1.7	–	–	–	–
0.6	0.9	0.4	–	–	–	–
42.3	*98.2*	*101.6*	*114.2*	*51.7*	*151.2*	*80.1*
–	–	–	–	–	–	–
2.2	*4.0*	*9.3*	*12.1*	*10.5*	*6.9*	*12.1*
82.5	**143.4**	**155.6**	**141.8**	**110.5**	**208.3**	**134.2**

11. TECH. COOP. GRANTS

1988	1989	1990	1987	1988	1989	1990
4.3	6.8	6.0	0.4	0.8	1.4	1.8
–	0.0	–	–	–	–	–
0.1	–	0.2	0.0	0.0	–	–
0.0	0.0	0.1	–	–	–	–
–	–	–	–	–	–	–
–	0.1	–	–	–	–	–
1.2	1.9	4.0	1.0	1.2	1.9	3.4
0.2	0.8	3.7	0.1	0.2	0.1	3.6
–	–	–	–	–	–	–
–	–	–	–	–	–	–
13.7	21.2	19.1	0.5	1.8	2.9	3.6
0.1	0.0	0.1	0.3	0.1	0.0	0.0
0.0	0.0	0.0	–	0.0	–	0.0
0.2	0.2	1.2	–	–	0.0	0.0
20.0	11.2	17.1	2.2	5.3	7.2	0.7
0.1	3.0	2.5	–	–	–	–
0.2	0.0	0.0	0.0	0.0	0.0	0.0
–	–	–	–	–	–	–
40.2	*45.2*	*54.0*	*4.5*	*9.4*	*13.6*	*13.2*
24.2	*28.5*	*23.4*	*16.4*	*14.3*	*20.2*	*18.1*
–	–	–	–	–	–	–
2.2	*4.0*	*9.3*	*1.4*	*1.8*	*2.0*	*7.1*
64.4	**73.7**	**77.4**	**20.9**	**23.6**	**33.8**	**31.3**

12. TOTAL OOF NET

1988	1989	1990	1987	1988	1989	1990
–	–	–	–	–	–	–
–	–	–	–	–	–	–
–	–	–	–	–	–	–
–	–	–	–	–	–	–
–	–	–	–	–	–	–
–	–	–	–	–	–	–
–	–	–	–	–	–	–
–	–	–	–	–	–	–
–	–	–	–	–	–	–
–	–	–	–	–	–	–
–	–	–	–	–	–	–
–	–	–	–	–	–	–
–	–	–	–	–	–	–
–	–	–	–	–	–	–
–	–	–	–	–	–	–
–	–	–	–	–	–	–
–	–	–	–	–	–	–
–	–	–	–	–	–	–

13. ODF COMMITMENTS: BY PURPOSE %

	1987	1988	1989	1990
Education	0	–	10	–
Health	–	–	–	–
Other Social Infrastr.	5	–	–	–
Water Sanitat. Sewage	–	–	0	–
Energy	11	21	11	–
Telecommunications	–	1	0	–
Transportation	24	9	5	–
Agriculture	5	13	21	–
Extractive Industries	–	–	–	–
Manufacturing	2	–	–	–
Trade Banking Tourism	–	6	–	–
Technical Cooperation	12	14	23	–
Multisector Aid	13	11	1	–
Programme	26	22	25	–
Debt Reorganisation	1	2	3	–
Food Aid	–	0	1	–
Emergency Aid	0	0	0	–
Unspecified	–	–	–	–
TOTAL	100	100	100	–

14. GRANT ELEMENT OF ODA %

DAC COUNTRIES	1987	1988	1989	1990
Australia	100.0	100.0	100.0	–
Austria	–	–	100.0	–
Belgium	100.0	–	–	–
Canada	100.0	–	100.0	–
Denmark	–	–	–	–
Finland	–	–	100.0	–
France	100.0	100.0	100.0	–
Germany	100.0	100.0	100.0	–
Ireland	–	–	–	–
Italy	–	100.0	–	–
Japan	100.0	100.0	100.0	–
Netherlands	100.0	100.0	100.0	–
New Zealand	100.0	–	–	–
Norway	–	–	–	–
Sweden	100.0	100.0	100.0	–
Switzerland	–	100.0	100.0	–
United Kingdom	100.0	100.0	100.0	–
United States	–	–	–	–
TOTAL	*100.0*	*100.0*	*100.0*	–
MULTILATERAL	*85.8*	*90.2*	*84.5*	–
ARAB COUNTRIES	–	–	–	–
E.E.C.+ MEMBERS	*100.0*	*100.0*	*100.0*	–
TOTAL	**89.3**	**94.8**	**90.1**	–

15. OTHER AGGREGATES

	1987	1988	1989	1990
OFFICIAL COMMITMENTS:				
TOTAL BILATERAL	88.8	111.0	57.1	54.2
of which:				
Arab Countries	–	–	–	–
C.E.E.C.	61.2	52.1	0.1	–
TOTAL MULTILATERAL	114.2	51.7	151.2	80.1
TOTAL BIL.& MULTIL.	203.0	162.6	208.3	134.3
of which:				
ODA Grants	89.7	124.4	82.6	75.5
ODA Loans	113.3	38.2	125.7	58.7
DISBURSEMENTS:				
DAC COUNTRIES COMBINED				
OFFICIAL & PRIVATE				
GROSS:				
Contractual Lending	–	1.1	8.1	–
Export Credits, Total	–	1.1	8.1	–
Export Credits, Priv.	–	1.1	8.1	–
NET:				
Contractual Lending	-3.2	-3.8	-1.9	-3.3
Export Credits Total	–	0.1	0.4	-0.5
PRIVATE SECTOR NET	0.1	0.3	0.5	–
Direct Investment	–	–	–	–
Portfolio Investment	0.1	0.2	0.2	0.5
Export Credits	–	0.1	0.4	-0.5
MARKET BORROWING:				
CHANGE IN CLAIMS				
Banks	1.0	-1.0	-3.0	1.0
MEMORANDUM ITEM:				
C.E.E.C. (Gross)	122.8	114.8	120.8	–

DISBURSEMENTS, UNLESS OTHERWISE STATED

1. TOTAL RECEIPTS NET / 4. TOTAL ODA NET / 7. TOTAL ODA GROSS

	1. TOTAL RECEIPTS NET 1987	1988	1989	1990	4. TOTAL ODA NET 1987	1988	1989	1990	7. TOTAL ODA GROSS 1987
DAC COUNTRIES									
Australia	0.0	0.2	0.4	0.2	0.0	0.2	0.4	0.2	0.0
Austria	17.4	0.0	1.9	-3.8	0.6	0.3	2.6	5.2	0.6
Belgium	-0.4	0.7	-4.3	-12.0	0.4	0.5	0.1	0.3	0.4
Canada	2.2	4.7	1.3	0.4	2.2	4.7	1.3	0.4	2.2
Denmark	–	–	–	–	–	–	–	–	–
Finland	1.5	0.2	0.3	0.4	0.6	0.2	0.3	0.4	0.6
France	3.2	41.4	33.4	8.8	19.2	31.6	27.3	25.9	19.9
Germany	6.1	12.9	9.4	-3.6	8.1	13.7	9.2	9.8	8.1
Ireland	–	–	0.0	0.0	–	–	0.0	0.0	–
Italy	10.0	51.2	16.3	2.4	8.8	21.1	16.3	11.9	8.8
Japan	0.1	0.2	1.1	0.1	0.1	0.2	1.1	0.1	0.1
Netherlands	1.8	1.2	1.2	1.2	0.8	1.1	1.3	1.0	0.8
New Zealand	–	–	–	–	–	–	–	–	–
Norway	0.3	1.7	0.7	1.0	0.3	0.7	0.7	1.0	0.3
Sweden	0.9	1.9	1.1	1.4	0.9	1.9	1.1	1.4	0.9
Switzerland	2.3	2.9	2.4	1.8	2.3	2.9	2.4	1.8	2.3
United Kingdom	-0.3	-0.4	-0.2	0.3	0.0	0.0	–	0.3	0.0
United States	21.0	20.0	19.0	12.0	21.0	20.0	19.0	12.0	22.0
TOTAL	*66.2*	*138.8*	*84.1*	*10.7*	*65.4*	*99.1*	*83.2*	*71.6*	*67.1*
MULTILATERAL									
AF.D.F.	–	–	–	–	–	–	–	–	–
AF.D.B.	–	–	–	–	–	–	–	–	–
AS.D.B	–	–	–	–	–	–	–	–	–
CAR.D.B.	–	–	–	–	–	–	–	–	–
E.E.C.	0.1	-1.2	13.7	13.7	6.6	5.4	19.1	19.1	6.6
IBRD	-1.5	-6.0	-2.0	-6.0	–	–	–	–	–
IDA	–	–	–	–	–	–	–	–	–
I.D.B.	–	–	–	–	–	–	–	–	–
IFAD	–	–	–	–	–	–	–	–	–
I.F.C.	–	–	–	–	–	–	–	–	–
IMF TRUST FUND	–	–	–	–	–	–	–	–	–
U.N. AGENCIES	–	–	–	–	–	–	–	–	–
UNDP	0.5	0.5	0.4	0.4	0.5	0.5	0.4	0.4	0.5
UNTA	0.7	0.5	0.8	0.5	0.7	0.5	0.8	0.5	0.7
UNICEF	5.1	5.0	4.3	3.4	5.1	5.0	4.3	3.4	5.1
UNRWA	–	–	–	–	–	–	–	–	–
WFP	4.5	18.8	5.7	4.8	4.5	18.8	5.7	4.8	4.5
UNHCR	0.1	0.1	0.1	0.1	0.1	0.1	0.1	0.1	0.1
Other Multilateral	0.1	0.1	1.8	0.3	0.1	0.1	1.8	0.3	0.1
Arab Agencies	–	-0.1	0.2	–	–	-0.1	0.2	–	–
TOTAL	*9.5*	*17.7*	*24.9*	*17.4*	*17.5*	*30.4*	*32.3*	*28.7*	*17.5*
ARAB COUNTRIES	*18.2*	*11.2*	*3.7*	*34.0*	*18.2*	*11.2*	*3.7*	*34.0*	*18.5*
E.E.C.+ MEMBERS	*20.6*	*105.8*	*69.6*	*10.8*	*43.9*	*73.5*	*73.3*	*68.1*	*44.7*
TOTAL	*94.0*	*167.6*	*112.8*	*62.1*	*101.1*	*140.7*	*119.1*	*134.3*	*103.1*

2. ODA LOANS GROSS / 5. ODA LOANS NET / 8. GRANTS

	2. ODA LOANS GROSS 1987	1988	1989	1990	5. ODA LOANS NET 1987	1988	1989	1990	8. GRANTS 1987
DAC COUNTRIES									
Australia	–	–	–	–	–	–	–	–	0.0
Austria	–	–	–	–	–	–	–	–	0.6
Belgium	–	–	–	–	–	–	–	–	0.4
Canada	–	–	–	–	–	–	–	–	2.2
Denmark	–	–	–	–	–	–	–	–	–
Finland	–	–	–	–	–	–	–	–	0.6
France	1.8	8.3	5.1	5.1	1.1	6.4	5.1	5.1	18.1
Germany	0.2	7.0	0.8	–	0.2	6.4	0.8	–	7.9
Ireland	–	–	–	–	–	–	–	–	–
Italy	–	–	–	2.5	–	–	–	2.5	8.8
Japan	–	–	–	–	–	–	–	–	0.1
Netherlands	–	–	–	–	–	–	–	–	0.8
New Zealand	–	–	–	–	–	–	–	–	–
Norway	–	–	–	–	–	–	–	–	0.3
Sweden	–	–	–	–	–	–	–	–	0.9
Switzerland	–	–	–	–	–	–	–	–	2.3
United Kingdom	–	–	–	–	–	–	–	–	0.0
United States	–	–	–	–	-1.0	–	–	–	22.0
TOTAL	*2.0*	*15.2*	*5.9*	*7.7*	*0.3*	*12.9*	*5.9*	*7.7*	*65.1*
MULTILATERAL	*–*	*1.0*	*–*	*–*	*–*	*-0.2*	*–*	*–*	*17.5*
ARAB COUNTRIES	*–*	*–*	*–*	*–*	*-0.2*	*-0.5*	*–*	*–*	*18.5*
E.E.C.+ MEMBERS	*2.0*	*15.2*	*5.9*	*7.7*	*1.3*	*12.9*	*5.9*	*7.7*	*42.6*
TOTAL	*2.0*	*16.2*	*5.9*	*7.7*	*0.0*	*12.2*	*5.9*	*7.7*	*101.1*

3. TOTAL OFFICIAL GROSS / 6. TOTAL OFFICIAL NET / 9. TOTAL OOF GROSS

	3. TOTAL OFFICIAL GROSS 1987	1988	1989	1990	6. TOTAL OFFICIAL NET 1987	1988	1989	1990	9. TOTAL OOF GROSS 1987
DAC COUNTRIES									
Australia	0.0	0.2	0.4	0.2	0.0	0.2	0.4	0.2	–
Austria	17.9	0.8	2.7	5.2	17.9	0.8	2.7	-2.9	17.3
Belgium	0.4	0.5	0.1	0.3	0.4	0.5	0.1	0.3	–
Canada	2.2	4.7	1.3	0.4	2.2	4.7	1.3	0.4	–
Denmark	–	–	–	–	–	–	–	–	–
Finland	0.6	0.2	0.3	0.4	0.6	0.2	0.3	0.4	–
France	19.9	33.5	27.3	25.9	19.2	31.6	27.3	25.9	–
Germany	8.1	14.3	9.2	10.0	8.1	13.7	9.2	4.2	–
Ireland	–	–	0.0	0.0	–	–	0.0	0.0	–
Italy	15.3	21.1	16.3	11.9	15.3	20.4	16.3	11.9	6.5
Japan	0.1	0.2	1.1	0.1	0.1	0.2	1.1	0.1	–
Netherlands	0.8	1.1	1.3	1.0	0.8	1.1	1.3	1.0	–
New Zealand	–	–	–	–	–	–	–	–	–
Norway	0.3	0.7	0.7	1.0	0.3	0.7	0.7	1.0	–
Sweden	0.9	1.9	1.1	1.4	0.9	1.9	1.1	1.4	–
Switzerland	2.3	2.9	2.4	1.8	2.3	2.9	2.4	1.8	–
United Kingdom	0.0	0.0	–	0.3	0.0	0.0	–	0.3	–
United States	22.0	20.0	19.0	12.0	21.0	20.0	19.0	12.0	–
TOTAL	*90.9*	*102.0*	*83.3*	*71.8*	*89.1*	*99.0*	*83.3*	*58.0*	*23.8*
MULTILATERAL	*17.5*	*31.5*	*32.3*	*28.8*	*9.5*	*17.7*	*24.9*	*17.4*	*–*
ARAB COUNTRIES	*18.5*	*11.7*	*3.7*	*34.0*	*18.2*	*11.2*	*3.7*	*34.0*	
E.E.C.+ MEMBERS	*51.2*	*75.9*	*73.3*	*68.3*	*44.0*	*66.2*	*68.0*	*57.2*	*6.5*
TOTAL	*126.9*	*145.2*	*119.2*	*134.6*	*116.9*	*127.9*	*111.9*	*109.4*	*23.8*

10. ODA COMMITMENTS

1988	1989	1990	1987	1988	1989	1990
0.2	0.4	0.2	0.2	0.2	0.5	0.5
0.3	2.6	5.2	0.6	0.3	2.6	5.2
0.5	0.1	0.3	0.2	0.4	0.1	0.3
4.7	1.3	0.4	2.1	4.7	1.2	0.4
–	–	–	–	–	–	–
0.2	0.3	0.4	–	–	0.3	0.2
33.5	27.3	25.9	18.1	46.5	21.4	21.3
14.3	9.2	9.8	9.4	14.1	7.5	10.1
–	0.0	0.0	–	–	0.0	0.0
21.1	16.3	11.9	7.8	25.9	17.8	12.6
0.2	1.1	0.1	0.1	0.2	0.2	0.1
1.1	1.3	1.0	0.8	1.1	1.1	1.0
–	–	–	–	–	–	–
0.7	0.7	1.0	–	–	–	–
1.9	1.1	1.4	0.9	1.9	1.1	–
2.9	2.4	1.8	2.2	2.8	2.4	1.7
0.0	–	0.3	0.0	0.0	–	0.3
20.0	19.0	12.0	23.9	12.3	17.0	23.3
101.5	*83.2*	*71.6*	*66.4*	*110.4*	*73.3*	*77.0*
–	–	–	–	–	–	–
–	–	–	–	–	–	–
–	–	–	–	–	–	–
5.4	19.1	19.1	11.1	11.8	24.9	24.9
–	–	–	–	–	–	–
–	–	–	–	–	–	–
–	–	–	–	–	–	–
–	–	–	10.9	25.0	13.1	9.6
0.5	0.4	0.4	–	–	–	–
0.5	0.8	0.5	–	–	–	–
5.0	4.3	3.4	–	–	–	–
–	–	–	–	–	–	–
18.8	5.7	4.8	–	–	–	–
0.1	0.1	0.1	–	–	–	–
0.1	1.8	0.3	–	–	–	–
1.1	0.2	0.2	–	0.3	0.1	0.2
31.5	*32.3*	*28.8*	*22.0*	*37.1*	*38.1*	*34.7*
11.7	*3.7*	*34.0*	*31.2*	*1.7*	*3.1*	*100.0*
75.9	*73.3*	*68.1*	*47.5*	*99.8*	*72.8*	*70.4*
144.7	*119.1*	*134.5*	*119.6*	*149.2*	*114.4*	*211.7*

11. TECH. COOP. GRANTS

1988	1989	1990	1987	1988	1989	1990
0.2	0.4	0.2	0.0	0.0	0.0	0.0
0.3	2.6	5.2	0.2	0.2	0.2	0.3
0.5	0.1	0.3	0.4	0.4	–	–
4.7	1.3	0.4	–	–	–	–
–	–	–	–	–	–	–
0.2	0.3	0.4	–	–	–	0.0
25.2	22.2	20.8	18.1	25.0	21.4	20.8
7.3	8.5	9.8	5.5	4.6	4.0	4.7
–	0.0	0.0	–	–	0.0	0.0
21.1	16.3	9.4	1.5	0.9	1.3	1.5
0.2	1.1	0.1	0.1	0.2	0.2	0.1
1.1	1.3	1.0	0.4	0.6	0.6	0.8
–	–	–	–	–	–	–
0.7	0.7	1.0	–	–	–	–
1.9	1.1	1.4	–	–	–	–
2.9	2.4	1.8	0.1	0.0	–	–
0.0	–	0.3	0.0	0.0	–	0.0
20.0	19.0	12.0	9.0	14.0	9.0	6.0
86.3	*77.3*	*63.9*	*35.3*	*46.1*	*36.8*	*34.2*
30.6	*32.3*	*28.8*	*8.4*	*9.0*	*7.4*	*4.8*
11.7	*3.7*	*34.0*	–	–	–	–
60.7	*67.4*	*60.5*	*28.0*	*34.4*	*27.3*	*27.7*
128.5	*113.2*	*126.8*	*43.7*	*55.1*	*44.1*	*39.0*

12. TOTAL OOF NET

1988	1989	1990	1987	1988	1989	1990
–	–	–	17.3	0.5	0.1	-8.0
0.5	0.1	–	–	–	–	–
–	–	–	–	–	–	–
–	–	–	–	–	–	–
–	–	–	–	–	–	–
–	–	–	–	–	–	–
–	–	0.2	–	–	–	-5.6
–	–	–	6.5	-0.6	–	–
–	–	–	–	–	–	–
–	–	–	–	–	–	–
–	–	–	–	–	–	–
–	–	–	–	–	–	–
–	–	–	–	–	–	–
–	–	–	–	–	–	–
–	–	–	–	–	–	–
0.5	*0.1*	*0.2*	*23.8*	*-0.1*	*0.1*	*-13.6*
–	–	–	*-8.0*	*-12.7*	*-7.3*	*-11.3*
–	–	–	–	–	–	–
–	–	0.2	*0.1*	*-7.3*	*-5.3*	*-10.9*
0.5	*0.1*	*0.2*	*15.8*	*-12.8*	*-7.2*	*-24.9*

13. ODF COMMITMENTS: BY PURPOSE %

	1987	1988	1989	1990
Education	3	4	4	–
Health	1	10	7	–
Other Social Infrastr.	1	4	4	–
Water Sanitat. Sewage	–	7	4	–
Energy	19	–	–	–
Telecommunications	–	8	6	–
Transportation	–	4	–	–
Agriculture	1	1	–	–
Extractive Industries	–	–	–	–
Manufacturing	–	0	–	–
Trade Banking Tourism	–	5	–	–
Technical Cooperation	34	28	50	–
Multisector Aid	2	–	0	–
Programme	3	8	–	–
Debt Reorganisation	–	–	–	–
Food Aid	28	10	20	–
Emergency Aid	9	11	4	–
Unspecified	–	–	–	–
TOTAL	100	100	100	–

14. GRANT ELEMENT OF ODA %

DAC COUNTRIES	1987	1988	1989	1990
Australia	100.0	100.0	100.0	–
Austria	100.0	100.0	100.0	–
Belgium	100.0	100.0	100.0	–
Canada	100.0	100.0	100.0	–
Denmark	–	–	–	–
Finland	–	–	100.0	–
France	100.0	84.0	100.0	–
Germany	100.0	100.0	100.0	–
Ireland	–	–	100.0	–
Italy	100.0	90.4	90.2	–
Japan	100.0	100.0	100.0	–
Netherlands	100.0	100.0	100.0	–
New Zealand	–	–	–	–
Norway	–	–	–	–
Sweden	100.0	100.0	100.0	–
Switzerland	100.0	100.0	100.0	–
United Kingdom	100.0	100.0	–	–
United States	100.0	100.0	100.0	–
TOTAL	*100.0*	*91.0*	*97.6*	–
MULTILATERAL	*100.0*	*99.5*	*100.0*	–
ARAB COUNTRIES	*100.0*	*100.0*	*100.0*	–
E.E.C.+ MEMBERS	*100.0*	*90.1*	*97.6*	–
TOTAL	*100.0*	*93.2*	*98.5*	–

15. OTHER AGGREGATES

OFFICIAL COMMITMENTS:	1987	1988	1989	1990
TOTAL BILATERAL	122.6	114.9	76.3	177.0
of which:				
Arab Countries	31.2	1.7	3.1	100.0
C.E.E.C.	25.0	–	–	–
TOTAL MULTILATERAL	22.0	37.1	38.1	34.7
TOTAL BIL.& MULTIL.	144.6	152.0	114.4	211.7
of which:				
ODA Grants	119.6	122.7	110.4	211.1
ODA Loans	25.0	26.5	4.0	0.6

DISBURSEMENTS:

DAC COUNTRIES COMBINED

OFFICIAL & PRIVATE	1987	1988	1989	1990
GROSS:				
Contractual Lending	15.6	37.5	3.0	4.4
Export Credits, Total	13.8	22.3	-2.9	-3.3
Export Credits, Priv.	-9.9	21.8	-3.0	-3.5
NET:				
Contractual Lending	6.3	30.4	2.0	-19.9
Export Credits Total	6.2	17.5	-3.9	-21.8
PRIVATE SECTOR NET	-22.9	39.8	0.9	-47.3
Direct Investment	1.3	-0.3	1.6	6.5
Portfolio Investment	-6.6	22.4	3.3	-39.8
Export Credits	-17.6	17.7	-4.0	-13.9

MARKET BORROWING:

CHANGE IN CLAIMS	1987	1988	1989	1990
Banks	–	–	–	–

MEMORANDUM ITEM:

	1987	1988	1989	1990
C.E.E.C. (Gross)	–	–	–	–

	1987	1988	1989	1990		1987	1988	1989	1990		1987
1. TOTAL RECEIPTS NET					**4. TOTAL ODA NET**					**7. TOTAL ODA GROSS**	
DAC COUNTRIES											
Australia	0.0	0.2	2.4	1.0		0.0	0.2	2.4	1.0	Australia	0.0
Austria	0.0	0.0	0.0	–		0.0	0.0	0.0	–	Austria	0.0
Belgium	0.0	0.0	0.0	0.0		0.0	0.0	0.0	0.0	Belgium	0.0
Canada	2.5	7.4	1.7	1.5		2.5	2.3	2.5	2.2	Canada	2.5
Denmark	1.6	4.7	3.3	8.2		1.6	4.7	3.3	8.2	Denmark	1.6
Finland	0.3	0.2	0.3	0.2		0.3	0.2	0.3	0.2	Finland	0.3
France	3.0	7.0	5.8	20.0		2.7	4.2	3.8	16.7	France	2.7
Germany	10.3	10.2	12.1	14.2		10.5	10.6	12.6	14.4	Germany	10.5
Ireland	4.4	3.5	3.2	3.4		4.4	3.5	3.2	3.4	Ireland	4.4
Italy	1.4	5.1	1.2	0.4		1.4	0.3	1.2	0.4	Italy	1.4
Japan	2.2	1.2	0.6	0.8		2.2	1.2	0.6	0.8	Japan	2.2
Netherlands	-5.1	0.7	0.5	1.3		1.7	0.7	0.5	1.3	Netherlands	1.7
New Zealand	–	–	–	–		–	–	–	–	New Zealand	–
Norway	0.3	4.5	1.1	1.5		0.3	4.5	1.1	1.5	Norway	0.3
Sweden	7.4	6.5	8.1	7.7		8.1	6.5	8.5	8.7	Sweden	8.1
Switzerland	1.4	1.6	0.9	2.0		1.4	1.6	0.9	2.0	Switzerland	1.4
United Kingdom	6.4	7.9	6.4	9.7		6.4	8.7	9.8	10.3	United Kingdom	6.4
United States	19.0	21.0	18.0	14.0		19.0	21.0	18.0	14.0	United States	19.0
TOTAL	*55.0*	*81.7*	*65.7*	*85.8*		*62.5*	*70.1*	*68.8*	*85.1*	**TOTAL**	*62.5*
MULTILATERAL											
AF.D.F.	10.8	7.2	11.0	13.4		10.8	7.2	11.0	13.4	AF.D.F.	11.1
AF.D.B.	0.7	1.6	-0.4	2.0		–	–	–	–	AF.D.B.	–
AS.D.B	–	–	–	–		–	–	–	–	AS.D.B	–
CAR.D.B.	–	–	–	–		–	–	–	–	CAR.D.B.	–
E.E.C.	7.3	13.9	12.1	12.1		7.3	13.9	12.1	12.1	E.E.C.	7.4
IBRD	–	–	–	–		–	–	–	–	IBRD	–
IDA	8.2	7.0	13.0	8.0		8.2	7.0	13.0	8.0	IDA	8.6
I.D.B.	–	–	–	–		–	–	–	–	I.D.B.	–
IFAD	2.8	0.6	1.1	1.2		2.8	0.6	1.1	1.2	IFAD	2.8
I.F.C.	–	–	–	–		–	–	–	–	I.F.C.	–
IMF TRUST FUND	–	–	–	–		–	–	–	–	IMF TRUST FUND	–
U.N. AGENCIES	–	–	–	–		–	–	–	–	U.N. AGENCIES	–
UNDP	3.2	3.1	5.2	4.4		3.2	3.1	5.2	4.4	UNDP	3.2
UNTA	1.1	1.0	1.3	1.2		1.1	1.0	1.3	1.2	UNTA	1.1
UNICEF	1.0	0.6	1.0	1.6		1.0	0.6	1.0	1.6	UNICEF	1.0
UNRWA	–	–	–	–		–	–	–	–	UNRWA	–
WFP	10.6	4.0	9.1	8.4		10.6	4.0	9.1	8.4	WFP	10.6
UNHCR	0.4	0.4	0.2	0.2		0.4	0.4	0.2	0.2	UNHCR	0.4
Other Multilateral	1.6	2.1	2.7	2.8		1.6	2.1	2.7	2.8	Other Multilateral	1.6
Arab Agencies	-1.6	-1.3	2.2	–		-1.6	-1.3	2.2	–	Arab Agencies	–
TOTAL	*46.2*	*40.1*	*58.4*	*55.1*		*45.5*	*38.5*	*58.8*	*53.1*	**TOTAL**	*47.8*
ARAB COUNTRIES	*-0.5*	*-0.7*	*-0.3*	*-0.4*		*-0.5*	*-0.7*	*-0.3*	*-0.4*	***ARAB COUNTRIES***	*–*
E.E.C.+ MEMBERS	*29.3*	*53.0*	*44.5*	*69.3*		*36.0*	*46.6*	*46.5*	*66.7*	*E.E.C.+ MEMBERS*	*36.2*
TOTAL	*100.7*	*121.1*	*123.7*	*140.5*		*107.5*	*108.0*	*127.2*	*137.8*	**TOTAL**	*110.3*
2. ODA LOANS GROSS					**5. ODA LOANS NET**					**8. GRANTS**	
DAC COUNTRIES											
Australia	–	–	–	–		–	–	–	–	Australia	0.0
Austria	–	–	–	–		–	–	–	–	Austria	0.0
Belgium	–	–	–	–		–	–	–	–	Belgium	0.0
Canada	–	–	–	–		–	–	–	–	Canada	2.5
Denmark	–	–	–	–		–	–	–	–	Denmark	1.6
Finland	–	–	–	–		–	–	–	–	Finland	0.3
France	1.2	2.0	2.8	11.6		1.2	2.0	2.8	11.6	France	1.4
Germany	–	–	1.6	–		–	–	1.6	–	Germany	10.5
Ireland	–	–	–	–		–	–	–	–	Ireland	4.4
Italy	–	–	–	–		–	–	–	–	Italy	1.4
Japan	–	–	–	–		–	–	–	–	Japan	2.2
Netherlands	–	–	–	–		–	–	–	–	Netherlands	1.7
New Zealand	–	–	–	–		–	–	–	–	New Zealand	–
Norway	–	–	–	–		–	–	–	–	Norway	0.3
Sweden	–	–	–	–		–	–	–	–	Sweden	8.1
Switzerland	–	–	–	–		–	–	–	–	Switzerland	1.4
United Kingdom	–	–	–	–		0.0	0.0	0.0	0.0	United Kingdom	6.4
United States	–	–	–	–		–	–	–	–	United States	19.0
TOTAL	*1.2*	*2.0*	*4.4*	*11.6*		*1.2*	*2.0*	*4.3*	*11.5*	**TOTAL**	*61.3*
MULTILATERAL	*23.1*	*17.2*	*31.5*	*25.9*		*20.8*	*15.7*	*28.3*	*22.4*	*MULTILATERAL*	*24.7*
ARAB COUNTRIES	*–*	*–*	*0.3*	*–*		*-0.5*	*-0.7*	*-0.3*	*-0.4*	***ARAB COUNTRIES***	*–*
E.E.C.+ MEMBERS	*1.9*	*4.4*	*5.9*	*13.1*		*1.8*	*4.2*	*5.6*	*12.9*	*E.E.C.+ MEMBERS*	*34.2*
TOTAL	*24.3*	*19.3*	*36.2*	*37.4*		*21.6*	*17.1*	*32.4*	*33.6*	**TOTAL**	*86.0*
3. TOTAL OFFICIAL GROSS					**6. TOTAL OFFICIAL NET**					**9. TOTAL OOF GROSS**	
DAC COUNTRIES											
Australia	0.0	0.2	2.4	1.0		0.0	0.2	2.4	1.0	Australia	–
Austria	0.0	0.0	0.0	–		0.0	0.0	0.0	–	Austria	–
Belgium	0.0	0.0	0.0	0.0		0.0	0.0	0.0	0.0	Belgium	–
Canada	2.5	7.4	2.5	2.2		2.5	7.4	1.7	1.5	Canada	–
Denmark	1.6	4.7	3.3	8.2		1.6	4.7	3.3	8.2	Denmark	–
Finland	0.3	0.2	0.3	0.2		0.3	0.2	0.3	0.2	Finland	–
France	2.7	4.2	3.8	16.7		2.7	4.2	3.8	16.7	France	–
Germany	10.6	10.6	12.6	14.4		10.1	10.1	12.1	14.1	Germany	0.0
Ireland	4.4	3.5	3.2	3.4		4.4	3.5	3.2	3.4	Ireland	–
Italy	1.4	0.3	1.2	0.4		1.4	0.3	1.2	0.4	Italy	–
Japan	2.2	1.2	0.6	0.8		2.2	1.2	0.6	0.8	Japan	–
Netherlands	1.7	0.7	0.5	1.3		1.7	0.7	0.5	1.3	Netherlands	–
New Zealand	–	–	–	–		–	–	–	–	New Zealand	–
Norway	0.3	4.5	1.1	1.5		0.3	4.5	1.1	1.5	Norway	–
Sweden	8.1	6.5	8.5	8.7		8.1	6.5	8.5	8.7	Sweden	–
Switzerland	1.4	1.6	0.9	2.0		1.4	1.6	0.9	2.0	Switzerland	–
United Kingdom	6.4	8.7	9.9	10.3		6.0	8.3	9.4	9.9	United Kingdom	–
United States	19.0	21.0	18.0	14.0		19.0	21.0	18.0	14.0	United States	–
TOTAL	*62.6*	*75.3*	*68.8*	*85.1*		*61.7*	*74.4*	*67.1*	*83.6*	**TOTAL**	*0.0*
MULTILATERAL	*50.0*	*42.8*	*64.8*	*59.2*		*46.2*	*40.1*	*58.4*	*55.1*	*MULTILATERAL*	*2.2*
ARAB COUNTRIES	*–*	*–*	*0.3*	*–*		*-0.5*	*-0.7*	*-0.3*	*-0.4*	***ARAB COUNTRIES***	*–*
E.E.C.+ MEMBERS	*36.2*	*46.8*	*46.8*	*67.0*		*35.2*	*45.7*	*45.6*	*66.0*	*E.E.C.+ MEMBERS*	*0.0*
TOTAL	*112.6*	*118.1*	*133.8*	*144.2*		*107.4*	*113.8*	*125.1*	*138.3*	**TOTAL**	*2.3*

1988	1989	1990		1987	1988	1989	1990

10. ODA COMMITMENTS

1988	1989	1990	1987	1988	1989	1990
0.2	2.4	1.0	0.1	2.1	1.6	1.1
0.0	0.0	–	0.0	0.0	0.0	–
0.0	0.0	0.0	0.0	0.1	0.0	0.0
2.3	2.5	2.2	0.6	4.7	2.8	0.2
4.7	3.3	8.2	3.8	–	7.4	3.2
0.2	0.3	0.2	–	0.2	0.2	0.4
4.2	3.8	16.7	9.6	0.3	10.2	16.7
10.6	12.6	14.4	14.3	3.7	15.7	11.4
3.5	3.2	3.4	4.4	3.5	3.2	3.4
0.3	1.2	0.4	1.6	2.8	1.2	1.1
1.2	0.6	0.8	3.2	0.6	0.8	0.8
0.7	0.5	1.3	1.1	2.1	1.2	0.2
–	–	–	–	–	–	–
4.5	1.1	1.5	0.2	2.8	–	0.2
6.5	8.5	8.7	8.1	6.5	8.5	5.9
1.6	0.9	2.0	0.1	4.9	0.8	4.5
8.7	9.9	10.3	3.6	5.7	12.7	9.0
21.0	18.0	14.0	10.0	30.7	14.5	8.2
70.2	*68.8*	*85.1*	*60.8*	*70.6*	*80.9*	*66.2*
7.3	11.8	13.9	16.6	23.1	3.4	24.3
–	–	–	–	–	–	–
–	–	–	–	–	–	–
14.1	12.3	12.3	9.3	27.0	10.3	10.3
–	–	–	–	–	–	–
7.0	13.0	9.0	–	36.0	12.0	21.0
–	–	–	–	–	–	–
0.6	1.1	1.2	–	8.3	–	–
–	–	–	–	–	–	–
–	–	–	17.9	11.1	19.5	18.5
3.1	5.2	4.4	–	–	–	–
1.0	1.3	1.2	–	–	–	–
0.6	1.0	1.6	–	–	–	–
–	–	–	–	–	–	–
4.0	9.1	8.4	–	–	–	–
0.4	0.2	0.2	–	–	–	–
2.1	2.7	2.8	–	–	–	–
–	4.3	0.3	–	12.2	–	–
40.0	*61.9*	*55.2*	*43.8*	*117.7*	*45.2*	*74.1*
–	*0.3*	–	*3.9*	–	*9.2*	–
46.8	*46.8*	*67.0*	*47.7*	*45.2*	*61.9*	*55.2*
110.2	*131.0*	*140.3*	*108.5*	*188.4*	*135.3*	*140.3*

11. TECH. COOP. GRANTS

1988	1989	1990	1987	1988	1989	1990
0.2	2.4	1.0	0.1	0.2	0.3	0.5
0.0	0.0	–	0.0	0.0	0.0	–
0.0	0.0	0.0	–	–	–	–
2.3	2.5	2.2	–	0.7	0.8	2.2
4.7	3.3	8.2	0.7	1.7	0.9	2.5
0.2	0.3	0.2	0.1	0.1	–	–
2.2	1.0	5.1	0.3	0.3	0.4	0.1
10.6	11.0	14.4	7.0	5.7	5.6	7.3
3.5	3.2	3.4	3.3	2.7	3.2	3.4
0.3	1.2	0.4	1.4	0.3	–	0.4
1.2	0.6	0.8	0.1	0.0	0.1	0.1
0.7	0.5	1.3	1.1	0.2	0.2	0.2
–	–	–	–	–	–	–
4.5	1.1	1.5	0.2	–	0.1	0.1
6.5	8.5	8.7	3.3	4.7	4.8	0.3
1.6	0.9	2.0	0.2	2.0	–	–
8.7	9.9	10.3	3.5	5.5	5.2	6.1
21.0	18.0	14.0	10.0	16.0	15.0	12.0
68.1	*64.4*	*73.5*	*31.2*	*40.1*	*36.5*	*35.2*
22.8	*30.4*	*29.4*	*7.6*	*9.6*	*10.4*	*10.1*
–	–	–	–	–	–	–
42.4	*40.9*	*53.9*	*17.6*	*18.9*	*15.4*	*20.0*
90.9	*94.8*	*102.9*	*38.8*	*49.7*	*46.8*	*45.3*

12. TOTAL OOF NET

1988	1989	1990	1987	1988	1989	1990
–	–	–	–	–	–	–
–	–	–	–	–	–	–
5.2	–	–	–	5.2	-0.7	-0.8
–	–	–	–	–	–	–
–	–	–	–	–	–	–
–	–	–	-0.5	-0.5	-0.5	-0.3
–	–	–	–	–	–	–
–	–	–	–	–	–	–
–	–	–	–	–	–	–
–	–	–	–	–	–	–
–	–	–	–	–	–	–
–	–	–	–	–	–	–
–	–	–	–	–	–	–
–	–	–	-0.3	-0.4	-0.4	-0.4
–	–	–	–	–	–	–
5.2	–	–	*-0.8*	*4.3*	*-1.7*	*-1.5*
2.8	*2.8*	*3.9*	*0.7*	*1.6*	*-0.4*	*2.0*
–	–	–	–	–	–	–
–	–	–	*-0.8*	*-0.9*	*-0.9*	*-0.7*
7.9	*2.8*	*3.9*	*-0.2*	*5.9*	*-2.0*	*0.5*

13. ODF COMMITMENTS: BY PURPOSE %

	1987	1988	1989	1990
Education	4	5	3	–
Health	22	1	13	–
Other Social Infrastr.	7	14	2	–
Water Sanitat. Sewage	5	2	1	–
Energy	9	2	6	–
Telecommunications	1	0	0	–
Transportation	2	9	26	–
Agriculture	8	29	7	–
Extractive Industries	–	–	–	–
Manufacturing	3	–	2	–
Trade Banking Tourism	–	–	3	–
Technical Cooperation	30	34	31	–
Multisector Aid	1	–	3	–
Programme	–	–	0	–
Debt Reorganisation	0	0	–	–
Food Aid	7	3	3	–
Emergency Aid	0	0	–	–
Unspecified	0	–	–	–
TOTAL	100	100	100	–

14. GRANT ELEMENT OF ODA %

DAC COUNTRIES

	1987	1988	1989	1990
Australia	100.0	100.0	100.0	–
Austria	100.0	100.0	100.0	–
Belgium	100.0	100.0	100.0	–
Canada	100.0	100.0	100.0	–
Denmark	100.0	–	100.0	–
Finland	–	100.0	100.0	–
France	75.9	100.0	58.5	–
Germany	100.0	100.0	100.0	–
Ireland	100.0	100.0	100.0	–
Italy	100.0	100.0	100.0	–
Japan	100.0	100.0	100.0	–
Netherlands	100.0	100.0	100.0	–
New Zealand	–	–	–	–
Norway	100.0	100.0	--	–
Sweden	100.0	100.0	100.0	–
Switzerland	100.0	100.0	100.0	–
United Kingdom	100.0	100.0	100.0	–
United States	100.0	100.0	100.0	–
TOTAL	*96.2*	*100.0*	*93.4*	–
MULTILATERAL	*92.3*	*83.3*	*89.9*	–
ARAB COUNTRIES	*52.8*	–	*56.8*	–
E.E.C.+ MEMBERS	*95.2*	*100.0*	*91.0*	–
TOTAL	*93.0*	*90.4*	*89.8*	–

15. OTHER AGGREGATES

	1987	1988	1989	1990
OFFICIAL COMMITMENTS:				
TOTAL BILATERAL	64.7	76.0	90.1	66.2
of which:				
Arab Countries	3.9	–	9.2	–
C.E.E.C.	–	–	–	–
TOTAL MULTILATERAL	43.8	117.7	45.2	74.1
TOTAL BIL.& MULTIL.	108.5	193.7	135.3	140.3
of which:				
ODA Grants	82.0	109.2	99.3	80.9
ODA Loans	26.5	79.2	36.0	59.4
DISBURSEMENTS:				
DAC COUNTRIES COMBINED				
OFFICIAL & PRIVATE				
GROSS:				
Contractual Lending	2.4	10.1	6.9	14.6
Export Credits, Total	1.1	8.0	2.6	3.0
Export Credits, Priv.	1.1	2.9	2.6	3.0
NET:				
Contractual Lending	-0.3	8.7	1.3	12.0
Export Credits Total	-1.2	7.1	-2.6	0.9
PRIVATE SECTOR NET	-6.6	7.3	-1.4	2.2
Direct Investment	0.1	4.7	–	–
Portfolio Investment	-6.1	0.1	0.0	0.3
Export Credits	-0.7	2.5	-1.4	1.9
MARKET BORROWING:				
CHANGE IN CLAIMS				
Banks	1.0	-1.0	5.0	-2.0
MEMORANDUM ITEM:				
C.E.E.C. (Gross)	–	–	–	–

1. TOTAL RECEIPTS NET

DAC COUNTRIES	1987	1988	1989	1990
Australia	–	–	-0.7	-0.7
Austria	–	–	–	0.0
Belgium	-98.8	-4.5	126.4	-51.7
Canada	5.6	2.3	1.1	-1.5
Denmark	4.3	5.1	1.1	0.6
Finland	–	33.5	–	0.5
France	76.2	-0.6	88.7	252.7
Germany	-49.7	51.5	-3.6	-3.6
Ireland	0.1	0.0	0.0	0.1
Italy	0.7	22.1	-6.1	0.1
Japan	-267.2	354.4	98.5	378.8
Netherlands	24.5	3.9	0.5	0.7
New Zealand	–	–	–	–
Norway	-1.4	0.1	0.1	-5.2
Sweden	-6.5	0.1	-2.5	0.7
Switzerland	0.0	0.0	–	0.2
United Kingdom	-32.0	-0.9	-76.5	1.0
United States	28.0	42.0	28.0	-16.0
TOTAL	-316.2	509.1	255.0	556.5
MULTILATERAL				
AF.D.F.	5.8	2.6	0.1	32.4
AF.D.B.	–	-0.1	–	-33.3
AS.D.B	–	–	–	–
CAR.D.B.	–	–	–	–
E.E.C.	5.0	4.2	10.6	10.6
IBRD	1.4	–	–	–
IDA	6.0	1.0	–	–
I.D.B.	–	–	–	–
IFAD	3.0	0.3	–	1.1
I.F.C.	–	7.5	-0.6	-0.4
IMF TRUST FUND	–	–	–	–
U.N. AGENCIES	–	–	–	–
UNDP	2.4	2.9	3.9	2.7
UNTA	1.0	0.9	1.2	0.8
UNICEF	0.6	0.6	0.9	0.5
UNRWA	–	–	–	–
WFP	1.3	1.5	0.8	22.9
UNHCR	–	0.4	0.4	0.2
Other Multilateral	0.4	1.2	1.3	1.0
Arab Agencies	–	–	–	–
TOTAL	27.0	22.9	18.7	38.4
ARAB COUNTRIES	–	0.0	–	–
E.E.C.+ MEMBERS	-69.8	80.8	141.0	210.4
TOTAL	-289.3	532.0	273.7	594.9

2. ODA LOANS GROSS

DAC COUNTRIES	1987	1988	1989	1990
Australia	–	–	–	–
Austria	–	–	–	–
Belgium	–	–	–	–
Canada	–	–	–	–
Denmark	3.9	4.8	0.7	–
Finland	–	–	–	–
France	–	–	–	–
Germany	0.2	0.0	–	–
Ireland	–	–	–	–
Italy	–	–	–	–
Japan	–	–	–	–
Netherlands	–	–	–	–
New Zealand	–	–	–	–
Norway	–	–	–	–
Sweden	–	–	–	–
Switzerland	–	–	–	–
United Kingdom	–	–	–	–
United States	11.0	–	–	–
TOTAL	15.0	4.8	0.7	–
MULTILATERAL	15.6	3.9	0.4	34.5
ARAB COUNTRIES	–	–	–	–
E.E.C.+ MEMBERS	4.7	4.8	0.7	–
TOTAL	30.6	8.7	1.2	34.5

3. TOTAL OFFICIAL GROSS

DAC COUNTRIES	1987	1988	1989	1990
Australia	–	–	–	–
Austria	–	–	–	0.0
Belgium	0.1	0.2	0.0	0.0
Canada	6.0	3.2	2.6	0.2
Denmark	4.5	5.1	1.1	0.6
Finland	–	–	–	0.5
France	0.8	0.7	1.9	1.8
Germany	8.7	61.1	9.0	7.3
Ireland	0.1	0.0	0.0	0.1
Italy	0.1	–	–	0.1
Japan	10.2	8.8	10.1	6.4
Netherlands	0.5	2.9	1.2	7.7
New Zealand	–	–	–	–
Norway	0.1	0.2	0.1	0.2
Sweden	–	0.1	–	0.1
Switzerland	0.0	0.0	–	0.2
United Kingdom	1.5	1.5	1.0	1.0
United States	28.0	26.0	19.0	19.0
TOTAL	60.7	109.9	46.1	45.1
MULTILATERAL	28.5	24.1	20.5	74.7
ARAB COUNTRIES	–	0.0	–	–
E.E.C.+ MEMBERS	22.4	76.8	25.9	30.2
TOTAL	89.2	134.0	66.6	119.8

4. TOTAL ODA NET

DAC COUNTRIES	1987	1988	1989	1990
Australia	–	–	–	–
Austria	–	–	–	0.0
Belgium	0.0	0.2	0.0	0.0
Canada	0.2	0.6	1.8	0.2
Denmark	4.5	5.1	1.1	0.6
Finland	–	–	–	0.5
France	0.8	0.7	1.2	1.0
Germany	8.5	7.9	9.0	7.3
Ireland	0.1	0.0	0.0	0.1
Italy	0.1	–	–	–
Japan	10.2	8.8	10.1	6.4
Netherlands	0.5	1.0	1.2	5.7
New Zealand	–	–	–	–
Norway	0.1	0.2	0.1	0.2
Sweden	–	0.1	–	0.1
Switzerland	0.0	0.0	–	0.2
United Kingdom	1.5	1.5	1.0	1.0
United States	25.0	22.0	13.0	19.0
TOTAL	51.7	48.3	38.5	42.2
MULTILATERAL				
AF.D.F.	5.8	2.6	0.1	32.4
AF.D.B.	–	–	–	–
AS.D.B	–	–	–	–
CAR.D.B.	–	–	–	–
E.E.C.	6.2	5.2	11.5	11.5
IBRD	–	–	–	–
IDA	6.0	1.0	–	–
I.D.B.	–	–	–	–
IFAD	3.0	0.3	–	1.1
I.F.C.	–	–	–	–
IMF TRUST FUND	–	–	–	–
U.N. AGENCIES	–	–	–	–
UNDP	2.4	2.9	3.9	2.7
UNTA	1.0	0.9	1.2	0.8
UNICEF	0.6	0.6	0.9	0.5
UNRWA	–	–	–	–
WFP	1.3	1.5	0.8	22.9
UNHCR	–	0.4	0.4	0.2
Other Multilateral	0.4	1.2	1.3	1.0
Arab Agencies	–	–	–	–
TOTAL	26.7	16.5	20.1	73.0
ARAB COUNTRIES	–	0.0	–	–
E.E.C.+ MEMBERS	22.2	21.7	25.1	27.2
TOTAL	78.4	64.8	58.7	115.2

5. ODA LOANS NET

DAC COUNTRIES	1987	1988	1989	1990
Australia	–	–	–	–
Austria	–	–	–	–
Belgium	–	–	–	–
Canada	–	–	–	–
Denmark	3.9	4.8	0.7	–
Finland	–	–	–	–
France	–	–	-0.7	-0.8
Germany	0.2	–	0.0	–
Ireland	–	–	–	–
Italy	–	–	–	–
Japan	–	–	–	–
Netherlands	–	-1.8	–	-2.0
New Zealand	–	–	–	–
Norway	–	–	–	–
Sweden	–	–	–	–
Switzerland	–	–	–	–
United Kingdom	–	–	–	–
United States	8.0	-4.0	-5.0	–
TOTAL	12.0	-1.0	-5.0	-2.8
MULTILATERAL	15.6	3.8	0.0	33.4
ARAB COUNTRIES	–	–	–	–
E.E.C.+ MEMBERS	4.7	2.9	-0.1	-2.9
TOTAL	27.6	2.7	-5.0	30.5

6. TOTAL OFFICIAL NET

DAC COUNTRIES	1987	1988	1989	1990
Australia	–	–	-0.7	-0.7
Austria	–	–	–	0.0
Belgium	0.1	0.2	0.0	0.0
Canada	5.6	2.3	1.1	-1.5
Denmark	4.5	5.1	1.1	0.6
Finland	–	–	–	0.5
France	0.8	0.7	1.2	1.0
Germany	-2.1	45.0	-3.9	2.1
Ireland	0.1	0.0	0.0	0.1
Italy	0.1	–	–	–
Japan	10.2	8.8	10.1	6.4
Netherlands	0.5	0.3	0.5	0.7
New Zealand	–	–	–	–
Norway	0.1	0.2	0.1	0.2
Sweden	–	0.1	–	0.1
Switzerland	0.0	0.0	–	0.2
United Kingdom	1.5	1.5	1.0	1.0
United States	25.0	21.0	13.0	19.0
TOTAL	46.5	85.3	23.6	29.6
MULTILATERAL	27.0	22.9	18.7	38.4
ARAB COUNTRIES	–	0.0	–	–
E.E.C.+ MEMBERS	10.5	57.0	10.5	16.2
TOTAL	73.5	108.2	42.2	68.0

7. TOTAL ODA GROSS

	1987
Australia	–
Austria	–
Belgium	0.0
Canada	0.2
Denmark	4.5
Finland	–
France	0.8
Germany	8.5
Ireland	0.1
Italy	0.1
Japan	10.2
Netherlands	0.5
New Zealand	–
Norway	0.1
Sweden	–
Switzerland	0.0
United Kingdom	1.5
United States	28.0
TOTAL	54.7
AF.D.F.	5.8
AF.D.B.	–
AS.D.B	–
CAR.D.B.	–
E.E.C.	6.2
IBRD	–
IDA	6.0
I.D.B.	–
IFAD	3.0
I.F.C.	–
IMF TRUST FUND	–
U.N. AGENCIES	–
UNDP	2.4
UNTA	1.0
UNICEF	0.6
UNRWA	–
WFP	1.3
UNHCR	–
Other Multilateral	0.4
Arab Agencies	–
TOTAL	26.7
ARAB COUNTRIES	–
E.E.C.+ MEMBERS	22.2
TOTAL	81.4

8. GRANTS

	1987
Australia	–
Austria	–
Belgium	0.0
Canada	0.2
Denmark	0.7
Finland	–
France	0.8
Germany	8.4
Ireland	0.1
Italy	0.1
Japan	10.2
Netherlands	0.5
New Zealand	–
Norway	0.1
Sweden	–
Switzerland	0.0
United Kingdom	1.5
United States	17.0
TOTAL	39.6
MULTILATERAL	11.2
ARAB COUNTRIES	–
E.E.C.+ MEMBERS	17.5
TOTAL	50.8

9. TOTAL OOF GROSS

	1987
Australia	–
Austria	–
Belgium	0.1
Canada	5.8
Denmark	–
Finland	–
France	–
Germany	0.1
Ireland	–
Italy	–
Japan	–
Netherlands	–
New Zealand	–
Norway	–
Sweden	–
Switzerland	–
United Kingdom	–
United States	–
TOTAL	6.0
MULTILATERAL	1.8
ARAB COUNTRIES	–
E.E.C.+ MEMBERS	0.2
TOTAL	7.8

10. ODA COMMITMENTS

1988	1989	1990	1987	1988	1989	1990
–	–	–	–	–	–	–
–	–	0.0	–	–	–	0.0
0.2	0.0	0.0	0.5	–	0.0	0.0
0.6	1.8	0.2	0.3	1.5	0.3	0.1
5.1	1.1	0.6	–	5.2	–	–
–	–	0.5	–	–	–	0.5
0.7	1.9	1.8	0.8	0.7	0.9	0.6
8.0	9.0	7.3	9.6	7.5	8.1	4.9
0.0	0.0	0.1	0.1	0.0	0.0	0.1
–	–	–	0.0	–	–	–
8.8	10.1	6.4	9.9	11.8	5.6	4.1
2.9	1.2	7.7	0.2	2.6	1.1	6.2
–	–	–	–	–	–	–
0.2	0.1	0.2	0.0	–	–	–
0.1	–	0.1	–	0.1	–	–
0.0	–	0.2	0.0	0.0	–	0.1
1.5	1.0	1.0	1.5	1.5	1.0	1.0
26.0	18.0	19.0	38.1	19.2	30.9	5.6
54.1	*44.3*	*45.0*	*61.1*	*50.2*	*47.9*	*23.4*
2.6	0.4	33.4	–	–	3.0	–
–	–	–	–	–	–	–
–	–	–	–	–	–	–
5.3	11.6	11.6	93.1	0.1	5.7	5.7
–	–	–	–	–	–	–
1.0	–	–	–	–	–	–
–	–	–	–	–	–	–
0.3	–	1.1	–	–	–	–
–	–	–	–	–	–	–
–	–	–	–	–	–	–
–	–	–	5.7	7.4	8.5	28.1
2.9	3.9	2.7	–	–	–	–
0.9	1.2	0.8	–	–	–	–
0.6	0.9	0.5	–	–	–	–
–	–	–	–	–	–	–
1.5	0.8	22.9	–	–	–	–
0.4	0.4	0.2	–	–	–	–
1.2	1.3	1.0	–	–	–	–
–	–	–	–	–	–	–
16.6	*20.5*	*74.1*	*98.9*	*7.5*	*17.2*	*33.8*
0.0	–	–	–	*0.0*	–	–
23.7	*25.9*	*30.1*	*105.9*	*17.6*	*16.8*	*18.6*
70.7	*64.8*	*119.1*	*160.0*	*57.7*	*65.1*	*57.2*

11. TECH. COOP. GRANTS

1988	1989	1990	1987	1988	1989	1990
–	–	–	–	–	–	–
–	–	0.0	–	–	–	–
0.2	0.0	0.0	0.0	0.0	–	–
0.6	1.8	0.2	–	–	–	0.2
0.3	0.4	0.6	0.7	0.6	–	0.0
–	–	0.5	–	–	–	–
0.7	1.9	1.8	0.8	0.7	0.9	0.6
7.9	9.0	7.3	8.4	7.9	8.8	3.3
0.0	0.0	0.1	0.1	0.0	0.0	0.1
–	–	–	0.1	–	–	–
8.8	10.1	6.4	3.1	2.7	2.8	2.3
2.9	1.2	7.7	0.2	1.2	1.1	1.1
–	–	–	–	–	–	–
0.2	0.1	0.2	0.0	0.1	0.0	0.0
0.1	–	0.1	–	–	–	–
0.0	–	0.2	–	–	–	–
1.5	1.0	1.0	1.5	1.5	1.0	0.5
26.0	18.0	19.0	11.0	18.0	14.0	8.0
49.3	*43.5*	*45.0*	*25.8*	*32.8*	*28.7*	*16.2*
12.7	*20.1*	*39.6*	*5.7*	*6.4*	*7.7*	*5.1*
0.0	–	–	–	–	–	–
18.9	*25.1*	*30.1*	*13.0*	*12.5*	*11.9*	*5.6*
62.0	*63.6*	*84.6*	*31.5*	*39.2*	*36.4*	*21.3*

12. TOTAL OOF NET

1988	1989	1990	1987	1988	1989	1990
–	–	–	–	–	-0.7	-0.7
–	–	–	–	–	–	–
–	–	–	0.1	–	–	–
2.6	0.8	–	5.4	1.7	-0.6	-1.7
–	–	–	–	–	–	–
–	–	–	–	–	–	–
53.2	–	0.0	-10.6	37.1	-13.0	-5.2
–	–	–	–	–	–	–
–	–	0.1	–	–	–	0.0
–	–	–	–	-0.7	-0.7	-5.0
–	–	–	–	–	–	–
–	–	–	–	–	–	–
–	–	–	–	–	–	–
–	1.0	–	–	-1.0	–	–
55.8	*1.8*	*0.1*	*-5.1*	*37.0*	*-15.0*	*-12.5*
7.5	–	*0.7*	*0.2*	*6.4*	*-1.5*	*-34.6*
–	–	–	–	–	–	–
53.2	–	*0.1*	*-11.7*	*35.3*	*-14.5*	*-11.0*
63.3	*1.8*	*0.8*	*-4.9*	*43.4*	*-16.4*	*-47.1*

13. ODF COMMITMENTS: BY PURPOSE %

	1987	1988	1989	1990
Education	1	2	8	–
Health	4	–	8	–
Other Social Infrastr.	0	1	1	–
Water Sanitat. Sewage	–	6	–	–
Energy	5	9	–	–
Telecommunications	–	–	–	–
Transportation	1	2	–	–
Agriculture	3	9	2	–
Extractive Industries	–	–	–	–
Manufacturing	–	–	–	–
Trade Banking Tourism	–	–	–	–
Technical Cooperation	51	53	59	–
Multisector Aid	0	0	1	–
Programme	23	6	11	–
Debt Reorganisation	–	–	–	–
Food Aid	11	12	10	–
Emergency Aid	0	–	–	–
Unspecified	–	–	–	–
TOTAL	100	100	100	–

14. GRANT ELEMENT OF ODA %

DAC COUNTRIES	1987	1988	1989	1990
Australia	–	–	–	–
Austria	–	–	–	–
Belgium	100.0	–	100.0	–
Canada	100.0	100.0	100.0	–
Denmark	–	91.0	–	–
Finland	–	–	–	–
France	100.0	100.0	100.0	–
Germany	100.0	100.0	100.0	–
Ireland	100.0	100.0	100.0	–
Italy	100.0	–	–	–
Japan	100.0	100.0	100.0	–
Netherlands	100.0	100.0	100.0	–
New Zealand	–	–	–	–
Norway	100.0	–	–	–
Sweden	–	100.0	–	–
Switzerland	100.0	100.0	–	–
United Kingdom	100.0	100.0	100.0	–
United States	91.4	100.0	100.0	–
TOTAL	*94.7*	*99.1*	*100.0*	–
MULTILATERAL	*100.0*	*100.0*	*100.0*	–
ARAB COUNTRIES	–	*100.0*	–	–
E.E.C.+ MEMBERS	*100.0*	*97.3*	*100.0*	–
TOTAL	*98.0*	*99.2*	*100.0*	–

15. OTHER AGGREGATES

	1987	1988	1989	1990
OFFICIAL COMMITMENTS:				
TOTAL BILATERAL	61.4	53.5	53.6	23.4
of which:				
Arab Countries	–	0.0	–	–
C.E.E.C.	–	–	–	–
TOTAL MULTILATERAL	107.4	7.5	17.2	33.8
TOTAL BIL.& MULTIL.	168.8	61.0	70.8	57.2
of which:				
ODA Grants	149.3	56.3	62.2	57.2
ODA Loans	10.7	1.5	3.0	–
DISBURSEMENTS:				
DAC COUNTRIES COMBINED				
OFFICIAL & PRIVATE				
GROSS:				
Contractual Lending	26.9	33.0	-69.1	115.8
Export Credits, Total	11.7	28.1	-70.9	115.8
Export Credits, Priv.	5.9	-27.6	-71.6	115.7
NET:				
Contractual Lending	-146.1	-43.8	-125.2	51.0
Export Credits Total	-149.7	-29.3	-108.7	62.8
PRIVATE SECTOR NET	-362.8	423.8	231.4	526.8
Direct Investment	0.8	290.2	656.0	276.2
Portfolio Investment	-210.7	213.4	-319.4	184.2
Export Credits	-152.9	-79.7	-105.2	66.4
MARKET BORROWING:				
CHANGE IN CLAIMS				
Banks	–	–	–	–
MEMORANDUM ITEM:				
C.E.E.C. (Gross)	–	–	–	–

1. TOTAL RECEIPTS NET

DAC COUNTRIES	1987	1988	1989	1990
Australia	–	–	–	–
Austria	-0.2	0.0	0.0	0.8
Belgium	2.1	0.5	2.3	1.8
Canada	8.2	4.3	0.9	0.9
Denmark	0.0	0.5	2.1	0.1
Finland	0.1	–	0.1	–
France	85.2	94.3	91.9	153.2
Germany	35.2	14.9	16.5	42.6
Ireland	–	–	–	–
Italy	27.6	-3.6	6.6	4.1
Japan	6.8	43.1	16.0	32.1
Netherlands	1.0	0.2	-0.7	1.2
New Zealand	–	–	–	–
Norway	6.1	5.6	4.3	5.4
Sweden	–	–	-0.9	-1.0
Switzerland	12.7	25.8	13.0	32.2
United Kingdom	-1.5	-2.0	-0.1	1.1
United States	16.0	12.0	6.0	22.0
TOTAL	199.2	195.5	157.9	296.3
MULTILATERAL				
AF.D.F.	16.4	8.2	18.8	20.5
AF.D.B.	16.9	10.2	3.9	1.1
AS.D.B	–	–	–	–
CAR.D.B.	–	–	–	–
E.E.C.	19.8	29.6	45.9	45.9
IBRD	-1.5	-2.0	-2.0	-3.0
IDA	89.8	49.0	68.0	40.0
I.D.B.	–	–	–	–
IFAD	4.7	0.9	1.3	2.8
I.F.C.	2.0	0.7	-1.3	5.6
IMF TRUST FUND	–	–	–	–
U.N. AGENCIES	–	–	–	–
UNDP	6.5	7.9	9.2	15.1
UNTA	1.3	0.9	1.2	1.5
UNICEF	2.5	4.2	3.2	4.0
UNRWA	–	–	–	–
WFP	6.5	1.7	4.1	0.8
UNHCR	–	–	–	–
Other Multilateral	1.9	2.7	2.7	2.3
Arab Agencies	-7.2	-7.3	-8.0	–
TOTAL	159.6	106.7	146.9	136.5
ARAB COUNTRIES	1.2	-7.8	-2.2	-0.7
E.E.C.+ MEMBERS	169.4	134.3	164.4	249.9
TOTAL	360.0	294.3	302.6	432.2

2. ODA LOANS GROSS

DAC COUNTRIES	1987	1988	1989	1990
Australia	–	–	–	–
Austria	–	–	–	–
Belgium	–	–	–	–
Canada	–	–	–	–
Denmark	–	–	–	–
Finland	–	–	–	–
France	74.3	67.7	42.8	32.5
Germany	13.9	3.1	1.8	9.9
Ireland	–	–	–	–
Italy	–	–	–	–
Japan	7.3	–	17.1	2.2
Netherlands	–	–	–	–
New Zealand	–	–	–	–
Norway	–	–	–	–
Sweden	–	–	–	–
Switzerland	–	–	–	–
United Kingdom	–	–	–	–
United States	8.0	–	1.0	–
TOTAL	103.5	70.9	62.7	44.7
MULTILATERAL	117.8	64.5	96.6	75.5
ARAB COUNTRIES	–	2.7	–	0.5
E.E.C.+ MEMBERS	93.3	74.4	50.3	48.1
TOTAL	221.3	138.0	159.4	120.7

3. TOTAL OFFICIAL GROSS

DAC COUNTRIES	1987	1988	1989	1990
Australia	–	–	0.0	–
Austria	0.0	0.0	0.0	0.8
Belgium	4.5	1.7	4.1	4.9
Canada	8.2	4.3	0.9	20.8
Denmark	0.0	0.6	2.1	0.1
Finland	0.1	–	0.1	–
France	118.4	113.0	148.4	195.8
Germany	37.6	17.0	19.6	156.2
Ireland	–	–	–	–
Italy	29.6	3.7	24.7	5.7
Japan	13.6	42.8	28.7	16.8
Netherlands	0.5	0.5	0.5	0.9
New Zealand	–	–	–	–
Norway	6.1	5.6	4.3	5.4
Sweden	–	–	0.1	–
Switzerland	12.7	25.8	13.0	32.2
United Kingdom	0.9	0.8	0.5	1.1
United States	16.0	13.0	7.0	28.0
TOTAL	248.2	228.7	253.8	468.5
MULTILATERAL	173.5	129.3	164.9	152.0
ARAB COUNTRIES	3.5	2.7	–	0.5
E.E.C.+ MEMBERS	212.3	167.8	246.6	411.4
TOTAL	425.1	360.7	418.8	620.9

4. TOTAL ODA NET

	1987	1988	1989	1990
Australia	–	–	–	–
Austria	0.0	0.0	0.0	0.8
Belgium	0.4	0.4	0.2	0.5
Canada	8.2	1.8	0.9	1.1
Denmark	0.0	0.6	2.1	0.1
Finland	0.1	–	0.1	–
France	102.4	107.4	107.1	143.0
Germany	23.4	14.3	12.6	41.6
Ireland	–	–	–	–
Italy	2.2	3.7	13.6	5.7
Japan	8.4	40.8	15.6	14.0
Netherlands	0.5	0.5	0.5	0.9
New Zealand	–	–	–	–
Norway	6.1	5.6	4.3	5.4
Sweden	–	–	0.1	–
Switzerland	12.7	25.8	13.0	32.2
United Kingdom	0.9	0.8	0.5	1.1
United States	16.0	12.0	5.0	22.0
TOTAL	181.3	213.5	175.4	268.2
AF.D.F.	16.4	8.2	18.8	20.5
AF.D.B.	–	–	–	–
AS.D.B	–	–	–	–
CAR.D.B.	–	–	–	–
E.E.C.	19.8	29.6	45.9	45.9
IBRD	–	–	–	–
IDA	89.8	49.0	68.0	40.0
I.D.B.	–	–	–	–
IFAD	4.7	0.9	1.3	2.8
I.F.C.	–	–	–	–
IMF TRUST FUND	–	–	–	–
U.N. AGENCIES	–	–	–	–
UNDP	6.5	7.9	9.2	15.1
UNTA	1.3	0.9	1.2	1.5
UNICEF	2.5	4.2	3.2	4.0
UNRWA	–	–	–	–
WFP	6.5	1.7	4.1	0.8
UNHCR	–	–	–	–
Other Multilateral	1.9	2.7	2.7	2.3
Arab Agencies	-7.0	-12.8	-7.3	–
TOTAL	142.4	92.2	147.0	132.8
ARAB COUNTRIES	-2.3	-1.5	-2.2	-0.7
E.E.C.+ MEMBERS	149.7	157.1	182.4	238.6
TOTAL	321.5	304.3	320.2	400.4

5. ODA LOANS NET

	1987	1988	1989	1990
Australia	–	–	–	–
Austria	–	–	–	–
Belgium	–	–	–	–
Canada	–	–	–	-19.7
Denmark	–	0.0	–	–
Finland	–	–	–	–
France	65.1	66.7	23.7	14.3
Germany	13.9	3.1	1.8	-99.0
Ireland	–	–	–	–
Italy	–	–	–	–
Japan	2.0	-2.0	4.0	-0.5
Netherlands	–	–	–	–
New Zealand	–	–	–	–
Norway	–	–	–	–
Sweden	–	–	–	–
Switzerland	–	–	–	–
United Kingdom	–	–	–	–
United States	8.0	-1.0	–	-6.0
TOTAL	89.0	66.8	29.5	-110.9
MULTILATERAL	108.0	47.8	85.5	63.8
ARAB COUNTRIES	-2.3	-1.5	-2.2	-0.7
E.E.C.+ MEMBERS	83.1	72.3	30.2	-79.9
TOTAL	194.7	113.1	112.8	-47.8

6. TOTAL OFFICIAL NET

	1987	1988	1989	1990
Australia	-0.2	0.0	0.0	–
Austria	4.5	1.7	4.1	4.8
Belgium	8.2	4.3	0.9	0.9
Canada	0.0	0.6	2.1	0.1
Denmark	0.1	–	0.1	–
Finland	104.6	106.2	119.5	145.3
France	37.6	15.7	16.2	46.4
Germany	–	–	–	–
Ireland	26.0	3.7	17.2	5.7
Italy	8.4	40.8	15.6	14.0
Japan	0.5	0.5	0.5	0.9
Netherlands	–	–	–	–
Norway	6.1	5.6	4.3	5.4
Sweden	–	–	0.1	–
Switzerland	12.7	25.8	13.0	32.2
United Kingdom	0.9	0.8	0.5	1.1
United States	16.0	12.0	6.0	22.0
TOTAL	225.4	217.6	199.9	279.4
MULTILATERAL	159.6	106.7	146.9	136.5
ARAB COUNTRIES	1.2	-7.8	-2.2	-0.7
E.E.C.+ MEMBERS	194.0	158.7	205.9	250.1
TOTAL	386.2	316.4	344.6	415.2

7. TOTAL ODA GROSS

	1987
Australia	–
Austria	0.0
Belgium	0.4
Canada	8.2
Denmark	0.0
Finland	0.1
France	111.7
Germany	23.4
Ireland	–
Italy	2.2
Japan	13.6
Netherlands	0.5
New Zealand	–
Norway	6.1
Sweden	–
Switzerland	12.7
United Kingdom	0.9
United States	16.0
TOTAL	195.8
AF.D.F.	16.6
AF.D.B.	–
AS.D.B	–
CAR.D.B.	–
E.E.C.	20.8
IBRD	–
IDA	91.3
I.D.B.	–
IFAD	4.8
I.F.C.	–
IMF TRUST FUND	–
U.N. AGENCIES	–
UNDP	6.5
UNTA	1.3
UNICEF	2.5
UNRWA	–
WFP	6.5
UNHCR	–
Other Multilateral	1.9
Arab Agencies	–
TOTAL	152.2
ARAB COUNTRIES	–
E.E.C.+ MEMBERS	159.9
TOTAL	348.0

8. GRANTS

	1987
Australia	–
Austria	0.0
Belgium	0.4
Canada	8.2
Denmark	0.0
Finland	0.1
France	37.4
Germany	9.5
Ireland	–
Italy	2.2
Japan	6.3
Netherlands	0.5
New Zealand	–
Norway	6.1
Sweden	–
Switzerland	12.7
United Kingdom	0.9
United States	8.0
TOTAL	92.3
MULTILATERAL	34.4
ARAB COUNTRIES	–
E.E.C.+ MEMBERS	66.6
TOTAL	126.7

9. TOTAL OOF GROSS

	1987
Australia	–
Austria	–
Belgium	4.1
Canada	–
Denmark	–
Finland	–
France	6.7
Germany	14.2
Ireland	–
Italy	27.5
Japan	–
Netherlands	–
New Zealand	–
Norway	–
Sweden	–
Switzerland	–
United Kingdom	–
United States	–
TOTAL	52.4
MULTILATERAL	21.3
ARAB COUNTRIES	3.5
E.E.C.+ MEMBERS	52.4
TOTAL	77.1

10. ODA COMMITMENTS

1988	1989	1990	1987	1988	1989	1990
–	–	–	–	–	–	–
0.0	0.0	0.8	0.0	0.0	0.0	7.8
0.4	0.2	0.5	0.1	0.9	0.2	0.5
1.8	0.9	20.8	8.3	1.5	2.0	0.8
0.6	2.1	0.1	–	4.5	–	–
–	0.1	–	–	–	–	–
108.5	126.2	161.2	141.3	136.7	112.2	82.3
14.3	12.6	150.5	9.8	24.6	14.0	28.3
–	–	–	–	–	–	–
3.7	13.6	5.7	2.0	20.9	5.1	2.4
42.8	28.7	16.8	20.8	45.5	29.4	12.4
0.5	0.5	0.9	0.5	0.6	0.5	0.9
–	–	–	–	–	–	–
5.6	4.3	5.4	4.3	4.3	1.2	13.8
–	0.1	–	–	0.1	–	–
25.8	13.0	32.2	8.9	41.5	21.7	32.8
0.8	0.5	1.1	0.9	0.8	0.5	3.2
13.0	6.0	28.0	23.4	26.2	18.1	26.8
217.6	*208.6*	*423.8*	*220.4*	*308.0*	*204.9*	*211.8*
8.7	19.6	21.6	13.9	16.9	54.1	17.8
–	–	–	–	–	–	–
–	–	–	–	–	–	–
–	–	–	–	–	–	–
30.6	46.8	46.8	73.1	57.1	8.7	8.7
–	–	–	–	–	–	–
51.0	70.0	43.0	134.0	203.0	27.0	149.0
–	–	–	–	–	–	–
0.9	1.4	3.0	0.0	13.8	–	0.1
–	–	–	–	–	–	–
–	–	–	–	–	–	–
–	–	–	18.7	17.4	20.4	23.7
7.9	9.2	15.1	–	–	–	–
0.9	1.2	1.5	–	–	–	–
4.2	3.2	4.0	–	–	–	–
–	–	–	–	–	–	–
1.7	4.1	0.8	–	–	–	–
–	–	–	–	–	–	–
2.7	2.7	2.3	–	–	–	–
0.4	–	2.2	5.4	10.0	–	5.0
108.9	*158.2*	*140.3*	*245.1*	*318.3*	*110.1*	*204.2*
2.7	*–*	*0.5*	*3.2*	*0.0*	*–*	*–*
159.2	*202.5*	*366.7*	*227.8*	*246.0*	*141.1*	*126.1*
329.2	*366.8*	*564.6*	*468.7*	*626.2*	*315.0*	*416.0*

11. TECH. COOP. GRANTS

1988	1989	1990	1987	1988	1989	1990
–	–	–	–	–	–	–
0.0	0.0	0.8	0.0	0.0	–	–
0.4	0.2	0.5	0.3	0.0	0.0	–
1.8	0.9	20.8	–	0.0	0.4	–
0.6	2.1	0.1	0.0	0.0	0.0	–
–	0.1	–	0.0	–	–	–
40.8	83.4	128.6	30.9	33.0	32.5	40.3
11.2	10.8	140.6	8.2	9.0	9.1	11.1
–	–	–	–	–	–	–
3.7	13.6	5.7	2.0	1.4	1.5	1.5
42.8	11.5	14.5	1.3	1.5	2.5	4.7
0.5	0.5	0.9	0.5	0.5	0.5	0.9
–	–	–	–	–	–	–
5.6	4.3	5.4	0.7	0.8	0.5	0.6
–	0.1	–	–	–	0.1	–
25.8	13.0	32.2	2.5	2.2	–	–
0.8	0.5	1.1	0.7	0.8	0.5	0.6
13.0	5.0	28.0	–	1.0	1.0	2.0
146.8	*145.9*	*379.1*	*47.2*	*50.2*	*48.7*	*61.7*
44.4	*61.5*	*64.8*	*13.2*	*18.4*	*16.3*	*22.9*
0.0	*–*	*–*	*–*	*–*	*–*	*–*
84.8	*152.2*	*318.6*	*43.6*	*47.4*	*44.2*	*54.4*
191.2	*207.4*	*444.0*	*60.3*	*68.6*	*65.0*	*84.6*

12. TOTAL OOF NET

1988	1989	1990	1987	1988	1989	1990
–	–	–	–	–	–	–
–	–	–	-0.2	–	–	–
1.4	3.9	4.4	4.1	1.4	3.9	4.3
2.5	–	–	–	2.5	–	-0.3
–	–	–	–	–	–	–
–	–	–	–	–	–	–
4.5	22.2	34.6	2.2	-1.2	12.4	2.3
2.7	7.0	5.7	14.2	1.4	3.5	4.9
–	–	–	–	–	–	–
–	11.0	–	23.8	–	3.6	–
–	–	–	–	–	–	–
–	–	–	–	–	–	–
–	–	–	–	–	–	–
–	–	–	–	–	–	–
–	–	–	–	–	–	–
–	–	–	–	–	–	–
–	–	–	–	–	–	–
–	1.0	–	–	–	1.0	–
11.1	*45.2*	*44.7*	*44.1*	*4.0*	*24.5*	*11.2*
20.4	*6.8*	*11.6*	*17.2*	*14.5*	*-0.1*	*3.7*
–	*–*	*–*	*3.5*	*-6.4*	*–*	*–*
8.6	*44.2*	*44.7*	*44.3*	*1.5*	*23.5*	*11.5*
31.5	*52.0*	*56.3*	*64.7*	*12.1*	*24.3*	*14.9*

13. ODF COMMITMENTS: BY PURPOSE %

	1987	1988	1989	1990
Education	1	0	1	–
Health	1	0	0	–
Other Social Infrastr.	1	4	5	–
Water Sanitat. Sewage	4	2	0	–
Energy	10	2	2	–
Telecommunications	–	1	6	–
Transportation	8	13	8	–
Agriculture	10	9	22	–
Extractive Industries	2	2	0	–
Manufacturing	3	7	2	–
Trade Banking Tourism	0	4	5	–
Technical Cooperation	17	15	22	–
Multisector Aid	0	–	1	–
Programme	31	39	14	–
Debt Reorganisation	7	1	10	–
Food Aid	5	2	1	–
Emergency Aid	0	0	–	–
Unspecified	0	0	0	–
TOTAL	100	100	100	–

14. GRANT ELEMENT OF ODA %

DAC COUNTRIES

	1987	1988	1989	1990
Australia	–	–	–	–
Austria	100.0	100.0	100.0	–
Belgium	100.0	100.0	100.0	–
Canada	100.0	100.0	100.0	–
Denmark	–	100.0	–	–
Finland	–	–	–	–
France	53.7	57.3	70.3	–
Germany	74.6	93.2	65.5	–
Ireland	–	–	–	–
Italy	100.0	100.0	100.0	–
Japan	74.2	92.7	61.0	–
Netherlands	100.0	100.0	100.0	–
New Zealand	–	–	–	–
Norway	100.0	100.0	100.0	–
Sweden	–	100.0	–	–
Switzerland	100.0	100.0	100.0	–
United Kingdom	100.0	100.0	100.0	–
United States	88.5	99.4	98.6	–
TOTAL	*67.6*	*79.4*	*75.9*	*–*
MULTILATERAL	*87.5*	*83.7*	*86.6*	*–*
ARAB COUNTRIES	*81.1*	*100.0*	*–*	*–*
E.E.C.+ MEMBERS	*70.2*	*74.9*	*72.9*	*–*
TOTAL	*78.4*	*81.5*	*80.1*	*–*

15. OTHER AGGREGATES

	1987	1988	1989	1990
OFFICIAL COMMITMENTS:				
TOTAL BILATERAL	299.2	327.2	301.7	248.5
of which:				
Arab Countries	6.7	0.0	–	–
C.E.E.C.	25.0	14.8	–	–
TOTAL MULTILATERAL	249.4	324.5	115.9	204.5
TOTAL BIL.& MULTIL.	548.6	651.7	417.6	452.9
of which:				
ODA Grants	171.8	265.8	140.1	204.3
ODA Loans	296.9	360.4	174.8	211.7
DISBURSEMENTS:				
DAC COUNTRIES COMBINED				
OFFICIAL & PRIVATE				
GROSS:				
Contractual Lending	151.8	72.1	104.6	67.7
Export Credits, Total	-3.6	-7.4	10.4	-21.5
Export Credits, Priv.	-3.6	-9.9	-3.1	-21.5
NET:				
Contractual Lending	112.5	42.8	32.7	-93.6
Export Credits Total	-20.3	-25.5	-15.1	6.0
PRIVATE SECTOR NET	-26.1	-22.1	-42.0	16.9
Direct Investment	3.5	2.9	2.3	3.9
Portfolio Investment	-9.5	3.0	-23.2	6.8
Export Credits	-20.1	-28.0	-21.1	6.3
MARKET BORROWING:				
CHANGE IN CLAIMS				
Banks	-26.0	-17.0	-27.0	3.0
MEMORANDUM ITEM:				
C.E.E.C. (Gross)	19.9	24.0	11.5	–

	1987	1988	1989	1990		1987	1988	1989	1990		1987
1. TOTAL RECEIPTS NET					**4. TOTAL ODA NET**					**7. TOTAL ODA GROSS**	
DAC COUNTRIES											
Australia	0.1	0.4	6.6	5.2		0.1	0.4	6.6	5.2	Australia	0.1
Austria	–	0.0	0.6	0.9		–	0.0	0.6	0.9	Austria	–
Belgium	0.1	1.1	-0.6	4.5		0.0	0.1	0.1	4.5	Belgium	0.0
Canada	7.5	5.7	10.4	7.8		7.5	5.7	10.4	7.8	Canada	7.5
Denmark	12.3	4.5	7.5	6.2		11.7	4.5	7.5	6.3	Denmark	34.9
Finland	0.2	0.1	0.3	0.1		0.2	0.1	0.3	0.1	Finland	0.2
France	11.4	4.3	2.5	-0.3		5.0	3.5	5.2	9.5	France	5.0
Germany	31.8	27.1	31.6	52.4		29.6	27.2	33.0	51.8	Germany	29.6
Ireland	0.0	0.1	0.0	0.1		0.0	0.1	0.0	0.1	Ireland	0.0
Italy	3.9	5.3	1.9	0.6		3.9	5.3	1.7	0.5	Italy	3.9
Japan	50.8	35.7	21.2	42.0		51.5	38.1	21.6	42.0	Japan	51.7
Netherlands	14.6	13.7	9.5	10.8		10.8	10.8	8.4	9.9	Netherlands	10.8
New Zealand	–	–	–	–		–	–	–	–	New Zealand	–
Norway	0.2	2.4	3.0	3.6		0.2	2.4	3.0	3.6	Norway	0.2
Sweden	–	0.1	-0.4	-0.2		0.3	0.1	–	0.3	Sweden	0.3
Switzerland	0.6	0.0	1.7	2.1		0.6	0.0	1.7	2.1	Switzerland	0.6
United Kingdom	57.6	87.7	43.2	60.3		31.7	53.1	51.8	50.7	United Kingdom	35.8
United States	17.0	30.0	32.0	21.0		17.0	30.0	30.0	21.0	United States	18.0
TOTAL	*208.2*	*218.2*	*170.6*	*216.9*		*170.2*	*181.4*	*181.7*	*216.0*	*TOTAL*	*198.7*
MULTILATERAL											
AF.D.F.	11.2	7.3	12.0	14.8		11.2	7.3	12.0	14.8	AF.D.F.	11.4
AF.D.B.	4.9	-1.7	-3.5	-2.6		–	–	–	–	AF.D.B.	–
AS.D.B	–	–	–	–		–	–	–	–	AS.D.B	–
CAR.D.B.	–	–	–	–		–	–	–	–	CAR.D.B.	–
E.E.C.	27.2	37.0	43.4	43.4		27.3	38.4	43.3	43.3	E.E.C.	27.5
IBRD	2.5	2.0	-5.0	-6.0		–	–	–	–	IBRD	–
IDA	43.9	60.0	77.0	95.0		43.9	60.0	77.0	95.0	IDA	45.2
I.D.B.	–	–	–	–		–	–	–	–	I.D.B.	–
IFAD	5.5	1.2	0.8	4.9		5.5	1.2	0.8	4.9	IFAD	5.9
I.F.C.	-1.1	2.3	-2.5	0.1		–	–	–	–	I.F.C.	–
IMF TRUST FUND	–	–	–	–		–	–	–	–	IMF TRUST FUND	–
U.N. AGENCIES	–	–	–	–		–	–	–	–	U.N. AGENCIES	–
UNDP	5.6	10.8	13.8	16.1		5.6	10.8	13.8	16.1	UNDP	5.6
UNTA	1.0	0.5	1.1	1.3		1.0	0.5	1.1	1.3	UNTA	1.0
UNICEF	2.0	2.5	3.1	3.4		2.0	2.5	3.1	3.4	UNICEF	2.0
UNRWA	–	–	–	–		–	–	–	–	UNRWA	–
WFP	6.2	25.0	31.2	43.3		6.2	25.0	31.2	43.3	WFP	6.2
UNHCR	6.2	37.5	29.0	36.3		6.2	37.5	29.0	36.3	UNHCR	6.2
Other Multilateral	1.3	1.5	18.5	4.3		1.3	1.5	18.5	4.3	Other Multilateral	1.3
Arab Agencies	-0.1	-0.1	0.1	–		-0.1	-0.1	0.1	–	Arab Agencies	–
TOTAL	*116.3*	*185.8*	*219.0*	*254.4*		*110.1*	*184.6*	*230.0*	*262.7*	*TOTAL*	*112.3*
ARAB COUNTRIES	*0.2*	*–*	*–*	*–*		*0.2*	*–*	*–*	*–*	*ARAB COUNTRIES*	*0.2*
E.E.C.+ MEMBERS	*158.9*	*180.8*	*138.8*	*178.0*		*120.0*	*143.0*	*150.9*	*176.5*	*E.E.C.+ MEMBERS*	*147.6*
TOTAL	*324.7*	*404.0*	*389.7*	*471.3*		*280.5*	*366.0*	*411.6*	*478.7*	*TOTAL*	*311.2*
2. ODA LOANS GROSS					**5. ODA LOANS NET**					**8. GRANTS**	
DAC COUNTRIES											
Australia	–	–	–	–		–	–	–	–	Australia	0.1
Austria	–	–	–	–		–	–	–	–	Austria	–
Belgium	–	–	–	–		–	–	–	–	Belgium	0.0
Canada	–	–	–	–		–	–	–	–	Canada	7.5
Denmark	0.3	–	-0.2	–		-22.9	–	-0.2	–	Denmark	34.6
Finland	–	–	–	–		–	–	–	–	Finland	0.2
France	2.8	1.9	3.2	3.6		2.8	1.9	3.1	3.6	France	2.2
Germany	–	–	1.6	–		–	–	1.6	–	Germany	29.6
Ireland	–	–	–	–		–	–	–	–	Ireland	0.0
Italy	–	–	–	–		–	–	–	–	Italy	3.9
Japan	40.0	24.0	6.9	30.1		39.8	24.0	5.9	25.3	Japan	11.7
Netherlands	1.3	0.5	1.3	0.7		1.3	0.5	1.3	0.7	Netherlands	9.5
New Zealand	–	–	–	–		–	–	–	–	New Zealand	–
Norway	–	–	–	–		–	–	–	–	Norway	0.2
Sweden	–	–	–	–		–	–	–	–	Sweden	0.3
Switzerland	–	–	–	–		–	–	–	–	Switzerland	0.6
United Kingdom	4.0	4.6	10.2	1.7		-0.1	-1.7	5.0	-2.8	United Kingdom	31.8
United States	–	–	–	–		-1.0	-1.0	-2.0	–	United States	18.0
TOTAL	*48.4*	*31.0*	*23.0*	*36.1*		*19.9*	*23.7*	*14.8*	*26.8*	*TOTAL*	*150.2*
MULTILATERAL	*68.8*	*73.9*	*93.1*	*119.2*		*66.6*	*70.5*	*90.2*	*115.0*	*MULTILATERAL*	*43.5*
ARAB COUNTRIES	*–*	*–*	*–*	*–*		*–*	*–*	*–*	*–*	*ARAB COUNTRIES*	*0.2*
E.E.C.+ MEMBERS	*14.8*	*10.2*	*17.1*	*7.1*		*-12.8*	*2.8*	*11.3*	*2.0*	*E.E.C.+ MEMBERS*	*132.8*
TOTAL	*117.2*	*104.9*	*116.0*	*155.3*		*86.5*	*94.2*	*105.0*	*141.8*	*TOTAL*	*194.0*
3. TOTAL OFFICIAL GROSS					**6. TOTAL OFFICIAL NET**					**9. TOTAL OOF GROSS**	
DAC COUNTRIES											
Australia	0.1	0.4	6.6	5.2		0.1	0.4	6.6	5.2	Australia	–
Austria	–	0.0	0.6	0.9		–	0.0	0.6	0.9	Austria	–
Belgium	0.0	0.1	0.1	4.5		0.0	0.1	0.1	4.5	Belgium	–
Canada	7.5	5.7	10.4	7.8		7.5	5.7	10.4	7.8	Canada	–
Denmark	35.5	4.5	7.5	6.3		12.3	4.5	7.5	6.2	Denmark	0.6
Finland	0.2	0.1	0.3	0.1		0.2	0.1	0.3	0.1	Finland	–
France	5.0	3.7	5.3	9.5		4.1	3.5	5.1	9.4	France	–
Germany	29.6	27.9	33.5	53.3		28.8	26.8	32.2	52.0	Germany	0.0
Ireland	0.0	0.1	0.0	0.1		0.0	0.1	0.0	0.1	Ireland	–
Italy	3.9	5.3	1.7	0.5		3.9	5.3	1.7	0.5	Italy	–
Japan	51.7	38.1	22.6	46.8		51.5	38.1	21.6	42.0	Japan	–
Netherlands	12.0	12.1	8.7	11.6		12.1	11.9	8.4	9.8	Netherlands	1.2
New Zealand	–	–	–	–		–	–	–	–	New Zealand	–
Norway	0.2	2.4	3.0	3.6		0.2	2.4	3.0	3.6	Norway	–
Sweden	0.3	0.1	–	0.3		0.3	0.1	–	0.3	Sweden	–
Switzerland	0.6	0.0	1.7	2.1		0.6	0.0	1.7	2.1	Switzerland	–
United Kingdom	40.8	71.7	69.3	66.1		32.5	67.4	39.6	44.9	United Kingdom	5.0
United States	18.0	31.0	34.0	21.0		17.0	30.0	32.0	21.0	United States	–
TOTAL	*205.5*	*203.2*	*205.1*	*239.6*		*171.2*	*196.5*	*170.6*	*210.3*	*TOTAL*	*6.8*
MULTILATERAL	*131.7*	*202.5*	*238.1*	*276.5*		*116.3*	*185.8*	*219.0*	*254.3*	*MULTILATERAL*	*19.4*
ARAB COUNTRIES	*0.2*	*–*	*–*	*–*		*0.2*	*–*	*–*	*–*	*ARAB COUNTRIES*	*–*
E.E.C.+ MEMBERS	*157.7*	*165.6*	*171.8*	*197.8*		*120.9*	*156.7*	*138.0*	*170.8*	*E.E.C.+ MEMBERS*	*10.2*
TOTAL	*337.4*	*405.7*	*443.2*	*516.1*		*287.7*	*382.3*	*389.7*	*464.6*	*TOTAL*	*26.2*

1988	1989	1990	1987	1988	1989	1990

10. ODA COMMITMENTS

1988	1989	1990	1987	1988	1989	1990
0.4	6.6	5.2	0.5	3.4	2.2	5.6
0.0	0.6	0.9	–	0.0	0.6	1.2
0.1	0.1	4.5	0.0	0.0	0.1	4.5
5.7	10.4	7.8	0.7	22.2	2.0	2.4
4.5	7.5	6.3	23.7	9.6	3.3	1.8
0.1	0.3	0.1	–	–	0.3	0.1
3.5	5.2	9.5	4.4	9.6	1.4	15.6
27.2	33.0	51.8	21.7	36.9	41.3	83.1
0.1	0.0	0.1	0.0	0.1	0.0	0.1
5.3	1.7	0.5	6.1	5.1	1.4	0.5
38.1	22.6	46.8	24.0	25.1	15.2	49.9
10.8	8.4	9.9	13.6	11.7	8.4	11.0
–	–	–	–	–	–	–
2.4	3.0	3.6	0.1	–	0.8	0.5
0.1	–	0.3	0.3	0.1	–	–
0.0	1.7	2.1	0.6	0.0	1.7	2.1
59.4	57.0	55.3	50.5	86.4	57.2	29.1
31.0	32.0	21.0	12.9	49.2	70.9	23.7
188.7	*189.9*	*225.4*	*159.0*	*259.2*	*206.7*	*230.9*
7.5	12.3	15.2	12.4	14.8	19.1	73.5
–	–	–	–	–	–	–
–	–	–	–	–	–	–
39.4	43.8	43.8	62.2	41.8	25.0	25.0
–	–	–	–	–	–	–
62.0	79.0	98.0	53.9	102.0	134.0	77.0
–	–	–	–	–	–	–
1.2	0.8	5.1	6.9	–	–	–
–	–	–	–	–	–	–
–	–	–	–	–	–	–
–	–	–	22.4	77.9	96.7	104.8
10.8	13.8	16.1	–	–	–	–
0.5	1.1	1.3	–	–	–	–
2.5	3.1	3.4	–	–	–	–
–	–	–	–	–	–	–
25.0	31.2	43.3	–	–	–	–
37.5	29.0	36.3	–	–	–	–
1.5	18.5	4.3	–	–	–	–
–	0.2	0.2	–	–	–	–
188.0	*232.8*	*267.0*	*157.7*	*236.4*	*274.8*	*280.3*
–	–	–	–	–	–	–
150.3	*156.6*	*181.6*	*182.1*	*201.0*	*138.2*	*170.7*
376.7	**422.7**	**492.4**	**316.7**	**495.6**	**481.5**	**511.2**

11. TECH. COOP. GRANTS

1988	1989	1990	1987	1988	1989	1990
0.4	6.6	5.2	0.1	0.3	0.5	1.0
0.0	0.6	0.9	–	0.0	–	0.0
0.1	0.1	4.5	0.0	0.1	0.1	–
5.7	10.4	7.8	–	0.3	0.5	0.5
4.5	7.7	6.3	0.5	1.1	2.2	0.9
0.1	0.3	0.1	0.1	–	–	–
1.7	2.1	5.9	1.1	1.0	1.4	0.9
27.2	31.4	51.8	8.8	8.3	8.4	11.5
0.1	0.0	0.1	0.0	0.1	0.0	0.1
5.3	1.7	0.5	1.6	–	–	–
14.1	15.7	16.7	4.8	5.1	4.7	4.6
10.3	7.0	9.1	0.8	1.4	1.3	2.1
–	–	–	–	–	–	–
2.4	3.0	3.6	0.1	0.1	0.0	0.0
0.1	–	0.3	–	–	–	–
0.0	1.7	2.1	0.0	0.0	–	–
54.8	46.8	53.5	12.5	17.4	15.7	16.0
31.0	32.0	21.0	8.0	9.0	16.0	14.0
157.7	*166.9*	*189.2*	*38.4*	*44.2*	*50.7*	*51.6*
114.1	*139.7*	*147.8*	*17.6*	*56.9*	*65.5*	*61.4*
–	–	–	–	–	–	–
140.2	*139.6*	*174.5*	*26.7*	*33.3*	*29.1*	*31.5*
271.9	**306.6**	**337.0**	**56.0**	**101.1**	**116.2**	**113.0**

12. TOTAL OOF NET

1988	1989	1990	1987	1988	1989	1990
–	–	–	–	–	–	–
–	–	–	–	–	–	–
–	–	–	–	–	–	–
–	–	–	0.6	–	0.0	0.0
–	–	–	–	–	–	–
0.2	0.1	–	-0.9	0.0	-0.1	-0.1
0.7	0.4	1.6	-0.7	-0.4	-0.8	0.2
–	–	–	–	–	–	–
–	–	–	–	–	–	–
1.2	0.4	1.8	1.2	1.1	0.0	-0.1
–	–	–	–	–	–	–
–	–	–	–	–	–	–
–	–	–	–	–	–	–
12.4	12.3	10.9	0.9	14.4	-12.2	-5.7
–	2.0	–	–	–	–	2.0
14.5	*15.2*	*14.2*	*1.1*	*15.1*	*-11.0*	*-5.7*
14.5	*5.3*	*9.6*	*6.2*	*1.2*	*-10.9*	*-8.4*
–	–	–	–	–	–	–
15.3	*15.2*	*16.2*	*1.0*	*13.7*	*-12.9*	*-5.7*
28.9	**20.5**	**23.8**	**7.2**	**16.3**	**-22.0**	**-14.1**

13. ODF COMMITMENTS: BY PURPOSE %

	1987	1988	1989	1990
Education	16	1	4	–
Health	5	0	3	–
Other Social Infrastr.	1	5	1	–
Water Sanitat. Sewage	7	2	1	–
Energy	1	–	15	–
Telecommunications	1	2	–	–
Transportation	5	18	5	–
Agriculture	12	8	8	–
Extractive Industries	–	0	–	–
Manufacturing	–	–	–	–
Trade Banking Tourism	1	1	9	–
Technical Cooperation	22	27	33	–
Multisector Aid	1	0	9	–
Programme	12	29	9	–
Debt Reorganisation	13	1	–	–
Food Aid	1	3	4	–
Emergency Aid	0	1	1	–
Unspecified	–	0	–	–
TOTAL	100	100	100	–

14. GRANT ELEMENT OF ODA %

DAC COUNTRIES

	1987	1988	1989	1990
Australia	100.0	100.0	100.0	–
Austria	–	100.0	100.0	–
Belgium	100.0	100.0	100.0	–
Canada	100.0	100.0	100.0	–
Denmark	100.0	100.0	100.0	–
Finland	–	–	100.0	–
France	81.0	64.4	100.0	–
Germany	100.0	100.0	100.0	–
Ireland	100.0	100.0	100.0	–
Italy	100.0	100.0	100.0	–
Japan	82.3	100.0	100.0	–
Netherlands	100.0	100.0	100.0	–
New Zealand	–	–	–	–
Norway	100.0	–	100.0	–
Sweden	100.0	100.0	–	–
Switzerland	100.0	100.0	100.0	–
United Kingdom	100.0	100.0	100.0	–
United States	99.9	100.0	100.0	–
TOTAL	*96.6*	*98.7*	*100.0*	–
MULTILATERAL	*90.8*	*90.3*	*89.8*	–
ARAB COUNTRIES	–	–	–	–
E.E.C.+ MEMBERS	*99.5*	*98.2*	*100.0*	–
TOTAL	*93.5*	*94.7*	*94.2*	–

15. OTHER AGGREGATES

OFFICIAL COMMITMENTS:

	1987	1988	1989	1990
TOTAL BILATERAL	184.7	268.5	217.0	235.4
of which:				
Arab Countries	–	–	–	–
C.E.E.C.	–	–	–	–
TOTAL MULTILATERAL	163.2	240.0	274.8	280.4
TOTAL BIL.& MULTIL.	347.9	508.4	491.8	515.8
of which:				
ODA Grants	216.2	355.9	316.4	318.7
ODA Loans	100.5	139.8	165.1	192.5

DISBURSEMENTS:

DAC COUNTRIES COMBINED

OFFICIAL & PRIVATE	1987	1988	1989	1990
GROSS:				
Contractual Lending	63.8	55.3	46.3	62.6
Export Credits, Total	8.6	9.9	8.2	12.2
Export Credits, Priv.	8.5	9.9	8.2	12.3
NET:				
Contractual Lending	23.2	41.0	-4.5	31.0
Export Credits Total	1.8	1.9	-8.6	9.6
PRIVATE SECTOR NET	37.0	21.7	0.0	6.7
Direct Investment	24.8	17.4	9.3	1.0
Portfolio Investment	9.9	2.0	-1.0	-4.4
Export Credits	2.2	2.3	-8.3	10.0

MARKET BORROWING:

CHANGE IN CLAIMS

	1987	1988	1989	1990
Banks	-13.0	-1.0	-11.0	-9.0

MEMORANDUM ITEM:

	1987	1988	1989	1990
C.E.E.C. (Gross)	–	–	–	–

1. TOTAL RECEIPTS NET

DAC COUNTRIES	1987	1988	1989	1990
Australia	232.6	6.5	66.3	72.8
Austria	12.7	-5.6	-7.0	-8.0
Belgium	-35.5	42.8	-32.3	-20.4
Canada	7.6	2.0	-4.2	6.0
Denmark	-0.5	2.0	29.9	3.7
Finland	0.7	0.8	2.7	27.2
France	-38.4	-156.0	-75.2	-100.3
Germany	-4.6	-10.7	-4.8	-82.1
Ireland	0.0	–	–	–
Italy	1.0	4.0	22.8	3.9
Japan	225.3	198.9	612.1	576.3
Netherlands	-8.2	1.9	1.9	7.3
New Zealand	0.2	0.2	0.1	3.4
Norway	3.3	0.8	0.1	1.5
Sweden	-6.4	0.6	-12.1	-12.1
Switzerland	0.4	0.7	0.3	0.6
United Kingdom	198.7	190.2	20.9	100.3
United States	-244.0	344.0	-122.0	664.0
TOTAL	344.8	622.9	499.3	1244.2
MULTILATERAL				
AF.D.F.	–	–	–	–
AF.D.B.	–	–	–	–
AS.D.B	24.3	13.5	7.5	32.6
CAR.D.B.	–	–	–	–
E.E.C.	0.3	–	0.6	0.6
IBRD	-7.4	-18.0	15.0	41.0
IDA	–	–	–	–
I.D.B.	–	–	–	–
IFAD	–	–	–	–
I.F.C.	13.6	-0.3	-8.6	4.7
IMF TRUST FUND	–	–	–	–
U.N. AGENCIES	–	–	–	–
UNDP	2.0	3.5	2.3	1.8
UNTA	1.4	1.2	1.4	1.5
UNICEF	0.2	0.1	0.2	0.4
UNRWA	–	–	–	–
WFP	–	–	–	–
UNHCR	4.9	5.5	7.1	6.9
Other Multilateral	1.1	0.5	1.1	0.7
Arab Agencies	4.5	4.1	-3.3	–
TOTAL	44.8	10.1	23.1	90.2
ARAB COUNTRIES	0.1	-5.2	-5.8	-2.9
E.E.C.+ MEMBERS	112.8	74.1	-36.3	-87.0
TOTAL	389.7	627.8	516.6	1331.5

4. TOTAL ODA NET

DAC COUNTRIES	1987	1988	1989	1990
Australia	38.6	37.1	21.4	26.9
Austria	0.0	0.0	0.1	0.1
Belgium	0.2	0.2	0.1	0.7
Canada	3.8	4.6	6.3	5.6
Denmark	-0.2	-0.2	-0.2	-0.3
Finland	0.3	0.3	0.2	0.5
France	8.1	6.4	3.2	2.5
Germany	7.7	7.3	8.2	8.6
Ireland	0.0	–	–	–
Italy	1.0	1.3	0.6	0.8
Japan	276.4	24.8	79.6	372.6
Netherlands	0.6	1.9	1.9	2.4
New Zealand	0.2	0.2	0.1	3.4
Norway	1.4	0.3	-0.1	-0.6
Sweden	2.9	0.6	0.9	5.0
Switzerland	0.4	0.7	0.3	0.6
United Kingdom	10.8	12.2	10.6	29.8
United States	–	-1.0	-1.0	–
TOTAL	352.2	96.7	131.9	458.6
MULTILATERAL				
AF.D.F.	–	–	–	–
AF.D.B.	–	–	–	–
AS.D.B	0.8	1.4	2.2	2.0
CAR.D.B.	–	–	–	–
E.E.C.	0.3	–	0.6	0.6
IBRD	–	–	–	–
IDA	–	–	–	–
I.D.B.	–	–	–	–
IFAD	–	–	–	–
I.F.C.	–	–	–	–
IMF TRUST FUND	–	–	–	–
U.N. AGENCIES	–	–	–	–
UNDP	2.0	3.5	2.3	1.8
UNTA	1.4	1.2	1.4	1.5
UNICEF	0.2	0.1	0.2	0.4
UNRWA	–	–	–	–
WFP	–	–	–	–
UNHCR	4.9	5.5	7.1	6.9
Other Multilateral	1.1	0.5	1.1	0.7
Arab Agencies	0.5	0.0	-0.7	–
TOTAL	11.1	12.2	14.1	13.9
ARAB COUNTRIES	0.1	-5.2	-5.8	-2.9
E.E.C.+ MEMBERS	28.5	29.1	24.9	45.0
TOTAL	363.4	103.7	140.2	469.6

7. TOTAL ODA GROSS

DAC COUNTRIES	1987
Australia	38.6
Austria	0.2
Belgium	0.2
Canada	4.3
Denmark	–
Finland	0.3
France	8.8
Germany	8.6
Ireland	0.0
Italy	1.0
Japan	349.3
Netherlands	0.6
New Zealand	0.2
Norway	1.5
Sweden	2.9
Switzerland	0.4
United Kingdom	14.3
United States	–
TOTAL	431.1
MULTILATERAL	
AF.D.F.	–
AF.D.B.	–
AS.D.B	1.0
CAR.D.B.	–
E.E.C.	0.3
IBRD	–
IDA	–
I.D.B.	–
IFAD	–
I.F.C.	–
IMF TRUST FUND	–
U.N. AGENCIES	–
UNDP	2.0
UNTA	1.4
UNICEF	0.2
UNRWA	–
WFP	–
UNHCR	4.9
Other Multilateral	1.1
Arab Agencies	1.7
TOTAL	12.4
ARAB COUNTRIES	8.6
E.E.C.+ MEMBERS	33.7
TOTAL	452.1

2. ODA LOANS GROSS

DAC COUNTRIES	1987	1988	1989	1990
Australia	–	–	–	–
Austria	–	–	–	–
Belgium	–	–	–	–
Canada	0.2	–	–	–
Denmark	–	–	–	–
Finland	–	–	–	0.3
France	6.8	5.1	0.3	0.7
Germany	–	–	–	–
Ireland	–	–	–	–
Italy	–	–	–	–
Japan	300.6	71.2	117.3	410.8
Netherlands	–	–	–	–
New Zealand	–	–	–	–
Norway	–	–	–	–
Sweden	–	–	–	–
Switzerland	–	–	–	–
United Kingdom	1.3	1.3	–	0.9
United States	–	–	–	–
TOTAL	308.9	77.6	117.6	412.8
MULTILATERAL	1.6	1.6	0.7	–
ARAB COUNTRIES	8.5	2.8	2.1	2.1
E.E.C.+ MEMBERS	8.2	6.4	0.3	1.7
TOTAL	319.1	82.0	120.4	414.9

5. ODA LOANS NET

DAC COUNTRIES	1987	1988	1989	1990
Australia	–	–	–	–
Austria	-0.1	-0.1	–	–
Belgium	–	–	–	–
Canada	-0.4	-0.6	-0.6	-0.6
Denmark	-0.2	-0.2	-0.2	-0.3
Finland	–	–	–	0.3
France	6.2	4.5	-0.3	0.2
Germany	-0.9	-0.9	-0.8	-1.1
Ireland	–	–	–	–
Italy	–	–	–	–
Japan	227.7	-32.8	20.9	312.3
Netherlands	–	–	–	–
New Zealand	–	–	–	–
Norway	-0.1	0.0	-0.2	-0.7
Sweden	–	–	–	–
Switzerland	–	–	–	–
United Kingdom	-2.1	-2.5	-3.6	-4.2
United States	–	-1.0	-1.0	–
TOTAL	230.0	-33.7	14.1	305.9
MULTILATERAL	0.3	-0.2	-0.9	-0.2
ARAB COUNTRIES	0.0	-5.2	-5.8	-2.9
E.E.C.+ MEMBERS	3.0	0.8	-4.9	-5.3
TOTAL	230.3	-39.2	7.4	302.8

8. GRANTS

DAC COUNTRIES	1987
Australia	38.6
Austria	0.2
Belgium	0.2
Canada	4.2
Denmark	–
Finland	0.3
France	1.9
Germany	8.6
Ireland	0.0
Italy	1.0
Japan	48.7
Netherlands	0.6
New Zealand	0.2
Norway	1.5
Sweden	2.9
Switzerland	0.4
United Kingdom	12.9
United States	–
TOTAL	122.2
MULTILATERAL	10.8
ARAB COUNTRIES	0.1
E.E.C.+ MEMBERS	25.6
TOTAL	133.1

3. TOTAL OFFICIAL GROSS

DAC COUNTRIES	1987	1988	1989	1990
Australia	38.6	37.1	21.4	28.5
Austria	0.2	0.1	0.1	0.1
Belgium	0.3	0.2	0.1	0.7
Canada	8.6	7.5	6.9	6.2
Denmark	0.3	2.3	0.1	1.0
Finland	0.3	0.3	0.2	0.5
France	8.8	7.0	3.7	3.0
Germany	14.2	8.5	9.6	24.3
Ireland	0.0	–	–	–
Italy	1.0	1.3	9.4	0.8
Japan	375.7	135.1	204.3	544.7
Netherlands	0.6	1.9	1.9	2.4
New Zealand	0.2	0.2	0.1	3.4
Norway	1.5	0.3	0.1	0.1
Sweden	2.9	0.6	0.9	5.0
Switzerland	0.4	0.7	0.3	0.6
United Kingdom	15.4	17.9	14.2	37.4
United States	1.0	–	–	–
TOTAL	469.8	221.1	273.0	658.8
MULTILATERAL	190.3	190.4	216.3	289.9
ARAB COUNTRIES	8.6	2.8	2.2	2.1
E.E.C.+ MEMBERS	40.8	39.2	39.5	70.1
TOTAL	668.6	414.3	491.5	950.7

6. TOTAL OFFICIAL NET

DAC COUNTRIES	1987	1988	1989	1990
Australia	38.6	37.1	21.4	28.5
Austria	0.0	0.0	0.1	0.1
Belgium	0.3	0.2	0.1	0.7
Canada	7.6	2.0	-4.2	-4.6
Denmark	-0.2	2.0	-0.3	0.7
Finland	0.3	0.3	0.2	0.5
France	8.1	6.4	3.2	2.5
Germany	9.9	3.4	3.1	-29.0
Ireland	0.0	–	–	–
Italy	1.0	1.3	6.6	-2.0
Japan	277.8	3.1	-56.0	415.0
Netherlands	0.6	1.9	1.9	2.4
New Zealand	0.2	0.2	0.1	3.4
Norway	1.4	0.2	-0.2	-0.6
Sweden	2.9	0.6	0.9	5.0
Switzerland	0.4	0.7	0.3	0.6
United Kingdom	8.4	13.5	9.9	29.3
United States	-8.0	-8.0	-36.0	–
TOTAL	349.3	65.0	-49.0	452.3
MULTILATERAL	44.8	10.1	23.1	90.2
ARAB COUNTRIES	0.1	-5.2	-5.8	-2.9
E.E.C.+ MEMBERS	28.4	28.7	25.1	5.0
TOTAL	394.2	69.9	-31.7	539.6

9. TOTAL OOF GROSS

DAC COUNTRIES	1987
Australia	–
Austria	–
Belgium	0.1
Canada	4.3
Denmark	0.3
Finland	–
France	–
Germany	5.6
Ireland	–
Italy	–
Japan	26.4
Netherlands	–
New Zealand	–
Norway	–
Sweden	–
Switzerland	–
United Kingdom	1.2
United States	1.0
TOTAL	38.7
MULTILATERAL	177.8
ARAB COUNTRIES	–
E.E.C.+ MEMBERS	7.0
TOTAL	216.5

1988	1989	1990		1987	1988	1989	1990

10. ODA COMMITMENTS

1988	1989	1990	1987	1988	1989	1990
37.1	21.4	26.9	36.1	19.7	31.4	36.4
0.1	0.1	0.1	0.1	0.1	0.1	0.1
0.2	0.1	0.7	–	–	0.1	0.7
5.2	6.9	6.2	2.7	7.4	3.8	20.7
0.0	0.1	–	–	–	–	–
0.3	0.2	0.5	–	0.1	0.2	6.2
7.0	3.7	3.0	1.9	1.9	3.5	2.3
8.2	9.0	9.7	4.0	13.7	6.0	16.0
–	–	–	0.0	–	–	–
1.3	0.6	0.8	0.7	3.1	0.6	0.7
128.8	176.0	471.2	50.7	680.7	67.3	495.9
1.9	1.9	2.4	0.6	1.9	1.9	2.4
0.2	0.1	3.4	0.1	0.2	–	–
0.3	0.1	0.1	0.3	–	–	1.3
0.6	0.9	5.0	3.7	2.3	0.8	7.1
0.7	0.3	0.6	0.1	0.3	0.0	0.1
16.0	14.2	34.9	3.9	12.5	8.5	72.9
–	–	–	–	–	1.0	–
208.0	*235.4*	*565.5*	*104.9*	*743.8*	*125.1*	*662.6*
–	–	–	–	–	–	–
1.6	2.4	2.2	–	–	–	–
–	0.6	0.6	0.6	0.6	1.2	1.2
–	–	–	–	–	–	–
–	–	–	–	–	–	–
–	–	–	–	–	–	–
–	–	–	9.5	10.8	11.9	11.4
3.5	2.3	1.8	–	–	–	–
1.2	1.4	1.5	–	–	–	–
0.1	0.2	0.4	–	–	–	–
–	–	–	–	–	–	–
–	–	–	–	–	–	–
5.5	7.1	6.9	–	–	–	–
0.5	1.1	0.7	–	–	–	–
1.6	0.8	–	–	–	–	–
14.0	*15.7*	*14.1*	*10.1*	*11.4*	*13.2*	*12.6*
2.8	2.2	2.1	0.0	–	–	–
34.7	30.1	52.0	11.7	33.7	21.8	96.1
224.8	*253.2*	*581.6*	*115.0*	*755.2*	*138.2*	*675.2*

11. TECH. COOP. GRANTS

1988	1989	1990	1987	1988	1989	1990
37.1	21.4	26.9	38.4	36.2	20.0	26.5
0.1	0.1	0.1	0.0	0.1	0.1	0.1
0.2	0.1	0.7	0.2	0.1	0.1	0.3
5.2	6.9	6.2	–	1.6	1.9	2.5
0.0	0.1	–	–	0.0	0.0	–
0.3	0.2	0.2	0.1	0.1	0.1	0.0
1.9	3.5	2.3	1.9	1.9	1.2	2.3
8.2	9.0	9.7	8.5	8.2	8.8	9.5
–	–	–	0.0	–	–	–
1.3	0.6	0.8	1.0	0.7	0.6	0.7
57.6	58.7	60.3	40.8	54.7	57.0	58.5
1.9	1.9	2.4	0.6	1.9	1.9	2.4
0.2	0.1	3.4	0.2	0.2	–	3.4
0.3	0.1	0.1	0.3	–	0.0	0.1
0.6	0.9	5.0	0.4	0.6	0.9	1.7
0.7	0.3	0.6	0.1	0.0	–	–
14.7	14.2	34.0	2.9	6.3	5.5	5.7
–	–	–	–	–	–	–
130.4	*117.8*	*152.7*	*95.3*	*112.6*	*98.0*	*113.5*
12.4	15.0	14.1	9.6	10.8	11.9	11.4
–	0.0	–	–	–	–	–
28.3	29.8	50.4	15.2	19.2	18.1	20.8
142.8	*132.8*	*166.8*	*104.9*	*123.4*	*110.0*	*124.9*

12. TOTAL OOF NET

1988	1989	1990	1987	1988	1989	1990
–	–	1.6	0.0	0.0	–	1.6
–	–	–	–	–	–	–
–	0.0	–	0.1	–	0.0	–
2.3	–	–	3.8	-2.5	-10.4	-10.2
2.3	–	1.0	0.1	2.3	-0.1	1.0
–	–	–	–	–	–	–
0.3	0.6	14.6	2.2	-3.9	-5.0	-37.6
–	–	–	–	–	–	–
–	8.8	–	–	–	6.0	-2.8
6.3	28.3	73.6	1.4	-21.7	-135.6	42.4
–	–	–	–	–	–	–
–	–	–	–	0.0	0.0	0.0
–	–	–	–	–	–	–
1.9	–	2.5	-2.4	1.3	-0.7	-0.6
–	–	–	-8.0	-7.0	-35.0	–
13.1	*37.7*	*93.3*	*-2.9*	*-31.7*	*-180.9*	*-6.3*
176.4	*200.6*	*275.8*	*33.7*	*-2.1*	*9.0*	*76.4*
–	–	–	–	–	–	–
4.5	9.4	18.1	-0.1	-0.4	0.2	-40.0
189.5	*238.3*	*369.1*	*30.8*	*-33.8*	*-171.9*	*70.0*

13. ODF COMMITMENTS: BY PURPOSE %

	1987	1988	1989	1990
Education	11	13	1	–
Health	11	–	–	–
Other Social Infrastr.	0	0	1	–
Water Sanitat. Sewage	0	–	–	–
Energy	35	38	2	–
Telecommunications	–	–	–	–
Transportation	0	–	0	–
Agriculture	3	8	25	–
Extractive Industries	–	–	–	–
Manufacturing	0	2	1	–
Trade Banking Tourism	15	28	28	–
Technical Cooperation	23	11	42	–
Multisector Aid	0	0	0	–
Programme	–	–	–	–
Debt Reorganisation	–	–	–	–
Food Aid	–	–	0	–
Emergency Aid	0	–	–	–
Unspecified	–	–	–	–
TOTAL	100	100	100	–

14. GRANT ELEMENT OF ODA %

DAC COUNTRIES

	1987	1988	1989	1990
Australia	100.0	100.0	100.0	–
Austria	100.0	100.0	100.0	–
Belgium	–	–	100.0	–
Canada	100.0	100.0	100.0	–
Denmark	–	–	–	–
Finland	–	100.0	100.0	–
France	100.0	100.0	100.0	–
Germany	100.0	100.0	100.0	–
Ireland	100.0	–	–	–
Italy	100.0	100.0	100.0	–
Japan	97.7	51.1	97.0	–
Netherlands	100.0	100.0	100.0	–
New Zealand	100.0	100.0	–	–
Norway	100.0	–	–	–
Sweden	100.0	100.0	100.0	–
Switzerland	100.0	100.0	100.0	–
United Kingdom	100.0	100.0	100.0	–
United States	–	–	100.0	–
TOTAL	*98.9*	*55.2*	*98.4*	*–*
MULTILATERAL	*100.0*	*100.0*	*100.0*	*–*
ARAB COUNTRIES	**100.0**	**–**	**–**	**–**
E.E.C.+ MEMBERS	*100.0*	*100.0*	*100.0*	*–*
TOTAL	**99.0**	**55.9**	**98.5**	**–**

15. OTHER AGGREGATES

OFFICIAL COMMITMENTS:

	1987	1988	1989	1990
TOTAL BILATERAL	108.2	776.6	207.1	752.4
of which:				
Arab Countries	0.0	–	–	–
C.E.E.C.	–	–	–	–
TOTAL MULTILATERAL	183.3	244.8	377.4	36.2
TOTAL BIL.& MULTIL.	291.5	1021.4	584.5	788.6
of which:				
ODA Grants	112.8	136.1	134.6	244.1
ODA Loans	2.2	619.1	3.6	431.1

DISBURSEMENTS:

DAC COUNTRIES COMBINED

OFFICIAL & PRIVATE

	1987	1988	1989	1990
GROSS:				
Contractual Lending	431.4	131.9	239.6	600.7
Export Credits, Total	119.7	46.5	95.7	111.4
Export Credits, Priv.	83.9	41.2	84.5	94.7
NET:				
Contractual Lending	116.4	-127.5	-200.3	234.7
Export Credits Total	-98.8	-85.2	-164.9	-143.9
PRIVATE SECTOR NET	-4.5	557.9	548.3	791.9
Direct Investment	384.3	674.2	562.8	1038.9
Portfolio Investment	-278.2	-54.2	19.0	-182.2
Export Credits	-110.7	-62.0	-33.4	-64.8

MARKET BORROWING:

CHANGE IN CLAIMS

	1987	1988	1989	1990
Banks	-1780.0	-1284.0	-535.0	-366.0

MEMORANDUM ITEM:

	1987	1988	1989	1990
C.E.E.C. (Gross)	–	–	–	–

1. TOTAL RECEIPTS NET

DAC COUNTRIES	1987	1988	1989	1990
Australia	–	–	0.0	0.0
Austria	0.3	0.2	0.2	0.2
Belgium	4.1	2.6	-0.5	4.5
Canada	21.6	12.5	21.2	20.9
Denmark	0.2	3.7	2.1	2.8
Finland	–	–	–	–
France	63.8	85.6	104.9	124.7
Germany	29.0	31.2	38.2	30.5
Ireland	0.0	0.0	–	–
Italy	20.9	33.2	28.1	16.3
Japan	8.9	9.8	27.6	12.3
Netherlands	22.4	21.8	28.6	34.1
New Zealand	–	–	–	–
Norway	2.4	10.3	13.6	11.0
Sweden	–	–	–	–
Switzerland	10.1	9.0	5.0	16.8
United Kingdom	-0.8	-1.5	-0.8	1.1
United States	33.0	36.0	24.0	30.0
TOTAL	*215.8*	*254.5*	*292.2*	*305.2*
MULTILATERAL				
AF.D.F.	22.1	38.9	31.9	20.3
AF.D.B.	-0.5	-0.4	-0.4	-0.5
AS.D.B	–	–	–	–
CAR.D.B.	–	–	–	–
E.E.C.	33.0	22.9	47.1	47.1
IBRD	–	–	–	–
IDA	42.1	59.0	46.0	41.0
I.D.B.	–	–	–	–
IFAD	6.7	3.4	3.9	4.0
I.F.C.	-0.2	-0.1	-0.1	-0.1
IMF TRUST FUND	–	–	–	–
U.N. AGENCIES	–	–	–	–
UNDP	11.7	11.8	12.3	14.1
UNTA	1.5	0.9	1.6	1.6
UNICEF	4.4	4.4	6.2	6.1
UNRWA	–	–	–	–
WFP	6.5	20.8	2.3	8.5
UNHCR	–	–	0.0	0.0
Other Multilateral	3.6	2.9	4.8	3.5
Arab Agencies	4.5	-1.7	-3.7	–
TOTAL	*135.4*	*162.8*	*152.0*	*145.6*
ARAB COUNTRIES	*8.6*	*5.4*	*2.8*	*15.4*
E.E.C.+ MEMBERS	*172.6*	*199.5*	*247.7*	*261.1*
TOTAL	*359.8*	*422.7*	*446.9*	*466.2*

2. ODA LOANS GROSS

DAC COUNTRIES	1987	1988	1989	1990
Australia	–	–	–	–
Austria	–	–	–	–
Belgium	–	–	–	–
Canada	–	–	–	–
Denmark	–	–	–	–
Finland	–	–	–	–
France	26.2	40.9	75.3	77.7
Germany	–	–	–	–
Ireland	–	–	–	–
Italy	–	1.8	1.5	3.7
Japan	–	–	18.7	3.3
Netherlands	–	–	–	–
New Zealand	–	–	–	–
Norway	–	–	–	–
Sweden	–	–	–	–
Switzerland	–	–	–	–
United Kingdom	–	–	–	–
United States	–	–	–	–
TOTAL	*26.2*	*42.7*	*95.5*	*84.6*
MULTILATERAL	*77.7*	*108.5*	*95.9*	*80.8*
ARAB COUNTRIES	*12.7*	*10.3*	*7.9*	*18.9*
E.E.C.+ MEMBERS	*26.5*	*44.3*	*79.8*	*84.2*
TOTAL	*116.6*	*161.5*	*199.4*	*184.3*

3. TOTAL OFFICIAL GROSS

DAC COUNTRIES	1987	1988	1989	1990
Australia	–	–	0.0	0.0
Austria	0.3	0.2	0.2	0.2
Belgium	4.2	2.1	0.9	4.4
Canada	21.6	12.5	21.2	20.9
Denmark	0.2	3.7	2.2	2.9
Finland	–	–	–	–
France	66.2	82.1	110.5	137.2
Germany	31.6	39.1	39.9	31.0
Ireland	0.0	0.0	–	–
Italy	20.9	34.4	29.2	16.3
Japan	8.9	9.8	27.6	12.3
Netherlands	22.4	23.2	29.2	35.5
New Zealand	–	–	–	–
Norway	2.4	10.3	13.6	11.0
Sweden	–	–	–	–
Switzerland	10.1	9.0	5.0	16.8
United Kingdom	1.6	2.1	1.9	1.7
United States	33.0	36.0	25.0	30.0
TOTAL	*223.4*	*264.6*	*306.3*	*320.2*
MULTILATERAL	*138.8*	*172.4*	*170.6*	*159.1*
ARAB COUNTRIES	*14.1*	*10.8*	*9.6*	*19.0*
E.E.C.+ MEMBERS	*180.4*	*209.9*	*261.0*	*276.3*
TOTAL	*376.3*	*447.8*	*486.5*	*498.3*

4. TOTAL ODA NET

DAC COUNTRIES	1987	1988	1989	1990
Australia	–	–	0.0	0.0
Austria	0.3	0.2	0.2	0.2
Belgium	4.2	2.1	0.9	4.4
Canada	21.6	12.5	21.2	20.9
Denmark	0.2	3.7	2.2	2.9
Finland	–	–	–	–
France	65.2	77.6	108.2	129.1
Germany	31.6	39.1	39.9	31.0
Ireland	0.0	0.0	–	–
Italy	20.9	34.3	27.8	16.3
Japan	8.9	9.8	27.6	12.3
Netherlands	22.4	23.2	29.2	35.5
New Zealand	–	–	–	–
Norway	2.4	10.3	13.6	11.0
Sweden	–	–	–	–
Switzerland	10.1	9.0	5.0	16.8
United Kingdom	1.6	2.1	1.9	1.7
United States	33.0	36.0	23.0	30.0
TOTAL	*222.4*	*260.0*	*300.6*	*312.2*
MULTILATERAL				
AF.D.F.	22.1	38.9	31.9	20.3
AF.D.B.	–	–	–	–
AS.D.B	–	–	–	–
CAR.D.B.	–	–	–	–
E.E.C.	33.0	22.9	47.1	47.1
IBRD	–	–	–	–
IDA	42.1	59.0	46.0	41.0
I.D.B.	–	–	–	–
IFAD	6.7	3.4	3.9	4.0
I.F.C.	–	–	–	–
IMF TRUST FUND	–	–	–	–
U.N. AGENCIES	–	–	–	–
UNDP	11.7	11.8	12.3	14.1
UNTA	1.5	0.9	1.6	1.6
UNICEF	4.4	4.4	6.2	6.1
UNRWA	–	–	–	–
WFP	6.5	20.8	2.3	8.5
UNHCR	–	–	0.0	0.0
Other Multilateral	3.6	2.9	4.8	3.5
Arab Agencies	4.5	-3.1	-5.7	–
TOTAL	*136.1*	*162.0*	*150.6*	*146.2*
ARAB COUNTRIES	*7.6*	*5.4*	*2.8*	*15.4*
E.E.C.+ MEMBERS	*179.1*	*205.0*	*257.2*	*268.1*
TOTAL	*366.0*	*427.4*	*453.9*	*473.8*

5. ODA LOANS NET

DAC COUNTRIES	1987	1988	1989	1990
Australia	–	–	–	–
Austria	–	–	–	–
Belgium	–	–	–	–
Canada	–	–	–	–
Denmark	–	–	–	–
Finland	–	–	–	–
France	25.2	39.8	73.0	72.7
Germany	–	–	–	–
Ireland	–	–	–	–
Italy	–	1.7	1.5	3.7
Japan	–	–	18.7	3.3
Netherlands	–	–	–	–
New Zealand	–	–	–	–
Norway	–	–	–	–
Sweden	–	–	–	–
Switzerland	–	–	–	–
United Kingdom	–	–	–	–
United States	–	–	-1.0	–
TOTAL	*25.2*	*41.5*	*92.2*	*79.6*
MULTILATERAL	*75.0*	*99.5*	*77.9*	*65.5*
ARAB COUNTRIES	*7.1*	*4.9*	*1.0*	*15.3*
E.E.C.+ MEMBERS	*25.2*	*42.8*	*77.3*	*79.1*
TOTAL	*107.3*	*145.9*	*171.2*	*160.4*

6. TOTAL OFFICIAL NET

DAC COUNTRIES	1987	1988	1989	1990
Australia	–	–	0.0	0.0
Austria	0.3	0.2	0.2	0.2
Belgium	4.2	2.1	0.9	4.4
Canada	21.6	12.5	21.2	20.9
Denmark	0.2	3.7	2.1	2.8
Finland	–	–	–	–
France	65.1	80.9	108.1	131.9
Germany	31.0	38.6	39.3	30.3
Ireland	0.0	0.0	–	–
Italy	20.9	34.3	28.1	16.3
Japan	8.9	9.8	27.6	12.3
Netherlands	22.4	23.2	29.2	35.5
New Zealand	–	–	–	–
Norway	2.4	10.3	13.6	11.0
Sweden	–	–	–	–
Switzerland	10.1	9.0	5.0	16.8
United Kingdom	1.6	2.1	1.9	1.7
United States	33.0	36.0	24.0	30.0
TOTAL	*221.7*	*262.8*	*301.1*	*314.1*
MULTILATERAL	*135.4*	*162.8*	*152.0*	*145.6*
ARAB COUNTRIES	*8.6*	*5.4*	*2.8*	*15.4*
E.E.C.+ MEMBERS	*178.5*	*207.8*	*256.6*	*270.0*
TOTAL	*365.7*	*431.0*	*455.8*	*475.2*

7. TOTAL ODA GROSS

	1987
Australia	–
Austria	0.3
Belgium	4.2
Canada	21.6
Denmark	0.2
Finland	–
France	66.2
Germany	31.6
Ireland	0.0
Italy	20.9
Japan	8.9
Netherlands	22.4
New Zealand	–
Norway	2.4
Sweden	–
Switzerland	10.1
United Kingdom	1.6
United States	33.0
TOTAL	*223.4*
AF.D.F.	22.4
AF.D.B.	–
AS.D.B	–
CAR.D.B.	–
E.E.C.	33.3
IBRD	–
IDA	43.5
I.D.B.	–
IFAD	6.7
I.F.C.	–
IMF TRUST FUND	–
U.N. AGENCIES	–
UNDP	11.7
UNTA	1.5
UNICEF	4.4
UNRWA	–
WFP	6.5
UNHCR	–
Other Multilateral	3.6
Arab Agencies	5.2
TOTAL	*138.8*
ARAB COUNTRIES	*13.1*
E.E.C.+ MEMBERS	*180.4*
TOTAL	*375.3*

8. GRANTS

	1987
Australia	–
Austria	0.3
Belgium	4.2
Canada	21.6
Denmark	0.2
Finland	–
France	40.0
Germany	31.6
Ireland	0.0
Italy	20.9
Japan	8.9
Netherlands	22.4
New Zealand	–
Norway	2.4
Sweden	–
Switzerland	10.1
United Kingdom	1.6
United States	33.0
TOTAL	*197.2*
MULTILATERAL	*61.1*
ARAB COUNTRIES	*0.4*
E.E.C.+ MEMBERS	*153.9*
TOTAL	*258.7*

9. TOTAL OOF GROSS

	1987
Australia	–
Austria	–
Belgium	–
Canada	–
Denmark	–
Finland	–
France	–
Germany	–
Ireland	–
Italy	–
Japan	–
Netherlands	–
New Zealand	–
Norway	–
Sweden	–
Switzerland	–
United Kingdom	–
United States	–
TOTAL	*–*
MULTILATERAL	*–*
ARAB COUNTRIES	*1.0*
E.E.C.+ MEMBERS	*–*
TOTAL	*1.0*

1988	1989	1990		1987	1988	1989	1990

10. ODA COMMITMENTS

1988	1989	1990		1987	1988	1989	1990
–	0.0	0.0		–	–	0.0	0.0
0.2	0.2	0.2		0.3	0.1	0.1	0.6
2.1	0.9	4.4		2.8	0.3	0.9	4.4
12.5	21.2	20.9		25.5	24.8	48.3	7.0
3.7	2.2	2.9		–	11.1	–	–
–	–	–		–	–	–	–
78.6	110.5	134.2		53.7	92.0	142.6	89.2
39.1	39.9	31.0		56.7	62.7	50.8	38.2
0.0	–	–		0.0	0.0	–	–
34.4	27.8	16.3		32.7	26.1	23.4	8.8
9.8	27.6	12.3		9.5	12.3	39.6	8.5
23.2	29.2	35.5		18.7	13.0	45.4	40.8
–	–	–		–	–	–	–
10.3	13.6	11.0		3.6	0.0	8.6	0.3
–	–	–		–	–	–	–
9.0	5.0	16.8		1.4	5.4	3.2	18.7
2.1	1.9	1.7		1.6	2.1	4.9	2.3
36.0	24.0	30.0		14.6	28.0	39.9	26.8
261.2	*303.9*	*317.2*		*221.0*	*278.0*	*407.5*	*245.4*
39.4	32.3	21.1		41.0	49.2	26.4	–
–	–	–		–	–	–	–
–	–	–		–	–	–	–
23.2	47.3	47.3		52.3	89.8	87.3	87.3
–	–	–		–	–	–	–
61.0	48.0	43.0		–	89.0	59.0	123.0
–	–	–		–	–	–	–
3.4	3.9	4.0		0.2	11.7	0.1	13.2
–	–	–		–	–	–	–
–	–	–		–	–	–	–
–	–	–		27.8	40.9	27.3	33.8
11.8	12.3	14.1		–	–	–	–
0.9	1.6	1.6		–	–	–	–
4.4	6.2	6.1		–	–	–	–
–	–	–		–	–	–	–
20.8	2.3	8.5		–	–	–	–
–	0.0	0.0		–	–	–	–
2.9	4.8	3.5		–	–	–	–
3.2	9.8	10.0		8.5	0.0	13.7	6.2
171.0	*168.6*	*159.1*		*129.8*	*280.5*	*213.8*	*263.5*
10.8	*9.6*	*19.0*		*5.9*	*9.8*	*20.8*	*8.2*
206.5	*259.6*	*273.3*		*218.6*	*297.1*	*355.3*	*270.9*
443.0	**482.1**	**495.3**		**356.7**	**568.3**	**642.1**	**517.1**

11. TECH. COOP. GRANTS

1988	1989	1990		1987	1988	1989	1990
–	0.0	0.0		–	–	–	–
0.2	0.2	0.2		0.1	0.1	0.1	0.1
2.1	0.9	4.4		1.6	0.8	0.5	0.2
12.5	21.2	20.9		–	1.8	1.5	0.8
3.7	2.2	2.9		–	0.1	0.1	0.3
–	–	–		–	–	–	–
37.8	35.2	56.5		20.8	21.6	22.0	28.6
39.1	39.9	31.0		13.5	14.8	15.5	16.5
0.0	–	–		0.0	0.0	–	–
32.6	26.3	12.6		3.6	2.1	0.4	0.0
9.8	8.9	9.0		0.3	0.8	0.6	1.0
23.2	29.2	35.5		3.2	3.2	2.9	4.0
–	–	–		–	–	–	–
10.3	13.6	11.0		0.2	0.7	0.7	0.7
–	–	–		–	–	–	–
9.0	5.0	16.8		0.5	2.2	–	–
2.1	1.9	1.7		1.1	1.9	1.4	0.9
36.0	24.0	30.0		20.0	19.0	17.0	21.0
218.5	*208.4*	*232.6*		*64.9*	*68.9*	*62.6*	*73.9*
62.5	*72.6*	*78.3*		*22.2*	*22.8*	*24.9*	*25.3*
0.5	*1.7*	*0.1*		–	–	–	–
162.2	*179.9*	*189.0*		*44.8*	*47.1*	*42.8*	*50.4*
281.5	**282.8**	**311.0**		**87.1**	**91.6**	**87.5**	**99.2**

12. TOTAL OOF NET

1988	1989	1990		1987	1988	1989	1990
–	–	–		–	–	–	–
–	–	–		–	–	–	–
–	–	–		–	–	–	–
–	–	–		–	0.0	-0.1	-0.1
–	–	–		–	–	–	–
3.4	–	3.0		0.0	3.3	-0.1	2.7
–	–	–		-0.6	-0.5	-0.6	-0.7
–	1.4	–		–	–	0.3	–
–	–	–		–	–	–	–
–	–	–		–	–	–	–
–	–	–		–	–	–	–
–	–	–		–	–	–	–
–	1.0	–		–	–	1.0	–
3.4	*2.4*	*3.0*		*-0.6*	*2.8*	*0.5*	*1.9*
1.4	*2.0*	–		*-0.7*	*0.9*	*1.4*	*-0.6*
–	–	–		*1.0*	–	–	–
3.4	*1.4*	*3.0*		*-0.6*	*2.8*	*-0.5*	*1.9*
4.8	**4.4**	**3.0**		**-0.3**	**3.6**	**1.9**	**1.4**

13. ODF COMMITMENTS: BY PURPOSE %

	1987	1988	1989	1990
Education	3	1	7	–
Health	7	2	1	–
Other Social Infrastr.	2	13	5	–
Water Sanitat. Sewage	2	11	3	–
Energy	3	4	9	–
Telecommunications	–	0	1	–
Transportation	–	1	3	–
Agriculture	25	18	21	–
Extractive Industries	–	0	–	–
Manufacturing	2	9	1	–
Trade Banking Tourism	0	0	5	–
Technical Cooperation	40	16	20	–
Multisector Aid	3	1	1	–
Programme	8	21	20	–
Debt Reorganisation	–	–	1	–
Food Aid	4	2	2	–
Emergency Aid	1	0	0	–
Unspecified	–	0	–	–
TOTAL	100	100	100	–

14. GRANT ELEMENT OF ODA %

DAC COUNTRIES

	1987	1988	1989	1990
Australia	–	–	100.0	–
Austria	100.0	100.0	100.0	–
Belgium	100.0	100.0	100.0	–
Canada	100.0	100.0	100.0	–
Denmark	–	100.0	–	–
Finland	–	–	–	–
France	99.2	78.8	77.9	–
Germany	100.0	100.0	100.0	–
Ireland	100.0	100.0	–	–
Italy	100.0	100.0	99.7	–
Japan	100.0	100.0	79.5	–
Netherlands	100.0	100.0	100.0	–
New Zealand	–	–	–	–
Norway	100.0	100.0	100.0	–
Sweden	–	–	–	–
Switzerland	100.0	100.0	100.0	–
United Kingdom	100.0	100.0	100.0	–
United States	100.0	100.0	100.0	–
TOTAL	*99.8*	*93.0*	*90.6*	–
MULTILATERAL	*91.1*	*89.5*	*88.3*	–
ARAB COUNTRIES	**80.8**	**60.4**	**63.1**	–
E.E.C.+ MEMBERS	*99.8*	*92.9*	*91.6*	–
TOTAL	**96.4**	**90.8**	**88.9**	–

15. OTHER AGGREGATES

OFFICIAL COMMITMENTS:

	1987	1988	1989	1990
TOTAL BILATERAL	232.8	309.5	443.5	263.7
of which:				
Arab Countries	5.9	9.8	20.8	8.2
C.E.E.C.	5.7	18.2	–	–
TOTAL MULTILATERAL	133.2	280.5	213.8	263.5
TOTAL BIL.& MULTIL.	366.0	590.1	657.4	527.2
of which:				
ODA Grants	291.2	330.5	388.3	323.0
ODA Loans	71.1	256.0	253.8	194.1

DISBURSEMENTS:

DAC COUNTRIES COMBINED

	1987	1988	1989	1990
OFFICIAL & PRIVATE				
GROSS:				
Contractual Lending	24.3	49.6	94.9	81.0
Export Credits, Total	-1.8	3.5	-3.0	-6.6
Export Credits, Priv.	-1.8	3.5	-3.0	-6.6
NET:				
Contractual Lending	19.0	40.9	85.7	72.9
Export Credits Total	-5.5	-3.5	-7.0	-8.6
PRIVATE SECTOR NET	-5.9	-8.3	-8.9	-8.9
Direct Investment	-0.5	-4.9	-1.3	0.1
Portfolio Investment	0.2	0.0	-0.6	-0.4
Export Credits	-5.5	-3.5	-7.0	-8.6

MARKET BORROWING:

CHANGE IN CLAIMS

	1987	1988	1989	1990
Banks	5.0	–	-4.0	-12.0

MEMORANDUM ITEM:

	1987	1988	1989	1990
C.E.E.C. (Gross)	4.9	1.0	2.0	–

MAURITANIA

1. TOTAL RECEIPTS NET

DAC COUNTRIES	1987	1988	1989	1990
Australia	–	–	–	–
Austria	0.2	0.2	0.1	0.3
Belgium	1.1	0.0	-0.2	0.3
Canada	1.7	3.4	0.6	0.6
Denmark	10.6	2.2	2.2	1.7
Finland	–	–	0.1	–
France	38.2	50.9	49.7	47.3
Germany	5.9	15.8	63.7	15.8
Ireland	–	–	–	–
Italy	10.8	10.4	10.0	10.1
Japan	4.5	3.9	6.6	2.2
Netherlands	6.4	1.6	0.4	9.9
New Zealand	–	–	–	–
Norway	1.9	0.5	0.6	0.9
Sweden	–	–	–	0.3
Switzerland	0.1	0.3	0.4	0.2
United Kingdom	-0.5	0.3	-8.6	0.1
United States	10.0	9.0	12.0	9.0
TOTAL	90.7	98.4	137.5	98.6
MULTILATERAL				
AF.D.F.	2.1	0.8	22.2	10.1
AF.D.B.	1.0	8.6	-2.5	1.2
AS.D.B	–	–	–	–
CAR.D.B.	–	–	–	–
E.E.C.	7.7	17.0	31.8	31.8
IBRD	3.9	-9.0	-10.0	-11.0
IDA	38.3	23.0	9.0	38.0
I.D.B.	–	–	–	–
IFAD	2.3	2.2	0.5	3.4
I.F.C.	–	–	–	1.1
IMF TRUST FUND	–	–	–	–
U.N. AGENCIES	–	–	–	–
UNDP	6.8	8.7	7.0	5.4
UNTA	1.0	0.9	1.0	1.4
UNICEF	2.0	0.9	1.7	2.3
UNRWA	–	–	–	–
WFP	2.7	4.0	4.5	6.1
UNHCR	–	–	0.5	1.0
Other Multilateral	2.7	3.3	3.2	2.1
Arab Agencies	4.5	13.5	2.2	–
TOTAL	75.1	73.9	71.1	92.7
ARAB COUNTRIES	13.1	-3.6	-10.1	0.3
E.E.C.+ MEMBERS	80.1	98.2	149.1	117.0
TOTAL	179.0	168.8	198.6	191.5

2. ODA LOANS GROSS

DAC COUNTRIES	1987	1988	1989	1990
Australia	–	–	–	–
Austria	–	–	–	–
Belgium	–	–	–	–
Canada	–	–	–	–
Denmark	10.4	–	–	–
Finland	–	–	–	–
France	7.3	15.2	10.7	8.5
Germany	0.6	1.9	–	–
Ireland	–	–	–	–
Italy	–	0.0	–	–
Japan	–	–	2.3	–
Netherlands	–	–	–	9.8
New Zealand	–	–	–	–
Norway	–	–	–	–
Sweden	–	–	–	–
Switzerland	–	–	–	–
United Kingdom	–	–	–	–
United States	–	–	–	–
TOTAL	18.3	17.1	13.0	18.2
MULTILATERAL	60.7	61.8	53.2	72.6
ARAB COUNTRIES	27.7	20.4	9.8	4.2
E.E.C.+ MEMBERS	20.6	27.8	18.3	25.8
TOTAL	106.7	99.2	76.1	95.0

3. TOTAL OFFICIAL GROSS

DAC COUNTRIES	1987	1988	1989	1990
Australia	–	–	–	–
Austria	0.2	0.2	0.1	0.3
Belgium	0.6	0.4	0.0	0.4
Canada	1.7	6.7	0.6	0.6
Denmark	11.1	2.2	2.2	1.7
Finland	–	–	0.1	–
France	53.9	62.5	62.0	60.4
Germany	8.3	18.7	64.9	17.1
Ireland	–	–	–	–
Italy	10.8	9.3	11.1	8.9
Japan	5.2	4.7	9.3	3.2
Netherlands	7.2	5.8	3.9	12.0
New Zealand	–	–	–	–
Norway	1.9	0.5	0.6	0.9
Sweden	–	–	–	0.3
Switzerland	0.1	0.3	0.4	0.2
United Kingdom	0.3	0.3	0.3	0.1
United States	10.0	9.0	12.0	12.0
TOTAL	111.3	120.6	167.5	117.9
MULTILATERAL	101.5	125.9	99.9	133.0
ARAB COUNTRIES	38.0	22.5	13.1	4.5
E.E.C.+ MEMBERS	102.3	119.0	178.9	135.0
TOTAL	250.8	268.9	280.5	255.4

4. TOTAL ODA NET

	1987	1988	1989	1990
Australia	–	–	–	–
	0.2	0.2	0.1	0.3
	0.6	0.4	0.0	0.4
	1.7	3.4	0.6	0.6
	10.6	2.2	2.2	1.7
	–	–	0.1	–
	42.2	60.0	60.3	52.5
	7.6	15.7	62.3	16.5
	–	–	–	–
	10.8	9.3	11.1	8.8
	4.5	3.9	6.6	1.9
	7.2	5.8	3.9	12.0
	–	–	–	–
	1.9	0.5	0.6	0.9
	–	–	–	0.3
	0.1	0.3	0.4	0.2
	0.3	0.3	0.3	0.1
	10.0	9.0	12.0	10.0
TOTAL	97.5	111.0	160.3	106.1
	2.1	0.8	22.2	10.1
	–	–	–	–
	–	–	–	–
	–	–	–	–
	10.2	19.7	34.5	34.5
	–	–	–	–
	38.3	23.0	9.0	38.0
	–	–	–	–
	2.3	2.2	0.5	3.4
	–	–	–	–
	–	–	–	–
	–	–	–	–
	6.8	8.7	7.0	5.4
	1.0	0.9	1.0	1.4
	2.0	0.9	1.7	2.3
	–	–	–	–
	2.7	4.0	4.5	6.1
	–	–	0.5	1.0
	2.7	3.3	3.2	2.1
	4.5	13.5	2.2	–
TOTAL	72.7	77.0	86.3	104.2
ARAB COUNTRIES	14.4	-3.6	-4.5	0.3
E.E.C.+ MEMBERS	89.3	113.5	174.6	126.6
TOTAL	184.6	184.4	242.1	210.6

5. ODA LOANS NET

	1987	1988	1989	1990
	–	–	–	–
	–	–	–	–
	–	–	–	–
	-0.1	-3.3	–	–
	9.8	–	–	–
	–	–	–	–
	6.5	13.9	9.0	5.4
	0.5	1.8	–	–
	–	–	–	–
	–	0.0	0.0	0.0
	-0.7	-0.8	-0.5	-1.3
	–	–	–	9.8
	–	–	–	–
	–	–	–	–
	–	–	–	–
	–	–	–	–
	–	–	–	–
	–	–	–	–
TOTAL	16.1	11.5	8.5	13.9
MULTILATERAL	49.0	47.5	41.0	63.3
ARAB COUNTRIES	6.0	-5.7	-7.8	-0.1
E.E.C.+ MEMBERS	19.1	26.3	16.6	22.8
TOTAL	71.0	53.4	41.7	77.1

6. TOTAL OFFICIAL NET

	1987	1988	1989	1990
	0.2	0.2	0.1	0.3
	0.6	0.4	0.0	0.4
	1.7	3.4	0.6	0.6
	10.6	2.2	2.2	1.7
	–	–	0.1	–
	51.5	59.3	60.1	54.1
	8.2	17.5	64.2	16.7
	–	–	–	–
	10.8	9.3	11.1	8.8
	4.5	3.9	6.6	1.9
	7.2	5.8	3.9	12.0
	–	–	–	–
	1.9	0.5	0.6	0.9
	–	–	–	0.3
	0.1	0.3	0.4	0.2
	0.3	0.3	0.3	0.1
	10.0	9.0	12.0	9.0
TOTAL	107.4	112.0	161.9	106.9
MULTILATERAL	75.1	73.9	71.1	92.7
ARAB COUNTRIES	13.1	-3.6	-10.1	0.3
E.E.C.+ MEMBERS	96.8	111.9	173.5	125.6
TOTAL	195.7	182.4	223.0	199.8

7. TOTAL ODA GROSS

	1987
Australia	–
Austria	0.2
Belgium	0.6
Canada	1.7
Denmark	11.1
Finland	–
France	43.1
Germany	7.6
Ireland	–
Italy	10.8
Japan	5.2
Netherlands	7.2
New Zealand	–
Norway	1.9
Sweden	–
Switzerland	0.1
United Kingdom	0.3
United States	10.0
TOTAL	99.7
AF.D.F.	2.1
AF.D.B.	–
AS.D.B	–
CAR.D.B.	–
E.E.C.	10.2
IBRD	–
IDA	38.7
I.D.B.	–
IFAD	2.3
I.F.C.	–
IMF TRUST FUND	–
U.N. AGENCIES	–
UNDP	6.8
UNTA	1.0
UNICEF	2.0
UNRWA	–
WFP	2.7
UNHCR	–
Other Multilateral	2.7
Arab Agencies	15.8
TOTAL	84.4
ARAB COUNTRIES	36.1
E.E.C.+ MEMBERS	90.8
TOTAL	220.2

8. GRANTS

	1987
Australia	–
Austria	0.2
Belgium	0.6
Canada	1.7
Denmark	0.7
Finland	–
France	35.8
Germany	7.0
Ireland	–
Italy	10.8
Japan	5.2
Netherlands	7.2
New Zealand	–
Norway	1.9
Sweden	–
Switzerland	0.1
United Kingdom	0.3
United States	10.0
TOTAL	81.4
MULTILATERAL	23.7
ARAB COUNTRIES	8.4
E.E.C.+ MEMBERS	70.2
TOTAL	113.6

9. TOTAL OOF GROSS

	1987
Australia	–
Austria	–
Belgium	–
Canada	–
Denmark	–
Finland	–
France	10.9
Germany	0.7
Ireland	–
Italy	–
Japan	–
Netherlands	–
New Zealand	–
Norway	–
Sweden	–
Switzerland	–
United Kingdom	–
United States	–
TOTAL	11.5
MULTILATERAL	17.1
ARAB COUNTRIES	1.9
E.E.C.+ MEMBERS	11.5
TOTAL	30.6

(continued table — row labels on facing page)

1988	1989	1990
–	–	–
0.2	0.1	0.3
0.4	0.0	0.4
6.7	0.6	0.6
2.2	2.2	1.7
–	0.1	–
61.4	62.0	55.6
15.8	62.3	16.5
–	–	–
9.3	11.1	8.9
4.7	9.3	3.2
5.8	3.9	12.0
–	–	–
0.5	0.6	0.9
–	–	0.3
0.3	0.4	0.2
0.3	0.3	0.1
9.0	12.0	10.0
116.5	*164.8*	*110.5*
1.0	22.4	10.4
–	–	–
–	–	–
19.7	34.5	34.5
–	–	–
24.0	10.0	39.0
–	–	–
2.2	0.5	3.4
–	–	–
–	–	–
–	–	–
8.7	7.0	5.4
0.9	1.0	1.4
0.9	1.7	2.3
–	–	–
4.0	4.5	6.1
–	0.5	1.0
3.3	3.2	2.1
26.6	13.3	12.4
91.3	*98.6*	*117.9*
22.5	*13.1*	*4.5*
114.9	*176.3*	*129.6*
230.2	*276.5*	*232.9*
–	–	–
0.2	0.1	0.3
0.4	0.0	0.4
6.7	0.6	0.6
2.2	2.2	1.7
–	0.1	–
46.2	51.3	47.1
13.9	62.3	16.5
–	–	–
9.3	11.1	8.9
4.7	7.0	3.2
5.8	3.9	2.2
–	–	–
0.5	0.6	0.9
–	–	0.3
0.3	0.4	0.2
0.3	0.3	0.1
9.0	12.0	10.0
99.4	*151.8*	*92.2*
29.5	*45.4*	*45.4*
2.1	*3.3*	*0.3*
87.2	*158.0*	*103.8*
131.0	*200.4*	*137.9*
–	–	–
–	0.0	0.0
–	–	–
–	–	–
1.1	–	4.8
2.9	2.6	0.6
–	–	–
–	–	–
–	–	–
–	–	–
–	–	–
–	–	–
–	–	–
–	–	2.0
4.1	2.6	7.4
34.6	1.3	15.1
–	–	–
4.1	2.6	5.4
38.6	*4.0*	*22.5*

10. ODA COMMITMENTS

1987	1988	1989	1990
–	–	–	–
0.2	0.2	0.0	1.5
0.5	0.3	0.0	0.4
4.5	3.6	0.4	0.2
–	–	1.7	–
–	–	0.1	–
52.5	48.6	63.1	72.3
3.3	20.1	57.5	30.5
–	–	–	–
20.3	5.8	9.3	8.2
–	6.8	5.9	10.8
21.2	1.2	6.1	1.4
–	–	–	–
0.4	–	–	–
–	–	–	–
0.0	0.2	0.4	0.2
0.3	0.3	0.3	0.7
8.8	8.7	8.3	7.3
111.9	*95.8*	*153.0*	*133.4*
14.6	41.9	16.7	–
–	–	–	–
–	–	–	–
39.6	69.5	5.2	5.2
52.4	18.0	–	79.0
–	–	–	–
–	–	11.4	0.3
–	–	–	–
–	–	–	–
15.3	17.8	17.9	18.2
–	–	–	–
–	–	–	–
–	–	–	–
–	–	–	–
–	–	–	–
–	–	–	–
–	–	–	–
11.3	9.1	59.7	3.9
133.2	*156.3*	*110.9*	*106.6*
15.2	*9.0*	*24.6*	*17.8*
137.6	*145.9*	*143.1*	*118.6*
260.3	*261.0*	*288.4*	*257.7*

11. TECH. COOP. GRANTS

1987	1988	1989	1990
–	–	–	–
0.2	0.2	0.0	0.1
0.1	–	–	0.1
–	0.0	0.0	0.6
0.2	0.3	0.2	0.0
–	–	–	–
22.4	21.9	20.8	25.5
3.3	4.4	4.6	6.6
–	–	–	–
2.1	0.4	0.3	–
0.0	0.0	0.1	0.0
0.4	1.2	1.1	1.4
–	–	–	–
–	0.1	0.1	0.0
0.4	–	–	–
0.1	0.0	–	–
0.3	0.3	0.2	0.1
5.0	5.0	6.0	6.0
34.3	*33.9*	*33.3*	*40.5*
13.0	14.4	13.4	12.2
–	–	–	–
29.1	29.1	27.2	33.7
47.3	*48.3*	*46.7*	*52.7*

12. TOTAL OOF NET

1987	1988	1989	1990
–	–	–	–
–	–	0.0	0.0
–	0.0	–	–
–	–	–	–
9.3	-0.7	-0.2	1.5
0.6	1.9	1.9	0.2
–	–	–	–
–	–	–	–
–	–	–	–
–	–	–	–
–	–	–	–
–	–	–	–
–	–	–	–
–	–	–	-1.0
9.9	1.1	1.6	0.8
2.5	-3.1	-15.2	-11.5
-1.3	–	-5.5	–
7.5	-1.6	-1.1	-1.0
11.1	*-2.0*	*-19.1*	*-10.7*

13. ODF COMMITMENTS: BY PURPOSE %

	1987	1988	1989	1990
Education	2	11	8	–
Health	0	–	1	–
Other Social Infrastr.	2	8	1	–
Water Sanitat. Sewage	6	8	1	–
Energy	4	0	11	–
Telecommunications	5	0	6	–
Transportation	0	0	9	–
Agriculture	18	12	7	–
Extractive Industries	3	6	1	–
Manufacturing	0	–	0	–
Trade Banking Tourism	0	–	6	–
Technical Cooperation	24	32	15	–
Multisector Aid	0	1	1	–
Programme	29	14	–	–
Debt Reorganisation	–	3	22	–
Food Aid	6	5	2	–
Emergency Aid	0	0	0	–
Unspecified	–	–	8	–
TOTAL	100	100	100	

14. GRANT ELEMENT OF ODA %

DAC COUNTRIES

	1987	1988	1989	1990
Australia	–	–	–	–
Austria	100.0	100.0	100.0	–
Belgium	100.0	100.0	100.0	–
Canada	100.0	100.0	100.0	–
Denmark	–	–	100.0	–
Finland	–	–	100.0	–
France	93.8	93.0	90.7	–
Germany	100.0	100.0	97.9	–
Ireland	–	–	–	–
Italy	100.0	100.0	100.0	–
Japan	–	75.4	100.0	–
Netherlands	71.5	100.0	100.0	–
New Zealand	–	–	–	–
Norway	100.0	–	–	–
Sweden	–	–	–	–
Switzerland	100.0	100.0	100.0	–
United Kingdom	100.0	100.0	100.0	–
United States	100.0	100.0	100.0	–
TOTAL	*91.6*	*94.7*	*95.7*	–
MULTILATERAL	*84.7*	*89.5*	*70.9*	–
ARAB COUNTRIES	*71.8*	*61.4*	*47.6*	–
E.E.C.+ MEMBERS	*92.2*	*97.6*	*95.4*	–
TOTAL	*87.1*	*90.4*	*81.4*	–

15. OTHER AGGREGATES

OFFICIAL COMMITMENTS:

	1987	1988	1989	1990
TOTAL BILATERAL	136.9	107.2	191.8	152.9
of which:				
Arab Countries	15.2	9.0	24.6	17.8
C.E.E.C.	–	0.4	–	–
TOTAL MULTILATERAL	133.2	156.3	110.9	173.2
TOTAL BIL.& MULTIL.	270.1	263.4	302.7	326.1
of which:				
ODA Grants	122.2	173.0	154.8	130.5
ODA Loans	138.0	88.4	133.6	127.3

DISBURSEMENTS:

DAC COUNTRIES COMBINED

	1987	1988	1989	1990
OFFICIAL & PRIVATE				
GROSS:				
Contractual Lending	20.1	16.2	-1.7	20.6
Export Credits, Total	-9.7	-5.0	-16.6	-4.9
Export Credits, Priv.	-9.7	-5.0	-17.3	-5.1
NET:				
Contractual Lending	11.9	1.8	-12.4	7.3
Export Credits Total	-14.1	-10.8	-21.7	-10.2
PRIVATE SECTOR NET	-16.7	-13.6	-24.4	-8.3
Direct Investment	-0.1	0.0	-0.1	–
Portfolio Investment	-2.5	-2.7	-1.8	-0.9
Export Credits	-14.1	-10.8	-22.5	-7.4

MARKET BORROWING:

CHANGE IN CLAIMS

	1987	1988	1989	1990
Banks	-22.0	34.0	-29.0	20.0

MEMORANDUM ITEM:

	1987	1988	1989	1990
C.E.E.C. (Gross)	–	0.4	–	–

	1987	1988	1989	1990		1987	1988	1989	1990		1987
1. TOTAL RECEIPTS NET					**4. TOTAL ODA NET**					**7. TOTAL ODA GROSS**	
DAC COUNTRIES											
Australia	1.6	3.1	3.5	4.2	Australia	1.6	3.1	3.5	4.2	Australia	1.6
Austria	0.0	0.0	0.0	0.0	Austria	0.0	0.0	0.0	0.0	Austria	0.0
Belgium	0.0	-0.6	-0.5	-0.5	Belgium	0.4	0.1	–	–	Belgium	0.4
Canada	0.3	0.3	0.3	0.3	Canada	0.3	0.3	0.3	0.3	Canada	0.3
Denmark	–	0.0	0.0	–	Denmark	–	–	–	–	Denmark	–
Finland	–	0.0	0.0	0.0	Finland	–	0.0	0.0	0.0	Finland	–
France	19.4	31.6	30.4	60.1	France	22.4	27.6	25.5	32.3	France	27.0
Germany	8.4	8.0	9.4	33.8	Germany	8.0	7.6	3.1	23.5	Germany	8.1
Ireland	–	–	–	–	Ireland	–	–	–	–	Ireland	–
Italy	0.2	0.6	0.6	–	Italy	0.2	0.6	–	–	Italy	0.2
Japan	8.7	4.8	18.1	15.1	Japan	6.4	3.3	15.1	6.5	Japan	6.7
Netherlands	0.1	0.1	0.1	0.1	Netherlands	0.1	0.1	0.1	0.1	Netherlands	0.1
New Zealand	–	–	–	–	New Zealand	–	–	–	–	New Zealand	–
Norway	0.0	0.0	0.0	0.0	Norway	0.0	0.0	0.0	0.0	Norway	0.0
Sweden	0.7	0.1	0.6	22.8	Sweden	0.4	0.1	0.6	5.8	Sweden	0.4
Switzerland	0.0	0.0	–	–	Switzerland	0.0	0.0	–	–	Switzerland	0.0
United Kingdom	42.2	20.0	44.4	4.2	United Kingdom	5.8	2.2	2.7	1.8	United Kingdom	7.7
United States	4.0	7.0	2.0	-4.0	United States	4.0	–	-1.0	1.0	United States	5.0
TOTAL	85.6	74.9	108.9	136.1	TOTAL	49.6	44.9	50.0	75.5	TOTAL	57.4
MULTILATERAL											
AF.D.F.	–	–	-0.2	-0.4	AF.D.F.	–	–	-0.2	-0.4	AF.D.F.	–
AF.D.B.	4.5	17.1	0.0	1.5	AF.D.B.	–	–	–	–	AF.D.B.	–
AS.D.B	–	–	–	–	AS.D.B	–	–	–	–	AS.D.B	–
CAR.D.B.	–	–	–	–	CAR.D.B.	–	–	–	–	CAR.D.B.	–
E.E.C.	11.1	13.8	10.0	10.0	E.E.C.	10.6	6.1	6.7	6.7	E.E.C.	10.6
IBRD	8.5	13.0	-7.0	-10.0	IBRD	–	–	–	–	IBRD	–
IDA	-0.2	–	–	–	IDA	-0.2	–	–	–	IDA	–
I.D.B.	–	–	–	–	I.D.B.	–	–	–	–	I.D.B.	–
IFAD	0.0	2.4	0.7	1.2	IFAD	0.0	2.4	0.7	1.2	IFAD	0.3
I.F.C.	1.0	2.5	1.8	5.5	I.F.C.	–	–	–	–	I.F.C.	–
IMF TRUST FUND	–	–	–	–	IMF TRUST FUND	–	–	–	–	IMF TRUST FUND	–
U.N. AGENCIES	–	–	–	–	U.N. AGENCIES	–	–	–	–	U.N. AGENCIES	–
UNDP	0.9	1.1	1.2	1.0	UNDP	0.9	1.1	1.2	1.0	UNDP	0.9
UNTA	0.5	0.2	0.5	0.5	UNTA	0.5	0.2	0.5	0.5	UNTA	0.5
UNICEF	0.2	0.2	0.3	0.4	UNICEF	0.2	0.2	0.3	0.4	UNICEF	0.2
UNRWA	–	–	–	–	UNRWA	–	–	–	–	UNRWA	–
WFP	0.5	2.0	1.3	2.5	WFP	0.5	2.0	1.3	2.5	WFP	0.5
UNHCR	–	–	–	–	UNHCR	–	–	–	–	UNHCR	–
Other Multilateral	0.2	0.3	0.3	0.8	Other Multilateral	0.2	0.3	0.3	0.8	Other Multilateral	0.2
Arab Agencies	-2.3	-1.9	-2.0	–	Arab Agencies	-0.7	-1.2	-1.2	–	Arab Agencies	–
TOTAL	25.0	50.8	6.7	13.0	TOTAL	12.0	11.2	9.5	12.6	TOTAL	13.2
ARAB COUNTRIES	3.5	3.2	-1.2	0.9	ARAB COUNTRIES	3.5	3.2	-1.2	0.9	ARAB COUNTRIES	5.3
E.E.C.+ MEMBERS	81.3	73.4	94.3	107.7	E.E.C.+ MEMBERS	47.4	44.2	38.0	64.3	E.E.C.+ MEMBERS	53.9
TOTAL	114.0	128.8	114.4	149.9	TOTAL	65.0	59.3	58.3	89.0	TOTAL	75.9
2. ODA LOANS GROSS					**5. ODA LOANS NET**					**8. GRANTS**	
DAC COUNTRIES											
Australia	–	–	–	–	Australia	–	–	–	–	Australia	1.6
Austria	–	–	–	–	Austria	–	–	–	–	Austria	0.0
Belgium	–	–	–	–	Belgium	–	–	–	–	Belgium	0.4
Canada	–	–	–	–	Canada	–	–	–	–	Canada	0.3
Denmark	–	–	–	–	Denmark	–	–	–	–	Denmark	–
Finland	–	–	–	–	Finland	–	–	–	–	Finland	–
France	14.8	20.3	23.1	27.2	France	10.3	16.4	15.6	20.4	France	12.1
Germany	7.6	7.5	3.2	23.6	Germany	7.5	7.1	2.5	22.6	Germany	0.5
Ireland	–	–	–	–	Ireland	–	–	–	–	Ireland	–
Italy	–	–	–	–	Italy	–	–	–	–	Italy	0.2
Japan	3.3	1.0	6.4	0.3	Japan	2.9	0.6	6.0	-0.6	Japan	3.5
Netherlands	–	–	–	–	Netherlands	–	–	–	–	Netherlands	0.1
New Zealand	–	–	–	–	New Zealand	–	–	–	–	New Zealand	–
Norway	–	–	–	–	Norway	–	–	–	–	Norway	0.0
Sweden	–	–	–	–	Sweden	–	–	–	–	Sweden	0.4
Switzerland	–	–	–	–	Switzerland	–	–	–	–	Switzerland	0.0
United Kingdom	2.1	0.6	1.4	0.8	United Kingdom	0.2	-1.5	-0.8	-1.3	United Kingdom	5.6
United States	–	–	–	–	United States	-1.0	-1.0	-1.0	-1.0	United States	5.0
TOTAL	27.8	29.4	34.1	51.9	TOTAL	19.9	21.6	22.3	40.1	TOTAL	29.7
MULTILATERAL	1.9	3.2	2.4	3.0	MULTILATERAL	0.7	1.6	0.6	0.7	MULTILATERAL	11.3
ARAB COUNTRIES	5.3	5.0	0.6	1.6	ARAB COUNTRIES	3.4	3.2	-1.2	0.9	ARAB COUNTRIES	–
E.E.C.+ MEMBERS	26.1	28.8	28.9	52.9	E.E.C.+ MEMBERS	19.6	22.3	18.5	42.9	E.E.C.+ MEMBERS	27.8
TOTAL	34.9	37.6	37.1	56.5	TOTAL	24.1	26.3	21.7	41.6	TOTAL	41.0
3. TOTAL OFFICIAL GROSS					**6. TOTAL OFFICIAL NET**					**9. TOTAL OOF GROSS**	
DAC COUNTRIES											
Australia	1.6	3.1	3.5	4.2	Australia	1.6	3.1	3.5	4.2	Australia	–
Austria	0.0	0.0	0.0	0.0	Austria	0.0	0.0	0.0	0.0	Austria	–
Belgium	0.4	0.1	–	–	Belgium	0.4	0.1	–	–	Belgium	0.0
Canada	0.3	0.3	0.3	0.3	Canada	0.3	0.3	0.3	0.3	Canada	–
Denmark	–	0.0	–	–	Denmark	–	0.0	0.0	–	Denmark	–
Finland	–	0.0	0.0	0.0	Finland	–	0.0	0.0	0.0	Finland	–
France	27.0	35.2	33.7	52.5	France	22.4	31.2	26.1	43.9	France	–
Germany	8.1	8.0	9.2	30.1	Germany	8.0	7.6	8.5	29.0	Germany	–
Ireland	–	–	–	–	Ireland	–	–	–	–	Ireland	–
Italy	0.2	0.6	–	–	Italy	0.2	0.6	–	–	Italy	–
Japan	6.7	3.7	15.5	7.4	Japan	6.4	3.3	15.1	6.5	Japan	–
Netherlands	0.1	0.1	0.1	0.1	Netherlands	0.1	0.1	0.1	0.1	Netherlands	–
New Zealand	–	–	–	–	New Zealand	–	–	–	–	New Zealand	–
Norway	0.0	0.0	0.0	0.0	Norway	0.0	0.0	0.0	0.0	Norway	–
Sweden	0.4	0.1	0.6	5.8	Sweden	0.4	0.1	0.6	5.8	Sweden	–
Switzerland	0.0	0.0	–	–	Switzerland	0.0	0.0	–	–	Switzerland	–
United Kingdom	13.2	11.4	20.0	8.9	United Kingdom	11.1	9.2	17.5	5.8	United Kingdom	5.6
United States	5.0	8.0	3.0	2.0	United States	4.0	7.0	2.0	-4.0	United States	–
TOTAL	63.0	70.5	86.0	111.2	TOTAL	55.0	62.5	73.8	91.7	TOTAL	5.6
MULTILATERAL	43.9	72.7	28.6	34.4	MULTILATERAL	25.0	50.8	6.7	13.0	MULTILATERAL	30.8
ARAB COUNTRIES	5.3	5.0	0.6	1.6	ARAB COUNTRIES	3.5	3.2	-1.2	0.9	ARAB COUNTRIES	–
E.E.C.+ MEMBERS	61.5	70.7	74.8	103.3	E.E.C.+ MEMBERS	53.3	62.5	62.2	88.9	E.E.C.+ MEMBERS	7.6
TOTAL	112.2	148.2	115.2	147.2	TOTAL	83.4	116.5	79.4	105.6	TOTAL	36.3

1988	1989	1990		1987	1988	1989	1990

10. ODA COMMITMENTS

1988	1989	1990		1987	1988	1989	1990
3.1	3.5	4.2		1.1	1.3	4.0	3.0
0.0	0.0	0.0		0.0	0.0	0.0	0.0
0.1	–	–		0.0	0.1	–	–
0.3	0.3	0.3		0.3	0.4	0.1	0.1
–	–	–		–	–	–	–
0.0	0.0	0.0		–	–	0.0	3.1
31.6	33.1	39.1		17.6	35.2	40.7	74.0
8.0	3.8	24.5		12.1	2.3	22.1	0.4
–	–	–		–	–	–	–
0.6	–	–		0.1	0.6	–	0.0
3.7	15.5	7.4		0.5	20.5	9.6	2.9
0.1	0.1	0.1		0.1	0.1	0.1	0.1
–	–	–		–	–	–	–
0.0	0.0	0.0		0.0	–	–	–
0.1	0.6	5.8		0.1	1.0	–	5.9
0.0	–	–		0.0	–	–	–
4.3	4.9	4.0		2.4	4.4	4.6	4.0
1.0	–	2.0		2.5	19.6	2.9	0.1
52.8	61.7	87.4		36.8	85.4	84.1	93.5
–	–	–		–	–	1.2	–
–	–	–		–	–	–	–
–	–	–		–	–	–	–
–	–	–		–	–	–	–
6.1	6.7	6.7		28.1	14.8	1.0	1.0
–	–	–		–	–	–	–
–	–	–		–	–	–	–
2.9	1.2	1.7		–	–	–	–
–	–	–		–	–	–	–
–	–	–		2.3	3.8	3.5	5.1
1.1	1.2	1.0		–	–	–	–
0.2	0.5	0.5		–	–	–	–
0.2	0.3	0.4		–	–	–	–
–	–	–		–	–	–	–
2.0	1.3	2.5		–	–	–	–
–	–	–		–	–	–	–
0.3	0.3	0.8		–	–	–	–
–	–	–		–	–	–	–
12.8	11.3	13.5		30.4	18.6	5.6	6.1
5.0	0.6	1.6		3.6	–	–	–
50.7	48.4	74.4		60.3	57.4	68.5	79.4
70.5	73.6	102.5		70.8	104.1	89.8	99.6

11. TECH. COOP. GRANTS

1988	1989	1990		1987	1988	1989	1990
3.1	3.5	4.2		0.4	0.6	0.9	1.1
0.0	0.0	0.0		0.0	0.0	0.0	0.0
0.1	–	–		0.1	0.0	–	0.0
0.3	0.3	0.3		–	–	–	0.0
–	–	–		–	–	–	–
0.0	0.0	0.0		–	–	–	–
11.2	9.9	11.9		17.3	7.3	7.7	8.9
0.5	0.6	0.9		0.5	0.5	0.6	0.9
–	–	–		–	–	–	–
0.6	–	–		0.2	0.6	–	–
2.7	9.1	7.1		0.5	2.0	3.1	2.9
0.1	0.1	0.1		0.1	0.1	0.1	0.1
–	–	–		–	–	–	–
0.0	0.0	0.0		0.0	0.0	0.0	0.0
0.1	0.6	5.8		–	0.1	0.6	0.3
0.0	–	–		–	0.0	–	–
3.7	3.5	3.2		2.3	3.6	3.4	3.1
1.0	–	2.0		–	–	–	–
23.3	27.7	35.5		21.3	14.9	16.4	17.2
9.6	8.9	10.6		2.1	2.2	2.2	2.7
–	–	–		–	–	–	–
21.9	19.5	21.5		20.6	12.6	11.7	12.8
32.9	36.6	46.1		23.4	17.2	18.5	19.8

12. TOTAL OOF NET

1988	1989	1990		1987	1988	1989	1990
–	–	–		–	–	–	–
–	–	–		0.0	–	–	–
–	–	–		–	–	–	–
0.0	–	–		–	0.0	0.0	–
–	–	–		–	–	–	–
3.6	0.7	13.4		–	3.6	0.6	11.6
–	5.4	5.5		–	–	5.4	5.5
–	–	–		–	–	–	–
–	–	–		–	–	–	–
–	–	–		–	–	–	–
–	–	–		–	–	–	–
–	–	–		–	–	–	–
7.1	15.2	4.9		5.4	7.0	14.8	4.0
7.0	3.0	–		–	7.0	3.0	-5.0
17.7	24.3	23.8		5.4	17.6	23.8	16.2
59.9	17.2	20.8		13.0	39.5	-2.7	0.4
–	–	–		–	–	–	–
20.1	26.4	28.9		5.9	18.3	24.2	24.5
77.6	41.5	44.7		18.3	57.2	21.1	16.6

13. ODF COMMITMENTS: BY PURPOSE %

	1987	1988	1989	1990
Education	0	0	0	–
Health	–	–	0	–
Other Social Infrastr.	1	–	0	–
Water Sanitat. Sewage	3	12	1	–
Energy	9	7	–	–
Telecommunications	2	14	39	–
Transportation	11	2	16	–
Agriculture	1	5	5	–
Extractive Industries	–	–	–	–
Manufacturing	8	1	0	–
Trade Banking Tourism	52	23	12	–
Technical Cooperation	10	30	16	–
Multisector Aid	–	1	2	–
Programme	1	1	3	–
Debt Reorganisation	–	–	–	–
Food Aid	2	5	3	–
Emergency Aid	–	–	–	–
Unspecified	–	–	–	–
TOTAL	100	100	100	–

14. GRANT ELEMENT OF ODA %

DAC COUNTRIES

	1987	1988	1989	1990
Australia	100.0	100.0	100.0	–
Austria	100.0	100.0	100.0	–
Belgium	100.0	100.0	–	–
Canada	100.0	100.0	100.0	–
Denmark	–	–	–	–
Finland	–	–	100.0	–
France	74.6	55.4	46.8	–
Germany	44.7	100.0	37.7	–
Ireland	–	–	–	–
Italy	100.0	100.0	–	–
Japan	100.0	68.8	100.0	–
Netherlands	100.0	100.0	100.0	–
New Zealand	–	–	–	–
Norway	100.0	–	–	–
Sweden	100.0	100.0	–	–
Switzerland	100.0	–	–	–
United Kingdom	100.0	100.0	100.0	–
United States	100.0	100.0	100.0	–
TOTAL	69.7	73.9	55.4	–
MULTILATERAL	100.0	100.0	97.8	–
ARAB COUNTRIES	46.9	–	–	–
E.E.C.+ MEMBERS	80.4	72.3	47.2	–
TOTAL	80.6	78.6	57.6	–

15. OTHER AGGREGATES

OFFICIAL COMMITMENTS:

	1987	1988	1989	1990
TOTAL BILATERAL	70.2	96.1	95.6	125.3
of which:				
Arab Countries	3.6	–	–	–
C.E.E.C.	–	–	–	–
TOTAL MULTILATERAL	118.8	38.9	35.6	24.8
TOTAL BIL.& MULTIL.	189.0	135.1	131.2	150.1
of which:				
ODA Grants	45.8	65.9	36.4	35.8
ODA Loans	25.0	38.1	53.3	63.8

DISBURSEMENTS:

DAC COUNTRIES COMBINED

	1987	1988	1989	1990
OFFICIAL & PRIVATE				
GROSS:				
Contractual Lending	43.3	61.0	64.7	93.3
Export Credits, Total	10.0	17.8	6.4	17.5
Export Credits, Priv.	10.0	13.8	6.4	17.5
NET:				
Contractual Lending	34.5	51.0	46.8	68.1
Export Credits Total	9.3	15.8	0.7	11.8
PRIVATE SECTOR NET	30.6	12.4	35.1	44.4
Direct Investment	23.6	7.4	32.5	15.0
Portfolio Investment	-2.2	-6.8	2.0	17.6
Export Credits	9.3	11.8	0.7	11.8

MARKET BORROWING:

CHANGE IN CLAIMS

	1987	1988	1989	1990
Banks	-8.0	-48.0	27.0	62.0

MEMORANDUM ITEM:

	1987	1988	1989	1990
C.E.E.C. (Gross)	–	–	–	–

DISBURSEMENTS, UNLESS OTHERWISE STAT

	1987	1988	1989	1990		1987	1988	1989	1990			1987

1. TOTAL RECEIPTS NET — DAC COUNTRIES / 4. TOTAL ODA NET — DAC COUNTRIES / 7. TOTAL ODA GROSS

	1987	1988	1989	1990		1987	1988	1989	1990		1987
1. TOTAL RECEIPTS NET					**4. TOTAL ODA NET**					**7. TOTAL ODA GROSS**	
DAC COUNTRIES					**DAC COUNTRIES**						
Australia	-2.6	-3.4	-3.6	-0.2	0.1	0.2	0.2	0.1	Australia	0.1
Austria	-3.6	0.4	0.4	21.6	-0.7	0.4	0.4	0.6	Austria	0.4
Belgium	-619.5	-169.5	76.4	104.1	0.6	0.9	0.6	3.9	Belgium	0.6
Canada	110.2	-6.2	-5.0	72.3	1.7	1.7	1.9	2.4	Canada	1.7
Denmark	-7.1	-10.5	30.1	6.7	–	0.0	0.1	–	Denmark	–
Finland	2.7	0.2	21.2	39.1	0.3	0.7	0.5	0.9	Finland	0.3
France	181.5	-638.4	-552.2	-2329.8	38.0	35.1	12.4	51.1	France	45.4
Germany	214.8	188.3	100.7	420.1	5.3	8.5	10.7	9.3	Germany	21.2
Ireland	–	–	–	–	–	–	–	–	Ireland	–
Italy	5.2	13.2	55.3	103.6	3.0	0.4	1.1	1.5	Italy	3.0
Japan	1425.5	642.7	1980.7	-3416.6	35.0	38.8	25.0	24.1	Japan	35.0
Netherlands	163.8	-10.9	3.0	34.3	3.6	3.4	3.0	5.2	Netherlands	4.3
New Zealand	0.0	0.1	0.1	0.1	0.0	0.1	0.1	0.1	New Zealand	0.0
Norway	0.4	-2.5	-1.8	-12.4	0.0	0.1	0.2	0.2	Norway	0.0
Sweden	-13.5	0.1	-9.7	29.1	0.1	0.1	0.1	0.1	Sweden	0.1
Switzerland	0.4	0.5	0.9	0.9	0.4	0.5	0.9	0.9	Switzerland	0.4
United Kingdom	195.1	58.8	157.6	-81.4	1.0	2.2	2.1	2.0	United Kingdom	1.0
United States	-182.0	-4120.0	1253.0	1041.0	62.0	47.0	18.0	23.0	United States	65.0
TOTAL	*1471.4*	*-4057.1*	*3107.0*	*-3967.5*	*150.3*	*140.1*	*77.2*	*125.2*	*TOTAL*	*178.5*
MULTILATERAL										
AF.D.F.	–	–	–	–	–	–	–	–	AF.D.F.	–
AF.D.B.	–	–	–	–	–	–	–	–	AF.D.B.	–
AS.D.B	–	–	–	–	–	–	–	–	AS.D.B	–
CAR.D.B.	–	–	–	–	–	–	–	–	CAR.D.B.	–
E.E.C.	0.9	5.8	4.5	4.5	0.9	5.8	4.5	4.5	E.E.C.	0.9
IBRD	415.9	674.0	620.0	2525.0	–	–	–	–	IBRD	–
IDA	–	–	–	–	–	–	–	–	IDA	–
I.D.B.	-40.5	81.5	94.2	71.5	-21.0	-5.9	-17.9	-22.1	I.D.B.	3.9
IFAD	2.8	-1.5	-1.3	-0.7	2.8	-1.5	-1.3	-0.7	IFAD	5.7
I.F.C.	3.6	57.3	21.6	219.3	–	–	–	–	I.F.C.	–
IMF TRUST FUND	–	–	–	–	–	–	–	–	IMF TRUST FUND	–
U.N. AGENCIES	–	–	–	–	–	–	–	–	U.N. AGENCIES	–
UNDP	3.3	5.7	1.3	3.6	3.3	5.7	1.3	3.6	UNDP	3.3
UNTA	1.3	1.0	1.3	1.7	1.3	1.0	1.3	1.7	UNTA	1.3
UNICEF	1.9	1.6	2.5	3.7	1.9	1.6	2.5	3.7	UNICEF	1.9
UNRWA	–	–	–	–	–	–	–	–	UNRWA	–
WFP	6.0	16.1	6.4	10.2	6.0	16.1	6.4	10.2	WFP	6.0
UNHCR	7.7	7.4	8.1	8.3	7.7	7.4	8.1	8.3	UNHCR	7.7
Other Multilateral	2.3	2.8	4.1	5.5	2.3	2.8	4.1	5.5	Other Multilateral	2.3
Arab Agencies	–	–	–	–	–	–	–	–	Arab Agencies	–
TOTAL	*405.2*	*851.5*	*762.7*	*2852.6*	*5.2*	*32.8*	*8.9*	*14.7*	*TOTAL*	*33.1*
ARAB COUNTRIES	2.8	–	–	–	–	–	–	–	**ARAB COUNTRIES**	–
E.E.C.+ MEMBERS	*134.9*	*-563.1*	*-124.7*	*-1737.9*	*52.5*	*56.4*	*34.5*	*77.3*	*E.E.C.+ MEMBERS*	*76.5*
TOTAL	**1879.4**	**-3205.5**	**3869.6**	**-1114.9**	**155.5**	**172.9**	**86.1**	**139.8**	**TOTAL**	**211.5**

2. ODA LOANS GROSS — DAC COUNTRIES / 5. ODA LOANS NET — DAC COUNTRIES / 8. GRANTS

	1987	1988	1989	1990		1987	1988	1989	1990		1987
2. ODA LOANS GROSS					**5. ODA LOANS NET**					**8. GRANTS**	
DAC COUNTRIES					**DAC COUNTRIES**						
Australia	–	–	–	–	–	–	–	–	Australia	0.1
Austria	–	–	–	0.0	-1.1	0.0	–	–	Austria	0.4
Belgium	–	–	–	–	–	–	–	–	Belgium	0.6
Canada	–	–	–	–	–	–	–	–	Canada	1.7
Denmark	–	–	–	–	–	–	–	–	Denmark	–
Finland	–	–	–	–	–	-0.1	–	–	Finland	0.3
France	34.1	34.3	12.4	44.2	26.7	24.6	5.0	35.1	France	11.3
Germany	8.8	–	–	–	-7.1	-4.2	-2.0	-5.9	Germany	12.4
Ireland	–	–	–	–	–	–	–	–	Ireland	–
Italy	–	–	–	–	–	-0.5	-1.2	–	Italy	3.0
Japan	17.6	20.9	6.5	–	17.6	20.9	3.9	0.0	Japan	17.4
Netherlands	0.8	–	–	1.2	0.2	-0.3	–	0.8	Netherlands	3.5
New Zealand	–	–	–	–	–	–	–	–	New Zealand	0.0
Norway	–	–	–	–	–	–	–	–	Norway	0.0
Sweden	–	–	–	–	–	–	–	–	Sweden	0.1
Switzerland	–	–	–	–	–	–	–	–	Switzerland	0.4
United Kingdom	–	–	–	–	–	–	–	–	United Kingdom	1.0
United States	–	–	–	–	-3.0	-4.0	-2.0	–	United States	65.0
TOTAL	*61.4*	*55.2*	*18.9*	*45.4*	*33.2*	*36.5*	*3.7*	*30.0*	*TOTAL*	*117.1*
MULTILATERAL	*9.6*	*18.5*	*6.9*	*4.6*	*-18.2*	*-8.3*	*-20.0*	*-23.3*	*MULTILATERAL*	*23.5*
ARAB COUNTRIES	–	–	–	–	–	–	–	–	**ARAB COUNTRIES**	–
E.E.C.+ MEMBERS	*43.8*	*34.3*	*12.4*	*45.4*	*19.7*	*19.6*	*1.8*	*30.0*	*E.E.C.+ MEMBERS*	*32.8*
TOTAL	**71.0**	**73.7**	**25.8**	**50.0**	**15.0**	**28.2**	**-16.3**	**6.8**	**TOTAL**	**140.6**

3. TOTAL OFFICIAL GROSS — DAC COUNTRIES / 6. TOTAL OFFICIAL NET — DAC COUNTRIES / 9. TOTAL OOF GROSS

	1987	1988	1989	1990		1987	1988	1989	1990		1987
3. TOTAL OFFICIAL GROSS					**6. TOTAL OFFICIAL NET**					**9. TOTAL OOF GROSS**	
DAC COUNTRIES					**DAC COUNTRIES**						
Australia	1.3	0.2	0.2	0.1	1.2	0.0	-0.1	-0.2	Australia	1.2
Austria	0.4	0.4	0.4	0.6	-0.7	0.4	0.4	0.6	Austria	–
Belgium	18.4	7.3	2.3	26.9	18.4	7.3	2.3	26.9	Belgium	17.8
Canada	53.0	18.4	54.5	98.8	47.1	-11.0	32.2	79.3	Canada	51.3
Denmark	0.5	0.0	8.2	0.2	0.4	0.0	8.2	0.2	Denmark	0.5
Finland	0.3	0.7	0.5	0.9	0.3	0.7	0.5	0.9	Finland	–
France	150.8	97.1	19.8	61.3	143.4	87.5	12.4	52.2	France	105.4
Germany	117.7	97.2	120.1	157.5	65.5	45.6	86.3	91.3	Germany	96.5
Ireland	–	–	–	–	–	–	–	–	Ireland	–
Italy	48.6	1.0	3.8	17.5	42.2	-1.3	0.7	16.7	Italy	45.6
Japan	515.5	380.3	403.0	1831.2	497.1	174.9	274.9	1745.2	Japan	480.6
Netherlands	5.3	4.0	3.0	22.0	4.6	3.7	3.0	21.6	Netherlands	1.0
New Zealand	0.0	0.1	0.1	0.1	0.0	0.1	0.1	0.1	New Zealand	–
Norway	0.0	0.1	0.2	0.2	0.0	0.1	0.2	0.2	Norway	–
Sweden	0.1	0.1	0.1	0.1	0.1	0.1	0.1	0.1	Sweden	–
Switzerland	0.4	0.5	0.9	0.9	0.4	0.5	0.9	0.9	Switzerland	–
United Kingdom	1.0	2.2	2.1	2.0	1.0	2.2	2.1	2.0	United Kingdom	–
United States	837.0	252.0	29.0	327.0	539.0	44.0	-124.0	122.0	United States	772.0
TOTAL	*1750.3*	*861.6*	*648.1*	*2547.3*	*1359.9*	*354.7*	*300.2*	*2160.0*	*TOTAL*	*1571.8*
MULTILATERAL	*1174.9*	*1845.1*	*1710.2*	*3941.1*	*405.2*	*851.5*	*762.7*	*2852.6*	*MULTILATERAL*	*1141.9*
ARAB COUNTRIES	3.3	–	–	–	2.8	–	–	–	**ARAB COUNTRIES**	3.3
E.E.C.+ MEMBERS	*343.2*	*214.7*	*163.7*	*291.8*	*276.4*	*150.8*	*119.5*	*215.4*	*E.E.C.+ MEMBERS*	*266.7*
TOTAL	**2928.6**	**2706.8**	**2358.4**	**6488.4**	**1768.0**	**1206.2**	**1062.9**	**5012.6**	**TOTAL**	**2717.0**

10. ODA COMMITMENTS

1988	1989	1990	1987	1988	1989	1990
0.2	0.2	0.1	0.1	0.1	0.1	0.1
0.4	0.4	0.6	0.4	0.4	0.4	1.1
0.9	0.6	3.9	3.0	0.7	0.6	3.9
1.7	1.9	2.4	1.5	1.3	2.1	3.0
0.0	0.1	–	–	–	–	–
0.7	0.5	0.9	0.1	0.7	0.2	15.7
44.8	19.7	60.2	40.3	18.5	63.1	33.8
12.7	12.7	15.1	15.5	8.9	18.4	17.6
–	–	–	–	–	–	–
0.9	2.4	1.5	3.0	1.8	2.6	2.4
38.9	27.6	24.1	19.5	27.9	24.7	542.6
3.8	3.0	5.5	4.1	3.7	3.0	6.1
0.1	0.1	0.1	0.0	0.1	–	–
0.1	0.2	0.2	0.0	–	–	–
0.1	0.1	0.1	0.1	0.1	–	0.1
0.5	0.9	0.9	0.2	0.3	0.7	0.5
2.2	2.1	2.0	1.0	2.2	2.1	2.0
51.0	20.0	23.0	52.6	17.7	22.1	18.7
158.8	*92.5*	*140.5*	*141.4*	*84.5*	*140.4*	*647.6*
–	–	–	–	–	–	–
–	–	–	–	–	–	–
–	–	–	–	–	–	–
5.8	4.5	4.5	0.5	2.2	10.4	10.4
–	–	–	–	–	–	–
19.4	7.6	3.6	–	–	–	–
–	–	1.5	–	–	–	30.8
–	–	–	–	–	–	–
–	–	–	22.5	34.5	23.7	33.0
5.7	1.3	3.6	–	–	–	–
1.0	1.3	1.7	–	–	–	–
1.6	2.5	3.7	–	–	–	–
–	–	–	–	–	–	–
16.1	6.4	10.2	–	–	–	–
7.4	8.1	8.3	–	–	–	–
2.8	4.1	5.5	–	–	–	–
–	–	–	–	–	–	–
59.6	*35.8*	*42.5*	*22.9*	*36.6*	*34.1*	*74.2*
–	–	–	–	–	–	–
71.0	*45.1*	*92.6*	*67.4*	*38.1*	*100.3*	*76.2*
218.4	**128.2**	**183.0**	**164.3**	**121.1**	**174.5**	**721.8**

11. TECH. COOP. GRANTS

1988	1989	1990	1987	1988	1989	1990
0.2	0.2	0.1	0.0	0.1	0.0	0.0
0.4	0.4	0.6	0.4	0.4	0.4	0.5
0.9	0.6	3.9	0.6	0.1	0.2	0.1
1.7	1.9	2.4	–	–	–	–
0.0	0.1	–	–	0.0	–	–
0.7	0.5	0.9	0.3	0.3	0.1	0.3
10.5	7.3	16.0	10.7	10.5	9.8	16.0
12.7	12.7	15.1	12.0	12.4	11.1	13.4
–	–	–	–	–	–	–
0.9	2.4	1.5	2.1	0.8	1.9	1.5
17.9	21.1	24.1	17.1	16.7	16.6	18.2
3.8	3.0	4.4	2.6	3.5	2.7	3.1
0.1	0.1	0.1	0.0	0.1	–	0.1
0.1	0.2	0.2	0.0	–	–	–
0.1	0.1	0.1	0.1	0.1	0.1	0.1
0.5	0.9	0.9	0.2	0.1	–	–
2.2	2.1	2.0	1.0	2.2	2.0	2.0
51.0	20.0	23.0	2.0	3.0	4.0	3.0
103.6	*73.6*	*95.1*	*49.0*	*50.2*	*49.0*	*58.3*
41.1	*28.9*	*37.9*	*16.9*	*19.0*	*17.3*	*22.8*
–	–	–	–	–	–	–
36.7	*32.7*	*47.2*	*29.3*	*30.2*	*27.8*	*36.0*
144.7	**102.4**	**133.1**	**65.9**	**69.2**	**66.3**	**81.1**

12. TOTAL OOF NET

1988	1989	1990	1987	1988	1989	1990
–	–	–	1.1	-0.2	-0.2	-0.2
–	–	–	–	–	–	–
6.4	1.7	23.0	17.8	6.4	1.7	23.0
16.8	52.6	96.4	45.5	-12.7	30.3	76.9
–	8.1	0.2	0.4	–	8.1	0.2
–	–	–	–	–	–	–
52.3	0.0	1.1	105.4	52.3	0.0	1.1
84.6	107.4	142.4	60.2	37.1	75.6	82.1
–	–	–	–	–	–	–
0.1	1.4	16.0	39.2	-1.7	-0.4	15.2
341.4	375.4	1807.1	462.2	136.1	249.9	1721.1
0.3	–	16.5	1.0	0.3	–	16.5
–	–	–	–	–	–	–
–	–	–	–	–	–	–
–	–	–	–	–	–	–
–	–	–	–	–	–	–
201.0	9.0	304.0	477.0	-3.0	-142.0	99.0
702.8	*555.7*	*2406.8*	*1209.6*	*214.6*	*223.0*	*2034.9*
1785.5	*1674.5*	*3898.6*	*400.0*	*818.7*	*753.8*	*2837.9*
			2.8	–	–	–
143.7	*118.7*	*199.3*	*223.9*	*94.4*	*85.0*	*138.1*
2488.3	**2230.1**	**6305.3**	**1612.4**	**1033.3**	**976.8**	**4872.8**

13. ODF COMMITMENTS: BY PURPOSE %

	1987	1988	1989	1990
Education	2	–	0	–
Health	0	–	0	–
Other Social Infrastr.	0	18	0	–
Water Sanitat. Sewage	–	–	0	–
Energy	–	–	9	–
Telecommunications	0	1	7	–
Transportation	7	–	1	–
Agriculture	11	38	4	–
Extractive Industries	19	–	–	–
Manufacturing	0	39	0	–
Trade Banking Tourism	37	–	35	–
Technical Cooperation	2	4	1	–
Multisector Aid	–	–	–	–
Programme	20	–	40	–
Debt Reorganisation	0	–	3	–
Food Aid	1	–	0	–
Emergency Aid	0	0	0	–
Unspecified	–	–	–	–
TOTAL	100	100	100	–

14. GRANT ELEMENT OF ODA %

DAC COUNTRIES

	1987	1988	1989	1990
Australia	100.0	100.0	100.0	–
Austria	100.0	100.0	100.0	–
Belgium	100.0	100.0	100.0	–
Canada	100.0	100.0	100.0	–
Denmark	–	–	–	–
Finland	100.0	100.0	100.0	–
France	77.0	75.6	79.6	–
Germany	100.0	100.0	100.0	–
Ireland	–	–	–	–
Italy	100.0	100.0	100.0	–
Japan	100.0	100.0	78.8	–
Netherlands	91.7	100.0	100.0	–
New Zealand	100.0	100.0	–	–
Norway	100.0	–	–	–
Sweden	100.0	100.0	–	–
Switzerland	100.0	100.0	100.0	–
United Kingdom	100.0	100.0	100.0	–
United States	100.0	100.0	100.0	–
TOTAL	*93.4*	*92.7*	*89.6*	–
MULTILATERAL	*100.0*	*100.0*	*100.0*	–
ARAB COUNTRIES	–	–	–	–
E.E.C.+ MEMBERS	*85.9*	*85.6*	*91.2*	–
TOTAL	**94.3**	**94.7**	**92.1**	–

15. OTHER AGGREGATES

	1987	1988	1989	1990
OFFICIAL COMMITMENTS:				
TOTAL BILATERAL	2388.5	526.5	3321.3	1776.2
of which:				
Arab Countries	5.9	–	–	–
C.E.E.C.	–	–	–	–
TOTAL MULTILATERAL	1990.3	1706.7	2992.7	3861.3
TOTAL BIL.& MULTIL.	4378.9	2233.2	6314.0	5637.5
of which:				
ODA Grants	133.9	113.1	114.7	150.8
ODA Loans	30.5	8.0	59.8	571.0
DISBURSEMENTS:				
DAC COUNTRIES COMBINED				
OFFICIAL & PRIVATE				
GROSS:				
Contractual Lending	2798.5	2215.4	3433.7	4811.1
Export Credits, Total	1468.9	1833.2	3099.6	2659.3
Export Credits, Priv.	1168.2	1460.0	2861.3	2358.7
NET:				
Contractual Lending	1536.2	805.6	1404.8	2600.5
Export Credits Total	250.3	443.4	1093.2	484.1
PRIVATE SECTOR NET	111.4	-4411.7	2806.8	-6127.5
Direct Investment	545.7	811.9	1236.3	2353.8
Portfolio Investment	-730.4	-5780.8	390.2	-9016.7
Export Credits	296.2	557.2	1180.3	535.4
MARKET BORROWING:				
CHANGE IN CLAIMS				
Banks	-376.0	-3574.0	-617.0	-15324.0
MEMORANDUM ITEM:				
C.E.E.C. (Gross)	–	–	1.0	–

1. TOTAL RECEIPTS NET

DAC COUNTRIES	1987	1988	1989	1990
Australia	–	–	–	–
Austria	–	–	–	–
Belgium	–	–	–	–
Canada	0.2	0.2	0.1	0.3
Denmark	–	–	–	–
Finland	–	–	–	–
France	1.0	–	–	–
Germany	–	–	–	–
Ireland	–	–	–	–
Italy	-0.2	–	–	–
Japan	–	–	–	–
Netherlands	–	–	–	–
New Zealand	–	–	–	–
Norway	–	–	–	–
Sweden	–	–	–	–
Switzerland	–	–	–	–
United Kingdom	2.2	4.1	6.6	7.6
United States	–	–	–	–
TOTAL	3.1	4.2	6.8	7.8
MULTILATERAL				
AF.D.F.	–	–	–	–
AF.D.B.	–	–	–	–
AS.D.B	–	–	–	–
CAR.D.B.	0.0	0.2	0.2	0.2
E.E.C.	1.2	1.4	0.0	0.0
IBRD	–	–	–	–
IDA	–	–	–	–
I.D.B.	–	–	–	–
IFAD	–	–	–	–
I.F.C.	–	–	–	–
IMF TRUST FUND	–	–	–	–
U.N. AGENCIES	–	–	–	–
UNDP	0.2	0.0	0.1	0.4
UNTA	–	–	–	–
UNICEF	–	–	–	–
UNRWA	–	–	–	–
WFP	–	–	–	–
UNHCR	–	–	–	–
Other Multilateral	0.0	–	0.0	0.0
Arab Agencies	–	–	–	–
TOTAL	1.4	1.6	0.3	0.6
ARAB COUNTRIES	–	–	–	–
E.E.C.+ MEMBERS	4.1	5.4	6.7	7.6
TOTAL	4.5	5.8	7.1	8.4

2. ODA LOANS GROSS

DAC COUNTRIES	1987	1988	1989	1990
Australia	–	–	–	–
Austria	–	–	–	–
Belgium	–	–	–	–
Canada	–	–	–	–
Denmark	–	–	–	–
Finland	–	–	–	–
France	–	–	–	–
Germany	–	–	–	–
Ireland	–	–	–	–
Italy	–	–	–	–
Japan	–	–	–	–
Netherlands	–	–	–	–
New Zealand	–	–	–	–
Norway	–	–	–	–
Sweden	–	–	–	–
Switzerland	–	–	–	–
United Kingdom	–	–	–	–
United States	–	–	–	–
TOTAL	–	–	–	–
MULTILATERAL	0.1	0.2	0.3	0.3
ARAB COUNTRIES	–	–	–	–
E.E.C.+ MEMBERS	0.1	0.1	0.1	0.1
TOTAL	0.1	0.2	0.3	0.3

3. TOTAL OFFICIAL GROSS

DAC COUNTRIES	1987	1988	1989	1990
Australia	–	–	–	–
Austria	–	–	–	–
Belgium	–	–	–	–
Canada	0.2	0.2	0.1	0.3
Denmark	–	–	–	–
Finland	–	–	–	–
France	–	–	–	–
Germany	–	–	–	–
Ireland	–	–	–	–
Italy	–	–	–	–
Japan	–	–	–	–
Netherlands	–	–	–	–
New Zealand	–	–	–	–
Norway	–	–	–	–
Sweden	–	–	–	–
Switzerland	–	–	–	–
United Kingdom	2.2	4.1	6.6	7.6
United States	–	–	–	–
TOTAL	2.3	4.3	6.8	7.8
MULTILATERAL	1.4	1.6	0.3	0.7
ARAB COUNTRIES	–	–	–	–
E.E.C.+ MEMBERS	3.3	5.5	6.7	7.6
TOTAL	3.8	5.8	7.1	8.5

4. TOTAL ODA NET

DAC COUNTRIES	1987	1988	1989	1990
Australia	–	–	–	–
Austria	–	–	–	–
Belgium	–	–	–	–
Canada	0.2	0.2	0.1	0.3
Denmark	–	–	–	–
Finland	–	–	–	–
France	–	–	–	–
Germany	–	–	–	–
Ireland	–	–	–	–
Italy	–	–	–	–
Japan	–	–	–	–
Netherlands	–	–	–	–
New Zealand	–	–	–	–
Norway	–	–	–	–
Sweden	–	–	–	–
Switzerland	–	–	–	–
United Kingdom	2.2	4.1	6.6	7.6
United States	–	–	–	–
TOTAL	2.3	4.2	6.8	7.8
MULTILATERAL				
AF.D.F.	–	–	–	–
AF.D.B.	–	–	–	–
AS.D.B	–	–	–	–
CAR.D.B.	0.0	0.2	0.2	0.2
E.E.C.	0.9	1.2	0.1	0.1
IBRD	–	–	–	–
IDA	–	–	–	–
I.D.B.	–	–	–	–
IFAD	–	–	–	–
I.F.C.	–	–	–	–
IMF TRUST FUND	–	–	–	–
U.N. AGENCIES	–	–	–	–
UNDP	0.2	0.0	0.1	0.4
UNTA	–	–	–	–
UNICEF	–	–	–	–
UNRWA	–	–	–	–
WFP	–	–	–	–
UNHCR	–	–	–	–
Other Multilateral	0.0	–	0.0	0.0
Arab Agencies	–	–	–	–
TOTAL	1.1	1.4	0.3	0.7
ARAB COUNTRIES	–	–	–	–
E.E.C.+ MEMBERS	3.0	5.3	6.7	7.6
TOTAL	3.4	5.7	7.1	8.5

5. ODA LOANS NET

DAC COUNTRIES	1987	1988	1989	1990
Australia	–	–	–	–
Austria	–	–	–	–
Belgium	–	–	–	–
Canada	0.0	0.0	0.0	0.0
Denmark	–	–	–	–
Finland	–	–	–	–
France	–	–	–	–
Germany	–	–	–	–
Ireland	–	–	–	–
Italy	–	–	–	–
Japan	–	–	–	–
Netherlands	–	–	–	–
New Zealand	–	–	–	–
Norway	–	–	–	–
Sweden	–	–	–	–
Switzerland	–	–	–	–
United Kingdom	–	0.0	–	–
United States	–	–	–	–
TOTAL	0.0	0.0	0.0	0.0
MULTILATERAL	0.1	0.2	0.3	0.3
ARAB COUNTRIES	–	–	–	–
E.E.C.+ MEMBERS	0.1	0.1	0.1	0.1
TOTAL	0.1	0.2	0.2	0.2

6. TOTAL OFFICIAL NET

DAC COUNTRIES	1987	1988	1989	1990
Australia	–	–	–	–
Austria	–	–	–	–
Belgium	–	–	–	–
Canada	0.2	0.2	0.1	0.3
Denmark	–	–	–	–
Finland	–	–	–	–
France	–	–	–	–
Germany	–	–	–	–
Ireland	–	–	–	–
Italy	–	–	–	–
Japan	–	–	–	–
Netherlands	–	–	–	–
New Zealand	–	–	–	–
Norway	–	–	–	–
Sweden	–	–	–	–
Switzerland	–	–	–	–
United Kingdom	2.2	4.1	6.6	7.6
United States	–	–	–	–
TOTAL	2.3	4.2	6.8	7.8
MULTILATERAL	1.4	1.6	0.3	0.6
ARAB COUNTRIES	–	–	–	–
E.E.C.+ MEMBERS	3.3	5.4	6.7	7.6
TOTAL	3.7	5.8	7.1	8.4

7. TOTAL ODA GROSS

	1987
Australia	–
Austria	–
Belgium	–
Canada	0.2
Denmark	–
Finland	–
France	–
Germany	–
Ireland	–
Italy	–
Japan	–
Netherlands	–
New Zealand	–
Norway	–
Sweden	–
Switzerland	–
United Kingdom	2.2
United States	–
TOTAL	2.3
AF.D.F.	–
AF.D.B.	–
AS.D.B	–
CAR.D.B.	0.0
E.E.C.	0.9
IBRD	–
IDA	–
I.D.B.	–
IFAD	–
I.F.C.	–
IMF TRUST FUND	–
U.N. AGENCIES	–
UNDP	0.2
UNTA	–
UNICEF	–
UNRWA	–
WFP	–
UNHCR	–
Other Multilateral	0.0
Arab Agencies	–
TOTAL	1.1
ARAB COUNTRIES	–
E.E.C.+ MEMBERS	3.0
TOTAL	3.4

8. GRANTS

	1987
Australia	–
Austria	–
Belgium	–
Canada	0.2
Denmark	–
Finland	–
France	–
Germany	–
Ireland	–
Italy	–
Japan	–
Netherlands	–
New Zealand	–
Norway	–
Sweden	–
Switzerland	–
United Kingdom	2.2
United States	–
TOTAL	2.3
MULTILATERAL	1.0
ARAB COUNTRIES	–
E.E.C.+ MEMBERS	3.0
TOTAL	3.3

9. TOTAL OOF GROSS

	1987
Australia	–
Austria	–
Belgium	–
Canada	–
Denmark	–
Finland	–
France	–
Germany	–
Ireland	–
Italy	–
Japan	–
Netherlands	–
New Zealand	–
Norway	–
Sweden	–
Switzerland	–
United Kingdom	–
United States	–
TOTAL	–
MULTILATERAL	0.3
ARAB COUNTRIES	–
E.E.C.+ MEMBERS	0.3
TOTAL	0.3

10. ODA COMMITMENTS

1988	1989	1990	1987	1988	1989	1990
–	–	–	–	–	–	–
–	–	–	–	–	–	–
0.2	0.1	0.3	0.2	3.2	0.3	0.3
–	–	–	–	–	–	–
–	–	–	–	–	–	–
–	–	–	–	–	–	–
–	–	–	–	–	–	–
–	–	–	–	–	–	–
–	–	–	–	–	–	–
–	–	–	–	–	–	–
–	–	–	–	–	–	–
–	–	–	–	–	–	–
–	–	–	–	–	–	–
4.1	6.6	7.6	2.2	4.1	6.6	3.8
–	–	–	–	–	–	–
4.3	*6.8*	*7.8*	*2.3*	*7.2*	*6.9*	*4.0*

1988	1989	1990	1987	1988	1989	1990
–	–	–	–	–	–	–
–	–	–	–	–	–	–
0.2	0.2	0.2	–	0.6	1.6	1.6
1.2	0.1	0.1	1.7	0.6	–	–
–	–	–	–	–	–	–
–	–	–	–	–	–	–
–	–	–	–	–	–	–
–	–	–	0.2	0.0	0.1	0.4
0.0	0.1	0.4	–	–	–	–
–	–	–	–	–	–	–
–	–	–	–	–	–	–
–	–	–	–	–	–	–
–	0.0	0.0	–	–	–	–
–	–	–	–	–	–	–
1.4	*0.3*	*0.7*	*1.9*	*1.2*	*1.7*	*2.1*
–	–	–	–	–	–	–
5.3	*6.7*	*7.6*	*3.9*	*4.7*	*6.6*	*3.8*
5.7	*7.1*	*8.5*	*4.2*	*8.5*	*8.6*	*6.1*

11. TECH. COOP. GRANTS

1988	1989	1990	1987	1988	1989	1990
–	–	–	–	–	–	–
–	–	–	–	–	–	–
0.2	0.1	0.3	–	0.4	0.1	0.2
–	–	–	–	–	–	–
–	–	–	–	–	–	–
–	–	–	–	–	–	–
–	–	–	–	–	–	–
–	–	–	–	–	–	–
–	–	–	–	–	–	–
–	–	–	–	–	–	–
–	–	–	–	–	–	–
–	–	–	–	–	–	–
4.1	6.6	7.6	0.5	0.9	1.3	3.8
–	–	–	–	–	–	–
4.3	*6.8*	*7.8*	*0.5*	*1.3*	*1.5*	*4.0*
1.2	0.1	0.4	0.2	0.0	0.1	0.4
–	–	–	–	–	–	–
5.2	6.6	7.6	0.5	0.9	1.3	3.8
5.5	*6.9*	*8.2*	*0.7*	*1.3*	*1.5*	*4.4*

12. TOTAL OOF NET

1988	1989	1990	1987	1988	1989	1990
–	–	–	–	–	–	–
–	–	–	–	–	–	–
–	–	–	–	–	–	–
–	–	–	–	–	–	–
–	–	–	–	–	–	–
–	–	–	–	–	–	–
–	–	–	–	–	–	–
–	–	–	–	–	–	–
–	–	–	–	–	–	–
–	–	–	–	–	–	–
–	–	–	–	–	–	–
–	–	–	–	–	–	–
–	–	–	–	–	–	–
–	–	–	–	–	–	–
–	–	–	–	–	–	–
–	–	–	–	–	–	–
–	–	–	–	–	–	–
–	–	–	–	–	–	–
0.2	–	–	0.3	0.1	0.0	0.0
–	–	–	–	–	–	–
0.2	–	–	0.3	0.1	0.0	0.0
0.2	*–*	*–*	*0.3*	*0.1*	*0.0*	*0.0*

13. ODF COMMITMENTS: BY PURPOSE %

	1987	1988	1989	1990
Education	–	–	–	–
Health	–	–	–	–
Other Social Infrastr.	–	–	–	–
Water Sanitat. Sewage	–	–	–	–
Energy	–	–	–	–
Telecommunications	–	–	–	–
Transportation	–	–	13	–
Agriculture	–	43	–	–
Extractive Industries	–	–	–	–
Manufacturing	–	–	–	–
Trade Banking Tourism	–	–	–	–
Technical Cooperation	36	13	87	–
Multisector Aid	64	44	–	–
Programme	–	–	–	–
Debt Reorganisation	–	–	–	–
Food Aid	–	–	–	–
Emergency Aid	–	–	–	–
Unspecified	–	–	–	–
TOTAL	100	100	100	–

14. GRANT ELEMENT OF ODA %

DAC COUNTRIES

	1987	1988	1989	1990
Australia	–	–	–	–
Austria	–	–	–	–
Belgium	–	–	–	–
Canada	100.0	100.0	100.0	–
Denmark	–	–	–	–
Finland	–	–	–	–
France	–	–	–	–
Germany	–	–	–	–
Ireland	–	–	–	–
Italy	–	–	–	–
Japan	–	–	–	–
Netherlands	–	–	–	–
New Zealand	–	–	–	–
Norway	–	–	–	–
Sweden	–	–	–	–
Switzerland	–	–	–	–
United Kingdom	100.0	100.0	100.0	–
United States	–	–	–	–
TOTAL	*100.0*	*100.0*	*100.0*	*–*
MULTILATERAL	*100.0*	*100.0*	*100.0*	*–*
ARAB COUNTRIES	**–**	**–**	**–**	**–**
E.E.C.+ MEMBERS	*100.0*	*100.0*	*100.0*	*–*
TOTAL	**100.0**	**100.0**	**100.0**	**–**

15. OTHER AGGREGATES

OFFICIAL COMMITMENTS:

	1987	1988	1989	1990
TOTAL BILATERAL	2.3	7.2	6.9	4.0
of which:				
Arab Countries	–	–	–	–
C.E.E.C.	–	–	–	–
TOTAL MULTILATERAL	1.9	1.2	1.7	2.1
TOTAL BIL.& MULTIL.	4.2	8.5	8.6	6.1
of which:				
ODA Grants	4.2	8.0	7.1	4.6
ODA Loans	–	0.5	1.5	1.5

DISBURSEMENTS:

DAC COUNTRIES COMBINED

	1987	1988	1989	1990
OFFICIAL & PRIVATE				
GROSS:				
Contractual Lending	–	–	–	–
Export Credits, Total	–	–	–	–
Export Credits, Priv.	–	–	–	–
NET:				
Contractual Lending	0.0	0.0	0.0	0.0
Export Credits Total	–	–	–	–
PRIVATE SECTOR NET	0.8	–	–	–
Direct Investment	–	–	–	–
Portfolio Investment	0.8	–	–	–
Export Credits	–	–	–	–

MARKET BORROWING:

CHANGE IN CLAIMS

	1987	1988	1989	1990
Banks	–	–	–	–

MEMORANDUM ITEM:

	1987	1988	1989	1990
C.E.E.C. (Gross)	–	–	–	–

1. TOTAL RECEIPTS NET

DAC COUNTRIES	1987	1988	1989	1990
Australia	–	–	–	–
Austria	0.1	0.1	-0.3	-0.3
Belgium	-13.4	9.3	8.6	-25.8
Canada	12.6	66.0	80.2	91.8
Denmark	2.0	-0.1	13.5	12.5
Finland	–	–	0.0	0.2
France	64.1	63.1	68.3	114.4
Germany	37.4	90.1	104.6	76.9
Ireland	–	–	–	–
Italy	38.5	60.0	124.7	136.5
Japan	52.6	37.1	-7.2	117.2
Netherlands	-2.4	1.2	6.4	8.2
New Zealand	–	–	–	–
Norway	0.0	1.9	0.5	0.0
Sweden	-1.6	–	17.2	9.5
Switzerland	0.1	1.2	0.5	1.6
United Kingdom	7.4	-39.6	170.0	18.4
United States	130.0	264.0	225.0	12.0
TOTAL	327.3	554.2	811.9	573.0
MULTILATERAL				
AF.D.F.	0.4	1.9	1.1	0.2
AF.D.B.	59.4	133.4	163.3	170.7
AS.D.B	–	–	–	–
CAR.D.B.	–	–	–	–
E.E.C.	22.6	8.2	26.6	26.6
IBRD	241.0	227.0	183.0	224.0
IDA	-0.7	-1.0	-1.0	-1.0
I.D.B.	–	–	–	–
IFAD	2.5	-2.2	-0.8	5.8
I.F.C.	27.7	-4.1	-7.2	92.2
IMF TRUST FUND	–	–	–	–
U.N. AGENCIES	–	–	–	–
UNDP	2.4	3.5	4.5	6.9
UNTA	1.1	1.1	1.6	1.5
UNICEF	1.7	1.6	3.7	2.6
UNRWA	–	–	–	–
WFP	11.4	21.8	28.8	25.8
UNHCR	–	0.1	0.1	0.1
Other Multilateral	1.9	3.3	2.9	2.7
Arab Agencies	-29.7	12.7	26.0	–
TOTAL	341.7	407.2	432.3	557.9
ARAB COUNTRIES	67.4	21.8	8.2	358.7
E.E.C.+ MEMBERS	156.2	192.2	522.5	367.6
TOTAL	736.4	983.2	1252.5	1489.6

2. ODA LOANS GROSS

DAC COUNTRIES	1987	1988	1989	1990
Australia	–	–	–	–
Austria	–	–	–	–
Belgium	–	2.6	–	–
Canada	0.0	8.5	16.0	14.5
Denmark	–	–	–	–
Finland	–	–	–	–
France	138.9	71.8	105.7	132.3
Germany	27.3	65.0	69.1	49.1
Ireland	–	–	–	–
Italy	0.0	12.7	1.1	32.1
Japan	12.8	10.3	11.7	89.8
Netherlands	0.5	0.3	–	–
New Zealand	–	–	–	–
Norway	–	–	–	–
Sweden	–	–	–	–
Switzerland	0.0	0.8	0.5	1.4
United Kingdom	–	–	–	–
United States	40.0	42.0	48.0	35.0
TOTAL	219.6	213.9	252.1	354.1
MULTILATERAL	15.4	29.7	26.1	35.2
ARAB COUNTRIES	62.0	35.6	18.9	19.7
E.E.C.+ MEMBERS	166.8	152.3	175.9	213.5
TOTAL	297.0	279.2	297.2	409.0

3. TOTAL OFFICIAL GROSS

DAC COUNTRIES	1987	1988	1989	1990
Australia	–	–	0.1	0.2
Austria	0.1	0.1	0.1	0.2
Belgium	10.5	12.1	4.9	4.8
Canada	14.2	66.9	83.3	75.1
Denmark	0.5	0.1	13.7	13.2
Finland	–	–	0.0	0.2
France	303.5	215.5	281.9	301.5
Germany	47.9	83.1	93.2	72.1
Ireland	–	–	–	–
Italy	102.8	85.3	152.4	177.6
Japan	25.3	43.7	25.7	111.6
Netherlands	0.6	1.2	0.7	8.8
New Zealand	–	–	–	–
Norway	–	0.5	0.3	–
Sweden	–	–	6.2	2.3
Switzerland	0.1	1.2	0.5	1.6
United Kingdom	0.3	1.2	0.8	18.7
United States	98.0	214.0	221.0	67.0
TOTAL	603.8	724.8	884.7	854.6
MULTILATERAL	636.8	758.9	752.7	841.7
ARAB COUNTRIES	90.9	48.6	33.2	369.8
E.E.C.+ MEMBERS	492.9	411.5	580.4	629.5
TOTAL	1331.4	1532.3	1670.6	2066.1

4. TOTAL ODA NET

	1987	1988	1989	1990
Australia	–	–	–	–
Austria	0.1	0.1	-0.3	-0.3
Belgium	4.2	6.2	1.9	3.1
Canada	5.9	35.5	29.1	30.3
Denmark	-0.1	-0.1	10.6	12.7
Finland	–	–	0.0	0.2
France	189.2	156.5	157.4	217.5
Germany	36.4	81.5	83.1	71.1
Ireland	–	–	–	–
Italy	7.8	21.8	8.2	36.1
Japan	20.4	28.1	23.0	111.4
Netherlands	0.6	1.2	0.7	0.5
New Zealand	–	–	–	–
Norway	–	–	–	–
Sweden	–	–	6.2	2.3
Switzerland	0.1	1.2	0.5	1.6
United Kingdom	0.3	1.2	0.8	18.7
United States	85.0	69.0	68.0	57.0
TOTAL	350.0	402.2	389.1	562.1
AF.D.F.	0.4	1.9	1.1	0.2
AF.D.B.	–	–	–	–
AS.D.B	–	–	–	–
CAR.D.B.	–	–	–	–
E.E.C.	9.6	2.8	4.5	4.5
IBRD	–	–	–	–
IDA	-0.7	-1.0	-1.0	-1.0
I.D.B.	–	–	–	–
IFAD	2.5	-2.2	-0.8	5.8
I.F.C.	–	–	–	–
IMF TRUST FUND	–	–	–	–
U.N. AGENCIES	–	–	–	–
UNDP	2.4	3.5	4.5	6.9
UNTA	1.1	1.1	1.6	1.5
UNICEF	1.7	1.6	3.7	2.6
UNRWA	–	–	–	–
WFP	11.4	21.8	28.8	25.8
UNHCR	–	0.1	0.1	0.1
Other Multilateral	1.9	3.3	2.9	2.7
Arab Agencies	5.5	24.4	18.3	–
TOTAL	35.8	57.2	63.6	49.1
ARAB COUNTRIES	61.5	21.4	-2.4	358.7
E.E.C.+ MEMBERS	248.1	271.1	267.1	364.1
TOTAL	447.2	480.7	450.3	969.9

5. ODA LOANS NET

	1987	1988	1989	1990
Australia	–	–	–	–
Austria	–	0.0	-0.4	-0.5
Belgium	–	2.6	–	–
Canada	-0.1	8.5	16.0	14.5
Denmark	-0.1	-0.1	-0.1	0.0
Finland	–	–	–	–
France	105.7	68.3	77.7	106.0
Germany	22.5	64.7	65.4	49.1
Ireland	–	–	–	–
Italy	0.0	12.7	1.1	32.1
Japan	9.2	10.2	9.0	89.6
Netherlands	0.5	0.3	–	–
New Zealand	–	–	–	–
Norway	–	–	–	–
Sweden	–	–	–	–
Switzerland	0.0	0.8	0.5	1.4
United Kingdom	–	–	–	–
United States	38.0	23.0	19.0	25.0
TOTAL	175.7	190.8	188.1	317.1
MULTILATERAL	7.6	22.2	16.5	26.7
ARAB COUNTRIES	49.4	10.8	-5.8	8.6
E.E.C.+ MEMBERS	128.6	148.4	143.4	186.5
TOTAL	232.7	223.8	198.8	352.4

6. TOTAL OFFICIAL NET

	1987	1988	1989	1990
Australia	–	–	-0.3	-0.3
Austria	0.1	0.1	-0.3	-0.3
Belgium	10.2	11.7	4.5	4.8
Canada	12.6	66.0	80.2	71.7
Denmark	0.4	-0.1	13.5	12.8
Finland	–	–	0.0	0.2
France	187.9	187.1	202.3	223.3
Germany	38.7	80.6	82.4	70.2
Ireland	–	–	–	–
Italy	97.3	79.1	146.9	142.0
Japan	21.0	43.5	22.7	110.7
Netherlands	0.6	1.2	0.7	8.8
New Zealand	–	–	–	–
Norway	–	0.5	0.3	0.0
Sweden	–	–	6.2	2.3
Switzerland	0.1	1.2	0.5	1.6
United Kingdom	0.3	1.2	0.8	18.7
United States	75.0	162.0	43.0	42.0
TOTAL	444.3	634.2	603.5	708.8
MULTILATERAL	341.7	407.2	432.3	557.9
ARAB COUNTRIES	67.4	21.8	8.2	358.7
E.E.C.+ MEMBERS	358.1	369.0	477.5	507.2
TOTAL	853.3	1063.1	1044.1	1625.4

7. TOTAL ODA GROSS

	1987
Australia	–
Austria	0.1
Belgium	4.2
Canada	6.0
Denmark	–
Finland	–
France	222.5
Germany	41.3
Ireland	–
Italy	7.8
Japan	24.0
Netherlands	0.6
New Zealand	–
Norway	–
Sweden	–
Switzerland	0.1
United Kingdom	0.3
United States	87.0
TOTAL	393.8
AF.D.F.	0.4
AF.D.B.	–
AS.D.B	–
CAR.D.B.	–
E.E.C.	9.6
IBRD	–
IDA	–
I.D.B.	–
IFAD	4.9
I.F.C.	–
IMF TRUST FUND	–
U.N. AGENCIES	–
UNDP	2.4
UNTA	1.1
UNICEF	1.7
UNRWA	–
WFP	11.4
UNHCR	–
Other Multilateral	1.9
Arab Agencies	10.1
TOTAL	43.6
ARAB COUNTRIES	74.1
E.E.C.+ MEMBERS	286.3
TOTAL	511.5

8. GRANTS

	1987
Australia	–
Austria	0.1
Belgium	4.2
Canada	6.0
Denmark	–
Finland	–
France	83.6
Germany	14.0
Ireland	–
Italy	7.8
Japan	11.3
Netherlands	0.2
New Zealand	–
Norway	–
Sweden	–
Switzerland	0.1
United Kingdom	0.3
United States	47.0
TOTAL	174.3
MULTILATERAL	28.1
ARAB COUNTRIES	12.1
E.E.C.+ MEMBERS	119.6
TOTAL	214.6

9. TOTAL OOF GROSS

	1987
Australia	–
Austria	–
Belgium	6.4
Canada	8.2
Denmark	0.5
Finland	–
France	81.0
Germany	6.6
Ireland	–
Italy	95.0
Japan	1.3
Netherlands	–
New Zealand	–
Norway	–
Sweden	–
Switzerland	–
United Kingdom	–
United States	11.0
TOTAL	210.0
MULTILATERAL	593.2
ARAB COUNTRIES	16.7
E.E.C.+ MEMBERS	206.6
TOTAL	819.9

1988	1989	1990		1987	1988	1989	1990

10. ODA COMMITMENTS

1988	1989	1990		1987	1988	1989	1990
–	–	–		–	–	–	–
0.1	0.1	0.2		0.1	0.1	0.1	0.9
6.2	1.9	3.1		10.3	5.8	1.9	3.1
35.5	29.1	30.3		12.9	86.5	23.2	92.3
0.0	10.7	12.7		–	26.0	–	8.7
–	0.0	0.2		–	–	0.0	3.7
160.0	185.4	243.7		223.2	202.5	190.2	365.1
81.8	86.9	71.1		43.2	80.1	145.6	41.6
–	–	–		–	–	–	–
21.8	8.2	36.1		34.4	30.4	5.0	88.4
28.3	25.7	111.6		31.2	17.2	32.7	113.7
1.2	0.7	0.5		0.4	0.8	0.6	0.5
–	–	–		–	–	–	–
–	–	–		–	–	–	–
–	6.2	2.3		–	–	6.1	2.3
1.2	0.5	1.6		–	0.3	0.0	0.1
1.2	0.8	18.7		0.3	1.2	0.8	24.5
88.0	97.0	67.0		91.1	133.6	48.9	86.7
425.3	*453.1*	*599.1*		*447.1*	*584.5*	*455.0*	*831.7*
1.9	1.1	0.2		–	–	–	30.9
–	–	–		–	–	–	–
–	–	–		–	–	–	–
2.8	5.2	5.2		0.9	15.4	132.5	132.5
–	–	–		–	–	–	–
–	2.0	10.0		–	–	0.2	15.4
–	–	–		–	–	–	–
–	–	–		18.5	31.3	41.5	39.6
3.5	4.5	6.9		–	–	–	–
1.1	1.6	1.5		–	–	–	–
1.6	3.7	2.6		–	–	–	–
–	–	–		–	–	–	–
21.8	28.8	25.8		–	–	–	–
0.1	0.1	0.1		–	–	–	–
3.3	2.9	2.7		–	–	–	–
28.7	23.5	25.1		61.0	12.9	71.5	1.1
64.7	*73.2*	*80.0*		*80.4*	*59.6*	*245.7*	*219.5*
46.2	*22.3*	*369.8*		*–*	*30.7*	*66.2*	*141.7*
275.0	*299.6*	*391.1*		*312.8*	*362.2*	*476.6*	*664.4*
536.2	*548.6*	*1048.9*		*527.5*	*674.8*	*766.8*	*1193.0*

11. TECH. COOP. GRANTS

1988	1989	1990		1987	1988	1989	1990
–	–	–		–	–	–	–
0.1	0.1	0.2		0.1	0.1	0.1	0.2
3.6	1.9	3.1		3.5	2.4	1.3	2.5
27.0	13.1	15.8		–	1.1	1.6	1.7
0.0	10.7	12.7		–	–	–	1.2
–	0.0	0.2		–	–	0.0	–
88.3	79.7	111.4		83.6	81.6	79.6	111.4
16.8	17.7	22.0		13.7	16.3	17.6	21.5
–	–	–		–	–	–	–
9.1	7.1	4.0		5.8	5.1	4.6	1.8
18.0	14.0	21.9		5.2	8.2	9.1	9.3
0.9	0.7	0.5		0.2	0.8	0.6	0.5
–	–	–		–	–	–	–
–	6.2	2.3		–	–	–	–
0.4	0.1	0.3		0.0	0.0	–	–
1.2	0.8	18.7		0.3	0.8	0.6	0.7
46.0	49.0	32.0		18.0	23.0	25.0	19.0
211.4	*201.0*	*245.0*		*130.2*	*139.4*	*140.1*	*169.8*
35.0	47.1	44.8		8.9	11.1	12.7	13.8
10.6	*3.4*	*350.1*		*–*	*–*	*–*	*–*
122.7	*123.7*	*177.6*		*108.8*	*108.6*	*104.3*	*139.6*
256.9	*251.5*	*639.9*		*139.1*	*150.5*	*152.9*	*183.6*

12. TOTAL OOF NET

1988	1989	1990		1987	1988	1989	1990
–	–	–		–	–	–	–
5.9	3.0	1.7		6.1	5.5	2.6	1.7
31.3	54.2	44.8		6.7	30.5	51.2	41.4
0.1	2.9	0.5		0.5	0.0	2.8	0.2
–	–	–		–	–	–	–
55.5	96.6	57.8		-1.3	30.6	44.9	5.9
1.3	6.3	1.0		2.3	-0.8	-0.7	-0.8
–	–	–		–	–	–	–
63.5	144.2	141.5		89.4	57.3	138.8	105.9
15.4	–	–		0.5	15.4	-0.3	-0.7
–	–	8.2		–	–	–	8.2
–	–	–		–	–	–	–
0.5	0.3	–		–	0.5	0.3	0.0
–	–	–		–	–	–	–
126.0	124.0	–		-10.0	93.0	-25.0	-15.0
299.6	*431.6*	*255.5*		*94.3*	*232.0*	*214.5*	*146.7*
694.2	*679.5*	*761.7*		*305.9*	*350.0*	*368.8*	*508.9*
2.4	*10.9*	*–*		*5.9*	*0.5*	*10.6*	*–*
136.5	*280.8*	*238.4*		*110.0*	*98.0*	*210.4*	*143.1*
996.2	*1122.0*	*1017.2*		*406.1*	*582.4*	*593.8*	*655.6*

13. ODF COMMITMENTS: BY PURPOSE %

	1987	1988	1989	1990
Education	8	0	8	–
Health	0	0	2	–
Other Social Infrastr.	2	1	5	–
Water Sanitat. Sewage	10	1	19	–
Energy	2	3	16	–
Telecommunications	9	1	1	–
Transportation	1	5	2	–
Agriculture	22	22	19	–
Extractive Industries	1	3	0	–
Manufacturing	–	7	0	–
Trade Banking Tourism	5	0	0	–
Technical Cooperation	11	14	10	–
Multisector Aid	17	0	1	–
Programme	4	17	11	–
Debt Reorganisation	4	–	4	–
Food Aid	4	9	1	–
Emergency Aid	–	0	–	–
Unspecified	–	6	–	–
TOTAL	100	100	100	–

14. GRANT ELEMENT OF ODA %

DAC COUNTRIES

	1987	1988	1989	1990
Australia	–	–	–	–
Austria	100.0	100.0	100.0	–
Belgium	100.0	100.0	100.0	–
Canada	100.0	91.9	100.0	–
Denmark	–	100.0	–	–
Finland	–	–	100.0	–
France	83.9	79.0	91.3	–
Germany	54.0	52.2	58.3	–
Ireland	–	–	–	–
Italy	84.8	73.1	89.1	–
Japan	69.8	100.0	70.4	–
Netherlands	100.0	100.0	100.0	–
New Zealand	–	–	–	–
Norway	–	–	–	–
Sweden	–	–	100.0	–
Switzerland	–	100.0	100.0	–
United Kingdom	100.0	100.0	100.0	–
United States	81.8	78.0	100.0	–
TOTAL	*78.3*	*78.4*	*76.7*	*–*
MULTILATERAL	*44.5*	*87.1*	*81.3*	*–*
ARAB COUNTRIES	*–*	*52.3*	*67.3*	*–*
E.E.C.+ MEMBERS	*77.3*	*75.2*	*79.6*	*–*
TOTAL	*72.5*	*78.0*	*77.3*	*–*

15. OTHER AGGREGATES

	1987	1988	1989	1990
OFFICIAL COMMITMENTS:				
TOTAL BILATERAL	469.5	1001.3	1232.6	1987.2
of which:				
Arab Countries	0.6	35.5	68.4	141.7
C.E.E.C.	–	–	190.8	–
TOTAL MULTILATERAL	1339.1	569.0	1226.9	931.1
TOTAL BIL.& MULTIL.	1808.7	1570.3	2459.5	2918.2
of which:				
ODA Grants	228.8	284.4	397.9	541.3
ODA Loans	298.7	390.4	559.7	651.7
DISBURSEMENTS:				
DAC COUNTRIES COMBINED				
OFFICIAL & PRIVATE				
GROSS:				
Contractual Lending	525.8	520.8	1058.6	782.9
Export Credits, Total	210.6	54.0	580.6	218.8
Export Credits, Priv.	97.4	7.3	375.5	173.5
NET:				
Contractual Lending	142.4	266.4	568.0	500.3
Export Credits Total	-44.5	-135.3	295.2	57.2
PRIVATE SECTOR NET	-116.9	-79.9	208.4	-135.8
Direct Investment	20.5	3.3	53.4	33.2
Portfolio Investment	-11.0	73.2	-11.1	-205.7
Export Credits	-126.4	-156.4	166.1	36.8
MARKET BORROWING:				
CHANGE IN CLAIMS				
Banks	–	-335.0	65.0	-97.0
MEMORANDUM ITEM:				
C.E.E.C. (Gross)	–	–	–	–

	1987	1988	1989	1990		1987	1988	1989	1990		1987

1. TOTAL RECEIPTS NET

DAC COUNTRIES

	1987	1988	1989	1990
Australia	4.7	11.0	12.0	8.2
Austria	4.2	1.3	5.2	4.1
Belgium	0.8	1.6	0.8	0.7
Canada	24.2	29.8	27.4	35.0
Denmark	14.9	16.0	15.5	24.0
Finland	9.7	18.2	30.3	26.5
France	16.1	48.8	-64.1	44.5
Germany	1.1	11.6	16.1	143.1
Ireland	0.0	0.1	0.0	0.1
Italy	82.8	191.5	65.5	58.0
Japan	16.5	15.9	51.8	15.5
Netherlands	52.1	49.4	35.3	40.8
New Zealand	–	–	0.0	–
Norway	35.3	44.7	49.4	52.3
Sweden	54.2	89.4	97.6	135.1
Switzerland	23.4	6.4	7.4	26.1
United Kingdom	31.6	47.6	7.0	42.9
United States	61.0	60.0	34.0	71.0
TOTAL	*432.6*	*643.4*	*391.2*	*727.8*

MULTILATERAL

	1987	1988	1989	1990
AF.D.F.	7.3	4.2	16.8	13.9
AF.D.B.	3.2	2.2	1.9	-0.3
AS.D.B	–	–	–	–
CAR.D.B.	–	–	–	–
E.E.C.	25.8	66.8	89.7	89.7
IBRD	–	–	–	–
IDA	48.8	41.0	50.0	69.0
I.D.B.	–	–	–	–
IFAD	4.1	–	–	1.6
I.F.C.	1.3	–	-0.2	–
IMF TRUST FUND	–	–	–	–
U.N. AGENCIES	–	–	–	–
UNDP	7.7	12.4	14.3	20.1
UNTA	1.5	0.7	1.2	1.3
UNICEF	6.5	11.2	9.8	15.6
UNRWA	–	–	–	–
WFP	12.1	18.5	24.1	33.9
UNHCR	–	3.0	4.6	4.5
Other Multilateral	3.9	4.3	15.6	6.0
Arab Agencies	-5.1	-1.9	-2.9	–
TOTAL	*117.2*	*162.5*	*224.7*	*255.2*
ARAB COUNTRIES	***3.0***	***3.1***	***3.3***	***–***
E.E.C.+ MEMBERS	*225.2*	*433.5*	*165.7*	*443.7*
TOTAL	***552.8***	***808.9***	***619.2***	***983.0***

2. ODA LOANS GROSS

DAC COUNTRIES

	1987	1988	1989	1990
Australia	–	–	–	–
Austria	4.0	–	3.2	–
Belgium	–	0.4	0.4	–
Canada	–	–	–	–
Denmark	–	–	–	3.6
Finland	2.1	4.0	13.1	3.6
France	34.4	20.0	27.0	37.9
Germany	16.9	13.4	12.2	16.7
Ireland	–	–	–	–
Italy	47.6	184.3	11.0	14.5
Japan	0.6	1.7	3.2	–
Netherlands	1.6	–	–	–
New Zealand	–	–	–	–
Norway	–	–	–	–
Sweden	–	–	–	–
Switzerland	–	–	–	–
United Kingdom	1.4	–	0.1	–
United States	–	–	–	–
TOTAL	*108.5*	*223.9*	*70.2*	*72.7*
MULTILATERAL	*61.4*	*47.1*	*68.6*	*87.1*
ARAB COUNTRIES	***3.9***	***3.8***	***4.7***	***–***
E.E.C.+ MEMBERS	*102.2*	*219.7*	*52.0*	*70.3*
TOTAL	***173.8***	***274.7***	***143.5***	***159.7***

3. TOTAL OFFICIAL GROSS

DAC COUNTRIES

	1987	1988	1989	1990
Australia	4.7	11.0	12.0	8.2
Austria	4.2	1.3	5.2	4.1
Belgium	1.0	1.7	1.8	0.7
Canada	24.2	29.8	27.4	35.0
Denmark	14.9	16.0	15.5	35.2
Finland	9.7	18.4	30.5	26.5
France	39.4	61.5	47.1	79.0
Germany	29.8	24.7	25.9	38.9
Ireland	0.0	0.1	0.0	0.1
Italy	135.3	298.0	81.9	107.4
Japan	18.1	15.4	51.6	17.5
Netherlands	51.0	66.7	48.7	64.9
New Zealand	–	–	0.0	–
Norway	35.3	44.7	49.4	52.3
Sweden	54.5	89.4	99.5	136.1
Switzerland	23.4	6.4	7.4	26.1
United Kingdom	37.4	54.4	36.8	45.2
United States	67.0	60.0	34.0	81.0
TOTAL	*549.7*	*799.3*	*574.6*	*758.2*
MULTILATERAL	*128.1*	*171.1*	*232.9*	*262.0*
ARAB COUNTRIES	***3.9***	***3.8***	***4.7***	***–***
E.E.C.+ MEMBERS	*334.4*	*589.8*	*347.2*	*461.1*
TOTAL	***681.8***	***974.1***	***812.2***	***1020.2***

4. TOTAL ODA NET

	1987	1988	1989	1990
Australia	4.7	11.0	12.0	8.2
Austria	4.2	1.3	5.2	4.1
Belgium	1.0	1.7	0.8	0.7
Canada	24.2	29.8	27.4	34.3
Denmark	14.9	16.0	15.5	24.0
Finland	9.7	18.4	30.5	26.5
France	39.4	24.8	42.2	71.8
Germany	29.7	24.6	21.1	37.4
Ireland	0.0	0.1	0.0	0.1
Italy	135.3	286.8	80.1	106.2
Japan	17.6	14.8	51.1	17.0
Netherlands	50.6	49.4	35.3	40.8
New Zealand	–	–	0.0	–
Norway	35.3	44.7	49.4	52.3
Sweden	54.5	89.4	99.5	136.1
Switzerland	23.4	6.4	7.4	26.1
United Kingdom	35.3	52.1	34.7	43.2
United States	55.0	60.0	34.0	62.0
TOTAL	*534.7*	*731.1*	*546.1*	*690.6*
AF.D.F.	7.3	4.2	16.8	13.9
AF.D.B.	–	–	–	–
AS.D.B	–	–	–	–
CAR.D.B.	–	–	–	–
E.E.C.	25.8	66.8	89.7	89.7
IBRD	–	–	–	–
IDA	48.8	41.0	50.0	69.0
I.D.B.	–	–	–	–
IFAD	4.1	–	–	1.6
I.F.C.	–	–	–	–
IMF TRUST FUND	–	–	–	–
U.N. AGENCIES	–	–	–	–
UNDP	7.7	12.4	14.3	20.1
UNTA	1.5	0.7	1.2	1.3
UNICEF	6.5	11.2	9.8	15.6
UNRWA	–	–	–	–
WFP	12.1	18.5	24.1	33.9
UNHCR	–	3.0	4.6	4.5
Other Multilateral	3.9	4.3	15.6	6.0
Arab Agencies	-4.6	-3.4	-3.7	–
TOTAL	*113.1*	*158.8*	*222.3*	*255.5*
ARAB COUNTRIES	***3.0***	***3.1***	***3.3***	***–***
E.E.C.+ MEMBERS	*331.9*	*522.2*	*319.2*	*413.7*
TOTAL	***650.8***	***893.0***	***771.7***	***946.1***

5. ODA LOANS NET

	1987	1988	1989	1990
Australia	–	–	–	–
Austria	4.0	–	3.2	–
Belgium	–	0.4	0.4	–
Canada	–	–	–	–
Denmark	–	–	–	-11.2
Finland	2.1	4.0	13.1	3.6
France	34.4	19.1	23.8	30.7
Germany	16.9	13.4	12.2	16.7
Ireland	–	–	–	–
Italy	47.6	173.1	9.3	13.3
Japan	0.1	1.2	2.7	-0.5
Netherlands	1.2	-17.4	-13.5	-24.2
New Zealand	–	–	–	–
Norway	–	–	–	–
Sweden	–	–	–	–
Switzerland	–	–	–	–
United Kingdom	-0.7	-2.2	-1.9	-2.0
United States	–	–	–	–
TOTAL	*105.6*	*191.6*	*49.2*	*26.4*
MULTILATERAL	*55.8*	*43.3*	*64.3*	*82.4*
ARAB COUNTRIES	***3.0***	***3.1***	***3.3***	***–***
E.E.C.+ MEMBERS	*99.8*	*188.0*	*31.5*	*24.6*
TOTAL	***164.4***	***238.0***	***116.7***	***108.8***

6. TOTAL OFFICIAL NET

	1987	1988	1989	1990
Australia	4.7	11.0	12.0	8.2
Austria	4.2	1.3	5.2	4.1
Belgium	1.0	1.7	1.8	0.7
Canada	24.2	29.8	27.4	35.0
Denmark	14.9	16.0	15.5	24.0
Finland	9.7	18.4	30.5	26.5
France	39.4	58.1	-44.1	71.8
Germany	1.3	11.6	16.2	31.0
Ireland	0.0	0.1	0.0	0.1
Italy	135.3	285.6	80.1	106.2
Japan	17.6	14.8	51.1	17.0
Netherlands	50.6	49.4	35.3	40.8
New Zealand	–	–	0.0	–
Norway	35.3	44.7	49.4	52.3
Sweden	54.5	89.4	99.5	136.1
Switzerland	23.4	6.4	7.4	26.1
United Kingdom	35.3	52.1	34.7	43.2
United States	61.0	60.0	34.0	71.0
TOTAL	*512.3*	*750.3*	*456.0*	*693.9*
MULTILATERAL	*117.2*	*162.5*	*224.7*	*255.2*
ARAB COUNTRIES	***3.0***	***3.1***	***3.3***	***–***
E.E.C.+ MEMBERS	*303.5*	*541.4*	*229.1*	*407.4*
TOTAL	***632.5***	***915.8***	***683.9***	***949.1***

7. TOTAL ODA GROSS

	1987
Australia	4.7
Austria	4.2
Belgium	1.0
Canada	24.2
Denmark	14.9
Finland	9.7
France	39.4
Germany	29.7
Ireland	0.0
Italy	135.3
Japan	18.1
Netherlands	51.0
New Zealand	–
Norway	35.3
Sweden	54.5
Switzerland	23.4
United Kingdom	37.4
United States	55.0
TOTAL	*537.6*
AF.D.F.	7.4
AF.D.B.	–
AS.D.B	–
CAR.D.B.	–
E.E.C.	25.8
IBRD	–
IDA	48.8
I.D.B.	–
IFAD	4.7
I.F.C.	–
IMF TRUST FUND	–
U.N. AGENCIES	–
UNDP	7.7
UNTA	1.5
UNICEF	6.5
UNRWA	–
WFP	12.1
UNHCR	–
Other Multilateral	3.9
Arab Agencies	0.3
TOTAL	*118.7*
ARAB COUNTRIES	***3.9***
E.E.C.+ MEMBERS	*334.3*
TOTAL	***660.2***

8. GRANTS

	1987
Australia	4.7
Austria	0.3
Belgium	1.0
Canada	24.2
Denmark	14.9
Finland	7.6
France	4.9
Germany	12.7
Ireland	0.0
Italy	87.8
Japan	17.5
Netherlands	49.4
New Zealand	–
Norway	35.3
Sweden	54.5
Switzerland	23.4
United Kingdom	36.0
United States	55.0
TOTAL	*429.1*
MULTILATERAL	*57.3*
ARAB COUNTRIES	***0.0***
E.E.C.+ MEMBERS	*232.1*
TOTAL	***486.4***

9. TOTAL OOF GROSS

	1987
Australia	–
Austria	–
Belgium	–
Canada	–
Denmark	–
Finland	–
France	–
Germany	0.2
Ireland	–
Italy	–
Japan	–
Netherlands	–
New Zealand	–
Norway	–
Sweden	–
Switzerland	–
United Kingdom	–
United States	12.0
TOTAL	*12.2*
MULTILATERAL	*9.4*
ARAB COUNTRIES	***–***
E.E.C.+ MEMBERS	*0.2*
TOTAL	***21.6***

10. ODA COMMITMENTS

1988	1989	1990	1987	1988	1989	1990
11.0	12.0	8.2	8.6	2.5	10.9	15.1
1.3	5.2	4.1	0.4	6.9	4.2	7.7
1.7	0.8	0.7	3.6	1.8	0.8	0.7
29.8	27.4	34.3	5.0	27.0	42.6	26.8
16.0	15.5	35.2	29.2	33.5	9.8	15.4
18.4	30.5	26.5	23.6	21.6	50.4	11.0
25.7	45.4	79.0	17.2	48.6	48.4	83.4
24.6	21.1	37.4	33.0	50.0	10.2	79.7
0.1	0.0	0.1	0.0	0.1	0.0	0.1
298.0	81.9	107.4	148.5	310.6	80.1	85.6
15.4	51.6	17.5	12.5	17.0	53.1	19.5
66.7	48.7	64.9	46.0	74.6	41.4	45.0
–	0.0	–	–	–	–	–
44.7	49.4	52.3	40.3	8.6	16.0	22.1
89.4	99.5	136.1	55.7	82.5	99.4	71.0
6.4	7.4	26.1	23.9	6.8	31.3	19.7
54.4	36.8	45.2	52.4	30.7	58.6	42.4
60.0	34.0	62.0	60.5	60.7	74.0	75.6
763.4	*567.2*	*736.9*	*560.5*	*783.6*	*631.2*	*620.8*
4.4	17.3	14.9	–	97.8	12.1	19.5
–	–	–	–	–	–	–
–	–	–	–	–	–	–
–	–	–	–	–	–	–
66.8	89.7	89.7	133.8	112.3	67.7	67.7
–	–	–	–	–	–	–
41.0	50.0	69.0	108.6	76.0	282.0	69.0
–	–	–	–	–	–	–
–	–	1.9	16.3	–	–	–
–	–	–	–	–	–	–
–	–	–	–	–	–	–
–	–	–	31.8	50.2	69.6	81.4
12.4	14.3	20.1	–	–	–	–
0.7	1.2	1.3	–	–	–	–
11.2	9.8	15.6	–	–	–	–
–	–	–	–	–	–	–
18.5	24.1	33.9	–	–	–	–
3.0	4.6	4.5	–	–	–	–
4.3	15.6	6.0	–	–	–	–
0.2	0.0	0.1	5.0	2.8	10.0	3.8
162.6	*226.6*	*256.9*	*295.5*	*339.2*	*441.4*	*241.4*
3.8	*4.7*	*–*	*10.8*	*–*	*3.7*	*–*
553.9	*339.8*	*459.5*	*463.7*	*662.3*	*317.1*	*420.1*
929.7	**798.4**	**993.8**	**866.7**	**1122.9**	**1076.4**	**862.2**

11. TECH. COOP. GRANTS

1988	1989	1990	1987	1988	1989	1990
11.0	12.0	8.2	0.1	0.0	0.1	0.1
1.3	2.0	4.1	0.3	0.1	0.0	0.4
1.2	0.4	0.7	0.1	–	–	–
29.8	27.4	34.3	–	0.3	1.0	1.3
16.0	15.5	35.2	2.5	4.0	4.1	6.4
14.3	17.4	23.0	0.1	0.8	2.1	2.5
5.8	18.4	41.2	3.3	4.1	2.7	2.5
11.2	8.9	20.7	1.8	4.0	3.9	5.8
0.1	0.0	0.1	0.0	0.0	0.0	0.1
113.7	70.8	92.9	23.2	11.4	7.0	5.3
13.6	48.4	17.5	0.2	0.3	0.5	0.5
66.7	48.7	64.9	3.8	4.3	4.0	5.1
–	0.0	–	–	–	–	–
44.7	49.4	52.3	3.4	3.7	4.4	5.0
89.4	99.5	136.1	9.6	12.6	19.1	1.5
6.4	7.4	26.1	0.5	1.7	–	–
54.4	36.6	45.2	3.5	11.0	4.3	4.5
60.0	34.0	62.0	–	–	1.0	7.0
539.5	*496.9*	*664.3*	*52.3*	*58.2*	*54.1*	*47.9*
115.5	*158.0*	*169.8*	*20.9*	*34.1*	*45.5*	*47.5*
–	–	–	–	–	–	–
334.2	*287.7*	*389.2*	*39.3*	*41.3*	*25.9*	*29.7*
655.0	**654.9**	**834.0**	**73.1**	**92.2**	**99.5**	**95.4**

12. TOTAL OOF NET

1988	1989	1990	1987	1988	1989	1990
–	–	–	–	–	–	–
–	1.0	–	–	–	1.0	–
–	–	0.7	–	–	–	0.7
0.0	–	0.1	–	0.0	–	0.1
–	–	–	–	–	–	–
35.8	1.7	–	0.0	33.3	-86.2	–
0.1	4.8	1.6	-28.4	-12.9	-4.9	-6.4
–	–	–	–	-1.2	–	–
–	–	–	–	–	–	–
–	–	–	–	–	–	–
–	–	–	–	–	–	–
–	–	–	–	–	–	–
–	–	–	–	–	–	–
–	–	19.0	6.0	–	–	9.0
35.9	*7.5*	*21.3*	*-22.4*	*19.2*	*-90.1*	*3.3*
8.5	*6.3*	*5.1*	*4.1*	*3.7*	*2.4*	*-0.3*
–	–	–	–	–	–	–
35.9	*7.5*	*1.6*	*-28.4*	*19.2*	*-90.1*	*-6.4*
44.4	**13.8**	**26.5**	**-18.3**	**22.9**	**-87.8**	**3.0**

13. ODF COMMITMENTS: BY PURPOSE %

	1987	1988	1989	1990
Education	1	2	2	–
Health	0	2	4	–
Other Social Infrastr.	8	7	7	–
Water Sanitat. Sewage	0	2	2	–
Energy	6	3	4	–
Telecommunications	0	1	2	–
Transportation	4	6	15	–
Agriculture	10	7	8	–
Extractive Industries	–	–	2	–
Manufacturing	1	5	1	–
Trade Banking Tourism	1	1	2	–
Technical Cooperation	13	10	12	–
Multisector Aid	1	1	1	–
Programme	40	21	27	–
Debt Reorganisation	0	20	1	–
Food Aid	10	9	5	–
Emergency Aid	4	3	4	–
Unspecified	0	0	0	–
TOTAL	100	100	100	–

14. GRANT ELEMENT OF ODA %

DAC COUNTRIES

	1987	1988	1989	1990
Australia	100.0	100.0	100.0	–
Austria	100.0	100.0	89.3	–
Belgium	100.0	100.0	100.0	–
Canada	100.0	100.0	100.0	–
Denmark	100.0	100.0	100.0	–
Finland	95.0	100.0	100.0	–
France	53.6	51.7	73.5	–
Germany	92.9	88.0	100.0	–
Ireland	100.0	100.0	100.0	–
Italy	98.9	66.3	100.0	–
Japan	96.8	92.9	95.8	–
Netherlands	100.0	100.0	100.0	–
New Zealand	–	–	–	–
Norway	100.0	100.0	100.0	–
Sweden	100.0	100.0	100.0	–
Switzerland	100.0	100.0	100.0	–
United Kingdom	100.0	100.0	100.0	–
United States	100.0	100.0	100.0	–
TOTAL	*97.6*	*82.3*	*97.5*	*–*
MULTILATERAL	*91.0*	*91.5*	*86.4*	*–*
ARAB COUNTRIES	*57.1*	*–*	*40.8*	*–*
E.E.C.+ MEMBERS	*97.4*	*79.4*	*96.0*	*–*
TOTAL	*94.8*	*84.7*	*93.0*	*–*

15. OTHER AGGREGATES

	1987	1988	1989	1990
OFFICIAL COMMITMENTS:				
TOTAL BILATERAL	805.3	914.0	711.3	826.7
of which:				
Arab Countries	10.8	–	3.7	–
C.E.E.C.	221.5	40.5	74.7	–
TOTAL MULTILATERAL	303.3	356.8	441.4	241.4
TOTAL BIL.& MULTIL.	1108.5	1270.7	1152.8	1068.1
of which:				
ODA Grants	858.0	699.3	747.0	743.8
ODA Loans	230.2	464.1	404.0	118.4
DISBURSEMENTS:				
DAC COUNTRIES COMBINED				
OFFICIAL & PRIVATE				
GROSS:				
Contractual Lending	110.0	251.2	54.1	73.6
Export Credits, Total	-10.6	-8.6	-23.5	-19.7
Export Credits, Priv.	-10.6	-8.6	-23.6	-20.4
NET:				
Contractual Lending	7.9	101.1	-101.5	-41.1
Export Credits	-109.9	-122.7	-69.7	-88.0
PRIVATE SECTOR NET	-79.7	-106.9	-64.7	33.9
Direct Investment	0.1	-0.3	1.1	-0.6
Portfolio Investment	-4.4	3.1	-5.3	105.2
Export Credits	-75.4	-109.7	-60.5	-70.7
MARKET BORROWING:				
CHANGE IN CLAIMS				
Banks	-27.0	-41.0	-40.0	220.0
MEMORANDUM ITEM:				
C.E.E.C. (Gross)	102.5	75.0	52.1	–

DISBURSEMENTS, UNLESS OTHERWISE STATED

	1987	1988	1989	1990		1987	1988	1989	1990		1987
1. TOTAL RECEIPTS NET					**4. TOTAL ODA NET**					**7. TOTAL ODA GROSS**	
DAC COUNTRIES											
Australia	7.3	8.0	4.2	2.2		8.3	8.2	4.2	2.2	Australia	8.3
Austria	-4.7	-4.8	-4.2	-4.5		0.0	–	–	0.0	Austria	0.0
Belgium	-1.3	-1.0	-1.6	-0.8		0.0	0.0	0.0	0.0	Belgium	0.0
Canada	1.0	2.4	0.7	1.7		1.0	2.4	0.7	1.7	Canada	1.0
Denmark	0.2	0.3	-0.2	–		0.2	0.3	-0.2	–	Denmark	0.2
Finland	1.3	2.5	4.7	1.1		1.3	2.5	4.7	1.1	Finland	1.3
France	15.9	5.2	-5.1	9.2		9.0	6.2	0.9	9.7	France	9.4
Germany	21.5	43.2	-55.4	31.0		25.7	37.1	4.6	2.4	Germany	41.5
Ireland	–	–	–	–		–	–	–	–	Ireland	–
Italy	1.1	0.4	0.7	-12.6		1.1	0.4	0.1	–	Italy	1.4
Japan	163.6	286.6	71.4	15.3		172.0	259.6	71.4	61.3	Japan	192.4
Netherlands	3.5	0.1	-2.5	0.9		1.6	1.1	0.0	0.8	Netherlands	1.8
New Zealand	0.0	–	–	–		0.0	–	–	–	New Zealand	0.0
Norway	-4.6	-0.7	-4.4	-10.2		0.1	0.1	0.1	0.1	Norway	0.1
Sweden	–	–	0.1	–		–	–	0.1	–	Sweden	–
Switzerland	1.6	0.7	0.4	2.5		1.6	0.7	0.4	2.5	Switzerland	1.6
United Kingdom	7.6	1.6	-17.8	-8.9		7.7	4.0	1.2	0.2	United Kingdom	7.7
United States	11.0	10.0	2.0	1.0		11.0	10.0	2.0	1.0	United States	11.0
TOTAL	*225.1*	*354.6*	*-7.0*	*27.9*		*240.7*	*332.7*	*89.9*	*83.1*	*TOTAL*	*277.7*
MULTILATERAL											
AF.D.F.	–	–	–	–		–	–	–	–	AF.D.F.	–
AF.D.B.	–	–	–	–		–	–	–	–	AF.D.B.	–
AS.D.B	35.7	35.5	24.9	5.9		36.0	35.7	25.3	6.2	AS.D.B	38.6
CAR.D.B.	–	–	–	–		–	–	–	–	CAR.D.B.	–
E.E.C.	0.1	0.3	1.2	1.2		0.1	0.3	1.2	1.2	E.E.C.	0.1
IBRD	–	–	–	–		–	–	–	–	IBRD	–
IDA	64.6	63.0	52.0	54.0		64.6	63.0	52.0	54.0	IDA	66.2
I.D.B.	–	–	–	–		–	–	–	–	I.D.B.	–
IFAD	–	–	–	–		–	–	–	–	IFAD	–
I.F.C.	–	–	–	–		–	–	–	–	I.F.C.	–
IMF TRUST FUND	–	–	–	–		–	–	–	–	IMF TRUST FUND	–
U.N. AGENCIES	–	–	–	–		–	–	–	–	U.N. AGENCIES	–
UNDP	11.2	11.3	7.4	13.3		11.2	11.3	7.4	13.3	UNDP	11.2
UNTA	2.4	1.2	3.1	1.7		2.4	1.2	3.1	1.7	UNTA	2.4
UNICEF	7.3	6.0	6.6	7.9		7.3	6.0	6.6	7.9	UNICEF	7.3
UNRWA	–	–	–	–		–	–	–	–	UNRWA	–
WFP	–	–	–	0.0		–	–	–	0.0	WFP	–
UNHCR	–	–	–	–		–	–	–	–	UNHCR	–
Other Multilateral	2.4	2.1	1.8	3.1		2.4	2.1	1.8	3.1	Other Multilateral	2.4
Arab Agencies	3.1	-1.5	-3.4	–		3.1	-1.5	-3.4	–	Arab Agencies	6.5
TOTAL	*126.7*	*117.9*	*93.6*	*87.1*		*127.0*	*118.2*	*94.0*	*87.4*	*TOTAL*	*134.6*
ARAB COUNTRIES	*0.0*	*–*	*0.0*	*–*		*0.0*	*–*	*0.0*	*–*	***ARAB COUNTRIES***	*0.0*
E.E.C.+ MEMBERS	*48.6*	*50.2*	*-80.7*	*20.0*		*45.4*	*49.5*	*7.7*	*14.3*	*E.E.C.+ MEMBERS*	*62.0*
TOTAL	*351.8*	*472.5*	*86.6*	*115.0*		*367.7*	*450.9*	*183.9*	*170.5*	*TOTAL*	*412.3*
2. ODA LOANS GROSS					**5. ODA LOANS NET**					**8. GRANTS**	
DAC COUNTRIES											
Australia	–	–	–	–		–	–	–	–	Australia	8.3
Austria	–	–	–	–		–	–	–	–	Austria	0.0
Belgium	–	–	–	–		–	–	–	–	Belgium	0.0
Canada	–	–	–	–		–	–	–	–	Canada	1.0
Denmark	–	0.2	-0.2	–		–	0.2	-0.2	–	Denmark	0.2
Finland	–	–	–	–		–	–	–	–	Finland	1.3
France	9.0	5.8	1.5	9.6		8.7	5.8	0.5	9.5	France	0.4
Germany	32.0	31.1	0.5	–		16.2	27.8	0.5	–	Germany	9.4
Ireland	–	–	–	–		–	–	–	–	Ireland	–
Italy	–	–	–	–		-0.3	–	–	–	Italy	1.4
Japan	125.1	187.4	37.7	28.0		104.7	168.3	27.5	28.0	Japan	67.3
Netherlands	–	–	–	–		-0.2	–	-0.9	-0.3	Netherlands	1.8
New Zealand	–	–	–	–		–	–	–	–	New Zealand	0.0
Norway	–	–	–	–		–	–	–	–	Norway	0.1
Sweden	–	–	–	–		–	–	–	–	Sweden	–
Switzerland	–	–	–	–		–	–	–	–	Switzerland	1.6
United Kingdom	–	–	–	–		–	–	–	–	United Kingdom	7.7
United States	–	–	–	–		–	–	–	–	United States	11.0
TOTAL	*166.2*	*224.6*	*39.6*	*37.5*		*129.1*	*202.1*	*27.5*	*37.3*	*TOTAL*	*111.5*
MULTILATERAL	*110.6*	*106.6*	*83.8*	*68.7*		*103.0*	*97.2*	*73.9*	*57.3*	*MULTILATERAL*	*24.0*
ARAB COUNTRIES	*–*	*–*	*–*	*–*		*–*	*–*	*–*	*–*	***ARAB COUNTRIES***	*0.0*
E.E.C.+ MEMBERS	*41.0*	*37.2*	*1.8*	*9.6*		*24.4*	*33.8*	*0.0*	*9.3*	*E.E.C.+ MEMBERS*	*21.0*
TOTAL	*276.8*	*331.2*	*123.4*	*106.2*		*232.1*	*299.3*	*101.4*	*94.6*	*TOTAL*	*135.5*
3. TOTAL OFFICIAL GROSS					**6. TOTAL OFFICIAL NET**					**9. TOTAL OOF GROSS**	
DAC COUNTRIES											
Australia	8.3	8.2	4.2	2.2		7.3	8.0	4.2	2.2	Australia	–
Austria	0.0	–	–	0.0		0.0	–	–	0.0	Austria	–
Belgium	0.2	0.0	0.1	0.2		0.2	0.0	0.1	0.2	Belgium	0.2
Canada	1.0	2.4	0.7	1.7		1.0	2.4	0.7	1.7	Canada	–
Denmark	0.2	0.3	-0.2	–		0.2	0.3	-0.2	–	Denmark	–
Finland	1.3	2.5	4.7	1.1		1.3	2.5	4.7	1.1	Finland	–
France	9.4	6.3	1.9	9.8		9.0	6.2	0.9	9.7	France	–
Germany	41.5	46.9	7.7	25.8		25.0	42.8	-62.1	25.8	Germany	–
Ireland	–	–	–	–		–	–	–	–	Ireland	–
Italy	1.4	0.4	0.1	–		1.1	0.4	0.1	–	Italy	–
Japan	192.4	278.6	81.6	61.3		172.0	259.6	71.4	61.3	Japan	–
Netherlands	1.8	1.1	0.9	1.0		1.6	1.1	0.0	0.8	Netherlands	–
New Zealand	0.0	–	–	–		0.0	–	–	–	New Zealand	–
Norway	0.1	0.1	0.1	0.1		0.1	0.1	0.1	0.1	Norway	–
Sweden	–	–	0.1	–		–	–	0.1	–	Sweden	–
Switzerland	1.6	0.7	0.4	2.5		1.6	0.7	0.4	2.5	Switzerland	–
United Kingdom	7.7	4.0	1.2	0.2		7.7	4.0	1.2	0.2	United Kingdom	–
United States	11.0	10.0	2.0	1.0		11.0	10.0	2.0	1.0	United States	–
TOTAL	*277.9*	*361.6*	*105.2*	*106.9*		*239.2*	*338.2*	*23.3*	*106.6*	*TOTAL*	*0.2*
MULTILATERAL	*134.6*	*127.6*	*103.9*	*95.9*		*126.7*	*117.9*	*93.6*	*87.1*	*MULTILATERAL*	*–*
ARAB COUNTRIES	*0.0*	*–*	*0.0*	*–*		*0.0*	*–*	*0.0*	*–*	***ARAB COUNTRIES***	*–*
E.E.C.+ MEMBERS	*62.2*	*59.3*	*12.8*	*38.1*		*44.9*	*55.2*	*-58.9*	*37.9*	*E.E.C.+ MEMBERS*	*0.2*
TOTAL	*412.5*	*489.2*	*209.1*	*202.8*		*365.9*	*456.1*	*117.0*	*193.7*	*TOTAL*	*0.2*

Left panel

1988	1989	1990
8.2	4.2	2.2
–	–	0.0
0.0	0.0	0.0
2.4	0.7	1.7
0.3	-0.2	–
2.5	4.7	1.1
6.3	1.9	9.8
40.4	4.6	2.4
–	–	–
0.4	0.1	–
278.6	81.6	61.3
1.1	0.9	1.0
–	–	–
0.1	0.1	0.1
–	0.1	–
0.7	0.4	2.5
4.0	1.2	0.2
10.0	2.0	1.0
355.2	102.0	83.3
–	–	–
–	–	–
39.1	29.6	11.5
–	–	–
0.3	1.2	1.2
–	–	–
65.0	54.0	57.0
–	–	–
–	–	–
–	–	–
11.3	7.4	13.3
1.2	3.1	1.7
6.0	6.6	7.9
–	–	–
–	–	0.0
–	–	–
2.1	1.8	3.1
2.5	0.2	0.2
127.5	103.9	95.9
–	0.0	–
52.9	9.6	14.6
482.7	205.9	179.3
8.2	4.2	2.2
–	–	0.0
0.0	0.0	0.0
2.4	0.7	1.7
0.1	–	–
2.5	4.7	1.1
0.4	0.3	0.2
9.3	4.1	2.4
–	–	–
0.4	0.1	–
91.3	43.9	33.3
1.1	0.9	1.0
–	–	–
0.1	0.1	0.1
–	0.1	–
0.7	0.4	2.5
4.0	1.2	0.2
10.0	2.0	1.0
130.6	62.4	45.8
20.9	20.1	27.2
–	0.0	–
15.7	7.7	5.0
151.5	82.5	73.0
–	–	–
–	–	–
–	0.1	0.2
–	–	–
–	–	–
–	–	–
6.5	3.1	23.4
–	–	–
–	–	–
–	–	–
–	–	–
–	–	–
–	–	–
–	–	–
6.5	3.2	23.6
0.1	–	–
–	–	–
6.5	3.2	23.6
6.5	3.2	23.6

Middle panel

10. ODA COMMITMENTS

1987	1988	1989	1990
8.2	3.4	0.5	1.9
0.0	–	–	0.0
–	–	0.0	0.0
0.2	4.8	7.6	–
–	15.6	–	–
4.6	1.7	0.2	0.7
0.4	0.4	0.3	0.2
74.2	4.4	1.3	1.1
–	–	–	–
1.4	2.3	0.1	–
290.0	69.5	3.8	27.4
0.8	0.9	0.9	1.0
–	–	–	–
0.1	–	–	–
–	0.4	0.1	–
1.8	–	1.2	–
1.5	2.8	1.1	0.2
16.5	10.7	0.1	–
399.6	117.0	17.2	32.5
–	–	–	–
–	–	–	–
20.6	–	–	–
–	–	–	–
4.0	0.9	1.0	1.0
–	–	–	–
63.0	–	–	–
–	–	–	–
–	–	–	–
23.3	20.6	18.9	26.0
–	–	–	–
–	–	–	–
–	–	–	–
–	–	–	–
–	–	–	–
–	–	–	–
–	–	–	–
110.9	21.5	19.8	34.3
–	–	–	–
82.3	27.4	4.7	3.5
510.5	138.5	37.0	66.8

11. TECH. COOP. GRANTS

1987	1988	1989	1990
3.5	3.1	1.3	0.8
0.0	–	–	0.0
0.0	–	–	–
–	0.0	–	–
0.2	0.1	–	0.1
0.1	0.0	0.0	0.1
0.4	0.4	0.3	0.2
9.3	7.9	3.9	2.3
–	–	–	–
1.4	–	–	–
11.8	9.6	3.5	3.2
0.8	0.9	0.9	1.0
0.0	–	–	–
0.1	0.1	0.1	0.1
–	–	–	–
0.0	0.1	–	–
1.5	2.6	1.0	0.1
3.0	9.0	2.0	1.0
32.1	33.8	13.0	8.8
23.3	20.8	18.9	26.0
–	–	–	–
13.5	12.2	6.1	3.6
55.4	54.6	31.8	34.8

12. TOTAL OOF NET

1987	1988	1989	1990
-1.0	-0.2	–	–
–	–	–	–
0.2	–	0.1	0.2
–	–	–	–
–	–	–	–
–	–	–	–
-0.7	5.7	-66.7	23.4
–	–	–	–
–	–	–	–
–	–	–	–
–	–	–	–
–	–	–	–
–	–	–	–
–	–	–	–
-1.5	5.5	-66.6	23.6
-0.3	-0.2	-0.3	-0.3
–	–	–	–
-0.5	5.7	-66.6	23.6
-1.8	5.3	-66.9	23.2

Right panel

13. ODF COMMITMENTS: BY PURPOSE %

	1987	1988	1989	1990
Education	1	1	–	–
Health	0	4	–	–
Other Social Infrastr.	2	–	–	–
Water Sanitat. Sewage	0	6	–	–
Energy	40	1	0	–
Telecommunications	1	–	–	–
Transportation	5	12	4	–
Agriculture	7	16	–	–
Extractive Industries	0	2	–	–
Manufacturing	3	1	2	–
Trade Banking Tourism	3	–	–	–
Technical Cooperation	12	33	93	–
Multisector Aid	–	1	0	–
Programme	26	–	–	–
Debt Reorganisation	0	22	–	–
Food Aid	–	–	–	–
Emergency Aid	–	0	0	–
Unspecified	–	–	–	–
TOTAL	100	100	100	–

14. GRANT ELEMENT OF ODA %

DAC COUNTRIES	1987	1988	1989	1990
Australia	100.0	100.0	100.0	–
Austria	100.0	–	–	–
Belgium	–	–	100.0	–
Canada	100.0	100.0	100.0	–
Denmark	–	100.0	–	–
Finland	68.6	100.0	100.0	–
France	100.0	100.0	100.0	–
Germany	84.0	100.0	100.0	–
Ireland	–	–	–	–
Italy	100.0	71.1	100.0	–
Japan	68.4	100.0	100.0	–
Netherlands	100.0	100.0	100.0	–
New Zealand	–	–	–	–
Norway	100.0	–	–	–
Sweden	–	100.0	100.0	–
Switzerland	100.0	–	100.0	–
United Kingdom	100.0	100.0	100.0	–
United States	100.0	100.0	100.0	–
TOTAL	73.7	99.4	100.0	–
MULTILATERAL	86.5	100.0	100.0	–
ARAB COUNTRIES	–	–	–	–
E.E.C.+ MEMBERS	85.6	97.6	100.0	–
TOTAL	76.1	99.5	100.0	–

15. OTHER AGGREGATES

OFFICIAL COMMITMENTS:	1987	1988	1989	1990
TOTAL BILATERAL	399.6	117.0	17.3	32.7
of which:				
Arab Countries	–	–	–	–
C.E.E.C.	–	0.1	–	–
TOTAL MULTILATERAL	110.9	21.5	19.8	34.3
TOTAL BIL.& MULTIL.	510.5	138.5	37.1	67.0
of which:				
ODA Grants	133.0	136.6	37.0	59.5
ODA Loans	377.5	1.9	–	7.3

DISBURSEMENTS:

DAC COUNTRIES COMBINED

OFFICIAL & PRIVATE	1987	1988	1989	1990
GROSS:				
Contractual Lending	210.3	348.4	43.2	84.2
Export Credits, Total	44.1	117.4	1.8	46.7
Export Credits, Priv.	44.1	117.4	0.9	23.3
NET:				
Contractual Lending	114.9	223.7	-73.6	-21.6
Export Credits Total	-14.2	15.2	-103.0	-58.9
PRIVATE SECTOR NET	-14.1	16.4	-30.3	-78.7
Direct Investment	-1.5	–	–	4.9
Portfolio Investment	0.0	0.3	3.7	-1.3
Export Credits	-12.6	16.1	-34.0	-82.3

MARKET BORROWING:

CHANGE IN CLAIMS	1987	1988	1989	1990
Banks	20.0	-64.0	-32.0	-6.0

MEMORANDUM ITEM:

	1987	1988	1989	1990
C.E.E.C. (Gross)	–	–	–	–

1. TOTAL RECEIPTS NET

DAC COUNTRIES	1987	1988	1989	1990
Australia	0.1	0.2	0.0	0.1
Austria	–	–	–	–
Belgium	–	–	–	1.3
Canada	–	–	–	–
Denmark	–	–	–	–
Finland	–	–	–	–
France	–	0.2	–	2.6
Germany	-2.9	-1.3	-1.5	-2.8
Ireland	–	–	–	–
Italy	–	–	–	–
Japan	3.7	27.8	-7.4	-0.1
Netherlands	–	–	–	–
New Zealand	–	–	–	0.0
Norway	–	–	–	–
Sweden	–	–	–	–
Switzerland	–	–	–	–
United Kingdom	–	–	–	–
United States	–	–	–	–
TOTAL	*0.8*	*26.8*	*-8.9*	*1.2*
MULTILATERAL				
AF.D.F.	–	–	–	–
AF.D.B.	–	–	–	–
AS.D.B	–	–	–	–
CAR.D.B.	–	–	–	–
E.E.C.	–	–	–	–
IBRD	–	–	–	–
IDA	–	–	–	–
I.D.B.	–	–	–	–
IFAD	–	–	–	–
I.F.C.	–	–	–	–
IMF TRUST FUND	–	–	–	–
U.N. AGENCIES	–	–	–	–
UNDP	–	–	–	–
UNTA	–	–	–	–
UNICEF	–	–	–	–
UNRWA	–	–	–	–
WFP	–	–	–	–
UNHCR	–	–	–	–
Other Multilateral	–	–	–	–
Arab Agencies	–	–	–	–
TOTAL	–	–	–	–
ARAB COUNTRIES	–	–	–	–
E.E.C.+ MEMBERS	-2.9	-1.1	-1.5	1.1
TOTAL	*0.8*	*26.8*	*-8.9*	*1.2*

2. ODA LOANS GROSS

DAC COUNTRIES	1987	1988	1989	1990
Australia	–	–	–	–
Austria	–	–	–	–
Belgium	–	–	–	–
Canada	–	–	–	–
Denmark	–	–	–	–
Finland	–	–	–	–
France	–	–	–	–
Germany	–	–	–	–
Ireland	–	–	–	–
Italy	–	–	–	–
Japan	–	–	–	–
Netherlands	–	–	–	–
New Zealand	–	–	–	–
Norway	–	–	–	–
Sweden	–	–	–	–
Switzerland	–	–	–	–
United Kingdom	–	–	–	–
United States	–	–	–	–
TOTAL	–	–	–	–
MULTILATERAL				
ARAB COUNTRIES	–	–	–	–
E.E.C.+ MEMBERS	–	–	–	–
TOTAL	–	–	–	–

3. TOTAL OFFICIAL GROSS

DAC COUNTRIES	1987	1988	1989	1990
Australia	0.1	0.2	0.0	0.1
Austria	–	–	–	–
Belgium	–	–	–	–
Canada	–	–	–	–
Denmark	–	–	–	–
Finland	–	–	–	–
France	–	–	–	–
Germany	–	–	–	–
Ireland	–	–	–	–
Italy	–	–	–	–
Japan	0.0	0.0	0.0	0.0
Netherlands	–	–	–	–
New Zealand	–	–	–	0.0
Norway	–	–	–	–
Sweden	–	–	–	–
Switzerland	–	–	–	–
United Kingdom	–	–	–	–
United States	–	–	–	–
TOTAL	*0.1*	*0.2*	*0.1*	*0.2*
MULTILATERAL				
ARAB COUNTRIES	–	–	–	–
E.E.C.+ MEMBERS	–	–	–	–
TOTAL	*0.1*	*0.2*	*0.1*	*0.2*

4. TOTAL ODA NET

	1987	1988	1989	1990
Australia	0.1	0.2	0.0	0.1
Austria	–	–	–	–
Belgium	–	–	–	–
Canada	–	–	–	–
Denmark	–	–	–	–
Finland	–	–	–	–
France	–	–	–	–
Germany	–	–	–	–
Ireland	–	–	–	–
Italy	–	–	–	–
Japan	0.0	0.0	0.0	0.0
Netherlands	–	–	–	–
New Zealand	–	–	–	0.0
Norway	–	–	–	–
Sweden	–	–	–	–
Switzerland	–	–	–	–
United Kingdom	–	–	–	–
United States	–	–	–	–
TOTAL	–	–	–	–
(MULTILATERAL)	–	–	–	–
ARAB COUNTRIES	–	–	–	–
E.E.C.+ MEMBERS	–	–	–	–
TOTAL	*0.1*	*0.2*	*0.1*	*0.2*

5. ODA LOANS NET

	1987	1988	1989	1990
Australia	–	–	–	–
Austria	–	–	–	–
Belgium	–	–	–	–
Canada	–	–	–	–
Denmark	–	–	–	–
Finland	–	–	–	–
France	–	–	–	–
Germany	–	–	–	–
Ireland	–	–	–	–
Italy	–	–	–	–
Japan	–	–	–	–
Netherlands	–	–	–	–
New Zealand	–	–	–	–
Norway	–	–	–	–
Sweden	–	–	–	–
Switzerland	–	–	–	–
United Kingdom	–	–	–	–
United States	–	–	–	–
TOTAL	–	–	–	–
ARAB COUNTRIES	–	–	–	–
E.E.C.+ MEMBERS	–	–	–	–
TOTAL	–	–	–	–

6. TOTAL OFFICIAL NET

	1987	1988	1989	1990
Australia	0.1	0.2	0.0	0.1
Austria	–	–	–	–
Belgium	–	–	–	–
Canada	–	–	–	–
Denmark	–	–	–	–
Finland	–	–	–	–
France	–	–	–	–
Germany	–	–	–	–
Ireland	–	–	–	–
Italy	–	–	–	–
Japan	0.0	0.0	0.0	0.0
Netherlands	–	–	–	–
New Zealand	–	–	–	0.0
Norway	–	–	–	–
Sweden	–	–	–	–
Switzerland	–	–	–	–
United Kingdom	–	–	–	–
United States	–	–	–	–
TOTAL	*0.1*	*0.2*	*0.1*	*0.2*
ARAB COUNTRIES	–	–	–	–
E.E.C.+ MEMBERS	–	–	–	–
TOTAL	*0.1*	*0.2*	*0.1*	*0.2*

7. TOTAL ODA GROSS

	1987
Australia	0.1
Austria	–
Belgium	–
Canada	–
Denmark	–
Finland	–
France	–
Germany	–
Ireland	–
Italy	–
Japan	0.0
Netherlands	–
New Zealand	–
Norway	–
Sweden	–
Switzerland	–
United Kingdom	–
United States	–
TOTAL	*0.1*
AF.D.F.	–
AF.D.B.	–
AS.D.B	–
CAR.D.B.	–
E.E.C.	–
IBRD	–
IDA	–
I.D.B.	–
IFAD	–
I.F.C.	–
IMF TRUST FUND	–
U.N. AGENCIES	–
UNDP	–
UNTA	–
UNICEF	–
UNRWA	–
WFP	–
UNHCR	–
Other Multilateral	–
Arab Agencies	–
TOTAL	–
ARAB COUNTRIES	–
E.E.C.+ MEMBERS	–
TOTAL	*0.1*

8. GRANTS

	1987
Australia	0.1
Austria	–
Belgium	–
Canada	–
Denmark	–
Finland	–
France	–
Germany	–
Ireland	–
Italy	–
Japan	0.0
Netherlands	–
New Zealand	–
Norway	–
Sweden	–
Switzerland	–
United Kingdom	–
United States	–
TOTAL	*0.1*
MULTILATERAL	–
ARAB COUNTRIES	–
E.E.C.+ MEMBERS	–
TOTAL	*0.1*

9. TOTAL OOF GROSS

	1987
Australia	–
Austria	–
Belgium	–
Canada	–
Denmark	–
Finland	–
France	–
Germany	–
Ireland	–
Italy	–
Japan	–
Netherlands	–
New Zealand	–
Norway	–
Sweden	–
Switzerland	–
United Kingdom	–
United States	–
TOTAL	–
MULTILATERAL	–
ARAB COUNTRIES	–
E.E.C.+ MEMBERS	–
TOTAL	

NAURU

Left section

1988	1989	1990		1987	1988	1989	1990

10. ODA COMMITMENTS

1988	1989	1990	1987	1988	1989	1990
0.2	0.0	0.1	0.1	0.1	0.1	0.0
–	–	–	–	–	–	–
–	–	–	–	–	–	–
–	–	–	–	–	–	–
–	–	–	–	–	–	–
–	–	–	–	–	–	–
–	–	–	–	–	–	–
–	–	–	–	–	–	–
0.0	0.0	0.0	0.0	0.0	0.0	0.0
–	–	0.0	–	–	–	–
–	–	–	–	–	–	–
–	–	–	–	–	–	–
–	–	–	–	–	–	–
0.2	**0.1**	**0.2**	**0.1**	**0.1**	**0.1**	**0.1**

1988	1989	1990	1987	1988	1989	1990
–	–	–	–	–	–	–
–	–	–	–	–	–	–
–	–	–	–	–	–	–
–	–	–	–	–	–	–
–	–	–	–	–	–	–
–	–	–	–	–	–	–
–	–	–	–	–	–	–
–	–	–	–	–	–	–
–	–	–	–	–	–	–
–	–	–	–	–	–	–
–	–	–	–	–	–	–
–	–	–	–	–	–	–
–	–	–	–	–	–	–
–	–	–	–	–	–	–
–	–	–	–	–	–	–
–	–	–	–	–	–	–
–	–	–	–	–	–	–
0.2	**0.1**	**0.2**	**0.1**	**0.1**	**0.1**	**0.1**

11. TECH. COOP. GRANTS

1988	1989	1990	1987	1988	1989	1990
0.2	0.0	0.1	0.1	0.1	0.1	0.1
–	–	–	–	–	–	–
–	–	–	–	–	–	–
–	–	–	–	–	–	–
–	–	–	–	–	–	–
–	–	–	–	–	–	–
–	–	–	–	–	–	–
–	–	–	–	–	–	–
0.0	0.0	0.0	0.0	0.0	0.0	0.0
–	–	0.0	–	–	–	0.0
–	–	–	–	–	–	–
–	–	–	–	–	–	–
–	–	–	–	–	–	–
0.2	**0.1**	**0.2**	**0.1**	**0.1**	**0.1**	**0.2**
–	–	–	–	–	–	–
–	–	–	–	–	–	–
0.2	**0.1**	**0.2**	**0.1**	**0.1**	**0.1**	**0.2**

12. TOTAL OOF NET

1988	1989	1990	1987	1988	1989	1990
–	–	–	–	–	–	–
–	–	–	–	–	–	–
–	–	–	–	–	–	–
–	–	–	–	–	–	–
–	–	–	–	–	–	–
–	–	–	–	–	–	–
–	–	–	–	–	–	–
–	–	–	–	–	–	–
–	–	–	–	–	–	–
–	–	–	–	–	–	–
–	–	–	–	–	–	–
–	–	–	–	–	–	–
–	–	–	–	–	–	–
–	–	–	–	–	–	–
–	–	–	–	–	–	–
–	–	–	–	–	–	–
–	–	–	–	–	–	–
–	–	–	–	–	–	–
–	–	–	–	–	–	–
–	–	–	–	–	–	–
–	–	–	–	–	–	–

Right section

13. ODF COMMITMENTS: BY PURPOSE %

	1987	1988	1989	1990
Education	–	–	–	–
Health	–	–	–	–
Other Social Infrastr.	–	–	–	–
Water Sanitat. Sewage	–	–	–	–
Energy	–	–	–	–
Telecommunications	–	–	–	–
Transportation	–	–	–	–
Agriculture	–	–	–	–
Extractive Industries	–	–	–	–
Manufacturing	–	–	–	–
Trade Banking Tourism	–	–	–	–
Technical Cooperation	100	100	100	–
Multisector Aid	–	–	–	–
Programme	–	–	–	–
Debt Reorganisation	–	–	–	–
Food Aid	–	–	–	–
Emergency Aid	–	–	–	–
Unspecified	–	–	–	–
TOTAL	100	100	100	–

14. GRANT ELEMENT OF ODA %

DAC COUNTRIES	1987	1988	1989	1990
Australia	100.0	100.0	100.0	–
Austria	–	–	–	–
Belgium	–	–	–	–
Canada	–	–	–	–
Denmark	–	–	–	–
Finland	–	–	–	–
France	–	–	–	–
Germany	–	–	–	–
Ireland	–	–	–	–
Italy	–	–	–	–
Japan	100.0	100.0	100.0	–
Netherlands	–	–	–	–
New Zealand	–	–	–	–
Norway	–	–	–	–
Sweden	–	–	–	–
Switzerland	–	–	–	–
United Kingdom	–	–	–	–
United States	–	–	–	–
TOTAL	*100.0*	*100.0*	*100.0*	–
MULTILATERAL	–	–	–	–
ARAB COUNTRIES	–	–	–	–
E.E.C.+ MEMBERS	–	–	–	–
TOTAL	**100.0**	**100.0**	**100.0**	–

15. OTHER AGGREGATES

	1987	1988	1989	1990
OFFICIAL COMMITMENTS:				
TOTAL BILATERAL	0.1	0.1	0.1	0.1
of which:				
Arab Countries	–	–	–	–
C.E.E.C.	–	–	–	–
TOTAL MULTILATERAL	–	–	–	–
TOTAL BIL.& MULTIL.	0.1	0.1	0.1	0.1
of which:				
ODA Grants	0.1	0.1	0.1	0.1
ODA Loans	–	–	–	–
DISBURSEMENTS:				
DAC COUNTRIES COMBINED				
OFFICIAL & PRIVATE				
GROSS:				
Contractual Lending	–	–	–	–
Export Credits, Total	–	–	–	–
Export Credits, Priv.	–	–	–	–
NET:				
Contractual Lending	–	–	–	–
Export Credits Total	–	–	–	–
PRIVATE SECTOR NET	0.7	26.7	-8.9	1.0
Direct Investment	-1.1	-1.1	–	-0.3
Portfolio Investment	1.8	27.8	-8.9	1.3
Export Credits	–	–	–	–
MARKET BORROWING:				
CHANGE IN CLAIMS				
Banks	4.0	-3.0	18.0	63.0
MEMORANDUM ITEM:				
C.E.E.C. (Gross)	–	–	–	–

1. TOTAL RECEIPTS NET

DAC COUNTRIES	1987	1988	1989	1990
Australia	2.8	3.4	3.6	1.2
Austria	0.6	0.3	1.5	6.4
Belgium	4.7	1.4	0.4	-5.0
Canada	7.8	12.5	10.6	8.4
Denmark	8.1	9.8	9.0	7.8
Finland	9.9	6.2	18.5	15.5
France	24.7	22.1	19.0	27.2
Germany	26.6	67.6	38.5	34.9
Ireland	0.0	0.0	0.0	0.0
Italy	0.8	1.1	2.2	0.1
Japan	72.6	61.5	76.9	63.6
Netherlands	4.4	5.1	4.3	5.7
New Zealand	0.1	0.1	0.1	0.1
Norway	3.1	3.8	5.0	9.8
Sweden	-0.2	–	–	–
Switzerland	9.7	12.8	19.5	16.0
United Kingdom	21.6	31.7	27.5	23.6
United States	19.0	15.0	14.0	17.0
TOTAL	216.3	254.2	250.4	232.3
MULTILATERAL				
AF.D.F.	–	–	–	–
AF.D.B.	–	–	–	–
AS.D.B	27.8	41.7	82.7	65.7
CAR.D.B.	–	–	–	–
E.E.C.	4.7	3.5	2.0	2.0
IBRD	–	–	–	–
IDA	78.4	82.0	107.0	65.0
I.D.B.	–	–	–	–
IFAD	8.6	6.2	7.7	10.0
I.F.C.	–	–	0.9	4.7
IMF TRUST FUND	–	–	–	–
U.N. AGENCIES	–	–	–	–
UNDP	13.5	18.0	20.9	22.8
UNTA	2.5	1.8	3.3	2.0
UNICEF	5.9	6.8	7.4	7.9
UNRWA	–	–	–	–
WFP	5.6	6.9	5.4	6.6
UNHCR	–	0.1	0.2	0.1
Other Multilateral	5.0	2.9	5.5	5.5
Arab Agencies	1.8	-0.1	0.3	–
TOTAL	153.6	169.9	243.3	192.4
ARAB COUNTRIES	3.6	4.3	2.3	2.3
E.E.C.+ MEMBERS	95.5	142.3	102.9	96.2
TOTAL	373.5	428.4	496.0	426.9

2. ODA LOANS GROSS

DAC COUNTRIES	1987	1988	1989	1990
Australia	–	–	–	–
Austria	–	–	–	5.3
Belgium	–	–	–	–
Canada	–	–	–	–
Denmark	–	–	–	–
Finland	–	–	–	–
France	1.1	4.1	6.7	25.9
Germany	–	–	–	1.2
Ireland	–	–	–	–
Italy	–	–	–	–
Japan	13.1	7.8	22.0	9.4
Netherlands	–	–	–	–
New Zealand	–	–	–	–
Norway	–	–	–	0.3
Sweden	–	–	–	–
Switzerland	–	–	–	–
United Kingdom	–	–	–	–
United States	–	–	–	–
TOTAL	14.1	11.8	28.7	42.1
MULTILATERAL	120.7	133.9	199.4	143.2
ARAB COUNTRIES	4.6	5.3	3.3	3.5
E.E.C.+ MEMBERS	1.1	4.1	6.7	27.1
TOTAL	139.4	151.0	231.4	188.8

3. TOTAL OFFICIAL GROSS

DAC COUNTRIES	1987	1988	1989	1990
Australia	2.8	3.4	3.6	1.2
Austria	0.6	0.3	1.5	6.4
Belgium	0.4	0.1	0.5	0.1
Canada	7.8	12.5	10.6	8.4
Denmark	8.1	9.8	9.1	7.9
Finland	9.9	6.2	18.5	15.5
France	2.2	5.5	17.6	34.0
Germany	27.1	68.5	38.0	35.6
Ireland	0.0	0.0	0.0	0.0
Italy	0.8	1.1	1.8	0.1
Japan	77.8	63.7	78.8	56.5
Netherlands	4.4	5.1	4.6	5.9
New Zealand	0.1	0.1	0.1	0.1
Norway	3.1	3.8	5.0	9.7
Sweden	–	–	–	–
Switzerland	9.7	12.8	19.5	16.0
United Kingdom	16.5	19.3	28.4	26.0
United States	20.0	15.0	14.0	17.0
TOTAL	191.3	227.1	251.5	240.5
MULTILATERAL	159.1	176.7	250.7	203.7
ARAB COUNTRIES	4.6	5.3	3.3	3.5
E.E.C.+ MEMBERS	64.1	113.0	102.0	111.6
TOTAL	355.0	409.0	505.5	447.7

4. TOTAL ODA NET

DAC COUNTRIES	1987	1988	1989	1990
Australia	2.8	3.4	3.6	1.2
Austria	0.6	0.3	1.5	6.4
Belgium	0.4	0.1	0.5	0.1
Canada	7.8	12.5	10.6	8.4
Denmark	8.0	9.2	8.1	7.8
Finland	9.9	6.2	18.5	15.5
France	2.2	5.5	17.6	34.0
Germany	26.7	68.5	38.0	35.6
Ireland	0.0	0.0	0.0	0.0
Italy	0.8	1.1	1.8	0.1
Japan	76.8	62.4	77.4	55.2
Netherlands	4.4	5.1	4.6	5.9
New Zealand	0.1	0.1	0.1	0.1
Norway	3.1	3.8	5.0	9.8
Sweden	–	–	–	–
Switzerland	9.7	12.8	19.5	16.0
United Kingdom	16.3	19.1	28.2	25.8
United States	20.0	15.0	14.0	17.0
TOTAL	189.6	224.9	248.9	238.8
MULTILATERAL				
AF.D.F.	–	–	–	–
AF.D.B.	–	–	–	–
AS.D.B	27.8	41.7	82.7	65.7
CAR.D.B.	–	–	–	–
E.E.C.	4.7	3.5	2.0	2.0
IBRD	–	–	–	–
IDA	78.4	82.0	107.0	65.0
I.D.B.	–	–	–	–
IFAD	8.6	6.2	7.7	10.0
I.F.C.	–	–	–	–
IMF TRUST FUND	–	–	–	–
U.N. AGENCIES	–	–	–	–
UNDP	13.5	18.0	20.9	22.8
UNTA	2.5	1.8	3.3	2.0
UNICEF	5.9	6.8	7.4	7.9
UNRWA	–	–	–	–
WFP	5.6	6.9	5.4	6.6
UNHCR	–	0.1	0.2	0.1
Other Multilateral	5.0	2.9	5.5	5.5
Arab Agencies	1.8	-0.1	0.3	–
TOTAL	153.6	169.9	242.4	187.6
ARAB COUNTRIES	3.6	4.3	2.3	2.3
E.E.C.+ MEMBERS	63.4	112.1	100.8	111.2
TOTAL	346.8	399.0	493.6	428.8

5. ODA LOANS NET

DAC COUNTRIES	1987	1988	1989	1990
Australia	–	–	–	–
Austria	–	–	–	5.3
Belgium	–	–	–	–
Canada	–	–	–	–
Denmark	–	–	–	–
Finland	–	–	–	–
France	1.1	4.1	6.7	25.9
Germany	-0.3	0.0	–	1.2
Ireland	–	–	–	–
Italy	–	–	–	–
Japan	12.0	6.4	20.6	8.0
Netherlands	–	–	–	–
New Zealand	–	–	–	–
Norway	–	–	–	0.3
Sweden	–	–	–	–
Switzerland	–	–	–	–
United Kingdom	-0.2	-0.2	-0.2	-0.2
United States	–	–	–	–
TOTAL	12.6	10.3	27.1	40.5
MULTILATERAL	115.1	127.1	192.0	135.2
ARAB COUNTRIES	3.6	4.3	2.3	2.3
E.E.C.+ MEMBERS	0.5	3.9	6.5	26.9
TOTAL	131.3	141.6	221.4	178.0

6. TOTAL OFFICIAL NET

DAC COUNTRIES	1987	1988	1989	1990
Australia	2.8	3.4	3.6	1.2
Austria	0.6	0.3	1.5	6.4
Belgium	0.4	0.1	0.5	0.1
Canada	7.8	12.5	10.6	8.4
Denmark	8.1	9.8	9.0	7.8
Finland	9.9	6.2	18.5	15.5
France	2.2	5.5	17.6	34.0
Germany	26.7	68.5	38.0	35.6
Ireland	0.0	0.0	0.0	0.0
Italy	0.8	1.1	1.8	0.1
Japan	76.8	62.4	77.4	55.2
Netherlands	4.4	5.1	4.6	5.9
New Zealand	0.1	0.1	0.1	0.1
Norway	3.1	3.8	5.0	9.8
Sweden	–	–	–	–
Switzerland	9.7	12.8	19.5	16.0
United Kingdom	16.3	19.1	28.2	25.8
United States	20.0	15.0	14.0	17.0
TOTAL	189.7	225.5	249.8	238.9
MULTILATERAL	153.6	169.9	243.3	192.4
ARAB COUNTRIES	3.6	4.3	2.3	2.3
E.E.C.+ MEMBERS	63.5	112.7	101.7	111.3
TOTAL	346.9	399.6	495.4	433.5

7. TOTAL ODA GROSS

	1987
Australia	2.8
Austria	0.6
Belgium	0.4
Canada	7.8
Denmark	8.0
Finland	9.9
France	2.2
Germany	27.1
Ireland	0.0
Italy	0.8
Japan	77.8
Netherlands	4.4
New Zealand	0.1
Norway	3.1
Sweden	–
Switzerland	9.7
United Kingdom	16.5
United States	20.0
TOTAL	191.2
AF.D.F.	–
AF.D.B.	–
AS.D.B	30.7
CAR.D.B.	–
E.E.C.	4.7
IBRD	–
IDA	79.5
I.D.B.	–
IFAD	8.6
I.F.C.	–
IMF TRUST FUND	–
U.N. AGENCIES	–
UNDP	13.5
UNTA	2.5
UNICEF	5.9
UNRWA	–
WFP	5.6
UNHCR	–
Other Multilateral	5.0
Arab Agencies	3.4
TOTAL	159.1
ARAB COUNTRIES	4.6
E.E.C.+ MEMBERS	64.0
TOTAL	354.9

8. GRANTS

	1987
Australia	2.8
Austria	0.6
Belgium	0.4
Canada	7.8
Denmark	8.0
Finland	9.9
France	1.1
Germany	27.1
Ireland	0.0
Italy	0.8
Japan	64.7
Netherlands	4.4
New Zealand	0.1
Norway	3.1
Sweden	–
Switzerland	9.7
United Kingdom	16.5
United States	20.0
TOTAL	177.0
MULTILATERAL	38.5
ARAB COUNTRIES	0.0
E.E.C.+ MEMBERS	62.9
TOTAL	215.5

9. TOTAL OOF GROSS

	1987
Australia	–
Austria	–
Belgium	–
Canada	–
Denmark	0.1
Finland	–
France	–
Germany	–
Ireland	–
Italy	–
Japan	–
Netherlands	–
New Zealand	–
Norway	–
Sweden	–
Switzerland	–
United Kingdom	–
United States	–
TOTAL	0.1
MULTILATERAL	–
ARAB COUNTRIES	–
E.E.C.+ MEMBERS	0.1
TOTAL	0.1

1988	1989	1990	1987	1988	1989	1990

10. ODA COMMITMENTS

1988	1989	1990	1987	1988	1989	1990
3.4	3.6	1.2	1.1	1.1	1.2	2.6
0.3	1.5	6.4	1.6	0.9	0.7	7.2
0.1	0.5	0.1	0.7	0.2	0.5	0.1
12.5	10.6	8.4	12.3	3.5	19.8	1.3
9.2	8.1	7.8	14.6	3.9	7.2	3.2
6.2	18.5	15.5	4.1	5.7	54.7	11.6
5.5	17.6	34.0	0.8	37.7	18.0	23.3
68.5	38.0	35.6	8.6	47.5	11.8	34.4
0.0	0.0	0.0	0.0	0.0	0.0	0.0
1.1	1.8	0.1	1.5	1.7	1.7	0.4
63.7	78.8	56.5	180.8	88.6	52.3	67.4
5.1	4.6	5.9	2.2	2.6	5.1	9.6
0.1	0.1	0.1	0.1	0.0	–	–
3.8	5.0	9.7	0.8	0.0	0.0	1.1
–	–	–	–	–	–	–
12.8	19.5	16.0	23.8	15.2	27.4	14.9
19.3	28.4	26.0	18.0	18.5	28.1	22.8
15.0	14.0	17.0	17.2	12.9	16.3	18.4
226.5	*250.5*	*240.4*	*288.0*	*240.1*	*244.9*	*218.2*
–	–	–	–	–	–	–
–	–	–	–	–	–	–
45.0	86.4	70.0	141.6	103.2	127.3	130.6
–	–	–	–	–	–	–
3.5	2.0	2.0	4.5	0.4	1.6	1.6
–	–	–	–	–	–	–
84.0	109.0	67.0	90.0	71.0	199.0	47.0
–	–	–	–	–	–	–
6.2	8.0	10.3	6.1	–	13.2	0.2
–	–	–	–	–	–	–
–	–	–	–	–	–	–
–	–	–	32.4	36.6	42.7	44.9
18.0	20.9	22.8	–	–	–	–
1.8	3.3	2.0	–	–	–	–
6.8	7.4	7.9	–	–	–	–
–	–	–	–	–	–	–
6.9	5.4	6.6	–	–	–	–
0.1	0.2	0.1	–	–	–	–
2.9	5.5	5.5	–	–	–	–
1.4	1.6	0.2	4.0	2.5	5.0	–
176.7	*249.8*	*194.4*	*278.5*	*213.7*	*388.7*	*224.2*
5.3	*3.3*	*3.5*	*8.0*	–	–	–
112.4	*101.0*	*111.5*	*50.7*	*112.6*	*74.1*	*95.3*
408.4	**503.6**	**438.3**	**574.5**	**453.8**	**633.6**	**442.4**

11. TECH. COOP. GRANTS

1988	1989	1990	1987	1988	1989	1990
3.4	3.6	1.2	0.1	0.4	1.8	-1.1
0.3	1.5	1.1	0.2	0.1	0.1	0.2
0.1	0.5	0.1	0.2	0.1	–	–
12.5	10.6	8.4	–	2.0	1.6	–
9.2	8.1	7.8	0.4	2.5	2.6	4.3
6.2	18.5	15.5	0.2	1.4	0.8	3.6
1.4	10.9	8.0	0.4	0.3	0.5	0.7
68.5	38.0	34.4	13.6	15.1	15.4	16.7
0.0	0.0	0.0	0.0	0.0	0.0	0.0
1.1	1.8	0.1	0.3	0.4	0.0	0.0
55.9	56.8	47.1	14.7	14.6	14.6	12.9
5.1	4.6	5.9	2.2	2.2	2.4	2.8
0.1	0.1	0.1	0.0	0.0	–	0.1
3.8	5.0	9.4	0.3	0.5	0.6	0.4
–	–	–	–	–	–	–
12.8	19.5	16.0	3.0	3.6	–	–
19.3	28.4	26.0	7.9	12.3	12.6	14.0
15.0	14.0	17.0	14.0	15.0	12.0	15.0
214.7	*221.8*	*198.3*	*57.5*	*70.3*	*64.8*	*69.6*
42.7	*50.4*	*51.2*	*27.3*	*29.9*	*37.2*	*38.4*
–	–	–	–	–	–	–
108.3	*94.3*	*84.4*	*25.4*	*33.0*	*33.4*	*38.5*
257.4	**272.2**	**249.5**	**84.7**	**100.2**	**102.1**	**107.9**

12. TOTAL OOF NET

1988	1989	1990	1987	1988	1989	1990
–	–	–	–	–	–	–
–	–	–	–	–	–	–
0.6	1.0	0.1	0.1	0.6	0.9	0.0
–	–	–	–	–	–	–
–	–	–	–	–	–	–
–	–	–	–	–	–	–
–	–	–	–	–	–	–
–	–	–	–	–	–	–
–	–	–	–	–	–	–
–	–	–	–	–	–	–
–	–	–	–	–	–	–
–	–	–	–	–	–	–
–	–	–	–	–	–	–
–	–	–	–	–	–	–
0.6	*1.0*	*0.1*	*0.1*	*0.6*	*0.9*	*0.0*
–	0.9	9.2	–	–	0.9	4.7
–	–	–	–	–	–	–
0.6	*1.0*	*0.1*	*0.1*	*0.6*	*0.9*	*0.0*
0.6	**1.9**	**9.4**	**0.1**	**0.6**	**1.8**	**4.7**

13. ODF COMMITMENTS: BY PURPOSE %

	1987	1988	1989	1990
Education	0	3	11	–
Health	4	1	1	–
Other Social Infrastr.	1	1	7	–
Water Sanitat. Sewage	2	4	5	–
Energy	2	8	9	–
Telecommunications	1	2	2	–
Transportation	10	11	18	–
Agriculture	23	45	16	–
Extractive Industries	–	0	–	–
Manufacturing	28	–	–	–
Trade Banking Tourism	0	1	1	–
Technical Cooperation	18	22	19	–
Multisector Aid	0	0	0	–
Programme	10	2	11	–
Debt Reorganisation	0	0	1	–
Food Aid	0	0	–	–
Emergency Aid	0	0	0	–
Unspecified	0	0	0	–
TOTAL	100	100	100	–

14. GRANT ELEMENT OF ODA %

DAC COUNTRIES

	1987	1988	1989	1990
Australia	100.0	100.0	100.0	–
Austria	100.0	100.0	100.0	–
Belgium	100.0	100.0	100.0	–
Canada	100.0	100.0	100.0	–
Denmark	100.0	100.0	100.0	–
Finland	100.0	100.0	100.0	–
France	100.0	69.4	71.0	–
Germany	100.0	100.0	100.0	–
Ireland	100.0	100.0	100.0	–
Italy	100.0	100.0	100.0	–
Japan	80.0	100.0	100.0	–
Netherlands	100.0	100.0	100.0	–
New Zealand	100.0	100.0	–	–
Norway	100.0	100.0	100.0	–
Sweden	–	–	–	–
Switzerland	100.0	100.0	100.0	–
United Kingdom	100.0	100.0	100.0	–
United States	100.0	100.0	100.0	–
TOTAL	*87.4*	*95.6*	*97.8*	–
MULTILATERAL	*82.9*	*81.5*	*81.5*	–
ARAB COUNTRIES	*43.4*	–	–	–
E.E.C.+ MEMBERS	*100.0*	*90.4*	*92.9*	–
TOTAL	*84.7*	*88.2*	*88.0*	–

15. OTHER AGGREGATES

	1987	1988	1989	1990
OFFICIAL COMMITMENTS:				
TOTAL BILATERAL	296.2	242.0	244.9	218.2
of which:				
Arab Countries	8.0	–	–	–
C.E.E.C.	–	–	–	–
TOTAL MULTILATERAL	278.5	213.7	388.7	226.3
TOTAL BIL.& MULTIL.	574.7	455.7	633.6	444.5
of which:				
ODA Grants	195.1	250.2	277.3	227.0
ODA Loans	379.5	203.6	356.3	215.5
DISBURSEMENTS:				
DAC COUNTRIES COMBINED				
OFFICIAL & PRIVATE				
GROSS:				
Contractual Lending	56.9	37.7	56.0	53.3
Export Credits, Total	42.6	25.3	26.3	11.1
Export Credits, Priv.	42.6	25.3	26.3	11.1
NET:				
Contractual Lending	39.7	29.0	46.9	29.8
Export Credits Total	27.0	18.1	18.9	-10.8
PRIVATE SECTOR NET	26.6	28.7	0.7	-6.6
Direct Investment	1.4	0.7	0.4	5.9
Portfolio Investment	-1.7	9.9	-18.7	-1.8
Export Credits	27.0	18.1	18.9	-10.8
MARKET BORROWING:				
CHANGE IN CLAIMS				
Banks	14.0	29.0	-10.0	-6.0
MEMORANDUM ITEM:				
C.E.E.C. (Gross)	–	25.5	–	–

DISBURSEMENTS, UNLESS OTHERWISE STATED

1. TOTAL RECEIPTS NET

DAC COUNTRIES	1987	1988	1989	1990
Australia	–	–	–	–
Austria	–	–	–	–
Belgium	-27.4	204.6	117.4	40.4
Canada	-0.4	–	–	0.1
Denmark	–	–	–	–
Finland	–	–	–	–
France	208.6	-75.9	367.4	1066.3
Germany	191.9	345.5	-56.9	-53.3
Ireland	–	–	–	–
Italy	1.7	709.7	9.7	-13.6
Japan	168.8	115.0	50.5	-50.3
Netherlands	-250.7	530.9	289.4	93.8
New Zealand	–	–	–	–
Norway	–	–	–	12.3
Sweden	-1.4	–	-1.4	-1.3
Switzerland	–	–	–	–
United Kingdom	-16.6	-4.2	75.5	–
United States	10.0	-8.0	38.0	79.0
TOTAL	*284.5*	*1817.5*	*889.6*	*1173.4*
MULTILATERAL				
AF.D.F.	–	–	–	–
AF.D.B.	–	–	–	–
AS.D.B	–	–	–	–
CAR.D.B.	–	–	–	–
E.E.C.	2.4	8.7	4.8	4.8
IBRD	–	–	–	–
IDA	–	–	–	–
I.D.B.	–	–	–	–
IFAD	–	–	–	–
I.F.C.	–	–	–	–
IMF TRUST FUND	–	–	–	–
U.N. AGENCIES	–	–	–	–
UNDP	0.4	0.3	0.3	0.4
UNTA	0.0	0.0	0.0	0.1
UNICEF	–	–	–	–
UNRWA	–	–	–	–
WFP	–	–	–	–
UNHCR	–	–	–	–
Other Multilateral	–	0.0	0.1	0.2
Arab Agencies	–	–	–	–
TOTAL	*2.8*	*9.1*	*5.3*	*5.4*
ARAB COUNTRIES	–	–	–	–
E.E.C.+ MEMBERS	*109.9*	*1719.2*	*807.3*	*1138.4*
TOTAL	*287.4*	*1826.6*	*895.0*	*1178.8*

2. ODA LOANS GROSS

DAC COUNTRIES	1987	1988	1989	1990
Australia	–	–	–	–
Austria	–	–	–	–
Belgium	–	–	–	–
Canada	–	–	–	–
Denmark	–	–	–	–
Finland	–	–	–	–
France	–	–	–	–
Germany	–	–	–	–
Ireland	–	–	–	–
Italy	–	–	–	–
Japan	–	–	–	–
Netherlands	20.1	15.8	18.5	4.9
New Zealand	–	–	–	–
Norway	–	–	–	–
Sweden	–	–	–	–
Switzerland	–	–	–	–
United Kingdom	–	–	–	–
United States	–	–	–	–
TOTAL	*20.1*	*15.8*	*18.5*	*4.9*
MULTILATERAL	–	0.3	0.2	0.2
ARAB COUNTRIES	–	–	–	–
E.E.C.+ MEMBERS	*20.1*	*16.2*	*18.7*	*5.1*
TOTAL	*20.1*	*16.2*	*18.7*	*5.1*

3. TOTAL OFFICIAL GROSS

DAC COUNTRIES	1987	1988	1989	1990
Australia	–	–	–	–
Austria	–	–	–	–
Belgium	0.0	–	–	–
Canada	–	–	–	0.1
Denmark	–	–	–	–
Finland	–	–	–	–
France	–	–	–	–
Germany	–	0.0	–	–
Ireland	–	–	–	–
Italy	–	–	10.3	23.1
Japan	0.0	0.0	–	0.0
Netherlands	72.7	63.5	69.9	52.9
New Zealand	–	–	–	–
Norway	–	–	–	–
Sweden	–	–	–	–
Switzerland	–	–	–	–
United Kingdom	–	–	–	–
United States	1.0	–	–	–
TOTAL	*73.8*	*63.5*	*80.2*	*76.1*
MULTILATERAL	*3.0*	*9.3*	*5.8*	*5.9*
ARAB COUNTRIES	–	–	–	–
E.E.C.+ MEMBERS	*75.4*	*72.4*	*85.5*	*81.3*
TOTAL	*76.8*	*72.8*	*86.0*	*82.0*

4. TOTAL ODA NET

DAC COUNTRIES	1987	1988	1989	1990
Australia	–	–	–	–
Austria	–	–	–	–
Belgium	0.0	–	–	–
Canada	–	–	–	0.1
Denmark	–	–	–	–
Finland	–	–	–	–
France	–	–	–	–
Germany	–	–	–	–
Ireland	–	–	–	–
Italy	–	–	–	–
Japan	0.0	0.0	–	0.0
Netherlands	61.9	51.0	57.0	52.9
New Zealand	–	–	–	–
Norway	–	–	–	–
Sweden	–	–	–	–
Switzerland	–	–	–	–
United Kingdom	–	–	–	–
United States	–	–	–	–
TOTAL	*61.9*	*51.0*	*57.0*	*53.0*
MULTILATERAL				
AF.D.F.	–	–	–	–
AF.D.B.	–	–	–	–
AS.D.B	–	–	–	–
CAR.D.B.	–	–	–	–
E.E.C.	2.2	2.1	3.8	3.8
IBRD	–	–	–	–
IDA	–	–	–	–
I.D.B.	–	–	–	–
IFAD	–	–	–	–
I.F.C.	–	–	–	–
IMF TRUST FUND	–	–	–	–
U.N. AGENCIES	–	–	–	–
UNDP	0.4	0.3	0.3	0.4
UNTA	0.0	0.0	0.0	0.1
UNICEF	–	–	–	–
UNRWA	–	–	–	–
WFP	–	–	–	–
UNHCR	–	–	–	–
Other Multilateral	–	0.0	0.1	0.2
Arab Agencies	–	–	–	–
TOTAL	*2.6*	*2.5*	*4.3*	*4.4*
ARAB COUNTRIES	–	–	–	–
E.E.C.+ MEMBERS	*64.1*	*53.1*	*60.8*	*56.7*
TOTAL	*64.5*	*53.4*	*61.3*	*57.4*

5. ODA LOANS NET

DAC COUNTRIES	1987	1988	1989	1990
Australia	–	–	–	–
Austria	–	–	–	–
Belgium	–	–	–	–
Canada	–	–	–	–
Denmark	–	–	–	–
Finland	–	–	–	–
France	–	–	–	–
Germany	–	–	–	–
Ireland	–	–	–	–
Italy	–	–	–	–
Japan	–	–	–	–
Netherlands	9.2	3.3	5.5	4.9
New Zealand	–	–	–	–
Norway	–	–	–	–
Sweden	–	–	–	–
Switzerland	–	–	–	–
United Kingdom	–	–	–	–
United States	–	–	–	–
TOTAL	*9.2*	*3.3*	*5.5*	*4.9*
MULTILATERAL	-0.2	0.1	0.0	0.0
ARAB COUNTRIES	–	–	–	–
E.E.C.+ MEMBERS	*9.0*	*3.5*	*5.5*	*5.0*
TOTAL	*9.0*	*3.5*	*5.5*	*5.0*

6. TOTAL OFFICIAL NET

DAC COUNTRIES	1987	1988	1989	1990
Australia	–	–	–	–
Austria	–	–	–	–
Belgium	0.0	–	–	–
Canada	-0.4	–	–	0.1
Denmark	–	–	–	–
Finland	–	–	–	–
France	–	–	–	–
Germany	–	0.0	–	–
Ireland	–	–	–	–
Italy	–	–	9.7	-9.9
Japan	0.0	0.0	–	0.0
Netherlands	61.9	51.0	57.0	52.9
New Zealand	–	–	–	–
Norway	–	–	–	–
Sweden	–	–	–	–
Switzerland	–	–	–	–
United Kingdom	–	–	–	–
United States	-19.0	-2.0	-2.0	-1.0
TOTAL	*42.5*	*49.0*	*64.7*	*42.1*
MULTILATERAL	*2.8*	*9.1*	*5.3*	*5.4*
ARAB COUNTRIES	–	–	–	–
E.E.C.+ MEMBERS	*64.3*	*59.7*	*71.5*	*47.9*
TOTAL	*45.4*	*58.1*	*70.0*	*47.5*

7. TOTAL ODA GROSS

	1987
Australia	–
Austria	–
Belgium	0.0
Canada	–
Denmark	–
France	–
Germany	–
Ireland	–
Italy	–
Japan	0.0
Netherlands	72.7
New Zealand	–
Norway	–
Sweden	–
Switzerland	–
United Kingdom	–
United States	–
TOTAL	*72.8*
AF.D.F.	–
AF.D.B.	–
AS.D.B	–
CAR.D.B.	–
E.E.C.	2.4
IBRD	–
IDA	–
I.D.B.	–
IFAD	–
I.F.C.	–
IMF TRUST FUND	–
U.N. AGENCIES	–
UNDP	0.4
UNTA	0.0
UNICEF	–
UNRWA	–
WFP	–
UNHCR	–
Other Multilateral	–
Arab Agencies	–
TOTAL	*2.8*
ARAB COUNTRIES	–
E.E.C.+ MEMBERS	*75.1*
TOTAL	*75.6*

8. GRANTS

	1987
Australia	–
Austria	–
Belgium	0.0
Canada	–
Denmark	–
Finland	–
France	–
Germany	–
Ireland	–
Italy	–
Japan	0.0
Netherlands	52.7
New Zealand	–
Norway	–
Sweden	–
Switzerland	–
United Kingdom	–
United States	–
TOTAL	*52.7*
MULTILATERAL	*2.8*
ARAB COUNTRIES	–
E.E.C.+ MEMBERS	*55.1*
TOTAL	*55.5*

9. TOTAL OOF GROSS

	1987
Australia	–
Austria	–
Belgium	–
Canada	–
Denmark	–
Finland	–
France	–
Germany	–
Ireland	–
Italy	–
Japan	–
Netherlands	–
New Zealand	–
Norway	–
Sweden	–
Switzerland	–
United Kingdom	–
United States	1.0
TOTAL	*1.0*
MULTILATERAL	*0.2*
ARAB COUNTRIES	–
E.E.C.+ MEMBERS	*0.2*
TOTAL	*1.2*

1988	1989	1990	1987	1988	1989	1990

10. ODA COMMITMENTS

1988	1989	1990	1987	1988	1989	1990
–	–	–	–	–	–	–
–	–	–	–	–	–	–
–	–	0.1	–	–	–	–
–	–	–	–	–	–	–
–	–	–	–	–	–	–
–	–	–	–	–	–	–
–	–	–	–	–	–	–
0.0	–	0.0	0.0	0.0	–	0.0
63.5	69.9	52.9	74.6	74.0	74.1	60.4
–	–	–	–	–	–	–
–	–	–	–	–	–	–
–	–	–	–	–	–	–
–	–	–	–	–	–	–
63.5	69.9	53.0	74.6	74.0	74.1	60.4
–	–	–	–	–	–	–
–	–	–	–	–	–	–
–	–	–	–	–	–	–
2.3	4.0	4.0	0.3	16.9	3.1	3.1
–	–	–	–	–	–	–
–	–	–	–	–	–	–
–	–	–	–	–	–	–
–	–	–	–	–	–	–
–	–	–	0.4	0.3	0.5	0.6
0.3	0.3	0.4	–	–	–	–
0.0	0.0	0.1	–	–	–	–
–	–	–	–	–	–	–
–	–	–	–	–	–	–
0.0	0.1	0.2	–	–	–	–
–	–	–	–	–	–	–
2.7	4.5	4.6	0.7	17.2	3.6	3.7
–	–	–	–	–	–	–
65.8	73.9	56.9	74.8	90.9	77.2	63.5
66.1	74.4	57.6	75.2	91.3	77.7	64.1

11. TECH. COOP. GRANTS

1988	1989	1990	1987	1988	1989	1990
–	–	–	–	–	–	–
–	–	–	–	–	–	–
–	–	0.1	–	–	–	–
–	–	–	–	–	–	–
–	–	–	–	–	–	–
–	–	–	–	–	–	–
–	–	–	–	–	–	–
0.0	–	0.0	0.0	0.0	–	0.0
47.6	51.5	48.0	5.6	7.7	5.7	6.7
–	–	–	–	–	–	–
–	–	–	–	–	–	–
–	–	–	–	–	–	–
–	–	–	–	–	–	–
47.6	51.5	48.1	5.6	7.7	5.7	6.7
2.3	4.3	4.4	0.5	0.6	0.5	0.6
–	–	–	–	–	–	–
49.6	55.3	51.8	5.7	8.0	5.7	6.7
50.0	55.8	52.5	6.2	8.3	6.2	7.3

12. TOTAL OOF NET

1988	1989	1990	1987	1988	1989	1990
–	–	–	–	–	–	–
–	–	–	–	–	–	–
–	–	–	-0.4	–	–	–
–	–	–	–	–	–	–
–	–	–	–	–	–	–
0.0	–	–	–	0.0	–	–
–	10.3	23.1	–	–	9.7	-9.9
–	–	–	–	–	–	–
–	–	–	–	–	–	–
–	–	–	–	–	–	–
–	–	–	–	–	–	–
–	–	–	-19.0	-2.0	-2.0	-1.0
0.0	10.3	23.1	-19.4	-2.0	7.7	-10.9
6.6	1.3	1.3	0.2	6.6	1.0	1.0
–	–	–	–	–	–	–
6.6	11.6	24.4	0.2	6.6	10.8	-8.9
6.6	11.6	24.4	-19.1	4.6	8.8	-9.9

13. ODF COMMITMENTS: BY PURPOSE %

	1987	1988	1989	1990
Education	1	1	1	–
Health	0	0	0	–
Other Social Infrastr.	28	29	29	–
Water Sanitat. Sewage	2	2	2	–
Energy	3	3	3	–
Telecommunications	2	2	2	–
Transportation	14	15	15	–
Agriculture	0	0	0	–
Extractive Industries	–	–	–	–
Manufacturing	–	–	–	–
Trade Banking Tourism	10	10	10	–
Technical Cooperation	12	8	10	–
Multisector Aid	28	30	28	–
Programme	–	–	–	–
Debt Reorganisation	–	–	–	–
Food Aid	0	0	0	–
Emergency Aid	–	–	–	–
Unspecified	–	–	–	–
TOTAL	100	100	100	–

14. GRANT ELEMENT OF ODA %

DAC COUNTRIES

	1987	1988	1989	1990
Australia	–	–	–	–
Austria	–	–	–	–
Belgium	–	–	–	–
Canada	–	–	–	–
Denmark	–	–	–	–
Finland	–	–	–	–
France	–	–	–	–
Germany	–	–	–	–
Ireland	–	–	–	–
Italy	–	–	–	–
Japan	100.0	100.0	–	–
Netherlands	88.3	86.8	88.6	–
New Zealand	–	–	–	–
Norway	–	–	–	–
Sweden	–	–	–	–
Switzerland	–	–	–	–
United Kingdom	–	–	–	–
United States	–	–	–	–
TOTAL	88.3	86.8	88.6	–
MULTILATERAL	100.0	100.0	100.0	–
ARAB COUNTRIES	–	–	–	–
E.E.C.+ MEMBERS	88.3	89.2	89.0	–
TOTAL	88.4	89.3	89.1	–

15. OTHER AGGREGATES

OFFICIAL COMMITMENTS:

	1987	1988	1989	1990
TOTAL BILATERAL	75.3	74.0	74.1	60.4
of which:				
Arab Countries	–	–	–	–
C.E.E.C.	–	–	–	–
TOTAL MULTILATERAL	0.7	20.9	6.5	6.6
TOTAL BIL.& MULTIL.	76.0	94.9	80.6	67.0
of which:				
ODA Grants	53.3	66.7	56.1	63.7
ODA Loans	21.9	24.5	21.7	0.4

DISBURSEMENTS:

DAC COUNTRIES COMBINED

OFFICIAL & PRIVATE

	1987	1988	1989	1990
GROSS:				
Contractual Lending	6.6	-1.8	46.9	-12.3
Export Credits, Total	-14.5	-17.7	28.4	-17.2
Export Credits, Priv.	-14.5	-17.7	18.1	-40.2
NET:				
Contractual Lending	-44.8	-24.4	18.5	-74.8
Export Credits Total	-55.0	-27.8	13.0	-79.8
PRIVATE SECTOR NET	242.0	1768.5	825.0	1131.3
Direct Investment	505.7	1182.6	207.5	381.9
Portfolio Investment	-229.0	611.7	612.1	818.1
Export Credits	-34.7	-25.8	5.3	-68.7

MARKET BORROWING:

CHANGE IN CLAIMS

	1987	1988	1989	1990
Banks	–	–	–	–

MEMORANDUM ITEM:

	1987	1988	1989	1990
C.E.E.C. (Gross)	–	–	–	–

DISBURSEMENTS, UNLESS OTHERWISE STATE

	1987	1988	1989	1990	1987	1988	1989	1990		1987
1. TOTAL RECEIPTS NET					**4. TOTAL ODA NET**				**7. TOTAL ODA GROSS**	
DAC COUNTRIES										
Australia	2.3	-0.3	0.1	-0.3	0.0	0.1	0.1	0.1	Australia	0.0
Austria	1.5	2.2	2.4	3.6	1.5	2.2	2.4	3.6	Austria	1.5
Belgium	0.7	0.9	0.9	2.3	0.8	1.2	0.9	1.7	Belgium	0.8
Canada	1.1	13.9	4.6	4.7	1.1	13.9	4.6	4.7	Canada	1.1
Denmark	11.4	10.4	7.8	14.5	11.4	10.4	7.8	14.5	Denmark	11.4
Finland	7.4	17.7	16.6	13.3	7.4	17.7	16.6	13.3	Finland	7.4
France	19.2	-4.8	-2.7	-3.8	9.2	2.3	3.6	4.5	France	9.2
Germany	5.3	11.9	3.9	30.5	6.2	6.8	11.0	20.4	Germany	6.2
Ireland	0.0	–	0.0	0.0	0.0	–	0.0	0.0	Ireland	0.0
Italy	6.5	29.4	-9.4	-3.7	10.3	16.7	15.9	10.0	Italy	10.6
Japan	-0.7	5.3	-5.4	0.9	0.3	0.4	0.5	0.9	Japan	0.3
Netherlands	32.6	28.2	23.0	29.6	19.8	25.7	23.4	29.9	Netherlands	19.8
New Zealand	–	0.0	0.1	0.0	–	0.0	0.1	0.0	New Zealand	–
Norway	14.4	20.0	22.3	35.1	14.4	20.0	22.3	35.1	Norway	14.4
Sweden	23.5	42.7	64.4	30.7	25.6	42.7	65.2	31.6	Sweden	25.6
Switzerland	3.2	6.2	8.5	6.3	3.2	6.2	8.5	6.3	Switzerland	3.2
United Kingdom	–	0.3	0.1	0.1	–	0.3	0.1	0.1	United Kingdom	–
United States	–	–	–	97.0	–	–	–	97.0	United States	–
TOTAL	128.3	184.0	137.1	260.8	111.1	166.6	182.8	273.7	TOTAL	111.4
MULTILATERAL										
AF.D.F.	–	–	–	–	–	–	–	–	AF.D.F.	–
AF.D.B.	–	–	–	–	–	–	–	–	AF.D.B.	–
AS.D.B	–	–	–	–	–	–	–	–	AS.D.B	–
CAR.D.B.	–	–	–	–	–	–	–	–	CAR.D.B.	–
E.E.C.	14.3	24.6	19.7	19.7	14.3	24.6	19.7	19.7	E.E.C.	14.3
IBRD	–	–	–	-1.0	–	–	–	–	IBRD	–
IDA	–	–	–	–	–	–	–	–	IDA	–
I.D.B.	17.8	11.0	2.3	-0.1	-0.6	-0.8	–	–	I.D.B.	4.1
IFAD	3.5	–	–	3.2	3.5	–	–	3.2	IFAD	3.5
I.F.C.	–	–	–	–	–	–	–	–	I.F.C.	–
IMF TRUST FUND	–	–	–	–	–	–	–	–	IMF TRUST FUND	–
U.N. AGENCIES	–	–	–	–	–	–	–	–	U.N. AGENCIES	–
UNDP	1.6	3.2	3.0	4.5	1.6	3.2	3.0	4.5	UNDP	1.6
UNTA	1.1	1.2	1.0	0.8	1.1	1.2	1.0	0.8	UNTA	1.1
UNICEF	1.8	2.1	2.8	3.6	1.8	2.1	2.8	3.6	UNICEF	1.8
UNRWA	–	–	–	–	–	–	–	–	UNRWA	
WFP	4.7	10.4	11.8	7.6	4.7	10.4	11.8	7.6	WFP	4.7
UNHCR	1.7	3.8	1.1	7.4	1.7	3.8	1.1	7.4	UNHCR	1.7
Other Multilateral	1.7	2.1	2.9	3.3	1.7	2.1	2.9	3.3	Other Multilateral	1.7
Arab Agencies	–	–	–	–	–	–	–	–	Arab Agencies	–
TOTAL	48.1	58.4	44.5	49.0	29.7	46.6	42.2	50.1	TOTAL	34.4
ARAB COUNTRIES	–	–	–	–	–	–	–	–	ARAB COUNTRIES	
E.E.C.+ MEMBERS	90.0	100.8	43.3	89.2	72.0	87.9	82.3	100.8	E.E.C.+ MEMBERS	72.3
TOTAL	176.4	242.4	181.7	309.8	140.8	213.1	225.0	323.8	TOTAL	145.8
2. ODA LOANS GROSS					**5. ODA LOANS NET**				**8. GRANTS**	
DAC COUNTRIES										
Australia	–	–	–	–	–	–	–	–	Australia	0.0
Austria	–	–	–	–	–	–	–	–	Austria	1.5
Belgium	–	–	–	–	–	–	–	–	Belgium	0.8
Canada	0.2	–	–	–	0.2	–	–	–	Canada	0.9
Denmark	8.5	8.2	1.5	-0.1	8.5	8.2	1.5	-0.1	Denmark	2.9
Finland	3.0	8.0	4.5	2.1	3.0	8.0	4.5	2.1	Finland	4.4
France	6.9	0.3	0.3	0.1	6.9	0.3	0.3	0.1	France	2.4
Germany	–	–	–	7.6	–	–	–	7.6	Germany	6.2
Ireland	–	–	–	–	–	–	–	–	Ireland	0.0
Italy	6.0	2.8	1.1	–	5.7	2.5	-0.9	–	Italy	4.6
Japan	–	–	–	–	–	–	–	–	Japan	0.3
Netherlands	6.4	3.4	0.7	0.3	6.4	3.4	0.7	0.3	Netherlands	13.4
New Zealand	–	–	–	–	–	–	–	–	New Zealand	–
Norway	–	–	–	–	–	–	–	–	Norway	14.4
Sweden	–	–	–	–	–	–	–	–	Sweden	25.6
Switzerland	–	–	–	–	–	–	–	–	Switzerland	3.2
United Kingdom	–	–	–	–	–	–	–	–	United Kingdom	–
United States	–	–	–	–	–	–	–	–	United States	–
TOTAL	31.0	22.6	8.2	9.9	30.7	22.4	6.1	9.9	TOTAL	80.4
MULTILATERAL	7.6	–	–	3.2	2.8	-1.0	–	3.2	MULTILATERAL	26.9
ARAB COUNTRIES	–	–	–	–	–	–	–	–	ARAB COUNTRIES	–
E.E.C.+ MEMBERS	27.8	14.6	3.7	7.9	27.5	14.4	1.6	7.9	E.E.C.+ MEMBERS	44.5
TOTAL	38.5	22.6	8.2	13.1	33.5	21.3	6.1	13.1	TOTAL	107.3
3. TOTAL OFFICIAL GROSS					**6. TOTAL OFFICIAL NET**				**9. TOTAL OOF GROSS**	
DAC COUNTRIES										
Australia	2.3	0.1	0.1	0.1	2.3	-0.3	0.1	-0.3	Australia	2.3
Austria	1.5	2.2	2.4	3.6	1.5	2.2	2.4	3.6	Austria	–
Belgium	0.8	1.2	0.9	1.7	0.8	1.2	0.9	1.7	Belgium	–
Canada	1.1	13.9	4.6	4.7	1.1	13.9	4.6	4.7	Canada	–
Denmark	11.4	10.4	7.8	14.5	11.4	10.4	7.8	14.5	Denmark	–
Finland	7.4	17.7	16.6	13.3	7.4	17.7	16.6	13.3	Finland	–
France	9.2	2.3	3.6	4.5	9.2	2.3	3.6	4.5	France	–
Germany	6.2	6.8	11.0	20.4	6.2	6.8	11.0	20.4	Germany	–
Ireland	0.0	–	0.0	0.0	0.0	–	0.0	0.0	Ireland	–
Italy	10.6	17.0	18.1	11.6	10.3	16.7	15.8	8.6	Italy	–
Japan	0.3	0.4	0.5	0.9	0.3	0.4	0.5	0.9	Japan	–
Netherlands	19.8	25.7	23.4	29.9	19.8	25.7	23.4	29.9	Netherlands	–
New Zealand	–	0.0	0.1	0.0	–	0.0	0.1	0.0	New Zealand	–
Norway	14.4	20.0	22.3	35.1	14.4	20.0	22.3	35.1	Norway	–
Sweden	25.6	42.7	65.2	31.6	25.6	42.7	65.2	31.6	Sweden	–
Switzerland	3.2	6.2	8.5	6.3	3.2	6.2	8.5	6.3	Switzerland	–
United Kingdom	–	0.3	0.1	0.1	–	0.3	0.1	0.1	United Kingdom	–
United States	–	–	–	97.0	–	–	–	97.0	United States	–
TOTAL	113.7	166.8	185.0	275.3	113.4	166.2	182.7	271.9	TOTAL	2.3
MULTILATERAL	53.0	59.7	44.5	50.0	48.1	58.4	44.5	49.0	MULTILATERAL	18.6
ARAB COUNTRIES	–	–	–	–	–	–	–	–	ARAB COUNTRIES	–
E.E.C.+ MEMBERS	72.3	88.2	84.5	102.4	72.0	87.9	82.2	99.4	E.E.C.+ MEMBERS	–
TOTAL	166.7	226.5	229.5	325.4	161.5	224.6	227.2	320.9	TOTAL	20.9

1988	1989	1990	1987	1988	1989	1990

10. ODA COMMITMENTS

1988	1989	1990	1987	1988	1989	1990
0.1	0.1	0.1	0.0	0.1	0.1	0.1
2.2	2.4	3.6	1.1	2.0	2.4	4.6
1.2	0.9	1.7	1.7	1.7	0.9	1.7
13.9	4.6	4.7	1.6	6.8	4.1	32.6
10.4	7.8	14.5	11.5	18.9	5.9	12.4
17.7	16.6	13.3	9.4	15.0	7.9	22.0
2.3	3.6	4.5	2.0	1.6	2.5	3.6
6.8	11.0	20.4	6.4	7.3	16.0	36.2
–	0.0	0.0	0.0	–	0.0	0.0
17.0	18.0	10.0	12.4	15.2	15.5	24.5
0.4	0.5	0.9	0.3	0.5	0.5	12.7
25.7	23.4	29.9	16.1	23.1	23.3	26.4
0.0	0.1	0.0	–	0.1	–	–
20.0	22.3	35.1	14.2	10.7	47.5	6.5
42.7	65.2	31.6	25.6	42.7	65.0	42.2
6.2	8.5	6.3	0.6	8.1	3.5	5.5
0.3	0.1	0.1	–	0.3	0.1	0.1
–	–	97.0	–	55.5	3.5	223.3
166.8	*184.9*	*273.7*	*102.8*	*209.4*	*198.7*	*454.7*
–	–	–	–	–	–	–
–	–	–	–	–	–	–
–	–	–	–	–	–	–
24.6	19.7	19.7	22.0	29.7	21.0	21.0
–	–	–	–	–	–	–
0.2	–	–	–	–	–	–
–	–	3.2	–	–	–	–
–	–	–	–	–	–	–
–	–	–	–	–	–	–
–	–	–	12.5	22.8	22.6	27.3
3.2	3.0	4.5	–	–	–	–
1.2	1.0	0.8	–	–	–	–
2.1	2.8	3.6	–	–	–	–
–	–	–	–	–	–	–
10.4	11.8	7.6	–	–	–	–
3.8	1.1	7.4	–	–	–	–
2.1	2.9	3.3	–	–	–	–
–	–	–	–	–	–	–
47.6	*42.2*	*50.1*	*34.5*	*52.5*	*43.6*	*48.3*
–	–	–	–	–	–	–
88.2	*84.4*	*100.8*	*72.0*	*97.8*	*85.1*	*126.0*
214.4	*227.1*	*323.8*	*137.3*	*262.0*	*242.3*	*503.0*

11. TECH. COOP. GRANTS

1988	1989	1990	1987	1988	1989	1990
0.1	0.1	0.1	0.0	–	0.0	0.0
2.2	2.4	3.6	1.4	1.5	0.6	1.6
1.2	0.9	1.7	0.5	0.0	–	0.2
13.9	4.6	4.7	–	0.2	0.2	0.1
2.2	6.3	14.6	1.4	0.5	1.2	2.9
9.7	12.0	11.3	0.0	0.7	0.3	1.6
2.0	3.2	4.4	1.8	1.3	1.7	3.1
6.8	11.0	12.8	5.6	5.6	7.5	9.1
–	0.0	0.0	0.0	–	0.0	0.0
14.2	16.8	10.0	2.7	3.1	3.5	2.0
0.4	0.5	0.9	0.3	0.4	0.5	0.9
22.3	22.7	29.6	7.0	15.2	16.3	19.8
0.0	0.1	0.0	–	0.0	–	0.0
20.0	22.3	35.1	0.6	1.4	2.3	2.8
42.7	65.2	31.6	6.3	6.1	8.3	3.7
6.2	8.5	6.3	0.8	1.1	–	–
0.3	0.1	0.1	–	–	–	0.0
–	–	97.0	–	–	–	7.0
144.2	*176.7*	*263.8*	*28.4*	*37.0*	*42.4*	*54.9*
47.6	*42.2*	*46.9*	*10.6*	*18.8*	*10.8*	*19.7*
–	–	–	–	–	–	–
73.6	*80.7*	*93.0*	*21.7*	*32.0*	*30.2*	*37.1*
191.8	*218.9*	*310.7*	*39.0*	*55.8*	*53.2*	*74.6*

12. TOTAL OOF NET

1988	1989	1990	1987	1988	1989	1990
–	–	–	2.3	-0.4	–	-0.4
–	–	–	–	–	–	–
–	–	–	–	–	–	–
–	–	–	–	–	–	–
–	–	–	–	–	–	–
–	–	–	–	–	–	–
–	–	–	–	–	–	–
–	0.1	1.6	–	–	-0.1	-1.4
–	–	–	–	–	–	–
–	–	–	–	–	–	–
–	–	–	–	–	–	–
–	–	–	–	–	–	–
–	–	–	–	–	–	–
–	–	–	–	–	–	–
–	0.1	1.6	2.3	-0.4	-0.1	-1.8
12.1	2.3	-0.1	18.4	11.9	2.3	-1.1
–	–	–	–	–	–	–
–	0.1	1.6	–	–	-0.1	-1.4
12.1	*2.4*	*1.5*	*20.7*	*11.5*	*2.2*	*-2.9*

13. ODF COMMITMENTS: BY PURPOSE %

	1987	1988	1989	1990
Education	0	1	1	–
Health	1	2	1	–
Other Social Infrastr.	1	2	2	–
Water Sanitat. Sewage	1	1	0	–
Energy	2	2	2	–
Telecommunications	–	–	–	–
Transportation	–	3	1	–
Agriculture	13	24	9	–
Extractive Industries	7	2	1	–
Manufacturing	18	0	1	–
Trade Banking Tourism	0	1	0	–
Technical Cooperation	13	25	11	–
Multisector Aid	8	3	0	–
Programme	26	26	65	–
Debt Reorganisation	–	–	–	–
Food Aid	7	3	0	–
Emergency Aid	2	4	5	–
Unspecified	1	1	0	–
TOTAL	100	100	100	–

14. GRANT ELEMENT OF ODA %

DAC COUNTRIES	1987	1988	1989	1990
Australia	100.0	100.0	100.0	–
Austria	100.0	100.0	100.0	–
Belgium	100.0	100.0	100.0	–
Canada	100.0	100.0	100.0	–
Denmark	78.0	100.0	100.0	–
Finland	77.8	86.5	100.0	–
France	100.0	100.0	100.0	–
Germany	100.0	100.0	100.0	–
Ireland	100.0	–	100.0	–
Italy	100.0	100.0	100.0	–
Japan	100.0	100.0	100.0	–
Netherlands	90.2	100.0	100.0	–
New Zealand	–	100.0	–	–
Norway	100.0	100.0	100.0	–
Sweden	100.0	100.0	100.0	–
Switzerland	100.0	100.0	100.0	–
United Kingdom	–	100.0	100.0	–
United States	–	100.0	100.0	–
TOTAL	*94.0*	*99.0*	*100.0*	*–*
MULTILATERAL	*100.0*	*100.0*	*100.0*	*–*
ARAB COUNTRIES	*–*	*–*	*–*	*–*
E.E.C.+ MEMBERS	*94.3*	*100.0*	*100.0*	*–*
TOTAL	*95.5*	*99.2*	*100.0*	*–*

15. OTHER AGGREGATES

	1987	1988	1989	1990
OFFICIAL COMMITMENTS:				
TOTAL BILATERAL	241.4	331.9	639.7	454.7
of which:				
Arab Countries	–	–	–	–
C.E.E.C.	136.4	122.5	441.0	–
TOTAL MULTILATERAL	34.5	52.5	43.6	48.3
TOTAL BIL.& MULTIL.	276.0	384.5	683.3	503.0
of which:				
ODA Grants	149.9	264.6	401.4	487.5
ODA Loans	123.8	65.4	267.8	15.5
DISBURSEMENTS:				
DAC COUNTRIES COMBINED				
OFFICIAL & PRIVATE				
GROSS:				
Contractual Lending	53.0	44.0	15.2	5.9
Export Credits, Total	22.1	21.4	7.0	-4.1
Export Credits, Priv.	19.8	21.4	6.9	-5.7
NET:				
Contractual Lending	28.7	31.9	-24.5	-10.9
Export Credits Total	-1.9	9.6	-30.7	-20.8
PRIVATE SECTOR NET	14.9	17.8	-45.5	-11.1
Direct Investment	2.4	-0.1	-6.9	0.7
Portfolio Investment	16.8	8.0	-8.1	7.2
Export Credits	-4.2	10.0	-30.5	-19.0
MARKET BORROWING:				
CHANGE IN CLAIMS				
Banks	-34.0	-177.0	-76.0	508.0
MEMORANDUM ITEM:				
C.E.E.C. (Gross)	116.9	60.0	219.6	–

DISBURSEMENTS, UNLESS OTHERWISE STAT[E]

	1987	1988	1989	1990		1987	1988	1989	1990		1987

1. TOTAL RECEIPTS NET

DAC COUNTRIES

	1987	1988	1989	1990
Australia	–	–	0.0	–
Austria	0.0	0.0	0.0	0.1
Belgium	4.9	5.9	4.6	4.8
Canada	28.4	14.5	18.9	13.3
Denmark	–	13.0	5.8	7.4
Finland	–	0.0	0.1	–
France	62.1	21.9	34.6	73.2
Germany	20.8	24.5	38.5	34.1
Ireland	–	–	–	–
Italy	15.2	33.6	21.6	20.0
Japan	84.6	41.8	0.3	35.7
Netherlands	7.9	12.9	13.3	13.9
New Zealand	–	–	–	–
Norway	1.7	2.4	2.3	1.5
Sweden	-0.2	–	–	–
Switzerland	5.2	7.3	6.6	5.8
United Kingdom	-1.6	-2.2	-0.4	0.5
United States	41.0	19.0	32.0	31.0
TOTAL	*270.0*	*194.5*	*178.1*	*241.3*

MULTILATERAL

	1987	1988	1989	1990
AF.D.F.	12.6	4.8	6.1	2.8
AF.D.B.	-2.5	-2.5	-1.5	–
AS.D.B	–	–	–	–
CAR.D.B.	–	–	–	–
E.E.C.	17.3	20.6	14.6	14.6
IBRD	–	–	–	–
IDA	63.9	60.0	33.0	47.0
I.D.B.	–	–	–	–
IFAD	2.1	–	–	0.6
I.F.C.	–	–	0.1	–
IMF TRUST FUND	–	–	–	–
U.N. AGENCIES	–	–	–	–
UNDP	10.3	13.4	11.4	12.0
UNTA	1.3	1.2	1.6	1.3
UNICEF	3.7	2.4	2.2	2.4
UNRWA	–	–	–	–
WFP	5.4	6.8	11.0	8.8
UNHCR	–	0.0	0.0	0.0
Other Multilateral	9.2	8.5	8.1	10.2
Arab Agencies	4.4	2.3	3.8	–
TOTAL	*127.6*	*117.5*	*90.6*	*99.8*
ARAB COUNTRIES	***8.6***	***6.3***	***2.4***	***2.9***
E.E.C.+ MEMBERS	*126.6*	*130.0*	*132.5*	*168.5*
TOTAL	**406.1**	**318.3**	**271.1**	**343.9**

2. ODA LOANS GROSS

DAC COUNTRIES

	1987	1988	1989	1990
Australia	–	–	–	–
Austria	–	–	–	–
Belgium	–	–	–	–
Canada	–	–	–	–
Denmark	–	–	–	–
Finland	–	–	–	–
France	41.1	36.2	21.2	7.4
Germany	–	–	–	–
Ireland	–	–	–	–
Italy	–	–	–	–
Japan	–	6.3	–	9.3
Netherlands	–	–	–	–
New Zealand	–	–	–	–
Norway	–	–	–	–
Sweden	–	–	–	–
Switzerland	–	–	–	–
United Kingdom	–	–	–	–
United States	–	–	–	–
TOTAL	*41.1*	*42.5*	*21.2*	*16.7*
MULTILATERAL	*85.6*	*73.5*	*45.0*	*52.4*
ARAB COUNTRIES	***4.7***	***8.3***	***2.2***	***2.9***
E.E.C.+ MEMBERS	*41.1*	*36.2*	*21.2*	*7.4*
TOTAL	**131.4**	**124.3**	**68.4**	**71.9**

3. TOTAL OFFICIAL GROSS

DAC COUNTRIES

	1987	1988	1989	1990
Australia	–	–	0.0	–
Austria	0.0	0.0	0.0	0.1
Belgium	5.4	6.4	4.9	4.6
Canada	28.4	14.5	18.9	13.3
Denmark	–	13.0	5.8	7.4
Finland	–	0.1	0.1	–
France	100.8	71.1	78.4	96.1
Germany	20.7	24.8	34.3	39.3
Ireland	–	–	–	–
Italy	15.2	33.5	21.6	20.0
Japan	26.8	45.0	15.2	38.7
Netherlands	7.9	12.8	13.3	13.9
New Zealand	–	–	–	–
Norway	1.7	2.4	2.3	1.5
Sweden	–	–	–	–
Switzerland	5.2	7.3	6.6	5.8
United Kingdom	0.3	0.7	0.5	0.5
United States	41.0	20.0	33.0	34.0
TOTAL	*253.5*	*251.5*	*234.9*	*275.1*
MULTILATERAL	*139.4*	*132.1*	*98.3*	*103.2*
ARAB COUNTRIES	***11.0***	***12.2***	***5.4***	***2.9***
E.E.C.+ MEMBERS	*169.0*	*184.3*	*174.4*	*197.5*
TOTAL	**403.8**	**395.8**	**338.5**	**381.1**

4. TOTAL ODA NET

	1987	1988	1989	1990
Australia	–	–	0.0	–
Austria	0.0	0.0	0.0	0.1
Belgium	5.4	6.4	4.8	4.6
Canada	28.4	14.5	18.9	13.3
Denmark	–	13.0	5.8	7.4
Finland	–	0.1	0.1	–
France	65.4	66.6	60.2	80.1
Germany	20.7	24.8	34.3	39.3
Ireland	–	–	–	–
Italy	15.2	33.5	21.6	20.0
Japan	23.7	41.8	0.3	36.9
Netherlands	7.9	12.8	13.3	13.9
New Zealand	–	–	–	–
Norway	1.7	2.4	2.3	1.5
Sweden	–	–	–	–
Switzerland	5.2	7.3	6.6	5.8
United Kingdom	0.3	0.7	0.5	0.5
United States	41.0	18.0	31.0	31.0
TOTAL	*214.9*	*241.9*	*199.7*	*254.3*

MULTILATERAL

	1987	1988	1989	1990
AF.D.F.	12.6	4.8	6.1	2.8
AF.D.B.	–	–	–	–
AS.D.B	–	–	–	–
CAR.D.B.	–	–	–	–
E.E.C.	18.6	22.0	15.8	15.8
IBRD	–	–	–	–
IDA	63.9	60.0	33.0	47.0
I.D.B.	–	–	–	–
IFAD	2.1	–	–	0.6
I.F.C.	–	–	–	–
IMF TRUST FUND	–	–	–	–
U.N. AGENCIES	–	–	–	–
UNDP	10.3	13.4	11.4	12.0
UNTA	1.3	1.2	1.6	1.3
UNICEF	3.7	2.4	2.2	2.4
UNRWA	–	–	–	–
WFP	5.4	6.8	11.0	8.8
UNHCR	–	0.0	0.0	0.0
Other Multilateral	9.2	8.5	8.1	10.2
Arab Agencies	2.6	4.5	5.0	–
TOTAL	*129.6*	*123.6*	*94.3*	*100.9*
ARAB COUNTRIES	***8.6***	***5.7***	***2.4***	***2.9***
E.E.C.+ MEMBERS	*133.6*	*179.7*	*156.2*	*181.5*
TOTAL	**353.1**	**371.2**	**296.4**	**358.1**

5. ODA LOANS NET

	1987	1988	1989	1990
Australia	–	–	–	–
Austria	–	–	–	–
Belgium	–	–	–	–
Canada	–	–	–	–
Denmark	–	–	–	–
Finland	–	–	–	–
France	36.6	33.7	15.5	-0.4
Germany	–	–	–	–
Ireland	–	–	–	–
Italy	–	–	–	–
Japan	-3.1	3.1	-14.9	7.5
Netherlands	–	–	–	–
New Zealand	–	–	–	–
Norway	–	–	–	–
Sweden	–	–	–	–
Switzerland	–	–	–	–
United Kingdom	–	–	–	–
United States	–	–	–	-3.0
TOTAL	*33.5*	*36.8*	*0.5*	*4.1*
MULTILATERAL	*81.2*	*68.6*	*41.1*	*50.3*
ARAB COUNTRIES	***2.3***	***4.5***	***-0.8***	***2.9***
E.E.C.+ MEMBERS	*36.5*	*33.6*	*15.4*	*-0.5*
TOTAL	**117.0**	**109.9**	**40.9**	**57.3**

6. TOTAL OFFICIAL NET

	1987	1988	1989	1990
Australia	–	–	0.0	–
Austria	0.0	0.0	0.0	0.1
Belgium	5.4	6.4	4.9	4.6
Canada	28.4	14.5	18.9	13.3
Denmark	–	13.0	5.8	7.4
Finland	–	0.1	0.1	–
France	86.7	59.8	69.9	86.8
Germany	20.7	24.8	34.3	39.3
Ireland	–	–	–	–
Italy	15.2	33.5	21.6	20.0
Japan	23.7	41.8	0.3	36.9
Netherlands	7.9	12.8	13.3	13.9
New Zealand	–	–	–	–
Norway	1.7	2.4	2.3	1.5
Sweden	–	–	–	–
Switzerland	5.2	7.3	6.6	5.8
United Kingdom	0.3	0.7	0.5	0.5
United States	41.0	19.0	32.0	31.0
TOTAL	*236.3*	*236.1*	*210.4*	*261.1*
MULTILATERAL	*127.6*	*117.5*	*90.6*	*99.8*
ARAB COUNTRIES	***8.6***	***6.3***	***2.4***	***2.9***
E.E.C.+ MEMBERS	*153.6*	*171.6*	*164.8*	*187.1*
TOTAL	**372.4**	**359.9**	**303.4**	**363.7**

7. TOTAL ODA GROSS

	1987
Australia	–
Austria	0.0
Belgium	5.4
Canada	28.4
Denmark	–
Finland	–
France	69.9
Germany	20.7
Ireland	–
Italy	15.2
Japan	26.8
Netherlands	7.9
New Zealand	–
Norway	1.7
Sweden	–
Switzerland	5.2
United Kingdom	0.3
United States	41.0
TOTAL	*222.5*
AF.D.F.	12.7
AF.D.B.	–
AS.D.B	–
CAR.D.B.	–
E.E.C.	18.6
IBRD	–
IDA	64.8
I.D.B.	–
IFAD	2.1
I.F.C.	–
IMF TRUST FUND	–
U.N. AGENCIES	–
UNDP	10.3
UNTA	1.3
UNICEF	3.7
UNRWA	–
WFP	5.4
UNHCR	–
Other Multilateral	9.2
Arab Agencies	6.0
TOTAL	*134.0*
ARAB COUNTRIES	***11.0***
E.E.C.+ MEMBERS	*138.1*
TOTAL	**367.5**

8. GRANTS

	1987
Australia	–
Austria	0.0
Belgium	5.4
Canada	28.4
Denmark	–
Finland	–
France	28.8
Germany	20.7
Ireland	–
Italy	15.2
Japan	26.8
Netherlands	7.9
New Zealand	–
Norway	1.7
Sweden	–
Switzerland	5.2
United Kingdom	0.3
United States	41.0
TOTAL	*181.4*
MULTILATERAL	*48.4*
ARAB COUNTRIES	***6.2***
E.E.C.+ MEMBERS	*97.0*
TOTAL	**236.1**

9. TOTAL OOF GROSS

	1987
Australia	–
Austria	0.0
Belgium	0.0
Canada	–
Denmark	–
Finland	–
France	30.9
Germany	–
Ireland	–
Italy	–
Japan	–
Netherlands	–
New Zealand	–
Norway	–
Sweden	–
Switzerland	–
United Kingdom	–
United States	–
TOTAL	*30.9*
MULTILATERAL	*5.4*
ARAB COUNTRIES	***–***
E.E.C.+ MEMBERS	*30.9*
TOTAL	**36.3**

1988	1989	1990	1987	1988	1989	1990

10. ODA COMMITMENTS

1988	1989	1990	1987	1988	1989	1990
–	0.0	–	–	–	0.1	0.1
0.0	0.0	0.1	0.0	0.0	0.0	0.1
6.4	4.8	4.6	0.3	2.5	4.8	4.6
14.5	18.9	13.3	13.2	15.5	13.5	33.8
13.0	5.8	7.4	–	9.0	–	2.7
0.1	0.1	–	–	–	0.1	–
69.1	66.0	87.9	52.6	68.2	60.0	73.2
24.8	34.3	39.3	42.5	29.8	42.2	24.5
–	–	–	–	–	–	–
33.5	21.6	20.0	60.3	14.9	7.6	17.4
45.0	15.2	38.7	16.5	35.8	28.1	23.3
12.8	13.3	13.9	10.4	7.9	5.8	11.7
–	–	–	–	–	–	–
2.4	2.3	1.5	5.3	1.5	–	–
–	–	–	–	–	–	–
7.3	6.6	5.8	4.1	26.2	1.9	5.4
0.7	0.5	0.5	0.3	0.7	1.0	0.4
18.0	31.0	34.0	28.5	38.4	27.5	28.9
247.6	*220.4*	*266.9*	*234.0*	*250.3*	*192.6*	*226.0*
4.9	6.4	2.8	3.9	10.0	24.2	3.1
–	–	–	–	–	–	–
–	–	–	–	–	–	–
22.1	15.8	15.8	63.4	107.2	7.2	7.2
–	–	–	–	–	–	–
61.0	34.0	49.0	85.5	41.0	–	20.0
–	–	0.6	14.7	–	5.3	0.2
–	–	–	–	–	–	–
–	–	–	29.8	32.3	34.4	34.8
13.4	11.4	12.0	–	–	–	–
1.2	1.6	1.3	–	–	–	–
2.4	2.2	2.4	–	–	–	–
–	–	–	–	–	–	–
6.8	11.0	8.8	–	–	–	–
0.0	0.0	0.0	–	–	–	–
8.5	8.1	10.2	–	–	–	–
8.2	7.6	0.2	8.4	5.7	4.0	1.5
128.4	*98.2*	*103.2*	*205.8*	*196.2*	*75.1*	*66.8*
9.5	*5.4*	*2.9*	*6.6*	*24.8*	*3.0*	*0.3*
182.4	*162.0*	*189.3*	*229.9*	*240.0*	*128.6*	*141.7*
385.5	*324.0*	*372.9*	*446.4*	*471.2*	*270.7*	*293.0*

11. TECH. COOP. GRANTS

1988	1989	1990	1987	1988	1989	1990
–	0.0	–	–	–	–	–
0.0	0.0	0.1	0.0	0.0	0.0	0.0
6.4	4.8	4.6	4.1	3.1	2.6	3.0
14.5	18.9	13.3	–	2.2	3.8	4.4
13.0	5.8	7.4	–	0.0	0.1	0.6
0.1	0.1	–	–	–	–	–
32.9	44.8	80.5	22.3	23.2	22.7	29.9
24.8	34.3	39.3	13.5	13.3	11.7	15.4
–	–	–	–	–	–	–
33.5	21.6	20.0	2.7	1.5	–	–
38.7	15.2	29.4	2.1	4.9	4.6	3.4
12.8	13.3	13.9	3.0	3.5	3.5	4.3
–	–	–	–	–	–	–
2.4	2.3	1.5	0.2	–	0.0	0.1
–	–	–	–	–	–	–
7.3	6.6	5.8	1.6	4.3	–	–
0.7	0.5	0.5	0.3	0.5	0.4	0.3
18.0	31.0	34.0	19.0	16.0	14.0	15.0
205.1	*199.2*	*250.2*	*68.7*	*72.7*	*63.6*	*76.5*
54.9	*53.2*	*50.7*	*25.4*	*26.5*	*23.4*	*26.0*
1.2	*3.2*	–	–	–	–	–
146.2	*140.8*	*181.9*	*46.8*	*46.3*	*41.0*	*53.6*
261.2	*255.5*	*301.0*	*94.1*	*99.2*	*87.0*	*102.4*

12. TOTAL OOF NET

1988	1989	1990	1987	1988	1989	1990
–	–	–	–	–	–	–
–	0.0	–	0.0	–	0.0	–
–	–	–	–	–	–	–
–	–	–	–	–	–	–
2.0	12.4	8.2	21.3	-6.8	9.7	6.7
–	–	–	–	–	–	–
–	–	–	–	–	–	–
–	–	–	–	–	–	–
–	–	–	–	–	–	–
–	–	–	–	–	–	–
–	–	–	–	–	–	–
2.0	2.0	–	–	1.0	1.0	–
4.0	*14.5*	*8.2*	*21.3*	*-5.8*	*10.7*	*6.7*
3.6	*0.1*	–	*-2.1*	*-6.1*	*-3.7*	*-1.1*
2.7	–	–	–	*0.6*	–	–
2.0	*12.5*	*8.2*	*20.0*	*-8.2*	*8.6*	*5.6*
10.3	*14.6*	*8.2*	*19.3*	*-11.3*	*7.0*	*5.6*

13. ODF COMMITMENTS: BY PURPOSE %

	1987	1988	1989	1990
Education	5	0	–	–
Health	2	3	5	–
Other Social Infrastr.	1	8	4	–
Water Sanitat. Sewage	12	7	7	–
Energy	1	10	4	–
Telecommunications	1	–	5	–
Transportation	3	12	5	–
Agriculture	15	16	14	–
Extractive Industries	0	3	2	–
Manufacturing	0	–	1	–
Trade Banking Tourism	–	0	0	–
Technical Cooperation	27	23	42	–
Multisector Aid	1	0	1	–
Programme	30	13	5	–
Debt Reorganisation	–	–	0	–
Food Aid	1	1	3	–
Emergency Aid	0	0	–	–
Unspecified	0	3	–	–
TOTAL	100	100	100	–

14. GRANT ELEMENT OF ODA %

DAC COUNTRIES

	1987	1988	1989	1990
Australia	–	–	100.0	–
Austria	100.0	100.0	100.0	–
Belgium	100.0	100.0	100.0	–
Canada	100.0	100.0	100.0	–
Denmark	–	100.0	–	–
Finland	–	–	100.0	–
France	73.8	87.0	81.8	–
Germany	100.0	100.0	100.0	–
Ireland	–	–	–	–
Italy	100.0	100.0	100.0	–
Japan	100.0	88.5	100.0	–
Netherlands	100.0	100.0	100.0	–
New Zealand	–	–	–	–
Norway	100.0	100.0	–	–
Sweden	–	–	–	–
Switzerland	100.0	100.0	100.0	–
United Kingdom	100.0	100.0	100.0	–
United States	100.0	100.0	100.0	–
TOTAL	*94.5*	*94.4*	*94.4*	–
MULTILATERAL	*88.9*	*93.3*	*91.2*	–
ARAB COUNTRIES	*100.0*	*59.3*	*100.0*	–
E.E.C.+ MEMBERS	*93.9*	*96.6*	*91.5*	–
TOTAL	*92.1*	*92.2*	*93.6*	–

15. OTHER AGGREGATES

	1987	1988	1989	1990
OFFICIAL COMMITMENTS:				
TOTAL BILATERAL	281.7	313.7	236.0	556.1
of which:				
Arab Countries	6.6	24.8	3.0	0.3
C.E.E.C.	–	–	–	–
TOTAL MULTILATERAL	205.8	204.6	122.5	115.8
TOTAL BIL.& MULTIL.	487.5	518.4	358.4	671.9
of which:				
ODA Grants	294.6	357.0	214.2	252.6
ODA Loans	151.8	114.3	56.5	40.4
DISBURSEMENTS:				
DAC COUNTRIES COMBINED				
OFFICIAL & PRIVATE				
GROSS:				
Contractual Lending	29.7	27.5	24.8	20.6
Export Credits, Total	-42.3	-19.0	-10.8	-4.2
Export Credits, Priv.	-42.3	-19.0	-10.8	-4.2
NET:				
Contractual Lending	10.3	8.5	-0.9	6.4
Export Credits Total	-44.5	-23.5	-13.0	-4.5
PRIVATE SECTOR NET	33.7	-41.6	-32.3	-19.8
Direct Investment	61.6	-1.4	-0.1	-1.2
Portfolio Investment	16.7	-17.7	-20.1	-14.1
Export Credits	-44.5	-22.5	-12.0	-4.5
MARKET BORROWING:				
CHANGE IN CLAIMS				
Banks	-61.0	-43.0	-39.0	-12.0
MEMORANDUM ITEM:				
C.E.E.C. (Gross)	–	–	–	–

1. TOTAL RECEIPTS NET

DAC COUNTRIES	1987	1988	1989	1990
Australia	0.3	0.7	0.5	1.3
Austria	-32.6	-10.8	-15.4	-17.4
Belgium	2.1	79.5	42.5	-9.5
Canada	1.2	2.6	2.8	2.5
Denmark	-13.2	-11.2	-10.5	-12.3
Finland	0.1	0.2	0.1	0.3
France	527.0	-374.6	205.5	-177.8
Germany	190.6	285.9	394.2	5.7
Ireland	0.0	0.0	0.0	0.2
Italy	-68.6	24.3	399.7	211.4
Japan	358.1	66.8	310.0	-63.4
Netherlands	16.6	-67.6	1.4	4.2
New Zealand	–	0.0	0.0	0.1
Norway	-4.7	-0.2	-0.1	0.4
Sweden	0.4	0.2	0.0	–
Switzerland	–	0.0	0.1	0.0
United Kingdom	-199.6	-391.0	640.1	-180.1
United States	628.0	295.0	-148.0	-67.0
TOTAL	1405.7	-100.4	1822.8	-301.4
MULTILATERAL				
AF.D.F.	–	–	–	–
AF.D.B.	0.5	10.6	163.8	151.8
AS.D.B	–	–	–	–
CAR.D.B.	–	–	–	–
E.E.C.	24.0	-4.8	1.4	1.4
IBRD	261.1	50.0	251.0	143.0
IDA	-1.2	-1.0	-1.0	6.0
I.D.B.	–	–	–	–
IFAD	–	–	0.7	3.1
I.F.C.	-3.5	2.2	3.0	16.3
IMF TRUST FUND	–	–	–	–
U.N. AGENCIES	–	–	–	–
UNDP	3.9	6.2	6.7	11.7
UNTA	1.7	1.7	1.9	2.5
UNICEF	7.5	9.5	15.0	25.5
UNRWA	–	–	–	–
WFP	–	0.3	–	–
UNHCR	–	0.3	0.3	0.4
Other Multilateral	2.4	4.2	5.0	5.4
Arab Agencies	–	–	–	–
TOTAL	296.3	78.9	447.7	367.1
ARAB COUNTRIES	0.0	0.1	–	–
E.E.C.+ MEMBERS	478.8	-459.6	1674.3	-156.7
TOTAL	1702.1	-21.4	2270.4	65.8

2. ODA LOANS GROSS

DAC COUNTRIES	1987	1988	1989	1990
Australia	–	–	–	–
Austria	–	–	–	–
Belgium	–	–	–	–
Canada	–	–	–	–
Denmark	–	–	–	–
Finland	–	–	–	–
France	–	–	–	–
Germany	3.7	2.6	2.6	7.3
Ireland	–	–	–	–
Italy	–	–	–	–
Japan	5.6	22.5	160.3	55.6
Netherlands	–	0.3	–	–
New Zealand	–	–	–	–
Norway	–	–	–	–
Sweden	–	–	–	–
Switzerland	–	–	–	–
United Kingdom	–	–	–	–
United States	–	–	–	–
TOTAL	9.2	25.5	162.9	62.9
MULTILATERAL	–	–	0.7	10.1
ARAB COUNTRIES	–	–	–	–
E.E.C.+ MEMBERS	3.7	3.0	2.6	7.3
TOTAL	9.2	25.5	163.6	73.1

3. TOTAL OFFICIAL GROSS

DAC COUNTRIES	1987	1988	1989	1990
Australia	0.3	0.7	0.5	1.3
Austria	0.8	0.8	0.8	1.3
Belgium	3.1	110.1	52.7	18.1
Canada	1.2	2.6	2.8	38.8
Denmark	0.1	0.2	0.0	0.1
Finland	0.1	0.2	0.1	0.3
France	563.5	7.2	5.4	170.3
Germany	391.6	1497.4	857.8	284.1
Ireland	0.0	0.0	0.0	0.2
Italy	2.9	5.8	430.4	324.1
Japan	18.7	55.4	178.9	82.8
Netherlands	3.7	3.7	2.5	4.2
New Zealand	–	0.0	0.0	0.1
Norway	0.1	0.2	0.3	0.4
Sweden	0.4	0.2	0.0	–
Switzerland	–	0.0	0.1	0.0
United Kingdom	8.8	13.4	103.2	24.9
United States	2.0	192.0	37.0	293.0
TOTAL	997.2	1889.6	1672.4	1244.1
MULTILATERAL	432.4	285.0	658.2	623.4
ARAB COUNTRIES	0.0	0.1	–	–
E.E.C.+ MEMBERS	1004.3	1641.9	1462.5	836.6
TOTAL	1429.6	2174.7	2330.7	1867.5

4. TOTAL ODA NET

DAC COUNTRIES	1987	1988	1989	1990
Australia	0.3	0.7	0.5	1.3
Austria	0.7	0.7	0.3	1.2
Belgium	0.4	0.4	0.0	0.8
Canada	1.2	2.6	2.8	2.5
Denmark	–	0.0	0.0	0.0
Finland	0.1	0.2	0.1	0.3
France	6.8	7.2	5.4	6.3
Germany	11.1	9.7	8.9	18.0
Ireland	0.0	0.0	0.0	0.2
Italy	2.9	5.8	14.3	12.5
Japan	18.0	53.8	165.9	78.7
Netherlands	3.5	3.7	2.2	3.7
New Zealand	–	0.0	0.0	0.1
Norway	0.1	0.2	0.3	0.4
Sweden	0.4	0.2	0.0	–
Switzerland	–	0.0	0.1	0.0
United Kingdom	4.6	13.0	103.2	24.7
United States	1.0	-1.0	6.0	22.0
TOTAL	51.0	97.0	309.8	172.6
MULTILATERAL				
AF.D.F.	–	–	–	–
AF.D.B.	–	–	–	–
AS.D.B	–	–	–	–
CAR.D.B.	–	–	–	–
E.E.C.	4.1	2.0	7.2	7.2
IBRD	–	–	–	–
IDA	-1.2	-1.0	-1.0	6.0
I.D.B.	–	–	–	–
IFAD	–	–	0.7	3.1
I.F.C.	–	–	–	–
IMF TRUST FUND	–	–	–	–
U.N. AGENCIES	–	–	–	–
UNDP	3.9	6.2	6.7	11.7
UNTA	1.7	1.7	1.9	2.5
UNICEF	7.5	9.5	15.0	25.5
UNRWA	–	–	–	–
WFP	–	0.3	–	–
UNHCR	–	0.3	0.3	0.4
Other Multilateral	2.4	4.2	5.0	5.4
Arab Agencies	–	–	–	–
TOTAL	18.3	23.0	35.6	61.8
ARAB COUNTRIES	0.0	0.1	–	–
E.E.C.+ MEMBERS	33.4	41.8	141.1	73.2
TOTAL	69.3	120.1	345.4	234.4

5. ODA LOANS NET

DAC COUNTRIES	1987	1988	1989	1990
Australia	–	–	–	–
Austria	-0.2	-0.1	-0.5	-0.1
Belgium	–	–	–	–
Canada	–	–	–	-36.3
Denmark	–	–	–	–
Finland	–	–	–	–
France	–	–	–	–
Germany	3.4	2.2	1.7	6.7
Ireland	–	–	–	–
Italy	–	–	–	–
Japan	4.9	20.9	147.3	51.6
Netherlands	-0.2	0.3	-0.2	–
New Zealand	–	–	–	–
Norway	–	–	–	–
Sweden	–	–	–	–
Switzerland	–	–	–	–
United Kingdom	-4.2	-0.4	0.0	-0.2
United States	-1.0	-3.0	-1.0	–
TOTAL	2.7	20.0	147.1	21.7
MULTILATERAL	-1.2	-1.0	-0.3	9.1
ARAB COUNTRIES	–	–	–	–
E.E.C.+ MEMBERS	-1.0	2.1	1.4	6.5
TOTAL	1.5	19.0	146.8	30.8

6. TOTAL OFFICIAL NET

DAC COUNTRIES	1987	1988	1989	1990
Australia	0.3	0.7	0.5	1.3
Austria	0.7	0.7	0.3	1.2
Belgium	3.1	110.1	52.7	0.7
Canada	1.2	2.6	2.8	2.5
Denmark	-13.2	-11.2	-10.5	0.0
Finland	0.1	0.2	0.1	0.3
France	563.5	5.5	5.4	155.9
Germany	388.1	472.1	409.7	163.2
Ireland	0.0	0.0	0.0	0.2
Italy	2.9	5.8	393.7	263.8
Japan	18.0	53.8	165.9	78.7
Netherlands	2.9	3.6	1.4	4.2
New Zealand	–	0.0	0.0	0.1
Norway	0.1	0.2	0.3	0.4
Sweden	0.4	0.2	0.0	–
Switzerland	–	0.0	0.1	0.0
United Kingdom	3.9	12.6	102.8	24.2
United States	1.0	169.0	36.0	155.0
TOTAL	972.9	825.6	1161.0	851.8
MULTILATERAL	296.3	78.9	447.7	367.1
ARAB COUNTRIES	0.0	0.1	–	–
E.E.C.+ MEMBERS	975.2	593.6	956.6	613.6
TOTAL	1269.3	904.7	1608.7	1218.9

7. TOTAL ODA GROSS

DAC COUNTRIES	1987
Australia	0.3
Austria	0.8
Belgium	0.4
Canada	1.2
Denmark	–
Finland	0.1
France	6.8
Germany	11.4
Ireland	0.0
Italy	2.9
Japan	18.7
Netherlands	3.7
New Zealand	–
Norway	0.1
Sweden	0.4
Switzerland	–
United Kingdom	8.8
United States	2.0
TOTAL	57.5
MULTILATERAL	
AF.D.F.	–
AF.D.B.	–
AS.D.B	–
CAR.D.B.	–
E.E.C.	4.1
IBRD	–
IDA	–
I.D.B.	–
IFAD	–
I.F.C.	–
IMF TRUST FUND	–
U.N. AGENCIES	–
UNDP	3.9
UNTA	1.7
UNICEF	7.5
UNRWA	–
WFP	–
UNHCR	–
Other Multilateral	2.4
Arab Agencies	–
TOTAL	19.5
ARAB COUNTRIES	0.0
E.E.C.+ MEMBERS	38.1
TOTAL	77.1

8. GRANTS

DAC COUNTRIES	1987
Australia	0.3
Austria	0.8
Belgium	0.4
Canada	1.2
Denmark	–
Finland	0.1
France	6.8
Germany	7.7
Ireland	0.0
Italy	2.9
Japan	13.1
Netherlands	3.7
New Zealand	–
Norway	0.1
Sweden	0.4
Switzerland	–
United Kingdom	8.8
United States	2.0
TOTAL	48.3
MULTILATERAL	19.5
ARAB COUNTRIES	0.0
E.E.C.+ MEMBERS	34.4
TOTAL	67.9

9. TOTAL OOF GROSS

	1987
Australia	–
Austria	–
Belgium	2.7
Canada	–
Denmark	0.1
Finland	–
France	556.7
Germany	380.3
Ireland	–
Italy	–
Japan	–
Netherlands	–
New Zealand	–
Norway	–
Sweden	–
Switzerland	–
United Kingdom	–
United States	–
TOTAL	939.7
MULTILATERAL	412.8
ARAB COUNTRIES	–
E.E.C.+ MEMBERS	966.3
TOTAL	1352.5

1988	1989	1990

10. ODA COMMITMENTS

1988	1989	1990	1987	1988	1989	1990
0.7	0.5	1.3	0.2	0.5	0.5	0.8
0.8	0.8	1.3	0.8	0.8	0.8	1.3
0.4	0.0	0.8	0.3	0.1	0.0	0.8
2.6	2.8	38.8	2.6	1.6	2.9	1.8
0.0	0.0	0.0	–	–	–	–
0.2	0.1	0.3	–	–	0.1	0.4
7.2	5.4	6.3	6.8	7.2	5.4	6.3
10.1	9.7	18.5	5.4	7.8	8.1	58.4
0.0	0.0	0.2	0.0	0.0	0.0	0.2
5.8	14.3	12.5	2.6	11.3	13.3	12.2
55.4	178.9	82.8	6.8	72.6	216.8	43.4
3.7	2.5	3.7	3.7	4.7	2.6	15.9
0.0	0.0	0.1	–	0.0	–	–
0.2	0.3	0.4	0.6	–	–	–
0.2	0.0	–	0.2	0.2	0.0	–
0.0	0.1	0.0	–	–	–	–
13.4	103.2	24.9	8.8	13.4	120.2	61.5
2.0	7.0	22.0	20.9	5.6	123.0	11.6
102.5	*325.6*	*213.9*	*59.6*	*125.6*	*493.6*	*214.6*
–	–	–	–	–	–	56.9
–	–	–	–	–	–	–
–	–	–	–	–	–	–
2.0	7.2	7.2	11.0	222.3	63.3	63.3
–	–	–	–	–	–	–
–	–	7.0	–	–	101.0	240.0
–	0.7	3.1	0.1	15.5	–	12.4
–	–	–	–	–	–	–
–	–	–	–	–	–	–
–	–	–	15.5	22.0	28.8	45.5
6.2	6.7	11.7	–	–	–	–
1.7	1.9	2.5	–	–	–	–
9.5	15.0	25.5	–	–	–	–
–	–	–	–	–	–	–
0.3	0.3	0.4	–	–	–	–
4.2	5.0	5.4	–	–	–	–
–	–	–	–	–	–	–
24.0	*36.6*	*62.8*	*26.6*	*259.7*	*193.0*	*418.0*
0.1	–	–	–	*0.1*	–	–
42.6	*142.3*	*74.0*	*38.5*	*266.7*	*212.8*	*218.5*
126.6	**362.1**	**276.7**	**86.2**	**385.4**	**686.7**	**632.6**

11. TECH. COOP. GRANTS

1988	1989	1990	1987	1988	1989	1990
0.7	0.5	1.3	0.2	0.6	0.4	1.2
0.8	0.8	1.3	0.7	0.8	0.7	1.1
0.4	0.0	0.8	0.4	0.3	0.0	0.5
2.6	2.8	38.8	–	0.1	0.9	0.0
0.0	0.0	0.0	–	0.0	–	–
0.2	0.1	0.3	0.1	–	–	0.0
7.2	5.4	6.3	6.8	7.2	5.4	6.3
7.5	7.2	11.2	7.7	7.5	6.6	9.6
0.0	0.0	0.2	0.0	0.0	0.0	0.2
5.8	14.3	12.5	2.5	0.7	2.2	3.1
32.8	18.6	27.2	5.6	7.6	6.3	6.8
3.4	2.5	3.7	3.1	1.8	2.2	2.5
0.0	0.0	0.1	–	0.0	–	0.1
0.2	0.3	0.4	0.1	0.1	0.1	0.1
0.2	0.0	–	0.2	–	–	–
0.0	0.1	0.0	–	0.0	–	–
13.4	103.2	24.9	7.6	9.0	10.2	14.1
2.0	7.0	22.0	1.0	2.0	7.0	4.0
77.1	*162.7*	*151.0*	*36.0*	*37.7*	*42.1*	*49.4*
24.0	*35.9*	*52.7*	*18.1*	*27.9*	*28.8*	*45.5*
0.1	–	–	–	–	–	–
39.7	*139.7*	*66.7*	*30.7*	*32.4*	*26.6*	*36.2*
101.1	**198.6**	**203.6**	**54.1**	**65.6**	**70.8**	**94.9**

12. TOTAL OOF NET

1988	1989	1990	1987	1988	1989	1990
–	–	–	–	–	–	–
–	–	–	–	–	–	–
109.7	52.7	17.3	2.7	109.7	52.7	0.0
–	–	–	–	–	–	–
0.1	–	0.1	-13.2	-11.3	-10.5	-0.1
–	–	–	–	–	–	–
–	–	164.0	556.7	-1.7	–	149.6
1487.3	848.1	265.6	377.1	462.5	400.8	145.2
–	–	–	–	–	–	–
–	416.1	311.6	–	–	379.3	251.4
–	–	–	–	–	–	–
–	–	0.6	-0.6	-0.2	-0.8	0.6
–	–	–	–	–	–	–
–	–	–	–	–	–	–
–	–	–	–	–	–	–
–	–	–	-0.7	-0.4	-0.3	-0.5
190.0	30.0	271.0	–	170.0	30.0	133.0
1787.1	*1346.9*	*1030.2*	*921.9*	*728.6*	*851.2*	*679.1*
261.0	*621.7*	*560.6*	*278.0*	*56.0*	*412.1*	*305.3*
–	–	–	–	–	–	–
1599.3	*1320.2*	*762.5*	*941.8*	*551.8*	*815.5*	*540.4*
2048.1	**1968.5**	**1590.8**	**1199.9**	**784.6**	**1263.3**	**984.4**

13. ODF COMMITMENTS: BY PURPOSE %

	1987	1988	1989	1990
Education	0	1	0	–
Health	0	0	3	–
Other Social Infrastr.	0	0	8	–
Water Sanitat. Sewage	8	0	10	–
Energy	–	–	–	–
Telecommunications	–	–	–	–
Transportation	–	–	10	–
Agriculture	63	0	8	–
Extractive Industries	–	–	–	–
Manufacturing	0	–	–	–
Trade Banking Tourism	12	12	14	–
Technical Cooperation	16	5	3	–
Multisector Aid	–	–	–	–
Programme	–	22	11	–
Debt Reorganisation	–	59	33	–
Food Aid	–	–	–	–
Emergency Aid	0	0	–	–
Unspecified	–	–	–	–
TOTAL	100	100	100	–

14. GRANT ELEMENT OF ODA %

DAC COUNTRIES

	1987	1988	1989	1990
Australia	100.0	100.0	100.0	–
Austria	100.0	100.0	100.0	–
Belgium	100.0	100.0	100.0	–
Canada	100.0	100.0	100.0	–
Denmark	–	–	–	–
Finland	–	–	100.0	–
France	100.0	100.0	100.0	–
Germany	100.0	50.6	100.0	–
Ireland	100.0	100.0	100.0	–
Italy	100.0	100.0	100.0	–
Japan	100.0	100.0	59.4	–
Netherlands	100.0	100.0	100.0	–
New Zealand	–	100.0	–	–
Norway	100.0	–	–	–
Sweden	100.0	100.0	100.0	–
Switzerland	–	–	–	–
United Kingdom	100.0	100.0	100.0	–
United States	100.0	100.0	100.0	–
TOTAL	*100.0*	*90.6*	*83.2*	–
MULTILATERAL	*80.8*	*100.0*	*88.7*	–
ARAB COUNTRIES	–	*100.0*	–	–
E.E.C.+ MEMBERS	100.0	96.2	100.0	–
TOTAL	*92.4*	*97.0*	*84.8*	–

15. OTHER AGGREGATES

OFFICIAL COMMITMENTS:

	1987	1988	1989	1990
TOTAL BILATERAL	1279.1	1901.3	1733.6	832.3
of which:				
Arab Countries	–	0.1	–	–
C.E.E.C.	300.0	100.0	–	–
TOTAL MULTILATERAL	449.2	1744.4	793.2	1072.9
TOTAL BIL.& MULTIL.	1728.3	3645.7	2526.8	1905.2
of which:				
ODA Grants	86.2	342.2	378.3	265.6
ODA Loans	–	43.2	308.4	367.0

DISBURSEMENTS:

DAC COUNTRIES COMBINED

OFFICIAL & PRIVATE

	1987	1988	1989	1990
GROSS:				
Contractual Lending	1538.0	2069.4	2868.8	1095.2
Export Credits, Total	606.3	306.1	1621.8	97.6
Export Credits, Priv.	606.3	266.0	1369.9	14.4
NET:				
Contractual Lending	654.2	-65.7	1683.8	-32.6
Export Credits Total	-266.3	-841.1	851.1	-807.5
PRIVATE SECTOR NET	432.8	-926.0	661.7	-1153.1
Direct Investment	570.2	68.3	289.8	-313.2
Portfolio Investment	115.8	-189.1	-324.4	-118.8
Export Credits	-253.2	-805.2	696.3	-721.1

MARKET BORROWING:

CHANGE IN CLAIMS

	1987	1988	1989	1990
Banks	-515.0	-1249.0	-1353.0	-1004.0

MEMORANDUM ITEM:

	1987	1988	1989	1990
C.E.E.C. (Gross)	–	–	–	–

	1987	1988	1989	1990	1987	1988	1989	1990		1987

1. TOTAL RECEIPTS NET

4. TOTAL ODA NET

7. TOTAL ODA GROSS

DAC COUNTRIES

	1987	1988	1989	1990	1987	1988	1989	1990		1987
Australia	0.2	0.3	0.3	0.5	0.2	0.3	0.3	0.5	Australia	0.2
Austria	–	–	–	–	–	–	–	–	Austria	–
Belgium	–	–	–	–	–	–	–	–	Belgium	–
Canada	–	–	–	–	–	–	–	–	Canada	–
Denmark	–	–	–	–	–	–	–	–	Denmark	–
Finland	–	–	–	–	–	–	–	–	Finland	–
France	–	–	–	–	–	–	–	–	France	–
Germany	–	–	–	2.2	–	–	–	–	Germany	–
Ireland	–	–	–	–	–	–	–	–	Ireland	–
Italy	–	–	–	–	–	–	–	–	Italy	–
Japan	0.0	0.1	0.0	0.0	0.0	0.1	0.0	0.0	Japan	0.0
Netherlands	–	–	–	–	–	–	–	–	Netherlands	–
New Zealand	6.4	4.7	5.2	6.4	6.4	4.7	5.2	6.4	New Zealand	6.4
Norway	–	–	–	–	–	–	–	–	Norway	–
Sweden	–	–	–	–	–	–	–	–	Sweden	–
Switzerland	–	–	–	–	–	–	–	–	Switzerland	–
United Kingdom	–	–	–	–	–	–	–	–	United Kingdom	–
United States	–	–	–	–	–	–	–	–	United States	–
TOTAL	*6.6*	*5.1*	*5.5*	*9.2*	*6.6*	*5.1*	*5.5*	*7.0*	*TOTAL*	*6.6*
MULTILATERAL										
AF.D.F.	–	–	–	–	–	–	–	–	AF.D.F.	–
AF.D.B.	–	–	–	–	–	–	–	–	AF.D.B.	–
AS.D.B	–	–	–	–	–	–	–	–	AS.D.B	–
CAR.D.B.	–	–	–	–	–	–	–	–	CAR.D.B.	–
E.E.C.	–	–	–	–	–	–	–	–	E.E.C.	–
IBRD	–	–	–	–	–	–	–	–	IBRD	–
IDA	–	–	–	–	–	–	–	–	IDA	–
I.D.B.	–	–	–	–	–	–	–	–	I.D.B.	–
IFAD	–	–	–	–	–	–	–	–	IFAD	–
I.F.C.	–	–	–	–	–	–	–	–	I.F.C.	–
IMF TRUST FUND	–	–	–	–	–	–	–	–	IMF TRUST FUND	–
U.N. AGENCIES	–	–	–	–	–	–	–	–	U.N. AGENCIES	–
UNDP	0.1	0.2	0.1	0.2	0.1	0.2	0.1	0.2	UNDP	0.1
UNTA	–	–	–	–	–	–	–	–	UNTA	–
UNICEF	–	–	–	–	–	–	–	–	UNICEF	–
UNRWA	–	–	–	–	–	–	–	–	UNRWA	–
WFP	–	–	–	–	–	–	–	–	WFP	–
UNHCR	–	–	–	–	–	–	–	–	UNHCR	–
Other Multilateral	–	–	–	–	–	–	–	–	Other Multilateral	–
Arab Agencies	–	–	–	–	–	–	–	–	Arab Agencies	–
TOTAL	*0.1*	*0.2*	*0.1*	*0.2*	*0.1*	*0.2*	*0.1*	*0.2*	*TOTAL*	*0.1*
ARAB COUNTRIES	–	–	–	–	–	–	–	–	**ARAB COUNTRIES**	–
E.E.C.+ MEMBERS	–	–	–	2.2	–	–	–	–	*E.E.C.+ MEMBERS*	–
TOTAL	**6.7**	**5.3**	**5.6**	**9.4**	**6.7**	**5.3**	**5.6**	**7.2**	**TOTAL**	**6.7**

2. ODA LOANS GROSS

5. ODA LOANS NET

8. GRANTS

DAC COUNTRIES

	1987	1988	1989	1990	1987	1988	1989	1990		1987
Australia	–	–	–	–	–	–	–	–	Australia	0.2
Austria	–	–	–	–	–	–	–	–	Austria	–
Belgium	–	–	–	–	–	–	–	–	Belgium	–
Canada	–	–	–	–	–	–	–	–	Canada	–
Denmark	–	–	–	–	–	–	–	–	Denmark	–
Finland	–	–	–	–	–	–	–	–	Finland	–
France	–	–	–	–	–	–	–	–	France	–
Germany	–	–	–	–	–	–	–	–	Germany	–
Ireland	–	–	–	–	–	–	–	–	Ireland	–
Italy	–	–	–	–	–	–	–	–	Italy	–
Japan	–	–	–	–	–	–	–	–	Japan	0.0
Netherlands	–	–	–	–	–	–	–	–	Netherlands	–
New Zealand	–	–	–	–	–	–	–	–	New Zealand	6.4
Norway	–	–	–	–	–	–	–	–	Norway	–
Sweden	–	–	–	–	–	–	–	–	Sweden	–
Switzerland	–	–	–	–	–	–	–	–	Switzerland	–
United Kingdom	–	–	–	–	–	–	–	–	United Kingdom	–
United States	–	–	–	–	–	–	–	–	United States	–
TOTAL	–	–	–	–	–	–	–	–	*TOTAL*	*6.6*
MULTILATERAL	–	–	–	–	–	–	–	–	*MULTILATERAL*	*0.1*
ARAB COUNTRIES	–	–	–	–	–	–	–	–	**ARAB COUNTRIES**	–
E.E.C.+ MEMBERS	–	–	–	–	–	–	–	–	*E.E.C.+ MEMBERS*	–
TOTAL	–	–	–	–	–	–	–	–	**TOTAL**	**6.7**

3. TOTAL OFFICIAL GROSS

6. TOTAL OFFICIAL NET

9. TOTAL OOF GROSS

DAC COUNTRIES

	1987	1988	1989	1990	1987	1988	1989	1990		1987
Australia	0.2	0.3	0.3	0.5	0.2	0.3	0.3	0.5	Australia	–
Austria	–	–	–	–	–	–	–	–	Austria	–
Belgium	–	–	–	–	–	–	–	–	Belgium	–
Canada	–	–	–	–	–	–	–	–	Canada	–
Denmark	–	–	–	–	–	–	–	–	Denmark	–
Finland	–	–	–	–	–	–	–	–	Finland	–
France	–	–	–	–	–	–	–	–	France	–
Germany	–	–	–	–	–	–	–	–	Germany	–
Ireland	–	–	–	–	–	–	–	–	Ireland	–
Italy	–	–	–	–	–	–	–	–	Italy	–
Japan	0.0	0.1	0.0	0.0	0.0	0.1	0.0	0.0	Japan	–
Netherlands	–	–	–	–	–	–	–	–	Netherlands	–
New Zealand	6.4	4.7	5.2	6.4	6.4	4.7	5.2	6.4	New Zealand	–
Norway	–	–	–	–	–	–	–	–	Norway	–
Sweden	–	–	–	–	–	–	–	–	Sweden	–
Switzerland	–	–	–	–	–	–	–	–	Switzerland	–
United Kingdom	–	–	–	–	–	–	–	–	United Kingdom	–
United States	–	–	–	–	–	–	–	–	United States	–
TOTAL	*6.6*	*5.1*	*5.5*	*7.0*	*6.6*	*5.1*	*5.5*	*7.0*	*TOTAL*	–
MULTILATERAL	*0.1*	*0.2*	*0.1*	*0.2*	*0.1*	*0.2*	*0.1*	*0.2*	*MULTILATERAL*	–
ARAB COUNTRIES	–	–	–	–	–	–	–	–	**ARAB COUNTRIES**	–
E.E.C.+ MEMBERS	–	–	–	–	–	–	–	–	*E.E.C.+ MEMBERS*	–
TOTAL	**6.7**	**5.3**	**5.6**	**7.2**	**6.7**	**5.3**	**5.6**	**7.2**	**TOTAL**	–

1988	1989	1990	1987	1988	1989	1990

10. ODA COMMITMENTS

1988	1989	1990	1987	1988	1989	1990
0.3	0.3	0.5	0.1	0.2	0.2	0.6
–	–	–	–	–	–	–
–	–	–	–	–	–	–
–	–	–	–	–	–	–
–	–	–	–	–	–	–
–	–	–	–	–	–	–
–	–	–	–	–	–	–
0.1	0.0	0.0	0.0	0.1	0.1	0.0
–	–	–	–	–	–	–
4.7	5.2	6.4	5.0	3.9	–	5.3
–	–	–	–	–	–	–
–	–	–	–	–	–	–
–	–	–	–	–	–	–
–	–	–	–	–	–	–
5.1	5.5	7.0	5.1	4.1	0.3	5.9
–	–	–	–	–	–	–
–	–	–	–	–	–	–
–	–	–	–	–	–	–
–	–	–	–	–	–	–
–	–	–	–	–	–	–
–	–	–	–	–	–	–
–	–	–	–	–	–	–
–	–	–	0.1	0.2	0.1	0.2
0.2	0.1	0.2	–	–	–	–
–	–	–	–	–	–	–
–	–	–	–	–	–	–
–	–	–	–	–	–	–
–	–	–	–	–	–	–
–	–	–	–	–	–	–
–	–	–	–	–	–	–
0.2	0.1	0.2	0.1	0.2	0.1	0.2
–	–	–	–	–	–	–
–	–	–	–	–	–	–
5.3	5.6	7.2	5.2	4.3	0.4	6.1

11. TECH. COOP. GRANTS

1988	1989	1990	1987	1988	1989	1990
0.3	0.3	0.5	0.1	0.0	0.1	0.2
–	–	–	–	–	–	–
–	–	–	–	–	–	–
–	–	–	–	–	–	–
–	–	–	–	–	–	–
–	–	–	–	–	–	–
–	–	–	–	–	–	–
0.1	0.0	0.0	0.0	0.1	0.0	0.0
–	–	–	–	–	–	–
4.7	5.2	6.4	0.2	0.2	–	0.2
–	–	–	–	–	–	–
–	–	–	–	–	–	–
–	–	–	–	–	–	–
5.1	5.5	7.0	0.3	0.3	0.1	0.4
0.2	0.1	0.2	0.1	0.2	0.1	0.2
–	–	–	–	–	–	–
–	–	–	–	–	–	–
5.3	5.6	7.2	0.4	0.4	0.2	0.6

12. TOTAL OOF NET

1988	1989	1990	1987	1988	1989	1990
–	–	–	–	–	–	–
–	–	–	–	–	–	–
–	–	–	–	–	–	–
–	–	–	–	–	–	–
–	–	–	–	–	–	–
–	–	–	–	–	–	–
–	–	–	–	–	–	–
–	–	–	–	–	–	–
–	–	–	–	–	–	–
–	–	–	–	–	–	–
–	–	–	–	–	–	–
–	–	–	–	–	–	–
–	–	–	–	–	–	–
–	–	–	–	–	–	–
–	–	–	–	–	–	–
–	–	–	–	–	–	–
–	–	–	–	–	–	–
–	–	–	–	–	–	–

13. ODF COMMITMENTS: BY PURPOSE %

	1987	1988	1989	1990
Education	–	–	–	–
Health	–	–	–	–
Other Social Infrastr.	–	–	–	–
Water Sanitat. Sewage	0	–	–	–
Energy	–	–	–	–
Telecommunications	–	–	–	–
Transportation	3	1	9	–
Agriculture	–	–	–	–
Extractive Industries	–	–	–	–
Manufacturing	–	–	–	–
Trade Banking Tourism	–	–	–	–
Technical Cooperation	97	95	65	–
Multisector Aid	–	3	27	–
Programme	–	–	–	–
Debt Reorganisation	–	–	–	–
Food Aid	–	–	–	–
Emergency Aid	–	–	–	–
Unspecified	–	–	–	–
TOTAL	100	100	100	–

14. GRANT ELEMENT OF ODA %

DAC COUNTRIES	1987	1988	1989	1990
Australia	100.0	100.0	100.0	–
Austria	–	–	–	–
Belgium	–	–	–	–
Canada	–	–	–	–
Denmark	–	–	–	–
Finland	–	–	–	–
France	–	–	–	–
Germany	–	–	–	–
Ireland	–	–	–	–
Italy	–	–	–	–
Japan	100.0	100.0	100.0	–
Netherlands	–	–	–	–
New Zealand	100.0	100.0	–	–
Norway	–	–	–	–
Sweden	–	–	–	–
Switzerland	–	–	–	–
United Kingdom	–	–	–	–
United States	–	–	–	–
TOTAL	*100.0*	*100.0*	*100.0*	*–*
MULTILATERAL	*100.0*	*100.0*	*100.0*	*–*
ARAB COUNTRIES	*–*	*–*	*–*	*–*
E.E.C.+ MEMBERS	*–*	*–*	*–*	*–*
TOTAL	*100.0*	*100.0*	*100.0*	*–*

15. OTHER AGGREGATES

	1987	1988	1989	1990
OFFICIAL COMMITMENTS:				
TOTAL BILATERAL	5.1	4.1	0.3	5.9
of which:				
Arab Countries	–	–	–	–
C.E.E.C.	–	–	–	–
TOTAL MULTILATERAL	0.1	0.2	0.1	0.2
TOTAL BIL.& MULTIL.	5.2	4.3	0.4	6.1
of which:				
ODA Grants	5.2	4.3	0.4	6.1
ODA Loans	–	–	–	–
DISBURSEMENTS:				
DAC COUNTRIES COMBINED				
OFFICIAL & PRIVATE				
GROSS:				
Contractual Lending	–	–	–	–
Export Credits, Total	–	–	–	–
Export Credits, Priv.	–	–	–	–
NET:				
Contractual Lending	–	–	–	–
Export Credits Total	–	–	–	–
PRIVATE SECTOR NET	–	–	–	2.2
Direct Investment	–	–	–	–
Portfolio Investment	–	–	–	2.2
Export Credits	–	–	–	–
MARKET BORROWING:				
CHANGE IN CLAIMS				
Banks	–	–	–	–
MEMORANDUM ITEM:				
C.E.E.C. (Gross)	–	–	–	–

1. TOTAL RECEIPTS NET

DAC COUNTRIES	1987	1988	1989	1990
Australia	–	–	–	-0.8
Austria	–	–	–	–
Belgium	-11.7	3.3	1.0	1.5
Canada	–	–	–	–
Denmark	–	–	–	–
Finland	–	–	–	–
France	-12.2	8.3	-4.0	-15.3
Germany	-4.6	-3.9	2.9	52.0
Ireland	–	–	–	–
Italy	0.1	0.9	8.0	0.0
Japan	5.6	2.0	31.9	-5.1
Netherlands	-2.5	5.3	0.5	47.2
New Zealand	–	–	–	–
Norway	–	–	–	–
Sweden	0.8	–	–	–
Switzerland	–	–	–	–
United Kingdom	73.1	-118.9	-375.7	-24.1
United States	13.0	8.0	8.0	4.0
TOTAL	61.4	-95.0	-327.5	59.4
MULTILATERAL				
AF.D.F.	–	–	–	–
AF.D.B.	–	–	–	–
AS.D.B	–	–	–	–
CAR.D.B.	–	–	–	–
E.E.C.	–	–	–	–
IBRD	2.9	-1.0	-2.0	-7.0
IDA	–	–	–	–
I.D.B.	–	–	–	–
IFAD	–	–	–	–
I.F.C.	–	–	–	–
IMF TRUST FUND	–	–	–	–
U.N. AGENCIES	–	–	–	–
UNDP	0.9	1.5	2.9	5.1
UNTA	0.5	0.4	0.5	0.6
UNICEF	0.4	0.1	0.5	0.5
UNRWA	–	–	–	–
WFP	–	–	–	–
UNHCR	–	–	–	–
Other Multilateral	0.0	0.1	0.3	0.3
Arab Agencies	-5.4	0.6	-1.3	–
TOTAL	-0.6	1.6	1.0	-0.6
ARAB COUNTRIES	-18.4	-30.7	-12.3	51.1
E.E.C.+ MEMBERS	42.1	-105.0	-367.3	61.3
TOTAL	42.4	-124.2	-338.9	109.9

2. ODA LOANS GROSS

DAC COUNTRIES	1987	1988	1989	1990
Australia	–	–	–	–
Austria	–	–	–	–
Belgium	–	–	–	–
Canada	–	–	–	–
Denmark	–	–	–	–
Finland	–	–	–	–
France	–	–	–	–
Germany	–	–	–	–
Ireland	–	–	–	–
Italy	–	–	–	–
Japan	–	–	–	–
Netherlands	–	–	–	–
New Zealand	–	–	–	–
Norway	–	–	–	–
Sweden	–	–	–	–
Switzerland	–	–	–	–
United Kingdom	–	–	–	–
United States	8.0	2.0	3.0	–
TOTAL	8.0	2.0	3.0	–
MULTILATERAL	1.2	–	3.2	–
ARAB COUNTRIES	13.8	2.2	12.5	2.9
E.E.C.+ MEMBERS	–	–	–	–
TOTAL	23.0	4.2	18.6	2.9

3. TOTAL OFFICIAL GROSS

DAC COUNTRIES	1987	1988	1989	1990
Australia	–	–	–	0.0
Austria	–	–	–	–
Belgium	–	–	–	0.0
Canada	–	–	–	–
Denmark	–	–	–	–
Finland	–	–	–	–
France	0.2	0.4	0.4	0.5
Germany	0.5	0.9	1.0	2.3
Ireland	–	–	–	–
Italy	0.1	0.0	0.0	0.0
Japan	0.6	2.0	24.9	9.4
Netherlands	–	–	–	–
New Zealand	–	–	–	–
Norway	–	–	–	–
Sweden	–	–	–	–
Switzerland	–	–	–	–
United Kingdom	0.8	1.7	1.5	1.2
United States	13.0	9.0	8.0	5.0
TOTAL	15.2	14.0	35.7	18.4
MULTILATERAL	23.3	27.1	26.6	15.5
ARAB COUNTRIES	13.8	2.2	12.5	58.5
E.E.C.+ MEMBERS	1.6	3.0	2.8	3.9
TOTAL	52.3	43.3	74.9	92.4

4. TOTAL ODA NET

DAC COUNTRIES	1987	1988	1989	1990
Australia	–	–	–	0.0
Austria	–	–	–	–
Belgium	–	–	–	0.0
Canada	–	–	–	–
Denmark	–	–	–	–
Finland	–	–	–	–
France	0.2	0.4	0.4	0.5
Germany	0.5	0.8	1.0	2.3
Ireland	–	–	–	–
Italy	0.1	0.0	0.0	0.0
Japan	0.6	2.0	6.1	3.4
Netherlands	–	–	–	–
New Zealand	–	–	–	–
Norway	–	–	–	–
Sweden	–	–	–	–
Switzerland	–	–	–	–
United Kingdom	0.8	1.7	1.5	1.2
United States	13.0	9.0	8.0	4.0
TOTAL	15.2	13.9	16.9	11.3
MULTILATERAL				
AF.D.F.	–	–	–	–
AF.D.B.	–	–	–	–
AS.D.B	–	–	–	–
CAR.D.B.	–	–	–	–
E.E.C.	–	–	–	–
IBRD	–	–	–	–
IDA	–	–	–	–
I.D.B.	–	–	–	–
IFAD	–	–	–	–
I.F.C.	–	–	–	–
IMF TRUST FUND	–	–	–	–
U.N. AGENCIES	–	–	–	–
UNDP	0.9	1.5	2.9	5.1
UNTA	0.5	0.4	0.5	0.6
UNICEF	0.4	0.1	0.5	0.5
UNRWA	–	–	–	–
WFP	–	–	–	–
UNHCR	–	–	–	–
Other Multilateral	0.0	0.1	0.3	0.3
Arab Agencies	0.5	-0.6	1.8	–
TOTAL	2.4	1.5	6.1	6.4
ARAB COUNTRIES	-1.6	-14.8	-4.8	51.1
E.E.C.+ MEMBERS	1.6	3.0	2.8	3.9
TOTAL	16.0	0.6	18.2	68.8

5. ODA LOANS NET

DAC COUNTRIES	1987	1988	1989	1990
Australia	–	–	–	–
Austria	–	–	–	–
Belgium	–	–	–	–
Canada	–	–	–	–
Denmark	–	–	–	–
Finland	–	–	–	–
France	–	–	–	–
Germany	0.0	0.0	–	–
Ireland	–	–	–	–
Italy	–	–	–	–
Japan	–	–	–	–
Netherlands	–	–	–	–
New Zealand	–	–	–	–
Norway	–	–	–	–
Sweden	–	–	–	–
Switzerland	–	–	–	–
United Kingdom	–	–	–	–
United States	8.0	2.0	3.0	-1.0
TOTAL	8.0	2.0	3.0	-1.0
MULTILATERAL	0.5	-0.8	1.8	–
ARAB COUNTRIES	-1.6	-14.8	-4.8	-4.6
E.E.C.+ MEMBERS	0.0	0.0	–	–
TOTAL	6.9	-13.6	-0.1	-5.6

6. TOTAL OFFICIAL NET

DAC COUNTRIES	1987	1988	1989	1990
Australia	–	–	–	0.0
Austria	–	–	–	–
Belgium	–	–	–	0.0
Canada	–	–	–	–
Denmark	–	–	–	–
Finland	–	–	–	–
France	0.2	0.4	0.4	0.5
Germany	0.5	0.9	1.0	2.3
Ireland	–	–	–	–
Italy	0.1	0.0	0.0	0.0
Japan	0.6	2.0	24.9	9.4
Netherlands	–	–	–	–
New Zealand	–	–	–	–
Norway	–	–	–	–
Sweden	–	–	–	–
Switzerland	–	–	–	–
United Kingdom	0.8	1.7	1.5	1.2
United States	13.0	9.0	8.0	4.0
TOTAL	15.2	14.0	35.7	17.4
MULTILATERAL	-0.6	1.6	1.0	-0.6
ARAB COUNTRIES	-18.4	-30.8	-12.3	51.1
E.E.C.+ MEMBERS	1.6	3.0	2.8	3.9
TOTAL	-3.9	-15.2	24.4	67.8

7. TOTAL ODA GROSS

	1987
Australia	–
Austria	–
Belgium	–
Canada	–
Denmark	–
Finland	–
France	0.2
Germany	0.5
Ireland	–
Italy	0.1
Japan	0.6
Netherlands	–
New Zealand	–
Norway	–
Sweden	–
Switzerland	–
United Kingdom	0.8
United States	13.0
TOTAL	15.2
AF.D.F.	–
AF.D.B.	–
AS.D.B	–
CAR.D.B.	–
E.E.C.	–
IBRD	–
IDA	–
I.D.B.	–
IFAD	–
I.F.C.	–
IMF TRUST FUND	–
U.N. AGENCIES	–
UNDP	0.9
UNTA	0.5
UNICEF	0.4
UNRWA	–
WFP	–
UNHCR	–
Other Multilateral	0.0
Arab Agencies	1.2
TOTAL	3.1
ARAB COUNTRIES	13.8
E.E.C.+ MEMBERS	1.6
TOTAL	32.1

8. GRANTS

	1987
Australia	–
Austria	–
Belgium	–
Canada	–
Denmark	–
Finland	–
France	0.2
Germany	0.5
Ireland	–
Italy	0.1
Japan	0.6
Netherlands	–
New Zealand	–
Norway	–
Sweden	–
Switzerland	–
United Kingdom	0.8
United States	5.0
TOTAL	7.2
MULTILATERAL	1.9
ARAB COUNTRIES	0.1
E.E.C.+ MEMBERS	1.6
TOTAL	9.1

9. TOTAL OOF GROSS

	1987
Australia	–
Austria	–
Belgium	–
Canada	–
Denmark	–
Finland	–
France	–
Germany	–
Ireland	–
Italy	–
Japan	–
Netherlands	–
New Zealand	–
Norway	–
Sweden	–
Switzerland	–
United Kingdom	–
United States	–
TOTAL	–
MULTILATERAL	20.2
ARAB COUNTRIES	–
E.E.C.+ MEMBERS	–
TOTAL	20.2

1988	1989	1990
–	–	0.0
–	–	–
–	–	0.0
–	–	–
–	–	–
0.4	0.4	0.5
0.9	1.0	2.3
–	–	–
0.0	0.0	0.0
2.0	6.1	3.4
–	–	–
–	–	–
–	–	–
1.7	1.5	1.2
9.0	8.0	5.0
13.9	*16.9*	*12.3*
–	–	–
–	–	–
–	–	–
–	–	–
–	–	–
–	–	–
–	–	–
–	–	–
–	–	–
1.5	2.9	5.1
0.4	0.5	0.6
0.1	0.5	0.5
–	–	–
–	–	–
0.1	0.3	0.3
0.2	3.2	–
2.2	*7.5*	*6.4*
2.2	*12.5*	*58.5*
3.0	*2.8*	*3.9*
18.3	*36.9*	*77.3*

10. ODA COMMITMENTS

1987	1988	1989	1990
–	–	–	–
–	–	–	0.0
–	–	–	–
–	–	–	–
0.2	0.4	0.4	18.8
4.6	0.9	0.4	1.0
–	–	–	–
0.1	0.0	0.0	0.0
0.7	2.2	6.3	3.4
–	–	–	–
–	–	–	–
–	–	–	–
0.8	1.7	1.5	1.2
14.9	13.0	15.0	12.6
21.4	*18.2*	*23.6*	*37.0*
–	–	–	–
–	–	–	–
–	–	–	–
–	–	–	–
–	–	–	–
–	–	–	–
–	–	–	–
–	–	–	–
1.8	2.0	4.3	6.4
–	–	–	–
–	–	–	–
–	–	–	–
–	–	–	–
–	–	–	–
–	–	–	–
–	–	7.6	–
1.8	*2.0*	*11.9*	*6.4*
–	–	*10.9*	*21.4*
5.7	*3.0*	*2.3*	*21.0*
23.2	*20.2*	*46.3*	*64.8*

11. TECH. COOP. GRANTS

Left (1988 / 1989 / 1990):

1988	1989	1990
–	–	0.0
–	–	–
–	–	0.0
–	–	–
–	–	–
0.4	0.4	0.5
0.9	1.0	2.3
–	–	–
0.0	0.0	0.0
2.0	6.1	3.4
–	–	–
–	–	–
–	–	–
1.7	1.5	1.2
7.0	5.0	5.0
11.9	*13.9*	*12.3*
2.2	4.3	6.4
–	0.0	55.6
3.0	2.8	3.9
14.2	*18.2*	*74.4*

1987	1988	1989	1990
–	–	–	0.0
–	–	–	–
–	–	–	–
–	–	–	–
–	–	–	–
0.2	0.4	0.4	0.5
0.5	0.9	1.0	2.3
–	–	–	–
0.1	0.0	0.0	0.0
0.6	2.0	3.3	3.4
–	–	–	–
–	–	–	–
–	–	–	–
0.8	1.7	1.5	1.2
4.0	7.0	5.0	4.0
6.2	*11.9*	*11.1*	*11.3*
1.8	2.0	4.3	6.4
–	–	–	–
1.6	3.0	2.8	3.9
8.0	*14.0*	*15.3*	*17.7*

12. TOTAL OOF NET

Left (1988 / 1989 / 1990):

1988	1989	1990
–	–	–
–	–	–
–	–	–
–	–	–
0.1	–	–
–	–	–
–	18.9	6.0
–	–	–
–	–	–
–	–	–
–	–	–
–	–	–
0.1	*18.9*	*6.0*
24.9	*19.2*	*9.1*
–	–	–
0.1	–	–
25.0	*38.0*	*15.1*

1987	1988	1989	1990
–	–	–	–
–	–	–	–
–	–	–	–
–	–	–	–
–	0.1	–	–
–	–	–	–
–	–	18.9	6.0
–	–	–	–
–	–	–	–
–	–	–	–
–	–	–	–
–	–	–	–
–	*0.1*	*18.9*	*6.0*
-3.0	*0.1*	*-5.1*	*-7.0*
-16.8	*-15.9*	*-7.5*	–
–	*0.1*	–	–
-19.8	*-15.8*	*6.2*	*-1.0*

13. ODF COMMITMENTS: BY PURPOSE %

	1987	1988	1989	1990
Education	–	–	–	–
Health	–	–	–	–
Other Social Infrastr.	–	–	–	–
Water Sanitat. Sewage	35	32	7	–
Energy	–	–	–	–
Telecommunications	–	–	–	–
Transportation	–	–	–	–
Agriculture	–	–	80	–
Extractive Industries	–	–	–	–
Manufacturing	–	–	–	–
Trade Banking Tourism	–	–	–	–
Technical Cooperation	47	48	10	–
Multisector Aid	0	–	–	–
Programme	18	20	2	–
Debt Reorganisation	–	–	–	–
Food Aid	–	–	–	–
Emergency Aid	–	–	1	–
Unspecified	–	–	–	–
TOTAL	100	100	100	–

14. GRANT ELEMENT OF ODA %

DAC COUNTRIES

	1987	1988	1989	1990
Australia	–	–	–	–
Austria	–	–	–	–
Belgium	–	–	–	–
Canada	–	–	–	–
Denmark	–	–	–	–
Finland	–	–	–	–
France	100.0	100.0	100.0	–
Germany	100.0	100.0	100.0	–
Ireland	–	–	–	–
Italy	100.0	100.0	100.0	–
Japan	100.0	100.0	100.0	–
Netherlands	–	–	–	–
New Zealand	–	–	–	–
Norway	–	–	–	–
Sweden	–	–	–	–
Switzerland	–	–	–	–
United Kingdom	100.0	100.0	100.0	–
United States	69.5	69.7	100.0	–
TOTAL	*78.6*	*78.3*	*100.0*	–
MULTILATERAL	*100.0*	*100.0*	*65.9*	–
ARAB COUNTRIES	–	–	*27.6*	–
E.E.C.+ MEMBERS	*100.0*	*100.0*	*100.0*	–
TOTAL	*80.3*	*80.5*	*74.2*	–

15. OTHER AGGREGATES

OFFICIAL COMMITMENTS:

	1987	1988	1989	1990
TOTAL BILATERAL	35.7	18.2	222.9	58.4
of which:				
Arab Countries	14.4	–	10.9	21.4
C.E.E.C.	–	–	–	–
TOTAL MULTILATERAL	56.0	23.6	42.6	6.4
TOTAL BIL.& MULTIL.	91.7	41.7	265.5	64.8
of which:				
ODA Grants	13.3	12.2	28.4	25.1
ODA Loans	9.9	8.0	18.0	39.7

DISBURSEMENTS:

DAC COUNTRIES COMBINED

OFFICIAL & PRIVATE

	1987	1988	1989	1990
GROSS:				
Contractual Lending	288.5	-0.4	-128.7	215.4
Export Credits, Total	280.5	-2.4	-150.6	209.4
Export Credits, Priv.	280.5	-2.4	-150.6	209.4
NET:				
Contractual Lending	62.1	-120.0	-347.1	40.9
Export Credits Total	54.1	-122.0	-368.9	35.9
PRIVATE SECTOR NET	46.3	-109.0	-363.2	42.1
Direct Investment	11.3	-3.9	4.9	2.3
Portfolio Investment	-19.1	17.0	0.8	3.8
Export Credits	54.1	-122.0	-368.9	35.9

MARKET BORROWING:

CHANGE IN CLAIMS

	1987	1988	1989	1990
Banks	-253.0	-108.0	29.0	-294.0

MEMORANDUM ITEM:

	1987	1988	1989	1990
C.E.E.C. (Gross)	–	–	–	–

1. TOTAL RECEIPTS NET

DAC COUNTRIES	1987	1988	1989	1990
Australia	0.1	0.8	5.4	8.3
Austria	0.5	0.3	0.6	2.7
Belgium	0.1	66.6	0.8	-9.6
Canada	36.1	74.1	47.3	30.7
Denmark	-1.2	-1.9	-1.0	-0.7
Finland	0.6	0.5	6.3	2.3
France	-14.7	77.0	9.5	8.8
Germany	47.3	75.8	46.4	123.3
Ireland	0.0	0.0	–	–
Italy	-1.1	32.4	32.8	3.8
Japan	150.1	323.8	178.5	268.0
Netherlands	31.7	30.4	33.5	36.1
New Zealand	0.0	0.0	0.0	0.1
Norway	10.5	10.6	7.2	14.8
Sweden	5.6	3.9	15.2	8.7
Switzerland	11.6	6.6	5.8	9.6
United Kingdom	46.1	51.2	24.6	59.1
United States	5.0	400.0	937.0	182.0
TOTAL	*328.2*	*1152.0*	*1349.9*	*747.6*
MULTILATERAL				
AF.D.F.	–	–	–	–
AF.D.B.	–	–	–	–
AS.D.B	186.1	275.4	424.7	408.6
CAR.D.B.	–	–	–	–
E.E.C.	4.6	1.9	12.9	12.9
IBRD	149.7	276.0	344.0	283.0
IDA	124.4	101.0	90.0	115.0
I.D.B.	–	–	–	–
IFAD	17.9	–	1.0	8.1
I.F.C.	-5.6	-18.0	11.0	1.3
IMF TRUST FUND	–	–	–	–
U.N. AGENCIES	–	–	–	–
UNDP	10.7	10.7	13.4	23.6
UNTA	3.1	1.9	2.7	1.9
UNICEF	10.0	7.8	10.7	13.4
UNRWA	–	–	–	–
WFP	66.8	61.1	32.9	62.8
UNHCR	79.4	52.4	58.5	51.2
Other Multilateral	6.8	3.6	37.6	5.1
Arab Agencies	22.4	-30.5	-19.5	–
TOTAL	*676.5*	*743.2*	*1019.8*	*986.8*
ARAB COUNTRIES	*-30.1*	*-19.6*	*-24.4*	*-13.3*
E.E.C.+ MEMBERS	*112.8*	*333.3*	*159.4*	*233.5*
TOTAL	*974.6*	*1875.6*	*2345.3*	*1721.1*

2. ODA LOANS GROSS

DAC COUNTRIES	1987	1988	1989	1990
Australia	–	–	–	–
Austria	–	–	–	–
Belgium	–	–	–	–
Canada	1.3	–	–	–
Denmark	–	–	–	–
Finland	–	–	–	–
France	35.4	64.0	22.1	15.9
Germany	57.8	88.6	82.1	120.7
Ireland	–	–	–	–
Italy	10.0	53.9	38.0	6.0
Japan	86.1	244.6	142.3	179.9
Netherlands	6.0	4.4	0.2	5.5
New Zealand	–	–	–	–
Norway	–	–	–	–
Sweden	–	–	–	–
Switzerland	–	–	–	–
United Kingdom	0.0	0.2	–	0.1
United States	59.0	168.0	129.0	93.0
TOTAL	*255.5*	*623.7*	*413.8*	*421.0*
MULTILATERAL	*307.9*	*304.7*	*325.4*	*366.2*
ARAB COUNTRIES	*6.5*	*7.3*	*1.9*	*0.2*
E.E.C.+ MEMBERS	*109.1*	*211.1*	*142.5*	*148.1*
TOTAL	*569.9*	*935.6*	*741.2*	*787.3*

3. TOTAL OFFICIAL GROSS

DAC COUNTRIES	1987	1988	1989	1990
Australia	0.6	0.8	5.4	8.3
Austria	0.7	0.4	0.7	2.8
Belgium	0.4	1.6	0.5	0.6
Canada	44.0	84.1	58.1	41.2
Denmark	0.3	0.2	0.2	1.8
Finland	0.6	0.5	0.9	2.3
France	38.8	65.4	23.5	17.4
Germany	88.1	120.1	121.3	193.6
Ireland	0.0	0.0	–	–
Italy	16.4	60.7	44.4	20.1
Japan	163.1	347.8	231.4	247.5
Netherlands	42.6	39.2	39.9	48.1
New Zealand	0.0	0.0	0.0	0.1
Norway	10.9	11.9	7.5	15.4
Sweden	4.2	3.9	11.0	2.2
Switzerland	11.6	6.7	5.9	9.8
United Kingdom	36.8	41.5	50.9	84.6
United States	156.0	403.0	344.0	237.0
TOTAL	*614.8*	*1187.6*	*945.7*	*932.6*
MULTILATERAL	*914.5*	*1015.8*	*1259.4*	*1149.1*
ARAB COUNTRIES	*7.5*	*7.4*	*3.4*	*0.2*
E.E.C.+ MEMBERS	*227.8*	*330.5*	*293.5*	*379.0*
TOTAL	*1536.8*	*2210.8*	*2208.5*	*2081.8*

4. TOTAL ODA NET

DAC COUNTRIES	1987	1988	1989	1990
Australia	0.6	0.8	5.4	8.3
Austria	0.5	0.3	0.6	2.7
Belgium	0.3	-1.6	-1.7	0.6
Canada	38.0	64.4	35.3	28.4
Denmark	-0.2	-0.3	-0.9	-0.8
Finland	0.6	0.5	0.9	2.3
France	34.1	60.7	19.5	5.7
Germany	50.5	96.6	54.2	124.1
Ireland	0.0	0.0	–	–
Italy	16.1	59.0	36.3	13.8
Japan	126.7	302.2	177.5	193.6
Netherlands	27.9	27.2	26.6	26.8
New Zealand	0.0	0.0	0.0	0.1
Norway	10.7	10.8	7.3	15.0
Sweden	4.2	3.9	11.0	2.2
Switzerland	11.6	6.6	5.8	9.6
United Kingdom	29.3	33.8	41.4	54.4
United States	90.0	339.0	263.0	167.0
TOTAL	*440.7*	*1003.7*	*682.2*	*653.5*
MULTILATERAL				
AF.D.F.	–	–	–	–
AF.D.B.	–	–	–	–
AS.D.B	148.6	188.3	217.2	218.3
CAR.D.B.	–	–	–	–
E.E.C.	4.6	1.9	12.9	12.9
IBRD	–	–	–	–
IDA	124.4	101.0	90.0	115.0
I.D.B.	–	–	–	–
IFAD	17.9	–	1.0	8.1
I.F.C.	–	–	–	–
IMF TRUST FUND	–	–	–	–
U.N. AGENCIES	–	–	–	–
UNDP	10.7	10.7	13.4	23.6
UNTA	3.1	1.9	2.7	1.9
UNICEF	10.0	7.8	10.7	13.4
UNRWA	–	–	–	–
WFP	66.8	61.1	32.9	62.8
UNHCR	79.4	52.4	58.5	51.2
Other Multilateral	6.8	3.6	37.6	5.1
Arab Agencies	-4.3	-6.0	-5.1	–
TOTAL	*468.2*	*422.5*	*471.7*	*512.1*
ARAB COUNTRIES	*-29.5*	*-18.1*	*-24.4*	*-13.3*
E.E.C.+ MEMBERS	*162.5*	*277.2*	*188.2*	*237.4*
TOTAL	*879.4*	*1408.1*	*1129.5*	*1152.3*

5. ODA LOANS NET

DAC COUNTRIES	1987	1988	1989	1990
Australia	–	–	–	–
Austria	-0.2	-0.1	-0.1	-0.1
Belgium	0.0	-3.2	-2.1	–
Canada	-4.7	-9.1	-10.8	-11.4
Denmark	-0.5	-0.5	-1.1	-1.3
Finland	–	–	–	–
France	30.7	59.3	18.2	4.2
Germany	18.7	66.6	18.7	64.3
Ireland	–	–	–	–
Italy	10.0	52.2	29.9	-0.4
Japan	53.9	199.0	88.4	126.0
Netherlands	-3.1	-4.5	-8.9	-8.5
New Zealand	–	–	–	–
Norway	-0.2	-1.1	-0.2	-0.4
Sweden	–	–	–	–
Switzerland	–	-0.1	-0.1	-0.2
United Kingdom	-7.5	-7.5	-6.9	-7.0
United States	-7.0	104.0	48.0	23.0
TOTAL	*90.0*	*455.0*	*172.9*	*188.2*
MULTILATERAL	*283.7*	*278.7*	*296.5*	*332.4*
ARAB COUNTRIES	*-30.6*	*-18.2*	*-26.0*	*-13.3*
E.E.C.+ MEMBERS	*48.2*	*162.4*	*47.7*	*51.3*
TOTAL	*343.2*	*715.4*	*443.4*	*507.2*

6. TOTAL OFFICIAL NET

DAC COUNTRIES	1987	1988	1989	1990
Australia	0.1	0.8	5.4	8.3
Austria	0.5	0.3	0.6	2.7
Belgium	0.3	-1.6	-1.7	0.6
Canada	36.1	74.1	47.3	29.8
Denmark	-1.2	-1.9	-1.0	-2.7
Finland	0.6	0.5	0.9	2.3
France	34.1	60.7	17.8	5.7
Germany	39.4	94.7	51.3	131.2
Ireland	0.0	0.0	–	–
Italy	15.4	58.3	36.3	13.1
Japan	130.8	302.2	177.5	192.7
Netherlands	32.3	29.4	29.3	32.0
New Zealand	0.0	0.0	0.0	0.1
Norway	10.7	10.8	7.3	15.0
Sweden	4.2	3.9	11.0	2.2
Switzerland	11.6	6.6	5.8	9.6
United Kingdom	29.3	33.8	44.0	77.5
United States	80.0	329.0	253.0	164.0
TOTAL	*424.1*	*1001.4*	*684.9*	*684.0*
MULTILATERAL	*676.4*	*743.2*	*1019.8*	*986.8*
ARAB COUNTRIES	*-30.1*	*-19.6*	*-24.4*	*-13.3*
E.E.C.+ MEMBERS	*154.2*	*275.2*	*188.9*	*270.3*
TOTAL	*1070.4*	*1725.1*	*1680.3*	*1657.4*

7. TOTAL ODA GROSS

	1987
Australia	0.6
Austria	0.7
Belgium	0.3
Canada	44.0
Denmark	0.2
Finland	0.6
France	38.8
Germany	89.6
Ireland	0.0
Italy	16.0
Japan	158.9
Netherlands	37.1
New Zealand	0.0
Norway	10.9
Sweden	4.2
Switzerland	11.6
United Kingdom	36.8
United States	156.0
TOTAL	*606.2*
AF.D.F.	–
AF.D.B.	–
AS.D.B	152.2
CAR.D.B.	–
E.E.C.	4.6
IBRD	–
IDA	139.9
I.D.B.	–
IFAD	18.6
I.F.C.	–
IMF TRUST FUND	–
U.N. AGENCIES	–
UNDP	10.7
UNTA	3.1
UNICEF	10.0
UNRWA	–
WFP	66.8
UNHCR	79.4
Other Multilateral	6.8
Arab Agencies	0.0
TOTAL	*492.3*
ARAB COUNTRIES	*7.5*
E.E.C.+ MEMBERS	*223.4*
TOTAL	*1106.1*

8. GRANTS

	1987
Australia	0.6
Austria	0.7
Belgium	0.3
Canada	42.7
Denmark	0.2
Finland	0.6
France	3.4
Germany	31.8
Ireland	0.0
Italy	6.1
Japan	72.8
Netherlands	31.1
New Zealand	0.0
Norway	10.9
Sweden	4.2
Switzerland	11.6
United Kingdom	36.8
United States	97.0
TOTAL	*350.7*
MULTILATERAL	*184.5*
ARAB COUNTRIES	*1.0*
E.E.C.+ MEMBERS	*114.3*
TOTAL	*536.2*

9. TOTAL OOF GROSS

	1987
Australia	–
Austria	–
Belgium	0.0
Canada	–
Denmark	0.0
Finland	–
France	–
Germany	-1.5
Ireland	–
Italy	0.4
Japan	4.2
Netherlands	5.5
New Zealand	–
Norway	–
Sweden	–
Switzerland	–
United Kingdom	–
United States	–
TOTAL	*8.6*
MULTILATERAL	*422.2*
ARAB COUNTRIES	*–*
E.E.C.+ MEMBERS	*4.4*
TOTAL	*430.8*

10. ODA COMMITMENTS

1988	1989	1990	1987	1988	1989	1990
0.8	5.4	8.3	6.0	0.7	5.7	1.8
0.4	0.7	2.8	0.7	0.5	0.9	2.8
1.6	0.5	0.6	0.1	2.6	0.5	0.6
73.6	46.1	39.9	56.2	56.7	38.5	27.9
0.2	0.2	0.5	1.4	–	–	–
0.5	0.9	2.3	–	0.3	4.6	9.7
65.4	23.5	17.4	83.1	1.3	49.0	45.5
118.6	117.6	180.5	151.8	127.7	141.0	101.2
0.0	–	–	0.0	0.0	–	–
60.7	44.4	20.1	118.1	6.9	4.1	13.3
347.8	231.4	247.5	320.9	377.6	530.5	215.2
36.1	35.7	40.8	50.1	51.6	39.9	30.7
0.0	0.0	0.1	0.0	0.0	–	–
11.9	7.5	15.4	9.6	4.2	2.6	37.5
3.9	11.0	2.2	4.3	4.0	10.4	1.1
6.7	5.9	9.8	37.6	2.1	21.7	12.7
41.5	48.3	61.5	15.9	27.8	95.3	30.8
403.0	344.0	237.0	332.5	543.6	275.4	357.2
1172.5	*923.2*	*886.4*	*1188.3*	*1207.6*	*1219.8*	*887.9*
–	–	–	–	–	–	–
–	–	–	–	–	–	–
194.0	223.5	226.2	466.4	327.9	401.2	380.0
–	–	–	–	–	–	–
1.9	12.9	12.9	45.3	27.9	20.5	20.5
–	–	–	–	–	–	–
115.0	106.0	134.0	194.1	190.0	238.0	171.0
–	–	–	–	–	–	–
–	1.3	9.6	11.3	16.8	–	48.7
–	–	–	–	–	–	–
–	–	–	–	–	–	–
–	–	–	177.0	137.4	155.8	157.9
10.7	13.4	23.6	–	–	–	–
1.9	2.7	1.9	–	–	–	–
7.8	10.7	13.4	–	–	–	–
–	–	–	–	–	–	–
61.1	32.9	62.8	–	–	–	–
52.4	58.5	51.2	–	–	–	–
3.6	37.6	5.1	–	–	–	–
0.1	1.2	0.7	6.6	8.9	8.0	9.0
448.5	*500.7*	*541.2*	*900.6*	*708.9*	*823.4*	*787.0*
7.4	*3.4*	*0.2*	*10.9*	*0.1*	*1.0*	*33.9*
325.9	*283.0*	*334.2*	*465.9*	*245.8*	*350.2*	*242.5*
1628.3	*1427.3*	*1427.7*	*2099.8*	*1916.6*	*2044.3*	*1708.9*

11. TECH. COOP. GRANTS

1988	1989	1990	1987	1988	1989	1990
0.8	5.4	8.3	0.5	0.6	0.8	1.0
0.4	0.7	2.8	0.4	0.1	0.1	0.2
1.6	0.5	0.6	0.1	0.1	–	0.0
73.6	46.1	39.9	–	5.8	6.7	2.0
0.2	0.2	0.5	0.1	–	0.1	0.5
0.5	0.9	2.3	0.0	0.2	0.1	0.0
1.4	1.3	1.5	1.2	1.3	1.1	1.3
30.0	35.5	59.8	21.6	22.0	21.1	28.2
0.0	–	–	0.0	0.0	–	–
6.8	6.4	14.2	4.6	3.5	0.7	0.9
103.2	89.0	67.6	11.0	13.8	14.3	11.5
31.7	35.5	35.3	12.8	19.2	18.1	21.5
0.0	0.0	0.1	0.0	0.0	–	0.1
11.9	7.5	15.4	0.3	1.0	0.6	0.5
3.9	11.0	2.2	1.0	2.3	0.8	0.7
6.7	5.9	9.8	0.8	1.6	–	–
41.3	48.3	61.4	7.6	18.5	18.8	22.4
235.0	215.0	144.0	63.0	102.0	99.0	133.0
548.8	*509.4*	*465.4*	*125.0*	*191.9*	*182.3*	*223.7*
143.8	*175.2*	*175.1*	*110.4*	*77.2*	*122.9*	*95.1*
0.1	*1.5*	–	–	–	–	–
114.8	*140.5*	*186.1*	*48.4*	*65.3*	*60.0*	*74.7*
692.7	*686.1*	*640.4*	*235.5*	*269.0*	*305.2*	*318.8*

12. TOTAL OOF NET

1988	1989	1990	1987	1988	1989	1990
–	–	–	-0.5	–	–	–
–	–	–	–	–	–	–
–	0.0	0.1	0.0	–	0.0	0.1
10.6	12.0	1.4	-1.9	9.7	12.0	1.4
–	–	1.3	-1.0	-1.7	0.0	-1.9
–	–	–	–	–	–	–
–	–	–	–	–	-1.7	–
1.5	3.6	13.1	-11.1	-1.9	-2.9	7.1
–	–	–	–	–	–	–
–	–	–	-0.7	-0.7	–	-0.7
–	–	–	4.2	–	–	-0.8
3.1	4.2	7.3	4.4	2.2	2.6	5.2
–	–	–	–	–	–	–
–	–	–	–	–	–	–
–	2.6	23.1	–	–	2.6	23.1
			-10.0	-10.0	-10.0	-3.0
15.1	*22.5*	*46.2*	*-16.6*	*-2.3*	*2.7*	*30.4*
567.3	*758.7*	*607.8*	*208.2*	*320.7*	*548.1*	*474.7*
–	–	–	*-0.6*	*-1.5*	–	–
4.6	*10.5*	*44.8*	*-8.4*	*-2.0*	*0.7*	*32.9*
582.5	*781.2*	*654.1*	*191.0*	*317.0*	*550.8*	*505.1*

13. ODF COMMITMENTS: BY PURPOSE %

	1987	1988	1989	1990
Education	7	1	5	–
Health	1	2	1	–
Other Social Infrastr.	3	3	2	–
Water Sanitat. Sewage	0	1	13	–
Energy	31	18	17	–
Telecommunications	2	2	0	–
Transportation	7	4	3	–
Agriculture	23	25	16	–
Extractive Industries	–	1	8	–
Manufacturing	3	0	5	–
Trade Banking Tourism	3	15	11	–
Technical Cooperation	11	11	13	–
Multisector Aid	0	0	2	–
Programme	3	7	4	–
Debt Reorganisation	0	0	0	–
Food Aid	3	6	1	–
Emergency Aid	1	1	0	–
Unspecified	1	0	0	–
TOTAL	100	100	100	–

14. GRANT ELEMENT OF ODA %

DAC COUNTRIES

	1987	1988	1989	1990
Australia	100.0	100.0	100.0	–
Austria	100.0	100.0	100.0	–
Belgium	100.0	100.0	100.0	–
Canada	100.0	100.0	100.0	–
Denmark	100.0	–	–	–
Finland	–	100.0	100.0	–
France	57.5	100.0	68.7	–
Germany	67.3	69.6	73.4	–
Ireland	100.0	100.0	–	–
Italy	68.1	100.0	100.0	–
Japan	69.5	71.3	67.2	–
Netherlands	100.0	100.0	100.0	–
New Zealand	100.0	100.0	–	–
Norway	100.0	100.0	100.0	–
Sweden	100.0	100.0	100.0	–
Switzerland	100.0	100.0	100.0	–
United Kingdom	100.0	100.0	100.0	–
United States	87.4	86.3	100.0	–
TOTAL	*76.9*	*81.6*	*81.4*	–
MULTILATERAL	*84.2*	*81.5*	*82.5*	–
ARAB COUNTRIES	*58.6*	*100.0*	*100.0*	–
E.E.C.+ MEMBERS	*71.8*	*84.2*	*84.9*	–
TOTAL	*79.7*	*81.6*	*81.8*	–

15. OTHER AGGREGATES

OFFICIAL COMMITMENTS:	1987	1988	1989	1990
TOTAL BILATERAL	1317.0	1226.8	1433.3	1228.9
of which:				
Arab Countries	10.9	2.6	1.0	33.9
C.E.E.C.	110.0	–	159.4	–
TOTAL MULTILATERAL	1673.8	1542.1	2071.6	1619.0
TOTAL BIL.& MULTIL.	2990.7	2768.9	3504.9	2847.9
of which:				
ODA Grants	731.8	793.7	817.8	774.5
ODA Loans	1478.0	1122.9	1335.9	934.4

DISBURSEMENTS:

DAC COUNTRIES COMBINED

OFFICIAL & PRIVATE	1987	1988	1989	1990
GROSS:				
Contractual Lending	264.6	928.8	726.3	706.1
Export Credits, Total	-1.0	302.0	305.7	248.9
Export Credits, Priv.	0.8	290.4	290.2	239.2
NET:				
Contractual Lending	19.4	641.5	240.9	257.4
Export Credits Total	-78.4	186.7	64.6	40.0
PRIVATE SECTOR NET	-95.9	150.6	665.0	63.7
Direct Investment	20.9	25.5	21.8	93.7
Portfolio Investment	-63.2	-64.3	577.7	-69.2
Export Credits	-53.6	189.3	65.5	39.2

MARKET BORROWING:

CHANGE IN CLAIMS	1987	1988	1989	1990
Banks	-29.0	492.0	97.0	402.0

MEMORANDUM ITEM:

	1987	1988	1989	1990
C.E.E.C. (Gross)	14.6	12.6	34.2	–

DISBURSEMENTS, UNLESS OTHERWISE STATE

	1987	1988	1989	1990		1987	1988	1989	1990		1987

1. TOTAL RECEIPTS NET

DAC COUNTRIES

	1987	1988	1989	1990	4. TOTAL ODA NET	1987	1988	1989	1990	7. TOTAL ODA GROSS	1987
Australia	–	0.0	–	–	Australia	–	0.0	–	–	Australia	–
Austria	–	–	–	–	Austria	–	–	–	–	Austria	–
Belgium	35.0	157.7	6.5	-56.9	Belgium	0.1	0.0	0.1	0.1	Belgium	0.1
Canada	-0.2	0.4	0.7	0.4	Canada	0.5	0.4	0.7	0.4	Canada	0.5
Denmark	2.2	–	–	–	Denmark	–	–	–	–	Denmark	–
Finland	1.8	11.0	-1.9	–	Finland	0.0	–	–	–	Finland	0.0
France	54.8	-88.1	677.6	-111.1	France	4.4	0.8	0.6	0.5	France	4.4
Germany	-28.3	-8.6	46.0	-48.4	Germany	1.3	1.5	1.3	1.9	Germany	1.6
Ireland	–	–	–	–	Ireland	–	–	–	–	Ireland	–
Italy	1.5	-39.6	3.5	-1.1	Italy	0.2	–	–	0.8	Italy	0.2
Japan	1621.7	833.5	875.7	814.8	Japan	5.6	4.5	2.9	2.3	Japan	5.6
Netherlands	126.7	-46.4	0.5	-14.8	Netherlands	0.5	0.5	0.5	-14.8	Netherlands	0.5
New Zealand	–	–	–	–	New Zealand	–	–	–	–	New Zealand	–
Norway	0.0	–	–	–	Norway	0.0	–	–	–	Norway	0.0
Sweden	49.3	0.1	-3.2	-4.1	Sweden	0.1	0.1	–	–	Sweden	0.1
Switzerland	–	0.0	–	0.5	Switzerland	–	0.0	–	0.5	Switzerland	–
United Kingdom	-68.1	317.1	-18.1	-12.9	United Kingdom	0.1	0.2	1.2	1.3	United Kingdom	0.1
United States	486.0	12.0	1016.0	566.0	United States	14.0	11.0	7.0	97.0	United States	16.0
TOTAL	2282.4	1149.1	2603.3	1132.4	TOTAL	26.7	19.2	14.2	90.1	TOTAL	29.0

MULTILATERAL

	1987	1988	1989	1990		1987	1988	1989	1990		1987
AF.D.F.	–	–	–	–		–	–	–	–	AF.D.F.	–
AF.D.B.	–	–	–	–		–	–	–	–	AF.D.B.	–
AS.D.B	–	–	–	–		–	–	–	–	AS.D.B	–
CAR.D.B.	–	–	–	–		–	–	–	–	CAR.D.B.	–
E.E.C.	0.1	0.4	0.1	0.1		0.1	0.4	0.1	0.1	E.E.C.	0.1
IBRD	-18.8	1.0	–	-41.0		–	–	–	–	IBRD	–
IDA	–	–	–	–		–	–	–	–	IDA	–
I.D.B.	-4.4	0.9	0.4	-0.2		2.2	-0.2	0.1	-0.4	I.D.B.	9.1
IFAD	7.2	–	-0.1	-0.4		7.2	–	-0.1	-0.4	IFAD	8.1
I.F.C.	4.9	–	–	–		–	–	–	–	I.F.C.	–
IMF TRUST FUND	–	–	–	–		–	–	–	–	IMF TRUST FUND	–
U.N. AGENCIES	–	–	–	–		–	–	–	–	U.N. AGENCIES	–
UNDP	2.4	1.6	1.2	1.1		2.4	1.6	1.2	1.1	UNDP	2.4
UNTA	1.1	0.6	0.7	0.6		1.1	0.6	0.7	0.6	UNTA	1.1
UNICEF	0.1	–	0.0	–		0.1	–	0.0	–	UNICEF	0.1
UNRWA	–	–	–	–		–	–	–	–	UNRWA	–
WFP	0.3	0.1	0.7	0.6		0.3	0.1	0.7	0.6	WFP	0.3
UNHCR	–	–	–	0.2		–	–	–	0.2	UNHCR	–
Other Multilateral	0.4	0.3	0.7	0.6		0.4	0.3	0.7	0.6	Other Multilateral	0.4
Arab Agencies	–	–	–	–		–	–	–	–	Arab Agencies	–
TOTAL	-6.7	4.8	3.7	-38.5		13.8	2.8	3.4	2.4	TOTAL	21.6
ARAB COUNTRIES	–	–	–	–		–	–	–	–	ARAB COUNTRIES	–
E.E.C.+ MEMBERS	123.8	292.4	716.1	-245.1		6.6	3.5	3.8	-10.1	E.E.C.+ MEMBERS	6.9
TOTAL	2275.7	1153.9	2606.9	1093.9		40.5	21.9	17.5	92.4	TOTAL	50.7

2. ODA LOANS GROSS

DAC COUNTRIES

	1987	1988	1989	1990	5. ODA LOANS NET	1987	1988	1989	1990	8. GRANTS	1987
Australia	–	–	–	–	Australia	–	–	–	–	Australia	–
Austria	–	–	–	–	Austria	–	–	–	–	Austria	–
Belgium	–	–	–	–	Belgium	–	–	–	–	Belgium	0.1
Canada	–	–	–	–	Canada	–	–	–	–	Canada	0.5
Denmark	–	–	–	–	Denmark	–	–	–	–	Denmark	–
Finland	–	–	–	–	Finland	–	–	–	–	Finland	0.0
France	3.8	0.2	0.2	–	France	3.8	0.2	0.2	–	France	0.6
Germany	–	–	–	–	Germany	-0.3	-0.3	-0.3	-0.4	Germany	1.6
Ireland	–	–	–	–	Ireland	–	–	–	–	Ireland	–
Italy	–	–	–	–	Italy	–	–	–	–	Italy	0.2
Japan	–	–	–	–	Japan	–	–	–	–	Japan	5.6
Netherlands	–	–	–	–	Netherlands	–	–	–	-15.4	Netherlands	0.5
New Zealand	–	–	–	–	New Zealand	–	–	–	–	New Zealand	–
Norway	–	–	–	–	Norway	–	–	–	–	Norway	0.0
Sweden	–	–	–	–	Sweden	–	–	–	–	Sweden	0.1
Switzerland	–	–	–	–	Switzerland	–	–	–	–	Switzerland	–
United Kingdom	–	–	–	–	United Kingdom	–	–	–	–	United Kingdom	0.1
United States	3.0	1.0	–	–	United States	1.0	1.0	–	–	United States	13.0
TOTAL	6.8	1.2	0.2	–	TOTAL	4.5	0.9	-0.2	-15.8	TOTAL	22.3
MULTILATERAL	16.0	0.5	0.4	1.5	MULTILATERAL	8.1	-0.2	0.0	-0.8	MULTILATERAL	5.7
ARAB COUNTRIES	–	–	–	–	ARAB COUNTRIES	–	–	–	–	ARAB COUNTRIES	–
E.E.C.+ MEMBERS	3.8	0.2	0.2	–	E.E.C.+ MEMBERS	3.5	-0.1	-0.2	-15.8	E.E.C.+ MEMBERS	3.2
TOTAL	22.8	1.7	0.5	1.5	TOTAL	12.6	0.7	-0.2	-16.6	TOTAL	27.9

3. TOTAL OFFICIAL GROSS

DAC COUNTRIES

	1987	1988	1989	1990	6. TOTAL OFFICIAL NET	1987	1988	1989	1990	9. TOTAL OOF GROSS	1987
Australia	–	0.0	–	–	Australia	–	0.0	–	–	Australia	–
Austria	–	–	–	–	Austria	–	–	–	–	Austria	–
Belgium	0.1	0.0	0.1	0.1	Belgium	0.1	0.0	0.1	0.1	Belgium	0.1
Canada	0.5	0.4	0.7	0.4	Canada	-0.2	0.4	0.7	0.4	Canada	–
Denmark	–	–	–	–	Denmark	–	–	–	–	Denmark	–
Finland	0.0	–	–	–	Finland	0.0	–	–	–	Finland	–
France	4.4	0.8	0.6	0.5	France	4.4	0.8	0.6	0.5	France	–
Germany	1.6	1.8	2.3	2.3	Germany	1.3	1.5	2.0	1.8	Germany	–
Ireland	–	–	–	–	Ireland	–	–	–	–	Ireland	–
Italy	0.2	–	–	0.8	Italy	0.2	–	–	0.8	Italy	–
Japan	5.6	4.5	2.9	2.3	Japan	5.6	4.5	2.9	2.3	Japan	–
Netherlands	0.5	0.5	0.5	0.6	Netherlands	0.5	0.5	0.5	-14.8	Netherlands	–
New Zealand	–	–	–	–	New Zealand	–	–	–	–	New Zealand	–
Norway	0.0	–	–	–	Norway	0.0	–	–	–	Norway	–
Sweden	0.1	0.1	–	–	Sweden	0.1	0.1	–	–	Sweden	–
Switzerland	–	0.0	–	0.5	Switzerland	–	0.0	–	0.5	Switzerland	–
United Kingdom	0.1	1.8	1.2	1.3	United Kingdom	0.1	1.8	1.2	1.3	United Kingdom	–
United States	463.0	468.0	474.0	568.0	United States	13.0	13.0	32.0	62.0	United States	447.0
TOTAL	476.1	478.0	482.2	576.9	TOTAL	25.1	22.7	39.9	55.1	TOTAL	447.1
MULTILATERAL	55.7	8.5	4.0	14.3	MULTILATERAL	-6.7	4.8	3.7	-38.5	MULTILATERAL	34.0
ARAB COUNTRIES	–	–	–	–	ARAB COUNTRIES	–	–	–	–	ARAB COUNTRIES	–
E.E.C.+ MEMBERS	7.0	5.3	4.8	5.8	E.E.C.+ MEMBERS	6.7	5.0	4.5	-10.1	E.E.C.+ MEMBERS	0.1
TOTAL	531.8	486.6	486.3	591.3	TOTAL	18.4	27.5	43.6	16.6	TOTAL	481.1

10. ODA COMMITMENTS

1988	1989	1990		1987	1988	1989	1990
0.0	–	–		0.0	0.0	–	–
–	–	–		–	–	–	–
0.0	0.1	0.1		0.0	0.0	0.1	0.1
0.4	0.7	0.4		0.4	0.4	0.7	0.1
–	–	–		–	–	–	–
0.8	0.6	0.5		5.6	0.7	0.5	0.5
1.8	1.6	2.3		0.7	1.4	1.8	2.8
–	–	–		–	–	–	–
–	–	0.8		0.2	–	–	0.8
4.5	2.9	2.3		6.2	4.9	3.1	2.4
0.5	0.5	0.6		0.5	0.5	0.5	0.6
–	–	–		–	–	–	–
–	–	–		0.0	–	–	–
0.1	–	–		0.1	–	–	–
0.0	–	0.5		–	–	–	0.5
0.2	1.2	1.3		10.8	–	0.2	0.2
11.0	7.0	97.0		10.2	–	–	398.8
19.5	*14.5*	*105.9*		*34.6*	*7.9*	*6.7*	*406.9*
–	–	–		–	–	–	–
–	–	–		–	–	–	–
–	–	–		–	–	–	–
0.4	0.1	0.1		0.1	0.7	–	–
–	–	–		–	–	–	–
0.5	0.1	–		–	–	–	–
–	0.3	1.5		–	–	–	–
–	–	–		–	–	–	–
–	–	–		4.4	2.6	3.3	3.0
1.6	1.2	1.1		–	–	–	–
0.6	0.7	0.6		–	–	–	–
–	0.0	–		–	–	–	–
0.1	0.7	0.6		–	–	–	–
–	–	0.2		–	–	–	–
0.3	0.7	0.6		–	–	–	–
–	–	–		–	–	–	–
3.4	*3.7*	*4.6*		*4.5*	*3.3*	*3.3*	*3.0*
–	–	–		–	–	–	–
3.8	*4.1*	*5.7*		*17.9*	*3.3*	*2.9*	*5.1*
22.9	*18.2*	*110.5*		*39.1*	*11.2*	*10.0*	*409.9*

11. TECH. COOP. GRANTS

1988	1989	1990		1987	1988	1989	1990
0.0	–	–		–	–	–	–
–	–	–		0.0	–	–	–
0.0	0.1	0.1		–	–	0.0	–
0.4	0.7	0.4		–	–	–	–
–	–	–		0.0	–	–	–
0.7	0.5	0.5		0.6	0.7	0.5	0.5
1.8	1.6	2.3		1.6	1.7	1.3	1.7
–	–	–		–	–	–	–
–	–	0.8		0.2	–	–	–
4.5	2.9	2.3		5.4	4.5	2.9	2.3
0.5	0.5	0.6		0.5	0.5	0.5	0.6
–	–	–		–	–	–	–
–	–	–		0.0	–	–	–
0.1	–	–		0.1	0.1	–	–
0.0	–	0.5		–	0.0	–	–
0.2	1.2	1.3		0.1	0.2	0.2	0.2
10.0	7.0	97.0		8.0	5.0	7.0	-24.0
18.3	*14.3*	*105.9*		*16.5*	*12.8*	*12.3*	*-18.6*
2.9	*3.4*	*3.1*		*4.2*	*2.7*	*2.7*	*2.5*
–	–	–		–	–	–	–
3.6	*3.9*	*5.7*		*3.1*	*3.4*	*2.4*	*3.1*
21.3	*17.7*	*109.0*		*20.7*	*15.5*	*14.9*	*-16.2*

12. TOTAL OOF NET

1988	1989	1990		1987	1988	1989	1990
–	–	–		–	–	–	–
–	0.0	0.0		0.1	–	0.0	0.0
–	–	–		-0.7	–	–	–
–	–	–		–	–	–	–
–	–	–		–	–	–	–
0.0	0.7	0.0		–	0.0	0.7	0.0
–	–	–		–	–	–	–
–	–	–		–	–	–	–
–	–	–		–	–	–	–
–	–	–		–	–	–	–
–	–	–		–	–	–	–
1.5	–	–		–	1.5	–	–
457.0	467.0	471.0		-1.0	2.0	25.0	-35.0
458.5	*467.8*	*471.1*		*-1.6*	*3.5*	*25.7*	*-35.0*
5.1	*0.3*	*9.7*		*-20.4*	*2.1*	*0.3*	*-40.8*
–	–	–		–	–	–	–
1.5	0.8	0.1		0.1	1.5	0.7	0.0
463.6	*468.1*	*480.8*		*-22.1*	*5.6*	*26.0*	*-75.8*

13. ODF COMMITMENTS: BY PURPOSE %

	1987	1988	1989	1990
Education	6	8	–	–
Health	4	–	–	–
Other Social Infrastr.	22	0	–	–
Water Sanitat. Sewage	0	–	–	–
Energy	28	–	–	–
Telecommunications	–	–	–	–
Transportation	20	–	–	–
Agriculture	1	1	5	–
Extractive Industries	–	–	–	–
Manufacturing	–	–	–	–
Trade Banking Tourism	–	–	–	–
Technical Cooperation	18	90	95	–
Multisector Aid	–	–	–	–
Programme	–	–	–	–
Debt Reorganisation	–	–	–	–
Food Aid	–	–	–	–
Emergency Aid	–	1	–	–
Unspecified	–	–	–	–
TOTAL	100	100	100	–

14. GRANT ELEMENT OF ODA %

DAC COUNTRIES

	1987	1988	1989	1990
Australia	100.0	100.0	–	–
Austria	–	–	–	–
Belgium	100.0	100.0	100.0	–
Canada	100.0	100.0	100.0	–
Denmark	–	–	–	–
Finland	–	–	–	–
France	71.6	100.0	100.0	–
Germany	100.0	100.0	100.0	–
Ireland	–	–	–	–
Italy	100.0	–	–	–
Japan	100.0	100.0	100.0	–
Netherlands	100.0	100.0	100.0	–
New Zealand	–	–	–	–
Norway	100.0	–	–	–
Sweden	100.0	–	–	–
Switzerland	–	–	–	–
United Kingdom	100.0	–	100.0	–
United States	100.0	–	–	–
TOTAL	*95.4*	*100.0*	*100.0*	–
MULTILATERAL	*93.5*	*100.0*	*100.0*	–
ARAB COUNTRIES	–	–	–	–
E.E.C.+ MEMBERS	*91.1*	*100.0*	*100.0*	–
TOTAL	*95.2*	*100.0*	*100.0*	–

15. OTHER AGGREGATES

	1987	1988	1989	1990
OFFICIAL COMMITMENTS:				
TOTAL BILATERAL	67.0	44.6	42.2	437.1
of which:				
Arab Countries	–	–	–	–
C.E.E.C.	–	–	–	–
TOTAL MULTILATERAL	26.2	3.3	3.3	3.0
TOTAL BIL.& MULTIL.	93.2	47.9	45.6	440.2
of which:				
ODA Grants	34.1	11.2	10.0	409.9
ODA Loans	5.0	–	–	–
DISBURSEMENTS:				
DAC COUNTRIES COMBINED				
OFFICIAL & PRIVATE				
GROSS:				
Contractual Lending	456.2	458.3	617.5	453.3
Export Credits, Total	2.4	0.2	150.3	-17.7
Export Credits, Priv.	2.4	0.2	149.6	-17.7
NET:				
Contractual Lending	-145.1	-113.9	131.0	-98.9
Export Credits Total	-151.6	-117.7	106.2	-48.0
PRIVATE SECTOR NET	2257.3	1126.4	2563.4	1077.3
Direct Investment	1937.9	1025.4	2025.2	812.7
Portfolio Investment	467.2	217.8	432.7	312.6
Export Credits	-147.8	-116.7	105.5	-48.0
MARKET BORROWING:				
CHANGE IN CLAIMS				
Banks	–	–	–	–
MEMORANDUM ITEM:				
C.E.E.C. (Gross)	–	–	–	–

1. TOTAL RECEIPTS NET

DAC COUNTRIES	1987	1988	1989	1990
Australia	212.9	232.6	375.6	319.9
Austria	0.6	0.5	0.5	0.6
Belgium	2.2	1.0	0.4	13.1
Canada	-6.1	-2.1	-1.9	-1.6
Denmark	0.0	–	–	–
Finland	0.1	-0.6	-0.7	0.1
France	7.4	5.2	7.9	23.0
Germany	16.6	-4.2	41.6	1.1
Ireland	0.0	0.0	–	0.0
Italy	0.0	–	7.8	–
Japan	18.1	32.8	70.8	43.2
Netherlands	0.4	0.5	1.0	7.1
New Zealand	2.1	2.6	3.4	2.6
Norway	0.0	–	–	–
Sweden	–	–	–	0.0
Switzerland	0.1	0.2	0.3	0.2
United Kingdom	-51.9	65.6	181.6	22.8
United States	1.0	1.0	1.0	1.0
TOTAL	203.7	335.1	689.4	432.9
MULTILATERAL				
AF.D.F.	–	–	–	–
AF.D.B.	–	–	–	–
AS.D.B	14.1	23.5	23.9	65.2
CAR.D.B.	–	–	–	–
E.E.C.	60.0	57.1	4.7	4.7
IBRD	23.4	24.0	14.0	50.0
IDA	-0.4	-1.0	-1.0	-1.0
I.D.B.	–	–	–	–
IFAD	0.9	-0.1	0.9	0.8
I.F.C.	–	–	–	–
IMF TRUST FUND	–	–	–	–
U.N. AGENCIES	–	–	–	–
UNDP	2.0	3.8	5.0	4.9
UNTA	1.4	1.0	1.5	1.4
UNICEF	0.2	0.3	0.6	1.0
UNRWA	–	–	–	–
WFP	–	–	–	–
UNHCR	–	2.2	1.9	1.3
Other Multilateral	0.3	0.7	1.0	1.0
Arab Agencies	0.2	-0.2	-0.2	–
TOTAL	102.1	111.3	52.3	129.2
ARAB COUNTRIES	-0.2	-0.2	-0.2	–
E.E.C.+ MEMBERS	34.8	125.1	245.0	71.7
TOTAL	305.6	446.2	741.5	562.1

4. TOTAL ODA NET

	1987	1988	1989	1990
Australia	217.2	240.9	254.0	262.2
Austria	0.6	0.5	0.5	0.6
Belgium	0.1	0.1	0.1	0.2
Canada	0.2	0.1	0.3	0.1
Denmark	–	–	–	–
Finland	0.1	0.2	0.0	0.1
France	0.2	0.5	0.5	0.8
Germany	8.6	6.7	6.4	8.0
Ireland	0.0	0.0	–	0.0
Italy	0.0	–	–	–
Japan	17.7	41.2	39.6	38.1
Netherlands	0.1	0.5	0.4	0.5
New Zealand	2.1	2.6	3.4	2.6
Norway	0.0	–	–	0.0
Sweden	–	–	–	0.0
Switzerland	0.1	0.2	0.3	0.2
United Kingdom	6.6	13.1	7.6	5.7
United States	1.0	1.0	1.0	1.0
TOTAL	254.8	307.4	314.3	320.0
AF.D.F.	–	–	–	–
AF.D.B.	–	–	–	–
AS.D.B	5.3	9.9	10.7	42.2
CAR.D.B.	–	–	–	–
E.E.C.	58.4	55.6	4.8	4.8
IBRD	–	–	–	–
IDA	-0.4	-1.0	-1.0	-1.0
I.D.B.	–	–	–	–
IFAD	0.9	-0.1	0.9	0.8
I.F.C.	–	–	–	–
IMF TRUST FUND	–	–	–	–
U.N. AGENCIES	–	–	–	–
UNDP	2.0	3.8	5.0	4.9
UNTA	1.4	1.0	1.5	1.4
UNICEF	0.2	0.3	0.6	1.0
UNRWA	–	–	–	–
WFP	–	–	–	–
UNHCR	–	2.2	1.9	1.3
Other Multilateral	0.3	0.7	1.0	1.0
Arab Agencies	0.1	0.0	0.0	–
TOTAL	68.2	72.4	25.3	56.4
ARAB COUNTRIES	-0.2	-0.2	-0.2	–
E.E.C.+ MEMBERS	74.2	76.4	19.8	19.9
TOTAL	322.7	379.6	339.3	376.3

7. TOTAL ODA GROSS

	1987
Australia	217.4
Austria	0.6
Belgium	0.1
Canada	0.2
Denmark	–
Finland	0.1
France	0.2
Germany	8.6
Ireland	0.0
Italy	0.0
Japan	18.3
Netherlands	0.1
New Zealand	2.1
Norway	0.0
Sweden	–
Switzerland	0.1
United Kingdom	7.6
United States	1.0
TOTAL	256.5
AF.D.F.	–
AF.D.B.	–
AS.D.B	6.4
CAR.D.B.	–
E.E.C.	58.5
IBRD	–
IDA	0.1
I.D.B.	–
IFAD	0.9
I.F.C.	–
IMF TRUST FUND	–
U.N. AGENCIES	–
UNDP	2.0
UNTA	1.4
UNICEF	0.2
UNRWA	–
WFP	–
UNHCR	–
Other Multilateral	0.3
Arab Agencies	0.4
TOTAL	70.3
ARAB COUNTRIES	–
E.E.C.+ MEMBERS	75.2
TOTAL	326.8

2. ODA LOANS GROSS

DAC COUNTRIES	1987	1988	1989	1990
Australia	–	–	–	–
Austria	–	–	–	–
Belgium	–	–	–	–
Canada	–	–	–	–
Denmark	–	–	–	–
Finland	–	–	–	–
France	–	–	–	–
Germany	2.0	0.3	0.5	0.2
Ireland	–	–	–	–
Italy	–	–	–	–
Japan	12.9	12.3	13.4	21.3
Netherlands	–	–	–	–
New Zealand	–	–	–	–
Norway	–	–	–	–
Sweden	–	–	–	–
Switzerland	–	–	–	–
United Kingdom	7.4	13.9	7.9	5.5
United States	–	–	–	–
TOTAL	22.3	26.5	21.8	27.0
MULTILATERAL	7.4	11.1	10.7	42.6
ARAB COUNTRIES	–	–	–	–
E.E.C.+ MEMBERS	9.4	14.2	8.4	5.7
TOTAL	29.8	37.7	32.5	69.6

5. ODA LOANS NET

	1987	1988	1989	1990
Australia	-0.2	–	–	–
Austria	–	–	–	–
Belgium	–	–	–	–
Canada	–	–	–	–
Denmark	–	–	–	–
Finland	–	–	–	–
France	–	–	–	–
Germany	2.0	0.3	0.5	-0.1
Ireland	–	–	–	–
Italy	–	–	–	–
Japan	12.3	10.7	11.9	18.5
Netherlands	–	–	–	–
New Zealand	–	–	–	–
Norway	–	–	–	–
Sweden	–	–	–	–
Switzerland	–	–	–	–
United Kingdom	6.5	12.9	7.4	5.5
United States	–	–	–	–
TOTAL	20.6	23.9	19.7	23.9
MULTILATERAL	5.3	7.9	7.5	38.9
ARAB COUNTRIES	-0.2	-0.2	-0.2	–
E.E.C.+ MEMBERS	8.3	13.1	7.7	5.3
TOTAL	25.6	31.5	27.0	62.8

8. GRANTS

	1987
Australia	217.4
Austria	0.6
Belgium	0.1
Canada	0.2
Denmark	–
Finland	0.1
France	0.2
Germany	6.6
Ireland	0.0
Italy	0.0
Japan	5.4
Netherlands	0.1
New Zealand	2.1
Norway	0.0
Sweden	–
Switzerland	0.1
United Kingdom	0.1
United States	1.0
TOTAL	234.2
MULTILATERAL	62.9
ARAB COUNTRIES	–
E.E.C.+ MEMBERS	65.8
TOTAL	297.1

3. TOTAL OFFICIAL GROSS

DAC COUNTRIES	1987	1988	1989	1990
Australia	217.4	242.3	261.6	265.6
Austria	0.6	0.5	0.5	0.6
Belgium	0.1	0.1	0.1	0.2
Canada	0.2	0.1	0.3	0.1
Denmark	0.0	–	–	–
Finland	0.1	0.2	0.0	0.1
France	0.2	0.5	0.5	0.8
Germany	8.6	6.7	8.0	11.8
Ireland	0.0	0.0	–	0.0
Italy	0.0	–	–	–
Japan	18.3	42.8	72.8	42.4
Netherlands	0.1	0.5	0.4	0.5
New Zealand	2.1	2.6	3.4	2.6
Norway	0.0	–	–	–
Sweden	–	–	–	0.0
Switzerland	0.1	0.2	0.3	0.2
United Kingdom	10.9	26.1	18.8	16.0
United States	1.0	1.0	1.0	1.0
TOTAL	259.9	323.5	367.8	341.8
MULTILATERAL	115.7	129.6	87.9	153.2
ARAB COUNTRIES	–	–	–	–
E.E.C.+ MEMBERS	81.3	92.2	36.2	37.5
TOTAL	375.5	453.1	455.7	495.0

6. TOTAL OFFICIAL NET

	1987	1988	1989	1990
Australia	208.8	232.6	256.0	253.7
Austria	0.6	0.5	0.5	0.6
Belgium	0.1	0.1	0.1	0.2
Canada	-6.1	-2.1	-1.9	-1.6
Denmark	0.0	–	–	–
Finland	0.1	0.2	0.0	0.1
France	0.2	0.5	0.5	0.8
Germany	8.6	6.7	-8.6	-6.8
Ireland	0.0	0.0	–	0.0
Italy	0.0	–	–	–
Japan	17.7	41.2	71.2	39.7
Netherlands	0.1	0.5	0.4	0.5
New Zealand	2.1	2.6	3.4	2.6
Norway	0.0	–	–	–
Sweden	–	–	–	0.0
Switzerland	0.1	0.2	0.3	0.2
United Kingdom	8.7	24.0	16.7	13.8
United States	1.0	1.0	1.0	1.0
TOTAL	242.2	307.9	339.6	304.7
MULTILATERAL	102.1	111.3	52.3	129.2
ARAB COUNTRIES	-0.2	-0.2	-0.2	–
E.E.C.+ MEMBERS	77.9	88.8	13.7	13.2
TOTAL	344.1	419.0	391.6	433.9

9. TOTAL OOF GROSS

	1987
Australia	–
Austria	–
Belgium	–
Canada	–
Denmark	0.0
Finland	–
France	–
Germany	–
Ireland	–
Italy	–
Japan	–
Netherlands	–
New Zealand	–
Norway	–
Sweden	–
Switzerland	–
United Kingdom	3.3
United States	–
TOTAL	3.4
MULTILATERAL	45.4
ARAB COUNTRIES	–
E.E.C.+ MEMBERS	6.1
TOTAL	48.7

1988	1989	1990		1987	1988	1989	1990

10. ODA COMMITMENTS

1988	1989	1990		1987	1988	1989	1990
240.9	254.0	262.2		236.5	485.2	19.0	42.0
0.5	0.5	0.6		0.6	0.5	0.8	0.5
0.1	0.1	0.2		0.1	0.3	0.1	0.2
0.1	0.3	0.1		0.4	0.2	0.2	0.2
–	–	–		–	–	–	–
0.2	0.0	0.1		–	–	0.0	0.1
0.5	0.5	0.8		0.2	0.5	0.5	0.8
6.7	6.4	8.3		7.1	7.9	10.0	15.5
0.0	–	0.0		0.0	0.0	–	0.0
–	–	–		0.0	–	–	–
42.8	41.1	40.9		81.8	128.3	24.0	21.8
0.5	0.4	0.5		0.1	0.5	0.4	0.5
2.6	3.4	2.6		2.4	1.2	–	2.7
–	–	–		0.0	–	–	–
–	–	0.0		–	–	–	–
0.2	0.3	0.2		–	–	0.2	–
14.1	8.1	5.7		7.6	14.1	8.1	5.7
1.0	1.0	1.0		0.8	1.1	1.2	1.1
310.1	*316.3*	*323.1*		*337.7*	*639.8*	*64.6*	*91.0*
–	–	–		–	–	–	–
–	–	–		–	–	–	–
11.0	11.9	43.9		14.9	–	62.8	19.5
–	–	–		–	–	–	–
55.7	4.9	4.9		67.2	75.0	7.3	7.3
–	–	–		–	–	–	–
–	–	–		–	–	–	–
0.7	1.5	1.5		–	–	0.2	–
–	–	–		–	–	–	–
–	–	–		4.0	8.1	10.0	9.6
3.8	5.0	4.9		–	–	–	–
1.0	1.5	1.4		–	–	–	–
0.3	0.6	1.0		–	–	–	–
–	–	–		–	–	–	–
2.2	1.9	1.3		–	–	–	–
0.7	1.0	1.0		–	–	–	–
0.2	0.2	0.0		–	–	–	–
75.6	*28.5*	*59.9*		*86.1*	*83.1*	*80.2*	*36.3*
–	*–*	*–*		*7.2*	*–*	*–*	*–*
77.6	*20.5*	*20.3*		*82.4*	*98.2*	*26.4*	*29.8*
385.8	*344.8*	*382.9*		*430.9*	*722.8*	*144.8*	*127.3*

11. TECH. COOP. GRANTS

1988	1989	1990		1987	1988	1989	1990
240.9	254.0	262.2		6.4	9.7	17.3	18.0
0.5	0.5	0.6		0.6	0.5	0.5	0.5
0.1	0.1	0.2		0.0	0.0	–	0.0
0.1	0.3	0.1		–	–	0.0	0.0
–	–	–		–	–	–	–
0.2	0.0	0.1		0.1	–	–	0.1
0.5	0.5	0.8		0.2	0.5	0.5	0.8
6.3	6.0	8.1		6.4	6.3	5.7	6.8
0.0	–	0.0		0.0	0.0	–	0.0
–	–	–		0.0	–	–	–
30.5	27.7	19.6		5.0	8.3	8.4	7.4
0.5	0.4	0.5		0.1	0.4	0.4	0.5
2.6	3.4	2.6		1.1	0.9	–	1.6
–	–	–		0.0	–	–	–
–	–	0.0		–	–	–	0.0
0.2	0.3	0.2		0.1	0.2	–	–
0.2	0.2	0.2		0.1	0.2	0.2	0.2
1.0	1.0	1.0		1.0	1.0	1.0	1.0
283.6	*294.5*	*296.1*		*21.3*	*28.1*	*34.0*	*36.8*
64.5	*17.8*	*17.3*		*4.8*	*12.9*	*10.0*	*9.5*
–	*–*	*–*		*–*	*–*	*–*	*–*
63.4	*12.1*	*14.6*		*7.8*	*12.3*	*6.8*	*8.2*
348.1	*312.4*	*313.3*		*26.1*	*41.1*	*44.0*	*46.3*

12. TOTAL OOF NET

1988	1989	1990		1987	1988	1989	1990
1.4	7.6	3.4		-8.4	-8.2	2.0	-8.6
–	–	–		–	–	–	–
–	–	–		-6.2	-2.2	-2.2	-1.7
–	–	–		0.0	–	–	–
–	–	–		–	–	–	–
–	1.6	3.5		–	–	-15.1	-14.8
–	–	–		–	–	–	–
–	31.6	1.6		–	–	31.6	1.6
–	–	–		–	–	–	–
–	–	–		–	–	–	–
–	–	–		–	–	–	–
12.0	10.7	10.3		2.1	10.9	9.0	8.2
–	*–*	*–*		*–*	*–*	*–*	*–*
13.4	*51.5*	*18.8*		*-12.5*	*0.5*	*25.3*	*-15.3*
54.0	*59.4*	*93.3*		*33.9*	*38.9*	*27.0*	*72.8*
–	*–*	*–*		*–*	*–*	*–*	*–*
14.7	*15.7*	*17.2*		*3.8*	*12.4*	*-6.1*	*-6.7*
67.4	*110.9*	*112.1*		*21.4*	*39.4*	*52.3*	*57.5*

13. ODF COMMITMENTS: BY PURPOSE %

	1987	1988	1989	1990
Education	0	0	3	–
Health	1	1	8	–
Other Social Infrastr.	1	0	0	–
Water Sanitat. Sewage	–	–	3	–
Energy	24	–	5	–
Telecommunications	1	0	0	–
Transportation	11	7	–	–
Agriculture	7	7	59	–
Extractive Industries	–	7	–	–
Manufacturing	–	1	–	–
Trade Banking Tourism	–	0	–	–
Technical Cooperation	12	5	20	–
Multisector Aid	–	0	0	–
Programme	42	71	–	–
Debt Reorganisation	–	–	–	–
Food Aid	0	–	–	–
Emergency Aid	0	0	–	–
Unspecified	–	–	–	–
TOTAL	100	100	100	–

14. GRANT ELEMENT OF ODA %

DAC COUNTRIES

	1987	1988	1989	1990
Australia	100.0	100.0	100.0	–
Austria	100.0	100.0	100.0	–
Belgium	100.0	100.0	100.0	–
Canada	100.0	100.0	100.0	–
Denmark	–	–	–	–
Finland	–	–	100.0	–
France	100.0	100.0	100.0	–
Germany	100.0	100.0	100.0	–
Ireland	100.0	100.0	–	–
Italy	100.0	–	–	–
Japan	58.2	72.5	98.6	–
Netherlands	100.0	100.0	100.0	–
New Zealand	100.0	100.0	–	–
Norway	100.0	–	–	–
Sweden	–	–	–	–
Switzerland	–	–	100.0	–
United Kingdom	100.0	100.0	100.0	–
United States	100.0	100.0	100.0	–
TOTAL	*89.7*	*94.4*	*99.4*	*–*
MULTILATERAL	*92.6*	*98.5*	*82.1*	*–*
ARAB COUNTRIES	*39.0*	*–*	*–*	*–*
E.E.C.+ MEMBERS	*100.0*	*100.0*	*100.0*	*–*
TOTAL	*89.5*	*94.9*	*89.6*	*–*

15. OTHER AGGREGATES

	1987	1988	1989	1990
OFFICIAL COMMITMENTS:				
TOTAL BILATERAL	345.0	692.8	80.2	152.2
of which:				
Arab Countries	7.2	–	–	–
C.E.E.C.	–	–	–	–
TOTAL MULTILATERAL	91.1	97.2	132.6	103.3
TOTAL BIL.& MULTIL.	436.0	790.1	212.8	255.5
of which:				
ODA Grants	334.6	617.3	73.4	96.1
ODA Loans	96.3	105.6	71.3	31.2
DISBURSEMENTS:				
DAC COUNTRIES COMBINED				
OFFICIAL & PRIVATE				
GROSS:				
Contractual Lending	-30.0	43.9	290.6	71.0
Export Credits, Total	-55.7	5.4	225.0	29.1
Export Credits, Priv.	-55.7	4.0	217.3	25.7
NET:				
Contractual Lending	-55.4	24.4	255.9	28.6
Export Credits Total	-78.1	-10.4	210.5	10.2
PRIVATE SECTOR NET	-38.5	27.2	349.9	128.3
Direct Investment	13.1	40.6	104.2	155.4
Portfolio Investment	11.8	-13.3	34.9	-47.6
Export Credits	-63.4	0.0	210.8	20.4
MARKET BORROWING:				
CHANGE IN CLAIMS				
Banks	-16.0	52.0	45.0	-130.0
MEMORANDUM ITEM:				
C.E.E.C. (Gross)	–	–	–	–

1. TOTAL RECEIPTS NET

DAC COUNTRIES	1987	1988	1989	1990
Australia	–	–	–	–
Austria	0.0	0.0	0.0	0.0
Belgium	2.6	-2.7	-6.6	0.0
Canada	0.3	0.3	0.4	0.3
Denmark	0.1	–	-0.1	–
Finland	0.0	–	–	–
France	-10.3	5.4	-34.5	-22.5
Germany	58.4	24.5	43.2	22.8
Ireland	–	–	0.0	0.0
Italy	0.3	4.3	2.9	1.3
Japan	26.5	36.9	71.5	23.2
Netherlands	-5.3	-3.9	-3.1	1.1
New Zealand	–	–	–	–
Norway	–	0.1	0.1	0.1
Sweden	-0.3	–	–	0.3
Switzerland	0.8	0.6	0.8	1.0
United Kingdom	-1.8	-2.2	0.4	-3.0
United States	1.0	–	2.0	–
TOTAL	*72.4*	*63.3*	*77.0*	*24.6*
MULTILATERAL				
AF.D.F.	–	–	–	–
AF.D.B.	–	–	–	–
AS.D.B	–	–	–	–
CAR.D.B.	–	–	–	–
E.E.C.	0.1	0.1	0.8	0.8
IBRD	-16.8	-25.0	-22.0	-24.0
IDA	-0.9	-1.0	-1.0	-1.0
I.D.B.	42.8	16.8	2.5	-6.5
IFAD	1.6	-0.6	-0.7	5.6
I.F.C.	–	-0.3	-0.7	–
IMF TRUST FUND	–	–	–	–
U.N. AGENCIES	–	–	–	–
UNDP	1.5	1.2	1.4	1.3
UNTA	0.3	0.2	0.4	0.4
UNICEF	0.3	0.3	0.3	0.7
UNRWA	–	–	–	–
WFP	2.7	1.1	1.7	2.1
UNHCR	–	–	–	0.0
Other Multilateral	0.6	0.6	0.8	1.2
Arab Agencies	-1.1	-0.7	-0.3	–
TOTAL	*31.0*	*-7.4*	*-16.9*	*-19.4*
ARAB COUNTRIES	–	–	–	–
E.E.C.+ MEMBERS	*44.2*	*25.5*	*2.9*	*0.6*
TOTAL	*103.5*	*55.8*	*60.1*	*5.2*

2. ODA LOANS GROSS

DAC COUNTRIES	1987	1988	1989	1990
Australia	–	–	–	–
Austria	–	–	–	–
Belgium	–	–	–	–
Canada	–	–	–	–
Denmark	–	–	–	–
Finland	–	–	–	–
France	0.6	4.2	0.4	2.4
Germany	5.2	5.2	2.0	3.9
Ireland	–	–	–	–
Italy	–	–	–	–
Japan	16.8	26.4	49.5	26.4
Netherlands	–	–	–	–
New Zealand	–	–	–	–
Norway	–	–	–	–
Sweden	–	–	–	–
Switzerland	–	–	–	–
United Kingdom	–	–	–	–
United States	–	–	–	–
TOTAL	*22.6*	*35.8*	*51.9*	*32.7*
MULTILATERAL	*30.2*	*20.3*	*10.9*	*14.5*
ARAB COUNTRIES	–	–	–	–
E.E.C.+ MEMBERS	*5.8*	*9.4*	*2.4*	*6.3*
TOTAL	*52.7*	*56.1*	*62.8*	*47.3*

3. TOTAL OFFICIAL GROSS

DAC COUNTRIES	1987	1988	1989	1990
Australia	–	–	–	–
Austria	0.0	0.0	0.0	0.0
Belgium	0.1	0.2	0.2	0.4
Canada	0.3	0.3	0.4	0.3
Denmark	0.1	–	–	–
Finland	0.0	–	–	–
France	1.2	4.8	1.1	3.2
Germany	33.9	16.8	28.9	41.6
Ireland	–	–	0.0	0.0
Italy	0.3	0.8	0.5	0.6
Japan	45.8	61.8	76.5	46.4
Netherlands	0.4	0.8	0.8	1.1
New Zealand	–	–	–	–
Norway	–	0.1	0.1	0.1
Sweden	–	–	–	0.3
Switzerland	0.8	0.6	0.8	1.0
United Kingdom	0.5	0.9	0.6	0.9
United States	2.0	1.0	2.0	2.0
TOTAL	*85.4*	*88.0*	*111.9*	*97.9*
MULTILATERAL	*79.0*	*51.4*	*38.3*	*39.2*
ARAB COUNTRIES	–	–	–	–
E.E.C.+ MEMBERS	*36.5*	*24.3*	*32.7*	*48.7*
TOTAL	*164.4*	*139.4*	*150.1*	*137.1*

4. TOTAL ODA NET

DAC COUNTRIES	1987	1988	1989	1990
Australia	–	–	–	–
Austria	0.0	0.0	0.0	0.0
Belgium	0.1	0.2	0.2	0.4
Canada	0.3	0.3	0.4	0.3
Denmark	–	–	–	–
Finland	0.0	–	–	–
France	1.2	4.8	1.1	3.2
Germany	10.6	11.1	10.7	12.3
Ireland	–	–	0.0	0.0
Italy	0.3	0.8	0.5	0.6
Japan	39.3	43.6	72.5	26.4
Netherlands	0.4	0.8	0.8	1.1
New Zealand	–	–	–	–
Norway	–	0.1	0.1	0.1
Sweden	–	–	–	0.3
Switzerland	0.8	0.6	0.8	1.0
United Kingdom	0.5	0.9	0.4	0.9
United States	1.0	–	1.0	–
TOTAL	*54.4*	*63.0*	*88.4*	*46.6*
MULTILATERAL				
AF.D.F.	–	–	–	–
AF.D.B.	–	–	–	–
AS.D.B	–	–	–	–
CAR.D.B.	–	–	–	–
E.E.C.	0.1	0.1	0.8	0.8
IBRD	–	–	–	–
IDA	-0.9	-1.0	-1.0	-1.0
I.D.B.	21.4	11.3	0.5	-1.1
IFAD	1.6	-0.6	-0.7	5.6
I.F.C.	–	–	–	–
IMF TRUST FUND	–	–	–	–
U.N. AGENCIES	–	–	–	–
UNDP	1.5	1.2	1.4	1.3
UNTA	0.3	0.2	0.4	0.4
UNICEF	0.3	0.3	0.3	0.7
UNRWA	–	–	–	–
WFP	2.7	1.1	1.7	2.1
UNHCR	–	–	–	0.0
Other Multilateral	0.6	0.6	0.8	1.2
Arab Agencies	-1.1	-0.7	-0.3	–
TOTAL	*26.5*	*12.4*	*3.8*	*9.9*
ARAB COUNTRIES	–	–	–	–
E.E.C.+ MEMBERS	*13.1*	*18.6*	*14.3*	*19.4*
TOTAL	*80.9*	*75.4*	*92.2*	*56.5*

5. ODA LOANS NET

DAC COUNTRIES	1987	1988	1989	1990
Australia	–	–	–	–
Austria	–	–	–	–
Belgium	–	–	–	–
Canada	0.0	0.0	0.0	0.0
Denmark	–	–	–	–
Finland	–	–	–	–
France	0.6	4.2	0.4	2.4
Germany	2.7	3.9	2.0	-0.5
Ireland	–	–	–	–
Italy	–	–	–	–
Japan	10.3	8.1	45.5	6.4
Netherlands	–	–	–	–
New Zealand	–	–	–	–
Norway	–	–	–	–
Sweden	–	–	–	–
Switzerland	–	–	–	–
United Kingdom	–	–	-0.2	–
United States	-1.0	-1.0	-1.0	-2.0
TOTAL	*12.6*	*15.2*	*46.7*	*6.3*
MULTILATERAL	*20.9*	*7.9*	*-2.0*	*2.8*
ARAB COUNTRIES	–	–	–	–
E.E.C.+ MEMBERS	*3.3*	*8.1*	*2.2*	*1.9*
TOTAL	*33.5*	*23.1*	*44.7*	*9.1*

6. TOTAL OFFICIAL NET

DAC COUNTRIES	1987	1988	1989	1990
Australia	–	–	–	–
Austria	0.0	0.0	0.0	0.0
Belgium	0.1	0.2	0.2	0.4
Canada	0.3	0.3	0.4	0.3
Denmark	0.1	–	-0.1	–
Finland	0.0	–	–	–
France	1.2	4.8	1.1	3.2
Germany	25.6	7.8	28.9	13.9
Ireland	–	–	0.0	0.0
Italy	0.3	0.8	0.5	0.6
Japan	28.5	39.5	72.5	26.4
Netherlands	0.4	0.8	0.8	1.1
New Zealand	–	–	–	–
Norway	–	0.1	0.1	0.1
Sweden	–	–	–	0.3
Switzerland	0.8	0.6	0.8	1.0
United Kingdom	0.5	0.9	0.4	0.9
United States	1.0	–	1.0	–
TOTAL	*58.8*	*55.7*	*106.5*	*48.2*
MULTILATERAL	*31.0*	*-7.4*	*-16.9*	*-19.4*
ARAB COUNTRIES	–	–	–	–
E.E.C.+ MEMBERS	*28.2*	*15.3*	*32.4*	*21.0*
TOTAL	*89.8*	*48.3*	*89.6*	*28.8*

7. TOTAL ODA GROSS

	1987
Australia	–
Austria	0.0
Belgium	0.1
Canada	0.3
Denmark	–
Finland	0.0
France	1.2
Germany	13.0
Ireland	–
Italy	0.3
Japan	45.8
Netherlands	0.4
New Zealand	–
Norway	–
Sweden	–
Switzerland	0.8
United Kingdom	0.5
United States	2.0
TOTAL	*64.4*
AF.D.F.	–
AF.D.B.	–
AS.D.B	–
CAR.D.B.	–
E.E.C.	0.1
IBRD	–
IDA	–
I.D.B.	27.6
IFAD	2.7
I.F.C.	–
IMF TRUST FUND	–
U.N. AGENCIES	–
UNDP	1.5
UNTA	0.3
UNICEF	0.3
UNRWA	–
WFP	2.7
UNHCR	–
Other Multilateral	0.6
Arab Agencies	0.0
TOTAL	*35.7*
ARAB COUNTRIES	
E.E.C.+ MEMBERS	*15.5*
TOTAL	*100.1*

8. GRANTS

	1987
Australia	–
Austria	0.0
Belgium	0.1
Canada	0.3
Denmark	–
Finland	0.0
France	0.6
Germany	7.8
Ireland	–
Italy	0.3
Japan	29.0
Netherlands	0.4
New Zealand	–
Norway	–
Sweden	–
Switzerland	0.8
United Kingdom	0.5
United States	2.0
TOTAL	*41.8*
MULTILATERAL	*5.5*
ARAB COUNTRIES	–
E.E.C.+ MEMBERS	*9.7*
TOTAL	*47.4*

9. TOTAL OOF GROSS

	1987
Australia	–
Austria	–
Belgium	–
Canada	–
Denmark	0.1
Finland	–
France	–
Germany	20.9
Ireland	–
Italy	–
Japan	–
Netherlands	–
New Zealand	–
Norway	–
Sweden	–
Switzerland	–
United Kingdom	–
United States	–
TOTAL	*21.0*
MULTILATERAL	*43.3*
ARAB COUNTRIES	–
E.E.C.+ MEMBERS	*21.0*
TOTAL	*64.3*

10. ODA COMMITMENTS

1988	1989	1990	1987	1988	1989	1990
–	–	–	–	–	–	–
0.0	0.0	0.0	0.0	0.0	0.0	0.0
0.2	0.2	0.4	0.1	0.2	0.2	0.4
0.3	0.4	0.3	0.4	0.6	0.4	0.1
–	–	–	–	–	–	–
4.8	1.1	3.2	0.6	0.6	0.7	0.9
12.4	10.7	16.7	14.0	8.5	11.8	12.1
–	0.0	0.0	–	–	0.0	0.0
0.8	0.5	0.6	1.0	0.3	0.4	1.4
61.8	76.5	46.4	116.0	41.7	30.1	96.6
0.8	0.8	1.1	0.4	0.8	0.8	0.9
–	–	–	–	–	–	–
0.1	0.1	0.1	–	–	–	–
–	–	0.3	–	–	–	–
0.6	0.8	1.0	0.5	0.3	0.3	0.6
0.9	0.6	0.9	0.5	0.9	0.6	0.9
1.0	2.0	2.0	1.8	1.6	2.7	2.4
83.6	*93.6*	*73.0*	*135.1*	*55.5*	*47.9*	*116.2*
–	–	–	–	–	–	–
–	–	–	–	–	–	–
–	–	–	–	–	–	–
0.1	0.8	0.8	0.7	0.1	0.7	0.7
–	–	–	–	–	–	–
21.3	10.0	7.0	12.1	47.8	18.8	30.0
–	1.4	7.5	–	–	–	–
–	–	–	–	–	–	–
–	–	–	5.3	3.4	4.6	5.7
1.2	1.4	1.3	–	–	–	–
0.2	0.4	0.4	–	–	–	–
0.3	0.3	0.7	–	–	–	–
–	–	–	–	–	–	–
1.1	1.7	2.1	–	–	–	–
–	–	0.0	–	–	–	–
0.6	0.8	1.2	–	–	–	–
–	–	–	–	–	–	–
24.8	*16.8*	*21.0*	*18.1*	*51.3*	*24.1*	*36.5*
–	–	–	–	–	–	–
19.9	14.5	23.7	17.0	11.3	15.2	17.3
108.4	*110.4*	*94.0*	*153.2*	*106.8*	*72.0*	*152.7*

11. TECH. COOP. GRANTS

1988	1989	1990	1987	1988	1989	1990
–	–	–	–	–	–	–
0.0	0.0	0.0	0.0	0.0	–	0.0
0.2	0.2	0.4	0.1	0.0	0.0	0.0
0.3	0.4	0.3	–	–	–	–
–	–	–	0.0	–	–	–
0.6	0.7	0.9	0.6	0.6	0.7	0.9
7.2	8.7	12.8	7.8	7.2	7.8	11.9
–	0.0	0.0	–	–	0.0	0.0
0.8	0.5	0.6	0.3	0.8	0.1	0.6
35.4	27.0	20.0	18.5	23.6	19.5	19.0
0.8	0.8	1.1	0.4	0.8	0.8	1.1
–	–	–	–	–	–	–
0.1	0.1	0.1	–	0.0	0.0	0.0
–	–	0.3	–	–	–	0.2
0.6	0.8	1.0	0.1	0.1	–	–
0.9	0.6	0.9	0.5	0.9	0.6	0.9
1.0	2.0	2.0	1.0	1.0	2.0	2.0
47.8	*41.7*	*40.3*	*29.2*	*35.0*	*31.5*	*36.6*
4.5	5.8	6.5	2.7	2.3	2.9	3.6
–	–	–	–	–	–	–
10.5	12.1	17.4	9.6	10.2	10.0	15.4
52.3	*47.6*	*46.8*	*32.0*	*37.3*	*34.4*	*40.2*

12. TOTAL OOF NET

1988	1989	1990	1987	1988	1989	1990
–	–	–	–	–	–	–
–	–	–	–	–	–	–
–	–	–	–	–	–	–
–	–	–	0.1	–	-0.1	–
–	–	–	–	–	–	–
–	–	–	–	–	–	–
4.4	18.2	24.9	15.0	-3.3	18.2	1.6
–	–	–	–	–	–	–
–	–	–	-10.7	-4.0	–	–
–	–	–	–	–	–	–
–	–	–	–	–	–	–
–	–	–	–	–	–	–
–	–	–	–	–	–	–
–	–	–	–	–	–	–
–	–	–	–	–	–	–
4.4	*18.2*	*24.9*	*4.4*	*-7.3*	*18.1*	*1.6*
26.6	*21.5*	*18.2*	*4.6*	*-19.8*	*-20.7*	*-29.3*
–	–	–	–	–	–	–
4.4	*18.2*	*24.9*	*15.1*	*-3.3*	*18.1*	*1.6*
31.0	*39.7*	*43.1*	*9.0*	*-27.2*	*-2.6*	*-27.7*

13. ODF COMMITMENTS: BY PURPOSE %

	1987	1988	1989	1990
Education	3	–	–	–
Health	0	–	1	–
Other Social Infrastr.	0	0	1	–
Water Sanitat. Sewage	–	35	–	–
Energy	4	19	1	–
Telecommunications	–	–	–	–
Transportation	–	–	–	–
Agriculture	66	16	18	–
Extractive Industries	–	–	–	–
Manufacturing	–	–	–	–
Trade Banking Tourism	0	–	–	–
Technical Cooperation	26	30	79	–
Multisector Aid	–	–	–	–
Programme	–	–	–	–
Debt Reorganisation	–	–	–	–
Food Aid	–	–	–	–
Emergency Aid	0	0	0	–
Unspecified	–	–	–	–
TOTAL	100	100	100	–

14. GRANT ELEMENT OF ODA %

DAC COUNTRIES

	1987	1988	1989	1990
Australia	–	–	–	–
Austria	100.0	100.0	100.0	–
Belgium	100.0	100.0	100.0	–
Canada	100.0	100.0	100.0	–
Denmark	–	–	–	–
Finland	–	–	–	–
France	100.0	100.0	100.0	–
Germany	73.5	100.0	100.0	–
Ireland	–	–	100.0	–
Italy	100.0	100.0	100.0	–
Japan	53.9	87.8	91.9	–
Netherlands	100.0	100.0	100.0	–
New Zealand	–	–	–	–
Norway	–	–	–	–
Sweden	–	–	–	–
Switzerland	100.0	100.0	100.0	–
United Kingdom	100.0	100.0	100.0	–
United States	100.0	100.0	100.0	–
TOTAL	*57.7*	*90.9*	*95.1*	–
MULTILATERAL	*100.0*	*77.5*	*100.0*	–
ARAB COUNTRIES	–	–	–	–
E.E.C.+ MEMBERS	*78.2*	*100.0*	*100.0*	–
TOTAL	*59.5*	*83.7*	*95.6*	–

15. OTHER AGGREGATES

OFFICIAL COMMITMENTS:

	1987	1988	1989	1990
TOTAL BILATERAL	135.7	83.7	47.9	118.1
of which:				
Arab Countries	–	–	–	–
C.E.E.C.	–	–	–	–
TOTAL MULTILATERAL	38.1	51.3	24.5	36.5
TOTAL BIL.& MULTIL.	173.8	135.0	72.4	154.6
of which:				
ODA Grants	47.9	52.1	47.4	50.5
ODA Loans	105.3	54.7	24.6	102.2

DISBURSEMENTS:

DAC COUNTRIES COMBINED

OFFICIAL & PRIVATE

	1987	1988	1989	1990
GROSS:				
Contractual Lending	52.9	69.1	78.0	57.7
Export Credits, Total	30.3	33.4	26.0	24.9
Export Credits, Priv.	9.4	29.0	7.8	0.0
NET:				
Contractual Lending	14.8	11.6	47.7	-25.4
Export Credits Total	2.3	-3.6	1.1	-14.7
PRIVATE SECTOR NET	13.6	7.6	-29.6	-23.6
Direct Investment	-0.1	0.7	4.2	2.1
Portfolio Investment	15.8	3.2	-16.6	7.6
Export Credits	-2.1	3.8	-17.1	-33.3

MARKET BORROWING:

CHANGE IN CLAIMS

	1987	1988	1989	1990
Banks	-7.0	-64.0	-10.0	25.0

MEMORANDUM ITEM:

	1987	1988	1989	1990
C.E.E.C. (Gross)	–	–	–	–

	1987	1988	1989	1990		1987	1988	1989	1990		1987

1. TOTAL RECEIPTS NET

DAC COUNTRIES

	1987	1988	1989	1990
Australia	–	-0.2	0.0	–
Austria	0.1	-0.1	-0.1	0.4
Belgium	2.7	6.4	1.5	0.1
Canada	15.4	22.5	19.5	23.2
Denmark	0.0	-0.2	0.4	1.9
Finland	4.3	5.2	3.7	3.8
France	-35.2	-145.6	-24.8	-20.7
Germany	72.6	70.5	79.8	77.0
Ireland	0.1	0.0	0.0	0.1
Italy	-46.9	5.6	51.4	19.5
Japan	3.2	32.4	-2.6	23.8
Netherlands	55.1	41.0	-4.3	7.6
New Zealand	0.2	0.1	0.1	0.1
Norway	0.4	0.4	-0.6	-9.9
Sweden	8.5	0.7	-12.1	-6.5
Switzerland	8.2	6.0	6.3	10.7
United Kingdom	19.8	-8.9	61.7	-4.8
United States	-159.0	-87.0	-190.0	-302.0
TOTAL	*-50.6*	*-51.2*	*-10.2*	*-175.8*

MULTILATERAL

	1987	1988	1989	1990
AF.D.F.	–	–	–	–
AF.D.B.	–	–	–	–
AS.D.B	–	–	–	–
CAR.D.B.	–	–	–	–
E.E.C.	12.8	15.1	19.7	19.7
IBRD	31.9	2.0	–	–
IDA	–	–	–	–
I.D.B.	96.1	37.9	2.3	3.2
IFAD	7.1	1.8	-0.7	4.3
I.F.C.	1.6	-2.9	-2.1	–
IMF TRUST FUND	–	–	–	–
U.N. AGENCIES	–	–	–	–
UNDP	6.1	6.4	5.0	3.7
UNTA	1.1	1.4	0.7	1.2
UNICEF	2.0	2.1	3.7	4.5
UNRWA	–	–	–	–
WFP	3.0	2.9	10.5	10.7
UNHCR	–	–	–	0.1
Other Multilateral	4.3	4.7	3.9	4.4
Arab Agencies	–	0.8	0.7	–
TOTAL	*165.9*	*72.1*	*43.8*	*51.7*
ARAB COUNTRIES	–	–	–	–
E.E.C.+ MEMBERS	*81.1*	*-16.1*	*185.2*	*100.3*
TOTAL	**115.3**	**21.0**	**33.5**	**-124.1**

2. ODA LOANS GROSS

DAC COUNTRIES

	1987	1988	1989	1990
Australia	–	–	–	–
Austria	–	–	–	–
Belgium	–	–	–	–
Canada	4.6	–	–	–
Denmark	–	–	–	–
Finland	0.4	1.2	1.4	1.2
France	0.0	–	–	–
Germany	34.8	11.5	16.6	15.4
Ireland	–	–	–	–
Italy	0.7	4.8	61.2	53.9
Japan	5.7	1.7	2.2	0.5
Netherlands	15.7	1.7	0.1	–
New Zealand	–	–	–	–
Norway	–	–	–	–
Sweden	–	–	–	–
Switzerland	2.7	–	–	–
United Kingdom	–	–	–	–
United States	30.0	25.0	14.0	21.0
TOTAL	*94.5*	*45.9*	*95.5*	*91.9*
MULTILATERAL	*14.7*	*3.8*	*3.6*	*5.7*
ARAB COUNTRIES	–	–	–	–
E.E.C.+ MEMBERS	*51.2*	*18.0*	*77.8*	*69.3*
TOTAL	**109.2**	**49.7**	**99.0**	**97.6**

3. TOTAL OFFICIAL GROSS

DAC COUNTRIES

	1987	1988	1989	1990
Australia	–	–	0.0	–
Austria	0.9	1.2	0.7	0.4
Belgium	4.0	4.1	2.4	3.9
Canada	15.5	22.6	22.4	23.2
Denmark	0.0	0.1	0.6	1.9
Finland	3.6	6.4	3.5	2.8
France	3.7	3.8	4.7	6.5
Germany	76.5	51.8	57.3	60.7
Ireland	0.1	0.0	0.0	0.1
Italy	19.2	35.8	77.9	80.6
Japan	37.6	28.6	28.0	39.9
Netherlands	31.5	22.5	23.5	30.0
New Zealand	0.2	0.1	0.1	0.1
Norway	0.8	0.9	0.7	1.4
Sweden	0.6	0.7	0.8	1.0
Switzerland	8.2	6.0	6.3	10.7
United Kingdom	1.7	2.4	1.8	2.1
United States	73.0	72.0	52.0	84.0
TOTAL	*277.0*	*258.9*	*282.5*	*349.4*
MULTILATERAL	*244.2*	*106.6*	*54.0*	*57.1*
ARAB COUNTRIES	–	–	–	–
E.E.C.+ MEMBERS	*149.6*	*135.5*	*187.8*	*205.5*
TOTAL	**521.3**	**365.6**	**336.5**	**406.5**

4. TOTAL ODA NET

	1987	1988	1989	1990
Australia	–	–	0.0	–
Austria	0.9	0.7	-0.1	0.4
Belgium	3.5	4.1	2.2	3.8
Canada	15.4	22.5	22.4	23.2
Denmark	0.0	0.1	0.6	1.9
Finland	3.6	6.4	3.5	2.8
France	3.7	3.8	4.7	6.5
Germany	71.4	48.7	55.3	60.4
Ireland	0.1	0.0	0.0	0.1
Italy	19.2	35.8	77.9	80.6
Japan	37.6	28.4	27.9	39.8
Netherlands	31.5	22.5	23.5	30.0
New Zealand	0.2	0.1	0.1	0.1
Norway	0.8	0.9	0.7	1.4
Sweden	0.6	0.7	0.8	1.0
Switzerland	8.2	6.0	6.3	10.7
United Kingdom	1.7	2.4	1.8	2.1
United States	63.0	61.0	36.0	79.0
TOTAL	*261.2*	*244.1*	*263.4*	*343.9*

	1987	1988	1989	1990
–	–	–	–	–
–	–	–	–	–
–	–	–	–	–
–	–	–	–	–
E.E.C.	12.8	15.1	19.7	19.7
–	–	–	–	–
–	–	–	–	–
I.D.B.	-5.4	-7.1	-2.0	-0.1
IFAD	7.1	1.8	-0.7	4.3
–	–	–	–	–
–	–	–	–	–
–	–	–	–	–
UNDP	6.1	6.4	5.0	3.7
UNTA	1.1	1.4	0.7	1.2
UNICEF	2.0	2.1	3.7	4.5
–	–	–	–	–
WFP	3.0	2.9	10.5	10.7
UNHCR	–	–	–	0.1
Other Multilateral	4.3	4.7	3.9	4.4
Arab Agencies	–	0.8	0.7	–
TOTAL	*31.0*	*28.0*	*41.5*	*48.4*
ARAB COUNTRIES	–	–	–	–
E.E.C.+ MEMBERS	*143.9*	*132.4*	*185.6*	*205.1*
TOTAL	**292.2**	**272.2**	**304.9**	**392.3**

5. ODA LOANS NET

DAC COUNTRIES

	1987	1988	1989	1990
Australia	–	–	–	–
Austria	–	-0.5	-0.8	–
Belgium	–	–	–	–
Canada	4.5	-0.1	–	0.0
Denmark	–	–	–	–
Finland	0.4	1.2	1.4	1.2
France	0.0	–	–	–
Germany	34.8	11.1	16.2	15.4
Ireland	–	–	–	–
Italy	0.7	4.8	61.2	53.9
Japan	5.7	1.6	2.1	0.4
Netherlands	15.7	1.7	0.1	–
New Zealand	–	–	–	–
Norway	–	–	–	–
Sweden	–	–	–	–
Switzerland	2.7	–	–	–
United Kingdom	–	–	–	–
United States	20.0	14.0	-2.0	16.0
TOTAL	*84.3*	*33.9*	*78.2*	*86.8*
MULTILATERAL	*1.7*	*-4.7*	*-2.0*	*4.5*
ARAB COUNTRIES	–	–	–	–
E.E.C.+ MEMBERS	*51.2*	*17.7*	*77.5*	*69.3*
TOTAL	**86.0**	**29.1**	**76.2**	**91.3**

6. TOTAL OFFICIAL NET

DAC COUNTRIES

	1987	1988	1989	1990
Australia	–	–	0.0	–
Austria	0.9	0.7	-0.1	0.4
Belgium	4.0	4.1	2.4	3.9
Canada	15.4	22.5	19.5	23.2
Denmark	0.0	0.1	0.6	1.9
Finland	3.6	6.4	3.5	2.8
France	3.7	3.8	4.7	6.5
Germany	76.5	51.4	56.7	60.5
Ireland	0.1	0.0	0.0	0.1
Italy	19.2	35.8	77.9	78.4
Japan	37.6	28.4	27.9	39.8
Netherlands	31.5	22.5	23.5	30.0
New Zealand	0.2	0.1	0.1	0.1
Norway	0.8	0.9	0.7	1.4
Sweden	0.6	0.7	0.8	1.0
Switzerland	8.2	6.0	6.3	10.7
United Kingdom	1.7	2.4	1.8	2.1
United States	63.0	61.0	34.0	79.0
TOTAL	*266.9*	*246.9*	*260.1*	*341.9*
MULTILATERAL	*165.9*	*72.1*	*43.8*	*51.7*
ARAB COUNTRIES	–	–	–	–
E.E.C.+ MEMBERS	*149.5*	*135.2*	*187.1*	*203.1*
TOTAL	**432.8**	**319.0**	**303.8**	**393.5**

7. TOTAL ODA GROSS

	1987
Australia	–
Austria	0.9
Belgium	3.5
Canada	15.5
Denmark	0.0
Finland	3.6
France	3.7
Germany	71.4
Ireland	0.1
Italy	19.2
Japan	37.6
Netherlands	31.5
New Zealand	0.2
Norway	0.8
Sweden	0.6
Switzerland	8.2
United Kingdom	1.7
United States	73.0
TOTAL	*271.4*

	1987
AF.D.F.	–
AF.D.B.	–
AS.D.B	–
CAR.D.B.	–
E.E.C.	12.8
IBRD	–
IDA	–
I.D.B.	6.6
IFAD	8.2
I.F.C.	–
IMF TRUST FUND	–
U.N. AGENCIES	–
UNDP	6.1
UNTA	1.1
UNICEF	2.0
UNRWA	–
WFP	3.0
UNHCR	–
Other Multilateral	4.3
Arab Agencies	–
TOTAL	*44.0*
ARAB COUNTRIES	–
E.E.C.+ MEMBERS	*143.9*
TOTAL	**315.4**

8. GRANTS

	1987
Australia	–
Austria	0.9
Belgium	3.5
Canada	10.9
Denmark	0.0
Finland	3.2
France	3.7
Germany	36.6
Ireland	0.1
Italy	18.5
Japan	31.9
Netherlands	15.8
New Zealand	0.2
Norway	0.8
Sweden	0.6
Switzerland	5.5
United Kingdom	1.7
United States	43.0
TOTAL	*176.9*
MULTILATERAL	*29.3*
ARAB COUNTRIES	–
E.E.C.+ MEMBERS	*92.7*
TOTAL	**206.2**

9. TOTAL OOF GROSS

	1987
Australia	–
Austria	–
Belgium	0.5
Canada	–
Denmark	0.0
Finland	–
France	–
Germany	5.2
Ireland	–
Italy	–
Japan	–
Netherlands	–
New Zealand	–
Norway	–
Sweden	–
Switzerland	–
United Kingdom	–
United States	–
TOTAL	*5.6*
MULTILATERAL	*200.2*
ARAB COUNTRIES	–
E.E.C.+ MEMBERS	*5.6*
TOTAL	**205.9**

10. ODA COMMITMENTS

1988	1989	1990	1987	1988	1989	1990
–	0.0	–	–	–	0.0	0.0
1.2	0.7	0.4	0.8	1.3	0.6	0.4
4.1	2.2	3.8	2.2	5.7	2.2	3.8
22.6	22.4	23.2	8.8	35.8	6.9	14.6
0.1	0.6	1.9	–	–	1.2	1.4
6.4	3.5	2.8	1.7	3.3	1.0	1.9
3.8	4.7	6.5	3.7	4.0	4.3	6.2
49.0	55.6	60.4	66.8	41.7	43.1	54.5
0.0	0.0	0.1	0.1	0.0	0.0	0.1
35.8	77.9	80.6	38.9	96.4	177.0	33.9
28.6	28.0	39.9	30.8	29.0	35.8	33.1
22.5	23.5	30.0	25.2	17.3	24.9	33.8
0.1	0.1	0.1	0.1	0.1	–	–
0.9	0.7	1.4	0.4	–	–	–
0.7	0.8	1.0	1.0	0.6	0.4	0.0
6.0	6.3	10.7	9.9	7.2	6.9	8.6
2.4	1.8	2.1	1.5	2.4	1.8	2.1
72.0	52.0	84.0	63.7	98.1	68.0	93.5
256.2	*280.6*	*349.0*	*255.3*	*342.9*	*374.0*	*288.0*
–	–	–	–	–	–	–
–	–	–	–	–	–	–
–	–	–	–	–	–	–
15.1	19.7	19.7	11.3	39.9	12.5	12.5
–	–	–	–	–	–	–
1.2	–	–	–	–	–	–
2.1	2.9	5.5	0.2	–	–	–
–	–	–	–	–	–	–
–	–	–	–	–	–	–
–	–	–	16.4	17.4	23.9	24.5
6.4	5.0	3.7	–	–	–	–
1.4	0.7	1.2	–	–	–	–
2.1	3.7	4.5	–	–	–	–
–	–	–	–	–	–	–
2.9	10.5	10.7	–	–	–	–
–	–	0.1	–	–	–	–
4.7	3.9	4.4	–	–	–	–
0.8	0.7	0.2	3.0	–	–	–
36.6	*47.1*	*49.9*	*30.8*	*57.3*	*36.4*	*37.0*
–	–	–	–	–	–	–
132.8	185.9	205.1	149.6	207.4	266.9	148.3
292.8	*327.8*	*398.9*	*286.2*	*400.3*	*410.3*	*324.9*

11. TECH. COOP. GRANTS

1988	1989	1990	1987	1988	1989	1990
–	0.0	–	–	–	–	–
1.2	0.7	0.4	0.9	1.1	0.3	0.3
4.1	2.2	3.8	3.0	2.1	1.1	1.5
22.6	22.4	23.2	–	0.7	1.7	0.3
0.1	0.6	1.9	0.0	0.0	–	0.0
5.2	2.1	1.6	0.0	4.8	0.3	0.2
3.8	4.7	6.5	3.7	3.6	3.7	5.8
37.5	39.1	45.0	34.9	33.1	29.4	32.3
0.0	0.0	0.1	0.1	0.0	0.0	0.1
31.0	16.7	26.8	7.8	3.0	3.3	3.5
26.8	25.8	39.4	18.3	19.3	19.7	19.1
20.8	23.4	30.0	9.8	14.0	15.8	26.2
0.1	0.1	0.1	0.1	0.1	–	0.1
0.9	0.7	1.4	0.2	0.2	0.1	0.2
0.7	0.8	1.0	0.5	0.7	0.5	0.2
6.0	6.3	10.7	1.7	1.8	–	–
2.4	1.8	2.1	1.5	2.3	1.5	1.6
47.0	38.0	63.0	15.0	17.0	20.0	22.0
210.3	*185.2*	*257.1*	*97.3*	*103.7*	*97.4*	*113.4*
32.8	*43.5*	*44.1*	*16.1*	*22.7*	*13.4*	*13.8*
–	–	–	–	–	–	–
114.8	108.1	135.9	63.4	66.2	54.8	71.1
243.0	*228.7*	*301.2*	*113.4*	*126.4*	*110.7*	*127.2*

12. TOTAL OOF NET

1988	1989	1990	1987	1988	1989	1990
–	–	–	–	–	–	–
–	–	–	–	–	–	–
–	0.2	0.1	0.5	–	0.2	0.1
–	–	–	–	–	-2.9	–
–	–	–	0.0	–	0.0	–
–	–	–	–	–	–	–
2.8	1.7	0.3	5.2	2.7	1.4	0.1
–	–	–	–	–	–	–
–	–	–	–	–	–	-2.2
–	–	–	–	–	–	–
–	–	–	–	–	–	–
–	–	–	–	–	–	–
–	–	–	–	–	–	–
–	–	–	–	–	-2.0	–
2.8	*1.9*	*0.4*	*5.6*	*2.7*	*-3.3*	*-2.0*
70.0	6.8	7.2	135.0	44.1	2.2	3.2
–	–	–	–	–	–	–
2.8	*1.9*	*0.4*	*5.6*	*2.7*	*1.5*	*-2.0*
72.8	*8.7*	*7.6*	*140.6*	*46.8*	*-1.1*	*1.2*

13. ODF COMMITMENTS: BY PURPOSE %

	1987	1988	1989	1990
Education	0	1	2	–
Health	5	2	2	–
Other Social Infrastr.	6	3	35	–
Water Sanitat. Sewage	–	0	0	–
Energy	21	–	4	–
Telecommunications	2	1	–	–
Transportation	–	6	–	–
Agriculture	18	24	17	–
Extractive Industries	–	–	–	–
Manufacturing	0	0	0	–
Trade Banking Tourism	1	–	0	–
Technical Cooperation	34	38	29	–
Multisector Aid	0	1	0	–
Programme	–	3	0	–
Debt Reorganisation	–	–	1	–
Food Aid	11	20	8	–
Emergency Aid	0	0	0	–
Unspecified	0	0	3	–
TOTAL	100	100	100	–

14. GRANT ELEMENT OF ODA %

DAC COUNTRIES	1987	1988	1989	1990
Australia	–	–	100.0	–
Austria	100.0	100.0	100.0	–
Belgium	100.0	100.0	100.0	–
Canada	100.0	100.0	100.0	–
Denmark	–	–	100.0	–
Finland	100.0	100.0	100.0	–
France	100.0	100.0	100.0	–
Germany	82.3	100.0	97.9	–
Ireland	100.0	100.0	100.0	–
Italy	95.4	84.9	68.3	–
Japan	100.0	100.0	100.0	–
Netherlands	88.3	100.0	100.0	–
New Zealand	100.0	100.0	–	–
Norway	100.0	–	–	–
Sweden	100.0	100.0	100.0	–
Switzerland	100.0	100.0	100.0	–
United Kingdom	100.0	100.0	100.0	–
United States	83.5	88.7	89.8	–
TOTAL	*89.4*	*92.5*	*82.9*	–
MULTILATERAL	*81.1*	*100.0*	*100.0*	–
ARAB COUNTRIES	–	–	–	–
E.E.C.+ MEMBERS	*88.9*	*93.0*	*78.6*	–
TOTAL	*88.3*	*93.6*	*84.4*	–

15. OTHER AGGREGATES

OFFICIAL COMMITMENTS:

	1987	1988	1989	1990
TOTAL BILATERAL	272.4	513.1	464.2	288.1
of which:				
Arab Countries	–	–	–	–
C.E.E.C.	–	170.0	–	–
TOTAL MULTILATERAL	100.7	57.3	36.4	37.6
TOTAL BIL.& MULTIL.	373.1	570.4	500.5	325.6
of which:				
ODA Grants	224.2	336.8	233.7	296.9
ODA Loans	62.0	63.4	176.6	28.0

DISBURSEMENTS:

DAC COUNTRIES COMBINED

OFFICIAL & PRIVATE	1987	1988	1989	1990
GROSS:				
Contractual Lending	133.2	66.7	203.5	59.7
Export Credits, Total	33.5	18.0	108.1	-32.2
Export Credits, Priv.	33.5	18.0	106.3	-32.5
NET:				
Contractual Lending	-8.5	-27.5	53.2	-38.2
Export Credits Total	-98.0	-64.1	-22.7	-124.8
PRIVATE SECTOR NET	-317.5	-298.0	-270.3	-517.6
Direct Investment	-58.7	-20.0	-112.7	-365.4
Portfolio Investment	-160.8	-213.9	-136.1	-29.3
Export Credits	-98.0	-64.1	-21.6	-122.9

MARKET BORROWING:

CHANGE IN CLAIMS

	1987	1988	1989	1990
Banks	-459.0	-417.0	-475.0	-358.0

MEMORANDUM ITEM:

	1987	1988	1989	1990
C.E.E.C. (Gross)	–	–	–	–

1. TOTAL RECEIPTS NET

DAC COUNTRIES

	1987	1988	1989	1990
Australia	23.7	35.5	42.1	24.7
Austria	-6.4	-6.5	-6.0	-7.0
Belgium	-29.3	2.9	-13.4	27.6
Canada	13.2	25.7	23.6	28.9
Denmark	1.5	3.9	7.7	2.8
Finland	0.7	-1.7	-1.4	1.1
France	-47.9	-26.6	9.1	87.1
Germany	98.6	11.9	41.1	53.3
Ireland	0.1	0.0	0.0	0.0
Italy	15.2	-7.5	6.9	42.9
Japan	409.4	493.8	701.3	886.3
Netherlands	22.2	31.8	37.4	13.4
New Zealand	1.1	0.9	1.3	1.6
Norway	4.0	4.7	4.5	4.9
Sweden	8.0	2.9	-0.5	0.9
Switzerland	1.5	1.7	1.8	9.4
United Kingdom	-15.2	28.0	54.0	16.2
United States	170.0	603.0	5.0	233.0
TOTAL	*670.4*	*1204.5*	*914.3*	*1427.2*

MULTILATERAL

	1987	1988	1989	1990
AF.D.F.	–	–	–	–
AF.D.B.	–	–	–	–
AS.D.B	88.3	105.8	141.3	319.4
CAR.D.B.	–	–	–	–
E.E.C.	2.9	4.8	7.2	7.2
IBRD	43.2	-25.0	195.0	205.0
IDA	7.3	2.0	–	-1.0
I.D.B.	–	–	–	–
IFAD	0.4	-2.1	-0.7	0.9
I.F.C.	14.4	1.2	-72.7	97.8
IMF TRUST FUND	–	–	–	–
U.N. AGENCIES	–	–	–	–
UNDP	5.3	6.1	8.4	8.8
UNTA	2.0	1.5	1.8	1.9
UNICEF	6.2	4.2	6.9	7.4
UNRWA	–	–	–	–
WFP	1.4	1.4	3.1	2.7
UNHCR	6.5	6.4	8.7	13.0
Other Multilateral	2.1	2.3	4.3	8.1
Arab Agencies	-1.8	-2.4	-2.1	–
TOTAL	*178.1*	*106.2*	*301.3*	*671.0*
ARAB COUNTRIES	*-0.4*	*-0.1*	*0.3*	*–*
E.E.C.+ MEMBERS	*48.1*	*49.2*	*149.9*	*250.5*
TOTAL	**848.0**	**1310.5**	**1215.8**	**2098.2**

2. ODA LOANS GROSS

DAC COUNTRIES

	1987	1988	1989	1990
Australia	–	–	–	–
Austria	–	–	–	–
Belgium	–	–	–	–
Canada	–	–	–	–
Denmark	2.6	4.2	0.7	–
Finland	–	–	–	–
France	–	1.5	7.6	30.4
Germany	5.3	4.5	12.7	15.4
Ireland	–	–	–	–
Italy	–	–	–	10.6
Japan	282.0	536.4	256.3	617.0
Netherlands	0.4	1.1	0.3	–
New Zealand	–	–	–	–
Norway	–	2.5	–	–
Sweden	–	–	–	–
Switzerland	–	–	–	–
United Kingdom	–	–	0.7	0.4
United States	–	30.0	-1.0	21.0
TOTAL	*290.3*	*580.1*	*277.4*	*694.8*
MULTILATERAL	*43.3*	*37.2*	*46.2*	*124.0*
ARAB COUNTRIES	*–*	*0.2*	*0.4*	*–*
E.E.C.+ MEMBERS	*8.3*	*11.2*	*22.1*	*56.8*
TOTAL	**333.6**	**617.5**	**323.9**	**818.8**

3. TOTAL OFFICIAL GROSS

DAC COUNTRIES

	1987	1988	1989	1990
Australia	16.3	31.0	24.5	28.9
Austria	0.2	0.2	0.2	0.3
Belgium	9.4	43.1	7.7	71.5
Canada	16.3	26.3	23.9	28.9
Denmark	2.8	4.8	0.8	3.3
Finland	0.3	0.7	1.1	1.1
France	1.3	42.9	11.9	34.0
Germany	51.6	50.5	53.1	124.3
Ireland	0.1	0.0	0.0	0.0
Italy	29.2	1.2	12.5	45.5
Japan	558.8	766.1	674.3	879.5
Netherlands	21.5	27.7	27.7	22.6
New Zealand	1.1	0.9	1.3	1.6
Norway	4.0	4.7	4.5	3.9
Sweden	1.5	2.9	0.7	1.0
Switzerland	1.5	1.7	1.8	9.4
United Kingdom	0.4	1.9	19.5	19.3
United States	246.0	366.0	287.0	452.0
TOTAL	*962.3*	*1372.5*	*1152.5*	*1727.0*
MULTILATERAL	*448.6*	*457.4*	*716.6*	*1037.1*
ARAB COUNTRIES	*0.1*	*0.4*	*0.8*	*–*
E.E.C.+ MEMBERS	*119.1*	*176.8*	*140.4*	*327.7*
TOTAL	**1411.1**	**1830.3**	**1869.9**	**2764.1**

4. TOTAL ODA NET

	1987	1988	1989	1990
Australia	16.3	30.4	21.9	28.6
Austria	0.2	0.1	0.2	0.3
Belgium	1.0	1.4	1.7	4.9
Canada	16.4	25.0	23.2	28.7
Denmark	2.7	4.4	0.8	3.3
Finland	0.3	0.7	1.1	1.1
France	1.2	1.4	9.4	32.2
Germany	24.9	30.0	36.4	44.0
Ireland	0.1	0.0	0.0	0.0
Italy	0.7	1.2	12.5	14.9
Japan	379.4	534.7	403.8	647.5
Netherlands	21.5	26.9	26.7	22.0
New Zealand	1.1	0.9	1.3	1.6
Norway	4.0	4.7	4.5	3.9
Sweden	1.5	2.9	0.7	1.0
Switzerland	1.5	1.7	1.8	9.4
United Kingdom	0.4	1.9	19.5	9.0
United States	230.0	121.0	192.0	248.0
TOTAL	*703.1*	*789.3*	*757.3*	*1100.3*
AF.D.F.	–	–	–	–
AF.D.B.	–	–	–	–
AS.D.B	35.3	40.9	49.3	127.5
CAR.D.B.	–	–	–	–
E.E.C.	2.9	4.8	7.2	7.2
IBRD	–	–	–	–
IDA	7.3	2.0	–	-1.0
I.D.B.	–	–	–	–
IFAD	0.4	-2.1	-0.7	0.9
I.F.C.	–	–	–	–
IMF TRUST FUND	–	–	–	–
U.N. AGENCIES	–	–	–	–
UNDP	5.3	6.1	8.4	8.8
UNTA	2.0	1.5	1.8	1.9
UNICEF	6.2	4.2	6.9	7.4
UNRWA	–	–	–	–
WFP	1.4	1.4	3.1	2.7
UNHCR	6.5	6.4	8.7	13.0
Other Multilateral	2.1	2.3	4.3	8.1
Arab Agencies	-1.8	-2.4	-2.1	–
TOTAL	*67.5*	*65.1*	*86.9*	*176.4*
ARAB COUNTRIES	*-0.4*	*-0.1*	*0.3*	*–*
E.E.C.+ MEMBERS	*55.3*	*72.0*	*114.0*	*137.6*
TOTAL	**770.2**	**854.3**	**844.5**	**1276.7**

5. ODA LOANS NET

	1987	1988	1989	1990
Australia	0.0	0.0	0.0	0.0
Austria	-0.4	-0.1	–	–
Belgium	–	–	–	–
Canada	–	–	–	–
Denmark	2.6	4.2	0.7	–
Finland	–	–	–	–
France	-0.1	0.4	7.6	28.6
Germany	1.3	-1.1	12.7	7.7
Ireland	–	–	–	–
Italy	–	–	–	10.6
Japan	267.6	403.6	227.7	494.3
Netherlands	0.4	1.1	0.3	–
New Zealand	–	–	–	–
Norway	–	2.5	–	–
Sweden	–	–	–	–
Switzerland	–	–	–	–
United Kingdom	–	–	0.7	0.4
United States	-1.0	11.0	-15.0	16.0
TOTAL	*270.3*	*421.6*	*234.7*	*557.5*
MULTILATERAL	*39.3*	*30.4*	*40.1*	*117.4*
ARAB COUNTRIES	*-0.5*	*-0.3*	*-0.2*	*–*
E.E.C.+ MEMBERS	*3.7*	*4.5*	*22.1*	*47.2*
TOTAL	**309.0**	**451.7**	**274.7**	**674.9**

6. TOTAL OFFICIAL NET

	1987	1988	1989	1990
Australia	15.3	29.3	23.9	28.6
Austria	0.2	0.1	0.2	0.3
Belgium	8.7	43.0	7.7	71.5
Canada	13.2	25.7	23.6	28.9
Denmark	2.3	4.7	0.7	2.8
Finland	0.3	0.7	1.1	1.1
France	-0.6	41.9	11.9	32.2
Germany	42.6	39.4	52.1	81.9
Ireland	0.1	0.0	0.0	0.0
Italy	24.6	1.2	12.5	41.7
Japan	534.2	624.7	636.5	740.9
Netherlands	21.5	27.7	27.7	22.6
New Zealand	1.1	0.9	1.3	1.6
Norway	4.0	4.7	4.5	3.9
Sweden	1.5	2.9	0.7	1.0
Switzerland	1.5	1.7	1.8	9.4
United Kingdom	-0.4	1.0	18.7	18.5
United States	226.0	333.0	263.0	423.0
TOTAL	*896.0*	*1182.6*	*1087.7*	*1509.7*
MULTILATERAL	*178.1*	*106.2*	*301.3*	*671.0*
ARAB COUNTRIES	*-0.4*	*-0.1*	*0.3*	*–*
E.E.C.+ MEMBERS	*101.6*	*163.7*	*138.4*	*278.3*
TOTAL	**1073.7**	**1288.7**	**1389.3**	**2180.7**

7. TOTAL ODA GROSS

	1987
Australia	16.3
Austria	0.2
Belgium	1.3
Canada	16.4
Denmark	2.7
Finland	0.3
France	1.3
Germany	29.0
Ireland	0.1
Italy	0.7
Japan	393.8
Netherlands	21.5
New Zealand	1.1
Norway	4.0
Sweden	1.5
Switzerland	1.5
United Kingdom	0.4
United States	231.0
TOTAL	*723.1*
AF.D.F.	–
AF.D.B.	–
AS.D.B	35.8
CAR.D.B.	–
E.E.C.	2.9
IBRD	–
IDA	7.6
I.D.B.	–
IFAD	1.4
I.F.C.	–
IMF TRUST FUND	–
U.N. AGENCIES	–
UNDP	5.3
UNTA	2.0
UNICEF	6.2
UNRWA	–
WFP	1.4
UNHCR	6.5
Other Multilateral	2.1
Arab Agencies	0.4
TOTAL	*71.5*
ARAB COUNTRIES	*0.1*
E.E.C.+ MEMBERS	*59.9*
TOTAL	**794.7**

8. GRANTS

	1987
Australia	16.3
Austria	0.2
Belgium	1.3
Canada	16.4
Denmark	0.1
Finland	0.3
France	1.3
Germany	23.7
Ireland	0.1
Italy	0.7
Japan	111.8
Netherlands	21.2
New Zealand	1.1
Norway	4.0
Sweden	1.5
Switzerland	1.5
United Kingdom	0.4
United States	231.0
TOTAL	*432.8*
MULTILATERAL	*28.2*
ARAB COUNTRIES	*0.1*
E.E.C.+ MEMBERS	*51.6*
TOTAL	**461.2**

9. TOTAL OOF GROSS

	1987
Australia	–
Austria	–
Belgium	8.1
Canada	0.0
Denmark	0.1
Finland	–
France	0.0
Germany	22.6
Ireland	–
Italy	28.5
Japan	165.0
Netherlands	–
New Zealand	–
Norway	–
Sweden	–
Switzerland	–
United Kingdom	–
United States	15.0
TOTAL	*239.3*
MULTILATERAL	*377.1*
ARAB COUNTRIES	*–*
E.E.C.+ MEMBERS	*59.3*
TOTAL	**616.4**

1988	1989	1990	1987	1988	1989	1990

10. ODA COMMITMENTS

1988	1989	1990	1987	1988	1989	1990
30.4	21.9	28.6	7.3	71.4	25.2	30.8
0.2	0.2	0.3	0.2	0.2	0.2	0.3
1.4	1.7	4.9	6.2	2.6	1.7	4.9
25.0	23.2	28.7	32.1	24.0	96.1	5.2
4.4	0.8	3.3	–	–	13.7	2.7
0.7	1.1	1.1	0.1	0.1	0.3	18.7
2.4	9.4	34.0	2.8	9.4	40.8	33.0
35.7	36.4	51.8	34.8	61.1	83.0	65.2
0.0	0.0	0.0	0.1	0.0	0.0	0.0
1.2	12.5	14.9	0.9	5.7	9.6	80.2
667.5	432.4	770.1	578.8	1305.7	694.1	1057.0
26.9	26.7	22.0	21.6	15.8	28.0	32.9
0.9	1.3	1.6	0.8	0.9	–	1.2
4.7	4.5	3.9	4.0	2.8	–	4.1
2.9	0.7	1.0	3.4	2.6	0.4	4.4
1.7	1.8	9.4	1.1	15.6	15.4	1.0
1.9	19.5	9.0	0.4	1.9	24.3	5.4
140.0	206.0	253.0	329.7	139.1	371.1	514.5
947.8	*800.0*	*1237.6*	*1024.2*	*1658.8*	*1403.8*	*1861.4*
–	–	–	–	–	–	–
–	–	–	–	–	–	–
41.5	50.2	128.5	1.9	177.8	137.5	236.8
–	–	–	–	–	–	–
4.8	7.2	7.2	24.7	4.6	36.3	36.3
–	–	–	–	–	–	–
3.0	1.0	–	–	–	–	–
–	–	–	–	–	–	–
0.4	1.1	3.2	–	–	–	–
–	–	–	–	–	–	–
–	–	–	23.3	22.0	33.3	41.8
6.1	8.4	8.8	–	–	–	–
1.5	1.8	1.9	–	–	–	–
4.2	6.9	7.4	–	–	–	–
–	–	–	–	–	–	–
1.4	3.1	2.7	–	–	–	–
6.4	8.7	13.0	–	–	–	–
2.3	4.3	8.1	–	–	–	–
0.2	0.3	0.8	–	7.3	0.4	–
71.8	*93.0*	*181.6*	*49.9*	*211.7*	*207.4*	*314.9*
0.4	*0.8*	*–*	*–*	*0.2*	*–*	*–*
78.7	*114.0*	*147.2*	*91.3*	*101.1*	*237.3*	*260.5*
1020.1	*893.8*	*1419.1*	*1074.1*	*1870.7*	*1611.2*	*2176.2*

11. TECH. COOP. GRANTS

1988	1989	1990	1987	1988	1989	1990
30.4	21.9	28.6	4.9	8.9	15.4	24.9
0.2	0.2	0.3	0.2	0.2	0.2	0.3
1.4	1.7	4.9	0.5	0.2	0.1	3.2
25.0	23.2	28.7	–	1.0	1.3	2.6
0.2	0.0	3.3	0.1	0.6	0.0	1.8
0.7	1.1	1.1	0.1	–	0.8	–
1.0	1.7	3.6	0.9	1.0	1.3	2.7
31.1	23.7	36.4	21.3	22.8	16.6	22.3
0.0	0.0	0.0	0.1	0.0	0.0	0.0
1.2	12.5	4.3	0.5	0.6	6.5	3.9
131.1	176.1	153.1	44.9	60.7	60.7	62.0
25.9	26.4	22.0	8.8	8.3	8.0	11.0
0.9	1.3	1.6	0.6	0.4	–	0.6
2.2	4.5	3.9	0.6	1.3	0.3	0.4
2.9	0.7	1.0	0.9	1.9	0.6	0.7
1.7	1.8	9.4	0.0	0.2	–	–
1.9	18.9	8.6	0.4	1.8	2.0	1.6
110.0	207.0	232.0	23.0	52.0	46.0	67.0
367.7	*522.6*	*542.8*	*107.8*	*162.0*	*159.7*	*205.0*
34.7	*46.8*	*57.6*	*22.7*	*22.1*	*30.2*	*39.1*
0.2	*0.4*	*–*	*–*	*–*	*–*	*–*
67.4	*92.0*	*90.3*	*33.4*	*36.9*	*34.5*	*46.6*
402.6	*569.8*	*600.3*	*130.5*	*184.1*	*189.9*	*244.1*

12. TOTAL OOF NET

1988	1989	1990	1987	1988	1989	1990
0.7	2.6	0.3	-1.0	-1.1	2.0	0.0
–	–	–	–	–	–	–
41.6	6.0	66.5	7.7	41.6	6.0	66.5
1.3	0.7	0.2	-3.2	0.7	0.3	0.2
0.4	0.0	–	-0.4	0.3	0.0	-0.5
–	–	–	–	–	–	–
40.5	2.6	–	-1.8	40.5	2.6	–
14.9	16.8	72.5	17.7	9.4	15.7	37.8
–	–	30.7	23.9	–	–	26.8
98.6	241.9	109.4	154.8	90.0	232.7	93.5
0.8	0.9	0.6	–	0.8	0.9	0.6
–	–	–	–	–	–	–
–	–	–	–	–	–	–
–	–	10.3	-0.8	-0.9	-0.8	9.5
226.0	81.0	199.0	-4.0	212.0	71.0	175.0
424.7	*352.6*	*489.5*	*192.8*	*393.3*	*330.4*	*409.4*
385.5	*623.6*	*855.5*	*110.7*	*41.1*	*214.4*	*494.6*
–	*–*	*–*	*–*	*–*	*–*	*–*
98.1	*26.3*	*180.5*	*46.3*	*91.7*	*24.4*	*140.7*
810.2	*976.2*	*1345.0*	*303.5*	*434.4*	*544.8*	*904.0*

13. ODF COMMITMENTS: BY PURPOSE %

	1987	1988	1989	1990
Education	0	4	0	–
Health	2	1	3	–
Other Social Infrastr.	22	9	2	–
Water Sanitat. Sewage	0	1	6	–
Energy	15	10	11	–
Telecommunications	0	2	1	–
Transportation	2	10	6	–
Agriculture	1	19	7	–
Extractive Industries	–	0	0	–
Manufacturing	–	0	2	–
Trade Banking Tourism	0	3	26	–
Technical Cooperation	13	10	9	–
Multisector Aid	0	4	2	–
Programme	39	15	25	–
Debt Reorganisation	2	7	0	–
Food Aid	4	3	1	–
Emergency Aid	0	0	0	–
Unspecified	0	1	0	–
TOTAL	100	100	100	

14. GRANT ELEMENT OF ODA %

DAC COUNTRIES

	1987	1988	1989	1990
Australia	100.0	100.0	100.0	–
Austria	100.0	100.0	100.0	–
Belgium	100.0	100.0	100.0	–
Canada	100.0	100.0	100.0	–
Denmark	–	–	100.0	–
Finland	100.0	100.0	100.0	–
France	100.0	63.2	70.3	–
Germany	94.2	80.4	79.5	–
Ireland	100.0	100.0	100.0	–
Italy	100.0	100.0	100.0	–
Japan	58.1	59.8	66.1	–
Netherlands	100.0	100.0	100.0	–
New Zealand	100.0	100.0	–	–
Norway	100.0	34.1	–	–
Sweden	100.0	100.0	100.0	–
Switzerland	100.0	100.0	100.0	–
United Kingdom	100.0	100.0	100.0	–
United States	100.0	90.9	100.0	–
TOTAL	*76.1*	*66.5*	*81.5*	*–*
MULTILATERAL	*94.1*	*76.3*	*84.5*	*–*
ARAB COUNTRIES	*–*	*100.0*	*–*	*–*
E.E.C.+ MEMBERS	*97.7*	*84.6*	*90.4*	*–*
TOTAL	*77.0*	*67.7*	*81.9*	*–*

15. OTHER AGGREGATES

OFFICIAL COMMITMENTS:

	1987	1988	1989	1990
TOTAL BILATERAL	1471.2	1967.4	2242.1	2416.6
of which:				
Arab Countries	–	0.2	–	–
C.E.E.C.	–	–	–	–
TOTAL MULTILATERAL	435.4	980.6	1575.6	1750.9
TOTAL BIL.& MULTIL.	1906.6	2948.0	3817.7	4167.5
of which:				
ODA Grants	580.8	523.8	845.1	873.8
ODA Loans	493.3	1346.9	766.1	1302.4

DISBURSEMENTS:

DAC COUNTRIES COMBINED

OFFICIAL & PRIVATE

	1987	1988	1989	1990
GROSS:				
Contractual Lending	566.0	998.4	724.8	1330.8
Export Credits, Total	90.2	2.4	185.2	230.4
Export Credits, Priv.	46.3	-3.5	102.5	154.9
NET:				
Contractual Lending	319.1	581.9	452.4	901.2
Export Credits Total	-126.0	-253.7	-41.5	-38.4
PRIVATE SECTOR NET	-225.6	21.8	-173.5	-82.5
Direct Investment	77.7	215.1	379.9	312.6
Portfolio Investment	-169.0	36.8	-448.3	-337.8
Export Credits	-134.3	-230.1	-105.1	-57.3

MARKET BORROWING:

CHANGE IN CLAIMS

	1987	1988	1989	1990
Banks	-436.0	-1834.0	-2541.0	-383.0

MEMORANDUM ITEM:

	1987	1988	1989	1990
C.E.E.C. (Gross)	–	–	–	–

	1987	1988	1989	1990	1987	1988	1989	1990		1987
1. TOTAL RECEIPTS NET					**4. TOTAL ODA NET**				**7. TOTAL ODA GROSS**	
DAC COUNTRIES										
Australia	–	–	–	–	–	–	–	–	Australia	–
Austria	2.4	2.7	2.4	7.2	2.4	2.7	2.4	7.2	Austria	2.4
Belgium	34.3	30.8	25.1	43.2	33.5	29.1	26.7	43.4	Belgium	33.5
Canada	6.0	7.6	12.7	13.8	6.0	7.6	12.7	13.8	Canada	6.0
Denmark	0.0	0.5	1.0	1.8	0.0	0.6	1.0	1.8	Denmark	0.0
Finland	1.1	1.1	1.7	0.2	1.1	1.1	1.7	0.2	Finland	1.1
France	41.6	23.9	15.9	32.2	31.8	22.1	17.8	33.9	France	33.2
Germany	22.1	23.3	30.7	33.0	22.0	25.0	27.2	31.8	Germany	22.0
Ireland	0.2	0.2	0.1	0.1	0.2	0.2	0.1	0.1	Ireland	0.2
Italy	2.2	0.9	1.5	1.3	2.2	0.9	1.5	1.3	Italy	2.2
Japan	7.6	10.0	19.2	10.4	7.6	10.0	16.5	13.8	Japan	8.0
Netherlands	6.8	8.5	7.1	10.5	6.6	7.2	5.6	10.7	Netherlands	6.6
New Zealand	–	–	–	–	–	–	–	–	New Zealand	–
Norway	0.2	0.1	–	0.0	0.2	0.1	–	0.0	Norway	0.2
Sweden	0.6	0.4	–	0.1	0.6	0.4	–	0.1	Sweden	0.6
Switzerland	9.4	12.8	9.1	10.2	9.4	12.8	9.1	10.2	Switzerland	9.4
United Kingdom	-0.4	0.4	-0.2	0.8	0.3	0.5	0.5	0.9	United Kingdom	0.3
United States	14.0	17.0	9.0	13.0	14.0	17.0	9.0	13.0	United States	14.0
TOTAL	*148.0*	*140.1*	*135.1*	*177.8*	*137.8*	*137.2*	*131.6*	*182.2*	*TOTAL*	*139.6*
MULTILATERAL										
AF.D.F.	20.6	20.7	16.4	18.5	20.6	20.7	16.4	18.5	AF.D.F.	20.7
AF.D.B.	-0.2	-0.3	-0.3	-0.5	–	–	–	–	AF.D.B.	–
AS.D.B	–	–	–	–	–	–	–	–	AS.D.B	–
CAR.D.B.	–	–	–	–	–	–	–	–	CAR.D.B.	–
E.E.C.	20.6	39.1	32.5	32.5	20.6	39.1	32.5	32.5	E.E.C.	20.6
IBRD	–	–	–	–	–	–	–	–	IBRD	–
IDA	38.4	24.0	26.0	21.0	38.4	24.0	26.0	21.0	IDA	39.0
I.D.B.	–	–	–	–	–	–	–	–	I.D.B.	–
IFAD	3.7	2.6	1.0	3.4	3.7	2.6	1.0	3.4	IFAD	3.9
I.F.C.	–	-0.5	0.0	-0.5	–	–	–	–	I.F.C.	–
IMF TRUST FUND	–	–	–	–	–	–	–	–	IMF TRUST FUND	–
U.N. AGENCIES	–	–	–	–	–	–	–	–	U.N. AGENCIES	–
UNDP	7.6	10.2	9.0	12.3	7.6	10.2	9.0	12.3	UNDP	7.6
UNTA	1.6	1.1	1.4	0.9	1.6	1.1	1.4	0.9	UNTA	1.6
UNICEF	1.4	2.0	2.3	2.8	1.4	2.0	2.3	2.8	UNICEF	1.4
UNRWA	–	–	–	–	–	–	–	–	UNRWA	–
WFP	1.8	1.6	1.0	2.0	1.8	1.6	1.0	2.0	WFP	1.8
UNHCR	0.8	3.9	1.5	1.5	0.8	3.9	1.5	1.5	UNHCR	0.8
Other Multilateral	3.6	4.8	5.1	4.0	3.6	4.8	5.1	4.0	Other Multilateral	3.6
Arab Agencies	1.3	2.0	-1.3	–	1.3	2.0	-1.3	–	Arab Agencies	3.1
TOTAL	*101.0*	*111.2*	*94.7*	*98.0*	*101.2*	*112.0*	*95.0*	*98.9*	*TOTAL*	*103.9*
ARAB COUNTRIES	***5.7***	***12.4***	***6.0***	***5.9***	***5.7***	***2.7***	***6.0***	***5.9***	***ARAB COUNTRIES***	***7.5***
E.E.C.+ MEMBERS	*127.4*	*127.6*	*113.6*	*155.5*	*117.2*	*124.7*	*112.8*	*156.4*	*E.E.C.+ MEMBERS*	*118.6*
TOTAL	*254.8*	*263.7*	*235.8*	*281.7*	*244.8*	*251.9*	*232.6*	*287.0*	*TOTAL*	*251.1*
2. ODA LOANS GROSS					**5. ODA LOANS NET**				**8. GRANTS**	
DAC COUNTRIES										
Australia	–	–	–	–	–	–	–	–	Australia	–
Austria	–	–	–	3.3	–	–	–	3.3	Austria	2.4
Belgium	–	–	–	–	–	–	–	–	Belgium	33.5
Canada	–	–	–	–	–	–	–	–	Canada	6.0
Denmark	–	–	–	–	–	–	–	–	Denmark	0.0
Finland	–	–	–	–	–	–	–	–	Finland	1.1
France	22.0	13.1	7.7	5.7	20.6	11.5	6.0	2.5	France	11.2
Germany	–	–	–	–	–	–	–	–	Germany	22.0
Ireland	–	–	–	–	–	–	–	–	Ireland	0.2
Italy	–	–	–	–	–	–	–	–	Italy	2.2
Japan	–	–	0.8	–	-0.4	-0.4	0.2	-0.5	Japan	8.0
Netherlands	–	–	–	–	–	–	–	–	Netherlands	6.6
New Zealand	–	–	–	–	–	–	–	–	New Zealand	–
Norway	–	–	–	–	–	–	–	–	Norway	0.2
Sweden	–	–	–	–	–	–	–	–	Sweden	0.6
Switzerland	–	–	–	–	–	-0.1	–	–	Switzerland	9.4
United Kingdom	–	–	–	–	–	–	–	–	United Kingdom	0.3
United States	–	–	–	–	–	–	–	–	United States	14.0
TOTAL	*22.0*	*13.1*	*8.5*	*9.0*	*20.2*	*11.0*	*6.2*	*5.2*	*TOTAL*	*117.6*
MULTILATERAL	*67.9*	*53.6*	*46.5*	*46.1*	*65.2*	*50.1*	*42.1*	*41.1*	*MULTILATERAL*	*36.0*
ARAB COUNTRIES	***7.5***	***4.6***	***8.3***	***6.9***	***5.7***	***2.7***	***6.0***	***5.9***	***ARAB COUNTRIES***	***0.1***
E.E.C.+ MEMBERS	*23.3*	*13.9*	*7.8*	*5.8*	*21.9*	*12.2*	*6.1*	*2.6*	*E.E.C.+ MEMBERS*	*95.3*
TOTAL	*97.4*	*71.3*	*63.3*	*62.1*	*91.1*	*63.7*	*54.2*	*52.3*	*TOTAL*	*153.7*
3. TOTAL OFFICIAL GROSS					**6. TOTAL OFFICIAL NET**				**9. TOTAL OOF GROSS**	
DAC COUNTRIES										
Australia	–	–	–	–	–	–	–	–	Australia	–
Austria	2.4	2.7	2.4	7.2	2.4	2.7	2.4	7.2	Austria	–
Belgium	33.5	29.1	26.7	43.4	33.5	29.1	26.7	43.4	Belgium	–
Canada	6.0	7.6	12.7	13.8	6.0	7.6	12.7	13.8	Canada	–
Denmark	0.0	0.6	1.0	1.8	0.0	0.5	1.0	1.8	Denmark	–
Finland	1.1	1.1	1.7	0.2	1.1	1.1	1.7	0.2	Finland	–
France	33.2	23.7	19.6	37.2	31.8	22.1	17.8	33.9	France	–
Germany	22.0	25.0	27.2	31.8	22.0	25.0	27.2	31.8	Germany	–
Ireland	0.2	0.2	0.1	0.1	0.2	0.2	0.1	0.1	Ireland	–
Italy	2.2	0.9	1.5	1.3	2.2	0.9	1.5	1.3	Italy	–
Japan	8.0	10.4	17.1	14.4	7.6	10.0	16.5	13.8	Japan	–
Netherlands	6.6	7.2	5.6	10.7	6.6	7.2	5.6	10.7	Netherlands	–
New Zealand	–	–	–	–	–	–	–	–	New Zealand	–
Norway	0.2	0.1	–	0.0	0.2	0.1	–	0.0	Norway	–
Sweden	0.6	0.4	–	0.1	0.6	0.4	–	0.1	Sweden	–
Switzerland	9.4	12.9	9.1	10.2	9.4	12.8	9.1	10.2	Switzerland	–
United Kingdom	0.3	0.5	0.5	0.9	0.3	0.5	0.5	0.9	United Kingdom	–
United States	14.0	17.0	9.0	13.0	14.0	17.0	9.0	13.0	United States	–
TOTAL	*139.6*	*139.4*	*133.9*	*186.0*	*137.8*	*137.1*	*131.6*	*182.1*	*TOTAL*	*–*
MULTILATERAL	*103.9*	*115.5*	*99.5*	*102.2*	*101.0*	*111.2*	*94.7*	*98.0*	*MULTILATERAL*	*–*
ARAB COUNTRIES	***7.5***	***14.3***	***8.3***	***6.9***	***5.7***	***12.4***	***6.0***	***5.9***	***ARAB COUNTRIES***	***–***
E.E.C.+ MEMBERS	*118.6*	*126.3*	*114.6*	*159.7*	*117.2*	*124.5*	*112.8*	*156.4*	*E.E.C.+ MEMBERS*	*–*
TOTAL	*251.1*	*269.2*	*241.7*	*295.1*	*244.6*	*260.6*	*232.3*	*286.0*	*TOTAL*	*–*

10. ODA COMMITMENTS

1988	1989	1990	1987	1988	1989	1990
–	–	–	–	–	–	–
2.7	2.4	7.2	1.2	6.3	5.6	13.2
29.1	26.7	43.4	37.3	21.1	26.7	43.4
7.6	12.7	13.8	22.0	8.7	25.8	17.1
0.6	1.0	1.8	–	–	–	0.3
1.1	1.7	0.2	4.1	1.1	0.0	0.4
23.7	19.6	37.2	34.4	11.9	14.0	33.4
25.0	27.2	31.8	37.8	30.5	32.4	50.7
0.2	0.1	0.1	0.2	0.2	0.1	0.1
0.9	1.5	1.3	5.6	0.8	0.6	1.2
10.4	17.1	14.4	5.2	17.1	39.0	8.5
7.2	5.6	10.7	3.7	4.1	7.3	11.3
–	–	–	–	–	–	–
0.1	–	0.0	0.2	–	–	–
0.4	–	0.1	0.6	0.4	–	–
12.9	9.1	10.2	18.3	17.7	11.2	9.3
0.5	0.5	0.9	0.3	0.5	0.5	0.9
17.0	9.0	13.0	17.1	13.1	7.5	13.2
139.4	*133.9*	*186.0*	*187.9*	*133.4*	*170.7*	*202.8*
21.0	16.7	19.4	24.6	–	9.3	27.0
–	–	–	–	–	–	–
–	–	–	–	–	–	–
39.1	32.5	32.5	68.0	31.4	34.4	34.4
–	–	–	–	–	–	–
25.0	27.0	22.0	36.5	–	52.0	57.0
–	–	–	–	–	–	–
2.6	1.0	3.5	0.2	11.6	–	9.0
–	–	–	–	–	–	–
–	–	–	–	–	–	–
–	–	–	16.7	23.6	20.3	23.4
10.2	9.0	12.3	–	–	–	–
1.1	1.4	0.9	–	–	–	–
2.0	2.3	2.8	–	–	–	–
–	–	–	–	–	–	–
1.6	1.0	2.0	–	–	–	–
3.9	1.5	1.5	–	–	–	–
4.8	5.1	4.0	–	–	–	–
4.2	2.0	1.3	7.3	3.5	9.5	5.0
115.5	*99.4*	*102.2*	*153.3*	*70.0*	*125.5*	*155.9*
4.6	*8.3*	*6.9*	*10.8*	–	–	*10.3*
126.3	*114.6*	*159.7*	*187.2*	*100.4*	*116.0*	*175.6*
259.5	*241.7*	*295.0*	*351.9*	*203.4*	*296.2*	*369.0*

11. TECH. COOP. GRANTS

1988	1989	1990	1987	1988	1989	1990
–	–	–	–	–	–	–
2.7	2.4	3.9	1.7	1.6	0.4	0.9
29.1	26.7	43.4	24.1	15.9	17.4	19.0
7.6	12.7	13.8	–	3.4	5.4	5.5
0.6	1.0	1.8	0.0	–	0.0	–
1.1	1.7	0.2	1.1	0.1	–	–
10.6	11.8	31.5	8.2	7.9	7.2	8.4
25.0	27.2	31.8	16.7	17.1	18.7	21.8
0.2	0.1	0.1	0.1	0.2	0.1	–
0.9	1.5	1.3	1.8	0.3	0.7	0.2
10.4	16.3	14.4	0.8	1.4	2.8	2.5
7.2	5.6	10.7	2.5	2.8	3.2	3.7
–	–	–	–	–	–	–
0.1	–	0.0	–	–	–	–
0.4	–	0.1	–	–	–	–
12.9	9.1	10.2	3.2	3.3	–	–
0.5	0.5	0.9	0.2	0.3	0.3	0.5
17.0	9.0	13.0	6.0	9.0	7.0	8.0
126.3	*125.4*	*177.0*	*66.3*	*63.3*	*63.2*	*70.6*
61.9	*52.9*	*56.0*	*17.0*	*24.4*	*19.3*	*21.5*
–	–	–	–	–	–	–
112.4	*106.7*	*153.9*	*55.6*	*46.7*	*47.6*	*53.7*
188.2	*178.4*	*233.0*	*83.3*	*87.6*	*82.5*	*92.1*

12. TOTAL OOF NET

1988	1989	1990	1987	1988	1989	1990
–	–	–	–	–	–	–
–	–	–	–	–	–	–
–	–	–	–	–	–	–
–	–	–	–	-0.1	–	–
–	–	–	–	–	–	–
–	–	–	–	–	–	0.0
–	–	–	–	–	–	–
–	–	–	–	–	–	–
–	–	–	–	–	–	–
–	–	–	–	–	–	–
–	–	–	–	–	–	–
–	–	–	–	–	–	–
–	–	–	–	–	–	–
–	–	0.0	–	–	–	0.0
–	–	–	–	–	–	–
–	–	–	–	–	–	–
–	–	0.0	–	-0.1	–	-0.1
–	0.1	0.1	-0.2	-0.8	-0.3	-0.9
9.7	–	–	–	*9.7*	–	–
–	–	–	–	-0.1	–	0.0
9.7	*0.1*	*0.0*	*-0.2*	*8.7*	*-0.3*	*-1.0*

13. ODF COMMITMENTS: BY PURPOSE %

	1987	1988	1989	1990
Education	11	0	10	–
Health	1	1	2	–
Other Social Infrastr.	4	5	15	–
Water Sanitat. Sewage	18	6	0	–
Energy	3	0	10	–
Telecommunications	2	2	0	–
Transportation	4	28	4	–
Agriculture	13	7	12	–
Extractive Industries	–	–	0	–
Manufacturing	0	0	0	–
Trade Banking Tourism	0	–	6	–
Technical Cooperation	35	41	29	–
Multisector Aid	5	2	4	–
Programme	1	2	6	–
Debt Reorganisation	0	0	1	–
Food Aid	3	3	1	–
Emergency Aid	0	1	–	–
Unspecified	–	1	0	–
TOTAL	100	100	100	–

14. GRANT ELEMENT OF ODA %

DAC COUNTRIES	1987	1988	1989	1990
Australia	–	–	–	–
Austria	100.0	100.0	100.0	–
Belgium	100.0	100.0	100.0	–
Canada	100.0	100.0	100.0	–
Denmark	–	–	–	–
Finland	100.0	100.0	100.0	–
France	69.5	100.0	93.0	–
Germany	100.0	100.0	100.0	–
Ireland	100.0	100.0	100.0	–
Italy	100.0	100.0	100.0	–
Japan	100.0	100.0	85.3	–
Netherlands	100.0	100.0	100.0	–
New Zealand	–	–	–	–
Norway	100.0	–	–	–
Sweden	100.0	100.0	–	–
Switzerland	100.0	100.0	100.0	–
United Kingdom	100.0	100.0	100.0	–
United States	100.0	100.0	100.0	–
TOTAL	*94.4*	*100.0*	*96.1*	–
MULTILATERAL	*90.3*	*92.7*	*84.2*	–
ARAB COUNTRIES	*51.5*	–	–	–
E.E.C.+ MEMBERS	*94.4*	*100.0*	*99.0*	–
TOTAL	*91.3*	*97.2*	*91.0*	–

15. OTHER AGGREGATES

OFFICIAL COMMITMENTS:	1987	1988	1989	1990
TOTAL BILATERAL	199.0	133.4	175.1	213.1
of which:				
Arab Countries	11.1	–	–	10.3
C.E.E.C.	–	–	–	–
TOTAL MULTILATERAL	153.3	70.2	130.8	155.9
TOTAL BIL.& MULTIL.	352.2	203.6	305.8	369.0
of which:				
ODA Grants	249.5	188.4	186.9	232.7
ODA Loans	102.4	15.1	109.3	136.3

DISBURSEMENTS:

DAC COUNTRIES COMBINED

OFFICIAL & PRIVATE	1987	1988	1989	1990
GROSS:				
Contractual Lending	23.3	15.8	10.3	7.5
Export Credits, Total	1.3	2.7	1.8	-1.5
Export Credits, Priv.	1.3	2.7	1.8	-1.5
NET:				
Contractual Lending	20.0	10.3	6.3	-0.4
Export Credits Total	-0.2	-0.5	0.1	-5.6
PRIVATE SECTOR NET	10.2	3.0	3.5	-4.3
Direct Investment	-0.4	3.7	3.4	-0.1
Portfolio Investment	10.7	-0.1	0.0	1.4
Export Credits	-0.2	-0.5	0.1	-5.6

MARKET BORROWING:

CHANGE IN CLAIMS	1987	1988	1989	1990
Banks	16.0	–	10.0	-6.0

MEMORANDUM ITEM:

	1987	1988	1989	1990
C.E.E.C. (Gross)	–	–	–	–

1. TOTAL RECEIPTS NET

DAC COUNTRIES	1987	1988	1989	1990
Australia	–	–	–	–
Austria	0.7	1.4	1.1	1.5
Belgium	5.0	4.9	6.7	16.2
Canada	25.5	23.9	28.7	31.6
Denmark	9.6	3.0	1.5	1.6
Finland	0.7	2.1	4.6	1.8
France	175.7	77.8	231.2	187.1
Germany	14.3	21.3	18.1	81.2
Ireland	–	–	–	–
Italy	48.5	50.2	73.0	48.3
Japan	23.8	35.0	78.8	81.5
Netherlands	16.1	22.8	12.4	26.9
New Zealand	–	–	–	–
Norway	-0.8	-2.3	-2.1	-1.4
Sweden	–	0.7	–	0.0
Switzerland	12.7	4.5	10.5	12.5
United Kingdom	1.7	0.7	0.3	-2.2
United States	49.0	35.0	42.0	59.0
TOTAL	*382.4*	*280.9*	*506.9*	*545.5*
MULTILATERAL				
AF.D.F.	36.1	23.3	5.4	25.9
AF.D.B.	-4.9	-1.5	4.6	0.0
AS.D.B	–	–	–	–
CAR.D.B.	–	–	–	–
E.E.C.	70.6	61.2	17.5	17.5
IBRD	-6.6	-10.0	-10.0	-13.0
IDA	114.7	57.0	48.0	112.0
I.D.B.	–	–	–	–
IFAD	2.1	1.8	0.7	1.4
I.F.C.	2.7	7.1	0.0	3.8
IMF TRUST FUND	–	–	–	–
U.N. AGENCIES	–	–	–	–
UNDP	8.9	10.0	8.3	11.6
UNTA	1.2	0.8	1.1	1.4
UNICEF	3.0	2.7	3.8	5.1
UNRWA	–	–	–	–
WFP	4.1	11.8	9.0	11.7
UNHCR	–	0.9	2.5	4.9
Other Multilateral	5.6	4.6	5.4	8.2
Arab Agencies	4.6	-0.7	-6.2	–
TOTAL	*242.1*	*168.9*	*89.9*	*190.4*
ARAB COUNTRIES	*35.4*	*17.7*	*9.2*	*3.5*
E.E.C.+ MEMBERS	*341.5*	*241.9*	*360.8*	*376.5*
TOTAL	**659.9**	**467.4**	**606.0**	**739.3**

4. TOTAL ODA NET

DAC COUNTRIES	1987	1988	1989	1990
Australia	–	–	–	–
Austria	0.7	1.4	1.1	1.5
Belgium	5.8	6.4	8.4	10.1
Canada	25.9	24.4	29.0	30.9
Denmark	5.8	1.0	1.3	1.5
Finland	0.5	0.8	1.7	1.8
France	154.1	167.3	255.0	230.3
Germany	15.2	19.2	20.2	80.4
Ireland	–	–	–	–
Italy	45.1	49.6	72.3	45.8
Japan	25.3	36.3	79.4	82.1
Netherlands	16.0	18.5	10.4	24.2
New Zealand	–	–	–	–
Norway	0.8	1.1	1.1	2.2
Sweden	–	0.7	–	0.0
Switzerland	12.7	4.5	10.5	12.5
United Kingdom	2.8	1.7	5.0	1.5
United States	48.0	35.0	41.0	57.0
TOTAL	*358.8*	*367.8*	*536.4*	*581.7*
MULTILATERAL				
AF.D.F.	36.1	23.3	5.4	25.9
AF.D.B.	–	–	–	–
AS.D.B	–	–	–	–
CAR.D.B.	–	–	–	–
E.E.C.	73.9	64.8	21.2	21.2
IBRD	0.4	–	–	–
IDA	114.7	57.0	48.0	112.0
I.D.B.	–	–	–	–
IFAD	2.1	1.8	0.7	1.4
I.F.C.	–	–	–	–
IMF TRUST FUND	–	–	–	–
U.N. AGENCIES	–	–	–	–
UNDP	8.9	10.0	8.3	11.6
UNTA	1.2	0.8	1.1	1.4
UNICEF	3.0	2.7	3.8	5.1
UNRWA	–	–	–	–
WFP	4.1	11.8	9.0	11.7
UNHCR	–	0.9	2.5	4.9
Other Multilateral	5.6	4.6	5.4	8.2
Arab Agencies	2.5	-0.8	-3.6	–
TOTAL	*252.4*	*176.8*	*101.7*	*203.3*
ARAB COUNTRIES	*30.4*	*24.0*	*11.6*	*3.5*
E.E.C.+ MEMBERS	*318.8*	*328.4*	*393.8*	*415.0*
TOTAL	**641.6**	**568.6**	**649.6**	**788.4**

7. TOTAL ODA GROSS

	1987
Australia	–
Austria	0.7
Belgium	5.8
Canada	25.9
Denmark	9.4
Finland	0.5
France	174.8
Germany	16.0
Ireland	–
Italy	45.4
Japan	25.3
Netherlands	16.1
New Zealand	–
Norway	0.8
Sweden	–
Switzerland	12.7
United Kingdom	3.0
United States	48.0
TOTAL	*384.3*
AF.D.F.	36.3
AF.D.B.	–
AS.D.B	–
CAR.D.B.	–
E.E.C.	74.4
IBRD	0.4
IDA	116.3
I.D.B.	–
IFAD	2.1
I.F.C.	–
IMF TRUST FUND	–
U.N. AGENCIES	–
UNDP	8.9
UNTA	1.2
UNICEF	3.0
UNRWA	–
WFP	4.1
UNHCR	–
Other Multilateral	5.6
Arab Agencies	9.1
TOTAL	*261.4*
ARAB COUNTRIES	*33.3*
E.E.C.+ MEMBERS	*344.8*
TOTAL	**679.0**

2. ODA LOANS GROSS

DAC COUNTRIES	1987	1988	1989	1990
Australia	–	–	–	–
Austria	–	–	–	–
Belgium	–	–	0.7	3.6
Canada	–	–	–	–
Denmark	5.7	0.1	0.8	–
Finland	0.1	–	0.9	–
France	105.9	118.1	147.2	53.0
Germany	4.7	7.3	7.3	14.2
Ireland	–	–	–	–
Italy	18.3	15.8	12.0	15.0
Japan	–	–	30.5	22.0
Netherlands	1.3	2.9	–	0.4
New Zealand	–	–	–	–
Norway	–	–	–	–
Sweden	–	–	–	–
Switzerland	0.3	–	0.0	–
United Kingdom	–	–	–	–
United States	8.0	7.0	5.0	5.0
TOTAL	*144.4*	*151.2*	*204.4*	*113.3*
MULTILATERAL	*166.0*	*96.9*	*64.5*	*152.7*
ARAB COUNTRIES	*30.8*	*21.3*	*14.3*	*6.1*
E.E.C.+ MEMBERS	*137.7*	*153.1*	*174.6*	*92.8*
TOTAL	**341.2**	**269.4**	**283.2**	**272.1**

5. ODA LOANS NET

DAC COUNTRIES	1987	1988	1989	1990
Australia	–	–	–	–
Austria	–	–	–	–
Belgium	–	–	0.7	3.6
Canada	–	–	–	-12.9
Denmark	2.1	0.1	0.8	-4.1
Finland	0.1	–	0.9	–
France	85.3	98.7	128.4	33.1
Germany	3.9	6.0	7.1	-142.6
Ireland	–	–	–	–
Italy	18.0	15.5	9.0	13.2
Japan	–	–	30.1	22.0
Netherlands	1.2	2.9	-0.1	0.4
New Zealand	–	–	–	–
Norway	–	–	–	–
Sweden	–	–	–	–
Switzerland	0.3	0.0	0.0	0.0
United Kingdom	-0.1	-0.1	-0.1	-0.1
United States	8.0	7.0	5.0	5.0
TOTAL	*118.9*	*130.1*	*181.8*	*-82.4*
MULTILATERAL	*157.0*	*89.6*	*56.1*	*142.7*
ARAB COUNTRIES	*27.9*	*18.7*	*9.5*	*3.5*
E.E.C.+ MEMBERS	*111.7*	*131.4*	*151.4*	*-90.8*
TOTAL	**303.8**	**238.4**	**247.4**	**63.7**

8. GRANTS

	1987
Australia	–
Austria	0.7
Belgium	5.8
Canada	25.9
Denmark	3.7
Finland	0.4
France	68.9
Germany	11.3
Ireland	–
Italy	27.1
Japan	25.3
Netherlands	14.8
New Zealand	–
Norway	0.8
Sweden	–
Switzerland	12.4
United Kingdom	3.0
United States	40.0
TOTAL	*239.9*
MULTILATERAL	*95.3*
ARAB COUNTRIES	*2.5*
E.E.C.+ MEMBERS	*207.1*
TOTAL	**337.8**

3. TOTAL OFFICIAL GROSS

DAC COUNTRIES	1987	1988	1989	1990
Australia	–	–	–	–
Austria	0.7	1.4	1.1	1.5
Belgium	5.8	6.4	8.4	10.8
Canada	25.9	24.4	29.0	44.6
Denmark	13.4	3.0	1.6	5.7
Finland	0.5	0.8	1.7	1.8
France	233.4	188.1	302.7	273.6
Germany	16.0	20.4	20.5	237.5
Ireland	–	–	–	–
Italy	46.7	51.6	79.0	55.0
Japan	25.3	36.3	79.7	82.1
Netherlands	16.1	21.4	10.7	25.6
New Zealand	–	–	–	–
Norway	0.8	1.1	1.1	2.2
Sweden	–	0.7	–	0.0
Switzerland	12.7	4.5	10.5	12.5
United Kingdom	3.0	1.8	5.1	1.6
United States	49.0	37.0	44.0	62.0
TOTAL	*449.3*	*398.8*	*595.1*	*816.6*
MULTILATERAL	*272.8*	*199.8*	*117.4*	*222.4*
ARAB COUNTRIES	*38.3*	*26.5*	*16.4*	*6.1*
E.E.C.+ MEMBERS	*408.7*	*358.0*	*450.1*	*632.0*
TOTAL	**760.4**	**625.2**	**728.8**	**1045.2**

6. TOTAL OFFICIAL NET

DAC COUNTRIES	1987	1988	1989	1990
Australia	–	–	–	–
Austria	0.7	1.4	1.1	1.5
Belgium	5.3	5.6	8.4	10.5
Canada	25.5	23.9	28.7	31.6
Denmark	9.8	3.0	1.5	1.6
Finland	0.5	0.8	1.7	1.8
France	184.9	127.0	258.3	249.5
Germany	15.2	19.1	20.2	80.7
Ireland	–	–	–	–
Italy	46.3	50.7	72.9	50.4
Japan	25.3	36.3	79.4	82.1
Netherlands	15.9	21.2	10.7	25.3
New Zealand	–	–	–	–
Norway	0.8	1.1	1.1	2.2
Sweden	–	0.7	–	0.0
Switzerland	12.7	4.5	10.5	12.5
United Kingdom	2.8	1.7	5.0	1.5
United States	49.0	35.0	42.0	59.0
TOTAL	*394.6*	*331.9*	*541.5*	*610.1*
MULTILATERAL	*242.1*	*168.9*	*89.9*	*190.4*
ARAB COUNTRIES	*35.4*	*17.7*	*9.2*	*3.5*
E.E.C.+ MEMBERS	*350.7*	*289.5*	*394.6*	*436.9*
TOTAL	**672.0**	**518.5**	**640.6**	**803.9**

9. TOTAL OOF GROSS

	1987
Australia	–
Austria	–
Belgium	0.0
Canada	0.1
Denmark	4.0
Finland	–
France	58.7
Germany	–
Ireland	–
Italy	1.3
Japan	–
Netherlands	–
New Zealand	–
Norway	–
Sweden	–
Switzerland	–
United Kingdom	–
United States	1.0
TOTAL	*65.0*
MULTILATERAL	*11.4*
ARAB COUNTRIES	*5.0*
E.E.C.+ MEMBERS	*64.0*
TOTAL	**81.4**

1988	1989	1990	1987	1988	1989	1990
			10. ODA COMMITMENTS			
–	–	–	–	–	–	–
1.4	1.1	1.5	1.0	1.7	1.7	1.8
6.4	8.4	10.1	6.3	2.8	8.4	10.1
24.4	29.0	43.8	33.8	47.6	24.5	16.0
1.0	1.3	5.6	3.6	–	–	–
0.8	1.7	1.8	0.1	7.1	0.6	2.6
186.6	273.9	250.2	216.0	176.3	179.5	149.1
20.4	20.5	237.3	40.5	28.4	20.8	90.3
–	–	–	–	–	–	–
50.0	75.3	47.6	85.0	46.1	65.0	46.2
36.3	79.7	82.1	35.5	74.3	57.9	100.8
18.5	10.5	24.1	16.9	16.8	25.1	15.6
–	–	–	–	–	–	–
1.1	1.1	2.2	0.7	–	2.0	0.8
0.7	–	0.0	–	0.7	–	–
4.5	10.5	12.5	8.6	12.2	6.9	1.3
1.8	5.1	1.6	1.7	1.8	5.3	1.9
35.0	41.0	57.0	47.2	36.9	54.5	44.6
388.9	*559.0*	*777.4*	*496.8*	*452.6*	*452.3*	*480.9*
23.4	5.5	26.4	63.4	–	4.1	56.5
–	–	–	–	–	–	–
–	–	–	–	–	–	–
65.4	22.1	22.1	194.0	49.8	6.3	6.3
–	–	–	–	–	–	–
59.0	50.0	115.0	151.6	63.0	87.0	127.0
–	–	–	–	–	–	–
1.8	0.7	1.8	–	11.6	7.2	0.2
–	–	–	–	–	–	–
–	–	–	–	–	–	–
–	–	–	22.7	30.7	30.0	42.8
10.0	8.3	11.6	–	–	–	–
0.8	1.1	1.4	–	–	–	–
2.7	3.8	5.1	–	–	–	–
–	–	–	–	–	–	–
11.8	9.0	11.7	–	–	–	–
0.9	2.5	4.9	–	–	–	–
4.6	5.4	8.2	–	–	–	–
3.9	1.8	2.9	6.7	16.2	29.1	–
184.1	*110.1*	*211.0*	*438.4*	*171.4*	*163.7*	*232.8*
26.5	*16.4*	*6.1*	*0.0*	*19.0*	*8.0*	*27.6*
350.1	*417.0*	*598.6*	*563.8*	*322.0*	*310.5*	*319.5*
599.6	*685.4*	*994.6*	*935.2*	*643.0*	*624.1*	*741.3*
			11. TECH. COOP. GRANTS			
–	–	–	–	–	–	–
1.4	1.1	1.5	0.7	1.4	0.1	0.4
6.4	7.7	6.5	4.8	3.6	3.8	3.1
24.4	29.0	43.8	–	2.3	5.5	5.2
0.9	0.6	5.6	0.1	0.2	0.2	0.0
0.8	0.7	1.8	–	–	–	0.1
68.6	126.7	197.2	59.8	56.8	57.5	79.5
13.2	13.1	223.0	9.0	9.7	9.5	12.7
–	–	–	–	–	–	–
34.1	63.3	32.6	7.8	2.6	2.3	3.7
36.3	49.3	60.1	6.2	7.8	9.1	10.0
15.6	10.5	23.7	1.8	2.7	2.7	13.2
–	–	–	–	–	–	–
1.1	1.1	2.2	–	0.1	0.1	0.2
0.7	–	0.0	–	0.7	–	0.0
4.5	10.5	12.5	4.2	3.0	–	–
1.8	5.1	1.6	1.1	1.4	1.3	1.4
28.0	36.0	52.0	16.0	18.0	19.0	19.0
237.7	*354.6*	*664.2*	*111.7*	*110.3*	*110.9*	*148.4*
87.2	*45.6*	*58.3*	*19.8*	*20.6*	*21.1*	*31.1*
5.2	*2.1*	–	–	–	–	–
197.0	*242.5*	*505.8*	*85.7*	*78.7*	*77.2*	*113.6*
330.1	*402.2*	*722.5*	*131.5*	*130.9*	*132.0*	*179.5*
			12. TOTAL OOF NET			
–	–	–	–	–	–	–
–	0.0	0.8	-0.5	-0.7	0.0	0.4
–	–	0.8	-0.4	-0.6	-0.3	0.7
2.0	0.3	0.1	3.9	2.0	0.2	0.1
–	–	–	–	–	–	–
1.4	28.9	23.4	30.8	-40.3	3.3	19.2
–	0.0	0.3	0.0	-0.1	0.0	0.3
–	–	–	–	–	–	–
1.6	3.6	7.4	1.1	1.1	0.6	4.6
–	–	–	–	–	–	–
2.9	0.3	1.4	-0.1	2.7	0.3	1.1
–	–	–	–	–	–	–
–	–	–	–	–	–	–
–	–	–	–	–	–	–
–	–	–	–	–	–	–
2.0	3.0	5.0	1.0	–	1.0	2.0
9.9	*36.1*	*39.2*	*35.8*	*-35.9*	*5.1*	*28.3*
15.7	*7.4*	*11.4*	*-10.3*	*-7.9*	*-11.7*	*-12.9*
–	–	–	*5.0*	*-6.3*	*-2.4*	–
7.9	*33.1*	*33.4*	*32.0*	*-38.9*	*0.8*	*22.0*
25.6	*43.4*	*50.6*	*30.5*	*-50.1*	*-9.0*	*15.5*

13. ODF COMMITMENTS: BY PURPOSE %

	1987	1988	1989	1990
Education	2	0	1	–
Health	0	1	2	–
Other Social Infrastr.	5	14	13	–
Water Sanitat. Sewage	7	8	4	–
Energy	9	0	2	–
Telecommunications	4	0	–	–
Transportation	1	5	8	–
Agriculture	17	19	7	–
Extractive Industries	–	–	–	–
Manufacturing	4	1	5	–
Trade Banking Tourism	0	6	9	–
Technical Cooperation	20	21	24	–
Multisector Aid	0	1	0	–
Programme	26	21	23	–
Debt Reorganisation	1	1	0	–
Food Aid	3	2	2	–
Emergency Aid	0	0	0	–
Unspecified	–	–	–	–
TOTAL	100	100	100	–

14. GRANT ELEMENT OF ODA %

DAC COUNTRIES

	1987	1988	1989	1990
Australia	–	–	–	–
Austria	100.0	100.0	100.0	–
Belgium	100.0	100.0	100.0	–
Canada	100.0	100.0	100.0	–
Denmark	100.0	–	–	–
Finland	–	100.0	100.0	–
France	56.6	78.3	80.3	–
Germany	87.2	65.2	92.4	–
Ireland	–	–	–	–
Italy	92.5	99.6	93.8	–
Japan	100.0	81.6	99.4	–
Netherlands	93.0	100.0	100.0	–
New Zealand	–	–	–	–
Norway	100.0	–	100.0	–
Sweden	–	100.0	–	–
Switzerland	100.0	100.0	100.0	–
United Kingdom	100.0	100.0	100.0	–
United States	93.1	95.6	97.0	–
TOTAL	*78.9*	*85.9*	*90.8*	–
MULTILATERAL	*91.4*	*84.6*	*78.8*	–
ARAB COUNTRIES	*100.0*	*71.5*	*54.2*	–
E.E.C.+ MEMBERS	*81.7*	*85.2*	*87.1*	–
TOTAL	*84.5*	*85.1*	*87.6*	–

15. OTHER AGGREGATES

OFFICIAL COMMITMENTS:

	1987	1988	1989	1990
TOTAL BILATERAL	609.0	519.0	550.5	596.0
of which:				
Arab Countries	5.0	19.0	8.0	27.6
C.E.E.C.	–	–	–	–
TOTAL MULTILATERAL	451.8	171.4	175.0	232.8
TOTAL BIL.& MULTIL.	1060.7	690.3	725.4	828.8
of which:				
ODA Grants	500.4	372.5	353.0	421.6
ODA Loans	434.8	270.4	271.1	319.8

DISBURSEMENTS:

DAC COUNTRIES COMBINED

	1987	1988	1989	1990
OFFICIAL & PRIVATE				
GROSS:				
Contractual Lending	200.9	150.7	210.9	129.4
Export Credits, Total	-8.4	-10.4	-29.5	-22.0
Export Credits, Priv.	-8.4	-10.4	-29.4	-22.8
NET:				
Contractual Lending	140.6	77.3	148.4	-88.0
Export Credits Total	-14.4	-18.5	-40.8	-34.0
PRIVATE SECTOR NET	-12.2	-51.1	-34.6	-64.6
Direct Investment	2.4	-0.6	10.1	2.7
Portfolio Investment	-0.5	-33.5	-6.3	-33.7
Export Credits	-14.0	-16.9	-38.4	-33.6

MARKET BORROWING:

CHANGE IN CLAIMS

	1987	1988	1989	1990
Banks	329.0	-49.0	-289.0	-74.0

MEMORANDUM ITEM:

	1987	1988	1989	1990
C.E.E.C. (Gross)	–	–	–	–

	1987	1988	1989	1990	1987	1988	1989	1990	1987
1. TOTAL RECEIPTS NET					**4. TOTAL ODA NET**				**7. TOTAL ODA GROSS**
DAC COUNTRIES									
Australia	1.0	1.5	2.0	1.1	1.0	1.5	2.0	1.1	Australia 1.0
Austria	0.3	–	0.0	0.0	0.3	–	0.0	0.0	Austria 0.3
Belgium	0.0	3.3	-7.1	12.0	0.9	0.6	0.4	5.2	Belgium 0.9
Canada	0.2	0.1	0.3	0.2	0.2	0.1	0.3	0.2	Canada 0.2
Denmark	-0.1	–	–	–	–	–	–	–	Denmark –
Finland	–	–	–	–	–	–	–	–	Finland –
France	14.4	4.0	2.7	10.3	10.0	8.1	4.4	12.7	France 10.7
Germany	0.3	0.6	1.8	1.9	0.5	0.4	1.2	1.5	Germany 0.5
Ireland	–	–	–	–	–	–	–	–	Ireland –
Italy	0.2	0.2	0.3	0.6	0.2	0.2	0.1	0.5	Italy 0.2
Japan	1.3	2.3	0.0	0.8	1.1	2.3	0.3	0.8	Japan 1.1
Netherlands	-0.4	0.0	0.1	0.3	0.1	0.1	0.2	0.3	Netherlands 0.1
New Zealand	0.0	0.0	0.0	0.0	0.0	0.0	0.0	0.0	New Zealand 0.0
Norway	1.0	0.3	0.2	0.2	1.0	0.3	0.2	0.2	Norway 1.0
Sweden	–	0.1	2.3	0.2	–	0.1	0.1	0.0	Sweden –
Switzerland	0.1	0.2	0.0	0.2	0.1	0.2	0.0	0.2	Switzerland 0.1
United Kingdom	-6.0	-7.0	2.6	0.9	2.7	3.0	1.8	1.0	United Kingdom 2.8
United States	1.0	1.0	4.0	8.0	1.0	1.0	4.0	8.0	United States 1.0
TOTAL	*13.1*	*6.6*	*9.3*	*36.7*	*18.8*	*17.8*	*15.1*	*31.6*	*TOTAL* *19.6*
MULTILATERAL									
AF.D.F.	1.5	1.0	2.0	0.5	1.5	1.0	2.0	0.5	AF.D.F. 1.5
AF.D.B.	3.2	0.7	1.3	-0.9	–	–	–	–	AF.D.B. –
AS.D.B	–	–	–	–	–	–	–	–	AS.D.B –
CAR.D.B.	–	–	–	–	–	–	–	–	CAR.D.B. –
E.E.C.	2.1	0.5	1.3	1.3	2.1	0.5	1.3	1.3	E.E.C. 2.1
IBRD	–	1.0	–	–	–	–	–	–	IBRD –
IDA	–	–	–	–	–	–	–	–	IDA –
I.D.B.	–	–	–	–	–	–	–	–	I.D.B. –
IFAD	–	–	–	–	–	–	–	–	IFAD –
I.F.C.	2.6	–	0.3	–	–	–	–	–	I.F.C. –
IMF TRUST FUND	–	–	–	–	–	–	–	–	IMF TRUST FUND –
U.N. AGENCIES	–	–	–	–	–	–	–	–	U.N. AGENCIES –
UNDP	0.5	0.4	0.3	0.3	0.5	0.4	0.3	0.3	UNDP 0.5
UNTA	0.4	0.5	0.5	0.6	0.4	0.5	0.5	0.6	UNTA 0.4
UNICEF	0.0	–	0.1	–	0.0	–	0.1	–	UNICEF 0.0
UNRWA	–	–	–	–	–	–	–	–	UNRWA –
WFP	–	0.1	0.3	0.5	–	0.1	0.3	0.5	WFP –
UNHCR	–	–	–	–	–	–	–	–	UNHCR –
Other Multilateral	0.2	0.2	0.3	0.4	0.2	0.2	0.3	0.4	Other Multilateral 0.2
Arab Agencies	-0.2	-0.9	-1.2	–	-0.1	-0.1	-0.1	–	Arab Agencies –
TOTAL	*10.3*	*3.4*	*5.2*	*2.6*	*4.7*	*2.5*	*4.8*	*3.5*	*TOTAL* *4.7*
ARAB COUNTRIES	***-0.7***	***0.2***	***0.0***	***-0.2***	***0.7***	***0.4***	***0.0***	***–***	***ARAB COUNTRIES*** ***0.7***
E.E.C.+ MEMBERS	*10.4*	*1.6*	*1.7*	*27.3*	*16.3*	*12.8*	*9.4*	*22.3*	*E.E.C.+ MEMBERS* *17.1*
TOTAL	***22.8***	***10.1***	***14.5***	***39.2***	***24.2***	***20.7***	***19.8***	***35.1***	***TOTAL*** ***25.1***
2. ODA LOANS GROSS					**5. ODA LOANS NET**				**8. GRANTS**
DAC COUNTRIES									
Australia	–	–	–	–	–	–	–	–	Australia 1.0
Austria	–	–	–	–	–	–	–	–	Austria 0.3
Belgium	–	–	–	5.1	–	–	–	5.1	Belgium 0.9
Canada	–	–	–	–	–	–	–	–	Canada 0.2
Denmark	–	–	–	–	–	–	–	–	Denmark –
Finland	–	–	–	–	–	–	–	–	Finland –
France	5.9	4.5	1.5	7.7	5.1	4.2	1.0	7.3	France 4.9
Germany	0.0	–	–	0.9	0.0	–	0.0	0.8	Germany 0.4
Ireland	–	–	–	–	–	–	–	–	Ireland –
Italy	–	–	–	–	–	–	–	–	Italy 0.2
Japan	–	–	–	–	–	–	–	–	Japan 1.1
Netherlands	–	–	–	–	–	–	–	–	Netherlands 0.1
New Zealand	–	–	–	–	–	–	–	–	New Zealand 0.0
Norway	–	–	–	–	–	–	–	–	Norway 1.0
Sweden	–	–	–	–	–	–	–	–	Sweden –
Switzerland	–	–	–	–	–	–	–	–	Switzerland 0.1
United Kingdom	0.9	0.6	0.0	0.2	0.9	0.5	0.0	-0.5	United Kingdom 1.9
United States	–	–	–	–	–	–	–	–	United States 1.0
TOTAL	*6.8*	*5.0*	*1.6*	*14.0*	*6.0*	*4.7*	*1.0*	*12.8*	*TOTAL* *12.8*
MULTILATERAL	*2.1*	*1.0*	*3.1*	*1.6*	*2.0*	*0.8*	*2.7*	*1.2*	*MULTILATERAL* *2.6*
ARAB COUNTRIES	***0.5***	***0.4***	***0.4***	***–***	***0.5***	***0.4***	***0.0***	***–***	***ARAB COUNTRIES*** ***0.2***
E.E.C.+ MEMBERS	*7.4*	*5.0*	*2.4*	*14.8*	*6.6*	*4.6*	*1.7*	*13.5*	*E.E.C.+ MEMBERS* *9.8*
TOTAL	***9.4***	***6.4***	***5.1***	***15.6***	***8.6***	***5.9***	***3.7***	***13.9***	***TOTAL*** ***15.7***
3. TOTAL OFFICIAL GROSS					**6. TOTAL OFFICIAL NET**				**9. TOTAL OOF GROSS**
DAC COUNTRIES									
Australia	1.0	1.5	2.0	1.1	1.0	1.5	2.0	1.1	Australia –
Austria	0.3	–	0.0	0.0	0.3	–	0.0	0.0	Austria –
Belgium	1.0	0.6	0.5	5.2	1.0	0.6	0.5	5.2	Belgium 0.1
Canada	0.2	0.1	0.3	0.2	0.2	0.1	0.3	0.2	Canada –
Denmark	–	–	–	–	–	–	–	–	Denmark –
Finland	–	–	–	–	–	–	–	–	Finland –
France	10.8	9.8	5.4	13.6	10.1	9.5	4.8	12.0	France 0.1
Germany	0.5	0.4	2.1	1.5	0.5	0.4	2.0	1.3	Germany –
Ireland	–	–	–	–	–	–	–	–	Ireland –
Italy	0.2	0.2	0.1	0.5	0.2	0.2	0.1	0.5	Italy –
Japan	1.1	2.3	0.3	0.8	1.1	2.3	0.3	0.8	Japan –
Netherlands	0.1	0.1	0.2	0.3	0.1	0.1	0.2	0.3	Netherlands –
New Zealand	0.0	0.0	0.0	0.0	0.0	0.0	0.0	0.0	New Zealand –
Norway	1.0	0.3	0.2	0.2	1.0	0.3	0.2	0.2	Norway –
Sweden	–	0.1	0.1	0.0	–	0.1	0.1	0.0	Sweden –
Switzerland	0.1	0.2	0.0	0.2	0.1	0.2	0.0	0.2	Switzerland –
United Kingdom	2.8	3.1	1.9	1.7	2.5	2.7	1.6	0.9	United Kingdom –
United States	1.0	1.0	4.0	8.0	1.0	1.0	4.0	8.0	United States –
TOTAL	*19.8*	*19.6*	*16.9*	*33.3*	*18.7*	*18.9*	*16.0*	*30.7*	*TOTAL* *0.2*
MULTILATERAL	*11.6*	*5.4*	*8.7*	*5.8*	*10.3*	*3.4*	*5.2*	*2.6*	*MULTILATERAL* *6.8*
ARAB COUNTRIES	***0.7***	***0.4***	***0.5***	***–***	***-0.7***	***0.2***	***0.0***	***-0.2***	***ARAB COUNTRIES*** ***–***
E.E.C.+ MEMBERS	*17.3*	*14.7*	*11.3*	*24.2*	*16.3*	*13.9*	*10.3*	*21.5*	*E.E.C.+ MEMBERS* *0.2*
TOTAL	***32.1***	***25.4***	***26.2***	***39.1***	***28.4***	***22.5***	***21.2***	***33.2***	***TOTAL*** ***7.0***

1988	1989	1990	1987	1988	1989	1990

10. ODA COMMITMENTS

1988	1989	1990	1987	1988	1989	1990
1.5	2.0	1.1	0.5	1.2	1.1	1.8
–	0.0	0.0	–	–	0.0	0.0
0.6	0.4	5.2	1.0	0.1	0.4	5.2
0.1	0.3	0.2	0.1	0.5	0.2	0.1
–	–	–	–	–	–	–
–	–	–	–	–	–	–
8.4	4.9	13.1	4.9	4.5	9.4	13.3
0.4	1.3	1.5	0.5	1.5	0.5	1.9
–	–	–	–	–	–	–
0.2	0.1	0.5	0.1	0.0	0.1	0.4
2.3	0.3	0.8	2.8	0.5	0.6	5.0
0.1	0.2	0.3	0.1	0.1	0.2	0.3
0.0	0.0	0.0	0.0	0.0	–	–
0.3	0.2	0.2	0.8	0.1	–	0.6
0.1	0.1	0.0	–	0.1	–	–
0.2	0.0	0.2	0.3	–	0.2	–
3.1	1.9	1.7	1.8	2.5	1.8	1.4
1.0	4.0	8.0	2.9	3.5	3.4	3.3
18.1	*15.6*	*32.8*	*15.8*	*14.6*	*17.8*	*33.2*
1.0	2.3	0.8	–	50.2	2.8	–
–	–	–	–	–	–	–
–	–	–	–	–	–	–
–	–	–	–	–	–	–
0.5	1.3	1.3	1.5	0.2	5.2	5.2
–	–	–	–	–	–	–
–	–	–	–	–	–	–
–	–	–	–	–	–	1.2
–	–	–	–	–	–	–
–	–	–	1.1	1.2	1.6	1.7
0.4	0.3	0.3	–	–	–	–
0.5	0.5	0.6	–	–	–	–
–	0.1	–	–	–	–	–
–	–	–	–	–	–	–
0.1	0.3	0.5	–	–	–	–
–	–	–	–	–	–	–
0.2	0.3	0.4	–	–	–	–
–	–	–	–	–	–	–
2.7	*5.2*	*3.9*	*2.6*	*51.6*	*9.6*	*8.1*
0.4	*0.4*	–	–	–	–	–
13.2	*10.0*	*23.6*	*9.8*	*8.9*	*17.5*	*27.7*
21.2	*21.3*	*36.6*	*18.4*	*66.2*	*27.4*	*41.4*

11. TECH. COOP. GRANTS

1988	1989	1990	1987	1988	1989	1990
1.5	2.0	1.1	0.9	1.0	0.9	0.8
–	0.0	0.0	0.3	–	0.0	0.0
0.6	0.4	0.1	0.4	0.5	0.4	0.1
0.1	0.3	0.2	–	–	–	0.0
–	–	–	–	–	–	–
3.9	3.4	5.4	4.0	3.0	2.9	4.1
0.4	1.3	0.6	0.4	0.4	1.3	0.6
–	–	–	–	–	–	–
0.2	0.1	0.5	0.2	0.2	0.1	0.0
2.3	0.3	0.8	0.3	0.3	0.3	0.6
0.1	0.2	0.3	0.1	0.1	0.2	0.3
0.0	0.0	0.0	0.0	0.0	–	0.0
0.3	0.2	0.2	0.2	0.3	–	–
0.1	0.1	0.0	–	0.1	0.1	–
0.2	0.0	0.2	0.0	0.1	–	–
2.5	1.8	1.4	1.8	2.5	1.8	1.4
1.0	4.0	8.0	–	–	–	1.0
13.1	*14.1*	*18.8*	*8.5*	*8.5*	*7.9*	*9.0*
1.7	*2.1*	*2.2*	*1.2*	*1.2*	*1.3*	*1.3*
–	–	–	–	–	–	–
8.2	*7.6*	*8.8*	*6.8*	*6.8*	*6.6*	*6.5*
14.8	*16.2*	*21.1*	*9.6*	*9.6*	*9.1*	*10.3*

12. TOTAL OOF NET

1988	1989	1990	1987	1988	1989	1990
–	–	–	–	–	–	–
–	0.1	0.1	0.1	–	0.1	0.1
–	–	–	–	–	–	–
–	–	–	–	–	–	–
1.5	0.4	0.5	0.1	1.5	0.4	-0.7
–	0.8	–	–	–	0.8	-0.1
–	–	–	–	–	–	–
–	–	–	–	–	–	–
–	–	–	–	–	–	–
–	–	–	–	–	–	–
–	–	–	–	–	–	–
–	–	–	–	–	–	–
–	–	–	-0.2	-0.3	-0.3	0.0
1.5	*1.3*	*0.6*	*-0.1*	*1.2*	*1.0*	*-0.8*
2.7	*3.5*	*1.9*	*5.7*	*0.9*	*0.4*	*-0.9*
–	*0.1*	–	*-1.4*	*-0.3*	*0.0*	*-0.2*
1.5	*1.3*	*0.6*	*-0.1*	*1.2*	*1.0*	*-0.8*
4.2	*4.9*	*2.5*	*4.2*	*1.8*	*1.3*	*-1.9*

13. ODF COMMITMENTS: BY PURPOSE %

	1987	1988	1989	1990
Education	1	3	25	–
Health	1	–	1	–
Other Social Infrastr.	0	0	4	–
Water Sanitat. Sewage	–	–	8	–
Energy	–	–	19	–
Telecommunications	–	3	–	–
Transportation	–	–	2	–
Agriculture	13	1	0	–
Extractive Industries	–	1	–	–
Manufacturing	–	–	–	–
Trade Banking Tourism	20	–	–	–
Technical Cooperation	45	53	28	–
Multisector Aid	–	7	1	–
Programme	11	31	11	–
Debt Reorganisation	–	–	–	–
Food Aid	–	1	1	–
Emergency Aid	–	–	–	–
Unspecified	8	–	–	–
TOTAL	100	100	100	–

14. GRANT ELEMENT OF ODA %

DAC COUNTRIES	1987	1988	1989	1990
Australia	100.0	100.0	100.0	–
Austria	–	–	100.0	–
Belgium	100.0	100.0	100.0	–
Canada	100.0	100.0	100.0	–
Denmark	–	–	–	–
Finland	–	–	–	–
France	74.9	100.0	63.5	–
Germany	100.0	100.0	100.0	–
Ireland	–	–	–	–
Italy	100.0	100.0	100.0	–
Japan	100.0	100.0	100.0	–
Netherlands	100.0	100.0	100.0	–
New Zealand	100.0	100.0	–	–
Norway	100.0	100.0	–	–
Sweden	–	100.0	–	–
Switzerland	100.0	–	100.0	–
United Kingdom	100.0	100.0	100.0	–
United States	100.0	100.0	100.0	–
TOTAL	*89.6*	*100.0*	*80.8*	–
MULTILATERAL	*100.0*	*100.0*	*97.6*	–
ARAB COUNTRIES	–	–	–	–
E.E.C.+ MEMBERS	*84.7*	*100.0*	*78.5*	–
TOTAL	*90.9*	*100.0*	*85.4*	–

15. OTHER AGGREGATES

	1987	1988	1989	1990
OFFICIAL COMMITMENTS:				
TOTAL BILATERAL	17.6	17.4	18.5	34.1
of which:				
Arab Countries	–	–	–	–
C.E.E.C.	–	2.0	–	–
TOTAL MULTILATERAL	13.8	52.6	18.4	9.8
TOTAL BIL.& MULTIL.	31.4	70.0	36.9	43.9
of which:				
ODA Grants	18.4	17.9	17.4	23.4
ODA Loans	–	50.2	9.9	18.0
DISBURSEMENTS:				
DAC COUNTRIES COMBINED				
OFFICIAL & PRIVATE				
GROSS:				
Contractual Lending	11.5	1.0	2.8	27.8
Export Credits, Total	4.6	-5.4	0.0	13.4
Export Credits, Priv.	4.6	-5.4	0.0	13.4
NET:				
Contractual Lending	0.0	-3.5	-4.5	22.2
Export Credits Total	-5.8	-9.4	-6.4	10.3
PRIVATE SECTOR NET	-5.6	-12.4	-6.7	6.0
Direct Investment	-0.1	-7.0	4.0	-1.5
Portfolio Investment	0.3	4.0	-4.3	-2.9
Export Credits	-5.8	-9.4	-6.4	10.3
MARKET BORROWING:				
CHANGE IN CLAIMS				
Banks	9.0	5.0	12.0	-16.0
MEMORANDUM ITEM:				
C.E.E.C. (Gross)	2.8	2.0	–	–

1. TOTAL RECEIPTS NET / 4. TOTAL ODA NET / 7. TOTAL ODA GROSS

	1. TOTAL RECEIPTS NET				4. TOTAL ODA NET				7. TOTAL ODA GROSS
	1987	1988	1989	1990	1987	1988	1989	1990	1987
DAC COUNTRIES									
Australia	5.0	-2.7	-2.8	-2.8	0.1	0.1	0.1	0.1	0.1
Austria	0.0	0.0	0.0	–	0.0	0.0	0.0	–	0.0
Belgium	2.3	0.1	0.7	-0.4	0.1	0.1	0.0	0.1	0.1
Canada	0.3	0.2	0.3	0.3	0.3	0.2	0.3	0.3	0.3
Denmark	6.9	1.3	0.5	2.4	6.9	1.3	0.5	2.4	6.9
Finland	0.0	–	0.0	0.1	0.0	–	0.0	0.1	0.0
France	5.3	5.7	3.1	4.0	1.2	2.6	2.4	2.5	2.3
Germany	20.5	20.4	23.8	11.1	11.1	21.3	24.4	11.6	11.4
Ireland	0.1	0.1	0.0	0.1	0.1	0.1	0.0	0.1	0.1
Italy	9.4	15.6	20.6	17.9	3.3	5.6	16.6	7.9	3.8
Japan	3.4	4.0	11.1	6.0	3.4	4.0	11.1	6.0	3.4
Netherlands	0.9	1.7	1.1	1.2	1.2	1.7	1.1	1.2	1.2
New Zealand	–	0.0	–	–	–	0.0	–	–	–
Norway	0.5	0.5	0.3	-2.8	0.5	0.6	0.3	0.5	0.5
Sweden	–	–	0.2	0.2	–	–	0.2	0.2	–
Switzerland	–	0.0	–	0.0	–	0.0	–	0.0	–
United Kingdom	7.6	12.0	11.0	4.0	3.6	6.0	4.1	4.0	4.3
United States	11.0	9.0	10.0	2.0	12.0	9.0	11.0	3.0	12.0
TOTAL	*73.2*	*67.9*	*79.9*	*43.2*	*43.8*	*52.5*	*72.2*	*39.9*	*46.4*
MULTILATERAL									
AF.D.F.	–	10.6	0.6	-0.3	–	10.6	0.6	-0.3	–
AF.D.B.	–	-4.1	–	-0.9	–	–	–	–	–
AS.D.B	–	–	–	–	–	–	–	–	–
CAR.D.B.	–	–	–	–	–	–	–	–	–
E.E.C.	4.7	17.0	13.8	13.8	4.7	17.0	13.8	13.8	4.7
IBRD	0.0	–	–	–	–	–	–	–	–
IDA	2.2	1.0	–	–	2.2	1.0	–	–	2.2
I.D.B.	–	–	–	–	–	–	–	–	–
IFAD	3.1	–	–	1.4	3.1	–	–	1.4	3.1
I.F.C.	–	–	–	–	–	–	–	–	–
IMF TRUST FUND	–	–	–	–	–	–	–	–	–
U.N. AGENCIES	–	–	–	–	–	–	–	–	–
UNDP	6.0	6.5	7.7	6.5	6.0	6.5	7.7	6.5	6.0
UNTA	0.8	0.8	1.0	0.7	0.8	0.8	1.0	0.7	0.8
UNICEF	1.7	1.8	2.2	2.7	1.7	1.8	2.2	2.7	1.7
UNRWA	–	–	–	–	–	–	–	–	–
WFP	0.4	0.5	0.6	1.3	0.4	0.5	0.6	1.3	0.4
UNHCR	–	0.2	0.1	2.5	–	0.2	0.1	2.5	–
Other Multilateral	1.3	1.5	1.4	1.8	1.3	1.5	1.4	1.8	1.3
Arab Agencies	0.7	0.0	0.4	–	0.7	0.0	0.4	–	0.8
TOTAL	*20.9*	*35.7*	*27.8*	*29.4*	*21.0*	*39.8*	*27.8*	*30.3*	*21.1*
ARAB COUNTRIES	*3.7*	*10.1*	*0.3*	*–*	*3.7*	*10.1*	*0.3*	*–*	*3.7*
E.E.C.+ MEMBERS	*57.7*	*73.8*	*74.6*	*54.0*	*32.2*	*55.5*	*62.9*	*43.5*	*34.8*
TOTAL	*97.8*	*113.7*	*108.0*	*72.5*	*68.4*	*102.4*	*100.3*	*70.1*	*71.1*

2. ODA LOANS GROSS / 5. ODA LOANS NET / 8. GRANTS

	2. ODA LOANS GROSS				5. ODA LOANS NET				8. GRANTS
	1987	1988	1989	1990	1987	1988	1989	1990	1987
DAC COUNTRIES									
Australia	–	–	–	–	–	–	–	–	0.1
Austria	–	–	–	–	–	–	–	–	0.0
Belgium	–	–	–	–	–	–	–	–	0.1
Canada	–	–	–	–	–	–	–	–	0.3
Denmark	–	–	–	–	–	–	–	–	6.9
Finland	–	–	–	–	–	–	–	–	0.0
France	–	–	–	–	-1.1	–	-0.6	-0.7	2.3
Germany	0.1	–	–	–	-0.2	–	–	–	11.3
Ireland	–	–	–	–	–	–	–	–	0.1
Italy	1.0	–	19.2	5.7	0.5	–	14.3	5.7	2.8
Japan	–	–	2.7	–	0.0	-0.4	1.6	–	3.4
Netherlands	–	–	–	–	–	–	–	–	1.2
New Zealand	–	–	–	–	–	–	–	–	–
Norway	–	–	–	–	–	–	–	–	0.5
Sweden	–	–	–	–	–	–	–	–	–
Switzerland	–	–	–	–	–	–	–	–	–
United Kingdom	–	–	–	–	-0.6	-0.6	-0.5	-0.6	4.3
United States	8.0	4.0	4.0	–	8.0	4.0	4.0	–	4.0
TOTAL	*9.2*	*4.0*	*25.9*	*5.7*	*6.5*	*3.1*	*18.8*	*4.4*	*37.2*
MULTILATERAL	*5.4*	*12.1*	*0.6*	*1.4*	*5.4*	*11.6*	*0.6*	*1.1*	*15.6*
ARAB COUNTRIES	*0.5*	*–*	*0.2*	*–*	*0.5*	*–*	*0.2*	*–*	*3.2*
E.E.C.+ MEMBERS	*1.2*	*–*	*19.2*	*5.7*	*-1.4*	*-0.6*	*13.2*	*4.4*	*33.6*
TOTAL	*15.1*	*16.1*	*26.8*	*7.1*	*12.4*	*14.6*	*19.6*	*5.4*	*56.0*

3. TOTAL OFFICIAL GROSS / 6. TOTAL OFFICIAL NET / 9. TOTAL OOF GROSS

	3. TOTAL OFFICIAL GROSS				6. TOTAL OFFICIAL NET				9. TOTAL OOF GROSS
	1987	1988	1989	1990	1987	1988	1989	1990	1987
DAC COUNTRIES									
Australia	5.8	0.1	0.1	0.1	5.0	-2.7	-2.8	-2.8	5.8
Austria	0.0	0.0	0.0	–	0.0	0.0	0.0	–	–
Belgium	2.8	0.1	0.0	0.1	2.8	0.1	0.0	0.1	2.7
Canada	0.3	0.2	0.3	0.3	0.3	0.2	0.3	0.3	–
Denmark	6.9	1.3	0.5	2.4	6.9	1.3	0.5	2.4	–
Finland	0.0	–	0.0	0.1	0.0	–	0.0	0.1	–
France	7.5	6.2	3.0	3.8	5.8	6.2	2.4	3.1	5.2
Germany	23.4	21.3	24.4	11.6	23.0	21.3	24.4	11.6	11.9
Ireland	0.1	0.1	0.0	0.1	0.1	0.1	0.0	0.1	–
Italy	10.8	5.6	31.7	7.9	9.4	5.6	20.8	7.9	7.0
Japan	3.4	4.4	12.2	6.0	3.4	4.0	11.1	6.0	–
Netherlands	1.2	1.7	1.1	1.2	1.2	1.4	1.1	1.2	–
New Zealand	–	0.0	–	–	–	0.0	–	–	–
Norway	0.5	0.6	0.3	0.5	0.5	0.6	0.3	0.5	–
Sweden	–	–	0.2	0.2	–	–	0.2	0.2	–
Switzerland	–	0.0	–	0.0	–	0.0	–	0.0	–
United Kingdom	4.3	6.6	4.6	4.5	3.6	6.0	4.1	4.0	–
United States	12.0	9.0	11.0	3.0	11.0	9.0	10.0	2.0	–
TOTAL	*78.9*	*57.0*	*89.5*	*41.8*	*72.9*	*53.0*	*72.4*	*36.5*	*32.5*
MULTILATERAL	*21.0*	*40.2*	*27.8*	*30.8*	*20.9*	*35.7*	*27.8*	*29.4*	*–*
ARAB COUNTRIES	*3.7*	*10.1*	*0.3*	*–*	*3.7*	*10.1*	*0.3*	*–*	*–*
E.E.C.+ MEMBERS	*61.6*	*59.7*	*79.1*	*45.4*	*57.4*	*58.8*	*67.1*	*44.1*	*26.8*
TOTAL	*103.6*	*107.4*	*117.6*	*72.5*	*97.5*	*98.9*	*100.5*	*65.9*	*32.5*

1988	1989	1990	1987	1988	1989	1990

10. ODA COMMITMENTS

1988	1989	1990	1987	1988	1989	1990
0.1	0.1	0.1	0.0	0.1	0.1	0.1
0.0	0.0	–	0.0	0.0	0.0	–
0.1	0.0	0.1	0.0	0.1	0.0	0.1
0.2	0.3	0.3	0.2	0.2	0.3	0.3
1.3	0.5	2.4	0.4	–	5.5	–
–	0.0	0.1	–	–	0.0	0.1
2.6	3.0	3.3	8.1	2.4	1.9	1.9
21.3	24.4	11.6	17.3	21.2	9.2	11.5
0.1	0.0	0.1	0.1	0.1	0.0	0.1
5.6	21.6	7.9	16.4	3.0	108.5	2.0
4.4	12.2	6.0	7.3	8.3	9.6	0.6
1.7	1.1	1.2	1.0	1.5	1.1	1.2
0.0	–	–	0.5	0.0	–	–
0.6	0.3	0.5	0.0	–	–	–
–	0.2	0.2	–	–	0.2	–
0.0	–	0.0	–	–	–	–
6.6	4.6	4.5	4.3	6.6	4.6	4.5
9.0	11.0	3.0	12.0	12.6	7.1	14.3
53.4	*79.3*	*41.2*	*67.6*	*56.0*	*147.9*	*36.6*
10.8	0.6	–	–	–	1.4	49.3
–	–	–	–	–	–	–
–	–	–	–	–	–	–
–	–	–	–	–	–	–
17.0	13.8	13.8	29.5	12.0	10.5	10.5
–	–	–	–	–	–	–
1.0	–	–	–	–	–	–
–	–	1.4	–	–	–	–
–	–	–	–	–	–	–
–	–	–	10.2	11.2	13.1	15.4
6.5	7.7	6.5	–	–	–	–
0.8	1.0	0.7	–	–	–	–
1.8	2.2	2.7	–	–	–	–
–	–	–	–	–	–	–
0.5	0.6	1.3	–	–	–	–
0.2	0.1	2.5	–	–	–	–
1.5	1.4	1.8	–	–	–	–
0.3	0.4	0.2	–	0.8	–	–
40.2	*27.8*	*30.8*	*39.8*	*24.0*	*25.0*	*75.2*
10.1	*0.3*	–	*23.0*	–	*10.6*	–
56.1	*69.0*	*44.8*	*77.1*	*46.8*	*141.2*	*31.7*
103.8	*107.4*	*72.0*	*130.3*	*80.0*	*183.5*	*111.8*

11. TECH. COOP. GRANTS

1988	1989	1990	1987	1988	1989	1990
0.1	0.1	0.1	0.1	0.1	0.1	0.1
0.0	0.0	–	0.0	0.0	0.0	–
0.1	0.0	0.1	0.1	0.0	–	–
0.2	0.3	0.3	–	–	–	0.1
1.3	0.5	2.4	0.0	0.2	0.1	0.2
–	0.0	0.1	–	–	–	–
2.6	3.0	3.3	1.4	1.9	1.2	1.3
21.3	24.4	11.6	8.3	8.5	7.8	7.8
0.1	0.0	0.1	0.1	0.1	0.0	0.1
5.6	2.3	2.3	1.0	0.8	0.6	0.8
4.4	9.5	6.0	0.3	0.2	0.5	0.3
1.7	1.1	1.2	1.0	1.0	1.0	1.2
0.0	–	–	–	0.0	–	–
0.6	0.3	0.5	0.0	0.0	0.1	0.1
–	0.2	0.2	–	–	–	–
0.0	–	0.0	–	–	–	–
6.6	4.6	4.5	3.4	5.2	3.3	2.4
5.0	7.0	3.0	2.0	2.0	2.0	1.0
49.4	*53.4*	*35.5*	*17.8*	*20.1*	*16.7*	*15.4*
28.2	*27.2*	*29.4*	*10.7*	*12.7*	*12.5*	*14.2*
10.1	*0.1*	–	–	–	–	–
56.1	*49.7*	*39.1*	*16.3*	*19.8*	*14.0*	*13.8*
87.7	*80.7*	*64.9*	*28.5*	*32.8*	*29.2*	*29.6*

12. TOTAL OOF NET

1988	1989	1990	1987	1988	1989	1990
–	–	–	4.9	-2.7	-2.9	-2.9
–	–	–	–	–	–	–
–	–	–	2.7	–	–	–
–	–	–	–	–	–	–
–	–	–	–	–	–	–
3.6	–	0.6	4.7	3.6	–	0.6
–	–	–	11.9	–	–	–
–	10.2	–	6.0	–	4.1	–
–	–	–	–	-0.3	–	–
–	–	–	–	–	–	–
–	–	–	–	–	–	–
–	–	–	–	–	–	–
–	–	–	–	–	–	–
–	–	–	-1.0	–	-1.0	-1.0
3.6	*10.2*	*0.6*	*29.2*	*0.6*	*0.2*	*-3.4*
–	–	–	*0.0*	*-4.1*	–	*-0.9*
–	–	–	–	–	–	–
3.6	*10.2*	*0.6*	*25.2*	*3.3*	*4.1*	*0.6*
3.6	*10.2*	*0.6*	*29.1*	*-3.5*	*0.2*	*-4.3*

13. ODF COMMITMENTS: BY PURPOSE %

	1987	1988	1989	1990
Education	0	–	–	–
Health	22	–	0	–
Other Social Infrastr.	13	–	0	–
Water Sanitat. Sewage	10	13	0	–
Energy	–	–	61	–
Telecommunications	–	–	–	–
Transportation	3	5	7	–
Agriculture	–	4	0	–
Extractive Industries	–	–	–	–
Manufacturing	–	–	2	–
Trade Banking Tourism	–	–	0	–
Technical Cooperation	22	61	16	–
Multisector Aid	–	–	0	–
Programme	5	–	1	–
Debt Reorganisation	15	1	9	–
Food Aid	9	15	3	–
Emergency Aid	0	–	–	–
Unspecified	–	–	–	–
TOTAL	100	100	100	–

14. GRANT ELEMENT OF ODA %
DAC COUNTRIES

	1987	1988	1989	1990
Australia	100.0	100.0	100.0	–
Austria	100.0	100.0	100.0	–
Belgium	100.0	100.0	100.0	–
Canada	100.0	100.0	100.0	–
Denmark	100.0	–	100.0	–
Finland	–	–	100.0	–
France	100.0	100.0	100.0	–
Germany	89.4	100.0	100.0	–
Ireland	100.0	100.0	100.0	–
Italy	96.2	100.0	65.0	–
Japan	100.0	100.0	83.5	–
Netherlands	100.0	100.0	100.0	–
New Zealand	100.0	100.0	–	–
Norway	100.0	–	–	–
Sweden	–	–	100.0	–
Switzerland	–	–	–	–
United Kingdom	100.0	100.0	–	–
United States	78.3	79.7	100.0	–
TOTAL	*91.6*	*95.4*	*73.3*	–
MULTILATERAL	*100.0*	*98.2*	*100.0*	–
ARAB COUNTRIES	*100.0*	–	*59.8*	–
E.E.C.+ MEMBERS	*96.2*	*100.0*	*73.1*	–
TOTAL	*95.7*	*96.3*	*75.9*	–

15. OTHER AGGREGATES

	1987	1988	1989	1990
OFFICIAL COMMITMENTS:				
TOTAL BILATERAL	125.8	56.0	169.4	36.6
of which:				
Arab Countries	23.0	–	10.6	–
C.E.E.C.	–	–	–	–
TOTAL MULTILATERAL	39.8	24.0	25.0	75.2
TOTAL BIL.& MULTIL.	165.6	80.0	194.4	111.8
of which:				
ODA Grants	115.1	71.3	63.2	53.5
ODA Loans	15.2	8.8	120.3	58.3
DISBURSEMENTS:				
DAC COUNTRIES COMBINED				
OFFICIAL & PRIVATE				
GROSS:				
Contractual Lending	41.4	17.2	40.8	16.3
Export Credits, Total	5.5	9.6	4.7	10.0
Export Credits, Priv.	-0.3	9.6	4.7	10.0
NET:				
Contractual Lending	33.0	13.0	18.4	7.7
Export Credits Total	1.2	6.7	-4.6	2.8
PRIVATE SECTOR NET	0.3	14.8	7.5	6.7
Direct Investment	4.0	6.3	7.4	–
Portfolio Investment	-1.0	-0.9	0.8	0.0
Export Credits	-2.7	9.4	-0.7	6.7
MARKET BORROWING:				
CHANGE IN CLAIMS				
Banks	15.0	-1.0	-13.0	-1.0
MEMORANDUM ITEM:				
C.E.E.C. (Gross)	–	–	–	–

1. TOTAL RECEIPTS NET

DAC COUNTRIES	1987	1988	1989	1990
Australia	-211.6	-40.2	487.7	415.5
Austria	–	-0.3	0.2	0.4
Belgium	72.1	-102.7	57.5	282.1
Canada	1.0	0.5	0.3	0.5
Denmark	–	–	-15.0	3.2
Finland	3.2	0.7	0.9	–
France	142.7	8.0	218.4	6.5
Germany	-69.1	141.5	107.4	-7.1
Ireland	–	–	–	–
Italy	0.8	2.6	32.4	-49.7
Japan	313.0	635.9	1165.8	1068.2
Netherlands	102.3	35.3	–	161.4
New Zealand	0.1	0.1	0.1	1.0
Norway	-1.1	1.3	0.1	3.4
Sweden	-0.3	–	2.9	10.3
Switzerland	–	–	–	–
United Kingdom	270.2	381.9	753.8	36.1
United States	320.0	616.0	168.0	864.0
TOTAL	*943.2*	*1680.7*	*2980.5*	*2795.8*
MULTILATERAL				
AF.D.F.	–	–	–	–
AF.D.B.	–	–	–	–
AS.D.B	-9.6	-9.1	-8.6	-14.4
CAR.D.B.	–	–	–	–
E.E.C.	0.1	–	0.1	0.1
IBRD	-22.2	-15.0	-10.0	-25.0
IDA	–	–	–	–
I.D.B.	–	–	–	–
IFAD	–	–	–	–
I.F.C.	–	–	–	–
IMF TRUST FUND	–	–	–	–
U.N. AGENCIES	–	–	–	–
UNDP	0.5	0.7	0.4	0.5
UNTA	0.4	0.3	0.4	0.7
UNICEF	–	–	–	–
UNRWA	–	–	–	–
WFP	–	–	–	–
UNHCR	–	0.3	0.4	0.3
Other Multilateral	0.0	–	0.0	0.0
Arab Agencies	0.3	–	–	–
TOTAL	*-30.6*	*-22.8*	*-17.3*	*-37.9*
ARAB COUNTRIES	–	–	–	–
E.E.C.+ MEMBERS	*519.1*	*466.6*	*1154.6*	*432.6*
TOTAL	*912.7*	*1657.9*	*2963.2*	*2757.9*

2. ODA LOANS GROSS

DAC COUNTRIES	1987	1988	1989	1990
Australia	–	–	–	–
Austria	–	0.2	–	–
Belgium	–	–	–	–
Canada	–	–	–	–
Denmark	–	–	–	–
Finland	–	–	–	–
France	–	–	–	–
Germany	–	–	75.1	–
Ireland	–	–	–	–
Italy	–	–	–	–
Japan	0.7	0.4	–	–
Netherlands	–	–	–	–
New Zealand	–	–	–	–
Norway	–	–	–	–
Sweden	–	–	–	–
Switzerland	–	–	–	–
United Kingdom	–	–	–	–
United States	–	–	–	–
TOTAL	*0.7*	*0.6*	*75.1*	*–*
MULTILATERAL	–	–	–	–
ARAB COUNTRIES	–	–	–	–
E.E.C.+ MEMBERS	*–*	*–*	*75.1*	*–*
TOTAL	*0.7*	*0.6*	*75.1*	*–*

3. TOTAL OFFICIAL GROSS

DAC COUNTRIES	1987	1988	1989	1990
Australia	3.6	3.7	1.9	2.0
Austria	0.0	0.3	0.1	0.1
Belgium	0.0	–	–	–
Canada	0.6	0.5	0.6	0.6
Denmark	–	–	–	–
Finland	0.0	–	–	–
France	2.9	2.1	2.6	2.4
Germany	4.6	3.8	79.8	4.7
Ireland	–	–	–	–
Italy	–	–	–	–
Japan	18.0	18.8	23.5	227.0
Netherlands	0.0	–	–	–
New Zealand	0.1	0.1	0.1	1.0
Norway	–	–	–	–
Sweden	–	–	–	–
Switzerland	–	–	–	–
United Kingdom	0.4	0.2	0.6	0.5
United States	1.0	1.0	1.0	2.0
TOTAL	*31.3*	*30.5*	*110.2*	*240.3*
MULTILATERAL	*1.3*	*1.4*	*1.3*	*1.5*
ARAB COUNTRIES	–	–	–	–
E.E.C.+ MEMBERS	*8.1*	*6.2*	*83.1*	*7.7*
TOTAL	*32.6*	*31.9*	*111.5*	*241.9*

4. TOTAL ODA NET

DAC COUNTRIES	1987	1988	1989	1990
Australia	3.6	3.7	1.9	2.0
Austria	–	-0.4	0.1	0.1
Belgium	–	–	–	–
Canada	0.6	0.5	0.6	0.6
Denmark	–	–	–	–
Finland	0.0	–	–	–
France	2.9	2.1	2.6	2.4
Germany	4.5	3.6	78.3	0.8
Ireland	–	–	–	–
Italy	–	–	–	–
Japan	11.2	11.2	10.7	-10.4
Netherlands	0.0	–	–	–
New Zealand	0.1	0.1	0.1	1.0
Norway	–	–	–	–
Sweden	–	–	–	–
Switzerland	–	–	–	–
United Kingdom	-1.8	-1.2	-1.5	-1.7
United States	1.0	1.0	1.0	2.0
TOTAL	*22.2*	*20.7*	*93.7*	*-3.2*
AF.D.F.	–	–	–	–
AF.D.B.	–	–	–	–
AS.D.B	-0.2	-0.2	-0.2	-1.4
CAR.D.B.	–	–	–	–
E.E.C.	0.1	–	0.1	0.1
IBRD	–	–	–	–
IDA	–	–	–	–
I.D.B.	–	–	–	–
IFAD	–	–	–	–
I.F.C.	–	–	–	–
IMF TRUST FUND	–	–	–	–
U.N. AGENCIES	–	–	–	–
UNDP	0.5	0.7	0.4	0.5
UNTA	0.4	0.3	0.4	0.7
UNICEF	–	–	–	–
UNRWA	–	–	–	–
WFP	–	–	–	–
UNHCR	–	0.3	0.4	0.3
Other Multilateral	0.0	–	0.0	0.0
Arab Agencies	0.3	–	–	–
TOTAL	*1.1*	*1.2*	*1.1*	*0.2*
ARAB COUNTRIES	–	–	–	–
E.E.C.+ MEMBERS	*5.8*	*4.5*	*79.5*	*1.6*
TOTAL	*23.3*	*21.9*	*94.8*	*-3.0*

5. ODA LOANS NET

DAC COUNTRIES	1987	1988	1989	1990
Australia	–	–	–	–
Austria	0.0	-0.4	–	–
Belgium	–	–	–	–
Canada	–	–	–	–
Denmark	–	–	–	–
Finland	–	–	–	–
France	–	–	–	–
Germany	–	-0.1	74.3	-3.8
Ireland	–	–	–	–
Italy	–	–	–	–
Japan	-6.1	-7.1	-5.6	-24.8
Netherlands	–	–	–	–
New Zealand	–	–	–	–
Norway	–	–	–	–
Sweden	–	–	–	–
Switzerland	–	–	–	–
United Kingdom	-2.1	-1.5	-2.1	-2.2
United States	–	–	–	–
TOTAL	*-8.2*	*-9.1*	*66.7*	*-30.8*
MULTILATERAL	*-0.2*	*-0.2*	*-0.2*	*-1.4*
ARAB COUNTRIES	–	–	–	–
E.E.C.+ MEMBERS	*-2.1*	*-1.5*	*72.2*	*-6.0*
TOTAL	*-8.4*	*-9.3*	*66.5*	*-32.2*

6. TOTAL OFFICIAL NET

DAC COUNTRIES	1987	1988	1989	1990
Australia	3.6	3.7	1.9	2.0
Austria	–	-0.4	0.1	0.1
Belgium	0.0	–	–	–
Canada	0.6	0.5	0.6	0.6
Denmark	–	–	–	–
Finland	0.0	–	–	–
France	2.9	2.1	2.6	2.4
Germany	-24.4	3.7	79.0	0.9
Ireland	–	–	–	–
Italy	–	–	–	–
Japan	11.2	-10.6	-2.4	182.9
Netherlands	0.0	–	–	–
New Zealand	0.1	0.1	0.1	1.0
Norway	–	-0.1	-0.1	-0.1
Sweden	–	–	–	–
Switzerland	–	–	–	–
United Kingdom	-2.2	-1.2	-1.5	-1.7
United States	1.0	1.0	1.0	2.0
TOTAL	*-7.1*	*-1.1*	*81.3*	*190.1*
MULTILATERAL	*-30.6*	*-22.8*	*-17.3*	*-37.9*
ARAB COUNTRIES	–	–	–	–
E.E.C.+ MEMBERS	*-23.6*	*4.6*	*80.2*	*1.7*
TOTAL	*-37.7*	*-23.9*	*64.0*	*152.2*

7. TOTAL ODA GROSS

DAC COUNTRIES	1987
Australia	3.6
Austria	0.0
Belgium	–
Canada	0.6
Denmark	–
Finland	0.0
France	2.9
Germany	4.5
Ireland	–
Italy	–
Japan	18.0
Netherlands	0.0
New Zealand	0.1
Norway	–
Sweden	–
Switzerland	–
United Kingdom	0.4
United States	1.0
TOTAL	*31.1*
AF.D.F.	–
AF.D.B.	–
AS.D.B	–
CAR.D.B.	–
E.E.C.	0.1
IBRD	–
IDA	–
I.D.B.	–
IFAD	–
I.F.C.	–
IMF TRUST FUND	–
U.N. AGENCIES	–
UNDP	0.5
UNTA	0.4
UNICEF	–
UNRWA	–
WFP	–
UNHCR	–
Other Multilateral	0.0
Arab Agencies	0.3
TOTAL	*1.3*
ARAB COUNTRIES	–
E.E.C.+ MEMBERS	*7.9*
TOTAL	*32.4*

8. GRANTS

	1987
Australia	3.6
Austria	0.0
Belgium	–
Canada	0.6
Denmark	–
Finland	0.0
France	2.9
Germany	4.5
Ireland	–
Italy	–
Japan	17.3
Netherlands	0.0
New Zealand	0.1
Norway	–
Sweden	–
Switzerland	–
United Kingdom	0.4
United States	1.0
TOTAL	*30.4*
MULTILATERAL	*1.3*
ARAB COUNTRIES	–
E.E.C.+ MEMBERS	*7.9*
TOTAL	*31.7*

9. TOTAL OOF GROSS

	1987
Australia	–
Austria	–
Belgium	0.0
Canada	–
Denmark	–
Finland	–
France	–
Germany	0.2
Ireland	–
Italy	–
Japan	–
Netherlands	–
New Zealand	–
Norway	–
Sweden	–
Switzerland	–
United Kingdom	–
United States	–
TOTAL	*0.2*
MULTILATERAL	*–*
ARAB COUNTRIES	*–*
E.E.C.+ MEMBERS	*0.2*
TOTAL	*0.2*

10. ODA COMMITMENTS

1988	1989	1990	1987	1988	1989	1990
3.7	1.9	2.0	3.0	1.8	2.1	1.8
0.3	0.1	0.1	0.0	0.3	0.1	0.1
–	–	–	–	–	–	–
0.5	0.6	0.6	0.4	0.4	0.5	0.4
–	–	–	–	–	–	–
2.1	2.6	2.4	2.9	2.1	2.6	2.4
3.7	79.1	4.6	5.3	84.8	1.8	4.7
–	–	–	–	–	–	–
18.8	16.2	14.3	18.8	21.2	16.8	14.5
–	–	–	0.0	–	–	–
0.1	0.1	1.0	0.1	0.1	–	–
–	–	–	–	–	–	–
–	–	–	–	–	–	–
0.2	0.6	0.5	0.4	0.2	0.6	0.9
1.0	1.0	2.0	–	–	–	–
30.4	102.2	27.7	31.0	110.9	24.5	24.9
–	–	–	–	–	–	–
–	–	–	–	–	–	–
–	0.1	0.1	–	–	0.0	0.0
–	–	–	–	–	–	–
–	–	–	–	–	–	–
–	–	–	–	–	–	–
–	–	–	–	–	–	–
–	–	–	0.9	1.4	1.2	1.4
0.7	0.4	0.5	–	–	–	–
0.3	0.4	0.7	–	–	–	–
–	–	–	–	–	–	–
0.3	0.4	0.3	–	–	–	–
–	0.0	0.0	–	–	–	–
–	–	–	–	–	–	–
1.4	1.3	1.5	0.9	1.4	1.2	1.5
–	–	–	–	–	–	–
6.1	82.4	7.7	8.7	87.1	5.1	8.1
31.8	103.5	29.2	31.9	112.3	25.8	26.4

11. TECH. COOP. GRANTS

1988	1989	1990	1987	1988	1989	1990
3.7	1.9	2.0	3.6	3.6	1.8	1.9
0.1	0.1	0.1	0.0	0.1	0.1	0.1
–	–	–	–	–	–	–
0.5	0.6	0.6	–	0.0	0.0	0.1
–	–	–	–	–	–	–
2.1	2.6	2.4	2.9	2.1	2.6	2.4
3.7	3.9	4.6	4.5	3.7	3.9	4.6
–	–	–	–	–	–	–
18.3	16.2	14.3	15.9	18.3	15.5	14.3
–	–	–	0.0	–	–	–
0.1	0.1	1.0	0.1	0.1	–	1.0
–	–	–	–	–	–	–
–	–	–	–	–	–	–
0.2	0.6	0.5	0.2	0.1	0.2	0.2
1.0	1.0	2.0	–	–	–	–
29.8	27.1	27.7	27.3	28.1	24.2	24.7
1.4	1.3	1.5	1.0	1.4	1.2	1.4
–	–	–	–	–	–	–
6.1	7.3	7.7	7.7	6.0	6.8	7.3
31.2	28.4	29.2	28.2	29.5	25.4	26.1

12. TOTAL OOF NET

1988	1989	1990	1987	1988	1989	1990
–	–	–	–	–	–	–
–	–	–	0.0	–	–	–
–	–	–	–	–	–	–
–	–	–	–	–	–	–
–	–	–	–	–	–	–
0.1	0.7	0.0	-28.9	0.1	0.7	0.0
–	–	–	–	–	–	–
–	7.3	212.6	–	-21.8	-13.1	193.3
–	–	–	–	–	–	–
–	–	–	–	-0.1	-0.1	-0.1
–	–	–	–	–	–	–
–	–	–	-0.4	–	–	–
–	–	–	–	–	–	–
0.1	8.0	212.7	-29.3	-21.8	-12.4	193.2
–	–	–	-31.7	-23.9	-18.4	-38.1
–	–	–	–	–	–	–
0.1	0.7	0.0	-29.3	0.1	0.7	0.0
0.1	8.0	212.7	-61.0	-45.8	-30.8	155.1

13. ODF COMMITMENTS: BY PURPOSE %

	1987	1988	1989	1990
Education	2	–	–	–
Health	–	–	–	–
Other Social Infrastr.	0	1	–	–
Water Sanitat. Sewage	–	–	–	–
Energy	–	–	–	–
Telecommunications	0	–	–	–
Transportation	–	–	–	–
Agriculture	–	–	–	–
Extractive Industries	–	–	–	–
Manufacturing	2	72	0	–
Trade Banking Tourism	–	0	59	–
Technical Cooperation	96	27	40	–
Multisector Aid	–	–	–	–
Programme	–	–	–	–
Debt Reorganisation	–	–	–	–
Food Aid	–	–	–	–
Emergency Aid	–	–	–	–
Unspecified	–	–	–	–
TOTAL	100	100	100	–

14. GRANT ELEMENT OF ODA %

DAC COUNTRIES

	1987	1988	1989	1990
Australia	100.0	100.0	100.0	–
Austria	100.0	60.4	100.0	–
Belgium	–	–	–	–
Canada	100.0	100.0	100.0	–
Denmark	–	–	–	–
Finland	–	–	–	–
France	100.0	100.0	100.0	–
Germany	100.0	36.6	100.0	–
Ireland	–	–	–	–
Italy	–	–	–	–
Japan	97.5	100.0	100.0	–
Netherlands	100.0	–	–	–
New Zealand	100.0	100.0	–	–
Norway	–	–	–	–
Sweden	–	–	–	–
Switzerland	–	–	–	–
United Kingdom	100.0	100.0	100.0	–
United States	–	–	–	–
TOTAL	98.5	51.2	100.0	–
MULTILATERAL	100.0	100.0	100.0	–
ARAB COUNTRIES	–	–	–	–
E.E.C.+ MEMBERS	100.0	38.3	100.0	–
TOTAL	98.5	51.8	100.0	–

15. OTHER AGGREGATES

	1987	1988	1989	1990
OFFICIAL COMMITMENTS:				
TOTAL BILATERAL	118.1	120.8	60.8	354.7
of which:				
Arab Countries	–	–	–	–
C.E.E.C.	–	–	–	–
TOTAL MULTILATERAL	0.9	1.4	1.2	1.5
TOTAL BIL.& MULTIL.	119.0	122.2	62.0	356.2
of which:				
ODA Grants	31.2	31.4	25.8	26.0
ODA Loans	0.7	80.9	–	0.4
DISBURSEMENTS:				
DAC COUNTRIES COMBINED				
OFFICIAL & PRIVATE				
GROSS:				
Contractual Lending	136.1	111.4	197.8	268.8
Export Credits, Total	135.4	110.8	114.7	56.1
Export Credits, Priv.	135.4	110.8	114.8	56.2
NET:				
Contractual Lending	-388.1	-27.7	34.8	118.3
Export Credits Total	-379.4	3.3	-19.5	-44.1
PRIVATE SECTOR NET	950.4	1681.8	2899.2	2605.7
Direct Investment	930.2	1677.9	2490.8	2006.6
Portfolio Investment	370.5	0.6	427.7	643.2
Export Credits	-350.3	3.3	-19.3	-44.1
MARKET BORROWING:				
CHANGE IN CLAIMS				
Banks	–	–	–	–
MEMORANDUM ITEM:				
C.E.E.C. (Gross)	–	–	–	–

DISBURSEMENTS, UNLESS OTHERWISE STAT

	1987	1988	1989	1990		1987	1988	1989	1990			1987

1. TOTAL RECEIPTS NET

DAC COUNTRIES

	1987	1988	1989	1990
Australia	18.4	10.9	9.9	9.5
Austria	–	–	–	–
Belgium	3.1	1.7	2.5	11.7
Canada	0.0	0.0	0.0	0.1
Denmark	–	–	–	–
Finland	–	–	–	–
France	–	–	–	–
Germany	-1.0	0.7	-0.1	1.5
Ireland	–	–	–	–
Italy	0.0	–	–	–
Japan	5.3	16.7	14.1	9.3
Netherlands	0.2	0.3	0.2	0.3
New Zealand	1.5	1.5	2.1	2.1
Norway	–	–	–	–
Sweden	–	–	–	–
Switzerland	–	–	–	–
United Kingdom	7.9	9.0	9.0	9.2
United States	–	1.0	1.0	–
TOTAL	*35.4*	*41.7*	*38.6*	*43.5*

MULTILATERAL

	1987	1988	1989	1990
AF.D.F.	–	–	–	–
AF.D.B.	–	–	–	–
AS.D.B	4.3	6.2	3.8	4.1
CAR.D.B.	–	–	–	–
E.E.C.	25.4	13.5	4.0	4.0
IBRD	–	–	–	–
IDA	1.4	1.0	2.0	3.0
I.D.B.	–	–	–	–
IFAD	0.6	0.4	0.1	0.4
I.F.C.	–	–	–	–
IMF TRUST FUND	–	–	–	–
U.N. AGENCIES	–	–	–	–
UNDP	1.0	1.2	0.9	0.8
UNTA	0.5	0.6	0.8	0.8
UNICEF	–	–	–	–
UNRWA	–	–	–	–
WFP	0.1	–	–	–
UNHCR	–	–	–	–
Other Multilateral	0.5	0.5	0.4	0.2
Arab Agencies	0.1	0.1	-0.3	–
TOTAL	*33.8*	*23.4*	*11.7*	*13.1*
ARAB COUNTRIES	**1.2**	**0.0**	**-0.4**	**–**
E.E.C.+ MEMBERS	*35.6*	*25.1*	*15.6*	*26.6*
TOTAL	**70.4**	**65.1**	**49.9**	**56.6**

2. ODA LOANS GROSS

DAC COUNTRIES

	1987	1988	1989	1990
Australia	–	–	–	–
Austria	–	–	–	–
Belgium	–	–	–	–
Canada	–	–	–	–
Denmark	–	–	–	–
Finland	–	–	–	–
France	–	–	–	–
Germany	–	–	–	–
Ireland	–	–	–	–
Italy	–	–	–	–
Japan	–	8.3	4.6	–
Netherlands	–	–	–	–
New Zealand	–	–	–	–
Norway	–	–	–	–
Sweden	–	–	–	–
Switzerland	–	–	–	–
United Kingdom	1.9	1.2	2.4	0.7
United States	–	–	–	–
TOTAL	*1.9*	*9.4*	*7.0*	*0.7*
MULTILATERAL	*5.4*	*7.6*	*6.1*	*5.9*
ARAB COUNTRIES	**1.2**	**0.2**	**–**	**–**
E.E.C.+ MEMBERS	*1.9*	*1.2*	*2.4*	*0.7*
TOTAL	**8.5**	**17.2**	**13.1**	**6.5**

3. TOTAL OFFICIAL GROSS

DAC COUNTRIES

	1987	1988	1989	1990
Australia	18.4	11.7	11.7	11.5
Austria	–	–	–	–
Belgium	0.0	0.1	–	–
Canada	0.0	0.0	0.0	0.1
Denmark	–	–	–	–
Finland	–	–	–	–
France	–	–	–	–
Germany	0.2	0.4	0.3	2.0
Ireland	–	–	–	–
Italy	0.0	–	–	–
Japan	4.7	13.9	14.3	8.7
Netherlands	0.2	0.3	0.2	0.3
New Zealand	1.5	1.5	2.1	2.1
Norway	–	–	–	–
Sweden	–	–	–	–
Switzerland	–	–	–	–
United Kingdom	8.1	9.3	9.2	9.4
United States	–	1.0	1.0	–
TOTAL	*33.1*	*38.0*	*38.7*	*34.0*
MULTILATERAL	*34.1*	*23.9*	*12.3*	*13.4*
ARAB COUNTRIES	**1.2**	**0.2**	**–**	**–**
E.E.C.+ MEMBERS	*33.9*	*23.5*	*13.7*	*15.7*
TOTAL	**68.4**	**62.1**	**51.0**	**47.4**

4. TOTAL ODA NET

	1987	1988	1989	1990
Australia	7.4	8.5	11.7	11.5
Austria	–	–	–	–
Belgium	–	0.1	–	–
Canada	0.0	0.0	0.0	0.1
Denmark	–	–	–	–
Finland	–	–	–	–
France	–	–	–	–
Germany	0.2	0.4	0.3	2.0
Ireland	–	–	–	–
Italy	0.0	–	–	–
Japan	4.7	13.8	14.3	8.7
Netherlands	0.2	0.3	0.2	0.3
New Zealand	1.5	1.5	2.1	2.1
Norway	–	–	–	–
Sweden	–	–	–	–
Switzerland	–	–	–	–
United Kingdom	8.1	9.3	8.4	6.6
United States	–	1.0	1.0	–
TOTAL	*22.1*	*34.8*	*37.9*	*31.1*

	1987	1988	1989	1990
AF.D.F.	–	–	–	–
AF.D.B.	–	–	–	–
AS.D.B	4.3	6.2	3.8	4.1
CAR.D.B.	–	–	–	–
E.E.C.	25.4	13.5	4.0	4.0
IBRD	–	–	–	–
IDA	1.4	1.0	2.0	3.0
I.D.B.	–	–	–	–
IFAD	0.6	0.4	0.1	0.4
I.F.C.	–	–	–	–
IMF TRUST FUND	–	–	–	–
U.N. AGENCIES	–	–	–	–
UNDP	1.0	1.2	0.9	0.8
UNTA	0.5	0.6	0.8	0.8
UNICEF	–	–	–	–
UNRWA	–	–	–	–
WFP	0.1	–	–	–
UNHCR	–	–	–	–
Other Multilateral	0.5	0.5	0.4	0.2
Arab Agencies	0.1	0.1	-0.3	–
TOTAL	*33.8*	*23.4*	*11.7*	*13.1*
ARAB COUNTRIES	**1.2**	**0.0**	**-0.4**	**–**
E.E.C.+ MEMBERS	*33.9*	*23.5*	*12.8*	*12.8*
TOTAL	**57.1**	**58.3**	**49.2**	**44.2**

5. ODA LOANS NET

	1987	1988	1989	1990
Australia	–	–	–	–
Austria	–	–	–	–
Belgium	–	–	–	–
Canada	–	–	–	–
Denmark	–	–	–	–
Finland	–	–	–	–
France	–	–	–	–
Germany	–	–	–	–
Ireland	–	–	–	–
Italy	–	–	–	–
Japan	0.0	8.2	4.6	-0.1
Netherlands	–	–	–	–
New Zealand	–	–	–	–
Norway	–	–	–	–
Sweden	–	–	–	–
Switzerland	–	–	–	–
United Kingdom	1.8	1.2	2.3	0.7
United States	–	–	–	–
TOTAL	*1.8*	*9.4*	*7.0*	*0.6*
MULTILATERAL	*5.1*	*7.1*	*5.5*	*5.2*
ARAB COUNTRIES	**1.2**	**0.0**	**-0.4**	**–**
E.E.C.+ MEMBERS	*1.9*	*1.2*	*2.3*	*0.6*
TOTAL	**8.2**	**16.5**	**12.1**	**5.8**

6. TOTAL OFFICIAL NET

	1987	1988	1989	1990
Australia	18.4	10.9	9.9	9.5
Austria	–	–	–	–
Belgium	0.0	0.1	–	–
Canada	0.0	0.0	0.0	0.1
Denmark	–	–	–	–
Finland	–	–	–	–
France	–	–	–	–
Germany	0.2	0.4	0.3	1.9
Ireland	–	–	–	–
Italy	0.0	–	–	–
Japan	4.7	13.8	14.3	8.7
Netherlands	0.2	0.3	0.2	0.3
New Zealand	1.5	1.5	2.1	2.1
Norway	–	–	–	–
Sweden	–	–	–	–
Switzerland	–	–	–	–
United Kingdom	7.9	9.0	9.0	9.2
United States	–	1.0	1.0	–
TOTAL	*32.9*	*36.9*	*36.6*	*31.6*
MULTILATERAL	*33.8*	*23.4*	*11.7*	*13.1*
ARAB COUNTRIES	**1.2**	**0.0**	**-0.4**	**–**
E.E.C.+ MEMBERS	*33.7*	*23.3*	*13.4*	*15.3*
TOTAL	**67.9**	**60.4**	**47.9**	**44.7**

7. TOTAL ODA GROSS

	1987
Australia	7.4
Austria	–
Belgium	–
Canada	0.0
Denmark	–
Finland	–
France	–
Germany	0.2
Ireland	–
Italy	0.0
Japan	4.7
Netherlands	0.2
New Zealand	1.5
Norway	–
Sweden	–
Switzerland	–
United Kingdom	8.1
United States	–
TOTAL	*22.1*
AF.D.F.	–
AF.D.B.	–
AS.D.B	4.3
CAR.D.B.	–
E.E.C.	25.4
IBRD	–
IDA	1.4
I.D.B.	–
IFAD	0.6
I.F.C.	–
IMF TRUST FUND	–
U.N. AGENCIES	–
UNDP	1.0
UNTA	0.5
UNICEF	–
UNRWA	–
WFP	0.1
UNHCR	–
Other Multilateral	0.5
Arab Agencies	0.3
TOTAL	*34.1*
ARAB COUNTRIES	**1.2**
E.E.C.+ MEMBERS	*33.9*
TOTAL	**57.4**

8. GRANTS

	1987
Australia	7.4
Austria	–
Belgium	–
Canada	0.0
Denmark	–
Finland	–
France	–
Germany	0.2
Ireland	–
Italy	0.0
Japan	4.7
Netherlands	0.2
New Zealand	1.5
Norway	–
Sweden	–
Switzerland	–
United Kingdom	6.3
United States	–
TOTAL	*20.2*
MULTILATERAL	*28.7*
ARAB COUNTRIES	**–**
E.E.C.+ MEMBERS	*32.0*
TOTAL	**48.9**

9. TOTAL OOF GROSS

	1987
Australia	11.0
Austria	–
Belgium	0.0
Canada	–
Denmark	–
Finland	–
France	–
Germany	–
Ireland	–
Italy	–
Japan	–
Netherlands	–
New Zealand	–
Norway	–
Sweden	–
Switzerland	–
United Kingdom	–
United States	–
TOTAL	*11.0*
MULTILATERAL	*–*
ARAB COUNTRIES	**–**
E.E.C.+ MEMBERS	*0.0*
TOTAL	**11.0**

10. ODA COMMITMENTS

1988	1989	1990	1987	1988	1989	1990
8.5	11.7	11.5	8.4	6.0	15.1	8.7
–	–	–	–	–	–	–
0.1	–	–	–	–	–	–
0.0	0.0	0.1	0.3	0.0	–	0.1
–	–	–	–	–	–	–
–	–	–	–	–	–	–
0.4	0.3	2.0	0.2	2.7	–	1.3
–	–	–	–	–	–	–
–	–	–	0.0	–	–	–
13.9	14.3	8.7	7.2	18.3	13.5	9.6
0.3	0.2	0.3	0.3	0.3	0.2	0.3
1.5	2.1	2.1	1.5	1.3	–	1.7
–	–	–	–	–	–	–
–	–	–	–	–	–	–
9.3	8.4	6.6	6.8	7.3	8.5	7.3
1.0	1.0	–	0.5	0.7	0.7	0.5
34.8	*37.9*	*31.2*	*25.0*	*36.5*	*38.1*	*29.5*
–	–	–	–	–	–	–
6.3	4.0	4.3	12.0	–	–	4.7
–	–	–	–	–	–	–
13.5	4.0	4.0	28.8	15.0	0.3	0.3
–	–	–	–	–	–	–
1.0	2.0	3.0	–	–	–	–
0.4	0.1	0.4	0.1	1.5	–	–
–	–	–	–	–	–	–
–	–	–	2.0	2.3	2.1	1.7
1.2	0.9	0.8	–	–	–	–
0.6	0.8	0.8	–	–	–	–
–	–	–	–	–	–	–
–	–	–	–	–	–	–
0.5	0.4	0.2	–	–	–	–
0.3	0.1	–	–	–	–	–
23.9	*12.3*	*13.4*	*42.9*	*18.9*	*2.4*	*6.7*
0.2	–	–	–	–	–	–
23.5	*12.9*	*12.9*	*36.1*	*25.3*	*9.0*	*9.2*
58.9	**50.2**	**44.6**	**67.8**	**55.4**	**40.4**	**36.2**

11. TECH. COOP. GRANTS

1988	1989	1990	1987	1988	1989	1990
8.5	11.7	11.5	3.6	5.3	8.6	8.0
–	–	–	–	–	–	–
0.1	–	–	–	–	–	–
0.0	0.0	0.1	–	–	–	–
–	–	–	–	–	–	–
–	–	–	–	–	–	–
0.4	0.3	2.0	0.2	0.4	0.3	–
–	–	–	–	–	–	–
–	–	–	0.0	–	–	–
5.6	9.6	8.7	1.3	2.0	2.1	3.3
0.3	0.2	0.3	0.2	0.3	0.2	0.3
1.5	2.1	2.1	0.7	1.1	–	1.1
–	–	–	–	–	–	–
–	–	–	–	–	–	–
8.1	6.0	5.9	5.2	6.2	5.3	5.0
1.0	1.0	–	–	–	1.0	–
25.4	*30.9*	*30.5*	*11.1*	*15.2*	*17.5*	*17.8*
16.3	*6.2*	*7.5*	*3.5*	*5.1*	*2.1*	*1.7*
–	–	–	–	–	–	–
22.3	*10.5*	*12.2*	*7.2*	*9.6*	*5.8*	*5.3*
41.7	**37.1**	**38.0**	**14.6**	**20.2**	**19.6**	**19.5**

12. TOTAL OOF NET

1988	1989	1990	1987	1988	1989	1990
3.2	–	–	11.0	2.4	-1.9	-2.0
–	–	–	0.0	–	–	–
–	–	–	–	–	–	–
–	–	–	–	–	–	–
–	–	–	–	–	–	–
–	–	–	–	–	–	–
–	–	–	–	–	–	-0.1
–	–	–	–	–	–	–
–	–	–	–	–	–	–
–	–	–	–	–	–	–
–	–	–	–	–	–	–
–	–	–	–	–	–	–
–	0.8	2.8	-0.2	-0.2	0.6	2.6
–	–	–	–	–	–	–
3.2	*0.8*	*2.8*	*10.8*	*2.1*	*-1.3*	*0.5*
–	–	–	–	–	–	–
–	–	–	–	–	–	–
–	0.8	2.8	-0.2	-0.2	0.6	2.5
3.2	**0.8**	**2.8**	**10.8**	**2.1**	**-1.3**	**0.5**

13. ODF COMMITMENTS: BY PURPOSE %

	1987	1988	1989	1990
Education	0	0	12	–
Health	12	1	1	–
Other Social Infrastr.	0	2	5	–
Water Sanitat. Sewage	–	2	1	–
Energy	13	0	0	–
Telecommunications	–	1	–	–
Transportation	16	9	0	–
Agriculture	19	3	34	–
Extractive Industries	–	–	–	–
Manufacturing	–	32	1	–
Trade Banking Tourism	–	–	–	–
Technical Cooperation	39	50	45	–
Multisector Aid	0	0	1	–
Programme	–	–	–	–
Debt Reorganisation	–	–	–	–
Food Aid	–	–	–	–
Emergency Aid	1	–	–	–
Unspecified	–	–	0	–
TOTAL	100	100	100	–

14. GRANT ELEMENT OF ODA %

DAC COUNTRIES

	1987	1988	1989	1990
Australia	100.0	100.0	100.0	–
Austria	–	–	–	–
Belgium	–	–	–	–
Canada	100.0	100.0	–	–
Denmark	–	–	–	–
Finland	–	–	–	–
France	–	–	–	–
Germany	100.0	100.0	–	–
Ireland	–	–	–	–
Italy	100.0	–	–	–
Japan	100.0	57.7	96.5	–
Netherlands	100.0	100.0	100.0	–
New Zealand	100.0	100.0	–	–
Norway	–	–	–	–
Sweden	–	–	–	–
Switzerland	–	–	–	–
United Kingdom	100.0	100.0	100.0	–
United States	100.0	100.0	100.0	–
TOTAL	*100.0*	*78.3*	*98.7*	–
MULTILATERAL	*92.9*	*100.0*	*100.0*	–
ARAB COUNTRIES	–	–	–	–
E.E.C.+ MEMBERS	*100.0*	*100.0*	*100.0*	–
TOTAL	*95.3*	*85.4*	*98.8*	–

15. OTHER AGGREGATES

OFFICIAL COMMITMENTS:

	1987	1988	1989	1990
TOTAL BILATERAL	25.0	37.5	42.0	49.9
of which:				
Arab Countries	–	–	–	–
C.E.E.C.	–	–	–	–
TOTAL MULTILATERAL	42.9	18.9	2.4	6.7
TOTAL BIL.& MULTIL.	67.8	56.3	44.4	56.6
of which:				
ODA Grants	54.4	40.4	37.5	30.9
ODA Loans	13.5	15.0	2.9	5.3

DISBURSEMENTS:

DAC COUNTRIES COMBINED

OFFICIAL & PRIVATE

	1987	1988	1989	1990
GROSS:				
Contractual Lending	13.0	13.3	7.8	3.5
Export Credits, Total	11.1	3.9	–	–
Export Credits, Priv.	0.1	0.7	–	–
NET:				
Contractual Lending	12.5	11.8	5.3	0.7
Export Credits Total	10.9	2.7	-2.2	-2.4
PRIVATE SECTOR NET	2.5	4.7	2.0	11.9
Direct Investment	1.0	2.9	-0.2	10.4
Portfolio Investment	1.7	1.6	2.5	1.9
Export Credits	-0.1	0.3	-0.4	-0.4

MARKET BORROWING:

CHANGE IN CLAIMS

	1987	1988	1989	1990
Banks	-29.0	-15.0	2.0	-2.0

MEMORANDUM ITEM:

	1987	1988	1989	1990
C.E.E.C. (Gross)	–	–	–	–

DISBURSEMENTS, UNLESS OTHERWISE STAT[E]

1. TOTAL RECEIPTS NET

DAC COUNTRIES	1987	1988	1989	1990
Australia	0.7	0.2	0.2	0.0
Austria	0.0	0.0	0.1	0.4
Belgium	4.9	0.1	0.1	8.2
Canada	0.4	0.5	0.8	0.9
Denmark	9.9	8.3	6.5	2.1
Finland	16.5	13.3	8.5	22.5
France	2.5	-3.0	-5.6	-3.2
Germany	115.2	-11.7	-6.3	20.1
Ireland	0.0	0.0	–	–
Italy	195.1	187.9	176.7	110.0
Japan	20.5	15.4	17.6	10.2
Netherlands	0.3	0.1	0.3	2.9
New Zealand	–	–	–	–
Norway	0.1	0.8	0.7	1.1
Sweden	1.9	1.9	1.7	2.5
Switzerland	1.3	1.0	1.9	1.8
United Kingdom	11.9	11.9	8.7	3.0
United States	52.0	54.0	28.0	72.0
TOTAL	433.3	280.6	239.7	254.6
MULTILATERAL				
AF.D.F.	13.2	3.6	13.4	19.1
AF.D.B.	-0.7	–	-2.2	-0.4
AS.D.B	–	–	–	–
CAR.D.B.	–	–	–	–
E.E.C.	9.4	14.9	35.3	35.3
IBRD	–	–	–	–
IDA	38.6	22.0	45.0	32.0
I.D.B.	–	–	–	–
IFAD	5.5	1.7	-0.1	1.5
I.F.C.	0.4	–	0.0	–
IMF TRUST FUND	–	–	–	–
U.N. AGENCIES	–	–	–	–
UNDP	7.0	9.7	9.9	8.8
UNTA	3.0	1.8	2.3	1.3
UNICEF	2.8	3.1	2.3	3.6
UNRWA	–	–	–	–
WFP	48.8	23.4	20.1	21.5
UNHCR	48.1	34.3	19.8	11.2
Other Multilateral	2.6	2.5	10.1	3.0
Arab Agencies	1.6	1.2	2.6	–
TOTAL	180.2	118.3	158.4	136.9
ARAB COUNTRIES	1.1	4.1	0.8	30.5
E.E.C.+ MEMBERS	349.2	208.5	215.6	178.4
TOTAL	614.6	402.9	398.9	421.9

2. ODA LOANS GROSS

DAC COUNTRIES	1987	1988	1989	1990
Australia	–	–	–	–
Austria	–	–	–	–
Belgium	–	–	–	–
Canada	–	–	–	–
Denmark	0.0	–	–	–
Finland	–	–	–	–
France	8.7	5.8	–	–
Germany	–	–	–	–
Ireland	–	–	–	–
Italy	80.6	–	–	–
Japan	7.1	5.2	1.2	1.7
Netherlands	–	–	–	–
New Zealand	–	–	–	–
Norway	–	–	–	–
Sweden	–	–	–	–
Switzerland	–	–	–	–
United Kingdom	–	–	–	–
United States	2.0	–	1.0	–
TOTAL	98.3	10.9	2.2	1.7
MULTILATERAL	59.9	28.8	67.7	59.9
ARAB COUNTRIES	0.2	10.2	2.7	11.1
E.E.C.+ MEMBERS	89.3	6.3	4.7	4.7
TOTAL	158.4	49.9	72.5	72.7

3. TOTAL OFFICIAL GROSS

DAC COUNTRIES	1987	1988	1989	1990
Australia	0.7	0.2	0.2	0.0
Austria	0.0	0.0	0.1	0.4
Belgium	4.2	0.3	0.3	8.0
Canada	0.4	0.5	0.8	0.9
Denmark	9.9	8.4	12.7	2.1
Finland	16.5	13.3	8.5	22.5
France	10.1	7.9	4.0	4.7
Germany	50.9	31.6	35.1	20.8
Ireland	0.0	0.0	–	–
Italy	232.5	197.2	177.6	111.3
Japan	22.7	15.4	17.5	10.2
Netherlands	0.3	0.1	0.3	0.2
New Zealand	–	–	–	–
Norway	0.7	0.8	0.7	1.1
Sweden	1.7	1.9	1.7	2.5
Switzerland	1.3	1.0	1.9	1.8
United Kingdom	11.9	11.9	8.7	3.0
United States	52.0	56.0	28.0	72.0
TOTAL	415.8	346.5	297.8	261.5
MULTILATERAL	182.0	119.6	164.7	140.4
ARAB COUNTRIES	1.1	11.4	2.9	34.9
E.E.C.+ MEMBERS	329.3	272.7	274.1	185.6
TOTAL	598.9	477.5	465.4	436.7

4. TOTAL ODA NET

DAC COUNTRIES	1987	1988	1989	1990
Australia	0.7	0.2	0.2	0.0
Austria	0.0	0.0	0.1	0.4
Belgium	4.2	0.3	0.3	8.0
Canada	0.4	0.5	0.8	0.9
Denmark	9.9	8.4	6.5	2.1
Finland	16.5	13.3	8.5	22.5
France	10.2	6.7	2.7	3.1
Germany	51.0	31.6	24.6	20.8
Ireland	0.0	0.0	–	–
Italy	215.1	197.2	164.5	111.3
Japan	22.7	15.4	17.6	10.2
Netherlands	0.3	0.1	0.3	0.2
New Zealand	–	–	–	–
Norway	0.7	0.8	0.7	1.1
Sweden	1.7	1.9	1.7	2.5
Switzerland	1.3	1.0	1.9	1.8
United Kingdom	11.9	11.9	8.7	3.0
United States	52.0	22.0	28.0	72.0
TOTAL	398.5	311.3	266.9	259.8
MULTILATERAL				
AF.D.F.	13.2	3.6	13.4	19.1
AF.D.B.	–	–	–	–
AS.D.B	–	–	–	–
CAR.D.B.	–	–	–	–
E.E.C.	9.4	14.9	35.3	35.3
IBRD	–	–	–	–
IDA	38.6	22.0	45.0	32.0
I.D.B.	–	–	–	–
IFAD	5.5	1.7	-0.1	1.5
I.F.C.	–	–	–	–
IMF TRUST FUND	–	–	–	–
U.N. AGENCIES	–	–	–	–
UNDP	7.0	9.7	9.9	8.8
UNTA	3.0	1.8	2.3	1.3
UNICEF	2.8	3.1	2.3	3.6
UNRWA	–	–	–	–
WFP	48.8	23.4	20.1	21.5
UNHCR	48.1	34.3	19.8	11.2
Other Multilateral	2.6	2.5	10.1	3.0
Arab Agencies	1.6	0.8	1.2	–
TOTAL	180.5	117.9	159.2	137.3
ARAB COUNTRIES	1.1	4.1	0.8	30.5
E.E.C.+ MEMBERS	311.9	271.2	242.9	183.7
TOTAL	580.1	433.2	426.9	427.6

5. ODA LOANS NET

DAC COUNTRIES	1987	1988	1989	1990
Australia	–	–	–	–
Austria	–	–	–	–
Belgium	–	–	–	–
Canada	–	–	–	–
Denmark	0.0	–	-6.1	–
Finland	–	–	–	–
France	8.7	4.6	-1.2	-1.7
Germany	0.1	–	–	–
Ireland	–	–	–	–
Italy	63.2	–	-13.1	–
Japan	7.1	5.2	1.2	1.7
Netherlands	–	–	–	–
New Zealand	–	–	–	–
Norway	–	–	–	–
Sweden	–	–	–	–
Switzerland	–	–	–	–
United Kingdom	–	–	–	–
United States	2.0	-2.0	1.0	–
TOTAL	81.0	7.7	-18.2	0.0
MULTILATERAL	58.8	27.5	63.6	57.0
ARAB COUNTRIES	0.2	2.9	0.6	6.7
E.E.C.+ MEMBERS	72.0	4.8	-16.1	2.7
TOTAL	139.9	38.1	45.9	63.7

6. TOTAL OFFICIAL NET

DAC COUNTRIES	1987	1988	1989	1990
Australia	0.7	0.2	0.2	0.0
Austria	0.0	0.0	0.1	0.4
Belgium	4.2	0.3	0.3	8.0
Canada	0.4	0.5	0.8	0.9
Denmark	9.9	8.4	6.5	2.1
Finland	16.5	13.3	8.5	22.5
France	10.2	5.4	2.7	3.1
Germany	51.0	31.6	34.6	20.0
Ireland	0.0	0.0	–	–
Italy	196.6	197.2	164.5	111.3
Japan	22.7	15.4	17.6	10.2
Netherlands	0.3	0.1	0.3	0.2
New Zealand	–	–	–	–
Norway	0.7	0.8	0.7	1.1
Sweden	1.7	1.9	1.7	2.5
Switzerland	1.3	1.0	1.9	1.8
United Kingdom	11.9	11.9	8.7	3.0
United States	52.0	54.0	28.0	72.0
TOTAL	380.0	342.0	276.8	259.0
MULTILATERAL	180.2	118.3	158.4	136.9
ARAB COUNTRIES	1.1	4.1	0.8	30.5
E.E.C.+ MEMBERS	293.4	269.9	252.8	182.9
TOTAL	561.3	464.3	436.0	426.3

7. TOTAL ODA GROSS

	1987
Australia	0.7
Austria	0.0
Belgium	4.2
Canada	0.4
Denmark	9.9
Finland	16.5
France	10.1
Germany	50.9
Ireland	0.0
Italy	232.5
Japan	22.7
Netherlands	0.3
New Zealand	–
Norway	0.7
Sweden	1.7
Switzerland	1.3
United Kingdom	11.9
United States	52.0
TOTAL	415.8
AF.D.F.	13.3
AF.D.B.	–
AS.D.B	–
CAR.D.B.	–
E.E.C.	9.4
IBRD	–
IDA	39.6
I.D.B.	–
IFAD	5.5
I.F.C.	–
IMF TRUST FUND	–
U.N. AGENCIES	–
UNDP	7.0
UNTA	3.0
UNICEF	2.8
UNRWA	–
WFP	48.8
UNHCR	48.1
Other Multilateral	2.6
Arab Agencies	1.6
TOTAL	181.6
ARAB COUNTRIES	1.1
E.E.C.+ MEMBERS	329.3
TOTAL	598.5

8. GRANTS

	1987
Australia	0.7
Austria	0.0
Belgium	4.2
Canada	0.4
Denmark	9.9
Finland	16.5
France	1.5
Germany	50.9
Ireland	0.0
Italy	151.9
Japan	15.6
Netherlands	0.3
New Zealand	–
Norway	0.7
Sweden	1.7
Switzerland	1.3
United Kingdom	11.9
United States	50.0
TOTAL	317.5
MULTILATERAL	121.7
ARAB COUNTRIES	1.0
E.E.C.+ MEMBERS	240.0
TOTAL	440.2

9. TOTAL OOF GROSS

	1987
Australia	–
Austria	–
Belgium	–
Canada	–
Denmark	–
Finland	–
France	–
Germany	–
Ireland	–
Italy	–
Japan	–
Netherlands	–
New Zealand	–
Norway	–
Sweden	–
Switzerland	–
United Kingdom	–
United States	–
TOTAL	–
MULTILATERAL	0.4
ARAB COUNTRIES	–
E.E.C.+ MEMBERS	–
TOTAL	0.4

1988	1989	1990		1987	1988	1989	1990

10. ODA COMMITMENTS

1988	1989	1990		1987	1988	1989	1990
0.2	0.2	0.0		0.1	0.5	0.2	0.2
0.0	0.1	0.4		0.0	0.0	0.1	0.4
0.3	0.3	8.0		10.3	7.1	0.3	8.0
0.5	0.8	0.9		0.6	0.3	0.4	0.5
8.4	12.7	2.1		–	8.9	–	–
13.3	8.5	22.5		–	8.7	20.5	1.2
7.9	3.9	4.7		5.0	6.0	1.2	0.9
31.6	24.6	20.8		33.3	44.8	6.7	22.9
0.0	–	–		0.0	0.0	–	–
197.2	177.6	111.3		328.3	260.6	158.0	113.9
15.4	17.5	10.2		24.4	14.8	7.0	13.5
0.1	0.3	0.2		0.2	0.1	0.2	0.2
–	–	–		–	–	–	–
0.8	0.7	1.1		0.1	–	1.8	–
1.9	1.7	2.5		1.7	2.3	1.5	0.7
1.0	1.9	1.8		1.3	1.0	1.8	1.8
11.9	8.7	3.0		16.9	8.7	6.1	2.8
24.0	28.0	72.0		46.5	15.6	20.3	2.2
314.5	287.3	261.5		468.7	379.4	226.1	169.3
3.6	13.8	19.3		33.9	–	10.4	38.9
–	–	–		–	–	–	–
–	–	–		–	–	–	–
15.2	35.5	35.5		32.6	25.2	93.7	93.7
–	–	–		–	–	–	–
23.0	48.0	34.0		44.1	19.0	99.0	26.0
–	–	–		–	–	–	–
1.7	–	2.0		0.2	–	11.9	–
–	–	–		–	–	–	–
–	–	–		112.3	74.9	64.5	49.4
9.7	9.9	8.8		–	–	–	–
1.8	2.3	1.3		–	–	–	–
3.1	2.3	3.6		–	–	–	–
–	–	–		–	–	–	–
23.4	20.1	21.5		–	–	–	–
34.3	19.8	11.2		–	–	–	–
2.5	10.1	3.0		–	–	–	–
0.8	1.5	0.2		–	2.5	0.1	–
119.1	163.3	140.4		223.1	121.5	279.6	208.0
11.4	2.9	34.9		8.7	1.0	–	70.0
272.7	263.6	185.6		426.6	361.5	266.1	242.5
445.1	453.5	436.7		700.5	502.0	505.7	447.3

11. TECH. COOP. GRANTS

1988	1989	1990		1987	1988	1989	1990
0.2	0.2	0.0		0.1	0.1	0.1	0.0
0.0	0.1	0.4		0.0	0.0	0.0	0.0
0.3	0.3	8.0		0.1	0.0	0.0	–
0.5	0.8	0.9		–	0.0	0.0	–
8.4	12.7	2.1		0.9	0.6	0.5	0.5
13.3	8.5	22.5		0.1	0.2	2.0	1.4
2.1	3.9	4.7		1.5	2.1	1.2	0.9
31.6	24.6	20.8		13.0	16.5	17.2	11.8
0.0	–	–		0.0	0.0	–	–
197.2	177.6	111.3		36.8	14.9	35.5	34.7
10.2	16.4	8.5		0.9	0.7	0.5	0.1
0.1	0.3	0.2		0.2	0.1	0.1	0.2
–	–	–		–	–	–	–
0.8	0.7	1.1		0.1	0.1	0.1	–
1.9	1.7	2.5		1.1	1.2	1.7	1.3
1.0	1.9	1.8		0.0	–	–	–
11.9	8.7	3.0		6.0	8.3	5.4	2.6
24.0	27.0	72.0		20.0	19.0	17.0	13.0
303.6	285.1	259.8		80.7	63.9	81.3	66.7
90.3	95.6	80.4		65.8	55.2	44.4	27.9
1.2	0.2	23.8		–	–	–	–
266.4	258.9	181.0		60.8	46.4	59.9	50.9
395.1	380.9	364.0		146.5	119.1	125.7	94.6

12. TOTAL OOF NET

1988	1989	1990		1987	1988	1989	1990
–	–	–		–	–	–	–
–	–	–		–	–	–	–
–	–	–		–	–	–	–
–	–	–		–	–	–	–
–	–	–		–	–	–	–
–	0.0	–		–	-1.3	0.0	–
–	10.5	–		–	–	9.9	-0.8
–	–	–		–	–	–	–
–	–	–		-18.5	–	–	–
–	–	–		–	–	–	–
–	–	–		–	–	–	–
–	–	–		–	–	–	–
–	–	–		–	–	–	–
–	–	–		–	–	–	–
32.0	–	–		–	32.0	–	–
32.0	10.5	–		-18.5	30.7	9.9	-0.8
0.4	1.4	0.0		-0.3	0.4	-0.8	-0.4
–	–	–		–	–	–	–
–	10.5	–		-18.5	-1.3	9.9	-0.8
32.4	11.9	0.0		-18.8	31.1	9.1	-1.2

13. ODF COMMITMENTS: BY PURPOSE %

	1987	1988	1989	1990
Education	0	1	5	–
Health	0	8	5	–
Other Social Infrastr.	0	0	0	–
Water Sanitat. Sewage	1	3	–	–
Energy	2	16	0	–
Telecommunications	–	9	–	–
Transportation	4	10	0	–
Agriculture	13	10	53	–
Extractive Industries	–	–	–	–
Manufacturing	0	4	–	–
Trade Banking Tourism	–	–	0	–
Technical Cooperation	22	34	22	–
Multisector Aid	29	–	0	–
Programme	5	1	10	–
Debt Reorganisation	16	0	2	–
Food Aid	5	3	1	–
Emergency Aid	1	0	0	–
Unspecified	0	–	0	–
TOTAL	100	100	100	–

14. GRANT ELEMENT OF ODA %

DAC COUNTRIES	1987	1988	1989	1990
Australia	100.0	100.0	100.0	–
Austria	100.0	100.0	100.0	–
Belgium	100.0	100.0	100.0	–
Canada	100.0	100.0	100.0	–
Denmark	–	100.0	–	–
Finland	–	100.0	100.0	–
France	100.0	80.6	100.0	–
Germany	100.0	100.0	100.0	–
Ireland	100.0	100.0	–	–
Italy	89.6	100.0	100.0	–
Japan	90.4	97.3	100.0	–
Netherlands	100.0	100.0	100.0	–
New Zealand	–	–	–	–
Norway	100.0	–	100.0	–
Sweden	100.0	100.0	100.0	–
Switzerland	100.0	100.0	100.0	–
United Kingdom	100.0	100.0	100.0	–
United States	98.8	99.3	97.9	–
TOTAL	91.9	99.6	99.8	–
MULTILATERAL	93.7	95.6	91.4	–
ARAB COUNTRIES	82.2	100.0	–	–
E.E.C.+ MEMBERS	91.5	99.7	100.0	–
TOTAL	92.3	98.6	95.1	–

15. OTHER AGGREGATES

	1987	1988	1989	1990
OFFICIAL COMMITMENTS:				
TOTAL BILATERAL	494.3	412.7	236.6	239.3
of which:				
Arab Countries	8.7	1.0	–	70.0
C.E.E.C.	–	–	–	–
TOTAL MULTILATERAL	229.1	126.2	279.6	208.0
TOTAL BIL.& MULTIL.	723.4	538.9	516.2	447.3
of which:				
ODA Grants	505.5	475.2	380.7	379.7
ODA Loans	195.0	26.7	125.0	67.7
DISBURSEMENTS:				
DAC COUNTRIES COMBINED				
OFFICIAL & PRIVATE				
GROSS:				
Contractual Lending	101.7	40.3	50.9	-0.1
Export Credits, Total	3.4	-2.7	48.7	-1.8
Export Credits, Priv.	3.4	-2.7	38.2	-1.8
NET:				
Contractual Lending	57.2	27.0	20.7	-6.9
Export Credits Total	-5.3	-11.4	39.0	-6.8
PRIVATE SECTOR NET	53.3	-61.4	-37.1	-4.4
Direct Investment	64.3	-43.4	-41.2	5.6
Portfolio Investment	-5.8	-6.6	-24.9	-3.9
Export Credits	-5.3	-11.4	29.0	-6.1
MARKET BORROWING:				
CHANGE IN CLAIMS				
Banks	-6.0	-19.0	38.0	-43.0
MEMORANDUM ITEM:				
C.E.E.C. (Gross)	–	–	–	–

1. TOTAL RECEIPTS NET / 4. TOTAL ODA NET / 7. TOTAL ODA GROSS

	1987	1988	1989	1990	1987	1988	1989	1990		1987
1. TOTAL RECEIPTS NET					**4. TOTAL ODA NET**				**7. TOTAL ODA GROSS**	
DAC COUNTRIES										
Australia	1.2	2.5	7.4	5.0	1.4	2.7	5.1	4.0	Australia	1.4
Austria	0.1	0.1	0.2	0.9	0.1	0.1	0.2	0.9	Austria	0.1
Belgium	0.8	1.6	0.4	1.5	0.8	1.0	0.5	1.1	Belgium	0.8
Canada	20.8	27.3	14.4	3.3	21.8	28.3	15.4	4.3	Canada	22.9
Denmark	4.4	7.8	9.1	6.4	4.6	7.7	9.1	6.4	Denmark	5.0
Finland	14.0	15.7	19.5	13.6	14.0	15.2	19.5	13.6	Finland	14.0
France	9.3	19.3	-7.0	8.2	7.1	12.6	1.3	11.0	France	8.0
Germany	38.3	37.7	38.0	31.3	39.7	37.2	40.8	26.2	Germany	45.8
Ireland	0.0	0.0	–	0.0	0.0	0.0	–	0.0	Ireland	0.0
Italy	3.8	4.1	5.2	5.0	3.7	4.1	5.1	4.8	Italy	3.7
Japan	153.4	205.1	185.3	162.1	118.3	199.8	185.2	176.1	Japan	129.6
Netherlands	26.0	38.6	17.2	18.9	23.5	28.4	18.0	22.3	Netherlands	27.0
New Zealand	0.1	–	0.1	0.1	0.1	–	0.1	0.1	New Zealand	0.1
Norway	15.6	16.4	13.3	24.0	15.6	16.4	13.3	22.5	Norway	15.6
Sweden	-5.9	7.2	-4.1	4.7	19.9	7.2	6.3	10.6	Sweden	19.9
Switzerland	4.3	4.0	3.6	3.6	4.3	4.0	3.6	3.6	Switzerland	4.4
United Kingdom	50.1	5.6	249.0	59.5	16.3	30.4	30.9	21.3	United Kingdom	18.9
United States	33.0	39.0	40.0	72.0	35.0	41.0	43.0	75.0	United States	43.0
TOTAL	*369.4*	*431.9*	*591.5*	*420.2*	*326.1*	*436.0*	*397.3*	*403.8*	*TOTAL*	*360.2*
MULTILATERAL										
AF.D.F.	–	–	–	–	–	–	–	–	AF.D.F.	–
AF.D.B.	–	–	–	–	–	–	–	–	AF.D.B.	–
AS.D.B	46.9	62.9	76.4	112.4	46.9	62.9	76.4	112.4	AS.D.B	49.8
CAR.D.B.	–	–	–	–	–	–	–	–	CAR.D.B.	–
E.E.C.	11.7	7.5	4.1	4.1	11.7	7.5	4.1	4.1	E.E.C.	11.7
IBRD	-0.1	2.0	1.0	-6.0	–	–	–	–	IBRD	–
IDA	81.4	55.0	51.0	123.0	81.4	55.0	51.0	123.0	IDA	82.4
I.D.B.	–	–	–	–	–	–	–	–	I.D.B.	–
IFAD	7.1	2.1	2.9	3.5	7.1	2.1	2.9	3.5	IFAD	7.1
I.F.C.	-0.8	-15.7	2.9	-2.4	–	–	–	–	I.F.C.	–
IMF TRUST FUND	–	–	–	–	–	–	–	–	IMF TRUST FUND	–
U.N. AGENCIES	–	–	–	–	–	–	–	–	U.N. AGENCIES	
UNDP	7.7	8.7	7.4	7.7	7.7	8.7	7.4	7.7	UNDP	7.7
UNTA	2.5	2.0	2.6	1.8	2.5	2.0	2.6	1.8	UNTA	2.5
UNICEF	4.3	5.3	3.6	4.5	4.3	5.3	3.6	4.5	UNICEF	4.3
UNRWA	–	–	–	–	–	–	–	–	UNRWA	–
WFP	10.1	6.6	1.9	3.7	10.1	6.6	1.9	3.7	WFP	10.1
UNHCR	–	6.5	2.9	2.2	–	6.5	2.9	2.2	UNHCR	–
Other Multilateral	1.6	2.7	3.0	2.5	1.6	2.7	3.0	2.5	Other Multilateral	1.6
Arab Agencies	-0.2	-3.3	-3.3	–	-0.2	-3.3	-3.3	–	Arab Agencies	3.1
TOTAL	*172.2*	*142.3*	*156.2*	*256.8*	*173.1*	*156.0*	*152.3*	*265.3*	*TOTAL*	*180.3*
ARAB COUNTRIES	*2.4*	*6.4*	*-2.8*	*-4.1*	*2.4*	*6.4*	*-2.8*	*-4.1*	***ARAB COUNTRIES***	*8.2*
E.E.C.+ MEMBERS	*144.5*	*122.2*	*316.0*	*134.9*	*107.3*	*128.8*	*109.7*	*97.2*	*E.E.C.+ MEMBERS*	*120.8*
TOTAL	***544.0***	***580.6***	***744.9***	***672.8***	***501.7***	***598.3***	***546.8***	***664.9***	***TOTAL***	***548.6***

2. ODA LOANS GROSS / 5. ODA LOANS NET / 8. GRANTS

	1987	1988	1989	1990	1987	1988	1989	1990		1987
2. ODA LOANS GROSS					**5. ODA LOANS NET**				**8. GRANTS**	
DAC COUNTRIES										
Australia	–	–	–	–	–	–	–	–	Australia	1.4
Austria	–	–	–	–	–	–	–	–	Austria	0.1
Belgium	–	–	–	–	–	–	–	–	Belgium	0.8
Canada	0.0	–	–	–	-1.1	-1.5	-1.7	-3.4	Canada	22.8
Denmark	2.8	5.0	1.9	0.0	2.3	4.6	1.4	-0.6	Denmark	2.3
Finland	–	–	–	–	–	–	–	–	Finland	14.0
France	7.0	12.8	1.5	10.8	6.1	11.9	0.6	10.2	France	1.0
Germany	29.5	27.8	32.1	21.2	23.4	21.5	25.8	10.0	Germany	16.3
Ireland	–	–	–	–	–	–	–	–	Ireland	0.0
Italy	–	–	–	–	–	–	–	–	Italy	3.7
Japan	63.0	127.7	107.0	104.2	51.6	113.0	91.6	85.1	Japan	66.6
Netherlands	0.6	3.5	0.6	0.0	-2.9	-0.7	-4.0	-5.2	Netherlands	26.4
New Zealand	–	–	–	–	–	–	–	–	New Zealand	0.1
Norway	0.3	–	–	–	0.3	–	0.0	0.0	Norway	15.3
Sweden	–	–	–	–	–	–	–	–	Sweden	19.9
Switzerland	–	–	0.4	0.0	-0.1	-0.1	0.3	0.0	Switzerland	4.4
United Kingdom	–	–	–	–	-2.6	-2.8	-2.6	-2.8	United Kingdom	18.9
United States	28.0	39.0	30.0	38.0	20.0	29.0	20.0	28.0	United States	15.0
TOTAL	*131.2*	*215.8*	*173.4*	*174.3*	*97.1*	*174.9*	*131.2*	*121.2*	*TOTAL*	*229.0*
MULTILATERAL	*141.1*	*123.2*	*133.2*	*241.5*	*133.9*	*114.9*	*123.6*	*230.1*	*MULTILATERAL*	*39.2*
ARAB COUNTRIES	*8.2*	*11.7*	*5.1*	*1.0*	*2.4*	*6.4*	*-2.9*	*-4.1*	***ARAB COUNTRIES***	*0.0*
E.E.C.+ MEMBERS	*39.8*	*49.1*	*36.0*	*32.1*	*26.4*	*34.5*	*21.1*	*11.6*	*E.E.C.+ MEMBERS*	*81.0*
TOTAL	***280.4***	***350.8***	***311.7***	***416.7***	***233.5***	***296.2***	***251.9***	***347.2***	***TOTAL***	***268.2***

3. TOTAL OFFICIAL GROSS / 6. TOTAL OFFICIAL NET / 9. TOTAL OOF GROSS

	1987	1988	1989	1990	1987	1988	1989	1990		1987
3. TOTAL OFFICIAL GROSS					**6. TOTAL OFFICIAL NET**				**9. TOTAL OOF GROSS**	
DAC COUNTRIES										
Australia	1.4	2.7	7.4	5.0	1.2	2.5	7.4	5.0	Australia	–
Austria	0.1	0.1	0.2	0.9	0.1	0.1	0.2	0.9	Austria	–
Belgium	0.8	1.0	0.5	1.1	0.8	1.0	0.5	1.1	Belgium	–
Canada	22.9	29.7	17.1	7.7	20.8	27.3	14.4	3.3	Canada	–
Denmark	5.0	8.3	9.6	7.1	4.4	7.8	9.1	6.4	Denmark	0.0
Finland	14.0	15.2	19.5	13.6	14.0	15.2	19.5	13.6	Finland	–
France	8.0	13.5	2.1	11.5	7.1	12.6	1.3	11.0	France	–
Germany	45.8	43.4	47.1	38.0	39.7	37.2	40.5	26.4	Germany	–
Ireland	0.0	0.0	–	0.0	0.0	0.0	–	0.0	Ireland	–
Italy	3.7	4.1	5.1	4.8	3.7	4.1	5.1	4.8	Italy	–
Japan	154.7	218.2	200.6	195.1	142.5	200.7	181.8	172.8	Japan	25.1
Netherlands	28.4	32.5	22.6	27.6	24.3	28.2	17.2	20.6	Netherlands	1.4
New Zealand	0.1	–	0.1	0.1	0.1	–	0.1	0.1	New Zealand	–
Norway	15.6	16.4	13.3	22.6	15.6	16.4	13.3	22.5	Norway	–
Sweden	19.9	7.2	6.3	10.6	19.9	7.2	6.3	10.6	Sweden	–
Switzerland	4.4	4.1	3.7	3.7	4.3	4.0	3.6	3.6	Switzerland	–
United Kingdom	30.6	38.7	38.6	30.3	26.7	35.9	36.0	27.5	United Kingdom	11.7
United States	43.0	51.0	53.0	85.0	33.0	39.0	41.0	72.0	United States	–
TOTAL	*398.4*	*486.1*	*446.8*	*464.7*	*358.2*	*439.0*	*397.0*	*402.2*	*TOTAL*	*38.2*
MULTILATERAL	*184.3*	*171.3*	*170.9*	*272.5*	*172.2*	*142.3*	*156.2*	*256.8*	*MULTILATERAL*	*4.0*
ARAB COUNTRIES	*8.2*	*11.7*	*5.2*	*1.0*	*2.4*	*6.4*	*-2.8*	*-4.1*	***ARAB COUNTRIES***	*–*
E.E.C.+ MEMBERS	*134.0*	*149.0*	*129.8*	*124.5*	*118.3*	*134.2*	*113.7*	*101.9*	*E.E.C.+ MEMBERS*	*13.1*
TOTAL	***590.9***	***669.1***	***622.9***	***738.2***	***532.8***	***587.7***	***550.5***	***654.9***	***TOTAL***	***42.3***

1988	1989	1990		1987	1988	1989	1990

10. ODA COMMITMENTS

1988	1989	1990		1987	1988	1989	1990
2.7	5.1	4.0		2.3	3.7	7.2	2.7
0.1	0.2	0.9		0.1	0.1	0.2	0.9
1.0	0.5	1.1		1.0	0.7	0.5	1.1
29.7	17.1	7.7		12.1	22.5	19.2	11.2
8.2	9.6	7.1		0.1	9.5	12.6	0.4
15.2	19.5	13.6		23.2	31.8	3.0	21.4
13.5	2.1	11.5		7.7	10.0	4.8	15.5
43.4	47.1	37.3		21.8	22.7	19.3	14.4
0.0	–	0.0		0.0	0.0	–	0.0
4.1	5.1	4.8		3.6	4.1	5.1	4.8
214.6	200.6	195.1		178.2	457.6	66.4	285.9
32.5	22.6	27.6		18.4	28.3	17.5	19.5
–	0.1	0.1		0.1	0.1	–	–
16.4	13.3	22.6		6.2	1.3	31.1	3.0
7.2	6.3	10.6		19.9	7.1	6.1	11.9
4.1	3.7	3.7		2.4	3.6	2.1	8.3
33.2	33.5	24.2		10.3	34.2	16.7	28.1
51.0	53.0	85.0		52.6	61.3	73.7	43.1
476.9	*439.4*	*456.8*		*360.0*	*698.4*	*285.3*	*472.2*
–	–	–		–	–	–	–
–	–	–		–	–	–	–
66.6	80.4	117.1		152.3	106.9	131.2	204.1
–	–	–		–	–	–	–
7.5	4.1	4.1		43.7	9.9	11.0	11.0
–	–	–		–	–	–	–
56.0	53.0	126.0		38.6	203.0	69.0	264.0
–	–	–		–	–	–	–
2.4	3.2	3.8		–	6.5	0.3	0.3
–	–	–		–	–	–	–
–	–	–		26.3	31.7	21.3	22.3
8.7	7.4	7.7		–	–	–	–
2.0	2.6	1.8		–	–	–	–
5.3	3.6	4.5		–	–	–	–
–	–	–		–	–	–	–
6.6	1.9	3.7		–	–	–	–
6.5	2.9	2.2		–	–	–	–
2.7	3.0	2.5		–	–	–	–
–	–	–		–	0.5	–	–
164.3	*162.0*	*273.3*		*260.9*	*358.6*	*232.7*	*501.6*
11.7	*5.2*	*1.0*		–	–	–	–
143.4	*124.6*	*117.7*		*106.6*	*119.3*	*87.3*	*94.7*
652.9	*606.6*	*731.1*		*620.9*	*1057.0*	*518.0*	*973.8*

11. TECH. COOP. GRANTS

1988	1989	1990		1987	1988	1989	1990
2.7	5.1	4.0		1.2	1.4	1.3	2.2
0.1	0.2	0.9		0.1	0.1	0.1	0.1
1.0	0.5	1.1		0.8	0.7	–	0.6
29.7	17.1	7.7		–	0.7	0.6	4.3
3.1	7.7	7.1		1.7	3.1	5.3	0.0
15.2	19.5	13.6		0.4	0.7	2.0	0.3
0.7	0.6	0.7		1.0	0.7	0.5	0.5
15.6	15.0	16.1		16.1	15.3	14.7	15.8
0.0	–	0.0		0.0	0.0	–	0.0
4.1	5.1	4.8		0.2	0.0	–	–
86.9	93.7	91.0		12.5	21.3	17.8	16.6
29.0	22.0	27.6		9.0	9.4	8.8	8.9
–	0.1	0.1		0.0	–	–	0.1
16.4	13.3	22.6		1.2	1.9	1.6	1.1
7.2	6.3	10.6		1.0	2.0	2.1	1.0
4.1	3.3	3.6		0.4	0.8	–	–
33.2	33.5	24.2		7.6	12.8	11.4	11.2
12.0	23.0	47.0		5.0	8.0	-14.0	23.0
261.1	*266.0*	*282.6*		*58.1*	*78.8*	*80.2*	*85.8*
41.0	*28.8*	*31.8*		*17.8*	*27.9*	*19.4*	*18.6*
–	*0.2*	–		–	–	–	–
94.3	*88.6*	*85.6*		*38.0*	*44.8*	*40.7*	*37.1*
302.1	*295.0*	*314.4*		*75.9*	*106.8*	*99.6*	*104.5*

12. TOTAL OOF NET

1988	1989	1990		1987	1988	1989	1990
–	2.3	1.0		-0.2	-0.2	2.3	1.0
–	–	–		–	–	–	–
–	–	–		-1.0	-1.0	-1.0	-1.0
0.1	–	–		-0.2	0.1	–	–
–	–	–		–	–	–	–
–	–	0.7		–	–	-0.3	0.3
–	–	–		–	–	–	–
–	–	–		–	–	–	–
3.7	–	–		24.3	0.9	-3.4	-3.3
–	–	–		0.8	-0.2	-0.8	-1.7
–	–	–		–	–	–	–
–	–	0.0		–	–	–	0.0
–	–	–		–	–	–	–
5.4	5.1	6.2		10.4	5.4	5.1	6.2
–	–	–		-2.0	-2.0	-2.0	-3.0
9.2	*7.4*	*7.9*		*32.1*	*3.1*	*-0.2*	*-1.6*
7.0	*8.9*	*-0.7*		*-0.9*	*-13.7*	*3.9*	*-8.4*
–	–	–		–	–	–	–
5.6	*5.1*	*6.8*		*11.0*	*5.4*	*4.0*	*4.7*
16.2	*16.3*	*7.1*		*31.1*	*-10.6*	*3.6*	*-10.0*

13. ODF COMMITMENTS: BY PURPOSE %

	1987	1988	1989	1990
Education	2	7	2	–
Health	1	5	4	–
Other Social Infrastr.	4	8	13	–
Water Sanitat. Sewage	9	7	5	–
Energy	21	10	0	–
Telecommunications	0	1	2	–
Transportation	4	20	1	–
Agriculture	17	13	28	–
Extractive Industries	–	–	–	–
Manufacturing	1	0	6	–
Trade Banking Tourism	0	10	–	–
Technical Cooperation	15	10	25	–
Multisector Aid	2	0	0	–
Programme	18	3	–	–
Debt Reorganisation	1	0	1	–
Food Aid	6	3	9	–
Emergency Aid	1	1	3	–
Unspecified	0	–	–	–
TOTAL	100	100	100	–

14. GRANT ELEMENT OF ODA %

DAC COUNTRIES

	1987	1988	1989	1990
Australia	100.0	100.0	100.0	–
Austria	100.0	100.0	100.0	–
Belgium	100.0	100.0	100.0	–
Canada	100.0	100.0	100.0	–
Denmark	100.0	100.0	100.0	–
Finland	100.0	100.0	100.0	–
France	66.7	67.9	67.1	–
Germany	100.0	89.3	100.0	–
Ireland	100.0	100.0	–	–
Italy	100.0	100.0	100.0	–
Japan	68.7	72.8	100.0	–
Netherlands	100.0	93.8	100.0	–
New Zealand	100.0	100.0	–	–
Norway	96.1	100.0	100.0	–
Sweden	100.0	100.0	100.0	–
Switzerland	100.0	100.0	100.0	–
United Kingdom	100.0	100.0	100.0	–
United States	79.7	83.0	83.5	–
TOTAL	*80.8*	*79.6*	*95.2*	–
MULTILATERAL	*87.3*	*81.2*	*82.3*	–
ARAB COUNTRIES	–	–	–	–
E.E.C.+ MEMBERS	*97.6*	*93.8*	*98.2*	–
TOTAL	*82.9*	*80.3*	*90.1*	–

15. OTHER AGGREGATES

OFFICIAL COMMITMENTS:

	1987	1988	1989	1990
TOTAL BILATERAL	441.3	698.4	290.6	477.5
of which:				
Arab Countries	–	–	–	–
C.E.E.C.	79.7	–	–	–
TOTAL MULTILATERAL	260.9	358.6	232.7	501.6
TOTAL BIL.& MULTIL.	702.2	1057.0	523.2	979.2
of which:				
ODA Grants	254.5	375.3	274.8	254.3
ODA Loans	446.2	681.7	243.2	719.5

DISBURSEMENTS:

DAC COUNTRIES COMBINED

OFFICIAL & PRIVATE	1987	1988	1989	1990
GROSS:				
Contractual Lending	212.5	257.3	606.5	307.1
Export Credits, Total	68.2	36.0	428.0	126.0
Export Credits, Priv.	43.1	32.3	425.8	125.0
NET:				
Contractual Lending	112.4	153.9	350.9	174.0
Export Credits Total	4.3	-26.4	215.7	48.1
PRIVATE SECTOR NET	11.2	-7.1	194.4	17.9
Direct Investment	25.7	12.6	3.2	7.1
Portfolio Investment	2.3	4.4	-28.7	-43.5
Export Credits	-16.8	-24.1	219.9	54.4

MARKET BORROWING:

CHANGE IN CLAIMS

	1987	1988	1989	1990
Banks	-177.0	-99.0	230.0	-214.0

MEMORANDUM ITEM:

	1987	1988	1989	1990
C.E.E.C. (Gross)	–	–	–	–

1. TOTAL RECEIPTS NET

	1987	1988	1989	1990
DAC COUNTRIES				
Australia	0.0	0.0	0.0	–
Austria	–	–	0.0	–
Belgium	–	–	–	–
Canada	1.7	3.7	2.3	1.4
Denmark	–	–	–	–
Finland	–	–	0.0	–
France	2.3	-4.7	11.3	-0.7
Germany	0.0	0.0	0.2	0.0
Ireland	–	–	–	–
Italy	–	–	–	0.0
Japan	0.0	0.1	0.2	0.0
Netherlands	–	–	–	–
New Zealand	–	–	–	–
Norway	–	–	–	–
Sweden	–	–	–	–
Switzerland	–	–	–	–
United Kingdom	3.2	2.0	1.4	1.4
United States	–	4.0	8.0	2.0
TOTAL	*7.3*	*5.1*	*23.4*	*4.2*
MULTILATERAL				
AF.D.F.	–	–	–	–
AF.D.B.	–	–	–	–
AS.D.B	–	–	–	–
CAR.D.B.	1.8	1.4	1.8	1.8
E.E.C.	1.1	1.3	0.4	0.4
IBRD	–	–	–	–
IDA	–	–	–	–
I.D.B.	–	–	–	–
IFAD	–	–	–	–
I.F.C.	–	–	–	–
IMF TRUST FUND	–	–	–	–
U.N. AGENCIES	–	–	–	–
UNDP	0.4	0.3	0.2	0.3
UNTA	0.2	0.1	0.1	0.2
UNICEF	–	–	–	–
UNRWA	–	–	–	–
WFP	0.1	0.6	–	–
UNHCR	–	–	–	–
Other Multilateral	0.0	0.1	0.0	0.0
Arab Agencies	–	–	–	–
TOTAL	*3.5*	*3.7*	*2.6*	*2.8*
ARAB COUNTRIES	–	–	–	–
E.E.C.+ MEMBERS	*6.6*	*-1.4*	*13.3*	*1.2*
TOTAL	*10.9*	*8.8*	*25.9*	*7.0*

2. ODA LOANS GROSS

	1987	1988	1989	1990
DAC COUNTRIES				
Australia	–	–	–	–
Austria	–	–	–	–
Belgium	–	–	–	–
Canada	–	–	–	–
Denmark	–	–	–	–
Finland	–	–	–	–
France	–	–	–	–
Germany	–	–	–	–
Ireland	–	–	–	–
Italy	–	–	–	–
Japan	–	–	–	–
Netherlands	–	–	–	–
New Zealand	–	–	–	–
Norway	–	–	–	–
Sweden	–	–	–	–
Switzerland	–	–	–	–
United Kingdom	–	–	–	0.0
United States	–	2.0	7.0	2.0
TOTAL	–	*2.0*	*7.0*	*2.0*
MULTILATERAL	*2.2*	*2.1*	*2.1*	*2.2*
ARAB COUNTRIES	–	–	–	–
E.E.C.+ MEMBERS	*0.5*	*0.7*	*0.4*	*0.4*
TOTAL	*2.2*	*4.1*	*9.1*	*4.2*

3. TOTAL OFFICIAL GROSS

	1987	1988	1989	1990
DAC COUNTRIES				
Australia	0.0	0.0	0.0	–
Austria	–	–	0.0	–
Belgium	–	–	–	–
Canada	1.7	3.7	2.3	1.4
Denmark	–	–	–	–
Finland	–	–	0.0	–
France	–	–	–	–
Germany	0.0	0.0	0.2	0.0
Ireland	–	–	–	–
Italy	–	–	–	0.0
Japan	0.0	0.1	0.2	0.0
Netherlands	–	–	–	–
New Zealand	–	–	–	–
Norway	–	–	–	–
Sweden	–	–	–	–
Switzerland	–	–	–	–
United Kingdom	2.3	3.7	1.2	1.7
United States	–	4.0	8.0	2.0
TOTAL	*4.1*	*11.5*	*11.8*	*5.1*
MULTILATERAL	*3.6*	*3.7*	*2.6*	*2.9*
ARAB COUNTRIES	–	–	–	–
E.E.C.+ MEMBERS	*3.5*	*5.1*	*1.8*	*2.2*
TOTAL	*7.7*	*15.3*	*14.5*	*8.1*

4. TOTAL ODA NET

	1987	1988	1989	1990
Australia	0.0	0.0	0.0	–
Austria	–	–	0.0	–
Belgium	–	–	–	–
Canada	1.7	3.7	2.3	1.4
Denmark	–	–	–	–
Finland	–	–	0.0	–
France	–	–	–	–
Germany	0.0	0.0	0.2	0.0
Ireland	–	–	–	–
Italy	–	–	–	0.0
Japan	0.0	0.1	0.2	0.0
Netherlands	–	–	–	–
New Zealand	–	–	–	–
Norway	–	–	–	–
Sweden	–	–	–	–
Switzerland	–	–	–	–
United Kingdom	2.2	3.6	1.0	1.5
United States	–	3.0	7.0	2.0
TOTAL	*4.0*	*10.4*	*10.7*	*5.0*
AF.D.F.	–	–	–	–
AF.D.B.	–	–	–	–
AS.D.B	–	–	–	–
CAR.D.B.	1.7	1.3	1.7	1.7
E.E.C.	1.1	1.3	0.4	0.4
IBRD	–	–	–	–
IDA	–	–	–	–
I.D.B.	–	–	–	–
IFAD	–	–	–	–
I.F.C.	–	–	–	–
IMF TRUST FUND	–	–	–	–
U.N. AGENCIES	–	–	–	–
UNDP	0.4	0.3	0.2	0.3
UNTA	0.2	0.1	0.1	0.2
UNICEF	–	–	–	–
UNRWA	–	–	–	–
WFP	0.1	0.6	–	–
UNHCR	–	–	–	–
Other Multilateral	0.0	0.1	0.0	0.0
Arab Agencies	–	–	–	–
TOTAL	*3.5*	*3.6*	*2.5*	*2.7*
ARAB COUNTRIES	–	–	–	–
E.E.C.+ MEMBERS	*3.3*	*4.8*	*1.6*	*2.0*
TOTAL	*7.5*	*14.0*	*13.2*	*7.7*

5. ODA LOANS NET

	1987	1988	1989	1990
Australia	–	–	–	–
Austria	–	–	–	–
Belgium	–	–	–	–
Canada	–	–	–	–
Denmark	–	–	–	–
Finland	–	–	–	–
France	–	–	–	–
Germany	–	–	–	–
Ireland	–	–	–	–
Italy	–	–	–	–
Japan	–	–	–	–
Netherlands	–	–	–	–
New Zealand	–	–	–	–
Norway	–	–	–	–
Sweden	–	–	–	–
Switzerland	–	–	–	–
United Kingdom	-0.1	-0.2	-0.1	-0.2
United States	–	2.0	7.0	2.0
TOTAL	*-0.1*	*1.8*	*6.9*	*1.8*
MULTILATERAL	*2.1*	*2.0*	*2.1*	*2.1*
ARAB COUNTRIES	–	–	–	–
E.E.C.+ MEMBERS	*0.3*	*0.5*	*0.2*	*0.2*
TOTAL	*2.0*	*3.8*	*8.9*	*4.0*

6. TOTAL OFFICIAL NET

	1987	1988	1989	1990
Australia	0.0	0.0	0.0	–
Austria	–	–	0.0	–
Belgium	–	–	–	–
Canada	1.7	3.7	2.3	1.4
Denmark	–	–	–	–
Finland	–	–	0.0	–
France	–	–	–	–
Germany	0.0	0.0	0.2	0.0
Ireland	–	–	–	–
Italy	–	–	–	0.0
Japan	0.0	0.1	0.2	0.0
Netherlands	–	–	–	–
New Zealand	–	–	–	–
Norway	–	–	–	–
Sweden	–	–	–	–
Switzerland	–	–	–	–
United Kingdom	2.2	3.6	1.0	1.5
United States	–	4.0	8.0	2.0
TOTAL	*4.0*	*11.4*	*11.7*	*5.0*
MULTILATERAL	*3.5*	*3.7*	*2.6*	*2.8*
ARAB COUNTRIES	–	–	–	–
E.E.C.+ MEMBERS	*3.3*	*4.8*	*1.6*	*2.0*
TOTAL	*7.5*	*15.0*	*14.3*	*7.7*

7. TOTAL ODA GROSS

	1987
Australia	0.0
Austria	–
Belgium	–
Canada	1.7
Denmark	–
Finland	–
France	–
Germany	0.0
Ireland	–
Italy	–
Japan	0.0
Netherlands	–
New Zealand	–
Norway	–
Sweden	–
Switzerland	–
United Kingdom	2.3
United States	–
TOTAL	*4.1*
AF.D.F.	–
AF.D.B.	–
AS.D.B	–
CAR.D.B.	1.7
E.E.C.	1.1
IBRD	–
IDA	–
I.D.B.	–
IFAD	–
I.F.C.	–
IMF TRUST FUND	–
U.N. AGENCIES	–
UNDP	0.4
UNTA	0.2
UNICEF	–
UNRWA	–
WFP	0.1
UNHCR	–
Other Multilateral	0.0
Arab Agencies	–
TOTAL	*3.5*
ARAB COUNTRIES	–
E.E.C.+ MEMBERS	*3.5*
TOTAL	*7.7*

8. GRANTS

	1987
Australia	0.0
Austria	–
Belgium	–
Canada	1.7
Denmark	–
Finland	–
France	–
Germany	0.0
Ireland	–
Italy	–
Japan	0.0
Netherlands	–
New Zealand	–
Norway	–
Sweden	–
Switzerland	–
United Kingdom	2.3
United States	–
TOTAL	*4.1*
MULTILATERAL	*1.4*
ARAB COUNTRIES	–
E.E.C.+ MEMBERS	*3.0*
TOTAL	*5.5*

9. TOTAL OOF GROSS

	1987
Australia	–
Austria	–
Belgium	–
Canada	–
Denmark	–
Finland	–
France	–
Germany	–
Ireland	–
Italy	–
Japan	–
Netherlands	–
New Zealand	–
Norway	–
Sweden	–
Switzerland	–
United Kingdom	–
United States	–
TOTAL	–
MULTILATERAL	*0.1*
ARAB COUNTRIES	–
E.E.C.+ MEMBERS	–
TOTAL	*0.1*

10. ODA COMMITMENTS

1988	1989	1990		1987	1988	1989	1990
0.0	0.0	–		–	0.0	0.0	–
–	0.0	–		–	–	0.0	–
–	–	–		–	–	–	–
3.7	2.3	1.4		2.9	8.7	0.1	0.4
–	–	–		–	–	–	–
–	0.0	–		–	–	0.0	–
–	–	–		–	–	–	–
0.0	0.2	0.0		0.0	0.0	0.2	0.0
–	–	–		–	–	–	–
–	–	0.0		–	–	–	0.0
0.1	0.2	0.0		0.1	0.1	0.2	0.0
–	–	–		–	–	–	–
–	–	–		–	–	–	–
–	–	–		–	–	–	–
–	–	–		–	–	–	–
3.7	1.2	1.7		0.6	0.6	8.9	1.3
3.0	7.0	2.0		8.1	1.6	0.6	–
10.5	*10.8*	*5.1*		*11.7*	*11.1*	*10.0*	*1.8*
–	–	–		–	–	–	–
–	–	–		–	–	–	–
1.3	1.7	1.7		1.4	5.2	3.7	3.7
1.3	0.5	0.5		1.7	0.1	3.0	3.0
–	–	–		–	–	–	–
–	–	–		–	–	–	–
–	–	–		–	–	–	–
–	–	–		–	–	–	–
–	–	–		0.7	1.0	0.3	0.5
0.3	0.2	0.3		–	–	–	–
0.1	0.1	0.2		–	–	–	–
–	–	–		–	–	–	–
0.6	–	–		–	–	–	–
0.1	0.0	0.0		–	–	–	–
–	–	0.1		0.5	–	–	–
3.7	2.6	2.8		4.3	6.3	7.0	7.2
–	–	–		–	–	–	–
5.1	1.8	2.2		2.4	0.8	12.2	4.4
14.2	*13.4*	*8.0*		*16.1*	*17.4*	*17.0*	*9.0*

11. TECH. COOP. GRANTS

1988	1989	1990		1987	1988	1989	1990
0.0	0.0	–		0.0	0.0	–	–
–	0.0	–		–	–	0.0	–
3.7	2.3	1.4		–	0.3	0.7	0.5
–	–	–		–	–	–	–
–	0.0	–		–	–	–	–
–	–	–		–	–	–	–
0.0	0.2	0.0		0.0	0.0	0.0	0.0
–	–	–		–	–	–	–
–	–	0.0		–	–	–	–
0.1	0.2	0.0		0.0	0.1	0.1	0.0
–	–	–		–	–	–	–
–	–	–		–	–	–	–
–	–	–		–	–	–	–
–	–	–		–	–	–	–
3.7	1.2	1.7		0.6	0.6	0.7	1.2
1.0	–	–		–	–	–	–
8.5	*3.8*	*3.1*		*0.7*	*1.1*	*1.5*	*1.7*
1.6	*0.4*	*0.6*		*0.6*	*0.4*	*0.3*	*0.5*
–	–	–		–	–	–	–
4.4	*1.5*	*1.8*		*0.7*	*0.7*	*0.8*	*1.2*
10.1	*4.3*	*3.8*		*1.3*	*1.5*	*1.9*	*2.3*

12. TOTAL OOF NET

1988	1989	1990		1987	1988	1989	1990
–	–	–		–	–	–	–
–	–	–		–	–	–	–
–	–	–		–	–	–	–
–	–	–		–	–	–	–
–	–	–		–	–	–	–
–	–	–		–	–	–	–
–	–	–		–	–	–	–
–	–	–		–	–	–	–
–	–	–		–	–	–	–
–	–	–		–	–	–	–
–	–	–		–	–	–	–
–	–	–		–	–	–	–
–	–	–		–	–	–	–
–	–	–		–	–	–	–
–	–	–		–	–	–	–
1.0	1.0	–		–	1.0	1.0	–
1.0	*1.0*	–		–	*1.0*	*1.0*	–
0.1	*0.1*	*0.1*		*0.1*	*0.1*	*0.1*	*0.1*
–	–	–		–	–	–	–
–	–	–		–	–	–	–
1.1	*1.1*	*0.1*		*0.1*	*1.1*	*1.1*	*0.1*

13. ODF COMMITMENTS: BY PURPOSE %

	1987	1988	1989	1990
Education	4	–	–	–
Health	2	–	–	–
Other Social Infrastr.	–	–	–	–
Water Sanitat. Sewage	0	75	–	–
Energy	–	–	–	–
Telecommunications	–	–	0.0	–
Transportation	–	–	–	–
Agriculture	8	1	–	–
Extractive Industries	–	–	–	–
Manufacturing	–	–	–	–
Trade Banking Tourism	1	–	–	–
Technical Cooperation	13	10	12	–
Multisector Aid	72	14	82	–
Programme	–	–	–	–
Debt Reorganisation	–	–	–	–
Food Aid	–	–	5	–
Emergency Aid	–	–	0	–
Unspecified	–	–	–	–
TOTAL	100	100	100	–

14. GRANT ELEMENT OF ODA %
DAC COUNTRIES

	1987	1988	1989	1990
Australia	–	100.0	100.0	–
Austria	–	–	100.0	–
Belgium	–	–	–	–
Canada	100.0	100.0	100.0	–
Denmark	–	–	–	–
Finland	–	–	100.0	–
France	–	–	–	–
Germany	100.0	100.0	100.0	–
Ireland	–	–	–	–
Italy	–	–	–	–
Japan	100.0	100.0	100.0	–
Netherlands	–	–	–	–
New Zealand	–	–	–	–
Norway	–	–	–	–
Sweden	–	–	–	–
Switzerland	–	–	–	–
United Kingdom	100.0	100.0	69.0	–
United States	46.4	60.1	100.0	–
TOTAL	*63.0*	*94.3*	*72.3*	–
MULTILATERAL	*70.3*	*100.0*	*100.0*	–
ARAB COUNTRIES	–	–	–	–
E.E.C.+ MEMBERS	*100.0*	*100.0*	*77.2*	–
TOTAL	*63.7*	*95.0*	*79.3*	–

15. OTHER AGGREGATES

	1987	1988	1989	1990
OFFICIAL COMMITMENTS:				
TOTAL BILATERAL	14.3	11.1	10.2	1.8
of which:				
Arab Countries	–	–	–	–
C.E.E.C.	–	–	–	–
TOTAL MULTILATERAL	4.3	6.8	7.0	7.2
TOTAL BIL.& MULTIL.	18.6	17.9	17.2	9.0
of which:				
ODA Grants	4.4	11.2	5.1	5.3
ODA Loans	11.7	6.2	11.9	3.7
DISBURSEMENTS:				
DAC COUNTRIES COMBINED				
OFFICIAL & PRIVATE				
GROSS:				
Contractual Lending	1.1	1.8	9.0	2.0
Export Credits, Total	1.1	-1.2	1.0	–
Export Credits, Priv.	1.1	-1.2	1.0	–
NET:				
Contractual Lending	0.9	0.1	8.2	1.8
Export Credits Total	1.0	-2.7	0.4	0.0
PRIVATE SECTOR NET	3.3	-6.3	11.7	-0.8
Direct Investment	0.3	–	–	–
Portfolio Investment	2.0	-3.5	11.3	-0.7
Export Credits	1.0	-2.7	0.4	0.0
MARKET BORROWING:				
CHANGE IN CLAIMS				
Banks	–	–	–	–
MEMORANDUM ITEM:				
C.E.E.C. (Gross)	–	–	–	–

DISBURSEMENTS, UNLESS OTHERWISE STATE

	1987	1988	1989	1990		1987	1988	1989	1990		1987

1. TOTAL RECEIPTS NET

DAC COUNTRIES

	1987	1988	1989	1990
Australia	0.0	0.0	0.0	0.0
Austria	–	–	–	–
Belgium	–	–	–	0.0
Canada	3.8	4.4	2.8	2.8
Denmark	–	–	–	–
Finland	–	–	–	–
France	0.0	0.0	3.3	1.9
Germany	0.1	0.2	0.1	0.0
Ireland	–	–	–	–
Italy	–	2.4	–	–
Japan	0.2	1.1	3.5	0.4
Netherlands	0.0	–	0.1	0.5
New Zealand	–	–	–	–
Norway	–	–	–	–
Sweden	–	–	–	–
Switzerland	–	–	–	–
United Kingdom	6.1	6.7	13.7	1.5
United States	–	–	–	–
TOTAL	*10.2*	*14.8*	*23.5*	*7.1*

MULTILATERAL

	1987	1988	1989	1990
AF.D.F.	–	–	–	–
AF.D.B.	–	–	–	–
AS.D.B	–	–	–	–
CAR.D.B.	2.4	6.0	3.7	3.7
E.E.C.	1.0	1.2	2.2	2.2
IBRD	–	–	–	–
IDA	–	–	–	–
I.D.B.	–	–	–	–
IFAD	0.2	–	0.2	–
I.F.C.	–	–	–	–
IMF TRUST FUND	–	–	–	–
U.N. AGENCIES	–	–	–	–
UNDP	0.7	0.8	0.3	0.3
UNTA	0.4	0.1	0.1	0.2
UNICEF	–	–	–	–
UNRWA	–	–	–	–
WFP	0.3	2.4	0.0	–
UNHCR	–	–	–	–
Other Multilateral	0.2	0.0	0.1	0.1
Arab Agencies	–	–	–	–
TOTAL	*5.1*	*10.5*	*6.6*	*6.5*
ARAB COUNTRIES	*–*	*–*	*–*	*–*
E.E.C.+ MEMBERS	*7.3*	*10.5*	*19.4*	*6.1*
TOTAL	***15.3***	***25.3***	***30.0***	***13.6***

2. ODA LOANS GROSS

DAC COUNTRIES

	1987	1988	1989	1990
Australia	–	–	–	–
Austria	–	–	–	–
Belgium	–	–	–	–
Canada	–	–	–	–
Denmark	–	–	–	–
Finland	–	–	–	–
France	–	–	–	–
Germany	–	–	–	–
Ireland	–	–	–	–
Italy	–	–	–	–
Japan	–	–	–	–
Netherlands	–	–	–	–
New Zealand	–	–	–	–
Norway	–	–	–	–
Sweden	–	–	–	–
Switzerland	–	–	–	–
United Kingdom	–	0.6	3.4	1.4
United States	–	–	–	–
TOTAL	*–*	*0.6*	*3.4*	*1.4*
MULTILATERAL	*2.7*	*6.0*	*5.6*	*5.5*
ARAB COUNTRIES	*–*	*–*	*–*	*–*
E.E.C.+ MEMBERS	*0.3*	*0.6*	*5.0*	*3.0*
TOTAL	***2.7***	***6.6***	***9.0***	***6.9***

3. TOTAL OFFICIAL GROSS

DAC COUNTRIES

	1987	1988	1989	1990
Australia	0.0	0.0	0.0	0.0
Austria	–	–	–	–
Belgium	–	–	–	0.0
Canada	3.8	4.4	2.8	2.3
Denmark	–	–	–	–
Finland	–	–	–	–
France	0.0	0.0	0.0	0.4
Germany	0.1	0.2	0.0	0.0
Ireland	–	–	–	–
Italy	–	–	–	–
Japan	0.2	1.1	3.5	0.4
Netherlands	0.0	–	–	–
New Zealand	–	–	–	–
Norway	–	–	–	–
Sweden	–	–	–	–
Switzerland	–	–	–	–
United Kingdom	5.2	5.1	14.6	4.2
United States	–	–	–	–
TOTAL	*9.3*	*10.8*	*20.9*	*7.4*
MULTILATERAL	*5.1*	*10.6*	*6.8*	*6.7*
ARAB COUNTRIES	*–*	*–*	*–*	*–*
E.E.C.+ MEMBERS	*6.4*	*6.6*	*16.9*	*6.9*
TOTAL	***14.4***	***21.4***	***27.7***	***14.2***

4. TOTAL ODA NET

	1987	1988	1989	1990
	0.0	0.0	0.0	0.0
	–	–	–	–
	–	–	–	0.0
	3.8	4.4	2.8	2.3
	–	–	–	–
	–	–	–	–
	0.0	0.0	0.0	0.1
	0.1	0.2	0.0	0.0
	–	–	–	–
	–	–	–	–
	0.2	1.1	3.5	0.4
	0.0	–	–	–
	–	–	–	–
	–	–	–	–
	–	–	–	–
	–	–	–	–
	1.8	1.5	5.5	3.2
	–	–	–	–
TOTAL	*6.0*	*7.2*	*11.8*	*6.2*

	1987	1988	1989	1990
	–	–	–	–
	–	–	–	–
	–	–	–	–
	2.2	6.0	3.7	3.7
	1.0	1.2	2.2	2.2
	–	–	–	–
	–	–	–	–
	–	–	–	–
	0.2	–	0.2	–
	–	–	–	–
	–	–	–	–
	–	–	–	–
	0.7	0.8	0.3	0.3
	0.4	0.1	0.1	0.2
	–	–	–	–
	–	–	–	–
	0.3	2.4	0.0	–
	–	–	–	–
	0.2	0.0	0.1	0.1
	–	–	–	–
TOTAL	*4.9*	*10.5*	*6.5*	*6.4*
ARAB COUNTRIES	*–*	*–*	*–*	*–*
E.E.C.+ MEMBERS	*3.0*	*2.9*	*7.7*	*5.6*
TOTAL	***10.9***	***17.6***	***18.3***	***12.6***

5. ODA LOANS NET

	1987	1988	1989	1990
	–	–	–	–
	–	–	–	–
	–	–	–	–
	–	0.0	0.0	–
	–	–	–	–
	–	–	–	–
	–	–	–	–
	–	–	–	–
	–	–	–	–
	–	–	–	–
	–	–	–	–
	–	–	–	–
	–	–	–	–
	–	–	–	–
	–	–	–	–
	–	–	–	–
	-0.1	0.6	3.3	1.3
	–	–	–	–
TOTAL	*-0.1*	*0.6*	*3.3*	*1.3*
MULTILATERAL	*2.6*	*5.8*	*5.4*	*5.2*
ARAB COUNTRIES	*–*	*–*	*–*	*–*
E.E.C.+ MEMBERS	*0.1*	*0.5*	*4.9*	*2.9*
TOTAL	***2.5***	***6.4***	***8.7***	***6.5***

6. TOTAL OFFICIAL NET

	1987	1988	1989	1990
	0.0	0.0	0.0	0.0
	–	–	–	–
	–	–	–	0.0
	3.8	4.4	2.8	2.3
	–	–	–	–
	–	–	–	–
	0.0	0.0	0.0	0.4
	0.1	0.2	0.0	0.0
	–	–	–	–
	–	–	–	–
	0.2	1.1	3.5	0.4
	0.0	–	–	–
	–	–	–	–
	–	–	–	–
	–	–	–	–
	–	–	–	–
	4.9	4.7	13.8	2.6
	–	–	–	–
TOTAL	*9.0*	*10.4*	*20.2*	*5.8*
MULTILATERAL	*5.1*	*10.5*	*6.6*	*6.5*
ARAB COUNTRIES	*–*	*–*	*–*	*–*
E.E.C.+ MEMBERS	*6.0*	*6.1*	*16.1*	*5.2*
TOTAL	***14.0***	***20.9***	***26.7***	***12.3***

7. TOTAL ODA GROSS

	1987
Australia	0.0
Austria	–
Belgium	–
Canada	3.8
Denmark	–
Finland	–
France	0.0
Germany	0.1
Ireland	–
Italy	–
Japan	0.2
Netherlands	0.0
New Zealand	–
Norway	–
Sweden	–
Switzerland	–
United Kingdom	1.9
United States	–
TOTAL	*6.0*

	1987
AF.D.F.	–
AF.D.B.	–
AS.D.B	–
CAR.D.B.	2.2
E.E.C.	1.0
IBRD	–
IDA	–
I.D.B.	–
IFAD	0.2
I.F.C.	–
IMF TRUST FUND	–
U.N. AGENCIES	–
UNDP	0.7
UNTA	0.4
UNICEF	–
UNRWA	–
WFP	0.3
UNHCR	–
Other Multilateral	0.2
Arab Agencies	–
TOTAL	*5.0*
ARAB COUNTRIES	*–*
E.E.C.+ MEMBERS	*3.1*
TOTAL	***11.0***

8. GRANTS

	1987
Australia	0.0
Austria	–
Belgium	–
Canada	3.8
Denmark	–
Finland	–
France	0.0
Germany	0.1
Ireland	–
Italy	–
Japan	0.2
Netherlands	0.0
New Zealand	–
Norway	–
Sweden	–
Switzerland	–
United Kingdom	1.9
United States	–
TOTAL	*6.0*
MULTILATERAL	*2.3*
ARAB COUNTRIES	*–*
E.E.C.+ MEMBERS	*2.8*
TOTAL	***8.4***

9. TOTAL OOF GROSS

	1987
Australia	–
Austria	–
Belgium	–
Canada	–
Denmark	–
Finland	–
France	–
Germany	–
Ireland	–
Italy	–
Japan	–
Netherlands	–
New Zealand	–
Norway	–
Sweden	–
Switzerland	–
United Kingdom	3.3
United States	–
TOTAL	*3.3*
MULTILATERAL	*0.1*
ARAB COUNTRIES	*–*
E.E.C.+ MEMBERS	*3.3*
TOTAL	***3.4***

10. ODA COMMITMENTS

1988	1989	1990	1987	1988	1989	1990
0.0	0.0	0.0	–	0.0	0.0	0.0
–	–	–	–	–	–	–
4.4	2.8	2.3	1.3	19.0	0.1	2.8
–	–	–	–	–	–	–
0.0	0.0	0.1	0.0	0.0	0.0	15.7
0.2	0.0	0.0	0.1	0.2	0.0	0.0
–	–	–	–	–	–	–
1.1	3.5	0.4	0.2	5.2	0.1	0.1
			0.0	–	–	–
–	–	–	–	–	–	–
–	–	–	–	–	–	–
–	–	–	–	–	–	–
–	–	–	–	–	–	–
1.5	5.5	3.3	0.8	0.7	1.6	1.4
–	–	–	–	–	–	–
7.2	*11.9*	*6.3*	*2.4*	*25.0*	*1.8*	*20.1*
–	–	–	–	–	–	–
–	–	–	–	–	–	–
6.0	3.7	3.7	6.5	2.8	4.2	4.2
1.3	2.3	2.3	0.7	4.3	1.5	1.5
–	–	–	–	–	–	5.0
–	–	–	–	–	–	–
–	0.3	0.2	–	–	–	–
–	–	–	–	–	–	–
–	–	–	1.6	3.3	0.5	0.6
0.8	0.3	0.3	–	–	–	–
0.1	0.1	0.2	–	–	–	–
–	–	–	–	–	–	–
2.4	0.0	–	–	–	–	–
–	–	–	–	–	–	–
0.0	0.1	0.1	–	–	–	–
–	–	–	0.5	–	–	1.9
10.6	*6.8*	*6.7*	*9.3*	*10.4*	*6.2*	*13.2*
–	–	–	–	–	–	–
3.0	*7.9*	*5.8*	*1.6*	*5.2*	*3.2*	*18.7*
17.8	*18.6*	*13.0*	*11.7*	*35.4*	*8.0*	*33.2*

11. TECH. COOP. GRANTS

1988	1989	1990	1987	1988	1989	1990
0.0	0.0	0.0	0.0	0.0	0.0	0.0
–	–	–	–	–	–	–
–	–	0.0	–	–	–	–
4.4	2.8	2.3	–	1.1	1.3	1.3
–	–	–	–	–	–	–
–	–	–	–	–	–	–
0.0	0.0	0.1	0.0	0.0	0.0	0.1
0.2	0.0	0.0	0.1	0.2	0.0	0.0
–	–	–	–	–	–	–
1.1	3.5	0.4	0.2	0.1	0.1	0.1
–	–	–	0.0	–	–	–
–	–	–	–	–	–	–
–	–	–	–	–	–	–
–	–	–	–	–	–	–
0.9	2.2	1.9	0.7	0.7	1.6	1.4
–	–	–	–	–	–	–
6.6	*8.5*	*4.9*	*1.1*	*2.1*	*3.0*	*2.9*
4.6	*1.1*	*1.2*	*1.3*	*1.1*	*0.5*	*0.6*
–	–	–	–	–	–	–
2.4	*2.9*	*2.7*	*0.9*	*1.1*	*1.6*	*1.5*
11.2	*9.7*	*6.1*	*2.4*	*3.3*	*3.5*	*3.5*

12. TOTAL OOF NET

1988	1989	1990	1987	1988	1989	1990
–	–	–	–	–	–	–
–	–	–	–	–	–	–
–	–	–	–	–	–	–
–	–	–	–	–	–	–
–	–	–	–	–	–	–
–	–	–	–	–	–	–
–	–	0.3	–	–	–	0.3
–	–	–	–	–	–	–
–	–	–	–	–	–	–
–	–	–	–	–	–	–
–	–	–	–	–	–	–
–	–	–	–	–	–	–
–	–	–	–	–	–	–
–	–	–	–	–	–	–
3.6	9.0	0.9	3.0	3.2	8.4	-0.7
–	–	–	–	–	–	–
3.6	*9.0*	*1.2*	*3.0*	*3.2*	*8.4*	*-0.4*
0.1	*0.0*	*0.0*	*0.1*	*0.1*	*0.0*	*0.0*
–	–	–	–	–	–	–
3.6	*9.0*	*1.2*	*3.0*	*3.2*	*8.4*	*-0.4*
3.6	*9.1*	*1.2*	*3.1*	*3.3*	*8.4*	*-0.3*

13. ODF COMMITMENTS: BY PURPOSE %

	1987	1988	1989	1990
Education	8	–	8	–
Health	–	1	3	–
Other Social Infrastr.	–	1	14	–
Water Sanitat. Sewage	–	71	–	–
Energy	77	–	–	–
Telecommunications	–	–	–	–
Transportation	–	–	–	–
Agriculture	1	19	7	–
Extractive Industries	–	–	–	–
Manufacturing	–	–	–	–
Trade Banking Tourism	–	–	17	–
Technical Cooperation	14	7	47	–
Multisector Aid	–	–	3	–
Programme	–	–	–	–
Debt Reorganisation	–	–	–	–
Food Aid	–	–	–	–
Emergency Aid	–	–	–	–
Unspecified	–	–	–	–
TOTAL	100	100	100	–

14. GRANT ELEMENT OF ODA %

DAC COUNTRIES

	1987	1988	1989	1990
Australia	–	100.0	100.0	–
Austria	–	–	–	–
Belgium	–	–	–	–
Canada	100.0	100.0	100.0	–
Denmark	–	–	–	–
Finland	–	–	–	–
France	100.0	100.0	100.0	–
Germany	100.0	100.0	100.0	–
Ireland	–	–	–	–
Italy	–	–	–	–
Japan	100.0	100.0	100.0	–
Netherlands	100.0	–	–	–
New Zealand	–	–	–	–
Norway	–	–	–	–
Sweden	–	–	–	–
Switzerland	–	–	–	–
United Kingdom	100.0	100.0	100.0	–
United States	–	–	–	–
TOTAL	*100.0*	*100.0*	*100.0*	–
MULTILATERAL	*87.4*	*100.0*	*100.0*	–
ARAB COUNTRIES	–	–	–	–
E.E.C.+ MEMBERS	*100.0*	*100.0*	*100.0*	–
TOTAL	*93.3*	*100.0*	*100.0*	–

15. OTHER AGGREGATES

OFFICIAL COMMITMENTS:

	1987	1988	1989	1990
TOTAL BILATERAL	15.5	25.0	5.9	20.1
of which:				
Arab Countries	–	–	–	–
C.E.E.C.	–	–	–	–
TOTAL MULTILATERAL	9.3	15.9	9.0	19.0
TOTAL BIL.& MULTIL.	24.8	41.0	14.9	39.0
of which:				
ODA Grants	4.7	33.3	3.8	6.6
ODA Loans	7.0	2.1	4.2	26.7

DISBURSEMENTS:

DAC COUNTRIES COMBINED

	1987	1988	1989	1990
OFFICIAL & PRIVATE				
GROSS:				
Contractual Lending	4.9	9.0	12.7	3.4
Export Credits, Total	1.6	4.9	0.3	0.9
Export Credits, Priv.	1.6	4.9	0.3	0.9
NET:				
Contractual Lending	4.2	8.2	11.5	0.3
Export Credits Total	1.3	4.4	-0.1	-0.7
PRIVATE SECTOR NET	1.3	4.4	3.3	1.3
Direct Investment	–	–	3.4	2.0
Portfolio Investment	–	–	0.1	0.0
Export Credits	1.3	4.4	-0.1	-0.7

MARKET BORROWING:

CHANGE IN CLAIMS

	1987	1988	1989	1990
Banks	–	–	–	–

MEMORANDUM ITEM:

	1987	1988	1989	1990
C.E.E.C. (Gross)	–	–	–	–

1. TOTAL RECEIPTS NET / 4. TOTAL ODA NET / 7. TOTAL ODA GROSS

	1. TOTAL RECEIPTS NET				4. TOTAL ODA NET				7. TOTAL ODA GROSS
	1987	1988	1989	1990	1987	1988	1989	1990	1987
DAC COUNTRIES									
Australia	0.0	–	–	–	0.0	–	–	–	0.0
Austria	–	–	–	–	–	–	–	–	–
Belgium	–	–	–	–	–	–	–	–	–
Canada	1.4	1.3	0.7	1.1	1.4	1.3	0.7	1.1	1.4
Denmark	–	–	–	–	–	–	–	–	–
Finland	–	–	–	–	–	–	–	–	–
France	0.0	0.0	0.0	0.0	0.0	0.0	0.0	0.0	0.0
Germany	0.2	-0.5	-0.6	0.1	0.0	0.1	0.1	0.1	0.0
Ireland	–	–	–	–	–	–	–	–	–
Italy	–	–	–	–	–	–	–	–	–
Japan	0.2	1.4	3.0	0.8	0.2	1.4	3.0	0.8	0.2
Netherlands	–	–	1.6	-0.7	–	–	–	–	–
New Zealand	–	–	–	–	–	–	–	–	–
Norway	–	0.0	–	–	–	0.0	–	–	–
Sweden	–	–	–	–	–	–	–	–	–
Switzerland	–	–	–	–	–	–	–	–	–
United Kingdom	1.5	1.4	1.3	2.3	1.6	1.4	1.6	2.3	1.8
United States	2.0	2.0	1.0	1.0	2.0	2.0	1.0	1.0	2.0
TOTAL	*5.2*	*5.6*	*7.0*	*4.5*	*5.3*	*6.2*	*6.4*	*5.2*	*5.4*
MULTILATERAL									
AF.D.F.	–	–	–	–	–	–	–	–	–
AF.D.B.	–	–	–	–	–	–	–	–	–
AS.D.B	–	–	–	–	–	–	–	–	–
CAR.D.B.	4.6	5.8	5.4	5.4	4.6	5.8	5.4	5.4	4.6
E.E.C.	2.0	1.3	1.5	1.5	2.0	1.3	1.5	1.5	2.0
IBRD	–	–	–	–	–	–	–	–	–
IDA	0.5	1.0	1.0	1.0	0.5	1.0	1.0	1.0	0.5
I.D.B.	–	–	–	–	–	–	–	–	–
IFAD	–	–	–	–	–	–	–	–	–
I.F.C.	–	–	–	–	–	–	–	–	–
IMF TRUST FUND	–	–	–	–	–	–	–	–	–
U.N. AGENCIES	–	–	–	–	–	–	–	–	–
UNDP	0.6	0.6	0.6	0.4	0.6	0.6	0.6	0.4	0.6
UNTA	0.2	0.1	0.1	0.1	0.2	0.1	0.1	0.1	0.2
UNICEF	–	–	–	–	–	–	–	–	–
UNRWA	–	–	–	–	–	–	–	–	–
WFP	0.2	1.8	–	0.1	0.2	1.8	–	0.1	0.2
UNHCR	–	–	–	–	–	–	–	–	–
Other Multilateral	0.1	0.1	0.1	0.1	0.1	0.1	0.1	0.1	0.1
Arab Agencies	-0.1	-0.1	-0.1	–	-0.1	-0.1	-0.1	–	–
TOTAL	*8.1*	*10.5*	*8.6*	*8.5*	*8.1*	*10.5*	*8.6*	*8.5*	*8.3*
ARAB COUNTRIES	–	–	–	–	–	–	–	–	–
E.E.C.+ MEMBERS	*3.7*	*2.3*	*3.8*	*3.2*	*3.7*	*2.8*	*3.2*	*3.9*	*3.9*
TOTAL	*13.4*	*16.1*	*15.6*	*13.0*	*13.4*	*16.6*	*15.0*	*13.7*	*13.7*

2. ODA LOANS GROSS / 5. ODA LOANS NET / 8. GRANTS

	2. ODA LOANS GROSS				5. ODA LOANS NET				8. GRANTS
	1987	1988	1989	1990	1987	1988	1989	1990	1987
DAC COUNTRIES									
Australia	–	–	–	–	–	–	–	–	0.0
Austria	–	–	–	–	–	–	–	–	–
Belgium	–	–	–	–	–	–	–	–	–
Canada	–	–	–	–	0.0	0.0	0.0	0.0	1.4
Denmark	–	–	–	–	–	–	–	–	–
Finland	–	–	–	–	–	–	–	–	–
France	–	–	–	–	–	–	–	–	0.0
Germany	–	–	–	–	–	–	–	–	0.0
Ireland	–	–	–	–	–	–	–	–	–
Italy	–	–	–	–	–	–	–	–	–
Japan	–	–	–	–	–	–	–	–	0.2
Netherlands	–	–	–	–	–	–	–	–	–
New Zealand	–	–	–	–	–	–	–	–	–
Norway	–	–	–	–	–	–	–	–	–
Sweden	–	–	–	–	–	–	–	–	–
Switzerland	–	–	–	–	–	–	–	–	–
United Kingdom	–	0.0	0.3	0.3	-0.2	-0.1	0.2	0.2	1.8
United States	2.0	2.0	1.0	1.0	2.0	2.0	1.0	1.0	–
TOTAL	*2.0*	*2.0*	*1.3*	*1.3*	*1.8*	*1.9*	*1.1*	*1.2*	*3.4*
MULTILATERAL	*6.9*	*7.5*	*6.6*	*6.7*	*6.8*	*7.4*	*6.5*	*6.5*	*1.4*
ARAB COUNTRIES	–	–	–	–	–	–	–	–	
E.E.C.+ MEMBERS	*1.8*	*0.7*	*0.6*	*0.5*	*1.6*	*0.6*	*0.4*	*0.4*	*2.1*
TOTAL	*8.9*	*9.5*	*8.0*	*8.0*	*8.6*	*9.2*	*7.6*	*7.7*	*4.8*

3. TOTAL OFFICIAL GROSS / 6. TOTAL OFFICIAL NET / 9. TOTAL OOF GROSS

	3. TOTAL OFFICIAL GROSS				6. TOTAL OFFICIAL NET				9. TOTAL OOF GROSS
	1987	1988	1989	1990	1987	1988	1989	1990	1987
DAC COUNTRIES									
Australia	0.0	–	–	–	0.0	–	–	–	–
Austria	–	–	–	–	–	–	–	–	–
Belgium	–	–	–	–	–	–	–	–	–
Canada	1.4	1.3	0.7	1.1	1.4	1.3	0.7	1.1	–
Denmark	–	–	–	–	–	–	–	–	–
Finland	–	–	–	–	–	–	–	–	–
France	0.0	0.0	0.0	0.0	0.0	0.0	0.0	0.0	–
Germany	0.0	0.1	0.1	0.1	0.0	0.1	-0.7	0.1	–
Ireland	–	–	–	–	–	–	–	–	–
Italy	–	–	–	–	–	–	–	–	–
Japan	0.2	1.4	3.0	0.8	0.2	1.4	3.0	0.8	–
Netherlands	–	–	–	–	–	–	–	–	–
New Zealand	–	–	–	–	–	–	–	–	–
Norway	–	0.0	–	–	–	0.0	–	–	–
Sweden	–	–	–	–	–	–	–	–	–
Switzerland	–	–	–	–	–	–	–	–	–
United Kingdom	1.8	1.5	1.8	2.4	1.6	1.4	1.3	2.3	–
United States	2.0	2.0	1.0	1.0	2.0	2.0	1.0	1.0	–
TOTAL	*5.4*	*6.3*	*6.5*	*5.3*	*5.3*	*6.1*	*5.3*	*5.2*	*–*
MULTILATERAL	*8.3*	*10.6*	*8.8*	*8.6*	*8.1*	*10.5*	*8.6*	*8.5*	*–*
ARAB COUNTRIES	–	–	–	–	–	–	–	–	–
E.E.C.+ MEMBERS	*3.9*	*2.9*	*3.4*	*4.0*	*3.7*	*2.8*	*2.1*	*3.9*	*–*
TOTAL	*13.7*	*17.0*	*15.3*	*13.9*	*13.4*	*16.6*	*13.9*	*13.7*	*TOTAL*

1988	1989	1990

10. ODA COMMITMENTS

1987	1988	1989	1990

1988	1989	1990	1987	1988	1989	1990
–	–	–	0.0	–	–	–
–	–	–	–	–	–	–
1.3	0.7	1.1	4.0	1.3	2.0	0.5
–	–	–	–	–	–	–
0.0	0.0	0.0	–	0.0	0.0	0.0
0.1	0.1	0.1	0.0	0.1	0.1	0.1
–	–	–	–	–	–	–
1.4	3.0	0.8	2.2	3.0	0.1	0.1
–	–	–	–	–	–	–
0.0	–	–	–	–	–	–
–	–	–	–	–	–	–
1.5	1.8	2.4	8.7	0.7	2.7	0.8
2.0	1.0	1.0	2.0	–	–	–
6.3	*6.5*	*5.3*	*16.9*	*5.1*	*4.8*	*1.4*
–	–	–	–	–	–	–
–	–	–	–	–	–	–
5.8	5.4	5.4	2.8	7.3	2.0	2.0
1.3	1.5	1.5	2.2	7.0	3.0	3.0
–	–	–	–	–	–	–
1.0	1.0	1.0	–	–	1.0	–
–	–	–	–	–	–	–
–	–	–	–	–	–	–
–	–	–	–	–	–	–
–	–	–	1.1	2.5	0.9	0.7
0.6	0.6	0.4	–	–	–	–
0.1	0.1	0.1	–	–	–	–
–	–	–	–	–	–	–
1.8	–	0.1	–	–	–	–
–	–	–	–	–	–	–
0.1	0.1	0.1	–	–	–	–
–	–	0.1	0.5	1.0	–	–
10.6	*8.8*	*8.6*	*6.6*	*17.7*	*6.9*	*5.7*
–	–	–	–	–	–	–
2.9	3.4	4.0	10.9	7.7	5.8	3.8
17.0	*15.3*	*13.9*	*23.5*	*22.8*	*11.7*	*7.1*

11. TECH. COOP. GRANTS

1988	1989	1990	1987	1988	1989	1990
–	–	–	–	–	–	–
–	–	–	–	–	–	–
1.3	0.7	1.1	–	0.9	0.7	1.0
–	–	–	–	–	–	–
0.0	0.0	0.0	0.0	0.0	0.0	0.0
0.1	0.1	0.1	0.0	0.0	0.1	0.1
–	–	–	–	–	–	–
1.4	3.0	0.8	0.2	0.3	0.1	0.1
–	–	–	–	–	–	–
0.0	–	–	–	–	–	–
–	–	–	–	–	–	–
1.5	1.5	2.1	0.5	0.7	0.9	0.8
–	–	–	–	–	–	–
4.3	5.2	4.0	0.7	1.9	1.7	1.9
3.1	2.1	1.9	1.1	1.3	0.9	0.6
–	–	–	–	–	–	–
2.2	2.8	3.4	0.7	1.3	0.9	0.8
7.4	*7.3*	*5.9*	*1.8*	*3.2*	*2.6*	*2.5*

12. TOTAL OOF NET

1988	1989	1990	1987	1988	1989	1990
–	–	–	–	–	–	–
–	–	–	–	–	–	–
–	–	–	–	–	–	–
–	–	–	–	–	–	–
–	–	–	–	–	–	–
–	–	–	–	–	-0.7	–
–	–	–	–	–	–	–
–	–	–	–	–	–	–
–	–	–	–	–	–	–
–	–	–	–	–	–	–
–	–	–	–	–	–	–
–	–	–	–	0.0	-0.4	–
–	–	–	–	–	–	–
–	–	–	–	0.0	-1.1	–
–	–	–	–	–	–	–
–	–	–	–	–	–	–
–	–	–	–	0.0	-1.1	–
–	–	–	–	*0.0*	*-1.1*	–

13. ODF COMMITMENTS: BY PURPOSE %

	1987	1988	1989	1990
Education	5	–	–	–
Health	–	–	–	–
Other Social Infrastr.	–	–	–	–
Water Sanitat. Sewage	–	–	–	–
Energy	–	–	–	–
Telecommunications	–	–	–	–
Transportation	–	20	25	–
Agriculture	38	–	39	–
Extractive Industries	–	–	–	–
Manufacturing	–	–	–	–
Trade Banking Tourism	20	54	9	–
Technical Cooperation	16	26	26	–
Multisector Aid	20	–	2	–
Programme	–	–	–	–
Debt Reorganisation	–	–	–	–
Food Aid	–	–	–	–
Emergency Aid	–	0	–	–
Unspecified	–	–	–	–
TOTAL	100	100	100	–

14. GRANT ELEMENT OF ODA %

DAC COUNTRIES

	1987	1988	1989	1990
Australia	100.0	–	–	–
Austria	–	–	–	–
Belgium	–	–	–	–
Canada	100.0	100.0	100.0	–
Denmark	–	–	–	–
Finland	–	–	–	–
France	–	100.0	100.0	–
Germany	100.0	100.0	100.0	–
Ireland	–	–	–	–
Italy	–	–	–	–
Japan	100.0	100.0	100.0	–
Netherlands	–	–	–	–
New Zealand	–	–	–	–
Norway	–	–	–	–
Sweden	–	–	–	–
Switzerland	–	–	–	–
United Kingdom	100.0	100.0	100.0	–
United States	46.4	–	–	–
TOTAL	*87.7*	*100.0*	*100.0*	–
MULTILATERAL	*91.1*	*91.7*	*94.2*	–
ARAB COUNTRIES	–	–	–	–
E.E.C.+ MEMBERS	*100.0*	*100.0*	*100.0*	–
TOTAL	**88.8**	**94.9**	**97.0**	–

15. OTHER AGGREGATES

	1987	1988	1989	1990
OFFICIAL COMMITMENTS:				
TOTAL BILATERAL	16.9	5.1	4.8	1.4
of which:				
Arab Countries	–	–	–	–
C.E.E.C.	–	–	–	–
TOTAL MULTILATERAL	6.6	21.3	8.9	6.7
TOTAL BIL.& MULTIL.	23.6	26.4	13.7	8.1
of which:				
ODA Grants	10.1	12.1	8.7	5.1
ODA Loans	13.5	10.8	3.0	2.0
DISBURSEMENTS:				
DAC COUNTRIES COMBINED				
OFFICIAL & PRIVATE				
GROSS:				
Contractual Lending	2.0	2.0	1.3	1.3
Export Credits, Total	–	–	–	–
Export Credits, Priv.	–	–	–	–
NET:				
Contractual Lending	1.7	1.8	0.0	1.2
Export Credits Total	-0.1	–	–	–
PRIVATE SECTOR NET	0.0	-0.5	1.7	-0.7
Direct Investment	–	–	–	–
Portfolio Investment	0.1	-0.5	1.7	-0.7
Export Credits	-0.1	–	–	–
MARKET BORROWING:				
CHANGE IN CLAIMS				
Banks	–	–	–	–
MEMORANDUM ITEM:				
C.E.E.C. (Gross)	–	–	–	–

	1987	1988	1989	1990		1987	1988	1989	1990		1987
1. TOTAL RECEIPTS NET					**4. TOTAL ODA NET**					**7. TOTAL ODA GROSS**	
DAC COUNTRIES											
Australia	0.1	1.0	2.3	0.5		0.1	1.0	2.3	0.5	Australia	0.1
Austria	-12.0	-3.0	0.3	1.2		0.2	0.3	0.3	1.2	Austria	0.2
Belgium	-36.9	0.9	2.3	1.1		2.5	0.9	0.7	0.8	Belgium	2.5
Canada	12.1	15.7	11.9	10.2		12.1	15.0	11.9	10.2	Canada	12.1
Denmark	9.2	8.1	18.6	13.3		9.2	8.1	18.6	13.4	Denmark	9.2
Finland	7.0	20.2	16.2	12.4		7.0	20.2	16.2	12.4	Finland	7.0
France	-16.4	6.3	-29.9	-35.0		4.9	7.3	10.4	6.4	France	4.9
Germany	54.2	32.0	47.2	47.7		47.4	51.1	48.3	47.7	Germany	47.4
Ireland	2.3	2.5	0.9	1.6		2.3	2.5	0.9	1.6	Ireland	2.3
Italy	62.0	114.6	62.9	20.4		79.5	75.4	49.0	21.9	Italy	79.5
Japan	63.2	55.4	41.8	38.9		77.7	59.6	41.8	38.9	Japan	77.7
Netherlands	52.9	66.0	57.1	62.6		58.9	67.0	57.3	62.5	Netherlands	58.9
New Zealand	–	–	–	–		–	–	–	–	New Zealand	–
Norway	2.1	8.3	5.4	5.3		3.1	9.5	7.5	9.7	Norway	3.2
Sweden	2.4	22.0	0.7	6.9		2.4	22.0	4.0	7.1	Sweden	2.4
Switzerland	1.5	6.7	4.5	4.2		1.5	6.7	4.5	4.2	Switzerland	1.5
United Kingdom	44.2	46.5	60.0	37.2		31.3	45.2	50.8	37.2	United Kingdom	33.1
United States	103.0	107.0	110.0	143.0		103.0	109.0	110.0	143.0	United States	103.0
TOTAL	350.9	510.1	412.0	371.3		442.9	500.6	434.3	418.7	TOTAL	444.8
MULTILATERAL											
AF.D.F.	5.3	19.3	24.6	61.6		5.3	19.3	24.6	61.6	AF.D.F.	5.3
AF.D.B.	0.6	-0.8	16.6	4.7		–	–	–	–	AF.D.B.	–
AS.D.B	–	–	–	–		–	–	–	–	AS.D.B	–
CAR.D.B.	–	–	–	–		–	–	–	–	CAR.D.B.	–
E.E.C.	55.0	56.3	67.9	67.9		55.0	56.3	67.9	67.9	E.E.C.	56.2
IBRD	-5.7	-8.0	-8.0	-10.0		–	–	–	–	IBRD	–
IDA	59.6	120.0	81.0	117.0		59.6	120.0	81.0	117.0	IDA	61.7
I.D.B.	–	–	–	–		–	–	–	–	I.D.B.	–
IFAD	12.8	4.6	4.5	6.6		12.8	4.6	4.5	6.6	IFAD	13.0
I.F.C.	–	–	–	0.1		–	–	–	–	I.F.C.	–
IMF TRUST FUND	–	–	–	–		–	–	–	–	IMF TRUST FUND	–
U.N. AGENCIES	–	–	–	–		–	–	–	–	U.N. AGENCIES	–
UNDP	2.4	5.2	12.4	13.5		2.4	5.2	12.4	13.5	UNDP	2.4
UNTA	3.0	2.0	2.9	2.8		3.0	2.0	2.9	2.8	UNTA	3.0
UNICEF	14.2	12.6	26.0	21.6		14.2	12.6	26.0	21.6	UNICEF	14.2
UNRWA	–	–	–	–		–	–	–	–	UNRWA	–
WFP	23.5	42.6	21.1	37.6		23.5	42.6	21.1	37.6	WFP	23.5
UNHCR	42.4	37.0	29.2	31.4		42.4	37.0	29.2	31.4	UNHCR	42.4
Other Multilateral	9.2	9.2	33.5	11.5		9.2	9.2	33.5	11.5	Other Multilateral	9.2
Arab Agencies	-5.9	18.5	4.6	–		20.1	24.0	9.0	–	Arab Agencies	29.8
TOTAL	216.6	318.6	316.4	366.4		247.6	332.8	312.2	371.6	TOTAL	260.8
ARAB COUNTRIES	207.2	99.4	25.2	1.8		207.5	103.4	25.2	1.8	ARAB COUNTRIES	232.5
E.E.C.+ MEMBERS	226.6	333.1	286.9	216.7		290.9	313.8	303.9	259.4	E.E.C.+ MEMBERS	293.9
TOTAL	774.7	928.0	753.6	739.5		898.1	936.9	771.8	792.1	TOTAL	938.5
2. ODA LOANS GROSS					**5. ODA LOANS NET**					**8. GRANTS**	
DAC COUNTRIES											
Australia	–	–	–	–		–	–	–	–	Australia	0.1
Austria	–	–	–	–		–	–	–	–	Austria	0.2
Belgium	–	–	–	–		–	–	–	–	Belgium	2.5
Canada	–	–	–	–		–	–	–	–	Canada	12.1
Denmark	–	–	–	-0.1		–	–	-20.5	-0.1	Denmark	9.2
Finland	–	–	–	–		–	–	-0.1	-0.1	Finland	7.0
France	1.2	–	–	–		1.2	–	-0.7	-0.9	France	3.7
Germany	–	–	0.1	–		–	-1.0	0.1	–	Germany	47.4
Ireland	–	–	–	–		–	–	–	–	Ireland	2.3
Italy	21.9	8.6	8.9	1.7		21.9	8.3	8.9	1.7	Italy	57.6
Japan	1.7	–	–	–		1.7	–	–	–	Japan	76.0
Netherlands	0.1	–	–	–		0.1	–	–	–	Netherlands	58.8
New Zealand	–	–	–	–		–	–	–	–	New Zealand	–
Norway	–	–	–	–		-0.1	–	–	–	Norway	3.2
Sweden	–	–	–	–		–	–	–	–	Sweden	2.4
Switzerland	–	–	–	–		–	–	–	–	Switzerland	1.5
United Kingdom	–	–	0.1	0.1		-1.8	-0.8	-0.7	-0.7	United Kingdom	33.1
United States	67.0	40.0	29.0	1.0		67.0	39.0	28.0	1.0	United States	36.0
TOTAL	91.9	48.6	38.1	2.7		90.1	45.5	15.1	1.0	TOTAL	352.9
MULTILATERAL	122.1	182.2	130.3	213.6		108.9	172.6	120.2	193.6	MULTILATERAL	138.7
ARAB COUNTRIES	12.3	66.4	30.2	8.0		-13.0	48.9	18.1	1.8	ARAB COUNTRIES	220.6
E.E.C.+ MEMBERS	36.3	15.2	12.9	5.5		33.3	11.9	-9.6	3.2	E.E.C.+ MEMBERS	257.6
TOTAL	226.4	297.3	198.6	224.3		185.9	267.0	153.4	196.4	TOTAL	712.1
3. TOTAL OFFICIAL GROSS					**6. TOTAL OFFICIAL NET**					**9. TOTAL OOF GROSS**	
DAC COUNTRIES											
Australia	0.1	1.0	2.3	0.5		0.1	1.0	2.3	0.5	Australia	–
Austria	0.2	0.3	0.3	1.2		-1.7	-1.7	0.3	1.2	Austria	–
Belgium	2.5	0.9	0.7	0.8		2.5	0.9	0.7	0.8	Belgium	0.1
Canada	12.1	15.7	11.9	10.2		12.1	15.7	11.9	10.2	Canada	–
Denmark	9.2	8.1	39.1	13.4		9.2	8.1	18.6	13.3	Denmark	0.1
Finland	7.0	20.2	16.2	12.4		7.0	20.2	16.2	12.4	Finland	–
France	4.9	19.2	13.6	10.3		4.9	19.2	12.9	9.4	France	–
Germany	56.4	54.1	50.0	47.7		56.4	37.3	50.0	47.7	Germany	9.0
Ireland	2.3	2.5	0.9	1.6		2.3	2.5	0.9	1.6	Ireland	–
Italy	79.5	75.7	49.0	21.9		79.5	75.4	49.0	21.9	Italy	–
Japan	77.7	59.6	41.8	38.9		77.7	59.6	41.8	38.9	Japan	–
Netherlands	58.9	67.0	57.3	62.5		58.9	67.0	57.3	62.5	Netherlands	–
New Zealand	–	–	–	–		–	–	–	–	New Zealand	–
Norway	3.2	9.5	7.5	9.7		3.1	9.5	7.5	9.7	Norway	–
Sweden	2.4	22.0	4.0	6.9		2.4	22.0	4.0	6.9	Sweden	–
Switzerland	1.5	6.7	4.5	4.2		1.5	6.7	4.5	4.2	Switzerland	–
United Kingdom	33.1	46.0	51.6	38.0		31.2	45.2	50.8	37.2	United Kingdom	–
United States	103.0	110.0	111.0	143.0		103.0	107.0	110.0	143.0	United States	–
TOTAL	454.0	518.5	461.6	423.3		450.2	495.6	438.6	421.4	TOTAL	9.2
MULTILATERAL	262.4	343.6	342.6	403.0		216.6	318.6	316.4	366.4	MULTILATERAL	1.6
ARAB COUNTRIES	232.9	120.9	37.3	8.0		207.2	99.4	25.2	1.8	ARAB COUNTRIES	–
E.E.C.+ MEMBERS	303.1	331.2	330.6	264.7		300.0	312.0	308.1	262.3	E.E.C.+ MEMBERS	9.2
TOTAL	949.3	983.0	841.4	834.3		873.9	913.6	780.2	789.6	TOTAL	10.8

1988	1989	1990	1987	1988	1989	1990

10. ODA COMMITMENTS

1988	1989	1990	1987	1988	1989	1990
1.0	2.3	0.5	0.3	1.0	3.2	1.1
0.3	0.3	1.2	0.2	0.2	0.3	1.2
0.9	0.7	0.8	1.1	5.1	0.7	0.8
15.0	11.9	10.2	11.1	11.7	8.8	7.9
8.1	39.1	13.4	0.2	23.1	14.7	2.5
20.2	16.2	12.4	20.9	18.3	40.2	3.4
7.3	11.1	7.2	3.1	9.8	5.3	4.2
52.1	48.3	47.7	51.2	64.2	28.7	45.9
2.5	0.9	1.6	2.3	2.5	0.9	1.6
75.7	49.0	21.9	109.4	61.0	34.0	9.7
59.6	41.8	38.9	47.7	74.8	39.4	53.7
67.0	57.3	62.5	64.2	74.0	68.7	51.3
–	–	–	–	–	–	–
9.5	7.5	9.7	1.1	0.3	0.2	1.3
22.0	4.0	7.1	2.2	3.0	4.5	0.5
6.7	4.5	4.2	1.1	6.6	4.5	4.1
46.0	51.6	38.0	22.7	73.4	35.3	24.5
110.0	111.0	143.0	88.2	64.5	59.8	25.9
503.7	*457.4*	*420.5*	*427.0*	*493.5*	*349.2*	*239.7*
19.5	25.0	62.2	22.0	81.8	2.3	56.8
–	–	–	–	–	–	–
–	–	–	–	–	–	–
57.6	68.5	68.5	53.3	123.3	74.2	74.2
–	–	–	–	–	–	–
123.0	84.0	121.0	151.7	55.0	157.0	–
–	–	–	–	–	–	–
4.6	4.6	7.1	–	10.1	–	10.7
–	–	–	–	–	–	–
–	–	–	–	–	–	–
–	–	–	94.8	108.6	125.2	118.5
5.2	12.4	13.5	–	–	–	–
2.0	2.9	2.8	–	–	–	–
12.6	26.0	21.6	–	–	–	–
–	–	–	–	–	–	–
42.6	21.1	37.6	–	–	–	–
37.0	29.2	31.4	–	–	–	–
9.2	33.5	11.5	–	–	–	–
29.1	15.0	19.7	1.0	85.0	43.1	8.2
342.4	*322.3*	*397.1*	*322.8*	*463.8*	*401.9*	*268.5*
120.9	*37.3*	*8.0*	*267.8*	*67.6*	*5.8*	*10.0*
317.2	*326.4*	*261.7*	*307.6*	*436.3*	*262.6*	*214.8*
967.1	*816.9*	*825.5*	*1017.6*	*1024.8*	*756.9*	*518.2*

11. TECH. COOP. GRANTS

1988	1989	1990	1987	1988	1989	1990
1.0	2.3	0.5	0.0	0.0	–	–
0.3	0.3	1.2	0.1	0.2	0.2	0.3
0.9	0.7	0.8	0.7	0.6	0.6	0.4
15.0	11.9	10.2	–	0.2	0.9	0.6
8.1	39.1	13.5	2.5	2.7	0.5	1.2
20.2	16.2	12.4	0.1	0.1	1.8	1.5
7.3	11.1	7.2	2.6	3.5	3.9	3.1
52.1	48.1	47.7	17.1	18.8	20.5	24.4
2.5	0.9	1.6	0.9	0.9	0.6	0.8
67.1	40.0	20.2	5.6	1.1	0.4	0.5
59.6	41.8	38.9	2.3	3.7	4.3	3.7
67.0	57.3	62.5	20.5	22.3	21.9	24.2
–	–	–	–	–	–	–
9.5	7.5	9.7	0.8	1.2	1.0	0.8
22.0	4.0	7.1	0.2	0.3	0.3	0.4
6.7	4.5	4.2	0.1	0.0	–	–
46.0	51.5	37.9	11.1	12.4	13.8	12.9
70.0	82.0	142.0	11.0	18.0	33.0	33.0
455.1	*419.2*	*417.8*	*75.5*	*85.8*	*103.6*	*107.8*
160.2	*192.0*	*183.5*	*72.2*	*70.0*	*104.1*	*80.9*
54.5	*7.1*	*0.0*	–	–	–	–
302.0	*313.5*	*256.2*	*61.9*	*66.2*	*62.2*	*67.5*
669.8	*618.3*	*601.3*	*147.7*	*155.8*	*207.7*	*188.6*

12. TOTAL OOF NET

1988	1989	1990	1987	1988	1989	1990
–	–	–	–	–	–	–
–	–	–	-1.9	-1.9	–	–
–	–	–	0.1	–	–	–
0.8	–	–	–	0.8	–	–
–	–	–	0.1	–	–	-0.2
–	–	–	–	–	–	–
12.0	2.5	3.1	–	12.0	2.5	3.1
2.1	1.8	–	9.0	-13.8	1.8	–
–	–	–	–	–	–	–
–	–	–	–	–	–	–
–	–	–	–	–	–	–
–	–	–	–	–	–	–
–	–	-0.2	–	–	–	-0.2
–	–	–	-0.1	–	–	–
–	–	–	–	-2.0	–	–
14.8	*4.2*	*2.9*	*7.2*	*-5.0*	*4.2*	*2.7*
1.2	*20.3*	*6.0*	*-31.0*	*-14.3*	*4.2*	*-5.2*
–	–	–	*-0.3*	*-4.0*	–	–
14.0	*4.2*	*3.1*	*9.1*	*-1.8*	*4.2*	*2.9*
16.0	*24.5*	*8.8*	*-24.1*	*-23.3*	*8.4*	*-2.5*

13. ODF COMMITMENTS: BY PURPOSE %

	1987	1988	1989	1990
Education	3	0	1	–
Health	2	1	1	–
Other Social Infrastr.	3	0	14	–
Water Sanitat. Sewage	3	9	7	–
Energy	9	9	1	–
Telecommunications	3	0	1	–
Transportation	7	12	15	–
Agriculture	5	35	13	–
Extractive Industries	–	–	–	–
Manufacturing	1	2	1	–
Trade Banking Tourism	1			–
Technical Cooperation	19	16	24	–
Multisector Aid	1	0	0	–
Programme	29	5	3	–
Debt Reorganisation	0	0	4	–
Food Aid	11	8	10	–
Emergency Aid	1	3	4	–
Unspecified	0	–	–	–
TOTAL	100	100	100	–

14. GRANT ELEMENT OF ODA %

DAC COUNTRIES

	1987	1988	1989	1990
Australia	100.0	100.0	100.0	–
Austria	100.0	100.0	100.0	–
Belgium	100.0	100.0	100.0	–
Canada	100.0	100.0	100.0	–
Denmark	100.0	100.0	100.0	–
Finland	100.0	100.0	100.0	–
France	100.0	100.0	100.0	–
Germany	100.0	100.0	100.0	–
Ireland	100.0	100.0	100.0	–
Italy	93.6	100.0	100.0	–
Japan	97.6	100.0	100.0	–
Netherlands	100.0	100.0	100.0	–
New Zealand	–	–	–	–
Norway	100.0	100.0	100.0	–
Sweden	100.0	100.0	100.0	–
Switzerland	100.0	100.0	100.0	–
United Kingdom	100.0	100.0	100.0	–
United States	75.7	80.0	83.7	–
TOTAL	*93.1*	*97.4*	*97.2*	–
MULTILATERAL	*95.9*	*82.7*	*87.3*	–
ARAB COUNTRIES	*76.6*	*61.2*	*100.0*	–
E.E.C.+ MEMBERS	*97.7*	*100.0*	*100.0*	–
TOTAL	*88.8*	*87.9*	*91.8*	–

15. OTHER AGGREGATES

OFFICIAL COMMITMENTS:

	1987	1988	1989	1990
TOTAL BILATERAL	695.5	561.8	355.1	249.5
of which:				
Arab Countries	267.8	67.6	5.8	10.0
C.E.E.C.	–	–	–	–
TOTAL MULTILATERAL	322.8	488.6	401.9	295.0
TOTAL BIL.& MULTIL.	1018.3	1050.4	756.9	544.5
of which:				
ODA Grants	648.7	683.0	532.5	443.6
ODA Loans	368.9	341.8	224.5	74.6

DISBURSEMENTS:

DAC COUNTRIES COMBINED

OFFICIAL & PRIVATE

	1987	1988	1989	1990
GROSS:				
Contractual Lending	93.1	88.3	40.7	-7.8
Export Credits, Total	-7.9	25.7	0.1	-13.4
Export Credits, Priv.	-7.9	25.0	-1.7	-13.4
NET:				
Contractual Lending	25.1	52.8	11.2	-15.7
Export Credits Total	-73.9	10.1	-6.3	-19.3
PRIVATE SECTOR NET	-99.2	14.4	-26.5	-50.1
Direct Investment	11.7	2.0	8.9	-1.1
Portfolio Investment	-38.8	0.2	-27.3	-29.6
Export Credits	-72.1	12.3	-8.1	-19.3

MARKET BORROWING:

CHANGE IN CLAIMS

	1987	1988	1989	1990
Banks	-182.0	-87.0	2.0	–

MEMORANDUM ITEM:

	1987	1988	1989	1990
C.E.E.C. (Gross)	4.0	–	–	–

	1987	1988	1989	1990		1987	1988	1989	1990		1987

1. TOTAL RECEIPTS NET

DAC COUNTRIES

	1987	1988	1989	1990	4. TOTAL ODA NET	1987	1988	1989	1990	7. TOTAL ODA GROSS	1987
Australia	–	–	–	–		–	–	–	–	Australia	–
Austria	–	–	–	–		–	–	–	–	Austria	–
Belgium	1.0	1.5	-9.9	4.9		1.2	1.4	1.3	4.8	Belgium	1.2
Canada	–	–	0.1	0.1		–	–	0.1	0.1	Canada	–
Denmark	–	–	–	–		–	–	–	–	Denmark	–
Finland	0.0	–	–	–		0.0	–	–	–	Finland	0.0
France	-1.5	0.6	-0.4	0.8		0.2	0.1	0.1	0.1	France	0.2
Germany	1.9	1.6	0.0	0.0		0.0	0.0	0.0	0.1	Germany	0.0
Ireland	–	–	–	–		–	–	–	–	Ireland	–
Italy	-9.0	–	0.2	–		-0.1	-0.4	0.2	0.6	Italy	–
Japan	-0.2	-0.4	-2.1	66.5		-0.1	-0.4	0.2	0.6	Japan	0.1
Netherlands	-39.1	-29.1	39.6	42.4		7.0	13.7	43.4	45.5	Netherlands	7.0
New Zealand	–	–	–	–		–	–	–	–	New Zealand	–
Norway	0.0	0.0	–	–		0.0	0.0	–	–	Norway	0.0
Sweden	–	–	-0.5	–		–	–	–	–	Sweden	–
Switzerland	0.3	–	–	–		0.3	–	–	–	Switzerland	0.3
United Kingdom	–	0.0	0.0	–		–	0.0	0.0	–	United Kingdom	–
United States	–	–	–	-1.0		–	–	–	–	United States	–
TOTAL	*-46.5*	*-25.7*	*26.9*	*113.7*		*8.6*	*14.7*	*45.0*	*51.2*	*TOTAL*	*8.8*

MULTILATERAL

	1987	1988	1989	1990		1987	1988	1989	1990		1987
AF.D.F.	–	–	–	–		–	–	–	–	AF.D.F.	–
AF.D.B.	–	–	–	–		–	–	–	–	AF.D.B.	–
AS.D.B	–	–	–	–		–	–	–	–	AS.D.B	–
CAR.D.B.	–	–	–	–		–	–	–	–	CAR.D.B.	–
E.E.C.	1.4	5.9	4.8	4.8		1.4	5.9	4.8	4.8	E.E.C.	1.6
IBRD	–	–	–	–		–	–	–	–	IBRD	–
IDA	–	–	–	–		–	–	–	–	IDA	–
I.D.B.	4.3	1.3	1.9	4.1		3.5	0.2	0.1	0.1	I.D.B.	3.5
IFAD	–	–	–	–		–	–	–	–	IFAD	–
I.F.C.	–	–	–	–		–	–	–	–	I.F.C.	–
IMF TRUST FUND	–	–	–	–		–	–	–	–	IMF TRUST FUND	–
U.N. AGENCIES	–	–	–	–		–	–	–	–	U.N. AGENCIES	–
UNDP	0.4	0.3	0.4	0.6		0.4	0.3	0.4	0.6	UNDP	0.4
UNTA	0.2	0.2	0.2	0.2		0.2	0.2	0.2	0.2	UNTA	0.2
UNICEF	–	–	–	–		–	–	–	–	UNICEF	–
UNRWA	–	–	–	–		–	–	–	–	UNRWA	–
WFP	–	–	–	–		–	–	–	–	WFP	–
UNHCR	–	–	0.2	0.1		–	–	0.2	0.1	UNHCR	–
Other Multilateral	0.2	0.0	0.2	0.6		0.2	0.0	0.2	0.6	Other Multilateral	0.2
Arab Agencies	–	–	–	–		–	–	–	–	Arab Agencies	–
TOTAL	*6.5*	*7.7*	*7.7*	*10.4*		*5.7*	*6.6*	*5.9*	*6.4*	*TOTAL*	*5.9*
ARAB COUNTRIES	***8.0***	***–***	***–***	***–***		***8.0***	***–***	***–***	***–***	***ARAB COUNTRIES***	***8.0***
E.E.C.+ MEMBERS	*-45.3*	*-19.5*	*34.2*	*52.9*		*9.8*	*21.0*	*49.5*	*55.2*	*E.E.C.+ MEMBERS*	*10.0*
TOTAL	***-31.9***	***-18.0***	***34.6***	***124.1***		***22.3***	***21.4***	***50.9***	***57.5***	***TOTAL***	***22.7***

2. ODA LOANS GROSS

DAC COUNTRIES

	1987	1988	1989	1990	5. ODA LOANS NET	1987	1988	1989	1990	8. GRANTS	1987
Australia	–	–	–	–		–	–	–	–	Australia	–
Austria	–	–	–	–		–	–	–	–	Austria	–
Belgium	–	–	–	–		–	–	–	–	Belgium	1.2
Canada	–	–	–	–		–	–	–	–	Canada	–
Denmark	–	–	–	–		–	–	–	–	Denmark	–
Finland	–	–	–	–		–	–	–	–	Finland	0.0
France	–	–	–	–		–	–	–	–	France	0.2
Germany	–	–	–	–		–	–	–	–	Germany	0.0
Ireland	–	–	–	–		–	–	–	–	Ireland	–
Italy	–	–	–	–		–	–	–	–	Italy	–
Japan	–	–	–	–		-0.2	-0.4	-0.1	-0.1	Japan	0.1
Netherlands	–	–	–	–		–	–	–	–	Netherlands	7.0
New Zealand	–	–	–	–		–	–	–	–	New Zealand	–
Norway	–	–	–	–		–	–	–	–	Norway	0.0
Sweden	–	–	–	–		–	–	–	–	Sweden	–
Switzerland	–	–	–	–		–	–	–	–	Switzerland	0.3
United Kingdom	–	–	–	–		–	–	–	–	United Kingdom	–
United States	–	–	–	–		–	–	–	–	United States	–
TOTAL	*–*	*–*	*–*	*–*		*-0.2*	*-0.4*	*-0.1*	*-0.1*	*TOTAL*	*8.8*
MULTILATERAL	*1.4*	*1.3*	*1.5*	*1.5*		*1.2*	*1.0*	*1.5*	*1.5*	*MULTILATERAL*	*4.6*
ARAB COUNTRIES	***–***	***–***	***–***	***–***		***–***	***–***	***–***	***–***	***ARAB COUNTRIES***	***8.0***
E.E.C.+ MEMBERS	*1.3*	*1.1*	*1.4*	*1.4*		*1.1*	*0.8*	*1.4*	*1.4*	*E.E.C.+ MEMBERS*	*8.7*
TOTAL	***1.4***	***1.3***	***1.5***	***1.5***		***0.9***	***0.6***	***1.4***	***1.4***	***TOTAL***	***21.4***

3. TOTAL OFFICIAL GROSS

DAC COUNTRIES

	1987	1988	1989	1990	6. TOTAL OFFICIAL NET	1987	1988	1989	1990	9. TOTAL OOF GROSS	1987
Australia	–	–	–	–		–	–	–	–	Australia	–
Austria	–	–	–	–		–	–	–	–	Austria	–
Belgium	1.2	1.4	1.3	4.8		1.2	1.4	1.3	4.8	Belgium	–
Canada	–	–	0.1	0.1		–	–	0.1	0.1	Canada	–
Denmark	–	–	–	–		–	–	–	–	Denmark	–
Finland	0.0	–	–	–		0.0	–	–	–	Finland	–
France	0.2	0.1	0.1	0.1		0.2	0.1	0.1	0.1	France	–
Germany	1.8	1.6	0.2	0.1		1.7	1.5	0.1	0.0	Germany	1.8
Ireland	–	–	–	–		–	–	–	–	Ireland	–
Italy	–	–	–	–		–	–	–	–	Italy	–
Japan	0.1	0.0	0.3	0.7		-0.1	-0.4	0.2	0.6	Japan	–
Netherlands	7.0	13.7	43.4	45.5		7.0	13.7	43.4	45.5	Netherlands	–
New Zealand	–	–	–	–		–	–	–	–	New Zealand	–
Norway	0.0	0.0	–	–		0.0	0.0	–	–	Norway	–
Sweden	–	–	–	–		–	–	–	–	Sweden	–
Switzerland	0.3	–	–	–		0.3	–	–	–	Switzerland	–
United Kingdom	–	0.0	0.0	–		–	0.0	0.0	–	United Kingdom	–
United States	–	–	–	–		–	–	–	–	United States	–
TOTAL	*10.6*	*16.7*	*45.2*	*51.2*		*10.3*	*16.2*	*45.1*	*51.1*	*TOTAL*	*1.8*
MULTILATERAL	*6.7*	*8.0*	*7.7*	*10.4*		*6.5*	*7.7*	*7.7*	*10.4*	*MULTILATERAL*	*0.8*
ARAB COUNTRIES	***8.0***	***–***	***–***	***–***		***8.0***	***–***	***–***	***–***	***ARAB COUNTRIES***	***–***
E.E.C.+ MEMBERS	*11.7*	*22.8*	*49.7*	*55.3*		*11.5*	*22.5*	*49.5*	*55.2*	*E.E.C.+ MEMBERS*	*1.8*
TOTAL	***25.3***	***24.7***	***52.9***	***61.6***		***24.8***	***23.9***	***52.7***	***61.5***	***TOTAL***	***2.6***

254

10. ODA COMMITMENTS

1988	1989	1990	1987	1988	1989	1990
–	–	–	–	–	–	–
1.4	1.3	4.8	0.5	6.7	1.3	4.8
–	0.1	0.1	–	0.1	0.1	0.1
–	–	–	–	–	–	–
0.1	0.1	0.1	0.2	0.1	0.1	0.1
0.0	0.0	0.1	0.0	0.0	0.0	0.1
–	–	–	–	–	–	–
0.0	0.3	0.7	0.1	0.0	0.3	4.3
13.7	43.4	45.5	6.7	35.5	35.1	24.6
–	–	–	–	–	–	–
0.0	–	–	0.0	–	–	–
–	–	–	–	–	–	–
–	–	–	0.3	–	–	–
0.0	0.0	–	–	0.0	0.0	–
–	–	–	–	–	–	–
15.1	*45.1*	*51.2*	*7.9*	*42.3*	*36.9*	*33.9*
–	–	–	–	–	–	–
–	–	–	–	–	–	–
–	–	–	–	–	–	–
6.2	4.8	4.8	14.7	1.5	15.5	15.5
–	–	–	–	–	–	–
–	–	–	–	–	–	–
0.2	0.1	0.1	1.5	–	–	–
–	–	–	–	–	–	–
–	–	–	–	–	–	–
–	–	–	0.8	0.5	1.0	1.5
0.3	0.4	0.6	–	–	–	–
0.2	0.2	0.2	–	–	–	–
–	–	–	–	–	–	–
–	–	–	–	–	–	–
–	0.2	0.1	–	–	–	–
0.0	0.2	0.6	–	–	–	–
–	–	–	–	–	–	–
6.9	*5.9*	*6.4*	*17.0*	*2.0*	*16.5*	*17.0*
–	–	–	–	–	–	–
21.3	49.5	55.3	22.2	43.7	52.0	45.1
22.0	**51.0**	**57.6**	**24.9**	**44.4**	**53.4**	**51.0**

11. TECH. COOP. GRANTS

1988	1989	1990	1987	1988	1989	1990
–	–	–	–	–	–	–
1.4	1.3	4.8	1.1	1.0	0.8	0.9
–	0.1	0.1	–	–	–	–
–	–	–	0.0	–	–	–
0.1	0.1	0.1	0.2	0.1	0.1	0.1
0.0	0.0	0.1	0.0	0.0	0.0	0.1
–	–	–	–	–	–	–
0.0	0.3	0.7	0.1	0.0	0.3	0.2
13.7	43.4	45.5	3.2	3.4	4.4	9.0
0.0	–	–	–	–	–	–
–	–	–	0.0	0.0	–	–
0.0	0.0	–	–	0.0	0.0	–
–	–	–	–	–	–	–
15.1	*45.1*	*51.2*	*4.6*	*4.5*	*5.6*	*10.2*
5.6	*4.4*	*4.9*	*0.8*	*0.7*	*1.0*	*1.5*
–	–	–	–	–	–	–
20.2	48.1	53.9	4.5	4.6	5.4	10.0
20.8	**49.5**	**56.1**	**5.5**	**5.2**	**6.6**	**11.7**

12. TOTAL OOF NET

1988	1989	1990	1987	1988	1989	1990
–	–	–	–	–	–	–
–	–	–	–	–	–	–
–	–	–	–	–	–	–
–	–	–	–	–	–	–
–	–	–	–	–	–	–
1.5	0.1	–	1.7	1.5	0.1	-0.1
–	–	–	–	–	–	–
–	–	–	–	–	–	–
–	–	–	–	–	–	–
–	–	–	–	–	–	–
–	–	–	–	–	–	–
–	–	–	–	–	–	–
–	–	–	–	–	–	–
1.5	*0.1*	–	*1.7*	*1.5*	*0.1*	*-0.1*
1.1	*1.8*	*4.0*	*0.8*	*1.1*	*1.8*	*4.0*
–	–	–	–	–	–	–
1.5	*0.1*	–	*1.7*	*1.5*	*0.1*	*-0.1*
2.6	**1.9**	**4.0**	**2.5**	**2.6**	**1.9**	**3.9**

13. ODF COMMITMENTS: BY PURPOSE %

	1987	1988	1989	1990
Education	–	–	–	–
Health	–	17	–	–
Other Social Infrastr.	–	–	–	–
Water Sanitat. Sewage	–	–	–	–
Energy	41	–	–	–
Telecommunications	–	–	–	–
Transportation	–	–	–	–
Agriculture	–	–	–	–
Extractive Industries	–	–	–	–
Manufacturing	–	–	–	–
Trade Banking Tourism	–	–	–	–
Technical Cooperation	37	15	16	–
Multisector Aid	–	–	–	–
Programme	–	65	84	–
Debt Reorganisation	–	–	–	–
Food Aid	–	–	–	–
Emergency Aid	22	4	0	–
Unspecified	–	–	–	–
TOTAL	100	100	100	–

14. GRANT ELEMENT OF ODA %

DAC COUNTRIES

	1987	1988	1989	1990
Australia	–	–	–	–
Austria	–	–	–	–
Belgium	100.0	100.0	100.0	–
Canada	–	100.0	100.0	–
Denmark	–	–	–	–
Finland	–	–	–	–
France	100.0	100.0	100.0	–
Germany	100.0	100.0	100.0	–
Ireland	–	–	–	–
Italy	–	–	–	–
Japan	100.0	100.0	100.0	–
Netherlands	100.0	100.0	100.0	–
New Zealand	–	–	–	–
Norway	100.0	–	–	–
Sweden	–	–	–	–
Switzerland	100.0	–	–	–
United Kingdom	–	100.0	100.0	–
United States	–	–	–	–
TOTAL	*100.0*	*100.0*	*100.0*	–
MULTILATERAL	*100.0*	*85.9*	*100.0*	–
ARAB COUNTRIES	–	–	–	–
E.E.C.+ MEMBERS	*100.0*	*100.0*	*100.0*	–
TOTAL	**100.0**	**98.9**	**100.0**	–

15. OTHER AGGREGATES

	1987	1988	1989	1990
OFFICIAL COMMITMENTS:				
TOTAL BILATERAL	7.9	42.3	36.9	33.9
of which:				
Arab Countries	–	–	–	–
C.E.E.C.	–	–	–	–
TOTAL MULTILATERAL	23.3	2.0	16.5	17.0
TOTAL BIL.& MULTIL.	31.2	44.4	53.4	51.0
of which:				
ODA Grants	23.4	41.6	50.1	47.6
ODA Loans	1.5	2.7	3.3	3.3
DISBURSEMENTS:				
DAC COUNTRIES COMBINED				
OFFICIAL & PRIVATE				
GROSS:				
Contractual Lending	2.5	1.7	4.1	9.1
Export Credits, Total	0.7	0.2	4.1	9.1
Export Credits, Priv.	0.7	0.2	4.0	9.1
NET:				
Contractual Lending	-9.0	1.2	3.9	6.9
Export Credits Total	-10.5	0.2	4.1	7.1
PRIVATE SECTOR NET	-56.8	-41.9	-18.2	62.6
Direct Investment	-43.9	-34.9	-0.6	-0.7
Portfolio Investment	-2.4	-7.2	-21.5	56.3
Export Credits	-10.5	0.2	3.9	7.1
MARKET BORROWING:				
CHANGE IN CLAIMS				
Banks	9.0	-17.0	4.0	14.0
MEMORANDUM ITEM:				
C.E.E.C. (Gross)	–	–	–	–

1. TOTAL RECEIPTS NET

DAC COUNTRIES	1987	1988	1989	1990
Australia	0.6	0.3	0.7	0.8
Austria	–	–	0.0	0.0
Belgium	0.2	–	0.4	0.0
Canada	1.4	1.4	1.5	1.8
Denmark	6.6	3.9	3.3	4.9
Finland	0.0	-0.3	-0.3	0.1
France	0.2	0.0	0.0	-0.2
Germany	3.8	3.3	1.5	1.0
Ireland	0.1	0.1	0.1	0.1
Italy	0.7	4.1	1.7	5.5
Japan	0.0	0.0	0.0	0.1
Netherlands	0.7	1.9	5.3	5.9
New Zealand	–	–	–	–
Norway	0.5	0.1	0.1	0.0
Sweden	0.3	–	–	–
Switzerland	0.1	–	–	0.1
United Kingdom	1.6	-0.5	-21.3	-1.6
United States	12.0	10.0	11.0	14.0
TOTAL	28.6	24.4	3.9	32.4
MULTILATERAL				
AF.D.F.	0.8	1.3	1.7	1.3
AF.D.B.	1.2	-9.1	-1.3	0.4
AS.D.B	–	–	–	–
CAR.D.B.	–	–	–	–
E.E.C.	1.9	1.9	5.0	5.0
IBRD	-0.9	-4.0	-4.0	-19.0
IDA	-0.1	–	–	–
I.D.B.	–	–	–	–
IFAD	1.8	0.6	–	1.0
I.F.C.	-0.2	1.0	1.4	–
IMF TRUST FUND	–	–	–	–
U.N. AGENCIES	–	–	–	–
UNDP	1.4	1.5	1.5	1.8
UNTA	0.6	0.6	0.8	0.6
UNICEF	0.3	0.4	0.6	0.9
UNRWA	–	–	–	–
WFP	3.8	2.4	3.4	3.6
UNHCR	1.8	3.7	1.5	1.3
Other Multilateral	0.8	0.5	0.7	0.6
Arab Agencies	-0.3	-0.3	-0.3	–
TOTAL	12.9	0.5	10.9	-2.6
ARAB COUNTRIES	–	–	–	–
E.E.C.+ MEMBERS	15.7	14.8	-4.1	20.5
TOTAL	41.5	24.9	14.8	29.7

2. ODA LOANS GROSS

DAC COUNTRIES	1987	1988	1989	1990
Australia	–	–	–	–
Austria	–	–	–	–
Belgium	–	–	–	–
Canada	–	–	–	–
Denmark	6.4	3.8	2.8	1.8
Finland	–	–	–	–
France	0.0	–	0.0	–
Germany	0.9	0.6	1.5	0.7
Ireland	–	–	–	–
Italy	–	0.8	–	4.4
Japan	–	–	–	–
Netherlands	–	0.4	4.1	–
New Zealand	–	–	–	–
Norway	–	–	–	–
Sweden	–	–	–	–
Switzerland	–	–	–	–
United Kingdom	0.3	0.5	1.7	3.5
United States	–	–	–	–
TOTAL	7.7	6.1	10.1	10.4
MULTILATERAL	2.7	4.2	6.1	6.8
ARAB COUNTRIES	–	–	–	–
E.E.C.+ MEMBERS	7.7	8.2	13.9	14.1
TOTAL	10.4	10.3	16.2	17.1

3. TOTAL OFFICIAL GROSS

DAC COUNTRIES	1987	1988	1989	1990
Australia	0.6	0.3	0.7	0.8
Austria	–	–	0.0	0.0
Belgium	0.3	–	0.4	0.0
Canada	1.8	1.7	1.9	3.1
Denmark	6.8	4.1	3.4	5.0
Finland	0.0	0.0	0.1	0.1
France	0.3	0.1	0.2	0.2
Germany	3.7	3.5	4.3	5.3
Ireland	0.1	0.1	0.1	0.1
Italy	0.7	4.1	1.7	5.6
Japan	0.2	0.0	0.0	0.1
Netherlands	0.7	1.9	5.3	1.4
New Zealand	–	–	–	–
Norway	0.5	0.1	0.1	0.0
Sweden	0.3	–	–	–
Switzerland	0.1	–	–	0.1
United Kingdom	5.7	9.0	10.0	8.8
United States	12.0	10.0	11.0	14.0
TOTAL	33.7	35.1	39.1	44.5
MULTILATERAL	26.2	21.1	26.2	26.4
ARAB COUNTRIES	–	–	–	–
E.E.C.+ MEMBERS	23.2	27.9	33.5	34.3
TOTAL	60.0	56.1	65.4	70.9

4. TOTAL ODA NET

	1987	1988	1989	1990
Australia	0.6	0.3	0.7	0.8
Austria	–	–	0.0	0.0
Belgium	0.3	–	0.4	0.0
Canada	1.7	1.7	1.9	1.9
Denmark	6.4	3.9	3.3	4.9
Finland	0.0	0.0	0.1	0.1
France	0.3	0.0	0.2	0.2
Germany	3.7	2.8	3.1	3.9
Ireland	0.1	0.1	0.1	0.1
Italy	0.7	4.1	1.7	5.5
Japan	0.2	0.0	0.0	0.1
Netherlands	0.7	1.9	5.3	1.4
New Zealand	–	–	–	–
Norway	0.5	0.1	0.1	0.0
Sweden	0.3	–	–	–
Switzerland	0.1	–	–	0.1
United Kingdom	2.0	-2.5	-16.1	3.1
United States	12.0	10.0	11.0	14.0
TOTAL	29.7	22.6	11.6	36.1
AF.D.F.	0.8	1.3	1.7	1.3
AF.D.B.	–	–	–	–
AS.D.B	–	–	–	–
CAR.D.B.	–	–	–	–
E.E.C.	4.7	5.0	8.0	8.0
IBRD	–	–	–	–
IDA	-0.1	–	–	–
I.D.B.	–	–	–	–
IFAD	1.8	0.6	–	1.0
I.F.C.	–	–	–	–
IMF TRUST FUND	–	–	–	–
U.N. AGENCIES	–	–	–	–
UNDP	1.4	1.5	1.5	1.8
UNTA	0.6	0.6	0.8	0.6
UNICEF	0.3	0.4	0.6	0.9
UNRWA	–	–	–	–
WFP	3.8	2.4	3.4	3.6
UNHCR	1.8	3.7	1.5	1.3
Other Multilateral	0.8	0.5	0.7	0.6
Arab Agencies	-0.3	-0.3	-0.3	–
TOTAL	15.7	15.6	17.8	19.0
ARAB COUNTRIES	–	–	–	–
E.E.C.+ MEMBERS	19.1	15.4	5.9	27.1
TOTAL	45.4	38.2	29.5	55.1

5. ODA LOANS NET

	1987	1988	1989	1990
Australia	–	–	–	–
Austria	–	–	–	–
Belgium	–	–	–	–
Canada	0.0	–	–	-1.2
Denmark	6.2	3.6	2.6	1.6
Finland	–	–	–	–
France	0.0	-0.1	0.0	–
Germany	0.9	-0.1	0.3	-0.7
Ireland	–	–	–	–
Italy	–	0.8	–	4.4
Japan	–	–	–	–
Netherlands	–	0.4	4.1	–
New Zealand	–	–	–	–
Norway	–	–	–	–
Sweden	–	–	–	–
Switzerland	–	–	–	–
United Kingdom	-2.5	-7.2	-20.9	-0.6
United States	–	–	–	–
TOTAL	4.6	-2.6	-13.9	3.6
MULTILATERAL	2.1	3.6	5.1	5.7
ARAB COUNTRIES	–	–	–	–
E.E.C.+ MEMBERS	4.5	-0.6	-10.2	8.4
TOTAL	6.7	1.0	-8.7	9.3

6. TOTAL OFFICIAL NET

	1987	1988	1989	1990
Australia	0.6	0.3	0.7	0.8
Austria	–	–	0.0	0.0
Belgium	0.3	–	0.4	0.0
Canada	1.4	1.4	1.5	1.8
Denmark	6.6	3.9	3.3	4.9
Finland	0.0	0.0	0.1	0.1
France	0.3	0.0	0.2	0.2
Germany	3.7	2.8	1.4	1.8
Ireland	0.1	0.1	0.1	0.1
Italy	0.7	4.1	1.7	5.5
Japan	0.2	0.0	0.0	0.1
Netherlands	0.7	1.9	5.3	1.4
New Zealand	–	–	–	–
Norway	0.5	0.1	0.1	0.0
Sweden	0.3	–	–	–
Switzerland	0.1	–	–	0.1
United Kingdom	0.2	-0.3	-15.2	0.1
United States	12.0	10.0	11.0	14.0
TOTAL	27.7	24.4	10.4	30.8
MULTILATERAL	12.9	0.5	10.8	-2.6
ARAB COUNTRIES	–	–	–	–
E.E.C.+ MEMBERS	14.6	14.5	2.1	18.9
TOTAL	40.5	24.9	21.3	28.2

7. TOTAL ODA GROSS

	1987
Australia	0.6
Austria	–
Belgium	0.3
Canada	1.8
Denmark	6.6
Finland	0.0
France	0.3
Germany	3.7
Ireland	0.1
Italy	0.7
Japan	0.2
Netherlands	0.7
New Zealand	–
Norway	0.5
Sweden	0.3
Switzerland	0.1
United Kingdom	4.8
United States	12.0
TOTAL	32.8
AF.D.F.	0.8
AF.D.B.	–
AS.D.B	–
CAR.D.B.	–
E.E.C.	4.9
IBRD	–
IDA	–
I.D.B.	–
IFAD	1.8
I.F.C.	–
IMF TRUST FUND	–
U.N. AGENCIES	–
UNDP	1.4
UNTA	0.6
UNICEF	0.3
UNRWA	–
WFP	3.8
UNHCR	1.8
Other Multilateral	0.8
Arab Agencies	–
TOTAL	16.2
ARAB COUNTRIES	–
E.E.C.+ MEMBERS	22.3
TOTAL	49.0

8. GRANTS

	1987
Australia	0.6
Austria	–
Belgium	0.3
Canada	1.8
Denmark	0.2
Finland	0.0
France	0.3
Germany	2.8
Ireland	0.1
Italy	0.7
Japan	0.2
Netherlands	0.7
New Zealand	–
Norway	0.5
Sweden	0.3
Switzerland	0.1
United Kingdom	4.6
United States	12.0
TOTAL	25.1
MULTILATERAL	13.5
ARAB COUNTRIES	–
E.E.C.+ MEMBERS	14.6
TOTAL	38.6

9. TOTAL OOF GROSS

	1987
Australia	–
Austria	–
Belgium	–
Canada	–
Denmark	0.2
Finland	–
France	–
Germany	–
Ireland	–
Italy	–
Japan	–
Netherlands	–
New Zealand	–
Norway	–
Sweden	–
Switzerland	–
United Kingdom	0.8
United States	–
TOTAL	1.0
MULTILATERAL	10.0
ARAB COUNTRIES	–
E.E.C.+ MEMBERS	1.0
TOTAL	11.0

10. ODA COMMITMENTS

1988	1989	1990	1987	1988	1989	1990
0.3	0.7	0.8	0.1	0.7	0.5	0.8
–	0.0	0.0	–	–	0.0	0.0
–	0.4	0.0	0.0	0.1	0.4	0.0
1.7	1.9	3.1	3.1	5.1	0.2	0.2
4.1	3.4	5.0	–	–	5.2	–
0.0	0.1	0.1	–	–	0.1	0.1
0.1	0.2	0.2	0.3	1.2	1.1	0.2
3.5	4.3	5.3	4.2	1.5	9.0	1.8
0.1	0.1	0.1	0.1	0.1	0.1	0.1
4.1	1.7	5.6	1.3	4.4	1.0	1.2
0.0	0.0	0.1	0.2	0.1	1.1	0.1
1.9	5.3	1.4	0.8	1.4	5.3	2.5
–	–	–	–	–	–	–
0.1	0.1	0.0	0.5	–	–	–
–	–	–	0.3	–	–	–
–	–	0.1	0.1	–	–	0.1
5.3	6.5	7.2	4.1	5.1	5.8	7.1
10.0	11.0	14.0	2.4	20.2	8.8	5.4
31.3	*35.6*	*42.9*	*17.3*	*39.9*	*38.5*	*19.5*
1.3	1.9	1.5	8.6	–	7.6	1.7
–	–	–	–	–	–	–
–	–	–	–	–	–	–
5.1	8.1	8.1	16.1	21.8	3.1	3.1
–	–	–	–	–	–	–
–	–	–	–	–	–	–
0.9	0.5	1.6	–	–	–	–
–	–	–	–	–	–	–
–	–	–	8.7	9.0	8.4	8.7
1.5	1.5	1.8	–	–	–	–
0.6	0.8	0.6	–	–	–	–
0.4	0.6	0.9	–	–	–	–
–	–	–	–	–	–	–
2.4	3.4	3.6	–	–	–	–
3.7	1.5	1.3	–	–	–	–
0.5	0.7	0.6	–	–	–	–
–	–	–	–	–	–	–
16.2	*18.8*	*19.9*	*33.4*	*30.8*	*19.0*	*13.4*
–	–	–	–	–	–	–
24.1	*30.0*	*32.7*	*26.9*	*35.5*	*30.9*	*15.9*
47.5	*54.4*	*62.7*	*50.7*	*70.7*	*57.6*	*33.0*

11. TECH. COOP. GRANTS

1988	1989	1990	1987	1988	1989	1990
0.3	0.7	0.8	0.2	0.3	0.7	0.8
–	0.0	0.0	–	–	0.0	–
–	0.4	0.0	0.3	–	0.4	–
1.7	1.9	3.1	–	0.5	0.9	1.4
0.3	0.6	3.2	0.2	0.8	0.4	0.5
0.0	0.1	0.1	0.0	–	–	–
0.1	0.2	0.2	0.3	0.1	0.2	0.2
2.9	2.8	4.6	2.7	2.8	2.6	3.8
0.1	0.1	0.1	0.0	0.1	0.1	0.1
3.3	1.7	1.1	0.1	1.0	1.6	0.4
0.0	0.0	0.1	0.2	0.0	0.0	0.1
1.5	1.2	1.4	0.6	1.0	1.2	0.7
–	–	–	–	–	–	–
0.1	0.1	0.0	–	–	0.0	0.0
–	–	–	–	–	–	–
–	–	0.1	–	–	–	–
4.8	4.8	3.7	3.5	4.5	4.3	3.4
10.0	11.0	14.0	7.0	10.0	9.0	12.0
25.2	*25.5*	*32.5*	*15.1*	*21.2*	*21.4*	*23.4*
12.0	*12.7*	*13.1*	*6.2*	*8.4*	*5.0*	*5.1*
–	–	–	–	–	–	–
16.0	*16.1*	*18.6*	*9.1*	*12.1*	*10.8*	*9.0*
37.2	*38.2*	*45.6*	*21.3*	*29.6*	*26.4*	*28.5*

12. TOTAL OOF NET

1988	1989	1990	1987	1988	1989	1990
–	–	–	–	–	–	–
–	–	–	–	–	–	–
–	–	–	-0.4	-0.4	-0.4	-0.2
–	–	–	0.2	–	–	–
–	–	–	–	–	–	–
–	–	–	–	–	-1.8	-2.1
–	–	–	–	–	–	–
–	–	–	–	–	–	–
–	–	–	–	–	–	–
–	–	–	–	–	–	–
–	–	–	–	–	–	–
–	–	–	–	–	–	–
–	–	–	–	–	–	–
3.8	3.5	1.6	-1.8	2.2	1.0	-3.0
–	–	–	–	–	–	–
3.8	*3.5*	*1.6*	*-2.0*	*1.8*	*-1.2*	*-5.3*
4.9	*7.4*	*6.5*	*-2.8*	*-15.1*	*-7.0*	*-21.7*
–	–	–	–	–	–	–
3.8	*3.5*	*1.6*	*-4.5*	*-0.9*	*-3.8*	*-8.1*
8.7	*10.9*	*8.1*	*-4.8*	*-13.3*	*-8.2*	*-27.0*

13. ODF COMMITMENTS: BY PURPOSE %

	1987	1988	1989	1990
Education	17	11	2	–
Health	4	3	8	–
Other Social Infrastr.	–	1	4	–
Water Sanitat. Sewage	–	1	–	–
Energy	–	–	2	–
Telecommunications	–	–	7	–
Transportation	27	9	20	–
Agriculture	1	3	7	–
Extractive Industries	–	–	–	–
Manufacturing	14	0	–	–
Trade Banking Tourism	0	0	–	–
Technical Cooperation	36	69	49	–
Multisector Aid	0	–	1	–
Programme	–	–	–	–
Debt Reorganisation	–	–	–	–
Food Aid	–	2	–	–
Emergency Aid	–	0	–	–
Unspecified	–	–	–	–
TOTAL	100	100	100	–

14. GRANT ELEMENT OF ODA %

DAC COUNTRIES

	1987	1988	1989	1990
Australia	100.0	100.0	100.0	–
Austria	–	–	100.0	–
Belgium	100.0	100.0	100.0	–
Canada	100.0	100.0	100.0	–
Denmark	–	–	100.0	–
Finland	–	–	100.0	–
France	100.0	100.0	100.0	–
Germany	100.0	100.0	89.7	–
Ireland	100.0	100.0	100.0	–
Italy	100.0	100.0	100.0	–
Japan	100.0	100.0	100.0	–
Netherlands	100.0	100.0	100.0	–
New Zealand	–	–	–	–
Norway	100.0	–	–	–
Sweden	100.0	–	–	–
Switzerland	100.0	–	–	–
United Kingdom	100.0	100.0	100.0	–
United States	100.0	100.0	100.0	–
TOTAL	*100.0*	*100.0*	*97.3*	–
MULTILATERAL	96.6	96.7	93.3	–
ARAB COUNTRIES	–	–	–	–
E.E.C.+ MEMBERS	100.0	100.0	96.3	–
TOTAL	*97.9*	*98.5*	*95.9*	–

15. OTHER AGGREGATES

	1987	1988	1989	1990
OFFICIAL COMMITMENTS:				
TOTAL BILATERAL	25.4	39.9	39.3	19.5
of which:				
Arab Countries	–	–	–	–
C.E.E.C.	–	–	–	–
TOTAL MULTILATERAL	43.4	30.8	29.9	23.8
TOTAL BIL.& MULTIL.	68.8	70.7	69.2	43.3
of which:				
ODA Grants	38.5	65.7	41.3	26.8
ODA Loans	12.2	4.9	16.2	6.2
DISBURSEMENTS:				
DAC COUNTRIES COMBINED				
OFFICIAL & PRIVATE				
GROSS:				
Contractual Lending	8.7	9.7	10.6	11.8
Export Credits, Total	–	-0.2	-3.0	-0.2
Export Credits, Priv.	–	-0.2	-3.0	-0.2
NET:				
Contractual Lending	-0.3	-3.4	-21.7	-3.6
Export Credits Total	-3.3	-3.0	-7.0	-2.1
PRIVATE SECTOR NET	0.9	0.0	-6.5	1.6
Direct Investment	3.8	2.0	–	3.7
Portfolio Investment	0.0	0.6	0.1	-0.2
Export Credits	-2.9	-2.7	-6.6	-1.9
MARKET BORROWING:				
CHANGE IN CLAIMS				
Banks	-21.0	6.0	-7.0	-14.0
MEMORANDUM ITEM:				
C.E.E.C. (Gross)	–	–	–	–

1. TOTAL RECEIPTS NET

DAC COUNTRIES	1987	1988	1989	1990
Australia	–	0.0	0.0	0.0
Austria	0.4	0.4	1.6	2.6
Belgium	-0.2	0.7	0.1	-0.3
Canada	0.7	0.7	0.4	0.2
Denmark	0.1	0.1	–	–
Finland	–	–	–	0.5
France	5.0	64.3	36.4	64.9
Germany	23.8	156.4	90.1	88.7
Ireland	–	–	–	–
Italy	-49.4	2.0	47.9	-2.5
Japan	123.4	136.6	42.2	-8.5
Netherlands	-5.4	0.4	0.2	0.9
New Zealand	–	–	–	–
Norway	–	–	–	–
Sweden	-0.8	–	–	–
Switzerland	0.2	0.2	0.2	0.3
United Kingdom	-2.4	-2.6	-21.7	–
United States	–	–	7.0	-5.0
TOTAL	*95.3*	*359.2*	*204.5*	*141.8*
MULTILATERAL				
AF.D.F.	–	–	–	–
AF.D.B.	–	–	–	–
AS.D.B	–	–	–	–
CAR.D.B.	–	–	–	–
E.E.C.	9.6	33.2	2.3	2.3
IBRD	1.3	-1.0	–	-1.0
IDA	–	–	–	-2.0
I.D.B.	–	–	–	–
IFAD	2.0	–	–	0.8
I.F.C.	–	–	–	–
IMF TRUST FUND	–	–	–	–
U.N. AGENCIES	–	–	–	–
UNDP	1.3	2.8	2.0	3.7
UNTA	1.6	1.0	2.2	1.4
UNICEF	1.1	0.6	0.7	0.7
UNRWA	–	–	–	–
WFP	13.3	17.0	18.4	22.7
UNHCR	–	–	–	0.2
Other Multilateral	0.9	1.2	1.6	1.1
Arab Agencies	20.5	19.3	22.2	–
TOTAL	*51.5*	*74.0*	*49.4*	*29.7*
ARAB COUNTRIES	**580.8**	**-8.5**	**-11.6**	**550.3**
E.E.C.+ MEMBERS	*-19.0*	*254.4*	*155.3*	*154.0*
TOTAL	**727.7**	**424.7**	**242.4**	**721.8**

4. TOTAL ODA NET

DAC COUNTRIES	1987	1988	1989	1990
Australia	–	0.0	0.0	0.0
Austria	0.4	0.4	1.6	2.6
Belgium	0.2	0.2	–	–
Canada	0.7	0.7	0.4	0.2
Denmark	0.1	0.1	–	–
Finland	–	–	–	0.5
France	13.0	10.1	11.4	15.9
Germany	28.5	49.2	52.6	44.2
Ireland	–	–	–	–
Italy	0.1	0.0	0.0	0.0
Japan	45.1	107.1	42.2	5.5
Netherlands	0.5	0.3	0.3	0.1
New Zealand	–	–	–	–
Norway	–	–	–	–
Sweden	–	–	–	–
Switzerland	0.2	0.2	0.2	0.3
United Kingdom	0.2	0.0	–	–
United States	–	–	–	–
TOTAL	*88.9*	*168.3*	*108.8*	*69.4*
MULTILATERAL				
AF.D.F.	–	–	–	–
AF.D.B.	–	–	–	–
AS.D.B	–	–	–	–
CAR.D.B.	–	–	–	–
E.E.C.	0.6	5.8	1.9	1.9
IBRD	–	–	–	–
IDA	–	–	–	-2.0
I.D.B.	–	–	–	–
IFAD	2.0	–	–	0.8
I.F.C.	–	–	–	–
IMF TRUST FUND	–	–	–	–
U.N. AGENCIES	–	–	–	–
UNDP	1.3	2.8	2.0	3.7
UNTA	1.6	1.0	2.2	1.4
UNICEF	1.1	0.6	0.7	0.7
UNRWA	–	–	–	–
WFP	13.3	17.0	18.4	22.7
UNHCR	–	–	–	0.2
Other Multilateral	0.9	1.2	1.6	1.1
Arab Agencies	-0.9	8.1	6.5	–
TOTAL	*19.8*	*36.4*	*33.3*	*30.3*
ARAB COUNTRIES	**575.2**	**-13.5**	**-14.9**	**550.3**
E.E.C.+ MEMBERS	*43.0*	*65.6*	*66.2*	*62.1*
TOTAL	**683.8**	**191.1**	**127.2**	**649.9**

7. TOTAL ODA GROSS

DAC COUNTRIES	1987
Australia	–
Austria	0.4
Belgium	0.2
Canada	0.7
Denmark	0.1
Finland	–
France	13.2
Germany	29.1
Ireland	–
Italy	0.1
Japan	49.1
Netherlands	0.5
New Zealand	–
Norway	–
Sweden	–
Switzerland	0.2
United Kingdom	0.2
United States	–
TOTAL	*93.7*
AF.D.F.	–
AF.D.B.	–
AS.D.B	–
CAR.D.B.	–
E.E.C.	0.6
IBRD	–
IDA	–
I.D.B.	–
IFAD	2.0
I.F.C.	–
IMF TRUST FUND	–
U.N. AGENCIES	–
UNDP	1.3
UNTA	1.6
UNICEF	1.1
UNRWA	–
WFP	13.3
UNHCR	–
Other Multilateral	0.9
Arab Agencies	6.1
TOTAL	*26.8*
ARAB COUNTRIES	**608.2**
E.E.C.+ MEMBERS	*43.8*
TOTAL	**728.6**

2. ODA LOANS GROSS

DAC COUNTRIES	1987	1988	1989	1990
Australia	–	–	–	–
Austria	–	–	–	–
Belgium	–	–	–	–
Canada	–	–	–	–
Denmark	–	–	–	–
Finland	–	–	–	–
France	1.8	0.9	2.0	3.5
Germany	25.1	46.4	52.2	39.0
Ireland	–	–	–	–
Italy	–	–	–	–
Japan	46.4	106.3	37.8	10.8
Netherlands	–	–	–	–
New Zealand	–	–	–	–
Norway	–	–	–	–
Sweden	–	–	–	–
Switzerland	–	–	–	–
United Kingdom	–	–	–	–
United States	–	–	–	–
TOTAL	*73.2*	*153.5*	*92.0*	*53.2*
MULTILATERAL	*8.1*	*9.2*	*17.4*	*2.1*
ARAB COUNTRIES	**39.9**	**5.9**	**6.5**	**–**
E.E.C.+ MEMBERS	*26.9*	*47.2*	*54.2*	*42.5*
TOTAL	**121.2**	**168.5**	**115.8**	**55.3**

5. ODA LOANS NET

DAC COUNTRIES	1987	1988	1989	1990
Australia	–	–	–	–
Austria	–	–	–	–
Belgium	–	–	–	–
Canada	–	–	–	–
Denmark	–	–	–	–
Finland	–	–	–	–
France	1.6	-0.5	1.2	2.8
Germany	24.5	41.8	47.5	36.8
Ireland	–	–	–	–
Italy	–	–	–	–
Japan	42.3	101.7	37.8	0.9
Netherlands	–	–	–	–
New Zealand	–	–	–	–
Norway	–	–	–	–
Sweden	–	–	–	–
Switzerland	–	–	–	–
United Kingdom	–	–	–	–
United States	–	–	–	–
TOTAL	*68.4*	*143.0*	*86.5*	*40.5*
MULTILATERAL	*1.1*	*8.1*	*6.1*	*-2.5*
ARAB COUNTRIES	**6.9**	**-13.5**	**-15.0**	**–**
E.E.C.+ MEMBERS	*26.1*	*41.3*	*48.6*	*39.4*
TOTAL	**76.4**	**137.6**	**77.7**	**38.0**

8. GRANTS

	1987
Australia	–
Austria	0.4
Belgium	0.2
Canada	0.7
Denmark	0.1
Finland	–
France	11.4
Germany	4.0
Ireland	–
Italy	0.1
Japan	2.8
Netherlands	0.5
New Zealand	–
Norway	–
Sweden	–
Switzerland	0.2
United Kingdom	0.2
United States	–
TOTAL	*20.5*
MULTILATERAL	*18.7*
ARAB COUNTRIES	**568.3**
E.E.C.+ MEMBERS	*17.0*
TOTAL	**607.5**

3. TOTAL OFFICIAL GROSS

DAC COUNTRIES	1987	1988	1989	1990
Australia	–	0.0	0.0	0.0
Austria	0.4	0.4	1.6	2.6
Belgium	0.2	0.2	–	–
Canada	0.7	0.7	0.4	0.2
Denmark	0.1	0.1	–	–
Finland	–	–	–	0.5
France	13.2	11.4	12.1	16.6
Germany	29.1	53.8	57.4	46.9
Ireland	–	–	–	–
Italy	0.1	0.0	0.0	0.0
Japan	49.1	160.3	42.2	15.4
Netherlands	0.5	0.3	0.3	0.1
New Zealand	–	–	–	–
Norway	–	–	–	–
Sweden	–	–	–	–
Switzerland	0.2	0.2	0.2	0.3
United Kingdom	0.2	0.0	–	–
United States	–	–	–	–
TOTAL	*93.7*	*227.4*	*114.4*	*82.6*
MULTILATERAL	*65.4*	*101.9*	*84.7*	*42.8*
ARAB COUNTRIES	**613.8**	**10.9**	**9.9**	**550.3**
E.E.C.+ MEMBERS	*53.7*	*100.5*	*75.6*	*69.4*
TOTAL	**772.9**	**340.2**	**208.9**	**675.7**

6. TOTAL OFFICIAL NET

DAC COUNTRIES	1987	1988	1989	1990
Australia	–	0.0	0.0	0.0
Austria	0.4	0.4	1.6	2.6
Belgium	0.2	0.2	–	–
Canada	0.7	0.7	0.4	0.2
Denmark	0.1	0.1	–	–
Finland	–	–	–	0.5
France	13.0	10.1	11.4	15.9
Germany	28.5	49.2	52.7	44.7
Ireland	–	–	–	–
Italy	0.1	0.0	0.0	0.0
Japan	45.1	155.8	42.2	5.5
Netherlands	0.5	0.3	0.3	0.1
New Zealand	–	–	–	–
Norway	–	–	–	–
Sweden	–	–	–	–
Switzerland	0.2	0.2	0.2	0.3
United Kingdom	0.2	0.0	–	–
United States	–	–	–	–
TOTAL	*88.9*	*217.0*	*108.9*	*69.9*
MULTILATERAL	*51.5*	*74.0*	*49.4*	*29.7*
ARAB COUNTRIES	**580.8**	**-8.5**	**-11.6**	**550.3**
E.E.C.+ MEMBERS	*52.1*	*93.0*	*66.7*	*63.0*
TOTAL	**721.2**	**282.5**	**146.7**	**649.8**

9. TOTAL OOF GROSS

	1987
Australia	–
Austria	–
Belgium	–
Canada	–
Denmark	–
Finland	–
France	–
Germany	–
Ireland	–
Italy	–
Japan	–
Netherlands	–
New Zealand	–
Norway	–
Sweden	–
Switzerland	–
United Kingdom	–
United States	–
TOTAL	*–*
MULTILATERAL	*38.7*
ARAB COUNTRIES	**5.7**
E.E.C.+ MEMBERS	*9.9*
TOTAL	**44.3**

10. ODA COMMITMENTS

1988	1989	1990		1987	1988	1989	1990
0.0	0.0	0.0		0.0	0.0	0.0	0.0
0.4	1.6	2.6		0.4	0.4	1.6	2.6
0.2	–	–		–	0.0	–	–
0.7	0.4	0.2		0.8	0.5	0.6	–
0.1	–	–		–	–	–	–
–	–	0.5		–	–	0.1	0.3
11.4	12.1	16.6		11.4	25.7	10.2	13.1
53.8	57.3	46.4		46.3	133.9	10.0	11.3
–	–	–		–	–	–	–
0.0	0.0	0.0		0.1	0.0	0.0	14.5
111.6	42.2	15.4		217.5	5.8	5.3	4.1
0.3	0.3	0.1		0.3	0.1	0.1	0.1
–	–	–		–	–	–	–
–	–	–		–	–	–	–
0.2	0.2	0.3		0.1	0.1	0.1	0.3
0.0	–	–		0.2	0.0	–	–
–	–	–		–	–	–	–
178.8	*114.3*	*82.1*		*277.1*	*166.5*	*27.9*	*46.3*
–	–	–		–	–	–	–
–	–	–		–	–	–	–
–	–	–		–	–	–	–
5.8	2.0	2.0		0.3	2.4	0.3	0.3
–	–	–		–	–	–	–
–	–	–		–	–	–	–
–	–	0.8		7.2	–	–	–
–	–	–		–	–	–	–
–	–	–		18.1	22.5	24.9	29.6
2.8	2.0	3.7		–	–	–	–
1.0	2.2	1.4		–	–	–	–
0.6	0.7	0.7		–	–	–	–
–	–	–		–	–	–	–
17.0	18.4	22.7		–	–	–	–
–	–	0.2		–	–	–	–
1.2	1.6	1.1		–	–	–	–
9.2	17.6	1.3		1.1	0.7	–	–
37.5	*44.5*	*33.8*		*26.7*	*25.6*	*25.2*	*29.9*
5.9	*6.5*	*550.3*		*538.6*	*8.4*	*21.1*	*602.8*
71.5	*71.8*	*65.1*		*58.6*	*162.0*	*20.6*	*39.3*
222.1	*165.3*	*666.1*		*842.4*	*200.5*	*74.3*	*679.1*

11. TECH. COOP. GRANTS

1988	1989	1990		1987	1988	1989	1990
0.0	0.0	0.0		–	0.0	–	0.0
0.4	1.6	2.6		0.4	0.4	0.5	0.7
0.2	–	–		0.2	0.1	–	–
0.7	0.4	0.2		–	–	–	–
0.1	–	–		–	0.1	–	–
–	–	0.5		–	–	–	0.1
10.5	10.2	13.1		10.3	10.5	10.2	13.1
7.4	5.1	7.4		4.0	4.5	3.3	6.7
–	–	–		–	–	–	–
0.0	0.0	0.0		0.1	0.0	0.0	0.0
5.3	4.4	4.6		2.5	5.0	4.4	4.1
0.3	0.3	0.1		0.2	0.1	0.1	0.1
–	–	–		–	–	–	–
–	–	–		–	–	–	–
0.2	0.2	0.3		0.2	0.2	–	–
0.0	–	–		0.2	0.0	–	–
–	–	–		–	–	–	–
25.2	*22.3*	*28.9*		*18.0*	*20.9*	*18.4*	*24.8*
28.3	*27.1*	*31.7*		*4.8*	*7.1*	*6.5*	*7.0*
–	*0.1*	*550.3*		–	–	–	–
24.3	*17.6*	*22.7*		*15.0*	*16.9*	*13.5*	*20.0*
53.6	*49.5*	*610.8*		*22.8*	*28.0*	*24.9*	*31.7*

12. TOTAL OOF NET

1988	1989	1990		1987	1988	1989	1990
–	–	–		–	–	–	–
–	–	–		–	–	–	–
–	–	–		–	–	–	–
–	–	–		–	–	–	–
–	–	–		–	–	–	–
–	0.1	0.5		–	–	0.1	0.5
–	–	–		–	–	–	–
48.7	–	–		–	48.7	–	–
–	–	–		–	–	–	–
–	–	–		–	–	–	–
–	–	–		–	–	–	–
–	–	–		–	–	–	–
–	–	–		–	–	–	–
48.7	*0.1*	*0.5*		–	*48.7*	*0.1*	*0.5*
64.3	*40.2*	*9.1*		*31.7*	*37.6*	*16.2*	*-0.5*
5.1	*3.4*	–		*5.7*	*5.1*	*3.4*	–
28.9	*3.8*	*4.2*		*9.0*	*27.4*	*0.5*	*0.9*
118.1	*43.7*	*9.6*		*37.4*	*91.4*	*19.6*	*-0.1*

13. ODF COMMITMENTS: BY PURPOSE %

	1987	1988	1989	1990
Education	0	–	0	–
Health	–	–	0	–
Other Social Infrastr.	3	0	1	–
Water Sanitat. Sewage	0	20	–	–
Energy	23	44	–	–
Telecommunications	–	0	–	–
Transportation	–	–	–	–
Agriculture	0	0	41	–
Extractive Industries	–	–	–	–
Manufacturing	1	–	–	–
Trade Banking Tourism	–	–	–	–
Technical Cooperation	3	17	57	–
Multisector Aid	–	9	–	–
Programme	69	6	–	–
Debt Reorganisation	–	–	–	–
Food Aid	1	2	–	–
Emergency Aid	0	0	–	–
Unspecified	–	–	–	–
TOTAL	100	100	100	–

14. GRANT ELEMENT OF ODA %

DAC COUNTRIES

	1987	1988	1989	1990
Australia	100.0	100.0	100.0	–
Austria	100.0	100.0	100.0	–
Belgium	–	100.0	–	–
Canada	100.0	100.0	100.0	–
Denmark	–	–	–	–
Finland	–	–	100.0	–
France	100.0	81.3	100.0	–
Germany	47.2	48.5	100.0	–
Ireland	–	–	–	–
Italy	100.0	100.0	100.0	–
Japan	35.2	100.0	100.0	–
Netherlands	100.0	100.0	100.0	–
New Zealand	–	–	–	–
Norway	–	–	–	–
Sweden	–	–	–	–
Switzerland	100.0	100.0	100.0	–
United Kingdom	100.0	100.0	–	–
United States	–	–	–	–
TOTAL	*40.3*	*55.7*	*100.0*	–
MULTILATERAL	*100.0*	*100.0*	*100.0*	–
ARAB COUNTRIES	*100.0*	*31.1*	*46.0*	–
E.E.C.+ MEMBERS	*58.2*	*54.5*	*100.0*	–
TOTAL	*80.2*	*60.4*	*84.7*	–

15. OTHER AGGREGATES

	1987	1988	1989	1990
OFFICIAL COMMITMENTS:				
TOTAL BILATERAL	891.6	174.9	49.0	649.1
of which:				
Arab Countries	548.0	8.4	21.1	602.8
C.E.E.C.	–	–	–	–
TOTAL MULTILATERAL	89.6	25.6	25.2	29.9
TOTAL BIL.& MULTIL.	981.2	200.5	74.3	679.1
of which:				
ODA Grants	577.3	58.0	53.2	561.8
ODA Loans	265.1	142.5	21.1	117.3
DISBURSEMENTS:				
DAC COUNTRIES COMBINED				
OFFICIAL & PRIVATE				
GROSS:				
Contractual Lending	162.4	218.4	154.3	56.6
Export Credits, Total	89.2	64.9	62.3	3.4
Export Credits, Priv.	89.2	16.2	62.3	2.9
NET:				
Contractual Lending	90.7	176.3	118.1	27.2
Export Credits Total	22.3	33.3	31.6	-13.3
PRIVATE SECTOR NET	6.4	142.2	95.6	71.9
Direct Investment	6.6	120.7	73.8	71.5
Portfolio Investment	-22.4	36.9	-9.7	14.3
Export Credits	22.3	-15.4	31.5	-13.8
MARKET BORROWING:				
CHANGE IN CLAIMS				
Banks	-114.0	-131.0	-49.0	-72.0
MEMORANDUM ITEM:				
C.E.E.C. (Gross)	75.1	64.6	39.9	–

1. TOTAL RECEIPTS NET

DAC COUNTRIES	1987	1988	1989	1990
Australia	0.0	-578.6	-49.0	-15.5
Austria	1.7	2.0	2.3	2.9
Belgium	-6.5	-1.5	1.8	-1.4
Canada	0.1	–	39.1	–
Denmark	-0.1	–	–	3.0
Finland	0.0	–	–	2.4
France	-19.2	12.1	8.6	16.4
Germany	5.9	3.9	-2.8	71.8
Ireland	–	–	–	–
Italy	0.1	-0.4	0.8	-2.2
Japan	325.2	446.7	368.3	495.2
Netherlands	-25.4	63.8	44.4	22.6
New Zealand	–	–	–	–
Norway	0.1	–	–	–
Sweden	3.8	–	9.0	41.6
Switzerland	0.0	0.0	–	–
United Kingdom	3.9	43.4	129.7	-13.6
United States	-454.0	-55.0	187.0	-320.0
TOTAL	*-164.3*	*-63.7*	*739.2*	*302.9*
MULTILATERAL				
AF.D.F.	–	–	–	–
AF.D.B.	–	–	–	–
AS.D.B	–	-5.7	-6.1	-3.6
CAR.D.B.	–	–	–	–
E.E.C.	–	–	–	–
IBRD	-131.0	-1.0	-1.0	-5.0
IDA	-0.5	–	–	–
I.D.B.	–	–	–	–
IFAD	–	–	–	–
I.F.C.	–	–	–	–
IMF TRUST FUND	–	–	–	–
U.N. AGENCIES	–	–	–	–
UNDP	–	–	–	–
UNTA	–	–	–	–
UNICEF	–	–	–	–
UNRWA	–	–	–	–
WFP	–	–	–	–
UNHCR	–	–	–	–
Other Multilateral	–	–	–	–
Arab Agencies	–	–	–	–
TOTAL	*-131.4*	*-6.7*	*-7.1*	*-8.6*
ARAB COUNTRIES	***-9.2***	***-8.8***	***–***	***30.0***
E.E.C.+ MEMBERS	*-41.2*	*121.2*	*182.6*	*96.3*
TOTAL	***-305.0***	***-79.2***	***732.1***	***324.3***

2. ODA LOANS GROSS

DAC COUNTRIES	1987	1988	1989	1990
Australia	–	–	–	–
Austria	–	–	–	–
Belgium	–	–	–	–
Canada	–	–	–	–
Denmark	–	–	–	–
Finland	–	–	–	–
France	–	–	–	–
Germany	–	–	–	–
Ireland	–	–	–	–
Italy	–	–	–	–
Japan	–	–	–	–
Netherlands	–	–	–	–
New Zealand	–	–	–	–
Norway	–	–	–	–
Sweden	–	–	–	–
Switzerland	–	–	–	–
United Kingdom	–	–	–	–
United States	–	–	–	–
TOTAL	*–*	*–*	*–*	*–*
MULTILATERAL	*–*			
ARAB COUNTRIES	***1.7***	***0.3***	***–***	***47.9***
E.E.C.+ MEMBERS	*–*	*–*	*–*	*–*
TOTAL	***1.7***	***0.3***	***–***	***47.9***

3. TOTAL OFFICIAL GROSS

DAC COUNTRIES	1987	1988	1989	1990
Australia	0.0	0.2	0.1	0.1
Austria	1.7	2.0	2.3	2.9
Belgium	0.7	0.2	0.3	0.2
Canada	0.1	–	45.5	–
Denmark	–	–	–	–
Finland	0.0	–	–	–
France	0.3	0.3	0.3	1.7
Germany	6.3	4.2	6.0	7.1
Ireland	–	–	–	–
Italy	–	–	–	–
Japan	87.1	–	–	–
Netherlands	–	–	–	–
New Zealand	–	–	–	–
Norway	–	–	–	–
Sweden	–	–	–	–
Switzerland	0.0	0.0	–	–
United Kingdom	–	–	–	–
United States	-4.0	-4.0	-5.0	-4.0
TOTAL	*92.2*	*2.9*	*49.5*	*8.0*
MULTILATERAL	*–*	*–*	*–*	*–*
ARAB COUNTRIES	***1.7***	***0.3***	***–***	***47.9***
E.E.C.+ MEMBERS	*7.2*	*4.7*	*6.6*	*8.9*
TOTAL	***93.9***	***3.2***	***49.5***	***55.9***

4. TOTAL ODA NET

DAC COUNTRIES	1987	1988	1989	1990
Australia	0.0	0.2	0.1	0.1
Austria	1.7	2.0	2.3	2.9
Belgium	0.2	0.2	0.1	0.1
Canada	0.1	–	0.0	–
Denmark	–	–	–	–
Finland	0.0	–	–	–
France	0.3	0.3	0.3	1.7
Germany	3.9	4.1	5.3	6.6
Ireland	–	–	–	–
Italy	–	–	–	–
Japan	–	–	–	–
Netherlands	–	–	–	–
New Zealand	–	–	–	–
Norway	–	–	–	–
Sweden	–	–	–	–
Switzerland	0.0	0.0	–	–
United Kingdom	–	–	–	–
United States	-5.0	-5.0	-6.0	-5.0
TOTAL	*1.2*	*1.9*	*2.1*	*6.3*
MULTILATERAL				
AF.D.F.	–	–	–	–
AF.D.B.	–	–	–	–
AS.D.B	–	–	–	–
CAR.D.B.	–	–	–	–
E.E.C.	–	–	–	–
IBRD	–	–	–	–
IDA	-0.5	–	–	–
I.D.B.	–	–	–	–
IFAD	–	–	–	–
I.F.C.	–	–	–	–
IMF TRUST FUND	–	–	–	–
U.N. AGENCIES	–	–	–	–
UNDP	–	–	–	–
UNTA	–	–	–	–
UNICEF	–	–	–	–
UNRWA	–	–	–	–
WFP	–	–	–	–
UNHCR	–	–	–	–
Other Multilateral	–	–	–	–
Arab Agencies	–	–	–	–
TOTAL	*-0.5*	*–*	*–*	*–*
ARAB COUNTRIES	***-9.2***	***-8.8***	***–***	***30.0***
E.E.C.+ MEMBERS	*4.3*	*4.7*	*5.7*	*8.3*
TOTAL	***-8.5***	***-6.9***	***2.1***	***36.3***

5. ODA LOANS NET

DAC COUNTRIES	1987	1988	1989	1990
Australia	–	–	–	–
Austria	–	–	–	–
Belgium	–	–	–	–
Canada	–	–	–	–
Denmark	–	–	–	–
Finland	–	–	–	–
France	–	–	–	–
Germany	-0.6	-0.1	–	–
Ireland	–	–	–	–
Italy	–	–	–	–
Japan	–	–	–	–
Netherlands	–	–	–	–
New Zealand	–	–	–	–
Norway	–	–	–	–
Sweden	–	–	–	–
Switzerland	–	–	–	–
United Kingdom	–	–	–	–
United States	-1.0	-1.0	-1.0	-1.0
TOTAL	*-1.6*	*-1.1*	*-1.0*	*-1.0*
MULTILATERAL	*-0.5*	*–*	*–*	*–*
ARAB COUNTRIES	***-9.2***	***-8.8***	***–***	***30.0***
E.E.C.+ MEMBERS	*-0.6*	*-0.1*	*–*	*–*
TOTAL	***-11.3***	***-9.8***	***-1.0***	***29.0***

6. TOTAL OFFICIAL NET

DAC COUNTRIES	1987	1988	1989	1990
Australia	0.0	0.2	0.1	0.1
Austria	1.7	2.0	2.3	2.9
Belgium	0.7	0.2	0.3	0.2
Canada	0.1	–	39.1	–
Denmark	–	–	–	–
Finland	0.0	–	–	–
France	0.3	0.3	0.3	1.7
Germany	-1.2	0.4	1.2	3.4
Ireland	–	–	–	–
Italy	–	–	–	–
Japan	87.1	–	–	–
Netherlands	–	–	–	–
New Zealand	–	–	–	–
Norway	–	–	–	–
Sweden				
Switzerland	0.0	0.0	–	–
United Kingdom	–	–	–	–
United States	-969.0	-6.0	-6.0	-5.0
TOTAL	*-880.2*	*-2.8*	*37.3*	*3.2*
MULTILATERAL	*-131.4*	*-6.7*	*-7.1*	*-8.6*
ARAB COUNTRIES	***-9.2***	***-8.8***	***–***	***30.0***
E.E.C.+ MEMBERS	*-0.2*	*1.0*	*1.8*	*5.2*
TOTAL	***-1020.9***	***-18.3***	***30.2***	***24.6***

7. TOTAL ODA GROSS

	1987
Australia	0.0
Austria	1.7
Belgium	0.2
Canada	0.1
Denmark	–
Finland	0.0
France	0.3
Germany	4.4
Ireland	–
Italy	–
Japan	–
Netherlands	–
New Zealand	–
Norway	–
Sweden	–
Switzerland	0.0
United Kingdom	–
United States	-4.0
TOTAL	*2.7*
AF.D.F.	–
AF.D.B.	–
AS.D.B	–
CAR.D.B.	–
E.E.C.	–
IBRD	–
IDA	–
I.D.B.	–
IFAD	–
I.F.C.	–
IMF TRUST FUND	–
U.N. AGENCIES	–
UNDP	–
UNTA	–
UNICEF	–
UNRWA	–
WFP	–
UNHCR	–
Other Multilateral	–
Arab Agencies	–
TOTAL	*–*
ARAB COUNTRIES	***1.7***
E.E.C.+ MEMBERS	*4.9*
TOTAL	***4.5***

8. GRANTS

	1987
Australia	0.0
Austria	1.7
Belgium	0.2
Canada	0.1
Denmark	–
Finland	0.0
France	0.3
Germany	4.4
Ireland	–
Italy	–
Japan	–
Netherlands	–
New Zealand	–
Norway	–
Sweden	–
Switzerland	0.0
United Kingdom	–
United States	-4.0
TOTAL	*2.7*
MULTILATERAL	
ARAB COUNTRIES	***–***
E.E.C.+ MEMBERS	*4.9*
TOTAL	***2.7***

9. TOTAL OOF GROSS

	1987
Australia	–
Austria	–
Belgium	0.5
Canada	–
Denmark	–
Finland	–
France	–
Germany	1.8
Ireland	–
Italy	–
Japan	87.1
Netherlands	–
New Zealand	–
Norway	–
Sweden	–
Switzerland	–
United Kingdom	–
United States	–
TOTAL	*89.5*
MULTILATERAL	*–*
ARAB COUNTRIES	***–***
E.E.C.+ MEMBERS	*2.3*
TOTAL	***89.5***

10. ODA COMMITMENTS

1988	1989	1990	1987	1988	1989	1990
0.2	0.1	0.1	–	0.1	0.1	0.2
2.0	2.3	2.9	1.7	2.0	2.3	2.9
0.2	0.1	0.1	0.1	0.2	0.1	0.1
–	0.0	–	–	–	–	–
–	–	–	–	–	–	–
0.3	0.3	1.7	0.3	0.3	0.3	0.6
4.2	5.3	6.6	4.5	4.0	5.8	6.1
–	–	–	–	–	–	–
–	–	–	–	–	–	–
–	–	–	–	–	–	–
–	–	–	–	–	–	–
–	–	–	–	–	–	–
0.0	–	–	–	–	–	–
–	–	–	–	–	–	–
-4.0	-5.0	-4.0	–	–	–	–
2.9	3.1	7.3	6.6	6.6	8.6	9.9
–	–	–	–	–	–	–
–	–	–	–	–	–	–
–	–	–	–	–	–	–
–	–	–	–	–	–	–
–	–	–	–	⌐	–	–
–	–	–	–	–	–	–
–	–	–	–	–	–	–
–	–	–	–	–	–	–
–	–	–	–	–	–	–
–	–	–	–	–	–	–
–	–	–	–	–	–	–
–	–	–	–	–	–	–
–	–	–	–	–	–	–
–	–	–	–	–	–	–
–	–	–	–	–	–	–
–	–	–	–	–	–	–
0.3	–	47.9	–	–	–	–
4.7	5.7	8.3	4.9	4.5	6.2	6.8
3.2	3.1	55.3	6.6	6.6	8.6	9.9

11. TECH. COOP. GRANTS

1988	1989	1990	1987	1988	1989	1990
0.2	0.1	0.1	–	0.2	0.1	0.1
2.0	2.3	2.9	1.7	2.0	2.2	2.9
0.2	0.1	0.1	0.1	0.1	–	–
–	0.0	–	–	–	–	–
–	–	–	0.0	–	–	–
0.3	0.3	1.7	0.3	0.3	0.3	0.6
4.2	5.3	6.6	4.4	4.2	4.3	5.5
–	–	–	–	–	–	–
–	–	–	–	–	–	–
–	–	–	–	–	–	–
–	–	–	–	–	–	–
0.0	–	–	0.0	0.0	–	–
–	–	–	–	–	–	–
-4.0	-5.0	-4.0	–	–	–	–
2.9	3.1	7.3	6.6	6.8	6.9	9.2
–	–	–	–	–	–	–
–	–	–	–	–	–	–
4.7	5.7	8.3	4.8	4.6	4.6	6.1
2.9	3.1	7.3	6.6	6.8	6.9	9.2

12. TOTAL OOF NET

1988	1989	1990	1987	1988	1989	1990
–	–	–	–	–	–	–
–	0.2	0.1	0.5	–	0.2	0.1
–	45.5	–	–	–	39.1	–
–	–	–	–	–	–	–
–	–	–	–	–	–	–
0.0	0.7	0.5	-5.0	-3.7	-4.1	-3.2
–	–	–	–	–	–	–
–	–	–	87.1	–	–	–
–	–	–	–	–	–	–
–	–	–	–	–	–	–
–	–	–	–	–	–	–
–	–	–	–	–	–	–
–	–	–	-964.0	-1.0	–	–
0.0	46.3	0.6	-881.4	-4.7	35.2	-3.1
–	–	–	-131.0	-6.7	-7.1	-8.6
–	–	–	–	–	–	–
0.0	0.9	0.6	-4.5	-3.7	-3.9	-3.1
0.0	46.4	0.6	-1012.3	-11.4	28.1	-11.7

13. ODF COMMITMENTS: BY PURPOSE %

	1987	1988	1989	1990
Education	–	–	–	–
Health	–	–	–	–
Other Social Infrastr.	–	–	–	–
Water Sanitat. Sewage	–	–	–	–
Energy	–	–	–	–
Telecommunications	–	–	–	–
Transportation	–	–	–	–
Agriculture	–	–	–	–
Extractive Industries	–	–	–	–
Manufacturing	–	4	–	–
Trade Banking Tourism	–	–	–	–
Technical Cooperation	100	96	100	–
Multisector Aid	–	–	–	–
Programme	–	–	–	–
Debt Reorganisation	–	–	–	–
Food Aid	–	–	–	–
Emergency Aid	–	–	–	–
Unspecified	–	–	–	–
TOTAL	100	100	100	

14. GRANT ELEMENT OF ODA %

DAC COUNTRIES

	1987	1988	1989	1990
Australia	–	100.0	100.0	–
Austria	100.0	100.0	100.0	–
Belgium	100.0	100.0	100.0	–
Canada	–	–	–	–
Denmark	–	–	–	–
Finland	–	–	–	–
France	100.0	100.0	100.0	–
Germany	100.0	100.0	100.0	–
Ireland	–	–	–	–
Italy	–	–	–	–
Japan	–	29.4	–	–
Netherlands	–	–	–	–
New Zealand	–	–	–	–
Norway	–	–	–	–
Sweden	–	–	–	–
Switzerland	–	–	–	–
United Kingdom	–	–	–	–
United States	–	–	–	–
TOTAL	100.0	98.1	100.0	–
MULTILATERAL	–	–	–	–
ARAB COUNTRIES	–	–	–	–
E.E.C.+ MEMBERS	100.0	100.0	100.0	–
TOTAL	100.0	98.1	100.0	–

15. OTHER AGGREGATES

	1987	1988	1989	1990
OFFICIAL COMMITMENTS:				
TOTAL BILATERAL	6.6	6.6	8.8	10.0
of which:				
Arab Countries	–	–	–	–
C.E.E.C.	–	–	–	–
TOTAL MULTILATERAL	–	–	–	–
TOTAL BIL.& MULTIL.	6.6	6.6	8.8	10.0
of which:				
ODA Grants	6.6	6.6	8.6	9.9
ODA Loans	–	–	–	–
DISBURSEMENTS:				
DAC COUNTRIES COMBINED				
OFFICIAL & PRIVATE				
GROSS:				
Contractual Lending	374.2	73.5	170.1	209.4
Export Credits, Total	287.1	73.5	170.1	209.4
Export Credits, Priv.	287.1	73.5	124.7	209.5
NET:				
Contractual Lending	-1026.5	14.3	19.5	8.4
Export Credits Total	-1112.1	15.3	20.6	9.4
PRIVATE SECTOR NET	715.9	-60.9	701.9	299.7
Direct Investment	765.9	186.0	804.4	740.0
Portfolio Investment	91.3	-266.9	-88.7	-453.5
Export Credits	-141.2	20.0	-13.8	13.2
MARKET BORROWING:				
CHANGE IN CLAIMS				
Banks	8270.0	-1690.0	-437.0	487.0
MEMORANDUM ITEM:				
C.E.E.C. (Gross)	–	–	–	–

DISBURSEMENTS, UNLESS OTHERWISE STATE[D]

1. TOTAL RECEIPTS NET / 4. TOTAL ODA NET / 7. TOTAL ODA GROSS

1. TOTAL RECEIPTS NET — DAC COUNTRIES

	1987	1988	1989	1990
Australia	1.8	3.0	4.2	8.0
Austria	1.6	0.7	-0.1	1.8
Belgium	27.6	5.7	15.6	33.0
Canada	36.0	48.9	37.1	34.7
Denmark	48.4	76.7	78.6	78.4
Finland	34.2	63.2	51.6	51.0
France	-9.0	-7.6	11.5	-4.5
Germany	129.6	67.4	62.3	59.2
Ireland	3.1	3.7	3.4	3.9
Italy	175.9	68.5	24.2	73.4
Japan	42.0	96.4	63.0	38.5
Netherlands	76.0	78.5	76.4	93.2
New Zealand	0.1	0.4	0.1	0.2
Norway	75.1	78.7	57.5	97.8
Sweden	76.8	103.6	89.7	148.9
Switzerland	17.0	14.5	23.5	19.0
United Kingdom	31.3	60.0	45.0	31.7
United States	27.0	14.0	12.0	39.0
TOTAL	*794.4*	*776.1*	*655.6*	*806.9*

MULTILATERAL

	1987	1988	1989	1990
AF.D.F.	9.8	16.7	18.3	24.9
AF.D.B.	-2.2	-0.3	-2.9	-2.3
AS.D.B	–	–	–	–
CAR.D.B.	–	–	–	–
E.E.C.	32.7	34.5	51.3	51.3
IBRD	-19.4	-22.0	-23.0	-26.0
IDA	87.0	98.0	111.0	181.0
I.D.B.	–	–	–	–
IFAD	0.3	1.5	0.5	0.4
I.F.C.	-0.3	–	-1.3	0.1
IMF TRUST FUND	–	–	–	–
U.N. AGENCIES	–	–	–	–
UNDP	8.6	10.6	16.0	16.9
UNTA	1.8	1.6	1.6	2.3
UNICEF	12.2	12.9	14.0	15.0
UNRWA	–	–	–	–
WFP	3.8	7.7	4.7	7.8
UNHCR	2.0	3.3	1.7	1.3
Other Multilateral	6.4	8.9	12.5	12.7
Arab Agencies	-1.9	–	-0.8	–
TOTAL	*140.9*	*173.3*	*203.7*	*285.3*
ARAB COUNTRIES	*–*	*0.3*	*1.0*	*3.7*
E.E.C.+ MEMBERS	*515.6*	*387.3*	*368.3*	*419.5*
TOTAL	*935.3*	*949.7*	*860.2*	*1095.9*

4. TOTAL ODA NET — DAC COUNTRIES

	1987	1988	1989	1990
Australia	2.0	3.0	4.2	8.0
Austria	2.7	1.8	1.0	3.1
Belgium	2.1	6.8	4.3	14.3
Canada	36.0	30.4	37.1	34.7
Denmark	49.2	77.8	78.7	78.6
Finland	34.2	67.2	55.4	51.0
France	5.2	2.6	18.3	4.5
Germany	60.2	68.1	51.8	61.4
Ireland	3.1	3.7	3.4	3.9
Italy	195.8	76.9	61.1	105.7
Japan	46.1	96.7	62.6	40.7
Netherlands	74.1	78.9	71.4	94.5
New Zealand	0.1	0.4	0.1	0.2
Norway	75.2	79.1	57.5	102.9
Sweden	76.5	103.6	90.4	149.6
Switzerland	17.0	14.5	23.5	19.0
United Kingdom	38.9	59.1	60.8	26.7
United States	1.0	15.0	6.0	39.0
TOTAL	*719.3*	*785.6*	*687.6*	*837.5*

MULTILATERAL

	1987	1988	1989	1990
AF.D.F.	9.8	16.7	18.3	24.9
AF.D.B.	–	–	–	–
AS.D.B	–	–	–	–
CAR.D.B.	–	–	–	–
E.E.C.	32.9	34.7	51.5	51.5
IBRD	–	–	–	–
IDA	87.0	98.0	111.0	181.0
I.D.B.	–	–	–	–
IFAD	0.3	1.5	0.5	0.4
I.F.C.	–	–	–	–
IMF TRUST FUND	–	–	–	–
U.N. AGENCIES	–	–	–	–
UNDP	8.6	10.6	16.0	16.9
UNTA	1.8	1.6	1.6	2.3
UNICEF	12.2	12.9	14.0	15.0
UNRWA	–	–	–	–
WFP	3.8	7.7	4.7	7.8
UNHCR	2.0	3.3	1.7	1.3
Other Multilateral	6.4	8.9	12.5	12.7
Arab Agencies	-1.9	–	-0.8	–
TOTAL	*163.0*	*195.9*	*231.1*	*313.8*
ARAB COUNTRIES	*–*	*0.3*	*1.0*	*3.7*
E.E.C.+ MEMBERS	*461.5*	*408.7*	*401.4*	*441.0*
TOTAL	*882.3*	*981.8*	*919.7*	*1154.9*

7. TOTAL ODA GROSS

	1987
Australia	2.0
Austria	2.7
Belgium	2.1
Canada	36.0
Denmark	49.2
Finland	34.2
France	5.2
Germany	60.2
Ireland	3.1
Italy	197.5
Japan	46.1
Netherlands	74.1
New Zealand	0.1
Norway	75.4
Sweden	76.5
Switzerland	17.0
United Kingdom	39.1
United States	10.0
TOTAL	*730.4*
AF.D.F.	10.1
AF.D.B.	–
AS.D.B	–
CAR.D.B.	–
E.E.C.	34.2
IBRD	–
IDA	90.0
I.D.B.	–
IFAD	0.3
I.F.C.	–
IMF TRUST FUND	–
U.N. AGENCIES	–
UNDP	8.6
UNTA	1.8
UNICEF	12.2
UNRWA	–
WFP	3.8
UNHCR	2.0
Other Multilateral	6.4
Arab Agencies	–
TOTAL	*169.4*
ARAB COUNTRIES	*–*
E.E.C.+ MEMBERS	*464.6*
TOTAL	*899.8*

2. ODA LOANS GROSS / 5. ODA LOANS NET / 8. GRANTS

2. ODA LOANS GROSS — DAC COUNTRIES

	1987	1988	1989	1990
Australia	–	–	–	–
Austria	–	–	–	–
Belgium	–	2.7	–	4.0
Canada	–	–	–	–
Denmark	–	–	–	–
Finland	1.0	–	–	–
France	2.8	–	1.6	1.5
Germany	–	–	–	0.4
Ireland	–	–	–	–
Italy	121.0	50.2	50.2	101.0
Japan	5.2	14.1	9.4	0.9
Netherlands	0.2	0.0	0.1	0.4
New Zealand	–	–	–	–
Norway	–	–	–	–
Sweden	–	–	–	–
Switzerland	–	–	–	–
United Kingdom	0.4	0.9	1.5	0.3
United States	1.0	1.0	1.0	–
TOTAL	*131.6*	*69.0*	*63.8*	*108.4*
MULTILATERAL	*100.4*	*122.3*	*135.4*	*213.3*
ARAB COUNTRIES	*–*	*0.3*	*0.8*	*2.7*
E.E.C.+ MEMBERS	*124.4*	*55.6*	*53.5*	*107.6*
TOTAL	*232.0*	*191.5*	*200.0*	*324.4*

5. ODA LOANS NET — DAC COUNTRIES

	1987	1988	1989	1990
Australia	0.0	0.0	0.0	0.0
Austria	–	–	–	–
Belgium	–	2.7	–	4.0
Canada	–	-12.3	–	–
Denmark	–	–	–	–
Finland	1.0	–	–	–
France	2.8	–	1.6	1.2
Germany	–	0.0	0.0	0.4
Ireland	–	–	–	–
Italy	119.2	49.4	47.7	89.6
Japan	5.2	14.1	5.9	-2.7
Netherlands	–	0.0	-0.4	0.0
New Zealand	–	–	–	–
Norway	-0.2	-0.2	-0.2	-0.2
Sweden	–	–	–	–
Switzerland	–	–	–	–
United Kingdom	0.3	0.5	0.6	-3.8
United States	-8.0	1.0	–	-39.0
TOTAL	*120.5*	*55.2*	*55.3*	*49.4*
MULTILATERAL	*94.0*	*116.7*	*127.7*	*200.6*
ARAB COUNTRIES	*–*	*0.3*	*0.8*	*2.7*
E.E.C.+ MEMBERS	*121.3*	*53.1*	*48.4*	*90.2*
TOTAL	*214.5*	*172.2*	*183.7*	*252.7*

8. GRANTS

	1987
Australia	2.0
Austria	2.7
Belgium	2.1
Canada	36.0
Denmark	49.2
Finland	33.2
France	2.4
Germany	60.2
Ireland	3.1
Italy	76.5
Japan	40.9
Netherlands	73.9
New Zealand	0.1
Norway	75.4
Sweden	76.5
Switzerland	17.0
United Kingdom	38.6
United States	9.0
TOTAL	*598.8*
MULTILATERAL	*69.0*
ARAB COUNTRIES	*–*
E.E.C.+ MEMBERS	*340.2*
TOTAL	*667.8*

3. TOTAL OFFICIAL GROSS / 6. TOTAL OFFICIAL NET / 9. TOTAL OOF GROSS

3. TOTAL OFFICIAL GROSS — DAC COUNTRIES

	1987	1988	1989	1990
Australia	2.0	3.0	4.2	8.0
Austria	2.7	1.8	1.0	3.1
Belgium	70.1	10.7	28.0	33.0
Canada	36.0	61.2	37.1	34.7
Denmark	49.3	77.8	78.7	78.6
Finland	34.2	67.2	55.4	51.0
France	5.2	2.6	18.4	4.7
Germany	141.1	68.4	64.4	61.8
Ireland	3.1	3.7	3.4	3.9
Italy	198.4	77.7	64.4	121.0
Japan	46.1	96.7	66.0	44.3
Netherlands	75.2	81.1	75.1	95.1
New Zealand	0.1	0.4	0.1	0.2
Norway	75.4	79.2	57.6	103.0
Sweden	76.5	103.6	90.4	149.7
Switzerland	17.0	14.5	23.5	19.0
United Kingdom	39.4	59.7	62.4	41.2
United States	46.0	15.0	17.0	78.0
TOTAL	*917.8*	*824.4*	*747.1*	*930.1*
MULTILATERAL	*178.3*	*205.0*	*241.1*	*324.7*
ARAB COUNTRIES	*–*	*0.3*	*1.0*	*3.7*
E.E.C.+ MEMBERS	*616.0*	*417.7*	*447.5*	*492.0*
TOTAL	*1096.1*	*1029.8*	*989.2*	*1258.5*

6. TOTAL OFFICIAL NET — DAC COUNTRIES

	1987	1988	1989	1990
Australia	1.8	3.0	4.2	8.0
Austria	2.7	1.8	1.0	3.1
Belgium	70.1	10.7	28.0	33.0
Canada	36.0	48.9	37.1	34.7
Denmark	48.4	76.7	78.6	78.4
Finland	34.2	67.2	55.4	51.0
France	5.2	2.6	18.4	4.5
Germany	141.1	68.4	63.1	61.3
Ireland	3.1	3.7	3.4	3.9
Italy	176.2	76.9	55.3	92.2
Japan	46.1	96.7	62.6	40.7
Netherlands	75.0	80.6	74.1	94.3
New Zealand	0.1	0.4	0.1	0.2
Norway	75.2	79.1	57.5	102.9
Sweden	76.5	103.6	90.4	149.7
Switzerland	17.0	14.5	23.5	19.0
United Kingdom	35.6	58.7	61.1	35.5
United States	27.0	14.0	12.0	39.0
TOTAL	*871.2*	*807.5*	*725.6*	*851.1*
MULTILATERAL	*140.9*	*173.3*	*203.7*	*285.3*
ARAB COUNTRIES	*–*	*0.3*	*1.0*	*3.7*
E.E.C.+ MEMBERS	*587.4*	*412.9*	*433.2*	*454.3*
TOTAL	*1012.1*	*981.2*	*930.2*	*1140.0*

9. TOTAL OOF GROSS

	1987
Australia	0.1
Austria	–
Belgium	68.0
Canada	–
Denmark	0.1
Finland	–
France	–
Germany	80.9
Ireland	–
Italy	0.9
Japan	–
Netherlands	1.1
New Zealand	–
Norway	–
Sweden	–
Switzerland	–
United Kingdom	0.3
United States	36.0
TOTAL	*187.4*
MULTILATERAL	*8.9*
ARAB COUNTRIES	*–*
E.E.C.+ MEMBERS	*151.4*
TOTAL	*196.3*

10. ODA COMMITMENTS

1988	1989	1990	1987	1988	1989	1990
3.0	4.2	8.0	2.1	8.3	1.8	0.7
1.8	1.0	3.1	1.4	0.6	0.8	11.1
6.8	4.3	14.3	1.9	12.3	4.3	14.3
42.7	37.1	34.7	34.2	22.3	4.5	29.3
77.8	78.7	78.6	50.1	50.0	98.9	57.3
67.2	55.4	51.0	22.0	80.3	64.0	51.5
2.6	18.3	4.7	4.2	1.9	16.4	1.4
68.1	51.9	61.4	105.9	47.9	59.1	88.0
3.7	3.4	3.9	3.1	3.7	3.4	3.9
77.7	63.6	117.1	265.2	57.8	28.6	79.3
96.7	66.0	44.3	54.8	85.6	68.1	62.1
78.9	71.9	95.0	80.0	77.0	73.3	80.0
0.4	0.1	0.2	0.1	0.2	–	–
79.2	57.6	103.0	68.5	24.4	29.6	54.7
103.6	90.4	149.6	52.6	100.2	89.5	92.7
14.5	23.5	19.0	12.8	33.4	10.2	26.1
59.6	61.7	30.8	58.1	48.1	33.4	76.3
15.0	7.0	78.0	66.8	15.6	11.5	118.2
799.4	696.1	896.5	883.7	669.6	597.3	846.9
17.0	18.8	25.5	125.5	17.1	18.2	91.2
–	–	–	–	–	–	–
–	–	–	–	–	–	–
–	–	–	–	–	–	–
36.0	52.7	52.7	146.4	48.3	20.3	20.3
–	–	–	–	–	–	–
102.0	116.0	187.0	23.0	203.0	66.0	519.0
–	–	–	–	–	–	–
1.5	0.6	0.9	–	0.2	26.9	0.3
–	–	–	–	–	–	–
–	–	–	–	–	–	–
–	–	–	34.8	44.9	50.6	56.0
10.6	16.0	16.9	–	–	–	–
1.6	1.6	2.3	–	–	–	–
12.9	14.0	15.0	–	–	–	–
–	–	–	–	–	–	–
7.7	4.7	7.8	–	–	–	–
3.3	1.7	1.3	–	–	–	–
8.9	12.5	12.7	–	–	–	–
–	0.2	0.2	4.6	–	–	14.5
201.4	238.8	322.2	334.3	313.4	181.9	701.3
0.3	1.0	3.7	4.0	–	0.1	19.2
411.2	406.5	458.4	714.9	347.1	337.6	420.8
1001.1	935.9	1222.4	1222.0	983.0	779.3	1567.4

11. TECH. COOP. GRANTS

1988	1989	1990	1987	1988	1989	1990
3.0	4.2	8.0	0.4	0.7	0.7	1.0
1.8	1.0	3.1	0.4	0.5	0.1	0.8
4.1	4.3	10.2	0.7	0.5	0.2	0.0
42.7	37.1	34.7	–	3.1	3.7	5.3
77.8	78.7	78.6	11.3	12.5	15.0	16.6
67.2	55.4	51.0	6.3	3.0	5.4	9.7
2.6	16.7	3.2	1.2	1.3	1.2	1.4
68.1	51.9	61.0	29.9	27.4	25.5	29.4
3.7	3.4	3.9	1.1	1.4	0.9	1.0
27.5	13.4	16.1	8.7	5.6	1.2	3.1
82.6	56.7	43.4	12.5	14.9	13.9	15.0
78.9	71.8	94.6	27.1	29.8	24.5	26.0
0.4	0.1	0.2	0.1	0.1	–	0.2
79.2	57.6	103.0	12.7	13.8	14.1	13.7
103.6	90.4	149.6	27.3	36.4	31.5	3.3
14.5	23.5	19.0	3.7	3.8	–	–
58.7	60.2	30.6	10.0	14.9	14.4	14.6
14.0	6.0	78.0	1.0	1.0	4.0	20.0
730.4	632.3	788.1	154.3	170.8	156.5	161.1
79.1	103.5	108.9	32.4	39.4	45.9	48.2
–	0.2	1.0	–	–	–	–
355.6	353.1	350.8	91.4	95.6	83.1	92.1
809.5	736.0	897.9	186.7	210.2	202.4	209.3

12. TOTAL OOF NET

1988	1989	1990	1987	1988	1989	1990
–	–	–	-0.2	0.0	–	–
–	–	–	–	–	–	–
3.9	23.6	18.7	68.0	3.9	23.6	18.7
18.6	–	–	–	18.6	–	–
–	–	–	-0.8	-1.1	-0.1	-0.1
–	–	–	–	–	–	–
–	0.1	–	–	–	0.1	–
0.3	12.5	0.5	80.9	0.3	11.2	0.0
–	–	–	–	–	–	–
–	0.8	3.9	-19.6	–	-5.8	-13.6
–	–	–	–	–	–	–
2.2	3.3	0.1	0.9	1.8	2.7	-0.3
–	–	–	–	–	–	–
–	–	0.1	–	–	–	0.1
–	–	–	–	–	–	–
0.1	0.7	10.4	-3.3	-0.5	0.3	8.8
–	10.0	–	26.0	-1.0	6.0	–
25.1	51.0	33.6	151.9	21.9	38.0	13.6
3.6	2.3	2.5	-22.1	-22.5	-27.4	-28.4
–	–	–	–	–	–	–
6.5	41.0	33.5	125.9	4.2	31.8	13.3
28.7	53.3	36.2	129.8	-0.6	10.5	-14.9

13. ODF COMMITMENTS: BY PURPOSE %

	1987	1988	1989	1990
Education	3	2	2	–
Health	1	1	2	–
Other Social Infrastr.	2	2	1	–
Water Sanitat. Sewage	2	5	2	–
Energy	9	2	4	–
Telecommunications	3	2	1	–
Transportation	12	5	19	–
Agriculture	9	16	13	–
Extractive Industries	0	2	0	–
Manufacturing	7	4	4	–
Trade Banking Tourism	2	2	5	–
Technical Cooperation	17	20	31	–
Multisector Aid	0	6	0	–
Programme	16	29	10	–
Debt Reorganisation	13	2	3	–
Food Aid	1	1	0	–
Emergency Aid	0	0	0	–
Unspecified	2	0	0	–
TOTAL	100	100	100	–

14. GRANT ELEMENT OF ODA %

DAC COUNTRIES	1987	1988	1989	1990
Australia	100.0	100.0	100.0	–
Austria	100.0	100.0	100.0	–
Belgium	100.0	100.0	100.0	–
Canada	100.0	100.0	100.0	–
Denmark	100.0	100.0	100.0	–
Finland	100.0	100.0	100.0	–
France	100.0	100.0	100.0	–
Germany	100.0	100.0	89.0	–
Ireland	100.0	100.0	100.0	–
Italy	68.6	75.4	80.1	–
Japan	100.0	89.3	100.0	–
Netherlands	100.0	100.0	100.0	–
New Zealand	100.0	100.0	–	–
Norway	100.0	100.0	100.0	–
Sweden	100.0	100.0	100.0	–
Switzerland	100.0	100.0	100.0	–
United Kingdom	100.0	100.0	100.0	–
United States	99.9	99.9	99.1	–
TOTAL	90.5	96.1	97.6	–
MULTILATERAL	94.0	85.8	88.2	–
ARAB COUNTRIES	81.0	–	100.0	–
E.E.C.+ MEMBERS	88.1	95.1	95.8	–
TOTAL	91.3	92.5	95.5	–

15. OTHER AGGREGATES

	1987	1988	1989	1990
OFFICIAL COMMITMENTS:				
TOTAL BILATERAL	1233.3	703.7	686.0	972.8
of which:				
Arab Countries	4.0	–	0.1	19.2
C.E.E.C.	63.2	10.4	–	–
TOTAL MULTILATERAL	334.4	314.3	181.9	703.3
TOTAL BIL.& MULTIL.	1567.6	1018.0	867.9	1676.1
of which:				
ODA Grants	868.5	704.6	622.6	849.5
ODA Loans	391.7	288.9	156.7	717.9
DISBURSEMENTS:				
DAC COUNTRIES COMBINED				
OFFICIAL & PRIVATE				
GROSS:				
Contractual Lending	333.3	113.6	102.6	132.5
Export Credits, Total	16.1	38.1	-10.3	-9.2
Export Credits, Priv.	15.1	19.6	-11.8	-9.4
NET:				
Contractual Lending	201.4	38.5	12.2	21.8
Export Credits Total	-80.2	-22.1	-89.9	-43.6
PRIVATE SECTOR NET	-76.8	-31.4	-70.0	-44.1
Direct Investment	-0.5	3.8	5.8	-2.3
Portfolio Investment	-6.1	3.4	4.9	-0.8
Export Credits	-70.2	-38.6	-80.8	-41.0
MARKET BORROWING:				
CHANGE IN CLAIMS				
Banks	20.0	-170.0	-33.0	-27.0
MEMORANDUM ITEM:				
C.E.E.C. (Gross)	8.9	–	–	–

1. TOTAL RECEIPTS NET

DAC COUNTRIES	1987	1988	1989	1990
Australia	42.8	18.6	66.8	62.8
Austria	-4.1	-3.3	-2.3	40.4
Belgium	79.5	25.3	-85.1	2.7
Canada	36.8	56.0	16.0	52.1
Denmark	-12.8	-12.3	2.1	-21.2
Finland	0.6	0.6	12.7	6.1
France	-15.6	34.7	82.9	159.6
Germany	-10.2	42.3	92.9	148.5
Ireland	0.0	0.0	0.0	0.0
Italy	9.5	4.7	66.1	5.4
Japan	531.7	595.2	1737.6	1995.9
Netherlands	44.4	35.2	81.0	-20.6
New Zealand	1.5	1.5	1.0	1.3
Norway	4.8	2.5	3.5	3.8
Sweden	-4.1	1.0	1.5	19.4
Switzerland	2.7	5.0	3.3	4.8
United Kingdom	25.1	67.9	105.7	10.2
United States	155.0	-127.0	214.0	292.0
TOTAL	*887.8*	*748.0*	*2399.8*	*2763.2*
MULTILATERAL				
AF.D.F.	–	–	–	–
AF.D.B.	–	–	–	–
AS.D.B	18.1	19.4	34.7	-77.4
CAR.D.B.	–	–	–	–
E.E.C.	17.7	13.9	8.0	8.0
IBRD	-26.9	-493.0	-246.0	-33.0
IDA	1.9	–	-1.0	-1.0
I.D.B.	–	–	–	–
IFAD	3.8	-2.4	-2.4	0.6
I.F.C.	-18.9	25.4	27.9	7.5
IMF TRUST FUND	–	–	–	–
U.N. AGENCIES	–	–	–	–
UNDP	4.9	5.7	8.1	6.8
UNTA	3.4	2.0	3.3	2.6
UNICEF	4.6	3.6	4.4	3.4
UNRWA	–	–	–	–
WFP	–	–	–	27.6
UNHCR	27.0	28.9	31.2	22.1
Other Multilateral	2.7	3.4	36.9	5.2
Arab Agencies	-3.2	-3.0	-3.2	–
TOTAL	*35.1*	*-396.2*	*-98.3*	*-27.6*
ARAB COUNTRIES	***-4.5***	***-6.8***	***-6.8***	***-3.1***
E.E.C.+ MEMBERS	*137.7*	*211.8*	*353.8*	*292.6*
TOTAL	**918.4**	**345.0**	**2294.7**	**2732.5**

2. ODA LOANS GROSS

DAC COUNTRIES	1987	1988	1989	1990
Australia	–	–	–	–
Austria	–	–	–	–
Belgium	0.3	–	–	0.5
Canada	1.6	4.2	1.1	0.2
Denmark	6.7	1.4	0.5	2.4
Finland	–	–	0.5	0.9
France	1.5	6.7	2.4	108.6
Germany	4.6	9.1	15.8	42.1
Ireland	–	–	–	–
Italy	–	–	–	–
Japan	235.2	298.5	360.8	330.8
Netherlands	1.7	0.6	0.9	1.3
New Zealand	–	–	–	–
Norway	1.3	–	–	–
Sweden	–	–	–	–
Switzerland	2.0	3.6	0.8	1.3
United Kingdom	0.6	–	2.0	2.1
United States	4.0	9.0	10.0	8.0
TOTAL	*259.5*	*333.3*	*394.7*	*498.1*
MULTILATERAL	*16.4*	*4.2*	*2.3*	*5.3*
ARAB COUNTRIES	***1.7***	***0.2***	***0.0***	***–***
E.E.C.+ MEMBERS	*15.5*	*17.9*	*21.6*	*156.9*
TOTAL	**277.6**	**337.6**	**397.1**	**503.5**

3. TOTAL OFFICIAL GROSS

DAC COUNTRIES	1987	1988	1989	1990
Australia	16.7	21.6	31.7	29.7
Austria	0.3	0.3	0.6	18.3
Belgium	6.3	3.1	5.2	7.2
Canada	43.1	52.4	24.4	84.5
Denmark	9.5	7.6	2.3	4.7
Finland	0.6	0.7	2.8	4.6
France	8.3	12.4	7.7	116.5
Germany	44.3	43.5	101.8	117.7
Ireland	0.0	0.0	0.0	0.0
Italy	6.1	5.2	3.5	1.1
Japan	401.8	496.7	809.1	940.4
Netherlands	12.6	13.1	10.6	18.0
New Zealand	1.5	1.5	1.0	1.3
Norway	4.7	2.3	3.0	2.7
Sweden	0.7	1.0	1.0	7.0
Switzerland	3.7	6.0	4.6	5.4
United Kingdom	8.8	41.4	16.8	19.2
United States	25.0	26.0	53.0	54.0
TOTAL	*594.1*	*734.8*	*1079.1*	*1432.5*
MULTILATERAL	*306.5*	*289.1*	*368.3*	*353.5*
ARAB COUNTRIES	***1.7***	***0.3***	***0.0***	***–***
E.E.C.+ MEMBERS	*113.7*	*140.2*	*155.8*	*292.5*
TOTAL	**902.3**	**1024.2**	**1447.4**	**1785.9**

4. TOTAL ODA NET

DAC COUNTRIES	1987	1988	1989	1990
Australia	16.6	21.1	30.8	29.7
Austria	-1.2	-0.4	-0.6	-0.3
Belgium	2.7	3.1	2.8	4.3
Canada	26.3	29.2	24.0	26.7
Denmark	6.8	1.9	1.0	3.0
Finland	0.6	0.6	2.8	4.5
France	7.7	11.7	7.1	115.4
Germany	21.9	35.1	38.8	61.5
Ireland	0.0	0.0	0.0	0.0
Italy	6.1	5.2	3.5	1.1
Japan	302.4	360.6	488.9	418.6
Netherlands	10.9	9.9	10.1	13.7
New Zealand	1.0	1.3	1.0	1.3
Norway	4.7	2.3	3.0	2.4
Sweden	0.7	1.0	1.0	7.0
Switzerland	2.7	5.0	3.3	4.8
United Kingdom	3.1	4.6	8.9	7.9
United States	23.0	22.0	31.0	30.0
TOTAL	*435.8*	*514.1*	*657.4*	*731.5*
MULTILATERAL				
AF.D.F.	–	–	–	–
AF.D.B.	–	–	–	–
AS.D.B	9.1	3.5	3.1	1.6
CAR.D.B.	–	–	–	–
E.E.C.	17.7	13.9	8.0	8.0
IBRD	–	–	–	–
IDA	1.9	–	-1.0	-1.0
I.D.B.	–	–	–	–
IFAD	3.8	-2.4	-2.4	0.6
I.F.C.	–	–	–	–
IMF TRUST FUND	–	–	–	–
U.N. AGENCIES	–	–	–	–
UNDP	4.9	5.7	8.1	6.8
UNTA	3.4	2.0	3.3	2.6
UNICEF	4.6	3.6	4.4	3.4
UNRWA	–	–	–	–
WFP	–	–	–	27.6
UNHCR	27.0	28.9	31.2	22.1
Other Multilateral	2.7	3.4	36.9	5.2
Arab Agencies	-2.8	-2.6	-2.8	–
TOTAL	*72.3*	*55.9*	*88.7*	*76.9*
ARAB COUNTRIES	***-4.5***	***-6.8***	***-6.8***	***-3.1***
E.E.C.+ MEMBERS	*76.8*	*85.3*	*80.2*	*214.8*
TOTAL	**503.6**	**563.2**	**739.2**	**805.4**

5. ODA LOANS NET

DAC COUNTRIES	1987	1988	1989	1990
Australia	-1.5	-0.6	-1.2	-1.4
Austria	0.3	–	–	0.5
Belgium	1.6	3.9	0.7	-0.2
Canada	6.0	0.0	-0.7	0.7
Denmark	–	0.0	0.5	0.9
Finland	0.9	6.1	1.8	107.4
France	-5.7	2.6	7.0	26.3
Germany	–	–	–	–
Japan	166.9	222.2	284.4	246.2
Netherlands	1.7	0.6	0.9	1.3
New Zealand	–	–	–	–
Norway	1.3	0.0	–	-0.3
Sweden	–	–	–	–
Switzerland	1.0	2.6	-0.5	0.6
United Kingdom	-0.4	-1.0	0.6	-1.1
United States	3.0	8.0	8.0	6.0
TOTAL	*175.0*	*244.3*	*301.4*	*386.9*
MULTILATERAL	*11.0*	*-2.5*	*-5.4*	*-3.6*
ARAB COUNTRIES	***-4.5***	***-6.8***	***-6.8***	***-3.1***
E.E.C.+ MEMBERS	*2.9*	*8.2*	*9.5*	*135.1*
TOTAL	**181.5**	**234.9**	**289.1**	**380.2**

6. TOTAL OFFICIAL NET

DAC COUNTRIES	1987	1988	1989	1990
Australia	14.0	18.6	28.8	26.8
Austria	-1.2	-0.4	-0.6	16.9
Belgium	6.3	3.1	5.2	7.2
Canada	36.8	45.8	24.0	52.1
Denmark	1.8	2.6	-2.9	2.6
Finland	0.6	0.6	2.8	4.5
France	7.7	11.7	7.1	115.4
Germany	6.3	11.0	62.6	71.9
Ireland	0.0	0.0	0.0	0.0
Italy	6.1	5.2	3.5	1.1
Japan	290.4	238.7	716.4	761.9
Netherlands	12.6	13.0	10.4	17.7
New Zealand	1.5	1.5	1.0	1.3
Norway	4.7	2.3	3.0	2.4
Sweden	0.7	1.0	1.0	7.0
Switzerland	2.7	5.0	3.3	4.8
United Kingdom	3.5	32.6	-11.8	11.1
United States	-2.0	5.0	41.0	40.0
TOTAL	*392.6*	*397.3*	*894.9*	*1144.7*
MULTILATERAL	*35.1*	*-396.2*	*-98.3*	*-27.6*
ARAB COUNTRIES	***-4.5***	***-6.8***	***-6.8***	***-3.1***
E.E.C.+ MEMBERS	*62.1*	*93.1*	*82.2*	*235.0*
TOTAL	**423.2**	**-5.7**	**789.8**	**1114.0**

7. TOTAL ODA GROSS

	1987
Australia	16.6
Austria	0.3
Belgium	2.7
Canada	26.3
Denmark	7.5
Finland	0.6
France	8.3
Germany	32.1
Ireland	0.0
Italy	6.1
Japan	370.8
Netherlands	10.9
New Zealand	1.0
Norway	4.7
Sweden	0.7
Switzerland	3.7
United Kingdom	4.0
United States	24.0
TOTAL	*520.3*
AF.D.F.	–
AF.D.B.	–
AS.D.B	9.3
CAR.D.B.	–
E.E.C.	17.7
IBRD	–
IDA	2.0
I.D.B.	–
IFAD	6.1
I.F.C.	–
IMF TRUST FUND	–
U.N. AGENCIES	–
UNDP	4.9
UNTA	3.4
UNICEF	4.6
UNRWA	–
WFP	–
UNHCR	27.0
Other Multilateral	2.7
Arab Agencies	0.0
TOTAL	*77.7*
ARAB COUNTRIES	***1.7***
E.E.C.+ MEMBERS	*89.4*
TOTAL	**599.7**

8. GRANTS

	1987
Australia	16.6
Austria	0.3
Belgium	2.4
Canada	24.7
Denmark	0.7
Finland	0.6
France	6.8
Germany	27.6
Ireland	0.0
Italy	6.1
Japan	135.6
Netherlands	9.1
New Zealand	1.0
Norway	3.5
Sweden	0.7
Switzerland	1.7
United Kingdom	3.4
United States	20.0
TOTAL	*260.8*
MULTILATERAL	*61.3*
ARAB COUNTRIES	***0.0***
E.E.C.+ MEMBERS	*73.9*
TOTAL	**322.1**

9. TOTAL OOF GROSS

	1987
Australia	0.2
Austria	–
Belgium	3.7
Canada	16.8
Denmark	2.0
Finland	–
France	–
Germany	12.2
Ireland	–
Italy	–
Japan	31.0
Netherlands	1.7
New Zealand	0.5
Norway	–
Sweden	–
Switzerland	–
United Kingdom	4.7
United States	1.0
TOTAL	*73.8*
MULTILATERAL	*228.8*
ARAB COUNTRIES	***–***
E.E.C.+ MEMBERS	*24.3*
TOTAL	**302.6**

1988	1989	1990		1987	1988	1989	1990

10. ODA COMMITMENTS

1988	1989	1990	1987	1988	1989	1990
21.1	30.8	29.7	13.3	18.7	13.6	43.0
0.3	0.6	1.1	0.3	0.3	0.6	1.9
3.1	2.8	4.3	3.7	5.3	2.8	4.3
29.5	24.4	27.1	29.2	32.4	34.6	48.3
3.3	2.2	4.7	–	–	0.2	3.0
0.7	2.8	4.6	–	1.2	12.5	10.0
12.4	7.7	116.5	11.9	5.6	4.9	184.4
41.6	47.7	77.4	42.2	55.3	77.4	117.1
0.0	0.0	0.0	0.0	0.0	0.0	0.0
5.2	3.5	1.1	8.1	1.8	3.4	1.6
437.0	565.3	503.1	450.4	885.1	298.9	793.9
9.9	10.1	13.6	12.6	8.8	8.1	13.0
1.3	1.0	1.3	0.8	0.9	–	0.6
2.3	3.0	2.7	4.7	–	4.3	–
1.0	1.0	7.0	1.2	1.2	0.8	6.6
6.0	4.6	5.4	1.4	2.1	3.4	2.8
5.6	10.3	11.1	3.6	4.5	12.6	6.1
23.0	33.0	32.0	29.3	30.8	30.3	19.9
603.1	*750.7*	*842.8*	*612.5*	*1054.1*	*508.3*	*1256.3*
–	–	–	–	–	–	–
–	–	–	–	–	–	–
3.6	3.5	2.3	–	–	–	–
–	–	–	–	–	–	–
13.9	8.0	8.0	10.6	17.0	56.7	56.7
–	–	–	–	–	–	–
1.0	–	–	–	–	–	–
–	–	–	–	–	–	–
0.3	1.1	5.0	10.1	–	–	–
–	–	–	–	–	–	–
–	–	–	–	–	–	–
–	–	–	42.6	43.5	83.9	67.7
5.7	8.1	6.8	–	–	–	–
2.0	3.3	2.6	–	–	–	–
3.6	4.4	3.4	–	–	–	–
–	–	–	–	–	–	–
–	–	27.6	–	–	–	–
28.9	31.2	22.1	–	–	–	–
3.4	36.9	5.2	–	–	–	–
0.2	–	0.2	3.0	–	–	–
62.6	*96.4*	*83.2*	*66.3*	*60.5*	*140.5*	*124.4*
0.3	**0.0**	**–**	**–**	**0.1**	**–**	**–**
95.0	*92.3*	*236.7*	*92.7*	*98.4*	*166.0*	*386.0*
666.0	**847.2**	**925.9**	**678.8**	**1114.7**	**648.9**	**1380.7**

11. TECH. COOP. GRANTS

1988	1989	1990	1987	1988	1989	1990
21.1	30.8	29.7	13.2	16.9	21.4	19.1
0.3	0.6	1.1	0.3	0.3	0.3	0.5
3.1	2.8	3.8	1.7	2.0	1.7	2.4
25.2	23.4	26.9	–	7.2	6.1	6.2
1.9	1.7	2.3	3.4	1.3	0.9	2.6
0.7	2.3	3.7	0.1	0.1	0.1	0.4
5.6	5.3	8.0	6.8	5.6	9.9	8.0
32.5	31.9	35.2	21.7	26.4	23.2	26.0
0.0	0.0	0.0	0.0	0.0	0.0	0.0
5.2	3.5	1.1	5.3	4.4	0.8	0.7
138.4	204.5	172.4	72.6	94.3	96.7	96.3
9.3	9.3	12.3	5.5	6.7	6.4	7.6
1.3	1.0	1.3	0.8	0.8	–	1.2
2.3	3.0	2.7	0.4	0.4	0.3	0.3
1.0	1.0	7.0	0.4	0.6	0.5	0.2
2.4	3.8	4.2	0.4	0.5	–	–
5.6	8.3	9.0	2.9	4.2	2.7	3.3
14.0	23.0	24.0	14.0	14.0	17.0	15.0
269.8	*356.0*	*344.7*	*149.7*	*185.5*	*187.9*	*189.9*
58.4	*94.1*	*77.8*	*43.5*	*47.8*	*83.9*	*40.1*
0.1	**0.0**	**–**	**–**	**–**	**–**	**–**
77.1	*70.7*	*79.7*	*48.3*	*54.8*	*45.5*	*50.7*
328.3	**450.1**	**422.5**	**193.2**	**233.3**	**271.8**	**230.1**

12. TOTAL OOF NET

1988	1989	1990	1987	1988	1989	1990
0.6	0.9	–	-2.6	-2.5	-2.0	-2.9
–	–	17.2	–	–	–	17.2
–	2.4	3.0	3.7	–	2.4	3.0
23.0	–	57.4	10.5	16.7	–	25.4
4.3	0.1	–	-5.0	0.8	-3.9	-0.4
–	–	–	–	–	–	–
1.9	54.1	40.4	-15.5	-24.1	23.8	10.4
–	–	–	–	–	–	–
59.8	243.9	437.3	-12.0	-121.9	227.6	343.3
3.1	0.5	4.4	1.7	3.1	0.3	4.1
0.2	–	–	0.5	0.2	–	–
–	–	–	–	–	–	–
–	–	–	–	–	–	–
35.9	6.5	8.1	0.4	28.1	-20.7	3.2
3.0	20.0	22.0	-25.0	-17.0	10.0	10.0
131.7	*328.4*	*589.7*	*-43.3*	*-116.8*	*237.5*	*413.2*
226.6	*271.8*	*270.3*	*-37.2*	*-452.1*	*-186.9*	*-104.5*
–	–	–	–	–	–	–
45.2	*63.6*	*55.8*	*-14.8*	*7.8*	*1.9*	*20.2*
358.2	**600.2**	**860.0**	**-80.4**	**-568.9**	**50.5**	**308.6**

13. ODF COMMITMENTS: BY PURPOSE %

	1987	1988	1989	1990
Education	3	1	0	–
Health	1	0	0	–
Other Social Infrastr.	8	2	4	–
Water Sanitat. Sewage	6	9	0	–
Energy	15	17	13	–
Telecommunications	8	20	10	–
Transportation	10	11	19	–
Agriculture	11	10	5	–
Extractive Industries	1	0	0	–
Manufacturing	6	2	26	–
Trade Banking Tourism	6	7	1	–
Technical Cooperation	25	18	21	–
Multisector Aid	0	4	0	–
Programme	–	–	–	–
Debt Reorganisation	–	–	–	–
Food Aid	0	0	0	–
Emergency Aid	1	0	1	–
Unspecified	–	0	–	–
TOTAL	100	100	100	

14. GRANT ELEMENT OF ODA %

DAC COUNTRIES

	1987	1988	1989	1990
Australia	100.0	100.0	100.0	–
Austria	100.0	100.0	100.0	–
Belgium	100.0	100.0	100.0	–
Canada	91.6	100.0	100.0	–
Denmark	–	–	100.0	–
Finland	–	100.0	100.0	–
France	83.9	100.0	100.0	–
Germany	86.5	89.0	84.1	–
Ireland	100.0	100.0	100.0	–
Italy	100.0	100.0	100.0	–
Japan	71.7	67.4	83.1	–
Netherlands	100.0	100.0	100.0	–
New Zealand	100.0	100.0	–	–
Norway	80.1	–	100.0	–
Sweden	100.0	100.0	100.0	–
Switzerland	100.0	100.0	100.0	–
United Kingdom	100.0	100.0	100.0	–
United States	92.1	98.6	100.0	–
TOTAL	*76.9*	*72.0*	*87.6*	*–*
MULTILATERAL	*87.1*	*100.0*	*100.0*	*–*
ARAB COUNTRIES	*–*	*100.0*	*–*	*–*
E.E.C.+ MEMBERS	*91.6*	*93.8*	*92.8*	*–*
TOTAL	*77.9*	*73.5*	*90.3*	*–*

15. OTHER AGGREGATES

	1987	1988	1989	1990
OFFICIAL COMMITMENTS:				
TOTAL BILATERAL	814.6	1470.1	890.1	1961.3
of which:				
Arab Countries	–	0.1	–	–
C.E.E.C.	–	–	–	–
TOTAL MULTILATERAL	150.3	401.9	480.2	327.6
TOTAL BIL.& MULTIL.	964.9	1872.0	1370.2	2288.8
of which:				
ODA Grants	332.7	416.0	492.6	476.0
ODA Loans	346.1	698.7	156.2	904.7
DISBURSEMENTS:				
DAC COUNTRIES COMBINED				
OFFICIAL & PRIVATE				
GROSS:				
Contractual Lending	570.2	746.1	1116.3	1654.9
Export Credits, Total	300.4	331.7	516.8	867.0
Export Credits, Priv.	242.4	283.2	396.5	571.0
NET:				
Contractual Lending	63.5	130.1	723.6	1037.0
Export Credits Total	-116.3	-186.3	251.5	381.7
PRIVATE SECTOR NET	495.2	350.7	1504.9	1618.5
Direct Investment	441.0	512.8	1406.9	1512.9
Portfolio Investment	116.8	-166.8	-90.0	-135.2
Export Credits	-62.7	4.7	188.0	240.8
MARKET BORROWING:				
CHANGE IN CLAIMS				
Banks	398.0	1406.0	1709.0	4662.0
MEMORANDUM ITEM:				
C.E.E.C. (Gross)	–	–	–	–

1. TOTAL RECEIPTS NET

DAC COUNTRIES	1987	1988	1989	1990
Australia	–	–	–	0.0
Austria	0.0	0.0	0.0	0.2
Belgium	-2.7	1.2	0.2	2.8
Canada	1.3	2.0	1.0	1.4
Denmark	8.4	5.2	1.3	2.7
Finland	–	–	–	0.0
France	17.0	90.1	12.3	89.6
Germany	24.7	24.6	31.6	37.3
Ireland	–	–	–	–
Italy	2.4	1.0	0.1	1.8
Japan	3.8	9.7	15.6	9.3
Netherlands	2.0	0.7	-0.6	1.0
New Zealand	–	–	–	–
Norway	0.2	–	0.1	–
Sweden	–	–	–	0.0
Switzerland	0.5	0.4	1.2	0.4
United Kingdom	0.2	0.5	0.5	0.6
United States	12.0	7.0	15.0	10.0
TOTAL	*69.6*	*142.3*	*78.3*	*157.4*
MULTILATERAL				
AF.D.F.	0.2	1.2	17.4	-0.7
AF.D.B.	-0.4	-2.0	-1.4	-1.6
AS.D.B	–	–	–	–
CAR.D.B.	–	–	–	–
E.E.C.	0.1	6.4	3.8	3.8
IBRD	-0.4	–	–	-1.0
IDA	19.9	49.0	38.0	30.0
I.D.B.	–	–	–	–
IFAD	3.6	0.9	1.2	3.4
I.F.C.	0.8	0.7	0.0	0.3
IMF TRUST FUND	–	–	–	–
U.N. AGENCIES	–	–	–	–
UNDP	3.9	6.8	6.9	8.0
UNTA	0.8	0.6	1.1	1.1
UNICEF	0.6	0.7	0.9	1.2
UNRWA	–	–	–	–
WFP	1.6	2.2	2.1	1.8
UNHCR	–	0.1	0.3	0.3
Other Multilateral	0.7	1.1	1.7	2.6
Arab Agencies	2.3	0.1	-1.5	–
TOTAL	*33.5*	*67.7*	*70.3*	*49.1*
ARAB COUNTRIES	*2.6*	*-1.5*	*-0.7*	*0.2*
E.E.C.+ MEMBERS	*52.0*	*129.6*	*49.1*	*139.7*
TOTAL	**105.6**	**208.4**	**147.9**	**206.7**

2. ODA LOANS GROSS

DAC COUNTRIES	1987	1988	1989	1990
Australia	–	–	–	–
Austria	–	–	–	–
Belgium	–	–	–	–
Canada	–	–	–	–
Denmark	–	–	–	–
Finland	–	–	–	–
France	15.0	63.6	10.3	29.5
Germany	–	–	–	–
Ireland	–	–	–	–
Italy	–	–	–	0.3
Japan	–	–	6.4	7.0
Netherlands	–	–	–	–
New Zealand	–	–	–	–
Norway	–	–	–	–
Sweden	–	–	–	–
Switzerland	–	–	–	–
United Kingdom	–	–	–	–
United States	–	–	–	–
TOTAL	*15.0*	*63.6*	*16.8*	*36.8*
MULTILATERAL	*27.9*	*52.5*	*58.4*	*34.5*
ARAB COUNTRIES	*3.6*	*0.3*	*0.0*	*–*
E.E.C.+ MEMBERS	*15.0*	*63.6*	*10.4*	*29.9*
TOTAL	**46.5**	**116.4**	**75.1**	**71.3**

3. TOTAL OFFICIAL GROSS

DAC COUNTRIES	1987	1988	1989	1990
Australia	–	–	–	0.0
Austria	0.0	0.0	0.0	0.2
Belgium	2.8	0.7	0.5	3.6
Canada	1.3	15.4	1.0	1.4
Denmark	8.4	5.4	1.3	3.0
Finland	–	–	–	0.0
France	33.3	107.8	53.8	115.7
Germany	29.0	33.7	31.1	37.5
Ireland	–	–	–	–
Italy	2.3	2.1	0.1	3.6
Japan	3.8	9.7	15.6	9.3
Netherlands	1.4	0.6	0.6	1.2
New Zealand	–	–	–	–
Norway	0.2	–	0.1	–
Sweden	–	–	–	0.0
Switzerland	0.5	0.4	1.2	0.4
United Kingdom	0.2	0.5	0.5	0.6
United States	12.0	8.0	15.0	10.0
TOTAL	*95.2*	*184.3*	*120.8*	*186.5*
MULTILATERAL	*41.1*	*74.9*	*79.0*	*57.5*
ARAB COUNTRIES	*3.6*	*0.6*	*0.6*	*0.7*
E.E.C.+ MEMBERS	*81.3*	*161.1*	*95.6*	*172.9*
TOTAL	**139.8**	**259.8**	**200.4**	**244.7**

4. TOTAL ODA NET

DAC COUNTRIES	1987	1988	1989	1990
Australia	–	–	–	0.0
Austria	0.0	0.0	0.0	0.2
Belgium	1.2	0.7	0.5	1.9
Canada	1.3	2.0	1.0	1.4
Denmark	5.8	4.8	1.3	1.2
Finland	–	–	–	0.0
France	31.1	76.7	41.6	91.0
Germany	26.8	24.5	30.6	36.6
Ireland	–	–	–	–
Italy	2.3	0.5	0.1	1.0
Japan	3.8	9.7	15.6	9.3
Netherlands	0.9	0.5	0.6	1.2
New Zealand	–	–	–	–
Norway	0.2	–	0.1	–
Sweden	–	–	–	0.0
Switzerland	0.5	0.4	1.2	0.4
United Kingdom	0.2	0.5	0.5	0.6
United States	12.0	8.0	15.0	10.0
TOTAL	*85.9*	*128.2*	*108.0*	*154.9*
MULTILATERAL				
AF.D.F.	0.2	1.2	17.4	-0.7
AF.D.B.	–	–	–	–
AS.D.B	–	–	–	–
CAR.D.B.	–	–	–	–
E.E.C.	3.5	10.0	7.5	7.5
IBRD	–	–	–	–
IDA	19.9	49.0	38.0	30.0
I.D.B.	–	–	–	–
IFAD	3.6	0.9	1.2	3.4
I.F.C.	–	–	–	–
IMF TRUST FUND	–	–	–	–
U.N. AGENCIES	–	–	–	–
UNDP	3.9	6.8	6.9	8.0
UNTA	0.8	0.6	1.1	1.1
UNICEF	0.6	0.7	0.9	1.2
UNRWA	–	–	–	–
WFP	1.6	2.2	2.1	1.8
UNHCR	–	0.1	0.3	0.3
Other Multilateral	0.7	1.1	1.7	2.6
Arab Agencies	2.3	0.1	-1.5	–
TOTAL	*36.9*	*72.6*	*75.5*	*55.1*
ARAB COUNTRIES	*2.6*	*-1.5*	*-0.7*	*0.2*
E.E.C.+ MEMBERS	*71.7*	*118.2*	*82.5*	*141.0*
TOTAL	**125.3**	**199.4**	**182.8**	**210.2**

5. ODA LOANS NET

DAC COUNTRIES	1987	1988	1989	1990
Australia	–	–	–	–
Austria	–	–	–	–
Belgium	–	–	–	–
Canada	–	-13.5	–	–
Denmark	–	–	–	–
Finland	–	–	–	–
France	13.7	58.1	3.9	23.6
Germany	-2.2	-2.2	–	–
Ireland	–	–	–	–
Italy	–	–	–	0.3
Japan	–	–	6.4	7.0
Netherlands	–	–	–	–
New Zealand	–	–	–	–
Norway	–	–	–	–
Sweden	–	–	–	–
Switzerland	–	–	–	–
United Kingdom	–	–	–	–
United States	–	–	–	–
TOTAL	*11.5*	*42.5*	*10.3*	*30.9*
MULTILATERAL	*25.6*	*50.9*	*54.9*	*31.2*
ARAB COUNTRIES	*2.6*	*-1.7*	*-1.2*	*-0.5*
E.E.C.+ MEMBERS	*11.2*	*55.7*	*3.7*	*23.7*
TOTAL	**39.7**	**91.6**	**64.0**	**61.6**

6. TOTAL OFFICIAL NET

DAC COUNTRIES	1987	1988	1989	1990
Australia	–	–	–	0.0
Austria	0.0	0.0	0.0	0.2
Belgium	2.8	0.4	0.4	2.6
Canada	1.3	2.0	1.0	1.4
Denmark	8.4	5.2	1.3	2.7
Finland	–	–	–	0.0
France	23.3	79.5	35.9	87.4
Germany	25.5	24.5	31.1	37.0
Ireland	–	–	–	–
Italy	2.3	1.0	0.1	1.8
Japan	3.8	9.7	15.6	9.3
Netherlands	1.4	0.6	0.6	1.1
New Zealand	–	–	–	–
Norway	0.2	–	0.1	–
Sweden	–	–	–	0.0
Switzerland	0.5	0.4	1.2	0.4
United Kingdom	0.2	0.5	0.5	0.6
United States	12.0	7.0	15.0	10.0
TOTAL	*81.5*	*130.7*	*102.9*	*154.7*
MULTILATERAL	*33.5*	*67.7*	*70.3*	*49.1*
ARAB COUNTRIES	*2.6*	*-1.5*	*-0.7*	*0.2*
E.E.C.+ MEMBERS	*63.9*	*118.0*	*73.7*	*137.0*
TOTAL	**117.5**	**196.9**	**172.6**	**204.0**

7. TOTAL ODA GROSS

	1987
Australia	–
Austria	0.0
Belgium	1.2
Canada	1.3
Denmark	5.8
Finland	–
France	32.3
Germany	29.0
Ireland	–
Italy	2.3
Japan	3.8
Netherlands	0.9
New Zealand	–
Norway	0.2
Sweden	–
Switzerland	0.5
United Kingdom	0.2
United States	12.0
TOTAL	*89.4*
AF.D.F.	0.3
AF.D.B.	–
AS.D.B	–
CAR.D.B.	–
E.E.C.	3.8
IBRD	–
IDA	20.3
I.D.B.	–
IFAD	3.6
I.F.C.	–
IMF TRUST FUND	–
U.N. AGENCIES	–
UNDP	3.9
UNTA	0.8
UNICEF	0.6
UNRWA	–
WFP	1.6
UNHCR	–
Other Multilateral	0.7
Arab Agencies	3.8
TOTAL	*39.2*
ARAB COUNTRIES	*3.6*
E.E.C.+ MEMBERS	*75.5*
TOTAL	**132.1**

8. GRANTS

	1987
Australia	–
Austria	0.0
Belgium	1.2
Canada	1.3
Denmark	5.8
Finland	–
France	17.4
Germany	29.0
Ireland	–
Italy	2.3
Japan	3.8
Netherlands	0.9
New Zealand	–
Norway	0.2
Sweden	–
Switzerland	0.5
United Kingdom	0.2
United States	12.0
TOTAL	*74.4*
MULTILATERAL	*11.3*
ARAB COUNTRIES	*–*
E.E.C.+ MEMBERS	*60.5*
TOTAL	**85.7**

9. TOTAL OOF GROSS

	1987
Australia	–
Austria	–
Belgium	1.6
Canada	–
Denmark	2.7
Finland	–
France	1.0
Germany	–
Ireland	–
Italy	–
Japan	–
Netherlands	0.5
New Zealand	–
Norway	–
Sweden	–
Switzerland	–
United Kingdom	–
United States	–
TOTAL	*5.8*
MULTILATERAL	*1.9*
ARAB COUNTRIES	*–*
E.E.C.+ MEMBERS	*5.8*
TOTAL	**7.7**

1988	1989	1990
–	–	0.0
0.0	0.0	0.2
0.7	0.5	1.9
15.4	1.0	1.4
4.8	1.3	1.2
–	–	0.0
82.2	48.1	96.9
26.8	30.6	36.6
–	–	–
0.5	0.1	1.0
9.7	15.6	9.3
0.5	0.6	1.2
–	–	–
–	0.1	–
–	–	0.0
0.4	1.2	0.4
0.5	0.5	0.6
8.0	15.0	10.0
149.4	*114.4*	*160.8*
1.4	18.1	0.1
–	–	–
–	–	–
10.3	7.7	7.7
–	–	–
49.0	39.0	31.0
–	–	–
0.9	1.2	3.4
–	–	–
–	–	–
–	–	–
6.8	6.9	8.0
0.6	1.1	1.1
0.7	0.9	1.2
–	–	–
2.2	2.1	1.8
0.1	0.3	0.3
1.1	1.7	2.6
1.3	0.0	–
74.2	*79.0*	*57.2*
0.6	*0.6*	*0.7*
126.1	*89.2*	*147.1*
224.1	*194.0*	*218.7*

10. ODA COMMITMENTS

1987	1988	1989	1990
–	–	–	–
0.0	0.0	0.0	4.4
1.5	0.6	0.5	1.9
2.3	13.9	0.8	1.3
–	–	–	–
42.1	60.0	53.7	68.4
18.7	52.9	27.1	36.3
–	–	–	–
3.5	0.5	0.2	1.0
2.6	27.5	5.8	8.8
0.9	0.5	0.7	1.3
–	–	–	–
–	–	–	–
–	–	–	–
0.1	0.9	0.1	0.5
0.2	0.5	0.5	1.8
9.2	9.5	11.5	10.3
81.2	*166.8*	*100.7*	*135.8*
–	18.6	–	11.8
–	–	–	–
–	–	–	–
1.6	44.7	56.9	56.9
–	–	–	–
61.2	60.0	26.0	79.0
–	–	–	–
6.1	–	–	9.8
–	–	–	–
–	–	–	–
7.5	11.4	13.0	15.0
–	–	–	–
–	–	–	–
–	–	–	–
–	–	–	–
–	–	–	–
–	–	–	–
–	–	–	–
–	–	–	–
76.4	*134.7*	*95.8*	*172.4*
–	–	–	–
68.6	*159.6*	*139.4*	*167.5*
157.6	*301.5*	*196.5*	*308.2*

11. TECH. COOP. GRANTS

1988	1989	1990		1987	1988	1989	1990
–	–	0.0		0.0	0.0	0.0	0.0
0.0	0.0	0.2		0.2	0.1	0.1	0.0
0.7	0.5	1.9		–	0.3	0.3	0.3
15.4	1.0	1.4		0.1	0.1	0.1	0.1
4.8	1.3	1.2		–	–	–	–
–	–	0.0		13.7	13.9	15.4	21.8
18.6	37.7	67.4		14.6	17.6	12.8	17.8
26.8	30.6	36.6		–	–	–	–
–	–	–		2.3	0.5	–	0.4
0.5	0.1	0.7		0.2	0.2	0.1	0.4
9.7	9.2	2.4		0.7	0.5	0.5	0.6
0.5	0.6	1.2		–	–	–	–
–	–	–		–	–	0.0	–
–	0.1	–		–	–	–	–
–	–	0.0		0.4	0.1	–	–
0.4	1.2	0.4		0.2	0.5	0.5	0.3
0.5	0.5	0.6		5.0	5.0	6.0	6.0
8.0	15.0	10.0		*37.2*	*38.9*	*35.7*	*47.7*
85.8	97.7	124.0		*7.3*	*11.6*	*10.8*	*13.2*
21.7	*20.6*	*22.6*		–	–	–	–
0.2	*0.6*	*0.7*		*33.1*	*35.6*	*29.3*	*40.9*
62.5	*78.8*	*117.3*		*44.5*	*50.5*	*46.6*	*60.9*
107.7	*118.8*	*147.3*					

12. TOTAL OOF NET

1988	1989	1990		1987	1988	1989	1990
–	–	–		–	–	–	–
–	–	1.7		1.6	-0.2	0.0	0.7
–	–	–		–	–	–	–
0.6	0.1	1.7		2.6	0.4	0.1	1.5
–	–	–		–	–	–	–
25.7	5.8	18.7		-7.8	2.8	-5.7	-3.6
7.0	0.6	0.9		-1.3	0.0	0.6	0.5
–	–	–		–	–	–	–
1.6	–	2.6		–	0.5	–	0.8
0.1	–	–		0.5	0.1	–	-0.1
–	–	–		–	–	–	–
–	–	–		–	–	–	–
–	–	–		–	–	–	–
–	–	–		–	–	–	–
–	–	–		–	-1.0	–	–
34.9	6.4	25.7		-4.4	2.5	-5.1	-0.2
0.7	*0.1*	*0.3*		-3.4	-4.9	-5.1	-6.0
–	–	–		–	–	–	–
34.9	*6.4*	*25.7*		*-7.8*	*-0.2*	*-8.8*	*-3.9*
35.6	*6.5*	*26.1*		*-7.8*	*-2.5*	*-10.2*	*-6.2*

13. ODF COMMITMENTS: BY PURPOSE %

	1987	1988	1989	1990
Education	0	0	0	–
Health	1	1	0	–
Other Social Infrastr.	1	1	4	–
Water Sanitat. Sewage	3	2	0	–
Energy	–	1	8	–
Telecommunications	2	–	11	–
Transportation	7	17	4	–
Agriculture	46	4	20	–
Extractive Industries	–	–	10	–
Manufacturing	8	–	0	–
Trade Banking Tourism	–	4	–	–
Technical Cooperation	29	21	28	–
Multisector Aid	–	0	4	–
Programme	2	45	3	–
Debt Reorganisation	–	2	5	–
Food Aid	2	2	3	–
Emergency Aid	–	–	–	–
Unspecified	–	–	–	–
TOTAL	100	100	100	–

14. GRANT ELEMENT OF ODA %

DAC COUNTRIES

	1987	1988	1989	1990
Australia	–	–	–	–
Austria	100.0	100.0	100.0	–
Belgium	100.0	100.0	100.0	–
Canada	100.0	100.0	100.0	–
Denmark	–	–	–	–
Finland	–	–	–	–
France	71.1	51.3	72.1	–
Germany	100.0	100.0	93.5	–
Ireland	–	–	–	–
Italy	100.0	100.0	100.0	–
Japan	100.0	85.0	100.0	–
Netherlands	100.0	100.0	100.0	–
New Zealand	–	–	–	–
Norway	–	–	–	–
Sweden	–	–	–	–
Switzerland	100.0	100.0	100.0	–
United Kingdom	100.0	100.0	100.0	–
United States	100.0	100.0	100.0	–
TOTAL	*85.0*	*80.6*	*84.1*	–
MULTILATERAL	*86.0*	*87.1*	*91.9*	–
ARAB COUNTRIES	–	–	–	–
E.E.C.+ MEMBERS	*82.2*	*82.3*	*87.6*	–
TOTAL	*85.4*	*83.9*	*88.0*	–

15. OTHER AGGREGATES

OFFICIAL COMMITMENTS:

	1987	1988	1989	1990
TOTAL BILATERAL	85.4	230.3	123.9	170.6
of which:				
Arab Countries	–	–	–	–
C.E.E.C.	–	–	–	–
TOTAL MULTILATERAL	85.5	135.9	95.9	174.0
TOTAL BIL.& MULTIL.	170.9	366.2	219.7	344.6
of which:				
ODA Grants	65.7	167.8	127.2	170.0
ODA Loans	91.9	133.8	69.3	138.3

DISBURSEMENTS:

DAC COUNTRIES COMBINED

OFFICIAL & PRIVATE

GROSS:	1987	1988	1989	1990
Contractual Lending	21.5	95.1	23.6	60.5
Export Credits, Total	1.0	-3.3	0.4	-2.0
Export Credits, Priv.	1.0	-3.3	0.4	-2.0
NET:				
Contractual Lending	-1.7	40.8	5.5	28.6
Export Credits Total	-8.5	-5.1	0.3	-2.3
PRIVATE SECTOR NET	-11.9	11.5	-24.7	2.7
Direct Investment	3.0	0.5	-6.9	-0.9
Portfolio Investment	-6.4	15.2	-17.9	5.7
Export Credits	-8.5	-4.1	0.2	-2.1

MARKET BORROWING:

CHANGE IN CLAIMS

	1987	1988	1989	1990
Banks	7.0	-6.0	-13.0	–

MEMORANDUM ITEM:

	1987	1988	1989	1990
C.E.E.C. (Gross)	–	–	–	–

1. TOTAL RECEIPTS NET

DAC COUNTRIES

	1987	1988	1989	1990
Australia	–	0.0	0.0	0.0
Austria	–	–	–	–
Belgium	0.0	–	–	–
Canada	–	–	–	–
Denmark	–	–	–	–
Finland	–	–	–	–
France	–	–	–	–
Germany	–	–	–	–
Ireland	–	–	–	–
Italy	–	–	–	–
Japan	–	–	–	–
Netherlands	–	–	–	–
New Zealand	1.6	3.4	4.3	4.4
Norway	–	0.0	–	–
Sweden	–	–	–	–
Switzerland	–	–	–	–
United Kingdom	–	–	–	–
United States	–	–	–	–
TOTAL	1.6	3.4	4.3	4.4

MULTILATERAL

	1987	1988	1989	1990
AF.D.F.	–	–	–	–
AF.D.B.	–	–	–	–
AS.D.B	–	–	–	–
CAR.D.B.	–	–	–	–
E.E.C.	–	–	–	–
IBRD	–	–	–	–
IDA	–	–	–	–
I.D.B.	–	–	–	–
IFAD	–	–	–	–
I.F.C.	–	–	–	–
IMF TRUST FUND	–	–	–	–
U.N. AGENCIES	–	–	–	–
UNDP	0.2	0.3	0.2	0.4
UNTA	0.0	–	–	–
UNICEF	–	–	–	–
UNRWA	–	–	–	–
WFP	–	–	–	–
UNHCR	–	–	–	–
Other Multilateral	–	–	0.0	–
Arab Agencies	–	–	–	–
TOTAL	0.2	0.3	0.3	0.4
ARAB COUNTRIES	–	–	–	–
E.E.C.+ MEMBERS	0.0	–	–	–
TOTAL	1.8	3.7	4.6	4.8

2. ODA LOANS GROSS

DAC COUNTRIES

	1987	1988	1989	1990
Australia	–	–	–	–
Austria	–	–	–	–
Belgium	–	–	–	–
Canada	–	–	–	–
Denmark	–	–	–	–
Finland	–	–	–	–
France	–	–	–	–
Germany	–	–	–	–
Ireland	–	–	–	–
Italy	–	–	–	–
Japan	–	–	–	–
Netherlands	–	–	–	–
New Zealand	–	–	–	–
Norway	–	–	–	–
Sweden	–	–	–	–
Switzerland	–	–	–	–
United Kingdom	–	–	–	–
United States	–	–	–	–
TOTAL	–	–	–	–
MULTILATERAL	–	–	–	–
ARAB COUNTRIES	–	–	–	–
E.E.C.+ MEMBERS	–	–	–	–
TOTAL	–	–	–	–

3. TOTAL OFFICIAL GROSS

DAC COUNTRIES

	1987	1988	1989	1990
Australia	–	0.0	0.0	0.0
Austria	–	–	–	–
Belgium	–	–	–	–
Canada	–	–	–	–
Denmark	–	–	–	–
Finland	–	–	–	–
France	–	–	–	–
Germany	–	–	–	–
Ireland	–	–	–	–
Italy	–	–	–	–
Japan	–	–	–	–
Netherlands	–	–	–	–
New Zealand	1.6	3.4	4.3	4.4
Norway	–	0.0	–	–
Sweden	–	–	–	–
Switzerland	–	–	–	–
United Kingdom	–	–	–	–
United States	–	–	–	–
TOTAL	1.6	3.4	4.3	4.4
MULTILATERAL	0.2	0.3	0.3	0.4
ARAB COUNTRIES	–	–	–	–
E.E.C.+ MEMBERS	–	–	–	–
TOTAL	1.8	3.7	4.6	4.8

4. TOTAL ODA NET

	1987	1988	1989	1990
Australia	–	0.0	0.0	0.0
Austria	–	–	–	–
Belgium	0.0	–	–	–
Canada	–	–	–	–
Denmark	–	–	–	–
Finland	–	–	–	–
France	–	–	–	–
Germany	–	–	–	–
Ireland	–	–	–	–
Italy	–	–	–	–
Japan	–	–	–	–
Netherlands	–	–	–	–
New Zealand	1.6	3.4	4.3	4.4
Norway	–	0.0	–	–
Sweden	–	–	–	–
Switzerland	–	–	–	–
United Kingdom	–	–	–	–
United States	–	–	–	–
TOTAL	1.6	3.4	4.3	4.4

	1987	1988	1989	1990
AF.D.F.	–	–	–	–
AF.D.B.	–	–	–	–
AS.D.B	–	–	–	–
CAR.D.B.	–	–	–	–
E.E.C.	–	–	–	–
IBRD	–	–	–	–
IDA	–	–	–	–
I.D.B.	–	–	–	–
IFAD	–	–	–	–
I.F.C.	–	–	–	–
IMF TRUST FUND	–	–	–	–
U.N. AGENCIES	–	–	–	–
UNDP	0.2	0.3	0.2	0.4
UNTA	0.0	–	–	–
UNICEF	–	–	–	–
UNRWA	–	–	–	–
WFP	–	–	–	–
UNHCR	–	–	–	–
Other Multilateral	–	–	0.0	–
Arab Agencies	–	–	–	–
TOTAL	0.2	0.3	0.3	0.4
ARAB COUNTRIES	–	–	–	–
E.E.C.+ MEMBERS	0.0	–	–	–
TOTAL	1.8	3.7	4.6	4.8

5. ODA LOANS NET

	1987	1988	1989	1990
	–	–	–	–
	–	–	–	–
	–	–	–	–
	–	–	–	–
	–	–	–	–
	–	–	–	–
	–	–	–	–
	–	–	–	–
	–	–	–	–
	–	–	–	–
	–	–	–	–
	–	–	–	–
	–	–	–	–
	–	–	–	–
	–	–	–	–
	–	–	–	–
	–	–	–	–
	–	–	–	–
	–	–	–	–
	–	–	–	–
	–	–	–	–
	–	–	–	–

6. TOTAL OFFICIAL NET

	1987	1988	1989	1990
Australia	–	0.0	0.0	0.0
Austria	–	–	–	–
Belgium	0.0	–	–	–
Canada	–	–	–	–
Denmark	–	–	–	–
Finland	–	–	–	–
France	–	–	–	–
Germany	–	–	–	–
Ireland	–	–	–	–
Italy	–	–	–	–
Japan	–	–	–	–
Netherlands	–	–	–	–
New Zealand	1.6	3.4	4.3	4.4
Norway	–	0.0	–	–
Sweden	–	–	–	–
Switzerland	–	–	–	–
United Kingdom	–	–	–	–
United States	–	–	–	–
TOTAL	1.6	3.4	4.3	4.4
MULTILATERAL	0.2	0.3	0.3	0.4
ARAB COUNTRIES	–	–	–	–
E.E.C.+ MEMBERS	0.0	–	–	–
TOTAL	1.8	3.7	4.6	4.8

7. TOTAL ODA GROSS

	1987
Australia	–
Austria	–
Belgium	–
Canada	–
Denmark	–
Finland	–
France	–
Germany	–
Ireland	–
Italy	–
Japan	–
Netherlands	–
New Zealand	1.6
Norway	–
Sweden	–
Switzerland	–
United Kingdom	–
United States	–
TOTAL	1.6
AF.D.F.	–
AF.D.B.	–
AS.D.B	–
CAR.D.B.	–
E.E.C.	–
IBRD	–
IDA	–
I.D.B.	–
IFAD	–
I.F.C.	–
IMF TRUST FUND	–
U.N. AGENCIES	–
UNDP	0.2
UNTA	0.0
UNICEF	–
UNRWA	–
WFP	–
UNHCR	–
Other Multilateral	–
Arab Agencies	–
TOTAL	0.2
ARAB COUNTRIES	–
E.E.C.+ MEMBERS	–
TOTAL	1.8

8. GRANTS

	1987
Australia	–
Austria	–
Belgium	–
Canada	–
Denmark	–
Finland	–
France	–
Germany	–
Ireland	–
Italy	–
Japan	–
Netherlands	–
New Zealand	1.6
Norway	–
Sweden	–
Switzerland	–
United Kingdom	–
United States	–
TOTAL	1.6
MULTILATERAL	0.2
ARAB COUNTRIES	–
E.E.C.+ MEMBERS	–
TOTAL	1.8

9. TOTAL OOF GROSS

	1987
Australia	–
Austria	–
Belgium	–
Canada	–
Denmark	–
Finland	–
France	–
Germany	–
Ireland	–
Italy	–
Japan	–
Netherlands	–
New Zealand	–
Norway	–
Sweden	–
Switzerland	–
United Kingdom	–
United States	–
TOTAL	–
MULTILATERAL	–
ARAB COUNTRIES	–
E.E.C.+ MEMBERS	–
TOTAL	–

10. ODA COMMITMENTS

(cont.) 1988	1989	1990		1987	1988	1989	1990
0.0	0.0	0.0		–	–	0.0	–
–	–	–		–	–	–	–
–	–	–		–	–	–	–
–	–	–		–	–	–	–
–	–	–		–	–	–	–
–	–	–		–	–	–	–
–	–	–		–	–	–	–
–	–	–		–	–	–	–
–	–	–		–	–	–	–
–	–	–		–	–	–	–
3.4	4.3	4.4		2.4	2.9	–	2.9
0.0	–	–		–	–	–	–
–	–	–		–	–	–	–
–	–	–		–	–	–	–
–	–	–		–	–	–	–
–	–	–		–	–	–	–
3.4	4.3	4.4		2.4	2.9	0.0	2.9
–	–	–		–	–	–	–
–	–	–		–	–	–	–
–	–	–		–	–	–	–
–	–	–		–	–	–	–
–	–	–		–	–	–	–
–	–	–		–	–	–	–
–	–	–		–	–	–	–
–	–	–		0.2	0.3	0.3	0.4
0.3	0.2	0.4		–	–	–	–
–	–	–		–	–	–	–
–	–	–		–	–	–	–
–	–	–		–	–	–	–
–	0.0	–		–	–	–	–
–	–	–		–	–	–	–
0.3	0.3	0.4		0.2	0.3	0.3	0.4
–	–	–		–	–	–	–
3.7	4.6	4.8		2.6	3.2	0.3	3.3

11. TECH. COOP. GRANTS

1988	1989	1990		1987	1988	1989	1990
0.0	0.0	0.0		–	0.0	0.0	0.0
–	–	–		0.0	–	–	–
–	–	–		–	–	–	–
–	–	–		–	–	–	–
–	–	–		–	–	–	–
–	–	–		–	–	–	–
–	–	–		–	–	–	–
–	–	–		–	–	–	–
–	–	–		–	–	–	–
–	–	–		–	–	–	–
3.4	4.3	4.4		0.0	0.0	–	0.0
0.0	–	–		–	–	–	–
–	–	–		–	–	–	–
–	–	–		–	–	–	–
3.4	4.3	4.4		0.0	0.0	0.0	0.0
0.3	0.3	0.4		0.2	0.3	0.3	0.4
–	–	–		–	–	–	–
–	–	–		0.0	–	–	–
3.7	4.6	4.8		0.2	0.3	0.3	0.4

12. TOTAL OOF NET

1988	1989	1990		1987	1988	1989	1990
–	–	–		–	–	–	–
–	–	–		–	–	–	–
–	–	–		–	–	–	–
–	–	–		–	–	–	–
–	–	–		–	–	–	–
–	–	–		–	–	–	–
–	–	–		–	–	–	–
–	–	–		–	–	–	–
–	–	–		–	–	–	–
–	–	–		–	–	–	–
–	–	–		–	–	–	–
–	–	–		–	–	–	–
–	–	–		–	–	–	–
–	–	–		–	–	–	–
–	–	–		–	–	–	–
–	–	–		–	–	–	–
–	–	–		–	–	–	–
–	–	–		–	–	–	–
–	–	–		–	–	–	–

13. ODF COMMITMENTS: BY PURPOSE %

	1987	1988	1989	1990
Education	–	–	–	–
Health	–	–	–	–
Other Social Infrastr.	–	–	–	–
Water Sanitat. Sewage	–	–	–	–
Energy	–	–	–	–
Telecommunications	–	–	–	–
Transportation	–	–	–	–
Agriculture	–	–	–	–
Extractive Industries	–	–	–	–
Manufacturing	–	–	–	–
Trade Banking Tourism	–	–	–	–
Technical Cooperation	100	100	100	–
Multisector Aid	–	–	–	–
Programme	–	–	–	–
Debt Reorganisation	–	–	–	–
Food Aid	–	–	–	–
Emergency Aid	–	–	–	–
Unspecified	–	–	–	–
TOTAL	100	100	100	–

14. GRANT ELEMENT OF ODA %

DAC COUNTRIES

	1987	1988	1989	1990
Australia	–	–	100.0	–
Austria	–	–	–	–
Belgium	–	–	–	–
Canada	–	–	–	–
Denmark	–	–	–	–
Finland	–	–	–	–
France	–	–	–	–
Germany	–	–	–	–
Ireland	–	–	–	–
Italy	–	–	–	–
Japan	–	–	–	–
Netherlands	–	–	–	–
New Zealand	100.0	100.0	–	–
Norway	–	–	–	–
Sweden	–	–	–	–
Switzerland	–	–	–	–
United Kingdom	–	–	–	–
United States	–	–	–	–
TOTAL	100.0	100.0	100.0	–
MULTILATERAL	100.0	100.0	100.0	–
ARAB COUNTRIES	–	–	–	–
E.E.C.+ MEMBERS	–	–	–	–
TOTAL	100.0	100.0	100.0	–

15. OTHER AGGREGATES

OFFICIAL COMMITMENTS:

	1987	1988	1989	1990
TOTAL BILATERAL	2.4	2.9	0.0	2.9
of which:				
Arab Countries	–	–	–	–
C.E.E.C.	–	–	–	–
TOTAL MULTILATERAL	0.2	0.3	0.3	0.4
TOTAL BIL.& MULTIL.	2.6	3.2	0.3	3.3
of which:				
ODA Grants	2.6	3.2	0.3	3.3
ODA Loans	–	–	–	–

DISBURSEMENTS:

DAC COUNTRIES COMBINED

	1987	1988	1989	1990
OFFICIAL & PRIVATE				
GROSS:				
Contractual Lending	–	–	–	–
Export Credits, Total	–	–	–	–
Export Credits, Priv.	–	–	–	–
NET:				
Contractual Lending	–	–	–	–
Export Credits Total	–	–	–	–
PRIVATE SECTOR NET	–	–	–	–
Direct Investment	–	–	–	–
Portfolio Investment	–	–	–	–
Export Credits	–	–	–	–

MARKET BORROWING:

CHANGE IN CLAIMS

	1987	1988	1989	1990
Banks	–	–	–	–

MEMORANDUM ITEM:

	1987	1988	1989	1990
C.E.E.C. (Gross)	–	–	–	–

1. TOTAL RECEIPTS NET

DAC COUNTRIES	1987	1988	1989	1990
Australia	7.2	5.5	9.1	8.5
Austria	–	–	–	–
Belgium	–	–	–	–
Canada	–	–	–	–
Denmark	–	–	0.0	0.0
Finland	–	–	–	–
France	14.0	-11.4	-2.0	0.3
Germany	0.8	0.0	11.1	0.9
Ireland	–	–	–	–
Italy	–	–	–	–
Japan	5.1	3.5	5.4	10.1
Netherlands	0.2	0.1	0.2	0.3
New Zealand	3.1	2.8	2.7	3.8
Norway	–	–	–	–
Sweden	–	–	–	–
Switzerland	–	–	–	–
United Kingdom	0.1	0.3	0.4	0.1
United States	–	–	–	–
TOTAL	*30.5*	*0.8*	*26.9*	*24.0*
MULTILATERAL				
AF.D.F.	–	–	–	–
AF.D.B.	–	–	–	–
AS.D.B	0.6	1.4	1.7	2.6
CAR.D.B.	–	–	–	–
E.E.C.	3.9	1.9	1.3	1.3
IBRD	–	–	–	–
IDA	–	1.0	–	1.0
I.D.B.	–	–	–	–
IFAD	0.5	–	0.9	0.7
I.F.C.	–	–	–	–
IMF TRUST FUND	–	–	–	–
U.N. AGENCIES	–	–	–	–
UNDP	0.5	0.4	0.2	0.4
UNTA	0.5	0.4	0.5	0.7
UNICEF	–	–	–	–
UNRWA	–	–	–	–
WFP	–	–	–	–
UNHCR	–	–	–	–
Other Multilateral	0.2	0.2	0.3	0.2
Arab Agencies	-0.1	-0.1	-0.1	–
TOTAL	*6.1*	*5.2*	*4.8*	*7.0*
ARAB COUNTRIES	–	–	–	–
E.E.C.+ MEMBERS	*19.0*	*-9.2*	*11.1*	*3.0*
TOTAL	**36.6**	**5.9**	**31.7**	**31.0**

2. ODA LOANS GROSS

DAC COUNTRIES	1987	1988	1989	1990
Australia	–	–	–	–
Austria	–	–	–	–
Belgium	–	–	–	–
Canada	–	–	–	–
Denmark	–	–	–	–
Finland	–	–	–	–
France	–	–	–	–
Germany	0.0	0.0	–	–
Ireland	–	–	–	–
Italy	–	–	–	–
Japan	–	–	–	–
Netherlands	–	–	–	–
New Zealand	–	–	–	–
Norway	–	–	–	–
Sweden	–	–	–	–
Switzerland	–	–	–	–
United Kingdom	–	–	–	–
United States	–	–	–	–
TOTAL	*0.0*	*0.0*	*–*	*–*
MULTILATERAL	*2.3*	*3.2*	*1.7*	*2.9*
ARAB COUNTRIES	–	–	–	–
E.E.C.+ MEMBERS	*1.1*	*0.7*	*0.2*	*0.2*
TOTAL	**2.3**	**3.2**	**1.7**	**2.9**

3. TOTAL OFFICIAL GROSS

DAC COUNTRIES	1987	1988	1989	1990
Australia	5.9	6.9	9.3	8.6
Austria	–	–	–	–
Belgium	0.0	–	–	–
Canada	–	–	–	–
Denmark	–	–	0.0	0.0
Finland	–	–	–	–
France	–	–	0.7	0.3
Germany	0.9	0.9	1.1	1.0
Ireland	–	–	–	–
Italy	–	–	–	–
Japan	5.1	3.5	5.4	10.1
Netherlands	0.2	0.1	0.2	0.3
New Zealand	3.1	2.8	2.7	3.8
Norway	–	–	–	–
Sweden	–	–	–	–
Switzerland	–	–	–	–
United Kingdom	0.4	0.5	0.6	0.4
United States	–	–	–	–
TOTAL	*15.6*	*14.8*	*19.9*	*24.6*
MULTILATERAL	*6.3*	*5.4*	*5.2*	*7.2*
ARAB COUNTRIES	–	–	–	–
E.E.C.+ MEMBERS	*5.5*	*3.5*	*4.0*	*3.6*
TOTAL	**22.0**	**20.2**	**25.1**	**31.8**

4. TOTAL ODA NET

DAC COUNTRIES	1987	1988	1989	1990
Australia	5.9	6.9	9.3	8.6
Austria	–	–	–	–
Belgium	–	–	–	–
Canada	–	–	–	–
Denmark	–	–	0.0	0.0
Finland	–	–	–	–
France	–	–	0.7	0.3
Germany	0.8	0.0	1.1	0.9
Ireland	–	–	–	–
Italy	–	–	–	–
Japan	5.1	3.5	5.4	10.1
Netherlands	0.2	0.1	0.2	0.3
New Zealand	3.1	2.8	2.7	3.8
Norway	–	–	–	–
Sweden	–	–	–	–
Switzerland	–	–	–	–
United Kingdom	0.1	0.3	0.4	0.1
United States	–	–	–	–
TOTAL	*15.2*	*13.6*	*19.7*	*24.2*
MULTILATERAL				
AF.D.F.	–	–	–	–
AF.D.B.	–	–	–	–
AS.D.B	0.6	1.4	1.7	2.6
CAR.D.B.	–	–	–	–
E.E.C.	3.9	1.9	1.3	1.3
IBRD	–	–	–	–
IDA	–	1.0	–	1.0
I.D.B.	–	–	–	–
IFAD	0.5	–	0.9	0.7
I.F.C.	–	–	–	–
IMF TRUST FUND	–	–	–	–
U.N. AGENCIES	–	–	–	–
UNDP	0.5	0.4	0.2	0.4
UNTA	0.5	0.4	0.5	0.7
UNICEF	–	–	–	–
UNRWA	–	–	–	–
WFP	–	–	–	–
UNHCR	–	–	–	–
Other Multilateral	0.2	0.2	0.3	0.2
Arab Agencies	-0.1	-0.1	-0.1	–
TOTAL	*6.1*	*5.2*	*4.8*	*7.0*
ARAB COUNTRIES	–	–	–	–
E.E.C.+ MEMBERS	*5.0*	*2.3*	*3.7*	*3.1*
TOTAL	**21.3**	**18.8**	**24.6**	**31.2**

5. ODA LOANS NET

DAC COUNTRIES	1987	1988	1989	1990
Australia	–	–	–	–
Austria	–	–	–	–
Belgium	–	–	–	–
Canada	–	–	–	–
Denmark	–	–	–	–
Finland	–	–	–	–
France	–	–	–	–
Germany	-0.1	-0.9	–	-0.1
Ireland	–	–	–	–
Italy	–	–	–	–
Japan	–	–	–	–
Netherlands	–	–	–	–
New Zealand	–	–	–	–
Norway	–	–	–	–
Sweden	–	–	–	–
Switzerland	–	–	–	–
United Kingdom	-0.2	-0.2	-0.2	-0.3
United States	–	–	–	–
TOTAL	*-0.4*	*-1.1*	*-0.2*	*-0.4*
MULTILATERAL	*2.0*	*2.9*	*1.3*	*2.5*
ARAB COUNTRIES	–	–	–	–
E.E.C.+ MEMBERS	*0.6*	*-0.5*	*-0.2*	*-0.4*
TOTAL	**1.6**	**1.8**	**1.1**	**2.1**

6. TOTAL OFFICIAL NET

DAC COUNTRIES	1987	1988	1989	1990
Australia	5.9	6.9	9.1	8.5
Austria	–	–	–	–
Belgium	–	–	–	–
Canada	–	–	–	–
Denmark	–	–	0.0	0.0
Finland	–	–	–	–
France	–	–	0.7	0.3
Germany	0.8	0.0	1.1	0.9
Ireland	–	–	–	–
Italy	–	–	–	–
Japan	5.1	3.5	5.4	10.1
Netherlands	0.2	0.1	0.2	0.3
New Zealand	3.1	2.8	2.7	3.8
Norway	–	–	–	–
Sweden	–	–	–	–
Switzerland	–	–	–	–
United Kingdom	0.1	0.3	0.4	0.1
United States	–	–	–	–
TOTAL	*15.2*	*13.6*	*19.6*	*24.0*
MULTILATERAL	*6.1*	*5.2*	*4.8*	*7.0*
ARAB COUNTRIES	–	–	–	–
E.E.C.+ MEMBERS	*5.0*	*2.3*	*3.7*	*3.1*
TOTAL	**21.3**	**18.8**	**24.4**	**31.0**

7. TOTAL ODA GROSS

	1987
Australia	5.9
Austria	–
Belgium	0.0
Canada	–
Denmark	–
Finland	–
France	–
Germany	0.9
Ireland	–
Italy	–
Japan	5.1
Netherlands	0.2
New Zealand	3.1
Norway	–
Sweden	–
Switzerland	–
United Kingdom	0.4
United States	–
TOTAL	*15.6*
AF.D.F.	–
AF.D.B.	–
AS.D.B	0.7
CAR.D.B.	–
E.E.C.	4.0
IBRD	–
IDA	–
I.D.B.	–
IFAD	0.5
I.F.C.	–
IMF TRUST FUND	–
U.N. AGENCIES	–
UNDP	0.5
UNTA	0.5
UNICEF	–
UNRWA	–
WFP	–
UNHCR	–
Other Multilateral	0.2
Arab Agencies	–
TOTAL	*6.3*
ARAB COUNTRIES	–
E.E.C.+ MEMBERS	*5.5*
TOTAL	**22.0**

8. GRANTS

	1987
Australia	5.9
Austria	–
Belgium	0.0
Canada	–
Denmark	–
Finland	–
France	–
Germany	0.9
Ireland	–
Italy	–
Japan	5.1
Netherlands	0.2
New Zealand	3.1
Norway	–
Sweden	–
Switzerland	–
United Kingdom	0.4
United States	–
TOTAL	*15.6*
MULTILATERAL	*4.1*
ARAB COUNTRIES	–
E.E.C.+ MEMBERS	*4.4*
TOTAL	**19.7**

9. TOTAL OOF GROSS

	1987
Australia	–
Austria	–
Belgium	–
Canada	–
Denmark	–
Finland	–
France	–
Germany	–
Ireland	–
Italy	–
Japan	–
Netherlands	–
New Zealand	–
Norway	–
Sweden	–
Switzerland	–
United Kingdom	–
United States	–
TOTAL	*–*
MULTILATERAL	*–*
ARAB COUNTRIES	–
E.E.C.+ MEMBERS	*–*
TOTAL	*–*

1988	1989	1990		1987	1988	1989	1990

10. ODA COMMITMENTS

1988	1989	1990		1987	1988	1989	1990
6.9	9.3	8.6		6.8	9.8	8.2	9.2
–	–	–		–	–	–	–
–	–	–		–	–	–	–
–	0.0	0.0		0.2	–	–	–
–	–	–		–	–	–	–
–	0.7	0.3		–	–	0.7	0.3
0.9	1.1	1.0		0.1	1.2	0.2	1.6
–	–	–		–	–	–	–
–	–	–		–	–	–	–
3.5	5.4	10.1		1.6	6.0	7.8	6.2
0.1	0.2	0.3		0.2	0.1	0.2	0.3
2.8	2.7	3.8		2.4	1.2	–	3.1
–	–	–		–	–	–	–
–	–	–		–	–	–	–
0.5	0.6	0.4		0.4	0.5	0.6	0.4
–	–	–		0.3	0.4	0.5	0.6
14.8	*19.9*	*24.6*		*11.9*	*19.3*	*18.1*	*21.7*
–	–	–		–	–	–	–
1.5	1.8	2.7		0.5	3.4	5.2	2.6
–	–	–		–	–	–	–
2.0	1.5	1.5		3.4	0.3	1.8	1.8
–	–	–		–	–	–	–
1.0	–	1.0		2.0	–	–	3.0
–	–	–		–	–	–	–
–	0.9	0.7		–	2.3	–	–
–	–	–		–	–	–	–
–	–	–		–	–	–	–
–	–	–		1.1	1.0	1.1	1.3
0.4	0.2	0.4		–	–	–	–
0.4	0.5	0.7		–	–	–	–
–	–	–		–	–	–	–
–	–	–		–	–	–	–
0.2	0.3	0.2		–	–	–	–
–	–	–		–	–	–	–
5.4	*5.2*	*7.2*		*7.0*	*6.9*	*8.1*	*8.7*
–	–	–		–	–	–	–
3.5	*4.0*	*3.6*		*4.0*	*2.1*	*3.5*	*4.5*
20.2	*25.1*	*31.8*		*18.9*	*26.2*	*26.2*	*30.4*

11. TECH. COOP. GRANTS

1988	1989	1990		1987	1988	1989	1990
6.9	9.3	8.6		2.6	2.6	5.7	4.6
–	–	–		–	–	–	–
–	–	–		–	–	–	–
–	0.0	0.0		–	–	0.1	–
–	–	–		–	–	–	–
–	0.7	0.3		–	–	0.7	0.3
0.9	1.1	1.0		0.9	0.9	1.1	1.0
–	–	–		–	–	–	–
–	–	–		–	–	–	–
3.5	5.4	10.1		1.4	1.5	2.0	1.7
0.1	0.2	0.3		0.2	0.1	0.2	0.3
2.8	2.7	3.8		1.1	1.0	–	1.3
–	–	–		–	–	–	–
–	–	–		–	–	–	–
0.5	0.6	0.4		0.4	0.5	0.6	0.4
–	–	–		–	–	–	–
14.8	*19.9*	*24.6*		*6.5*	*6.6*	*10.2*	*9.6*
2.3	*3.5*	*4.3*		*1.1*	*1.1*	*1.1*	*1.3*
–	–	–		–	–	–	–
2.8	*3.9*	*3.4*		*1.4*	*1.6*	*2.6*	*2.0*
17.0	*23.4*	*28.9*		*7.6*	*7.6*	*11.3*	*10.9*

12. TOTAL OOF NET

1988	1989	1990		1987	1988	1989	1990
–	–	–		–	–	-0.2	-0.2
–	–	–		–	–	–	–
–	–	–		–	–	–	–
–	–	–		–	–	–	–
–	–	–		–	–	–	–
–	–	–		–	–	–	–
–	–	–		–	–	–	–
–	–	–		–	–	–	–
–	–	–		–	–	–	–
–	–	–		–	–	–	–
–	–	–		–	–	–	–
–	–	–		–	–	–	–
–	–	–		–	–	–	–
–	–	–		–	–	-0.2	-0.2
–	–	–		–	–	–	–
–	–	–		–	–	–	–
–	–	–		–	–	-0.2	-0.2

	1987	1988	1989	1990

13. ODF COMMITMENTS: BY PURPOSE %

	1987	1988	1989	1990
Education	–	–	–	–
Health	3	–	0	–
Other Social Infrastr.	–	–	–	–
Water Sanitat. Sewage	2	0	–	–
Energy	–	–	–	–
Telecommunications .	1	0	–	–
Transportation	23	20	37	–
Agriculture	–	22	–	–
Extractive Industries	–	–	–	–
Manufacturing	–	–	–	–
Trade Banking Tourism	15	–	–	–
Technical Cooperation	50	41	59	–
Multisector Aid	3	14	1	–
Programme	4	2	3	–
Debt Reorganisation	–	–	–	–
Food Aid	–	–	–	–
Emergency Aid	–	–	–	–
Unspecified	–	–	–	–
TOTAL	100	100	100	–

14. GRANT ELEMENT OF ODA %

DAC COUNTRIES

	1987	1988	1989	1990
Australia	100.0	100.0	100.0	–
Austria	–	–	–	–
Belgium	–	–	–	–
Canada	100.0	–	–	–
Denmark	–	–	–	–
Finland	–	–	–	–
France	–	–	100.0	–
Germany	100.0	100.0	100.0	–
Ireland	–	–	–	–
Italy	–	–	–	–
Japan	100.0	100.0	100.0	–
Netherlands	100.0	100.0	100.0	–
New Zealand	100.0	100.0	–	–
Norway	–	–	–	–
Sweden	–	–	–	–
Switzerland	–	–	–	–
United Kingdom	100.0	100.0	100.0	–
United States	100.0	100.0	100.0	–
TOTAL	*100.0*	*100.0*	*100.0*	–
MULTILATERAL	*92.9*	*83.1*	*100.0*	–
ARAB COUNTRIES	–	–	–	–
E.E.C.+ MEMBERS	*100.0*	*100.0*	*100.0*	–
TOTAL	*98.0*	*95.5*	*100.0*	–

15. OTHER AGGREGATES

OFFICIAL COMMITMENTS:

	1987	1988	1989	1990
TOTAL BILATERAL	11.9	19.3	19.5	21.7
of which:				
Arab Countries	–	–	–	–
C.E.E.C.	–	–	–	–
TOTAL MULTILATERAL	7.0	6.9	10.3	10.9
TOTAL BIL.& MULTIL.	18.9	26.2	29.8	32.6
of which:				
ODA Grants	14.7	20.6	20.6	24.5
ODA Loans	4.2	5.6	5.5	5.9

DISBURSEMENTS:

DAC COUNTRIES COMBINED

OFFICIAL & PRIVATE	1987	1988	1989	1990
GROSS:				
Contractual Lending	1.3	-11.4	–	–
Export Credits, Total	1.3	-11.4	–	–
Export Credits, Priv.	1.3	-11.4	–	–
NET:				
Contractual Lending	0.9	-14.0	-0.4	-0.6
Export Credits Total	1.3	-12.8	-0.2	-0.2
PRIVATE SECTOR NET	15.3	-12.9	7.3	0.0
Direct Investment	–	–	–	–
Portfolio Investment	14.0	0.0	7.3	0.0
Export Credits	1.3	-12.8	–	–

MARKET BORROWING:

CHANGE IN CLAIMS

	1987	1988	1989	1990
Banks	16.0	-11.0	-3.0	–

MEMORANDUM ITEM:

	1987	1988	1989	1990
C.E.E.C. (Gross)	–	–	–	–

	1987	1988	1989	1990		1987	1988	1989	1990		1987

1. TOTAL RECEIPTS NET
DAC COUNTRIES

	1987	1988	1989	1990
Australia	–	–	–	–
Austria	-1.8	-1.9	-1.7	-2.0
Belgium	-5.5	-7.6	0.3	0.4
Canada	0.2	-5.9	8.3	3.6
Denmark	-0.2	-0.2	-0.2	-0.2
Finland	–	0.1	–	–
France	-20.1	-2.7	13.2	-11.7
Germany	37.4	5.0	2.9	6.2
Ireland	0.0	–	–	–
Italy	–	-29.4	-31.8	-6.9
Japan	79.9	21.4	-23.0	-16.5
Netherlands	0.3	0.7	0.7	0.8
New Zealand	–	–	–	–
Norway	–	0.1	0.1	–
Sweden	–	–	–	–
Switzerland	0.1	0.1	0.2	0.1
United Kingdom	-7.7	-2.8	-8.6	-4.0
United States	-67.0	-25.0	107.0	-86.0
TOTAL	15.5	-48.3	67.4	-116.3

MULTILATERAL

	1987	1988	1989	1990
AF.D.F.	–	–	–	–
AF.D.B.	–	–	–	–
AS.D.B	–	–	–	–
CAR.D.B.	1.3	2.9	3.4	3.4
E.E.C.	5.5	-0.9	1.7	1.7
IBRD	-7.5	-6.0	-6.0	13.0
IDA	–	–	–	–
I.D.B.	-0.6	9.7	7.6	9.4
IFAD	–	–	–	–
I.F.C.	41.1	19.6	-2.5	-3.2
IMF TRUST FUND	–	–	–	–
U.N. AGENCIES	–	–	–	–
UNDP	1.3	2.3	1.4	1.0
UNTA	0.5	0.4	0.6	0.5
UNICEF	–	–	–	–
UNRWA	–	–	–	–
WFP	–	–	–	–
UNHCR	–	–	–	–
Other Multilateral	0.2	0.2	0.3	0.4
Arab Agencies	–	–	–	–
TOTAL	41.8	28.2	6.4	26.2
ARAB COUNTRIES	–	–	–	–
E.E.C.+ MEMBERS	9.6	-38.0	-21.7	-13.8
TOTAL	57.3	-20.1	73.8	-90.1

2. ODA LOANS GROSS
DAC COUNTRIES

	1987	1988	1989	1990
Australia	–	–	–	–
Austria	–	–	–	–
Belgium	–	–	–	–
Canada	0.0	–	–	–
Denmark	–	–	–	–
Finland	–	–	–	–
France	–	–	–	–
Germany	31.3	–	0.3	–
Ireland	–	–	–	–
Italy	–	–	–	–
Japan	–	–	–	–
Netherlands	–	0.5	0.1	–
New Zealand	–	–	–	–
Norway	–	–	–	–
Sweden	–	–	–	–
Switzerland	–	–	–	–
United Kingdom	–	–	0.5	–
United States	–	–	–	–
TOTAL	31.3	0.5	0.9	–
MULTILATERAL	0.0	1.1	1.2	1.3
ARAB COUNTRIES	–	–	–	–
E.E.C.+ MEMBERS	31.3	0.5	0.9	–
TOTAL	31.3	1.6	2.1	1.3

3. TOTAL OFFICIAL GROSS
DAC COUNTRIES

	1987	1988	1989	1990
Australia	–	–	–	–
Austria	0.0	0.0	–	0.0
Belgium	–	0.1	–	–
Canada	0.5	5.4	9.0	3.6
Denmark	–	–	–	–
Finland	–	0.1	–	–
France	0.3	0.3	20.4	8.0
Germany	31.6	0.4	9.3	4.2
Ireland	0.0	–	–	–
Italy	–	–	11.0	3.5
Japan	10.6	0.3	0.8	14.9
Netherlands	0.2	0.7	0.3	0.4
New Zealand	–	–	–	–
Norway	–	0.1	0.1	–
Sweden	–	–	–	–
Switzerland	0.1	0.1	0.2	0.1
United Kingdom	0.3	0.3	1.1	1.3
United States	–	8.0	55.0	9.0
TOTAL	43.6	15.7	107.0	45.0
MULTILATERAL	52.7	37.8	20.1	57.5
ARAB COUNTRIES	–	–	–	–
E.E.C.+ MEMBERS	40.5	3.8	47.3	22.7
TOTAL	96.3	53.5	127.1	102.4

4. TOTAL ODA NET

	1987	1988	1989	1990
Australia	–	–	–	–
Austria	0.0	0.0	–	0.0
Belgium	–	0.1	–	–
Canada	0.2	0.0	3.3	2.1
Denmark	–	–	–	–
Finland	–	0.1	–	–
France	0.3	0.3	0.3	0.4
Germany	31.5	-1.1	-4.3	0.3
Ireland	0.0	–	–	–
Italy	–	–	–	–
Japan	0.2	0.3	0.8	1.6
Netherlands	0.2	0.7	0.3	0.4
New Zealand	–	–	–	–
Norway	–	0.1	0.1	–
Sweden	–	–	–	–
Switzerland	0.1	0.1	0.2	0.1
United Kingdom	0.2	0.2	1.0	1.3
United States	–	2.0	–	–
TOTAL	32.8	2.7	1.6	6.1

MULTILATERAL

	1987	1988	1989	1990
AF.D.F.	–	–	–	–
AF.D.B.	–	–	–	–
AS.D.B	–	–	–	–
CAR.D.B.	0.0	0.4	0.3	0.3
E.E.C.	0.3	0.4	1.2	1.2
IBRD	–	–	–	–
IDA	–	–	–	–
I.D.B.	-0.8	2.2	0.6	0.7
IFAD	–	–	–	–
I.F.C.	–	–	–	–
IMF TRUST FUND	–	–	–	–
U.N. AGENCIES	–	–	–	–
UNDP	1.3	2.3	1.4	1.0
UNTA	0.5	0.4	0.6	0.5
UNICEF	–	–	–	–
UNRWA	–	–	–	–
WFP	–	–	–	–
UNHCR	–	–	–	–
Other Multilateral	0.2	0.2	0.3	0.4
Arab Agencies	–	–	–	–
TOTAL	1.6	5.9	4.4	4.1
ARAB COUNTRIES	–	–	–	–
E.E.C.+ MEMBERS	32.6	0.6	-1.5	3.5
TOTAL	34.4	8.6	6.0	10.3

5. ODA LOANS NET

	1987	1988	1989	1990
Australia	–	–	–	–
Austria	–	–	–	–
Belgium	–	–	–	–
Canada	-0.3	-0.7	-0.7	0.0
Denmark	–	–	–	–
Finland	–	–	–	–
France	–	–	–	–
Germany	31.3	-1.4	-4.5	–
Ireland	–	–	–	–
Italy	–	–	–	–
Japan	–	–	–	–
Netherlands	–	0.5	0.1	–
New Zealand	–	–	–	–
Norway	–	–	–	–
Sweden	–	–	–	–
Switzerland	–	–	–	–
United Kingdom	-0.1	-0.1	0.4	0.0
United States	–	–	–	–
TOTAL	30.9	-1.7	-4.7	-0.1
MULTILATERAL	-0.7	0.3	0.5	0.5
ARAB COUNTRIES	–	–	–	–
E.E.C.+ MEMBERS	31.2	-1.1	-4.0	0.0
TOTAL	30.2	-1.4	-4.2	0.5

6. TOTAL OFFICIAL NET

	1987	1988	1989	1990
Australia	–	–	–	–
Austria	0.0	0.0	–	0.0
Belgium	–	0.1	–	–
Canada	0.2	-5.9	8.3	3.6
Denmark	–	–	–	–
Finland	–	0.1	–	–
France	0.3	0.3	20.4	8.0
Germany	31.6	-1.0	4.4	4.2
Ireland	0.0	–	–	–
Italy	–	–	9.6	1.3
Japan	8.5	-2.0	0.8	14.9
Netherlands	0.2	0.7	0.3	0.4
New Zealand	–	–	–	–
Norway	–	0.1	0.1	–
Sweden	–	–	–	–
Switzerland	0.1	0.1	0.2	0.1
United Kingdom	0.2	0.2	1.0	1.3
United States	-34.0	-11.0	15.0	5.0
TOTAL	7.1	-18.5	60.1	38.7
MULTILATERAL	41.8	28.2	6.4	26.2
ARAB COUNTRIES	–	–	–	–
E.E.C.+ MEMBERS	37.8	-0.6	37.4	16.7
TOTAL	48.9	9.7	66.5	64.9

7. TOTAL ODA GROSS

	1987
Australia	–
Austria	0.0
Belgium	–
Canada	0.5
Denmark	–
Finland	–
France	0.3
Germany	31.5
Ireland	0.0
Italy	–
Japan	0.2
Netherlands	0.2
New Zealand	–
Norway	–
Sweden	–
Switzerland	0.1
United Kingdom	0.3
United States	–
TOTAL	33.2

	1987
AF.D.F.	–
AF.D.B.	–
AS.D.B	–
CAR.D.B.	0.0
E.E.C.	0.3
IBRD	–
IDA	–
I.D.B.	–
IFAD	–
I.F.C.	–
IMF TRUST FUND	–
U.N. AGENCIES	–
UNDP	1.3
UNTA	0.5
UNICEF	–
UNRWA	–
WFP	–
UNHCR	–
Other Multilateral	0.2
Arab Agencies	–
TOTAL	2.4
ARAB COUNTRIES	–
E.E.C.+ MEMBERS	32.7
TOTAL	35.6

8. GRANTS

	1987
Australia	–
Austria	0.0
Belgium	–
Canada	0.5
Denmark	–
Finland	–
France	0.3
Germany	0.2
Ireland	0.0
Italy	–
Japan	0.2
Netherlands	0.2
New Zealand	–
Norway	–
Sweden	–
Switzerland	0.1
United Kingdom	0.3
United States	–
TOTAL	1.9
MULTILATERAL	2.4
ARAB COUNTRIES	–
E.E.C.+ MEMBERS	1.4
TOTAL	4.2

9. TOTAL OOF GROSS

	1987
Australia	–
Austria	–
Belgium	–
Canada	–
Denmark	–
Finland	–
France	–
Germany	0.0
Ireland	–
Italy	–
Japan	10.4
Netherlands	–
New Zealand	–
Norway	–
Sweden	–
Switzerland	–
United Kingdom	–
United States	–
TOTAL	10.4
MULTILATERAL	50.3
ARAB COUNTRIES	–
E.E.C.+ MEMBERS	7.8
TOTAL	60.7

10. ODA COMMITMENTS

1988	1989	1990	1987	1988	1989	1990
–	–	–	–	–	–	–
0.0	–	0.0	0.0	0.0	–	0.0
0.1	–	–	–	–	–	–
0.7	4.0	2.1	0.4	5.3	0.8	0.6
–	–	–	–	–	–	–
0.1	–	–	–	–	–	–
0.3	0.3	0.4	0.3	0.3	26.8	0.4
0.3	0.6	0.3	0.5	0.2	0.4	0.1
			0.0	–	–	–
–	–	–	–	–	–	–
0.3	0.8	1.6	0.3	0.3	0.9	1.6
0.7	0.3	0.4	0.6	0.2	0.2	0.4
–	–	–	–	–	–	–
0.1	0.1	–	–	–	–	–
–	–	–	–	–	–	–
0.1	0.2	0.1	–	–	–	–
0.3	1.1	1.3	0.3	0.3	1.1	1.3
2.0	–	–	–	–	–	–
5.0	7.2	6.2	2.5	6.6	30.1	4.4
–	–	–	–	–	–	–
–	–	–	–	–	–	–
0.4	0.3	0.3	0.3	0.1	0.5	0.5
0.4	1.2	1.2	0.0	8.2	19.8	19.8
–	–	–	–	–	–	–
2.9	1.4	1.5	–	–	–	–
–	–	–	–	–	–	–
–	–	–	–	–	–	–
			2.0	2.9	2.3	1.9
2.3	1.4	1.0	–	–	–	–
0.4	0.6	0.5	–	–	–	–
–	–	–	–	–	–	–
–	–	–	–	–	–	–
–	–	–	–	–	–	–
0.2	0.3	0.4	–	–	–	–
–	–	–	–	–	–	–
6.6	5.2	4.9	2.3	11.1	22.5	22.2
–	–	–	–	–	–	–
2.2	3.3	3.6	1.8	9.1	48.2	22.0
11.6	12.4	11.1	4.8	17.7	52.6	26.6

11. TECH. COOP. GRANTS

1988	1989	1990	1987	1988	1989	1990
0.0	–	0.0	0.0	0.0	–	0.0
0.1	–	–	–	–	–	–
0.7	4.0	2.1	–	0.1	0.1	0.3
–	–	–	–	–	–	–
0.1	–	–	–	–	–	–
0.3	0.3	0.4	0.3	0.3	0.3	0.4
0.3	0.2	0.3	0.2	0.3	0.1	0.1
			0.0	–	–	–
–	–	–	–	–	–	–
0.3	0.8	1.6	0.2	0.3	0.8	1.6
0.2	0.2	0.4	0.2	0.2	0.2	0.4
–	–	–	–	–	–	–
0.1	0.1	–	–	0.1	–	–
–	–	–	–	–	–	–
0.1	0.2	0.1	–	–	–	–
0.3	0.6	1.3	0.2	0.1	0.1	0.1
2.0	–	–	–	–	–	–
4.5	6.3	6.2	1.1	1.5	1.7	2.9
5.5	4.0	3.6	2.4	3.6	2.3	1.9
–	–	–	–	–	–	–
1.7	2.4	3.6	1.3	1.7	0.7	1.1
10.0	10.2	9.8	3.6	5.1	4.0	4.8

12. TOTAL OOF NET

1988	1989	1990	1987	1988	1989	1990
–	–	–	–	–	–	–
–	–	–	–	–	–	–
4.7	5.0	1.5	–	-5.9	5.0	1.5
–	–	–	–	–	–	–
–	20.1	7.5	–	–	20.1	7.5
0.1	8.7	3.9	0.0	0.1	8.7	3.9
–	–	–	–	–	–	–
–	11.0	3.5	–	–	9.6	1.3
–	–	13.4	8.3	-2.3	–	13.4
–	–	–	–	–	–	–
–	–	–	–	–	–	–
–	–	–	–	–	–	–
–	–	–	–	–	–	–
6.0	55.0	9.0	-34.0	-13.0	15.0	5.0
10.8	99.8	38.8	-25.7	-21.2	58.5	32.6
31.2	14.9	52.6	40.2	22.3	2.0	22.1
–	–	–	–	–	–	–
1.6	44.0	19.1	5.2	-1.2	39.0	13.2
42.0	114.7	91.4	14.5	1.1	60.5	54.6

13. ODF COMMITMENTS: BY PURPOSE %

	1987	1988	1989	1990
Education	72	–	–	–
Health	–	–	–	–
Other Social Infrastr.	–	–	2	–
Water Sanitat. Sewage	–	–	–	–
Energy	–	–	–	–
Telecommunications	–	–	0	–
Transportation	–	38	–	–
Agriculture	1	17	–	–
Extractive Industries	–	–	–	–
Manufacturing	–	–	–	–
Trade Banking Tourism	20	–	–	–
Technical Cooperation	7	45	27	–
Multisector Aid	–	–	1	–
Programme	–	–	–	–
Debt Reorganisation	–	–	69	–
Food Aid	–	–	–	–
Emergency Aid	–	–	–	–
Unspecified	–	–	–	–
TOTAL	100	100	100	–

14. GRANT ELEMENT OF ODA %

DAC COUNTRIES

	1987	1988	1989	1990
Australia	–	–	–	–
Austria	100.0	100.0	–	–
Belgium	–	–	–	–
Canada	100.0	100.0	100.0	–
Denmark	–	–	–	–
Finland	–	–	–	–
France	100.0	100.0	100.0	–
Germany	100.0	100.0	100.0	–
Ireland	100.0	–	–	–
Italy	–	–	–	–
Japan	100.0	100.0	100.0	–
Netherlands	73.0	100.0	100.0	–
New Zealand	–	–	–	–
Norway	–	–	–	–
Sweden	–	–	–	–
Switzerland	–	–	–	–
United Kingdom	100.0	100.0	100.0	–
United States	–	–	–	–
TOTAL	93.1	100.0	100.0	–
MULTILATERAL	75.0	95.2	100.0	–
ARAB COUNTRIES	–	–	–	–
E.E.C.+ MEMBERS	90.5	100.0	100.0	–
TOTAL	78.8	96.8	100.0	–

15. OTHER AGGREGATES

OFFICIAL COMMITMENTS:

	1987	1988	1989	1990
TOTAL BILATERAL	36.1	12.6	85.8	61.0
of which:				
Arab Countries	–	–	–	–
C.E.E.C.	–	–	–	–
TOTAL MULTILATERAL	2.3	41.8	116.5	94.0
TOTAL BIL.& MULTIL.	38.5	54.4	202.2	155.0
of which:				
ODA Grants	4.4	17.7	21.9	22.9
ODA Loans	0.4	–	30.7	3.7

DISBURSEMENTS:

DAC COUNTRIES COMBINED

	1987	1988	1989	1990
OFFICIAL & PRIVATE				
GROSS:				
Contractual Lending	53.7	15.7	151.8	64.4
Export Credits, Total	12.0	15.2	80.0	34.5
Export Credits, Priv.	12.0	4.6	51.1	25.7
NET:				
Contractual Lending	-10.5	-74.9	67.2	-2.7
Export Credits Total	-51.7	-73.2	1.1	-30.3
PRIVATE SECTOR NET	8.4	-29.8	7.3	-155.0
Direct Investment	-12.9	17.5	68.8	-84.6
Portfolio Investment	37.0	4.6	-74.9	-35.3
Export Credits	-15.7	-51.9	13.5	-35.1

MARKET BORROWING:

CHANGE IN CLAIMS

	1987	1988	1989	1990
Banks	-105.0	16.0	-49.0	-60.0

MEMORANDUM ITEM:

	1987	1988	1989	1990
C.E.E.C. (Gross)	–	–	–	–

1. TOTAL RECEIPTS NET

DAC COUNTRIES	1987	1988	1989	1990
Australia	–	–	–	–
Austria	-6.4	-7.0	-8.6	-9.2
Belgium	-17.5	-14.9	-2.9	15.2
Canada	7.3	11.9	12.0	-0.2
Denmark	-0.4	-0.4	-0.4	-0.5
Finland	–	0.3	0.0	0.3
France	-23.3	-36.7	28.3	11.0
Germany	2.7	37.7	15.4	23.4
Ireland	–	–	–	–
Italy	63.6	55.4	43.6	68.0
Japan	-20.3	18.0	11.1	14.8
Netherlands	-1.1	1.8	17.0	-0.2
New Zealand	–	–	–	–
Norway	–	–	–	0.1
Sweden	-6.3	1.6	-2.5	28.4
Switzerland	3.3	0.5	0.1	0.5
United Kingdom	0.2	3.9	-5.9	9.0
United States	16.0	25.0	12.0	24.0
TOTAL	*17.8*	*97.1*	*119.3*	*184.4*
MULTILATERAL				
AF.D.F.	–	–	–	–
AF.D.B.	45.6	74.5	96.3	115.3
AS.D.B	–	–	–	–
CAR.D.B.	–	–	–	–
E.E.C.	41.3	63.9	48.4	48.4
IBRD	67.1	62.0	156.0	102.0
IDA	-1.3	-1.0	-1.0	-1.0
I.D.B.	–	–	–	–
IFAD	6.6	-0.1	0.7	1.0
I.F.C.	0.9	6.5	-2.0	2.2
IMF TRUST FUND	–	–	–	–
U.N. AGENCIES	–	–	–	–
UNDP	2.1	2.6	2.9	2.7
UNTA	1.3	1.1	1.7	1.4
UNICEF	0.6	0.3	0.4	0.4
UNRWA	–	–	–	–
WFP	0.8	15.7	8.3	13.6
UNHCR	–	0.1	0.1	0.1
Other Multilateral	0.7	1.3	1.4	1.3
Arab Agencies	17.8	-4.2	1.9	–
TOTAL	*183.4*	*222.7*	*315.1*	*287.4*
ARAB COUNTRIES	*2.8*	*-1.1*	*-19.6*	*51.4*
E.E.C.+ MEMBERS	*65.5*	*110.6*	*143.5*	*174.2*
TOTAL	*204.1*	*318.6*	*414.9*	*523.1*

2. ODA LOANS GROSS

DAC COUNTRIES	1987	1988	1989	1990
Australia	–	–	–	–
Austria	–	–	–	–
Belgium	–	–	0.0	3.0
Canada	0.3	–	–	–
Denmark	–	–	–	–
Finland	–	–	0.0	0.3
France	33.6	14.1	25.4	41.4
Germany	28.0	41.7	31.0	40.2
Ireland	–	–	–	–
Italy	48.9	36.0	23.3	31.5
Japan	2.9	39.0	31.9	29.7
Netherlands	2.0	0.4	3.9	4.1
New Zealand	–	–	–	–
Norway	–	–	–	–
Sweden	–	–	–	–
Switzerland	3.1	0.1	–	–
United Kingdom	–	–	–	–
United States	24.0	26.0	27.0	6.0
TOTAL	*142.9*	*157.5*	*142.5*	*156.3*
MULTILATERAL	*25.0*	*22.8*	*23.6*	*40.8*
ARAB COUNTRIES	*54.9*	*39.9*	*35.2*	*18.0*
E.E.C.+ MEMBERS	*117.0*	*98.6*	*85.7*	*122.4*
TOTAL	*222.8*	*220.2*	*201.3*	*215.1*

3. TOTAL OFFICIAL GROSS

DAC COUNTRIES	1987	1988	1989	1990
Australia	–	–	–	–
Austria	0.9	0.8	0.5	0.6
Belgium	3.8	3.0	4.4	8.3
Canada	11.3	15.0	15.5	5.1
Denmark	0.1	–	–	–
Finland	–	0.1	0.0	0.3
France	66.0	53.4	64.7	89.9
Germany	44.9	57.4	49.4	79.2
Ireland	–	–	–	–
Italy	96.7	83.4	47.1	77.7
Japan	5.7	42.0	36.5	48.3
Netherlands	7.1	1.6	5.0	5.4
New Zealand	–	–	–	–
Norway	–	–	–	0.1
Sweden	0.5	2.7	0.1	19.0
Switzerland	3.3	0.5	0.2	0.6
United Kingdom	1.2	0.8	1.4	0.7
United States	46.0	49.0	51.0	44.0
TOTAL	*287.5*	*309.5*	*275.8*	*379.2*
MULTILATERAL	*353.6*	*403.5*	*481.7*	*464.5*
ARAB COUNTRIES	*66.3*	*41.2*	*35.2*	*68.2*
E.E.C.+ MEMBERS	*264.8*	*267.7*	*225.2*	*314.5*
TOTAL	*707.4*	*754.2*	*792.7*	*911.9*

4. TOTAL ODA NET

DAC COUNTRIES	1987	1988	1989	1990
Australia	–	–	–	–
Austria	-4.6	-6.6	-7.1	-8.6
Belgium	3.1	2.6	3.5	7.4
Canada	8.1	10.5	11.8	1.2
Denmark	-0.4	-0.4	-0.4	-0.5
Finland	–	0.1	0.0	0.3
France	56.4	43.0	54.6	76.2
Germany	10.2	36.4	20.2	-8.0
Ireland	–	–	–	–
Italy	86.7	74.9	27.0	65.2
Japan	1.0	36.7	28.8	27.0
Netherlands	1.5	-1.2	1.6	1.7
New Zealand	–	–	–	–
Norway	–	–	–	0.1
Sweden	-0.5	1.6	-0.8	19.0
Switzerland	3.3	0.5	0.1	0.5
United Kingdom	1.2	0.8	1.3	0.7
United States	35.0	37.0	37.0	31.0
TOTAL	*200.9*	*235.8*	*177.7*	*213.1*
MULTILATERAL				
AF.D.F.	–	–	–	–
AF.D.B.	–	–	–	–
AS.D.B	–	–	–	–
CAR.D.B.	–	–	–	–
E.E.C.	27.4	47.4	31.6	31.6
IBRD	–	–	–	–
IDA	-1.3	-1.0	-1.0	-1.0
I.D.B.	–	–	–	–
IFAD	6.6	-0.1	0.7	1.0
I.F.C.	–	–	–	–
IMF TRUST FUND	–	–	–	–
U.N. AGENCIES	–	–	–	–
UNDP	2.1	2.6	2.9	2.7
UNTA	1.3	1.1	1.7	1.4
UNICEF	0.6	0.3	0.4	0.4
UNRWA	–	–	–	–
WFP	0.8	15.7	8.3	13.6
UNHCR	–	0.1	0.1	0.1
Other Multilateral	0.7	1.3	1.4	1.3
Arab Agencies	8.3	9.8	14.7	–
TOTAL	*46.4*	*77.1*	*60.8*	*51.1*
ARAB COUNTRIES	*27.1*	*3.4*	*-4.7*	*51.4*
E.E.C.+ MEMBERS	*186.0*	*203.4*	*139.5*	*174.2*
TOTAL	*274.4*	*316.3*	*233.8*	*315.6*

5. ODA LOANS NET

DAC COUNTRIES	1987	1988	1989	1990
Australia	–	–	–	–
Austria	-5.5	-7.3	-7.7	-9.2
Belgium	–	-0.4	-0.4	2.6
Canada	-2.0	-1.3	-1.3	-2.7
Denmark	-0.4	-0.4	-0.4	-0.5
Finland	–	–	0.0	0.3
France	24.0	3.7	15.3	27.7
Germany	-6.7	21.2	2.0	-28.8
Ireland	–	–	–	–
Italy	46.3	32.8	8.8	25.8
Japan	-1.8	33.7	24.2	21.1
Netherlands	-3.6	-2.4	0.9	0.4
New Zealand	–	–	–	–
Norway	–	–	–	–
Sweden	-1.0	-1.1	-0.9	–
Switzerland	3.1	0.1	0.0	-0.1
United Kingdom	-0.1	-0.1	0.0	-0.1
United States	13.0	14.0	13.0	-7.0
TOTAL	*65.2*	*92.6*	*53.6*	*29.5*
MULTILATERAL	*18.0*	*14.5*	*15.7*	*34.4*
ARAB COUNTRIES	*20.5*	*2.4*	*-4.7*	*1.2*
E.E.C.+ MEMBERS	*63.9*	*60.8*	*28.3*	*29.2*
TOTAL	*103.7*	*109.5*	*64.6*	*65.1*

6. TOTAL OFFICIAL NET

DAC COUNTRIES	1987	1988	1989	1990
Australia	–	–	–	–
Austria	-6.4	-7.0	-8.6	-8.8
Belgium	3.8	2.6	4.0	7.9
Canada	7.3	11.9	12.0	-0.2
Denmark	-0.4	-0.4	-0.4	-0.5
Finland	–	0.1	0.0	0.3
France	56.4	43.0	54.6	76.2
Germany	9.2	35.8	18.6	7.2
Ireland	–	–	–	–
Italy	63.9	48.8	21.8	64.6
Japan	-9.9	16.5	13.8	25.4
Netherlands	1.5	-1.2	2.1	-0.2
New Zealand	–	–	–	–
Norway	–	–	–	0.1
Sweden	-0.5	1.6	-0.8	19.0
Switzerland	3.3	0.5	0.1	0.5
United Kingdom	1.2	0.8	1.3	0.7
United States	16.0	25.0	28.0	24.0
TOTAL	*145.5*	*177.9*	*146.6*	*216.0*
MULTILATERAL	*183.4*	*222.7*	*315.1*	*287.4*
ARAB COUNTRIES	*2.8*	*-1.1*	*-19.6*	*51.4*
E.E.C.+ MEMBERS	*176.9*	*193.2*	*150.4*	*204.2*
TOTAL	*331.7*	*399.4*	*442.1*	*554.7*

7. TOTAL ODA GROSS

	1987
Australia	–
Austria	0.9
Belgium	3.1
Canada	10.4
Denmark	–
Finland	–
France	66.0
Germany	44.9
Ireland	–
Italy	89.4
Japan	5.7
Netherlands	7.1
New Zealand	–
Norway	–
Sweden	0.5
Switzerland	3.3
United Kingdom	1.2
United States	46.0
TOTAL	*278.6*
AF.D.F.	–
AF.D.B.	–
AS.D.B	–
CAR.D.B.	–
E.E.C.	27.4
IBRD	–
IDA	–
I.D.B.	–
IFAD	8.1
I.F.C.	–
IMF TRUST FUND	–
U.N. AGENCIES	–
UNDP	2.1
UNTA	1.3
UNICEF	0.6
UNRWA	–
WFP	0.8
UNHCR	–
Other Multilateral	0.7
Arab Agencies	12.5
TOTAL	*53.4*
ARAB COUNTRIES	*61.5*
E.E.C.+ MEMBERS	*239.1*
TOTAL	*393.5*

8. GRANTS

	1987
Australia	–
Austria	0.9
Belgium	3.1
Canada	10.1
Denmark	–
Finland	–
France	32.4
Germany	16.9
Ireland	–
Italy	40.4
Japan	2.7
Netherlands	5.1
New Zealand	–
Norway	–
Sweden	0.5
Switzerland	0.2
United Kingdom	1.2
United States	22.0
TOTAL	*135.7*
MULTILATERAL	*28.4*
ARAB COUNTRIES	*6.6*
E.E.C.+ MEMBERS	*122.1*
TOTAL	*170.7*

9. TOTAL OOF GROSS

	1987
Australia	–
Austria	–
Belgium	0.7
Canada	0.9
Denmark	0.1
Finland	–
France	–
Germany	–
Ireland	–
Italy	7.3
Japan	–
Netherlands	–
New Zealand	–
Norway	–
Sweden	–
Switzerland	–
United Kingdom	–
United States	–
TOTAL	*8.9*
MULTILATERAL	*300.2*
ARAB COUNTRIES	*4.8*
E.E.C.+ MEMBERS	*25.6*
TOTAL	*313.9*

1988	1989	1990	1987	1988	1989	1990

10. ODA COMMITMENTS

1988	1989	1990	1987	1988	1989	1990
–	–	–	–	–	–	–
0.8	0.5	0.6	0.1	0.1	0.2	0.5
3.0	3.9	7.8	5.9	7.4	3.9	7.8
11.8	13.1	3.9	20.7	9.7	5.8	9.8
–	–	–	–	–	–	–
0.1	0.0	0.3	0.1	–	–	0.3
53.4	64.7	89.9	34.9	125.7	87.7	90.4
57.0	49.2	61.1	60.0	24.8	27.2	117.8
–	–	–	–	–	–	–
78.1	41.5	70.9	114.3	73.6	112.0	97.0
42.0	36.5	35.6	3.4	57.8	77.1	6.3
1.6	4.5	5.4	5.2	8.7	0.9	4.5
–	–	–	–	–	–	–
–	–	0.1	–	–	–	–
2.7	0.1	19.0	1.0	3.1	0.1	17.1
0.5	0.2	0.6	0.1	0.2	0.0	0.5
0.8	1.4	0.7	1.3	0.8	1.7	2.1
49.0	51.0	44.0	46.9	54.9	40.2	61.9
300.7	*266.7*	*339.8*	*293.8*	*366.8*	*356.7*	*416.0*
–	–	–	–	–	–	–
–	–	–	–	–	–	–
–	–	–	–	–	–	–
47.4	31.6	31.6	5.1	67.8	44.5	44.5
–	–	–	–	–	–	–
–	–	–	–	–	–	–
1.1	2.9	3.9	–	12.5	–	–
–	–	–	–	–	–	–
–	–	–	5.4	21.1	14.8	19.5
2.6	2.9	2.7	–	–	–	–
1.1	1.7	1.4	–	–	–	–
0.3	0.4	0.4	–	–	–	–
–	–	–	–	–	–	–
15.7	8.3	13.6	–	–	–	–
0.1	0.1	0.1	–	–	–	–
1.3	1.4	1.3	–	–	–	–
15.9	19.4	34.9	25.1	31.7	54.5	–
85.5	*68.7*	*89.9*	*35.6*	*133.0*	*113.8*	*64.0*
40.8	*35.2*	*68.2*	*22.6*	*160.0*	*47.4*	*84.3*
241.3	*196.9*	*267.4*	*226.8*	*308.7*	*277.9*	*364.1*
427.0	*370.5*	*497.9*	*352.0*	*659.7*	*517.9*	*564.3*

11. TECH. COOP. GRANTS

1988	1989	1990	1987	1988	1989	1990
–	–	–	–	–	–	–
0.8	0.5	0.6	0.9	0.1	0.1	0.5
3.0	3.9	4.8	2.9	2.3	3.3	4.2
11.8	13.1	3.9	–	0.8	1.3	1.2
–	–	–	–	–	–	–
0.1	–	0.0	–	–	–	–
39.3	39.3	48.5	32.4	34.6	30.1	42.7
15.3	18.2	20.9	15.6	13.5	17.6	19.4
–	–	–	–	–	–	–
42.1	18.2	39.4	10.8	4.9	5.8	5.0
3.0	4.6	5.9	2.7	2.3	4.3	5.6
1.1	0.7	1.3	0.4	0.3	0.3	0.3
–	–	0.1	–	–	–	–
2.7	0.1	19.0	0.5	0.5	0.2	2.5
0.3	0.2	0.6	0.1	0.1	–	–
0.8	1.4	0.7	0.3	0.5	0.3	0.3
23.0	24.0	38.0	13.0	13.0	13.0	13.0
143.2	*124.2*	*183.5*	*79.6*	*73.0*	*76.1*	*94.7*
62.7	*45.1*	*49.0*	*8.3*	*10.8*	*6.5*	*5.9*
0.9	–	*50.2*	–	–	–	–
142.7	*111.2*	*145.0*	*66.1*	*61.6*	*57.3*	*72.0*
206.8	*169.3*	*282.8*	*87.9*	*83.8*	*82.7*	*100.7*

12. TOTAL OOF NET

1988	1989	1990	1987	1988	1989	1990
–	–	–	–	–	–	–
–	–	–	-1.7	-0.5	-1.5	-0.2
–	0.5	0.5	0.7	–	0.5	0.5
3.2	2.4	1.2	-0.8	1.4	0.2	-1.4
–	–	–	0.0	0.0	–	–
–	–	–	–	–	–	–
0.4	0.1	18.2	-0.9	-0.6	-1.6	15.2
–	–	–	–	–	–	–
5.3	5.6	6.8	-22.7	-26.1	-5.2	-0.6
–	–	12.7	-10.8	-20.2	-15.1	-1.6
–	0.5	0.1	–	–	0.5	-1.9
–	–	–	–	–	–	–
–	–	–	–	–	–	–
–	–	–	-19.0	-12.0	-9.0	-7.0
8.9	*9.1*	*39.4*	*-55.4*	*-58.0*	*-31.1*	*2.9*
318.0	*413.1*	*374.6*	*137.0*	*145.5*	*254.3*	*236.2*
0.3	–	–	*-24.3*	*-4.5*	*-14.9*	–
26.4	*28.3*	*47.1*	*-9.1*	*-10.2*	*10.9*	*29.9*
327.2	*422.2*	*414.0*	*57.3*	*83.1*	*208.3*	*239.1*

13. ODF COMMITMENTS: BY PURPOSE %

	1987	1988	1989	1990
Education	1	1	9	–
Health	0	–	0	–
Other Social Infrastr.	9	3	18	–
Water Sanitat. Sewage	8	0	1	–
Energy	–	–	4	–
Telecommunications	–	4	0	–
Transportation	4	8	3	–
Agriculture	38	9	16	–
Extractive Industries	–	1	8	–
Manufacturing	0	2	0	–
Trade Banking Tourism	18	12	6	–
Technical Cooperation	13	10	7	–
Multisector Aid	0	0	0	–
Programme	3	28	24	–
Debt Reorganisation	1	–	–	–
Food Aid	5	5	3	–
Emergency Aid	–	0	–	–
Unspecified	–	17	0	–
TOTAL	100	100	100	–

14. GRANT ELEMENT OF ODA %

DAC COUNTRIES

	1987	1988	1989	1990
Australia	–	–	–	–
Austria	100.0	100.0	100.0	–
Belgium	100.0	100.0	100.0	–
Canada	100.0	100.0	100.0	–
Denmark	–	–	–	–
Finland	–	–	–	–
France	100.0	74.8	82.0	–
Germany	51.8	76.8	87.1	–
Ireland	–	–	–	–
Italy	70.7	79.5	62.3	–
Japan	100.0	49.3	55.8	–
Netherlands	100.0	49.8	100.0	–
New Zealand	–	–	–	–
Norway	–	–	–	–
Sweden	100.0	100.0	100.0	–
Switzerland	100.0	100.0	100.0	–
United Kingdom	100.0	100.0	100.0	–
United States	74.6	65.0	66.0	–
TOTAL	*74.7*	*71.3*	*69.3*	–
MULTILATERAL	*47.0*	*83.3*	*70.0*	–
ARAB COUNTRIES	*39.4*	*46.8*	*40.6*	–
E.E.C.+ MEMBERS	*72.4*	*81.4*	*77.8*	–
TOTAL	*69.6*	*67.4*	*66.8*	–

15. OTHER AGGREGATES

	1987	1988	1989	1990
OFFICIAL COMMITMENTS:				
TOTAL BILATERAL	868.8	547.8	441.4	537.4
of which:				
Arab Countries	22.6	160.0	47.4	84.3
C.E.E.C.	–	15.0	–	–
TOTAL MULTILATERAL	460.7	486.9	700.8	239.8
TOTAL BIL.& MULTIL.	1329.5	1034.7	1142.2	777.2
of which:				
ODA Grants	154.8	227.1	172.7	328.9
ODA Loans	197.3	432.6	345.2	235.4
DISBURSEMENTS:				
DAC COUNTRIES COMBINED				
OFFICIAL & PRIVATE				
GROSS:				
Contractual Lending	173.7	178.4	181.9	328.1
Export Credits, Total	30.7	20.6	38.8	159.1
Export Credits, Priv.	22.5	12.2	30.8	132.9
NET:				
Contractual Lending	-44.1	14.6	-17.0	86.2
Export Credits Total	-109.3	-78.3	-70.3	47.7
PRIVATE SECTOR NET	-127.7	-80.7	-27.2	-31.6
Direct Investment	17.4	17.3	14.6	25.3
Portfolio Investment	-91.8	-78.1	-2.9	-111.1
Export Credits	-53.2	-20.0	-38.9	54.2
MARKET BORROWING:				
CHANGE IN CLAIMS				
Banks	-98.0	-62.0	-178.0	-183.0
MEMORANDUM ITEM:				
C.E.E.C. (Gross)	0.3	1.8	3.5	–

DISBURSEMENTS, UNLESS OTHERWISE STAT[ED]

	1987	1988	1989	1990	1987	1988	1989	1990		1987
1. TOTAL RECEIPTS NET					**4. TOTAL ODA NET**				**7. TOTAL ODA GROSS**	
DAC COUNTRIES										
Australia	-3.5	-3.6	-1.6	–	–	–	0.1	–	Australia	–
Austria	-0.1	93.8	47.4	14.9	8.8	21.4	35.8	18.9	Austria	10.3
Belgium	271.5	86.3	142.3	-91.9	-0.8	7.8	3.6	2.6	Belgium	0.4
Canada	48.1	0.5	-59.7	-54.4	-0.8	-0.9	-1.8	1.6	Canada	0.8
Denmark	-0.2	5.4	0.7	1.2	-0.3	–	-0.1	–	Denmark	–
Finland	31.5	8.9	10.4	5.3	0.6	5.5	1.2	2.9	Finland	0.6
France	19.3	227.8	169.8	302.6	10.4	19.9	37.4	65.0	France	14.8
Germany	716.9	1274.8	474.6	715.3	248.8	185.9	133.3	241.5	Germany	307.5
Ireland	–	–	–	–	–	–	–	–	Ireland	–
Italy	-123.0	-51.4	31.3	-253.1	-0.3	0.2	-5.7	21.9	Italy	2.3
Japan	545.8	893.1	259.1	624.9	162.4	134.5	66.3	324.2	Japan	174.2
Netherlands	1.3	-28.5	-18.9	-8.9	-0.5	0.5	0.2	0.4	Netherlands	0.4
New Zealand	–	–	–	–	–	–	–	–	New Zealand	–
Norway	-3.6	-2.4	0.7	0.7	0.1	0.1	0.4	1.6	Norway	0.1
Sweden	77.2	-2.0	3.7	1.6	-2.0	-2.0	-1.1	0.7	Sweden	–
Switzerland	-10.6	-8.2	-3.3	-4.9	-0.8	-0.8	3.0	1.1	Switzerland	0.8
United Kingdom	272.7	669.1	29.7	56.9	-3.1	-12.2	-7.4	-8.2	United Kingdom	5.0
United States	-156.0	1099.0	333.0	-165.0	-37.0	-57.0	-76.0	-76.0	United States	21.0
TOTAL	*1687.3*	*4262.7*	*1419.1*	*1145.2*	*385.5*	*302.6*	*189.2*	*598.2*	*TOTAL*	*538.1*
MULTILATERAL										
AF.D.F.	–	–	–	–	–	–	–	–	AF.D.F.	–
AF.D.B.	–	–	–	–	–	–	–	–	AF.D.B.	–
AS.D.B	–	–	–	–	–	–	–	–	AS.D.B	–
CAR.D.B.	–	–	–	–	–	–	–	–	CAR.D.B.	–
E.E.C.	0.7	-9.8	-27.0	-27.0	8.6	-1.2	-18.1	-18.1	E.E.C.	27.0
IBRD	470.6	360.0	-82.0	7.0	–	–	–	–	IBRD	–
IDA	-3.6	-4.0	-5.0	-4.0	-3.6	-4.0	-5.0	-4.0	IDA	–
I.D.B.	–	–	–	–	–	–	–	–	I.D.B.	–
IFAD	2.5	0.3	–	2.2	2.5	0.3	–	2.2	IFAD	4.8
I.F.C.	4.5	58.2	50.0	114.0	–	–	–	–	I.F.C.	–
IMF TRUST FUND	–	–	–	–	–	–	–	–	IMF TRUST FUND	–
U.N. AGENCIES									U.N. AGENCIES	
UNDP	2.9	4.6	4.6	3.8	2.9	4.6	4.6	3.8	UNDP	2.9
UNTA	1.2	0.7	0.9	0.9	1.2	0.7	0.9	0.9	UNTA	1.2
UNICEF	0.1	0.4	1.0	1.3	0.1	0.4	1.0	1.3	UNICEF	0.1
UNRWA	–	–	–	–	–	–	–	–	UNRWA	–
WFP	0.9	1.4	2.1	2.7	0.9	1.4	2.1	2.7	WFP	0.9
UNHCR	2.8	4.3	3.8	1.9	2.8	4.3	3.8	1.9	UNHCR	2.8
Other Multilateral	230.3	236.2	165.3	189.1	4.0	2.2	5.6	6.1	Other Multilateral	4.6
Arab Agencies	38.3	-33.3	-46.5	–	0.0	0.3	0.3	–	Arab Agencies	2.5
TOTAL	*751.1*	*619.1*	*67.1*	*291.9*	*19.2*	*9.1*	*-4.8*	*-3.1*	*TOTAL*	*46.7*
ARAB COUNTRIES	***-23.1***	***-193.5***	***-39.0***	***669.6***	***-25.9***	***-42.7***	***-42.5***	***669.6***	***ARAB COUNTRIES***	***45.3***
E.E.C.+ MEMBERS	*1159.2*	*2173.7*	*802.4*	*695.2*	*262.8*	*200.8*	*143.1*	*305.2*	*E.E.C.+ MEMBERS*	*357.3*
TOTAL	***2415.3***	***4688.3***	***1447.2***	***2106.7***	***378.8***	***269.0***	***141.9***	***1264.7***	***TOTAL***	***630.1***
2. ODA LOANS GROSS					**5. ODA LOANS NET**				**8. GRANTS**	
DAC COUNTRIES										
Australia	–	–	–	–	–	–	–	–	Australia	–
Austria	3.1	17.5	20.9	5.4	1.6	13.6	17.0	-1.1	Austria	7.2
Belgium	–	8.2	5.1	6.0	-1.1	6.7	3.6	2.5	Belgium	0.4
Canada	–	–	–	–	-1.6	-1.7	-3.1	–	Canada	0.8
Denmark	–	–	–	–	-0.3	–	-0.1	–	Denmark	–
Finland	0.6	6.8	1.1	0.3	0.6	5.2	1.0	0.3	Finland	–
France	7.3	17.1	33.3	61.8	2.9	12.2	27.6	53.2	France	7.5
Germany	246.1	214.0	161.2	266.5	187.5	120.4	67.3	78.9	Germany	61.4
Ireland	–	–	–	–	–	–	–	–	Ireland	–
Italy	–	3.5	6.9	16.6	-2.5	-3.8	-16.5	10.6	Italy	2.3
Japan	169.0	147.0	81.3	329.9	157.3	125.6	55.6	308.6	Japan	5.1
Netherlands	–	2.4	2.3	–	-0.9	0.2	-0.3	-3.5	Netherlands	0.4
New Zealand	–	–	–	–	–	–	–	–	New Zealand	–
Norway	–	–	–	–	–	–	–	–	Norway	0.1
Sweden	–	–	–	–	-2.0	-2.0	-1.1	–	Sweden	–
Switzerland	–	–	–	–	-1.6	-1.2	–	–	Switzerland	0.8
United Kingdom	3.3	1.6	0.3	–	-4.9	-13.9	-10.9	-13.2	United Kingdom	1.7
United States	1.0	–	–	–	-57.0	-89.0	-136.0	-89.0	United States	20.0
TOTAL	*430.4*	*417.9*	*312.4*	*686.4*	*277.9*	*172.1*	*4.0*	*347.3*	*TOTAL*	*107.7*
MULTILATERAL	*20.6*	*16.5*	*8.3*	*8.1*	*-7.0*	*-12.3*	*-20.4*	*-21.4*	*MULTILATERAL*	*26.2*
ARAB COUNTRIES	***44.9***	***12.7***	***14.2***	***3.8***	***-26.3***	***-46.7***	***-46.8***	***-12.4***	***ARAB COUNTRIES***	***0.4***
E.E.C.+ MEMBERS	*266.2*	*255.8*	*210.1*	*351.9*	*171.7*	*111.4*	*52.4*	*110.4*	*E.E.C.+ MEMBERS*	*91.1*
TOTAL	***495.8***	***447.1***	***334.9***	***698.3***	***244.5***	***113.0***	***-63.2***	***313.5***	***TOTAL***	***134.3***
3. TOTAL OFFICIAL GROSS					**6. TOTAL OFFICIAL NET**				**9. TOTAL OOF GROSS**	
DAC COUNTRIES										
Australia	–	–	0.1	–	0.0	0.0	0.0	–	Australia	–
Austria	10.3	25.2	39.7	25.4	8.8	21.4	35.8	18.9	Austria	–
Belgium	2.7	9.2	7.0	7.7	-3.0	3.6	3.8	2.3	Belgium	2.3
Canada	83.4	65.7	3.5	1.6	41.6	1.2	-53.2	-54.4	Canada	82.6
Denmark	0.1	2.2	0.9	1.0	-0.2	2.2	0.7	0.9	Denmark	0.1
Finland	0.6	7.1	1.4	2.9	0.6	5.5	1.2	2.9	Finland	–
France	15.2	24.9	43.1	74.1	-17.0	-34.0	37.4	31.8	France	0.4
Germany	438.8	406.8	276.7	455.2	303.2	227.2	128.8	186.6	Germany	131.3
Ireland	–	–	–	–	–	–	–	–	Ireland	–
Italy	2.3	7.5	33.5	62.0	-10.8	-11.1	-0.6	47.2	Italy	–
Japan	239.4	378.2	116.6	533.2	169.1	285.3	21.0	456.0	Japan	65.2
Netherlands	1.0	2.7	2.8	9.6	-7.3	-7.0	-7.1	-2.5	Netherlands	0.5
New Zealand	–	–	–	–	–	–	–	–	New Zealand	–
Norway	0.1	0.1	0.6	1.6	0.1	0.1	0.6	1.6	Norway	–
Sweden	–	–	–	0.7	-2.0	-2.0	-1.1	0.7	Sweden	–
Switzerland	0.8	0.4	3.0	1.1	-10.6	-8.2	-3.3	-4.9	Switzerland	–
United Kingdom	5.0	4.5	6.0	5.0	-4.1	-12.1	-5.2	-8.2	United Kingdom	–
United States	40.0	42.0	61.0	13.0	-90.0	-249.0	-187.0	-169.0	United States	19.0
TOTAL	*839.4*	*976.6*	*595.8*	*1193.9*	*378.5*	*222.9*	*-28.0*	*509.7*	*TOTAL*	*301.4*
MULTILATERAL	*1225.0*	*1298.3*	*836.2*	*1056.1*	*751.1*	*619.1*	*67.1*	*291.9*	*MULTILATERAL*	*1178.3*
ARAB COUNTRIES	***93.6***	***137.8***	***22.0***	***685.8***	***-23.1***	***-193.5***	***-39.0***	***669.6***	***ARAB COUNTRIES***	***48.3***
E.E.C.+ MEMBERS	*491.9*	*476.0*	*371.0*	*615.7*	*261.6*	*159.0*	*130.8*	*231.0*	*E.E.C.+ MEMBERS*	*134.6*
TOTAL	***2158.0***	***2413.2***	***1454.0***	***2935.8***	***1106.4***	***648.6***	***0.0***	***1471.2***	***TOTAL***	***1528.0***

10. ODA COMMITMENTS

1988	1989	1990	1987	1988	1989	1990
–	0.1	–	–	–	–	–
25.2	39.7	25.4	16.3	8.4	19.2	20.0
9.2	5.1	6.0	0.5	8.2	5.1	6.0
0.8	1.3	1.6	0.7	0.7	1.3	1.7
7.1	1.4	2.9	1.4	–	0.8	1.9
24.8	43.1	73.6	21.5	59.7	92.8	21.2
279.5	227.2	429.2	426.3	160.6	259.0	199.2
–	–	–	–	–	–	–
7.5	17.7	27.9	14.2	39.1	20.5	9.3
155.8	92.0	345.5	263.6	9.7	266.7	216.9
2.7	2.8	3.9	0.4	2.8	2.8	1.2
–	–	–	–	–	–	–
0.1	0.4	1.6	0.1	–	–	–
–	–	0.7	–	–	–	–
0.4	3.0	1.1	–	–	3.7	–
3.3	3.8	5.0	3.5	98.4	1.9	0.7
32.0	60.0	13.0	21.3	32.4	60.4	14.7
548.4	497.6	937.3	769.8	419.9	734.1	492.8
–	–	–	–	–	–	–
–	–	–	–	–	–	–
–	–	–	–	–	–	–
18.2	1.0	1.0	26.0	24.7	–	–
–	–	–	–	–	–	–
–	–	–	–	–	–	–
2.7	2.3	5.3	–	–	20.4	16.4
–	–	–	–	–	–	–
–	–	–	8.7	12.3	15.5	16.7
4.6	4.6	3.8	–	–	–	–
0.7	0.9	0.9	–	–	–	–
0.4	1.0	1.3	–	–	–	–
–	–	–	–	–	–	–
1.4	2.1	2.7	–	–	–	–
4.3	3.8	1.9	–	–	–	–
2.8	6.0	7.9	3.8	2.0	2.8	1.8
2.8	2.1	–	2.7	–	–	–
37.8	23.8	24.9	41.1	38.9	38.7	34.9
16.8	18.5	685.8	29.5	0.0	–	1560.0
345.2	300.8	546.7	492.3	393.5	382.1	237.7
603.0	539.9	1647.9	840.5	458.8	772.8	2087.7

11. TECH. COOP. GRANTS

1988	1989	1990	1987	1988	1989	1990
–	0.1	–	–	–	–	–
7.8	18.8	20.0	6.2	7.7	7.9	10.7
1.1	0.1	0.1	–	0.0	–	–
0.8	1.3	1.6	–	–	–	–
–	–	–	–	–	–	–
0.3	0.3	2.6	–	–	0.0	0.1
7.7	9.8	11.8	7.5	7.3	9.3	11.2
65.5	66.0	162.7	61.1	63.8	64.6	89.8
–	–	–	–	–	–	–
4.0	10.8	11.3	2.2	2.4	3.3	3.8
8.9	10.7	15.6	4.8	8.6	10.7	15.3
0.3	0.5	3.9	0.2	0.3	0.3	0.4
–	–	–	–	–	–	–
0.1	0.4	1.6	0.1	0.1	0.1	0.1
–	–	0.7	–	–	–	–
0.4	3.0	1.1	0.1	0.2	–	–
1.7	3.5	5.0	0.8	1.1	0.9	0.7
32.0	60.0	13.0	–	–	–	–
130.5	185.2	250.9	83.1	91.4	97.1	132.0
21.4	15.6	16.8	9.6	15.7	13.4	14.0
4.1	4.3	682.0	–	–	–	–
89.4	90.7	194.8	73.7	79.7	78.4	105.8
155.9	205.0	949.7	92.7	107.1	110.4	146.0

12. TOTAL OOF NET

1988	1989	1990	1987	1988	1989	1990
–	–	–	0.0	0.0	0.0	–
–	1.9	1.7	-2.2	-4.2	0.2	-0.3
64.9	2.2	–	42.4	2.1	-51.4	-56.1
2.2	0.9	1.0	0.1	2.2	0.8	0.9
–	–	–	–	–	–	–
0.1	–	0.5	-27.3	-53.9	–	-33.2
127.3	49.5	26.1	54.4	41.3	-4.4	-55.0
–	–	–	–	–	–	–
–	15.8	34.1	-10.6	-11.2	5.1	25.3
222.4	24.6	187.6	6.7	150.9	-45.3	131.8
–	–	5.7	-6.8	-7.5	-7.3	-2.9
–	–	–	–	–	–	–
–	0.2	–	–	–	0.2	–
–	–	–	–	–	–	–
–	–	–	-9.8	-7.4	-6.2	-6.0
1.2	2.2	–	-0.9	0.2	2.2	–
10.0	1.0	–	-53.0	-192.0	-111.0	-93.0
428.1	98.2	256.6	-7.1	-79.6	-217.2	-88.5
1261.1	812.4	1031.3	731.9	610.1	71.9	295.0
121.0	3.5	–	2.8	-150.8	3.5	–
130.9	70.2	69.0	-1.2	-41.8	-12.4	-74.2
1810.2	914.1	1287.9	727.7	379.6	-141.8	206.5

13. ODF COMMITMENTS: BY PURPOSE %

	1987	1988	1989	1990
Education	4	6	–	–
Health	0	0	0	–
Other Social Infrastr.	6	0	–	–
Water Sanitat. Sewage	27	2	0	–
Energy	27	9	6	–
Telecommunications	–	–	–	–
Transportation	20	1	2	–
Agriculture	0	2	53	–
Extractive Industries	0	–	0	–
Manufacturing	1	0	0	–
Trade Banking Tourism	0	42	23	–
Technical Cooperation	5	6	9	–
Multisector Aid	–	–	0	–
Programme	7	32	7	–
Debt Reorganisation	0	–	–	–
Food Aid	–	–	–	–
Emergency Aid	–	0	–	–
Unspecified	0	–	–	–
TOTAL	100	100	100	–

14. GRANT ELEMENT OF ODA %

DAC COUNTRIES

	1987	1988	1989	1990
Australia	–	–	–	–
Austria	61.1	95.5	98.3	–
Belgium	100.0	100.0	100.0	–
Canada	100.0	100.0	100.0	–
Denmark	–	–	–	–
Finland	–	–	100.0	–
France	77.6	76.1	57.5	–
Germany	50.5	76.3	71.2	–
Ireland	–	–	–	–
Italy	77.5	80.3	89.4	–
Japan	41.8	100.0	55.0	–
Netherlands	100.0	100.0	100.0	–
New Zealand	–	–	–	–
Norway	100.0	–	–	–
Sweden	–	–	–	–
Switzerland	–	–	100.0	–
United Kingdom	100.0	100.0	100.0	–
United States	99.2	100.0	100.0	–
TOTAL	*50.7*	*85.2*	*68.3*	*–*
MULTILATERAL	*94.2*	*100.0*	*100.0*	*–*
ARAB COUNTRIES	**39.7**	**100.0**	**–**	**–**
E.E.C.+ MEMBERS	*54.4*	*84.3*	*71.3*	*–*
TOTAL	**51.6**	**86.5**	**69.1**	**–**

15. OTHER AGGREGATES

	1987	1988	1989	1990
OFFICIAL COMMITMENTS:				
TOTAL BILATERAL	1447.0	1175.5	755.1	2088.3
of which:				
Arab Countries	198.2	64.0	–	1560.0
C.E.E.C.	–	–	–	–
TOTAL MULTILATERAL	1366.8	1437.0	1366.4	596.7
TOTAL BIL.& MULTIL.	2813.8	2612.5	2121.5	2685.0
of which:				
ODA Grants	142.8	302.2	217.1	1813.6
ODA Loans	697.6	156.6	555.7	274.1
DISBURSEMENTS:				
DAC COUNTRIES COMBINED				
OFFICIAL & PRIVATE				
GROSS:				
Contractual Lending	1664.9	1852.1	1255.1	1700.1
Export Credits, Total	1181.7	1248.8	938.5	824.5
Export Credits, Priv.	935.5	1007.3	848.8	759.2
NET:				
Contractual Lending	691.7	607.1	-50.4	112.1
Export Credits Total	466.3	528.5	46.7	-302.6
PRIVATE SECTOR NET	1308.8	4039.7	1447.1	635.5
Direct Investment	370.6	862.1	435.2	304.8
Portfolio Investment	514.9	2661.7	844.8	475.3
Export Credits	423.3	515.9	167.2	-144.5
MARKET BORROWING:				
CHANGE IN CLAIMS				
Banks	1596.0	-55.0	40.0	3392.0
MEMORANDUM ITEM:				
C.E.E.C. (Gross)	1.6	1.1	–	–

	1987	1988	1989	1990		1987	1988	1989	1990		1987
1. TOTAL RECEIPTS NET					**4. TOTAL ODA NET**					**7. TOTAL ODA GROSS**	
DAC COUNTRIES											
Australia	–	–	–	–		–	–	–	–	Australia	–
Austria	–	–	–	–		–	–	–	–	Austria	–
Belgium	–	–	–	-0.9		–	–	–	–	Belgium	–
Canada	-7.6	0.2	0.1	0.1		0.3	0.2	0.1	0.1	Canada	0.3
Denmark	–	–	–	–		–	–	–	–	Denmark	–
Finland	–	–	–	–		–	–	–	–	Finland	–
France	-0.2	0.2	-0.2	-0.4		–	–	–	–	France	–
Germany	-1.7	–	0.0	-0.2		–	–	–	–	Germany	–
Ireland	–	–	–	–		–	–	–	–	Ireland	–
Italy	–	–	–	–		–	–	–	–	Italy	–
Japan	–	–	–	–		–	–	–	–	Japan	–
Netherlands	–	–	0.3	0.3		–	–	–	–	Netherlands	–
New Zealand	–	–	–	–		–	–	–	–	New Zealand	–
Norway	–	–	–	–		–	–	–	–	Norway	–
Sweden	–	–	–	–		–	–	–	–	Sweden	–
Switzerland	–	–	–	–		–	–	–	–	Switzerland	–
United Kingdom	8.8	7.5	8.6	8.7		8.8	7.5	8.6	8.7	United Kingdom	8.8
United States	–	–	–	–		–	–	–	–	United States	–
TOTAL	-0.7	7.9	8.8	7.7		9.1	7.7	8.7	8.9	TOTAL	9.1
MULTILATERAL											
AF.D.F.	–	–	–	–		–	–	–	–	AF.D.F.	–
AF.D.B.	–	–	–	–		–	–	–	–	AF.D.B.	–
AS.D.B	–	–	–	–		–	–	–	–	AS.D.B	–
CAR.D.B.	0.1	0.0	0.1	0.1		0.1	0.0	0.0	0.0	CAR.D.B.	0.1
E.E.C.	–	–	–	–		–	–	–	–	E.E.C.	–
IBRD	–	–	–	–		–	–	–	–	IBRD	–
IDA	–	–	–	–		–	–	–	–	IDA	–
I.D.B.	–	–	–	–		–	–	–	–	I.D.B.	–
IFAD	–	–	–	–		–	–	–	–	IFAD	–
I.F.C.	–	–	–	–		–	–	–	–	I.F.C.	–
IMF TRUST FUND	–	–	–	–		–	–	–	–	IMF TRUST FUND	–
U.N. AGENCIES	–	–	–	–		–	–	–	–	U.N. AGENCIES	–
UNDP	0.4	0.2	0.0	0.9		0.4	0.2	0.0	0.9	UNDP	0.4
UNTA	–	–	0.0	–		–	–	0.0	–	UNTA	–
UNICEF	–	–	–	–		–	–	–	–	UNICEF	–
UNRWA	–	–	–	–		–	–	–	–	UNRWA	–
WFP	–	–	–	–		–	–	–	–	WFP	–
UNHCR	–	–	–	–		–	–	–	–	UNHCR	–
Other Multilateral	0.1	0.1	0.1	0.3		0.1	0.1	0.1	0.3	Other Multilateral	0.1
Arab Agencies	–	–	–	–		–	–	–	–	Arab Agencies	–
TOTAL	0.6	0.3	0.2	1.3		0.6	0.3	0.1	1.3	TOTAL	0.6
ARAB COUNTRIES	–	–	–	–		–	–	–	–	ARAB COUNTRIES	–
E.E.C.+ MEMBERS	6.9	7.7	8.8	7.5		8.8	7.5	8.6	8.7	E.E.C.+ MEMBERS	8.8
TOTAL	-0.1	8.2	9.0	9.0		9.7	8.0	8.8	10.1	TOTAL	9.7
2. ODA LOANS GROSS					**5. ODA LOANS NET**					**8. GRANTS**	
DAC COUNTRIES											
Australia	–	–	–	–		–	–	–	–	Australia	–
Austria	–	–	–	–		–	–	–	–	Austria	–
Belgium	–	–	–	–		–	–	–	–	Belgium	–
Canada	–	–	–	–		–	–	–	–	Canada	0.3
Denmark	–	–	–	–		–	–	–	–	Denmark	–
Finland	–	–	–	–		–	–	–	–	Finland	–
France	–	–	–	–		–	–	–	–	France	–
Germany	–	–	–	–		–	–	–	–	Germany	–
Ireland	–	–	–	–		–	–	–	–	Ireland	–
Italy	–	–	–	–		–	–	–	–	Italy	–
Japan	–	–	–	–		–	–	–	–	Japan	–
Netherlands	–	–	–	–		–	–	–	–	Netherlands	–
New Zealand	–	–	–	–		–	–	–	–	New Zealand	–
Norway	–	–	–	–		–	–	–	–	Norway	–
Sweden	–	–	–	–		–	–	–	–	Sweden	–
Switzerland	–	–	–	–		–	–	–	–	Switzerland	–
United Kingdom	–	–	–	–		–	–	–	–	United Kingdom	8.8
United States	–	–	–	–		–	–	–	–	United States	–
TOTAL	–	–	–	–		–	–	–	–	TOTAL	9.1
MULTILATERAL	0.1	0.0	0.0	0.0		0.1	0.0	0.0	0.0	MULTILATERAL	0.5
ARAB COUNTRIES	–	–	–	–		–	–	–	–	ARAB COUNTRIES	–
E.E.C.+ MEMBERS	–	–	–	–		–	–	–	–	E.E.C.+ MEMBERS	8.8
TOTAL	0.1	0.0	0.0	0.0		0.1	0.0	0.0	0.0	TOTAL	9.6
3. TOTAL OFFICIAL GROSS					**6. TOTAL OFFICIAL NET**					**9. TOTAL OOF GROSS**	
DAC COUNTRIES											
Australia	–	–	–	–		–	–	–	–	Australia	–
Austria	–	–	–	–		–	–	–	–	Austria	–
Belgium	–	–	–	–		–	–	–	–	Belgium	–
Canada	12.2	0.2	0.1	0.1		-7.6	0.2	0.1	0.1	Canada	11.9
Denmark	–	–	–	–		–	–	–	–	Denmark	–
Finland	–	–	–	–		–	–	–	–	Finland	–
France	–	–	–	–		–	–	–	–	France	–
Germany	–	–	–	–		–	–	–	–	Germany	–
Ireland	–	–	–	–		–	–	–	–	Ireland	–
Italy	–	–	–	–		–	–	–	–	Italy	–
Japan	–	–	–	–		–	–	–	–	Japan	–
Netherlands	–	–	–	–		–	–	–	–	Netherlands	–
New Zealand	–	–	–	–		–	–	–	–	New Zealand	–
Norway	–	–	–	–		–	–	–	–	Norway	–
Sweden	–	–	–	–		–	–	–	–	Sweden	–
Switzerland	–	–	–	–		–	–	–	–	Switzerland	–
United Kingdom	8.8	7.5	8.6	8.7		8.8	7.5	8.6	8.7	United Kingdom	–
United States	–	–	–	–		–	–	–	–	United States	–
TOTAL	21.0	7.7	8.7	8.9		1.2	7.7	8.7	8.9	TOTAL	11.9
MULTILATERAL	0.6	0.3	0.2	1.3		0.6	0.3	0.2	1.3	MULTILATERAL	–
ARAB COUNTRIES	–	–	–	–		–	–	–	–	ARAB COUNTRIES	–
E.E.C.+ MEMBERS	8.8	7.5	8.6	8.7		8.8	7.5	8.6	8.7	E.E.C.+ MEMBERS	–
TOTAL	21.5	8.0	8.9	10.2		1.8	8.0	8.9	10.2	TOTAL	11.9

10. ODA COMMITMENTS

1988	1989	1990	1987	1988	1989	1990
–	–	–	–	–	–	–
–	–	–	–	–	–	–
0.2	0.1	0.1	0.3	0.2	0.1	0.1
–	–	–	–	–	–	–
–	–	–	–	–	–	–
–	–	–	–	–	–	–
–	–	–	–	–	–	–
–	–	–	–	–	–	–
–	–	–	–	–	–	–
–	–	–	–	–	–	–
–	–	–	–	–	–	–
–	–	–	–	–	–	–
7.5	8.6	8.7	8.8	7.5	8.6	4.0
–	–	–	–	–	–	–
7.7	8.7	8.9	9.1	7.7	8.7	4.0
–	–	–	–	–	–	–
–	–	–	–	–	–	–
0.0	0.0	0.0	–	0.1	1.1	1.1
–	–	–	–	–	3.8	3.8
–	–	–	–	–	–	–
–	–	–	–	–	–	–
–	–	–	–	–	–	–
–	–	–	–	–	–	–
–	–	–	–	–	–	–
–	–	–	0.5	0.3	0.1	1.2
0.2	0.0	0.9	–	–	–	–
–	0.0	–	–	–	–	–
–	–	–	–	–	–	–
–	–	–	–	–	–	–
0.1	0.1	0.3	–	–	–	–
–	–	–	–	–	–	–
0.3	0.1	1.3	0.5	0.4	5.0	6.2
–	–	–	–	–	–	–
7.5	8.6	8.7	8.8	7.5	12.4	7.7
8.0	8.8	10.1	9.6	8.1	13.7	10.2

11. TECH. COOP. GRANTS

1988	1989	1990	1987	1988	1989	1990
–	–	–	–	–	–	–
–	–	–	–	–	–	–
0.2	0.1	0.1	–	0.0	0.0	0.0
–	–	–	–	–	–	–
–	–	–	–	–	–	–
–	–	–	–	–	–	–
–	–	–	–	–	–	–
–	–	–	–	–	–	–
–	–	–	–	–	–	–
–	–	–	–	–	–	–
–	–	–	–	–	–	–
–	–	–	–	–	–	–
7.5	8.6	8.7	2.1	2.8	2.8	4.0
–	–	–	–	–	–	–
7.7	8.7	8.9	2.1	2.8	2.8	4.0
0.3	0.1	1.2	0.5	0.3	0.1	1.2
–	–	–	–	–	–	–
7.5	8.6	8.7	2.1	2.8	2.8	4.0
8.0	8.8	10.1	2.6	3.1	3.0	5.2

12. TOTAL OOF NET

1988	1989	1990	1987	1988	1989	1990
–	–	–	–	–	–	–
–	–	–	–	–	–	–
–	–	–	-7.9	–	–	–
–	–	–	–	–	–	–
–	–	–	–	–	–	–
–	–	–	–	–	–	–
–	–	–	–	–	–	–
–	–	–	–	–	–	–
–	–	–	–	–	–	–
–	–	–	–	–	–	–
–	–	–	–	–	–	–
–	–	–	–	–	–	–
–	–	–	–	–	–	–
–	–	–	–	–	–	–
–	–	–	-7.9	–	–	–
–	0.0	0.0	–	–	0.0	0.0
–	–	–	–	–	–	–
–	–	–	–	–	–	–
–	0.0	0.0	-7.9	–	0.0	0.0

13. ODF COMMITMENTS: BY PURPOSE %

	1987	1988	1989	1990
Education	–	–	–	–
Health	–	–	–	–
Other Social Infrastr.	–	–	–	–
Water Sanitat. Sewage	–	–	–	–
Energy	–	–	–	–
Telecommunications	–	–	–	–
Transportation	–	–	–	–
Agriculture	–	–	–	–
Extractive Industries	–	–	–	–
Manufacturing	–	–	–	–
Trade Banking Tourism	–	–	6	–
Technical Cooperation	28	39	94	–
Multisector Aid	41	58	–	–
Programme	31	3	–	–
Debt Reorganisation	–	–	–	–
Food Aid	–	–	–	–
Emergency Aid	–	–	–	–
Unspecified	–	–	–	–
TOTAL	100	100	100	–

14. GRANT ELEMENT OF ODA %

DAC COUNTRIES

	1987	1988	1989	1990
Australia	–	–	–	–
Austria	–	–	–	–
Belgium	–	–	–	–
Canada	100.0	100.0	100.0	–
Denmark	–	–	–	–
Finland	–	–	–	–
France	–	–	–	–
Germany	–	–	–	–
Ireland	–	–	–	–
Italy	–	–	–	–
Japan	–	–	–	–
Netherlands	–	–	–	–
New Zealand	–	–	–	–
Norway	–	–	–	–
Sweden	–	–	–	–
Switzerland	–	–	–	–
United Kingdom	100.0	100.0	100.0	–
United States	–	–	–	–
TOTAL	100.0	100.0	100.0	–
MULTILATERAL	100.0	100.0	100.0	–
ARAB COUNTRIES	–	–	–	–
E.E.C.+ MEMBERS	100.0	100.0	100.0	–
TOTAL	100.0	100.0	100.0	–

15. OTHER AGGREGATES

OFFICIAL COMMITMENTS:

	1987	1988	1989	1990
TOTAL BILATERAL	9.1	7.7	8.7	4.0
of which:				
Arab Countries	–	–	–	–
C.E.E.C.	–	–	–	–
TOTAL MULTILATERAL	0.5	0.4	5.3	6.5
TOTAL BIL.& MULTIL.	9.6	8.1	14.0	10.5
of which:				
ODA Grants	9.6	8.1	12.7	9.2
ODA Loans	–	–	1.0	1.0

DISBURSEMENTS:

DAC COUNTRIES COMBINED

OFFICIAL & PRIVATE

GROSS:	1987	1988	1989	1990
Contractual Lending	11.9	-0.2	-0.3	-0.4
Export Credits, Total	11.9	-0.2	-0.3	-0.4
Export Credits, Priv.	–	-0.2	-0.3	-0.4
NET:				
Contractual Lending	-7.9	-0.2	-0.3	-0.4
Export Credits Total	-7.9	-0.2	-0.3	-0.4
PRIVATE SECTOR NET	-1.8	0.2	0.2	-1.2
Direct Investment	-1.7	0.3	0.2	–
Portfolio Investment	-0.2	–	0.3	-0.8
Export Credits	–	-0.2	-0.3	-0.4

MARKET BORROWING:

CHANGE IN CLAIMS

	1987	1988	1989	1990
Banks	58.0	-15.0	9.0	-31.0

MEMORANDUM ITEM:

	1987	1988	1989	1990
C.E.E.C. (Gross)	–	–	–	–

DISBURSEMENTS, UNLESS OTHERWISE STATED

	1987	1988	1989	1990		1987	1988	1989	1990		1987

1. TOTAL RECEIPTS NET

DAC COUNTRIES

	1987	1988	1989	1990
Australia	6.4	1.6	1.0	1.7
Austria	–	–	–	–
Belgium	–	–	–	–
Canada	–	–	–	–
Denmark	–	–	–	–
Finland	–	–	–	–
France	–	–	–	–
Germany	0.1	0.1	0.1	0.1
Ireland	–	–	–	–
Italy	–	–	–	–
Japan	0.2	0.3	3.0	1.0
Netherlands	–	0.0	–	–
New Zealand	6.5	1.2	1.1	1.1
Norway	–	–	–	–
Sweden	–	–	–	–
Switzerland	–	–	–	–
United Kingdom	11.7	10.1	0.6	0.9
United States	–	–	–	–
TOTAL	*24.9*	*13.3*	*5.7*	*4.8*

MULTILATERAL

	1987	1988	1989	1990
AF.D.F.	–	–	–	–
AF.D.B.	–	–	–	–
AS.D.B	–	–	–	–
CAR.D.B.	–	–	–	–
E.E.C.	0.3	0.2	0.2	0.2
IBRD	–	–	–	–
IDA	–	–	–	–
I.D.B.	–	–	–	–
IFAD	–	–	–	–
I.F.C.	–	–	–	–
IMF TRUST FUND	–	–	–	–
U.N. AGENCIES	–	–	–	–
UNDP	0.5	0.4	1.0	0.0
UNTA	0.0	0.0	0.0	0.0
UNICEF	–	–	–	–
UNRWA	–	–	–	–
WFP	–	–	–	–
UNHCR	–	–	–	–
Other Multilateral	0.0	0.0	0.0	0.0
Arab Agencies	–	–	–	–
TOTAL	*0.8*	*0.7*	*1.2*	*0.2*
ARAB COUNTRIES	–	–	–	–
E.E.C.+ MEMBERS	*12.0*	*10.4*	*0.8*	*1.1*
TOTAL	*25.7*	*14.0*	*6.9*	*5.0*

2. ODA LOANS GROSS

DAC COUNTRIES

	1987	1988	1989	1990
Australia	–	–	–	–
Austria	–	–	–	–
Belgium	–	–	–	–
Canada	–	–	–	–
Denmark	–	–	–	–
Finland	–	–	–	–
France	–	–	–	–
Germany	–	–	–	–
Ireland	–	–	–	–
Italy	–	–	–	–
Japan	–	–	–	–
Netherlands	–	–	–	–
New Zealand	–	–	–	–
Norway	–	–	–	–
Sweden	–	–	–	–
Switzerland	–	–	–	–
United Kingdom	–	–	–	–
United States	–	–	–	–
TOTAL	–	–	–	–
MULTILATERAL	–	–	–	–
ARAB COUNTRIES	–	–	–	–
E.E.C.+ MEMBERS	–	–	–	–
TOTAL	–	–	–	–

3. TOTAL OFFICIAL GROSS

DAC COUNTRIES

	1987	1988	1989	1990
Australia	6.4	1.6	1.0	1.7
Austria	–	–	–	–
Belgium	–	–	–	–
Canada	–	–	–	–
Denmark	–	–	–	–
Finland	–	–	–	–
France	–	–	–	–
Germany	0.1	0.1	0.1	0.1
Ireland	–	–	–	–
Italy	–	–	–	–
Japan	0.2	0.3	3.0	1.0
Netherlands	–	0.0	–	–
New Zealand	6.5	1.2	1.1	1.1
Norway	–	–	–	–
Sweden	–	–	–	–
Switzerland	–	–	–	–
United Kingdom	11.7	10.1	0.6	0.9
United States	–	–	–	–
TOTAL	*24.9*	*13.3*	*5.7*	*4.8*
MULTILATERAL	*0.8*	*0.7*	*1.2*	*0.2*
ARAB COUNTRIES	–	–	–	–
E.E.C.+ MEMBERS	*12.0*	*10.4*	*0.8*	*1.1*
TOTAL	*25.7*	*14.0*	*6.9*	*5.0*

4. TOTAL ODA NET

DAC COUNTRIES

	1987	1988	1989	1990
Australia	6.4	1.6	1.0	1.7
Austria	–	–	–	–
Belgium	–	–	–	–
Canada	–	–	–	–
Denmark	–	–	–	–
Finland	–	–	–	–
France	–	–	–	–
Germany	0.1	0.1	0.1	0.1
Ireland	–	–	–	–
Italy	–	–	–	–
Japan	0.2	0.3	3.0	1.0
Netherlands	–	0.0	–	–
New Zealand	6.5	1.2	1.1	1.1
Norway	–	–	–	–
Sweden	–	–	–	–
Switzerland	–	–	–	–
United Kingdom	11.7	10.1	0.6	0.9
United States	–	–	–	–
TOTAL	*24.9*	*13.3*	*5.7*	*4.8*

MULTILATERAL

	1987	1988	1989	1990
AF.D.F.	–	–	–	–
AF.D.B.	–	–	–	–
AS.D.B	–	–	–	–
CAR.D.B.	–	–	–	–
E.E.C.	0.3	0.2	0.2	0.2
IBRD	–	–	–	–
IDA	–	–	–	–
I.D.B.	–	–	–	–
IFAD	–	–	–	–
I.F.C.	–	–	–	–
IMF TRUST FUND	–	–	–	–
U.N. AGENCIES	–	–	–	–
UNDP	0.5	0.4	1.0	0.0
UNTA	0.0	0.0	0.0	0.0
UNICEF	–	–	–	–
UNRWA	–	–	–	–
WFP	–	–	–	–
UNHCR	–	–	–	–
Other Multilateral	0.0	0.0	0.0	0.0
Arab Agencies	–	–	–	–
TOTAL	*0.8*	*0.7*	*1.2*	*0.2*
ARAB COUNTRIES	–	–	–	–
E.E.C.+ MEMBERS	*12.0*	*10.4*	*0.8*	*1.1*
TOTAL	*25.7*	*14.0*	*6.9*	*5.0*

5. ODA LOANS NET

DAC COUNTRIES

	1987	1988	1989	1990
Australia	–	–	–	–
Austria	–	–	–	–
Belgium	–	–	–	–
Canada	–	–	–	–
Denmark	–	–	–	–
Finland	–	–	–	–
France	–	–	–	–
Germany	–	–	–	–
Ireland	–	–	–	–
Italy	–	–	–	–
Japan	–	–	–	–
Netherlands	–	–	–	–
New Zealand	–	–	–	–
Norway	–	–	–	–
Sweden	–	–	–	–
Switzerland	–	–	–	–
United Kingdom	–	–	–	–
United States	–	–	–	–
TOTAL	–	–	–	–
MULTILATERAL	–	–	–	–
ARAB COUNTRIES	–	–	–	–
E.E.C.+ MEMBERS	–	–	–	–
TOTAL	–	–	–	–

6. TOTAL OFFICIAL NET

DAC COUNTRIES

	1987	1988	1989	1990
Australia	6.4	1.6	1.0	1.7
Austria	–	–	–	–
Belgium	–	–	–	–
Canada	–	–	–	–
Denmark	–	–	–	–
Finland	–	–	–	–
France	–	–	–	–
Germany	0.1	0.1	0.1	0.1
Ireland	–	–	–	–
Italy	–	–	–	–
Japan	0.2	0.3	3.0	1.0
Netherlands	–	0.0	–	–
New Zealand	6.5	1.2	1.1	1.1
Norway	–	–	–	–
Sweden	–	–	–	–
Switzerland	–	–	–	–
United Kingdom	11.7	10.1	0.6	0.9
United States	–	–	–	–
TOTAL	*24.9*	*13.3*	*5.7*	*4.8*
MULTILATERAL	*0.8*	*0.7*	*1.2*	*0.2*
ARAB COUNTRIES	–	–	–	–
E.E.C.+ MEMBERS	*12.0*	*10.4*	*0.8*	*1.1*
TOTAL	*25.7*	*14.0*	*6.9*	*5.0*

7. TOTAL ODA GROSS

	1987
Australia	6.4
Austria	–
Belgium	–
Canada	–
Denmark	–
Finland	–
France	–
Germany	0.1
Ireland	–
Italy	–
Japan	0.2
Netherlands	–
New Zealand	6.5
Norway	–
Sweden	–
Switzerland	–
United Kingdom	11.7
United States	–
TOTAL	*24.9*
AF.D.F.	–
AF.D.B.	–
AS.D.B	–
CAR.D.B.	–
E.E.C.	0.3
IBRD	–
IDA	–
I.D.B.	–
IFAD	–
I.F.C.	–
IMF TRUST FUND	–
U.N. AGENCIES	–
UNDP	0.5
UNTA	0.0
UNICEF	–
UNRWA	–
WFP	–
UNHCR	–
Other Multilateral	0.0
Arab Agencies	–
TOTAL	*0.8*
ARAB COUNTRIES	–
E.E.C.+ MEMBERS	*12.0*
TOTAL	*25.7*

8. GRANTS

	1987
Australia	6.4
Austria	–
Belgium	–
Canada	–
Denmark	–
Finland	–
France	–
Germany	0.1
Ireland	–
Italy	–
Japan	0.2
Netherlands	–
New Zealand	6.5
Norway	–
Sweden	–
Switzerland	–
United Kingdom	11.7
United States	–
TOTAL	*24.9*
MULTILATERAL	*0.8*
ARAB COUNTRIES	–
E.E.C.+ MEMBERS	*12.0*
TOTAL	*25.7*

9. TOTAL OOF GROSS

	1987
Australia	–
Austria	–
Belgium	–
Canada	–
Denmark	–
Finland	–
France	–
Germany	–
Ireland	–
Italy	–
Japan	–
Netherlands	–
New Zealand	–
Norway	–
Sweden	–
Switzerland	–
United Kingdom	–
United States	–
TOTAL	–
MULTILATERAL	–
ARAB COUNTRIES	–
E.E.C.+ MEMBERS	–
TOTAL	–

TUVALU

10. ODA COMMITMENTS

1988	1989	1990		1987	1988	1989	1990
1.6	1.0	1.7		1.3	1.2	2.3	0.6
–	–	–		–	–	–	–
–	–	–		–	–	–	–
–	–	–		0.1	–	–	–
–	–	–		–	–	–	–
–	–	–		–	–	–	–
–	–	–		–	–	–	–
0.1	0.1	0.1		0.1	0.1	0.1	0.1
–	–	–		–	–	–	–
–	–	–		–	–	–	–
0.3	3.0	1.0		0.2	2.3	2.3	0.2
0.0	–	–		–	–	–	–
1.2	1.1	1.1		3.3	1.0	–	1.0
–	–	–		–	–	–	–
–	–	–		–	–	–	–
10.1	0.6	0.9		8.6	7.9	0.6	1.1
–	–	–		0.0	0.0	0.0	0.0
13.3	*5.7*	*4.8*		*13.7*	*12.4*	*5.2*	*3.1*
–	–	–		–	–	–	–
–	–	–		–	–	–	–
0.2	0.2	0.2		0.9	0.0	–	–
–	–	–		–	–	–	–
–	–	–		–	–	–	–
–	–	–		–	–	–	–
–	–	–		0.5	0.4	1.1	0.1
0.4	1.0	0.0		–	–	–	–
0.0	0.0	0.0		–	–	–	–
–	–	–		–	–	–	–
–	–	–		–	–	–	–
0.0	0.0	0.0		–	–	–	–
–	–	–		–	–	–	–
0.7	*1.2*	*0.2*		*1.4*	*0.5*	*1.1*	*0.1*
–	–	–		–	–	–	–
10.4	*0.8*	*1.1*		*9.6*	*8.0*	*0.6*	*1.2*
14.0	*6.9*	*5.0*		*15.1*	*12.9*	*6.2*	*3.1*

11. TECH. COOP. GRANTS

1988	1989	1990		1987	1988	1989	1990
1.6	1.0	1.7		0.5	0.7	0.7	0.8
–	–	–		–	–	–	–
–	–	–		–	–	–	–
–	–	–		–	–	–	–
–	–	–		–	–	–	–
0.1	0.1	0.1		0.1	0.1	0.1	0.1
–	–	–		–	–	–	–
0.3	3.0	1.0		0.2	0.2	1.1	0.2
0.0	–	–		–	0.0	–	–
1.2	1.1	1.1		0.5	0.1	–	0.2
–	–	–		–	–	–	–
–	–	–		–	–	–	–
10.1	0.6	0.9		0.7	0.9	0.4	0.6
–	–	–		–	–	–	–
13.3	*5.7*	*4.8*		*2.0*	*2.0*	*2.3*	*1.9*
0.7	*1.2*	*0.2*		*0.6*	*0.4*	*1.1*	*0.1*
–	–	–		–	–	–	–
10.4	*0.8*	*1.1*		*0.9*	*1.0*	*0.5*	*0.7*
14.0	*6.9*	*5.0*		*2.6*	*2.5*	*3.4*	*1.9*

12. TOTAL OOF NET

1988	1989	1990		1987	1988	1989	1990
–	–	–		–	–	–	–
–	–	–		–	–	–	–
–	–	–		–	–	–	–
–	–	–		–	–	–	–
–	–	–		–	–	–	–
–	–	–		–	–	–	–
–	–	–		–	–	–	–
–	–	–		–	–	–	–
–	–	–		–	–	–	–
–	–	–		–	–	–	–
–	–	–		–	–	–	–
–	–	–		–	–	–	–
–	–	–		–	–	–	–
–	–	–		–	–	–	–
–	–	–		–	–	–	–
–	–	–		–	–	–	–
–	–	–		–	–	–	–
–	–	–		–	–	–	–
–	–	–		–	–	–	–

13. ODF COMMITMENTS: BY PURPOSE %

	1987	1988	1989	1990
Education	0	3	–	–
Health	–	–	–	–
Other Social Infrastr.	–	1	–	–
Water Sanitat. Sewage	–	–	–	–
Energy	–	–	–	–
Telecommunications	1	–	–	–
Transportation	21	0	–	–
Agriculture	–	16	21	–
Extractive Industries	–	–	–	–
Manufacturing	–	–	–	–
Trade Banking Tourism	–	0	0	–
Technical Cooperation	60	25	75	–
Multisector Aid	5	1	1	–
Programme	13	52	3	–
Debt Reorganisation	–	–	–	–
Food Aid	–	–	–	–
Emergency Aid	–	–	–	–
Unspecified	–	–	–	–
TOTAL	100	100	100	–

14. GRANT ELEMENT OF ODA %

DAC COUNTRIES

	1987	1988	1989	1990
Australia	100.0	100.0	100.0	–
Austria	–	–	–	–
Belgium	–	–	–	–
Canada	100.0	–	–	–
Denmark	–	–	–	–
Finland	–	–	–	–
France	–	–	–	–
Germany	100.0	100.0	100.0	–
Ireland	–	–	–	–
Italy	–	–	–	–
Japan	100.0	100.0	100.0	–
Netherlands	–	–	–	–
New Zealand	100.0	100.0	–	–
Norway	–	–	–	–
Sweden	–	–	–	–
Switzerland	–	–	–	–
United Kingdom	100.0	100.0	100.0	–
United States	100.0	100.0	100.0	–
TOTAL	*100.0*	*100.0*	*100.0*	–
MULTILATERAL	*100.0*	*100.0*	*100.0*	–
ARAB COUNTRIES	–	–	–	–
E.E.C.+ MEMBERS	*100.0*	*100.0*	*100.0*	–
TOTAL	*100.0*	*100.0*	*100.0*	–

15. OTHER AGGREGATES

OFFICIAL COMMITMENTS:

	1987	1988	1989	1990
TOTAL BILATERAL	13.7	12.4	5.2	3.1
of which:				
Arab Countries	–	–	–	–
C.E.E.C.	–	–	–	–
TOTAL MULTILATERAL	1.4	0.5	1.1	0.1
TOTAL BIL.& MULTIL.	15.1	12.9	6.2	3.1
of which:				
ODA Grants	15.1	12.9	6.2	3.1
ODA Loans	–	–	–	–

DISBURSEMENTS:

DAC COUNTRIES COMBINED

	1987	1988	1989	1990
OFFICIAL & PRIVATE				
GROSS:				
Contractual Lending	–	–	–	–
Export Credits, Total	–	–	–	–
Export Credits, Priv.	–	–	–	–
NET:				
Contractual Lending	–	–	–	–
Export Credits Total	–	–	–	–
PRIVATE SECTOR NET	–	–	–	–
Direct Investment	–	–	–	–
Portfolio Investment	–	–	–	–
Export Credits	–	–	–	–

MARKET BORROWING:

CHANGE IN CLAIMS

	1987	1988	1989	1990
Banks	–	–	–	1.0

MEMORANDUM ITEM:

	1987	1988	1989	1990
C.E.E.C. (Gross)	–	–	–	–

	1987	1988	1989	1990		1987	1988	1989	1990		1987

1. TOTAL RECEIPTS NET / 4. TOTAL ODA NET / 7. TOTAL ODA GROSS

DAC COUNTRIES

	1987	1988	1989	1990		1987	1988	1989	1990		1987
Australia	0.1	0.6	0.6	0.5		0.1	0.6	0.6	0.5	Australia	0.1
Austria	0.1	7.7	4.8	7.8		0.1	7.7	4.8	7.8	Austria	0.1
Belgium	1.7	1.0	-0.1	10.0		0.5	0.5	0.4	10.6	Belgium	0.5
Canada	2.1	11.6	6.6	7.1		2.1	11.6	6.6	7.1	Canada	2.1
Denmark	4.9	12.0	16.0	25.7		4.9	11.6	15.8	25.4	Denmark	4.9
Finland	0.7	7.6	0.8	1.5		0.7	7.6	0.8	1.5	Finland	0.7
France	0.8	-5.8	0.5	5.0		1.1	2.6	5.7	7.2	France	1.1
Germany	16.1	18.1	19.6	27.1		15.8	18.7	19.9	27.0	Germany	15.8
Ireland	0.1	0.2	0.1	0.1		0.1	0.2	0.1	0.1	Ireland	0.1
Italy	30.7	23.5	32.5	29.0		25.1	21.8	14.0	44.6	Italy	25.1
Japan	0.5	10.4	0.2	8.2		0.5	9.5	1.1	8.0	Japan	0.6
Netherlands	1.9	19.4	1.9	2.6		2.2	6.3	5.4	3.8	Netherlands	2.2
New Zealand	0.0	–	–	–		0.0	–	–	–	New Zealand	0.0
Norway	2.7	3.5	4.5	7.4		2.7	3.5	4.5	7.4	Norway	2.7
Sweden	4.0	11.2	16.3	14.5		4.0	11.2	16.3	14.5	Sweden	4.0
Switzerland	1.8	9.0	3.1	12.5		1.8	9.0	3.1	12.5	Switzerland	1.8
United Kingdom	15.5	51.8	47.5	49.3		11.2	48.8	39.8	35.5	United Kingdom	12.7
United States	14.0	18.0	20.0	30.0		14.0	17.0	20.0	30.0	United States	14.0
TOTAL	*97.7*	*199.7*	*175.0*	*238.2*		*86.8*	*188.0*	*158.9*	*243.4*	*TOTAL*	*88.4*

MULTILATERAL

AF.D.F.	0.9	19.1	21.4	23.2		0.9	19.1	21.4	23.2	AF.D.F.	0.9
AF.D.B.	13.3	2.0	-7.6	-5.7		–	–	–	–	AF.D.B.	–
AS.D.B	–	–	–	–		–	–	–	–	AS.D.B	–
CAR.D.B.	–	–	–	–		–	–	–	–	CAR.D.B.	–
E.E.C.	31.7	39.3	35.7	35.7		31.7	39.3	35.7	35.7	E.E.C.	31.8
IBRD	-2.5	-3.0	-5.0	-4.0		–	–	–	–	IBRD	–
IDA	110.6	67.0	91.0	191.0		110.6	67.0	91.0	191.0	IDA	111.3
I.D.B.	–	–	–	–		–	–	–	–	I.D.B.	–
IFAD	4.3	1.3	1.5	5.7		4.3	1.3	1.5	5.7	IFAD	5.0
I.F.C.	3.3	2.8	–	–		–	–	–	–	I.F.C.	–
IMF TRUST FUND	–	–	–	–		–	–	–	–	IMF TRUST FUND	–
U.N. AGENCIES	–	–	–	–		–	–	–	–	U.N. AGENCIES	–
UNDP	8.8	12.7	15.6	16.2		8.8	12.7	15.6	16.2	UNDP	8.8
UNTA	1.5	1.2	1.8	1.3		1.5	1.2	1.8	1.3	UNTA	1.5
UNICEF	7.0	9.4	12.5	11.8		7.0	9.4	12.5	11.8	UNICEF	7.0
UNRWA	–	–	–	–		–	–	–	–	UNRWA	–
WFP	14.3	15.4	15.0	16.5		14.3	15.4	15.0	16.5	WFP	14.3
UNHCR	7.5	5.8	6.2	2.5		7.5	5.8	6.2	2.5	UNHCR	7.5
Other Multilateral	1.5	6.6	8.1	8.0		1.5	6.6	8.1	8.0	Other Multilateral	1.5
Arab Agencies	0.0	-0.3	7.6	–		0.4	-2.3	3.8	–	Arab Agencies	3.4
TOTAL	*202.1*	*179.3*	*203.7*	*302.1*		*188.5*	*175.4*	*212.5*	*311.8*	*TOTAL*	*193.0*
ARAB COUNTRIES	**4.9**	**-0.1**	**31.2**	**2.3**		**4.9**	**-0.1**	**31.2**	**2.3**	**ARAB COUNTRIES**	**5.9**
E.E.C.+ MEMBERS	*103.5*	*159.5*	*153.8*	*184.5*		*92.5*	*149.8*	*136.9*	*189.9*	*E.E.C.+ MEMBERS*	*94.2*
TOTAL	**304.8**	**378.8**	**409.8**	**542.5**		**280.2**	**363.3**	**402.6**	**557.5**	**TOTAL**	**287.3**

2. ODA LOANS GROSS / 5. ODA LOANS NET / 8. GRANTS

DAC COUNTRIES

	1987	1988	1989	1990		1987	1988	1989	1990		1987
Australia	–	–	–	–		–	–	–	–	Australia	0.1
Austria	–	7.5	4.3	6.6		–	7.5	4.3	6.6	Austria	0.1
Belgium	–	–	–	–		–	–	–	–	Belgium	0.5
Canada	–	–	–	–		–	-10.0	–	–	Canada	2.1
Denmark	–	–	–	–		–	–	–	–	Denmark	4.9
Finland	–	7.2	–	–		–	7.2	–	–	Finland	0.7
France	0.0	1.7	3.5	3.2		0.0	1.5	3.5	3.0	France	1.1
Germany	–	–	–	–		–	–	–	–	Germany	15.8
Ireland	–	–	–	–		–	–	–	–	Ireland	0.1
Italy	6.7	3.7	3.4	29.3		6.7	3.7	3.4	28.9	Italy	18.4
Japan	–	–	–	–		-0.1	–	–	-1.4	Japan	0.6
Netherlands	–	2.8	2.3	–		–	2.8	2.3	–	Netherlands	2.2
New Zealand	–	–	–	–		–	–	–	–	New Zealand	0.0
Norway	–	–	–	–		–	–	–	–	Norway	2.7
Sweden	–	–	–	–		–	–	–	–	Sweden	4.0
Switzerland	–	–	–	–		–	–	–	–	Switzerland	1.8
United Kingdom	–	0.3	–	–		-1.6	-0.9	-0.9	-0.6	United Kingdom	12.7
United States	–	4.0	6.0	-2.0		–	3.0	5.0	-11.0	United States	14.0
TOTAL	*6.7*	*27.0*	*19.6*	*37.0*		*5.1*	*14.7*	*17.6*	*25.5*	*TOTAL*	*81.6*
MULTILATERAL	*121.2*	*91.5*	*118.2*	*222.6*		*116.7*	*86.0*	*116.1*	*214.1*	*MULTILATERAL*	*71.8*
ARAB COUNTRIES	**5.9**	**1.0**	**31.7**	**2.3**		**4.9**	**-0.1**	**31.0**	**2.3**	**ARAB COUNTRIES**	**0.0**
E.E.C.+ MEMBERS	*7.3*	*10.1*	*9.3*	*32.5*		*5.6*	*8.1*	*7.6*	*30.7*	*E.E.C.+ MEMBERS*	*86.9*
TOTAL	**133.8**	**119.5**	**169.4**	**261.9**		**126.7**	**100.6**	**164.8**	**241.8**	**TOTAL**	**153.5**

3. TOTAL OFFICIAL GROSS / 6. TOTAL OFFICIAL NET / 9. TOTAL OOF GROSS

DAC COUNTRIES

	1987	1988	1989	1990		1987	1988	1989	1990		1987
Australia	0.1	0.6	0.6	0.5		0.1	0.6	0.6	0.5	Australia	–
Austria	0.1	7.7	4.8	7.8		0.1	7.7	4.8	7.8	Austria	–
Belgium	0.5	0.5	0.4	10.6		0.5	0.5	0.4	10.6	Belgium	–
Canada	2.1	21.6	6.6	7.1		2.1	11.6	6.6	7.1	Canada	–
Denmark	4.9	12.0	16.0	25.7		4.9	12.0	16.0	25.7	Denmark	0.0
Finland	0.7	7.6	0.8	1.5		0.7	7.6	0.8	1.5	Finland	–
France	1.1	2.8	5.8	7.4		1.0	-2.7	5.7	7.2	France	–
Germany	15.8	18.7	19.9	27.0		15.8	18.1	19.8	26.8	Germany	–
Ireland	0.1	0.2	0.1	0.1		0.1	0.2	0.1	0.1	Ireland	–
Italy	25.1	21.8	54.1	48.5		25.1	21.8	27.3	32.3	Italy	–
Japan	0.6	9.5	1.1	9.5		0.5	9.5	1.1	8.0	Japan	–
Netherlands	2.2	11.9	5.4	3.8		2.0	11.8	5.0	3.2	Netherlands	–
New Zealand	0.0	–	–	–		0.0	–	–	–	New Zealand	–
Norway	2.7	3.5	4.5	7.4		2.7	3.5	4.5	7.4	Norway	–
Sweden	4.0	11.2	16.3	14.5		4.0	11.2	16.3	14.5	Sweden	–
Switzerland	1.8	9.0	3.1	12.5		1.8	9.0	3.1	12.5	Switzerland	–
United Kingdom	17.0	50.9	46.6	42.6		15.5	49.8	45.7	42.0	United Kingdom	4.3
United States	14.0	20.0	21.0	39.0		14.0	18.0	20.0	30.0	United States	–
TOTAL	*92.7*	*209.4*	*207.0*	*265.3*		*90.8*	*189.9*	*177.9*	*237.1*	*TOTAL*	*4.3*
MULTILATERAL	*214.5*	*198.8*	*221.9*	*326.1*		*202.1*	*179.3*	*203.7*	*302.1*	*MULTILATERAL*	*21.5*
ARAB COUNTRIES	**5.9**	**1.0**	**31.8**	**2.3**		**4.9**	**-0.1**	**31.2**	**2.3**	**ARAB COUNTRIES**	**–**
E.E.C.+ MEMBERS	*98.5*	*158.9*	*184.7*	*202.0*		*96.6*	*150.7*	*155.8*	*183.6*	*E.E.C.+ MEMBERS*	*4.3*
TOTAL	**313.1**	**409.2**	**460.7**	**593.6**		**297.9**	**369.1**	**412.7**	**541.4**	**TOTAL**	**25.8**

10. ODA COMMITMENTS

1988	1989	1990	1987	1988	1989	1990
0.6	0.6	0.5	0.2	0.4	0.7	0.6
7.7	4.8	7.8	0.1	8.2	5.0	19.6
0.5	0.4	10.6	0.9	1.7	0.4	10.6
21.6	6.6	7.1	15.3	14.5	4.7	14.1
11.6	15.8	25.4	30.1	14.6	22.2	56.0
7.6	0.8	1.5	0.0	7.2	1.9	1.1
2.8	5.8	7.4	1.5	10.5	8.2	13.0
18.7	19.9	27.0	14.1	25.0	16.5	43.7
0.2	0.1	0.1	0.1	0.2	0.1	0.1
21.8	14.0	45.1	29.5	16.8	8.0	43.0
9.5	1.1	9.5	2.0	10.6	6.0	16.0
6.3	5.4	3.8	2.1	6.2	5.3	4.0
–	–	–	0.0	–	–	–
3.5	4.5	7.4	1.4	–	5.7	4.0
11.2	16.3	14.5	4.0	6.3	16.3	–
9.0	3.1	12.5	1.7	2.6	11.7	1.7
49.9	40.7	36.0	22.1	64.2	36.4	37.8
18.0	21.0	39.0	13.7	29.4	21.1	67.7
200.3	160.8	255.0	138.9	218.3	170.2	333.0
19.1	21.4	23.2	37.8	–	3.8	86.0
–	–	–	–	–	–	–
–	–	–	–	–	–	–
40.0	36.4	36.4	83.2	34.9	33.0	33.0
–	–	–	–	–	–	–
68.0	92.0	193.0	120.0	132.0	88.0	336.0
–	–	–	–	–	–	–
1.3	1.5	6.0	12.1	–	–	–
–	–	–	–	–	–	–
–	–	–	–	–	–	–
–	–	–	40.5	51.1	59.2	56.2
12.7	15.6	16.2	–	–	–	–
1.2	1.8	1.3	–	–	–	–
9.4	12.5	11.8	–	–	–	–
–	–	–	–	–	–	–
15.4	15.0	16.5	–	–	–	–
5.8	6.2	2.5	–	–	–	–
6.6	8.1	8.0	–	–	–	–
1.5	4.2	0.7	5.6	14.8	0.2	0.0
180.9	214.6	315.6	299.2	232.7	184.2	511.3
1.0	31.8	2.3	2.2	7.5	130.0	–
151.7	138.4	191.7	183.6	174.1	130.1	241.2
382.2	407.2	572.8	440.2	458.5	484.4	844.2

11. TECH. COOP. GRANTS

1988	1989	1990	1987	1988	1989	1990
0.6	0.6	0.5	0.1	0.4	0.4	0.4
0.1	0.5	1.2	0.1	0.1	0.1	0.9
0.5	0.4	10.6	0.3	0.3	0.2	0.0
21.6	6.6	7.1	–	0.2	0.5	1.4
11.6	15.8	25.4	0.3	0.4	0.2	2.5
0.4	0.8	1.5	0.1	0.1	–	–
1.1	2.2	4.2	1.1	0.9	1.0	1.5
18.7	19.9	27.0	4.9	11.6	10.5	14.2
0.2	0.1	0.1	0.1	0.2	0.1	0.1
18.1	10.6	15.8	9.3	3.2	1.3	1.4
9.5	1.1	9.5	0.2	0.4	0.4	0.6
3.5	3.1	3.8	0.7	2.6	2.5	3.3
–	–	–	0.0	–	–	–
3.5	4.5	7.4	0.2	0.2	0.6	0.4
11.2	16.3	14.5	0.9	–	0.3	1.5
9.0	3.1	12.5	0.1	0.0	–	–
49.7	40.7	36.0	5.6	10.8	11.4	9.4
14.0	15.0	41.0	4.0	7.0	14.0	16.0
173.3	141.2	218.0	27.8	38.5	43.4	53.7
89.5	96.4	93.0	29.2	37.4	44.2	39.7
–	0.1	–	–	–	–	–
141.6	129.2	159.3	25.2	31.7	27.2	32.5
262.7	237.8	311.0	57.0	75.9	87.6	93.4

12. TOTAL OOF NET

1988	1989	1990	1987	1988	1989	1990
–	–	–	–	–	–	–
–	0.0	–	–	–	0.0	–
–	–	–	–	–	–	–
0.5	0.3	0.3	0.0	0.5	0.3	0.2
–	–	–	–	–	–	–
–	–	–	0.0	-5.3	–	–
–	–	–	–	-0.6	-0.1	-0.2
–	–	–	–	–	–	–
–	40.1	3.4	–	–	13.3	-12.3
–	–	–	–	–	–	–
5.7	–	–	-0.2	5.5	-0.4	-0.6
–	–	–	–	–	–	–
–	–	–	–	–	–	–
–	–	–	–	–	–	–
1.0	5.9	6.6	4.3	1.0	5.9	6.6
2.0	–	–	–	1.0	–	–
9.1	46.2	10.3	4.1	2.0	19.0	-6.3
17.9	7.3	10.5	13.6	3.8	-8.8	-9.7
–	–	–	–	–	–	–
7.1	46.2	10.3	4.1	1.0	19.0	-6.3
27.0	53.5	20.8	17.7	5.8	10.2	-16.1

13. ODF COMMITMENTS: BY PURPOSE %

	1987	1988	1989	1990
Education	0	5	0	–
Health	6	10	3	–
Other Social Infrastr.	31	4	2	–
Water Sanitat. Sewage	1	1	1	–
Energy	–	–	2	–
Telecommunications	2	–	12	–
Transportation	6	9	7	–
Agriculture	23	16	3	–
Extractive Industries	–	–	3	–
Manufacturing	2	2	29	–
Trade Banking Tourism	–	8	0	–
Technical Cooperation	18	17	22	–
Multisector Aid	–	2	0	–
Programme	6	24	11	–
Debt Reorganisation	1	0	1	–
Food Aid	2	1	2	–
Emergency Aid	2	2	2	–
Unspecified	0	–	–	–
TOTAL	100	100	100	–

14. GRANT ELEMENT OF ODA %

DAC COUNTRIES

	1987	1988	1989	1990
Australia	100.0	100.0	100.0	–
Austria	100.0	100.0	93.4	–
Belgium	100.0	100.0	100.0	–
Canada	100.0	100.0	100.0	–
Denmark	100.0	100.0	100.0	–
Finland	100.0	83.8	100.0	–
France	100.0	64.4	100.0	–
Germany	100.0	100.0	100.0	–
Ireland	100.0	100.0	100.0	–
Italy	100.0	100.0	100.0	–
Japan	100.0	100.0	100.0	–
Netherlands	100.0	100.0	100.0	–
New Zealand	100.0	–	–	–
Norway	100.0	–	100.0	–
Sweden	100.0	100.0	100.0	–
Switzerland	100.0	100.0	100.0	–
United Kingdom	100.0	100.0	100.0	–
United States	100.0	95.6	90.9	–
TOTAL	100.0	97.0	98.6	–
MULTILATERAL	87.4	84.5	89.4	–
ARAB COUNTRIES	47.8	80.6	30.7	–
E.E.C.+ MEMBERS	100.0	97.8	100.0	–
TOTAL	91.1	89.4	76.7	–

15. OTHER AGGREGATES

OFFICIAL COMMITMENTS:

	1987	1988	1989	1990
TOTAL BILATERAL	152.1	234.8	368.8	342.0
of which:				
Arab Countries	2.2	7.5	155.0	–
C.E.E.C.	0.1	–	–	–
TOTAL MULTILATERAL	308.9	246.9	191.6	539.7
TOTAL BIL.& MULTIL.	460.9	481.8	560.4	881.7
of which:				
ODA Grants	260.4	274.0	242.8	363.4
ODA Loans	179.9	184.5	241.6	480.8

DISBURSEMENTS:

DAC COUNTRIES COMBINED

OFFICIAL & PRIVATE	1987	1988	1989	1990
GROSS:				
Contractual Lending	17.2	38.6	74.4	65.4
Export Credits, Total	6.1	2.5	8.7	18.1
Export Credits, Priv.	6.1	2.5	8.7	18.1
NET:				
Contractual Lending	12.6	17.6	42.5	32.6
Export Credits Total	3.4	-0.1	5.9	13.4
PRIVATE SECTOR NET	6.9	9.7	-2.9	1.1
Direct Investment	–	4.7	-1.8	0.1
Portfolio Investment	3.5	4.1	-7.0	-12.4
Export Credits	3.4	0.9	5.9	13.4

MARKET BORROWING:

CHANGE IN CLAIMS

	1987	1988	1989	1990
Banks	-17.0	6.0	7.0	7.0

MEMORANDUM ITEM:

	1987	1988	1989	1990
C.E.E.C. (Gross)	0.1	–	–	–

DISBURSEMENTS, UNLESS OTHERWISE STATE

	1987	1988	1989	1990		1987	1988	1989	1990		1987
1. TOTAL RECEIPTS NET					**4. TOTAL ODA NET**					**7. TOTAL ODA GROSS**	
DAC COUNTRIES											
Australia	–	–	–	–		–	–	–	–	Australia	–
Austria	0.0	0.0	0.0	0.1		0.0	0.0	0.0	0.1	Austria	0.0
Belgium	-8.6	-3.6	-0.2	7.0		0.1	0.2	0.2	0.7	Belgium	0.1
Canada	1.0	1.3	1.4	1.3		1.0	1.3	1.4	1.3	Canada	1.0
Denmark	0.4	0.0	-0.1	0.0		–	–	–	–	Denmark	–
Finland	0.0	-0.3	-0.3	0.0		0.0	0.0	0.0	0.0	Finland	0.0
France	18.1	18.4	48.0	44.5		2.3	3.5	4.7	7.4	France	2.3
Germany	13.7	14.3	3.2	51.1		6.3	6.3	8.0	8.7	Germany	6.3
Ireland	–	–	–	–		–	–	–	–	Ireland	–
Italy	-2.3	9.7	5.7	4.9		1.0	3.8	6.4	8.6	Italy	1.0
Japan	5.8	7.7	23.7	9.9		2.1	3.2	4.4	4.5	Japan	2.3
Netherlands	42.5	18.0	1.2	17.1		1.0	1.3	1.2	1.5	Netherlands	1.0
New Zealand	–	–	–	–		–	–	–	–	New Zealand	–
Norway	0.1	0.0	0.0	0.1		0.1	0.1	0.0	0.1	Norway	0.1
Sweden	1.8	1.0	1.8	0.1		1.0	1.0	1.2	2.0	Sweden	1.0
Switzerland	0.0	0.1	0.1	0.1		0.0	0.1	0.1	0.1	Switzerland	0.0
United Kingdom	1.6	3.2	-2.3	0.7		0.1	0.0	0.0	0.1	United Kingdom	0.1
United States	92.0	-417.0	228.0	-241.0		-3.0	9.0	-2.0	–	United States	–
TOTAL	*166.2*	*-347.3*	*310.4*	*-104.4*		*12.1*	*29.8*	*25.7*	*34.9*	*TOTAL*	*15.3*
MULTILATERAL											
AF.D.F.	–	–	–	–		–	–	–	–	AF.D.F.	–
AF.D.B.	–	–	–	–		–	–	–	–	AF.D.B.	–
AS.D.B	–	–	–	–		–	–	–	–	AS.D.B	–
CAR.D.B.	–	–	–	–		–	–	–	–	CAR.D.B.	–
E.E.C.	1.3	0.9	1.0	1.0		1.3	0.9	1.0	1.0	E.E.C.	1.3
IBRD	37.7	24.0	36.0	8.0		–	–	–	–	IBRD	–
IDA	–	–	–	–		–	–	–	–	IDA	–
I.D.B.	45.9	39.4	44.8	28.3		1.4	6.6	7.5	6.5	I.D.B.	4.0
IFAD	–	–	–	–		–	–	–	–	IFAD	–
I.F.C.	0.1	12.9	-0.3	3.3		–	–	–	–	I.F.C.	–
IMF TRUST FUND	–	–	–	–		–	–	–	–	IMF TRUST FUND	–
U.N. AGENCIES	–	–	–	–		–	–	–	–	U.N. AGENCIES	–
UNDP	2.1	2.8	2.9	2.7		2.1	2.8	2.9	2.7	UNDP	2.1
UNTA	0.6	0.4	0.6	0.6		0.6	0.4	0.6	0.6	UNTA	0.6
UNICEF	–	–	0.0	0.2		–	–	0.0	0.2	UNICEF	–
UNRWA	–	–	–	–		–	–	–	–	UNRWA	–
WFP	–	–	–	–		–	–	–	–	WFP	–
UNHCR	–	–	–	0.1		–	–	–	0.1	UNHCR	–
Other Multilateral	0.3	0.4	0.7	0.7		0.3	0.4	0.7	0.7	Other Multilateral	0.3
Arab Agencies	–	–	–	–		–	–	–	–	Arab Agencies	–
TOTAL	*88.0*	*80.8*	*85.6*	*44.8*		*5.7*	*11.0*	*12.7*	*11.8*	*TOTAL*	*8.3*
ARAB COUNTRIES	–	–	–	–		–	–	–	–	*ARAB COUNTRIES*	–
E.E.C.+ MEMBERS	*66.7*	*60.8*	*56.5*	*126.1*		*12.1*	*16.0*	*21.4*	*27.9*	*E.E.C.+ MEMBERS*	*12.1*
TOTAL	**254.2**	**-266.6**	**396.0**	**-59.6**		**17.8**	**40.8**	**38.4**	**46.6**	**TOTAL**	**23.6**
2. ODA LOANS GROSS					**5. ODA LOANS NET**					**8. GRANTS**	
DAC COUNTRIES											
Australia	–	–	–	–		–	–	–	–	Australia	–
Austria	–	–	–	–		–	–	–	–	Austria	0.0
Belgium	–	–	–	–		–	–	–	–	Belgium	0.1
Canada	–	–	–	–		–	–	–	–	Canada	1.0
Denmark	–	–	–	–		–	–	–	–	Denmark	–
Finland	–	–	–	–		–	–	–	–	Finland	0.0
France	0.1	1.2	2.1	3.9		0.1	1.2	2.1	3.9	France	2.3
Germany	0.4	0.6	1.1	0.7		0.4	0.5	1.0	0.6	Germany	5.9
Ireland	–	–	–	–		–	–	–	–	Ireland	–
Italy	–	–	1.0	3.0		–	–	1.0	3.0	Italy	1.0
Japan	0.1	–	–	–		-0.2	-0.3	-0.3	-0.4	Japan	2.3
Netherlands	–	–	–	–		–	–	–	–	Netherlands	1.0
New Zealand	–	–	–	–		–	–	–	–	New Zealand	–
Norway	–	–	–	–		–	–	–	–	Norway	0.1
Sweden	–	–	–	–		–	–	–	–	Sweden	1.0
Switzerland	–	–	–	–		–	–	–	–	Switzerland	0.0
United Kingdom	–	–	–	–		–	–	–	–	United Kingdom	0.1
United States	–	–	–	–		-3.0	-3.0	-2.0	-2.0	United States	–
TOTAL	*0.5*	*1.8*	*4.1*	*7.7*		*-2.7*	*-1.6*	*1.8*	*5.2*	*TOTAL*	*14.8*
MULTILATERAL	*3.9*	*8.1*	*10.0*	*7.0*		*1.3*	*5.6*	*7.5*	*5.7*	*MULTILATERAL*	*4.4*
ARAB COUNTRIES	–	–	–	–		–	–	–	–	*ARAB COUNTRIES*	–
E.E.C.+ MEMBERS	*0.5*	*1.8*	*4.1*	*7.7*		*0.5*	*1.7*	*4.1*	*7.6*	*E.E.C.+ MEMBERS*	*11.7*
TOTAL	**4.4**	**9.9**	**14.1**	**14.7**		**-1.4**	**3.9**	**9.3**	**11.0**	**TOTAL**	**19.2**
3. TOTAL OFFICIAL GROSS					**6. TOTAL OFFICIAL NET**					**9. TOTAL OOF GROSS**	
DAC COUNTRIES											
Australia	–	–	–	–		–	–	–	–	Australia	–
Austria	0.0	0.0	0.0	0.1		0.0	0.0	0.0	0.1	Austria	–
Belgium	0.1	0.2	0.2	0.7		0.1	0.2	0.2	0.7	Belgium	0.0
Canada	1.0	1.3	1.4	1.3		1.0	1.3	1.4	1.3	Canada	–
Denmark	0.2	–	–	–		0.2	–	–	–	Denmark	0.2
Finland	0.0	0.0	0.0	0.0		0.0	0.0	0.0	0.0	Finland	–
France	2.3	3.5	4.7	7.4		2.3	3.5	4.7	7.4	France	–
Germany	6.3	6.4	8.2	8.9		6.3	6.3	8.1	8.8	Germany	–
Ireland	–	–	–	–		–	–	–	–	Ireland	–
Italy	1.0	3.8	6.4	8.6		-2.3	2.6	6.4	7.5	Italy	–
Japan	2.3	3.5	13.8	10.9		2.1	3.2	13.5	10.6	Japan	–
Netherlands	1.0	1.3	1.2	1.5		1.0	1.3	1.2	1.5	Netherlands	–
New Zealand	–	–	–	–		–	–	–	–	New Zealand	–
Norway	0.1	0.1	0.0	0.1		0.1	0.1	0.0	0.1	Norway	–
Sweden	1.0	1.0	1.2	2.0		1.0	1.0	1.2	2.0	Sweden	–
Switzerland	0.0	0.1	0.1	0.1		0.0	0.1	0.1	0.1	Switzerland	–
United Kingdom	0.1	0.0	0.0	0.1		0.1	0.0	0.0	0.1	United Kingdom	–
United States	–	12.0	–	2.0		-3.0	9.0	-6.0	-4.0	United States	–
TOTAL	*15.6*	*33.2*	*37.3*	*43.6*		*9.0*	*28.7*	*30.9*	*36.0*	*TOTAL*	*0.2*
MULTILATERAL	*123.4*	*123.9*	*132.3*	*114.5*		*88.0*	*80.8*	*85.6*	*44.8*	*MULTILATERAL*	*115.1*
ARAB COUNTRIES	–	–	–	–		–	–	–	–	*ARAB COUNTRIES*	–
E.E.C.+ MEMBERS	*12.4*	*16.1*	*21.6*	*28.1*		*9.1*	*14.9*	*21.5*	*26.9*	*E.E.C.+ MEMBERS*	*0.2*
TOTAL	**138.9**	**157.1**	**169.6**	**158.1**		**97.0**	**109.4**	**116.5**	**80.8**	**TOTAL**	**115.3**

1988	1989	1990		1987	1988	1989	1990

10. ODA COMMITMENTS

1988	1989	1990	1987	1988	1989	1990
–	–	–	–	–	–	–
0.0	0.0	0.1	0.0	0.0	0.0	0.1
0.2	0.2	0.7	0.1	0.2	0.2	0.7
1.3	1.4	1.3	1.2	2.7	1.1	1.5
–	–	–	–	–	–	–
0.0	0.0	0.0	–	–	0.1	0.0
3.5	4.7	7.4	2.3	2.3	9.7	3.5
6.4	8.0	8.8	9.0	8.4	14.1	8.5
–	–	–	–	–	–	–
3.8	6.4	8.6	1.1	10.1	34.5	3.4
3.5	4.7	4.8	2.3	4.4	56.7	4.8
1.3	1.2	1.5	0.9	1.3	1.2	1.5
–	–	–	–	–	–	–
0.1	0.0	0.1	–	–	–	–
1.0	1.2	2.0	0.6	1.5	0.9	0.5
0.1	0.1	0.1	–	–	–	–
0.0	0.0	0.1	0.1	0.0	0.0	0.1
12.0	–	2.0	12.2	–	0.2	5.1
33.2	*28.1*	*37.3*	*29.6*	*30.9*	*118.6*	*29.5*

1988	1989	1990	1987	1988	1989	1990
–	–	–	–	–	–	–
–	–	–	–	–	–	–
–	–	–	–	–	–	–
0.9	1.0	1.0	1.0	1.1	0.7	0.7
–	–	–	–	–	–	–
9.1	10.0	7.8	2.1	–	–	–
–	–	–	–	–	–	–
–	–	–	3.1	3.6	4.2	4.3
2.8	2.9	2.7	–	–	–	–
0.4	0.6	0.6	–	–	–	–
–	0.0	0.2	–	–	–	–
–	–	–	–	–	–	–
–	–	0.1	–	–	–	–
0.4	0.7	0.7	–	–	–	–
–	–	–	–	–	–	–
13.6	*15.1*	*13.0*	*6.1*	*4.7*	*4.9*	*5.0*
–	–	–	–	–	–	–
16.1	*21.5*	*27.9*	*14.3*	*23.4*	*60.4*	*18.2*
46.8	*43.2*	*50.4*	*35.7*	*35.5*	*123.5*	*34.5*

11. TECH. COOP. GRANTS

1988	1989	1990	1987	1988	1989	1990
–	–	–	–	–	–	–
0.0	0.0	0.1	0.0	0.0	0.0	0.1
0.2	0.2	0.7	0.1	0.0	–	0.1
1.3	1.4	1.3	–	0.0	0.2	0.2
–	–	–	–	–	–	–
0.0	0.0	0.0	0.0	–	–	–
2.3	2.6	3.5	2.3	2.3	2.6	3.5
5.9	7.0	8.1	5.9	5.9	6.1	7.5
–	–	–	–	–	–	–
3.8	5.4	5.5	1.0	1.9	3.3	2.8
3.5	4.7	4.8	1.9	3.5	4.1	4.5
1.3	1.2	1.5	0.9	1.3	1.2	1.5
–	–	–	–	–	–	–
0.1	0.0	0.1	–	–	–	–
1.0	1.2	2.0	1.0	1.0	1.0	1.3
0.1	0.1	0.1	0.0	0.1	–	–
0.0	0.0	0.1	0.0	0.0	0.0	0.1
12.0	–	2.0	–	–	–	–
31.4	*23.9*	*29.6*	*13.1*	*16.0*	*18.6*	*21.4*
5.5	*5.1*	*6.1*	*3.5*	*3.5*	*4.2*	*4.3*
–	–	–	–	–	–	–
14.4	*17.4*	*20.3*	*10.6*	*11.4*	*13.2*	*15.4*
36.9	*29.1*	*35.7*	*16.6*	*19.5*	*22.7*	*25.7*

12. TOTAL OOF NET

1988	1989	1990	1987	1988	1989	1990
–	–	–	–	–	–	–
–	–	–	0.0	–	–	–
–	–	–	–	–	–	–
–	–	–	0.2	–	–	–
–	–	–	–	–	–	–
–	–	–	–	–	–	–
–	0.1	0.1	–	–	0.1	0.1
–	–	–	–	–	–	–
–	–	0.0	-3.3	-1.1	–	-1.1
–	9.1	6.1	–	–	9.1	6.1
–	–	–	–	–	–	–
–	–	–	–	–	–	–
–	–	–	–	–	–	–
–	–	–	–	–	–	–
–	–	–	–	–	-4.0	-4.0
–	9.2	6.3	-3.1	-1.1	5.2	1.1
110.3	117.2	101.5	82.3	69.7	72.9	33.1
–	–	–	–	–	–	–
–	0.1	0.2	-3.1	-1.1	0.1	-0.9
110.3	*126.4*	*107.7*	*79.2*	*68.6*	*78.1*	*34.2*

	1987	1988	1989	1990

13. ODF COMMITMENTS: BY PURPOSE %

	1987	1988	1989	1990
Education	0	4	0	–
Health	–	–	0	–
Other Social Infrastr.	0	1	10	–
Water Sanitat. Sewage	–	19	–	–
Energy	–	–	–	–
Telecommunications	–	–	3	–
Transportation	33	–	32	–
Agriculture	20	29	13	–
Extractive Industries	0	–	–	–
Manufacturing	8	29	2	–
Trade Banking Tourism	–	–	7	–
Technical Cooperation	7	18	6	–
Multisector Aid	0	–	–	–
Programme	31	–	27	–
Debt Reorganisation	–	–	–	–
Food Aid	–	–	–	–
Emergency Aid	–	–	–	–
Unspecified	–	–	0	–
TOTAL	100	100	100	–

14. GRANT ELEMENT OF ODA %

DAC COUNTRIES

	1987	1988	1989	1990
Australia	–	–	–	–
Austria	100.0	100.0	100.0	–
Belgium	100.0	100.0	100.0	–
Canada	100.0	100.0	100.0	–
Denmark	–	–	–	–
Finland	–	–	100.0	–
France	100.0	100.0	76.8	–
Germany	100.0	100.0	100.0	–
Ireland	–	–	–	–
Italy	100.0	100.0	62.5	–
Japan	98.4	100.0	49.2	–
Netherlands	100.0	100.0	100.0	–
New Zealand	–	–	–	–
Norway	–	–	–	–
Sweden	100.0	100.0	100.0	–
Switzerland	–	–	–	–
United Kingdom	100.0	100.0	100.0	–
United States	100.0	–	100.0	–
TOTAL	*99.9*	*100.0*	*62.9*	–
MULTILATERAL	*100.0*	*89.1*	*100.0*	–
ARAB COUNTRIES	–	–	–	–
E.E.C.+ MEMBERS	*100.0*	*100.0*	*74.8*	–
TOTAL	*99.9*	*98.0*	*64.4*	–

15. OTHER AGGREGATES

OFFICIAL COMMITMENTS:

	1987	1988	1989	1990
TOTAL BILATERAL	29.6	107.5	190.7	29.5
of which:				
Arab Countries	–	–	–	–
C.E.E.C.	–	–	–	–
TOTAL MULTILATERAL	260.7	39.2	323.4	107.5
TOTAL BIL.& MULTIL.	290.3	146.7	514.0	137.0
of which:				
ODA Grants	33.5	35.5	34.5	34.5
ODA Loans	2.2	–	89.0	–

DISBURSEMENTS:

DAC COUNTRIES COMBINED

	1987	1988	1989	1990
OFFICIAL & PRIVATE				
GROSS:				
Contractual Lending	14.4	15.7	37.9	29.5
Export Credits, Total	13.7	13.9	24.7	15.7
Export Credits, Priv.	13.7	13.9	24.6	15.5
NET:				
Contractual Lending	1.4	6.7	22.1	12.5
Export Credits Total	3.9	8.3	11.3	1.2
PRIVATE SECTOR NET	157.2	-376.0	279.5	-140.4
Direct Investment	1.4	10.4	37.7	38.9
Portfolio Investment	148.5	-395.8	226.6	-185.4
Export Credits	7.2	9.5	15.1	6.1

MARKET BORROWING:

CHANGE IN CLAIMS

	1987	1988	1989	1990
Banks	94.0	1215.0	-1249.0	-31.0

MEMORANDUM ITEM:

	1987	1988	1989	1990
C.E.E.C. (Gross)	–	–	–	–

DISBURSEMENTS, UNLESS OTHERWISE STATED

	1987	1988	1989	1990		1987	1988	1989	1990		1987
1. TOTAL RECEIPTS NET					**4. TOTAL ODA NET**					**7. TOTAL ODA GROSS**	
DAC COUNTRIES											
Australia	9.1	9.0	13.8	11.4		9.1	9.0	13.8	11.7	Australia	9.1
Austria	–	–	–	–		–	–	–	–	Austria	–
Belgium	-0.3	6.3	–	5.6		–	–	–	–	Belgium	–
Canada	0.1	0.1	0.0	0.1		0.1	0.1	0.0	0.1	Canada	0.1
Denmark	–	–	–	–		–	–	–	–	Denmark	–
Finland	–	0.0	-0.1	–		–	–	–	–	Finland	–
France	-4.7	-13.0	25.9	75.9		8.4	5.2	5.0	9.2	France	9.0
Germany	0.1	0.0	0.0	–		0.1	0.0	0.0	–	Germany	0.1
Ireland	–	–	–	–		–	–	–	–	Ireland	–
Italy	–	–	–	–		–	–	–	–	Italy	–
Japan	2.1	13.5	27.7	33.5		5.6	3.7	2.9	8.1	Japan	5.6
Netherlands	–	0.4	-6.9	0.6		–	–	–	–	Netherlands	–
New Zealand	1.6	2.2	1.3	2.1		1.6	2.2	1.3	2.1	New Zealand	1.6
Norway	–	–	–	–		–	–	–	–	Norway	–
Sweden	–	–	–	–		–	–	–	–	Sweden	–
Switzerland	–	–	–	3.2		–	–	–	3.2	Switzerland	–
United Kingdom	8.9	9.8	9.5	8.6		7.7	8.8	8.7	7.7	United Kingdom	7.7
United States	–	–	–	–		–	–	–	–	United States	–
TOTAL	*16.7*	*28.3*	*71.2*	*140.9*		*32.5*	*29.0*	*31.8*	*42.1*	*TOTAL*	*33.1*
MULTILATERAL											
AF.D.F.	–	–	–	–		–	–	–	–	AF.D.F.	–
AF.D.B.	–	–	–	–		–	–	–	–	AF.D.B.	–
AS.D.B	1.4	1.2	3.5	2.7		1.4	1.2	3.5	2.7	AS.D.B	1.4
CAR.D.B.	–	–	–	–		–	–	–	–	CAR.D.B.	–
E.E.C.	14.4	6.5	1.2	1.2		14.4	6.5	1.2	1.2	E.E.C.	14.5
IBRD	–	–	–	–		–	–	–	–	IBRD	–
IDA	0.8	–	1.0	1.0		0.8	–	1.0	1.0	IDA	0.8
I.D.B.	–	–	–	–		–	–	–	–	I.D.B.	–
IFAD	–	–	–	–		–	–	–	–	IFAD	–
I.F.C.	–	–	–	–		–	–	–	–	I.F.C.	–
IMF TRUST FUND	–	–	–	–		–	–	–	–	IMF TRUST FUND	–
U.N. AGENCIES	–	–	–	–		–	–	–	–	U.N. AGENCIES	
UNDP	0.6	1.6	1.1	0.8		0.6	1.6	1.1	0.8	UNDP	0.6
UNTA	0.7	0.5	0.6	0.5		0.7	0.5	0.6	0.5	UNTA	0.7
UNICEF	–	–	–	–		–	–	–	–	UNICEF	–
UNRWA	–	–	–	–		–	–	–	–	UNRWA	–
WFP	0.4	–	0.0	–		0.4	–	0.0	–	WFP	0.4
UNHCR	–	–	–	–		–	–	–	–	UNHCR	–
Other Multilateral	0.3	0.6	0.5	0.5		0.3	0.6	0.5	0.5	Other Multilateral	0.3
Arab Agencies	–	–	–	–		–	–	–	–	Arab Agencies	–
TOTAL	*18.5*	*10.3*	*8.0*	*6.8*		*18.5*	*10.3*	*8.0*	*6.8*	*TOTAL*	*18.6*
ARAB COUNTRIES	*–*	*–*	*–*	*–*		*–*	*–*	*–*	*–*	***ARAB COUNTRIES***	
E.E.C.+ MEMBERS	*18.4*	*10.1*	*29.7*	*91.9*		*30.6*	*20.5*	*15.0*	*18.1*	*E.E.C.+ MEMBERS*	*31.3*
TOTAL	**35.2**	**38.6**	**79.2**	**147.7**		**51.0**	**39.3**	**39.8**	**48.8**	**TOTAL**	**51.7**

	1987	1988	1989	1990		1987	1988	1989	1990		1987
2. ODA LOANS GROSS					**5. ODA LOANS NET**					**8. GRANTS**	
DAC COUNTRIES											
Australia	–	–	–	–		–	–	–	–	Australia	9.1
Austria	–	–	–	–		–	–	–	–	Austria	–
Belgium	–	–	–	–		–	–	–	–	Belgium	–
Canada	–	–	–	–		–	–	–	–	Canada	0.1
Denmark	–	–	–	–		–	–	–	–	Denmark	–
Finland	–	–	–	–		–	–	–	–	Finland	–
France	2.5	1.5	0.6	3.2		1.9	1.1	0.2	2.8	France	6.5
Germany	–	–	–	–		–	–	–	–	Germany	0.1
Ireland	–	–	–	–		–	–	–	–	Ireland	–
Italy	–	–	–	–		–	–	–	–	Italy	–
Japan	–	–	0.5	0.4		–	–	0.5	0.4	Japan	5.6
Netherlands	–	–	–	–		–	–	–	–	Netherlands	–
New Zealand	–	–	–	–		–	–	–	–	New Zealand	1.6
Norway	–	–	–	–		–	–	–	–	Norway	–
Sweden	–	–	–	–		–	–	–	–	Sweden	–
Switzerland	–	–	–	–		–	–	–	–	Switzerland	–
United Kingdom	0.4	0.5	0.7	0.4		0.3	0.4	0.7	-1.8	United Kingdom	7.4
United States	–	–	–	–		–	–	–	–	United States	–
TOTAL	*2.9*	*1.9*	*1.8*	*4.0*		*2.2*	*1.6*	*1.4*	*1.4*	*TOTAL*	*30.2*
MULTILATERAL	*1.8*	*0.8*	*4.7*	*4.3*		*1.7*	*0.7*	*4.7*	*4.2*	*MULTILATERAL*	*16.8*
ARAB COUNTRIES	*–*	*–*	*–*	*–*		*–*	*–*	*–*	*–*	***ARAB COUNTRIES***	*–*
E.E.C.+ MEMBERS	*2.9*	*1.9*	*1.9*	*4.2*		*2.2*	*1.5*	*1.5*	*1.6*	*E.E.C.+ MEMBERS*	*28.5*
TOTAL	**4.7**	**2.7**	**6.5**	**8.2**		**4.0**	**2.2**	**6.1**	**5.6**	**TOTAL**	**47.0**

	1987	1988	1989	1990		1987	1988	1989	1990		1987
3. TOTAL OFFICIAL GROSS					**6. TOTAL OFFICIAL NET**					**9. TOTAL OOF GROSS**	
DAC COUNTRIES											
Australia	9.1	9.0	13.8	11.7		9.1	9.0	13.8	11.4	Australia	–
Austria	–	–	–	–		–	–	–	–	Austria	–
Belgium	–	–	–	3.2		–	–	–	3.2	Belgium	–
Canada	0.1	0.1	0.0	0.1		0.1	0.1	0.0	0.1	Canada	–
Denmark	–	–	–	–		–	–	–	–	Denmark	–
Finland	–	–	–	–		–	–	–	–	Finland	–
France	9.0	5.5	5.4	10.5		8.4	5.1	5.0	10.0	France	–
Germany	0.1	0.0	0.0	–		0.1	0.0	0.0	–	Germany	–
Ireland	–	–	–	–		–	–	–	–	Ireland	–
Italy	–	–	–	–		–	–	–	–	Italy	–
Japan	5.6	3.7	2.9	8.1		5.6	3.7	2.9	8.1	Japan	–
Netherlands	–	–	–	–		–	–	–	–	Netherlands	–
New Zealand	1.6	2.2	1.3	2.1		1.6	2.2	1.3	2.1	New Zealand	–
Norway	–	–	–	–		–	–	–	–	Norway	–
Sweden	–	–	–	–		–	–	–	–	Sweden	–
Switzerland	–	–	–	3.2		–	–	–	3.2	Switzerland	–
United Kingdom	9.1	10.0	9.5	10.8		9.1	10.0	9.5	8.6	United Kingdom	1.3
United States	–	–	–	–		–	–	–	–	United States	–
TOTAL	*34.4*	*30.5*	*32.9*	*49.7*		*33.8*	*30.1*	*32.5*	*46.7*	*TOTAL*	*1.3*
MULTILATERAL	*18.6*	*10.4*	*8.1*	*6.8*		*18.5*	*10.3*	*8.0*	*6.8*	*MULTILATERAL*	*–*
ARAB COUNTRIES	*–*	*–*	*–*	*–*		*–*	*–*	*–*	*–*	***ARAB COUNTRIES***	*–*
E.E.C.+ MEMBERS	*32.7*	*22.1*	*16.2*	*25.8*		*32.0*	*21.6*	*15.8*	*23.0*	*E.E.C.+ MEMBERS*	*1.3*
TOTAL	**53.0**	**40.9**	**41.0**	**56.5**		**52.3**	**40.4**	**40.5**	**53.4**	**TOTAL**	**1.3**

10. ODA COMMITMENTS

1988	1989	1990	1987	1988	1989	1990
9.0	13.8	11.7	11.0	6.8	21.4	4.8
–	–	–	–	–	–	–
–	–	–	–	–	–	–
0.1	0.0	0.1	0.3	0.1	–	0.2
–	–	–	–	–	–	–
–	–	–	–	–	–	–
5.5	5.4	9.6	6.5	4.1	10.3	6.5
0.0	0.0	–	0.1	0.0	0.0	–
–	–	–	–	–	–	–
–	–	–	–	–	–	–
3.7	2.9	8.1	3.6	2.5	9.4	4.8
–	–	–	0.1	0.0	–	–
2.2	1.3	2.1	1.5	1.5	–	2.0
–	–	–	–	–	–	–
–	–	3.2	–	–	–	3.2
8.8	8.8	9.9	6.0	8.6	6.7	8.5
–	–	–	–	–	–	0.0
29.3	*32.2*	*44.6*	*29.0*	*23.6*	*47.9*	*30.0*
–	–	–	–	–	–	–
–	–	–	–	–	–	–
1.2	3.5	2.7	6.9	–	–	–
–	–	–	–	–	–	–
6.6	1.3	1.3	16.0	8.1	2.8	2.8
–	1.0	1.0	–	8.0	–	–
–	–	–	–	–	–	–
–	–	–	–	–	–	–
–	–	–	2.0	2.7	2.3	1.8
1.6	1.1	0.8	–	–	–	–
0.5	0.6	0.5	–	–	–	–
–	–	–	–	–	–	–
–	0.0	–	–	–	–	–
–	–	–	–	–	–	–
0.6	0.5	0.5	–	–	–	–
–	–	–	–	–	–	–
10.4	*8.1*	*6.8*	*24.8*	*18.7*	*5.1*	*4.6*
–	–	–	–	–	–	–
20.9	*15.5*	*20.8*	*28.6*	*20.7*	*19.8*	*17.7*
39.7	*40.2*	*51.5*	*53.9*	*42.3*	*52.9*	*34.6*

11. TECH. COOP. GRANTS

1988	1989	1990	1987	1988	1989	1990
9.0	13.8	11.7	2.2	3.6	4.5	5.2
–	–	–	–	–	–	–
0.1	0.0	0.1	–	–	–	–
–	–	–	–	–	–	–
4.1	4.8	6.5	6.5	4.1	4.8	6.5
0.0	0.0	–	0.0	0.0	0.0	–
–	–	–	–	–	–	–
3.7	2.4	7.7	0.4	1.2	0.6	1.1
–	–	–	–	–	–	–
2.2	1.3	2.1	0.5	0.8	–	0.6
–	–	–	–	–	–	–
–	–	3.2	–	–	–	–
8.4	8.0	9.5	4.3	5.0	5.7	7.2
–	–	–	–	–	–	–
27.4	*30.4*	*40.7*	*13.9*	*14.7*	*15.8*	*20.5*
9.6	3.3	2.6	1.5	2.7	2.3	1.8
–	–	–	–	–	–	–
19.0	*13.5*	*16.6*	*10.9*	*9.1*	*10.6*	*13.7*
37.0	*33.7*	*43.2*	*15.5*	*17.4*	*18.0*	*22.3*

12. TOTAL OOF NET

1988	1989	1990	1987	1988	1989	1990
–	–	–	–	–	–	-0.3
–	–	3.2	–	–	–	3.2
–	–	–	–	–	–	–
–	–	–	–	–	–	–
–	–	0.9	–	0.0	–	0.8
–	–	–	–	–	–	–
–	–	–	–	–	–	–
–	–	–	–	–	–	–
–	–	–	–	–	–	–
–	–	–	–	–	–	–
1.2	0.7	0.9	1.3	1.2	0.7	0.9
–	–	–	–	–	–	–
1.2	*0.7*	*5.0*	*1.3*	*1.2*	*0.7*	*4.6*
–	–	–	–	–	–	–
–	–	–	–	–	–	–
1.2	*0.7*	*5.0*	*1.3*	*1.2*	*0.7*	*4.9*
1.2	*0.7*	*5.0*	*1.3*	*1.2*	*0.7*	*4.6*

13. ODF COMMITMENTS: BY PURPOSE %

	1987	1988	1989	1990
Education	0	2	13	–
Health	0	1	1	–
Other Social Infrastr.	–	2	8	–
Water Sanitat. Sewage	1	1	0	–
Energy	–	–	1	–
Telecommunications	–	2	9	–
Transportation	3	20	27	–
Agriculture	10	11	3	–
Extractive Industries	–	–	–	–
Manufacturing	–	–	–	–
Trade Banking Tourism	11	–	–	–
Technical Cooperation	64	58	37	–
Multisector Aid	1	1	0	–
Programme	5	3	–	–
Debt Reorganisation	–	–	–	–
Food Aid	–	–	–	–
Emergency Aid	5	1	–	–
Unspecified	–	–	–	–
TOTAL	100	100	100	–

14. GRANT ELEMENT OF ODA %

DAC COUNTRIES

	1987	1988	1989	1990
Australia	100.0	100.0	100.0	–
Austria	–	–	–	–
Belgium	–	–	–	–
Canada	100.0	100.0	–	–
Denmark	–	–	–	–
Finland	–	–	–	–
France	100.0	100.0	83.9	–
Germany	100.0	100.0	100.0	–
Ireland	–	–	–	–
Italy	–	–	–	–
Japan	100.0	100.0	97.3	–
Netherlands	100.0	100.0	–	–
New Zealand	100.0	100.0	–	–
Norway	–	–	–	–
Sweden	–	–	–	–
Switzerland	–	–	–	–
United Kingdom	100.0	100.0	100.0	–
United States	–	–	–	–
TOTAL	*100.0*	*100.0*	*95.9*	*–*
MULTILATERAL	*100.0*	*92.2*	*88.1*	*–*
ARAB COUNTRIES	*–*	*–*	*–*	*–*
E.E.C.+ MEMBERS	*100.0*	*100.0*	*91.3*	*–*
TOTAL	*100.0*	*96.7*	*94.2*	*–*

15. OTHER AGGREGATES

	1987	1988	1989	1990
OFFICIAL COMMITMENTS:				
TOTAL BILATERAL	32.8	24.2	48.8	33.8
of which:				
Arab Countries	–	–	–	–
C.E.E.C.	–	–	–	–
TOTAL MULTILATERAL	24.8	18.7	5.1	4.6
TOTAL BIL.& MULTIL.	57.6	42.9	53.9	38.4
of which:				
ODA Grants	46.6	33.8	46.1	33.9
ODA Loans	7.3	8.5	6.9	0.7
DISBURSEMENTS:				
DAC COUNTRIES COMBINED				
OFFICIAL & PRIVATE				
GROSS:				
Contractual Lending	-5.4	-5.6	21.7	0.1
Export Credits, Total	-9.6	-8.7	19.1	-5.7
Export Credits, Priv.	-9.6	-8.7	19.1	-5.7
NET:				
Contractual Lending	-6.3	-6.2	13.9	-2.9
Export Credits Total	-9.9	-8.9	11.8	-5.9
PRIVATE SECTOR NET	-17.1	-1.8	38.7	94.3
Direct Investment	-3.8	10.2	24.9	71.0
Portfolio Investment	-3.4	-3.1	2.0	29.0
Export Credits	-9.9	-8.9	11.8	-5.7
MARKET BORROWING:				
CHANGE IN CLAIMS				
Banks	–	–	–	–
MEMORANDUM ITEM:				
C.E.E.C. (Gross)	–	–	–	–

1. TOTAL RECEIPTS NET

DAC COUNTRIES	1987	1988	1989	1990
Australia	0.1	1.2	11.1	0.8
Austria	-9.9	-5.1	-0.2	1.5
Belgium	-1.5	0.3	-4.4	-0.8
Canada	–	–	–	0.0
Denmark	–	–	–	0.2
Finland	11.9	12.4	11.8	16.1
France	-3.9	18.2	1.2	17.1
Germany	2.5	6.1	5.9	19.7
Ireland	–	–	–	0.0
Italy	1.6	7.7	–	0.8
Japan	-6.4	0.6	18.8	-8.3
Netherlands	1.8	1.5	1.2	1.5
New Zealand	–	–	–	0.0
Norway	-0.3	-1.2	-0.6	0.1
Sweden	38.4	54.4	34.1	53.7
Switzerland	0.0	0.1	0.5	0.8
United Kingdom	-0.9	–	1.8	0.0
United States	1.0	1.0	2.0	2.0
TOTAL	*34.4*	*97.3*	*83.3*	*105.1*
MULTILATERAL				
AF.D.F.	–	–	–	–
AF.D.B.	–	–	–	–
AS.D.B	-0.1	-0.2	-0.1	-0.1
CAR.D.B.	–	–	–	–
E.E.C.	0.6	0.4	2.3	2.3
IBRD	–	–	–	–
IDA	0.4	–	-1.0	-1.0
I.D.B.	–	–	–	–
IFAD	–	–	–	–
I.F.C.	–	–	–	–
IMF TRUST FUND	–	–	–	–
U.N. AGENCIES	–	–	–	–
UNDP	16.4	21.3	19.4	34.1
UNTA	3.7	2.4	3.4	4.2
UNICEF	5.8	7.2	10.6	10.2
UNRWA	–	–	–	–
WFP	17.1	26.8	8.1	12.2
UNHCR	2.4	2.5	4.4	7.7
Other Multilateral	4.4	5.0	9.9	12.9
Arab Agencies	-1.0	-0.9	–	–
TOTAL	*49.7*	*64.4*	*57.0*	*82.5*
ARAB COUNTRIES	*-0.4*	*-0.7*	*7.2*	*–*
E.E.C.+ MEMBERS	0.1	34.1	8.1	40.9
TOTAL	**83.7**	**161.0**	**147.4**	**187.6**

2. ODA LOANS GROSS

DAC COUNTRIES	1987	1988	1989	1990
Australia	–	–	–	–
Austria	–	–	–	–
Belgium	–	–	–	–
Canada	–	–	–	–
Denmark	–	–	–	–
Finland	–	–	–	–
France	–	–	–	–
Germany	–	–	–	–
Ireland	–	–	–	–
Italy	–	–	–	–
Japan	–	–	–	–
Netherlands	–	–	–	–
New Zealand	–	–	–	–
Norway	–	–	–	–
Sweden	–	–	–	–
Switzerland	–	–	–	–
United Kingdom	–	–	–	–
United States	1.0	1.0	1.0	1.0
TOTAL	*1.0*	*1.0*	*1.0*	*1.0*
MULTILATERAL	*0.5*	*–*	*–*	*–*
ARAB COUNTRIES	*0.2*	*0.4*	*8.2*	*–*
E.E.C.+ MEMBERS	–	–	–	–
TOTAL	**1.6**	**1.4**	**9.2**	**1.0**

3. TOTAL OFFICIAL GROSS

DAC COUNTRIES	1987	1988	1989	1990
Australia	0.1	1.2	11.1	1.9
Austria	0.1	0.1	0.5	1.6
Belgium	2.8	0.4	0.8	0.9
Canada	–	–	–	0.0
Denmark	–	–	–	0.2
Finland	11.9	12.4	11.8	16.1
France	5.9	4.9	6.1	11.9
Germany	4.9	5.8	7.1	16.4
Ireland	–	–	–	0.0
Italy	0.0	0.0	0.0	0.8
Japan	0.3	4.8	1.6	1.3
Netherlands	1.8	1.5	1.2	1.5
New Zealand	–	–	–	0.0
Norway	0.4	0.2	0.0	0.1
Sweden	38.4	54.4	34.1	53.7
Switzerland	0.0	0.1	0.5	0.8
United Kingdom	–	–	–	0.0
United States	1.0	1.0	2.0	2.0
TOTAL	*67.5*	*86.9*	*76.7*	*109.1*
MULTILATERAL	*50.9*	*65.5*	*58.1*	*83.6*
ARAB COUNTRIES	*0.2*	*0.4*	*8.2*	*–*
E.E.C.+ MEMBERS	16.0	13.0	17.4	34.0
TOTAL	**118.5**	**152.8**	**143.0**	**192.7**

4. TOTAL ODA NET

DAC COUNTRIES	1987	1988	1989	1990
Australia	0.1	1.2	1.0	1.4
Austria	-4.3	-2.3	-0.2	1.5
Belgium	1.8	0.4	0.1	0.3
Canada	–	–	–	0.0
Denmark	–	–	–	0.2
Finland	11.9	12.4	11.8	16.1
France	5.9	4.9	6.1	11.9
Germany	4.3	5.3	6.6	16.1
Ireland	–	–	–	0.0
Italy	0.0	0.0	0.0	0.8
Japan	0.3	4.8	1.6	1.3
Netherlands	1.8	1.5	1.2	1.5
New Zealand	–	–	–	0.0
Norway	0.4	0.2	0.0	0.1
Sweden	38.4	54.4	34.1	53.7
Switzerland	0.0	0.1	0.5	0.8
United Kingdom	–	–	–	0.0
United States	1.0	1.0	2.0	2.0
TOTAL	*61.6*	*84.0*	*64.7*	*107.7*
MULTILATERAL				
AF.D.F.	–	–	–	–
AF.D.B.	–	–	–	–
AS.D.B	0.1	-0.1	–	–
CAR.D.B.	–	–	–	–
E.E.C.	0.6	0.4	2.3	2.3
IBRD	–	–	–	–
IDA	0.4	–	-1.0	-1.0
I.D.B.	–	–	–	–
IFAD	–	–	–	–
I.F.C.	–	–	–	–
IMF TRUST FUND	–	–	–	–
U.N. AGENCIES	–	–	–	–
UNDP	16.4	21.3	19.4	34.1
UNTA	3.7	2.4	3.4	4.2
UNICEF	5.8	7.2	10.6	10.2
UNRWA	–	–	–	–
WFP	17.1	26.8	8.1	12.2
UNHCR	2.4	2.5	4.4	7.7
Other Multilateral	4.4	5.0	9.9	12.9
Arab Agencies	-1.0	-0.9	–	–
TOTAL	*49.9*	*64.4*	*57.1*	*82.6*
ARAB COUNTRIES	*-0.4*	*-0.7*	*7.2*	*–*
E.E.C.+ MEMBERS	14.4	12.4	16.3	33.2
TOTAL	**111.0**	**147.8**	**129.0**	**190.3**

5. ODA LOANS NET

DAC COUNTRIES	1987	1988	1989	1990
Australia	–	–	–	–
Austria	-4.4	-2.4	-0.7	-0.1
Belgium	–	–	–	–
Canada	–	–	–	–
Denmark	–	–	–	–
Finland	–	–	–	–
France	–	–	–	–
Germany	–	–	–	–
Ireland	–	–	–	–
Italy	–	–	–	–
Japan	–	–	–	–
Netherlands	–	–	–	–
New Zealand	–	–	–	–
Norway	–	–	–	–
Sweden	–	–	–	–
Switzerland	–	–	–	–
United Kingdom	–	–	–	–
United States	1.0	1.0	1.0	1.0
TOTAL	*-3.4*	*-1.4*	*0.3*	*0.9*
MULTILATERAL	*-0.5*	*-1.0*	*-1.0*	*-1.0*
ARAB COUNTRIES	*-0.4*	*-0.7*	*7.2*	*–*
E.E.C.+ MEMBERS	–	–	–	–
TOTAL	**-4.3**	**-3.1**	**6.5**	**-0.1**

6. TOTAL OFFICIAL NET

DAC COUNTRIES	1987	1988	1989	1990
Australia	0.1	1.2	11.1	0.8
Austria	-4.3	-2.3	-0.2	1.5
Belgium	2.8	0.4	0.8	0.9
Canada	–	–	–	0.0
Denmark	–	–	–	0.2
Finland	11.9	12.4	11.8	16.1
France	5.9	4.9	6.1	11.9
Germany	4.9	5.8	7.1	16.4
Ireland	–	–	–	0.0
Italy	0.0	0.0	0.0	0.8
Japan	0.3	4.8	1.6	1.3
Netherlands	1.8	1.5	1.2	1.5
New Zealand	–	–	–	0.0
Norway	0.4	0.2	0.0	0.1
Sweden	38.4	54.4	34.1	53.7
Switzerland	0.0	0.1	0.5	0.8
United Kingdom	–	–	–	0.0
United States	1.0	1.0	2.0	2.0
TOTAL	*63.1*	*84.5*	*76.0*	*107.9*
MULTILATERAL	*49.7*	*64.4*	*57.0*	*82.5*
ARAB COUNTRIES	*-0.4*	*-0.7*	*7.2*	*–*
E.E.C.+ MEMBERS	16.0	13.0	17.4	34.0
TOTAL	**112.5**	**148.3**	**140.2**	**190.4**

7. TOTAL ODA GROSS

	1987
Australia	0.1
Austria	0.1
Belgium	1.8
Canada	–
Denmark	–
Finland	11.9
France	5.9
Germany	4.3
Ireland	–
Italy	0.0
Japan	0.3
Netherlands	1.8
New Zealand	–
Norway	0.4
Sweden	38.4
Switzerland	0.0
United Kingdom	–
United States	1.0
TOTAL	*65.9*
AF.D.F.	–
AF.D.B.	–
AS.D.B	0.1
CAR.D.B.	–
E.E.C.	0.6
IBRD	–
IDA	0.4
I.D.B.	–
IFAD	–
I.F.C.	–
IMF TRUST FUND	–
U.N. AGENCIES	–
UNDP	16.4
UNTA	3.7
UNICEF	5.8
UNRWA	–
WFP	17.1
UNHCR	2.4
Other Multilateral	4.4
TOTAL	*50.9*
ARAB COUNTRIES	*0.2*
E.E.C.+ MEMBERS	14.4
TOTAL	**116.9**

8. GRANTS

	1987
Australia	0.1
Austria	0.1
Belgium	1.8
Canada	–
Denmark	–
Finland	11.9
France	5.9
Germany	4.3
Ireland	–
Italy	0.0
Japan	0.3
Netherlands	1.8
New Zealand	–
Norway	0.4
Sweden	38.4
Switzerland	0.0
United Kingdom	–
United States	–
TOTAL	*64.9*
MULTILATERAL	*50.4*
ARAB COUNTRIES	*–*
E.E.C.+ MEMBERS	14.4
TOTAL	**115.3**

9. TOTAL OOF GROSS

	1987
Australia	–
Austria	–
Belgium	1.0
Canada	–
Denmark	–
Finland	–
France	–
Germany	0.6
Ireland	–
Italy	–
Japan	–
Netherlands	–
New Zealand	–
Norway	–
Sweden	–
Switzerland	–
United Kingdom	–
United States	–
TOTAL	*1.6*
MULTILATERAL	*–*
ARAB COUNTRIES	*–*
E.E.C.+ MEMBERS	1.6
TOTAL	**1.6**

1988	1989	1990

10. ODA COMMITMENTS

1988	1989	1990	1987	1988	1989	1990
1.2	1.0	1.4	0.8	1.0	0.9	2.4
0.1	0.5	1.6	0.1	0.1	0.5	1.6
0.4	0.1	0.3	0.1	1.0	0.1	0.3
–	–	0.0	–	–	–	0.1
–	–	0.2	–	–	–	1.0
12.4	11.8	16.1	–	11.8	22.6	5.3
4.9	6.1	11.9	5.0	4.7	3.4	10.2
5.3	6.6	16.1	4.3	5.4	7.4	21.3
–	–	0.0	–	–	–	0.0
0.0	0.0	0.8	0.0	0.0	0.0	0.9
4.8	1.6	1.3	0.3	5.0	1.5	1.5
1.5	1.2	1.5	1.4	1.5	1.2	1.5
–	–	0.0	–	–	–	–
0.2	0.0	0.1	0.8	–	–	–
54.4	34.1	53.7	39.2	54.4	33.8	50.7
0.1	0.5	0.8	–	0.1	0.4	0.7
–	–	0.0	–	–	–	0.0
1.0	2.0	2.0	0.7	0.8	0.8	0.8
86.4	*65.4*	*107.8*	*52.7*	*85.7*	*72.5*	*98.3*
–	–	–	–	–	–	–
–	–	–	–	–	–	–
–	–	–	–	–	–	–
0.4	2.3	2.3	0.3	0.4	5.2	5.2
–	–	–	–	–	–	–
–	–	–	–	–	–	–
–	–	–	–	–	–	–
			49.8	65.1	55.8	81.4
21.3	19.4	34.1	–	–	–	–
2.4	3.4	4.2	–	–	–	–
7.2	10.6	10.2	–	–	–	–
–	–	–	–	–	–	–
26.8	8.1	12.2	–	–	–	–
2.5	4.4	7.7	–	–	–	–
5.0	9.9	12.9	–	–	–	–
–	–	–	–	–	–	–
65.5	58.1	83.6	50.1	65.5	61.0	86.5
0.4	8.2	–	14.7	–	–	–
12.4	16.3	33.2	11.2	12.8	17.3	40.4
152.3	*131.8*	*191.4*	*117.6*	*151.2*	*133.5*	*184.9*

11. TECH. COOP. GRANTS

1988	1989	1990	1987	1988	1989	1990
1.2	1.0	1.4	0.0	0.6	0.1	0.3
0.1	0.5	1.6	0.1	0.1	0.1	0.1
0.4	0.1	0.3	0.1	0.1	–	–
–	–	0.0	–	–	–	–
–	–	0.2	–	–	–	–
12.4	11.8	16.1	0.0	2.3	1.9	1.0
4.9	6.1	11.9	4.5	3.5	5.0	9.4
5.3	6.6	16.1	4.0	4.6	4.6	14.0
–	–	0.0	–	–	–	0.0
0.0	0.0	0.8	0.0	0.0	0.0	0.0
4.8	1.6	1.3	0.3	4.6	1.2	1.3
1.5	1.2	1.5	1.4	1.2	0.9	1.5
–	–	0.0	–	–	–	0.0
0.2	0.0	0.1	0.3	0.2	–	0.0
54.4	34.1	53.7	30.8	16.0	16.7	2.1
0.1	0.5	0.8	0.0	0.0	–	–
–	–	0.0	–	–	–	–
–	1.0	1.0	–	–	–	–
85.4	64.4	106.8	41.6	33.2	30.6	29.8
65.5	58.1	83.6	32.7	38.3	47.7	69.1
–	–	–	–	–	–	–
12.4	16.3	33.2	10.1	9.4	10.6	24.9
150.8	*122.5*	*190.4*	*74.3*	*71.5*	*78.3*	*98.9*

12. TOTAL OOF NET

1988	1989	1990	1987	1988	1989	1990
–	10.2	0.4	–	–	10.2	-0.6
–	–	–	–	–	–	–
–	0.6	0.6	1.0	–	0.6	0.6
–	–	–	–	–	–	–
–	–	–	–	–	–	–
–	–	–	–	–	–	0.0
0.6	0.5	0.3	0.6	0.6	0.5	0.3
–	–	–	–	–	–	–
–	–	–	–	–	–	0.0
–	–	–	–	–	–	–
–	–	–	–	–	–	–
–	–	–	–	–	–	–
–	–	–	–	–	–	–
–	–	–	–	–	–	–
–	–	–	–	–	–	–
0.6	*11.3*	*1.2*	*1.6*	*0.6*	*11.3*	*0.2*
–	–	–	*-0.1*	*-0.1*	*-0.1*	*-0.1*
–	–	–	–	–	–	–
0.6	*1.1*	*0.8*	*1.6*	*0.6*	*1.1*	*0.8*
0.6	*11.3*	*1.2*	*1.5*	*0.5*	*11.1*	*0.0*

13. ODF COMMITMENTS: BY PURPOSE %

	1987	1988	1989	1990
Education	0	0	8	–
Health	2	2	4	–
Other Social Infrastr.	0	0	1	–
Water Sanitat. Sewage	3	5	12	–
Energy	0	1	1	–
Telecommunications	–	–	–	–
Transportation	1	0	3	–
Agriculture	0	0	1	–
Extractive Industries	–	–	–	–
Manufacturing	–	4	11	–
Trade Banking Tourism	–	–	–	–
Technical Cooperation	10	15	49	–
Multisector Aid	32	39	0	–
Programme	36	32	10	–
Debt Reorganisation	0	0	1	–
Food Aid	–	1	–	–
Emergency Aid	0	1	0	–
Unspecified	14	–	0	–
TOTAL	100	100	100	–

14. GRANT ELEMENT OF ODA %

DAC COUNTRIES

	1987	1988	1989	1990
Australia	100.0	100.0	100.0	–
Austria	100.0	100.0	100.0	–
Belgium	100.0	100.0	100.0	–
Canada	–	–	–	–
Denmark	–	–	–	–
Finland	–	100.0	100.0	–
France	100.0	100.0	100.0	–
Germany	100.0	100.0	100.0	–
Ireland	–	–	–	–
Italy	100.0	100.0	100.0	–
Japan	100.0	100.0	100.0	–
Netherlands	100.0	100.0	100.0	–
New Zealand	–	–	–	–
Norway	100.0	–	–	–
Sweden	100.0	100.0	100.0	–
Switzerland	–	100.0	100.0	–
United Kingdom	–	–	–	–
United States	67.1	67.1	67.1	–
TOTAL	*99.5*	*99.7*	*99.6*	–
MULTILATERAL	*100.0*	*100.0*	*100.0*	–
ARAB COUNTRIES	*47.5*	–	–	–
E.E.C.+ MEMBERS	100.0	100.0	100.0	–
TOTAL	*93.2*	*99.8*	*99.8*	–

15. OTHER AGGREGATES

OFFICIAL COMMITMENTS:

	1987	1988	1989	1990
TOTAL BILATERAL	411.6	425.2	106.2	98.9
of which:				
Arab Countries	14.7	–	–	–
C.E.E.C.	344.1	339.5	22.4	–
TOTAL MULTILATERAL	50.1	65.5	61.0	86.5
TOTAL BIL.& MULTIL.	461.7	490.7	167.2	185.4
of which:				
ODA Grants	252.1	299.9	155.1	184.0
ODA Loans	209.6	190.8	0.8	0.8

DISBURSEMENTS:

DAC COUNTRIES COMBINED

OFFICIAL & PRIVATE

	1987	1988	1989	1990
GROSS:				
Contractual Lending	0.6	-8.1	5.7	-7.1
Export Credits, Total	-1.0	-9.7	4.7	-8.1
Export Credits, Priv.	-1.0	-9.7	-5.9	-8.8
NET:				
Contractual Lending	-19.9	-19.7	-0.9	-8.3
Export Credits Total	-17.2	-18.9	-1.2	-9.2
PRIVATE SECTOR NET	-28.8	12.7	7.3	-2.7
Direct Investment	–	7.7	4.1	16.4
Portfolio Investment	-11.6	24.0	15.1	-10.4
Export Credits	-17.2	-18.9	-11.9	-8.8

MARKET BORROWING:

CHANGE IN CLAIMS

	1987	1988	1989	1990
Banks	-8.0	51.0	4.0	290.0

MEMORANDUM ITEM:

	1987	1988	1989	1990
C.E.E.C. (Gross)	1955.1	1802.1	1620.3	–

1. TOTAL RECEIPTS NET

DAC COUNTRIES

	1987	1988	1989	1990
Australia	–	–	–	–
Austria	–	–	–	–
Belgium	-0.9	1.0	4.6	3.5
Canada	0.1	0.1	0.1	0.0
Denmark	–	–	–	–
Finland	–	–	45.4	–
France	3.3	154.3	-201.3	7.7
Germany	46.4	5.2	-7.0	30.2
Ireland	–	–	–	–
Italy	–	3.1	26.5	0.9
Japan	38.8	94.3	46.4	129.8
Netherlands	-0.6	-0.1	4.2	2.4
New Zealand	–	–	–	–
Norway	–	–	–	–
Sweden	-0.3	–	–	–
Switzerland	–	–	–	–
United Kingdom	0.9	4.8	7.2	5.4
United States	–	-6.0	–	–
TOTAL	*87.7*	*256.7*	*-73.8*	*179.9*

MULTILATERAL

	1987	1988	1989	1990
AF.D.F.	–	–	–	–
AF.D.B.	–	–	–	–
AS.D.B	–	–	–	–
CAR.D.B.	1.0	0.8	4.2	4.2
E.E.C.	0.0	–	–	–
IBRD	–	–	–	–
IDA	–	–	–	–
I.D.B.	–	–	–	–
IFAD	–	–	–	–
I.F.C.	–	–	–	–
IMF TRUST FUND	–	–	–	–
U.N. AGENCIES	–	–	–	–
UNDP	0.1	0.1	0.1	0.0
UNTA	0.0	–	–	0.1
UNICEF	–	–	–	–
UNRWA	–	–	–	–
WFP	–	–	–	–
UNHCR	–	–	–	–
Other Multilateral	0.2	0.0	–	0.0
Arab Agencies	–	–	–	–
TOTAL	*1.3*	*0.9*	*4.3*	*4.3*
ARAB COUNTRIES	–	–	–	–
E.E.C.+ MEMBERS	*49.1*	*168.3*	*-165.8*	*50.1*
TOTAL	**89.0**	**257.6**	**-69.4**	**184.2**

2. ODA LOANS GROSS

DAC COUNTRIES

	1987	1988	1989	1990
Australia	–	–	–	–
Austria	–	–	–	–
Belgium	–	–	–	–
Canada	–	–	–	–
Denmark	–	–	–	–
Finland	–	–	–	–
France	–	–	–	–
Germany	–	–	–	–
Ireland	–	–	–	–
Italy	–	–	–	–
Japan	–	–	–	–
Netherlands	–	–	–	–
New Zealand	–	–	–	–
Norway	–	–	–	–
Sweden	–	–	–	–
Switzerland	–	–	–	–
United Kingdom	–	–	–	–
United States	–	–	–	–
TOTAL	–	–	–	–
MULTILATERAL	*1.0*	*0.8*	*1.9*	*1.9*
ARAB COUNTRIES	–	–	–	–
E.E.C.+ MEMBERS	–	–	–	–
TOTAL	**1.0**	**0.8**	**1.9**	**1.9**

3. TOTAL OFFICIAL GROSS

DAC COUNTRIES

	1987	1988	1989	1990
Australia	–	–	–	–
Austria	0.0	0.0	0.0	0.0
Belgium	0.0	0.0	0.0	0.0
Canada	0.1	0.1	0.1	0.0
Denmark	–	–	–	–
Finland	–	–	–	–
France	–	–	–	–
Germany	1.2	–	–	–
Ireland	–	–	–	–
Italy	–	–	–	–
Japan	–	–	–	–
Netherlands	–	–	–	–
New Zealand	–	–	–	–
Norway	–	–	–	–
Sweden	–	–	–	–
Switzerland				
United Kingdom	0.9	4.8	7.2	4.6
United States	–	–	–	–
TOTAL	*2.2*	*4.9*	*7.3*	*4.7*
MULTILATERAL	*1.3*	*0.9*	*4.3*	*4.3*
ARAB COUNTRIES	–	–	–	–
E.E.C.+ MEMBERS	*2.2*	*4.8*	*7.2*	*4.6*
TOTAL	**3.5**	**5.9**	**11.7**	**9.0**

4. TOTAL ODA NET

	1987	1988	1989	1990
Australia	–	–	–	–
Austria	–	–	–	–
Belgium	0.0	0.0	0.0	0.0
Canada	0.1	0.1	0.1	0.0
Denmark	–	–	–	–
Finland	–	–	–	–
France	–	–	–	–
Germany	–	–	–	–
Ireland	–	–	–	–
Italy	–	–	–	–
Japan	–	–	–	–
Netherlands	–	–	–	–
New Zealand	–	–	–	–
Norway	–	–	–	–
Sweden	–	–	–	–
Switzerland	–	–	–	–
United Kingdom	0.9	0.9	3.6	3.0
United States	–	–	–	–
TOTAL	*1.0*	*1.0*	*3.7*	*3.0*

MULTILATERAL

	1987	1988	1989	1990
AF.D.F.	–	–	–	–
AF.D.B.	–	–	–	–
AS.D.B	–	–	–	–
CAR.D.B.	1.0	0.8	1.9	1.9
E.E.C.	0.0	–	–	–
IBRD	–	–	–	–
IDA	–	–	–	–
I.D.B.	–	–	–	–
IFAD	–	–	–	–
I.F.C.	–	–	–	–
IMF TRUST FUND	–	–	–	–
U.N. AGENCIES	–	–	–	–
UNDP	0.1	0.1	0.1	0.0
UNTA	0.0	–	–	0.1
UNICEF	–	–	–	–
UNRWA	–	–	–	–
WFP	–	–	–	–
UNHCR	–	–	–	–
Other Multilateral	0.2	0.0	–	0.0
Arab Agencies	–	–	–	–
TOTAL	*1.3*	*0.9*	*2.1*	*2.0*
ARAB COUNTRIES	–	–	–	–
E.E.C.+ MEMBERS	*1.0*	*0.9*	*3.6*	*3.0*
TOTAL	**2.3**	**2.0**	**5.8**	**5.1**

5. ODA LOANS NET

	1987	1988	1989	1990
Australia	–	–	–	–
Austria	–	–	–	–
Belgium	–	–	–	–
Canada	–	–	–	–
Denmark	–	–	–	–
Finland	–	–	–	–
France	–	–	–	–
Germany	–	–	–	–
Ireland	–	–	–	–
Italy	–	–	–	–
Japan	–	–	–	–
Netherlands	–	–	–	–
New Zealand	–	–	–	–
Norway	–	–	–	–
Sweden	–	–	–	–
Switzerland	–	–	–	–
United Kingdom	–	–	0.0	0.0
United States	–	–	–	–
TOTAL	–	–	0.0	0.0
MULTILATERAL	*1.0*	*0.8*	*1.9*	*1.9*
ARAB COUNTRIES	–	–	–	–
E.E.C.+ MEMBERS	–	–	0.0	0.0
TOTAL	**1.0**	**0.8**	**1.9**	**1.9**

6. TOTAL OFFICIAL NET

	1987	1988	1989	1990
Australia	–	–	–	–
Austria	0.0	0.0	0.0	0.0
Belgium	0.0	0.0	0.0	0.0
Canada	0.1	0.1	0.1	0.0
Denmark	–	–	–	–
Finland	–	–	–	–
France	–	–	–	–
Germany	1.2	-0.2	–	–
Ireland	–	–	–	–
Italy	–	–	–	–
Japan	–	–	–	–
Netherlands	–	–	–	–
New Zealand	–	–	–	–
Norway	–	–	–	–
Sweden	–	–	–	–
Switzerland				
United Kingdom	0.9	4.8	7.2	4.6
United States	–	–	–	–
TOTAL	*2.2*	*4.7*	*7.3*	*4.6*
MULTILATERAL	*1.3*	*0.9*	*4.3*	*4.3*
ARAB COUNTRIES	–	–	–	–
E.E.C.+ MEMBERS	*2.2*	*4.6*	*7.2*	*4.6*
TOTAL	**3.5**	**5.6**	**11.7**	**9.0**

7. TOTAL ODA GROSS

	1987
Australia	–
Austria	–
Belgium	0.0
Canada	0.1
Denmark	–
Finland	–
France	–
Germany	–
Ireland	–
Italy	–
Japan	–
Netherlands	–
New Zealand	–
Norway	–
Sweden	–
Switzerland	–
United Kingdom	0.9
United States	–
TOTAL	*1.0*
AF.D.F.	–
AF.D.B.	–
AS.D.B	–
CAR.D.B.	1.0
E.E.C.	0.0
IBRD	–
IDA	–
I.D.B.	–
IFAD	–
I.F.C.	–
IMF TRUST FUND	–
U.N. AGENCIES	–
UNDP	0.1
UNTA	0.0
UNICEF	–
UNRWA	–
WFP	–
UNHCR	–
Other Multilateral	0.2
Arab Agencies	–
TOTAL	*1.3*
ARAB COUNTRIES	–
E.E.C.+ MEMBERS	*1.0*
TOTAL	**2.3**

8. GRANTS

	1987
Australia	–
Austria	–
Belgium	0.0
Canada	0.1
Denmark	–
Finland	–
France	–
Germany	–
Ireland	–
Italy	–
Japan	–
Netherlands	–
New Zealand	–
Norway	–
Sweden	–
Switzerland	–
United Kingdom	0.9
United States	–
TOTAL	*1.0*
MULTILATERAL	*0.3*
ARAB COUNTRIES	–
E.E.C.+ MEMBERS	*1.0*
TOTAL	**1.3**

9. TOTAL OOF GROSS

	1987
Australia	–
Austria	–
Belgium	–
Canada	–
Denmark	–
Finland	–
France	–
Germany	1.2
Ireland	–
Italy	–
Japan	–
Netherlands	–
New Zealand	–
Norway	–
Sweden	–
Switzerland	–
United Kingdom	–
United States	–
TOTAL	*1.2*
MULTILATERAL	*0.0*
ARAB COUNTRIES	–
E.E.C.+ MEMBERS	*1.2*
TOTAL	**1.2**

10. ODA COMMITMENTS   11. TECH. COOP. GRANTS   12. TOTAL OOF NET

1988	1989	1990	1987	1988	1989	1990
–	–	–	–	–	–	–
–	–	–	–	–	–	–
0.0	0.0	0.0	–	–	0.0	0.0
0.1	0.1	0.0	0.1	0.0	0.1	0.1
–	–	–	–	–	–	–
–	–	–	–	–	–	–
–	–	–	–	–	–	–
–	–	–	–	–	–	–
–	–	–	–	–	0.0	–
–	–	–	–	–	–	–
–	–	–	–	–	–	–
–	–	–	–	–	–	–
–	–	–	–	–	–	–
0.9	3.6	3.0	0.9	0.9	3.7	1.3
–	–	–	–	–	–	–
1.0	3.7	3.1	1.0	0.9	3.8	1.4
–	–	–	–	–	–	–
–	–	–	–	–	–	–
0.8	1.9	1.9	0.7	0.2	5.6	5.6
–	–	–	0.0	1.0	1.1	1.1
–	–	–	–	–	–	–
–	–	–	–	–	–	–
–	–	–	–	–	–	–
–	–	–	–	–	–	–
–	–	–	–	–	–	–
–	–	–	0.3	0.1	0.1	0.1
0.1	0.1	0.0	–	–	–	–
–	–	0.1	–	–	–	–
–	–	–	–	–	–	–
–	–	–	–	–	–	–
0.0	–	0.0	–	–	–	–
–	–	–	–	–	–	–
0.9	2.1	2.0	1.1	1.3	6.9	6.8
–	–	–	–	–	–	–
0.9	3.6	3.0	1.0	2.0	4.8	2.4
2.0	5.8	5.1	2.1	2.3	10.6	8.2

11. TECH. COOP. GRANTS

1988	1989	1990	1987	1988	1989	1990
–	–	–	–	–	–	–
0.0	0.0	0.0	–	–	–	–
0.1	0.1	0.0	–	0.1	0.1	0.0
–	–	–	–	–	–	–
–	–	–	–	–	–	–
–	–	–	–	–	–	–
–	–	–	–	–	–	–
–	–	–	–	–	–	–
–	–	–	–	–	–	–
–	–	–	–	–	–	–
–	–	–	–	–	–	–
–	–	–	–	–	–	–
0.9	3.6	3.0	0.4	0.4	0.5	1.3
–	–	–	–	–	–	–
1.0	3.7	3.1	0.4	0.5	0.6	1.3
0.1	0.1	0.1	0.3	0.1	0.1	0.1
–	–	–	–	–	–	–
0.9	3.6	3.0	0.4	0.4	0.5	1.3
1.1	3.9	3.2	0.7	0.6	0.7	1.4

12. TOTAL OOF NET

1988	1989	1990	1987	1988	1989	1990
–	–	–	–	–	–	–
–	–	–	–	–	–	–
–	–	–	–	–	–	–
–	–	–	–	–	–	–
–	–	–	–	–	–	–
–	–	–	1.2	-0.2	–	–
–	–	–	–	–	–	–
–	–	–	–	–	–	–
–	–	–	–	–	–	–
–	–	–	–	–	–	–
–	–	–	–	–	–	–
3.9	3.6	1.6	0.0	3.9	3.6	1.6
–	–	–	–	–	–	–
3.9	3.6	1.6	1.2	3.7	3.6	1.6
–	2.3	2.3	0.0	–	2.3	2.3
–	–	–	–	–	–	–
3.9	3.6	1.6	1.2	3.7	3.6	1.6
3.9	5.9	3.9	1.2	3.7	5.9	3.9

13. ODF COMMITMENTS: BY PURPOSE %

	1987	1988	1989	1990
Education	–	–	–	–
Health	–	–	–	–
Other Social Infrastr.	–	–	–	–
Water Sanitat. Sewage	–	–	–	–
Energy	–	90	–	–
Telecommunications	–	–	–	–
Transportation	–	–	–	–
Agriculture	–	–	–	–
Extractive Industries	–	–	–	–
Manufacturing	–	–	–	–
Trade Banking Tourism	–	–	0.0	–
Technical Cooperation	56	5	100	–
Multisector Aid	44	5	–	–
Programme	–	–	–	–
Debt Reorganisation	–	–	–	–
Food Aid	–	–	–	–
Emergency Aid	–	–	–	–
Unspecified	–	–	–	–
TOTAL	100	100	100	–

14. GRANT ELEMENT OF ODA %

DAC COUNTRIES

	1987	1988	1989	1990
Australia	–	–	–	–
Austria	–	–	–	–
Belgium	–	–	100.0	–
Canada	100.0	100.0	100.0	–
Denmark	–	–	–	–
Finland	–	–	–	–
France	–	–	–	–
Germany	–	–	–	–
Ireland	–	–	–	–
Italy	–	–	–	–
Japan	–	–	100.0	–
Netherlands	–	–	–	–
New Zealand	–	–	–	–
Norway	–	–	–	–
Sweden	–	–	–	–
Switzerland	–	–	–	–
United Kingdom	100.0	100.0	100.0	–
United States	–	–	–	–
TOTAL	100.0	100.0	100.0	–
MULTILATERAL	100.0	100.0	100.0	–
ARAB COUNTRIES	–	–	–	–
E.E.C.+ MEMBERS	100.0	100.0	100.0	–
TOTAL	100.0	100.0	100.0	–

15. OTHER AGGREGATES

	1987	1988	1989	1990
OFFICIAL COMMITMENTS:				
TOTAL BILATERAL	1.0	10.4	3.8	1.4
of which:				
Arab Countries	–	–	–	–
C.E.E.C.	–	–	–	–
TOTAL MULTILATERAL	3.2	1.3	17.6	17.6
TOTAL BIL.& MULTIL.	4.2	11.7	21.4	18.9
of which:				
ODA Grants	1.3	2.3	4.2	1.8
ODA Loans	0.7	–	6.4	6.4
DISBURSEMENTS:				
DAC COUNTRIES COMBINED				
OFFICIAL & PRIVATE				
GROSS:				
Contractual Lending	1.2	3.9	3.6	2.5
Export Credits, Total	1.2	–	–	0.9
Export Credits, Priv.	–	–	–	0.9
NET:				
Contractual Lending	0.1	3.7	3.6	2.4
Export Credits Total	0.1	-0.2	0.0	0.8
PRIVATE SECTOR NET	85.5	252.0	-81.1	175.3
Direct Investment	37.9	90.4	117.4	147.8
Portfolio Investment	48.7	161.7	-198.5	26.6
Export Credits	-1.1	–	0.0	0.8
MARKET BORROWING:				
CHANGE IN CLAIMS				
Banks	–	–	–	–
MEMORANDUM ITEM:				
C.E.E.C. (Gross)	–	–	–	–

1. TOTAL RECEIPTS NET

DAC COUNTRIES	1987	1988	1989	1990
Australia	6.0	7.3	7.3	8.9
Austria	–	–	–	–
Belgium	–	0.1	0.0	0.0
Canada	-0.1	0.0	-0.1	-0.1
Denmark	–	–	–	–
Finland	–	–	–	–
France	1.1	–	0.2	0.4
Germany	2.4	3.0	1.8	1.8
Ireland	–	–	–	–
Italy	–	–	–	–
Japan	6.9	7.7	6.0	15.8
Netherlands	0.1	0.0	0.0	0.2
New Zealand	3.9	4.0	3.5	5.8
Norway	–	–	–	–
Sweden	–	–	–	–
Switzerland	–	–	–	–
United Kingdom	0.0	0.1	0.1	0.3
United States	1.0	–	1.0	1.0
TOTAL	21.3	22.1	19.8	33.9
MULTILATERAL				
AF.D.F.	–	–	–	–
AF.D.B.	–	–	–	–
AS.D.B	1.5	1.7	3.7	11.6
CAR.D.B.	–	–	–	–
E.E.C.	6.7	3.6	2.7	2.7
IBRD	–	–	–	–
IDA	1.4	1.0	1.0	4.0
I.D.B.	–	–	–	–
IFAD	0.2	–	–	0.2
I.F.C.	–	–	–	–
IMF TRUST FUND	–	–	–	–
U.N. AGENCIES	–	–	–	–
UNDP	1.4	2.0	2.0	1.9
UNTA	0.7	0.3	0.9	1.1
UNICEF	–	–	–	–
UNRWA	–	–	–	–
WFP	–	–	–	1.0
UNHCR	–	–	–	–
Other Multilateral	0.1	0.4	0.2	0.3
Arab Agencies	-0.7	-0.8	-0.6	–
TOTAL	11.3	8.2	10.0	22.8
ARAB COUNTRIES	2.1	0.5	0.9	0.2
E.E.C.+ MEMBERS	10.2	6.8	4.8	5.2
TOTAL	34.7	30.8	30.6	56.9

2. ODA LOANS GROSS

DAC COUNTRIES	1987	1988	1989	1990
Australia	–	–	–	–
Austria	–	–	–	–
Belgium	–	–	–	–
Canada	–	–	–	–
Denmark	–	–	–	–
Finland	–	–	–	–
France	–	–	–	–
Germany	–	–	–	–
Ireland	–	–	–	–
Italy	–	–	–	–
Japan	–	–	–	–
Netherlands	–	–	–	–
New Zealand	–	–	–	–
Norway	–	–	–	–
Sweden	–	–	–	–
Switzerland	–	–	–	–
United Kingdom	–	–	–	–
United States	–	–	–	–
TOTAL	–	–	–	–
MULTILATERAL	3.5	3.0	4.0	15.8
ARAB COUNTRIES	2.1	0.5	0.9	0.2
E.E.C.+ MEMBERS	–	–	0.5	0.5
TOTAL	5.5	3.5	4.8	16.0

3. TOTAL OFFICIAL GROSS

DAC COUNTRIES	1987	1988	1989	1990
Australia	6.0	7.3	7.6	8.9
Austria	–	–	–	–
Belgium	–	0.1	0.0	–
Canada	–	0.0	–	–
Denmark	–	–	–	–
Finland	–	–	–	–
France	1.1	–	0.2	0.4
Germany	2.7	2.9	2.2	2.0
Ireland	–	–	–	–
Italy	–	–	–	–
Japan	6.9	7.7	6.0	9.2
Netherlands	0.1	0.0	0.0	0.2
New Zealand	3.9	4.0	3.5	5.8
Norway	–	–	–	–
Sweden	–	–	–	–
Switzerland	–	–	–	–
United Kingdom	0.0	0.1	0.1	0.3
United States	1.0	–	1.0	1.0
TOTAL	21.8	22.1	20.5	27.8
MULTILATERAL	12.7	9.8	11.7	23.9
ARAB COUNTRIES	2.1	0.5	0.9	0.2
E.E.C.+ MEMBERS	10.8	6.9	5.3	5.7
TOTAL	36.6	32.4	33.1	51.9

4. TOTAL ODA NET

DAC COUNTRIES	1987	1988	1989	1990
Australia	6.0	7.3	7.6	8.9
Austria	–	–	–	–
Belgium	–	0.1	0.0	–
Canada	–	0.0	–	–
Denmark	–	–	–	–
Finland	–	–	–	–
France	1.1	–	0.2	0.4
Germany	2.7	2.8	2.2	2.0
Ireland	–	–	–	–
Italy	–	–	–	–
Japan	6.9	7.7	6.0	9.2
Netherlands	0.1	0.0	0.0	0.2
New Zealand	3.9	4.0	3.5	5.8
Norway	–	–	–	–
Sweden	–	–	–	–
Switzerland	–	–	–	–
United Kingdom	0.0	0.1	0.1	0.3
United States	1.0	–	1.0	1.0
TOTAL	21.8	22.0	20.5	27.7
AF.D.F.	–	–	–	–
AF.D.B.	–	–	–	–
AS.D.B	1.5	1.7	3.7	11.6
CAR.D.B.	–	–	–	–
E.E.C.	6.7	3.6	2.7	2.7
IBRD	–	–	–	–
IDA	1.4	1.0	1.0	4.0
I.D.B.	–	–	–	–
IFAD	0.2	–	–	0.2
I.F.C.	–	–	–	–
IMF TRUST FUND	–	–	–	–
U.N. AGENCIES	–	–	–	–
UNDP	1.4	2.0	2.0	1.9
UNTA	0.7	0.3	0.9	1.1
UNICEF	–	–	–	–
UNRWA	–	–	–	–
WFP	–	–	–	1.0
UNHCR	–	–	–	–
Other Multilateral	0.1	0.4	0.2	0.3
Arab Agencies	-0.7	-0.8	-0.6	–
TOTAL	11.3	8.2	10.0	22.8
ARAB COUNTRIES	2.1	0.5	0.9	0.2
E.E.C.+ MEMBERS	10.5	6.6	5.1	5.5
TOTAL	35.2	30.7	31.3	50.7

5. ODA LOANS NET

DAC COUNTRIES	1987	1988	1989	1990
Australia	–	–	–	–
Austria	–	–	–	–
Belgium	–	–	–	–
Canada	–	–	–	–
Denmark	–	–	–	–
Finland	–	–	–	–
France	–	–	–	–
Germany	–	-0.1	–	–
Ireland	–	–	–	–
Italy	–	–	–	–
Japan	–	–	–	–
Netherlands	–	–	–	–
New Zealand	–	–	–	–
Norway	–	–	–	–
Sweden	–	–	–	–
Switzerland	–	–	–	–
United Kingdom	0.0	0.0	0.0	0.0
United States	–	–	–	–
TOTAL	0.0	-0.1	0.0	0.0
MULTILATERAL	2.1	1.5	2.2	14.2
ARAB COUNTRIES	2.1	0.5	0.9	0.2
E.E.C.+ MEMBERS	-0.2	-0.3	0.3	0.3
TOTAL	4.1	1.8	3.1	14.4

6. TOTAL OFFICIAL NET

DAC COUNTRIES	1987	1988	1989	1990
Australia	6.0	7.3	7.3	8.9
Austria	–	–	–	–
Belgium	–	0.1	0.0	–
Canada	-0.1	0.0	-0.1	-0.1
Denmark	–	–	–	–
Finland	–	–	–	–
France	1.1	–	0.2	0.4
Germany	2.2	2.3	2.1	2.0
Ireland	–	–	–	–
Italy	–	–	–	–
Japan	6.9	7.7	6.0	9.2
Netherlands	0.1	0.0	0.0	0.2
New Zealand	3.9	4.0	3.5	5.8
Norway	–	–	–	–
Sweden	–	–	–	–
Switzerland	–	–	–	–
United Kingdom	0.0	0.1	0.1	0.3
United States	1.0	–	1.0	1.0
TOTAL	21.1	21.4	20.0	27.6
MULTILATERAL	11.3	8.2	10.0	22.8
ARAB COUNTRIES	2.1	0.5	0.9	0.2
E.E.C.+ MEMBERS	10.1	6.1	5.0	5.5
TOTAL	34.5	30.1	30.8	50.6

7. TOTAL ODA GROSS

	1987
Australia	6.0
Austria	–
Belgium	–
Canada	–
Denmark	–
Finland	–
France	1.1
Germany	2.7
Ireland	–
Italy	–
Japan	6.9
Netherlands	0.1
New Zealand	3.9
Norway	–
Sweden	–
Switzerland	–
United Kingdom	0.0
United States	1.0
TOTAL	21.8
AF.D.F.	–
AF.D.B.	–
AS.D.B	1.9
CAR.D.B.	–
E.E.C.	6.9
IBRD	–
IDA	1.5
I.D.B.	–
IFAD	0.2
I.F.C.	–
IMF TRUST FUND	–
U.N. AGENCIES	–
UNDP	1.4
UNTA	0.7
UNICEF	–
UNRWA	–
WFP	–
UNHCR	–
Other Multilateral	0.1
Arab Agencies	–
TOTAL	12.7
ARAB COUNTRIES	2.1
E.E.C.+ MEMBERS	10.8
TOTAL	36.6

8. GRANTS

	1987
Australia	6.0
Austria	–
Belgium	–
Canada	–
Denmark	–
Finland	–
France	1.1
Germany	2.7
Ireland	–
Italy	–
Japan	6.9
Netherlands	0.1
New Zealand	3.9
Norway	–
Sweden	–
Switzerland	–
United Kingdom	0.0
United States	1.0
TOTAL	21.8
MULTILATERAL	9.2
ARAB COUNTRIES	0.0
E.E.C.+ MEMBERS	10.8
TOTAL	31.0

9. TOTAL OOF GROSS

	1987
Australia	–
Austria	–
Belgium	–
Canada	–
Denmark	–
Finland	–
France	–
Germany	–
Ireland	–
Italy	–
Japan	–
Netherlands	–
New Zealand	–
Norway	–
Sweden	–
Switzerland	–
United Kingdom	–
United States	–
TOTAL	–
MULTILATERAL	–
ARAB COUNTRIES	–
E.E.C.+ MEMBERS	–
TOTAL	–

10. ODA COMMITMENTS

1988	1989	1990	1987	1988	1989	1990
7.3	7.6	8.9	3.5	13.2	5.2	11.9
–	–	–	–	–	–	–
0.1	0.0	–	–	–	0.0	–
0.0	–	–	0.2	0.0	–	–
–	–	–	–	–	–	–
–	0.2	0.4	1.1	–	0.2	0.8
2.9	2.2	2.0	0.2	4.2	1.5	0.4
–	–	–	–	–	–	–
7.7	6.0	9.2	7.6	8.0	8.8	7.2
0.0	0.0	0.2	0.1	0.0	0.0	0.2
4.0	3.5	5.8	3.4	4.0	–	3.3
–	–	–	–	–	–	–
–	–	–	–	–	–	–
0.1	0.1	0.3	0.0	0.1	0.1	0.3
–	1.0	1.0	0.6	0.8	0.9	0.8
22.1	*20.5*	*27.8*	*16.6*	*30.4*	*16.7*	*24.8*
–	–	–	–	–	–	–
2.3	4.4	12.4	2.3	6.2	23.2	0.6
–	–	–	–	–	–	–
3.8	2.9	2.9	5.7	9.4	2.4	2.4
–	–	–	–	–	–	–
1.0	1.0	4.0	3.0	–	5.0	14.0
–	–	–	–	–	–	–
–	–	0.2	–	–	–	–
–	–	–	–	–	–	–
–	–	–	–	–	–	–
–	–	–	2.2	2.7	3.2	4.3
2.0	2.0	1.9	–	–	–	–
0.3	0.9	1.1	–	–	–	–
–	–	–	–	–	–	–
–	–	1.0	–	–	–	–
–	–	–	–	–	–	–
0.4	0.2	0.3	–	–	–	–
–	0.2	0.2	–	–	0.7	–
9.8	*11.7*	*23.9*	*13.2*	*18.3*	*34.5*	*21.2*
0.5	*0.9*	*0.2*	–	–	–	–
6.9	*5.3*	*5.7*	*7.1*	*13.8*	*4.2*	*4.0*
32.4	*33.1*	*51.9*	*29.8*	*48.7*	*51.1*	*46.0*

11. TECH. COOP. GRANTS

1988	1989	1990	1987	1988	1989	1990
7.3	7.6	8.9	3.0	3.3	5.0	5.4
–	–	–	–	–	–	–
0.1	0.0	–	–	–	–	–
0.0	–	–	–	–	–	–
–	–	–	–	–	–	–
–	0.2	0.4	1.1	–	0.2	0.4
2.9	2.2	2.0	1.1	0.9	1.1	0.4
–	–	–	–	–	–	–
7.7	6.0	9.2	2.5	2.4	2.1	2.5
0.0	0.0	0.2	0.1	0.0	0.0	0.1
4.0	3.5	5.8	1.8	1.2	–	1.0
–	–	–	–	–	–	–
–	–	–	–	–	–	–
0.1	0.1	0.3	0.0	0.1	0.1	0.1
–	1.0	1.0	1.0	–	1.0	1.0
22.1	*20.5*	*27.8*	*10.6*	*7.9*	*9.3*	*10.7*
6.7	*7.8*	*8.1*	*2.7*	*2.7*	*3.2*	*3.2*
–	–	–	–	–	–	–
6.9	*4.8*	*5.2*	*2.8*	*1.0*	*1.3*	*0.9*
28.9	*28.3*	*35.9*	*13.3*	*10.6*	*12.5*	*13.9*

12. TOTAL OOF NET

1988	1989	1990	1987	1988	1989	1990
–	–	–	–	–	-0.2	–
–	–	–	–	–	–	–
–	–	–	-0.1	0.0	-0.1	-0.1
–	–	–	–	–	–	–
–	–	–	–	–	–	–
–	–	–	-0.5	-0.5	-0.1	–
–	–	–	–	–	–	–
–	–	–	–	–	–	–
–	–	–	–	–	–	–
–	–	–	–	–	–	–
–	–	–	–	–	–	–
–	–	–	–	–	–	–
–	–	–	–	–	–	–
–	–	–	*-0.6*	*-0.5*	*-0.5*	*-0.1*
–	–	–	–	–	–	–
–	–	–	–	–	–	–
–	–	–	-0.5	-0.5	-0.1	–
–	–	–	*-0.6*	*-0.5*	*-0.5*	*-0.1*

13. ODF COMMITMENTS: BY PURPOSE %

	1987	1988	1989	1990
Education	–	–	–	–
Health	–	–	–	–
Other Social Infrastr.	1	18	–	–
Water Sanitat. Sewage	0	5	–	–
Energy	16	–	–	–
Telecommunications	–	–	22	–
Transportation	24	14	16	–
Agriculture	7	0	31	–
Extractive Industries	–	–	–	–
Manufacturing	–	–	1	–
Trade Banking Tourism	–	–	–	–
Technical Cooperation	51	53	17	–
Multisector Aid	1	0	11	–
Programme	–	9	2	–
Debt Reorganisation	0	0	–	–
Food Aid	–	–	–	–
Emergency Aid	–	–	–	–
Unspecified	–	–	–	–
TOTAL	100	100	100	

14. GRANT ELEMENT OF ODA %

DAC COUNTRIES

	1987	1988	1989	1990
Australia	100.0	100.0	100.0	–
Austria	–	–	–	–
Belgium	–	–	100.0	–
Canada	100.0	100.0	–	–
Denmark	–	–	–	–
Finland	–	–	–	–
France	100.0	–	100.0	–
Germany	100.0	100.0	100.0	–
Ireland	–	–	–	–
Italy	–	–	–	–
Japan	100.0	100.0	100.0	–
Netherlands	100.0	100.0	100.0	–
New Zealand	100.0	100.0	–	–
Norway	–	–	–	–
Sweden	–	–	–	–
Switzerland	–	–	–	–
United Kingdom	100.0	100.0	100.0	–
United States	100.0	100.0	100.0	–
TOTAL	*100.0*	*100.0*	*100.0*	–
MULTILATERAL	*95.3*	*100.0*	*81.1*	–
ARAB COUNTRIES	–	–	–	–
E.E.C.+ MEMBERS	*100.0*	*100.0*	*100.0*	–
TOTAL	*98.1*	*100.0*	*86.6*	–

15. OTHER AGGREGATES

OFFICIAL COMMITMENTS:

	1987	1988	1989	1990
TOTAL BILATERAL	16.6	30.4	18.8	24.8
of which:				
Arab Countries	–	–	–	–
C.E.E.C.	–	–	–	–
TOTAL MULTILATERAL	13.2	18.3	34.5	21.2
TOTAL BIL.& MULTIL.	29.8	48.7	53.3	46.0
of which:				
ODA Grants	24.5	37.5	22.3	31.1
ODA Loans	5.3	11.2	28.9	15.0

DISBURSEMENTS:

DAC COUNTRIES COMBINED

	1987	1988	1989	1990
OFFICIAL & PRIVATE				
GROSS:				
Contractual Lending	–	1.7	–	–
Export Credits, Total	–	1.7	–	–
Export Credits, Priv.	–	1.7	–	–
NET:				
Contractual Lending	-0.7	-0.1	-0.7	-0.4
Export Credits Total	-0.7	0.1	-0.7	-0.4
PRIVATE SECTOR NET	0.2	0.7	-0.2	6.3
Direct Investment	0.6	0.1	–	6.6
Portfolio Investment	-0.3	0.0	0.0	0.0
Export Credits	-0.1	0.6	-0.2	-0.2

MARKET BORROWING:

CHANGE IN CLAIMS

	1987	1988	1989	1990
Banks	–	–	–	–

MEMORANDUM ITEM:

	1987	1988	1989	1990
C.E.E.C. (Gross)	–	–	–	–

1. TOTAL RECEIPTS NET

DAC COUNTRIES

	1987	1988	1989	1990
Australia	26.7	-12.9	23.9	-3.1
Austria	0.1	0.1	0.1	0.1
Belgium	-0.8	-2.5	-1.4	-1.5
Canada	-0.8	-0.3	0.4	0.4
Denmark	6.1	13.0	12.6	13.1
Finland	0.1	0.1	0.1	0.2
France	9.4	7.0	9.4	26.6
Germany	30.0	31.4	30.7	48.0
Ireland	–	–	–	–
Italy	25.6	-26.5	-86.4	-25.0
Japan	15.1	30.2	69.7	20.3
Netherlands	29.9	34.1	33.6	33.7
New Zealand	–	–	–	–
Norway	0.2	0.2	0.1	0.4
Sweden	–	5.5	0.5	-0.3
Switzerland	0.3	2.5	1.1	2.2
United Kingdom	4.1	14.8	-7.0	9.0
United States	43.0	27.0	40.0	41.0
TOTAL	*188.9*	*123.6*	*127.3*	*164.9*

MULTILATERAL

	1987	1988	1989	1990
AF.D.F.	–	–	–	–
AF.D.B.	–	–	–	–
AS.D.B	–	–	–	–
CAR.D.B.	–	–	–	–
E.E.C.	2.5	5.6	1.9	1.9
IBRD	–	–	–	–
IDA	38.9	48.0	40.0	30.0
I.D.B.	–	–	–	–
IFAD	9.8	2.1	4.4	6.6
I.F.C.	0.4	-3.6	-3.3	–
IMF TRUST FUND	–	–	–	–
U.N. AGENCIES	–	–	–	–
UNDP	4.9	9.3	14.6	17.2
UNTA	3.8	2.5	4.0	2.7
UNICEF	3.1	3.2	4.7	4.3
UNRWA	–	–	–	–
WFP	18.5	19.3	27.0	21.0
UNHCR	–	0.3	0.3	0.4
Other Multilateral	4.9	4.2	8.4	7.0
Arab Agencies	11.8	-1.2	15.7	–
TOTAL	*98.6*	*89.7*	*117.6*	*91.0*
ARAB COUNTRIES	**151.9**	**24.6**	**33.9**	**132.1**
E.E.C.+ MEMBERS	*106.9*	*76.8*	*-6.6*	*105.7*
TOTAL	**439.4**	**237.9**	**278.8**	**388.0**

2. ODA LOANS GROSS

DAC COUNTRIES

	1987	1988	1989	1990
Australia	–	–	–	–
Austria	–	–	–	–
Belgium	–	–	–	–
Canada	–	–	–	–
Denmark	0.1	0.0	–	–
Finland	–	–	–	–
France	–	4.7	–	11.7
Germany	–	–	–	–
Ireland	–	–	–	–
Italy	5.6	4.3	1.4	0.2
Japan	14.9	15.1	53.6	4.9
Netherlands	1.9	1.6	3.0	–
New Zealand	–	–	–	–
Norway	–	–	–	–
Sweden	–	–	–	–
Switzerland	–	–	–	–
United Kingdom	–	–	–	–
United States	15.0	10.0	16.0	20.0
TOTAL	*37.4*	*35.8*	*73.9*	*36.7*
MULTILATERAL	*93.0*	*88.7*	*89.1*	*60.5*
ARAB COUNTRIES	**33.7**	**20.6**	**31.6**	**16.2**
E.E.C.+ MEMBERS	*7.5*	*10.6*	*4.4*	*11.9*
TOTAL	**164.1**	**145.1**	**194.6**	**113.5**

3. TOTAL OFFICIAL GROSS

DAC COUNTRIES

	1987	1988	1989	1990
Australia	–	–	–	–
Austria	0.1	0.1	0.1	0.1
Belgium	0.3	0.0	0.2	0.2
Canada	0.4	0.4	0.4	0.4
Denmark	8.6	16.3	12.7	13.2
Finland	0.1	0.1	0.1	0.2
France	4.3	9.0	3.5	16.7
Germany	32.4	33.1	27.5	38.2
Ireland	–	–	–	–
Italy	10.6	7.0	5.4	2.7
Japan	27.7	29.1	72.2	23.0
Netherlands	28.5	35.0	31.3	33.7
New Zealand	–	–	–	–
Norway	0.2	0.2	0.1	0.4
Sweden	–	5.5	0.6	–
Switzerland	0.3	2.5	1.1	2.2
United Kingdom	10.4	12.6	10.6	9.9
United States	45.0	27.0	40.0	43.0
TOTAL	*168.7*	*177.8*	*205.6*	*183.7*
MULTILATERAL	*173.3*	*222.1*	*199.1*	*119.4*
ARAB COUNTRIES	**192.2**	**66.5**	**80.1**	**161.8**
E.E.C.+ MEMBERS	*97.5*	*118.5*	*93.0*	*116.3*
TOTAL	**534.2**	**466.4**	**484.9**	**464.9**

4. TOTAL ODA NET

DAC COUNTRIES

	1987	1988	1989	1990
Australia	–	–	–	–
Austria	0.1	0.1	0.1	0.1
Belgium	0.0	0.0	–	–
Canada	0.4	0.4	0.4	0.4
Denmark	7.2	13.9	12.7	13.2
Finland	0.1	0.1	0.1	0.2
France	3.9	8.8	3.2	16.5
Germany	32.4	33.1	27.4	38.0
Ireland	–	–	–	–
Italy	10.0	4.9	-2.0	-0.2
Japan	25.2	25.6	69.9	16.7
Netherlands	28.5	35.0	30.9	30.4
New Zealand	–	–	–	–
Norway	0.2	0.2	0.1	0.4
Sweden	–	5.5	0.6	–
Switzerland	0.3	2.5	1.1	2.2
United Kingdom	10.4	12.6	10.6	9.9
United States	44.0	26.0	40.0	41.0
TOTAL	*162.4*	*168.6*	*195.1*	*168.8*

MULTILATERAL

	1987	1988	1989	1990
AF.D.F.	–	–	–	–
AF.D.B.	–	–	–	–
AS.D.B	–	–	–	–
CAR.D.B.	–	–	–	–
E.E.C.	2.5	5.6	1.9	1.9
IBRD	–	–	–	–
IDA	38.9	48.0	40.0	30.0
I.D.B.	–	–	–	–
IFAD	9.8	2.1	4.4	6.6
I.F.C.	–	–	–	–
IMF TRUST FUND	–	–	–	–
U.N. AGENCIES	–	–	–	–
UNDP	4.9	9.3	14.6	17.2
UNTA	3.8	2.5	4.0	2.7
UNICEF	3.1	3.2	4.7	4.3
UNRWA	–	–	–	–
WFP	18.5	19.3	27.0	21.0
UNHCR	–	0.3	0.3	0.4
Other Multilateral	4.9	4.2	8.4	7.0
Arab Agencies	21.3	15.3	23.9	–
TOTAL	*107.7*	*109.9*	*129.1*	*91.0*
ARAB COUNTRIES	**151.9**	**24.6**	**33.9**	**132.1**
E.E.C.+ MEMBERS	*94.8*	*113.9*	*84.8*	*109.8*
TOTAL	**422.1**	**303.1**	**358.1**	**392.0**

5. ODA LOANS NET

DAC COUNTRIES

	1987	1988	1989	1990
Australia	–	–	–	–
Austria	–	–	–	–
Belgium	–	–	–	–
Canada	–	–	–	–
Denmark	-1.4	-2.4	–	–
Finland	–	–	–	–
France	-0.4	4.6	-0.3	11.5
Germany	–	–	–	–
Ireland	–	–	–	–
Italy	5.0	2.2	-6.0	-2.7
Japan	12.3	11.6	51.3	-1.4
Netherlands	1.9	1.6	3.0	–
New Zealand	–	–	–	–
Norway	–	–	–	–
Sweden	–	–	–	–
Switzerland	–	–	–	–
United Kingdom	–	–	–	–
United States	14.0	9.0	16.0	18.0
TOTAL	*31.4*	*26.6*	*64.0*	*25.4*
MULTILATERAL	*69.0*	*64.2*	*67.5*	*41.6*
ARAB COUNTRIES	**-6.6**	**-21.3**	**-14.6**	**-13.5**
E.E.C.+ MEMBERS	*5.1*	*6.0*	*-3.3*	*8.9*
TOTAL	**93.8**	**69.5**	**116.8**	**53.6**

6. TOTAL OFFICIAL NET

DAC COUNTRIES

	1987	1988	1989	1990
Australia	–	–	-0.1	–
Austria	0.1	0.1	0.1	0.1
Belgium	0.3	0.0	0.2	0.2
Canada	-0.8	-0.3	0.4	0.4
Denmark	7.2	13.9	12.7	13.2
Finland	0.1	0.1	0.1	0.2
France	3.9	8.8	3.2	16.5
Germany	32.4	33.1	27.5	37.4
Ireland	–	–	–	–
Italy	10.0	4.9	-2.0	-0.2
Japan	25.2	25.6	69.9	16.7
Netherlands	28.5	35.0	31.3	33.7
New Zealand	–	–	–	–
Norway	0.2	0.2	0.1	0.4
Sweden	–	5.5	0.6	–
Switzerland	0.3	2.5	1.1	2.2
United Kingdom	10.4	12.6	10.6	9.9
United States	44.0	26.0	40.0	41.0
TOTAL	*161.5*	*168.0*	*195.6*	*171.6*
MULTILATERAL	*98.6*	*89.7*	*117.6*	*91.0*
ARAB COUNTRIES	**151.9**	**24.6**	**33.9**	**132.1**
E.E.C.+ MEMBERS	*95.1*	*113.9*	*85.4*	*112.6*
TOTAL	**411.9**	**282.3**	**347.0**	**394.7**

7. TOTAL ODA GROSS

	1987
Australia	–
Austria	0.1
Belgium	0.0
Canada	0.4
Denmark	8.6
Finland	0.1
France	4.3
Germany	32.4
Ireland	–
Italy	10.6
Japan	27.7
Netherlands	28.5
New Zealand	–
Norway	0.2
Sweden	–
Switzerland	0.3
United Kingdom	10.4
United States	45.0
TOTAL	*168.4*
AF.D.F.	–
AF.D.B.	–
AS.D.B	–
CAR.D.B.	–
E.E.C.	2.5
IBRD	–
IDA	40.4
I.D.B.	–
IFAD	10.0
I.F.C.	–
IMF TRUST FUND	–
U.N. AGENCIES	–
UNDP	4.9
UNTA	3.8
UNICEF	3.1
UNRWA	–
WFP	18.5
UNHCR	–
Other Multilateral	4.9
Arab Agencies	43.6
TOTAL	*131.7*
ARAB COUNTRIES	**192.2**
E.E.C.+ MEMBERS	*97.3*
TOTAL	**492.3**

8. GRANTS

	1987
Australia	–
Austria	0.1
Belgium	0.0
Canada	0.4
Denmark	8.6
Finland	0.1
France	4.3
Germany	32.4
Ireland	–
Italy	5.0
Japan	12.8
Netherlands	26.7
New Zealand	–
Norway	0.2
Sweden	–
Switzerland	0.3
United Kingdom	10.4
United States	30.0
TOTAL	*131.0*
MULTILATERAL	*38.7*
ARAB COUNTRIES	**158.5**
E.E.C.+ MEMBERS	*89.8*
TOTAL	**328.2**

9. TOTAL OOF GROSS

	1987
Australia	–
Austria	–
Belgium	0.3
Canada	–
Denmark	–
Finland	–
France	–
Germany	–
Ireland	–
Italy	–
Japan	–
Netherlands	–
New Zealand	–
Norway	–
Sweden	–
Switzerland	–
United Kingdom	–
United States	–
TOTAL	*0.3*
MULTILATERAL	*41.6*
ARAB COUNTRIES	**–**
E.E.C.+ MEMBERS	*0.3*
TOTAL	**41.9**

10. ODA COMMITMENTS

1988	1989	1990	1987	1988	1989	1990
–	–	–	–	–	–	–
0.1	0.1	0.1	0.1	0.1	0.1	0.1
0.0	–	–	–	0.0	–	–
0.4	0.4	0.4	0.4	0.4	0.3	0.4
16.3	12.7	13.2	1.5	4.9	9.8	20.5
0.1	0.1	0.2	–	–	0.1	0.1
9.0	3.5	16.7	4.7	59.2	3.0	4.2
33.1	27.4	38.0	50.5	25.0	48.7	33.6
–	–	–	–	–	–	–
7.0	5.4	2.7	4.6	9.9	10.1	5.9
29.1	72.2	23.0	14.8	193.5	14.5	23.8
35.0	30.9	30.4	35.8	14.4	13.1	31.1
–	–	–	–	–	–	–
0.2	0.1	0.4	0.2	–	–	–
5.5	0.6	–	–	5.5	0.6	–
2.5	1.1	2.2	8.8	–	0.3	0.8
12.6	10.6	9.9	10.4	13.8	9.4	9.8
27.0	40.0	43.0	26.2	38.4	35.4	43.3
177.8	*205.0*	*180.1*	*157.8*	*365.1*	*145.4*	*173.5*
–	–	–	–	–	–	–
–	–	–	–	–	–	–
–	–	–	–	–	–	–
5.6	1.9	1.9	12.2	0.1	1.4	1.4
–	–	–	–	–	–	–
49.0	43.0	33.0	57.5	35.0	48.0	88.0
–	–	–	–	–	–	–
2.1	4.4	6.8	2.7	10.9	15.5	7.4
–	–	–	–	–	–	–
–	–	–	35.2	38.9	58.9	52.5
9.3	14.6	17.2	–	–	–	–
2.5	4.0	2.7	–	–	–	–
3.2	4.7	4.3	–	–	–	–
–	–	–	–	–	–	–
19.3	27.0	21.0	–	–	–	–
0.3	0.3	0.4	–	–	–	–
4.2	8.4	7.0	–	–	–	–
38.8	42.6	21.5	48.0	143.3	10.0	9.0
134.4	150.8	115.8	155.6	228.2	133.8	158.3
66.5	*80.1*	*161.8*	*174.5*	*51.7*	*43.6*	*50.0*
118.5	92.4	112.8	119.6	127.2	95.4	106.4
378.7	***435.9***	***457.7***	***487.9***	***644.9***	***322.8***	***381.8***

11. TECH. COOP. GRANTS

1988	1989	1990	1987	1988	1989	1990
–	–	–	–	–	–	–
0.1	0.1	0.1	0.1	0.1	0.1	0.1
0.0	–	–	0.0	0.0	–	–
0.4	0.4	0.4	–	–	–	–
16.3	12.7	13.2	0.1	0.1	–	–
0.1	0.1	0.2	0.0	–	–	0.0
4.3	3.5	5.0	4.1	3.8	3.0	2.9
33.1	27.4	38.0	12.5	32.9	14.6	14.3
–	–	–	–	–	–	–
2.7	4.0	2.5	5.0	0.1	1.3	1.7
14.0	18.6	18.2	1.8	3.4	3.4	3.4
33.4	27.9	30.4	20.0	27.1	23.3	27.0
–	–	–	–	–	–	–
0.2	0.1	0.4	0.0	0.1	0.0	0.0
5.5	0.6	–	–	–	–	–
2.5	1.1	2.2	–	0.0	–	–
12.6	10.6	9.9	8.5	10.1	7.7	8.8
17.0	24.0	23.0	18.0	17.0	20.0	18.0
142.1	*131.1*	*143.4*	*70.0*	*94.6*	*73.5*	*76.3*
45.7	*61.7*	*55.2*	*16.7*	*21.0*	*31.9*	*31.6*
45.9	***48.5***	***145.6***	–	–	–	–
107.9	*88.1*	*100.9*	*50.1*	*75.5*	*50.0*	*54.7*
233.6	***241.3***	***344.2***	***86.7***	***115.6***	***105.4***	***107.9***

12. TOTAL OOF NET

1988	1989	1990	1987	1988	1989	1990
–	–	–	–	–	-0.1	–
–	–	–	–	–	–	–
–	0.2	0.2	0.3	–	0.2	0.2
–	–	–	-1.2	-0.6	–	–
–	–	–	–	–	–	–
–	–	–	–	–	–	–
–	–	–	–	–	–	–
–	0.1	0.1	–	–	0.1	-0.6
–	–	–	–	–	–	–
–	–	–	–	–	–	–
–	0.4	3.3	–	–	0.4	3.3
–	–	–	–	–	–	–
–	–	–	–	–	–	–
–	–	–	–	–	–	–
–	–	–	–	–	–	–
–	0.6	3.5	-1.0	-0.6	0.5	2.8
87.7	48.4	3.7	-9.2	-20.1	-11.5	–
–	–	–	–	–	–	–
–	0.6	3.5	0.3	–	0.6	2.8
87.7	**49.0**	**7.2**	**-10.1**	**-20.8**	**-11.1**	**2.8**

13. ODF COMMITMENTS: BY PURPOSE %

	1987	1988	1989	1990
Education	8	3	11	–
Health	7	4	2	–
Other Social Infrastr.	1	–	3	–
Water Sanitat. Sewage	12	7	–	–
Energy	0	14	2	–
Telecommunications	–	2	5	–
Transportation	10	7	9	–
Agriculture	8	15	20	–
Extractive Industries	18	0	–	–
Manufacturing	0	30	1	–
Trade Banking Tourism	–	–	1	–
Technical Cooperation	13	13	36	–
Multisector Aid	0	–	–	–
Programme	19	1	1	–
Debt Reorganisation	1	1	2	–
Food Aid	2	2	4	–
Emergency Aid	0	0	3	–
Unspecified	1	2	–	–
TOTAL	100	100	100	–

14. GRANT ELEMENT OF ODA %

DAC COUNTRIES	1987	1988	1989	1990
Australia	–	–	–	–
Austria	100.0	100.0	100.0	–
Belgium	–	100.0	–	–
Canada	100.0	100.0	100.0	–
Denmark	100.0	100.0	100.0	–
Finland	–	–	100.0	–
France	100.0	58.1	100.0	–
Germany	100.0	100.0	100.0	–
Ireland	–	–	–	–
Italy	100.0	100.0	82.1	–
Japan	100.0	73.3	100.0	–
Netherlands	98.1	88.7	100.0	–
New Zealand	–	–	–	–
Norway	100.0	–	–	–
Sweden	–	100.0	100.0	–
Switzerland	100.0	–	100.0	–
United Kingdom	100.0	100.0	100.0	–
United States	74.6	83.3	86.9	–
TOTAL	*95.4*	*76.8*	*95.6*	–
MULTILATERAL	*74.1*	*63.7*	*89.6*	–
ARAB COUNTRIES	***93.2***	***80.1***	***90.3***	–
E.E.C.+ MEMBERS	*99.4*	*79.2*	*98.1*	–
TOTAL	***87.6***	***72.5***	***92.7***	–

15. OTHER AGGREGATES

OFFICIAL COMMITMENTS:	1987	1988	1989	1990
TOTAL BILATERAL	454.0	416.7	192.3	223.7
of which:				
Arab Countries	174.5	51.7	43.6	50.0
C.E.E.C.	121.6	–	–	–
TOTAL MULTILATERAL	186.9	267.8	184.7	158.3
TOTAL BIL.& MULTIL.	640.8	684.5	377.0	382.0
of which:				
ODA Grants	344.6	188.8	221.4	257.6
ODA Loans	264.9	456.1	101.4	124.2

DISBURSEMENTS:

DAC COUNTRIES COMBINED

OFFICIAL & PRIVATE	1987	1988	1989	1990
GROSS:				
Contractual Lending	141.9	97.8	177.8	138.4
Export Credits, Total	104.5	62.1	103.5	98.4
Export Credits, Priv.	104.5	62.1	103.4	98.3
NET:				
Contractual Lending	79.9	-6.4	-3.9	1.4
Export Credits Total	48.5	-33.0	-68.3	-26.6
PRIVATE SECTOR NET	27.5	-44.4	-68.2	-6.7
Direct Investment	5.5	8.2	13.7	12.5
Portfolio Investment	-27.7	-20.2	-13.7	7.5
Export Credits	49.7	-32.4	-68.2	-26.7

MARKET BORROWING:

CHANGE IN CLAIMS	1987	1988	1989	1990
Banks	-148.0	45.0	77.0	23.0

MEMORANDUM ITEM:

	1987	1988	1989	1990
C.E.E.C. (Gross)	155.3	131.9	30.4	–

	1987	1988	1989	1990		1987	1988	1989	1990		1987
1. TOTAL RECEIPTS NET					**4. TOTAL ODA NET**					**7. TOTAL ODA GROSS**	
DAC COUNTRIES											
Australia	-0.4	-0.2	–	0.0		–	0.0	–	0.0	Australia	–
Austria	-10.0	-8.3	-1.3	46.7		2.4	2.6	5.5	8.8	Austria	2.5
Belgium	-2.2	-32.5	30.6	-91.7		0.1	0.0	–	0.0	Belgium	0.1
Canada	-5.4	8.5	18.2	23.4		–	–	–	–	Canada	–
Denmark	12.3	-0.3	-0.1	4.0		–	–	–	–	Denmark	–
Finland	17.3	–	0.0	8.5		–	–	0.0	1.9	Finland	–
France	-312.0	-33.0	-265.5	-182.1		3.4	3.3	3.4	4.4	France	3.4
Germany	-99.6	73.4	37.6	92.6		6.4	23.4	17.6	-2.0	Germany	10.7
Ireland	–	–	–	–		–	–	–	–	Ireland	–
Italy	138.8	11.6	41.8	-28.4		16.1	4.0	1.8	25.5	Italy	16.5
Japan	-3.8	37.5	50.9	31.4		0.5	1.3	7.1	-0.3	Japan	5.8
Netherlands	-24.0	-49.2	-48.6	-21.1		1.0	1.5	1.2	1.6	Netherlands	1.0
New Zealand	–	–	–	–		–	–	–	–	New Zealand	–
Norway	1.8	-34.9	-3.6	-12.6		–	–	-0.3	-0.6	Norway	–
Sweden	11.7	–	-1.6	0.9		–	–	–	–	Sweden	–
Switzerland	–	–	0.1	0.1		–	–	0.1	0.1	Switzerland	–
United Kingdom	-31.5	-113.8	111.5	-51.6		–	–	–	0.0	United Kingdom	–
United States	142.0	-34.0	-137.0	-314.0		–	–	–	–	United States	–
TOTAL	-165.2	-175.2	-167.0	-494.0		29.9	36.2	36.5	39.5	TOTAL	40.1
MULTILATERAL											
AF.D.F.	–	–	–	–		–	–	–	–	AF.D.F.	–
AF.D.B.	–	–	–	–		–	–	–	–	AF.D.B.	–
AS.D.B	–	–	–	–		–	–	–	–	AS.D.B	–
CAR.D.B.	–	–	–	–		–	–	–	–	CAR.D.B.	–
E.E.C.	33.9	7.3	53.8	53.8		0.7	3.1	2.2	2.2	E.E.C.	0.7
IBRD	-127.2	-312.0	-244.0	-136.0		–	–	–	–	IBRD	–
IDA	–	–	–	–		–	–	–	–	IDA	–
I.D.B.	–	–	–	–		–	–	–	–	I.D.B.	–
IFAD	–	–	–	–		–	–	–	–	IFAD	–
I.F.C.	12.6	-27.0	0.2	23.5		–	–	–	–	I.F.C.	–
IMF TRUST FUND	–	–	–	–		–	–	–	–	IMF TRUST FUND	–
U.N. AGENCIES	–	–	–	–		–	–	–	–	U.N. AGENCIES	–
UNDP	1.2	1.8	1.5	1.3		1.2	1.8	1.5	1.3	UNDP	1.2
UNTA	0.9	0.2	0.4	1.1		0.9	0.2	0.4	1.1	UNTA	0.9
UNICEF	–	–	–	–		–	–	–	–	UNICEF	–
UNRWA	–	–	–	–		–	–	–	–	UNRWA	–
WFP	–	–	–	–		–	–	–	–	WFP	–
UNHCR	2.1	2.0	2.1	3.0		2.1	2.0	2.1	3.0	UNHCR	2.1
Other Multilateral	21.2	16.9	17.6	9.6		0.3	0.3	0.2	0.7	Other Multilateral	0.3
Arab Agencies	–	–	–	–		–	–	–	–	Arab Agencies	–
TOTAL	-55.3	-310.9	-168.4	-43.7		5.2	7.4	6.4	8.2	TOTAL	5.2
ARAB COUNTRIES	*-29.7*	*-6.0*	*–*	*–*		*–*	*0.3*	*–*	*–*	*ARAB COUNTRIES*	*–*
E.E.C.+ MEMBERS	*-284.4*	*-136.5*	*-38.9*	*-224.6*		*27.7*	*35.4*	*26.2*	*31.7*	*E.E.C.+ MEMBERS*	*32.4*
TOTAL	*-250.2*	*-492.1*	*-335.4*	*-537.8*		*35.1*	*43.9*	*42.9*	*47.7*	*TOTAL*	*45.4*
2. ODA LOANS GROSS					**5. ODA LOANS NET**					**8. GRANTS**	
DAC COUNTRIES											
Australia	–	–	–	–		–	–	–	–	Australia	–
Austria	0.1	–	–	–		-0.1	-0.1	-0.1	-0.2	Austria	2.5
Belgium	–	–	–	–		–	–	–	–	Belgium	0.1
Canada	–	–	–	–		–	–	–	–	Canada	–
Denmark	–	–	–	–		–	–	–	–	Denmark	–
Finland	–	–	–	–		–	–	–	–	Finland	–
France	–	–	–	–		–	–	–	–	France	3.4
Germany	–	11.6	5.2	–		-4.4	11.5	5.2	-17.6	Germany	10.7
Ireland	–	–	–	–		–	–	–	–	Ireland	–
Italy	14.5	4.0	3.8	27.9		14.1	3.2	-0.9	24.4	Italy	2.0
Japan	4.5	4.2	6.2	–		-0.8	-0.3	5.3	-1.6	Japan	1.3
Netherlands	–	–	–	–		–	–	–	–	Netherlands	1.0
New Zealand	–	–	–	–		–	–	–	–	New Zealand	–
Norway	–	–	–	–		–	–	-0.3	-0.6	Norway	–
Sweden	–	–	–	–		–	–	–	–	Sweden	–
Switzerland	–	–	–	–		–	–	–	–	Switzerland	–
United Kingdom	–	–	–	–		–	–	–	–	United Kingdom	–
United States	–	–	–	–		–	–	–	–	United States	–
TOTAL	19.1	19.8	15.1	27.9		8.8	14.2	9.1	4.3	TOTAL	21.0
MULTILATERAL	–	–	–	–		–	–	–	–	MULTILATERAL	5.2
ARAB COUNTRIES	*–*	*–*	*–*	*–*		*–*	*–*	*–*	*–*	*ARAB COUNTRIES*	*–*
E.E.C.+ MEMBERS	*14.5*	*15.6*	*9.0*	*27.9*		*9.8*	*14.7*	*4.3*	*6.7*	*E.E.C.+ MEMBERS*	*17.9*
TOTAL	*19.1*	*19.8*	*15.1*	*27.9*		*8.8*	*14.2*	*9.1*	*4.3*	*TOTAL*	*26.3*
3. TOTAL OFFICIAL GROSS					**6. TOTAL OFFICIAL NET**					**9. TOTAL OOF GROSS**	
DAC COUNTRIES											
Australia	–	0.0	–	0.0		-0.4	-0.2	–	0.0	Australia	–
Austria	2.5	2.8	5.7	9.0		2.4	2.6	5.5	8.8	Austria	–
Belgium	0.4	0.0	0.2	0.2		0.4	0.0	0.2	0.2	Belgium	0.3
Canada	2.1	13.7	23.4	26.5		-5.5	8.5	17.9	22.1	Canada	2.1
Denmark	1.2	–	–	–		1.2	-0.3	-0.1	–	Denmark	1.2
Finland	–	–	0.0	1.9		–	–	0.0	1.9	Finland	–
France	123.7	59.9	62.6	4.4		123.7	59.9	27.0	-9.7	France	120.3
Germany	95.2	139.3	54.9	50.1		39.4	67.0	-3.0	-12.0	Germany	84.5
Ireland	–	–	–	–		–	–	–	–	Ireland	–
Italy	135.4	27.2	70.7	44.4		108.9	7.8	29.3	1.6	Italy	118.9
Japan	14.7	28.4	69.3	1.3		8.4	19.3	61.5	-6.9	Japan	8.9
Netherlands	1.0	11.2	1.2	1.6		-9.9	-0.1	-8.1	-9.2	Netherlands	–
New Zealand	–	–	–	–		–	–	–	–	New Zealand	–
Norway	–	–	–	–		–	–	-0.3	-0.6	Norway	–
Sweden	–	–	–	–		–	–	–	–	Sweden	–
Switzerland	–	–	0.1	0.1		–	–	0.1	0.1	Switzerland	–
United Kingdom	–	–	–	0.0		–	–	–	0.0	United Kingdom	–
United States	63.0	130.0	87.0	2.0		-40.0	-1.0	12.0	-38.0	United States	63.0
TOTAL	439.4	412.4	375.2	141.6		228.7	163.6	142.1	-41.7	TOTAL	399.3
MULTILATERAL	306.3	224.4	261.1	451.3		-55.3	-310.9	-168.4	-43.7	MULTILATERAL	301.1
ARAB COUNTRIES	*–*	*0.3*	*–*	*–*		*-29.7*	*-6.0*	*–*	*–*	*ARAB COUNTRIES*	*–*
E.E.C.+ MEMBERS	*396.2*	*253.9*	*253.4*	*164.4*		*297.6*	*141.6*	*99.1*	*24.6*	*E.E.C.+ MEMBERS*	*363.7*
TOTAL	*745.7*	*637.2*	*636.3*	*592.9*		*143.8*	*-153.3*	*-26.3*	*-85.4*	*TOTAL*	*700.4*

10. ODA COMMITMENTS

1988	1989	1990	1987	1988	1989	1990
0.0	–	0.0	–	–	–	0.0
2.8	5.7	9.0	2.5	2.8	5.7	9.0
0.0	–	0.0	–	–	–	0.0
–	–	–	–	–	–	–
–	0.0	1.9	–	–	–	0.1
3.3	3.4	4.4	3.4	3.3	3.4	4.4
23.5	17.6	15.6	10.7	29.1	12.5	15.9
–	–	–	–	–	–	–
4.8	6.5	29.0	0.8	62.3	1.0	59.9
5.8	8.1	1.3	5.6	6.2	8.0	1.4
1.5	1.2	1.6	1.0	1.5	1.2	1.6
–	–	–	–	–	–	–
–	–	–	–	–	–	–
–	0.1	0.1	–	–	–	–
–	–	0.0	–	–	0.0	0.0
–	–	–	–	–	–	–
41.8	*42.5*	*63.1*	*24.0*	*105.1*	*31.7*	*92.3*
–	–	–	–	–	–	–
–	–	–	–	–	–	–
3.1	2.2	2.2	0.8	0.8	2.9	2.9
–	–	–	–	–	–	–
–	–	–	–	–	–	–
–	–	–	–	–	–	–
–	–	–	4.5	4.3	4.2	6.0
1.8	1.5	1.3	–	–	–	–
0.2	0.4	1.1	–	–	–	–
–	–	–	–	–	–	–
2.0	2.1	3.0	–	–	–	–
0.3	0.2	0.7	–	–	–	–
–	–	–	–	–	–	–
7.4	*6.4*	*8.2*	*5.3*	*5.1*	*7.1*	*8.9*
0.3	–	–	–	–	–	–
36.2	*30.9*	*52.9*	*16.7*	*96.9*	*20.9*	*84.7*
49.5	*48.9*	*71.3*	*29.3*	*110.2*	*38.8*	*101.2*

11. TECH. COOP. GRANTS

1988	1989	1990	1987	1988	1989	1990
0.0	–	0.0	–	0.0	–	0.0
2.8	5.7	9.0	2.5	2.8	3.5	4.8
0.0	–	0.0	–	0.0	–	0.0
–	–	–	–	–	–	–
–	0.0	1.9	–	–	0.0	0.1
3.3	3.4	4.4	3.4	3.3	3.4	4.4
11.9	12.5	15.6	10.7	12.0	12.5	15.6
–	–	–	–	–	–	–
0.8	2.7	1.1	0.7	0.8	1.0	1.1
1.6	1.9	1.3	1.0	1.6	1.7	1.3
1.5	1.2	1.6	1.0	1.5	1.2	1.6
–	–	–	–	–	–	–
–	0.1	0.1	–	–	–	–
–	–	0.0	–	–	–	0.0
–	–	–	–	–	–	–
22.0	*27.4*	*35.1*	*19.3*	*22.0*	*23.2*	*29.0*
7.4	*6.4*	*8.2*	*4.5*	*4.5*	*4.2*	*6.0*
0.3	–	–	–	–	–	–
20.7	*21.9*	*24.9*	*15.9*	*17.8*	*18.0*	*22.7*
29.7	*33.8*	*43.4*	*23.9*	*26.5*	*27.4*	*35.0*

12. TOTAL OOF NET

1988	1989	1990	1987	1988	1989	1990
–	–	–	-0.4	-0.2	–	–
–	–	–	–	–	–	–
–	0.2	0.2	0.3	–	0.2	0.2
13.7	23.4	26.5	-5.5	8.5	17.9	22.1
–	–	–	1.2	-0.3	-0.1	–
–	–	–	–	–	–	–
56.6	59.3	–	120.3	56.6	23.6	-14.1
115.8	37.3	34.5	33.0	43.6	-20.6	-10.0
–	–	–	–	–	–	–
22.3	64.3	15.4	92.8	3.8	27.5	-23.9
22.6	61.2	–	7.9	18.0	54.3	-6.6
9.6	–	–	-11.0	-1.6	-9.3	-10.8
–	–	–	–	–	–	–
–	–	–	–	–	–	–
–	–	–	–	–	–	–
130.0	87.0	2.0	-40.0	-1.0	12.0	-38.0
370.6	*332.7*	*78.5*	*198.9*	*127.4*	*105.6*	*-81.2*
217.1	*254.7*	*443.1*	*-60.5*	*-318.2*	*-174.8*	*-52.0*
–	–	–	*-29.7*	*-6.3*	–	–
217.7	*222.5*	*111.5*	*270.0*	*106.2*	*72.9*	*-7.0*
587.7	*587.4*	*521.6*	*108.7*	*-197.2*	*-69.2*	*-133.1*

13. ODF COMMITMENTS: BY PURPOSE %

	1987	1988	1989	1990
Education	–	0	–	–
Health	–	–	–	–
Other Social Infrastr.	–	–	–	–
Water Sanitat. Sewage	–	–	–	–
Energy	38	–	–	–
Telecommunications	–	–	–	–
Transportation	52	18	–	–
Agriculture	–	–	–	–
Extractive Industries	–	–	–	–
Manufacturing	–	–	–	–
Trade Banking Tourism	–	–	–	–
Technical Cooperation	10	7	100	–
Multisector Aid	–	–	–	–
Programme	–	21	–	–
Debt Reorganisation	–	53	–	–
Food Aid	–	–	–	–
Emergency Aid	–	–	–	–
Unspecified	–	–	–	–
TOTAL	100	100	100	–

14. GRANT ELEMENT OF ODA %

DAC COUNTRIES

	1987	1988	1989	1990
Australia	–	–	–	–
Austria	100.0	100.0	100.0	–
Belgium	–	–	–	–
Canada	–	–	–	–
Denmark	–	–	–	–
Finland	–	–	–	–
France	100.0	100.0	100.0	–
Germany	100.0	50.2	100.0	–
Ireland	–	–	–	–
Italy	100.0	57.4	100.0	–
Japan	100.0	100.0	100.0	–
Netherlands	100.0	100.0	100.0	–
New Zealand	–	–	–	–
Norway	–	–	–	–
Sweden	–	–	–	–
Switzerland	–	–	–	–
United Kingdom	–	–	100.0	–
United States	–	–	–	–
TOTAL	*100.0*	*56.7*	*100.0*	–
MULTILATERAL	*100.0*	*100.0*	*100.0*	–
ARAB COUNTRIES	–	–	–	–
E.E.C.+ MEMBERS	*100.0*	*55.5*	*100.0*	–
TOTAL	*100.0*	*58.2*	*100.0*	–

15. OTHER AGGREGATES

	1987	1988	1989	1990
OFFICIAL COMMITMENTS:				
TOTAL BILATERAL	205.9	634.1	117.3	98.9
of which:				
Arab Countries	–	–	–	–
C.E.E.C.	–	–	–	–
TOTAL MULTILATERAL	249.5	399.1	339.8	776.4
TOTAL BIL.& MULTIL.	455.4	1033.1	457.1	875.4
of which:				
ODA Grants	24.8	27.4	32.6	46.7
ODA Loans	4.5	82.8	6.2	54.5
DISBURSEMENTS:				
DAC COUNTRIES COMBINED				
OFFICIAL & PRIVATE				
GROSS:				
Contractual Lending	663.0	667.1	926.3	303.6
Export Credits, Total	341.8	350.4	652.2	275.7
Export Credits, Priv.	245.1	276.8	578.7	197.4
NET:				
Contractual Lending	81.6	-107.4	288.3	-232.6
Export Credits Total	-200.9	-370.0	110.3	-185.2
PRIVATE SECTOR NET	-393.9	-338.8	-309.1	-452.3
Direct Investment	7.2	22.1	9.1	67.2
Portfolio Investment	-275.4	-112.0	-492.0	-363.9
Export Credits	-125.7	-248.9	173.8	-155.7
MARKET BORROWING:				
CHANGE IN CLAIMS				
Banks	-981.0	-678.0	-1425.0	-938.0
MEMORANDUM ITEM:				
C.E.E.C. (Gross)	–	–	–	–

1. TOTAL RECEIPTS NET

DAC COUNTRIES	1987	1988	1989	1990
Australia	–	0.1	0.1	0.1
Austria	-0.9	-0.9	-0.3	2.0
Belgium	152.3	126.6	145.8	128.6
Canada	17.1	24.7	23.4	15.0
Denmark	–	0.2	0.1	–
Finland	0.1	0.1	0.1	0.4
France	32.9	151.4	88.3	189.6
Germany	49.3	80.7	52.3	176.0
Ireland	–	–	–	–
Italy	108.7	134.0	-8.9	174.4
Japan	-27.0	19.1	68.8	36.3
Netherlands	2.7	7.2	3.2	-3.7
New Zealand	–	–	–	–
Norway	0.9	1.0	0.4	-1.1
Sweden	–	–	6.4	-2.5
Switzerland	1.7	1.2	0.9	1.0
United Kingdom	7.1	4.1	12.2	7.9
United States	79.0	110.0	57.0	250.0
TOTAL	*423.8*	*659.4*	*449.8*	*974.0*
MULTILATERAL				
AF.D.F.	29.6	26.8	30.3	38.0
AF.D.B.	46.4	73.5	59.8	114.3
AS.D.B	–	–	–	–
CAR.D.B.	–	–	–	–
E.E.C.	19.1	35.9	51.3	51.3
IBRD	-8.1	-8.0	-4.0	16.0
IDA	211.8	87.0	89.0	70.0
I.D.B.	–	–	–	–
IFAD	4.5	0.3	3.0	3.0
I.F.C.	-0.7	-1.5	2.5	4.9
IMF TRUST FUND	–	–	–	–
U.N. AGENCIES	–	–	–	–
UNDP	7.6	9.7	11.0	12.2
UNTA	1.4	1.4	1.5	1.5
UNICEF	4.0	5.6	6.6	7.0
UNRWA	–	–	–	–
WFP	0.7	–	0.4	3.2
UNHCR	6.8	6.4	4.5	3.4
Other Multilateral	1.3	1.9	2.2	2.5
Arab Agencies	-0.3	-0.6	-0.7	–
TOTAL	*324.0*	*238.3*	*257.3*	*327.1*
ARAB COUNTRIES	**-11.6**	**-12.6**	**–**	**–**
E.E.C.+ MEMBERS	*372.0*	*540.0*	*344.3*	*723.9*
TOTAL	**736.2**	**885.1**	**707.1**	**1301.1**

2. ODA LOANS GROSS

DAC COUNTRIES	1987	1988	1989	1990
Australia	–	–	–	–
Austria	–	–	–	–
Belgium	11.0	24.5	19.9	9.4
Canada	0.7	–	–	–
Denmark	–	–	–	–
Finland	–	–	–	–
France	18.6	53.7	52.5	42.9
Germany	27.8	27.1	21.1	92.9
Ireland	–	–	–	–
Italy	24.6	39.4	28.5	138.2
Japan	24.1	–	31.3	51.6
Netherlands	–	–	–	–
New Zealand	–	–	–	–
Norway	–	–	–	–
Sweden	–	–	–	–
Switzerland	–	–	–	–
United Kingdom	–	–	–	–
United States	17.0	22.0	25.0	19.0
TOTAL	*123.6*	*166.7*	*178.1*	*354.0*
MULTILATERAL	*256.1*	*120.7*	*126.6*	*115.9*
ARAB COUNTRIES	**–**	**–**	**–**	**–**
E.E.C.+ MEMBERS	*89.6*	*148.8*	*123.4*	*284.9*
TOTAL	**379.7**	**287.4**	**304.7**	**469.9**

3. TOTAL OFFICIAL GROSS

DAC COUNTRIES	1987	1988	1989	1990
Australia	–	0.1	0.1	0.1
Austria	0.2	0.2	0.2	2.0
Belgium	165.2	141.4	196.5	95.6
Canada	17.4	24.8	24.4	41.1
Denmark	–	0.2	0.1	0.0
Finland	0.1	0.1	0.1	0.4
France	56.2	170.8	106.2	358.4
Germany	62.8	112.9	53.2	212.7
Ireland	–	–	–	–
Italy	126.5	59.2	42.1	208.2
Japan	28.0	23.4	90.8	69.8
Netherlands	1.4	3.4	3.2	3.9
New Zealand	–	–	–	–
Norway	0.9	1.0	0.4	0.2
Sweden	–	–	–	–
Switzerland	1.7	1.2	0.9	1.0
United Kingdom	5.1	1.1	1.2	3.4
United States	172.0	223.0	54.0	409.0
TOTAL	*637.4*	*762.6*	*573.3*	*1405.9*
MULTILATERAL	*356.6*	*275.8*	*302.7*	*359.2*
ARAB COUNTRIES	**–**	**–**	**–**	**–**
E.E.C.+ MEMBERS	*439.4*	*528.3*	*459.3*	*939.2*
TOTAL	**994.0**	**1038.4**	**876.0**	**1765.1**

4. TOTAL ODA NET

	1987	1988	1989	1990
Australia	–	0.1	0.1	0.1
Austria	0.0	–	0.1	2.0
Belgium	121.6	136.4	95.9	95.4
Canada	17.4	12.0	24.4	14.3
Denmark	–	–	–	0.0
Finland	0.1	0.1	0.1	0.4
France	40.2	78.0	99.5	174.2
Germany	52.3	51.8	44.6	112.4
Ireland	–	–	–	–
Italy	31.4	56.0	33.1	145.1
Japan	26.5	23.4	76.6	44.1
Netherlands	1.4	3.4	3.2	3.9
New Zealand	–	–	–	–
Norway	0.9	1.0	0.4	0.2
Sweden	–	–	–	–
Switzerland	1.7	1.2	0.9	1.0
United Kingdom	5.1	1.1	1.2	3.4
United States	40.0	36.0	53.0	32.0
TOTAL	*338.5*	*400.3*	*432.9*	*628.5*
AF.D.F.	29.6	26.8	30.3	38.0
AF.D.B.	–	–	–	–
AS.D.B	–	–	–	–
CAR.D.B.	–	–	–	–
E.E.C.	21.1	37.0	53.7	53.7
IBRD	–	–	–	–
IDA	211.8	87.0	89.0	70.0
I.D.B.	–	–	–	–
IFAD	4.5	0.3	3.0	3.0
I.F.C.	–	–	–	–
IMF TRUST FUND	–	–	–	–
U.N. AGENCIES	–	–	–	–
UNDP	7.6	9.7	11.0	12.2
UNTA	1.4	1.4	1.5	1.5
UNICEF	4.0	5.6	6.6	7.0
UNRWA	–	–	–	–
WFP	0.7	–	0.4	3.2
UNHCR	6.8	6.4	4.5	3.4
Other Multilateral	1.3	1.9	2.2	2.5
Arab Agencies	-0.3	-0.6	-0.7	–
TOTAL	*288.4*	*175.4*	*201.5*	*194.4*
ARAB COUNTRIES	**–**	**–**	**–**	**–**
E.E.C.+ MEMBERS	*273.0*	*363.5*	*331.0*	*588.0*
TOTAL	**626.9**	**575.7**	**634.4**	**822.9**

5. ODA LOANS NET

	1987	1988	1989	1990
Australia	–	–	–	–
Austria	-0.2	-0.2	-0.1	–
Belgium	11.0	24.0	19.9	9.4
Canada	0.7	–	–	-26.8
Denmark	–	–	–	–
Finland	–	–	–	–
France	16.7	51.6	48.5	37.0
Germany	27.2	26.4	21.1	90.0
Ireland	–	–	–	–
Italy	23.6	36.1	19.5	137.0
Japan	22.5	–	17.0	25.9
Netherlands	–	–	–	–
New Zealand	–	–	–	–
Norway	–	–	–	–
Sweden	–	–	–	–
Switzerland	–	–	–	–
United Kingdom	–	–	–	–
United States	1.0	5.0	24.0	-1.0
TOTAL	*102.5*	*142.9*	*149.8*	*271.4*
MULTILATERAL	*251.9*	*116.3*	*119.8*	*109.2*
ARAB COUNTRIES	**–**	**–**	**–**	**–**
E.E.C.+ MEMBERS	*84.9*	*140.9*	*107.2*	*271.6*
TOTAL	**354.4**	**259.2**	**269.6**	**380.5**

6. TOTAL OFFICIAL NET

	1987	1988	1989	1990
Australia	–	0.1	0.1	0.1
Austria	0.0	–	0.1	2.0
Belgium	164.1	140.9	195.8	95.6
Canada	17.1	24.7	23.4	12.6
Denmark	–	0.2	0.1	–
Finland	0.1	0.1	0.1	0.4
France	52.4	147.9	101.2	210.7
Germany	57.2	84.3	52.7	177.0
Ireland	–	–	–	–
Italy	113.1	56.0	33.1	179.3
Japan	26.5	23.4	76.6	44.1
Netherlands	1.4	3.4	3.2	3.9
New Zealand	–	–	–	–
Norway	0.9	1.0	0.4	0.2
Sweden	–	–	–	–
Switzerland	1.7	1.2	0.9	1.0
United Kingdom	5.1	1.1	1.2	3.4
United States	103.0	146.0	53.0	251.0
TOTAL	*542.5*	*630.1*	*541.7*	*981.5*
MULTILATERAL	*324.0*	*238.3*	*257.3*	*327.1*
ARAB COUNTRIES	**-11.6**	**-12.6**	**–**	**–**
E.E.C.+ MEMBERS	*412.2*	*469.5*	*438.4*	*721.3*
TOTAL	**854.9**	**855.8**	**799.0**	**1308.6**

7. TOTAL ODA GROSS

	1987
Australia	–
Austria	0.2
Belgium	121.6
Canada	17.4
Denmark	–
Finland	0.1
France	42.0
Germany	52.9
Ireland	–
Italy	32.4
Japan	28.0
Netherlands	1.4
New Zealand	–
Norway	0.9
Sweden	–
Switzerland	1.7
United Kingdom	5.1
United States	56.0
TOTAL	*359.7*
AF.D.F.	30.1
AF.D.B.	–
AS.D.B	–
CAR.D.B.	–
E.E.C.	22.3
IBRD	–
IDA	213.9
I.D.B.	–
IFAD	4.5
I.F.C.	–
IMF TRUST FUND	–
U.N. AGENCIES	–
UNDP	7.6
UNTA	1.4
UNICEF	4.0
UNRWA	–
WFP	0.7
UNHCR	6.8
Other Multilateral	1.3
Arab Agencies	–
TOTAL	*292.6*
ARAB COUNTRIES	**–**
E.E.C.+ MEMBERS	*277.6*
TOTAL	*652.2*

8. GRANTS

	1987
Australia	–
Austria	0.2
Belgium	110.6
Canada	16.7
Denmark	–
Finland	0.1
France	23.5
Germany	25.1
Ireland	–
Italy	7.9
Japan	4.0
Netherlands	1.4
New Zealand	–
Norway	0.9
Sweden	–
Switzerland	1.7
United Kingdom	5.1
United States	39.0
TOTAL	*236.1*
MULTILATERAL	*36.5*
ARAB COUNTRIES	**–**
E.E.C.+ MEMBERS	*188.1*
TOTAL	*272.6*

9. TOTAL OOF GROSS

	1987
Australia	–
Austria	–
Belgium	43.7
Canada	–
Denmark	–
Finland	–
France	14.1
Germany	9.9
Ireland	–
Italy	94.1
Japan	–
Netherlands	–
New Zealand	–
Norway	–
Sweden	–
Switzerland	–
United Kingdom	–
United States	116.0
TOTAL	*277.8*
MULTILATERAL	*64.0*
ARAB COUNTRIES	**–**
E.E.C.+ MEMBERS	*161.8*
TOTAL	*341.8*

10. ODA COMMITMENTS

1988	1989	1990	1987	1988	1989	1990
0.1	0.1	0.1	–	0.1	0.1	0.1
0.2	0.2	2.0	0.2	0.2	0.2	11.5
136.9	95.9	95.4	111.4	141.7	95.9	95.4
12.0	24.4	41.1	18.1	11.4	16.7	11.6
–	–	0.0	–	–	–	–
0.1	0.1	0.4	–	–	0.1	0.4
80.1	103.4	180.2	83.2	72.6	53.4	51.0
52.5	44.6	115.3	41.5	62.3	114.3	43.1
–	–	–	–	–	–	–
59.2	42.1	146.3	58.8	85.8	23.7	130.8
23.4	90.8	69.8	50.4	42.6	74.1	64.0
3.4	3.2	3.9	1.3	3.3	3.2	3.9
–	–	–	–	–	–	–
1.0	0.4	0.2	1.0	–	–	–
–	–	–	–	–	–	–
1.2	0.9	1.0	1.3	0.8	0.5	0.5
1.1	1.2	3.4	4.0	1.1	0.8	13.9
53.0	54.0	52.0	52.7	61.3	255.4	56.5
424.1	461.2	711.1	423.8	483.2	638.2	482.6
27.3	31.0	39.2	14.8	45.7	134.6	2.3
–	–	–	–	–	–	–
–	–	–	–	–	–	–
38.3	56.9	56.9	136.5	31.5	50.1	50.1
–	–	–	–	–	–	–
89.0	91.0	72.0	229.3	65.0	95.0	49.0
–	–	–	–	–	–	–
0.3	3.0	3.2	7.8	–	–	0.2
–	–	–	–	–	–	–
–	–	–	21.9	25.0	26.3	29.8
9.7	11.0	12.2	–	–	–	–
1.4	1.5	1.5	–	–	–	–
5.6	6.6	7.0	–	–	–	–
–	–	–	–	–	–	–
–	0.4	3.2	–	–	–	–
6.4	4.5	3.4	–	–	–	–
1.9	2.2	2.5	–	–	–	–
–	–	–	–	–	–	–
179.8	208.3	201.1	410.2	167.2	306.0	131.4
–	–	–	–	–	–	–
371.4	347.2	601.4	436.6	398.4	341.2	388.1
603.9	669.4	912.2	834.0	650.3	944.1	614.0

11. TECH. COOP. GRANTS

1988	1989	1990	1987	1988	1989	1990
0.1	0.1	0.1	–	–	–	–
0.2	0.2	2.0	0.2	0.2	0.2	0.2
112.4	76.0	86.0	83.6	68.6	54.0	44.6
12.0	24.4	41.1	–	4.5	3.8	2.5
–	–	0.0	–	–	–	0.0
0.1	0.1	0.4	–	–	–	–
26.5	51.0	137.3	16.5	17.9	14.2	19.6
25.4	23.5	22.4	24.1	24.9	19.1	20.5
–	–	–	–	–	–	–
19.8	13.6	8.1	7.7	8.1	2.3	2.2
23.4	59.6	18.2	3.6	3.9	3.0	3.3
3.4	3.2	3.9	1.3	3.2	3.1	3.9
–	–	–	–	–	–	–
1.0	0.4	0.2	0.2	0.3	0.2	0.2
–	–	–	–	–	–	–
1.2	0.9	1.0	0.4	0.4	–	–
1.1	1.2	3.4	0.7	1.1	0.6	0.7
31.0	29.0	33.0	14.0	26.0	24.0	22.0
257.4	283.1	357.1	152.3	159.0	124.4	119.8
59.1	81.7	85.2	23.3	29.8	25.8	26.6
–	–	–	–	–	–	–
222.6	223.8	316.5	136.1	128.6	93.2	91.6
316.5	364.7	442.3	175.6	188.8	150.3	146.4

12. TOTAL OOF NET

1988	1989	1990	1987	1988	1989	1990
–	–	–	–	–	–	–
4.5	100.6	0.3	42.6	4.5	99.9	0.3
12.8	–	–	-0.3	12.8	-0.9	-1.7
0.2	0.1	–	–	0.2	0.1	0.0
–	–	–	–	–	–	–
90.7	2.8	178.2	12.1	69.9	1.7	36.5
60.4	8.7	97.5	4.9	32.5	8.2	64.7
–	–	61.9	81.6	–	–	34.3
–	–	–	–	–	–	–
–	–	–	–	–	–	–
–	–	–	–	–	–	–
–	–	–	–	–	–	–
–	–	–	–	–	–	–
170.0	–	357.0	63.0	110.0	–	219.0
338.5	112.1	694.8	203.9	229.8	108.8	353.0
96.0	94.4	158.1	35.6	62.9	55.9	132.8
–	–	–	-11.6	-12.6	–	–
156.9	112.1	337.8	139.3	106.0	107.4	133.3
434.5	206.5	852.9	228.0	280.1	164.7	485.7

13. ODF COMMITMENTS: BY PURPOSE %

	1987	1988	1989	1990
Education	2	0	6	–
Health	2	2	1	–
Other Social Infrastr.	2	1	4	–
Water Sanitat. Sewage	5	11	14	–
Energy	13	6	9	–
Telecommunications	0	1	–	–
Transportation	13	14	36	–
Agriculture	7	7	2	–
Extractive Industries	–	–	2	–
Manufacturing	–	15	2	–
Trade Banking Tourism	4	–	0	–
Technical Cooperation	23	27	11	–
Multisector Aid	0	0	1	–
Programme	23	1	5	–
Debt Reorganisation	3	9	3	–
Food Aid	3	4	4	–
Emergency Aid	0	0	–	–
Unspecified	–	–	–	–
TOTAL	100	100	100	–

14. GRANT ELEMENT OF ODA %

DAC COUNTRIES

	1987	1988	1989	1990
Australia	–	100.0	100.0	–
Austria	100.0	100.0	100.0	–
Belgium	100.0	100.0	100.0	–
Canada	100.0	100.0	100.0	–
Denmark	–	–	–	–
Finland	–	–	100.0	–
France	53.4	60.9	51.6	–
Germany	90.7	80.1	72.8	–
Ireland	–	–	–	–
Italy	71.0	79.4	77.1	–
Japan	61.8	91.4	67.6	–
Netherlands	100.0	100.0	100.0	–
New Zealand	–	–	–	–
Norway	100.0	–	–	–
Sweden	–	–	–	–
Switzerland	100.0	100.0	100.0	–
United Kingdom	100.0	100.0	100.0	–
United States	90.0	86.9	96.9	–
TOTAL	80.0	84.4	83.0	–
MULTILATERAL	88.7	86.9	86.5	–
ARAB COUNTRIES	–	–	–	–
E.E.C.+ MEMBERS	86.5	83.9	77.8	–
TOTAL	84.7	85.1	84.1	–

15. OTHER AGGREGATES

OFFICIAL COMMITMENTS:

	1987	1988	1989	1990
TOTAL BILATERAL	840.7	726.2	1088.6	1023.5
of which:				
Arab Countries	–	–	–	–
C.E.E.C.				
TOTAL MULTILATERAL	410.2	288.6	578.3	216.9
TOTAL BIL.& MULTIL.	1250.9	1014.8	1666.9	1240.5
of which:				
ODA Grants	408.0	343.7	507.4	326.2
ODA Loans	426.0	306.6	436.7	287.8

DISBURSEMENTS:

DAC COUNTRIES COMBINED

	1987	1988	1989	1990
OFFICIAL & PRIVATE				
GROSS:				
Contractual Lending	401.9	604.0	329.0	1062.0
Export Credits, Total	3.5	111.6	47.6	24.8
Export Credits, Priv.	0.7	98.8	39.0	13.5
NET:				
Contractual Lending	263.8	432.6	214.7	606.1
Export Credits Total	-96.5	16.3	-36.1	-149.2
PRIVATE SECTOR NET	-118.7	29.3	-91.9	-7.5
Direct Investment	-55.1	-3.9	-6.1	-12.5
Portfolio Investment	-21.2	-26.7	-42.1	22.9
Export Credits	-42.4	59.9	-43.7	-18.0

MARKET BORROWING:

CHANGE IN CLAIMS

	1987	1988	1989	1990
Banks	39.0	164.0	–	-95.0

MEMORANDUM ITEM:

	1987	1988	1989	1990
C.E.E.C. (Gross)	–	–	–	–

1. TOTAL RECEIPTS NET / 4. TOTAL ODA NET / 7. TOTAL ODA GROSS

	1. TOTAL RECEIPTS NET				4. TOTAL ODA NET				7. TOTAL ODA GROSS
	1987	1988	1989	1990	1987	1988	1989	1990	1987
DAC COUNTRIES									
Australia	0.4	3.1	0.7	2.2	0.4	3.1	0.7	2.2	0.4
Austria	2.3	0.7	0.4	0.2	2.3	0.7	0.4	0.2	2.3
Belgium	7.4	5.0	3.5	3.6	7.3	5.2	3.6	3.7	7.3
Canada	25.0	29.8	18.8	12.2	25.7	30.4	15.9	14.0	25.7
Denmark	3.5	8.3	6.4	17.4	3.5	8.3	6.4	17.4	3.5
Finland	26.3	23.8	25.3	24.9	26.3	23.8	25.1	24.9	26.3
France	-46.2	-8.3	-6.4	35.2	1.6	1.5	1.4	21.4	1.6
Germany	23.3	52.5	39.4	80.8	37.2	52.0	28.2	78.6	37.2
Ireland	3.3	2.8	3.0	3.3	3.3	2.8	3.0	3.3	3.3
Italy	36.5	40.7	18.9	17.9	36.1	39.5	23.1	12.3	36.1
Japan	17.6	72.8	45.0	18.7	41.7	90.6	63.0	40.1	41.7
Netherlands	28.3	28.2	25.4	54.4	29.6	25.8	23.2	43.0	29.6
New Zealand	–	0.0	0.0	0.1	–	0.0	0.0	0.1	–
Norway	31.9	40.2	34.9	55.3	31.9	40.2	34.9	55.3	31.9
Sweden	24.8	35.8	37.1	36.7	25.4	35.8	36.1	37.2	25.4
Switzerland	1.6	0.2	0.6	0.4	1.6	0.2	0.6	0.4	1.6
United Kingdom	49.3	25.8	220.0	28.7	38.5	29.6	30.6	42.9	40.1
United States	34.0	18.0	20.0	58.0	34.0	18.0	18.0	12.0	34.0
TOTAL	*269.4*	*379.3*	*493.1*	*449.9*	*346.3*	*407.4*	*314.2*	*408.9*	*347.9*
MULTILATERAL									
AF.D.F.	3.9	10.1	11.0	15.5	3.9	10.1	11.0	15.5	3.9
AF.D.B.	11.2	33.3	23.1	28.0	–	–	–	–	–
AS.D.B	–	–	–	–	–	–	–	–	–
CAR.D.B.	–	–	–	–	–	–	–	–	–
E.E.C.	15.4	29.7	29.1	29.1	19.9	34.6	34.0	34.0	20.0
IBRD	-3.5	1.0	–	-3.0	–	–	–	–	–
IDA	40.4	5.0	4.0	3.0	40.4	5.0	4.0	3.0	40.4
I.D.B.	–	–	–	–	–	–	–	–	–
IFAD	4.1	2.5	4.1	4.8	4.1	2.5	4.1	4.8	4.1
I.F.C.	4.2	5.0	-1.9	-0.8	–	–	–	–	–
IMF TRUST FUND	–	–	–	–	–	–	–	–	–
U.N. AGENCIES	–	–	–	–	–	–	–	–	–
UNDP	1.7	3.6	6.1	7.3	1.7	3.6	6.1	7.3	1.7
UNTA	2.4	1.8	1.9	1.5	2.4	1.8	1.9	1.5	2.4
UNICEF	2.4	2.2	3.4	2.8	2.4	2.2	3.4	2.8	2.4
UNRWA	–	–	–	–	–	–	–	–	–
WFP	2.2	2.9	0.6	2.6	2.2	2.9	0.6	2.6	2.2
UNHCR	3.6	4.0	4.1	3.5	3.6	4.0	4.1	3.5	3.6
Other Multilateral	4.1	4.2	8.6	7.8	4.1	4.2	8.6	7.8	4.1
Arab Agencies	-1.3	-0.2	-0.1	–	-1.3	-0.2	-0.1	–	–
TOTAL	*90.7*	*105.1*	*93.9*	*101.9*	*83.3*	*70.8*	*77.7*	*82.7*	*84.7*
ARAB COUNTRIES	–	–	–	–	–	–	–	–	–
E.E.C.+ MEMBERS	*120.8*	*184.6*	*339.4*	*270.3*	*176.9*	*199.1*	*153.5*	*256.5*	*178.6*
TOTAL	*360.1*	*484.4*	*586.9*	*551.8*	*429.6*	*478.2*	*391.9*	*491.6*	*432.7*

2. ODA LOANS GROSS / 5. ODA LOANS NET / 8. GRANTS

	2. ODA LOANS GROSS				5. ODA LOANS NET				8. GRANTS
	1987	1988	1989	1990	1987	1988	1989	1990	1987
DAC COUNTRIES									
Australia	–	–	–	–	–	–	–	–	0.4
Austria	–	–	–	–	–	–	–	–	2.3
Belgium	–	2.5	–	–	–	2.5	–	–	7.3
Canada	0.2	–	–	–	0.2	–	–	-73.8	25.5
Denmark	0.9	0.3	0.0	0.0	0.9	-2.9	0.0	-4.7	2.7
Finland	10.2	–	–	–	10.2	–	–	–	16.1
France	0.4	0.1	–	–	0.4	0.1	–	–	1.2
Germany	20.4	37.2	13.1	8.2	20.4	37.2	13.0	-251.1	16.8
Ireland	–	–	–	–	–	–	–	–	3.3
Italy	20.7	28.9	11.4	3.7	20.7	28.9	11.4	3.7	15.5
Japan	9.8	42.8	0.1	–	9.8	19.2	0.1	–	31.9
Netherlands	1.2	1.4	2.1	0.1	1.2	1.4	2.1	-17.6	28.4
New Zealand	–	–	–	–	–	–	–	–	–
Norway	–	–	–	–	–	–	–	–	31.9
Sweden	–	–	–	–	–	–	–	–	25.4
Switzerland	–	–	–	–	–	–	–	–	1.6
United Kingdom	1.2	0.1	3.0	0.3	-0.4	0.0	3.0	0.3	38.9
United States	3.0	13.0	13.0	7.0	3.0	12.0	11.0	5.0	31.0
TOTAL	*67.9*	*126.3*	*42.7*	*19.3*	*66.3*	*98.3*	*40.7*	*-338.2*	*280.0*
MULTILATERAL	*48.7*	*17.6*	*29.9*	*37.6*	*47.2*	*17.1*	*29.4*	*36.0*	*36.1*
ARAB COUNTRIES	–	–	–	–	–	–	–	–	–
E.E.C.+ MEMBERS	*45.0*	*70.5*	*40.3*	*23.1*	*43.2*	*66.9*	*40.0*	*-258.9*	*133.6*
TOTAL	*116.6*	*143.9*	*72.6*	*56.9*	*113.5*	*115.5*	*70.1*	*-302.2*	*316.0*

3. TOTAL OFFICIAL GROSS / 6. TOTAL OFFICIAL NET / 9. TOTAL OOF GROSS

	3. TOTAL OFFICIAL GROSS				6. TOTAL OFFICIAL NET				9. TOTAL OOF GROSS
	1987	1988	1989	1990	1987	1988	1989	1990	1987
DAC COUNTRIES									
Australia	0.4	3.1	0.7	2.2	0.4	3.1	0.7	2.2	–
Austria	2.3	0.7	0.4	0.2	2.3	0.7	0.4	0.2	–
Belgium	7.3	5.2	3.6	3.7	7.3	5.2	3.6	3.7	–
Canada	25.7	30.4	19.1	87.8	25.0	29.8	18.8	12.2	–
Denmark	3.5	11.4	6.4	22.1	3.5	8.3	6.4	17.4	–
Finland	26.3	23.8	25.1	24.9	26.3	23.8	25.1	24.9	–
France	1.6	1.5	1.4	21.4	1.6	1.5	1.4	21.4	–
Germany	40.9	66.5	41.0	337.9	40.6	66.5	40.9	78.2	3.6
Ireland	3.3	2.8	3.0	3.3	3.3	2.8	3.0	3.3	–
Italy	36.1	39.5	28.7	18.9	36.1	39.5	25.9	14.8	–
Japan	41.7	114.2	63.0	40.1	41.7	90.6	63.0	40.1	–
Netherlands	29.7	27.6	24.4	66.6	29.7	27.4	23.9	48.0	0.1
New Zealand	–	0.0	0.0	0.1	–	0.0	0.0	0.1	–
Norway	31.9	40.2	34.9	55.3	31.9	40.2	34.9	55.3	–
Sweden	25.4	35.8	36.1	37.2	25.4	35.8	36.1	37.2	–
Switzerland	1.6	0.2	0.6	0.4	1.6	0.2	0.6	0.4	–
United Kingdom	40.7	29.7	32.3	43.5	36.4	26.6	29.1	38.7	0.6
United States	34.0	19.0	22.0	77.0	34.0	18.0	20.0	58.0	–
TOTAL	*352.3*	*451.6*	*342.7*	*842.6*	*347.1*	*419.8*	*333.8*	*456.1*	*4.3*
MULTILATERAL	*123.8*	*125.5*	*111.8*	*135.2*	*90.7*	*105.1*	*93.9*	*101.9*	*39.0*
ARAB COUNTRIES	–	–	–	–	–	–	–	–	–
E.E.C.+ MEMBERS	*183.0*	*219.1*	*175.1*	*551.7*	*173.8*	*207.3*	*163.3*	*254.5*	*4.3*
TOTAL	*476.0*	*577.2*	*454.5*	*977.8*	*437.8*	*524.9*	*427.7*	*558.0*	*43.4*

10. ODA COMMITMENTS

1988	1989	1990	1987	1988	1989	1990
3.1	0.7	2.2	1.4	0.9	0.5	3.5
0.7	0.4	0.2	0.6	0.3	0.7	2.1
5.2	3.6	3.7	0.2	10.1	3.6	3.7
30.4	15.9	87.8	44.9	4.1	6.7	33.7
11.4	6.4	22.1	26.3	3.2	6.1	18.2
23.8	25.1	24.9	5.9	18.9	12.4	20.5
1.5	1.4	21.4	1.2	1.4	1.3	1.0
52.0	28.3	337.9	18.6	15.7	19.9	96.0
2.8	3.0	3.3	3.3	2.8	3.0	3.3
39.5	23.1	12.3	75.3	8.2	14.9	5.8
114.2	63.0	40.1	42.5	122.5	68.4	29.2
25.8	23.2	60.7	36.3	30.3	22.8	53.6
0.0	0.0	0.1	–	0.1	–	–
40.2	34.9	55.3	29.8	10.7	26.8	38.7
35.8	36.1	37.2	25.4	35.8	36.1	40.6
0.2	0.6	0.4	2.2	0.1	0.2	0.4
29.7	30.6	42.9	37.0	30.5	31.5	76.4
19.0	20.0	14.0	22.3	25.7	23.4	12.4
435.3	*316.3*	*766.5*	*373.1*	*321.0*	*278.4*	*438.8*
10.1	11.1	15.6	0.9	24.8	30.8	27.8
–	–	–	–	–	–	–
–	–	–	–	–	–	–
–	–	–	–	–	–	–
34.9	34.3	34.3	83.9	33.7	5.7	5.7
–	–	–	–	–	–	–
5.0	4.0	3.0	10.0	–	–	–
–	–	–	–	–	–	–
2.5	4.1	5.6	21.0	–	–	–
–	–	–	–	–	–	–
–	–	–	16.3	18.7	24.8	25.4
3.6	6.1	7.3	–	–	–	–
1.8	1.9	1.5	–	–	–	–
2.2	3.4	2.8	–	–	–	–
–	–	–	–	–	–	–
2.9	0.6	2.6	–	–	–	–
4.0	4.1	3.5	–	–	–	–
4.2	8.6	7.8	–	–	–	–
–	–	2.7	–	5.0	–	–
71.2	*78.2*	*86.5*	*132.2*	*82.2*	*61.2*	*58.9*
–	–	–	–	–	–	–
202.8	*153.8*	*538.5*	*282.1*	*135.7*	*108.8*	*263.6*
506.6	**394.4**	**853.0**	**505.2**	**403.2**	**339.6**	**497.7**

11. TECH. COOP. GRANTS

1988	1989	1990	1987	1988	1989	1990
3.1	0.7	2.2	0.3	0.6	0.5	1.1
0.7	0.4	0.2	0.6	0.4	0.0	0.1
2.7	3.6	3.7	1.6	2.2	2.3	1.9
30.4	15.9	87.8	–	1.7	2.5	3.1
11.2	6.4	22.1	2.1	7.1	1.7	5.2
23.8	25.1	24.9	3.9	1.6	3.9	8.4
1.4	1.4	21.4	1.2	1.4	1.3	1.0
14.8	15.2	329.7	16.0	14.4	14.3	16.4
2.8	3.0	3.3	2.4	2.3	2.4	2.6
10.6	11.7	8.6	4.9	1.6	1.3	0.9
71.4	62.9	40.1	9.2	11.8	13.4	15.7
24.4	21.1	60.6	8.3	10.7	11.2	15.9
0.0	0.0	0.1	–	0.0	–	0.1
40.2	34.9	55.3	7.7	8.0	7.6	6.6
35.8	36.1	37.2	5.4	7.9	11.4	1.0
0.2	0.6	0.4	0.1	0.1	–	–
29.6	27.6	42.6	19.9	23.8	23.5	21.4
6.0	7.0	7.0	4.0	5.0	6.0	5.0
309.1	*273.6*	*747.2*	*87.6*	*100.5*	*103.3*	*106.3*
53.6	*48.3*	*48.9*	*15.1*	*20.1*	*24.1*	*22.8*
–	–	–	–	–	–	–
132.3	*113.5*	*515.5*	*57.3*	*67.7*	*58.0*	*65.3*
362.7	**321.8**	**796.1**	**102.7**	**120.6**	**127.5**	**129.1**

12. TOTAL OOF NET

1988	1989	1990	1987	1988	1989	1990
–	–	–	–	–	–	–
–	–	–	–	–	–	–
–	3.2	–	-0.6	-0.6	2.9	-1.7
–	–	–	–	–	–	–
–	–	–	–	–	–	–
14.5	12.7	–	3.4	14.5	12.7	-0.5
–	–	–	–	–	–	–
–	5.6	6.7	–	–	2.8	2.5
–	–	–	–	–	–	–
1.8	1.2	5.8	0.1	1.6	0.7	5.0
–	–	–	–	–	–	–
–	–	–	–	–	–	–
–	–	–	–	–	–	–
–	1.8	0.6	-2.1	-3.0	-1.5	-4.2
–	2.0	63.0	–	–	2.0	46.0
16.3	*26.5*	*76.1*	*0.8*	*12.4*	*19.6*	*47.2*
54.3	*33.7*	*48.6*	*7.4*	*34.3*	*16.2*	*19.2*
–	–	–	–	–	–	–
16.3	*21.3*	*13.1*	*-3.1*	*8.1*	*9.8*	*-2.0*
70.6	**60.1**	**124.8**	**8.2**	**46.8**	**35.8**	**66.4**

13. ODF COMMITMENTS: BY PURPOSE %

	1987	1988	1989	1990
Education	2	4	8	–
Health	0	2	5	–
Other Social Infrastr.	4	7	6	–
Water Sanitat. Sewage	9	3	7	–
Energy	6	1	8	–
Telecommunications	0	0	0	–
Transportation	6	8	5	–
Agriculture	20	17	12	–
Extractive Industries	0	1	0	–
Manufacturing	8	2	4	–
Trade Banking Tourism	13	–	0	–
Technical Cooperation	19	32	31	–
Multisector Aid	0	0	1	–
Programme	5	12	9	–
Debt Reorganisation	0	5	0	–
Food Aid	4	5	6	–
Emergency Aid	0	0	0	–
Unspecified	3	–	0	–
TOTAL	100	100	100	–

14. GRANT ELEMENT OF ODA %

DAC COUNTRIES

	1987	1988	1989	1990
Australia	100.0	100.0	100.0	–
Austria	100.0	100.0	100.0	–
Belgium	100.0	100.0	100.0	–
Canada	100.0	100.0	100.0	–
Denmark	100.0	100.0	100.0	–
Finland	89.4	100.0	100.0	–
France	100.0	100.0	100.0	–
Germany	100.0	100.0	89.8	–
Ireland	100.0	100.0	100.0	–
Italy	70.9	100.0	100.0	–
Japan	100.0	87.0	100.0	–
Netherlands	97.8	100.0	100.0	–
New Zealand	–	100.0	–	–
Norway	100.0	100.0	100.0	–
Sweden	100.0	100.0	100.0	–
Switzerland	100.0	100.0	100.0	–
United Kingdom	100.0	100.0	100.0	–
United States	99.1	87.4	75.9	–
TOTAL	*93.6*	*94.6*	*97.2*	–
MULTILATERAL	*91.5*	*92.7*	*89.6*	–
ARAB COUNTRIES	–	–	–	–
E.E.C.+ MEMBERS	*91.6*	*100.0*	*98.0*	–
TOTAL	**93.0**	**94.3**	**95.5**	–

15. OTHER AGGREGATES

	1987	1988	1989	1990
OFFICIAL COMMITMENTS:				
TOTAL BILATERAL	419.4	326.6	316.2	636.9
of which:				
Arab Countries	–	–	–	–
C.E.E.C.	–	–	–	–
TOTAL MULTILATERAL	158.9	90.6	76.9	129.1
TOTAL BIL.& MULTIL.	578.3	417.2	393.0	766.0
of which:				
ODA Grants	396.3	302.5	280.5	446.6
ODA Loans	108.9	100.8	59.1	51.1
DISBURSEMENTS:				
DAC COUNTRIES COMBINED				
OFFICIAL & PRIVATE				
GROSS:				
Contractual Lending	66.5	139.5	229.3	94.1
Export Credits, Total	-5.8	-3.1	181.7	5.3
Export Credits, Priv.	-5.8	-3.1	160.1	-1.4
NET:				
Contractual Lending	18.5	69.9	181.9	-307.1
Export Credits Total	-49.2	-41.5	140.0	-32.2
PRIVATE SECTOR NET	-77.6	-40.5	159.2	-6.2
Direct Investment	7.5	0.9	37.6	-9.4
Portfolio Investment	-36.6	-0.5	0.1	19.3
Export Credits	-48.6	-40.9	121.6	-16.0
MARKET BORROWING:				
CHANGE IN CLAIMS				
Banks	-221.0	25.0	-109.0	84.0
MEMORANDUM ITEM:				
C.E.E.C. (Gross)	–	0.2	0.0	–

1. TOTAL RECEIPTS NET

DAC COUNTRIES	1987	1988	1989	1990
Australia	0.8	1.4	8.7	10.6
Austria	0.3	0.3	0.5	9.4
Belgium	-1.9	-1.0	-0.6	0.2
Canada	9.8	15.3	23.8	23.5
Denmark	8.2	12.4	19.5	14.3
Finland	7.6	2.7	9.7	10.4
France	12.8	20.0	-11.1	12.4
Germany	42.7	39.3	22.1	62.3
Ireland	1.1	0.6	0.5	0.5
Italy	26.8	6.5	-33.0	-8.5
Japan	8.7	25.4	21.0	27.6
Netherlands	42.3	24.3	17.7	28.5
New Zealand	0.1	–	0.1	0.2
Norway	21.6	23.7	17.3	24.1
Sweden	31.2	23.1	21.1	35.7
Switzerland	1.0	1.2	1.6	4.9
United Kingdom	134.3	114.1	159.1	20.0
United States	30.0	5.0	13.0	10.0
TOTAL	*377.3*	*314.1*	*291.0*	*286.1*
MULTILATERAL				
AF.D.F.	1.9	2.9	1.2	2.2
AF.D.B.	18.6	25.2	4.6	3.3
AS.D.B	–	–	–	–
CAR.D.B.	–	–	–	–
E.E.C.	7.8	27.2	29.3	29.3
IBRD	23.3	5.0	17.0	7.0
IDA	3.8	5.0	3.0	–
I.D.B.	–	–	–	–
IFAD	1.1	2.6	0.6	0.9
I.F.C.	-3.5	-1.8	6.2	71.4
IMF TRUST FUND	–	–	–	–
U.N. AGENCIES	–	–	–	–
UNDP	3.8	3.6	4.3	6.1
UNTA	1.2	1.0	1.4	1.3
UNICEF	2.9	2.1	2.1	2.4
UNRWA	–	–	–	–
WFP	2.5	4.8	2.0	3.4
UNHCR	1.1	3.3	3.3	3.8
Other Multilateral	3.0	2.7	4.3	6.1
Arab Agencies	1.8	-0.6	-2.8	–
TOTAL	*69.3*	*82.9*	*76.4*	*137.2*
ARAB COUNTRIES	**0.5**	**-3.2**	**-1.6**	**1.7**
E.E.C.+ MEMBERS	*274.2*	*243.3*	*203.6*	*159.1*
TOTAL	**447.0**	**393.8**	**365.8**	**425.1**

2. ODA LOANS GROSS

DAC COUNTRIES	1987	1988	1989	1990
Australia	–	–	–	–
Austria	–	–	–	8.8
Belgium	–	–	–	–
Canada	0.6	–	–	–
Denmark	4.7	5.7	11.9	6.6
Finland	6.0	2.7	9.3	10.1
France	12.9	9.3	9.3	15.7
Germany	18.0	17.5	5.4	21.4
Ireland	–	–	–	–
Italy	18.8	6.1	7.1	3.5
Japan	6.3	0.2	1.1	7.8
Netherlands	5.1	3.0	1.7	1.6
New Zealand	–	–	–	–
Norway	–	–	–	–
Sweden	–	–	–	–
Switzerland	0.2	–	0.3	0.1
United Kingdom	3.7	2.5	0.6	0.1
United States	–	–	–	–
TOTAL	*76.1*	*47.0*	*46.6*	*75.7*
MULTILATERAL	*8.8*	*13.1*	*6.2*	*4.9*
ARAB COUNTRIES	**3.9**	**0.2**	**1.7**	**2.1**
E.E.C.+ MEMBERS	*64.1*	*44.1*	*36.0*	*48.9*
TOTAL	**88.8**	**60.3**	**54.5**	**82.6**

3. TOTAL OFFICIAL GROSS

DAC COUNTRIES	1987	1988	1989	1990
Australia	0.8	1.4	8.7	10.6
Austria	0.3	0.3	0.5	9.4
Belgium	1.4	1.2	0.8	1.3
Canada	10.1	15.7	24.8	50.4
Denmark	8.2	12.4	19.5	14.6
Finland	7.1	3.3	9.8	10.7
France	14.7	11.0	10.9	17.3
Germany	46.3	42.1	29.3	60.6
Ireland	1.1	0.6	0.5	0.5
Italy	27.8	12.7	11.4	7.5
Japan	8.8	26.1	20.4	25.8
Netherlands	35.3	22.0	18.5	28.0
New Zealand	0.1	–	0.1	0.2
Norway	22.0	23.7	17.3	24.1
Sweden	32.9	23.1	21.8	37.5
Switzerland	1.0	1.2	1.6	4.9
United Kingdom	20.5	43.0	35.1	36.7
United States	35.0	10.0	17.0	15.0
TOTAL	*273.3*	*249.7*	*247.8*	*355.1*
MULTILATERAL	*83.9*	*109.6*	*117.9*	*182.7*
ARAB COUNTRIES	**3.9**	**0.2**	**1.7**	**2.1**
E.E.C.+ MEMBERS	*163.9*	*174.0*	*157.2*	*197.8*
TOTAL	**361.1**	**359.5**	**367.5**	**540.0**

4. TOTAL ODA NET

DAC COUNTRIES	1987	1988	1989	1990
Australia	0.8	1.4	8.7	10.6
Austria	0.3	0.3	0.5	9.4
Belgium	1.0	1.2	0.6	1.0
Canada	10.1	15.7	24.8	24.0
Denmark	8.2	12.4	19.5	14.3
Finland	7.1	3.1	9.7	10.4
France	14.7	11.0	10.9	16.5
Germany	44.5	40.1	27.4	49.2
Ireland	1.1	0.6	0.5	0.5
Italy	26.1	11.1	7.1	5.7
Japan	8.8	26.1	20.4	25.8
Netherlands	35.3	21.8	18.3	24.5
New Zealand	0.1	–	0.1	0.2
Norway	22.0	23.7	17.3	24.1
Sweden	32.9	23.1	21.8	36.4
Switzerland	1.0	1.2	1.6	4.9
United Kingdom	16.4	30.4	21.5	23.4
United States	35.0	10.0	17.0	15.0
TOTAL	*265.3*	*233.1*	*227.5*	*295.8*
AF.D.F.	1.9	2.9	1.2	2.2
AF.D.B.	–	–	–	–
AS.D.B	–	–	–	–
CAR.D.B.	–	–	–	–
E.E.C.	6.9	15.9	19.5	19.5
IBRD	–	–	–	–
IDA	3.8	5.0	3.0	–
I.D.B.	–	–	–	–
IFAD	1.1	2.6	0.6	0.9
I.F.C.	–	–	–	–
IMF TRUST FUND	–	–	–	–
U.N. AGENCIES	–	–	–	–
UNDP	3.8	3.6	4.3	6.1
UNTA	1.2	1.0	1.4	1.3
UNICEF	2.9	2.1	2.1	2.4
UNRWA	–	–	–	–
WFP	2.5	4.8	2.0	3.4
UNHCR	1.1	3.3	3.3	3.8
Other Multilateral	3.0	2.7	4.3	6.1
Arab Agencies	0.0	-0.9	-2.7	–
TOTAL	*28.2*	*42.8*	*38.9*	*45.7*
ARAB COUNTRIES	**0.5**	**-3.2**	**-1.6**	**1.7**
E.E.C.+ MEMBERS	*154.1*	*144.3*	*125.3*	*154.7*
TOTAL	**293.9**	**272.7**	**264.9**	**343.2**

5. ODA LOANS NET

DAC COUNTRIES	1987	1988	1989	1990
Australia	–	–	–	–
Austria	–	–	–	8.8
Belgium	–	–	–	–
Canada	0.6	–	–	-26.4
Denmark	4.7	5.7	11.9	6.4
Finland	6.0	2.5	9.2	9.7
France	12.9	9.3	9.3	14.9
Germany	16.2	15.5	3.5	18.5
Ireland	–	–	–	–
Italy	18.1	4.5	2.8	1.7
Japan	6.3	0.2	1.1	7.8
Netherlands	5.1	2.8	1.5	-0.1
New Zealand	–	–	–	–
Norway	–	–	–	–
Sweden	–	–	–	–
Switzerland	0.2	–	0.3	0.1
United Kingdom	3.4	1.6	-0.4	-2.3
United States	–	–	–	–
TOTAL	*73.3*	*42.2*	*39.1*	*39.1*
MULTILATERAL	*7.7*	*9.4*	*2.0*	*0.1*
ARAB COUNTRIES	**0.5**	**-3.2**	**-1.6**	**1.7**
E.E.C.+ MEMBERS	*61.2*	*39.3*	*28.5*	*39.0*
TOTAL	**81.4**	**48.3**	**39.5**	**40.9**

6. TOTAL OFFICIAL NET

DAC COUNTRIES	1987	1988	1989	1990
Australia	0.8	1.4	8.7	10.6
Austria	0.3	0.3	0.5	9.4
Belgium	1.4	1.2	0.8	1.3
Canada	9.5	15.1	24.1	23.4
Denmark	8.2	12.4	19.5	14.3
Finland	7.1	3.1	9.7	10.4
France	14.7	11.0	10.9	16.5
Germany	43.6	39.3	26.6	56.8
Ireland	1.1	0.6	0.5	0.5
Italy	27.2	11.1	7.1	5.7
Japan	8.8	26.1	20.4	25.8
Netherlands	35.3	21.8	18.3	26.4
New Zealand	0.1	–	0.1	0.2
Norway	22.0	23.7	17.3	24.1
Sweden	32.9	23.1	21.8	37.5
Switzerland	1.0	1.2	1.6	4.9
United Kingdom	12.3	33.6	31.7	33.1
United States	30.0	5.0	12.0	10.0
TOTAL	*256.2*	*229.8*	*231.5*	*310.8*
MULTILATERAL	*69.2*	*82.9*	*76.4*	*137.2*
ARAB COUNTRIES	**0.5**	**-3.2**	**-1.6**	**1.7**
E.E.C.+ MEMBERS	*151.5*	*158.0*	*144.8*	*183.9*
TOTAL	**325.9**	**309.5**	**306.3**	**449.7**

7. TOTAL ODA GROSS

	1987
Australia	0.8
Austria	0.3
Belgium	1.0
Canada	10.1
Denmark	8.2
Finland	7.1
France	14.7
Germany	46.3
Ireland	1.1
Italy	26.7
Japan	8.8
Netherlands	35.3
New Zealand	0.1
Norway	22.0
Sweden	32.9
Switzerland	1.0
United Kingdom	16.7
United States	35.0
TOTAL	*268.1*
AF.D.F.	1.9
AF.D.B.	–
AS.D.B	–
CAR.D.B.	–
E.E.C.	7.0
IBRD	–
IDA	3.8
I.D.B.	–
IFAD	1.1
I.F.C.	–
IMF TRUST FUND	–
U.N. AGENCIES	–
UNDP	3.8
UNTA	1.2
UNICEF	2.9
UNRWA	–
WFP	2.5
UNHCR	1.1
Other Multilateral	3.0
Arab Agencies	1.0
TOTAL	*29.3*
ARAB COUNTRIES	**3.9**
E.E.C.+ MEMBERS	*157.0*
TOTAL	**301.3**

8. GRANTS

	1987
Australia	0.8
Austria	0.3
Belgium	1.0
Canada	9.5
Denmark	3.5
Finland	1.2
France	1.8
Germany	28.3
Ireland	1.1
Italy	8.0
Japan	2.6
Netherlands	30.2
New Zealand	0.1
Norway	22.0
Sweden	32.9
Switzerland	0.8
United Kingdom	13.0
United States	35.0
TOTAL	*192.0*
MULTILATERAL	*20.5*
ARAB COUNTRIES	**–**
E.E.C.+ MEMBERS	*92.9*
TOTAL	**212.5**

9. TOTAL OOF GROSS

	1987
Australia	–
Austria	–
Belgium	0.4
Canada	–
Denmark	–
Finland	–
France	–
Germany	–
Ireland	–
Italy	1.1
Japan	–
Netherlands	–
New Zealand	–
Norway	–
Sweden	–
Switzerland	–
United Kingdom	3.8
United States	–
TOTAL	*5.2*
MULTILATERAL	*54.6*
ARAB COUNTRIES	**–**
E.E.C.+ MEMBERS	*6.9*
TOTAL	**59.8**

1988	1989	1990		1987	1988	1989	1990

10. ODA COMMITMENTS

1988	1989	1990		1987	1988	1989	1990
1.4	8.7	10.6		10.8	6.5	4.3	14.7
0.3	0.5	9.4		0.3	0.3	0.6	9.3
1.2	0.6	1.0		0.6	0.8	0.6	1.0
15.7	24.8	50.4		6.4	41.4	6.6	6.3
12.4	19.5	14.6		5.2	26.5	6.2	13.8
3.3	9.8	10.7		7.1	9.6	13.1	0.5
11.0	10.9	17.3		1.8	36.6	1.4	3.3
42.1	29.3	52.1		38.3	37.8	61.8	51.8
0.6	0.5	0.5		1.1	0.6	0.5	0.5
12.7	11.4	7.5		28.6	20.1	1.8	2.8
26.1	20.4	25.8		5.4	28.4	68.2	12.1
22.0	18.5	26.1		35.7	33.6	18.9	9.7
–	0.1	0.2		0.1	0.1	–	–
23.7	17.3	24.1		40.9	21.2	6.5	8.1
23.1	21.8	36.4		32.9	23.5	22.3	32.5
1.2	1.6	4.9		0.0	1.4	7.2	19.0
31.2	22.5	25.9		19.8	26.3	22.9	22.4
10.0	17.0	15.0		6.0	16.0	30.1	28.5
238.0	235.0	332.4		241.0	330.5	273.1	236.2
2.9	1.2	2.2		–	–	2.9	16.4
–	–	–		–	–	–	–
–	–	–		–	–	–	–
16.0	19.6	19.6		22.3	39.5	38.8	38.8
–	–	–		–	–	–	–
5.0	3.0	–		–	–	–	–
–	–	–		–	–	–	–
3.3	2.0	2.6		–	0.2	15.9	–
–	–	–		–	–	–	–
–	–	–		–	–	–	–
–	–	–		14.5	17.5	17.3	23.1
3.6	4.3	6.1		–	–	–	–
1.0	1.4	1.3		–	–	–	–
2.1	2.1	2.4		–	–	–	–
–	–	–		–	–	–	–
4.8	2.0	3.4		–	–	–	–
3.3	3.3	3.8		–	–	–	–
2.7	4.3	6.1		–	–	–	–
1.9	–	–		–	–	–	10.0
46.5	43.2	47.5		36.8	57.1	75.0	88.3
0.2	1.7	2.1		5.0	–	–	–
149.1	132.8	164.6		153.3	221.7	153.0	144.1
284.7	279.9	382.1		282.8	387.6	348.0	324.5

11. TECH. COOP. GRANTS

1988	1989	1990		1987	1988	1989	1990
1.4	8.7	10.6		0.7	1.1	1.6	2.0
0.3	0.5	0.6		0.3	0.3	0.4	0.5
1.2	0.6	1.0		0.8	0.6	0.2	0.2
15.7	24.8	50.4		–	3.6	5.2	4.3
6.7	7.7	7.9		1.5	3.3	3.5	3.7
0.6	0.5	0.7		0.2	0.1	0.9	3.5
1.7	1.6	1.6		1.8	1.7	1.4	1.6
24.6	23.9	30.6		26.0	23.9	20.4	26.2
0.6	0.5	0.5		0.9	0.6	0.5	0.5
6.6	4.3	4.0		6.8	2.3	2.8	3.7
26.0	19.3	18.0		1.9	2.7	3.0	2.4
19.0	16.8	24.6		5.0	6.5	7.2	8.2
–	0.1	0.2		0.1	–	–	0.1
23.7	17.3	24.1		0.9	1.7	2.5	2.4
23.1	21.8	36.4		4.8	6.8	9.1	2.2
1.2	1.4	4.9		0.3	0.9	–	–
28.8	22.0	25.7		8.6	11.9	12.2	13.4
10.0	17.0	15.0		15.0	10.0	11.0	9.0
191.0	188.5	256.7		75.4	77.9	81.7	84.1
33.4	36.9	42.7		13.0	15.2	15.4	19.7
–	–	–		–	–	–	–
105.0	96.8	115.6		52.3	53.4	48.1	57.6
224.4	225.4	299.4		88.3	93.1	97.1	103.8

12. TOTAL OOF NET

1988	1989	1990		1987	1988	1989	1990
–	–	–		–	–	–	–
–	0.3	0.3		0.4	–	0.3	0.3
–	–	–		-0.6	-0.6	-0.6	-0.6
–	–	–		–	–	–	–
–	–	–		–	–	–	–
–	–	8.5		-0.8	-0.9	-0.8	7.6
–	–	–		–	–	–	–
–	–	–		1.1	–	–	–
–	–	1.9		–	–	–	1.9
–	–	–		–	–	–	–
–	–	1.1		–	–	–	1.1
–	–	–		–	–	–	–
11.7	12.5	10.9		-4.1	3.2	10.2	9.7
–	–	–		-5.0	-5.0	-5.0	-5.0
11.7	12.8	22.7		-9.1	-3.3	4.0	14.9
63.1	74.8	135.2		41.1	40.1	37.5	91.6
–	–	–		–	–	–	–
24.9	24.5	33.2		-2.6	13.6	19.5	29.3
74.8	87.6	157.9		32.0	36.8	41.5	106.5

13. ODF COMMITMENTS: BY PURPOSE %

	1987	1988	1989	1990
Education	2	5	2	–
Health	3	2	1	–
Other Social Infrastr.	4	1	3	–
Water Sanitat. Sewage	22	1	6	–
Energy	1	19	2	–
Telecommunications	3	1	14	–
Transportation	4	9	11	–
Agriculture	5	9	6	–
Extractive Industries	–	–	–	–
Manufacturing	1	9	4	–
Trade Banking Tourism	0	6	0	–
Technical Cooperation	26	18	37	–
Multisector Aid	3	1	0	–
Programme	25	16	14	–
Debt Reorganisation	0	0	–	–
Food Aid	1	0	–	–
Emergency Aid	1	0	0	–
Unspecified	0	0	0	–
TOTAL	100	100	100	–

14. GRANT ELEMENT OF ODA %

DAC COUNTRIES

	1987	1988	1989	1990
Australia	100.0	100.0	100.0	–
Austria	100.0	100.0	100.0	–
Belgium	100.0	100.0	100.0	–
Canada	100.0	100.0	100.0	–
Denmark	100.0	79.3	100.0	–
Finland	69.8	–	100.0	–
France	100.0	65.6	100.0	–
Germany	90.5	91.2	79.2	–
Ireland	100.0	100.0	100.0	–
Italy	73.2	96.7	100.0	–
Japan	100.0	100.0	73.9	–
Netherlands	94.5	90.2	100.0	–
New Zealand	100.0	100.0	–	–
Norway	100.0	100.0	100.0	–
Sweden	100.0	100.0	100.0	–
Switzerland	100.0	100.0	100.0	–
United Kingdom	100.0	100.0	100.0	–
United States	99.7	100.0	100.0	–
TOTAL	93.5	92.1	88.2	–
MULTILATERAL	100.0	100.0	100.0	–
ARAB COUNTRIES	44.7	–	–	–
E.E.C.+ MEMBERS	91.2	88.5	91.6	–
TOTAL	93.5	93.3	90.3	–

15. OTHER AGGREGATES

	1987	1988	1989	1990
OFFICIAL COMMITMENTS:				
TOTAL BILATERAL	250.6	370.1	284.0	249.2
of which:				
Arab Countries	5.0	–	–	–
C.E.E.C.	–	–	–	–
TOTAL MULTILATERAL	123.1	161.1	224.0	502.5
TOTAL BIL.& MULTIL.	373.7	531.2	508.0	751.7
of which:				
ODA Grants	231.4	302.2	242.7	274.1
ODA Loans	51.4	85.3	105.3	50.4
DISBURSEMENTS:				
DAC COUNTRIES COMBINED				
OFFICIAL & PRIVATE				
GROSS:				
Contractual Lending	188.2	71.4	237.1	126.3
Export Credits, Total	108.3	12.7	178.0	28.2
Export Credits, Priv.	107.2	12.7	178.0	28.2
NET:				
Contractual Lending	117.9	1.4	99.6	15.0
Export Credits Total	48.7	-44.0	50.3	-45.4
PRIVATE SECTOR NET	121.1	84.3	59.4	-24.6
Direct Investment	119.4	102.3	79.8	5.3
Portfolio Investment	-52.4	19.6	-77.1	8.9
Export Credits	54.1	-37.5	56.8	-38.8
MARKET BORROWING:				
CHANGE IN CLAIMS				
Banks	-23.0	32.0	-35.0	159.0
MEMORANDUM ITEM:				
C.E.E.C. (Gross)	–	–	–	–

1. TOTAL RECEIPTS NET

DAC COUNTRIES	1987	1988	1989	1990
Australia	93.0	45.7	146.8	89.0
Austria	-3.0	25.2	25.9	49.5
Belgium	-1.8	78.1	239.1	115.2
Canada	324.9	371.3	301.6	332.4
Denmark	204.0	248.5	263.3	290.1
Finland	99.0	196.8	166.2	167.9
France	811.2	840.8	833.4	1472.7
Germany	814.1	759.2	737.3	1005.6
Ireland	11.0	11.2	8.2	10.6
Italy	864.7	1143.5	615.7	593.7
Japan	754.7	1574.9	1136.6	1293.2
Netherlands	450.9	487.5	417.6	525.5
New Zealand	14.4	9.7	8.0	11.2
Norway	176.4	195.8	218.0	250.8
Sweden	290.1	394.6	326.9	465.1
Switzerland	118.5	137.4	148.0	181.2
United Kingdom	312.7	510.2	424.1	422.4
United States	896.0	844.0	786.0	975.0
TOTAL	*6230.6*	*7874.5*	*6802.9*	*8251.0*
MULTILATERAL				
AF.D.F.	252.5	246.4	380.1	454.8
AF.D.B.	64.4	8.0	22.2	-14.2
AS.D.B	247.6	312.6	471.0	443.6
CAR.D.B.	–	–	–	–
E.E.C.	597.0	843.4	916.4	916.4
IBRD	-42.9	-64.0	-77.0	-91.0
IDA	1474.5	1457.0	1499.0	1910.0
I.D.B.	2.4	5.8	9.9	11.7
IFAD	145.9	51.8	57.3	108.3
I.F.C.	-0.6	14.8	-10.2	5.1
IMF TRUST FUND	–	–	–	–
U.N. AGENCIES	–	–	–	–
UNDP	294.5	337.2	372.1	404.6
UNTA	60.1	41.0	59.9	51.5
UNICEF	134.4	146.6	176.0	202.0
UNRWA	–	–	–	–
WFP	299.8	353.7	401.1	469.0
UNHCR	142.0	207.3	190.9	182.1
Other Multilateral	102.8	115.4	238.8	152.4
Arab Agencies	25.2	5.4	15.5	–
TOTAL	*3799.6*	*4082.4*	*4722.9*	*5206.3*
ARAB COUNTRIES	**517.0**	**182.5**	**105.9**	**216.6**
E.E.C.+ MEMBERS	*4063.7*	*4922.5*	*4455.2*	*5352.2*
TOTAL	**10547.2**	**12139.4**	**11631.7**	**13673.9**

2. ODA LOANS GROSS

DAC COUNTRIES	1987	1988	1989	1990
Australia	–	–	–	–
Austria	4.0	21.3	14.5	27.1
Belgium	4.6	8.9	7.8	6.6
Canada	–	–	–	–
Denmark	15.0	5.2	1.2	-0.1
Finland	3.1	11.2	13.1	3.6
France	386.6	417.1	387.6	447.2
Germany	52.2	47.0	29.7	20.9
Ireland	–	–	–	–
Italy	315.6	328.3	142.6	234.1
Japan	448.5	556.6	441.2	370.9
Netherlands	7.5	6.1	11.5	14.6
New Zealand	–	–	–	–
Norway	–	2.2	2.2	3.7
Sweden	–	–	–	–
Switzerland	–	–	–	–
United Kingdom	6.2	7.9	13.5	6.4
United States	128.0	97.0	69.0	54.0
TOTAL	*1371.2*	*1508.8*	*1133.9*	*1189.1*
MULTILATERAL	*2389.2*	*2336.1*	*2661.1*	*3162.1*
ARAB COUNTRIES	**222.3**	**206.6**	**192.2**	**111.8**
E.E.C.+ MEMBERS	*825.3*	*883.5*	*645.7*	*781.6*
TOTAL	**3982.7**	**4051.5**	**3987.2**	**4463.0**

3. TOTAL OFFICIAL GROSS

DAC COUNTRIES	1987	1988	1989	1990
Australia	78.9	73.0	130.8	97.1
Austria	16.1	35.4	31.8	55.9
Belgium	174.6	170.1	148.3	183.9
Canada	338.2	417.0	307.0	334.1
Denmark	263.4	257.1	296.0	298.9
Finland	97.7	167.9	170.5	168.0
France	883.3	993.0	1072.4	1403.4
Germany	899.7	911.7	917.4	910.2
Ireland	11.0	11.2	8.2	10.6
Italy	960.7	1161.7	802.3	778.3
Japan	1071.2	1264.8	1107.3	952.4
Netherlands	433.1	504.1	442.4	558.1
New Zealand	14.4	9.7	8.0	11.2
Norway	200.8	242.7	227.5	306.2
Sweden	279.2	394.6	343.4	477.0
Switzerland	118.5	137.5	148.0	181.2
United Kingdom	361.0	518.5	486.9	476.6
United States	948.0	855.0	809.0	1102.0
TOTAL	*7149.8*	*8124.9*	*7457.3*	*8304.9*
MULTILATERAL	*4276.4*	*4606.3*	*5189.8*	*5669.3*
ARAB COUNTRIES	**661.8**	**343.6**	**265.8**	**298.5**
E.E.C.+ MEMBERS	*4606.3*	*5396.4*	*5113.0*	*5558.9*
TOTAL	**12088.0**	**13074.8**	**12912.9**	**14272.8**

4. TOTAL ODA NET

DAC COUNTRIES	1987	1988	1989	1990
Australia	73.1	72.7	118.1	87.6
Austria	16.1	35.3	31.8	55.9
Belgium	100.1	87.7	72.8	159.6
Canada	324.7	349.3	306.2	331.7
Denmark	199.6	249.4	262.5	281.6
Finland	97.7	167.9	170.5	167.9
France	812.6	885.1	992.4	1276.2
Germany	741.8	809.7	840.3	851.1
Ireland	11.0	11.2	8.2	10.6
Italy	931.1	1112.3	698.6	722.6
Japan	1015.8	1195.7	1023.9	878.8
Netherlands	425.7	472.5	419.2	508.2
New Zealand	14.4	9.7	8.0	11.2
Norway	200.5	242.6	227.3	306.1
Sweden	279.2	394.6	343.4	477.0
Switzerland	118.5	137.4	148.0	181.2
United Kingdom	327.9	487.0	448.7	425.4
United States	859.0	798.0	761.0	984.0
TOTAL	*6549.0*	*7518.1*	*6880.8*	*7716.7*
MULTILATERAL				
AF.D.F.	252.5	246.4	380.1	454.8
AF.D.B.	–	–	–	–
AS.D.B	248.5	313.0	471.5	444.1
CAR.D.B.	–	–	–	–
E.E.C.	600.2	856.4	920.7	920.7
IBRD	–	–	–	–
IDA	1474.5	1457.0	1499.0	1910.0
I.D.B.	2.4	5.8	9.9	11.7
IFAD	145.9	51.8	57.3	108.3
I.F.C.	–	–	–	–
IMF TRUST FUND	–	–	–	–
U.N. AGENCIES	–	–	–	–
UNDP	294.5	337.2	372.1	404.6
UNTA	60.1	41.0	59.9	51.5
UNICEF	134.4	146.6	176.0	202.0
UNRWA	–	–	–	–
WFP	299.8	353.7	401.1	469.0
UNHCR	142.0	207.3	190.9	182.1
Other Multilateral	102.8	115.4	238.8	152.4
Arab Agencies	75.9	37.2	25.2	–
TOTAL	*3833.5*	*4168.8*	*4802.4*	*5311.2*
ARAB COUNTRIES	**517.8**	**176.3**	**108.4**	**216.6**
E.E.C.+ MEMBERS	*4150.2*	*4971.3*	*4663.3*	*5156.1*
TOTAL	**10900.2**	**11863.1**	**11791.6**	**13244.5**

5. ODA LOANS NET

DAC COUNTRIES	1987	1988	1989	1990
Australia	–	–	–	–
Austria	3.9	21.3	14.5	27.0
Belgium	4.6	7.7	6.9	6.6
Canada	-0.1	-39.1	–	–
Denmark	-41.7	-0.3	-31.0	-11.5
Finland	3.1	11.2	13.0	3.5
France	365.8	392.8	330.8	371.7
Germany	22.5	30.0	22.0	14.4
Ireland	–	–	–	–
Italy	293.8	312.5	100.3	213.5
Japan	393.1	487.5	357.8	297.3
Netherlands	7.0	-13.1	-3.5	-17.4
New Zealand	–	–	–	–
Norway	-0.2	2.1	2.0	3.6
Sweden	–	–	–	–
Switzerland	–	-0.1	–	–
United Kingdom	-9.0	-8.9	-2.0	-13.2
United States	101.0	76.0	41.0	-19.0
TOTAL	*1143.9*	*1279.4*	*851.8*	*876.5*
MULTILATERAL	*2219.5*	*2148.2*	*2453.6*	*2935.8*
ARAB COUNTRIES	**81.2**	**51.6**	**37.8**	**29.8**
E.E.C.+ MEMBERS	*673.5*	*773.9*	*467.9*	*608.6*
TOTAL	**3444.6**	**3479.2**	**3343.3**	**3842.2**

6. TOTAL OFFICIAL NET

DAC COUNTRIES	1987	1988	1989	1990
Australia	76.8	70.0	126.8	92.0
Austria	14.2	33.4	31.8	55.9
Belgium	173.1	168.7	147.2	181.5
Canada	324.9	371.3	300.5	327.2
Denmark	205.7	250.1	263.4	286.3
Finland	97.7	167.9	170.5	167.9
France	839.2	922.3	909.3	1297.4
Germany	822.6	809.8	762.8	878.7
Ireland	11.0	11.2	8.2	10.6
Italy	899.1	1129.4	719.5	713.2
Japan	1015.8	1195.7	1023.9	878.8
Netherlands	431.0	482.9	424.5	517.5
New Zealand	14.4	9.7	8.0	11.2
Norway	200.5	242.6	227.3	306.1
Sweden	279.2	394.6	343.4	477.0
Switzerland	118.5	137.4	148.0	181.2
United Kingdom	336.3	500.2	443.9	434.2
United States	894.0	822.0	770.0	1010.0
TOTAL	*6754.1*	*7719.0*	*6829.0*	*7826.6*
MULTILATERAL	*3799.6*	*4082.4*	*4722.9*	*5206.3*
ARAB COUNTRIES	**517.0**	**182.5**	**105.9**	**216.6**
E.E.C.+ MEMBERS	*4315.0*	*5118.0*	*4595.3*	*5235.9*
TOTAL	**11070.7**	**11983.9**	**11657.7**	**13249.5**

7. TOTAL ODA GROSS

DAC COUNTRIES	1987
Australia	73.1
Austria	16.1
Belgium	100.1
Canada	324.8
Denmark	256.4
Finland	97.7
France	833.4
Germany	771.5
Ireland	11.0
Italy	952.8
Japan	1071.2
Netherlands	426.2
New Zealand	14.4
Norway	200.8
Sweden	279.2
Switzerland	118.5
United Kingdom	343.1
United States	886.0
TOTAL	*6776.3*
AF.D.F.	255.4
AF.D.B.	–
AS.D.B	260.2
CAR.D.B.	–
E.E.C.	607.5
IBRD	–
IDA	1508.1
I.D.B.	5.0
IFAD	149.9
I.F.C.	–
IMF TRUST FUND	–
U.N. AGENCIES	–
UNDP	294.5
UNTA	60.1
UNICEF	134.4
UNRWA	–
WFP	299.8
UNHCR	142.0
Other Multilateral	102.8
Arab Agencies	183.4
TOTAL	*4003.1*
ARAB COUNTRIES	**658.9**
E.E.C.+ MEMBERS	*4302.1*
TOTAL	**11438.4**

8. GRANTS

	1987
Australia	73.1
Austria	12.2
Belgium	95.5
Canada	324.8
Denmark	241.4
Finland	94.6
France	446.8
Germany	719.3
Ireland	11.0
Italy	637.3
Japan	622.7
Netherlands	418.7
New Zealand	14.4
Norway	200.8
Sweden	279.2
Switzerland	118.5
United Kingdom	336.9
United States	758.0
TOTAL	*5405.1*
MULTILATERAL	*1614.0*
ARAB COUNTRIES	**436.6**
E.E.C.+ MEMBERS	*3476.8*
TOTAL	**7455.7**

9. TOTAL OOF GROSS

	1987
Australia	5.8
Austria	–
Belgium	74.4
Canada	13.5
Denmark	7.0
Finland	–
France	49.9
Germany	128.2
Ireland	–
Italy	7.9
Japan	–
Netherlands	6.9
New Zealand	–
Norway	–
Sweden	–
Switzerland	–
United Kingdom	17.9
United States	62.0
TOTAL	*373.5*
MULTILATERAL	*273.3*
ARAB COUNTRIES	**2.9**
E.E.C.+ MEMBERS	*304.3*
TOTAL	**649.7**

1988	1989	1990	1987	1988	1989	1990

10. ODA COMMITMENTS

1988	1989	1990	1987	1988	1989	1990
72.7	118.1	87.6	68.5	83.5	98.4	88.2
35.4	31.8	55.9	15.5	49.6	32.5	107.4
88.9	73.6	159.6	108.5	114.0	73.6	159.6
388.5	306.2	331.7	309.8	375.1	339.4	287.1
254.9	294.7	293.0	215.3	269.2	284.2	255.5
167.9	170.5	168.0	120.3	166.6	276.4	103.4
909.4	1049.2	1351.7	811.4	984.9	1112.8	1162.5
826.8	848.0	857.6	915.0	920.2	899.1	1070.4
11.2	8.2	10.6	11.0	11.2	8.2	10.6
1128.1	740.9	743.2	1485.5	1110.9	669.2	597.8
1264.8	1107.3	952.4	1117.0	1350.4	869.8	929.0
491.7	434.1	540.3	476.0	444.5	441.6	593.0
9.7	8.0	11.2	10.4	9.7	–	8.0
242.7	227.5	306.2	166.3	71.0	105.9	146.0
394.6	343.4	477.0	258.9	361.1	343.1	277.1
137.5	148.0	181.2	150.1	186.3	194.0	175.4
503.8	464.1	445.0	392.6	521.5	518.0	387.2
819.0	789.0	1057.0	925.6	888.1	891.8	1011.7
7747.5	7162.9	8029.3	7557.9	7917.9	7158.0	7370.0
250.8	389.6	468.5	596.0	520.1	620.8	717.1
–	–	–	–	–	–	–
327.9	490.6	466.6	654.6	398.8	564.1	531.7
–	–	–	–	–	–	–
866.0	928.1	928.1	1549.9	1643.0	1051.0	1051.0
–	–	–	–	–	–	–
1496.0	1548.0	1967.0	1666.3	1934.0	2242.0	2661.0
9.4	14.1	15.6	–	–	–	56.0
52.4	59.2	114.4	107.8	90.3	122.5	71.7
–	–	–	–	–	–	–
–	–	–	1033.5	1201.3	1438.7	1461.6
337.2	372.1	404.6	–	–	–	–
41.0	59.9	51.5	–	–	–	–
146.6	176.0	202.0	–	–	–	–
–	–	–	–	–	–	–
353.7	401.1	469.0	–	–	–	–
207.3	190.9	182.1	–	–	–	–
115.4	238.8	152.4	–	–	–	–
152.9	141.6	104.1	161.5	317.5	248.0	138.7
4356.7	5009.1	5525.8	5769.6	6104.9	6287.2	6688.7
331.3	262.8	298.5	612.5	210.7	354.8	235.5
5080.9	4841.1	5329.1	5965.4	6019.4	5057.7	5287.6
2435.4	12435.5	13853.6	13939.9	14233.4	13800.0	14294.1

11. TECH. COOP. GRANTS

1988	1989	1990	1987	1988	1989	1990
72.7	118.1	87.6	13.3	17.1	22.7	20.6
14.1	17.3	28.8	6.0	6.3	2.2	7.3
80.0	65.9	153.0	54.9	40.5	38.9	39.9
388.5	306.2	331.7	–	26.6	31.7	39.9
249.7	293.5	293.1	33.5	42.3	41.2	48.1
156.7	157.5	164.4	8.7	7.4	15.3	23.6
492.3	661.6	904.5	342.4	262.4	263.7	335.1
779.8	818.3	836.7	316.5	356.3	317.6	360.6
11.2	8.2	10.6	6.3	6.1	5.4	6.4
799.0	598.3	509.1	159.1	76.9	97.0	142.6
708.2	666.1	581.5	82.5	97.8	94.4	94.1
485.6	422.6	525.7	137.5	164.5	160.9	186.0
9.7	8.0	11.2	3.5	3.3	–	3.2
240.5	225.3	302.5	27.0	27.8	29.5	31.2
394.6	343.4	477.0	68.5	84.2	91.6	14.8
137.5	148.0	181.2	24.9	34.4	–	–
495.9	450.7	438.6	122.3	177.5	155.8	159.4
722.0	720.0	1003.0	264.0	334.0	373.0	402.0
6238.7	6029.0	6840.2	1670.9	1765.2	1740.8	1914.6
2020.6	2348.8	2363.7	767.4	923.4	1037.6	992.6
124.7	70.6	186.7	–	–	–	–
4197.4	4195.3	4547.5	1206.2	1202.3	1080.6	1278.0
8383.9	8448.3	9390.7	2438.3	2688.5	2778.5	2907.2

12. TOTAL OOF NET

1988	1989	1990	1987	1988	1989	1990
0.2	12.6	9.5	3.7	-2.8	8.7	4.4
–	–	–	-1.9	-1.9	–	–
81.2	74.7	24.3	73.0	81.0	74.4	21.9
28.5	0.8	2.3	0.2	22.0	-5.7	-4.6
2.2	1.4	5.8	6.0	0.7	1.0	4.7
–	–	–	–	–	–	–
83.7	23.2	51.6	26.6	37.2	-83.1	21.2
85.0	69.4	52.6	80.8	0.0	-77.5	27.6
–	–	–	–	–	–	–
33.6	61.4	35.1	-32.0	17.1	20.9	-9.5
–	–	–	–	–	–	–
12.3	8.3	17.8	5.2	10.4	5.3	9.3
–	–	–	–	–	–	–
–	–	0.0	–	–	–	0.0
–	–	–	–	–	–	–
14.7	22.7	31.6	8.4	13.2	-4.7	8.9
36.0	20.0	45.0	35.0	24.0	9.0	26.0
377.4	294.4	275.7	205.1	200.9	-51.8	109.9
249.6	180.0	143.5	-33.9	-86.4	-79.5	-104.9
12.4	3.0	–	-0.8	6.3	-2.5	–
315.5	271.9	229.8	164.8	146.7	-68.0	79.8
639.3	477.4	419.1	170.4	120.8	-133.9	5.0

13. ODF COMMITMENTS: BY PURPOSE %

	1987	1988	1989	1990
Education	3	3	4	–
Health	3	3	3	–
Other Social Infrastr.	5	5	5	–
Water Sanitat. Sewage	4	4	4	–
Energy	7	5	10	–
Telecommunications	1	1	2	–
Transportation	9	10	12	–
Agriculture	13	16	15	–
Extractive Industries	1	1	0	–
Manufacturing	4	5	3	–
Trade Banking Tourism	2	2	2	–
Technical Cooperation	20	22	22	–
Multisector Aid	3	1	1	–
Programme	15	13	10	–
Debt Reorganisation	3	3	2	–
Food Aid	5	5	3	–
Emergency Aid	1	2	1	–
Unspecified	1	0	1	–
TOTAL	100	100	100	–

14. GRANT ELEMENT OF ODA %

DAC COUNTRIES	1987	1988	1989	1990
Australia	100.0	100.0	100.0	–
Austria	100.0	96.8	95.8	–
Belgium	99.6	100.0	100.0	–
Canada	100.0	100.0	100.0	–
Denmark	100.0	99.8	100.0	–
Finland	97.8	99.3	100.0	–
France	82.6	78.7	82.8	–
Germany	97.8	98.5	98.7	–
Ireland	100.0	100.0	100.0	–
Italy	90.5	87.2	88.1	–
Japan	82.8	87.8	91.6	–
Netherlands	98.6	99.6	100.0	–
New Zealand	100.0	100.0	–	–
Norway	99.1	100.0	98.5	–
Sweden	100.0	100.0	100.0	–
Switzerland	100.0	100.0	100.0	–
United Kingdom	100.0	100.0	100.0	–
United States	95.4	96.0	97.9	–
TOTAL	92.8	92.7	94.8	–
MULTILATERAL	88.8	87.4	86.7	–
ARAB COUNTRIES	81.8	65.5	52.2	–
E.E.C.+ MEMBERS	94.8	93.8	94.4	–
TOTAL	90.7	90.0	89.9	–

15. OTHER AGGREGATES

	1987	1988	1989	1990
OFFICIAL COMMITMENTS:				
TOTAL BILATERAL	9519.0	8721.8	8133.6	8597.9
of which:				
Arab Countries	612.8	210.7	387.3	235.5
C.E.E.C.	855.2	236.3	86.7	–
TOTAL MULTILATERAL	5987.9	6395.1	6476.7	7071.2
TOTAL BIL.& MULTIL.	15506.9	15116.9	14610.3	15669.1
of which:				
ODA Grants	9379.5	9328.1	8507.2	8976.3
ODA Loans	5390.6	5141.6	5379.5	5317.9
DISBURSEMENTS:				
DAC COUNTRIES COMBINED				
OFFICIAL & PRIVATE				
GROSS:				
Contractual Lending	2053.3	2296.0	1956.6	1758.2
Export Credits, Total	332.2	491.8	591.8	342.0
Export Credits, Priv.	312.0	409.9	530.1	297.6
NET:				
Contractual Lending	911.5	1077.8	599.5	662.9
Export Credits Total	-493.0	-363.2	-246.9	-325.7
PRIVATE SECTOR NET	-523.5	155.5	-26.0	424.4
Direct Investment	177.3	326.2	701.2	460.6
Portfolio Investment	-266.6	231.7	-528.5	283.0
Export Credits	-434.1	-402.4	-198.7	-319.3
MARKET BORROWING:				
CHANGE IN CLAIMS				
Banks	-324.0	-353.0	-79.0	249.0
MEMORANDUM ITEM:				
C.E.E.C. (Gross)	786.1	713.0	362.5	–

1. TOTAL RECEIPTS NET

	1987	1988	1989	1990
DAC COUNTRIES				
Australia	166.4	194.2	239.2	255.9
Austria	14.4	39.3	43.9	210.1
Belgium	172.4	263.1	323.9	244.6
Canada	528.3	552.8	468.9	739.1
Denmark	189.2	113.6	151.5	123.6
Finland	110.8	166.5	198.4	163.8
France	1472.6	462.5	1516.7	1359.6
Germany	1643.4	1729.5	2096.5	2249.8
Ireland	5.2	3.5	4.1	4.5
Italy	-50.3	897.8	839.9	778.1
Japan	6253.2	6287.6	7563.7	5175.2
Netherlands	660.1	588.3	608.3	944.9
New Zealand	5.5	5.8	6.9	9.3
Norway	171.2	187.3	146.4	220.7
Sweden	520.3	313.1	870.1	916.2
Switzerland	121.7	152.2	124.0	152.3
United Kingdom	979.7	543.6	3376.6	897.5
United States	1973.0	4396.0	3206.0	1880.0
TOTAL	*14937.0*	*16897.0*	*21784.6*	*16325.2*
MULTILATERAL				
AF.D.F.	113.7	98.4	101.1	135.6
AF.D.B.	160.2	220.3	416.8	356.9
AS.D.B	644.7	989.5	1429.4	1815.6
CAR.D.B.	0.0	–	–	–
E.E.C.	509.0	665.8	608.9	608.9
IBRD	2340.8	3132.0	3111.0	2171.0
IDA	2056.1	2114.0	1778.0	2021.0
I.D.B.	108.6	117.8	93.2	113.8
IFAD	148.2	47.9	56.3	95.4
I.F.C.	-9.4	34.8	-14.8	397.3
IMF TRUST FUND	–	–	–	–
U.N. AGENCIES	–	–	–	–
UNDP	187.9	211.2	216.5	284.5
UNTA	46.1	31.5	46.2	41.9
UNICEF	143.8	155.9	195.0	218.0
UNRWA	–	–	–	–
WFP	280.0	338.0	189.4	218.2
UNHCR	113.9	103.2	111.2	117.3
Other Multilateral	81.9	93.4	164.1	130.1
Arab Agencies	1.5	-22.9	34.9	–
TOTAL	*6927.2*	*8330.7*	*8537.1*	*8725.5*
ARAB COUNTRIES	**71.5**	**-18.8**	**-17.8**	**2346.1**
E.E.C.+ MEMBERS	*5581.2*	*5267.9*	*9526.3*	*7211.5*
TOTAL	**21935.7**	**25208.8**	**30303.9**	**27396.8**

2. ODA LOANS GROSS

	1987	1988	1989	1990
DAC COUNTRIES				
Australia	–	–	–	–
Austria	38.0	35.3	82.4	143.0
Belgium	36.4	47.4	29.5	25.8
Canada	13.3	9.1	8.0	34.9
Denmark	107.3	60.7	37.8	15.9
Finland	25.2	28.0	33.3	30.9
France	533.0	635.8	700.2	644.9
Germany	652.7	813.6	791.8	1171.1
Ireland	–	–	–	–
Italy	265.9	386.0	373.9	343.7
Japan	2224.9	3104.5	3266.0	2939.5
Netherlands	191.2	231.6	197.1	262.0
New Zealand	–	–	–	–
Norway	3.5	2.5	–	–
Sweden	–	–	–	–
Switzerland	17.6	27.5	25.9	13.9
United Kingdom	11.9	6.5	11.3	9.6
United States	458.0	628.0	453.0	443.0
TOTAL	*4578.7*	*6016.3*	*6010.2*	*6078.0*
MULTILATERAL	*2774.7*	*2818.4*	*2637.4*	*3144.5*
ARAB COUNTRIES	**114.3**	**133.1**	**124.9**	**73.4**
E.E.C.+ MEMBERS	*1818.0*	*2203.4*	*2167.9*	*2499.4*
TOTAL	**7467.7**	**8967.8**	**8772.4**	**9295.9**

3. TOTAL OFFICIAL GROSS

	1987	1988	1989	1990
DAC COUNTRIES				
Australia	120.8	216.4	291.8	416.5
Austria	87.0	57.8	98.4	254.0
Belgium	319.7	401.6	347.5	271.9
Canada	566.3	646.1	560.5	1162.2
Denmark	194.1	173.7	177.1	191.0
Finland	97.8	133.0	152.5	163.3
France	1416.8	1064.0	1199.5	1720.0
Germany	1767.5	3428.0	2339.5	4015.3
Ireland	5.2	3.5	4.1	4.5
Italy	642.1	829.7	1095.6	1113.7
Japan	4400.0	5445.6	6209.0	5657.6
Netherlands	638.4	720.4	688.4	902.7
New Zealand	5.5	5.8	6.9	9.3
Norway	184.6	205.1	173.2	233.9
Sweden	251.9	313.1	502.0	342.1
Switzerland	121.7	152.5	124.2	153.1
United Kingdom	425.5	656.9	776.4	674.3
United States	2366.0	4633.0	2485.0	4960.0
TOTAL	*13611.1*	*19086.1*	*17231.2*	*22245.5*
MULTILATERAL	*9098.0*	*10647.3*	*11033.7*	*11619.1*
ARAB COUNTRIES	**227.7**	**140.5**	**135.8**	**2416.7**
E.E.C.+ MEMBERS	*5962.4*	*7994.8*	*7289.8*	*9555.2*
TOTAL	**22936.7**	**29873.9**	**28400.6**	**36281.2**

4. TOTAL ODA NET

	1987	1988	1989	1990
DAC COUNTRIES				
Australia	102.6	149.0	188.9	223.6
Austria	40.4	29.4	71.8	139.6
Belgium	178.9	179.0	128.1	152.6
Canada	345.0	436.7	371.1	407.4
Denmark	175.1	155.1	158.0	170.9
Finland	97.8	132.6	152.2	162.9
France	716.2	866.3	1069.2	1213.9
Germany	802.9	936.0	939.0	1748.6
Ireland	5.2	3.5	4.1	4.5
Italy	455.7	631.4	600.1	554.1
Japan	2557.1	3582.0	3858.7	3354.7
Netherlands	552.0	625.4	588.8	743.4
New Zealand	5.3	5.3	6.9	9.3
Norway	184.3	203.9	172.1	232.3
Sweden	251.9	313.1	502.0	340.8
Switzerland	121.7	152.2	124.0	152.3
United Kingdom	309.8	515.5	613.3	493.7
United States	1781.0	1669.0	1808.0	3283.0
TOTAL	*8682.8*	*10585.4*	*11356.2*	*13387.4*
MULTILATERAL				
AF.D.F.	113.7	98.4	101.1	135.6
AF.D.B.	–	–	–	–
AS.D.B	268.2	366.6	416.0	591.3
CAR.D.B.	0.0	–	–	–
E.E.C.	465.8	663.7	591.2	591.2
IBRD	0.4	–	–	–
IDA	2056.1	2114.0	1778.0	2021.0
I.D.B.	29.5	14.2	16.3	63.9
IFAD	148.2	47.9	56.3	95.4
I.F.C.	–	–	–	–
IMF TRUST FUND	–	–	–	–
U.N. AGENCIES	–	–	–	–
UNDP	187.9	211.2	216.5	284.5
UNTA	46.1	31.5	46.2	41.9
UNICEF	143.8	155.9	195.0	218.0
UNRWA	–	–	–	–
WFP	280.0	338.0	189.4	218.2
UNHCR	113.9	103.2	111.2	117.3
Other Multilateral	81.9	93.4	164.1	130.1
Arab Agencies	-31.1	-23.5	38.3	–
TOTAL	*3904.6*	*4214.4*	*3919.5*	*4508.4*
ARAB COUNTRIES	**75.5**	**7.0**	**-17.8**	**2346.1**
E.E.C.+ MEMBERS	*3661.6*	*4575.9*	*4691.9*	*5672.7*
TOTAL	**12662.9**	**14806.8**	**15258.0**	**20241.9**

5. ODA LOANS NET

	1987	1988	1989	1990
DAC COUNTRIES				
Australia	–	–	–	–
Austria	27.4	18.3	57.6	110.4
Belgium	32.9	32.3	22.8	12.7
Canada	-6.8	-30.6	-19.8	-350.3
Denmark	99.6	53.4	31.4	-1.9
Finland	25.2	27.6	33.1	30.4
France	471.3	578.7	626.4	539.4
Germany	341.7	457.9	464.9	-331.6
Ireland	–	–	–	–
Italy	259.0	371.1	326.6	312.9
Japan	1802.1	2477.1	2730.8	2239.4
Netherlands	117.4	147.5	112.1	130.7
New Zealand	–	–	–	–
Norway	3.1	1.2	-0.9	-1.5
Sweden	–	–	–	–
Switzerland	17.4	27.3	25.7	13.0
United Kingdom	-77.6	-76.0	-67.0	-69.8
United States	174.0	262.0	88.0	-54.0
TOTAL	*3286.9*	*4347.9*	*4431.6*	*2579.6*
MULTILATERAL	*2585.0*	*2603.7*	*2395.1*	*2864.6*
ARAB COUNTRIES	**-29.4**	**0.9**	**-26.4**	**2.8**
E.E.C.+ MEMBERS	*1261.0*	*1583.4*	*1537.8*	*612.9*
TOTAL	**5842.4**	**6952.5**	**6800.4**	**5447.0**

6. TOTAL OFFICIAL NET

	1987	1988	1989	1990
DAC COUNTRIES				
Australia	112.5	204.1	280.9	402.2
Austria	70.6	35.0	73.0	220.9
Belgium	314.2	385.8	340.1	240.9
Canada	497.3	562.5	483.9	730.6
Denmark	143.6	128.8	140.7	168.5
Finland	97.8	132.6	152.2	162.9
France	1318.7	936.8	1087.2	1416.1
Germany	1149.6	1750.9	1475.4	2238.4
Ireland	5.2	3.5	4.1	4.5
Italy	601.6	797.8	978.3	931.6
Japan	2668.0	4633.4	5480.2	4370.6
Netherlands	560.5	631.7	597.0	759.8
New Zealand	5.5	5.8	6.9	9.3
Norway	184.3	203.7	172.0	232.1
Sweden	251.9	313.1	502.0	342.1
Switzerland	121.7	152.2	124.0	152.3
United Kingdom	314.8	554.1	680.1	578.6
United States	1824.0	3981.0	1922.0	2540.0
TOTAL	*10241.9*	*15412.8*	*14500.0*	*15501.4*
MULTILATERAL	*6927.2*	*8330.7*	*8537.1*	*8725.5*
ARAB COUNTRIES	**71.5**	**-18.8**	**-17.8**	**2346.1**
E.E.C.+ MEMBERS	*4917.3*	*5855.1*	*5911.8*	*6947.4*
TOTAL	**17240.6**	**23724.6**	**23019.3**	**26573.0**

7. TOTAL ODA GROSS

	1987
Australia	102.6
Austria	51.0
Belgium	182.4
Canada	365.1
Denmark	182.7
Finland	97.8
France	777.8
Germany	1113.8
Ireland	5.2
Italy	462.6
Japan	2979.9
Netherlands	625.8
New Zealand	5.3
Norway	184.6
Sweden	251.9
Switzerland	121.8
United Kingdom	399.3
United States	2065.0
TOTAL	*9974.7*
AF.D.F.	115.7
AF.D.B.	–
AS.D.B	279.6
CAR.D.B.	0.0
E.E.C.	469.0
IBRD	0.4
IDA	2161.8
I.D.B.	41.4
IFAD	152.2
I.F.C.	–
IMF TRUST FUND	–
U.N. AGENCIES	–
UNDP	187.9
UNTA	46.1
UNICEF	143.8
UNRWA	–
WFP	280.0
UNHCR	113.9
Other Multilateral	81.9
Arab Agencies	20.8
TOTAL	*4094.3*
ARAB COUNTRIES	**219.2**
E.E.C.+ MEMBERS	*4218.6*
TOTAL	**14288.2**

8. GRANTS

	1987
Australia	102.6
Austria	13.0
Belgium	146.0
Canada	351.8
Denmark	75.4
Finland	72.7
France	244.9
Germany	461.2
Ireland	5.2
Italy	196.7
Japan	755.0
Netherlands	434.6
New Zealand	5.3
Norway	181.1
Sweden	251.9
Switzerland	104.3
United Kingdom	387.4
United States	1607.0
TOTAL	*5396.0*
MULTILATERAL	*1319.6*
ARAB COUNTRIES	**104.9**
E.E.C.+ MEMBERS	*2400.6*
TOTAL	**6820.5**

9. TOTAL OOF GROSS

	1987
Australia	18.2
Austria	35.9
Belgium	137.3
Canada	201.2
Denmark	11.5
Finland	–
France	639.0
Germany	653.7
Ireland	–
Italy	179.5
Japan	1420.1
Netherlands	12.6
New Zealand	0.2
Norway	–
Sweden	–
Switzerland	–
United Kingdom	26.2
United States	301.0
TOTAL	*3636.4*
MULTILATERAL	*5003.7*
ARAB COUNTRIES	**8.5**
E.E.C.+ MEMBERS	*1743.8*
TOTAL	**8648.5**

10. ODA COMMITMENTS

1988	1989	1990	1987	1988	1989	1990
149.0	188.9	223.6	96.9	213.3	216.1	186.6
46.3	96.6	172.2	46.0	106.8	196.7	119.8
194.1	134.7	165.7	159.8	212.9	134.7	165.7
476.4	398.9	792.7	629.7	535.7	546.7	348.8
162.3	164.4	188.7	168.0	180.3	183.2	110.8
133.0	152.5	163.3	68.0	155.3	181.5	234.3
923.4	1143.0	1319.4	838.5	1183.2	1390.7	929.1
1291.5	1265.9	3251.3	1339.4	1828.2	1670.0	2364.4
3.5	4.1	4.5	5.2	3.5	4.1	4.5
646.2	647.4	584.9	929.7	738.0	470.8	538.7
4209.4	4393.9	4054.8	3996.4	7720.8	4817.9	4837.2
709.5	673.8	874.7	749.9	848.9	782.4	764.0
5.3	6.9	9.3	4.8	6.5	–	6.4
205.1	173.0	233.9	233.3	87.0	144.9	177.2
313.1	502.0	340.8	259.1	319.9	502.6	346.3
152.5	124.2	153.1	171.4	163.1	152.9	153.4
598.0	691.6	573.0	622.6	610.7	769.2	965.9
2035.0	2173.0	3780.0	2204.1	2436.7	2677.7	14226.8
2253.8	*12934.8*	*16885.8*	*12522.9*	*17351.0*	*14842.2*	*26479.8*
100.2	103.7	139.7	119.3	119.6	311.6	328.4
–	–	–	–	–	–	–
381.4	432.5	610.7	778.7	692.0	776.1	962.2
–	–	–	–	0.2	–	–
667.2	597.0	597.0	1240.8	1113.0	551.6	551.6
–	–	–	–	–	–	–
2228.0	1916.0	2188.0	2566.0	2418.0	2680.0	3578.0
23.9	29.8	79.7	10.5	48.6	150.3	97.9
54.2	64.6	113.2	71.6	84.4	96.1	132.1
–	–	–	–	–	–	–
–	–	–	853.7	933.1	922.3	1010.0
211.2	216.5	284.5	–	–	–	–
31.5	46.2	41.9	–	–	–	–
155.9	195.0	218.0	–	–	–	–
–	–	–	–	–	–	–
338.0	189.4	218.2	–	–	–	–
103.2	111.2	117.3	–	–	–	–
93.4	164.1	130.1	–	–	–	–
41.2	94.8	24.9	34.1	69.7	323.3	35.6
4429.2	4160.6	4763.2	5674.6	5478.6	5811.3	6695.8
139.2	*133.4*	*2416.7*	*272.8*	*136.9*	*164.3*	*2977.2*
5195.9	*5322.0*	*7559.1*	*6053.9*	*6718.9*	*5956.8*	*6394.7*
6822.1	*17228.8*	*24065.6*	*18470.3*	*22966.5*	*20817.9*	*36152.9*

11. TECH. COOP. GRANTS

1988	1989	1990	1987	1988	1989	1990
149.0	188.9	223.6	58.2	76.4	92.1	103.9
11.1	14.2	29.2	8.9	8.7	6.3	11.0
146.7	105.3	139.9	104.1	84.5	64.3	60.3
467.3	390.9	757.8	–	55.7	75.9	55.8
101.6	126.6	172.7	38.8	50.5	52.4	39.5
105.0	119.2	132.5	5.8	7.2	16.0	41.8
287.7	442.8	674.5	327.9	196.4	184.6	243.2
478.0	474.1	2080.2	401.9	419.1	364.2	446.5
3.5	4.1	4.5	4.1	3.1	3.5	3.9
260.3	273.5	241.2	109.8	66.3	53.0	48.0
1104.9	1127.9	1115.3	302.7	405.1	413.8	491.2
477.9	476.7	612.7	181.5	228.1	241.6	292.7
5.3	6.9	9.3	2.8	3.1	–	6.5
202.7	173.0	233.9	23.8	28.4	26.2	24.1
313.1	502.0	340.8	62.8	62.3	144.6	21.5
125.0	98.3	139.9	17.2	21.2	–	–
591.5	680.3	563.4	137.1	210.4	202.5	234.3
1407.0	1720.0	3337.0	635.0	785.0	948.0	1097.0
6237.5	6924.6	10807.8	2422.1	2711.6	2889.0	3221.3
1610.8	*1523.2*	*1618.7*	*608.9*	*679.7*	*732.9*	*791.8*
6.1	*8.6*	*2343.3*	–	–	–	–
2992.5	*3154.1*	*5059.7*	*1340.3*	*1343.0*	*1166.1*	*1368.4*
7854.3	*8456.4*	*14769.8*	*3031.1*	*3391.2*	*3621.9*	*4013.1*

12. TOTAL OOF NET

1988	1989	1990	1987	1988	1989	1990
67.3	102.9	192.9	10.0	55.1	92.0	178.6
11.4	1.8	81.8	30.3	5.6	1.2	81.3
207.5	212.7	106.2	135.3	206.7	212.0	88.3
169.7	161.6	369.5	152.3	125.8	112.9	323.2
11.4	12.6	2.3	-31.5	-26.3	-17.2	-2.3
–	–	–	–	–	–	–
140.6	56.5	400.6	602.6	70.5	18.0	202.3
2136.4	1073.6	764.0	346.7	814.9	536.4	489.9
–	–	–	–	–	–	–
183.4	448.2	528.9	145.9	166.3	378.3	377.5
1236.2	1815.1	1602.8	110.9	1051.4	1621.5	1015.9
11.0	14.5	28.0	8.5	6.3	8.2	16.4
0.5	–	–	0.2	0.5	–	–
–	0.1	–	–	-0.2	-0.1	-0.2
–	–	1.3	–	–	–	1.3
–	–	–	–	–	–	–
58.9	84.8	101.3	5.0	38.6	66.8	85.0
2598.0	312.0	1180.0	43.0	2312.0	114.0	-743.0
6832.4	*4296.4*	*5359.6*	*1559.0*	*4827.4*	*3143.8*	*2114.0*
6218.1	*6873.1*	*6855.9*	*3022.6*	*4116.3*	*4617.6*	*4217.1*
1.3	*2.3*	–	*-4.0*	*-25.8*	*0.0*	–
2798.9	*1967.8*	*1996.1*	*1255.7*	*1279.2*	*1220.0*	*1274.7*
3051.8	*11171.8*	*12215.5*	*4577.7*	*8917.8*	*7761.3*	*6331.1*

13. ODF COMMITMENTS: BY PURPOSE %

	1987	1988	1989	1990
Education	2	2	3	–
Health	1	2	2	–
Other Social Infrastr.	5	6	4	–
Water Sanitat. Sewage	4	2	5	–
Energy	16	24	18	–
Telecommunications	2	2	2	–
Transportation	10	8	10	–
Agriculture	13	9	9	–
Extractive Industries	3	1	4	–
Manufacturing	6	5	5	–
Trade Banking Tourism	4	8	12	–
Technical Cooperation	12	10	11	–
Multisector Aid	1	3	2	–
Programme	15	10	10	–
Debt Reorganisation	2	4	3	–
Food Aid	2	2	1	–
Emergency Aid	1	0	0	–
Unspecified	1	0	0	–
TOTAL	100	100	100	–

14. GRANT ELEMENT OF ODA %

DAC COUNTRIES

	1987	1988	1989	1990
Australia	100.0	100.0	100.0	–
Austria	55.0	50.8	49.5	–
Belgium	100.0	100.0	100.0	–
Canada	100.0	99.1	100.0	–
Denmark	98.5	97.0	100.0	–
Finland	91.7	96.9	100.0	–
France	58.4	70.6	68.6	–
Germany	78.2	75.4	76.0	–
Ireland	100.0	100.0	100.0	–
Italy	76.4	85.1	81.9	–
Japan	62.8	65.8	69.2	–
Netherlands	87.0	84.3	87.3	–
New Zealand	100.0	100.0	–	–
Norway	98.9	97.9	100.0	–
Sweden	100.0	100.0	100.0	–
Switzerland	100.0	100.0	100.0	–
United Kingdom	100.0	100.0	100.0	–
United States	95.2	91.0	97.7	–
TOTAL	*79.4*	*77.1*	*82.0*	–
MULTILATERAL	*87.7*	*85.6*	*82.8*	–
ARAB COUNTRIES	*63.9*	*42.7*	*46.6*	–
E.E.C.+ MEMBERS	*83.7*	*84.2*	*82.7*	–
TOTAL	*81.7*	*79.0*	*81.9*	–

15. OTHER AGGREGATES

OFFICIAL COMMITMENTS:

	1987	1988	1989	1990
TOTAL BILATERAL	22848.5	31181.4	23946.6	34923.5
of which:				
Arab Countries	335.3	147.5	169.0	3277.2
C.E.E.C.	2929.9	6330.8	2782.5	–
TOTAL MULTILATERAL	13405.5	14939.6	16436.5	15956.3
TOTAL BIL.& MULTIL.	36253.9	46121.0	40383.1	50879.8
of which:				
ODA Grants	9054.7	9648.0	9735.8	24249.5
ODA Loans	11482.7	19199.0	13483.3	11903.4

DISBURSEMENTS:

DAC COUNTRIES COMBINED

	1987	1988	1989	1990
OFFICIAL & PRIVATE				
GROSS:				
Contractual Lending	13716.7	16139.0	18369.8	15870.5
Export Credits, Total	6268.1	3959.1	9187.4	5833.0
Export Credits, Priv.	5565.9	3334.6	8105.5	4480.8
NET:				
Contractual Lending	5434.8	8277.6	11125.1	4508.5
Export Credits Total	686.6	-859.0	4162.3	457.4
PRIVATE SECTOR NET	4695.1	1484.2	7284.6	823.8
Direct Investment	1557.0	525.7	2978.7	946.8
Portfolio Investment	2485.0	1811.9	713.9	14.1
Export Credits	653.2	-853.4	3592.0	-137.1

MARKET BORROWING:

CHANGE IN CLAIMS

	1987	1988	1989	1990
Banks	4996.0	6524.0	-1912.0	15915.0

MEMORANDUM ITEM:

	1987	1988	1989	1990
C.E.E.C. (Gross)	2589.8	2397.3	2448.0	–

	1987	1988	1989	1990		1987	1988	1989	1990		1987

1. TOTAL RECEIPTS NET / 4. TOTAL ODA NET / 7. TOTAL ODA GROSS

DAC COUNTRIES	1987	1988	1989	1990	DAC COUNTRIES	1987	1988	1989	1990		1987
Australia	259.0	253.5	453.1	394.3	Australia	241.5	271.7	297.3	305.0	Australia	241.7
Austria	-13.5	115.0	33.7	49.2	Austria	7.9	19.1	32.9	19.9	Austria	16.5
Belgium	277.0	159.3	85.8	-47.1	Belgium	37.9	47.6	35.5	39.0	Belgium	39.6
Canada	191.6	314.9	271.6	290.3	Canada	121.6	195.5	198.1	177.8	Canada	128.2
Denmark	23.3	7.5	15.9	-7.7	Denmark	16.2	5.6	15.9	24.7	Denmark	18.2
Finland	52.2	22.5	33.4	23.5	Finland	11.8	17.4	16.8	18.5	Finland	11.8
France	-172.7	64.9	-337.2	912.4	France	700.5	631.4	668.9	1301.5	France	776.5
Germany	1121.3	2118.8	1393.7	1701.1	Germany	638.5	671.4	632.9	716.6	Germany	765.1
Ireland	0.3	0.2	0.1	0.3	Ireland	0.3	0.2	0.1	0.3	Ireland	0.3
Italy	-73.1	198.4	660.6	61.4	Italy	200.5	243.9	322.9	346.5	Italy	208.0
Japan	1470.5	2058.1	2305.1	3509.4	Japan	769.3	914.5	955.0	1278.8	Japan	884.3
Netherlands	272.2	106.6	169.7	162.3	Netherlands	90.7	105.2	116.7	156.9	Netherlands	105.3
New Zealand	16.9	19.3	21.5	20.7	New Zealand	16.4	19.1	21.5	20.7	New Zealand	16.4
Norway	7.5	14.2	-6.8	-10.0	Norway	15.3	10.5	21.7	25.7	Norway	15.3
Sweden	94.7	7.5	11.6	56.9	Sweden	4.6	7.5	15.0	38.3	Sweden	7.7
Switzerland	24.9	22.8	29.7	33.4	Switzerland	34.7	30.2	36.0	39.3	Switzerland	37.5
United Kingdom	234.6	797.3	703.4	89.6	United Kingdom	43.5	46.6	29.1	66.9	United Kingdom	61.8
United States	907.0	778.0	694.0	389.0	United States	1217.0	1049.0	992.0	935.0	United States	1341.0
TOTAL	4693.7	7058.8	6538.9	7628.7	TOTAL	4168.0	4286.4	4408.3	5511.5	TOTAL	4675.1
MULTILATERAL					MULTILATERAL						
AF.D.F.	3.3	4.5	2.8	4.2	AF.D.F.	3.3	4.5	2.8	4.2	AF.D.F.	3.3
AF.D.B.	166.8	356.6	321.6	515.6	AF.D.B.	–	–	–	–	AF.D.B.	–
AS.D.B	33.3	44.5	60.7	-7.8	AS.D.B	15.4	15.0	15.9	48.3	AS.D.B	16.8
CAR.D.B.	10.5	15.2	16.0	16.0	CAR.D.B.	7.6	8.2	10.5	10.5	CAR.D.B.	7.6
E.E.C.	261.5	475.8	427.8	427.8	E.E.C.	210.7	418.1	398.5	398.5	E.E.C.	234.5
IBRD	1311.7	456.0	137.0	237.0	IBRD	–	–	–	–	IBRD	–
IDA	-1.6	-6.0	-11.0	-17.0	IDA	-1.6	-6.0	-11.0	-17.0	IDA	9.9
I.D.B.	503.6	442.2	413.3	333.7	I.D.B.	71.2	94.4	118.7	82.4	I.D.B.	142.3
IFAD	54.2	3.8	4.1	37.9	IFAD	54.2	3.8	4.1	37.9	IFAD	66.7
I.F.C.	32.7	87.5	72.8	288.3	I.F.C.	–	–	–	–	I.F.C.	–
IMF TRUST FUND	–	–	–	–	IMF TRUST FUND	–	–	–	–	IMF TRUST FUND	–
U.N. AGENCIES	–	–	–	–	U.N. AGENCIES	–	–	–	–	U.N. AGENCIES	
UNDP	71.7	88.7	93.1	101.3	UNDP	71.7	88.7	93.1	101.3	UNDP	71.7
UNTA	27.2	21.7	29.6	27.1	UNTA	27.2	21.7	29.6	27.1	UNTA	27.2
UNICEF	20.3	16.9	27.2	35.9	UNICEF	20.3	16.9	27.2	35.9	UNICEF	20.3
UNRWA	–	–	–	–	UNRWA	–	–	–	–	UNRWA	–
WFP	91.8	122.6	121.6	181.5	WFP	91.8	122.6	121.6	181.5	WFP	91.8
UNHCR	49.4	58.1	68.6	49.5	UNHCR	49.4	58.1	68.6	49.5	UNHCR	49.4
Other Multilateral	263.9	265.4	230.8	225.7	Other Multilateral	37.6	31.4	71.1	42.7	Other Multilateral	38.2
Arab Agencies	32.0	-12.9	1.5	–	Arab Agencies	4.5	38.3	39.4	–	Arab Agencies	31.6
TOTAL	2932.3	2440.5	2017.5	2456.7	TOTAL	663.3	915.6	990.1	1002.8	TOTAL	811.2
ARAB COUNTRIES	615.4	-196.9	-68.2	1624.8	ARAB COUNTRIES	633.8	-42.1	-70.7	1624.8	ARAB COUNTRIES	794.2
E.E.C.+ MEMBERS	1944.4	3928.8	3119.7	3299.9	E.E.C.+ MEMBERS	1938.7	2170.0	2220.5	3050.9	E.E.C.+ MEMBERS	2209.3
TOTAL	8241.3	9302.4	8488.2	11710.2	TOTAL	5465.0	5159.8	5327.8	8139.0	TOTAL	6280.5

2. ODA LOANS GROSS / 5. ODA LOANS NET / 8. GRANTS

DAC COUNTRIES	1987	1988	1989	1990	DAC COUNTRIES	1987	1988	1989	1990		1987
Australia	–	–	–	–	Australia	-0.2	–	–	–	Australia	241.7
Austria	3.1	17.5	20.9	5.4	Austria	-5.6	5.0	6.9	-12.2	Austria	13.4
Belgium	8.7	14.1	7.0	9.4	Belgium	6.9	11.6	4.7	4.4	Belgium	31.0
Canada	10.2	12.7	17.1	19.3	Canada	3.6	7.2	8.3	-197.9	Canada	118.0
Denmark	13.8	5.2	3.3	4.2	Denmark	11.8	2.7	1.0	1.5	Denmark	4.4
Finland	1.1	8.0	3.1	2.6	Finland	1.1	6.0	2.9	2.6	Finland	10.7
France	474.8	396.0	386.4	1002.0	France	398.8	334.5	325.2	823.6	France	301.7
Germany	463.7	478.7	455.0	523.7	Germany	337.1	330.8	302.9	226.3	Germany	301.4
Ireland	–	–	–	–	Ireland	–	–	–	–	Ireland	0.3
Italy	71.7	102.6	213.2	208.0	Italy	64.2	90.7	170.5	194.5	Italy	136.3
Japan	594.3	709.3	672.5	1013.6	Japan	479.3	572.1	533.8	848.5	Japan	290.0
Netherlands	34.0	18.8	33.5	27.7	Netherlands	19.4	11.6	18.9	11.6	Netherlands	71.3
New Zealand	–	–	–	–	New Zealand	–	–	–	–	New Zealand	16.4
Norway	1.3	–	–	–	Norway	1.3	0.0	–	-0.3	Norway	14.0
Sweden	–	–	–	–	Sweden	-3.1	-3.1	-2.1	–	Sweden	7.7
Switzerland	9.3	7.4	3.9	5.8	Switzerland	6.5	5.0	2.6	5.1	Switzerland	28.2
United Kingdom	18.7	26.1	15.3	13.9	United Kingdom	0.4	-4.4	-24.2	-7.5	United Kingdom	43.0
United States	271.0	252.0	292.0	245.0	United States	147.0	51.0	22.0	50.0	United States	1070.0
TOTAL	1975.6	2048.3	2123.2	3080.5	TOTAL	1468.5	1420.5	1373.4	1950.2	TOTAL	2699.5
MULTILATERAL	296.8	312.1	333.8	375.1	MULTILATERAL	148.9	142.0	161.6	194.8	MULTILATERAL	514.4
ARAB COUNTRIES	206.8	94.9	75.7	41.6	ARAB COUNTRIES	46.3	-57.7	-78.4	-7.8	ARAB COUNTRIES	587.4
E.E.C.+ MEMBERS	1105.7	1060.3	1127.6	1802.8	E.E.C.+ MEMBERS	835.2	771.9	788.8	1244.2	E.E.C.+ MEMBERS	1103.6
TOTAL	2479.2	2455.3	2532.7	3497.2	TOTAL	1663.7	1504.8	1456.5	2137.1	TOTAL	3801.3

3. TOTAL OFFICIAL GROSS / 6. TOTAL OFFICIAL NET / 9. TOTAL OOF GROSS

DAC COUNTRIES	1987	1988	1989	1990	DAC COUNTRIES	1987	1988	1989	1990		1987
Australia	241.9	273.7	305.9	308.4	Australia	228.4	258.6	297.0	292.1	Australia	0.2
Austria	16.5	31.6	47.0	54.6	Austria	5.1	15.5	29.6	36.8	Austria	–
Belgium	87.7	104.0	58.1	93.9	Belgium	81.1	95.8	53.5	86.9	Belgium	48.1
Canada	286.6	444.8	387.9	613.4	Canada	183.7	291.0	291.3	272.8	Canada	158.5
Denmark	37.8	23.4	29.1	29.0	Denmark	24.7	14.5	19.3	24.6	Denmark	19.6
Finland	11.8	19.4	17.0	18.6	Finland	11.8	17.4	16.8	18.5	Finland	–
France	1070.0	846.2	868.4	1676.9	France	872.4	647.6	720.8	1292.0	France	293.5
Germany	1020.9	1063.0	1034.8	1317.3	Germany	730.4	724.2	731.7	751.4	Germany	255.7
Ireland	0.3	0.2	0.1	0.3	Ireland	0.3	0.2	0.1	0.3	Ireland	–
Italy	335.3	359.1	690.7	687.2	Italy	274.8	296.5	606.1	557.2	Italy	127.2
Japan	1058.4	1444.5	1536.6	2097.2	Japan	747.4	969.2	1195.3	1710.1	Japan	174.0
Netherlands	117.2	115.9	138.9	195.3	Netherlands	90.8	97.2	114.7	160.3	Netherlands	11.9
New Zealand	16.9	19.3	21.5	20.7	New Zealand	16.9	19.3	21.5	20.7	New Zealand	0.5
Norway	15.3	11.0	22.2	26.0	Norway	15.3	11.0	22.2	25.7	Norway	–
Sweden	7.7	10.6	17.1	38.3	Sweden	4.6	7.5	15.0	38.3	Sweden	–
Switzerland	37.5	32.6	37.3	40.1	Switzerland	24.9	22.8	29.7	33.4	Switzerland	–
United Kingdom	86.5	168.6	134.4	153.6	United Kingdom	52.5	122.7	59.6	118.0	United Kingdom	24.7
United States	1450.0	1512.0	1496.0	1218.0	United States	1142.0	990.0	850.0	815.0	United States	109.0
TOTAL	5898.2	6479.9	6842.8	8588.7	TOTAL	4507.0	4600.9	5074.3	6253.9	TOTAL	1223.1
MULTILATERAL	5115.4	5514.0	4859.3	5420.9	MULTILATERAL	2932.3	2440.5	2017.5	2456.7	MULTILATERAL	4304.2
ARAB COUNTRIES	869.8	239.3	101.2	1674.2	ARAB COUNTRIES	615.4	-196.9	-68.2	1624.8	ARAB COUNTRIES	75.6
E.E.C.+ MEMBERS	3080.8	3225.2	3456.6	4655.6	E.E.C.+ MEMBERS	2388.5	2474.5	2733.6	3418.4	E.E.C.+ MEMBERS	871.5
TOTAL	11883.4	12233.2	11803.3	15683.7	TOTAL	8054.7	6844.6	7023.6	10335.3	TOTAL	5602.9

1988	1989	1990	1987	1988	1989	1990

10. ODA COMMITMENTS

1988	1989	1990	1987	1988	1989	1990
271.7	297.3	305.0	257.9	516.9	43.3	98.1
31.6	47.0	37.4	21.5	14.1	26.5	34.6
50.1	37.8	44.1	50.9	45.7	37.8	44.1
201.1	206.9	395.1	140.7	274.0	172.2	290.6
8.1	18.2	27.4	0.5	26.0	7.3	27.3
19.4	17.0	18.6	3.2	15.5	25.1	36.1
692.8	730.1	1479.9	722.4	828.1	918.5	1785.2
819.4	785.0	1014.0	959.2	812.9	865.9	881.5
0.2	0.1	0.3	0.3	0.2	0.1	0.3
255.7	365.6	359.9	323.8	422.9	535.2	378.1
1051.8	1093.7	1443.9	1294.8	1554.2	926.9	1647.5
112.4	131.3	173.0	107.3	112.8	149.4	170.0
19.1	21.5	20.7	16.1	19.4	–	18.5
10.5	21.7	26.0	11.5	0.8	5.7	9.9
10.6	17.1	38.3	10.2	14.2	15.0	41.1
32.6	37.3	40.1	31.0	22.0	37.2	42.7
77.1	68.7	88.3	73.6	170.7	68.0	80.5
1250.0	1262.0	1130.0	1307.2	1623.9	1208.5	1316.8
4914.2	5158.2	6641.9	5332.0	6474.2	5042.4	6902.6
4.5	3.3	4.7	9.2	9.1	31.3	50.7
–	–	–	–	–	–	–
16.3	17.6	50.8	18.5	3.4	68.0	27.2
8.2	10.5	10.5	2.8	28.7	8.6	8.6
442.5	422.6	422.6	294.0	764.4	530.7	530.7
–	–	–	–	–	–	–
8.0	3.0	2.0	2.0	–	1.0	3.0
189.0	200.0	173.8	287.4	71.3	137.0	323.4
18.2	26.6	63.5	47.4	26.2	45.4	56.6
–	–	–	–	–	–	–
–	–	–	294.8	338.0	408.8	438.0
88.7	93.1	101.3	–	–	–	–
21.7	29.6	27.1	–	–	–	–
16.9	27.2	35.9	–	–	–	–
–	–	–	–	–	–	–
122.6	121.6	181.5	–	–	–	–
58.1	68.6	49.5	–	–	–	–
32.0	71.6	44.5	3.8	2.0	2.8	1.8
59.1	67.3	63.6	100.4	47.0	135.0	1.1
1085.6	1162.3	1231.2	1060.3	1290.1	1368.5	1441.1
110.6	83.5	1674.2	597.9	199.2	134.7	2388.8
2458.4	2559.3	3609.4	2531.9	3183.8	3112.8	3897.5
6110.4	6404.0	9547.2	6990.2	7963.5	6545.6	10732.6

11. TECH. COOP. GRANTS

1988	1989	1990	1987	1988	1989	1990
271.7	297.3	305.0	23.0	30.6	46.6	44.9
14.1	26.1	32.1	12.2	13.3	12.6	17.3
36.0	30.8	34.6	22.8	17.5	14.7	17.4
188.3	189.8	375.8	–	21.3	24.5	27.5
3.0	14.8	23.2	5.0	2.5	1.5	4.7
11.4	13.9	15.9	1.7	7.7	2.4	4.0
296.8	343.7	477.9	280.1	264.6	300.3	398.3
340.6	330.0	490.3	277.6	289.7	274.7	348.8
0.2	0.1	0.3	0.3	0.2	0.1	0.3
153.2	152.5	151.9	69.0	46.2	40.7	43.5
342.5	421.2	430.3	158.3	207.0	209.9	222.7
93.6	97.8	145.3	49.2	70.6	74.2	96.3
19.1	21.5	20.7	3.8	4.2	–	4.9
10.5	21.7	26.0	2.4	1.4	1.3	2.9
10.6	17.1	38.3	6.3	6.6	6.5	8.8
25.2	33.4	34.3	7.2	8.0	–	–
51.0	53.4	74.4	24.9	38.4	32.8	34.5
998.0	970.0	885.0	240.0	298.0	359.0	349.0
2865.9	3035.0	3561.3	1183.5	1327.6	1401.9	1625.7
773.6	828.5	856.1	222.3	259.2	287.2	256.5
15.6	7.8	1632.6	–	–	–	–
1398.1	1431.8	1806.7	748.1	773.3	739.1	943.7
3655.1	3871.2	6050.0	1405.8	1586.7	1689.1	1882.2

12. TOTAL OOF NET

1988	1989	1990	1987	1988	1989	1990
2.0	8.6	3.4	-13.1	-13.1	-0.3	-12.9
–	–	17.2	-2.7	-3.5	-3.3	16.9
53.9	20.4	49.9	43.2	48.2	18.0	47.8
243.7	181.0	218.4	62.1	95.5	93.1	95.0
15.3	10.9	1.5	8.5	8.9	3.4	-0.1
–	–	–	–	–	–	–
153.4	138.3	197.0	172.0	16.2	51.9	-9.5
243.6	249.8	303.3	91.9	52.8	98.9	34.8
–	–	–	–	–	–	–
103.3	325.0	327.3	74.3	52.6	283.2	210.7
392.7	442.9	653.4	-21.9	54.7	240.3	431.2
3.5	7.6	22.4	0.1	-8.0	-2.0	3.4
0.2	–	–	0.5	0.2	–	–
0.5	0.5	–	–	0.5	0.5	0.0
–	–	–	–	–	–	–
–	–	–	-9.8	-7.4	-6.2	-6.0
91.5	65.7	65.3	9.0	76.1	30.5	51.1
262.0	234.0	88.0	-75.0	-59.0	-142.0	-120.0
1565.7	1684.6	1946.8	339.1	314.6	666.0	742.4
4428.4	3697.0	4189.7	2269.0	1525.0	1027.4	1453.9
128.8	17.8	–	-18.4	-154.8	2.5	–
766.8	897.3	1046.2	449.7	304.5	513.1	367.5
6122.8	5399.4	6136.5	2589.7	1684.8	1695.9	2196.3

13. ODF COMMITMENTS: BY PURPOSE %

	1987	1988	1989	1990
Education	3	2	4	–
Health	1	1	2	–
Other Social Infrastr.	7	2	8	–
Water Sanitat. Sewage	8	5	6	–
Energy	10	13	10	–
Telecommunications	2	5	2	–
Transportation	10	6	4	–
Agriculture	12	12	18	–
Extractive Industries	0	1	1	–
Manufacturing	2	1	3	–
Trade Banking Tourism	5	8	7	–
Technical Cooperation	15	15	16	–
Multisector Aid	4	3	1	–
Programme	15	18	13	–
Debt Reorganisation	1	1	2	–
Food Aid	3	4	2	–
Emergency Aid	2	1	1	–
Unspecified	0	2	0	–
TOTAL	100	100	100	–

14. GRANT ELEMENT OF ODA %

DAC COUNTRIES

	1987	1988	1989	1990
Australia	100.0	100.0	100.0	–
Austria	70.6	97.3	98.8	–
Belgium	98.8	100.0	100.0	–
Canada	98.3	97.5	100.0	–
Denmark	100.0	100.0	100.0	–
Finland	100.0	86.0	100.0	–
France	71.6	71.0	73.7	–
Germany	62.4	74.8	76.9	–
Ireland	100.0	100.0	100.0	–
Italy	79.5	81.6	71.9	–
Japan	57.9	69.6	74.1	–
Netherlands	87.1	90.3	94.5	–
New Zealand	100.0	100.0	–	–
Norway	91.9	100.0	100.0	–
Sweden	100.0	100.0	100.0	–
Switzerland	100.0	100.0	100.0	–
United Kingdom	80.3	100.0	62.5	–
United States	92.3	92.5	95.6	–
TOTAL	75.2	82.4	81.9	–
MULTILATERAL	83.7	93.3	90.0	–
ARAB COUNTRIES	94.0	47.0	54.6	–
E.E.C.+ MEMBERS	73.4	83.1	79.9	–
TOTAL	78.1	83.4	82.9	–

15. OTHER AGGREGATES

OFFICIAL COMMITMENTS:

	1987	1988	1989	1990
TOTAL BILATERAL	8227.4	9641.0	7482.8	12571.5
of which:				
Arab Countries	776.5	267.9	136.9	2388.8
C.E.E.C.	206.0	417.3	192.7	–
TOTAL MULTILATERAL	6387.5	5362.1	6067.7	5233.1
TOTAL BIL.& MULTIL.	14615.0	15003.1	13550.4	17804.6
of which:				
ODA Grants	3908.0	4936.5	3932.2	6542.3
ODA Loans	3288.2	3222.9	2806.1	4190.3

DISBURSEMENTS:

DAC COUNTRIES COMBINED

OFFICIAL & PRIVATE	1987	1988	1989	1990
GROSS:				
Contractual Lending	4775.7	5328.2	6646.4	7245.5
Export Credits, Total	2218.2	2357.0	3581.1	2985.3
Export Credits, Priv.	1595.5	1720.8	2849.8	2236.5
NET:				
Contractual Lending	1265.2	1663.6	2691.9	2575.6
Export Credits Total	-537.3	-234.2	771.9	-83.7
PRIVATE SECTOR NET	186.6	2457.8	1464.6	1374.8
Direct Investment	843.6	366.2	2499.9	2124.9
Portfolio Investment	-133.1	2156.5	-1699.1	-651.5
Export Credits	-523.9	-64.8	663.8	-98.6

MARKET BORROWING:

CHANGE IN CLAIMS

	1987	1988	1989	1990
Banks	223.0	313.0	451.0	6465.0

MEMORANDUM ITEM:

	1987	1988	1989	1990
C.E.E.C. (Gross)	1790.7	1697.9	1598.4	–

1. TOTAL RECEIPTS NET

DAC COUNTRIES	1987	1988	1989	1990
Australia	497.6	-70.7	236.1	1194.6
Austria	164.2	-85.1	-81.3	85.1
Belgium	-1272.3	1017.3	276.8	-821.1
Canada	122.7	-56.9	222.5	314.4
Denmark	-141.5	-187.2	-115.5	-125.7
Finland	72.4	47.9	166.2	124.1
France	3748.5	2940.4	2871.8	1866.5
Germany	2919.6	4475.3	2860.5	4497.5
Ireland	0.1	0.1	0.1	0.5
Italy	-104.4	1383.2	1359.6	-402.1
Japan	7756.8	8442.7	10206.5	4890.1
Netherlands	419.4	446.4	386.4	1035.2
New Zealand	10.7	7.1	8.1	17.6
Norway	8.8	-60.7	31.0	-11.7
Sweden	-71.2	25.9	77.2	133.1
Switzerland	12.3	12.4	19.1	15.7
United Kingdom	2181.9	1384.4	2721.0	-19.6
United States	3945.0	4844.0	5025.0	-844.0
TOTAL	*20270.6*	*24566.3*	*26271.0*	*11950.0*
MULTILATERAL				
AF.D.F.	1.5	1.0	1.8	0.1
AF.D.B.	23.2	29.9	49.9	128.2
AS.D.B	-139.5	-50.9	-385.1	29.7
CAR.D.B.	32.7	40.0	45.8	45.8
E.E.C.	205.8	217.0	276.8	276.8
IBRD	797.2	-99.0	140.0	2702.0
IDA	-2.2	-3.0	-1.0	-2.0
I.D.B.	343.6	662.1	637.5	573.2
IFAD	17.6	-1.8	-0.6	3.6
I.F.C.	175.2	218.7	316.2	694.1
IMF TRUST FUND	–	–	–	–
U.N. AGENCIES	–	–	–	–
UNDP	87.4	99.8	88.7	99.7
UNTA	25.8	19.5	27.0	28.1
UNICEF	13.7	11.9	24.8	23.7
UNRWA	–	–	–	–
WFP	44.9	57.9	45.8	57.1
UNHCR	57.7	75.7	85.6	75.1
Other Multilateral	205.5	227.4	289.7	98.7
Arab Agencies	-98.9	-3.7	42.0	–
TOTAL	*1791.2*	*1502.3*	*1685.0*	*4834.0*
ARAB COUNTRIES	*350.2*	*217.6*	*140.6*	*703.4*
E.E.C.+ MEMBERS	*7957.2*	*11676.8*	*10637.4*	*6308.0*
TOTAL	*22412.0*	*26286.1*	*28096.5*	*17487.4*

2. ODA LOANS GROSS

DAC COUNTRIES	1987	1988	1989	1990
Australia	–	–	–	–
Austria	69.9	39.2	27.9	32.8
Belgium	–	–	–	5.1
Canada	1.9	–	–	0.0
Denmark	–	–	–	–
Finland	0.6	0.5	0.0	5.7
France	226.1	160.2	144.0	275.8
Germany	406.9	187.8	237.1	338.3
Ireland	–	–	–	–
Italy	14.5	33.9	77.5	102.9
Japan	679.6	360.0	461.3	842.0
Netherlands	32.1	27.7	27.4	19.2
New Zealand	–	–	–	–
Norway	–	–	–	–
Sweden	–	–	–	–
Switzerland	–	–	3.0	–
United Kingdom	11.6	11.8	20.3	14.2
United States	56.0	30.0	40.0	18.0
TOTAL	*1499.2*	*851.0*	*1038.4*	*1654.0*
MULTILATERAL	*176.1*	*171.2*	*148.2*	*133.2*
ARAB COUNTRIES	*89.2*	*64.1*	*58.1*	*80.6*
E.E.C.+ MEMBERS	*698.2*	*427.2*	*518.5*	*767.7*
TOTAL	*1764.5*	*1086.3*	*1244.7*	*1867.9*

3. TOTAL OFFICIAL GROSS

DAC COUNTRIES	1987	1988	1989	1990
Australia	66.5	74.2	82.1	74.1
Austria	149.8	67.6	62.1	98.1
Belgium	108.0	50.2	50.1	98.2
Canada	250.6	168.5	483.2	488.8
Denmark	10.3	11.6	15.4	8.8
Finland	2.4	3.6	4.0	19.9
France	3937.9	3653.1	4267.8	4293.6
Germany	2186.8	1600.7	2073.4	2988.3
Ireland	0.1	0.1	0.1	0.5
Italy	1113.4	218.8	357.5	509.9
Japan	1675.9	1535.3	1543.4	3721.5
Netherlands	146.9	161.6	189.0	220.3
New Zealand	10.7	7.1	8.1	17.6
Norway	7.2	4.5	6.6	10.8
Sweden	26.0	27.2	16.8	67.0
Switzerland	12.3	12.4	19.1	15.7
United Kingdom	100.6	116.1	126.4	138.5
United States	3236.0	2548.0	2318.0	3435.0
TOTAL	*13041.5*	*10260.3*	*11623.2*	*16206.4*
MULTILATERAL	*6949.1*	*7956.2*	*7465.6*	*10648.7*
ARAB COUNTRIES	*609.3*	*442.6*	*259.5*	*774.1*
E.E.C.+ MEMBERS	*7877.0*	*6152.1*	*7488.4*	*8666.6*
TOTAL	*20599.8*	*18659.1*	*19348.2*	*27629.2*

4. TOTAL ODA NET

DAC COUNTRIES	1987	1988	1989	1990
Australia	65.2	74.1	53.9	63.6
Austria	76.8	52.2	51.0	64.4
Belgium	15.6	15.9	10.8	27.8
Canada	64.2	77.3	68.9	76.4
Denmark	-1.2	-1.1	0.0	4.5
Finland	2.4	3.2	4.0	19.9
France	2167.6	2369.1	2522.5	3244.7
Germany	596.4	391.7	406.0	656.8
Ireland	0.1	0.1	0.1	0.5
Italy	70.6	135.1	207.1	207.0
Japan	581.4	255.9	418.8	705.9
Netherlands	128.8	136.6	173.5	185.2
New Zealand	10.7	7.1	8.1	17.6
Norway	5.4	2.0	2.4	7.0
Sweden	24.7	25.9	15.8	66.4
Switzerland	12.3	12.4	19.1	15.7
United Kingdom	70.6	75.6	74.4	89.4
United States	1514.0	1469.0	1396.0	1565.0
TOTAL	*5405.6*	*5102.0*	*5432.4*	*7017.9*
MULTILATERAL				
AF.D.F.	1.5	1.0	1.8	0.1
AF.D.B.	–	–	–	–
AS.D.B	0.7	2.9	3.9	0.7
CAR.D.B.	20.0	22.3	26.2	26.2
E.E.C.	154.7	206.9	197.7	197.7
IBRD	–	–	–	–
IDA	-2.2	-3.0	-1.0	-2.0
I.D.B.	-11.1	0.8	-40.9	-46.2
IFAD	17.6	-1.8	-0.6	3.6
I.F.C.	–	–	–	–
IMF TRUST FUND	–	–	–	–
U.N. AGENCIES	–	–	–	–
UNDP	87.4	99.8	88.7	99.7
UNTA	25.8	19.5	27.0	28.1
UNICEF	13.7	11.9	24.8	23.7
UNRWA	–	–	–	–
WFP	44.9	57.9	45.8	57.1
UNHCR	57.7	75.7	85.6	75.1
Other Multilateral	16.9	28.2	68.1	69.9
Arab Agencies	11.6	-2.0	16.1	–
TOTAL	*439.2*	*520.0*	*543.3*	*533.7*
ARAB COUNTRIES	*470.9*	*299.1*	*129.0*	*704.2*
E.E.C.+ MEMBERS	*3203.2*	*3329.9*	*3592.1*	*4613.7*
TOTAL	*6315.7*	*5921.2*	*6104.7*	*8255.9*

5. ODA LOANS NET

DAC COUNTRIES	1987	1988	1989	1990
Australia	–	–	–	–
Austria	54.2	29.0	16.9	12.9
Belgium	–	–	–	5.1
Canada	-2.0	-4.8	-4.1	-10.3
Denmark	-1.3	-1.7	-0.5	-0.9
Finland	0.6	0.4	0.0	5.7
France	120.0	88.0	67.5	178.3
Germany	226.5	37.6	67.8	129.9
Ireland	–	–	–	–
Italy	11.8	29.2	62.5	93.3
Japan	359.0	-21.5	122.3	387.7
Netherlands	18.6	13.0	12.8	1.6
New Zealand	–	–	–	–
Norway	-1.8	-1.9	-2.6	-3.8
Sweden	-1.3	-1.3	-1.0	–
Switzerland	–	–	3.0	–
United Kingdom	-4.7	-6.8	8.8	-0.8
United States	-100.0	-96.0	-125.0	-145.0
TOTAL	*679.5*	*63.3*	*228.4*	*653.7*
MULTILATERAL	*32.8*	*16.7*	*7.2*	*-4.8*
ARAB COUNTRIES	*-12.8*	*-40.1*	*-51.9*	*10.7*
E.E.C.+ MEMBERS	*376.2*	*162.9*	*228.4*	*415.9*
TOTAL	*699.4*	*39.9*	*183.7*	*659.7*

6. TOTAL OFFICIAL NET

DAC COUNTRIES	1987	1988	1989	1990
Australia	62.5	70.2	78.3	69.3
Austria	133.8	28.7	7.8	68.2
Belgium	104.0	48.3	46.3	98.2
Canada	63.0	-86.9	235.5	183.3
Denmark	-31.6	-80.8	-55.8	7.2
Finland	2.4	3.5	4.0	19.9
France	3472.1	3272.8	3785.7	3879.2
Germany	1473.9	805.6	898.4	2164.3
Ireland	0.1	0.1	0.1	0.5
Italy	896.8	152.5	271.8	283.3
Japan	995.2	534.5	508.4	2727.9
Netherlands	119.0	131.9	162.0	191.8
New Zealand	10.7	7.1	8.1	17.6
Norway	3.4	2.4	3.9	6.7
Sweden	24.7	25.9	15.8	67.0
Switzerland	12.3	12.4	19.1	15.7
United Kingdom	74.0	87.5	103.5	108.4
United States	-270.0	1065.0	859.0	1857.0
TOTAL	*7146.4*	*6080.6*	*6951.9*	*11765.3*
MULTILATERAL	*1791.2*	*1502.3*	*1685.0*	*4834.0*
ARAB COUNTRIES	*350.2*	*217.6*	*140.6*	*703.4*
E.E.C.+ MEMBERS	*6314.1*	*4634.8*	*5488.9*	*7009.7*
TOTAL	*9287.8*	*7800.4*	*8777.5*	*17302.7*

7. TOTAL ODA GROSS

	1987
Australia	65.2
Austria	92.6
Belgium	15.6
Canada	68.1
Denmark	0.1
Finland	2.4
France	2273.7
Germany	776.9
Ireland	0.1
Italy	73.3
Japan	901.9
Netherlands	142.3
New Zealand	10.7
Norway	7.2
Sweden	26.0
Switzerland	12.3
United Kingdom	86.9
United States	1670.0
TOTAL	*6225.4*
AF.D.F.	1.5
AF.D.B.	–
AS.D.B	1.3
CAR.D.B.	20.0
E.E.C.	156.2
IBRD	–
IDA	1.8
I.D.B.	103.9
IFAD	25.3
I.F.C.	–
IMF TRUST FUND	–
U.N. AGENCIES	–
UNDP	87.4
UNTA	25.8
UNICEF	13.7
UNRWA	–
WFP	44.9
UNHCR	57.7
Other Multilateral	18.3
Arab Agencies	24.5
TOTAL	*582.4*
ARAB COUNTRIES	*572.9*
E.E.C.+ MEMBERS	*3525.1*
TOTAL	*7380.7*

8. GRANTS

	1987
Australia	65.2
Austria	22.6
Belgium	15.6
Canada	66.2
Denmark	0.1
Finland	1.9
France	2047.6
Germany	369.9
Ireland	0.1
Italy	58.8
Japan	222.4
Netherlands	110.2
New Zealand	10.7
Norway	7.2
Sweden	26.0
Switzerland	12.3
United Kingdom	75.3
United States	1614.0
TOTAL	*4726.2*
MULTILATERAL	*406.4*
ARAB COUNTRIES	*483.7*
E.E.C.+ MEMBERS	*2827.0*
TOTAL	*5616.3*

9. TOTAL OOF GROSS

	1987
Australia	1.3
Austria	57.2
Belgium	92.3
Canada	182.5
Denmark	10.2
Finland	–
France	1664.2
Germany	1410.0
Ireland	–
Italy	1040.1
Japan	773.9
Netherlands	4.6
New Zealand	–
Norway	–
Sweden	–
Switzerland	–
United Kingdom	13.8
United States	1566.0
TOTAL	*6816.1*
MULTILATERAL	*6366.7*
ARAB COUNTRIES	*36.4*
E.E.C.+ MEMBERS	*4351.9*
TOTAL	*13219.1*

1988	1989	1990	1987	1988	1989	1990

10. ODA COMMITMENTS

1988	1989	1990	1987	1988	1989	1990
74.1	53.9	63.6	61.5	50.3	57.3	61.5
62.4	62.0	84.3	48.1	149.9	137.5	57.9
15.9	10.8	27.8	12.2	24.2	10.8	27.8
82.1	73.1	86.8	75.2	114.8	48.7	101.8
0.6	0.5	5.4	0.5	–	3.4	10.5
3.3	4.0	19.9	1.9	11.3	3.6	40.3
2441.2	2599.0	3342.2	2207.7	2263.3	2879.8	3467.3
541.9	575.3	865.2	704.0	830.0	702.3	882.7
0.1	0.1	0.5	0.1	0.1	0.1	0.5
139.8	222.2	216.6	123.7	378.7	332.4	257.3
637.4	757.8	1160.1	593.3	1190.0	704.1	2266.4
151.3	188.1	202.8	139.3	193.4	179.8	186.1
7.1	8.1	17.6	8.3	7.4	–	8.1
3.9	5.0	10.8	2.1	0.1	0.2	1.9
27.2	16.8	66.4	31.5	34.3	16.8	33.6
12.4	19.1	15.7	11.0	9.7	12.8	41.4
94.1	85.9	104.5	101.0	82.5	83.3	128.9
1595.0	1561.0	1728.0	1687.1	1502.2	1461.7	1967.1
5889.7	6242.5	8018.2	5808.5	6842.1	6634.4	9541.2
1.0	2.3	0.8	–	81.6	4.8	2.2
–	–	–	–	–	–	–
3.5	4.6	2.5	–	–	–	–
22.3	26.2	26.2	22.8	29.1	23.9	23.9
209.2	200.4	200.4	253.4	249.0	291.6	291.6
–	–	–	–	–	–	–
1.0	3.0	2.0	6.0	–	–	5.0
121.1	73.3	64.8	48.6	–	–	–
4.1	4.7	13.8	–	40.8	9.3	67.4
–	–	–	–	–	–	–
–	–	–	247.5	283.6	337.7	354.1
99.8	88.7	99.7	–	–	–	–
19.5	27.0	28.1	–	–	–	–
11.9	24.8	23.7	–	–	–	–
–	–	–	–	–	–	–
57.9	45.8	57.1	–	–	–	–
75.7	85.6	75.1	–	–	–	–
29.6	69.9	71.5	0.4	10.8	4.1	1.1
18.0	28.0	17.1	4.4	112.3	94.0	3.2
674.5	684.2	682.9	583.1	807.2	765.4	748.7
403.4	239.0	774.1	501.1	413.0	323.4	583.4
3594.2	3882.3	4965.4	3541.9	4021.1	4483.4	5252.8
6967.6	7165.7	9475.2	6892.7	8062.3	7723.2	10873.2

11. TECH. COOP. GRANTS

1988	1989	1990	1987	1988	1989	1990
74.1	53.9	63.6	58.3	60.3	41.4	49.2
23.2	34.1	51.5	20.9	22.9	23.8	29.6
15.9	10.8	22.8	10.2	7.0	4.1	4.8
82.1	73.1	86.7	–	11.4	12.7	11.9
0.6	0.5	5.4	0.0	0.6	0.3	0.5
2.8	3.9	14.1	0.7	0.6	1.0	1.2
2281.0	2455.1	3066.4	1121.3	1181.5	1361.3	1923.9
354.1	338.2	526.9	364.3	348.7	307.4	361.2
0.1	0.1	0.5	0.1	0.1	0.1	0.5
105.9	144.6	113.7	45.0	45.4	69.4	66.8
277.3	296.5	318.2	195.7	247.6	254.5	288.4
123.6	160.7	183.6	44.0	58.6	53.7	73.3
7.1	8.1	17.6	1.6	1.5	–	11.2
3.9	5.0	10.8	1.0	0.8	1.2	0.7
27.2	16.8	66.4	3.7	6.0	6.3	11.2
12.4	16.1	15.7	1.6	1.8	–	–
82.4	65.6	90.3	26.9	38.6	36.0	39.8
1565.0	1521.0	1710.0	69.0	88.0	93.0	88.0
5038.7	5204.1	6364.2	1964.2	2121.3	2266.1	2962.4
503.3	536.1	549.7	218.6	265.4	291.9	297.0
339.3	180.9	693.5	–	–	–	–
3167.0	3363.8	4197.7	1627.9	1720.1	1832.3	2470.9
5881.3	5921.0	7607.3	2182.8	2386.7	2557.9	3259.4

12. TOTAL OOF NET

1988	1989	1990	1987	1988	1989	1990
0.1	28.2	10.5	-2.7	-3.9	24.4	5.7
5.2	0.1	13.8	57.1	-23.4	-43.2	3.8
34.3	39.3	70.3	88.3	32.3	35.6	70.3
86.4	410.2	402.0	-1.2	-164.2	166.6	106.9
11.0	14.9	3.4	-30.4	-79.7	-55.8	2.7
0.3	–	–	–	0.3	–	–
1211.9	1668.8	951.4	1304.5	903.7	1263.1	634.5
1058.8	1498.1	2123.1	877.5	413.9	492.4	1507.5
–	–	–	–	–	–	–
78.9	135.3	293.2	826.2	17.3	64.7	76.3
897.9	785.7	2561.4	413.9	278.6	89.5	2021.9
10.3	0.9	17.5	-9.8	-4.7	-11.5	6.6
–	–	–	–	–	–	–
0.5	1.6	–	-2.0	0.4	1.5	-0.4
–	–	0.6	–	–	–	0.6
–	–	–	–	–	–	–
22.0	40.5	34.0	3.4	12.0	29.1	19.0
953.0	757.0	1707.0	-1784.0	-404.0	-537.0	292.0
4370.6	5380.7	8188.3	1740.8	978.6	1519.5	4747.4
7281.7	6781.4	9965.8	1352.0	982.3	1141.7	4300.3
39.2	20.5	–	-120.7	-81.6	11.6	-0.8
2557.9	3606.1	3701.2	3110.9	1304.9	1896.7	2396.0
11691.5	12182.5	18154.0	2972.1	1879.2	2672.8	9046.9

13. ODF COMMITMENTS: BY PURPOSE %

	1987	1988	1989	1990
Education	3	2	1	–
Health	1	3	1	–
Other Social Infrastr.	7	6	6	–
Water Sanitat. Sewage	3	4	1	–
Energy	6	10	15	–
Telecommunications	0	0	2	–
Transportation	9	8	9	–
Agriculture	8	12	10	–
Extractive Industries	5	3	1	–
Manufacturing	1	6	1	–
Trade Banking Tourism	16	5	13	–
Technical Cooperation	15	17	12	–
Multisector Aid	1	1	1	–
Programme	20	18	22	–
Debt Reorganisation	5	4	6	–
Food Aid	1	0	0	–
Emergency Aid	0	0	0	–
Unspecified	0	–	0	–
TOTAL	100	100	100	–

14. GRANT ELEMENT OF ODA %

DAC COUNTRIES	1987	1988	1989	1990
Australia	100.0	100.0	100.0	–
Austria	62.0	40.6	47.9	–
Belgium	100.0	100.0	100.0	–
Canada	100.0	96.3	100.0	–
Denmark	100.0	–	100.0	–
Finland	38.5	100.0	100.0	–
France	97.4	97.2	95.1	–
Germany	70.7	63.5	69.6	–
Ireland	100.0	100.0	100.0	–
Italy	79.7	74.4	72.7	–
Japan	71.3	60.0	73.5	–
Netherlands	91.2	93.4	93.2	–
New Zealand	100.0	100.0	–	–
Norway	100.0	100.0	100.0	–
Sweden	100.0	100.0	100.0	–
Switzerland	100.0	100.0	100.0	–
United Kingdom	89.1	94.2	89.1	–
United States	98.6	99.1	99.9	–
TOTAL	91.2	84.4	88.8	–
MULTILATERAL	96.9	86.9	88.7	–
ARAB COUNTRIES	94.2	94.3	67.7	–
E.E.C.+ MEMBERS	90.9	87.7	89.1	–
TOTAL	91.8	85.1	87.9	–

15. OTHER AGGREGATES

	1987	1988	1989	1990
OFFICIAL COMMITMENTS:				
TOTAL BILATERAL	14026.2	12486.1	18168.2	15802.2
of which:				
Arab Countries	894.6	506.5	323.4	597.1
C.E.E.C.	85.0	2.0	2003.0	–
TOTAL MULTILATERAL	8719.9	9108.2	11322.6	10952.7
TOTAL BIL.& MULTIL.	22746.1	21594.3	29490.8	26754.9
of which:				
ODA Grants	5795.2	5900.7	5930.7	7832.6
ODA Loans	1182.5	2163.6	3745.4	3040.6
DISBURSEMENTS:				
DAC COUNTRIES COMBINED				
OFFICIAL & PRIVATE				
GROSS:				
Contractual Lending	17365.2	14006.7	21174.0	21345.7
Export Credits, Total	10554.7	9926.3	16547.7	14478.4
Export Credits, Priv.	9093.2	8806.2	14796.6	11528.7
NET:				
Contractual Lending	-681.2	1158.7	3887.8	5085.7
Export Credits Total	-5536.2	-959.2	1420.0	320.4
PRIVATE SECTOR NET	13124.2	18485.7	19319.1	184.7
Direct Investment	17845.9	18366.3	16671.9	16744.4
Portfolio Investment	-1663.5	-18.4	465.4	-16269.5
Export Credits	-3058.2	137.9	2181.7	-290.3
MARKET BORROWING:				
CHANGE IN CLAIMS				
Banks	-4439.0	-4686.0	-11337.0	-29264.0
MEMORANDUM ITEM:				
C.E.E.C. (Gross)	82.3	90.8	64.5	–

1. TOTAL RECEIPTS NET

DAC COUNTRIES	1987	1988	1989	1990
Australia	-172.3	2624.8	62.1	-563.4
Austria	16.9	44.6	22.0	57.9
Belgium	101.0	90.9	147.8	210.2
Canada	491.1	412.3	475.7	471.8
Denmark	175.5	110.0	133.9	253.0
Finland	53.0	58.5	92.1	128.7
France	929.5	849.0	885.5	930.7
Germany	2.7	23.4	2121.7	811.8
Ireland	10.7	-15.8	37.0	7.0
Italy	317.2	419.5	571.8	433.7
Japan	-2.4	-1130.8	-519.8	475.7
Netherlands	144.2	409.2	351.9	176.7
New Zealand	46.0	81.3	31.9	22.3
Norway	137.0	113.1	125.3	169.7
Sweden	335.3	978.7	399.1	461.0
Switzerland	-987.3	1652.9	1917.7	3674.2
United Kingdom	-1301.1	-399.6	-5572.2	-7771.4
United States	1678.0	2021.0	4403.0	2084.0
TOTAL	*1974.8*	*8342.9*	*5686.4*	*2033.6*
MULTILATERAL				
AF.D.F.	2.5	0.6	6.7	8.3
AF.D.B.	1.0	10.0	4.4	14.9
AS.D.B	6.6	9.1	11.5	16.9
CAR.D.B.	9.0	3.0	2.1	2.1
E.E.C.	314.0	441.0	363.9	965.6
IBRD	-11.6	-8.0	-9.0	-10.0
IDA	3.4	5.0	1.0	–
I.D.B.	90.6	-1.7	247.4	182.0
IFAD	–	–	–	–
I.F.C.	10.2	–	23.9	–
IMF TRUST FUND	–	–	–	–
U.N. AGENCIES	–	–	–	–
UNDP	144.7	177.4	205.9	239.6
UNTA	155.1	154.7	81.1	81.9
UNICEF	52.7	68.3	78.3	104.6
UNRWA	207.4	230.9	265.0	292.5
WFP	3.1	6.2	3.7	6.8
UNHCR	34.5	32.4	33.4	41.9
Other Multilateral	295.1	349.9	368.2	465.8
Arab Agencies	11.8	10.3	19.7	–
TOTAL	*1330.2*	*1489.1*	*1707.2*	*2412.8*
ARAB COUNTRIES	*1233.5*	*1447.1*	*1167.7*	*1263.9*
E.E.C.+ MEMBERS	*693.7*	*1927.5*	*-958.8*	*-3982.8*
TOTAL	*4538.5*	*11279.1*	*8561.3*	*5710.2*

2. ODA LOANS GROSS

DAC COUNTRIES	1987	1988	1989	1990
Australia	–	–	–	–
Austria	–	–	–	–
Belgium	0.6	0.1	2.8	0.2
Canada	–	–	–	–
Denmark	–	–	–	–
Finland	–	–	0.0	0.1
France	62.7	31.9	60.1	8.9
Germany	25.1	32.5	3.2	31.5
Ireland	–	–	–	–
Italy	–	–	–	–
Japan	–	0.2	12.1	–
Netherlands	–	–	–	–
New Zealand	–	–	–	–
Norway	–	–	–	–
Sweden	–	–	–	–
Switzerland	2.0	0.0	0.0	0.0
United Kingdom	7.9	–	–	–
United States	8.0	5.0	10.0	5.0
TOTAL	*106.3*	*69.7*	*88.3*	*45.7*
MULTILATERAL	*29.1*	*22.3*	*20.1*	*49.7*
ARAB COUNTRIES	–	–	–	–
E.E.C.+ MEMBERS	*98.5*	*70.9*	*72.5*	*76.6*
TOTAL	*135.4*	*92.0*	*108.4*	*95.3*

3. TOTAL OFFICIAL GROSS

DAC COUNTRIES	1987	1988	1989	1990
Australia	52.7	54.8	47.8	73.2
Austria	15.7	26.4	13.4	19.7
Belgium	95.5	88.1	109.1	168.7
Canada	404.1	524.4	636.8	698.3
Denmark	69.6	69.0	86.0	213.4
Finland	53.3	58.5	92.1	128.7
France	942.6	849.3	912.5	969.8
Germany	377.8	427.8	361.4	636.2
Ireland	10.7	6.9	6.6	7.0
Italy	219.9	285.0	506.2	448.8
Japan	218.2	475.1	537.8	575.3
Netherlands	221.4	212.5	213.0	307.6
New Zealand	19.5	52.2	31.9	22.3
Norway	122.0	112.9	131.5	184.4
Sweden	335.3	292.7	399.1	461.0
Switzerland	101.8	113.7	96.3	162.2
United Kingdom	496.2	490.5	298.4	400.0
United States	1840.0	1792.0	1870.0	1597.0
TOTAL	*5596.3*	*5931.8*	*6349.8*	*7073.7*
MULTILATERAL	*1371.4*	*1542.8*	*1785.7*	*2490.0*
ARAB COUNTRIES	*1233.5*	*1447.1*	*1167.7*	*1273.9*
E.E.C.+ MEMBERS	*2749.4*	*2870.9*	*2858.6*	*4118.6*
TOTAL	*8201.1*	*8921.7*	*9303.2*	*10837.5*

4. TOTAL ODA NET

DAC COUNTRIES	1987	1988	1989	1990
Australia	52.7	54.8	47.8	73.2
Austria	15.7	26.4	13.4	19.6
Belgium	95.1	85.0	109.1	168.7
Canada	404.1	524.3	636.7	696.8
Denmark	69.4	68.7	86.0	213.3
Finland	53.0	58.5	92.1	128.7
France	929.5	849.0	881.7	792.3
Germany	310.6	363.2	356.6	505.8
Ireland	10.7	6.9	6.6	7.0
Italy	219.9	285.0	360.4	282.0
Japan	211.2	473.8	522.1	568.2
Netherlands	221.4	212.5	213.0	307.6
New Zealand	19.5	52.2	31.9	22.3
Norway	122.0	112.9	131.5	184.4
Sweden	335.3	292.7	399.1	461.0
Switzerland	101.4	112.4	96.3	162.2
United Kingdom	256.1	305.6	297.0	399.1
United States	1783.0	1780.0	1869.0	1600.0
TOTAL	*5210.5*	*5664.0*	*6150.4*	*6592.1*
MULTILATERAL				
AF.D.F.	2.5	0.6	6.7	8.3
AF.D.B.	–	–	–	–
AS.D.B	6.6	9.1	11.5	16.9
CAR.D.B.	8.2	3.0	2.1	2.1
E.E.C.	315.7	441.8	364.7	788.0
IBRD	–	–	–	–
IDA	3.4	5.0	1.0	–
I.D.B.	28.9	18.6	39.7	42.7
IFAD	–	–	–	–
I.F.C.	–	–	–	–
IMF TRUST FUND	–	–	–	–
U.N. AGENCIES	–	–	–	–
UNDP	144.7	177.4	205.9	239.6
UNTA	155.1	154.7	81.1	81.9
UNICEF	52.7	68.3	78.3	104.6
UNRWA	207.4	230.9	265.0	292.5
WFP	3.1	6.2	3.7	6.8
UNHCR	34.5	32.4	33.4	41.9
Other Multilateral	295.1	349.9	368.2	465.8
Arab Agencies	11.8	10.3	19.7	–
TOTAL	*1269.7*	*1508.1*	*1481.0*	*2090.9*
ARAB COUNTRIES	*1233.5*	*1447.1*	*1167.7*	*1263.9*
E.E.C.+ MEMBERS	*2428.4*	*2617.7*	*2675.0*	*3463.6*
TOTAL	*7713.6*	*8619.2*	*8799.1*	*9946.9*

5. ODA LOANS NET

DAC COUNTRIES	1987	1988	1989	1990
Australia	–	–	–	–
Austria	–	–	–	–
Belgium	0.6	-3.1	2.8	0.2
Canada	0.0	-0.1	-0.1	-1.5
Denmark	0.0	-0.2	–	–
Finland	-0.3	–	0.0	0.1
France	49.6	31.6	34.3	-30.2
Germany	-3.4	10.7	-0.3	-85.0
Ireland	–	–	–	–
Italy	–	–	–	–
Japan	-6.9	-1.0	-3.5	-0.5
Netherlands	–	–	–	–
New Zealand	–	–	–	–
Norway	–	–	–	–
Sweden	–	–	–	–
Switzerland	1.5	-1.2	0.0	0.0
United Kingdom	6.0	-1.5	-1.4	-0.8
United States	-2.0	–	9.0	6.0
TOTAL	*45.0*	*35.2*	*40.9*	*-111.9*
MULTILATERAL	*24.9*	*15.5*	*7.0*	*37.4*
ARAB COUNTRIES	–	–	–	*-10.0*
E.E.C.+ MEMBERS	*54.9*	*43.8*	*41.1*	*-80.6*
TOTAL	*69.8*	*50.6*	*48.0*	*-84.5*

6. TOTAL OFFICIAL NET

DAC COUNTRIES	1987	1988	1989	1990
Australia	52.7	54.8	47.8	73.2
Austria	15.7	26.4	13.4	19.7
Belgium	95.5	85.0	109.1	168.7
Canada	404.1	524.3	636.7	696.8
Denmark	69.5	68.7	85.9	212.5
Finland	53.0	58.5	92.1	128.7
France	929.5	849.0	885.5	930.7
Germany	331.8	374.2	332.0	518.2
Ireland	10.7	6.9	6.6	7.0
Italy	219.9	285.0	506.2	448.8
Japan	211.2	473.8	522.1	568.9
Netherlands	221.4	212.5	213.0	322.8
New Zealand	19.5	52.2	31.9	22.3
Norway	122.0	112.9	131.5	184.4
Sweden	335.3	292.7	399.1	461.0
Switzerland	101.4	112.4	96.3	162.2
United Kingdom	494.1	489.1	296.9	399.1
United States	1771.0	1776.0	1859.0	1594.0
TOTAL	*5458.1*	*5854.5*	*6265.2*	*6919.1*
MULTILATERAL	*1330.2*	*1489.1*	*1707.2*	*2412.8*
ARAB COUNTRIES	*1233.5*	*1447.1*	*1167.7*	*1263.9*
E.E.C.+ MEMBERS	*2686.3*	*2811.4*	*2799.1*	*3973.4*
TOTAL	*8021.8*	*8790.7*	*9140.1*	*10595.7*

7. TOTAL ODA GROSS

DAC COUNTRIES	1987
Australia	52.7
Austria	15.7
Belgium	95.1
Canada	404.1
Denmark	69.4
Finland	53.3
France	942.6
Germany	339.1
Ireland	10.7
Italy	219.9
Japan	218.2
Netherlands	221.4
New Zealand	19.5
Norway	122.0
Sweden	335.3
Switzerland	101.8
United Kingdom	258.1
United States	1793.0
TOTAL	*5271.9*
MULTILATERAL	
AF.D.F.	2.6
AF.D.B.	–
AS.D.B	6.6
CAR.D.B.	8.2
E.E.C.	315.7
IBRD	–
IDA	3.4
I.D.B.	33.0
IFAD	–
I.F.C.	–
IMF TRUST FUND	–
U.N. AGENCIES	–
UNDP	144.7
UNTA	155.1
UNICEF	52.7
UNRWA	207.4
WFP	3.1
UNHCR	34.5
Other Multilateral	295.1
Arab Agencies	11.8
TOTAL	*1273.9*
ARAB COUNTRIES	*1233.5*
E.E.C.+ MEMBERS	*2472.0*
TOTAL	*7779.2*

8. GRANTS

	1987
Australia	52.7
Austria	15.7
Belgium	94.5
Canada	404.1
Denmark	69.4
Finland	53.3
France	880.0
Germany	314.0
Ireland	10.7
Italy	219.9
Japan	218.2
Netherlands	221.4
New Zealand	19.5
Norway	122.0
Sweden	335.3
Switzerland	99.8
United Kingdom	250.2
United States	1785.0
TOTAL	*5165.5*
MULTILATERAL	*1244.0*
ARAB COUNTRIES	*1233.5*
E.E.C.+ MEMBERS	*2373.6*
TOTAL	*7643.8*

9. TOTAL OOF GROSS

	1987
Australia	–
Austria	–
Belgium	0.4
Canada	–
Denmark	0.2
Finland	–
France	–
Germany	38.7
Ireland	–
Italy	–
Japan	0.0
Netherlands	–
New Zealand	–
Norway	–
Sweden	–
Switzerland	–
United Kingdom	238.1
United States	47.0
TOTAL	*324.4*
MULTILATERAL	*97.5*
ARAB COUNTRIES	–
E.E.C.+ MEMBERS	*277.0*
TOTAL	*421.9*

1988	1989	1990	1987	1988	1989	1990

10. ODA COMMITMENTS

1988	1989	1990	1987	1988	1989	1990
54.8	47.8	73.2	42.3	62.7	62.7	65.0
26.4	13.4	19.6	15.6	20.5	14.5	16.1
88.2	109.1	168.7	72.7	51.3	109.1	168.7
524.4	636.8	698.3	488.3	611.4	768.3	773.9
68.9	86.0	213.3	31.3	166.3	13.5	195.2
58.5	92.1	128.7	28.7	64.7	129.4	195.6
849.3	907.4	831.3	912.6	1107.0	870.6	851.5
385.1	360.0	622.3	385.7	450.2	459.2	658.9
6.9	6.6	7.0	10.7	6.9	6.6	7.0
285.0	360.4	282.0	272.4	389.8	301.5	321.0
475.1	537.8	568.7	341.2	510.4	551.1	552.2
212.5	213.0	307.6	236.5	209.0	211.4	323.5
52.2	31.9	22.3	11.1	35.3	89.2	7.5
112.9	131.5	184.4	100.9	154.5	170.6	288.5
292.7	399.1	461.0	229.0	348.9	397.2	650.5
113.7	96.3	162.2	98.6	137.5	112.1	203.3
307.1	298.4	400.0	251.5	306.0	299.1	397.1
1785.0	1870.0	1599.0	1288.3	1477.4	1630.9	1923.9
5698.5	*6197.7*	*6749.7*	*4817.4*	*6109.6*	*6196.8*	*7599.3*
1.1	8.1	10.0	44.9	32.5	23.1	24.8
–	–	–	–	–	–	–
9.1	11.5	16.9	–	–	–	–
3.0	2.1	2.1	0.5	2.8	0.2	0.2
441.8	365.4	788.8	507.8	665.9	682.0	264.9
–	–	–	–	–	–	–
5.0	1.0	–	6.0	–	–	–
22.9	46.0	49.4	–	–	–	–
–	–	–	6.4	8.2	7.6	9.8
–	–	–	–	–	–	–
–	–	–	892.6	1019.8	1035.6	1233.0
177.4	205.9	239.6	–	–	–	–
154.7	81.1	81.9	–	–	–	–
68.3	78.3	104.6	–	–	–	–
230.9	265.0	292.5	–	–	–	–
6.2	3.7	6.8	–	–	–	–
32.4	33.4	41.9	–	–	–	–
349.9	368.2	465.8	–	–	–	–
12.1	24.4	9.5	13.3	32.7	15.5	13.1
1514.9	*1494.1*	*2109.6*	*1471.4*	*1761.8*	*1764.0*	*1545.9*
1447.1	*1167.7*	*1273.9*	*1267.2*	*1525.6*	*1194.6*	*1826.6*
2644.7	*2706.4*	*3620.9*	*2681.0*	*3352.4*	*2952.9*	*3187.9*
8660.5	*8859.5*	*10133.1*	*7556.0*	*9397.0*	*9155.4*	*10971.7*

11. TECH. COOP. GRANTS

1988	1989	1990	1987	1988	1989	1990
54.8	47.8	73.2	27.4	18.3	9.0	16.8
26.4	13.4	19.6	0.1	2.0	0.0	1.0
88.1	106.3	168.5	34.3	18.0	30.9	86.0
524.4	636.8	698.3	–	160.5	11.0	201.7
68.9	86.0	213.3	0.2	11.5	6.2	16.0
58.5	92.0	128.7	34.4	2.4	30.9	31.6
817.4	847.3	822.5	528.3	516.9	497.5	543.6
352.5	356.8	590.8	174.9	180.3	187.5	281.6
6.9	6.6	7.0	2.5	3.3	2.1	0.3
285.0	360.4	282.0	106.0	113.9	138.6	96.1
474.9	525.6	568.7	327.9	199.3	234.9	249.2
212.5	213.0	307.6	130.8	109.5	113.0	131.0
52.2	31.9	22.3	3.6	36.3	–	9.5
112.9	131.5	184.4	30.0	27.9	28.2	38.9
292.7	399.1	461.0	43.4	47.6	67.1	121.7
113.7	96.3	162.2	24.1	36.1	–	–
307.1	298.4	400.0	151.1	177.5	179.9	240.8
1780.0	1860.0	1594.0	545.0	608.0	378.0	778.0
5628.8	*6109.4*	*6704.0*	*2164.0*	*2269.3*	*1914.7*	*2843.9*
1492.6	*1473.9*	*2060.0*	*922.8*	*1163.2*	*1031.9*	*1226.2*
1447.1	*1167.7*	*1273.9*	*–*	*–*	*–*	*–*
2573.8	*2633.9*	*3544.2*	*1161.4*	*1280.6*	*1155.7*	*1395.3*
8568.6	*8751.1*	*10037.8*	*3086.8*	*3432.6*	*2946.6*	*4070.1*

12. TOTAL OOF NET

1988	1989	1990	1987	1988	1989	1990
–	–	–	–	–	–	–
–	–	0.1	–	–	–	0.1
–	–	–	0.4	–	–	–
0.0	–	0.1	0.1	0.0	-0.1	-0.8
–	–	–	–	–	–	–
–	5.0	138.5	–	–	3.9	138.5
42.7	1.3	13.9	21.2	11.0	-24.6	12.4
–	–	–	–	–	–	–
–	145.8	166.9	–	–	145.8	166.9
–	–	6.6	0.0	–	–	0.7
–	–	–	–	–	–	15.2
–	–	–	–	–	–	–
–	–	–	–	–	–	–
–	–	–	–	–	–	–
183.5	–	–	237.9	183.5	-0.1	–
7.0	–	-2.0	-12.0	-4.0	-10.0	-6.0
233.2	*152.1*	*324.1*	*247.6*	*190.5*	*114.8*	*326.9*
28.0	*291.6*	*380.4*	*60.6*	*-19.0*	*226.2*	*321.8*
–	*–*	*–*	*–*	*–*	*–*	*–*
226.2	*152.1*	*497.7*	*257.9*	*193.7*	*124.0*	*509.7*
261.2	*443.7*	*704.4*	*308.1*	*171.5*	*341.0*	*648.8*

	1987	1988	1989	1990

13. ODF COMMITMENTS: BY PURPOSE %

	1987	1988	1989	1990
Education	9	7	8	–
Health	2	3	3	–
Other Social Infrastr.	2	2	2	–
Water Sanitat. Sewage	0	0	0	–
Energy	1	4	0	–
Telecommunications	0	0	1	–
Transportation	2	1	1	–
Agriculture	3	3	3	–
Extractive Industries	0	0	0	–
Manufacturing	0	0	0	–
Trade Banking Tourism	0	1	0	–
Technical Cooperation	53	50	52	–
Multisector Aid	3	4	6	–
Programme	21	21	19	–
Debt Reorganisation	0	0	–	–
Food Aid	1	1	2	–
Emergency Aid	2	3	2	–
Unspecified	2	1	1	–
TOTAL	100	100	100	

14. GRANT ELEMENT OF ODA %

DAC COUNTRIES

	1987	1988	1989	1990
Australia	100.0	100.0	100.0	–
Austria	100.0	100.0	100.0	–
Belgium	100.0	100.0	100.0	–
Canada	100.0	100.0	100.0	–
Denmark	100.0	100.0	100.0	–
Finland	100.0	100.0	100.0	–
France	100.0	100.0	100.0	–
Germany	100.0	100.0	100.0	–
Ireland	100.0	100.0	100.0	–
Italy	100.0	100.0	100.0	–
Japan	100.0	100.0	100.0	–
Netherlands	100.0	100.0	100.0	–
New Zealand	100.0	100.0	100.0	–
Norway	100.0	100.0	100.0	–
Sweden	100.0	100.0	100.0	–
Switzerland	100.0	100.0	100.0	–
United Kingdom	100.0	100.0	100.0	–
United States	100.0	100.0	100.0	–
TOTAL	*100.0*	*100.0*	*100.0*	*–*
MULTILATERAL	*100.0*	*99.9*	*100.0*	*–*
ARAB COUNTRIES	*100.0*	*100.0*	*100.0*	*–*
E.E.C.+ MEMBERS	*100.0*	*100.0*	*100.0*	*–*
TOTAL	*100.0*	*100.0*	*100.0*	*–*

15. OTHER AGGREGATES

OFFICIAL COMMITMENTS:

	1987	1988	1989	1990
TOTAL BILATERAL	6691.7	8258.8	8238.4	10322.9
of which:				
Arab Countries	1267.2	1525.6	1194.6	1826.6
C.E.E.C.	329.0	329.0	294.0	–
TOTAL MULTILATERAL	1514.9	2082.3	2047.1	1722.8
TOTAL BIL.& MULTIL.	8206.6	10341.2	10285.5	12045.6
of which:				
ODA Grants	7797.4	9627.5	9365.2	10898.4
ODA Loans	87.7	98.6	77.9	73.3

DISBURSEMENTS:

DAC COUNTRIES COMBINED

	1987	1988	1989	1990
OFFICIAL & PRIVATE				
GROSS:				
Contractual Lending	805.3	2071.0	964.9	645.4
Export Credits, Total	586.9	1959.6	870.2	455.4
Export Credits, Priv.	561.9	1951.5	870.2	442.6
NET:				
Contractual Lending	-1015.7	-1607.3	-1397.1	-519.8
Export Credits Total	-1095.9	-1649.4	-1412.1	-564.4
PRIVATE SECTOR NET	-3483.2	2488.5	-578.8	-4880.1
Direct Investment	458.3	5289.8	6882.1	6977.9
Portfolio Investment	-2820.7	-1151.9	-6053.7	-11290.0
Export Credits	-1120.8	-1649.5	-1407.1	-567.9

MARKET BORROWING:

CHANGE IN CLAIMS

	1987	1988	1989	1990
Banks	–	–	–	–

MEMORANDUM ITEM:

	1987	1988	1989	1990
C.E.E.C. (Gross)	330.0	328.3	306.7	–

DISBURSEMENTS, UNLESS OTHERWISE STAT[ED]

1. TOTAL RECEIPTS NET

DAC COUNTRIES	1987	1988	1989	1990
Australia	843.6	3047.5	1137.4	1370.3
Austria	179.0	139.1	44.2	451.7
Belgium	-723.8	1608.7	1073.3	-298.3
Canada	1658.5	1594.4	1740.3	2148.1
Denmark	450.5	292.4	449.0	533.2
Finland	387.4	492.3	656.2	608.0
France	6789.1	5157.6	5770.3	6541.8
Germany	6501.1	9106.3	9209.7	10265.7
Ireland	27.3	-0.8	49.5	22.9
Italy	954.2	4042.4	4047.5	1464.8
Japan	16232.8	17232.6	20692.1	15343.5
Netherlands	1946.8	2038.0	1933.9	2844.6
New Zealand	93.3	123.1	76.5	81.0
Norway	500.8	449.7	513.9	619.5
Sweden	1169.2	1719.7	1684.9	2032.4
Switzerland	-709.9	1977.7	2238.5	4056.7
United Kingdom	2407.7	2835.9	1652.8	-6381.5
United States	9399.0	12883.0	14114.0	4484.0
TOTAL	*48106.7*	*64739.4*	*67083.9*	*46188.4*
MULTILATERAL				
AF.D.F.	373.5	350.8	492.5	603.0
AF.D.B.	415.8	624.8	814.9	1001.5
AS.D.B	792.7	1304.7	1587.5	2298.0
CAR.D.B.	52.2	58.2	63.9	63.9
E.E.C.	1887.3	2643.0	2593.9	3195.6
IBRD	4395.3	3417.0	3302.0	5009.0
IDA	3530.2	3567.0	3266.0	3912.0
I.D.B.	1048.7	1226.3	1401.3	1214.4
IFAD	365.9	101.7	117.1	245.1
I.F.C.	208.1	355.8	387.9	1384.8
IMF TRUST FUND	–	–	–	–
U.N. AGENCIES				
UNDP	786.3	914.3	976.4	1129.6
UNTA	314.3	268.5	243.8	230.5
UNICEF	364.8	399.6	501.2	584.1
UNRWA	207.4	230.9	265.0	292.5
WFP	719.6	878.4	761.5	932.7
UNHCR	397.6	476.6	489.6	466.0
Other Multilateral	949.1	1051.4	1291.6	1072.8
Arab Agencies	-28.3	-23.9	113.6	–
TOTAL	*16780.5*	*17844.9*	*18669.6*	*23635.3*
ARAB COUNTRIES	***2787.5***	***1631.5***	***1328.2***	***6154.7***
E.E.C.+ MEMBERS	*20240.2*	*27723.5*	*26779.8*	*18188.8*
TOTAL	***67674.7***	***84215.8***	***87081.7***	***75978.4***

2. ODA LOANS GROSS

DAC COUNTRIES	1987	1988	1989	1990
Australia	–	–	–	–
Austria	115.1	113.2	145.7	208.2
Belgium	50.4	70.5	47.0	47.1
Canada	25.4	21.8	25.1	54.3
Denmark	136.0	71.1	42.3	20.0
Finland	29.9	47.7	49.5	42.9
France	1683.1	1640.9	1678.3	2378.8
Germany	1600.5	1559.6	1516.9	2085.6
Ireland	–	–	–	–
Italy	667.7	850.7	807.2	888.6
Japan	3947.3	4730.7	4853.1	5165.9
Netherlands	264.8	284.2	269.5	323.5
New Zealand	–	–	–	–
Norway	4.7	4.7	2.2	3.7
Sweden	–	–	–	–
Switzerland	28.9	35.0	32.8	19.6
United Kingdom	56.4	52.3	60.4	44.1
United States	921.0	1012.0	864.0	765.0
TOTAL	*9531.0*	*10494.2*	*10393.9*	*12047.3*
MULTILATERAL	*5665.4*	*5660.1*	*5800.0*	*6864.5*
ARAB COUNTRIES	***632.6***	***498.8***	***450.9***	***307.3***
E.E.C.+ MEMBERS	*4545.6*	*4645.1*	*4532.3*	*5928.0*
TOTAL	***15829.4***	***16653.0***	***16645.4***	***19219.2***

3. TOTAL OFFICIAL GROSS

DAC COUNTRIES	1987	1988	1989	1990
Australia	560.7	692.0	858.4	969.4
Austria	285.1	218.7	252.6	482.3
Belgium	785.5	814.1	713.1	816.5
Canada	1845.9	2200.8	2375.3	3296.8
Denmark	575.3	534.8	603.6	741.0
Finland	263.0	382.4	436.0	498.5
France	8250.6	7405.6	8320.5	10063.6
Germany	6252.7	7431.2	6726.5	9867.4
Ireland	27.3	21.9	19.1	22.9
Italy	3271.4	2854.2	3452.2	3537.9
Japan	8423.6	10165.2	10934.0	13004.1
Netherlands	1557.1	1714.5	1671.7	2184.0
New Zealand	66.8	94.0	76.5	81.0
Norway	529.9	576.3	560.9	761.3
Sweden	900.1	1038.1	1278.5	1385.4
Switzerland	391.9	448.6	424.9	552.3
United Kingdom	1469.8	1950.6	1822.5	1842.8
United States	9840.0	11340.0	8978.0	12312.0
TOTAL	*45296.8*	*49883.0*	*49504.3*	*62419.2*
MULTILATERAL	*26810.4*	*30266.6*	*30334.1*	*35847.9*
ARAB COUNTRIES	***3602.0***	***2613.2***	***1930.0***	***6437.3***
E.E.C.+ MEMBERS	*24276.0*	*25639.3*	*26206.3*	*32554.9*
TOTAL	***75709.1***	***82762.7***	***81768.3***	***104704.4***

4. TOTAL ODA NET

DAC COUNTRIES	1987	1988	1989	1990
Australia	535.0	622.4	706.0	753.0
Austria	156.9	162.4	200.9	299.4
Belgium	427.7	415.3	356.2	547.7
Canada	1259.6	1583.2	1581.0	1690.3
Denmark	459.0	477.7	522.3	695.0
Finland	262.7	379.6	435.5	497.9
France	5326.3	5600.8	6134.7	7828.5
Germany	3090.2	3172.1	3174.8	4478.9
Ireland	27.3	21.9	19.1	22.9
Italy	1877.9	2407.8	2189.1	2112.1
Japan	5134.8	6421.9	6778.5	6786.5
Netherlands	1418.7	1552.2	1511.2	1901.2
New Zealand	66.2	93.3	76.5	81.0
Norway	527.6	571.8	555.0	755.6
Sweden	895.7	1033.7	1275.4	1383.6
Switzerland	388.5	444.6	423.4	550.7
United Kingdom	1007.9	1430.2	1462.5	1474.4
United States	7154.0	6765.0	6826.0	8367.0
TOTAL	*30015.9*	*33155.9*	*34228.1*	*40225.7*
MULTILATERAL				
AF.D.F.	373.5	350.8	492.5	603.0
AF.D.B.	–	–	–	–
AS.D.B	539.5	706.6	918.8	1101.2
CAR.D.B.	35.8	33.6	38.7	38.7
E.E.C.	1747.2	2586.8	2472.8	2896.2
IBRD	0.4	–	–	–
IDA	3530.2	3567.0	3266.0	3912.0
I.D.B.	120.9	133.7	143.8	154.5
IFAD	365.9	101.7	117.1	245.1
I.F.C.	–	–	–	–
IMF TRUST FUND	–	–	–	–
U.N. AGENCIES	–	–	–	–
UNDP	786.3	914.3	976.4	1129.6
UNTA	314.3	268.5	243.8	230.5
UNICEF	364.8	399.6	501.2	584.1
UNRWA	207.4	230.9	265.0	292.5
WFP	719.6	878.4	761.5	932.7
UNHCR	397.6	476.6	489.6	466.0
Other Multilateral	534.2	618.2	910.3	860.9
Arab Agencies	72.7	60.4	138.7	–
TOTAL	*10110.2*	*11326.9*	*11736.3*	*13447.1*
ARAB COUNTRIES	***2931.4***	***1887.4***	***1316.7***	***6155.5***
E.E.C.+ MEMBERS	*15382.2*	*17664.8*	*17842.9*	*21956.9*
TOTAL	***43057.5***	***46370.1***	***47281.1***	***59828.2***

5. ODA LOANS NET

DAC COUNTRIES	1987	1988	1989	1990
Australia	-0.2	–	–	–
Austria	80.0	73.6	95.8	138.2
Belgium	45.1	48.5	37.2	28.9
Canada	-5.4	-67.4	-15.7	-560.1
Denmark	68.3	53.9	0.9	-12.8
Finland	29.5	45.2	49.0	42.3
France	1405.4	1425.7	1384.2	1882.8
Germany	924.4	867.0	857.4	-46.0
Ireland	–	–	–	–
Italy	628.9	803.5	659.8	814.2
Japan	3026.5	3514.2	3741.3	3772.5
Netherlands	162.4	158.9	140.3	126.5
New Zealand	–	–	–	–
Norway	2.3	1.3	-1.5	-2.0
Sweden	-4.4	-4.4	-3.1	–
Switzerland	25.5	30.9	31.3	18.1
United Kingdom	-84.9	-97.6	-85.9	-92.2
United States	320.0	293.0	35.0	-162.0
TOTAL	*6623.6*	*7146.3*	*6926.1*	*5948.2*
MULTILATERAL	*5011.5*	*4926.1*	*5024.6*	*6027.8*
ARAB COUNTRIES	***85.3***	***-45.4***	***-118.8***	***25.5***
E.E.C.+ MEMBERS	*3200.7*	*3336.0*	*3064.0*	*2801.1*
TOTAL	***11719.9***	***12027.0***	***11831.8***	***12001.5***

6. TOTAL OFFICIAL NET

DAC COUNTRIES	1987	1988	1989	1990
Australia	532.8	657.7	830.9	928.8
Austria	239.6	139.1	155.6	401.5
Belgium	767.9	783.5	696.2	776.1
Canada	1472.9	1662.2	1947.9	2210.7
Denmark	411.8	381.3	453.5	699.1
Finland	262.7	379.9	435.5	497.9
France	7432.0	6628.4	7388.4	8815.4
Germany	4508.3	4464.7	4200.4	6551.1
Ireland	27.3	21.9	19.1	22.9
Italy	2892.3	2661.2	3081.9	2934.1
Japan	5637.7	7806.6	8729.9	10256.2
Netherlands	1422.7	1556.2	1511.2	1952.1
New Zealand	66.8	94.0	76.5	81.0
Norway	525.6	572.6	556.9	755.0
Sweden	895.7	1033.7	1275.4	1385.4
Switzerland	378.8	437.2	417.1	544.7
United Kingdom	1271.6	1753.6	1584.0	1638.3
United States	5361.0	8634.0	6260.0	7816.0
TOTAL	*34107.4*	*39667.8*	*39620.4*	*48266.3*
MULTILATERAL	*16780.5*	*17844.9*	*18669.6*	*23635.3*
ARAB COUNTRIES	***2787.5***	***1631.5***	***1328.2***	***6154.7***
E.E.C.+ MEMBERS	*20621.2*	*20893.8*	*21528.6*	*26584.7*
TOTAL	***53675.5***	***59144.2***	***59618.2***	***78056.3***

7. TOTAL ODA GROSS

	1987
Australia	535.1
Austria	192.0
Belgium	433.0
Canada	1290.3
Denmark	526.7
Finland	263.0
France	5604.0
Germany	3766.4
Ireland	27.3
Italy	1916.7
Japan	6055.5
Netherlands	1521.0
New Zealand	66.2
Norway	529.9
Sweden	900.1
Switzerland	391.9
United Kingdom	1149.1
United States	7755.0
TOTAL	*32923.3*
AF.D.F.	378.5
AF.D.B.	–
AS.D.B	564.6
CAR.D.B.	35.8
E.E.C.	1782.9
IBRD	0.4
IDA	3684.7
I.D.B.	325.5
IFAD	394.1
I.F.C.	–
IMF TRUST FUND	–
U.N. AGENCIES	–
UNDP	786.3
UNTA	314.3
UNICEF	364.8
UNRWA	207.4
WFP	719.6
UNHCR	397.6
Other Multilateral	536.3
Arab Agencies	272.2
TOTAL	*10765.0*
ARAB COUNTRIES	***3478.7***
E.E.C.+ MEMBERS	*16727.1*
TOTAL	***47167.0***

8. GRANTS

	1987
Australia	535.1
Austria	76.9
Belgium	382.6
Canada	1264.9
Denmark	390.7
Finland	233.2
France	3920.9
Germany	2165.8
Ireland	27.3
Italy	1249.0
Japan	2108.2
Netherlands	1256.3
New Zealand	66.2
Norway	525.2
Sweden	900.1
Switzerland	363.0
United Kingdom	1092.8
United States	6834.0
TOTAL	*23392.3*
MULTILATERAL	*5099.2*
ARAB COUNTRIES	***2846.1***
E.E.C.+ MEMBERS	*12181.5*
TOTAL	***31337.6***

9. TOTAL OOF GROSS

	1987
Australia	25.5
Austria	93.1
Belgium	352.5
Canada	555.6
Denmark	48.6
Finland	–
France	2646.6
Germany	2486.3
Ireland	–
Italy	1354.7
Japan	2368.0
Netherlands	36.1
New Zealand	0.7
Norway	–
Sweden	–
Switzerland	–
United Kingdom	320.7
United States	2085.0
TOTAL	*12373.5*
MULTILATERAL	*16045.4*
ARAB COUNTRIES	***123.3***
E.E.C.+ MEMBERS	*7548.9*
TOTAL	***28542.1***

1988	1989	1990
622.4	706.0	753.0
202.0	250.8	369.4
437.3	366.0	565.8
1672.4	1621.8	2304.7
494.9	563.8	727.8
382.1	436.0	498.5
5816.1	6428.8	8324.6
3864.6	3834.3	6610.4
21.9	19.1	22.9
2455.0	2336.6	2186.6
7638.3	7890.3	8179.9
1677.4	1640.4	2098.3
93.3	76.5	81.0
575.2	558.6	761.3
1038.1	1278.5	1383.6
448.6	424.9	552.3
1580.1	1608.7	1610.7
7484.0	7655.0	9294.0
36503.7	37696.0	46324.8
357.5	506.9	623.7
–	–	–
738.2	956.7	1147.5
33.6	38.7	38.7
2626.7	2513.5	2936.8
–	–	–
3738.0	3471.0	4159.0
366.2	363.2	383.3
128.8	155.1	304.9
–	–	–
–	–	–
914.3	976.4	1129.6
268.5	243.8	230.5
399.6	501.2	584.1
230.9	265.0	292.5
878.4	761.5	932.7
476.6	489.6	466.0
620.2	912.5	864.3
283.4	356.1	219.1
12060.9	12511.1	14312.7
2431.5	1886.4	6437.3
8973.9	19311.1	25083.9
50996.1	52093.5	67074.8
622.4	706.0	753.0
88.8	105.1	161.2
366.8	319.0	518.8
1650.6	1596.7	2250.4
423.8	521.5	707.8
334.4	386.5	455.6
4175.1	4750.5	5945.7
2305.0	2317.4	4524.9
21.9	19.1	22.9
1604.3	1529.3	1297.9
2907.7	3037.2	3014.0
1393.3	1370.9	1774.8
93.3	76.5	81.0
570.5	556.5	757.6
1038.1	1278.5	1383.6
413.6	392.1	532.6
1527.8	1548.1	1566.6
6472.0	6791.0	8529.0
26009.5	27302.1	34277.5
6400.8	6710.5	7448.2
1932.8	1435.5	6130.0
4328.8	14778.8	19155.9
34343.1	35448.0	47855.6
69.7	152.4	216.3
16.7	1.9	112.9
376.9	347.1	250.7
528.4	753.5	992.2
39.9	39.8	13.1
0.3	–	–
1589.5	1891.8	1739.1
3566.5	2892.2	3257.0
–	–	–
399.3	1115.6	1351.3
2526.9	3043.7	4824.2
37.1	31.3	85.7
0.7	–	–
1.1	2.3	–
–	–	1.9
–	–	–
370.5	213.8	232.2
3856.0	1323.0	3018.0
3379.3	11808.3	16094.4
8205.7	17823.0	21535.2
181.6	43.6	–
6665.4	6895.2	7471.0
24766.6	29674.9	37629.6

10. ODA COMMITMENTS

1987	1988	1989	1990
527.0	926.6	477.8	499.4
146.7	340.8	407.6	335.8
404.1	448.2	366.0	565.8
1643.7	1911.0	1875.3	1802.1
415.7	641.8	491.5	599.4
222.2	413.3	616.0	609.7
5492.6	6366.5	7172.4	8195.6
4303.3	4841.4	4596.4	5857.9
27.3	21.9	19.1	22.9
3135.1	3040.4	2309.1	2092.7
7342.6	12325.8	7869.8	10232.3
1709.1	1808.6	1764.5	2036.6
50.8	78.3	89.2	48.4
514.2	313.5	427.3	623.5
788.7	1078.5	1274.6	1348.6
462.0	518.5	509.1	616.2
1441.3	1691.4	1737.6	1959.7
7412.4	7928.2	7870.5	20446.3
36038.6	44694.7	39873.9	57892.8
769.4	762.9	991.5	1123.2
–	–	–	–
1451.8	1094.1	1408.2	1521.1
26.1	60.8	32.7	32.7
3845.8	4435.4	3106.9	2689.8
–	–	–	–
4246.3	4352.0	4923.0	6247.0
346.5	119.9	287.3	477.3
233.2	249.8	281.0	337.6
–	–	–	–
3322.1	3775.7	4143.0	4496.7
–	–	–	–
–	–	–	–
–	–	–	–
–	–	–	–
–	–	–	–
4.2	12.7	6.9	3.0
313.7	579.2	815.8	191.7
14559.1	15442.5	15996.4	17120.2
3251.5	2485.4	2171.8	8011.5
20774.2	23295.6	21563.6	24020.4
53849.2	62622.7	58042.1	83024.5

11. TECH. COOP. GRANTS

1987	1988	1989	1990
180.1	202.7	211.8	235.5
48.1	53.2	44.9	66.3
226.2	167.4	152.9	208.3
–	275.4	155.7	336.8
77.5	107.4	101.6	108.7
51.2	25.3	65.7	102.3
2600.0	2421.8	2607.4	3444.1
1535.2	1594.1	1451.5	1798.7
13.3	12.7	11.2	11.4
488.7	348.8	398.8	396.9
1067.0	1156.7	1207.3	1345.7
542.9	631.3	643.3	779.3
15.3	48.4	–	35.3
84.2	86.3	86.4	97.8
184.6	206.6	316.1	178.0
74.9	101.6	–	–
462.4	642.4	607.0	708.9
1753.0	2113.0	2151.0	2714.0
9404.7	10194.9	10212.6	12567.9
2740.1	3290.8	3381.5	3564.1
–	–	–	–
6083.9	6319.2	5973.8	7456.3
12144.8	13485.7	13594.1	16132.0

12. TOTAL OOF NET

1987	1988	1989	1990
-2.1	35.3	124.9	175.7
82.7	-23.2	-45.3	102.1
340.2	368.2	340.0	228.4
213.4	79.0	366.9	520.4
-47.2	-96.4	-68.8	4.1
–	0.3	–	–
2105.7	1027.6	1253.7	986.9
1418.1	1292.6	1025.5	2072.2
–	–	–	–
1014.4	253.4	892.8	822.0
502.9	1384.7	1951.4	3469.7
4.0	4.0	0.0	50.9
0.7	0.7	–	–
-2.0	0.7	1.9	-0.6
–	–	–	1.9
-9.8	-7.4	-6.2	-6.0
263.7	323.4	121.6	163.9
-1793.0	1869.0	-566.0	-551.0
4091.6	6511.9	5392.3	8040.7
6670.3	6518.0	6933.3	10188.2
-143.9	-255.9	11.5	-0.8
5239.0	3229.0	3685.8	4627.7
10618.0	12774.0	12337.1	18228.1

13. ODF COMMITMENTS: BY PURPOSE %

	1987	1988	1989	1990
Education	3	3	3	–
Health	2	2	2	–
Other Social Infrastr.	5	5	5	–
Water Sanitat. Sewage	4	3	4	–
Energy	10	16	14	–
Telecommunications	2	2	2	–
Transportation	9	8	9	–
Agriculture	11	10	11	–
Extractive Industries	2	1	2	–
Manufacturing	4	4	3	–
Trade Banking Tourism	6	6	9	–
Technical Cooperation	18	17	17	–
Multisector Aid	2	3	2	–
Programme	16	14	14	–
Debt Reorganisation	3	3	3	–
Food Aid	2	3	2	–
Emergency Aid	1	1	1	–
Unspecified	1	0	0	–
TOTAL	100	100	100	–

14. GRANT ELEMENT OF ODA %

DAC COUNTRIES	1987	1988	1989	1990
Australia	100.0	100.0	100.0	–
Austria	69.1	56.3	57.6	–
Belgium	99.7	100.0	100.0	–
Canada	99.9	99.2	100.0	–
Denmark	99.4	99.1	100.0	–
Finland	95.9	98.0	100.0	–
France	86.3	86.7	86.3	–
Germany	79.4	79.7	81.6	–
Ireland	100.0	100.0	100.0	–
Italy	85.6	86.0	82.4	–
Japan	67.4	69.6	74.7	–
Netherlands	92.4	91.2	93.2	–
New Zealand	100.0	100.0	100.0	–
Norway	99.0	99.4	99.6	–
Sweden	100.0	100.0	100.0	–
Switzerland	100.0	100.0	100.0	–
United Kingdom	98.4	99.7	97.2	–
United States	96.3	95.1	98.3	–
TOTAL	86.2	84.9	88.2	–
MULTILATERAL	89.4	88.6	87.2	–
ARAB COUNTRIES	91.5	88.7	80.5	–
E.E.C.+ MEMBERS	89.0	89.4	88.7	–
TOTAL	87.4	86.0	87.6	–

15. OTHER AGGREGATES

	1987	1988	1989	1990
OFFICIAL COMMITMENTS:				
TOTAL BILATERAL	61312.8	70289.1	65969.6	82217.9
of which:				
Arab Countries	3886.3	2658.3	2211.2	8325.2
C.E.E.C.	4405.1	7315.5	5358.9	–
TOTAL MULTILATERAL	36015.7	37887.3	42350.6	40936.0
TOTAL BIL.& MULTIL.	97328.5	108176.4	108320.2	123154.0
of which:				
ODA Grants	35934.8	39440.8	37471.1	58499.1
ODA Loans	21431.8	29825.7	25492.3	24525.5
DISBURSEMENTS:				
DAC COUNTRIES COMBINED				
OFFICIAL & PRIVATE				
GROSS:				
Contractual Lending	38716.2	39840.9	49111.7	46865.2
Export Credits, Total	19960.2	18693.8	30778.2	24094.2
Export Credits, Priv.	17418.4	16223.0	27152.3	18986.2
NET:				
Contractual Lending	5914.6	10570.4	16907.2	12313.0
Export Credits Total	-6975.9	-4065.0	4695.2	-196.1
PRIVATE SECTOR NET	13999.2	25071.7	27463.5	-2072.4
Direct Investment	20882.0	24874.2	29733.8	27254.7
Portfolio Investment	-2398.9	3029.8	-7102.0	-27913.9
Export Credits	-4483.9	-2832.3	4831.7	-1413.2
MARKET BORROWING:				
CHANGE IN CLAIMS				
Banks	456.0	1798.0	-12877.0	-6635.0
MEMORANDUM ITEM:				
C.E.E.C. (Gross)	5578.9	5227.3	4780.1	–

1. TOTAL RECEIPTS NET

DAC COUNTRIES	1987	1988	1989	1990
Australia	259.4	239.9	386.0	344.9
Austria	11.4	64.5	69.8	259.6
Belgium	170.6	341.2	563.0	359.8
Canada	853.2	924.2	770.5	1071.6
Denmark	393.2	362.1	414.8	413.7
Finland	209.8	363.4	364.6	331.7
France	2283.8	1303.3	2350.1	2832.3
Germany	2457.5	2488.8	2833.9	3255.4
Ireland	16.3	14.8	12.3	15.1
Italy	814.4	2041.4	1455.6	1371.8
Japan	7007.9	7862.6	8700.3	6468.3
Netherlands	1111.0	1075.2	1025.9	1470.4
New Zealand	19.8	15.5	14.9	20.5
Norway	347.5	383.1	364.4	471.5
Sweden	810.4	707.7	1197.0	1381.4
Switzerland	240.2	289.6	272.0	333.4
United Kingdom	1292.3	1053.8	3800.6	1319.9
United States	2869.0	5240.0	3992.0	2855.0
TOTAL	*21167.5*	*24770.8*	*28587.6*	*24576.2*
MULTILATERAL				
AF.D.F.	366.2	344.8	481.1	590.4
AF.D.B.	224.7	228.3	439.0	342.7
AS.D.B	892.3	1302.0	1900.4	2259.2
CAR.D.B.	0.0	–	–	–
E.E.C.	1105.9	1509.2	1525.4	1525.4
IBRD	2298.0	3068.0	3034.0	2080.0
IDA	3530.6	3571.0	3277.0	3931.0
I.D.B.	111.0	123.6	103.1	125.5
IFAD	294.1	99.7	113.6	203.7
I.F.C.	-10.0	49.6	-25.1	402.4
IMF TRUST FUND	–	–	–	–
U.N. AGENCIES	–	–	–	–
UNDP	482.4	548.4	588.6	689.1
UNTA	106.2	72.5	106.1	93.4
UNICEF	278.2	302.6	370.9	420.0
UNRWA	–	–	–	–
WFP	579.8	691.7	590.4	687.3
UNHCR	256.0	310.4	302.0	299.4
Other Multilateral	184.6	208.7	402.8	282.5
Arab Agencies	26.8	-17.5	50.4	–
TOTAL	*10726.8*	*12413.0*	*13260.0*	*13931.9*
ARAB COUNTRIES	**588.5**	**163.7**	**88.1**	**2562.6**
E.E.C.+ MEMBERS	*9644.9*	*10189.7*	*13981.5*	*12563.7*
TOTAL	**32482.9**	**37347.5**	**41935.6**	**41070.7**

2. ODA LOANS GROSS

DAC COUNTRIES	1987	1988	1989	1990
Australia	–	–	–	–
Austria	42.0	56.6	96.9	170.1
Belgium	41.1	56.3	37.2	32.4
Canada	13.3	9.1	8.0	34.9
Denmark	122.2	65.9	39.0	15.8
Finland	28.3	39.2	46.4	34.4
France	919.5	1052.9	1087.8	1092.2
Germany	704.8	860.6	821.5	1192.1
Ireland	–	–	–	–
Italy	581.4	714.2	516.5	577.8
Japan	2673.4	3661.1	3707.2	3310.3
Netherlands	198.7	237.7	208.6	276.6
New Zealand	–	–	–	–
Norway	3.5	4.7	2.2	3.7
Sweden	–	–	–	–
Switzerland	17.6	27.5	25.9	13.9
United Kingdom	18.1	14.4	24.8	16.0
United States	586.0	725.0	522.0	497.0
TOTAL	*5949.9*	*7525.1*	*7144.0*	*7267.1*
MULTILATERAL	*5163.9*	*5154.5*	*5298.5*	*6306.6*
ARAB COUNTRIES	**336.6**	**339.7**	**317.1**	**185.1**
E.E.C.+ MEMBERS	*2643.3*	*3086.8*	*2813.6*	*3281.0*
TOTAL	**11450.4**	**13019.4**	**12759.6**	**13758.8**

3. TOTAL OFFICIAL GROSS

DAC COUNTRIES	1987	1988	1989	1990
Australia	199.7	289.3	422.6	513.6
Austria	103.1	93.1	130.1	309.9
Belgium	494.3	571.7	495.8	455.8
Canada	904.6	1063.1	867.5	1496.8
Denmark	457.5	430.8	473.1	489.8
Finland	195.5	300.9	323.0	331.3
France	2300.1	2057.0	2271.9	3123.3
Germany	2667.2	4339.7	3256.9	4925.5
Ireland	16.3	14.8	12.3	15.1
Italy	1602.8	1991.4	1897.8	1892.0
Japan	5471.2	6710.4	7316.2	6610.0
Netherlands	1071.5	1224.5	1130.8	1460.8
New Zealand	19.8	15.5	14.9	20.5
Norway	385.4	447.8	400.7	540.1
Sweden	531.1	707.7	845.4	819.1
Switzerland	240.3	290.0	272.2	334.3
United Kingdom	786.5	1175.4	1263.3	1150.9
United States	3314.0	5488.0	3294.0	6062.0
TOTAL	*20760.9*	*27211.0*	*24688.5*	*30550.4*
MULTILATERAL	*13374.4*	*15253.6*	*16223.5*	*17288.4*
ARAB COUNTRIES	**889.5**	**484.1**	**401.6**	**2715.2**
E.E.C.+ MEMBERS	*10568.7*	*13391.1*	*12402.8*	*15114.1*
TOTAL	**35024.8**	**42948.7**	**41313.5**	**50553.9**

4. TOTAL ODA NET

DAC COUNTRIES	1987	1988	1989	1990
Australia	175.7	221.8	307.0	311.2
Austria	56.5	64.7	103.6	195.5
Belgium	279.0	266.7	200.9	312.1
Canada	669.7	786.1	677.3	739.2
Denmark	374.7	404.5	420.5	452.5
Finland	195.5	300.5	322.7	330.8
France	1528.8	1751.4	2061.6	2490.1
Germany	1544.8	1745.7	1779.4	2599.7
Ireland	16.3	14.8	12.3	15.1
Italy	1386.8	1743.7	1298.6	1276.7
Japan	3572.9	4777.7	4882.6	4233.5
Netherlands	977.8	1097.9	1008.0	1251.6
New Zealand	19.7	15.0	14.9	20.5
Norway	384.8	446.4	399.4	538.4
Sweden	531.1	707.7	845.4	817.8
Switzerland	240.2	289.6	272.0	333.4
United Kingdom	637.7	1002.5	1062.0	919.0
United States	2640.0	2467.0	2569.0	4267.0
TOTAL	*15231.8*	*18103.5*	*18237.0*	*21104.1*
MULTILATERAL				
AF.D.F.	366.2	344.8	481.1	590.4
AF.D.B.	–	–	–	–
AS.D.B	516.7	679.6	887.5	1035.4
CAR.D.B.	0.0	–	–	–
E.E.C.	1066.0	1520.1	1512.0	1512.0
IBRD	0.4	–	–	–
IDA	3530.6	3571.0	3277.0	3931.0
I.D.B.	31.9	19.9	26.2	75.6
IFAD	294.1	99.7	113.6	203.7
I.F.C.	–	–	–	–
IMF TRUST FUND	–	–	–	–
U.N. AGENCIES	–	–	–	–
UNDP	482.4	548.4	588.6	689.1
UNTA	106.2	72.5	106.1	93.4
UNICEF	278.2	302.6	370.9	420.0
UNRWA	–	–	–	–
WFP	579.8	691.7	590.4	687.3
UNHCR	256.0	310.4	302.0	299.4
Other Multilateral	184.6	208.7	402.8	282.5
Arab Agencies	44.8	13.7	63.5	–
TOTAL	*7738.1*	*8383.2*	*8721.9*	*9819.7*
ARAB COUNTRIES	**593.3**	**183.2**	**90.6**	**2562.6**
E.E.C.+ MEMBERS	*7811.8*	*9547.2*	*9355.2*	*10828.7*
TOTAL	**23563.2**	**26669.9**	**27049.6**	**33486.4**

5. ODA LOANS NET

DAC COUNTRIES	1987	1988	1989	1990
Australia	–	–	–	–
Austria	31.3	39.6	72.0	137.4
Belgium	37.5	40.0	29.7	19.3
Canada	-6.9	-69.7	-19.8	-350.3
Denmark	57.9	53.2	0.3	-13.4
Finland	28.3	38.8	46.1	33.9
France	837.1	971.5	957.2	911.1
Germany	364.2	487.9	486.9	-317.2
Ireland	–	–	–	–
Italy	552.8	683.6	426.8	526.4
Japan	2195.2	2964.6	3088.6	2536.7
Netherlands	124.5	134.3	108.6	113.2
New Zealand	–	–	–	–
Norway	2.9	3.3	1.1	2.0
Sweden	–	–	–	–
Switzerland	17.4	27.2	25.7	13.0
United Kingdom	-86.6	-84.9	-69.0	-83.0
United States	275.0	338.0	129.0	-73.0
TOTAL	*4430.7*	*5627.4*	*5283.4*	*3456.2*
MULTILATERAL	*4804.5*	*4751.9*	*4848.8*	*5800.4*
ARAB COUNTRIES	**51.8**	**52.5**	**11.5**	**32.6**
E.E.C.+ MEMBERS	*1934.4*	*2357.3*	*2005.8*	*1221.5*
TOTAL	**9287.0**	**10431.7**	**10143.6**	**9289.2**

6. TOTAL OFFICIAL NET

DAC COUNTRIES	1987	1988	1989	1990
Australia	189.3	274.1	407.7	494.2
Austria	84.9	68.4	104.8	276.8
Belgium	487.3	554.4	487.3	422.4
Canada	822.2	933.8	784.4	1057.8
Denmark	349.2	378.9	404.2	454.8
Finland	195.5	300.5	322.7	330.8
France	2158.0	1859.1	1996.5	2713.5
Germany	1972.3	2560.6	2238.2	3117.1
Ireland	16.3	14.8	12.3	15.1
Italy	1500.7	1927.2	1697.8	1644.8
Japan	3683.8	5829.1	6504.1	5249.4
Netherlands	991.5	1114.0	1021.5	1277.3
New Zealand	19.8	15.5	14.9	20.5
Norway	384.8	446.2	399.4	538.2
Sweden	531.1	707.7	845.4	819.1
Switzerland	240.2	289.6	272.0	333.4
United Kingdom	651.1	1054.3	1124.0	1012.9
United States	2718.0	4803.0	2692.0	3550.0
TOTAL	*16995.9*	*23131.1*	*21329.0*	*23328.1*
MULTILATERAL	*10726.8*	*12413.0*	*13260.0*	*13931.9*
ARAB COUNTRIES	**588.5**	**163.7**	**88.1**	**2562.6**
E.E.C.+ MEMBERS	*9232.3*	*10972.4*	*10507.1*	*12183.3*
TOTAL	**28311.3**	**35707.9**	**34677.0**	**39822.5**

7. TOTAL ODA GROSS

	1987
Australia	175.7
Austria	67.2
Belgium	282.6
Canada	689.9
Denmark	439.0
Finland	195.5
France	1611.2
Germany	1885.3
Ireland	16.3
Italy	1415.4
Japan	4051.1
Netherlands	1052.0
New Zealand	19.7
Norway	385.4
Sweden	531.1
Switzerland	240.3
United Kingdom	742.4
United States	2951.0
TOTAL	*16751.0*
AF.D.F.	371.1
AF.D.B.	–
AS.D.B	539.8
CAR.D.B.	0.0
E.E.C.	1076.5
IBRD	0.4
IDA	3669.7
I.D.B.	46.4
IFAD	302.1
I.F.C.	–
IMF TRUST FUND	–
U.N. AGENCIES	–
UNDP	482.4
UNTA	106.2
UNICEF	278.2
UNRWA	–
WFP	579.8
UNHCR	256.0
Other Multilateral	184.6
Arab Agencies	204.3
TOTAL	*8097.4*
ARAB COUNTRIES	**878.1**
E.E.C.+ MEMBERS	*8520.7*
TOTAL	**25726.5**

8. GRANTS

	1987
Australia	175.7
Austria	25.2
Belgium	241.5
Canada	676.6
Denmark	316.8
Finland	167.3
France	691.7
Germany	1180.5
Ireland	16.3
Italy	834.0
Japan	1377.7
Netherlands	853.3
New Zealand	19.7
Norway	381.9
Sweden	531.1
Switzerland	222.7
United Kingdom	724.3
United States	2365.0
TOTAL	*10801.1*
MULTILATERAL	*2933.6*
ARAB COUNTRIES	**541.5**
E.E.C.+ MEMBERS	*5877.4*
TOTAL	**14276.2**

9. TOTAL OOF GROSS

	1987
Australia	24.0
Austria	35.9
Belgium	211.7
Canada	214.7
Denmark	18.5
Finland	–
France	688.9
Germany	781.9
Ireland	–
Italy	187.4
Japan	1420.1
Netherlands	19.5
New Zealand	0.2
Norway	–
Sweden	–
Switzerland	–
United Kingdom	44.1
United States	363.0
TOTAL	*4009.9*
MULTILATERAL	*5277.0*
ARAB COUNTRIES	**11.4**
E.E.C.+ MEMBERS	*2048.1*
TOTAL	**9298.2**

1988	1989	1990	1987	1988	1989	1990

10. ODA COMMITMENTS

1988	1989	1990	1987	1988	1989	1990
221.8	307.0	311.2	165.4	296.8	314.5	274.8
81.7	128.4	228.1	61.5	156.4	229.2	227.2
283.1	208.4	325.2	268.3	327.0	208.4	325.2
864.9	705.1	1124.5	939.5	910.8	886.1	635.8
417.2	459.1	481.7	383.3	449.5	467.4	366.4
300.9	323.0	331.3	188.4	321.9	457.9	337.7
1832.8	2192.2	2671.1	1649.9	2168.1	2503.5	2091.6
2118.3	2113.9	4108.9	2254.4	2748.4	2569.1	3434.8
14.8	12.3	15.1	16.3	14.8	12.3	15.1
1774.4	1388.3	1328.1	2415.2	1848.9	1140.0	1136.4
5474.2	5501.1	5007.2	5113.3	9071.2	5687.7	5766.2
1201.2	1108.0	1415.0	1225.9	1293.4	1224.1	1357.0
15.0	14.9	20.5	15.2	16.2	–	14.4
447.8	400.5	540.1	399.6	158.0	250.8	323.2
707.7	845.4	817.8	518.1	681.1	845.7	623.4
290.0	272.2	334.3	321.4	349.4	347.0	328.8
1101.8	1155.7	1018.0	1015.2	1132.3	1287.2	1353.1
2854.0	2962.0	4837.0	3129.7	3324.7	3569.5	15238.6
0001.2	20097.6	24915.1	20080.7	25268.8	22000.3	33849.8
351.0	493.2	608.2	715.3	639.7	932.4	1045.5
–	–	–	–	–	–	–
709.3	923.1	1077.2	1433.3	1090.8	1340.3	1493.9
–	–	–	–	0.2	–	–
1533.3	1525.1	1525.1	2790.6	2756.0	1602.6	1602.6
–	–	–	–	–	–	–
3724.0	3464.0	4155.0	4232.3	4352.0	4922.0	6239.0
33.2	43.9	95.3	10.5	48.6	150.3	153.9
106.6	123.8	227.7	179.4	174.6	218.6	203.7
–	–	–	–	–	–	–
–	–	–	1887.3	2134.4	2361.0	2471.6
548.4	588.6	689.1	–	–	–	–
72.5	106.1	93.4	–	–	–	–
302.6	370.9	420.0	–	–	–	–
–	–	–	–	–	–	–
691.7	590.4	687.3	–	–	–	–
310.4	302.0	299.4	–	–	–	–
208.7	402.8	282.5	–	–	–	–
194.2	236.4	129.0	195.6	387.2	571.3	174.3
8785.9	9170.4	10289.0	11444.2	11583.5	12098.5	13384.5
470.5	396.2	2715.2	885.3	347.6	519.1	3212.7
0276.7	10163.0	12888.2	12019.2	12738.3	11014.5	11682.3
9257.6	29664.3	37919.3	32410.2	37199.9	34617.9	50447.0

11. TECH. COOP. GRANTS

1988	1989	1990	1987	1988	1989	1990
221.8	307.0	311.2	71.4	93.5	114.8	124.5
25.1	31.5	58.0	14.9	15.0	8.5	18.3
226.7	171.1	292.8	159.0	125.0	103.2	100.2
855.8	697.1	1089.5	–	82.3	107.6	95.7
351.3	420.1	465.9	72.3	92.8	93.6	87.6
261.7	276.6	296.9	14.5	14.5	31.4	65.4
779.9	1104.4	1579.0	670.3	458.8	448.3	578.3
1257.8	1292.4	2916.0	718.4	775.4	681.8	807.1
14.8	12.3	15.1	10.4	9.1	8.9	10.3
1060.2	871.8	750.3	268.8	143.2	150.0	190.6
1813.1	1794.0	1696.8	385.2	502.8	508.2	585.3
963.5	899.3	1138.4	319.0	392.6	402.4	478.7
15.0	14.9	20.5	6.4	6.4	–	9.7
443.1	398.4	536.4	50.8	56.2	55.7	55.3
707.7	845.4	817.8	131.3	146.5	236.2	36.3
262.4	246.3	320.4	42.1	55.6	–	–
1087.4	1131.0	1002.0	259.4	387.9	358.4	393.7
2129.0	2440.0	4340.0	899.0	1119.0	1321.0	1499.0
2476.1	12953.6	17648.0	4093.0	4476.7	4629.8	5136.0
3631.3	3871.9	3982.4	1376.4	1603.0	1770.5	1784.4
130.8	79.2	2530.0	–	–	–	–
7189.9	7349.4	9607.3	2546.5	2545.2	2246.6	2646.4
6238.2	16904.7	24160.4	5469.4	6079.8	6400.4	6920.3

12. TOTAL OOF NET

1988	1989	1990	1987	1988	1989	1990
67.6	115.6	202.4	13.7	52.3	100.7	183.0
11.4	1.8	81.8	28.4	3.7	1.2	81.3
288.7	287.4	130.5	208.3	287.7	286.4	110.3
198.2	162.4	371.8	152.5	147.8	107.1	318.6
13.6	14.0	8.1	-25.4	-25.6	-16.3	2.3
–	–	–	–	–	–	–
224.3	79.7	452.2	629.2	107.7	-65.1	223.5
2221.4	1142.9	816.6	427.5	815.0	458.9	517.4
–	–	–	–	–	–	–
217.0	509.5	563.9	113.9	183.4	399.1	368.1
1236.2	1815.1	1602.8	110.9	1051.4	1621.5	1015.9
23.3	22.8	45.8	13.7	16.1	13.5	25.7
0.5	–	–	0.2	0.5	–	–
–	0.1	–	–	-0.2	-0.1	-0.2
–	–	1.3	–	–	–	1.3
–	–	–	–	–	–	–
73.6	107.6	132.9	13.4	51.8	62.0	93.8
2634.0	332.0	1225.0	78.0	2336.0	123.0	-717.0
7209.8	4590.9	5635.3	1764.1	5027.6	3092.0	2223.9
6467.7	7053.1	6999.4	2988.8	4029.8	4538.0	4112.2
13.7	5.3	–	-4.7	-19.5	-2.5	–
3114.4	2239.8	2225.9	1420.5	1425.2	1151.9	1354.5
3691.1	11649.3	12634.7	4748.1	9037.9	7627.5	6336.1

1987	1988	1989	1990

13. ODF COMMITMENTS: BY PURPOSE %

	1987	1988	1989	1990
Education	2	3	3	–
Health	2	2	2	–
Other Social Infrastr.	5	5	4	–
Water Sanitat. Sewage	4	3	5	–
Energy	13	20	16	–
Telecommunications	2	2	2	–
Transportation	10	9	11	–
Agriculture	13	11	10	–
Extractive Industries	2	1	3	–
Manufacturing	6	5	4	–
Trade Banking Tourism	3	6	9	–
Technical Cooperation	14	13	14	–
Multisector Aid	2	3	2	–
Programme	15	10	10	–
Debt Reorganisation	3	4	3	–
Food Aid	3	3	2	–
Emergency Aid	1	1	0	–
Unspecified	1	0	0	–
TOTAL	100	100	100	–

14. GRANT ELEMENT OF ODA %

DAC COUNTRIES

	1987	1988	1989	1990
Australia	100.0	100.0	100.0	–
Austria	66.3	62.4	56.1	–
Belgium	99.8	100.0	100.0	–
Canada	100.0	99.4	100.0	–
Denmark	99.3	98.7	100.0	–
Finland	95.4	98.2	100.0	–
France	69.8	74.3	74.8	–
Germany	86.1	83.1	83.8	–
Ireland	100.0	100.0	100.0	–
Italy	85.2	86.4	85.6	–
Japan	67.2	69.2	72.6	–
Netherlands	91.5	89.5	91.9	–
New Zealand	100.0	100.0	–	–
Norway	99.0	98.8	99.4	–
Sweden	100.0	100.0	100.0	–
Switzerland	100.0	100.0	100.0	–
United Kingdom	100.0	100.0	100.0	–
United States	95.2	92.4	97.7	–
TOTAL	84.4	82.0	86.1	–
MULTILATERAL	88.3	86.5	84.9	–
ARAB COUNTRIES	76.3	56.5	50.4	–
E.E.C.+ MEMBERS	89.2	88.7	88.0	–
TOTAL	85.5	83.2	85.2	–

15. OTHER AGGREGATES

OFFICIAL COMMITMENTS:

	1987	1988	1989	1990
TOTAL BILATERAL	32367.5	39903.2	32080.2	43521.4
of which:				
Arab Countries	948.0	358.3	556.3	3512.7
C.E.E.C.	3785.1	6567.2	2869.2	–
TOTAL MULTILATERAL	19393.4	21334.7	22913.2	23027.5
TOTAL BIL.& MULTIL.	51760.8	61237.9	54993.4	66548.9
of which:				
ODA Grants	18434.2	18976.1	18243.0	33225.8
ODA Loans	16873.4	24340.6	18862.8	17221.2

DISBURSEMENTS:

DAC COUNTRIES COMBINED

OFFICIAL & PRIVATE

GROSS:	1987	1988	1989	1990
Contractual Lending	15770.0	18434.9	20326.4	17628.6
Export Credits, Total	6600.3	4450.9	9779.2	6175.1
Export Credits, Priv.	5877.9	3744.5	8635.5	4778.4
NET:				
Contractual Lending	6346.3	9355.4	11724.6	5171.5
Export Credits Total	193.5	-1222.2	3915.4	131.7
PRIVATE SECTOR NET	4171.6	1639.7	7258.6	1248.2
Direct Investment	1734.2	851.9	3679.9	1407.5
Portfolio Investment	2218.3	2043.6	185.5	297.2
Export Credits	219.1	-1255.8	3393.3	-456.5

MARKET BORROWING:

CHANGE IN CLAIMS

	1987	1988	1989	1990
Banks	4672.0	6171.0	-1991.0	16164.0

MEMORANDUM ITEM:

	1987	1988	1989	1990
C.E.E.C. (Gross)	3375.9	3110.3	2810.5	–

1. TOTAL RECEIPTS NET

	1987	1988	1989	1990
DAC COUNTRIES				
Australia	31.8	28.9	60.8	68.4
Austria	-31.7	45.0	14.0	37.4
Belgium	191.8	378.1	549.8	388.6
Canada	372.4	482.1	529.0	501.3
Denmark	265.1	284.0	256.6	276.7
Finland	148.3	238.3	230.3	236.9
France	3114.3	2383.8	2461.2	3449.6
Germany	1213.3	1331.1	1500.6	1700.4
Ireland	16.6	15.1	12.4	15.2
Italy	1142.8	1559.7	1296.6	1274.3
Japan	618.3	1272.2	1294.5	1112.9
Netherlands	556.2	503.3	327.9	666.0
New Zealand	0.5	0.8	0.9	1.3
Norway	280.0	264.3	252.3	303.3
Sweden	402.0	510.7	450.8	602.3
Switzerland	147.2	161.5	150.8	233.9
United Kingdom	424.5	324.7	3209.0	383.1
United States	1715.0	1129.0	744.0	1455.0
TOTAL	*10608.3*	*10912.6*	*13341.8*	*12706.5*
MULTILATERAL				
AF.D.F.	369.1	346.5	484.4	591.8
AF.D.B.	268.7	351.6	462.7	593.6
AS.D.B	–	–	–	–
CAR.D.B.	–	–	–	–
E.E.C.	839.3	1477.5	1583.5	1583.5
IBRD	543.0	-39.0	216.0	93.0
IDA	1630.7	1415.0	1543.0	1902.0
I.D.B.	–	–	–	–
IFAD	129.7	49.7	45.9	91.8
I.F.C.	22.3	52.3	77.3	233.0
IMF TRUST FUND	–	–	–	–
U.N. AGENCIES	–	–	–	–
UNDP	262.2	311.3	334.4	383.8
UNTA	56.7	44.1	56.0	54.6
UNICEF	129.5	138.4	178.8	210.4
UNRWA	–	–	–	–
WFP	259.3	314.8	310.8	435.5
UNHCR	161.6	234.1	226.2	211.8
Other Multilateral	124.1	130.2	233.0	169.1
Arab Agencies	29.2	21.0	-6.4	–
TOTAL	*4825.3*	*4847.6*	*5745.6*	*6553.9*
ARAB COUNTRIES	*363.0*	*176.2*	*92.2*	*106.9*
E.E.C.+ MEMBERS	*7763.8*	*8257.4*	*11197.8*	*9737.3*
TOTAL	*15796.6*	*15936.4*	*19179.6*	*19367.3*

2. ODA LOANS GROSS

	1987	1988	1989	1990
DAC COUNTRIES				
Australia	–	–	–	–
Austria	12.8	21.3	22.1	30.6
Belgium	22.5	39.3	31.0	28.4
Canada	5.6	–	–	1.6
Denmark	45.6	24.1	18.8	11.4
Finland	20.8	13.9	23.3	13.6
France	910.1	1015.4	948.4	1332.3
Germany	205.3	200.3	172.0	276.5
Ireland	–	–	–	–
Italy	428.9	451.1	287.1	478.1
Japan	175.4	290.6	481.7	300.3
Netherlands	32.2	39.9	31.5	40.8
New Zealand	–	–	–	–
Norway	–	2.2	2.2	3.4
Sweden	–	–	–	–
Switzerland	2.0	3.5	2.2	1.3
United Kingdom	18.7	15.8	21.8	11.2
United States	155.0	107.0	112.0	70.0
TOTAL	*2034.9*	*2224.4*	*2154.0*	*2599.5*
MULTILATERAL	*2355.0*	*2051.3*	*2307.8*	*2841.0*
ARAB COUNTRIES	*198.0*	*220.7*	*173.5*	*103.6*
E.E.C.+ MEMBERS	*1721.1*	*1877.3*	*1603.3*	*2271.4*
TOTAL	*4587.9*	*4496.4*	*4635.3*	*5544.1*

3. TOTAL OFFICIAL GROSS

	1987	1988	1989	1990
DAC COUNTRIES				
Australia	40.8	42.0	68.4	72.3
Austria	30.0	38.8	41.0	66.0
Belgium	449.2	552.6	476.6	419.2
Canada	403.9	545.7	551.6	1093.2
Denmark	318.7	302.4	308.5	321.7
Finland	145.1	208.9	221.9	237.3
France	3843.9	3585.6	3618.6	5181.7
Germany	1572.5	2701.0	2033.6	3271.8
Ireland	16.6	15.1	12.4	15.2
Italy	1355.9	1470.1	1603.5	1702.8
Japan	613.5	986.2	1154.4	887.1
Netherlands	527.6	591.9	501.4	704.7
New Zealand	0.5	0.8	0.9	1.3
Norway	306.9	312.5	285.1	375.1
Sweden	380.1	510.7	464.5	621.7
Switzerland	147.5	161.8	150.8	218.8
United Kingdom	465.4	702.0	812.1	651.8
United States	1090.0	1294.0	862.0	1967.0
TOTAL	*11708.0*	*14022.0*	*13167.4*	*17808.8*
MULTILATERAL	*5683.3*	*5913.7*	*6913.0*	*7813.4*
ARAB COUNTRIES	*476.6*	*316.7*	*196.0*	*153.3*
E.E.C.+ MEMBERS	*9476.2*	*11492.5*	*11043.5*	*13945.5*
TOTAL	*17867.9*	*20252.4*	*20276.4*	*25775.5*

4. TOTAL ODA NET

	1987	1988	1989	1990
DAC COUNTRIES				
Australia	35.0	41.8	66.4	72.1
Austria	29.5	38.4	39.5	65.9
Belgium	286.9	286.9	213.5	298.2
Canada	364.8	384.0	445.3	426.7
Denmark	233.4	282.3	266.3	295.7
Finland	145.1	208.7	221.7	236.9
France	2420.6	2688.0	3042.1	4049.7
Germany	943.1	961.8	1023.3	1393.8
Ireland	16.6	15.1	12.4	15.2
Italy	1148.1	1364.5	1029.3	1090.2
Japan	592.8	943.2	1080.3	830.5
Netherlands	510.9	550.4	473.6	619.5
New Zealand	0.5	0.8	0.9	1.3
Norway	306.6	312.3	284.9	374.9
Sweden	380.1	510.7	464.5	620.7
Switzerland	147.2	161.5	150.8	218.8
United Kingdom	381.3	601.1	676.0	534.4
United States	783.0	772.0	730.0	1002.0
TOTAL	*8725.5*	*10123.5*	*10220.7*	*12146.3*
MULTILATERAL				
AF.D.F.	369.1	346.5	484.4	591.8
AF.D.B.	–	–	–	–
AS.D.B	–	–	–	–
CAR.D.B.	–	–	–	–
E.E.C.	816.6	1484.9	1575.3	1575.3
IBRD	0.4	–	–	–
IDA	1630.7	1415.0	1543.0	1902.0
I.D.B.	–	–	–	–
IFAD	129.7	49.7	45.9	91.8
I.F.C.	–	–	–	–
IMF TRUST FUND	–	–	–	–
U.N. AGENCIES	–	–	–	–
UNDP	262.2	311.3	334.4	383.8
UNTA	56.7	44.1	56.0	54.6
UNICEF	129.5	138.4	178.8	210.4
UNRWA	–	–	–	–
WFP	259.3	314.8	310.8	435.5
UNHCR	161.6	234.1	226.2	211.8
Other Multilateral	124.1	130.2	233.0	169.1
Arab Agencies	43.7	13.3	-4.3	–
TOTAL	*3983.6*	*4482.4*	*4983.5*	*5626.1*
ARAB COUNTRIES	*368.5*	*195.7*	*100.1*	*107.1*
E.E.C.+ MEMBERS	*6757.4*	*8235.1*	*8311.7*	*9871.8*
TOTAL	*13077.5*	*14801.6*	*15304.3*	*17879.4*

5. ODA LOANS NET

	1987	1988	1989	1990
DAC COUNTRIES				
Australia	–	–	–	–
Austria	12.3	20.9	20.6	30.5
Belgium	22.4	38.5	31.0	27.2
Canada	3.6	-55.4	-0.3	-573.9
Denmark	-14.7	16.4	-15.6	-12.1
Finland	20.8	13.7	23.1	13.2
France	815.4	915.5	820.7	1047.7
Germany	177.0	162.3	158.8	-955.7
Ireland	–	–	–	–
Italy	401.9	431.8	232.3	446.2
Japan	154.7	247.6	407.6	243.7
Netherlands	27.5	14.7	11.0	-21.4
New Zealand	–	–	–	–
Norway	-0.2	2.1	2.0	3.2
Sweden	–	–	–	–
Switzerland	1.7	3.2	2.1	1.2
United Kingdom	-24.5	-33.0	-33.7	-28.7
United States	105.0	57.0	77.0	-96.0
TOTAL	*1702.7*	*1835.3*	*1736.6*	*125.1*
MULTILATERAL	*2210.9*	*1890.1*	*2128.8*	*2635.9*
ARAB COUNTRIES	*101.2*	*112.0*	*77.6*	*57.4*
E.E.C.+ MEMBERS	*1446.8*	*1619.5*	*1279.3*	*578.1*
TOTAL	*4014.8*	*3837.4*	*3943.0*	*2818.4*

6. TOTAL OFFICIAL NET

	1987	1988	1989	1990
DAC COUNTRIES				
Australia	39.7	39.2	64.9	67.5
Austria	27.4	36.5	39.5	65.9
Belgium	446.0	549.6	475.6	397.8
Canada	370.7	467.3	532.5	494.6
Denmark	239.5	274.5	257.0	295.2
Finland	145.1	208.7	221.7	236.9
France	3534.9	3183.5	3210.4	4511.5
Germany	1470.2	1492.6	1477.1	1732.8
Ireland	16.6	15.1	12.4	15.2
Italy	1264.0	1430.5	1456.9	1470.4
Japan	592.8	943.2	1080.3	830.5
Netherlands	519.9	561.0	476.2	632.5
New Zealand	0.5	0.8	0.9	1.3
Norway	306.6	312.3	284.9	374.9
Sweden	380.1	510.7	464.5	621.7
Switzerland	147.2	161.5	150.8	218.8
United Kingdom	390.2	631.9	711.6	572.9
United States	915.0	1106.0	764.0	1432.0
TOTAL	*10806.5*	*11924.9*	*11681.2*	*13972.3*
MULTILATERAL	*4825.3*	*4847.6*	*5745.6*	*6553.9*
ARAB COUNTRIES	*363.0*	*176.2*	*92.2*	*106.9*
E.E.C.+ MEMBERS	*8720.5*	*9616.2*	*9660.7*	*11211.7*
TOTAL	*15994.8*	*16948.7*	*17519.0*	*20633.1*

7. TOTAL ODA GROSS

	1987
Australia	35.0
Austria	30.0
Belgium	287.1
Canada	366.7
Denmark	293.7
Finland	145.1
France	2515.3
Germany	971.5
Ireland	16.6
Italy	1175.2
Japan	613.5
Netherlands	515.6
New Zealand	0.5
Norway	306.9
Sweden	380.1
Switzerland	147.5
United Kingdom	424.6
United States	833.0
TOTAL	*9057.7*
AF.D.F.	374.0
AF.D.B.	–
AS.D.B	–
CAR.D.B.	–
E.E.C.	832.3
IBRD	0.4
IDA	1662.1
I.D.B.	–
IFAD	133.0
I.F.C.	–
IMF TRUST FUND	–
U.N. AGENCIES	–
UNDP	262.2
UNTA	56.7
UNICEF	129.5
UNRWA	–
WFP	259.3
UNHCR	161.6
Other Multilateral	124.1
Arab Agencies	132.6
TOTAL	*4127.7*
ARAB COUNTRIES	*465.2*
E.E.C.+ MEMBERS	*7031.7*
TOTAL	*13650.6*

8. GRANTS

	1987
Australia	35.0
Austria	17.1
Belgium	264.6
Canada	361.1
Denmark	248.1
Finland	124.3
France	1605.2
Germany	766.2
Ireland	16.6
Italy	746.2
Japan	438.2
Netherlands	483.4
New Zealand	0.5
Norway	306.9
Sweden	380.1
Switzerland	145.5
United Kingdom	405.9
United States	678.0
TOTAL	*7022.8*
MULTILATERAL	*1772.7*
ARAB COUNTRIES	*267.2*
E.E.C.+ MEMBERS	*5310.6*
TOTAL	*9062.7*

9. TOTAL OOF GROSS

	1987
Australia	5.8
Austria	–
Belgium	162.1
Canada	37.2
Denmark	25.1
Finland	–
France	1328.6
Germany	601.0
Ireland	–
Italy	180.7
Japan	–
Netherlands	12.0
New Zealand	–
Norway	–
Sweden	–
Switzerland	–
United Kingdom	40.8
United States	257.0
TOTAL	*2650.4*
MULTILATERAL	*1555.5*
ARAB COUNTRIES	*11.4*
E.E.C.+ MEMBERS	*2444.5*
TOTAL	*4217.3*

1988	1989	1990

10. ODA COMMITMENTS

1988	1989	1990		1987	1988	1989	1990
41.8	66.4	72.1		47.0	41.1	43.8	80.9
38.8	41.0	66.0		18.1	54.5	42.8	133.6
287.6	213.5	299.3		263.9	298.1	213.5	299.3
439.4	445.6	1002.1		487.7	557.2	447.7	426.7
290.0	300.8	319.3		265.9	276.4	231.0	258.7
208.9	221.9	237.3		118.7	229.6	337.7	204.2
2788.0	3169.8	4334.3		2613.1	2758.4	3107.2	3909.0
999.8	1036.5	2626.0		1063.0	1205.4	1078.0	1709.6
15.1	12.4	15.2		16.6	15.1	12.4	15.2
1383.8	1084.1	1122.0		1844.5	1520.0	904.2	889.9
986.2	1154.4	887.1		680.3	1176.8	1371.6	1143.4
575.5	494.1	681.7		581.1	578.2	535.5	615.9
0.8	0.9	1.3		1.0	1.8	–	0.2
312.5	285.1	375.1		269.5	120.3	124.3	242.2
510.7	464.5	620.7		359.4	478.3	463.9	478.5
161.8	150.8	218.8		158.9	228.3	195.3	238.1
650.0	731.4	574.3		504.5	676.4	696.7	648.3
822.0	765.0	1168.0		826.0	891.8	1326.7	1200.7
10512.5	10638.1	14620.6		10119.1	11107.8	11132.3	12494.4
352.7	497.4	610.6		724.5	730.4	929.6	1067.5
–	–	–		–	–	–	–
–	–	–		–	–	–	–
1503.2	1593.1	1593.1		2360.2	2911.3	1773.7	1773.7
1451.0	1585.0	1954.0		1915.0	2293.0	2329.0	3016.0
–	–	–		–	–	–	–
51.9	50.2	102.7		123.4	121.3	154.9	115.8
–	–	–		–	–	–	–
–	–	–		993.4	1173.0	1339.1	1465.1
311.3	334.4	383.8		–	–	–	–
44.1	56.0	54.6		–	–	–	–
138.4	178.8	210.4		–	–	–	–
–	–	–		–	–	–	–
314.8	310.8	435.5		–	–	–	–
234.1	226.2	211.8		–	–	–	–
130.2	233.0	169.1		–	–	–	–
112.0	96.5	85.0		107.7	208.7	267.3	125.4
4643.7	5161.3	5810.5		6224.1	7437.6	6793.6	7563.5
304.4	195.9	153.3		431.4	210.9	305.8	203.4
8492.9	8635.7	11565.2		9512.8	10239.4	8552.3	10119.7
15460.5	15995.3	20584.4		16774.5	18756.4	18231.7	20261.2

11. TECH. COOP. GRANTS

1988	1989	1990		1987	1988	1989	1990
41.8	66.4	72.1		6.8	10.0	13.3	18.8
17.5	18.9	35.4		9.4	9.6	3.6	9.1
248.3	182.5	270.9		164.1	129.8	111.9	97.6
439.4	445.6	1000.6		–	51.5	67.4	71.9
265.9	281.9	307.9		38.6	57.5	38.1	54.4
194.9	198.6	223.7		15.1	12.4	28.1	48.8
1772.6	2221.4	3002.0		1016.7	955.5	1103.9	1550.1
799.4	864.5	2349.5		435.4	466.3	426.6	497.3
15.1	12.4	15.2		10.7	9.9	9.0	10.3
932.7	797.0	644.0		204.8	112.9	124.0	178.6
695.6	672.7	586.8		91.4	113.8	116.6	128.4
535.7	462.6	640.8		159.1	183.6	180.5	217.8
0.8	0.9	1.3		0.3	0.4	–	0.8
310.2	282.9	371.7		46.5	44.4	45.8	47.0
510.7	464.5	620.7		79.9	109.0	121.0	20.4
158.3	148.7	217.5		31.6	39.0	–	–
634.1	709.6	563.1		159.3	234.8	217.0	220.5
715.0	653.0	1098.0		247.0	311.0	341.0	366.0
8288.1	8484.1	12021.1		2716.7	2851.3	2947.8	3537.7
2592.4	2853.5	2969.5		780.5	986.9	1028.3	1029.6
83.6	22.5	49.7		–	–	–	–
6615.6	7032.5	9293.8		2235.1	2279.0	2211.1	2826.5
10964.2	11360.0	15040.3		3497.2	3838.2	3976.1	4567.3

12. TOTAL OOF NET

1988	1989	1990		1987	1988	1989	1990
0.2	2.0	0.2		4.7	-2.5	-1.5	-4.6
–	–	–		-2.1	-1.9	–	–
265.0	263.1	119.9		159.0	262.7	262.1	99.6
106.3	106.0	91.1		6.0	83.3	87.3	67.9
12.5	7.7	2.4		6.1	-7.8	-9.3	-0.5
–	–	–		–	–	–	–
797.6	448.8	847.4		1114.3	495.4	168.3	461.9
1701.2	997.1	645.8		527.1	530.8	453.8	339.0
–	–	–		–	–	–	–
86.3	519.5	580.8		115.9	66.0	427.6	380.2
–	–	–		–	–	–	–
16.4	7.3	23.1		9.0	10.7	2.6	13.1
–	–	–		–	–	–	–
–	–	–		–	–	–	–
–	–	1.0		–	–	–	1.0
–	–	–		–	–	–	–
52.1	80.7	77.5		8.9	30.8	35.7	38.5
472.0	97.0	799.0		132.0	334.0	34.0	430.0
3509.5	2529.3	3188.1		2081.0	1801.4	1460.5	1826.0
1270.0	1751.7	2003.0		841.7	365.1	762.1	927.9
12.4	0.1	–		-5.5	-19.5	-7.9	-0.2
2999.7	2407.7	2380.3		1963.1	1381.2	1349.0	1339.9
4791.9	4281.1	5191.1		2917.3	2147.1	2214.7	2753.7

13. ODF COMMITMENTS: BY PURPOSE %

	1987	1988	1989	1990
Education	3	3	3	–
Health	2	2	3	–
Other Social Infrastr.	6	4	6	–
Water Sanitat. Sewage	4	4	6	–
Energy	5	4	5	–
Telecommunications	2	2	2	–
Transportation	9	9	11	–
Agriculture	14	12	13	–
Extractive Industries	0	1	1	–
Manufacturing	3	3	2	–
Trade Banking Tourism	2	4	6	–
Technical Cooperation	23	22	20	–
Multisector Aid	2	1	1	–
Programme	16	15	12	–
Debt Reorganisation	3	10	6	–
Food Aid	4	3	2	–
Emergency Aid	1	1	1	–
Unspecified	1	0	0	–
TOTAL	100	100	100	–

14. GRANT ELEMENT OF ODA %

DAC COUNTRIES	1987	1988	1989	1990
Australia	100.0	100.0	100.0	–
Austria	100.0	97.2	95.5	–
Belgium	99.8	100.0	100.0	–
Canada	100.0	100.0	100.0	–
Denmark	100.0	97.9	100.0	–
Finland	96.1	98.4	100.0	–
France	80.5	82.9	84.3	–
Germany	92.7	92.5	90.8	–
Ireland	100.0	100.0	100.0	–
Italy	89.1	85.6	88.4	–
Japan	83.5	88.0	79.1	–
Netherlands	95.2	97.6	97.6	–
New Zealand	100.0	100.0	–	–
Norway	99.4	100.0	98.7	–
Sweden	100.0	100.0	100.0	–
Switzerland	100.0	100.0	100.0	–
United Kingdom	100.0	100.0	94.5	–
United States	93.9	96.0	97.6	–
TOTAL	90.4	91.2	90.5	–
MULTILATERAL	91.1	89.9	87.9	–
ARAB COUNTRIES	77.1	58.1	46.7	–
E.E.C.+ MEMBERS	91.4	92.1	91.3	–
TOTAL	90.3	90.3	88.8	–

15. OTHER AGGREGATES

	1987	1988	1989	1990
OFFICIAL COMMITMENTS:				
TOTAL BILATERAL	14350.0	15344.2	14992.7	16840.1
of which:				
Arab Countries	440.1	210.9	330.8	203.4
C.E.E.C.	793.0	270.4	82.3	–
TOTAL MULTILATERAL	7534.7	10508.8	9051.3	9857.2
TOTAL BIL.& MULTIL.	21884.7	25853.1	24044.0	26697.2
of which:				
ODA Grants	11610.6	12814.8	11700.5	13095.0
ODA Loans	5607.0	6097.2	6613.5	7166.2
DISBURSEMENTS:				
DAC COUNTRIES COMBINED				
OFFICIAL & PRIVATE				
GROSS:				
Contractual Lending	5518.1	6399.2	7277.2	6037.5
Export Credits, Total	1013.4	912.1	3101.4	610.6
Export Credits, Priv.	860.0	674.5	2610.5	268.4
NET:				
Contractual Lending	2693.4	2033.5	3722.5	662.6
Export Credits Total	-1142.0	-1622.6	818.8	-1470.8
PRIVATE SECTOR NET	-198.2	-1012.2	1660.6	-1265.8
Direct Investment	1174.2	522.9	2518.0	290.3
Portfolio Investment	-309.3	58.9	-1399.4	-286.1
Export Credits	-1063.2	-1594.0	542.0	-1270.0
MARKET BORROWING:				
CHANGE IN CLAIMS				
Banks	-1062.0	-1313.0	-2212.0	-1042.0
MEMORANDUM ITEM:				
C.E.E.C. (Gross)	312.5	232.1	130.0	–

SECTION C

ECONOMIC INDICATORS

INDICATEURS ECONOMIQUES

	1984	1985	1986	1987	1988	1989	1990
EUROPE							
Albania							
Cyprus	3720	3770	4110	4870	5750	–	–
Gibraltar							
Greece	3800	3610	3650	3990	4770	5340	–
Malta	3440	3390	3580	4170	5180	5820	–
Turkey	1100	1080	1110	1220	1280	1370	–
Yugoslavia	2270	2040	2290	2510	2720	2920	–
Other Europe	2000	1970	2270	2850	3640	4260	–
Europe Unallocated							
TOTAL	*1770*	*1670*	*1780*	*1980*	*2200*	*2460*	–
NORTH OF SAHARA							
Algeria	2460	2580	2650	2680	2430	2220	–
Egypt	640	660	670	690	660	630	–
Libya	7230	6560	5500	5340	5410	–	–
Morocco	660	610	650	680	830	880	–
Tunisia	1210	1170	1110	1180	1230	1260	–
North of Sahara Unall.							
TOTAL	*1320*	*1320*	*1310*	*1330*	*1300*	*1090*	–
SOUTH OF SAHARA							
Angola							
Benin	260	260	280	310	370	380	–
Botswana	1080	960	970	1030	940	–	–
Burkina Faso	190	190	210	240	300	310	–
Burundi	240	250	240	250	240	220	–
Cameroon	820	810	890	920	980	1000	–
Cape Verde	450	440	470	550	680	760	–
Central African Rep.	280	270	290	320	370	390	–
Chad	130	150	150	140	180	190	–
Comoros	310	300	320	370	440	450	–
Congo	1150	1040	910	910	890	940	–
Cote d'Ivoire	690	650	710	790	880	790	–
Djibouti							
Equatorial Guinea							
Ethiopia	120	110	120	120	120	120	–
Gabon	3580	3560	3630	2890	2780	2960	–
Gambia	250	210	170	190	210	240	–
Ghana	370	370	390	390	400	390	–
Guinea	370	390	380	390	400	430	–
Guinea-Bissau	190	190	160	170	170	180	–
Kenya	330	310	330	340	370	370	–
Lesotho	480	390	340	340	410	470	–
Liberia							
Madagascar	340	310	290	270	250	230	–
Malawi	180	170	160	150	160	180	–
Mali	160	150	180	200	240	270	–
Mauritania	410	400	420	410	460	490	--
Mauritius	1080	1100	1230	1490	1790	1950	–
Mayotte							
Mozambique	180	180	220	150	100	80	–
Namibia							
Niger	240	230	240	250	300	290	–
Nigeria	900	930	710	370	280	250	–
Reunion							
Rwanda	260	270	300	310	330	320	–
St. Helena							
Sao Tome & Principe	340	320	370	370	400	340	–
Senegal	380	380	430	520	650	650	–
Seychelles	2330	2520	2660	3040	3640	4170	–
Sierra Leone	360	360	280	260	230	200	–
Somalia	150	160	150	170	170	–	–
Sudan	350	320	370	380	380	470	–
Swaziland	890	740	660	640	820	900	–
Tanzania	290	290	260	200	150	120	–
Togo	260	250	270	310	370	390	–
Uganda	160	190	230	260	280	–	–
Zaire	340	270	240	240	260	260	–
Zambia	460	370	260	240	290	390	–
Zimbabwe	730	620	560	540	570	650	–
East African Community							
DOM/TOM Unallocated							
EAMA Unallocated							
South of Sahara Unall.							
TOTAL	*490*	*480*	*440*	*360*	*310*	*320*	–
Africa Unspecified	–	–	–	–	–	–	–
AFRICA TOTAL	*650*	*650*	*610*	*550*	*500*	*470*	–
N.& C. AMERICA							
Aruba							
Bahamas	8190	8950	9530	10370	10680	11370	–

	1984	1985
Barbados	4420	4640
Belize	1100	1150
Bermuda	17160	18370
Costa Rica	1250	1400
Cuba		
Dominican Republic	1010	790
El Salvador	820	840
Guadeloupe		
Guatemala	1180	1200
Haiti	290	310
Honduras	720	740
Jamaica	1150	910
Martinique		
Mexico	2130	2180
Netherlands Antilles	6420	6360
Nicaragua	780	760
Panama	1980	2060
St. Pierre & Miquelon		
Trinidad & Tobago	6400	5940
Anguilla		
Antigua and Barbuda	2250	2550
Cayman Islands		
Dominica	1070	1120
Grenada	1080	1200
Montserrat		
St. Kitts-Nevis	1620	1750
St. Lucia	1140	1230
St. Vincent and Gr.	910	1000
Turks & Caicos Isl.		
Virgin Islands		
West Indies Unall.		
DOM/TOM Unallocated		
N.& C. America Unall.		
TOTAL	*1770*	*1800*
SOUTH AMERICA		
Argentina	2150	2140
Bolivia	450	420
Brazil	1730	1670
Chile	1680	1450
Colombia	1370	1280
Ecuador	1160	1170
Falkland Islands		
Guiana		
Guyana	500	510
Paraguay	1490	1170
Peru	1120	980
Suriname	2500	2450
Uruguay	1940	1680
Venezuela	4250	3830
South America Unall.		
TOTAL	*1800*	*1700*
America Unspecified	–	--
AMERICA TOTAL	*1790*	*1730*
MIDDLE EAST		
Bahrain	9680	8380
Iran	3920	4210
Iraq		
Israel	6680	6570
Jordan	1200	1160
Kuwait	17500	15010
Lebanon		
Oman	7280	7550
Qatar	15770	14430
Saudi Arabia	10840	9390
Syria	1580	1610
United Arab Emirates	24250	22220
Yemen	460	450
Middle East Unall.		
TOTAL	*4420*	*4320*
SOUTH ASIA		
Afghanistan		
Bangladesh	140	150
Bhutan		
India	280	290
Maldives	250	280
Myanmar (Burma)	180	180
Nepal	170	170
Pakistan	350	340
Sri Lanka	350	390

1986	1987	1988	1989	1990
5180	5350	5910	6370	–
1240	1390	1560	1720	–
20870	22530	24370	–	–
1550	1650	1680	1780	–
750	750	720	790	–
830	860	960	1070	–
1050	950	900	910	–
340	350	360	360	–
760	820	860	900	–
870	960	1080	1260	–
1890	1770	1750	1990	–
6340	6380	–	–	–
720	830	630	500	–
2170	2210	1810	1760	–
4970	4060	3410	3230	–
2980	3310	3810	–	–
1280	1480	1690	–	–
1360	1500	1710	1900	–
2030	2440	2860	–	–
1360	1490	1670	1810	–
1060	1140	1350	–	–
1610	*1540*	*1390*	*1670*	–
2380	2400	2570	2160	–
440	510	590	620	–
1810	1960	2120	2540	–
1350	1370	1510	1770	–
1220	1180	1180	1190	–
1140	1060	1090	1020	–
500	400	400	340	–
950	890	970	1030	–
1080	1170	1040	1010	–
2380	2260	2600	3020	–
1910	2210	2440	2620	–
3570	3180	3130	2450	–
1780	*1830*	*1940*	*2070*	–
–	–	–	–	–
1730	*1740*	*1760*	*1950*	–
7710	6840	6360	–	–
4180	4920	6360	7970	–
6780	7600	8940	9750	–
1150	1170	1130	–	–
15710	14680	14630	16380	–
6660	5810	4980	5220	–
12860	10940	9920	–	–
8540	6750	6480	6390	–
1630	1650	1680	–	–
16320	16700	16420	18430	–
610	580	600	650	–
4170	*4310*	*4490*	*7180*	–
160	160	170	180	–
290	310	340	340	–
310	350	380	420	–
190	210	250	–	–
160	160	180	180	–
340	330	350	360	–
410	410	420	430	–

	1984	1985	1986	1987	1988	1989	1990
SOUTH ASIA UNALL.							
TOTAL	*270*	*270*	*280*	*290*	*310*	*330*	–
FAR EAST ASIA							
BRUNEI							
CHINA	320	330	310	310	330	360	–
HONG KONG	6330	6080	6900	8190	9250	10320	–
INDONESIA	580	540	520	490	480	500	–
KAMPUCHEA							
KOREA	2240	2320	2570	2950	3600	4400	–
KOREA, DEM.							
LAOS	150	170	420	310	220	180	–
MACAO							
MALAYSIA	2040	1970	1850	1830	1930	2160	–
MONGOLIA							
PHILIPPINES	630	570	560	590	630	700	–
SINGAPORE	7740	7600	7440	7870	9050	10450	–
TAIWAN	3030	3100	3670	4410	5300	–	–
THAILAND	840	800	790	850	1030	1230	–
VIET NAM							
FAR EAST ASIA UNALL.							
TOTAL	*530*	*520*	*520*	*550*	*580*	*620*	–
Asia Unspecified	–	–	–	–	–	–	–
ASIA TOTAL	*580*	*580*	*580*	*600*	*640*	*710*	–
OCEANIA							
COOK ISLANDS							
FIJI	1770	1640	1760	1590	1500	1640	–
KIRIBATI	480	570	630	550	650	700	–
NAURU							
NEW CALEDONIA							
NIUE							
PACIF. ISL.(TRUST TR.)							
PAPUA NEW GUINEA	750	740	740	760	850	890	–
POLYNESIA, FRENCH							
SOLOMON ISLANDS	620	520	580	550	550	570	–
TOKELAU							
TONGA	790	750	760	760	800	910	–
TUVALU							
VANUATU	1020	930	910	780	830	860	–
WALLIS & FUTUNA							
WESTERN SAMOA							
TOM OCEANIA UNALL.							
Oceania Unallocated							
TOTAL	*1270*	*1240*	*1260*	*1250*	*830*	*970*	–
LDCs Unspecified	–	–	–	–	–	–	–
TOTAL,ALL LDCS	*750*	*740*	*740*	*760*	*780*	*860*	–
INCOME GROUPS							
LLDCS	210	210	220	220	210	230	–
OTHER LOW-INCOME	370	370	350	340	350	380	–
LOW MIDDLE-INCOME	1030	990	990	1020	890	1150	–
UPPER MIDDLE-INCOME	2730	2680	2700	2840	3020	3460	–
UNALLOCATED	–	–	–	–	–	–	–

EUROPE

	1984	1985	1986	1987	1988	1989	1990
Albania	2901	2962	3022	3083	3143	3204	–
Cyprus	660	666	673	680	687	694	–
Gibraltar	29	29	29	29	30	–	–
Greece	9896	9934	9964	9990	10013	10039	–
Malta	351	344	345	346	348	351	–
Turkey	49166	50310	51466	52623	53772	54899	–
Yugoslavia	22963	23123	23271	23411	23559	23707	–
Other Europe	10089	10157	10208	10250	10291	10333	–
Europe Unallocated							
TOTAL	*96055*	*97525*	*98978*	*100412*	*101843*	*103227*	–

NORTH OF SAHARA

	1984	1985	1986	1987	1988	1989	1990
Algeria	21173	21848	22497	23124	23753	24453	–
Egypt	45287	46497	47713	48935	50161	51390	–
Libya	3630	3786	3942	4095	4245	4395	–
Morocco	21475	22061	22706	23376	23960	24567	–
Tunisia	7082	7261	7441	7622	7804	7988	–
North of Sahara Unall.							
TOTAL	*98647*	*101453*	*104299*	*107152*	*109923*	*112793*	–

SOUTH OF SAHARA

	1984	1985	1986	1987	1988	1989	1990
Angola	8555	8754	8960	9179	9421	9694	–
Benin	3915	4043	4174	4310	4449	4593	–
Botswana	1035	1070	1106	1143	1180	1217	–
Burkina Faso	7688	7888	8096	8312	8539	8776	–
Burundi	4562	4696	4837	4986	5140	5299	–
Cameroon	9855	10166	10491	10830	11184	11554	–
Cape Verde	325	334	343	352	360	369	–
Central African Rep.	2578	2646	2717	2791	2869	2951	–
Chad	4901	5018	5140	5267	5398	5537	–
Comoros	381	395	410	426	442	459	–
Congo	1873	1938	2004	2071	2139	2208	–
Cote d'Ivoire	9551	9933	10337	10767	11225	11713	–
Djibouti	343	354	366	379	394	410	–
Equatorial Guinea	296	315	322	329	336	344	–
Ethiopia	42169	43350	44605	45939	47356	48861	–
Gabon	957	997	1023	1050	1077	1105	–
Gambia	724	748	772	797	822	848	–
Ghana	12168	12620	13073	13526	13977	14425	–
Guinea	4863	4987	5119	5258	5401	5547	–
Guinea-Bissau	870	886	903	921	940	960	–
Kenya	19358	20096	20856	21640	22446	23277	–
Lesotho	1505	1545	1587	1630	1676	1722	–
Liberia	2130	2199	2268	2337	2406	2475	–
Madagascar	9716	9985	10265	10556	10859	11174	–
Malawi	6948	7188	7437	7695	7960	8230	–
Mali	7215	7389	7574	7771	7983	8212	–
Mauritania	1721	1766	1812	1859	1906	1954	–
Mauritius	1014	1020	1030	1040	1051	1062	–
Mayotte							
Mozambique	13435	13791	14160	14544	14943	15357	–
Namibia	1106	1143	1181	1219	1259	1300	–
Niger	6356	6593	6813	7033	7256	7479	–
Nigeria	96432	99669	103011	106497	110068	113665	–
Reunion	538	547	557	566	576	585	–
Rwanda	5836	6026	6225	6434	6656	6893	–
St. Helena							
Sao Tome & Principe	105	108	112	115	119	122	–
Senegal	6211	6395	6589	6789	6996	7211	–
Seychelles	66	66	67	67	68	68	–
Sierra Leone	3570	3657	3747	3841	3938	4040	–
Somalia	5227	5384	5549	5721	5902	6089	–
Sudan	21169	21822	22475	23127	23777	24423	–
Swaziland	642	664	687	710	735	761	–
Tanzania	21482	22242	23036	23864	24728	25627	–
Togo	2933	3038	3147	3261	3381	3507	–
Uganda	14222	14680	15164	15675	16211	16772	–
Zaire	29489	30398	31346	32334	33366	34442	–
Zambia	6506	6753	7011	7280	7555	7837	–
Zimbabwe	8101	8406	8714	9017	9303	9567	–
East African Community							
DOM/TOM Unallocated							
EAMA Unallocated							
South of Sahara Unall.							
TOTAL	*410698*	*423766*	*437276*	*451315*	*465772*	*480721*	–
Africa Unspecified	–	–	–	–	–	–	–
AFRICA TOTAL	*509345*	*525219*	*541575*	*558467*	*575695*	*593514*	–

N.& C. AMERICA

	1984	1985	1986	1987	1988	1989	1990
Aruba							
Bahamas	229	232	236	240	244	248	–

	1984	1985
Barbados	253	253
Belize	162	166
Bermuda		
Costa Rica	2432	2489
Cuba	9992	10090
Dominican Republic	6268	6416
El Salvador	4707	4767
Guadeloupe	331	333
Guatemala	7739	7963
Haiti	5815	5922
Honduras	4232	4383
Jamaica	2279	2311
Martinique	330	331
Mexico	76896	78524
Netherlands Antilles	190	190
Nicaragua	3161	3272
Panama	2134	2180
St. Pierre & Miquelon		
Trinidad & Tobago	1157	1178
Anguilla		
Antigua and Barbuda	76	76
Cayman Islands		
Dominica	78	80
Grenada	93	94
Montserrat	12	12
St. Kitts-Nevis	44	43
St. Lucia	134	137
St. Vincent and Gr.	108	109
Turks & Caicos Isl.		
Virgin Islands		
West Indies Unall.		
DOM/TOM Unallocated		
N.& C. America Unall.		
TOTAL	*129020*	*131721*

SOUTH AMERICA

	1984	1985
Argentina	29925	30331
Bolivia	6200	6371
Brazil	132650	135564
Chile	11919	12121
Colombia	29281	29879
Ecuador	9071	9317
Falkland Islands		
Guiana	79	82
Guyana	785	790
Paraguay	3579	3693
Peru	18965	19383
Suriname	387	398
Uruguay	2989	3008
Venezuela	16851	17317
South America Unall.		
TOTAL	*262683*	*268256*
America Unspecified	–	–
AMERICA TOTAL	*391703*	*399977*

MIDDLE EAST

	1984	1985
Bahrain	407	425
Iran	42925	44212
Iraq	15351	15898
Israel	4170	4233
Jordan	3380	3506
Kuwait	1655	1712
Lebanon	2644	2668
Oman	1187	1242
Qatar	338	355
Saudi Arabia	11143	11595
Syria	10097	10458
United Arab Emirates	1299	1349
Yemen	9501	9811
Middle East Unall.		
TOTAL	*104097*	*107464*

SOUTH ASIA

	1984	1985
Afghanistan	17593	18100
Bangladesh	97776	100593
Bhutan	1261	1286
India	749677	765147
Maldives	177	183
Myanmar (Burma)	36735	37544
Nepal	16255	16682
Pakistan	93177	96180
Sri Lanka	15599	15837

1986	1987	1988	1989	1990
254	254	254	255	–
171	175	180	184	–
2547	2608	2670	2735	–
10194	10288	10391	10495	–
6564	6712	6859	7002	–
4846	4934	5032	5143	–
335	337	338	340	–
8195	8436	8686	8946	–
6031	6142	6254	6368	–
4535	4687	4837	4981	–
2338	2361	2379	2396	–
332	333	335	336	–
80199	81909	83656	85440	–
190	190	183	191	–
3387	3504	3623	3740	–
2227	2274	2322	2370	–
1199	1220	1241	1261	–
76	77	78	79	–
81	81	82	82	–
90	94	94	94	–
12	12	12	–	–
42	42	42	41	–
140	142	145	147	–
110	111	112	114	–
134504	137338	140105	142988	–
30730	31121	31506	31883	–
6547	6729	6917	7110	–
138494	141433	144369	147294	–
12330	12543	12760	12980	–
30481	31090	31707	32335	–
9566	9819	10073	10329	–
84	86	88	–	–
794	797	799	800	–
3808	3925	4042	4161	–
19806	20237	20681	21142	–
409	418	427	436	–
3025	3042	3060	3077	–
17791	18272	18751	19244	–
273867	*279514*	*285180*	*290791*	–
–	–	–	–	–
408371	*416851*	*425285*	*433779*	–
442	458	473	489	–
45578	47029	48569	50204	–
16463	17046	17649	18271	–
4305	4375	4444	4525	–
3635	3767	3903	4041	–
1791	1873	1958	2020	–
2666	2664	2661	–	–
1299	1359	1421	1486	–
373	391	411	431	–
12057	13610	14016	14435	–
10836	11232	11647	12082	–
1399	1448	1496	1544	–
10135	10475	10830	11200	–
110979	*115727*	*119478*	*120728*	–
18530	18980	19433	–	–
103348	106103	108860	111590	–
1313	1343	1373	1403	–
781893	798680	815590	832535	–
189	195	202	209	–
38358	39171	39983	40796	–
17098	17529	17976	18431	–
99399	102738	106261	109950	–
16117	16361	16587	16779	–

	1984	1985	1986	1987	1988	1989	1990
SOUTH ASIA UNALL.							
TOTAL	*1028250*	*1051552*	*1076245*	*1101100*	*1126265*	*1131693*	–
FAR EAST ASIA							
BRUNEI	212	219	226	233	241	249	–
CHINA	1033185	1044583	1057839	1072981	1088408	1105066	–
HONG KONG	5370	5456	5533	5613	5681	5735	–
INDONESIA	161319	164630	168044	171443	174832	178211	–
KAMPUCHEA	7070	7282	7474	7670	7865	–	–
KOREA	40406	40806	41184	41575	41975	42380	–
KOREA, DEM.	19566	19888	20208	20525	20837	21143	–
LAOS	3495	3594	3701	3813	3931	4055	–
MACAO	380	392	410	429	442	454	–
MALAYSIA	15272	15682	16109	16528	16921	17340	–
MONGOLIA	1857	1909	1962	2016	2071	2128	–
PHILIPPINES	54504	55819	57149	58493	59851	61224	–
SINGAPORE	2529	2558	2586	2613	2647	2684	–
TAIWAN	19072	19408	19694	19974	20234	–	–
THAILAND	50720	51683	52654	53605	54469	55200	–
VIET NAM	58592	59903	61272	62703	64197	65758	–
FAR EAST ASIA UNALL.							
TOTAL	*1473549*	*1493812*	*1516045*	*1540214*	*1564602*	*1561627*	–
Asia Unspecified	–	–	–	–	–	–	–
ASIA TOTAL	*2605896*	*2652828*	*2703269*	*2757041*	*2810345*	*2814048*	–
OCEANIA							
COOK ISLANDS							
FIJI	686	700	711	722	732	743	–
KIRIBATI	63	64	65	66	67	69	–
NAURU							
NEW CALEDONIA	149	152	154	156	158	160	–
NIUE							
PACIF. ISL.(TRUST TR.)	150	154	157	161	165	169	–
PAPUA NEW GUINEA	3377	3460	3546	3633	3722	3812	–
POLYNESIA, FRENCH	168	171	176	181	186	191	–
SOLOMON ISLANDS	265	274	284	293	303	314	–
TOKELAU							
TONGA	95	95	95	96	97	98	–
TUVALU							
VANUATU	132	136	139	143	147	152	–
WALLIS & FUTUNA							
WESTERN SAMOA	157	157	157	158	159	159	–
TOM OCEANIA UNALL.							
Oceania Unallocated							
TOTAL	*5296*	*5419*	*5540*	*5665*	*5736*	*5867*	–
LDCs Unspecified	–	–	–	–	–	–	–
TOTAL,ALL LDCS	*3608295*	*3680968*	*3757733*	*3838436*	*3918903*	*3950434*	–
INCOME GROUPS							
LLDCS	375341	386040	396821	407907	419276	411029	–
OTHER LOW-INCOME	2437945	2482617	2531110	2581945	2633442	2678538	–
LOW MIDDLE-INCOME	246482	252073	257769	263524	269229	274935	–
UPPER MIDDLE-INCOME	548527	560238	572033	585061	596956	585931	–
UNALLOCATED	–	–	–	–	–	–	–

DEFINITION OF CONCEPTS USED IN THIS REPORT

A1.   Disbursements represent the actual international transfer of financial resources. They may be recorded at one of several stages: provision of goods and services, placing of funds at the disposal of the recipient in an earmarked fund or account, withdrawal of funds by the recipient from an earmarked fund or account, payment by the donor of invoices on behalf of the recipient, etc. The disbursement mechanism used tends to vary as a function of the type of financial (or technical) co-operation flow involved. Disbursements may be recorded gross (the actual amounts disbursed) or net (i.e., less repayments of principal in respect of earlier loans).

A2.   A commitment is a firm obligation expressed in an agreement or equivalent contract and supported by the availability of public funds, undertaken by the government, an official agency of the reporting country or an international organisation, to furnish assistance of a specified amount under agreed financial terms and conditions and for specific purposes, for the benefit of a recipient country.

A3.   Grant Element: Reflects the financial terms of a transaction: interest rate, maturity (interval to final repayment) and grace period (interval to first repayment of capital). It is a measure of the concessionality (i.e., softness) of a loan. The extent of the benefit depends on the difference between the interest rate and the market rate of interest, and the length of time the funds are available to the borrower. To calculate this benefit, the present value at the market rate of interest of each repayment is ascertained. The excess of the loan's face value over the sum of these present values, expressed as a percentage of the face value, is the "grant element" of the loan. For operating purposes, the market rate is taken as 10 per cent. Thus, the grant element is nil for a loan carrying an interest rate of 10 per cent; it is 100 per cent for a grant; and it lies between these two limits for a soft loan. Generally speaking, a loan will not convey a grant element of over 25 per cent if its maturity is less than 10 years, unless its interest rate is well below 5 per cent. If the face value of a loan is multiplied by its grant element, the result is referred to as the grant equivalent of that loan.

Aggregates and Resource Flow Categories

A4.   *Official Development Assistance* is defined as those flows to developing countries and multilateral institutions provided by official agencies, including state and local governments, or by their executive agencies, each transaction of which meets the following tests:

  a) It is administered with the promotion of the economic development and welfare of developing countries as its main objective, and

  b) It is concessional in character and conveys a grant element (see paragraph A3) of at least 25 per cent.

A5.   *Grants*:   This heading covers transfers, in money or in kind, for which no repayment is required. It includes grants for technical co-operation, grant-like flows, i.e., loans repayable in recipients' currencies, extended by governments or official agencies in currencies of the donor countries, for which repayment is required in the currencies of the recipient countries, and transfer of resources through sales of commodities for recipients' currencies, less local currency balances used by the donor for other than development purposes (for example, to defray the local costs of embassy operations). In the case of overseas territories, grants are shown after deduction of tax receipts. The following are excluded: reparations and indemnification payments to private individuals, insurance and similar payments to residents of less-developed countries, and loans extended in and repayable in recipients' currencies.

A6.   *Technical Co-operation Grants*:   these data relate to free-standing technical cooperation (FTC); essentially activities involving the supply of human resources (teachers, volunteers, and experts: "technical co-operation personnel") or action targeted on human resources (education, training, advice), as distinct from investment related Technical Co-operation (IRTC). Used without qualification, the term technical co-operation (sometimes referred to as technical assistance) is a generic term covering contributions to development primarily through the medium of education and training and may relate to FTC and IRTC combined. The respective definitions are:

  a) Free-standing technical co-operation: Activities financed by a donor country whose primary purpose is to augment the level of knowledge, skills, technical know-how or productive aptitudes of the population of developing countries, i.e., increasing their stock of human intellectual capital, or their capacity for more effective use of their existing factor endowment.

  b) Investment-related technical co-operation (not included under this heading): financing of services by a donor country with the primary purpose of contributing to the design and/or implementation of a project or programme aiming to increase the physical capital stock of the recipient country.

A7.   *ODA Loans*: Loans with maturities of over one year and meeting the criteria set out in paragraph A4, extended by governments or official agencies, and for which repayment is required in convertible currencies or in kind. Rescheduling (maturity extension of loans originally made by a government or official agency) and loans made by a government or an official agency to refinance indebtedness due to the private or official sector, are included if reported as Official Development Assistance, otherwise as "Other Official Flows". The net data are reported after deduction of amortisation payments and the impact of other measures reducing debt (e.g. forgiveness).

A8.   *Other Official Flows*: Transactions by the official sector whose main objective is other than development-motivated, or, if development-motivated, whose grant element is below the 25 per cent threshold which would make them eligible to be recorded as ODA. The main classes of transactions included here are official export credits, official sector equity and portfolio investment,and debt reorganisation undertaken by the official sector at non-concessional terms (irrespective of the nature or the identity of the original creditor).

A9.   *Total Official Flows*: The sum of Official Development Assistance (ODA) and Other Official Flows (OOF) represents the total (gross or net) disbursements by the official sector at large to the recipient country shown.

A10.   Funds provided by the official sector to support export credits or direct investment by the private sector are treated in this report as an indistinguishable part of the relevant private sector transactions. This approach differs from that in the aggregate statistics presented in other approach DAC reviews, where these amounts are included as part of the official sector total, and the aggregate amounts for the private sector reduced correspondingly. For purposes of geographical allocation, the pertinent concept is the transactor dealing with a developing country; this latter is not concerned with the sources of the transactor's funds, as its indebtedness is to the transactor, not his sources of finance. By contrast, the aggregate statistics for individual donor countries place emphasis on the source of funds, which governs the extent to which official policy can determine the amount, terms and distribution of transactions in which official sector resources form part of the total financing package.

A11.   *Official Development Financing,* measured for recipient countries only, is defined as the sum of their receipts of bilateral ODA, concessional and non-concessional resources from multilateral sources, and bilateral other official flows made available for reasons unrelated to trade, in particular loans to refinance debt.

A12.   *Total Contractual Lending:* Bilateral ODA and OOF loans plus officially guaranteed private export credits i.e., all official and officially supported borrowing at fixed terms. Excludes unguaranteed loans and credits extended by the banking sector.

A13.   *Multilateral Agencies*:   The list of multilateral agencies for which data are shown separately in this report is given in the Introduction. To the extent possible, a distinction has been made between concessional and non-concessional flows from multilateral agencies. Loan disbursements for which it was not possible to make this distinction on a transaction by transaction basis have been treated as non-concessional if made from "ordinary capital" resources and as concessional if made from a "soft window". Thus, for some agencies "total loans" are significantly larger than loans on concessional terms, and the volume of loans on concessional terms actually received by the borrowing country is correspondingly understated. The "net" multilateral disbursements concept used in this report, like the net bilateral concept, is defined as gross disbursements of grants and loans to developing countries minus repayments on earlier loans. Capital subscription payments to multilateral agencies by their developing country Members are not subtracted out.

A14.   *Total Receipts, Net*:   In addition to Official Development Assistance, this heading includes in particular: other official bilateral transactions which are not concessional or which, even though they have concessional elements, are primarily trade facilitating in character (i.e., "Other Official Flows"); changes in bilateral long-term assets of the private non-monetary and monetary sectors, in particular guaranteed export credits, private direct investment, portfolio investment and, to the extent they are not covered in the preceding headings, loans by private banks. Flows from the multilateral sector which are not classified as concessional are also included here.

Relationships Between the Categories Shown in the Report

A15.   The total net resource flow data presented for a recipient country ("total net receipts") is the sum of items (1 + 2 + 3 = 4) in the table below.

CATEGORIES	DAC DONORS	MULTILATERAL DONORS	ARAB DONORS	CEEC DONORS
1. ODA, Net	By country	By agency	As a group	Not available
2. OOF, Net	By country	As a group	As a group	Not available
3. Private Sector Flows, Net	As a group	Not applicable	Not available	Not available
4. Total Resource Flows, Net	By country	By agency	Incomplete	Not available
Memo:				
ODA Gross	By country	By agency	As a group	As a group
ODA Commitments	By country	By agency	As a group	As a group

A16.   For any given recipient country, the DAC total for "private sector net" can be broken down by country of origin, by subtracting (ODA + OOF net) for the donor country concerned from the total receipts figure against its name.

A17.   "Private sector, net" is broken down, for DAC Members combined, into direct investment, portfolio investment and export credits (net). The transactions covered are those undertaken by residents of DAC Member countries. Portfolio investment corresponds largely, but not wholly, to transactions by the private monetary sector, adjusted where necessary and possible to transfer export credit claims to the corresponding heading. Accordingly, the coverage of portfolio investment differs in these regards from the coverage of (bank sector loans), which includes indistinguishably export credit lending by banks. The (bank sector loan) data represent the net change in banks' claims after adjustment to eliminate the effect of changes in exchange rates. They are therefore a proxy for net flow data, but are not themselves a net flow figure. They differ in three further regards from the other data in the report. First, they relate to loans by banks resident in countries which report quarterly to the Bank for International Settlements (BIS) i.e., DAC Members other than Australia, New Zealand and Spain and a number of offshore financial centres (see the BIS quarterly survey *International Banking and Financial Market Developments*). Second, for offshore centres viewed as debtor countries, the standard OECD/BIS approach is not to take account of borrowing by their resident banks, most of which operate as intermediaries relending internationally. Finally, no adjustment has been made to exclude short-term claims.

A18. It has recently become possible to reconcile valuation-adjusted data derived from banking system statistics of outstanding claims with valuation-adjusted data on guaranteed trade credits extended by banks. Semi-annual figures are shown in the OECD/BIS survey *Statistics on External Indebtedness: Bank and Trade-Related Non-Bank External Claims on Individual Borrowing Countries and Territories,* (No. 8, issued in January 1992).

NOTES ON THE INTERPRETATION OF CERTAIN DATA

A19. In establishing the statistical data in the present report, the aim is to present the fullest possible record of the resources put at the disposal of each country covered. However, there are some inconsistencies in Members' reporting. Although they are of marginal impact at aggregate level, it was nevertheless necessary to make estimates which in some instances affect the data shown, and in others were intended to fill gaps in the data originally submitted.

A20. The following list sets out the main areas in which particularities of the data stemming from these causes could have some influence on their understanding or use by the reader.

Data for Country Groups

a) Contents of the Groups

A21. Low-Income Countries (LICs) are those whose per capita GNP in 1989, as shown in the World Bank Atlas, was below approximately $750. Two sub-groups of Low-Income Countries are shown separately: those on the UN list of Least-developed Countries (LLDCs), some of which have a per capita income of over $750, and all other Low-Income Countries. A further two tables located at the end of Section B give the figures for Low-Income countries combined, including the lower-middle income LLDCs, and for sub-Saharan Africa. The remaining countries are subdivided into Lower Middle-Income Countries (LMICs) i.e., those with a per capita GNP in 1989 between $750 and $1 500, and Upper Middle-Income Countries (UMICs), with a per capita GNP exceeding $1 500. These groups have been defined purely for analytical purposes and, except for the Least-developed Countries, are not internationally agreed lists.

b) Treatment of Unallocated Amounts

A22. Some reporting countries are unable to supply a full geographical distribution. One element here is that some commitments or disbursements in fact relate to expenditures in a given region (e.g., West Africa) or group of countries (e.g., the Least-developed Countries). The data shown for countries and for groups are restricted to those which are available broken down by recipient. Amounts reported as provided to a region or group are included as "unallocated". The problem of the large proportion of unallocated amounts of Arab aid has already been referred to in the Introduction. Unallocated amounts also include commitments and disbursements concerning expenditures on the territory of the donor country for research specific to some developing countries' problems (e.g., tropical diseases) or in the form of subsidies to nationals of developing countries, e.g., for apprenticeships, or school or university tuition; there are obvious statistical difficulties in assigning these amounts to the countries of origin of the people concerned.

A23. In computing the share of a given country or group in a total for developing countries, the usual practice is to use as denominator the total excluding unallocated amounts. Implicit in this approach is the assumption that the percentage geographical distribution of allocated and unallocated amounts is the same.

A24. Negative Grants: In describing the recording methodology for grants, it was noted that the total of new grants is reduced by the amounts of a donor's local currency balances used by the donor for its own purposes. If the latter exceeds the volume of new grants, a "negative grant" is shown.

A25. Cancellations of Commitments: The data on commitments concern new commitments entered into during the calendar year. They exclude commitments that were cancelled in the year they were made, but are not adjusted to allow for cancellations during the year reported on of commitments made in earlier years.

A26. ODA Commitments of International Financial Institutions: As a general rule, international financial institutions report their commitments on an "approval basis" and these are the data shown in the "ODA commitments" panel. However, in order to calculate their "grant element" (shown under "All Source Commitments") the terms of each individual transaction must be ascertained. To do this, the "signature date" of each commitment is used. This normally post-dates the approval date. This explains why an entry may be found under the heading loan commitments accompanied by a nil entry under grant element (or vice versa). Discrepancies in either direction in any one year due to this cause are balanced by a counterpart entry in an adjacent year.

A27.   A figure for grant element may also appear in the absence of an amount under commitments if the amount concerned is less than $50 000 i.e., too small to be shown separately.

A28.   Partial Components of a Total: In the "All Sources Commitments" block, certain components only are shown. The presentation of full detail would have lengthened processing time so greatly as to delay the appearance of the report. The total of the missing components can be established by direct subtraction from the grand total of which they are part.

A29.   Commitments and Disbursements of the UN Agencies: Disbursement data are shown separately for each UN agency. Comparable commitment data are not available for the UN family. In the commitments table, gross disbursement data are shown as a proxy for the UN family as a group, with no entries against the individual agencies. This procedure was necessary to provide an order of magnitude of the commitments of multilateral organisations combined.

A30.   Effect of Changes in Exchange Rates: The currency unit used throughout this report is the US dollar. Loans are often denominated in another currency. If that currency strengthens vis-à-vis the dollar, repayments on the loan are reflected in the statistics by an increased number of dollars. This accounts for a number of cases in which cumulative repayments appear to exceed the original amount of a loan. Similarly, the weakening of a currency produces cases in which repayments, expressed in dollars, appear to be less than the original amount lent. In comparing data on changes in debt (e.g., in *The Financing and External Debt of Developing Countries* or the semi-annual OECD/BIS survey) with the figures shown for net resource flows in this report, it should be borne in mind that the debt data are converted to dollars at the end-of-period rate, whereas the flow data are converted at the annual average rate. (See Annex, paragraph A17.)

A31.   Unusually high amortisation entries: These relate in practically all cases to forgiveness of the outstanding principal on loans. The effect of cancellation is to extend a grant which is applied to pay off the loans concerned (see paragraph A7). Exceptionally large negative net loans on ODA account for the Least-Developed Countries will for this reason be found to be accompanied by exceptionally high entries for the same donor, in the same year, for disbursements of grants.

A32.   ODA from IBRD: Most IBRD lending is recorded as "Other Official Flows". The principal agency of the World Bank group for ODA is the International Development Association (IDA). Small amounts listed against IBRD correspond in the main to "Third Window" lending.

A33.   Belgium's Data for Commitments: By reason of the institutional procedures used, there is no stage at which it is possible for the Belgian authorities to identify the commitment of a grant (no problem arises with respect to loan reporting). In order not to leave blank entries in the commitments data for Belgium, the Secretariat has made estimates by distributing the total budget allocation for grants among recipient countries in proportion to each country's receipts of gross disbursements of grants in the same year. The errors involved are too small in any way to distort the figure for a recipient country's total receipts from DAC Members combined or from all sources. If analysing Belgium's commitment figures in isolation, a still closer approximation to the order of magnitude is obtained by taking an average over several years of the commitments data shown for Belgian grants.

A34.   Resource Flows from the European Economic Community: The figures shown pertain to outflows from the EEC, including outflows from the European Investment Bank at market terms. The latter can be ascertained from the data in the present volume as the difference between a country's Total Net Receipts from the EEC and its receipts of Total Net ODA from the EEC.

DÉFINITION DES CONCEPTS UTILISÉS DANS LE PRÉSENT RAPPORT

A1.   Les versements, tels que définis dans le présent rapport, représentent le transfert effectif de ressources financières au niveau international. Ils peuvent être saisis à l'un des stades suivants : fourniture de biens et services, dépôt de sommes mises à la disposition du bénéficiaire dans un fonds ou un compte réservé, retrait de fonds par le bénéficiaire sur un compte ou un fonds réservé, paiement de factures par le donneur pour le compte du bénéficiaire, etc. Les modalités de versement tendent à varier en fonction du type d'apport de coopération financière (ou technique) en cause. Les versements sont comptabilisés soit bruts (c'est-à-dire les montants effectivement versés), soit nets (c'est-à-dire moins le remboursement du capital au titre de prêts antérieurs).

A2.   Un engagement s'entend d'une obligation ferme, stipulée dans un contrat ou un accord similaire et étayée par la mise à disposition de fonds publics ; par cette obligation, le gouvernement, un organisme public du pays déclarant ou un organisme multilatéral s'engage à fournir, au profit du pays bénéficiaire, une aide d'un montant spécifié, assortie de conditions financières déterminées et destinées à des fins données.

A3.   Elément de libéralité : résume les conditions financières d'une opération : taux d'intérêt, durée de remboursement (délai jusqu'au remboursement final) et différé d'amortissement (délai jusqu'au premier remboursement du capital). Il s'agit d'une mesure de la libéralité d'un prêt. Le bénéfice qu'en retire l'emprunteur dépend de la différence entre le taux d'intérêt octroyé et le taux du marché, ainsi que de la durée pendant laquelle les fonds sont à sa disposition. Pour calculer cet avantage, on détermine la valeur actualisée, au taux d'intérêt du marché, de chaque remboursement. La différence, par excès, entre le montant nominal du prêt et le total de ces valeurs actualisées, exprimée en pourcentage de ce montant nominal, est « l'élément de libéralité » du prêt. Le taux du marché est conventionnellement fixé à 10 pour cent. Par conséquent, l'élément de libéralité d'un prêt de 10 pour cent est nul ; il est de 100 pour cent dans le cas d'un don ; et il se situe entre ces deux extrêmes pour un prêt libéral. En général, l'élément de libéralité d'un prêt remboursable en moins de 10 ans ne dépassera pas 25 pour cent, sauf si son taux d'intérêt est très inférieur à 5 pour cent. En multipliant la valeur nominale d'un prêt par son élément de libéralité, on obtient « l'équivalent-don » de ce prêt.

Agrégats et apports de ressource par catégories

A4.   Par *aide publique au développement,* on entend l'ensemble des apports de ressources qui sont fournis aux pays en développement et aux institutions multilatérales par des organismes officiels, y compris les collectivités locales, ou par leurs agents d'exécution et qui, considérés au niveau de chaque opération, répondent aux critères suivants :

   a) Etre dispensés dans le but essentiel de favoriser le développement économique et l'amélioration du niveau de vie dans les pays en développement, et

   b) Revêtir un caractère de faveur et comporter un élément de libéralité (voir paragraphe A3) d'au moins 25 pour cent.

A5.   *Dons :*   cette rubrique couvre les transferts, en espèces ou en nature, qui n'impliquent aucun remboursement. Elle inclut les dons au titre de la coopération technique, les apports assimilables à des dons, c'est-à-dire les prêts remboursables dans la monnaie du bénéficiaire, consentis par les pouvoirs publics ou des organismes publics dans la monnaie du pays donneur, ainsi que le transfert de ressources opéré par le biais de la vente de biens payables dans la monnaie du bénéficiaire, déduction faite du montant de ses avoirs en monnaie locale que le pays donneur a utilisés à des fins autres que le développement du pays bénéficiaire (par exemple pour le financement des dépenses locales afférentes au fonctionnement des ambassades). Dans le cas des territoires d'Outre-Mer les dons sont présentés nets des recettes d'impôts. Sont également exclus les paiements de réparation et d'indemnisation à des particuliers, les paiements d'assurances et autres paiements similaires à des résidents de pays en développement, et les prêts accordés et remboursables dans les monnaies des bénéficiaires.

A6.   *Dons de coopération technique :*   Ils concernent la coopération technique pure, c'est-à-dire essentiellement les activités comportant l'apport de ressources humaines (enseignants, volontaires et experts : « personnel de coopération technique ») ou des actions ciblées sur les ressources humaines (enseignement, formation, avis). Quand elle n'est pas qualifiée, l'expression « coopération technique » (pour laquelle on utilise quelquefois « assistance technique ») est une appellation générique qui désigne les contributions au développement fournies principalement par le biais de l'enseignement et de la formation. Il convient toutefois de faire une distinction entre la coopération technique pure (CTP) et la coopération technique associée à un projet d'équipement (CTAPE).

   a) Coopération technique pure : Activités financées par un pays donneur et ayant pour but essentiel d'élever le niveau des connaissances, des qualifications, du savoir-faire technique ou des aptitudes productives de la population des pays en développement, c'est-à-dire d'accroître le stock de capital intellectuel de ces pays, ou leur aptitude à utiliser plus efficacement leur dotation de facteurs.

  b) *Coopération technique associée à un projet d'équipement :* Financement de services par un pays donneur, dans le but essentiel de contribuer à la conception à la mise en œuvre d'un projet ou programme destiné à accroître le stock de capital physique du pays bénéficiaire.

A7. *Prêts d'APD :* ce sont les prêts à plus d'un an accordés par des gouvernements et des organismes publics, remboursables en monnaies convertibles ou en nature, qui satisfont aux critères énoncés dans le paragraphe A4 ci-dessus. Les opérations de rééchelonnement des échéances (allongement de la durée de prêts initialement accordés par un gouvernement ou un organisme public) et les prêts octroyés par un gouvernement ou un organisme public pour refinancer une dette contractée auprès du secteur privé ou du secteur public sont inclus dans cette catégorie s'ils sont notifiés comme aide publique au développement ; sinon, ils sont classés dans les « autres apports du secteur public ». Les montants nets sont indiqués après déduction des remboursements et d'autres moyens de réduction de l'encours par exemple l'effacement de la dette.

A8. *Autres apports du secteur public (AASP) :* il s'agit des opérations du secteur public dont le but essentiel est autre que le développement ou qui, tout en visant à favoriser le développement, sont assorties d'un élément de libéralité inférieur au seuil de 25 pour cent à partir duquel elles auraientpu être notifiées comme de l'APD. Les principales catégories d'opérations couvertes dans les AASP sont les crédits publics à l'exportation, les prises de participation et les investissements de portefeuille du secteur public et le réaménagement de la dette effectué par le secteur public aux conditions du marché (et ce, quelle que soit la nature ou l'identité du créancier initial).

A9. *Apports totaux du secteur public :* il s'agit du total de l'aide publique au développement (APD) et des autres apports du secteur public (AASP). Cet agrégat correspond aux versements (bruts ou nets) effectués par le secteur public dans son ensemble aux pays bénéficiaires considérés.

A10. Les ressources fournies par le secteur public pour soutenir les crédits à l'exportation ou les investissements directs du secteur privé sont comptabilisées dans le présent rapport avec les opérations correspondantes du secteur privé. Cette approche diffère de celle utilisée dans les données statistiques agrégées présentées dans certains autres documents établis par le CAD, où les montants en cause sont inclus dans les totaux afférents au secteur public et où les montants relatifs au secteur privé sont réduits proportionnellement. Dans l'optique de la répartition géographique, il convient de retenir comme unité statistique l'opérateur qui est en relation avec un pays en développement ; l'emprunteur ne s'intéresse pas à l'origine des capitaux que cet opérateur lui fournit, son endettement étant envers cet opérateur et non envers les sources de financement de ce dernier. Dans les statistiques agrégées pour les pays donneurs, en revanche, l'accent est mis sur les sources des fonds, car ce sont elles qui déterminent la mesure dans laquelle les politiques mises en œuvre par le secteur public peuvent déterminer sur les montants totaux, les conditions financières et la

répartition géographique des apports, dès lors que ceux-ci englobent des ressources en provenance du secteur public.

A11. *Financement public du développement* (agrégat calculé pour les seuls pays bénéficiaires) : le total pour chaque bénéficiaire des apports d'APD bilatérale, des ressources mises à disposition par le secteur multilatéral, qu'elles comportent ou non un élément de libéralité, et des AASP fournies pour des raisons n'ayant pas trait au commerce international, plus particulièrement les prêts dont l'objet est de refinancer l'endettement.

A12. *Total des prêts contractuels :* il s'agit du total des prêts bilatéraux au titre de l'APD ou des AASP, et des crédits privés garantis à l'exportation, c'est-à-dire la totalité des emprunts en provenance du secteur public ou garantis par celui-ci effectués à conditions fixes. Les prêts non garantis et les crédits financiers accordés par le secteur bancaire sont exclus.

A13. *Organismes multilatéraux :* la liste des organismes multilatéraux auxquels se réfèrent les données dans le présent rapport a été présentée dans l'introduction. Dans la mesure du possible, on a distingué, dans les apports fournis par ces organismes, ceux qui sont assortis de conditions libérales de ceux qui sont assortis des conditions du marché. Les versements de prêts pour lesquels il n'a pas été possible d'opérer cette distinction sur la base des différentes opérations ont été considérés comme non libéraux lorsqu'ils étaient effectués à l'aide de ressources en capital ordinaire et comme libéraux lorsqu'ils venaient de « guichets spéciaux ». Ainsi, pour certains organismes, les « prêts totaux » sont beaucoup plus élevés que les prêts à des conditions libérales, et le volume des prêts à des conditions libérales effectivement reçus par le pays emprunteur est proportionnellement sous-évalué. Dans le cas des apports des organismes multilatéraux comme dans celui des apports bilatéraux, on entend par « versements nets » le montant brut des dons et prêts versés aux pays en développement, diminué des remboursments de prêts antérieurs. Les paiements effectués par les pays en développement à titre de souscription au capital des organismes multilatéraux dont ils sont membres ne sont pas déduits.

A14. *Recettes totales nettes :* outre l'aide publique au développement, cette rubrique comprend en particulier : les autres transactions publiques bilatérales qui ne sont pas assorties de conditions libérales ou qui, dans le cas contraire, restent néanmoins de nature essentiellement commerciale (« autres apports du secteur public ») ; les variations des actifs bilatéraux à long terme du secteur privé monétaire et non monétaire, en particulier les crédits à l'exportation garantis, les investissements privés directs et, dans la mesure où ils ne sont pas repris dans les rubriques précédentes, les prêts des banques privées. Les apports en provenance des organismes multilatéraux qui ne sont pas considérés comme assortis de conditions libérales sont aussi inclus dans cette rubrique.

Liens entre les catégories d'apports présentées dans le rapport

A15. Pour un pays bénéficiaire donné, le total net des apports de ressources (« recettes totales nettes ») est la somme des rubriques (1 + 2 + 3 = 4) figurant dans le tableau ci-après.

CATÉGORIES	DONNEURS DU CAD	DONNEURS MULTILATÉRAUX	DONNEURS ARABES	DONNEURS DU PECO
1. APD, montants nets	Par pays	Par organisme	En tant que groupe	Non disponible
2. AASP, montants nets	Par pays	En tant que groupe	En tant que groupe	Non disponible
3. Apports nets du secteur privé	En tant que groupe	Sans objet	Non disponible	Non disponible
4. Total net des apports de ressources	Par pays	Par organisme	Incomplet	Non disponible
Pour mémoire :				
ADP, montants bruts	Par pays	Par organisme	En tant que groupe	En tant que groupe
ADP, engagements	Par pays	Par organisme	En tant que groupe	En tant que groupe

A16. Le total, pour l'ensemble des pays du CAD, des « apports nets du secteur privé » peut être ventilé par pays d'origine en soustrayant du total net des apports en provenance du pays concerné le total (APD + AASP) que l'on lira en regard de son nom dans le tableau se rapportant au pays bénéficiaire.

A17. La rubrique « apports nets du secteur privé » est ventilée, pour l'ensemble des Membres du CAD, en investissements directs, investissements de portefeuille et crédits à l'exportation (nets). Les opérations recensées dans chaque catégorie sont celles qui sont entreprises par des opérateurs résidents des pays Membres du CAD. Les investissements de portefeuille correspondent, dans une grande mesure mais pas dans leur totalité, aux opérations du secteur monétaire privé, ajustées si nécessaire et, dans la mesure du possible, de façon à transférer les créances au titre de crédits à l'exportation à la rubrique correspondante. Le champ de couverture des investissements de portefeuille diffère donc à ces deux égards de celui de la rubrique « prêts du secteur bancaire » laquelle englobe les crédits à l'exportation consentis par les banques. Les données sur les « prêts du secteur bancaire » correspondent à la variation des créances des banques après correction pour l'effet des variations des taux de change. Il s'agit donc d'un indicateur des apports nets, et non d'une mesure des apports nets. Il existe trois autres différences par rapport aux autres données dans le rapport. En premier lieu, sont compris les prêts octroyés par des succursales établies dans des centres financiers de banques mères résidant dans des pays qui effectuent tous les trimestres des déclarations statistiques auprès de la BRI, c'est-à-dire les Membres du CAD autres que l'Australie, l'Espagne, la Nouvelle-Zélande, y compris un certain nombre de centres financiers (voir l'enquête trimestrielle de la BRI « *Evolution de l'activité bancaire internationale et des marchés financiers internationaux* »). En second lieu, pour les centres financiers en tant que débiteurs, sont omis des données établies conjointement par l'OCDE et la BRI, les emprunts des banques qui y résident, dont la plupart agissent comme des intermédiaires qui prêtent sur le plan international. Enfin, aucun ajustement n'a été opéré en vue d'exclure les créances à court terme.

A18. Les derniers développements statistiques permettent de réconcilier les données corrigées tirées des statistiques bancaires sur l'encours des créances avec les données corrigées sur les crédits commerciaux garantis consentis par les banques. Les résultats sont présentés dans l'étude semestrielle de l'OCDE/BRI *Statistiques sur l'endettement extérieur : créances extérieures bancaires et créances extérieures non bancaires liées au commerce, ventilées par pays et territoire emprunteur* (n° 8 paru en janvier 1992).

NOTE SUR L'INTERPRÉTATION DE CERTAINES DONNÉES

A19. L'élaboration des données statistiques présentées dans ce rapport a pour but de dresser un tableau aussi complet que possible des ressources mises à la disposition de chaque pays visé. Les déclarations des pays Membres comportent néanmoins certaines incohérences ou lacunes qui, bien que n'ayant qu'une incidence marginale sur les données agrégées, ont obligé à recourir à des estimations influant, dans certains cas, sur le contenu des données ou permettant, dans d'autres, de combler les lacunes constatées.

A20. On trouvera ci-après la liste des principaux domaines où certaines particularités des données dues à ces facteurs pourraient gêner leur compréhension ou utilisation par le lecteur.

Données par groupes de pays

a) Groupes retenus

A21. Les pays à faible revenu sont ceux dont le PNB par habitant en 1989, tel qu'il figure dans l'Atlas de la Banque mondiale, était inférieur à environ 750 dollars. Deux sous-catégories de pays à faible revenu sont présentées séparément : les pays figurant sur la liste des pays les moins avancés (PMA) établie par l'ONU dont certains disposent d'un PNB par habitant supérieur à 750 dollars, et les autres pays à faible revenu. Deux autres tableaux, figurant à la fin de la section B, donnent d'une part l'ensemble des chiffres pour des pays à faible revenu, y compris les PMA faisant partie de la catégorie immédiatement supérieure, et, d'autre part, pour l'Afrique subsaharienne. Les pays à revenu intermédiaire sont subdivisés en deux catégories : ceux de la tranche inférieure (PRITI), soit les pays dont le PNB moyen par habitant en 1989 était compris entre 750 et 1 500 dollars, et ceux de la tranche supérieure (PRITS), dont le PNB par habitant dépassait 1 500 dollars. Ces groupes ont été définis uniquement à des fins analytiques et, à l'exception des « pays les moins avancés », ils ne correspondent pas à des classifications agréées sur le plan international.

b) Traitement des montants non ventilés

A22. Certains pays déclarants ne sont pas en mesure de ventiler la totalité de leurs apports par pays de destination, dans la mesure où les engagements ou les versements concernent des dépenses à entreprendre soit dans une région donnée (par exemple, l'Afrique de l'Ouest), soit dans un groupe de pays donnés (par exemple, les pays les moins avancés). Dans ce rapport, les données présentées pour les pays et pour les groupes sont limitées à celles pouvant être ventilées par bénéficiaires. Les montants notifiés comme ayant été versésà une région ou à un groupe sont inscrits à la rubrique des montants « non ventilés ». Le problème des montants importants non ventilés de l'aide des pays arabes membres de l'OPEP a déjà été abordé dans l'introduction. A la rubrique des montants non ventilés sont inscrites par ailleurs les ressources engagées ou versées sur le territoire du pays donneur soit pour des recherches consacrées à certains problèmes propres aux pays en développement (maladies tropicales, par exemple), soit sous la forme de subventions à des ressortissants de pays en développement, par exemple pour des stages d'apprentissage ou des cours dans des établissements scolaires ou universitaires ; pour des raisons statistiques évidentes, ces sommes ne peuvent être réparties entre les pays bénéficiaires.

A23. S'agissant du calcul de la part d'un pays ou d'un groupe donné dans le total des pays en développement, il est d'usage d'utiliser comme dénominateur le total hors montants non ventilés. On suppose, ce faisant, que la répartition géographique en pourcentage des montants non ventilés est la même que celles des montants ventilés.

A24. Dons négatifs : en décrivant la méthode de comptabilisation des dons, il a été noté que les montants inscrits dans les statistiques ont été minorés pour tenir compte des dépenses engagées pour son propre compte par un pays donneur en utilisant les avoirs en monnaie locale dont il dispose. Il peut arriver que ces montants dépassent celui des nouveaux dons accordés, d'où inscription de « dons négatifs ».

A25. Annulation des engagements : les données relatives aux engagements concernent les nouveaux engagements souscrits dans l'année. Elles excluent les engagements annulés dans l'année où ils ont été souscrits, mais aucune défalcation n'est faite pour tenir compte des annulations au cours de l'année d'engagements souscrits pendant des années antérieures.

A26. Engagements d'APD des institutions financières internationales : en règle générale, ces institutions notifient les « autorisations d'engagement », qui sont reprises en tant qu'engagements dans le pavé « engagements d'APD ». Toutefois, aux fins du calcul de l'élément de libéralité (présenté sous la rubrique « engagements de toutes provenances »), il convient de déterminer les conditions dont sont assortis les différents engagements, et la date retenue est alors celle de la signature, laquelle est normalement postérieure à celle de l'autorisation. C'est pourquoi, il peut arriver qu'une écriture sous la rubrique « engagements de prêts » ne soit pas assortie d'une écriture pour l'élément de libéralité correspondant (ou vice versa). Des déséquilibres dans un sens ou dans l'autre dus à cette cause sont compensés par un déséquilibre dans le sens inverse pour une année voisine.

A27. Au cas où un chiffre d'élément de libéralité est présenté sans être accompagné d'un montant d'engagement, cela est dû au fait que le montant en cause est inférieur à 50 000 dollars, c'est-à-dire trop petit pour être repris dans le tableau.

A28. Composantes manquantes : il convient de mentionner que dans le sous-pavé « engagements de toutes provenances », seules certaines composantes des totaux apparaissent, pour éviter certains traitements complexes qui auraient retardé la parution du rapport. Le total des composantes manquantes peut être établi par la soustraction des composantes qui sont présentées du total dont elles font partie.

A29. Engagements et versements des organismes des Nations Unies : les données sur les versements sont indiquées séparément pour chaque organisme des Nations Unies. Des données comparables sur les engagements n'étant pas disponibles pour l'ensemble de ces organismes, on a inscrit dans les tableaux des engagements les données relatives aux versements bruts des organismes des Nations Unies, avec inscription d'un montant nul en regard des différents organismes. Ce procédé répond à la nécessité de fournir un ordre de grandeur des engagements souscrits par l'ensemble du secteur multilatéral.

A30. Effet des variations des taux de change : l'unité monétaire utilisée dans le présent rapport est le dollar des Etats-Unis. Or, les prêts sont souvent libellés dans une autre monnaie. Si celle-ci se raffermit par rapport au dollar, le montant des remboursements apparaissant dans les statistiques représente un chiffre en dollars plus important. Il est ainsi des cas où le total des remboursements paraît dépasser le montant primitif du prêt. De même, l'affaiblissement d'une monnaie se traduit dans les statistiques par des remboursements dont le total, estimé en dollars, paraît être inférieur au principal. Si on effectue une comparaison des variations de la dette (par exemple à partir du rapport *Financement et dette extérieure des pays en développement* ou l'étude semestrielle OCDE/BRI) avec les chiffres présentés pour les apports totaux nets de ressources dans le présent rapport, il faut garder à l'esprit que les données relatives à la dette sont converties en dollars au taux s'appliquant en fin de période, tandis que les données relatives aux apports sont converties au taux annuel moyen (Voir aussi l'annexe paragraphe A17).

A31. Des montants exceptionnellement élevés d'amortissement tiennent, dans la quasi-totalité des cas, à la mise en œuvre de «l'ajustement rétroactif des conditions» sous la forme de l'annulation de l'endettement au titre des prêts antérieurs. L'annulation correspond à l'octroi d'un don, dont l'objet est de permettre le remboursement du principal des prêts en cours (voir paragraphe A7). La comptabilisation d'un montant exceptionnellement élevé d'amortissement (soit des prêts nets négatifs) dans les statistiques de l'aide publique au développement consentie aux pays les moins avancés s'accompagne, dans tous les cas, de la comptabilisation d'un montant exceptionnellement élevé de dons versés par le même donneur, la même année.

A32. APD en provenance de la BIRD : la plupart des prêts de la BIRD sont classés sous la rubrique «autres apports du secteur public»; en effet, l'APD est en règle générale dispensée par l'Association internationale du développement (IDA). Certains montants inscrits en regard de la BIRD correspondent aux prêts consentis par le biais du mécanisme du «troisième guichet».

A33. Données concernant les engagements de la Belgique : en raison des procédures administratives utilisées, les autorités belges ne peuvent déterminer les engagements de dons (ce problème n'existe pas pour la notification des prêts). Afin d'éviter de laisser en blanc les lignes relatives aux engagements de la Belgique, le Secrétariat a fait des estimations, en répartissant l'enveloppe budgétaire affectée aux dons au prorata de la part de chaque bénéficiaire dans les versements bruts de chaque année. Les petites erreurs ainsi induites ne sauraient fausser le chiffre des données pour le total des engagements de toutes provenances, ou en provenance de l'ensemble des Membres du CAD. Cependant, s'il s'agit d'analyser les seuls chiffres de la Belgique, une meilleure estimation consisterait à faire une moyenne pluriannuelle des engagements de dons de la Belgique.

A34. Apports de ressources en provenance de la Communauté économique européenne : les chiffres présentés englobent les dons et les prêts de la CEE ainsi que les fonds mis à disposition par la Banque européenne d'investissement aux conditions du marché. Ces derniers montants peuvent être déterminés à partir des données figurant dans le présent volume en calculant la différence entre le total des apports de la CEE reçus par un pays et le montant de ses recettes d'APD en provenance de la CEE.

ALSO AVAILABLE

Development Co-operation

Efforts and Policies of the Members of the Development Assistance Committee. 1991 Report. (1991)
(43 91 05 1) ISBN 92-64-13593-6   FF150   £18.00   US$32.00   DM62

External Debt Statistics

The Debt and other External Liabilities of Developing, Central and Eastern European and certain other Countries and Territories at end-December 1990 and end-December 1989 (1991)
(43 91 04 1) ISBN 92-64-13588-X   FF90   £12.50   US$22.00   DM38

Financing and External Debt of Developing Countries

1990 Survey (1991)
(43 91 02 1) ISBN 92-64-13494-8   FF150   £19.50   US$36.00   DM58

Promoting Private Enterprise in Developing Countries (1990)
(43 90 02 1) ISBN 92-64-13359-3   FF90   £11.00   US$19.00   DM35

Prices charged at the OECD Bookshop.
THE OECD CATALOGUE OF PUBLICATIONS and supplements will be sent free of charge
on request addressed either to OECD Publications Service,
or to the OECD Distributor in your country.

MAIN SALES OUTLETS OF OECD PUBLICATIONS – PRINCIPAUX POINTS DE VENTE DES PUBLICATIONS DE L'OCDE

Argentina – Argentine
Carlos Hirsch S.R.L.
Galería Güemes, Florida 165, 4° Piso
1333 Buenos Aires   Tel. (1) 331.1787 y 331.2391
                             Telefax: (1) 331.1787

Australia – Australie
D.A. Book (Aust.) Pty. Ltd.
648 Whitehorse Road, P.O.B 163
Mitcham, Victoria 3132   Tel. (03) 873.4411
                             Telefax: (03) 873.5679

Austria – Autriche
OECD Publications and Information Centre
Schedestrasse 7
D-W 5300 Bonn 1 (Germany)   Tel. (49.228) 21.60.45
                             Telefax: (49.228) 26.11.04
Gerold & Co.
Graben 31
Wien I   Tel. (0222) 533.50.14

Belgium – Belgique
Jean De Lannoy
Avenue du Roi 202
B-1060 Bruxelles   Tel. (02) 538.51.69/538.08.41
                             Telefax: (02) 538.08.41

Canada
Renouf Publishing Company Ltd.
1294 Algoma Road
Ottawa, ON K1B 3W8   Tel. (613) 741.4333
                             Telefax: (613) 741.5439
Stores:
61 Sparks Street
Ottawa, ON K1P 5R1   Tel. (613) 238.8985
211 Yonge Street
Toronto, ON M5B 1M4   Tel. (416) 363.3171
Federal Publications
165 University Avenue
Toronto, ON M5H 3B8   Tel. (416) 581.1552
                             Telefax: (416)581.1743
Les Éditions La Liberté Inc.
3020 Chemin Sainte-Foy
Sainte-Foy, PQ G1X 3V6   Tel. (418) 658.3763
                             Telefax: (418) 658.3763

China – Chine
China National Publications Import
 Export Corporation (CNPIEC)
P.O. Box 88
Beijing   Tel. 44.0731
                             Telefax: 401.5661

Denmark – Danemark
Munksgaard Export and Subscription Service
35, Nørre Søgade, P.O. Box 2148
DK-1016 København K   Tel. (33) 12.85.70
                             Telefax: (33) 12.93.87

Finland – Finlande
Akateeminen Kirjakauppa
Keskuskatu 1, P.O. Box 128
00100 Helsinki   Tel. (358 0) 12141
                             Telefax: (358 0) 121.4441

France
OECD/OCDE
Mail Orders/Commandes par correspondance:
2, rue André-Pascal
75775 Paris Cédex 16   Tel. (33-1) 45.24.82.00
                             Telefax: (33-1) 45.24.85.00
                             or (33-1) 45.24.81.76
                             Telex: 620 160 OCDE
Bookshop/Librairie:
33, rue Octave-Feuillet
75016 Paris   Tel. (33-1) 45.24.81.67
                             (33-1) 45.24.81.81
Librairie de l'Université
12a, rue Nazareth
13100 Aix-en-Provence   Tel. 42.26.18.08
                             Telefax: 42.26.63.26

Germany – Allemagne
OECD Publications and Information Centre
Schedestrasse 7
D-W 5300 Bonn 1   Tel. (0228) 21.60.45
                             Telefax: (0228) 26.11.04

Greece – Grèce
Librairie Kauffmann
Mavrokordatou 9
106 78 Athens   Tel. 322.21.60
                             Telefax: 363.39.67

Hong Kong
Swindon Book Co. Ltd.
13 - 15 Lock Road
Kowloon, Hong Kong   Tel. 366.80.31
                             Telefax: 739.49.75

Iceland – Islande
Mál Mog Menning
Laugavegi 18, Pósthólf 392
121 Reykjavik   Tel. 162.35.23

India – Inde
Oxford Book and Stationery Co.
Scindia House
New Delhi 110001   Tel.(11) 331.5896/5308
                             Telefax: (11) 332.5993
17 Park Street
Calcutta 700016   Tel. 240832

Indonesia – Indonésie
Pdii-Lipi
P.O. Box 269/JKSMG/88
Jakarta 12790   Tel. 583467
                             Telex: 62 875

Ireland – Irlande
TDC Publishers – Library Suppliers
12 North Frederick Street
Dublin 1   Tel. 74.48.35/74.96.77
                             Telefax: 74.84.16

Israel
Electronic Publications only
Publications électroniques seulement
Sophist Systems Ltd.
71 Allenby Street
Tel-Aviv 65134   Tel. 3-29.00.21
                             Telefax: 3-29.92.39

Italy – Italie
Libreria Commissionaria Sansoni
Via Duca di Calabria 1/1
50125 Firenze   Tel. (055) 64.54.15
                             Telefax: (055) 64.12.57
Via Bartolini 29
20155 Milano   Tel. (02) 36.50.83
Editrice e Libreria Herder
Piazza Montecitorio 120
00186 Roma   Tel. 679.46.28
                             Telex: NATEL I 621427
Libreria Hoepli
Via Hoepli 5
20121 Milano   Tel. (02) 86.54.46
                             Telefax: (02) 805.28.86
Libreria Scientifica
Dott. Lucio de Biasio 'Aeiou'
Via Meravigli 16
20123 Milano   Tel. (02) 805.68.98
                             Telefax: (02) 80.01.75

Japan – Japon
OECD Publications and Information Centre
Landic Akasaka Building
2-3-4 Akasaka, Minato-ku
Tokyo 107   Tel. (81.3) 3586.2016
                             Telefax: (81.3) 3584.7929

Korea – Corée
Kyobo Book Centre Co. Ltd.
P.O. Box 1658, Kwang Hwa Moon
Seoul   Tel. 730.78.91
                             Telefax: 735.00.30

Malaysia – Malaisie
Co-operative Bookshop Ltd.
University of Malaya
P.O. Box 1127, Jalan Pantai Baru
59700 Kuala Lumpur
Malaysia   Tel. 756.5000/756.5425
                             Telefax: 757.3661

Netherlands – Pays-Bas
SDU Uitgeverij
Christoffel Plantijnstraat 2
Postbus 20014
2500 EA's-Gravenhage   Tel. (070 3) 78.99.11
Voor bestellingen: Tel. (070 3) 78.98.80
                             Telefax: (070 3) 47.63.51

New Zealand – Nouvelle-Zélande
GP Publications Ltd.
Customer Services
33 The Esplanade - P.O. Box 38-900
Petone, Wellington   Tel. (04) 5685.555
                             Telefax: (04) 5685.333

Norway – Norvège
Narvesen Info Center - NIC
Bertrand Narvesens vei 2
P.O. Box 6125 Etterstad
0602 Oslo 6   Tel. (02) 57.33.00
                             Telefax: (02) 68.19.01

Pakistan
Mirza Book Agency
65 Shahrah Quaid-E-Azam
Lahore 3   Tel. 66.839
                             Telex: 44886 UBL PK. Attn: MIRZA BK

Portugal
Livraria Portugal
Rua do Carmo 70-74
Apart. 2681
1117 Lisboa Codex   Tel.: (01) 347.49.82/3/4/5
                             Telefax: (01) 347.02.64

Singapore – Singapour
Information Publications Pte. Ltd.
Pei-Fu Industrial Building
24 New Industrial Road No. 02-06
Singapore 1953   Tel. 283.1786/283.1798
                             Telefax: 284.8875

Spain – Espagne
Mundi-Prensa Libros S.A.
Castelló 37, Apartado 1223
Madrid 28001   Tel. (91) 431.33.99
                             Telefax: (91) 575.39.98
Libreria Internacional AEDOS
Consejo de Ciento 391
08009 - Barcelona   Tel. (93) 488.34.92
                             Telefax: (93) 487.76.59
Llibreria de la Generalitat
Palau Moja
Rambla dels Estudis, 118
08002 - Barcelona   Tel. (93) 318.80.12 (Subscripcions)
                         (93) 302.67.23 (Publicacions)
                         Telefax: (93) 412.18.54

Sri Lanka
Centre for Policy Research
c/o Colombo Agencies Ltd.
No. 300-304, Galle Road
Colombo 3   Tel. (1) 574240, 573551-2
                             Telefax: (1) 575394, 510711

Sweden – Suède
Fritzes Fackboksföretaget
Box 16356
Regeringsgatan 12
103 27 Stockholm   Tel. (08) 23.89.00
                             Telefax: (08) 20.50.21
Subscription Agency/Abonnements:
Wennergren-Williams AB
Nordenflychtsvägen 74
Box 30004
104 25 Stockholm   Tel. (08) 13.67.00
                             Telefax: (08) 618.62.32

Switzerland – Suisse
OECD Publications and Information Centre
Schedestrasse 7
D-W 5300 Bonn 1 (Germany)   Tel. (49.228) 21.60.45
                             Telefax: (49.228) 26.11.04
Suisse romande
Maditec S.A.
Chemin des Palettes 4
1020 Renens/Lausanne   Tel. (021) 635.08.65
                             Telefax: (021) 635.07.80
Librairie Payot
6 rue Grenus
1211 Genève 11   Tel. (022) 731.89.50
                             Telex: 28356
Subscription Agency – Service des Abonnements
Naville S.A.
7, rue Lévrier
1201 Genève   Tél.: (022) 732.24.00
                             Telefax: (022) 738.87.13

Taiwan – Formose
Good Faith Worldwide Int'l. Co. Ltd.
9th Floor, No. 118, Sec. 2
Chung Hsiao E. Road
Taipei   Tel. (02) 391.7396/391.7397
                             Telefax: (02) 394.9176

Thailand – Thaïlande
Suksit Siam Co. Ltd.
113, 115 Fuang Nakhon Rd.
Opp. Wat Rajbopith
Bangkok 10200   Tel. (662) 251.1630
                             Telefax: (662) 236.7783

Turkey – Turquie
Kültur Yayinlari Is-Türk Ltd. Sti.
Atatürk Bulvari No. 191/Kat. 21
Kavaklidere/Ankara   Tel. 25.07.60
Dolmabahce Cad. No. 29
Besiktas/Istanbul   Tel. 160.71.88
                             Telex: 43482B

United Kingdom – Royaume-Uni
HMSO
Gen. enquiries   Tel. (071) 873 0011
Postal orders only:
P.O. Box 276, London SW8 5DT
Personal Callers HMSO Bookshop
49 High Holborn, London WC1V 6HB
                             Telefax: 071 873 2000
Branches at: Belfast, Birmingham, Bristol, Edinburgh,
                             Manchester

United States – États-Unis
OECD Publications and Information Centre
2001 L Street N.W., Suite 700
Washington, D.C. 20036-4910 Tel. (202) 785.6323
                             Telefax: (202) 785.0350

Venezuela
Libreria del Este
Avda F. Miranda 52, Aptdo. 60337
Edificio Galipán
Caracas 106   Tel. 951.1705/951.2307/951.1297
                             Telegram: Libreste Caracas

Yugoslavia – Yougoslavie
Jugoslovenska Knjiga
Knez Mihajlova 2, P.O. Box 36
Beograd   Tel. (011) 621.992
                             Telefax: (011) 625.970

Orders and inquiries from countries where Distributors have
not yet been appointed should be sent to: OECD Publications Service, 2 rue André-Pascal, 75775 Paris Cédex 16,
France.

Les commandes provenant de pays où l'OCDE n'a pas
encore désigné de distributeur devraient être adressées à :
OCDE, Service des Publications, 2, rue André-Pascal, 75775
Paris Cédex 16, France.

OECD PUBLICATIONS, 2 rue André Pascal, 75775 PARIS CEDEX 16
PRINTED IN FRANCE
(43 92 01 3) ISBN 92-64-03526-5 No. 45930 1992
ISSN 1015-3934

ENQUIRY FORM
FORMULAIRE D'INFORMATION

This publication is drawn from the OECD/DAC computerised data base and is available both on magnetic tape and in the form of microfiches. The full data base, which likewise is available on magnetic tape, contains annual financial flow data going back to 1969. For the period 1960 to 1968 the data are available in published form only and with no distinction between Official Development Assistance (ODA) and Other Official Flows (OOF).

Aggregate annual data by donor country and type of resource flow are discussed in the DAC Chairman's Annual Report, *Development Co-operation - Efforts and Policies of Members of the Development Assistance Committee*, and presented in detail in the statistical Annex to that report. These publications are also available from OECD Publications Distributors.

Detailed data of external debt and debt service, by debtor country are contained in successive OECD surveys of the *Financing and External Debt of Developing Countries.*

Cette publication est tirée de la base de données informatisée OCDE/CAD, et est disponible soit sur bande magnétique, soit sous forme de microfiches. La base, qui est également disponible sur bande magnétique, contient des données annuelles sur les flux financiers remontant jusqu'en 1969. Pour la période allant de 1960 à 1968 les données ne sont disponibles que sous forme de publication, et ce, sans distinction entre l'Aide Publique au Développement (APD) et les Autres Apports du Secteur Public (AASP).

Les données agrégées par pays donneur et par type de flux sont présentées et analysées dans le rapport annuel du Président du CAD, *Coopération pour le développement — Efforts et politiques poursuivis par les membres du Comité d'Aide au Développement,* qui comporte une annexe statistique ; ces publications sont également en vente chez les distributeurs des publications de l'OCDE.

Des données détaillées de la dette et du service de la dette extérieure par pays débiteurs sont inclues dans la série de publications de l'OCDE *Financement et Dette Extérieure des Pays en Développement* .

Please send me more information about and prices for:
Veuillez me faire parvenir des informations complémentaires
et des indications sur les prix des :

PUBLICATIONS

☐ DAC CHAIRMAN'S REPORT
RAPPORT DU PRÉSIDENT DU CAD

☐ FINANCING AND EXTERNAL DEBT OF DEVELOPING COUNTRIES
FINANCEMENT ET DETTE EXTÉRIEURE DES PAYS EN DÉVELOPPEMENT

☐ EXTERNAL DEBT STATISTICS AT END DECEMBER 1983-1987 (DISKETTE)
STATISTIQUES DE LA DETTE EXTÉRIEURE A FIN DÉCEMBRE 1983-1987 (DISQUETTE)

☐ DAC AID PERFORMANCE

GEOGRAPHICAL DATA - DONNÉES GÉOGRAPHIQUES

☐ MICROFICHES

☐ MAGNETIC TAPES
BANDES MAGNÉTIQUES

☐ MICRO COMPUTER DISKETTE
(contains Section A)
(contient la Section A)

☐ MICRO COMPUTER DISKETTE

Name/Nom _____

Title/Fonction _____

Organisation _____

Address/Adresse _____

_____ Tél. _____

DIVISION DES SYSTÈMES STATISTIQUES
DIRECTION DE LA COOPÉRATION POUR LE DÉVELOPPEMENT

2, rue André-Pascal
75775 Paris Cedex 16 - France